SHIPS' ROUTEING

2013 EDITION

This edition includes amendments adopted up to December 2013

The chartlets contained herein are not to be used for navigation

IMO
INTERNATIONAL
MARITIME
ORGANIZATION
London, 2013

First published in 1970 by the
INTERNATIONAL MARITIME ORGANIZATION
4 Albert Embankment, London SE1 7SR
www.imo.org

Eleventh edition 2013

Printed by CPI Group (UK) Ltd, Croydon, CR0 4YY

PEFC
PEFC/06-37-03

ISBN: 978-92-801-1554-3

IMO PUBLICATION
Sales number: IE927E

J4655

Note

This edition supersedes all previous editions and includes all routeing measures adopted by IMO up to and including the ninety-second session (June 2013) of the Maritime Safety Committee and the twenty-eighth session (December 2013) of IMO Assembly. The expected dates of implementation of those revisions that have entered into force since the 2010 edition or were not in force on the date of publication of this edition are shown in footnotes.

With regard to the dates of implementation of the routeing measures, reference should be made to relevant Notices to Mariners. Users of this publication should note that there may be a delay between amendment to the General Provisions on Ships' Routeing and to routeing measures and the publication of a new edition.

The numbers of reference charts in the description of individual systems are those applicable at the time of adoption. Where amendments have been made to existing systems but from charts that are based on a different geodetic datum, this has been highlighted in this edition.

Hydrographic services promulgate, by appropriate means, full details of routeing systems adopted by IMO and such General Provisions on Ships' Routeing, as amended, as are relevant to the mariner.

Contents

Page

Section II – Western European waters

Section III – Mediterranean Sea and Black Sea

Page

Page

Page

Part E — Other routeing measures

Page

Part F — Associated rules and recommendations on navigation

Part G — Mandatory ship reporting systems, mandatory routeing systems and mandatory no anchoring areas

Section I – Mandatory ship reporting systems

Introduction

The practice of following predetermined routes originated in about 1898 and was adopted, for reasons of safety, by shipping companies operating passenger ships across the North Atlantic. Related provisions were subsequently incorporated into the International Conventions for the Safety of Life at Sea.

The 1960 Safety Convention referred to the same practice in converging areas on both sides of the North Atlantic. The Contracting Governments undertook the responsibility of using their influence to induce the owners of all passenger ships crossing the Atlantic to follow the recognized routes and to do everything in their power to ensure adherence to such routes in converging areas by all ships, so far as circumstances permit.

In 1961 the institutes of navigation of the Federal Republic of Germany, France and the United Kingdom undertook a study of measures for separating traffic in the Strait of Dover and, subsequently, in certain other areas where statistics indicated an increased risk of collision. Their studies resulted in proposals for the separation of traffic in those areas as well as for certain basic principles of ships' routeing. These proposals were submitted to the International Maritime Organization (IMO), the specialized agency of the United Nations responsible for maritime safety, efficiency of navigation and prevention of marine pollution, and were generally adopted. This initial step was further developed by IMO and the basic concept of separating opposing traffic was applied to many areas throughout the world.

The increase in recent years in the size and draught of ships has produced problems in certain shallow-water areas and led to the establishment of deep-water routes.

Similarly, the hazards to navigation in certain areas and the associated dangers to the marine environment and ecology have resulted in the establishment and adoption of "areas to be avoided" by certain ships.

Today, in accordance with regulation 10.2 of the revised chapter V of the International Convention for the Safety of Life at Sea, 1974 (1974 SOLAS Convention), IMO is recognized as the only international body for establishing and adopting measures on an international level concerning routeing and areas to be avoided by ships or certain classes of ships; whilst, in accordance with regulation 11.2 of the revised chapter V of the International Convention for the Safety of Life at Sea, 1974, IMO is recognized as the only international body for developing guidelines, criteria and regulations on an international level, including adoption of ship reporting systems.

Ships' Routeing is intended primarily for Administrations responsible for planning and supporting routeing systems for use by international shipping.

There are two categories of routeing systems. The first category of routeing systems includes traffic separation schemes, two-way routes, recommended tracks, areas to be avoided, inshore traffic zones, roundabouts, precautionary areas and deep-water routes. The second category is archipelagic sea lanes. Part A consists of General Provisions on Ships' Routeing which have been developed to ensure that all adopted routeing systems conform to the same general criteria and principles. Parts B to F include descriptions of routeing systems and associated rules and recommendations on navigation which have been adopted by the Organization. Part G includes descriptions of mandatory ship reporting systems and mandatory routeing measures which have been adopted by the Organization. Part H takes into account the unique character of achipelagic sea lanes as a routeing system and provides guidance for the preparation, consideration and adoption of proposals for the adoption, designation and substitution of archipelagic sea lanes.

Rule 10 of the International Regulations for Preventing Collisions at Sea, 1972 (COLREG 1972), as amended by Assembly resolutions A.464(XII), A.626(15), A.678(16), A.910(22) and A.1004(25), prescribes the conduct of vessels within or near traffic separation schemes adopted by IMO. The text of rule 10 is reproduced in part B.

Through its appropriate bodies, IMO keeps the subject of ships' routeing under continuous review by adopting new routeing systems and amending or, when necessary, withdrawing existing systems.

A Government intending to establish a new or amended routeing system should be guided by this publication and follow all recommended consultative procedures to ensure that a proposed system will comply with the relevant General Provisions on Ships' Routeing in part A and with part H.

Proposed routeing measures should be submitted to the Sub-Committee on Navigation, Communications and Search and Rescue at least three months before a scheduled meeting. The Sub-Committee will evaluate a proposal for technical compliance with the General Provisions and make a recommendation regarding its adoption. Submissions should include, in addition to the description of the routeing measure and associated chartlet, the reference chart or charts listed in the description of the routeing measure with the proposed routeing system delineated thereon. Member Governments should also take into account MSC/Circ. 1060 "Guidance notes on the preparation of proposals on ships' routeing systems and ship reporting systems for submission to the Sub-Committee on Safety of Navigation*" and its amendment in MSC.1/Circ.1060/Add.1.

The Maritime Safety Committee will adopt routeing measures in accordance with Assembly resolutions A.572(14), as amended, and A.858(20).

* After 1 January 2014, the Sub-Committee on Safety of Navigation and the Sub-Committee on Radiocommunications and Search and Rescue will be replaced by the Sub-Committee on Navigation, Communications and Search and Rescue.

INTERNATIONAL CONVENTION FOR THE SAFETY OF LIFE AT SEA, 1974, AS AMENDED

Regulation V/10 – Ships' routeing

1 Ships' routeing systems contribute to safety of life at sea, safety and efficiency of navigation, and/or protection of the marine environment. Ships' routeing systems are recommended for use by, and may be made mandatory for, all ships, certain categories of ships or ships carrying certain cargoes, when adopted and implemented in accordance with the guidelines and criteria developed by the Organization*.

2 The Organization is recognized as the only international body for developing guidelines, criteria and regulations on an international level for ships' routeing systems. Contracting Governments shall refer proposals for the adoption of ships' routeing systems to the Organization. The Organization will collate and disseminate to Contracting Governments all relevant information with regard to any adopted ships' routeing systems.

3 The initiation of action for establishing a ships' routeing system is the responsibility of the Government or Governments concerned. In developing such systems for adoption by the Organization*, the guidelines and criteria developed by the Organization* shall be taken into account.

4 Ships' routeing systems should be submitted to the Organization for adoption. However, a Government or Governments implementing ships' routeing systems not intended to be submitted to the Organization for adoption or which have not been adopted by the Organization are encouraged to take into account, wherever possible, the guidelines and criteria developed by the Organization*.

5 Where two or more Governments have a common interest in a particular area, they should formulate joint proposals for the delineation and use of a routeing system therein on the basis of an agreement between them. Upon receipt of such proposal and before proceeding with the consideration of it for adoption, the Organization shall ensure that details of the proposal are disseminated to the Governments which have a common interest in the area, including countries in the vicinity of the proposed ships' routeing system.

6 Contracting Governments shall adhere to the measures adopted by the Organization concerning ships' routeing. They shall promulgate all information necessary for the safe and effective use of adopted ships' routeing systems. A Government or Governments concerned may monitor traffic in those systems. Contracting Governments shall do everything in their power to secure the appropriate use of ships' routeing systems adopted by the Organization.

7 A ship shall use a mandatory ships' routeing system adopted by the Organization as required for its category or cargo carried and in accordance with the relevant provisions in force unless there are compelling reasons not to use a particular ships' routeing system. Any such reason shall be recorded in the ship's log.

8 Mandatory ships' routeing systems shall be reviewed by the Contracting Government or Governments concerned in accordance with the guidelines and criteria developed by the Organization*.

9 All adopted ships' routeing systems and actions taken to enforce compliance with those systems shall be consistent with international law, including the relevant provisions of the 1982 United Nations Convention on the Law of the Sea.

10 Nothing in this regulation nor its associated guidelines and criteria* shall prejudice the rights and duties of Governments under international law or the legal regimes of straits used for international navigation and archipelagic sea lanes.

* Refer to the General provisions on ships' routeing adopted by the Organization by resolution A.572(14), as amended.

Part A

General provisions on ships' routeing

A

GENERAL PROVISIONS ON SHIPS' ROUTEING

Introduction

The General Provisions on Ships' Routeing are established pursuant to regulation V/10 of the SOLAS Convention.

1 Objectives

1.1 The purpose of ships' routeing is to improve the safety of navigation in converging areas and in areas where the density of traffic is great or where freedom of movement of shipping is inhibited by restricted sea-room, the existence of obstructions to navigation, limited depths or unfavourable meteorological conditions. Ships' routeing may also be used for the purpose of preventing or reducing the risk of pollution or other damage to the marine environment caused by ships colliding or grounding or anchoring in or near environmentally sensitive areas.

1.2 The precise objectives of any routeing system will depend upon the particular hazardous circumstances which it is intended to alleviate, but may include some or all of the following:

.1 the separation of opposing streams of traffic so as to reduce the incidence of head-on encounters;

.2 the reduction of dangers of collision between crossing traffic and shipping in established traffic lanes;

.3 the simplification of the patterns of traffic flow in converging areas;

.4 the organization of safe traffic flow in areas of concentrated offshore exploration or exploitation;

.5 the organization of traffic flow in or around areas where navigation by all ships or by certain classes of ship is dangerous or undesirable;

.6 the organization of safe traffic flow in or around or at a safe distance from environmentally sensitive areas;

.7 the reduction of risk of grounding by providing special guidance to vessels in areas where water depths are uncertain or critical; and

.8 the guidance of traffic clear of fishing grounds or the organization of traffic through fishing grounds.

2 Definitions

2.1 The following terms are used in connection with matters related to ships' routeing:

.1 *Routeing system*

Any system of one or more routes or routeing measures aimed at reducing the risk of casualties; it includes traffic separation schemes, two-way routes, recommended tracks, areas to be avoided, no anchoring areas, inshore traffic zones, roundabouts, precautionary areas and deep-water routes.

.2 *Mandatory routeing system*

A routeing system adopted by the Organization, in accordance with the requirements of regulation V/10 of the International Convention for the Safety of Life at Sea 1974, for mandatory use by all ships, certain categories of ships or ships carrying certain cargoes.

.3 *Traffic separation scheme**

A routeing measure aimed at the separation of opposing streams of traffic by appropriate means and by the establishment of traffic lanes.

.4 *Separation zone or line**

A zone or line separating the traffic lanes in which ships are proceeding in opposite or nearly opposite directions; or separating a traffic lane from the adjacent sea area; or separating traffic lanes designated for particular classes of ship proceeding in the same direction.

* These terms are used in the 1972 Collision Regulations.

.5 *Traffic lane*[*]

An area within defined limits in which one-way traffic is established. Natural obstacles, including those forming separation zones, may constitute a boundary.

.6 *Roundabout*

A routeing measure comprising a separation point or circular separation zone and a circular traffic lane within defined limits. Traffic within the roundabout is separated by moving in a counterclockwise direction around the separation point or zone.

.7 *Inshore traffic zone*[*]

A routeing measure comprising a designated area between the landward boundary of a traffic separation scheme and the adjacent coast, to be used in accordance with the provisions of rule 10(d), as amended, of the International Regulations for Preventing Collisions at Sea, 1972 (Collision Regulations).

.8 *Two-way route*

A route within defined limits inside which two-way traffic is established, aimed at providing safe passage of ships through waters where navigation is difficult or dangerous.

.9 *Recommended route*

A route of undefined width, for the convenience of ships in transit, which is often marked by centreline buoys.

.10 *Recommended track*

A route which has been specially examined to ensure so far as possible that it is free of dangers and along which ships are advised to navigate.

.11 *Deep-water route*

A route within defined limits which has been accurately surveyed for clearance of sea bottom and submerged obstacles as indicated on the chart.

.12 *Precautionary area*

A routeing measure comprising an area within defined limits where ships must navigate with particular caution and within which the direction of traffic flow may be recommended.

.13 *Area to be avoided*

A routeing measure comprising an area within defined limits in which either navigation is particularly hazardous or it is exceptionally important to avoid casualties and which should be avoided by all ships, or certain classes of ship.

.14 *No anchoring area*

A routeing measure comprising an area within defined limits where anchoring is hazardous or could result in unacceptable damage to the marine environment. Anchoring in a no anchoring area should be avoided by all ships or certain classes of ships, except in case of immediate danger to the ship or the persons on board.

.15 *Established direction of traffic flow*

A traffic flow pattern indicating the directional movement of traffic as established within a traffic separation scheme.

.16 *Recommended direction of traffic flow*

A traffic flow pattern indicating a recommended directional movement of traffic where it is impractical or unnecessary to adopt an established direction of traffic flow.

[*] These terms are used in the 1972 Collision Regulations.

A

3 Procedures and responsibilities

Procedures and functions of IMO

3.1 IMO is recognized as the only international body responsible for establishing and adopting measures on an international level concerning ships' routeing systems for use by all ships, certain categories of ships or ships carrying certain cargoes or types and quantities of bunker fuel.

3.2 In deciding whether or not to adopt or amend a traffic separation scheme, IMO will consider whether:

- .1 the aids to navigation proposed will enable mariners to determine their position with sufficient accuracy to navigate in the scheme in accordance with rule 10 of the 1972 Collision Regulations, as amended;
- .2 the state of hydrographic surveys in the area is adequate;*
- .3 the scheme takes account of the accepted planning considerations and complies with the design criteria for traffic separation schemes and with established methods of routeing.

3.3 In deciding whether or not to adopt or amend a routeing system other than a traffic separation scheme, IMO will consider whether the aids to navigation and the state of hydrographic surveys are adequate for the purpose of the system.*

3.4 IMO shall not adopt or amend any routeing system without the agreement of the interested coastal States, where that system may affect:

- .1 their rights and practices in respect of the exploitation of living and mineral resources;
- .2 the environment, traffic pattern or established routeing systems in the waters concerned; and
- .3 demands for improvements or adjustments in the navigational aids or hydrographic surveys in the waters concerned.

3.5 In deciding whether or not to adopt or amend a mandatory routeing system, IMO will, in addition to the provisions of paragraphs 3.2, 3.3, as appropriate, and 3.4, consider whether:

- .1 proper and sufficient justification for the establishment of a mandatory routeing system has been provided by the sponsoring Government or Governments; and
- .2 ports or harbours of littoral States would be adversely affected.

3.6 In deciding whether or not to adopt or amend a routeing system which is intended to protect the marine environment, IMO will consider whether:

- .1 the proposed routeing system can reasonably be expected to significantly prevent or reduce the risk of pollution or other damage to the marine environment of the area concerned;
- .2 given the overall size of the area to be protected, or the aggregate number of environmentally sensitive areas established or identified in the geographical region concerned, the use of routeing systems – particularly areas to be avoided – could have the effect of unreasonably limiting the sea area available for navigation; and
- .3 the proposed routeing system meets the requirements of these General Provisions.

3.7 IMO will not adopt a proposed routeing system until is is satisfied that the proposed system will not impose unnecessary constraints on shipping and is completely in accordance with the requirements of regulation V/10, paragraph 9 of the SOLAS Convention. In particular, an area to be avoided will not be adopted if it would impede the passage of ships through an international strait.

Responsibilities of Governments and recommended and compulsory practices

3.8 A new or amended routeing system adopted by IMO shall not come into force as an IMO adopted system before an effective date promulgated by the Government that proposed the system, which shall be

* The minimum standards to which hydrographic surveys are to be conducted, to verify the accuracy of charted depths in the traffic lanes of a proposed or amended traffic separation scheme or in a deep-water route or other routeing measure, are those defined in Special Publication No. 44 of the International Hydrographic Organization, *IHO Standards for Hydrographic Surveys*.

communicated to IMO by the responsible Government. That date shall not be earlier than six months after the date of adoption of a routeing system by IMO but, when new chart editions necessitate a substantially longer period between adoption and implementation, IMO shall set a later date as required by the circumstances of the case. If the Government that proposed the system is unable at the time of adoption by IMO to declare a definite date of implementation, this information should be communicated to IMO as soon as possible thereafter and the implementation date then declared should not be earlier than four months after the date on which the declaration is made; in the case of a traffic separation scheme the exact time of implementation should also be stated. If there is a protracted delay in making such a declaration, the Government concerned should periodically inform IMO of the situation and forecast when implementation is likely to be possible. Either Notices to Mariners to amend charts, or revised charts to depict the system, shall be made available in ample time before the system comes into force.

3.9 The responsible Government implementing a new or amended routeing system should ensure that full and final details of planned changes to aids to navigation, anchorage areas or pilot boarding areas which are closely associated with the system and important to its effective utilization by the mariner are provided to the appropriate hydrographic authority at least six months prior to the date of implementation.

3.10 When establishing or amending a routeing system in a particular area where two or more Governments have a common interest, they should formulate joint proposals for adoption by IMO in accordance with SOLAS chapter V, regulation 10.5.

3.11 A Government, or Governments jointly, proposing a new routeing system or an amendment to an adopted system, any part of which lies beyond its or their territorial sea, should consult IMO so that such system may be adopted or amended by IMO for international use. Such Government or Governments should furnish all relevant information, in particular with regard to:

.1 the objectives of the proposed routeing system and a demonstrated need for its establishment, including the consideration of alternative routeing measures and the reasons why the proposed routeing system is preferred;

.2 the traffic pattern, hazards to navigation, aids to navigation and the state of hydrographic surveys;

.3 marine environmental considerations;

.4 the application to all ships, certain categories of ships or ships carrying certain cargoes or types and quantities of bunker fuel of a routeing system or any part thereof;

.5 any alternative routeing measure, if necessary, for all ships, certain categories of ships or ships carrying certain cargoes which may be excluded from using a routeing system or any part thereof; and

.6 the delineation of the routeing system as shown on a nautical chart (type of nautical chart as appropriate) and a description of the system including the geographical co-ordinates. The co-ordinates should be given in the WGS 84 datum; in addition, geographical co-ordinates should also be given in the same datum as the nautical chart, if this chart is based on a datum other than WGS 84.

3.12 Governments are recommended to ensure, as far as practicable, that drilling rigs (MODUs), exploration platforms and other similar structures are not established within the traffic lanes of routeing systems adopted by IMO or near their terminations. When the temporary positioning of a drilling rig or a similar structure in a traffic lane of an adopted traffic separation scheme cannot be avoided, the system should, if necessary, be amended temporarily in accordance with the guidelines given in section 7. In the case of mandatory routeing systems, Governments should ensure that drilling rigs (MODUs), exploration platforms and other structures obstructing navigation and not being an aid to navigation will not be established within the traffic lanes of a traffic separation scheme being part of a mandatory routeing system.

3.13 If the above exploration activities lead to the finding of important exploitation prospects, the effect of subsequent exploitation on the safety of marine traffic should be considered carefully. If the establishment of permanent installations within a traffic separation scheme is unavoidable, permanent amendments to the scheme, if deemed necessary, should be submitted to IMO for adoption.

3.14 Governments establishing routeing systems, no part of which lies beyond their territorial seas or in straits used for international navigation, are requested to design them in accordance with IMO guidelines and criteria for such schemes and submit them to IMO for adoption.

3.15 Where, for whatever reason, a Government decides not to submit a routeing system to IMO, it should, in promulgating the system to mariners, ensure that there are clear indications on charts and in nautical publications as to what rules apply to the system.

3.16 Governments establishing routeing systems, other than traffic separation schemes, no parts of which lie beyond their territorial seas, are recommended to follow the same procedure as that set out in paragraphs 3.14 and 3.15 above.

3.17 A routeing system, when adopted by IMO, shall not be amended or suspended before consultation with and agreement by IMO unless local conditions or the urgency of the case, as described in paragraph 3.19, require that earlier action be taken. In considering the proposal, IMO shall take account of the objectives, procedures, responsibilities, methods and criteria for routeing systems as set out in these General Provisions. A mandatory routeing system, when adopted by IMO, shall not be temporarily amended or suspended except in urgent cases as described in paragraph 3.19.

3.18 Mandatory routeing systems should be reviewed, as necessary, by the Government or Governments concerned, taking into account pertinent comments, reports and observations on the routeing system. Elements under review might include variations to traffic patterns, offshore exploration and exploitation, hydrographical changes, effectiveness of aids to navigation and other developments.

3.19 In an emergency such as might result from the unexpected blocking or obstruction of a traffic lane or any other part of a routeing system by a wreck or other hazard, immediate temporary changes in the use of the affected traffic separation scheme or other routeing system may be made by the responsible and sponsoring Government or Governments, with the objective of directing traffic flow clear of the new hazard. In such cases, every possible measure shall be taken by the Government or Governments concerned to immediately inform shipping of the hazard and of the temporary changes which have been made.

The responsible and sponsoring Government or Governments should inform IMO as soon as possible of any such changes and their justification.

3.20 By rules 10(k) and 10(l) respectively of the 1972 Collision Regulations, a vessel restricted in its ability to manoeuvre when engaged in an operation for either the maintenance of safety of navigation or the laying, servicing or picking up of a submarine cable in a traffic separation scheme is exempted from complying with rule 10 to the extent necessary to carry out the operation. The Government or authority responsible for safety of navigation in a traffic separation scheme should ensure that:

.1 the intention of undertaking such an operation is first notified to each Government or appropriate authority concerned;

.2 information about such ships working in a traffic separation scheme is, as far as practicable, promulgated in advance by Notice to Mariners, and subsequently by radionavigation warnings broadcast before and at regular intervals during the operations; and

.3 such operations are, as far as possible, avoided in conditions of restricted visibility.

4 Methods

In meeting the objectives set out in section 1, the following are among the methods which may be used:

4.1 *The separation of opposing streams of traffic by separation zones, or lines where zones are not possible*

In this method, streams of traffic proceeding in opposite or nearly opposite directions are separated by separation zones (4) or lines (3); the use of zones is to be preferred, but in narrow passages and restricted waters it may be necessary to use a separation line rather than a zone so as to allow more navigable space in the traffic lanes. A length of separation line may also be substituted for a zone in positions where this may encourage and facilitate correct procedures by crossing traffic. The outside limits (6) of such traffic separation schemes are the outer boundaries of the traffic lanes. The arrows (1) indicate the established direction of traffic flow.

4.2 *The separation of opposing streams of traffic by natural obstructions and geographically defined objects*

This method is used where there is a defined area with obstructions such as islands, shoals or rocks restricting free movement and providing a natural division for opposing traffic streams.

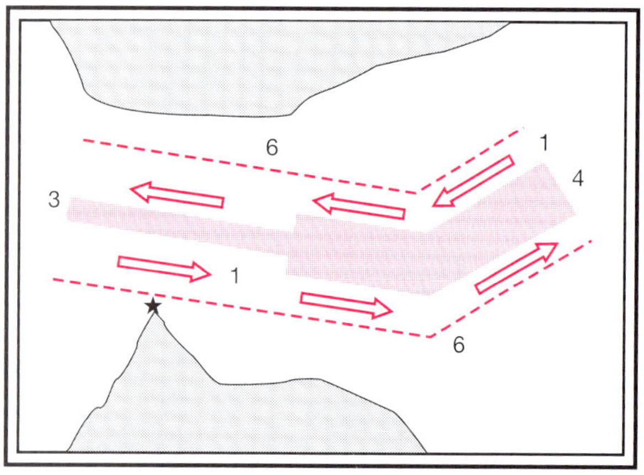

Figure 1 – *Traffic separation by separation zone and line*

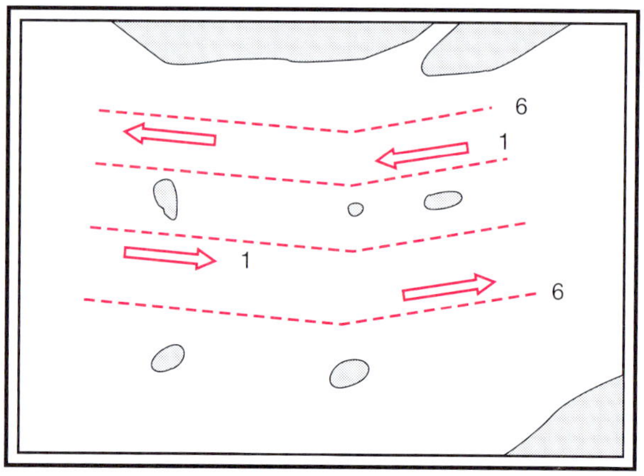

Figure 2 – *Separation of traffic by natural obstructions*

4.3 *The separation of through and local traffic by providing inshore traffic zones*

Beyond the outside limits of traffic separation schemes, ships may navigate in any direction. Where such areas lie between the traffic separation scheme and the coast they may be designated as inshore traffic zones (see also figures 4 and 10), with the purpose of keeping local traffic clear of the traffic separation scheme which should be used by through traffic.

Traffic in inshore traffic zones is separated from traffic in the adjacent traffic lane by separation zones (4) or by separation lines (3) (see also figures 4 and 10).

4.4 *The sectorial division of adjacent traffic separation schemes at approaches to focal points*

This method is used where ships converge at a focal point or a small area from various directions. Port approaches, sea pilot stations, positions where landfall buoys or lightvessels are located, entrances to channels, canals, estuaries, etc., may be considered as such focal points.

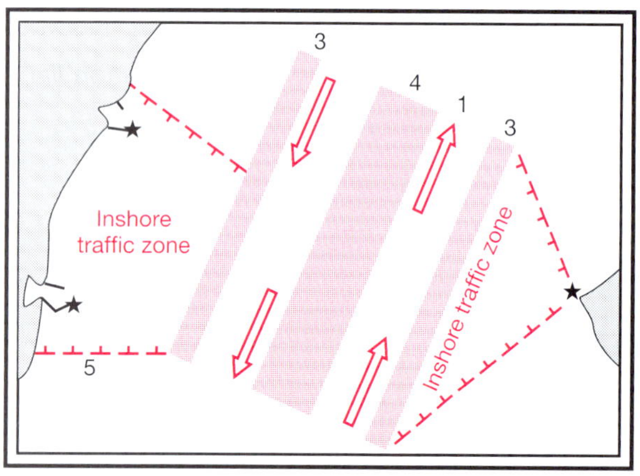

Figure 3 – *Inshore traffic zones*

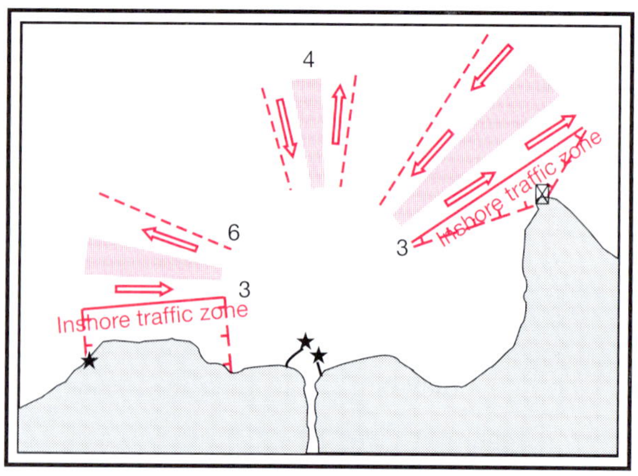

Figure 4 – *Sectorial division of adjacent traffic separation schemes at approaches to focal points*

4.5 *The routeing of traffic at focal points and route junctions where traffic separation schemes meet*

The routeing measure to be utilized at focal points, route junctions and intersections should be selected from the most appropriate of the following methods:

.1 *Roundabouts*

If the need can be demonstrated, a roundabout may be used to guide traffic counterclockwise round a circular separation zone (4) or specified point, as illustrated in figure 5.

.2 *Junctions*

These methods are used where two routes join or cross. The directions of traffic flow are established in the lanes of the adjoining schemes; the separation zone may be interrupted, as shown in figures 6 and 7, or replaced by a separation line, as shown in figure 8, in order to emphasize the correct method of crossing by traffic changing from one scheme to the other.

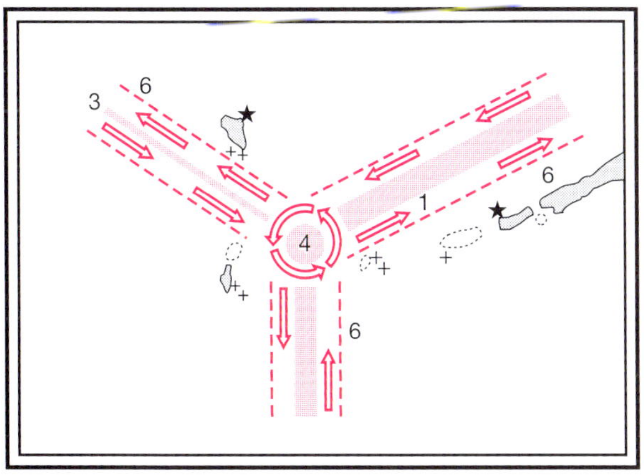

Figure 5 – *Separation of traffic at a roundabout*

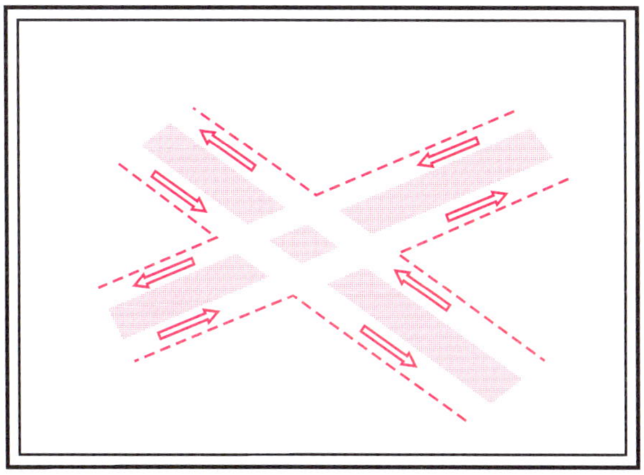

Figure 6 – *Separation of traffic at a crossing*

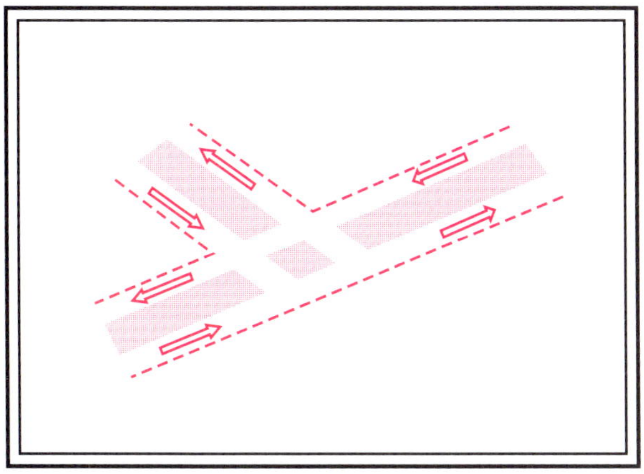

Figure 7 – *Separation of traffic at a junction*

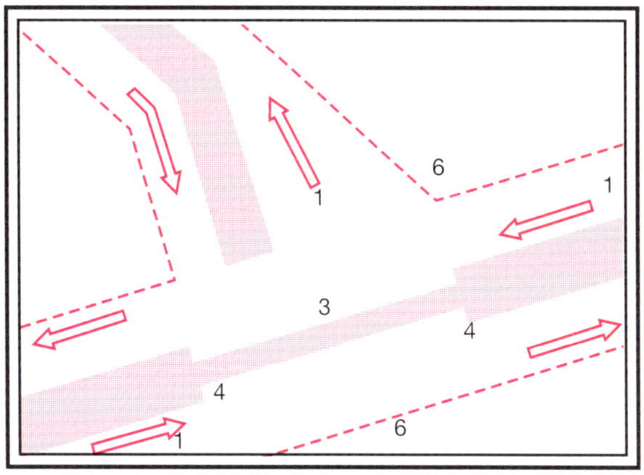

Figure 8 – *A junction, showing a separation line substituted for a zone, where there will be crossing traffic*

.3 *Precautionary areas*

It may be best, when routes converge, to terminate them clear of their potential joining points and in such a case a precautionary area (9) can be instituted so as to emphasize the need for care in navigation. Figures 9 and 10 illustrate the use of such an area at focal points; a direction of traffic flow may be recommended (2) around the focal point, as shown in figure 10.

Figure 11 gives an example of how a precautionary area (9) can be used at a junction with crossing traffic. The traffic lanes are terminated short of the point where traffic is expected to cross and replaced by a precautionary area within which the recommended directions of traffic flow (2) are indicated.

Precautionary areas may also be used at the termination of any single route.

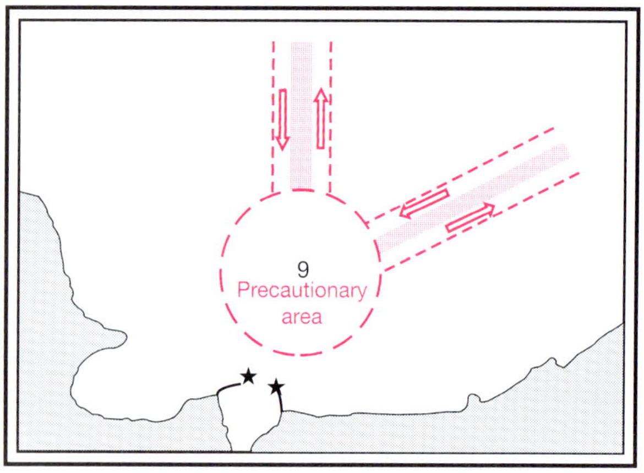

Figure 9 – *Precautionary area at a focal point*

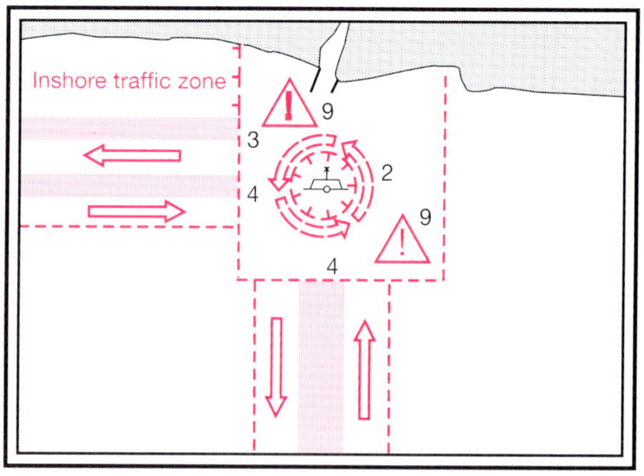

Figure 10 – *Precautionary area with recommended direction of traffic flow around an area to be avoided*

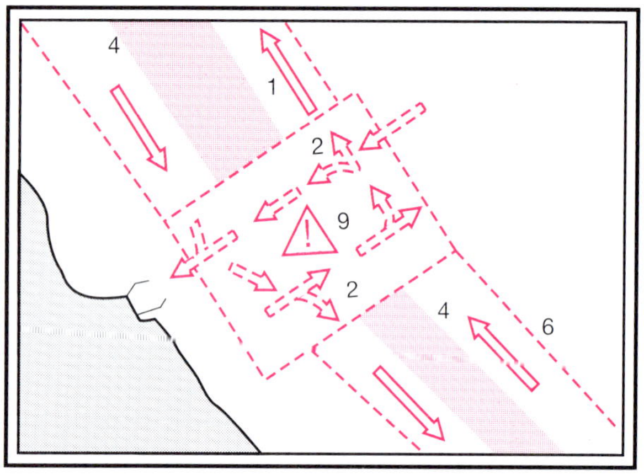

Figure 11 – *Precautionary area at a junction with recommended directions of traffic flow*

4.6 *Other routeing methods*

Other routeing methods which may be used are as shown in the figures below:

.1 *Deep-water routes* (figures 12 and 13);

.2 *Areas to be avoided* (figures 10 and 18);

.3 *Recommended directions of traffic flow* (figure 14), *two-way routes* (figure 15) and *recommended routes and tracks through areas where navigation is difficult or dangerous* (figures 16 and 17);

.4 *No anchoring areas* (figure 19).

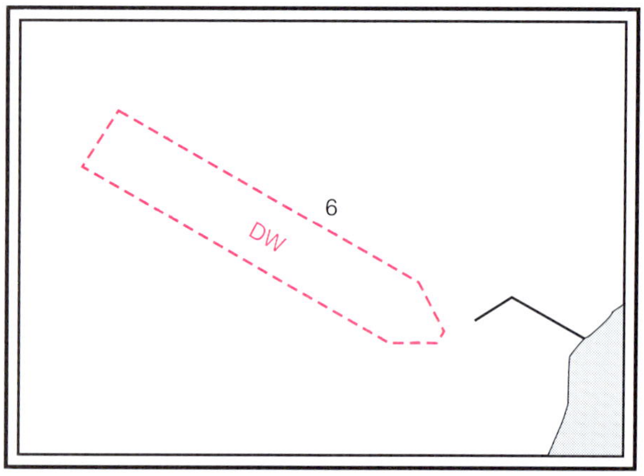

Figure 12 – *Deep-water route (two-way)*

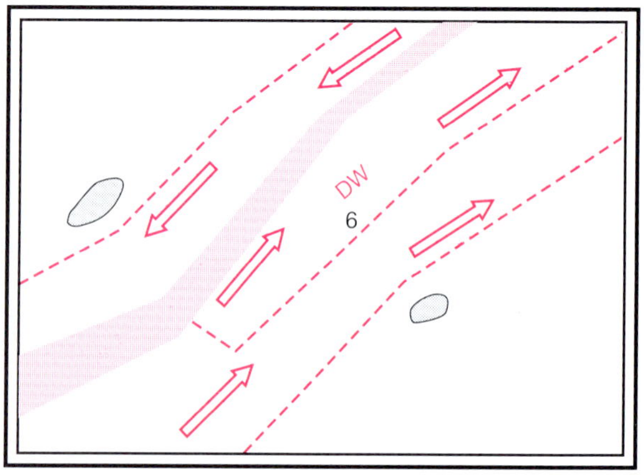

Figure 13 – *One-way deep-water route (within a traffic lane)*

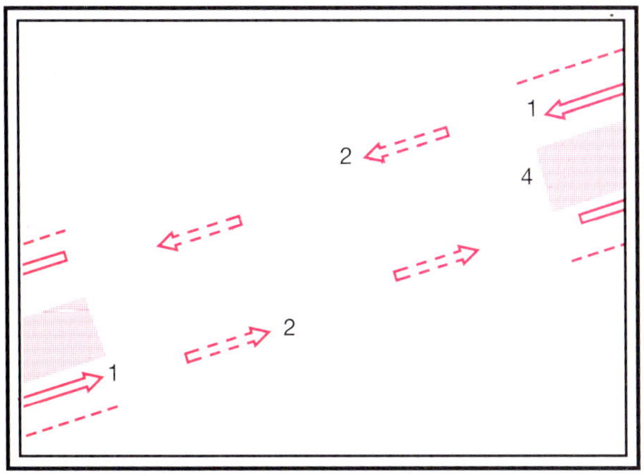

Figure 14 – *Recommended directions of traffic flow between two traffic separation schemes*

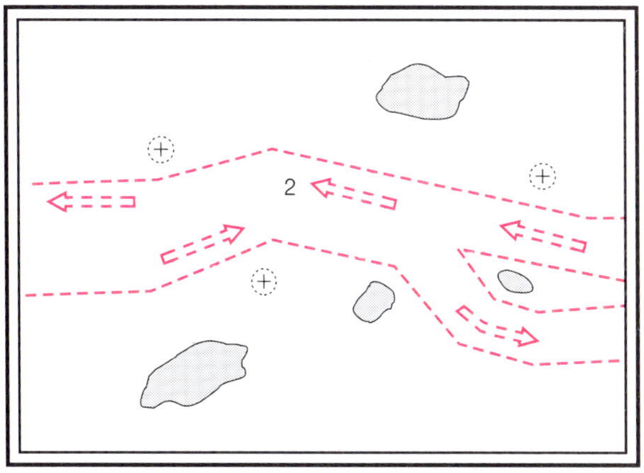

Figure 15 – *Two-way route (with one-way sections)*

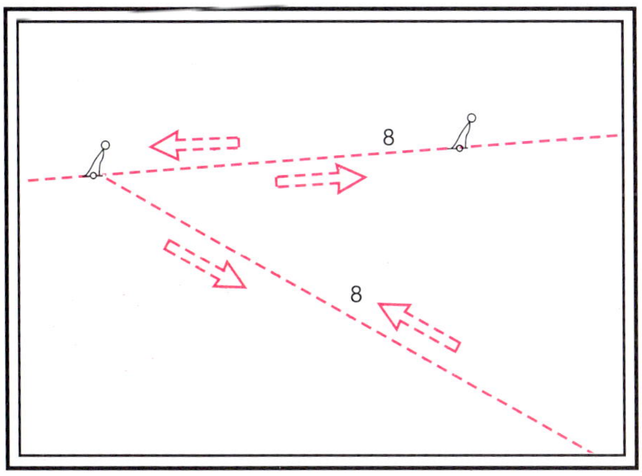

Figure 16 – *Recommended routes*

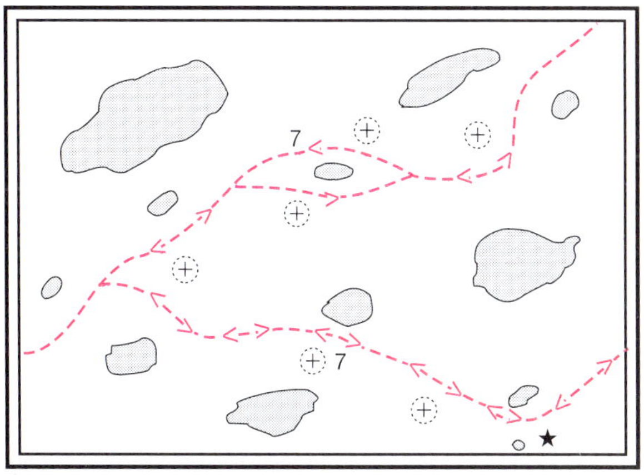

Figure 17 – *Recommended tracks (in black)*

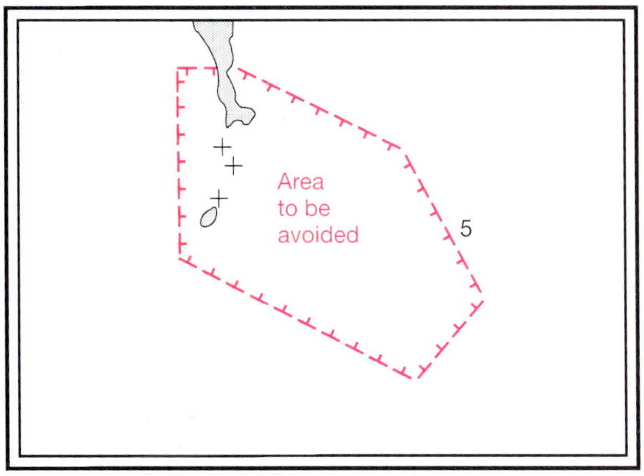

Figure 18 – *Area to be avoided*

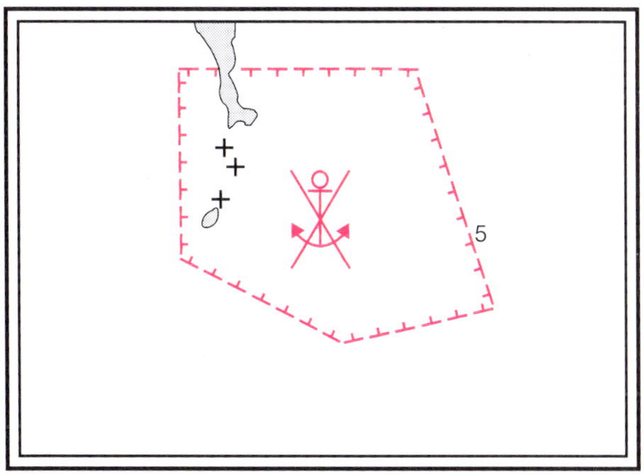

Figure 19 – *No anchoring area*

5 Planning

5.1 The routeing system selected for a particular area should aim at providing safe passage for ships through the area without unduly restricting legitimate rights and practices, and taking account of anticipated or existing navigational hazards.

5.2 When planning, establishing, reviewing or adjusting a routeing system, the following factors shall be among those taken into account by a Government:

.1 their rights and practices in respect of the exploitation of living and mineral resources;

.2 previously established routeing systems in adjacent waters, whether or not under the proposing Government's jurisdiction;

.3 the existing traffic pattern in the area concerned, including coastal traffic, crossing traffic, naval exercise areas and anchorage areas;

.4 foreseeable changes in the traffic pattern resulting from port or offshore terminal developments;

.5 the presence of fishing grounds;

.6 existing activities and foreseeable developments of offshore exploration or exploitation of the sea-bed and subsoil;

.7 the adequacy of existing aids to navigation, hydrographic surveys and nautical charts of the area;

.8 environmental factors, including prevailing weather conditions, tidal streams and currents and the possibility of ice concentrations; and

.9 the existence of environmental conservation areas and foreseeable developments in the establishment of such areas.

5.3 A Government or Governments planning, implementing and maintaining mandatory routeing systems should consider whether, because of the particular circumstances in the area or parts of the area concerned, an associated monitoring service, a reporting service or VTS should be established in accordance with the guidelines adopted by IMO for such services*, as appropriate.

5.4 Routeing systems should not be established in areas where the instability of the sea-bed is such that frequent changes in the alignment and positions of the main channels, and thus of the routeing system itself, are likely.

5.5 When establishing areas to be avoided by all ships or by certain classes of ship, the necessity for creating such areas should be well demonstrated and the reasons stated. In general, these areas should be established only in places where inadequate survey or insufficient provision of aids to navigation may lead to danger of stranding, or where local knowledge is considered essential for safe passage, or where there is the possibility that unacceptable damage to the environment could result from a casualty, or where there might be hazard to a vital aid to navigation. These areas shall not be regarded as prohibited areas unless specifically so stated; the classes of ship which should avoid the areas should be considered in each particular case.

5.6 When establishing a no anchoring area for all ships or certain classes of ships, the necessity for creating such an area should be well demonstrated and the reasons stated. In general, these areas should be established only in areas where anchoring is hazardous, or where there is a possibility that unacceptable damage to the marine environment could result. The classes of ships which should avoid anchoring in an area should be considered and clearly identified in each particular case.

5.7 Governments considering establishing a new routeing system or amending an existing one should consult at an early stage with:

.1 mariners using the area;

.2 authorities responsible for aids to navigation and for hydrographic surveys and nautical publications;

.3 port authorities; and

.4 organizations concerned with fishing, offshore exploration or exploitation and environmental protection, as appropriate.

This consultation process is implied in paragraphs 3.4, 3.11, 5.2, 5.5 and 6.2.

6 Design criteria

6.1 The following standards should, so far as the circumstances allow, be applied in the design of ships' routeing measures.

---

* Refer to resolution MSC.43(64), Guidelines and criteria for ship reporting systems, as amended by resolutions MSC.111(73) and MSC.189(79), and resolution A.857(20), Guidelines for vessel traffic services, as amended.

General

6.2 Routes should follow as closely as possible the existing patterns of traffic flow in the areas as determined by traffic surveys.

6.3 The configuration and length of routeing systems which are established to provide for an unobstructed passage through offshore exploration and exploitation areas may differ from the dimensions of normally established systems if the purpose of safeguarding a clear passage warrants such a special feature.

6.4 Course alterations along a route should be as few as possible and should be avoided in the approaches to convergence areas and route junctions or where crossing traffic may be expected to be heavy.

6.5 The number of convergence areas and route junctions should be kept to a minimum, and should be as widely separated from each other as possible. Adjacent traffic separation schemes should be placed such that nearly opposing streams of traffic in the adjacent schemes are separated as widely as possible. Route junctions should not be located where concentrated crossing traffic, not following established routes, may be expected, e.g. ferry traffic.

6.6 Routes should be designed to allow optimum use of aids to navigation in the area, and of such shipborne navigational aids as are required or recommended to be fitted by international conventions or by IMO resolutions and recommendations.

6.7 The state of hydrographic surveys within the limits of a routeing system and in the approaches thereto should be such that full information on existing depths of water and hazards to surface navigation is available to nautical charting authorities.

Traffic separation schemes

6.8 Traffic separation schemes shall be designed so as to enable ships using them to fully comply at all times with the International Regulations for Preventing Collisions at Sea, 1972, as amended.

6.9 A traffic separation scheme (TSS) may be part of a routeing system, including other routes or routeing measures. However, for compliance with the International Regulations for Preventing Collisions at Sea, 1972, as amended, it is essential to describe each TSS or part of TSS separately and under its own specific heading. Any other routeing measure or route forming part of a routeing system, including one or more traffic separation scheme(s), should also be described separately under its own specific heading.

6.10 The extent of a traffic separation scheme should be limited to what is essential in the interests of safe navigation.

6.11 Traffic lanes should be designed to make optimum use of available depths of water and the safe navigable areas, taking into account the maximum depth of water attainable along the length of the route. The width of lanes should take account of the traffic density, the general usage of the area and the sea-room available.

6.12 Where there is sufficient space, separation zones should be used in preference to separation lines to separate opposing streams of traffic and to segregate inshore traffic zones from adjacent traffic lanes. Separation zones or lines may also be used to separate a traffic lane from adjacent sea areas other than inshore traffic zones, in appropriate circumstances, taking into account traffic density and the available means of fixing ships' positions.

6.13 *Position fixing*

6.13.1 It should be possible for ships to fix their position anywhere within the limits of and in the immediate approaches to a traffic separation scheme by one or more of the following means, both by day and by night:

.1 visual bearing of readily identifiable objects;

.2 radar bearings and ranges of readily identifiable objects;

.3 D/F bearings; and

.4 other radionavigation equipment suitable for use throughout the intended voyage.

A

6.13.2 The position fixing of ships may be supplemented or substituted by shore-based radar and radio direction-finder systems to assist ships which have difficulty to accurately establish their position with the means prescribed under 6.13.1. Such shore-based systems should be approved by IMO before they are recognized as a position-fixing system for supporting the safety of navigation in or near traffic separation schemes.

6.14 When it is considered essential to provide within a traffic separation scheme an additional lane for ships carrying hazardous liquid substances in bulk, as specified in the International Convention for the Prevention of Pollution from Ships, 1973, as modified by the Protocol of 1978 relating thereto, in circumstances where it is not possible for ships to fix their position as set out in paragraph 6.13 over the whole area of that lane and an electronic position-fixing system covers that area, the existence of that system may be taken into account when designing the scheme.

6.15 The minimum widths of traffic lanes and of traffic separation zones should be related to the accuracy of the available position-fixing methods, accepting the appropriate performance standards for shipborne equipment as set out in IMO resolutions and recommendations.

6.16 Where space allows the use of traffic separation zones, the width of the zone should, if possible, be not less than three times the transverse component of the standard error (measured across the separation zone) of the most appropriate of the position-fixing methods listed in paragraph 6.13. Where necessary or desirable, and where practicable, additional separation should be provided to ensure that there will be adequate early indication that traffic proceeding in the opposite direction will pass on the correct side.

6.17 If there is doubt as to the ability of ships to fix their positions positively and without ambiguity in relation to separation lines or zones, serious consideration should be given to providing adequate marking by buoys.

Mandatory routeing systems

6.18 The extent of a mandatory routeing system should be limited to what is essential in the interest of safety of navigation and the protection of the marine environment.

6.19 It shall be possible for ships to fix their positions in relation to a mandatory routeing system by one or more of the means mentioned in paragraph 6.13 of this section.

Converging and junction areas

6.20 Whichever of the several available routeing methods is chosen for use at a route junction or in a converging area, it must be a cardinal principle that any ambiguity or possible source of confusion in the application of the 1972 Collision Regulations must be avoided. This principle should be particularly borne in mind when establishing or recommending the direction of traffic flow in such areas. If recommended directions of traffic flow are adopted, these should take full account of the existing pattern of traffic flow in the area concerned, and also of all other applicable provisions of ships' routeing.

6.21 At route junctions the following particular considerations apply:

.1 the need to encourage the crossing of traffic lanes as nearly as possible at right angles;

.2 the need to give ships which may be required to give way under the 1972 Collision Regulations as much room to manoeuvre as possible;

.3 the need to enable a stand-on vessel to maintain a steady course, as required by the 1972 Collision Regulations, for as long as possible before the route junction; and

.4 the need to encourage traffic not following an established route to avoid crossing at or near route junctions.

Deep-water routes

6.22 In designing deep-water routes, consideration should be given to marking critical turning points. Any wrecks or sea-bed obstructions which lie within the limits of a deep-water route and which have less depth of water over them than the minimum depth of water for the route as indicated on the charts, should be marked.

7 Temporary adjustments and suspensions

Traffic separation schemes

7.1 When the temporary positioning of an exploration rig is unavoidable, the design criteria and the provisions for planning should be taken into account before permitting the positioning of the rig or subsequently adjusting a traffic separation scheme.

7.2 The said adjustments should be made in accordance with the following:

.1 when the drilling location is situated near the boundary of a traffic lane or separation zone, a relatively slight adjustment of the scheme could have such effect that the drilling rig and its associated safety zone are sufficiently clear of the traffic lane;

Example

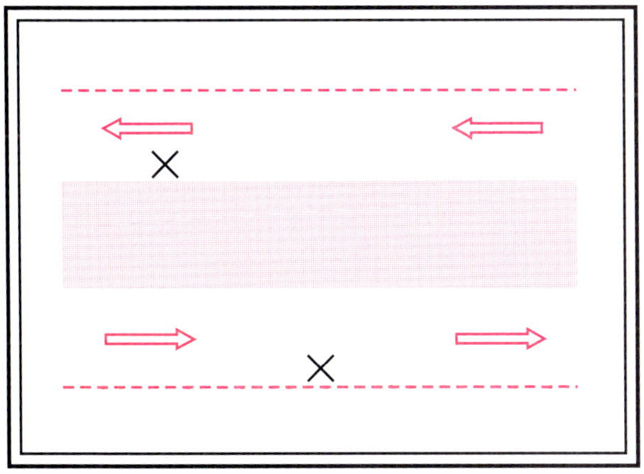

Original situation

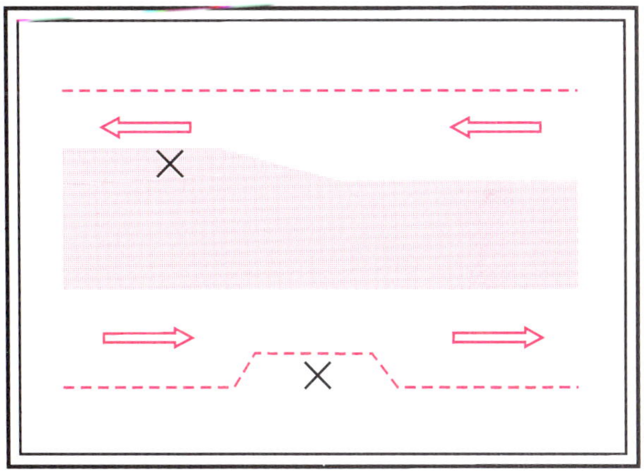

Adapted situation

.2 if a small temporary adjustment of the traffic lane is not possible the whole or part of the scheme could be temporarily shifted away from the drilling area so that traffic connected with the drilling operations will stay clear of the lane;

Example

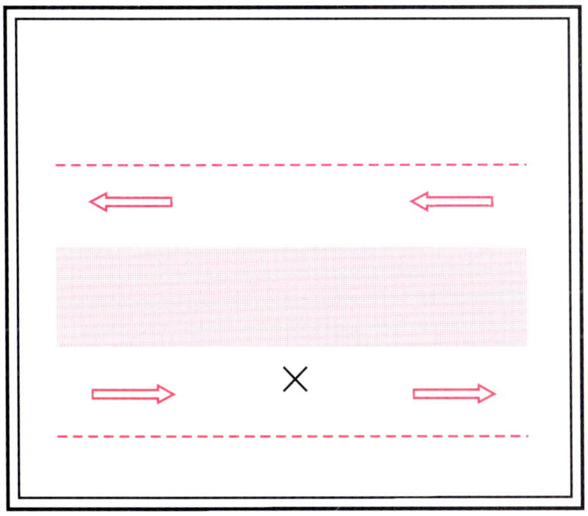

Original situation

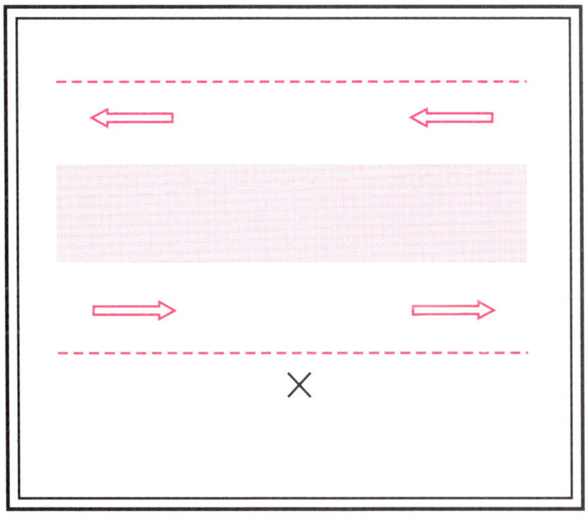

Adapted situation

.3 temporary local interruption of the scheme or part of the scheme in the area of location of the drilling rig. Such an interruption could be made a precautionary area;

Example

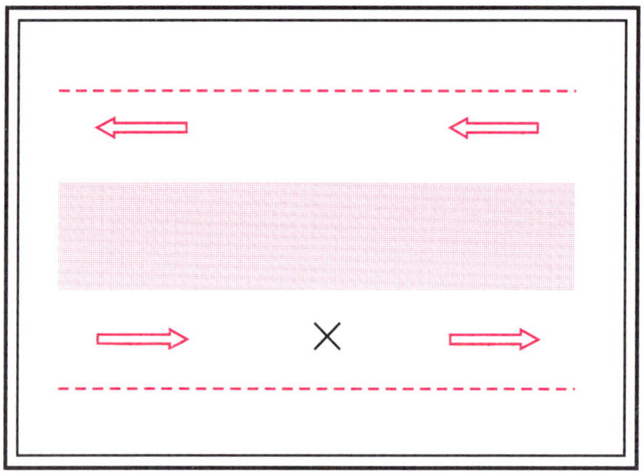

Original situation

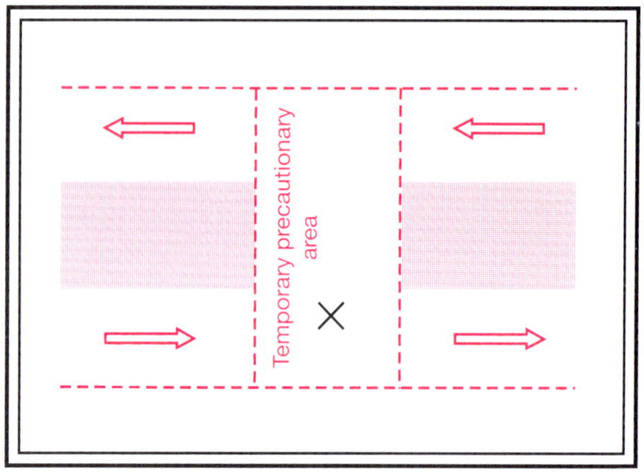

Adapted situation

.4 temporary suspension of the whole scheme.

7.3 In each case, exploration sites should be reviewed and such conditions specified as the responsible Government may deem necessary to ensure safety of navigation in the area.

7.4 Details of these temporary adjustments should be forwarded to IMO and to appropriate hydrographic offices at least four months before the rig is positioned within an adopted traffic separation scheme so as to allow ample time to inform shipping. When the duration of such temporary adjustments is expected to be six months or more, this should be made known to the relevant hydrographic authorities in order to allow appropriate action to be taken in notifying mariners.

7.5 In the event of a temporary adjustment to a traffic separation scheme remaining in force for more than one year, the responsible Government should consider whether permanent amendments to the scheme may ultimately become necessary and, if appropriate, initiate timely procedures for IMO to adopt such amendments.

Mandatory routeing systems

7.6 Mandatory routeing systems should not be temporarily adjusted. If necessary for the safety of navigation in the area concerned, a mandatory routeing system may be entirely or partly suspended by the Contracting Government or Governments which have implemented such systems. The responsible Government or Governments should inform IMO of such a suspension and promulgate details of the suspension by all appropriate means.

8 Use of routeing systems

8.1 Unless stated otherwise, routeing systems are recommended for use by all ships and may be made mandatory for all ships, certain categories of ships or ships carrying certain cargoes or types and quantities of bunker fuel.

8.2 Routeing systems are intended for use by day and by night in all weathers, in ice-free waters or under light ice conditions where no extraordinary manoeuvres or ice-breaker assistance are required.

8.3 Bearing in mind the need for adequate under-keel clearance, a decision to use a routeing system must take into account the charted depth, the possibility of changes in the sea-bed since the time of the last survey, and the effects of meteorological and tidal conditions on water depths.

8.4 A ship navigating in or near a traffic separation scheme adopted by IMO shall in particular comply with rule 10 of the 1972 Collision Regulations to minimize the development of risk of collision with another ship. The other rules of the 1972 Collision Regulations apply in all respects, and particularly the rules of part B, sections II and III, if risk of collision with another ship is deemed to exist.

8.5 At junction points where traffic from various directions meets, a true separation of traffic is not really possible, as ships may need to cross routes or change to another route. Ships should therefore navigate with great caution in such areas and be aware that the mere fact that a ship is proceeding along a through-going route gives that ship no special privilege or right of way.

8.6 A deep-water route is primarily intended for use by ships which, because of their draught in relation to the available depth of water in the area concerned, require the use of such a route. Through traffic to which the above consideration does not apply should, as far as practicable, avoid using deep-water routes.

8.7 Precautionary areas should be avoided, if practicable, by passing ships not making use of the associated traffic separation schemes or deep-water routes, or entering or leaving adjacent ports.

8.8 In two-way routes, including two-way deep-water routes, ships should as far as practicable keep to the starboard side.

8.9 Arrows printed on charts in connection with routeing systems merely indicate the general direction of established or recommended traffic flow; ships need not set their courses strictly along the arrows.

8.10 The signal *YG*, meaning *You appear not to be complying with the traffic separation scheme*, is provided in the International Code of Signals for appropriate use.

9 Representation on charts

9.1 The legends, symbols and notes appearing in paragraphs 9.2, 9.3, 9.4 and 9.5 are recommended by the International Hydrographic Organization as guidance for the representation of details of routeing systems and associated measures on nautical charts. They are included to illustrate the information likely to be found on charts and as an aid to those designing proposed routeing systems for adoption by IMO.

9.2 *Use of legends on charts and in notes*

Legend	Use of legend
Traffic separation scheme	Not usually shown on charts. Referred to in notes.
Inshore traffic zone	Shown on charts and referred to in notes.
Precautionary area	May be shown on charts in lieu of the symbol and referred to in notes.
Deep-water route	DW is shown on charts to indicate the deep water; *DW* or *deep-water route* is referred to in notes.
Area to be avoided	Shown on charts and referred to in notes.
Two-way route	Not usually shown on charts but referred to in notes.
Recommended route	Not usually shown on charts but referred to in notes.
Recommended track	Not usually shown on charts but referred to in notes.
Mandatory routeing system	Not usually shown on charts but referred to in notes.
No anchoring area	Shown on charts and referred to in notes.

9.3 *Symbols for basic elements of routeing measures*

Unless otherwise specified, symbols are printed on charts in colour, usually magenta.

Routeing term	Symbol	Description	Applications	Notes and paragraph references
1 Established direction of traffic flow		Outlined arrow	Traffic separation schemes and deep-water routes (when part of a traffic lane)	(1), (2)
2 Recommended direction of traffic flow		Dashed outlined arrow	Precautionary areas, two-way routes, recommended routes and deep-water routes	(1)
3 Separation lines		Tint, 3 mm wide	Traffic separation schemes and between traffic separation schemes and inshore traffic zones	(3), (4) and paragraph 9.4
4 Separation zones		Tint, may be any shape	Traffic separation schemes and between traffic separation schemes and inshore traffic zones	(4), (5) and paragraph 9.4
5 Limits of restricted areas (charting term)		T-shaped dashes	Areas to be avoided, no anchoring areas and ends of inshore traffic zones	(6) and paragraph 9.4
6 General maritime limits (charting term)		Dashed line	Traffic separation schemes, precautionary areas, two-way routes and deep-water routes	
7 Recommended tracks: one-way two-way	--<------- --<--->---	Dashed lines with arrowheads (colour black)	Generally reserved for use by charting authorities	(7)
8 Recommended routes		Dashed line and dashed outlined arrows	Recommended routes	
9 Precautionary areas		Precautionary symbol	Precautionary areas	(8)

Notes

(1) Arrows dispersed over width of route. Arrows may be curved. Where the traffic lane is converging, arrows should be oriented to the approximate average directions of the side boundaries.

(2) Arrow omitted at intersections (other than roundabouts) to avoid implying priority of one lane.

(3) Separation line 3 mm wide where chart scale permits.

(4) Tint light enough not to obscure detail beneath it.

(5) If traffic lanes are separated by natural obstacles, may be replaced by the symbol for general maritime limits at the boundaries of the lanes.

(6) Stems of dashes point towards the area in question.

(7) Symbol intended for tracks to be followed closely through inadequately surveyed areas.

(8) Legend Precautionary area may also be used within the precautionary area instead of the symbol.

For examples of routeing measures using these basic symbols see figures 1 to 19 in section 4.

9.4 *Boundary symbols in detail*

Example: Boundary symbol 8 means that the boundary, indicated by the line, between a precautionary area and an inshore traffic zone is to be shown by T-shaped dashes, with the stems of the T's pointing towards the ITZ.

1	Traffic separation scheme (ends) / Open sea	No boundary
2	Traffic separation scheme (sides) / Open sea	- - - - - - - - - - - - - - or  or  (zone)
3	Traffic separation scheme / Inshore traffic zone	 or 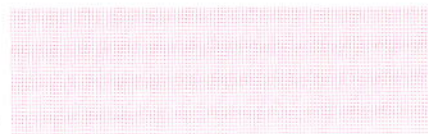 (zone)
4	Traffic separation scheme next to traffic separation scheme	No boundary
5	Inshore traffic zone (ends) / Open sea	⊥ ⊥ ⊥ ⊥ ⊥ ⊥ ⊥ ⊥ or no symbol (limits undefined)
6	Precautionary area / Open sea	- - - - - - - - - - - - - -
7	Precautionary area / Traffic separation scheme	- - - - - - - - - - - - - -
8	Precautionary area / Inshore traffic zone	⊤ ⊤ ⊤ ⊤ ⊤ ⊤ ⊤ ⊤
9	Deep-water route (sides) / Open sea	- - - - - - - - - - - - - -
10	Deep-water route (ends) / Open sea	- - - - - - - - - - - - - -
11	Deep-water route (ends) / Traffic separation scheme	- - - - - - - - - - - - - -
12	Deep-water route next to deep-water route	No boundary
13	Deep-water route (ends) / Precautionary area	- - - - - - - - - - - - - -
14	Deep-water route / Separation zone/line	 (Separation zone/line acts as boundary)
15	Two-way route / All other areas	Same rules as for deep-water route
16	Area to be avoided / All other areas	⊥ ⊥ ⊥ ⊥ ⊥ ⊥ ⊥ ⊥
17	No anchoring area / All other areas	⊥ ⊥ ⊥ ⊥ ⊥ ⊥ ⊥ ⊥

9.5 *Cautionary and explanatory notes on charts*

9.5.1 Traffic separation schemes and other routeing measures

The existence of special provisions applying to particular measures should be mentioned on the charts affected, if necessary referring mariners to the full text in Sailing Directions.

9.5.2 Deep-water routes

Where maintenance of a minimum depth can be guaranteed, the least depth (e.g. 22 m) may be given after the abbreviation DW. In other cases charted soundings will indicate the least depth, preferably in conjunction with a note giving the date of the latest survey.

9.5.3 Areas to be avoided

Notes on conditions governing avoidance of areas (classes and sizes of ships, nature of cargoes, etc.) should preferably be given on charts and should always be given in Sailing Directions.

9.5.4 No anchoring areas

Notes on conditions governing no anchoring areas (classes and sizes of ships, etc.) should preferably be given on charts and should always be given in Sailing Directions.

B

Part B

Traffic Separation Schemes and Inshore Traffic Zones

B

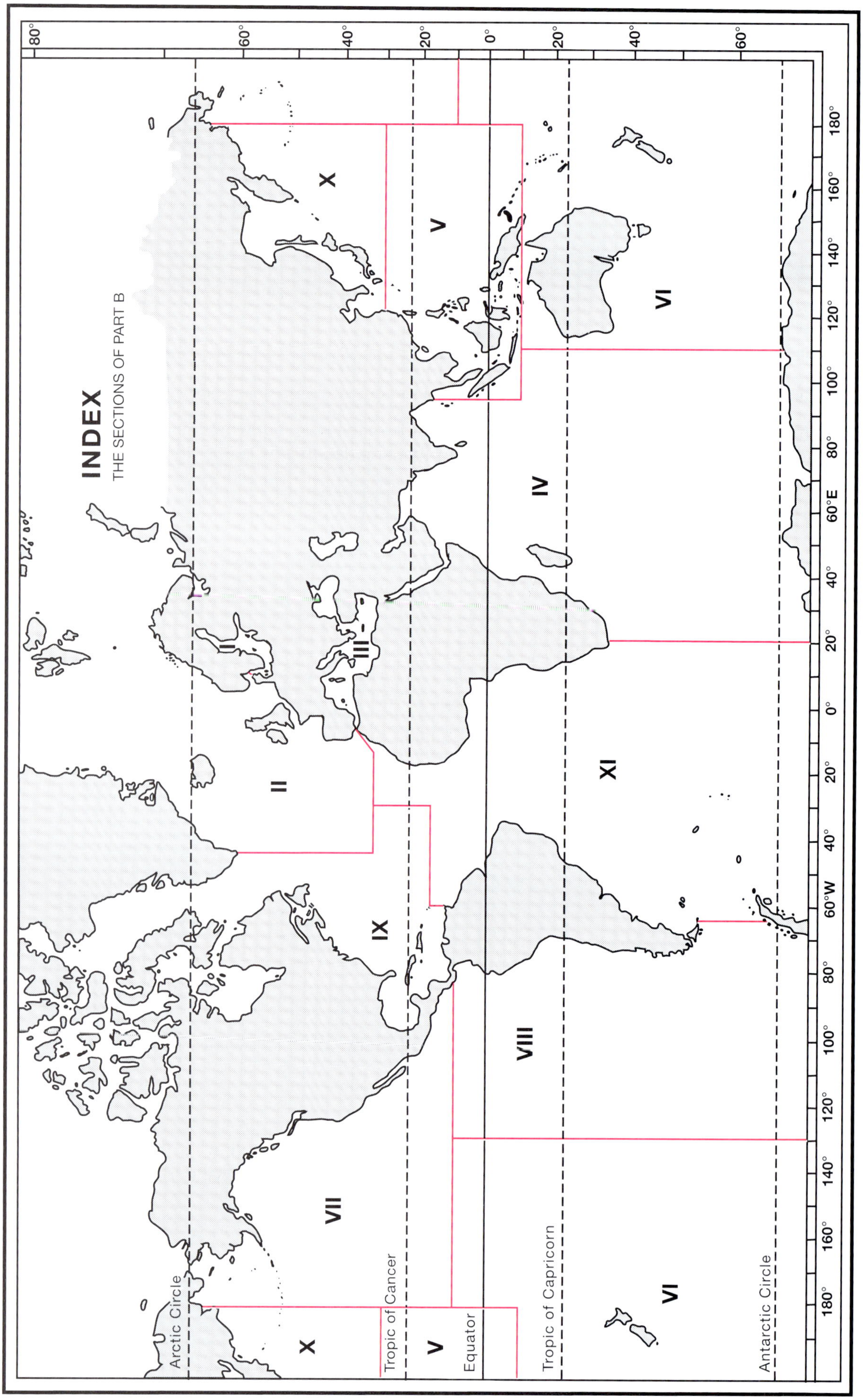
INDEX
THE SECTIONS OF PART B
Arctic Circle
Tropic of Cancer
Equator
Tropic of Capricorn
Antarctic Circle
I
II
III
IV
V
VI
VII
VIII
IX
X
XI
80°
60°
40°
20°
0°
180°
160°
140°
120°
100°
80°
60°W
60°E

Rule 10 of COLREG 1972

Rule 10 of the International Regulations for Preventing Collisions at Sea, 1972, as amended on 19 November 1981 by Assembly resolution A.464(XII), on 19 November 1987 by Assembly resolution A.626(15) and on 19 October 1989 by Assembly resolution A.678(16), is applicable to all traffic separation schemes contained in this part. The text is given below.

B

Rule 10

Traffic separation schemes

(a) This rule applies to traffic separation schemes adopted by the Organization and does not relieve any vessel of her obligation under any other rule.

(b) A vessel using a traffic separation scheme shall:

(i) proceed in the appropriate traffic lane in the general direction of traffic flow for that lane;

(ii) so far as practicable keep clear of a traffic separation line or separation zone;

(iii) normally join or leave a traffic lane at the termination of the lane, but when joining or leaving from either side shall do so at as small an angle to the general direction of traffic flow as practicable.

(c) A vessel shall, so far as practicable, avoid crossing traffic lanes but if obliged to do so shall cross on a heading as nearly as practicable at right angles to the general direction of traffic flow.

(d) (i) A vessel shall not use an inshore traffic zone when she can safely use the appropriate traffic lane within the adjacent traffic separation scheme. However, vessels of less than 20 metres in length, sailing vessels and vessels engaged in fishing may use the inshore traffic zone.

(ii) Notwithstanding subparagraph (d)(i), a vessel may use an inshore traffic zone when *en route* to or from a port, offshore installation or structure, pilot station or any other place situated within the inshore traffic zone, or to avoid immediate danger.

(e) A vessel other than a crossing vessel or a vessel joining or leaving a lane shall not normally enter a separation zone or cross a separation line except:

(i) in cases of emergency to avoid immediate danger;

(ii) to engage in fishing within a separation zone.

(f) A vessel navigating in areas near the terminations of traffic separation schemes shall do so with particular caution.

(g) A vessel shall so far as practicable avoid anchoring in a traffic separation scheme or in areas near its terminations.

(h) A vessel not using a traffic separation scheme shall avoid it by as wide a margin as is practicable.

(i) A vessel engaged in fishing shall not impede the passage of any vessel following a traffic lane.

(j) A vessel of less than 20 metres in length or a sailing vessel shall not impede the safe passage of a power-driven vessel following a traffic lane.

(k) A vessel restricted in her ability to manoeuvre when engaged in an operation for the maintenance of safety of navigation in a traffic separation scheme is exempted from complying with this rule to the extent necessary to carry out the operation.

(l) A vessel restricted in her ability to manoeuvre when engaged in an operation for the laying, servicing or picking up of a submarine cable, within a traffic separation scheme, is exempted from complying with this rule to the extent necessary to carry out the operation.

Section I

Baltic Sea and adjacent waters

Caution: The chartlets are for illustrative purposes only and must not be used for navigation. Mariners should consult the appropriate nautical publications and charts for up-to-date details on aids to navigation and other relevant information.

Warning: The geographical positions given in the descriptions of the routeing systems are only correct for charts using the same geodetic datum as the reference charts indicated under each scheme. Charts published by other hydrographic offices may use a different geodetic datum, as may new editions of the reference charts published after the adoption of the routeing system. Where amendments to existing systems are not based on the same geodetic datum as the original system, this is emphasized by the use of different colours for definitions of positions.

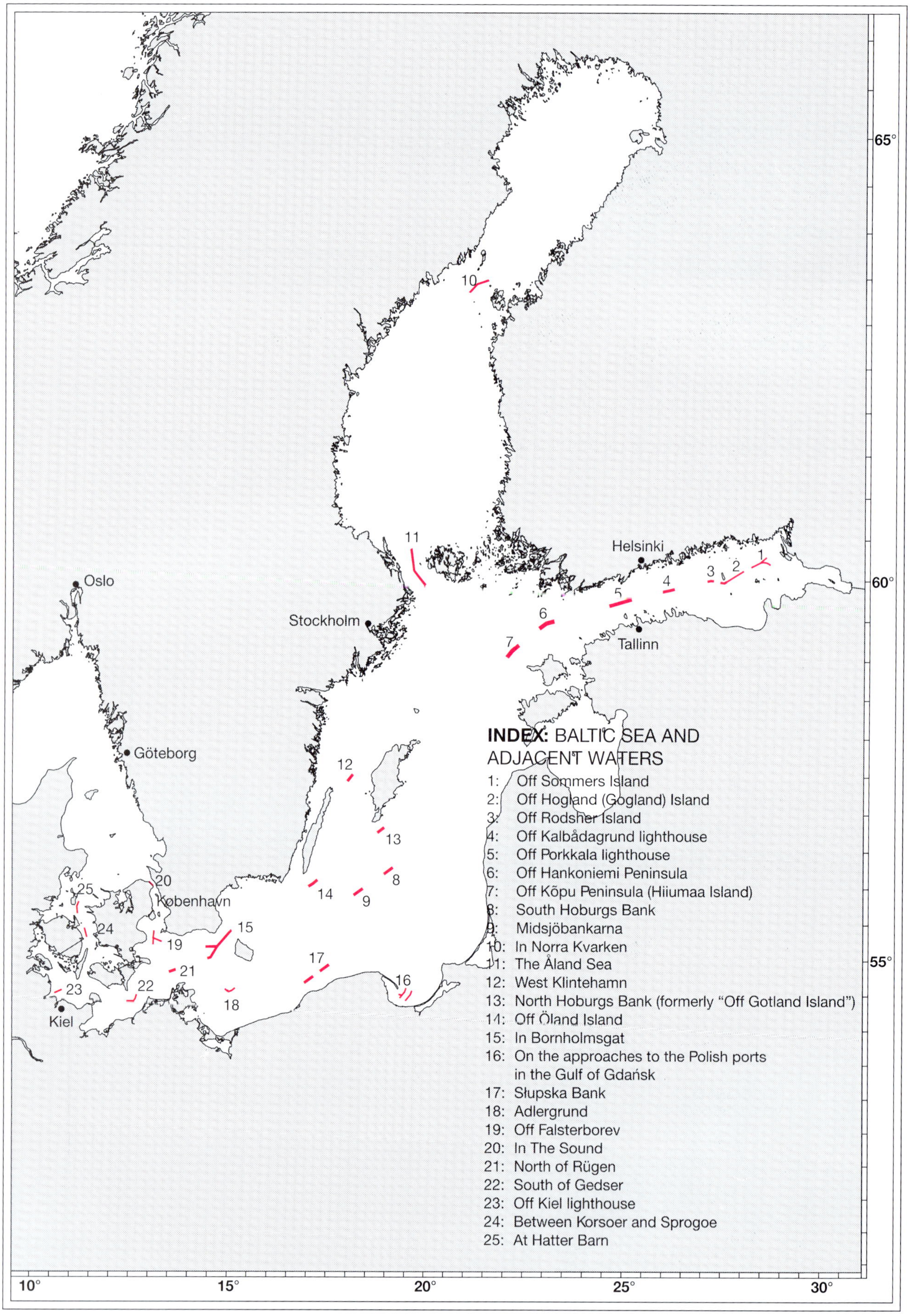
INDEX: BALTIC SEA AND ADJACENT WATERS
1: Off Sommers Island
2: Off Hogland (Gogland) Island
3: Off Rodsher Island
4: Off Kalbådagrund lighthouse
5: Off Porkkala lighthouse
6: Off Hankoniemi Peninsula
7: Off Kõpu Peninsula (Hiiumaa Island)
8: South Hoburgs Bank
9: Midsjöbankarna
10: In Norra Kvarken
11: The Åland Sea
12: West Klintehamn
13: North Hoburgs Bank (formerly "Off Gotland Island")
14: Off Öland Island
15: In Bornholmsgat
16: On the approaches to the Polish ports in the Gulf of Gdańsk
17: Słupska Bank
18: Adlergrund
19: Off Falsterborev
20: In The Sound
21: North of Rügen
22: South of Gedser
23: Off Kiel lighthouse
24: Between Korsoer and Sprogoe
25: At Hatter Barn
Helsinki
Tallinn
Stockholm
Oslo
Göteborg
København
Kiel
65°
60°
55°
10°
15°
20°
25°
30°

OFF SOMMERS ISLAND

(Reference chart: INT 1214.
Note: Geodetic datum of the year 1942 (Pulkovo). For obtaining position in WGS datum, such position should be moved 0′.14 (8″.3) westward.)

The traffic separation scheme consists of four parts:

Part I consists of a roundabout around the separation zone 0.5 miles in diameter centred on the geographical position 60°11′.50 N, 027°46′.20 E. The roundabout lane is 1 mile wide.

Part II consists of two traffic lanes separated by a zone with a centre line connecting the following geographical positions:

(1)	60°07′.55 N,	027°32′.80 E	(2)	60°10′.77 N,	027°43′.62 E

The traffic separation zone is 0.5 miles wide.
The traffic lanes on both sides of the traffic separation zone are 1 mile wide.

Part III consists of two traffic lanes separated by a line connecting the following geographical positions:

(3)	60°11′.15 N,	027°49′.05 E	(4)	60°07′.70 N,	028°16′.10 E

The traffic lanes on both sides of the traffic separation line are 1 mile wide.

Part IV consists of two traffic lanes separated by a line connecting the following geographical positions:

(5)	60°12′.70 N,	027°47′.90 E	(6)	60°24′.54 N,	028°05′.05 E

The traffic lanes on both sides of the traffic separation line are 0.5 miles wide.

Note: The roundabout serves the purpose of facilitating manoeuvring in the area where traffic to and from Leningrad, Vyborg and the western Baltic meets.

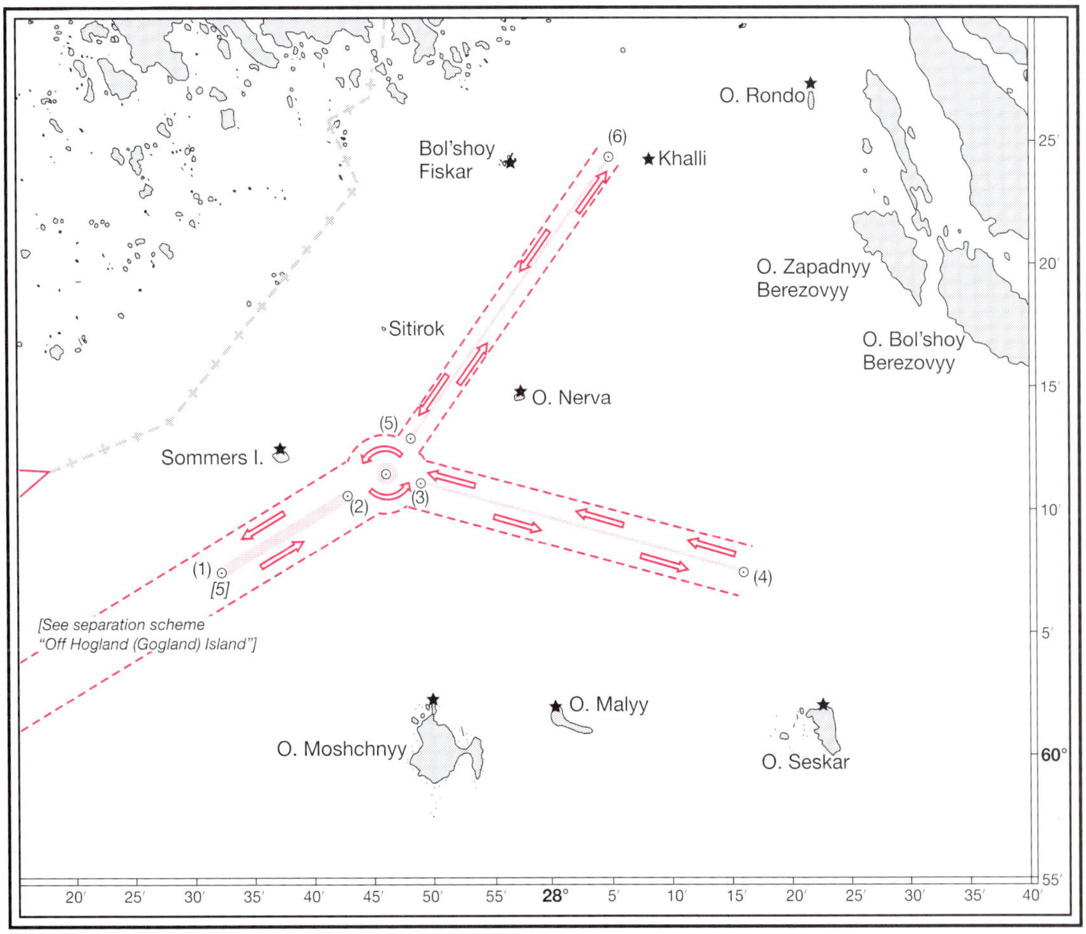

OFF SOMMERS ISLAND

OFF HOGLAND (GOGLAND) ISLAND*

(Reference chart: INT 1214.
Note: Geodetic datum of the year 1942 (Pulkovo). For obtaining position in WGS datum, such position should be moved 0′.14 (8″.3) westward.)

Description of the traffic separation scheme

The traffic separation scheme consists of two parts:

Part I consists of two traffic lanes separated by a zone with a centre line connecting the following geographical positions:

(1)	59°59′.00 N,	026°57′.40 E	(3)	59°59′.47 N,	027°06′.30 E
(2)	59°58′.52 N,	027°03′.10 E			

The traffic separation zone is 0.5 miles wide.

The traffic lanes on both sides of the traffic separation zone are 1 mile wide.

Part II consists of two traffic lanes separated by a line connecting the following geographical positions:

(4)	59°59′.47 N,	027°06′.30 E	(5)	60°07′.55 N,	027°32′.80 E

The traffic lanes on both sides of the traffic separation line are 1.25 miles wide.

OFF RODSHER ISLAND*

Note: See "Recommended tracks and traffic separation line between traffic separation schemes "Off Rodsher Island" and "Off Gogland Island"" in part E.

(Positions are based on World Geodetic System 1984 datum (WGS 84). The Russian Federation reference chart is 23004 (Pulkovo 1942 datum). For obtaining position in WGS 84 datum, charted positions should be moved 0′.14 (8″.3) westward.)

Description of the traffic separation scheme

(a) A separation zone is bounded by a line connecting the following geographical positions:

(1)	60° 00′.43 N,	026° 30′.16 E	(4)	59° 59′.85 N,	026° 44′.08 E
(2)	60° 01′.05 N,	026° 34′.86 E	(5)	60° 00′.15 N,	026° 40′.21 E
(3)	60° 00′.35 N,	026° 44′.24 E	(6)	59° 58′.76 N,	026° 30′.16 E

(b) A traffic lane, one mile wide, is established on each side of the separation zone.

* Date of implementation of amended scheme: 0000 hours UTC on 1 June 2013.

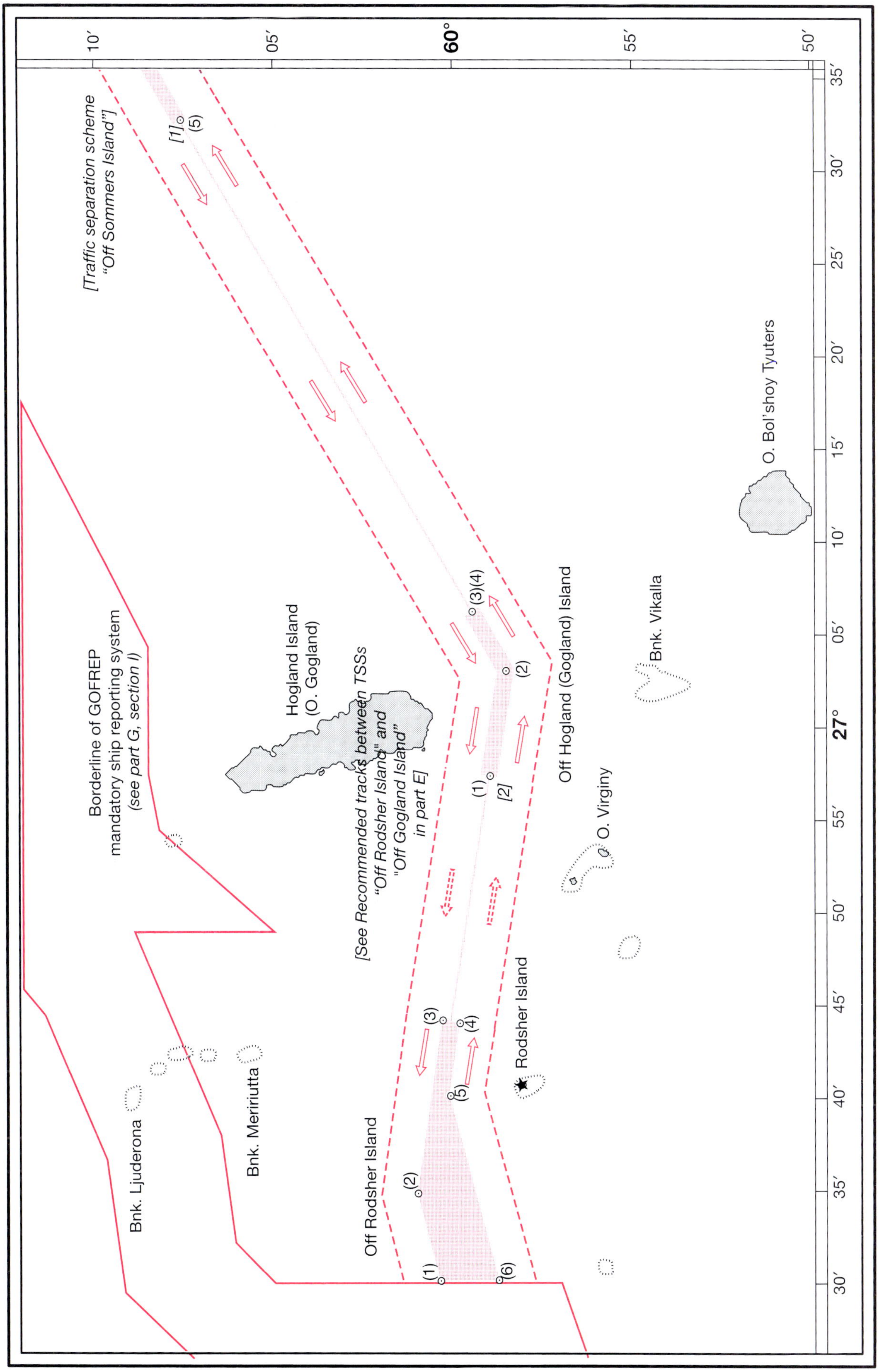

OFF HOGLAND (GOGLAND) ISLAND + OFF RODSHER ISLAND

OFF KALBÅDAGRUND LIGHTHOUSE

Note: See mandatory ship reporting system "In the Gulf of Finland" in part G, section I, and "Recommendations on navigation through the Gulf of Finland Traffic area" in part F.

(Reference charts: Estonian 300 (edition 2006-15-12) and 302 (edition 2004-24-11); Finnish 952 (edition 2008-11-10) and 953 (2008-06-10); and Russian 23069 (edition 2005).)
Note: Finnish and Estonian charts are based on World Geodetic System 1984 datum (WGS 84); Russian chart is based on Geodetic datum of the year 1942 (Pulkovo). For obtaining positions in WGS datum, such positions should be moved 0′.13 westward.

Description of the traffic separation scheme

Note: All positions are referred to WGS 84 datum

(a) A separation zone is bounded by lines connecting the following geographical positions:

(1)	59°52′.35 N,	025°40′.06 E	(4)	59°54′.75 N,	025°51′.14 E
(2)	59°52′.84 N,	025°46′.03 E	(5)	59°53′.81 N,	025°45′.55 E
(3)	59°53′.81 N,	025°51′.77 E	(6)	59°53′.34 N,	025°39′.73 E

(b) A traffic lane for eastbound traffic, 2.0 nautical miles wide, is established between the separation zone described in paragraph (a) above and a line connecting the following geographical positions:

(7)	59°50′.37 N,	025°40′.70 E	(9)	59°51′.91 N,	025°53′.04 E
(8)	59°50′.89 N,	025°46′.99 E			

(c) A traffic lane for westbound traffic, 2.0 nautical miles wide, is established between the separation zone described in paragraph (a) above and a line connecting the following geographical positions:

(10)	59°56′.65 N,	025°49′.88 E	(12)	59°55′.31 N,	025°39′.09 E
(11)	59°55′.76 N,	025°44′.59 E			

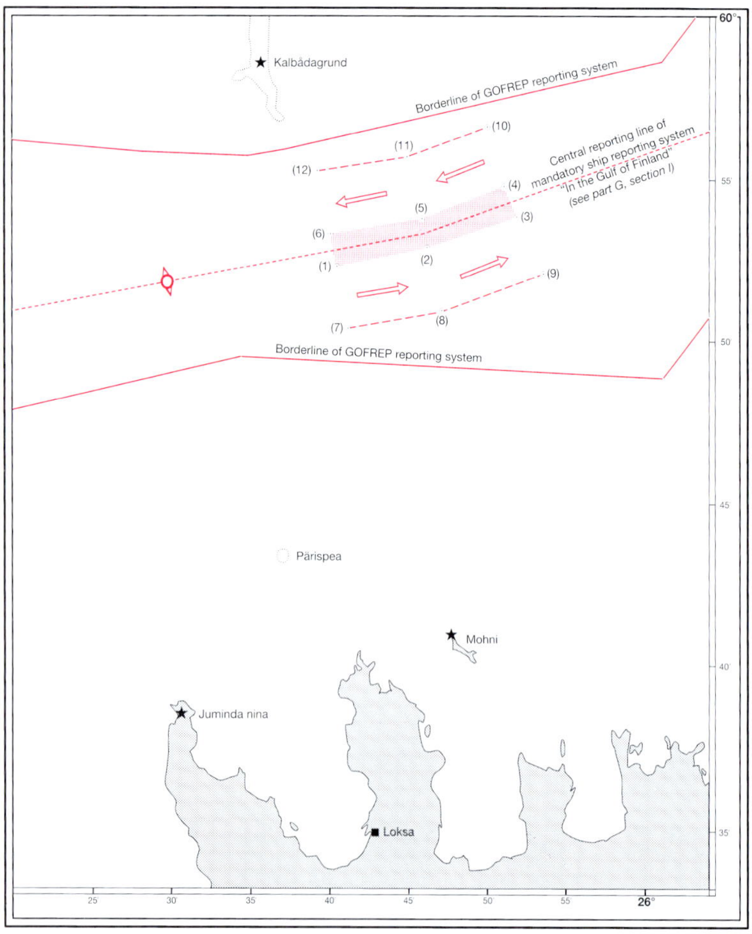

OFF KALBÅDAGRUND LIGHTHOUSE

OFF PORKKALA LIGHTHOUSE

Note: See mandatory ship reporting system "In the Gulf of Finland" in part G, section I, and "Recommendations on navigation through the Gulf of Finland Traffic area" in part F.

(Reference charts: Estonian 300 (edition 2006-15-12) and 302 (edition 2004-24-11); Finnish 952 (edition 2008-11-10) and 953 (2008-06-10); and Russian 23068 (edition 2001).)
Note: Finnish and Estonian charts are based on World Geodetic System 1984 datum (WGS 84); Russian chart is based on Geodetic datum of the year 1942 (Pulkovo). For obtaining positions in WGS datum, such positions should be moved 0′.13 westward.

Description of the traffic separation scheme

Note: All positions are referred to WGS 84 datum.

(a) A separation zone, 0.7 nautical miles wide, is bounded by lines connecting the following geographical positions.

(1)	59°43′.51 N,	024°18′.16 E	(4)	59°45′.47 N,	024°27′.97 E
(2)	59°44′.08 N,	024°21′.96 E	(5)	59°44′.76 N,	024°21′.61 E
(3)	59°44′.94 N,	024°29′.64 E	(6)	59°44′.19 N,	024°17′.77 E

(b) A separation zone is bounded by lines connecting the following geographical positions:

(7)	59°47′.33 N,	024°35′.39 E	(10)	59°46′.48 N,	024°29′.65 E
(8)	59°45′.74 N,	024°21′.11 E	(11)	59°45′.34 N,	024°33′.21 E
(9)	59°45′.54 N,	024°21′.21 E	(12)	59°45′.67 N,	024°36′.13 E

(c) A separation zone, 1.7 nautical miles wide, is bounded by lines connecting the following geographical positions:

(20)	59°49′.14 N,	025°07′.23 E	(22)	59°51′.24 N,	025°10′.39 E
(21)	59°49′.58 N,	025°11′.12 E	(23)	59°50′.80 N,	025°06′.50 E

(d) A traffic lane for eastbound traffic, 2.0 nautical miles wide, is bounded by a line connecting the following geographical positions:

(1)	59°43′.51 N,	024°18′.16 E	(15)	59°42′.98 N,	024°30′.50 E
(2)	59°44′.08 N,	024°21′.96 E	(14)	59°42′.13 N,	024°22′.96 E
(3)	59°44′.94 N,	024°29′.64 E	(13)	59°41′.58 N,	024°19′.29 E

(e) A traffic lane for westbound traffic, 1.0 nautical mile wide, is bounded by a line connecting the following geographical positions:

(3)	59°44′.94 N,	024°29′.64 E	(9)	59°45′.54 N,	024°21′.21 E
(4)	59°45′.47 N,	024°27′.97 E	(10)	59°46′.48 N,	024°29′.65 E
(5)	59°44′.76 N,	024°21′.61 E	(11)	59°45′.34 N,	024°33′.21 E
(6)	59°44′.19 N,	024°17′.77 E			

(f) A traffic lane for westbound traffic, 2.0 nautical miles wide, is bounded by lines connecting the following geographical positions:

(7)	59°47′.33 N,	024°35′.39 E	(18)	59°47′.68 N,	024°20′.11 E
(8)	59°45′.74 N,	024°21′.11 E	(17)	59°49′.29 N,	024°34′.53 E
(19)	59°47′.08 N,	024°16′.07 E			

(g) A traffic lane for eastbound traffic, 2.0 nautical miles wide, is bounded by lines connecting the following geographical positions:

(20)	59°49′.14 N,	025°07′.23 E	(25)	59°47′.62 N,	025°11′.99 E
(21)	59°49′.58 N,	025°11′.12 E	(24)	59°47′.18 N,	025°08′.10 E

(h) A traffic lane for westbound traffic, 2.0 nautical miles wide, is bounded by lines connecting the following geographical positions:

(22)	59°51′.24 N,	025°10′.39 E	(27)	59°52′.76 N,	025°05′.64 E
(23)	59°50′.80 N,	025°06′.50 E	(26)	59°53′.19 N,	025°09′.53 E

(i) An amended precautionary area with recommended direction of traffic flow is established connecting the following geographical positions:

(15)	59°42′.98 N,	024°30′.50 E	(17)	59°49′.29 N,	024°34′.53 E
(16)	59°43′.70 N,	024°36′.99 E	(7)	59°47′.33 N,	024°35′.39 E
(24)	59°47′.18 N,	025°08′.10 E	(12)	59°45′.67 N,	024°36′.13 E
(20)	59°49′.14 N,	025°07′.23 E	(11)	59°45′.34 N,	024°33′.21 E
(23)	59°50′.80 N,	025°06′.50 E	(3)	59°44′.94 N,	024°29′.64 E
(27)	59°52′.76 N,	025°05′.64 E			

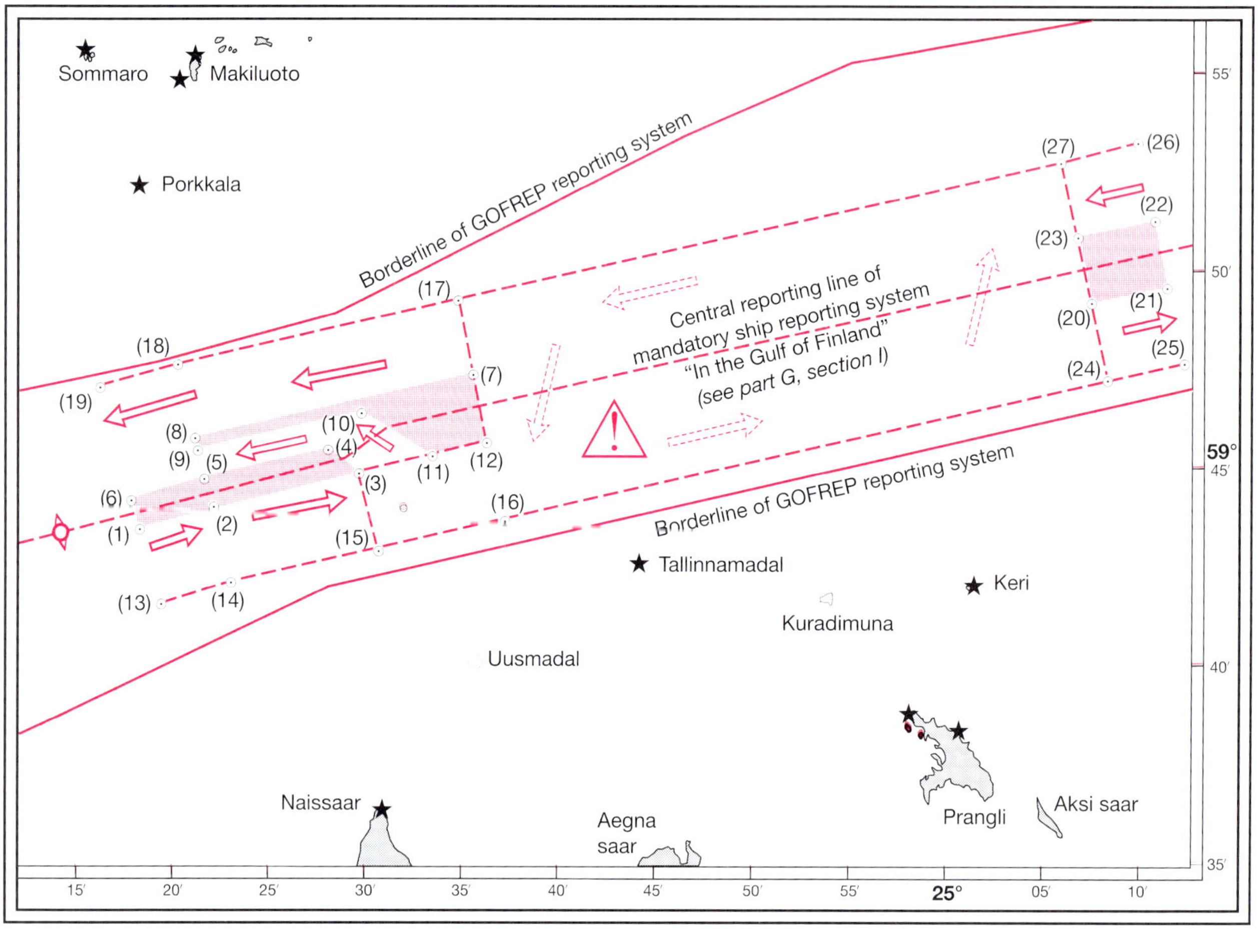

OFF PORKKALA LIGHTHOUSE

OFF HANKONIEMI PENINSULA

Note: See mandatory ship reporting system "In the Gulf of Finland" in part G, section I, and "Recommendations on navigation through the Gulf of Finland Traffic area" in part F.

Description of the traffic separation scheme

(Reference chart: FIN 912, 1999 edition.
Note: this chart is based on the national Finnish geodetic chart co-ordinate system (KKJ).
WGS 84 correction: latitude correction is –0′.01; longitude correction is +0′.20.)
Note: These positions are referred to KKJ datum.

(a) A separation zone, two miles wide, is centred upon the following geographical positions:

(1)	59°24′.50 N,	022°25′.00 E	(3)	59°30′.00 N,	022°45′.00 E
(2)	59°28′.00 N,	022°34′.00 E			

(b) A traffic lane, four miles wide, is established on each side of the separation zone.

Precautionary area

(Reference charts: Estonian 302 (edition 2004-24-11); Finnish 952 (edition 2008-11-10) and 953 (2008-06-10); and Russian 23067 (edition 2001).
Note: Finnish and Estonian charts are based on World Geodetic System 1984 datum (WGS 84);
Russian chart is based on Geodetic datum of the year 1942 (Pulkovo). For obtaining positions in WGS datum, such positions should be moved 0.13′ westward.)
Note: These positions are referred to WGS 84 datum.

(c) A precautionary area adjacent to the traffic separation scheme is bounded by a line connecting the following geographical positions:

(4)	59°25′.31 N,	022°48′.07 E	(7)	59°39′.31 N,	023°21′.16 E
(5)	59°34′.24 N,	023°37′.70 E	(8)	59°34′.71 N,	022°41′.52 E
(6)	59°40′.99 N,	023°32′.98 E			

(chartlet overleaf)

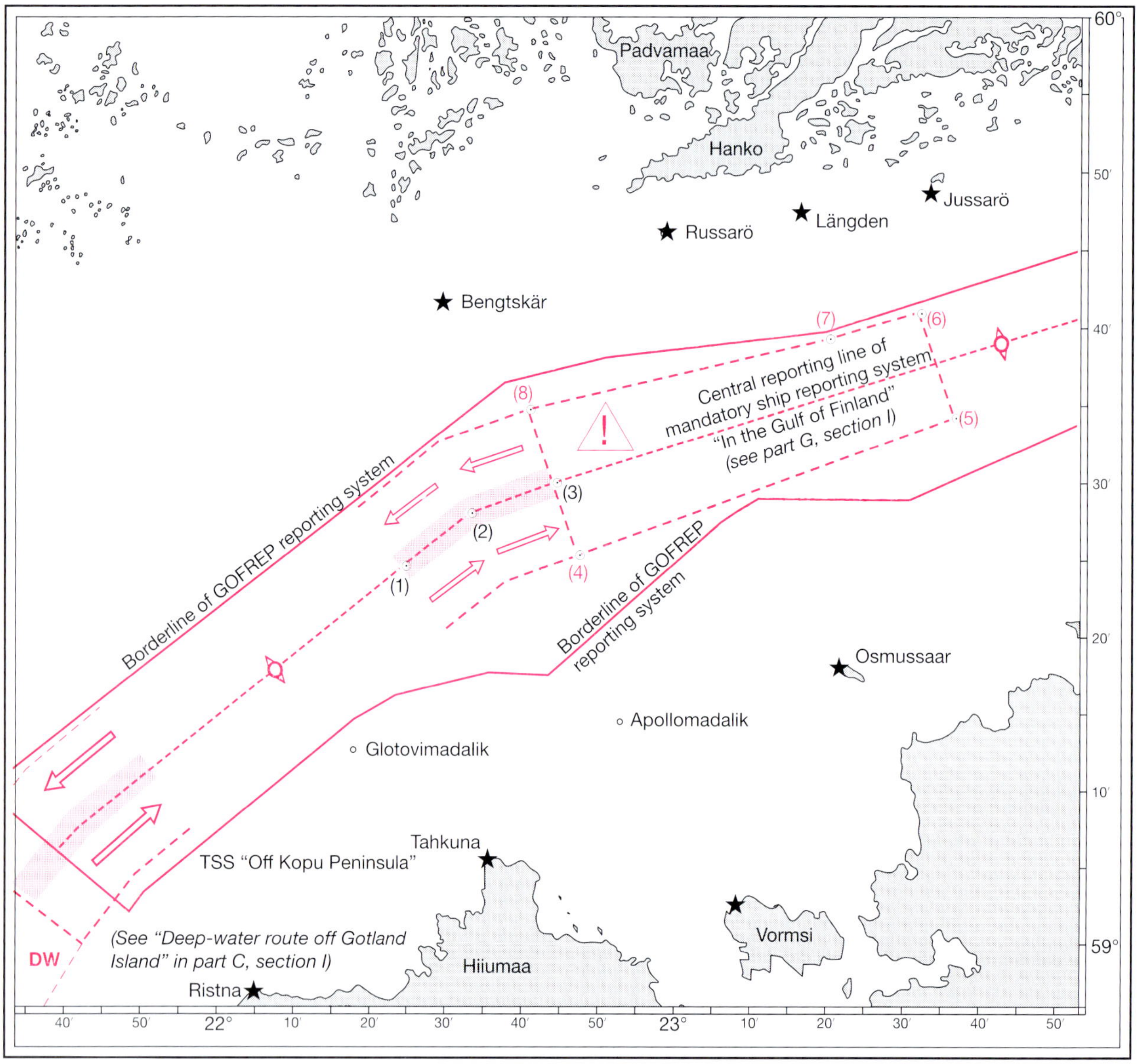

OFF HANKONIEMI PENINSULA

OFF KÕPU PENINSULA (HIIUMAA ISLAND)

Note: See mandatory ship reporting system "In the Gulf of Finland" in part G, section I and "Recommendations on navigation through the Gulf of Finland Traffic Area" in part F.

(Reference chart: USSR 444, 1988 edition.
Note: This chart is based on the single geodetic datum for Soviet nautical charts.)

Description of the traffic separation scheme

(a) A separation zone, two miles wide, is centred upon the following geographical positions:

(1)	59°02′.90 N,	021°35′.80 E	(3)	59°11′.60 N,	021°52′.00 E
(2)	59°07′.70 N,	021°42′.60 E			

(b) A traffic lane, four miles wide, is established on each side of the separation zone

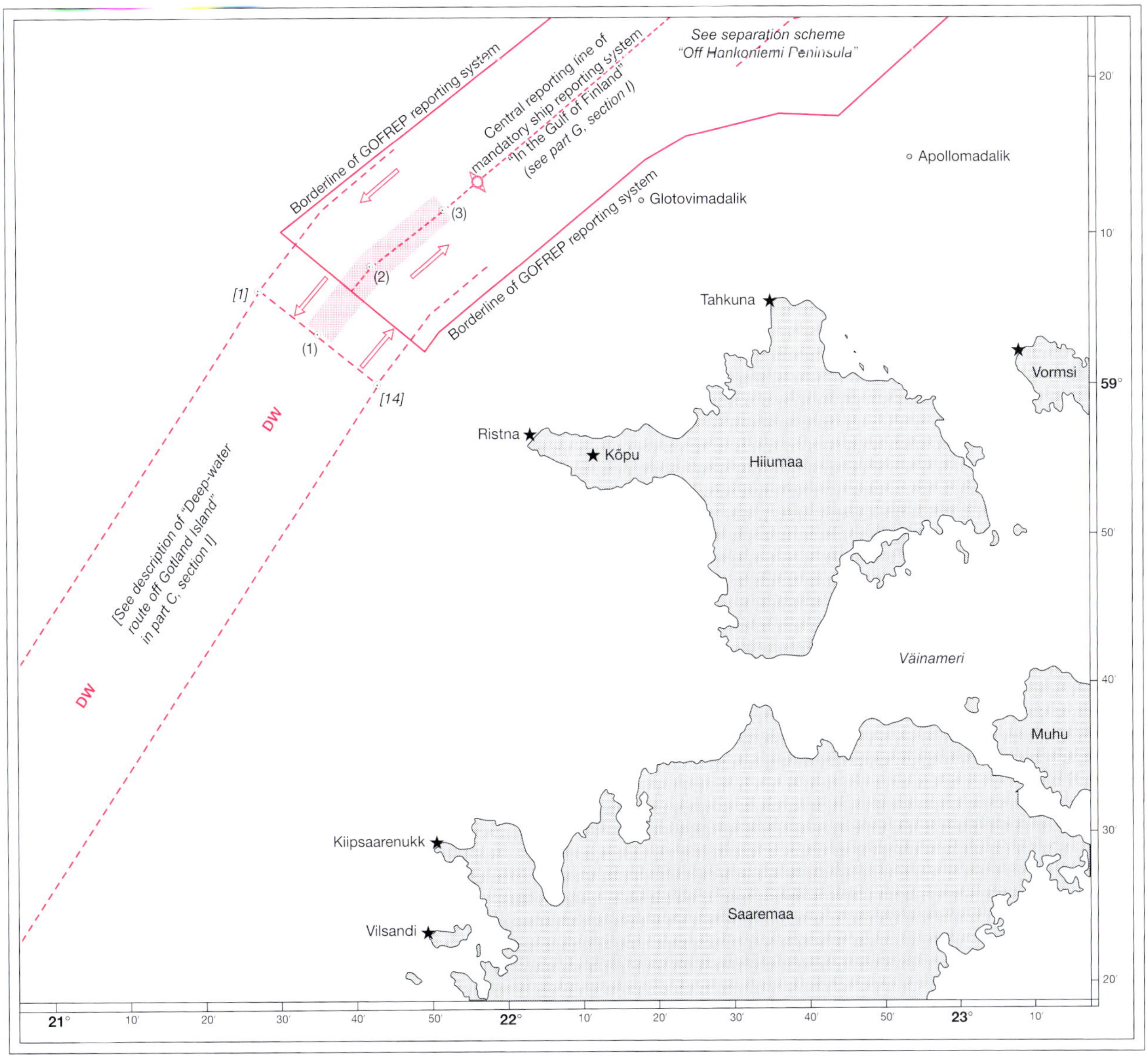

OFF KÕPU PENINSULA (HIIUMAA ISLAND)

SOUTH HOBURGS BANK

(Reference chart: Swedish SE7, edition 5/6-2008.
Note: This chart is based on World Geodetic System 1984 datum (WGS 84).)

Description of the traffic separation scheme

(a) A traffic separation zone is established upon the following geographical positions:

(1)	56°17′.57 N,	018°39′.09 E	(4)	56°24′.20 N,	018°52′.31 E
(2)	56°20′.23 N,	018°46′.82 E	(5)	56°19′.64 N,	018°47′.81 E
(3)	56°24′.58 N,	018°51′.02 E	(6)	56°16′.89 N,	018°39′.88 E

(b) A traffic lane for the southbound traffic is established between the traffic separation zone and a line connecting the following geographical positions:

(7)	56°20′.23 N,	018°36′.02 E	(9)	56°26′.04 N,	018°46′.14 E
(8)	56°22′.64 N,	018°42′.82 E			

(c) A traffic lane for the northbound traffic is established between the traffic separation zone and a line connecting the following geographical positions:

(10)	56°14′.21 N,	018°42′.96 E	(12)	56°22′.74 N,	018°57′.19 E
(11)	56°17′.23 N,	018°51′.80 E			

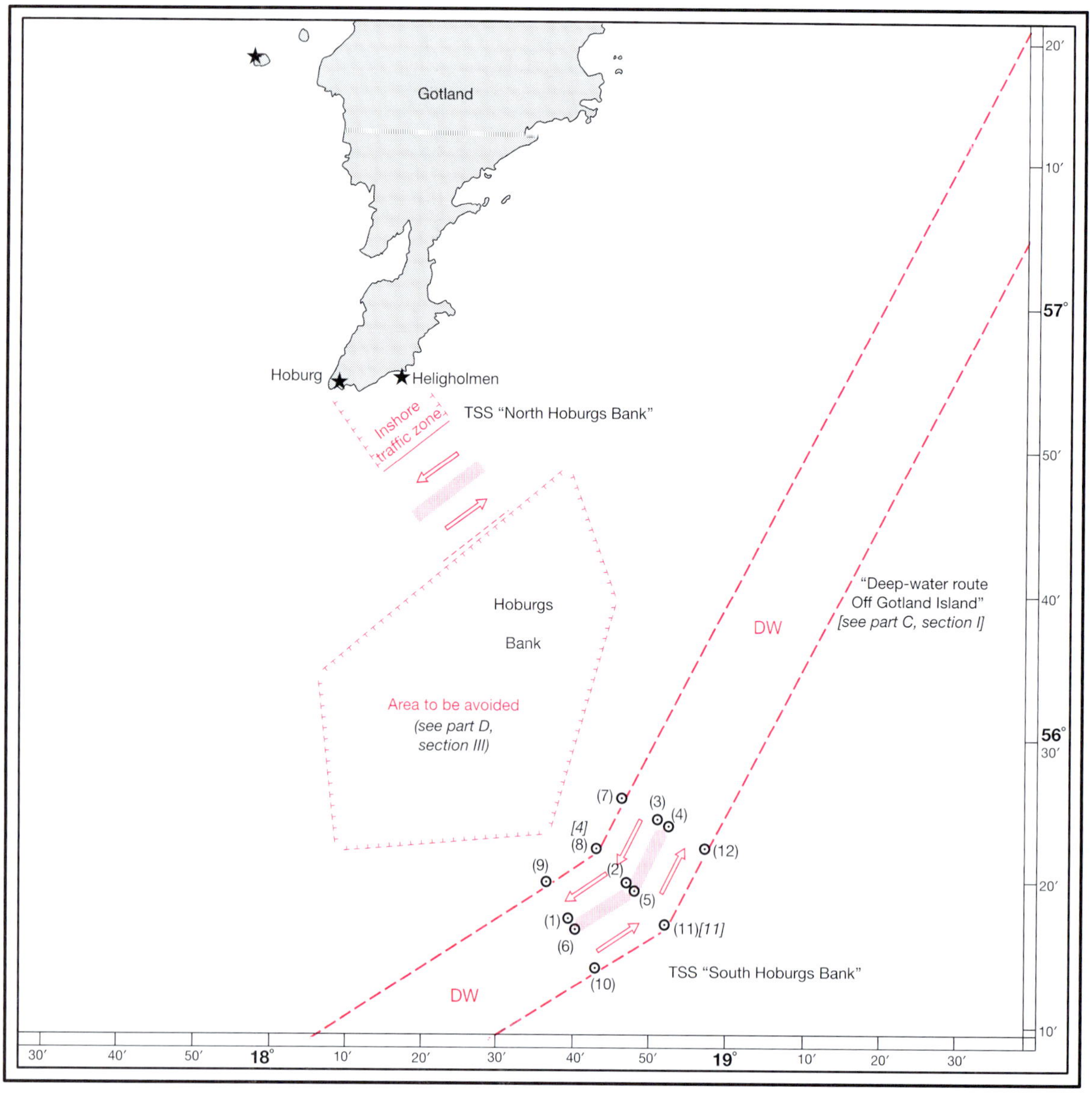

SOUTH HOBURGS BANK

MIDSJÖBANKARNA

(Reference chart: Swedish SE7, edition 5/6-2008.
Note: This chart is based on World Geodetic System 1984 datum (WGS 84).)

Description of the traffic separation scheme

(a) A traffic separation zone is established upon the following geographical positions:

(1)	55°56′.16 N,	017°32′.41 E	(3)	55°56′.68 N,	017°42′.13 E
(2)	55°57′.45 N,	017°41′.68 E	(4)	55°55′.38 N,	017°32′.71 E

(b) A traffic lane for the southbound traffic is established between the traffic separation zone and a line connecting the following geographical positions:

(5)	55°59′.07 N,	017°31′.27 E	(6)	56°00′.30 N,	017°40′.04 E

(c) A traffic lane for the northbound traffic is established between the traffic separation zone and a line connecting the following geographical positions:

(7)	55°52′.47 N,	017°33′.85 E	(8)	55°53′.85 N,	017°43′.75 E

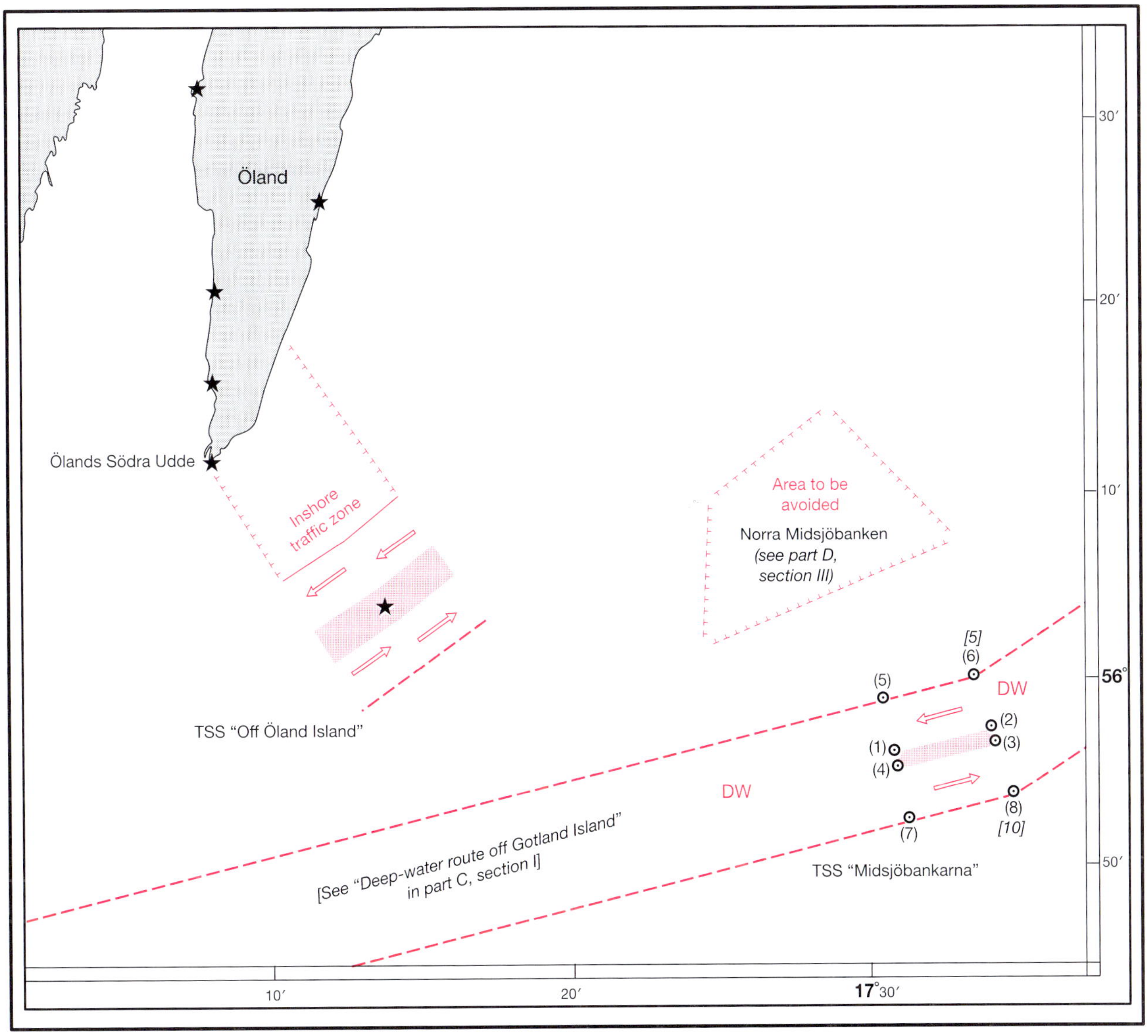

MIDSJÖBANKARNA

IN NORRA KVARKEN*

Note: See two-way routes "In Norra Kvarken" in part E.
(Reference chart: Finnish 47, edition 2005 V.
Note: This chart is based on World Geodetic System 1984 datum (WGS 84).)

Part I

(a) A traffic separation zone 0.1 mile wide is centred upon the following geographical positions:
(1) 63°27′.22 N, 020°37′.58 E (2) 63°27′.94 N, 020°38′.61 E

(b) A traffic lane for the northbound traffic is established between the traffic separation zone described in paragraph (a) and a line connecting the following geographical positions:
(3) 63°27′.03 N, 020°38′.32 E (4) 63°27′.77 N, 020°39′.28 E

(c) A traffic lane for the southbound traffic is established between the traffic separation zone described in paragraph (a) and a line connecting the following geographical positions:
(5) 63°28′.12 N, 020°37′.93 E (6) 63°27′.42 N, 020°36′.84 E

Part II

(d) A traffic separation zone 0.1 mile wide is centred upon the following geographical positions:
(7) 63°31′.60 N, 020°42′.72 E (9) 63°32′.50 N, 020°45′.82 E
(8) 63°31′.84 N, 020°43′.00 E

(e) A traffic lane for the northbound traffic is established between the traffic separation zone described in paragraph (d) and a line connecting the following geographical positions:
(10) 63°31′.19 N, 020°43′.77 E (11) 63°32′.29 N, 020°46′.24 E

(f) A traffic lane for the southbound traffic is established between the traffic separation zone described in paragraph (d) and a line connecting the following geographical positions:
(12) 63°32′.71 N, 020°45′.40 E (13) 63°32′.23 N, 020°41′.09 E

Part III

(g) A traffic separation zone 0.1 mile wide is centred upon the following geographical positions:
(14) 63°34′.73 N, 021°01′.51 E (15) 63°35′.06 N, 021°03′.60 E

(h) A traffic lane for the northbound traffic is established between the traffic separation zone described in paragraph (g) and a line connecting the following geographical positions:
(16) 63°34′.42 N, 021°01′.76 E (17) 63°34′.72 N, 021°03′.88 E

(i) A traffic lane for the southbound traffic is established between the traffic separation zone described in paragraph (g) and a line connecting the following geographical positions:
(18) 63°35′.40 N, 021°03′.33 E (19) 63°35′.04 N, 021°01′.26 E

* Date of implementation of new scheme: 0000 hours UTC on 1 May 2013.

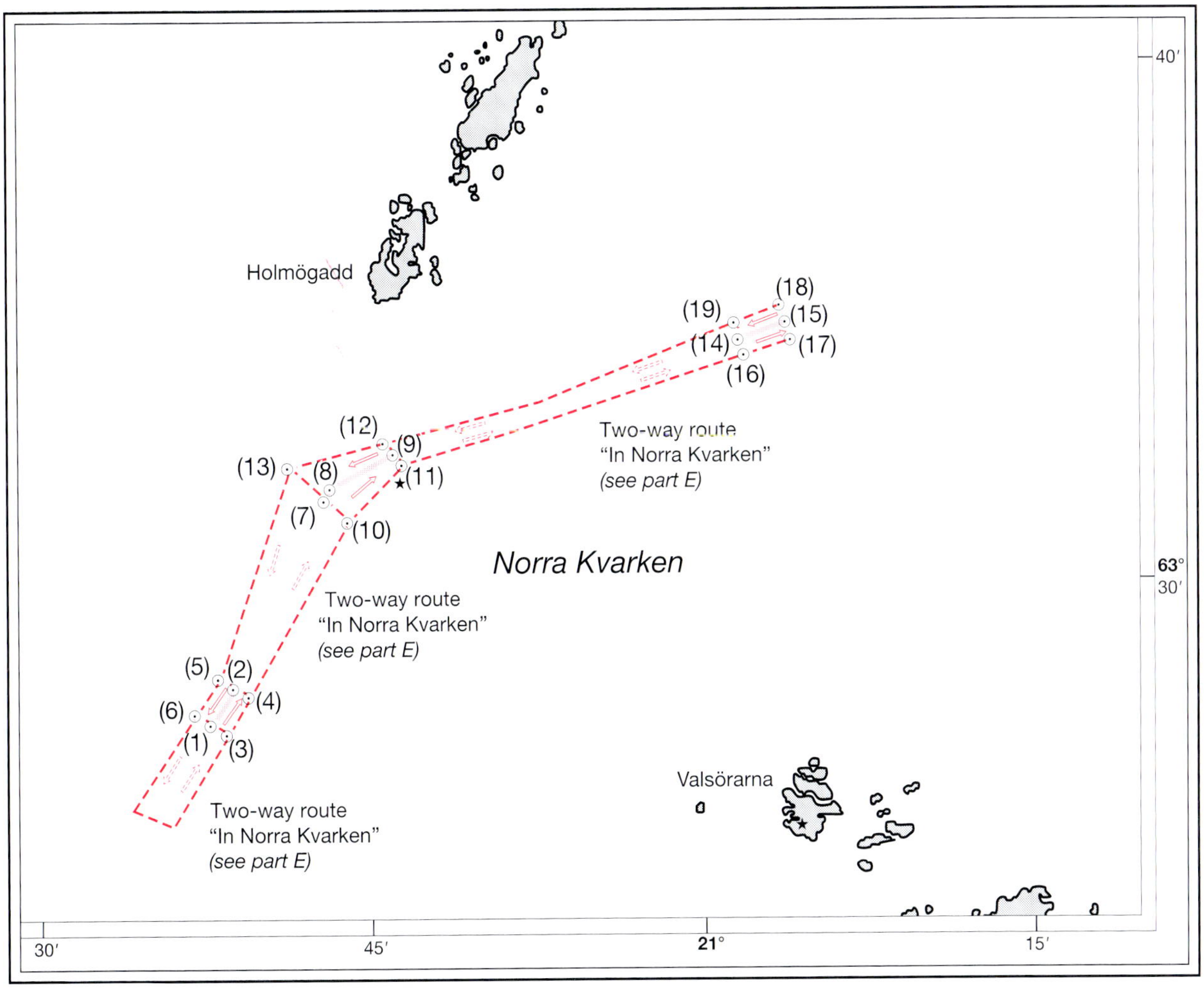

IN NORRA KVARKEN

THE ÅLAND SEA

Note: See "Deep-water routes leading to the Åland Sea" in part C, section I and "Recommended two-way route leading to the Åland Sea" in part E.

(Reference charts: Finnish 953, edition 2007 V, and Swedish chart SE61 (INT 1205), edition 21/2-2008.
Note: These charts are based on World Geodetic System 1984 datum (WGS 84).)

Description of the traffic separation schemes

North Åland Sea

Part I

(a) A separation line connecting the following geographical positions:

(1) 60°29′.52 N, 019°00′.30 E (2) 60°26′.94 N, 019°00′.36 E

(b) A traffic lane for southbound traffic is established between the separation line and a line connecting the following geographical positions:

(3) 60°29′.54 N, 018°56′.36 E (4) 60°26′.89 N, 018°57′.05 E

(c) A traffic lane for northbound traffic is established between the separation line and a line connecting the following geographical positions:

(5) 60°26′.89 N, 019°03′.88 E (6) 60°29′.51 N, 019°04′.56 E

Part II

(d) A separation zone, 1.1 mile wide, is centred upon the following geographical positions:

(7) 60°11′.06 N, 019°03′.21 E (8) 60°10′.09 N, 019°04′.80 E

(e) A traffic lane for southbound traffic is established between the separation zone and a line connecting the following geographical positions:

(9) 60°09′.79 N, 019°00′.12 E (10) 60°08′.83 N, 019°01′.71 E

(f) A traffic lane for northbound traffic is established between the separation zone and a line connecting the following geographical positions:

(11) 60°11′.36 N, 019°07′.89 E (12) 60°12′.33 N, 019°06′.30 E

South Åland Sea

Part I

(g) A separation zone, 1.1 mile wide, is centred upon the following geographical positions:

(13) 59°47′.28 N, 019°42′.44 E (14) 59°46′.30 N, 019°44′.04 E

(h) A traffic lane for southbound traffic is established between the separation zone and a line connecting the following geographical positions:

(15) 59°46′.01 N, 019°39′.39 E (16) 59°45′.04 N, 019°40′.99 E

(i) A traffic lane for northbound traffic is established between the separation zone and a line connecting the following geographical positions:

(17) 59°47′.57 N, 019°47′.10 E (18) 59°48′.55 N, 019°45′.50 E

Part II

(j) A separation zone is bounded by a line connecting the following geographical positions:

(19) 59°46′.03 N, 019°52′.85 E (21) 59°45′.36 N, 019°58′.85 E
(20) 59°45′.96 N, 019°58′.87 E (22) 59°45′.42 N, 019°53′.83 E

(k) A traffic lane for eastbound traffic is established between the separation zone and a line connecting the following geographical positions:

(23) 59°44′.24 N, 019°55′.74 E (24) 59°44′.25 N, 019°58′.80 E

(l) A traffic lane for westbound traffic is established between the separation zone and a line connecting the following geographical positions:

(25) 59°46′.96 N, 019°58′.92 E (26) 59°47′.37 N, 019°50′.68 E

Part III

(m) A separation line connecting the following geographical positions:

(27) 59°41′.22 N, 020°31′.98 E (29) 59°44′.76 N, 020°23′.10 E
(28) 59°43′.32 N, 020°28′.38 E

(n) A traffic lane for eastbound traffic is established between the separation line and a line connecting the following geographical positions:

(30) 59°44′.32 N, 020°19′.60 E (32) 59°40′.56 N, 020°30′.34 E
(31) 59°42′.87 N, 020°27′.57 E

(o) A traffic lane for westbound traffic is established between the separation line and a line connecting the following geographical positions:

(33) 59°41′.93 N, 020°33′.72 E (34) 59°45′.68 N, 020°24′.51 E

Part IV

(p) A separation line connecting the following geographical positions:

(35) 59°42′.26 N, 019°51′.55 E (37) 59°34′.26 N, 020°08′.40 E
(36) 59°39′.70 N, 019°55′.19 E (38) 59°30′.27 N, 020°08′.40 E

(q) A separation line connecting the following geographical positions:

(39) 59°30′.27 N, 020°06′.51 E (41) 59°39′.44 N, 019°54′.13 E
(40) 59°33′.75 N, 020°06′.51 E (42) 59°41′.91 N, 019°50′.60 E

(r) A traffic lane for southbound traffic is established between the separation line described in paragraph (q) and a line connecting the following geographical positions:

(43) 59°40′.89 N, 019°47′.83 E (45) 59°34′.89 N, 019°57′.20 E
(44) 59°39′.57 N, 019°51′.58 E (46) 59°30′.27 N, 019°54′.70 E

(s) A traffic lane for northbound traffic is established between the separation line described in paragraph (p) and the following two lines connecting the following geographical positions:

Line 1

(47) 59°30′.27 N, 020°15′.79 E (49) 59°33′.90 N, 020°30′.13 E
(48) 59°33′.90 N, 020°15′.79 E

Line 2

(50) 59°37′.92 N, 020°30′.13 E (52) 59°43′.59 N, 019°55′.17 E
(51) 59°37′.92 N, 020°06′.72 E

(t) The traffic is separated by natural obstructions (Svenska Björn lighthouse in geographical position 59°32′.86 N, 020°01′.24 E and two shallow waters) inside the traffic lane for southbound traffic by a line connecting the following geographical positions:

(53) 59°30′.27 N, 020°01′.84 E (55) 59°34′.15 N, 019°59′.68 E
(54) 59°34′.15 N, 020°01′.84 E (56) 59°30′.27 N, 019°59′.68 E

Precautionary areas

(u) A precautionary area is bounded by a line connecting the following geographical positions:

(16) 59°46′.01 N, 019°39′.39 E (23) 59°44′.24 N, 019°55′.74 E
(17) 59°47′.57 N, 019°47′.10 E (52) 59°43′.59 N, 019°55′.17 E
(26) 59°46′.96 N, 019°58′.92 E (43) 59°40′.89 N, 019°47′.83 E

(v) A circular precautionary area of radius 6.5 nautical miles is centred upon the following geographical position:

(57) 59°52′.03 N, 019°34′.66 E

(chartlets overleaf)

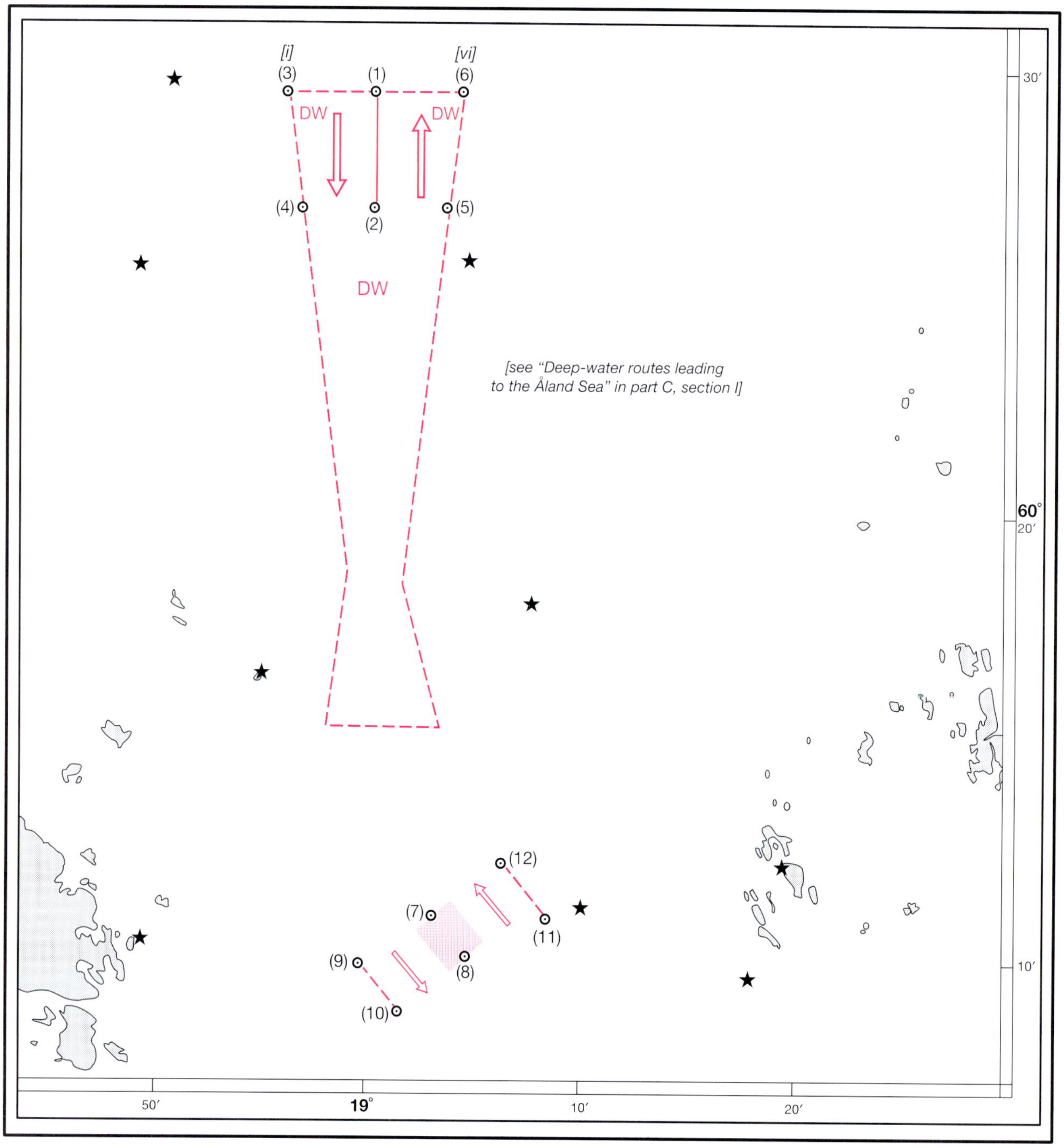

THE ÅLAND SEA: NORTH ÅLAND SEA

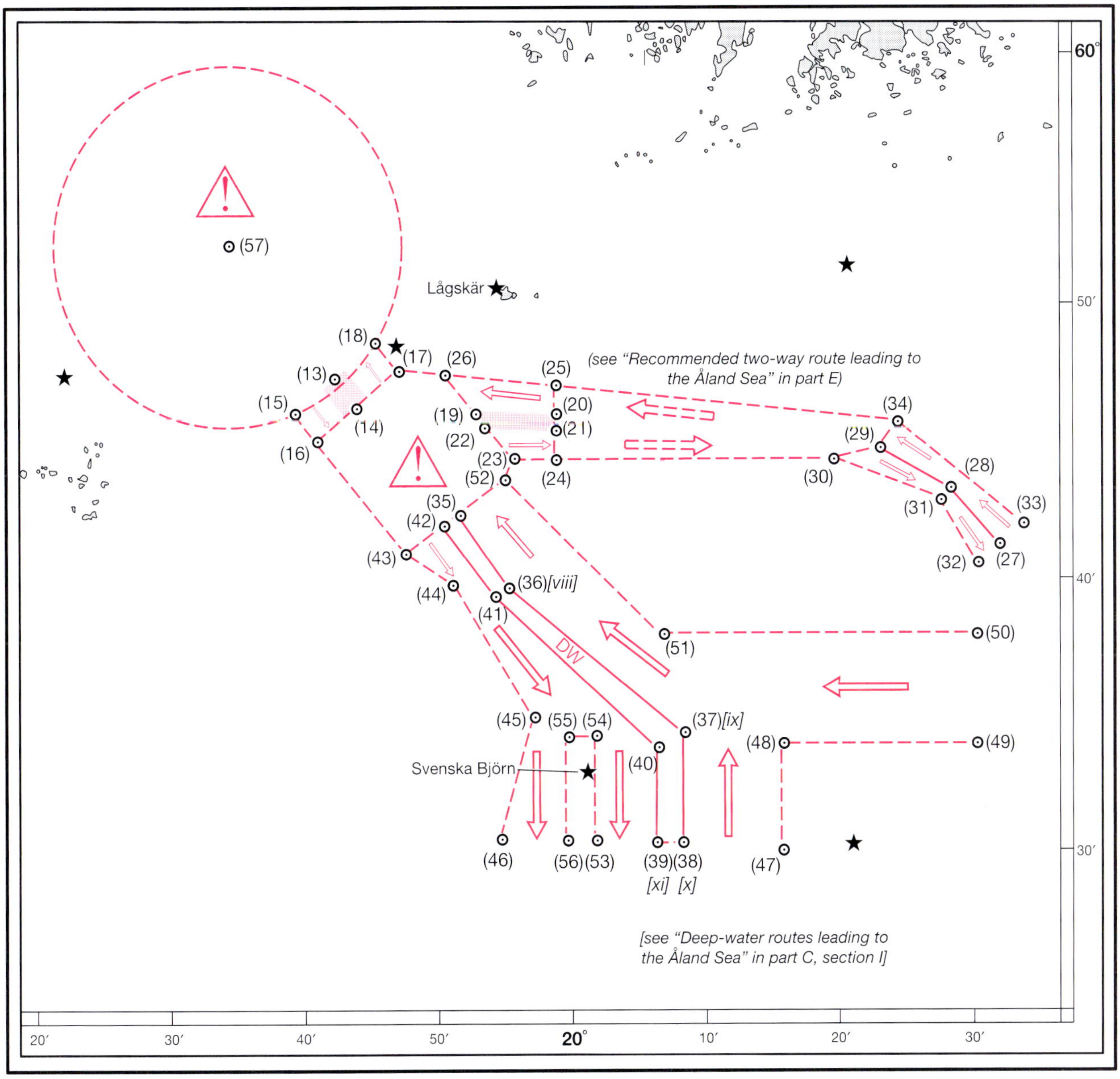

THE ÅLAND SEA: SOUTH ÅLAND SEA

B

WEST KLINTEHAMN

(Reference chart: Swedish SE72, edition 19/3-2008.
Note: This chart is based on World Geodetic System 1984 datum (WGS 84).)

Description of the traffic separation scheme

(a) A traffic separation zone is established upon the following geographical positions:

(1)	57°28′.00 N,	017°45′.67 E	(4)	57°26′.49 N,	017°42′.26 E
(2)	57°27′.09 N,	017°44′.75 E	(5)	57°27′.49 N,	017°43′.06 E
(3)	57°26′.10 N,	017°43′.97 E	(6)	57°28′.49 N,	017°44′.05 E

(b) A traffic lane for the northbound traffic is established between the traffic separation zone and a traffic separation line connecting the following geographical positions:

(7)	57°26′.55 N,	017°50′.52 E	(9)	57°24′.95 N,	017°49′.09 E
(8)	57°25′.87 N,	017°49′.82 E			

(c) A traffic lane for the southbound traffic is established between the traffic separation zone and a line connecting the following geographical positions:

(10)	57°29′.93 N,	017°39′.18 E	(12)	57°27′.63 N,	017°37′.13 E
(11)	57°28′.71 N,	017°37′.98 E			

(d) The limits of an inshore traffic zone along the coastline of Gotland Island lie between the following positions:

(13)	57°26′.46 N,	018°07′.15 E	(9)	57°24′.95 N,	017°49′.09 E
(7)	57°26′.55 N,	017°50′.52 E	(14)	57°20′.07 N,	018°10′.49 E
(8)	57°25′.87 N,	017°49′.82 E			

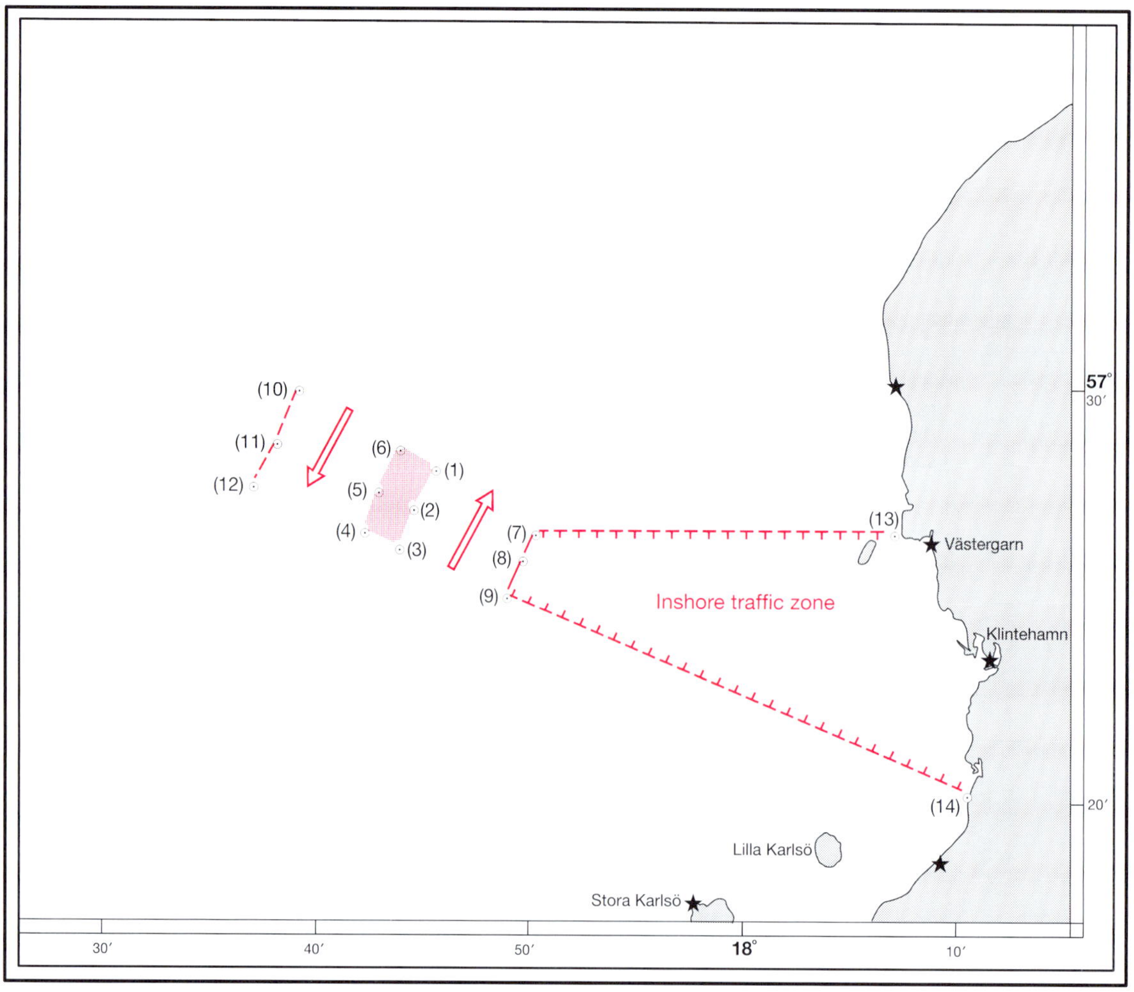

WEST KLINTEHAMN

NORTH HOBURGS BANK

(Reference chart: British Admiralty 2288)

Description of the traffic separation scheme

(a) A separation zone, one mile wide, is centred upon the following geographical positions:

(1)	56°46′.00 N,	018°19′.00 E	
(2)	56°49′.50 N,	018°27′.50 E	

(b) A traffic lane, three miles wide, is established on each side of the separation zone.

Inshore traffic zone

The area between the landward boundary of the traffic separation scheme and Gotland Island and between lines drawn in a direction of 324° from positions (1) and (2) is designated as an inshore traffic zone.

Note: The maximum draught in the traffic separation scheme is 12 metres. All ships bound to or from the north-eastern Baltic Sea with a draught of more than 12 metres are recommended to use the deep-water route Off Gotland Island.

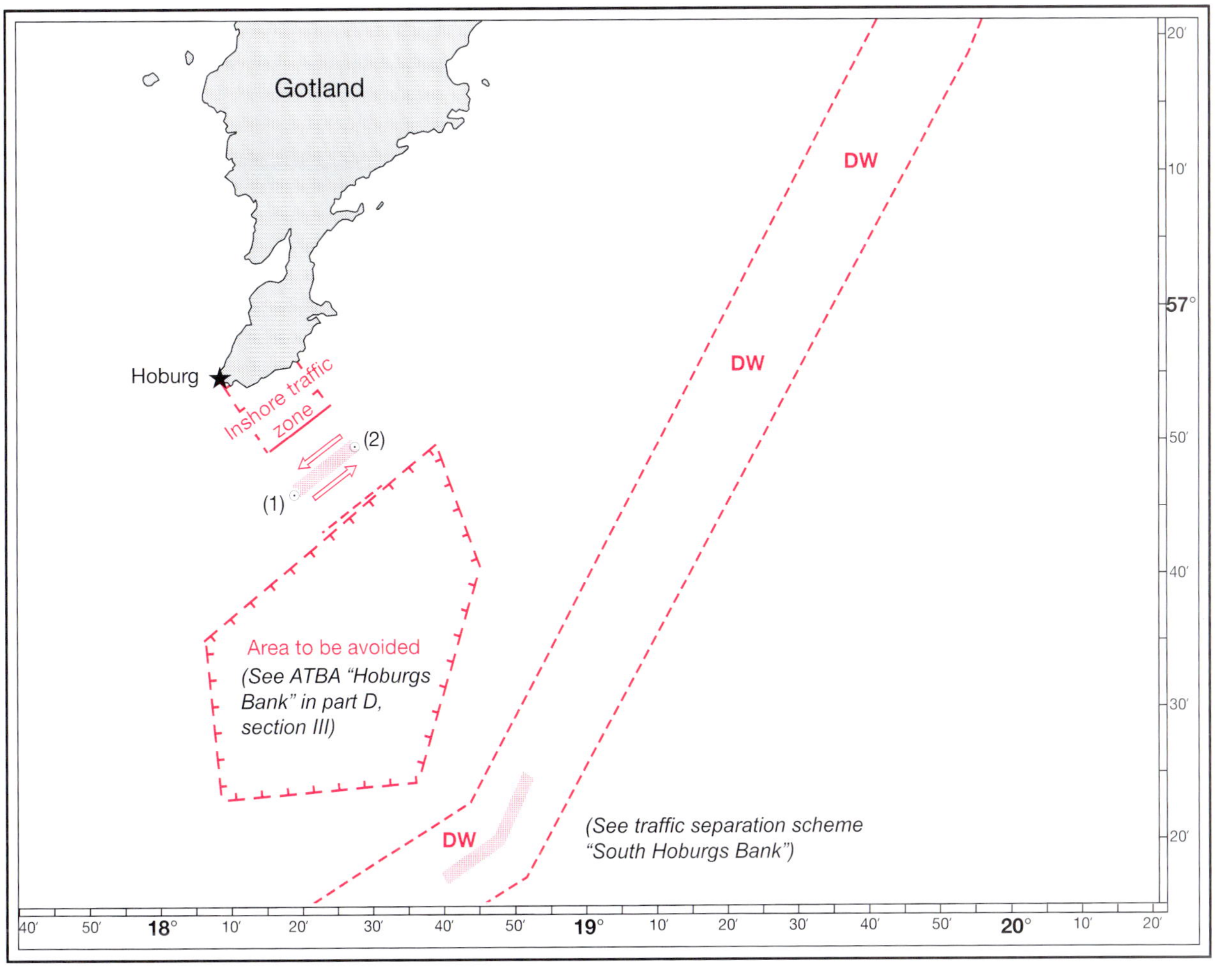

NORTH HOBURGS BANK

OFF ÖLAND ISLAND

(Reference chart: British Admiralty 2251)

Description of the traffic separation scheme

(a) A separation zone, two miles wide, is centred upon the following geographical positions:

(1) 56°02′.00 N,	016°35′.00 E	(3) 56°06′.70 N,	016°46′.90 E
(2) Ölands Södra Grund lighthouse			

(b) A traffic lane, three miles wide, is established on each side of the separation zone.

Inshore traffic zone

The area between the landward boundary of the traffic separation scheme and Öland Island and between a line drawn in an approximate direction of 328° from position (1) to Ölands Södra Udde lighthouse and a line drawn in a direction of 323° from position (3) to the shoreline is designated as an inshore traffic zone.

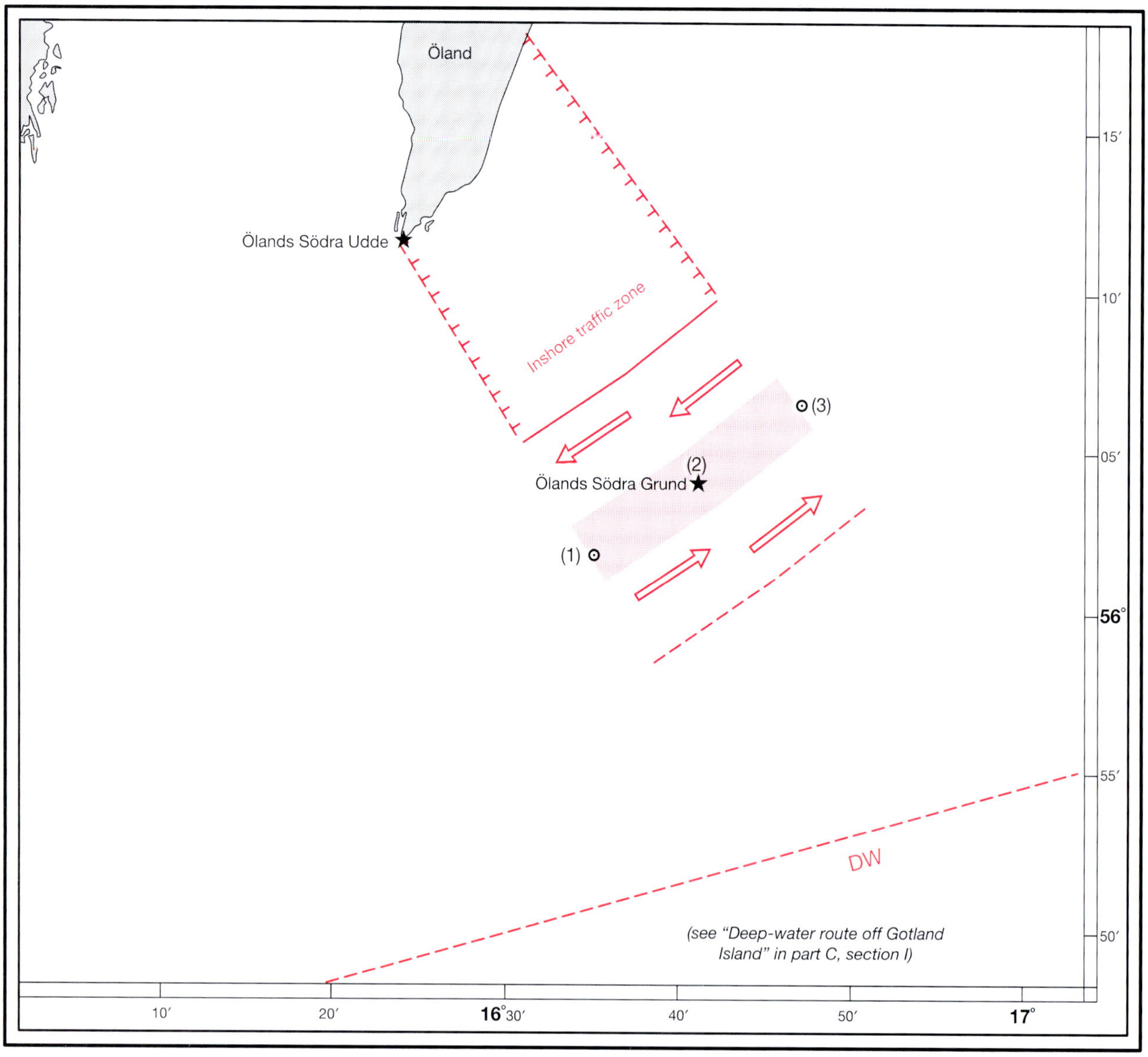

OFF ÖLAND ISLAND

IN BORNHOLMSGAT

(Reference chart: German 40, 6th edition, 1998.
Note: This chart is based on World Geodetic System 1984 datum (WGS 84).)

Description of the traffic separation scheme

Main part:

(a) A separation zone is bounded by a line connecting the following geographical positions:

(1)	55°24′.58 N,	014°37′.35 E	(3)	55°12′.53 N,	014°18′.95 E
(2)	55°25′.25 N,	014°36′.48 E	(4)	55°12′.03 N,	014°20′.04 E

(b) A traffic lane for eastbound traffic between the separation zone and a line connecting the following geographical positions:

(5)	55°22′.34 N,	014°40′.28 E	(6)	55°10′.37 N,	014°23′.76 E

(c) A traffic lane for westbound traffic between the separation zone and a line connecting the following geographical positions:

(7)	55°27′.55 N,	014°33′.62 E	(8)	55°14′.19 N,	014°15′.22 E

South-west part:

(d) A separation zone bounded by a line connecting the following geographical positions:

(9)	55°06′.06 N,	014°11′.90 E	(12)	55°02′.30 N,	014°02′.42 E
(10)	55°06′.56 N,	014°10′.80 E	(13)	55°01′.54 N,	014°02′.88 E
(11)	55°02′.99 N,	014°05′.97 E	(14)	55°02′.32 N,	014°06′.81 E

(e) A traffic lane for eastbound traffic between the separation zone and a line connecting the following geographical positions:

(15)	55°04′.40 N,	014°15′.60 E	(17)	54°58′.99 N,	014°04′.40 E
(16)	55°00′.02 N,	014°09′.65 E			

(f) A traffic lane for westbound traffic between the separation zone and a line connecting the following geographical positions:

(18)	55°08′.22 N,	014°07′.09 E	(20)	55°04′.85 N,	014°00′.89 E
(19)	55°05′.29 N,	014°03′.11 E			

West part:

(g) A separation zone bounded by a line connecting the following geographical positions:

(21)	55°10′.97 N,	014°05′.67 E	(23)	55°11′.93 N,	014°00′.00 E
(22)	55°11′.76 N,	014°05′.74 E	(24)	55°11′.13 N,	014°00′.00 E

(h) A traffic lane for eastbound traffic between the separation zone and a line connecting the following geographical positions:

(25)	55°08′.22 N,	014°07′.09 E	(26)	55°08′.43 N,	014°00′.00 E

(i) A traffic lane for westbound traffic between the separation zone and a line connecting the following geographical positions:

(27)	55°14′.46 N,	014°05′.99 E	(28)	55°14′.63 N,	014°00′.00 E

Precautionary area

(j) A precautionary area is established by a line connecting the following geographical positions:

(29)	55°10′.37 N,	014°23′.76 E	(32)	55°10′.97 N,	014°05′.67 E
(30)	55°14′.19 N,	014°15′.22 E	(33)	55°08′.22 N,	014°07′.09 E
(31)	55°14′.46 N,	014°05′.99 E	(34)	55°04′.40 N,	014°15′.60 E

Inshore traffic zone – Sweden

(k) The limits of the inshore traffic zone along the Swedish coastline lie between the following geographical positions:

(35)	55°23′.18 N,	014°27′.57 E	(37)	55°23′.20 N,	014°11′.58 E
(36)	55°28′.41 N,	014°17′.04 E	(38)	55°14′.19 N,	014°15′.22 E

Inshore traffic zone – Denmark (Bornholm)

(l) The limits of the inshore traffic zone along the Danish coastline lie between the following geographical positions:

(39)	55°17′.88 N,	014°46′.42 E	(41)	55°13′.76 N,	014°28′.42 E
(40)	55°22′.34 N,	014°40′.28 E	(42)	55°11′.35 N,	014°42′.14 E

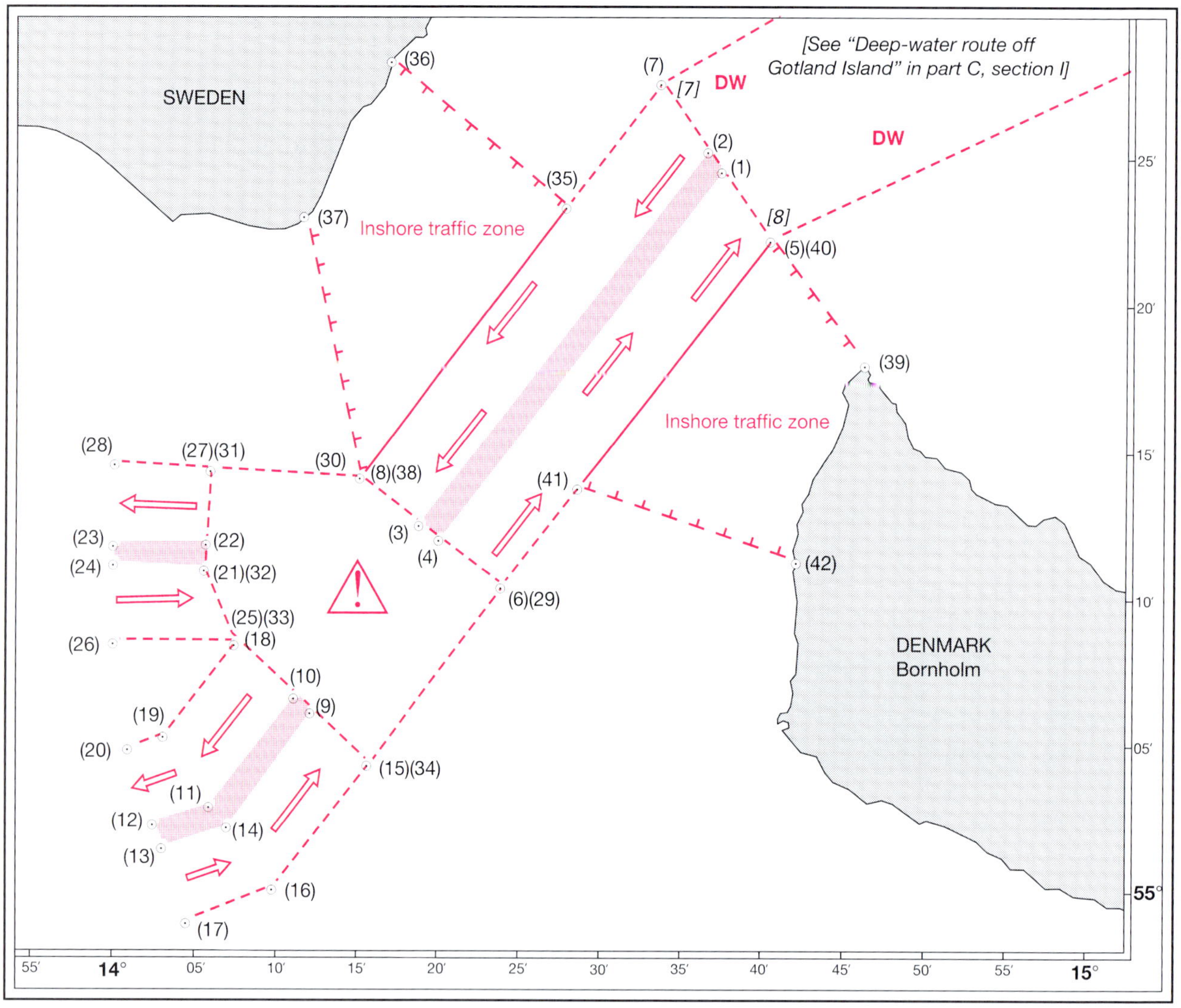

IN BORNHOLMSGAT

ON THE APPROACHES TO THE POLISH PORTS IN THE GULF OF GDAŃSK

Note: See "Recommendations on navigation to the Polish ports through the Gulf of Gdańsk Traffic area" in part F and the mandatory ship reporting system "On the approaches to the Polish ports in the Gulf of Gdańsk" in part G, section I.

(Reference chart: Polish 73 (INT 1288), 2004 edition.
Note: This chart is based on World Geodetic System 1984 datum (WGS 84).)

Traffic separation scheme "East"

Description of the traffic separation scheme

(a) A north-east separation zone is bounded by a line connecting the following geographical positions:

(1)	54°40′.43 N,	019°03′.79 E	(3)	54°37′.33 N,	019°06′.28 E
(2)	54°40′.57 N,	019°04′.61 E	(4)	54°37′.19 N,	019°05′.46 E

(b) A south-west separation zone is bounded by a line connecting the following geographical positions:

(5)	54°36′.47 N,	019°05′.36 E	(7)	54°26′.45 N,	018°58′.03 E
(6)	54°36′.26 N,	019°06′.13 E	(8)	54°26′.67 N,	018°57′.25 E

(c) A traffic separation line connects the following geographical positions:

(9)	54°37′.26 N,	019°05′.87 E	(11)	54°36′.36 N,	019°05′.74 E
(10)	54°36′.80 N,	019°06′.10 E (buoy ZN)			

(d) A traffic lane for inbound traffic is established between the separation zones/line and a line connecting the following geographical positions:

(12)	54°40′.15 N,	019°02′.15 E	(14)	54°27′.10 N,	018°55′.71 E
(13)	54°36′.90 N,	019°03′.81 E			

(e) A traffic lane for outbound traffic is established between the separation zone/line and a line connecting the following geographical positions:

(15)	54°40′.86 N,	019°06′.26 E	(17)	54°26′.02 N,	018°59′.57 E
(16)	54°36′.69 N,	019°08′.39 E			

Traffic separation scheme "West"

Description of the traffic separation scheme

North-east part:

(f) A separation line connects the following geographical positions:

(18)	54°40′.00 N,	018°57′.00 E	(21)	54°35′.10 N,	018°52′.80 E
(19)	54°36′.30 N,	018°54′.00 E	(22)	54°32′.40 N,	018°48′.74 E
(20)	54°35′.43 N,	018°53′.29 E (buoy HEL)			

(g) A traffic lane for inbound traffic is established between the separation line and a line connecting the following geographical positions:

(23)	54°40′.32 N,	018°55′.84 E	(25)	54°35′.43 N,	018°52′.15 E
(24)	54°36′.62 N,	018°52′.84 E	(26)	54°32′.73 N,	018°48′.09 E

(h) A traffic lane for outbound traffic is established between the separation line and a line connecting the following geographical positions:

(27)	54°39′.68 N,	018°58′.16 E	(29)	54°34′.77 N,	018°53′.45 E
(28)	54°35′.98 N,	018°55′.16 E	(30)	54°32′.07 N,	018°49′.39 E

Precautionary area

(i) A precautionary area is bounded by a line connecting the following geographical positions:

(31) 54°32′.07 N, 018°49′.39 E
(32) 54°32′.40 N, 018°48′.74 E
(33) 54°32′.73 N, 018°48′.09 E
(34) 54°32′.44 N, 018°46′.22 E
(35) 54°31′.94 N, 018°46′.20 E
(36) 54°31′.45 N, 018°46′.17 E
(37) 54°31′.12 N, 018°46′.81 E
(38) 54°30′.79 N, 018°47′.46 E
(39) 54°31′.56 N, 018°48′.61 E

South-west part:

(j) A separation line connects the following geographical positions:

(40) 54°31′.12 N, 018°46′.81 E
(41) 54°28′.48 N, 018°42′.84 E

(k) A traffic lane for inbound traffic is established between the separation line and a line connecting the following geographical positions:

(42) 54°31′.45 N, 018°46′.17 E
(43) 54°28′.81 N, 018°42′.20 E

(l) A traffic lane for outbound traffic is established between the separation line and a line connecting the following geographical positions:

(44) 54°30′.79 N, 018°47′.46 E
(45) 54°28′.15 N, 018°43′.49 E

West part:

(m) A separation line connects the following geographical positions:

(46) 54°31′.94 N, 018°46′.20 E
(47) 54°32′.04 N, 018°41′.10 E

(n) A traffic lane for inbound traffic is established between the separation line and a line connecting the following geographical positions:

(48) 54°32′.44 N, 018°46′.22 E
(49) 54°32′.54 N, 018°41′.13 E

(o) A traffic lane for outbound traffic is established between the separation line and a line connecting the following geographical positions:

(50) 54°31′.45 N, 018°46′.17 E
(51) 54°31′.54 N, 018°41′.07 E

Inshore traffic zone

(p) The inshore traffic zone is established in the waters between the inner limit of the north-eastern and western part of the traffic separation scheme "West" and the adjacent Polish coast and limited:

from the north by a line connecting the following geographical positions:

(23) 54°40′.32 N, 018°55′.84 E
(52) 54°40′.32 N, 018°44′.85 E

from the west by a line connecting the following geographical positions:

(49) 54°32′.54 N, 018°41′.13 E
(53) 54°41′.66 N, 018°41′.13 E

Recommended tracks between GD and NP buoys and between GN and PP buoys

See part E for description of recommended tracks on the approaches to the Polish ports in the Gulf of Gdańsk.

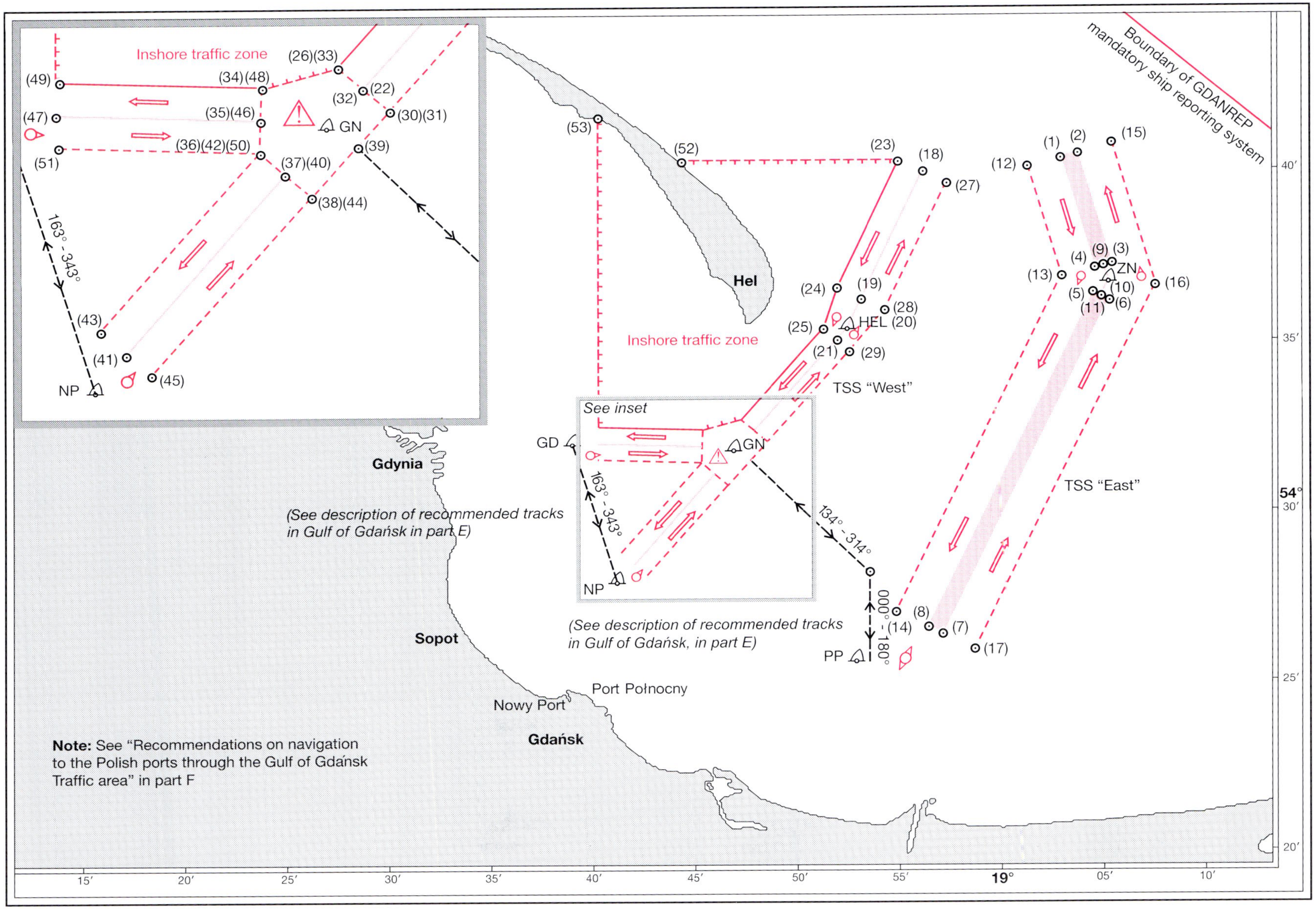

ON THE APPROACHES TO THE POLISH PORTS IN THE GULF OF GDAŃSK

SŁUPSKA BANK

(Reference chart: Polish 252 (INT 1219) published by the Hydrographic Office of the Polish Navy (BHMW), edition 12/2004.
Note: This chart is based on World Geodetic System 1984 datum (WGS 84).)

Description of the traffic separation scheme

The traffic separation scheme consists of:

- two traffic lanes, 1.75 miles wide, in two parts;
- one intermediate traffic separation zone, 0.5 mile wide, in two parts;
- one inshore traffic zone associated with the eastern part of the traffic separation scheme.

West part

(a) A separation zone bounded by a line connecting the following geographical positions:

(1)	54°47′.93 N,	016°29′.41 E	(3)	54°48′.80 N,	016°45′.90 E
(2)	54°47′.43 N,	016°29′.53 E	(4)	54°49′.28 N,	016°45′.78 E

(b) A traffic lane for eastbound traffic between the separation zone and a line connecting the following geographical positions:

(5)	54°45′.70 N,	016°29′.97 E	(6)	54°47′.06 N,	016°46′.32 E

(c) A traffic lane for westbound traffic between the separation zone and a line connecting the following geographical positions:

(7)	54°51′.01 N,	016°45′.35 E	(8)	54°49′.66 N,	016°28′.97 E

East part

(d) A separation zone bounded by a line connecting the following geographical positions:

(9)	54°50′.74 N,	016°56′.58 E	(11)	54°53′.72 N,	017°21′.59 E
(10)	54°50′.26 N,	016°56′.79 E	(12)	54°54′.21 N,	017°21′.39 E

(e) A traffic lane for eastbound traffic between the separation zone and a line connecting the following geographical positions:

(13)	54°48′.56 N,	016°57′.51 E	(14)	54°52′.02 N,	017°22′.29 E

(f) A traffic lane for westbound traffic between the separation zone and a line connecting the following geographical positions:

(15)	54°55′.91 N,	017°20′.68 E	(16)	54°52′.44 N,	016°55′.86 E

Inshore traffic zone

The area between the southern boundary of the eastern part of the traffic separation scheme and the Polish coast, which lies between a line drawn from position (13) above in a direction of 158° to the coast and a line drawn from position (14) above in a direction of 135° to the coast, is designated an inshore traffic zone.

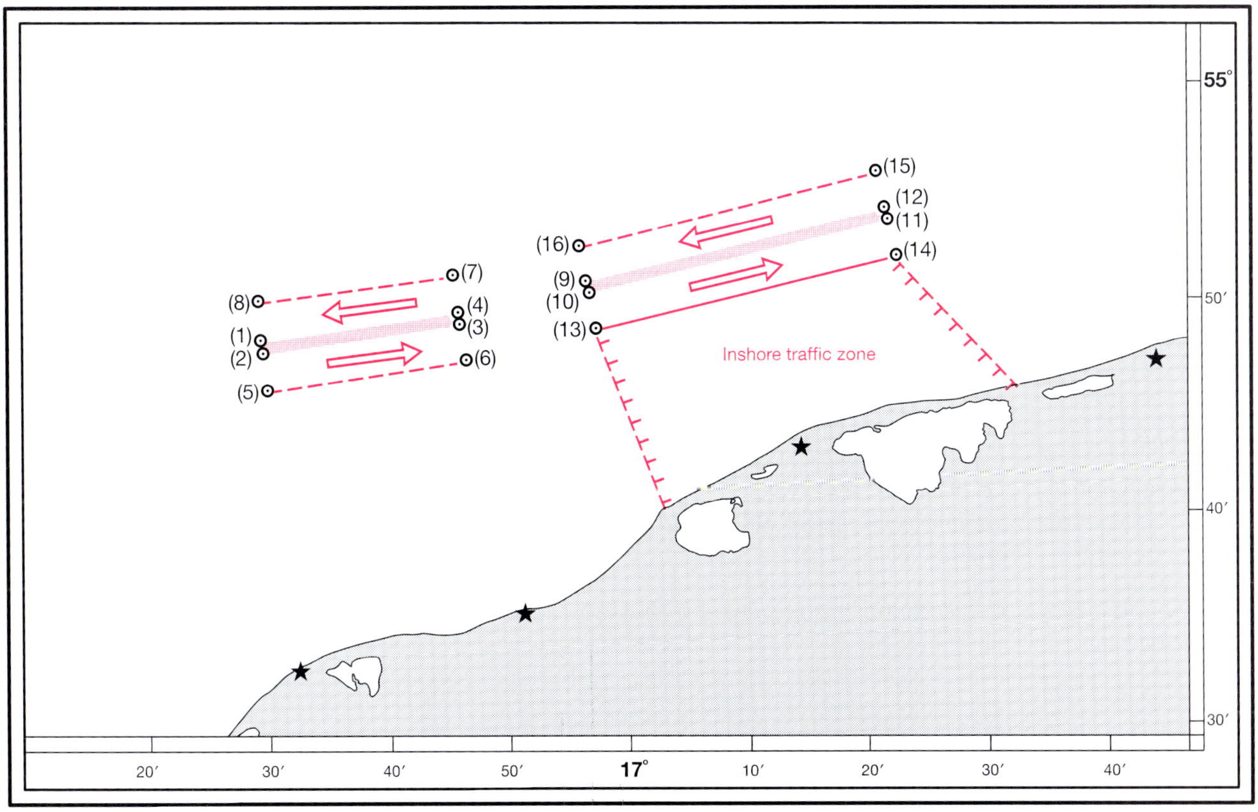

SŁUPSKA BANK

ADLERGRUND

(Reference chart: German 40 (INT 1201) published by the German Federal Maritime and Hydrographic Agency (BSH), 7th edition, 2006.
Note: This chart is based on World Geodetic System 1984 datum (WGS 84).)

Description of the traffic separation scheme

The traffic separation scheme consists of:

- two traffic lanes 2.0 miles wide;
- one intermediate traffic separation zone 0.5 mile wide.

(a) A separation zone, half a mile wide, centred upon the following geographical positions:

(1) 54°38′.00 N, 014°15′.50 E
(2) 54°36′.50 N, 014°24′.00 E
(3) 54°37′.00 N, 014°30′.00 E

(b) A traffic lane for eastbound traffic between the separation zone and a line connecting the following geographical positions:

(4) 54°36′.00 N, 014°14′.50 E
(5) 54°34′.50 N, 014°24′.00 E
(6) 54°35′.00 N, 014°30′.50 E

(c) A traffic lane for westbound traffic between the separation zone and a line connecting the following geographical positions:

(7) 54°40′.00 N, 014°16′.50 E
(8) 54°38′.50 N, 014°24′.30 E
(9) 54°39′.00 N, 014°29′.50 E

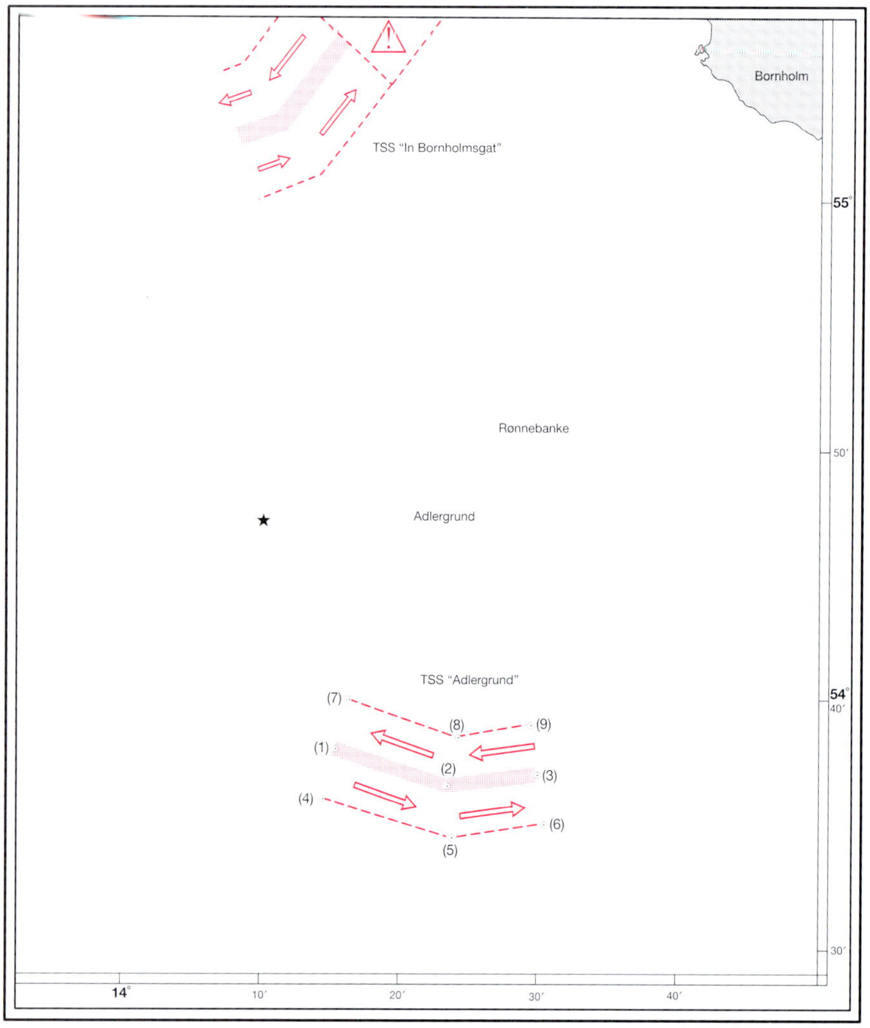

ADLERGRUND

OFF FALSTERBOREV

Note: See mandatory ship reporting system "In the Sound between Denmark and Sweden (SOUNDREP)" in part G, section I.

(Reference charts: Swedish Administration of Shipping and Navigation 921, 1980 edition; 929, 1980 edition. **Note:** These charts are based on Swedish National geodetic datum.)

Description of the traffic separation scheme

The traffic separation scheme "Off Falsterborev" consists of four parts:

Part I:

(a) A roundabout with a circular traffic separation zone half a mile in diameter is centred upon the following geographical position:
(1) 55°18′.60 N, 012°39′.50 E

(b) A circular traffic lane, one and three quarter miles wide, is established around the circular separation zone.

Part II:

(a) A separation line connects the following geographical positions:
(2) 55°15′.50 N, 012°52′.20 E (3) 55°17′.50 N, 012°42′.50 E

(b) A traffic lane, 1.1 miles wide, is established on each side of the separation line and the outside limits of the traffic lanes are extended to intersect with the outside limit of the roundabout.

Part III:

(a) A separation line connects the following geographical positions:
(4) 55°13′.10 N, 012°39′.10 E (5) 55°16′.60 N, 012°38′.90 E

(b) A traffic lane, one mile wide, is established on each side of the separation line and the outside limits of the traffic lanes are extended to intersect with the outside limit of the roundabout.

Part IV:

(a) A separation line connects the following geographical positions:
(6) 55°20′.50 N, 012°39′.40 E (7) 55°25′.00 N, 012°40′.70 E

(b) A traffic lane, one and a half miles wide, is established on each side of the separation line and the outside limits of the traffic lanes are extended to intersect with the outside limit of the roundabout.

Inshore traffic zone

The area between the eastern landward boundaries of the roundabout and the traffic separation scheme and the Swedish coast, and lying between a line drawn from position (2) to Falsterbokanalen No. 2 lighthouse (approximate position 55°23′.60 N, 012°57′.00 E) and a line drawn from position (7) to Skanör lighthouse (approximate position 55°25′.00 N, 012°49′.70 E), is designated as an inshore traffic zone.

Note: The roundabout serves the purpose of facilitating manoeuvring in the area where traffic to and from the Baltic Sea, the Kiel Canal and The Sound meets.

(chartlet overleaf)

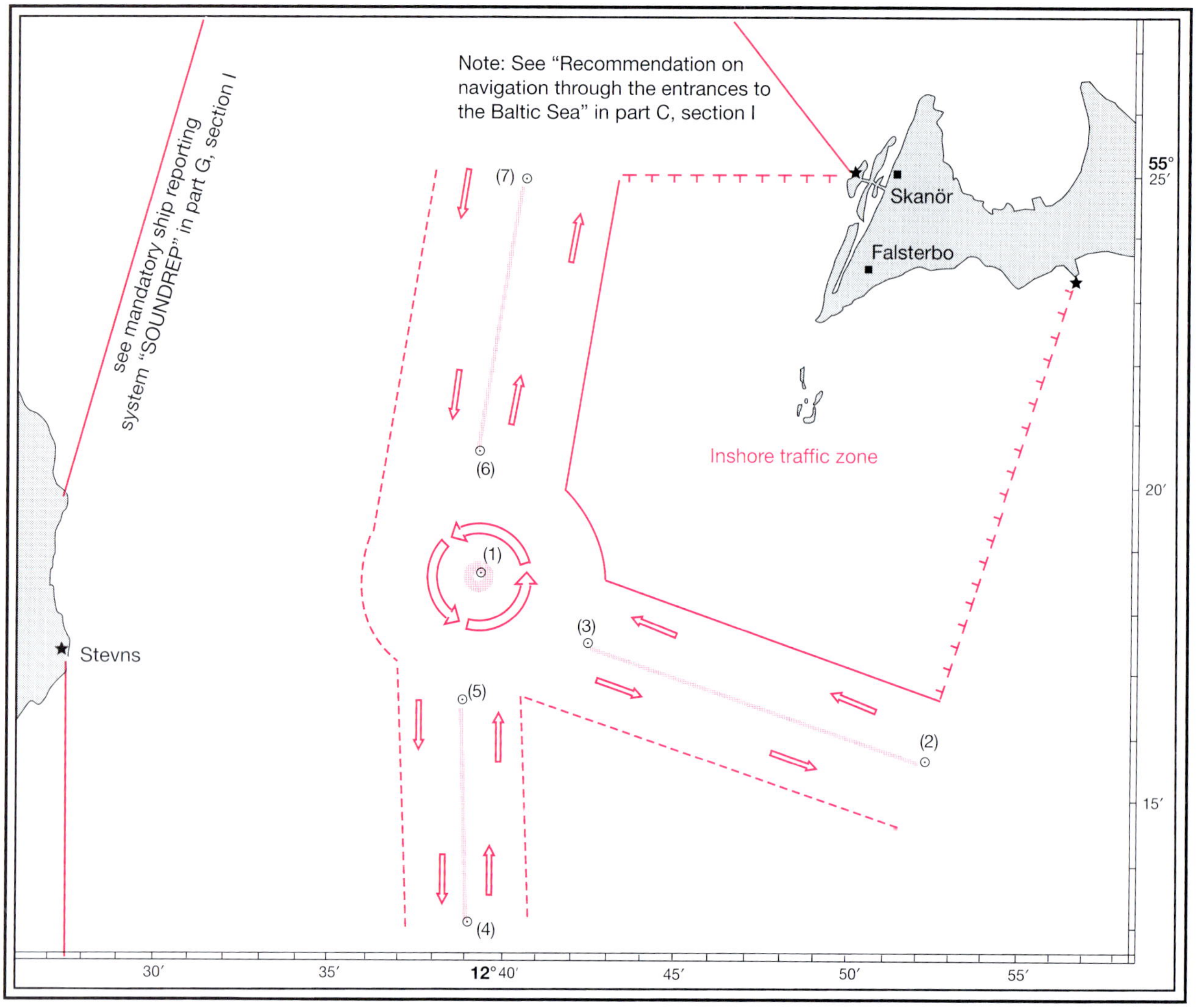

OFF FALSTERBOREV

IN THE SOUND

Note: See "Recommendation on navigation through the entrances to the Baltic Sea" in part C, section I and mandatory ship reporting system "In the Sound between Denmark and Sweden (SOUNDREP)" in part G, section I.

(Reference charts: Danish 131 (INT 1331), February 2006 edition; Swedish 922, January 2007 edition.
Note: These charts are based on World Geodetic System 1984 datum (WGS 84).)

Description of the traffic separation scheme

(a) A separation line connects the following geographical positions:

(1)	56°07′.30 N,	012°31′.46 E	(3)	55°58′.88 N,	012°41′.23 E
(2)	56°03′.27 N,	012°39′.01 E			

(b) A traffic lane for northbound traffic is established between the separation line and a separation line connecting the following geographic positions:

(4)	56°08′.03 N,	012°32′.69 E	(6)	56°03′.35 N,	012°39′.97 E
(5)	56°06′.39 N,	012°34′.74 E	(7)	55°59′.08 N,	012°42′.37 E

(c) A traffic lane for southbound traffic is established between the separation line and a separation line connecting the following geographical positions:

(8)	56°06′.58 N,	012°30′.22 E	(10)	56°03′.10 N,	012°38′.21 E
(9)	56°05′.50 N,	012°33′.22 E	(11)	56°01′.66 N,	012°37′.79 E

(d) In the southern part of this traffic lane the southbound traffic is divided into two lanes by a separation zone, bounded by a line connecting the following geographical positions:

(12)	56°00′.80 N,	012°38′.20 E	(14)	56°00′.80 N,	012°39′.35 E
(13)	56°01′.66 N,	012°38′.82 E			

(e) A traffic lane eastern most for southbound traffic is established between the separation line and a separation line connecting the following geographic positions:

(15)	56°00′.80 N,	012°39′.35 E	(17)	55°58′.82 N,	012°39′.98 E
(16)	55°59′.98 N,	012°39′.87 E			

Inshore traffic zones

Western inshore traffic zone

The area between the western landward boundary of the traffic separation scheme and the Danish coast and between a line drawn in the direction 224° from position (8) to position (20) and a line drawn in the direction of 257° from position (11) to position (21) is designated as an inshore traffic zone.

(8)	56°06′.58 N,	012°30′.22 E	(11)	56°01′.66 N,	012°37′.79 E
(20)	56°05′.64 N,	012°28′.64 E	(21)	56°01′.47 N,	012°36′.37 E

Eastern inshore traffic zone

The area between the eastern landward boundary of the traffic separation scheme and the Swedish coast and between a line drawn in a direction 049° from position (4) to position (18) and a line drawn in a direction of 060° from position (6) to position (19) is designated as an inshore traffic zone.

(4)	56°08′.03 N,	012°32′.69 E	(6)	56°03′.35 N,	012°39′.97 E
(18)	56°08′.72 N,	012°34′.09 E	(19)	56°03′.66 N,	012°40′.82 E

Note:
Cross-channel traffic
All precautions, including if necessary a reduction of speed, should be taken in the area between Helsingborg and Helsingør, which is widely used by local cross-channel ferry traffic.

(chartlet overleaf)

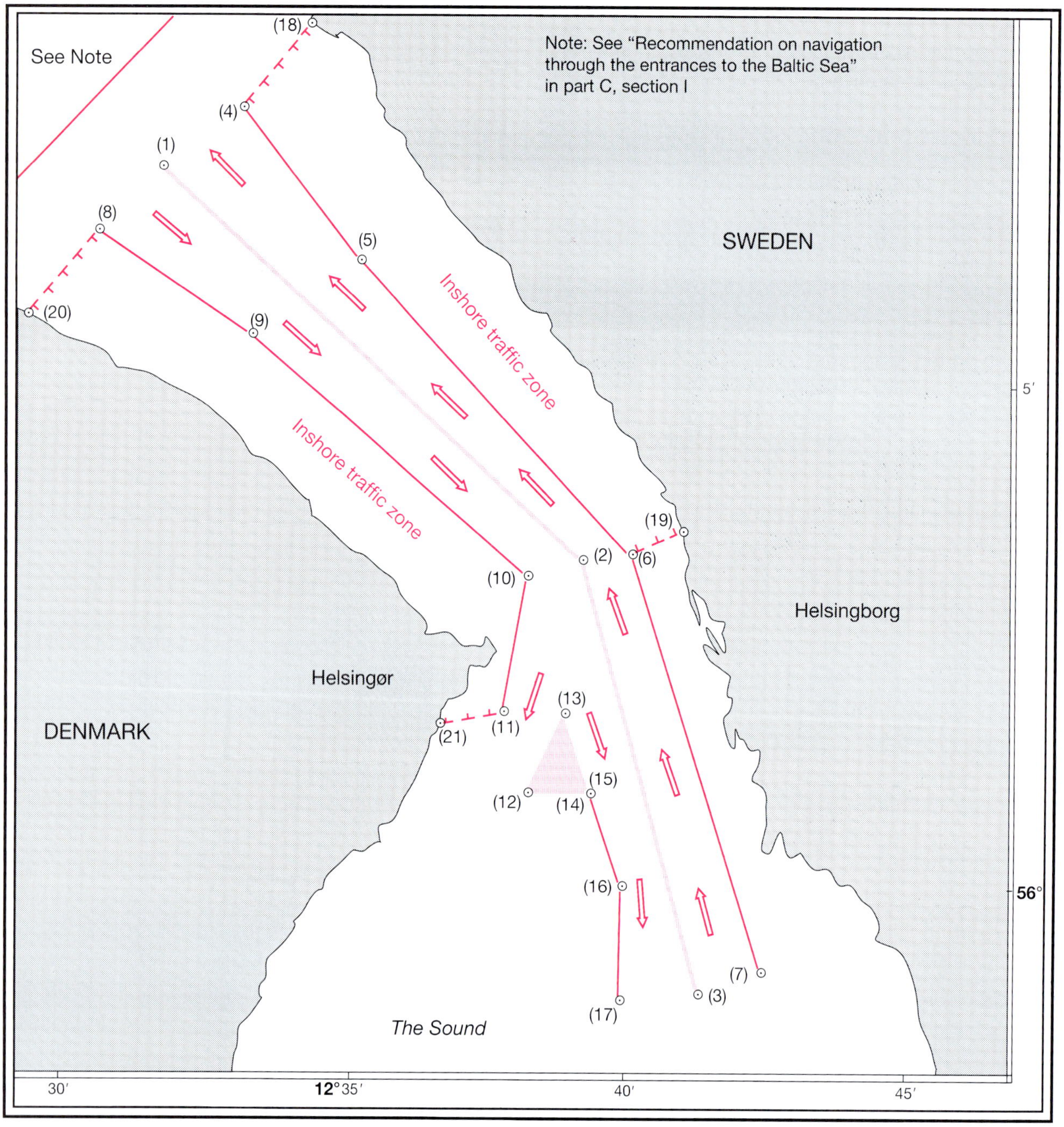

See Note
Note: See "Recommendation on navigation through the entrances to the Baltic Sea" in part C, section I
(18)
(4)
(1)
(8)
(5)
(20)
(9)
SWEDEN
Inshore traffic zone
Inshore traffic zone
5′
(19)
(2)
(6)
(10)
Helsingborg
Helsingør
(13)
(11)
DENMARK
(21)
(15)
(12)
(14)
(16)
56°
(7)
(3)
(17)
The Sound
30′
12°35′
40′
45′

IN THE SOUND

NORTH OF RÜGEN

(Reference chart: German 40, 6th edition, 1998.
Note: This chart is based on World Geodetic System 1984 datum (WGS 84).)

Description of the traffic separation scheme

(a) North traffic separation line connecting the following geographical positions:

(1)	54°54′.43 N,	013°11′.33 E	(2)	54°52′.80 N,	013°03′.12 E

(b) A separation zone is bounded by a line connecting the following geographical positions:

(3)	54°51′.59 N,	013°13′.03 E	(5)	54°50′.91 N,	013°04′.25 E
(4)	54°52′.54 N,	013°12′.47 E	(6)	54°49′.96 N,	013°04′.82 E

(c) South traffic separation line connecting the following geographical positions:

(7)	54°49′.70 N,	013°14′.16 E	(8)	54°48′.07 N,	013°05′.95 E

(d) A traffic lane for westbound traffic is situated between the separation zone and the north traffic separation line.

(e) A traffic lane for eastbound traffic is situated between the separation zone and the south traffic separation line.

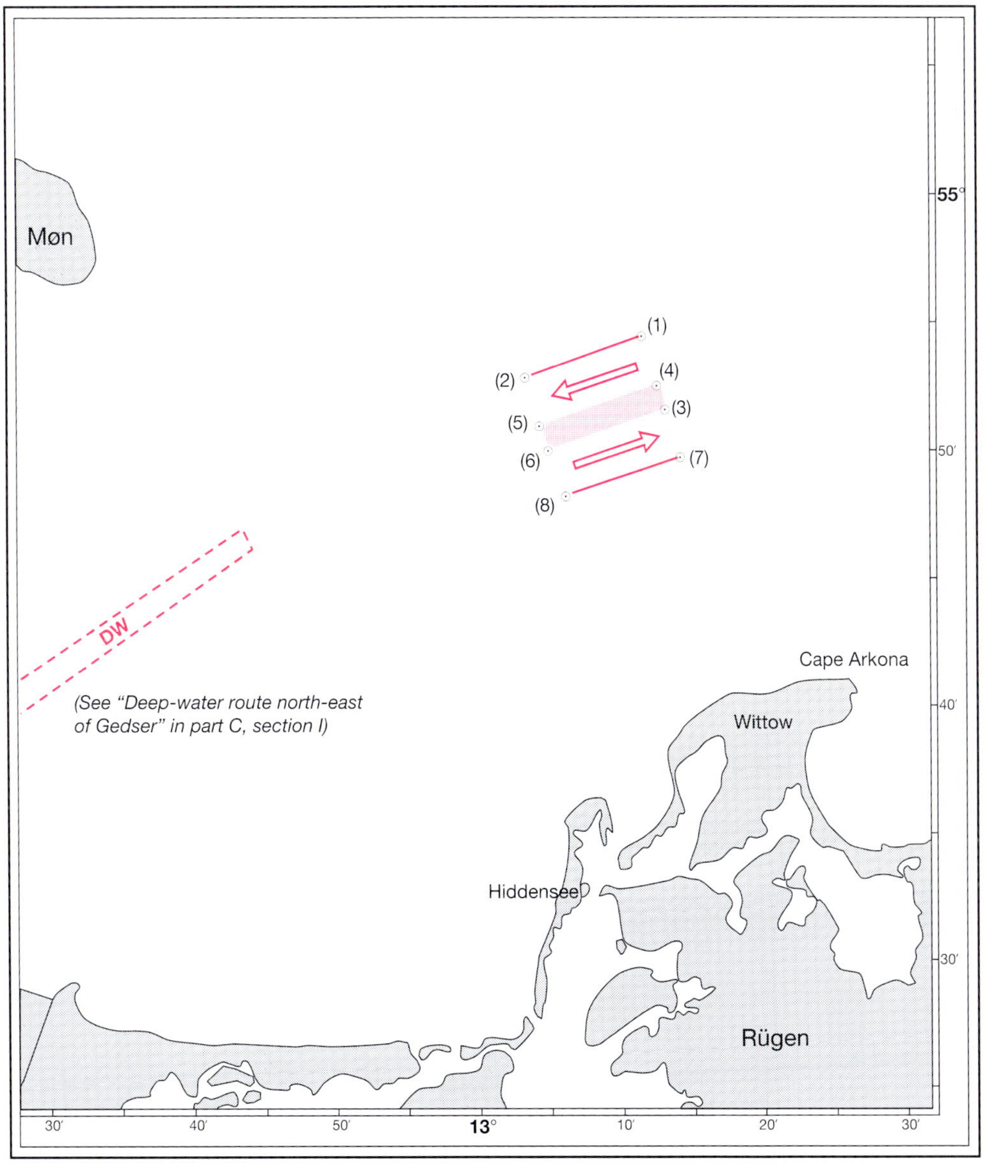

NORTH OF RÜGEN

B

SOUTH OF GEDSER

(Reference chart for all except the inshore traffic zone: Danish 186, 1984 edition.
Note: This chart is based on European datum. Locations relative to this datum are shown in black.)

Description of the traffic separation scheme

(a) A separation line connects the following geographical positions:

(1)	54°31′.20 N,	012°14′.10 E	3)	54°25′.30 N,	012°09′.40 E
(2)	54°27′.60 N,	012°12′.30 E	(4)	54°25′.30 N,	012°07′.00 E

(b) A separation zone, half a mile wide, is centred upon the following geographical positions:

(4)	54°25′.30 N,	012°07′.00 E	(5)	54°25′.30 N,	012°00′.00 E

(c) A traffic lane for westbound traffic is established between the separation line, the separation zone and a line connecting the following geographical positions:

(6)	54°31′.60 N,	012°10′.70 E	(8)	54°27′.10 N,	012°05′.20 E
(7)	54°28′.10 N,	012°09′.50 E	(9)	54°27′.10 N,	012°00′.00 E

(d) A traffic lane for eastbound traffic is established between the separation line, the separation zone and a line connecting the following geographical positions:

(10)	54°30′.80 N,	012°17′.60 E	(13)	54°23′.40 N,	012°05′.10 E
(11)	54°27′.20 N,	012°15′.20 E	(14)	54°23′.40 N,	012°00′.00 E
(12)	54°23′.40 N,	012°09′.80 E			

Description of the inshore traffic zone

(Reference chart: German 163, 11th edition, 2003.
Note: This chart is based on World Geodetic System 1984 datum (WGS 84). Locations relative to this datum are shown in colour.)

(e) The limits of the inshore traffic zone along the German coastline lie between the following geographical positions:

(15)	54°28′.41 N,	012°29′.94 E	(18)	54°23′.33 N,	012°09′.70 E
(16)	54°30′.76 N,	012°17′.53 E	(19)	54°12′.88 N,	012°09′.70 E
(17)	54°27′.16 N,	012°15′.13 E			

Note: The northern termination of the traffic separation scheme is connected to the deep-water route "North-east of Gedser" (see part C, section I).

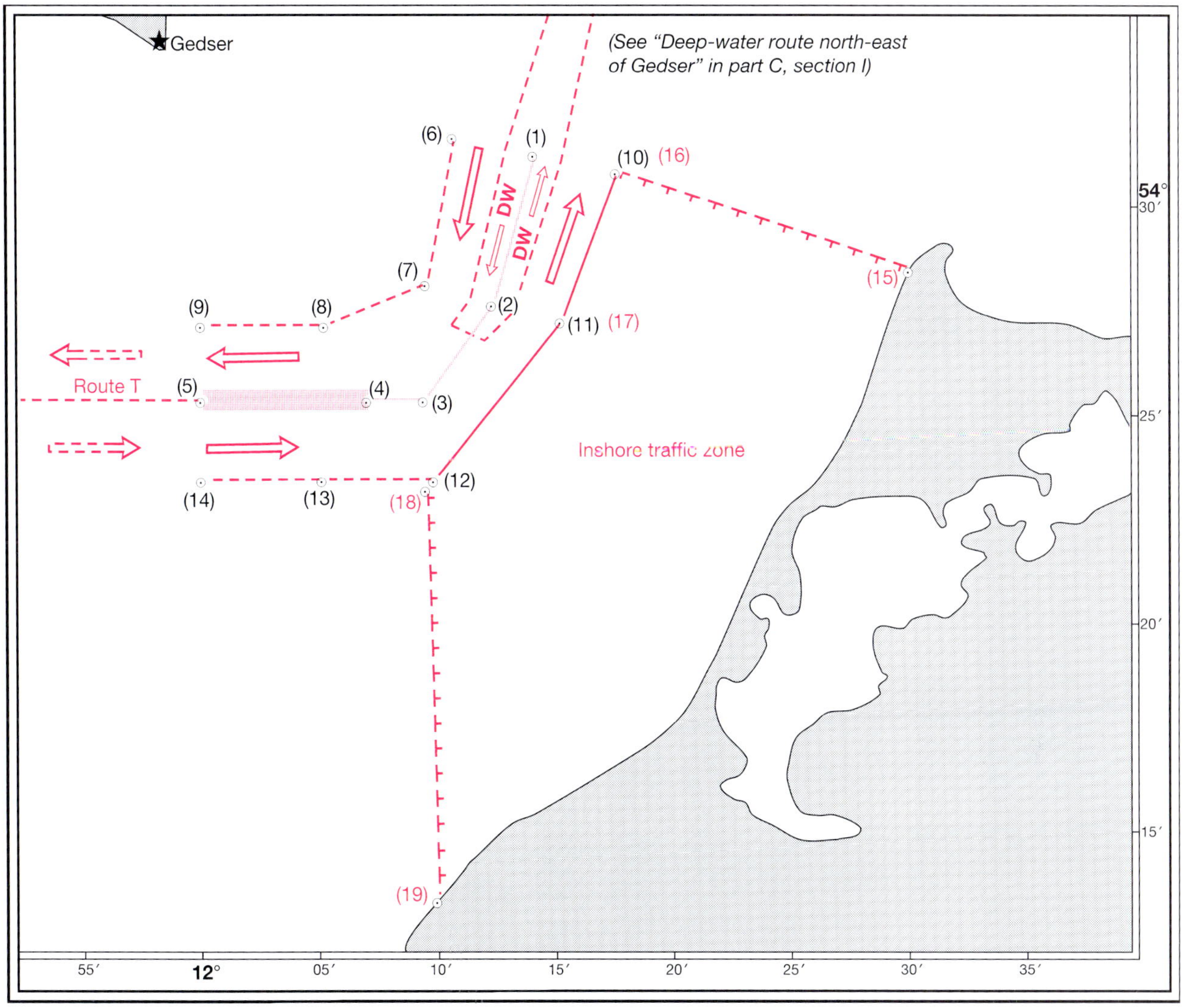

SOUTH OF GEDSER

OFF KIEL LIGHTHOUSE

(Reference chart: German Hydrographic Office 32, 1986 edition.
Note: This chart is based on European datum.)

Description of the traffic separation scheme

(a) A separation zone is bounded by a line connecting the following geographical positions:

(1)	54°29′.97 N,	010°18′.52 E	(3)	54°29′.02 N,	010°16′.57 E
(2)	54°29′.78 N,	010°18′.72 E	(4)	54°29′.18 N,	010°16′.53 E

(b) A traffic lane for north-eastbound traffic is established between the separation zone and a line connecting the following geographical positions:

(5)	54°28′.15 N,	010°17′.57 E	(6)	54°29′.20 N,	010°19′.40 E

(c) A traffic lane for south-westbound traffic is established between the separation zone and a line connecting the following geographical positions:

(7)	54°29′.65 N,	010°15′.78 E	(8)	54°30′.48 N,	010°17′.90 E

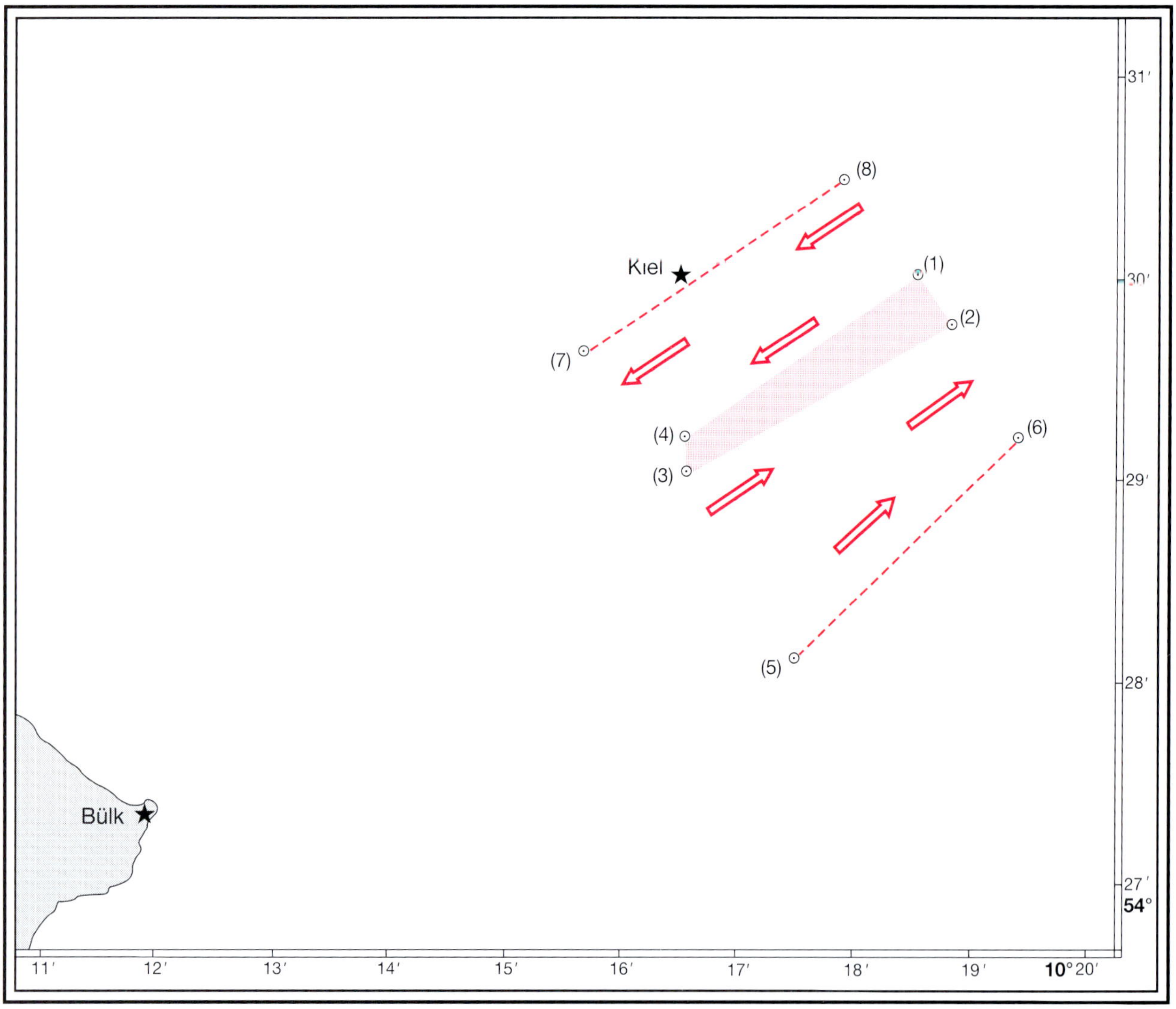

OFF KIEL LIGHTHOUSE

BETWEEN KORSOER AND SPROGOE

(Reference chart: Danish 143 (INT 1369), 14th edition, 1999.
Note: This chart is based on World Geodetic System 1984 datum (WGS 84).)

Description of the traffic separation scheme

(a) A separation line connects the following geographical positions:

(1)	55°21′.75 N,	011°02′.13 E	(2)	55°19′.23 N,	011°02′.19 E

(b) A traffic lane for northbound traffic is established between the separation line and a line connecting the following geographical positions:

(3)	55°21′.70 N,	011°02′.77 E	(4)	55°19′.49 N,	011°02′.80 E

(c) A traffic lane for southbound traffic is established between the separation line and a line connecting the following geographical positions:

(5)	55°21′.81 N,	011°01′.35 E	(7)	55°20′.43 N,	011°01′.51 E
(6)	55°21′.02 N,	011°01′.59 E	(8)	55°18′.91 N,	011°01′.42 E

Notes:

1 See mandatory ship reporting system "In the Storebælt (Great Belt) Traffic Area" in part G, section I.

2 The minimum free water depth in the northbound traffic lane is 17 metres and in the southbound traffic lane 19 metres.

3 Ships should reduce speed to maximum of 20 knots before entering the appropriate lane of the scheme.

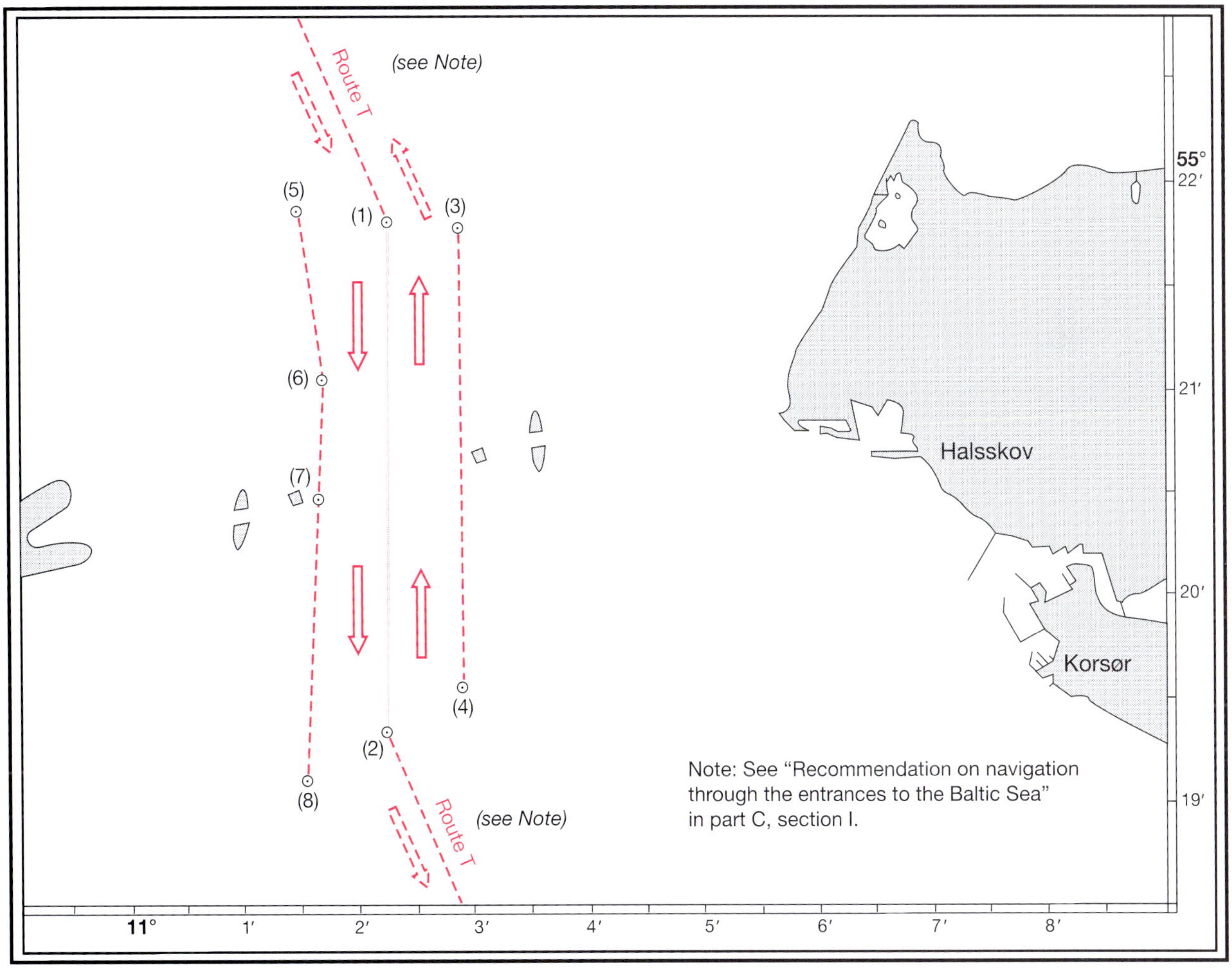

BETWEEN KORSOER AND SPROGOE

AT HATTER BARN

Note: See mandatory ship reporting system "In the Storebælt (Great Belt) Traffic Area (BELTREP)" in part G, section I.

(Reference chart: Danish 128, 9th edition, October 2007.
Note: This chart is based on World Geodetic System 1984 datum (WGS 84).)

Description of the traffic separation scheme

(a) A separation line connects the following geographical positions:

(1)	55°54′.67 N,	010°56′.40 E	(2)	55°50′.03 N,	010°49′.58 E

(b) A traffic lane, 675 metres wide at the narrowest part, for north-eastbound traffic is established between the separation line and a separation zone bounded by a line connecting the following geographical positions:

(3)	55°54′.75 N,	010°57′.87 E	(7)	55°47′.89 N,	010°50′.24 E
(4)	55°53′.88 N,	010°56′.08 E	(8)	55°47′.89 N,	010°51′.64 E
(5)	55°52′.42 N,	010°53′.93 E	(9)	55°53′.27 N,	010°59′.53 E
(6)	55°49′.64 N,	010°50′.24 E	(10)	55°54′.75 N,	011°00′.00 E

(c) A traffic lane, 800 metres wide, for south-westbound traffic is established between the separation line and a separation line connecting the following geographical positions:

(11)	55°54′.61 N,	010°55′.31 E	(12)	55°50′.54 N,	010°49′.34 E

Notes:

1 The minimum depth of water below mean sea level in the traffic separation scheme is 15 metres.

2 Ships with a draught of more than 13 metres should use the deep-water route which lies north-west of the traffic separation scheme.

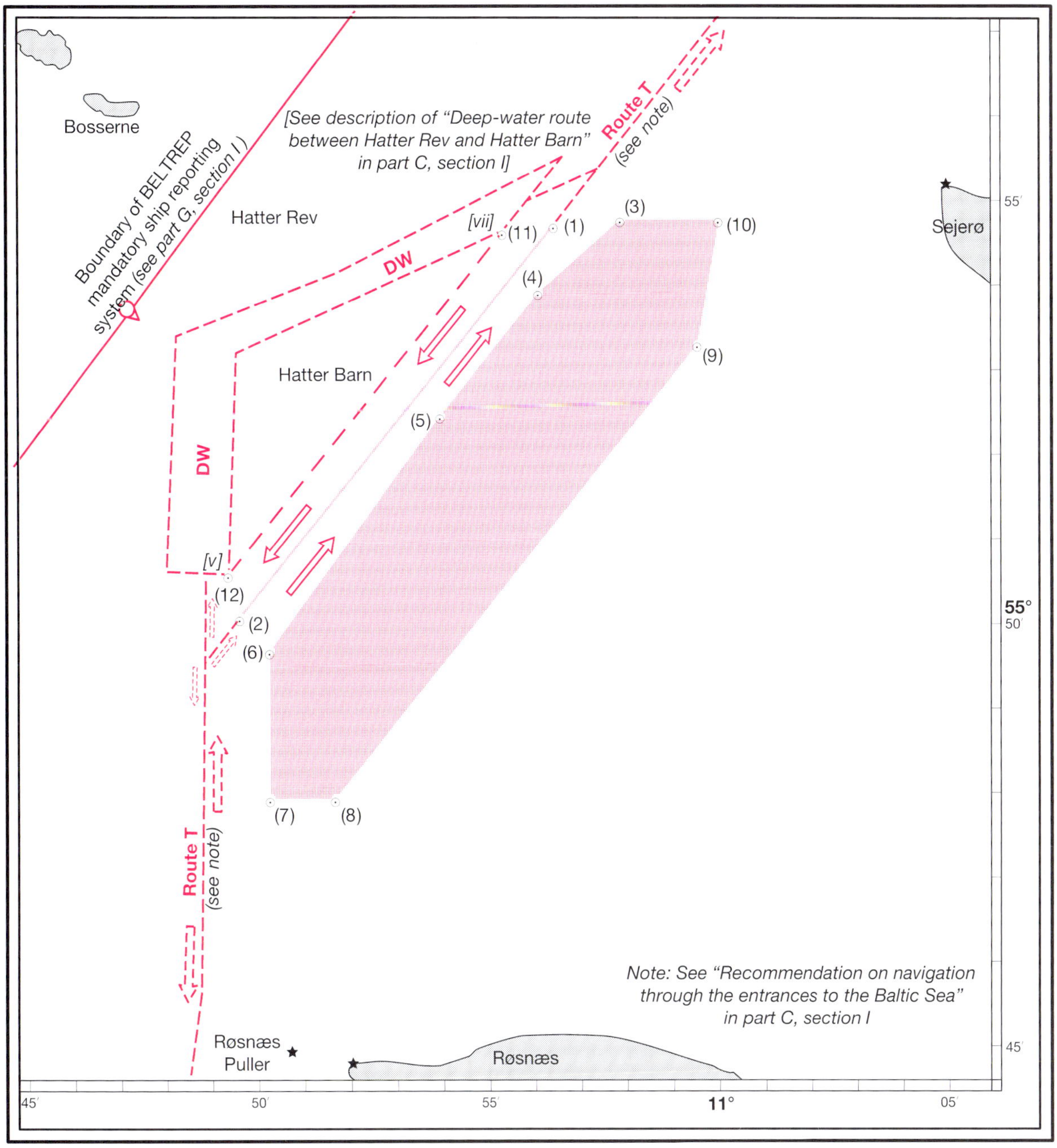

AT HATTER BARN

B

Section II

Western European waters

Caution: The chartlets are for illustrative purposes only and must not be used for navigation. Mariners should consult the appropriate nautical publications and charts for up-to-date details on aids to navigation and other relevant information.

Warning: The geographical positions given in the descriptions of the routeing systems are only correct for charts using the same geodetic datum as the reference charts indicated under each scheme. Charts published by other hydrographic offices may use a different geodetic datum, as may new editions of the reference charts published after the adoption of the routeing system. Where amendments to existing systems are not based on the same geodetic datum as the original system, this is emphasized by the use of different colours for definitions of positions.

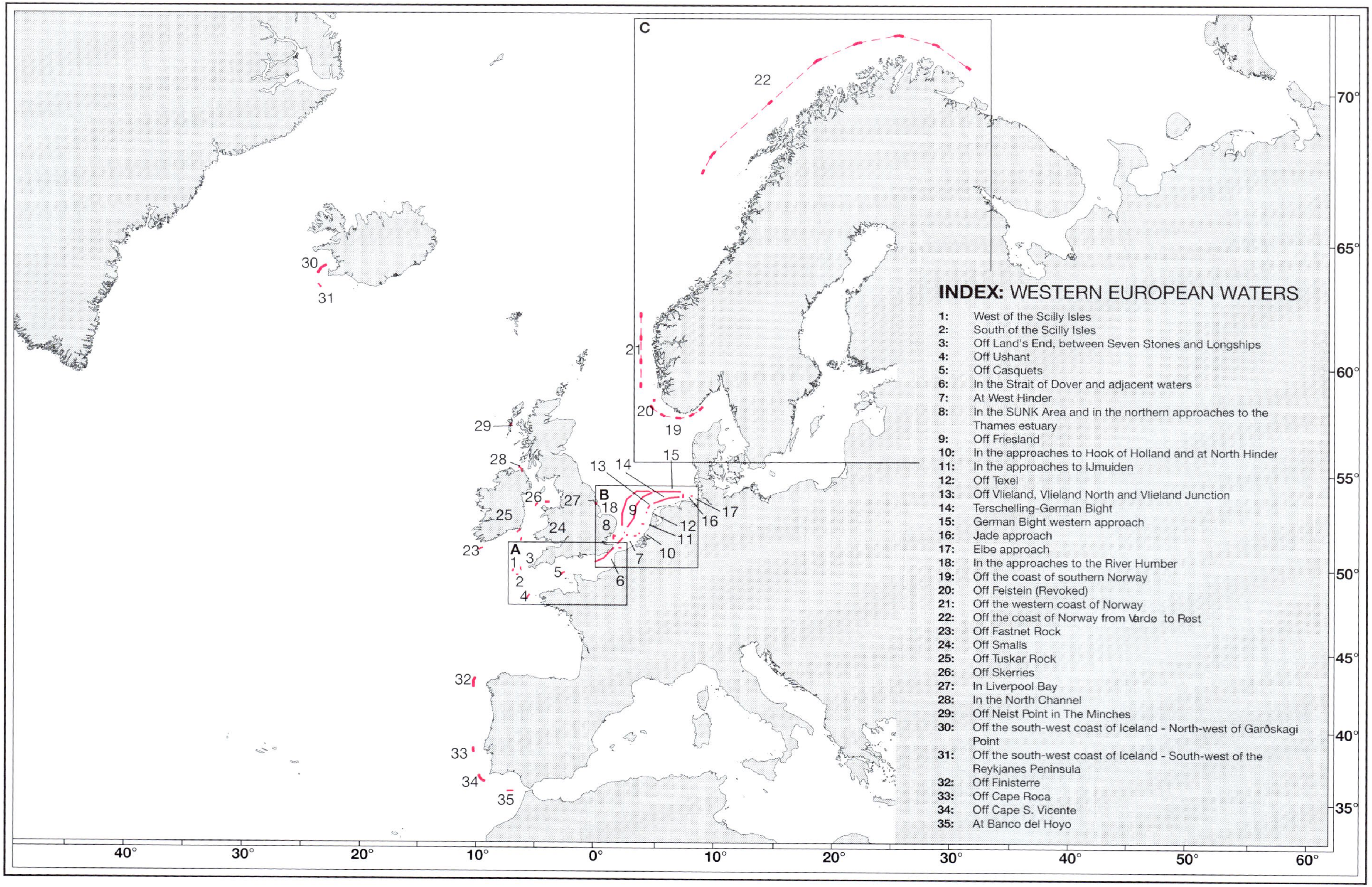
INDEX: WESTERN EUROPEAN WATERS
1: West of the Scilly Isles
2: South of the Scilly Isles
3: Off Land's End, between Seven Stones and Longships
4: Off Ushant
5: Off Casquets
6: In the Strait of Dover and adjacent waters
7: At West Hinder
8: In the SUNK Area and in the northern approaches to the Thames estuary
9: Off Friesland
10: In the approaches to Hook of Holland and at North Hinder
11: In the approaches to IJmuiden
12: Off Texel
13: Off Vlieland, Vlieland North and Vlieland Junction
14: Terschelling-German Bight
15: German Bight western approach
16: Jade approach
17: Elbe approach
18: In the approaches to the River Humber
19: Off the coast of southern Norway
20: Off Feistein (Revoked)
21: Off the western coast of Norway
22: Off the coast of Norway from Vardø to Røst
23: Off Fastnet Rock
24: Off Smalls
25: Off Tuskar Rock
26: Off Skerries
27: In Liverpool Bay
28: In the North Channel
29: Off Neist Point in The Minches
30: Off the south-west coast of Iceland - North-west of Garðskagi Point
31: Off the south-west coast of Iceland - South-west of the Reykjanes Peninsula
32: Off Finisterre
33: Off Cape Roca
34: Off Cape S. Vicente
35: At Banco del Hoyo
A
B
C
70°
65°
60°
55°
50°
45°
40°
35°
40°
30°
20°
10°
0°
10°
20°
30°
40°
50°
60°

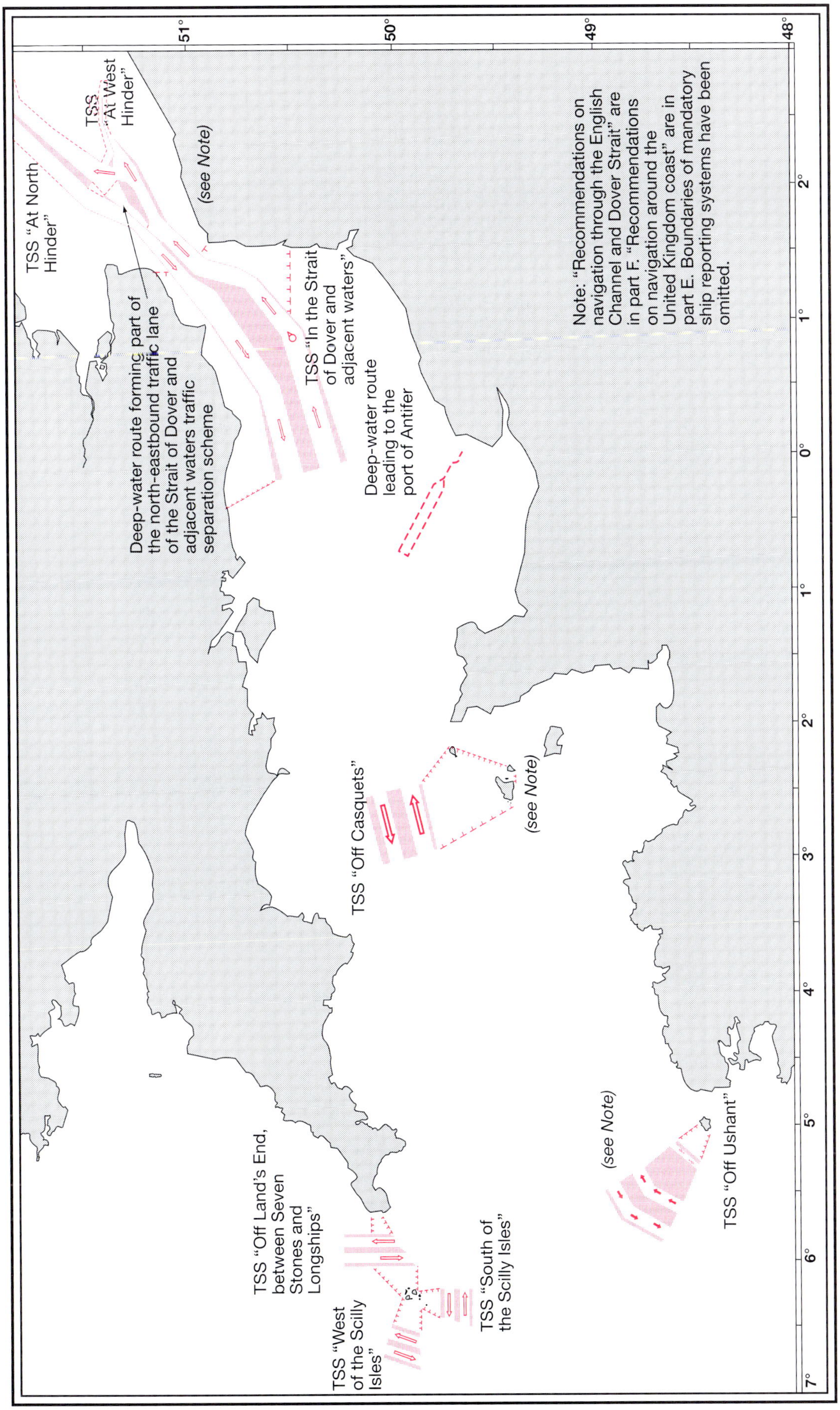

SUMMARY CHARTLET A

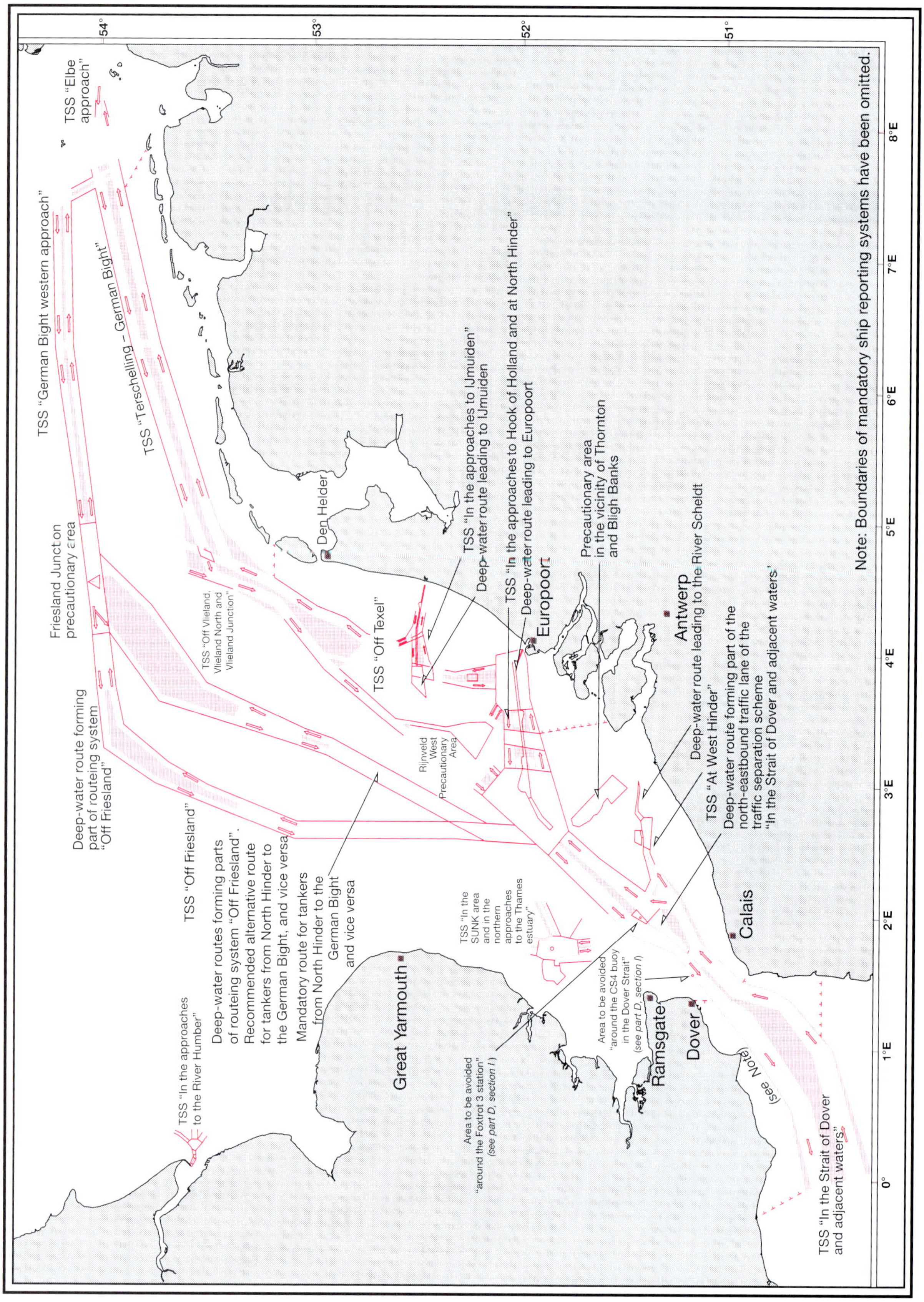

SUMMARY CHARTLET B

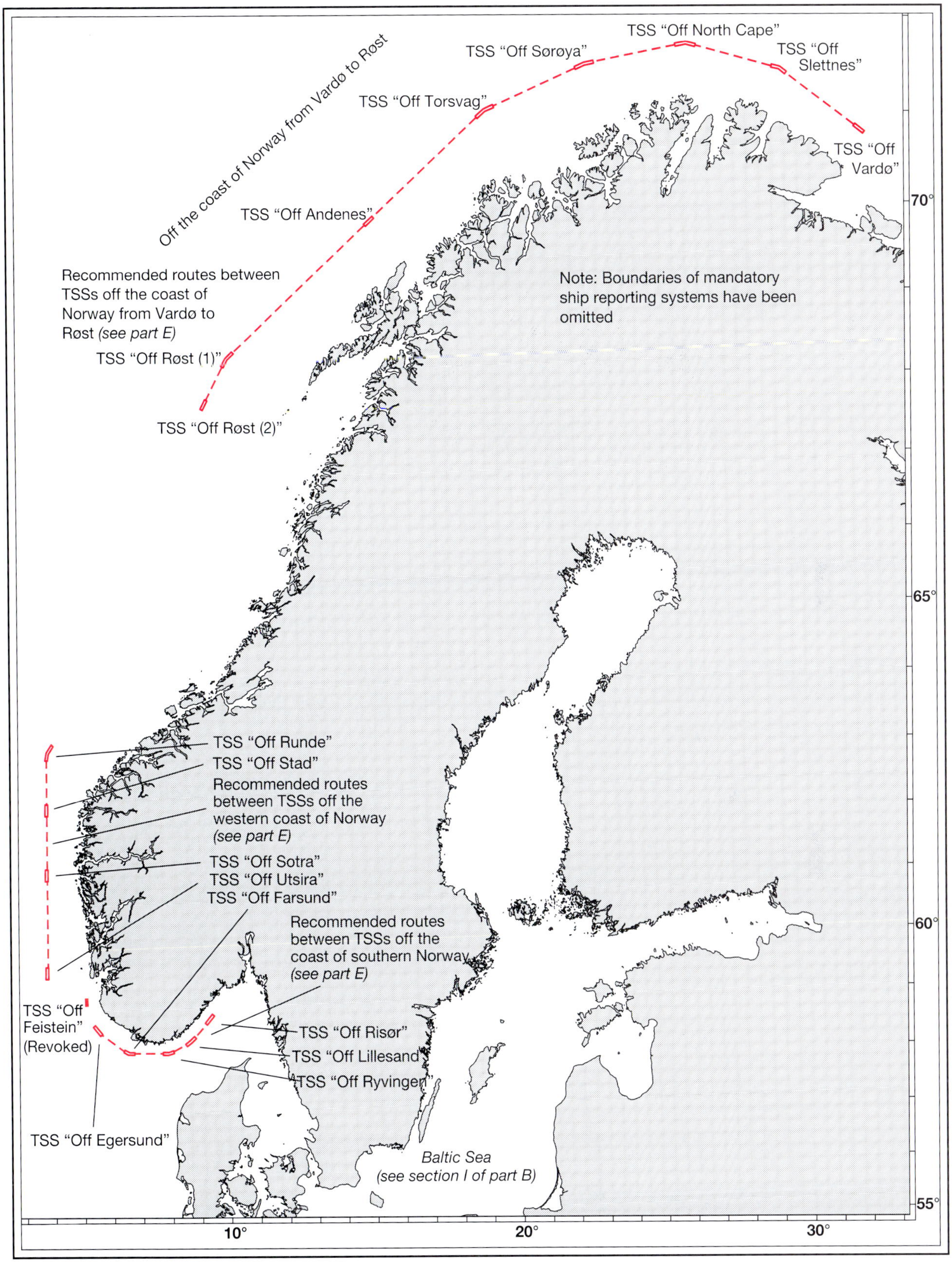

SUMMARY CHARTLET C

B

WEST OF THE SCILLY ISLES

Note: See mandatory ship reporting system "West European Tanker Reporting System" in part G, section I, and "Recommendations on navigation through the English Channel and the Dover Strait" in part F.

(Reference chart: British Admiralty 2565, 1982 edition.
Note: This chart is based on Ordnance Survey of Great Britain 1936 datum.)

Description of the traffic separation scheme

(a) A separation zone, two miles wide, is bounded by lines connecting the following geographical positions:

(1)	49°52′.33 N,	006°44′.00 W	(3)	50°02′.98 N,	006°42′.50 W
(2)	50°02′.43 N,	006°39′.50 W	(4)	49°52′.33 N,	006°47′.25 W

(b) A separation zone, one and a half miles wide, is bounded by lines connecting the following geographical positions:

(5)	49°52′.33 N,	006°36′.73 W	(7)	50°01′.57 N,	006°35′.03 W
(6)	50°01′.18 N,	006°32′.78 W	(8)	49°52′.33 N,	006°39′.17 W

(c) A separation zone, one mile wide, is bounded by lines connecting the following geographical positions:

(9)	49°52′.33 N,	006°52′.13 W	(11)	50°04′.07 N,	006°48′.53 W
(10)	50°03′.80 N,	006°47′.00 W	(12)	49°52′.33 N,	006°53′.78 W

(d) A traffic lane for north-eastbound ships, three miles wide, is established between the separation zones described in paragraphs (a) and (b) above.

(e) A traffic lane for south-westbound ships, three miles wide, is established between the separation zones described in paragraphs (a) and (c) above.

Inshore traffic zone

The area between the eastern boundary of the traffic separation scheme and the Scilly Isles and lying between a line drawn in a direction of 270° from Bishop Rock lighthouse and a line drawn in a direction of 286° from Round Island lighthouse is designated as an inshore traffic zone.

(chartlet is on page 1-2/2-2/3-2)

SOUTH OF THE SCILLY ISLES

Note: See mandatory ship reporting system "West European Tanker Reporting System" in part G, section I, and "Recommendations on navigation through the English Channel and the Dover Strait" in part F.

(Reference chart: British Admiralty 2565, 1982 edition.
Note: This chart is based on Ordnance Survey of Great Britain 1936 datum.)

Description of the traffic separation scheme

(a) A separation zone, two miles wide, is bounded by lines connecting the following geographical positions:

(1)	49°41′.50 N,	006°16′.50 W	(3)	49°39′.50 N,	006°32′.38 W
(2)	49°41′.50 N,	006°31′.50 W	(4)	49°39′.50 N,	006°16′.50 W

(b) A separation zone, one and a half miles wide, is bounded by lines connecting the following geographical positions:

(5)	49°46′.00 N,	006°16′.50 W	(7)	49°44′.50 N,	006°30′.15 W
(6)	49°46′.00 N,	006°29′.50 W	(8)	49°44′.50 N,	006°16′.50 W

(c) A separation zone, one mile wide, is bounded by lines connecting the following geographical positions:

(9)	49°36′.50 N,	006°16′.50 W	(11)	49°35′.50 N,	006°34′.15 W
(10)	49°36′.50 N,	006°33′.67 W	(12)	49°35′.50 N,	006°16′.50 W

(d) A traffic lane for eastbound ships, three miles wide, is established between the separation zones described in paragraphs (a) and (c) above.

(e) A traffic lane for westbound ships, three miles wide, is established between the separation zones described in paragraphs (a) and (b) above.

Inshore traffic zone

The area between the northern boundary of the traffic separation scheme and the Scilly Isles and lying between a line drawn in a direction of 196° from the Bishop Rock lighthouse and a line drawn in a direction of 180° from the eastern extremity of St. Mary's Island is designated as an inshore traffic zone.

(chartlet is on page 1-2/2-2/3-2)

OFF LAND'S END, BETWEEN SEVEN STONES AND LONGSHIPS

Note: See mandatory ship reporting system "West European Tanker Reporting System" in part G, section I, and "Recommendations on navigation around the United Kingdom coast" in part E and "Recommendations on navigation through the English Channel and the Dover Strait" in part F.

(Reference charts: British Admiralty 1148 (published 06/2001), 2565 (published 06/2001).
Note: These charts are based on World Geodetic System 1984 datum (WGS 84).)

Description of the traffic separation scheme

(a) A separation zone, two miles wide, is bounded by lines connecting the following geographical positions:

(1)	49°58′.02 N,	005°55′.76 W	(3)	50°20′.03 N,	005°58′.88 W
(2)	50°20′.03 N,	005°55′.76 W	(4)	49°56′.52 N,	005°58′.88 W

(b) A separation zone, one mile wide, is bounded by lines connecting the following geographical positions:

(5)	50°00′.99 N,	005°49′.58 W	(7)	50°20′.03 N,	005°51′.11 W
(6)	50°20′.03 N,	005°49′.58 W	(8)	50°00′.22 N,	005°51′.11 W

(c) A separation zone, one mile wide, is bounded by lines connecting the following geographical positions:

(9)	49°54′.29 N,	006°03′.56 W	(11)	50°20′.03 N,	006°05′.06 W
(10)	50°20′.03 N,	006°03′.56 W	(12)	49°53′.54 N,	006°05′.06 W

(d) A traffic lane for northbound traffic, three miles wide, is established between the separation zones described in paragraphs (a) and (b) above.

(e) A traffic lane for southbound traffic, three miles wide, is established between the separation zones described in paragraphs (a) and (c) above.

Inshore traffic zones

(f) The area between the eastern boundary of the traffic separation scheme and Land's End, and which lies between a line drawn from position (5) in a direction of 078° to the coast and a line drawn from position (13) 50°10′.00 N, 005°49′.58 W in a direction of 090° to the coast at Pendeen Point, is designated an inshore traffic zone.

(g) The area between the western boundary of the traffic separation scheme and the Isles of Scilly, and which lies between a line drawn from position (12) in a direction of 270° to the islands and a line drawn from position (14) 50°08′.00 N, 006°05′.06 W in a direction of 225° to Round Island lighthouse, is designated an inshore traffic zone.

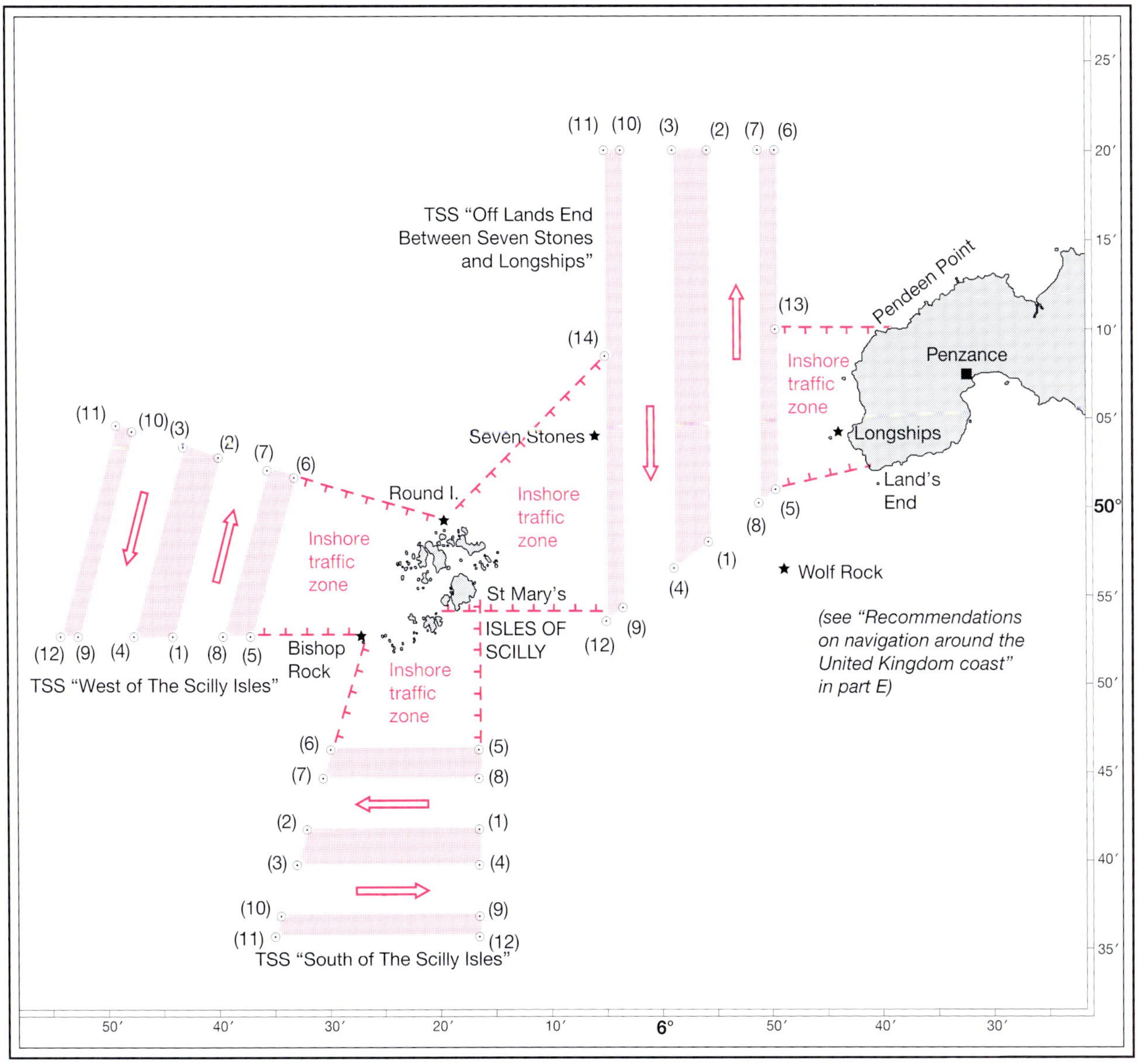

WEST OF THE SCILLY ISLES + SOUTH OF THE SCILLY ISLES + OFF LAND'S END, BETWEEN SEVEN STONES AND LONGSHIPS

OFF USHANT

Note: See mandatory ship reporting systems "West European Tanker Reporting System" and "Off Ushant" in part G, section I.

(Reference chart: French 6989.
Note: All positions are referred to World Geodetic System 1984 datum (WGS 84).)

Description of the traffic separation scheme

(a) A separation zone bounded by a line connecting the following geographical positions:

(1)	48°57′.00 N,	005°32′.50 W	(4)	48°37′.40 N,	005°48′.60 W
(2)	48°52′.75 N,	005°28′.60 W	(5)	48°39′.70 N,	005°55′.20 W
(3)	48°48′.60 N,	005°39′.60 W	(6)	48°52′.05 N,	005°45′.00 W

(b) A traffic lane for ships leaving the English Channel between the above separation zone and the following geographical positions:

(7)	48°42′.00 N,	006°01′.60 W	(9)	49°01′.10 N,	005°36′.05 W
(8)	48°55′.60 N,	005°50′.60 W			

(c) A traffic lane for ships entering the English Channel between that separation zone and the following geographical positions:

(10)	48°35′.10 N,	005°42′.30 W	(12)	48°48′.60 N,	005°25′.10 W
(11)	48°45′.00 N,	005°34′.30 W			

(d) An outer separation zone, seaward of the Ouessant traffic separation scheme, bounded by a line connecting points (7), (8), (9) and the following geographical positions:

(17)	48°42′.60 N,	006°02′.80 W	(19)	49°02′.00 N,	005°36′.80 W
(18)	48°56′.40 N,	005°51′.60 W			

(e) A separation zone bounded by a line connecting points (10), (11), (12) and the following geographical positions:

(13)	48°39′.70 N,	005°14′.70 W	(14)	48°30′.60 N,	005°26′.30 W

(f) A separation zone bounded by a line connecting the following geographical positions:

(15)	48°29′.80 N,	005°23′.50 W	(20)	48°37′.20 N,	005°11′.90 W
(16)	48°38′.00 N,	005°12′.90 W	(21)	48°29′.39 N,	005°22′.05 W

(g) An inshore traffic zone bounded by a line connecting points (20), (21), and the following geographical positions:

Men Korn light	48°28′.00 N,	005°01′.40 W
Jument light	48°25′.35 N,	005°08′.00 W

(h)* A two-way traffic route 2 miles wide established between the separation zones described in paragraphs (e) and (f), for passenger ships operating regular schedules to or from a Channel port situated west of meridian 1° W, and for ships sailing between ports situated between Cape de la Hague and Cape Finisterre, except for ships carrying oils listed in appendix I of Annex I of the International Convention for the Prevention of Pollution from Ships, 1973, as modified by the Protocol of 1978 (MARPOL 73/78), and ships carrying in bulk the substances listed in categories A and B listed in appendices I and II of Annex II of that Convention.

Special provision

North-eastbound traffic lane in (c):

Ships carrying oils listed in appendix I of Annex I of the International Convention for the Prevention of Pollution from Ships, 1973, as modified by the Protocol of 1978 (MARPOL 73/78), and ships carrying in bulk the substances listed in categories A and B listed in appendices I and II of Annex II of that Convention must, as far as possible, sail in the outer part of this lane.

* An amendment to this paragraph (see COLREG.2/Circ.64) that was adopted by the Maritime Safety Committee in December 2012 has not been included in this book. Its text will be reconsidered by that Committee at its 93rd session in May 2014.

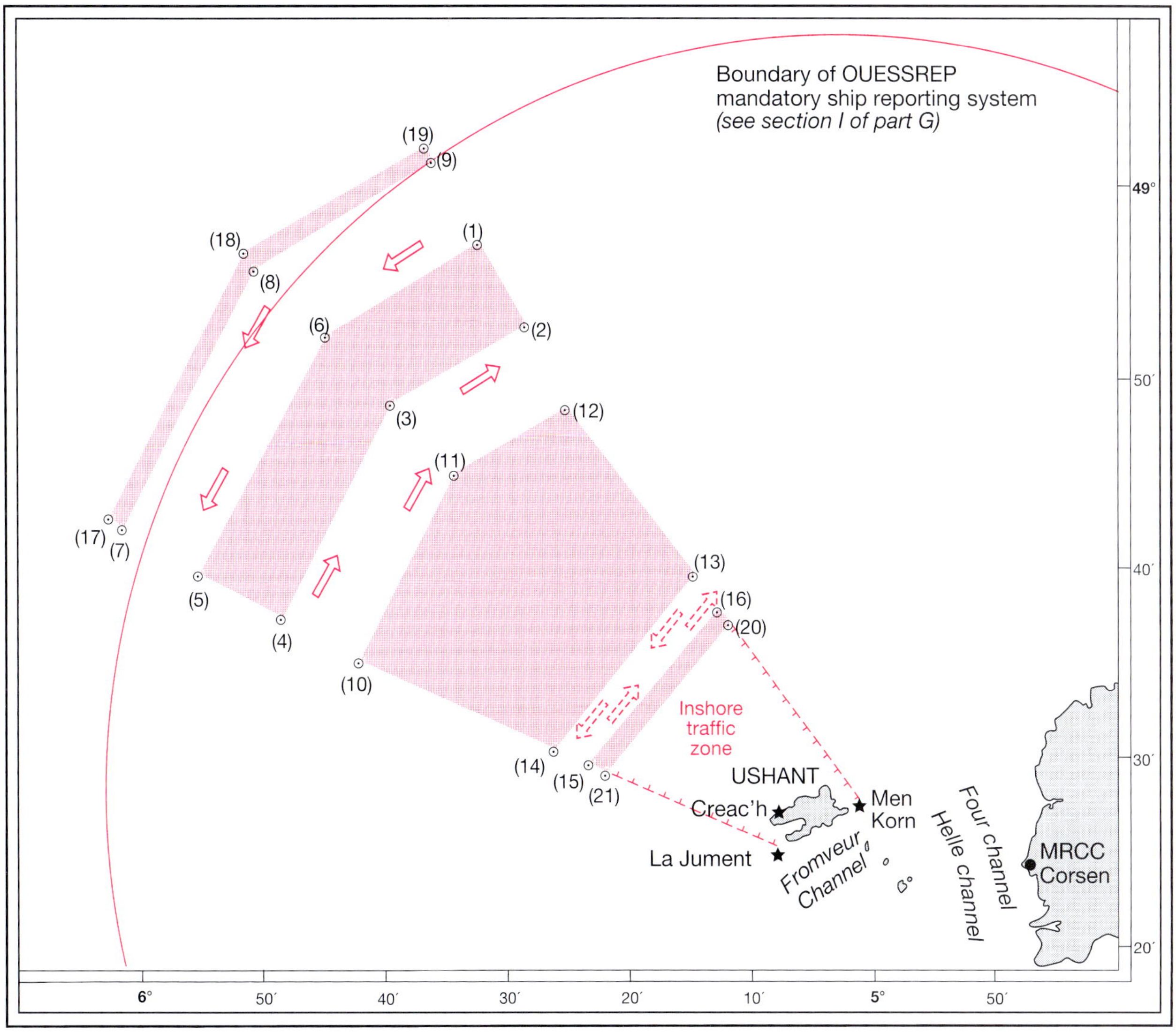
Boundary of OUESSREP
mandatory ship reporting system
(see section I of part G)
(19)
(9)
(18)
(8)
(1)
(6)
(2)
(3)
(12)
(11)
(17)
(7)
(5)
(4)
(10)
(13)
(16)
(20)
Inshore
traffic
zone
(14)
(15)
(21)
USHANT
Creac'h
Men
Korn
La Jument
Fromveur
Channel
Four channel
Helle channel
MRCC
Corsen
49°
50′
40′
30′
20′
6°
50′
40′
30′
20′
10′
5°
50′

OFF USHANT

B

OFF CASQUETS

Note: See "Recommendations on navigation through the English Channel and the Dover Strait" in part F and mandatory ship reporting systems "West European Tanker Reporting System" and "Off Les Casquets and the adjacent coastal area" in part G, section I.

(Reference charts: British Admiralty 2669, 1989 edition; French 6966, 1984 edition.
Note: These charts are based on European datum.)

Description of the traffic separation scheme

(a) A separation zone, five miles wide, is centred upon the following geographical positions:

(1)	49°54′.55 N,	002°53′.66 W	(2)	49°59′.55 N,	002°24′.41 W

(b) A separation zone, two miles wide, is centred upon the following geographical positions:

(3)	50°02′.65 N,	002°57′.01 W	(4)	50°07′.70 N,	002°27′.81 W

(c) A separation zone, one mile wide, is centred upon the following geographical positions:

(5)	49°46′.80 N,	002°50′.41 W	(6)	49°51′.80 N,	002°21′.24 W

(d) A traffic lane for westbound ships, five miles wide, is established between the separation zones described in paragraphs (a) and (b) above.

(e) A traffic lane for eastbound ships, five miles wide, is established between the separation zones described in paragraphs (a) and (c) above.

Inshore traffic zone

The area between the southern boundary of the traffic separation scheme and the Channel Islands, bounded by lines drawn from the south-west corner of the scheme to Les Hanois lighthouse, from St. Martin's Point light to the southern extremity of Sark, from the eastern extremity of Sark to Quenard Point and from Quenard Point to the south-east corner of the scheme, is designated as an inshore traffic zone.

Notes:

1 It is important that ships passing in this area listen to the appropriate VHF broadcasts by the Channel Navigation Information Service which provide information concerning traffic, navigation and visibility conditions in this area.

2 The Race of Alderney is not recommended for use by ships other than those proceeding to or from ports in the Channel Islands, ports located on the French coast between Cherbourg and Ushant or inshore routes at Ushant.

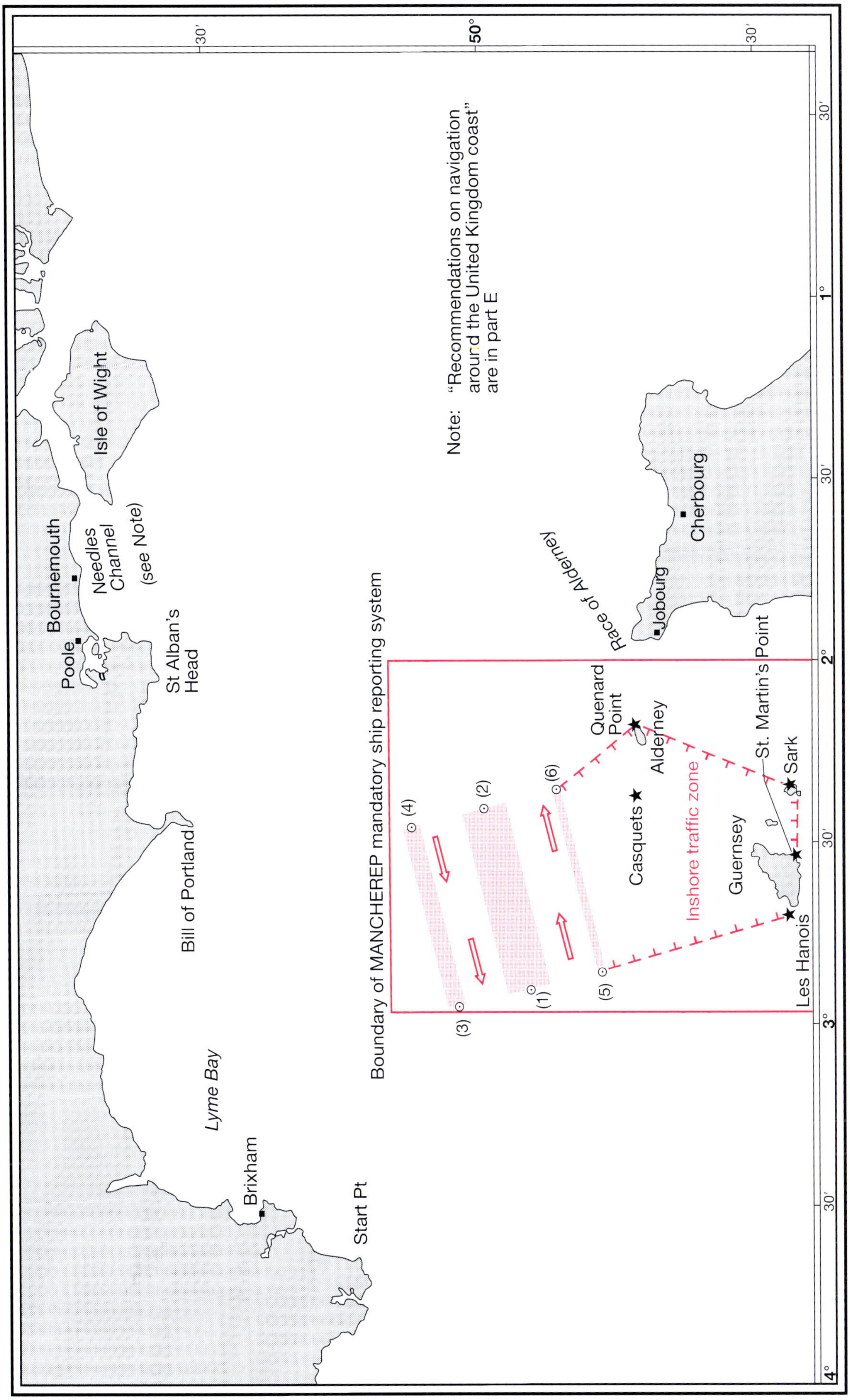

OFF CASQUETS

IN THE STRAIT OF DOVER AND ADJACENT WATERS*

Note: See "Recommendations on navigation through the English Channel and the Dover Strait" in part F and the mandatory ship reporting systems "The Dover Strait/Pas de Calais" and "West European Tanker Reporting System" in part G, section I.

(Reference charts: British Admiralty 2449, 2450, 2451; June 2007 editions.
Note: These charts are based on World Geodetic System 1984 datum (WGS 84).)

B

Description of the traffic separation scheme

(a) A separation zone is bounded by lines connecting the following geographical positions:

(1)	51°25′.31 N,	002°04′.03 E	(3)	51°31′.07 N,	002°07′.90 E
(2)	51°26′.77 N,	002°01′.48 E	(4)	51°29′.84 N,	002°10′.62 E

(b) A separation line connects the following geographical positions:

(5)	51°26′.97 N,	002°16′.95 E	(6)	51°22′.83 N,	002°12′.29 E

(c) A separation zone is bounded by lines connecting the following geographical positions:

(7)	51°22′.03 N,	001°58′.39 E	(9)	51°16′.53 N,	001°52′.29 E
(8)	51°22′.49 N,	001°57′.61 E			

(d) A precautionary area with recommended directions of traffic flow is established connecting geographical positions (1), (2), (8) and (7) above.

(e) A separation line connects the following geographical positions:

(10)	51°16′.53 N,	001°52′.29 E	(11)	51°06′.13 N,	001°38′.10 E

(f) A separation zone is bounded by lines connecting the following geographical positions:

(12)	51°05′.77 N,	001°38′.65 E	(17)	50°26′.91 N,	000°01′.09 W
(13)	51°06′.49 N,	001°37′.55 E	(18)	50°22′.12 N,	000°00′.91 E
(14)	50°57′.59 N,	001°23′.00 E	(19)	50°32′.71 N,	000°57′.73 E
(15)	50°51′.14 N,	001°17′.20 E	(20)	50°42′.87 N,	001°18′.30 E
(16)	50°33′.37 N,	000°36′.50 E	(21)	50°56′.87 N,	001°24′.03 E

(g) A traffic lane for south-westbound traffic is established between the separation zones/lines described in paragraphs (a), (c), (e) and (f) above and the following separation line/zone:

a separation line connecting the following geographical positions:

(22)	51°33′.66 N,	002°02′.17 E	(25)	51°06′.93 N,	001°30′.90 E
(23)	51°27′.35 N,	001°52′.76 E	(26)	50°52′.29 N,	001°02′.65 E
(24)	51°14′.13 N,	001°43′.99 E			

a separation zone bounded by lines connecting the following geographical positions:

(27)	50°52′.47 N,	001°02′.45 E	(30)	50°32′.71 N,	000°03′.49 W
(28)	50°39′.37 N,	000°32′.50 E	(31)	50°38′.91 N,	000°32′.70 E
(29)	50°34′.64 N,	000°04′.29 W	(32)	50°52′.09 N,	001°02′.85 E

(h) A traffic lane for north-eastbound traffic is established between the separation zones/lines described in paragraphs (a), (c), (e) and (f) above and the following separation line/zone:

a separation zone is bounded by lines connecting the following geographical positions:

(33)	50°16′.34 N,	000°03′.31 E	(36)	50°39′.29 N,	001°22′.63 E
(34)	50°14′.49 N,	000°04′.11 E	(37)	50°39′.69 N,	001°22′.20 E
(35)	50°26′.37 N,	001°00′.20 E	(38)	50°26′.94 N,	000°59′.90 E

a separation line connects the following geographical positions:

(39)	50°39′.49 N,	001°22′.40 E	(41)	50°53′.64 N,	001°30′.70 E
(40)	50°44′.54 N,	001°26′.90 E	(42)	51°04′.34 N,	001°45′.89 E

* Date of implementation of amended scheme: 0000 hours UTC on 1 June 2011.

a separation zone is bounded by lines connecting the following geographical positions:

(43)	51°04′.34 N,	001°45′.89 E	(45)	51°11′.23 N,	002°04′.09 E
(44)	51°06′.44 N,	001°48′.89 E	(46)	51°09′.84 N,	002°03′.12 E

an uncharted line representing the junction of the scheme with the adjacent scheme "At West Hinder" and joining the following geographical positions:

(47)	51°11′.23 N,	002°04′.09 E	(6)	51°22′.83 N,	002°12′.29 E

A separation zone is established within this lane as described in paragraph (i) below.

(i) A separation zone is bounded by lines connecting the following geographical positions:

(48)	51°18′.43 N,	002°04′.69 E	(52)	51°09′.75 N,	001°45′.61 E
(49)	51°16′.03 N,	002°04′.19 E	(53)	51°12′.35 N,	001°51′.03 E
(50)	51°13′.71 N,	002°00′.99 E	(54)	51°15′.05 N,	001°54′.40 E
(51)	51°09′.35 N,	001°47′.10 E			

(j) A deep-water route forming part of the north-eastbound traffic lane between the separation zone described in paragraph (i) above and the separation zone/line described in paragraphs (c) and (e) above has been established between a line connecting the following geographical positions:

(i)	51°09′.75 N,	001°45′.61 E	(ii)	51°10′.26 N,	001°43′.74 E

and a line connecting:

(iii)	51°22′.03 N,	001°58′.39 E	(iv)	51°18′.43 N,	002°04′.69 E

Note: An area to be avoided around the Foxtrot 3 station (51°24′.15 N, 002°00′.38 E) is described in part D, section I.

There is an uncharted line representing the junction of the scheme with the adjacent scheme "In the Approaches to Hook of Holland and At North Hinder" and joining the following geographical positions:

(5)	51°26′.97 N,	002°16′.95 E	(3)	51°31′.07 N,	002°07′.90 E
(4)	51°29′.84 N,	002°10′.62 E	(22)	51°33′.66 N,	002°02′.17 E

Inshore traffic zones

The area between the outer boundary of the traffic separation scheme and the English coast which lies between a line:

(v)	51°08′.42 N,	001°22′.24 E	(vi)	51°02′.53 N,	001°22′.24 E

and a line between:

(vii)	50°34′.64 N,	000°04′.29 W	(viii)	50°49′.60 N,	000°16′.86 W

is designated as an inshore traffic zone.

The area between the outer boundary of the traffic separation scheme and the French coast which lies between:

(ix)	50°53′.64 N,	001°30′.70 E	(x)	50°52′.10 N,	001°34′.96 E

and a line between:

(xi)	50°30′.09 N,	001°06′.66 E	(xii)	50°30′.09 N,	001°34′.59 E

is designated as an inshore traffic zone.

Warnings

1 A deep-water route forming part of the north-eastbound traffic lane is established to the north-west of the Sandettie Bank, and masters considering the use of this route should take into account the proximity of traffic using the south-westbound lane.

2 The main traffic lane for north-eastbound traffic lies to the south-east of the Sandettie Bank and shall be followed by all such ships as can safely navigate therein having regard to their draught.

3 In the area of the deep-water route east of the separation line, ships are recommended to avoid overtaking where traffic and navigation do not allow sufficient sea room and passing distance. If overtaking is performed then a safe distance must be maintained and COLREG Rule 13 observed.

4 Mariners leaving the north-east-going lane and planning to cross the south-west-going lane, between the Varne (51° 01′.3 N, 001° 23′.9 E) and F1 (51° 11′.2 N, 001°45′.0 E) light-buoys, should be aware of heavy traffic in the south-west-going lane, as well as ferry traffic, and alter course and/or speed at an appropriate point.

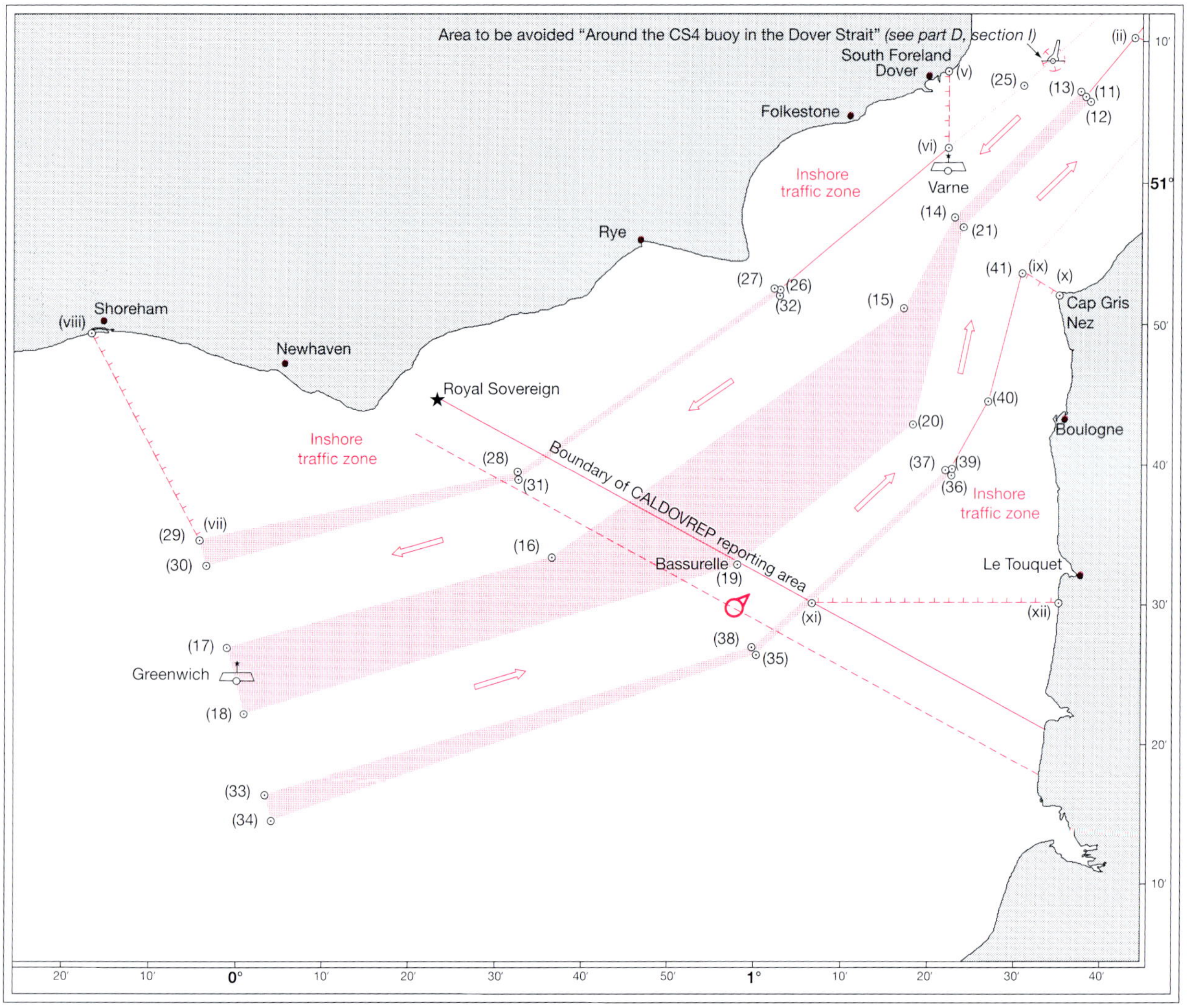

IN THE STRAIT OF DOVER AND ADJACENT WATERS – WEST

TERSCHELLING–GERMAN BIGHT

(Reference charts: German Federal Maritime and Hydrographic Agency 84, 1987 edition; 87 (INT 1413), 1991 edition; Netherlands Hydrographic Office 1352, 1988 edition; 1353, 1988 edition.
Note: These charts are based on European datum.)

Description of the traffic separation scheme

(a) A separation zone is bounded by a line connecting the following geographical positions:

(1)	54°00′.55 N,	007°39′.77 E	(3)	53°58′.17 N,	007°44′.85 E
(2)	54°01′.00 N,	007°43′.08 E	(4)	53°57′.82 N,	007°42′.23 E

(b) A separation zone is bounded by a line connecting the following geographical positions:

(5)	53°58′.78 N,	007°37′.53 E	(7)	53°57′.58 N,	007°40′.53 E
(6)	53°58′.90 N,	007°39′.33 E	(8)	53°57′.35 N,	007°38′.82 E

(c) A separation zone is bounded by a line connecting the following geographical positions:

(9)	53°48′.77 N,	006°23′.72 E	(12)	53°57′.12 N,	007°37′.10 E
(10)	53°58′.27 N,	007°30′.52 E	(13)	53°46′.73 N,	006°23′.83 E
(11)	53°58′.65 N,	007°35′.73 E			

(d) A separation line connects the following geographical positions:

(14)	53°47′.75 N,	006°23′.78 E	(16)	53°47′.26 N,	006°20′.43 E
(15)	53°47′.50 N,	006°22′.10 E			

(e) A separation zone is bounded by a line connecting the following geographical positions:

(17)	53°34′.30 N,	005°08′.60 E	(19)	53°46′.22 N,	006°20′.48 E
(18)	53°48′.29 N,	006°20′.37 E	(20)	53°32′.37 N,	005°09′.70 E

(f) A traffic lane for westbound traffic is established between the separation zones/line described in paragraphs (a), (b), (c), (d) and (e) and a line connecting the following geographical positions:

(21)	54°02′.89 N,	007°41′.89 E	(24)	53°51′.58 N,	006°21′.87 E
(22)	54°02′.38 N,	007°38′.13 E	(25)	53°37′.13 N,	005°07′.00 E
(23)	54°01′.68 N,	007°33′.00 E			

(g) A traffic lane for eastbound traffic is established between the separation zones/line described in paragraphs (a), (b), (c), (d) and (e) and a line connecting the following geographical positions:

(26)	53°29′.57 N,	005°11′.28 E	(28)	53°53′.51 N,	007°33′.20 E
(27)	53°43′.42 N,	006°22′.33 E	(29)	53°55′.33 N,	007°46′.61 E

Inshore traffic zone

The area between the coast and the landward boundary of the traffic separation scheme is designated as an inshore traffic zone. The eastern limit of the inshore traffic zone is bounded by a line connecting geographical positions 53°53′.51 N, 007°33′.20 E (28) and 53°47′.45 N, 007°51′.51 E (Wangerooge lighthouse).

Notes:

1 The gaps in the separation zones of this scheme indicate the areas where a concentration of crossing traffic is likely to be met.

2 The following classes of ships are referred to the provisions being part of the description of the "Mandatory route for tankers from North Hinder to the German Bight and vice versa" (see part G, section II):

(a) tankers of 10,000 tons gross tonnage and upwards, carrying oil as defined under Annex I to the International Convention for the Prevention of Pollution from Ships, 1973, as modified by the Protocol of 1978 relating thereto (MARPOL 73/78);

(b) chemical tankers of 5000 tons gross tonnage and upwards, carrying noxious liquid substances in bulk assessed or provisionally assessed as Category X or Y of Annex II to the International Convention for the Prevention of Pollution from Ships, 1973, as modified by the Protocol of 1978 relating thereto (MARPOL 73/78);

(c) chemical tankers and NLS tankers of 10,000 tons gross tonnage and upwards, carrying noxious liquid substances in bulk assessed or provisionally assessed as Category Z of Annex II to the International Convention for the Prevention of Pollution from Ships, 1973, as modified by the Protocol of 1978 relating thereto (MARPOL 73/78);

(d) ships of 10,000 tons gross tonnage and upwards, carrying liquefied gases in bulk.

(chartlet is on page 14-3/15-3)

GERMAN BIGHT WESTERN APPROACH

(Reference chart: German Federal Maritime and Hydrographic Agency 87 (INT 1413), 1991 edition.
Note: This chart is based on European datum.)

Description of the traffic separation scheme

(a) A separation zone is bounded by a line connecting the following geographical positions:

(1)	54°10′.53 N,	006°22′.47 E	(3)	54°10′.29 N,	007°25′.17 E
(2)	54°11′.28 N,	007°24′.27 E	(4)	54°09′.53 N,	006°22′.53 E

(b) A separation line connects the following geographical positions:

(5)	54°10′.03 N,	006°22′.50 E	(7)	54°09′.87 N,	006°19′.11 E
(6)	54°10′.00 N,	006°20′.80 E			

(c) A separation zone is bounded by a line connecting the following geographical positions:

(8)	54°08′.97 N,	006°01′.33 E	(10)	54°09′.37 N,	006°19′.14 E
(9)	54°10′.37 N,	006°19′.08 E	(11)	54°08′.00 N,	006°01′.90 E

(d) A traffic lane for westbound traffic is established between the separation zones/line described in paragraphs (a), (b) and (c) and a line connecting the following geographical positions:

(12)	54°13′.27 N,	007°22′.46 E	(14)	54°10′.90 N,	006°00′.20 E
(13)	54°12′.50 N,	006°20′.65 E			

(e) A traffic lane for eastbound traffic is established between the separation zones/line described in paragraphs (a), (b) and (c) and a line connecting the following geographical positions:

(15)	54°06′.10 N,	006°03′.00 E	(17)	54°08′.31 N,	007°26′.98 E
(16)	54°07′.51 N,	006°20′.95 E			

Notes:

1 This traffic separation scheme forms part of the "Mandatory route for tankers from North Hinder to the German Bight and vice versa" (see part G, section II).

Application and use of the route

2 The following classes of ships are referred to the provisions being part of the description of the "Mandatory route for tankers from North Hinder to the German Bight and vice versa" (see part G, section II):

(a) tankers of 10,000 tons gross tonnage and upwards, carrying oil as defined under Annex I to the International Convention for the Prevention of Pollution from Ships, 1973, as modified by the Protocol of 1978 relating thereto (MARPOL 73/78);

(b) chemical tankers of 5000 tons gross tonnage and upwards, carrying noxious liquid substances in bulk assessed or provisionally assessed as Category X or Y of Annex II to the International Convention for the Prevention of Pollution from Ships, 1973, as modified by the Protocol of 1978 relating thereto (MARPOL 73/78);

(c) chemical tankers and NLS tankers of 10,000 tons gross tonnage and upwards, carrying noxious liquid substances in bulk assessed or provisionally assessed as Category Z of Annex II to the International Convention for the Prevention of Pollution from Ships, 1973, as modified by the Protocol of 1978 relating thereto (MARPOL 73/78);

(d) ships of 10,000 tons gross tonnage and upwards, carrying liquefied gases in bulk.

These ships shall avoid the sea area between the mandatory route and the adjacent Frisian Islands' coast, except when joining or leaving the route at the nearest point of the route to the port of departure or destination which permits a safe passage from or to that port.

The classes of ships referred to above shall use the mandatory route or part of it:

(i) when sailing from North Hinder to the Baltic or to North Sea ports of Norway, Sweden, Denmark, Germany or the Netherlands north of latitude 53° N and vice versa;

B

(ii) when sailing between North Sea ports of the Netherlands and/or Germany, except in cases of adjacent port areas;

(iii) when sailing between United Kingdom or Continental North Sea ports south of 53° N and Scandinavian or Baltic ports; and

(iv) when sailing between North Hinder, United Kingdom or Continental North Sea ports south of 53° N and offshore and shore-based oil loading facilities in the North Sea area.

These ships shall use the appropriate traffic lanes of the traffic separation schemes forming part of the route, should follow the recommended direction of traffic flow in the precautionary area (indicated by dashed open-outlined arrows in the charts) and shall, as far as practicable, keep to the starboard side of the deep-water routes forming part of the mandatory route.

Joining or leaving the route

3 The classes of ships referred to above, when joining or leaving the route:

(a) shall do so at the nearest point of the route to the port of departure or destination which permits a safe passage from or to that port; and

(b) should be aware that oil and gas production facilities and mobile offshore drilling units may be encountered in the proximity of the route; safety zones of 500 m (0.27 nautical miles) radius are established around all offshore structures.

Pilotage

4 Ships required to use the "Mandatory route for tankers from North Hinder to the German Bight and vice versa" are referred to resolution A.486(XII), adopted on 19 November 1981, concerning the "Recommendation on the use of adequately qualified deep-sea pilots in the North Sea, English Channel and Skagerrak".

5 It is recommended that an efficient electronic position-fixing device appropriate for the area should be carried on board.

6 Numerous offshore structures situated within the limits of the separation zones and/or situated in the proximity of the route are equipped with X- and S-band racons.

Least water depth

7 The area of this scheme is surveyed to a least water depth of 30 m at LWS once every 5 years.

8 The gap in the separation zone of this scheme indicates the area where a concentration of crossing traffic is likely to be met.

(chartlet is on page 14-3/15-3)

B

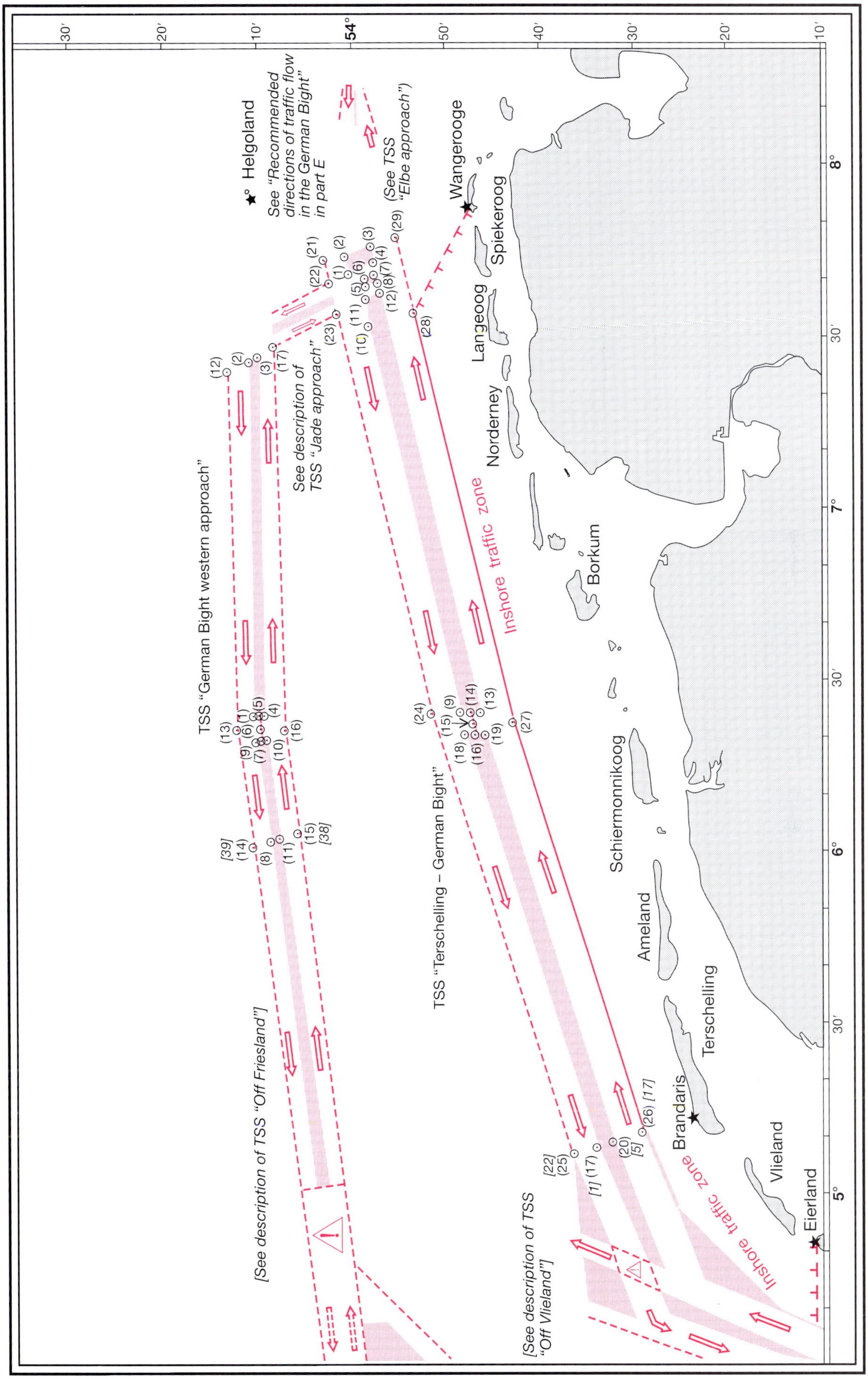

TERSCHELLING–GERMAN BIGHT + GERMAN BIGHT WESTERN APPROACH

JADE APPROACH

(Reference charts: German Federal Maritime and Hydrographic Agency 87 (INT 1413), 1991 edition; Netherlands Hydrographic Office 1352 and 1353 (INT 1413), 1988 edition.
Note: These charts are based on European datum.)

Description of the traffic separation scheme

(a) A separation zone is bounded by a line connecting the following geographical positions:

(1)	54°08′.34 N,	007°30′.81 E	(3)	54°01′.92 N,	007°34′.71 E
(2)	54°02′.15 N,	007°36′.42 E	(4)	54°08′.33 N,	007°28′.89 E

(b) A traffic lane for northbound traffic is established between the separation zone described in paragraph (a) and a line connecting the following geographical positions:

(5)	54°02′.38 N,	007°38′.13 E	(6)	54°08′.35 N,	007°32′.72 E

(c) A traffic lane for southbound traffic is established between the separation zone described in paragraph (a) and a line connecting the following geographical positions:

(7)	54°08′.31 N,	007°26′.98 E	(8)	54°01′.68 N,	007°33′.00 E

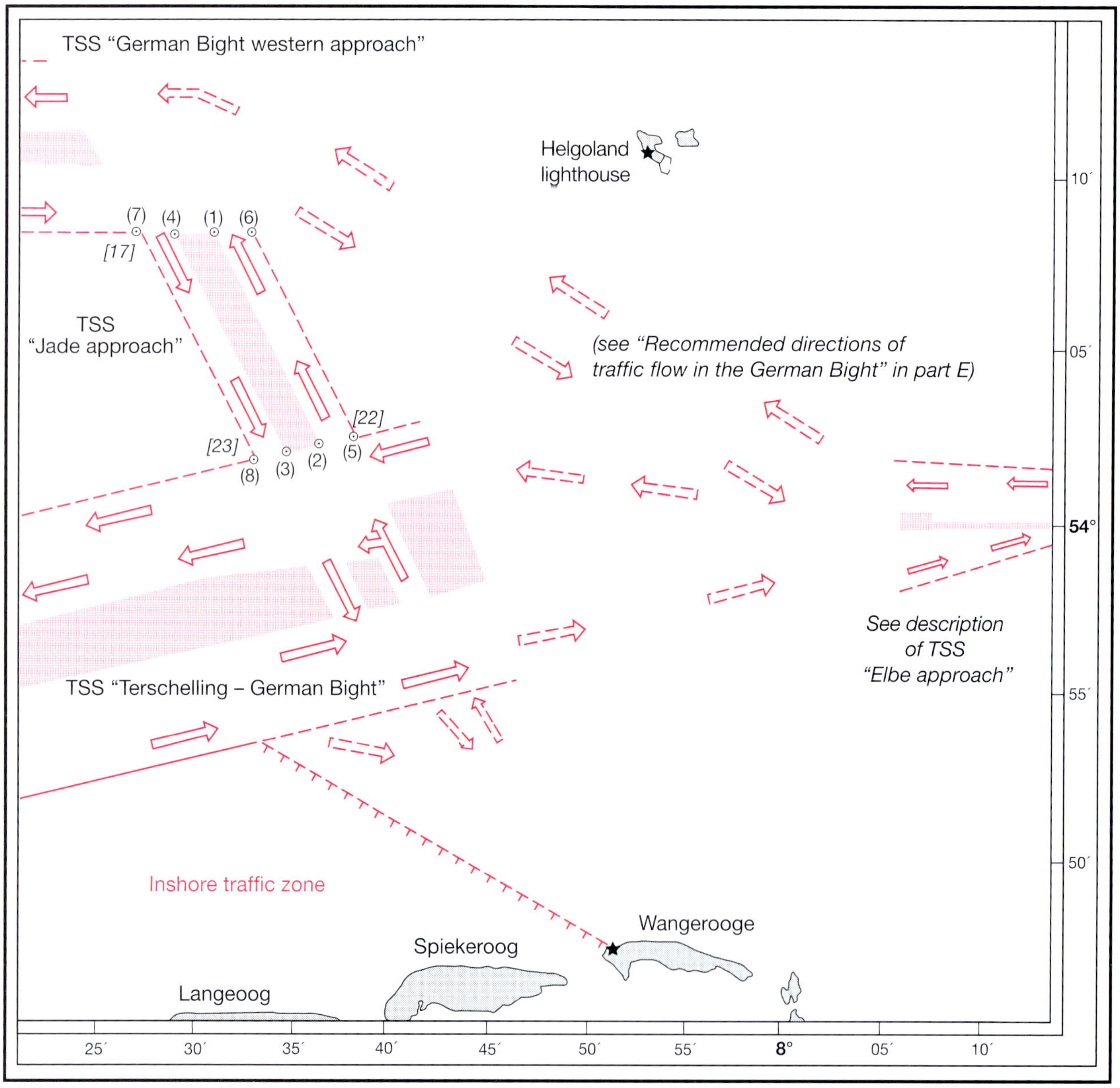

JADE APPROACH

ELBE APPROACH

(Reference charts: German Hydrographic Office 44; 49 (INT 1452), 1989 edition; 87 (INT 1413), 1989 edition.
Note: These charts are based on European datum.)

Description of the traffic separation scheme

(a) A separation zone, half a mile wide, is centred upon the following geographical positions:

(1)	54°00′.00 N,	008°05′.47 E	(2)	54°00′.00 N,	008°07′.15 E

(b) A separation line connects the following geographical positions:

(3)	54°00′.00 N,	008°07′.15 E	(4)	53°59′.95 N,	008°13′.37 E

(c) A traffic lane for eastbound traffic is established between the separation zone/line and a line connecting the following geographical positions:

(5)	53°58′.00 N,	008°05′.47 E	(6)	53°59′.38 N,	008°13′.28 E

(d) A traffic lane for westbound traffic is established between the separation zone/line and a line connecting the following geographical positions:

(7)	54°01′.85 N,	008°05′.47 E	(8)	54°01′.63 N,	008°13′.57 E

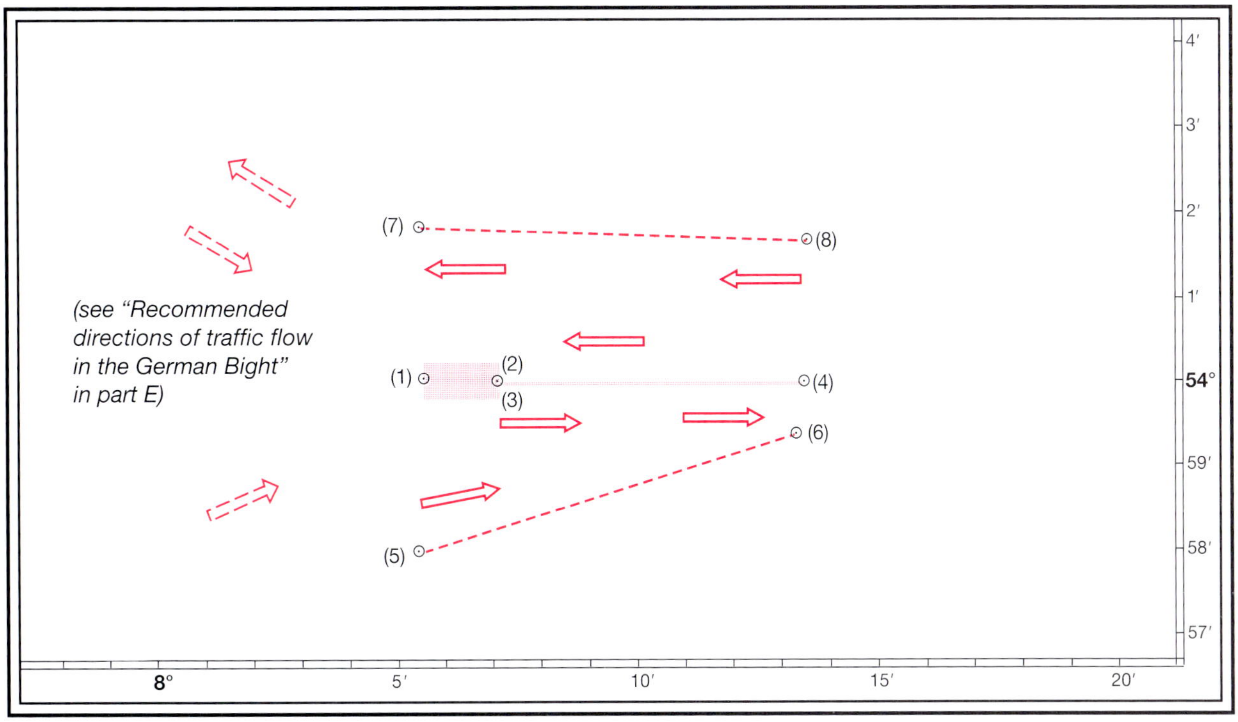

ELBE APPROACH

B

IN THE APPROACHES TO THE RIVER HUMBER

(Reference charts: British Admiralty 109 (published 06/2006), 107 (published 09/2004).
Note: These charts are based on World Geodetic System 1984 datum (WGS 84).)

Description of the traffic separation scheme

Part I

Entrance to River Humber within port area

(a) A precautionary area established by a line connecting the following geographical positions:

(1)	53°34′.22 N,	000°06′.32 E	
(2)	53°33′.54 N,	000°05′.70 E	
(3)	53°33′.14 N,	000°06′.80 E	(Hobo)
(4)	53°33′.92 N,	000°07′.43 E	(No. 3A Binks)
(1)	53°34′.22 N,	000°06′.32 E	

(b) A separation line connecting the following geographical positions:

(5)	53°33′.54 N,	000°07′.13 E	(Delta)
(6)	53°32′.73 N,	000°09′.65 E	(Charlie)

(c) A traffic lane for inbound traffic established between the separation line specified in paragraph (b) above and a straight line connecting the following geographical positions:

(4)	53°33′.92 N,	000°07′.43 E	(No. 3A Binks)
(7)	53°33′.16 N,	000°10′.27 E	

(d) A traffic lane for outbound traffic established between the separation line specified in paragraph (b) above and a straight line connecting the following geographical positions:

(3)	53°33′.14 N,	000°06′.80 E	(Hobo)
(8)	53°32′.34 N,	000°09′.11 E	(No. 2B)

(e) A precautionary area established by a line connecting the following geographical positions:

(7)	53°33′.16 N,	000°10′.27 E	
(8)	53°32′.34 N,	000°09′.11 E	(No. 2B)
(9)	53°32′.38 N,	000°11′.12 E	
(10)	53°33′.16 N,	000°11′.17 E	
(11)	53°33′.07 N,	000°10′.63 E	(No. 3 Chequer)
(7)	53°33′.16 N,	000°10′.27 E	

(f) A separation line connecting the following geographical positions:

(12)	53°32′.67 N,	000°11′.15 E	(Bravo)
(13)	53°32′.82 N,	000°13′.20 E	(Alpha)

(g) A traffic lane for inbound traffic established between the separation line specified in paragraph (f) above and a straight line connecting the following geographical positions:

(10)	53°33′.16 N,	000°11′.17 E
(14)	53°33′.52 N,	000°13′.80 E

(h) A traffic lane for outbound traffic established between the separation line specified in paragraph (f) above and a straight line connecting the following geographical positions:

(9)	53°32′.38 N,	000°11′.12 E
(15)	53°32′.41 N,	000°12′.80 E

Part II

River Humber approaches

(i) A precautionary area established by a line connecting the following geographical positions:

(15) 53°32′.41 N, 000°12′.80 E
(16) 53°32′.42 N, 000°13′.18 E (No. 2 Haile Sand)
(17) 53°30′.59 N, 000°16′.61 E
(18) 53°31′.90 N, 000°18′.29 E (Hotspur)
(19) 53°33′.57 N, 000°18′.29 E
(20) 53°34′.22 N, 000°17′.59 E (South Haile)
(21) 53°34′.74 N, 000°16′.54 E (South Binks)
(22) 53°33′.56 N, 000°14′.19 E (Spurn Light Float)
(14) 53°33′.52 N, 000°13′.80 E
(15) 53°32′.41 N, 000°12′.80 E

Eastern approaches (Sea Reach)

(j) A separation line connecting the following geographical positions:

(23) 53°32′.72 N, 000°18′.29 E (Inner Sea Reach)
(24) 53°32′.72 N, 000°22′.95 E (Outer Sea Reach)

(k) A traffic lane for inbound traffic established between the separation line specified in paragraph (j) above and a straight line connecting the following geographical positions:

(19) 53°33′.57 N, 000°18′.29 E
(25) 53°33′.57 N, 000°22′.95 E

(l) A traffic lane for outbound traffic established between the separation line specified in paragraph (j) above and a straight line connecting the following geographical positions:

(18) 53°31′.90 N, 000°18′.29 E (Hotspur)
(26) 53°31′.90 N, 000°22′.95 E

South-east approaches (Rosse Reach)

(m) A separation line connecting the following geographical positions:

(27) 53°31′.24 N, 000°17′.44 E (Inner Rosse Reach)
(28) 53°29′.89 N, 000°20′.79 E (Outer Rosse Reach)

(n) A traffic lane for inbound traffic established between the separation line specified in paragraph (m) above and a straight line connecting the following geographical positions:

(18) 53°31′.90 N, 000°18′.29 E (Hotspur)
(29) 53°30′.56 N, 000°21′.57 E

(o) A traffic lane for outbound traffic established between the separation line specified in paragraph (m) above and a straight line connecting the following geographical positions:

(17) 53°30′.59 N, 000°16′.61 E
(30) 53°29′.19 N, 000°19′.97 E

Part III

North-east approaches (New Sand Hole)

(p) A separation line connecting the following geographical positions:

(31) 53°34′.48 N, 000°17′.06 E
(32) 53°36′.99 N, 000°20′.64 E
(35) 53°38′.52 N, 000°21′.87 E

(q) A traffic lane for inbound traffic established between the separation line specified in paragraph (p) above and a straight line connecting the following geographical positions:

(21) 53°34′.74 N, 000°16′.54 E (South Binks)
(33) 53°37′.27 N, 000°20′.10 E (Outer Binks)
(36) 53°38′.70 N, 000°21′.24 E

(r) A traffic lane for outbound traffic established between the separation line specified in paragraph (p) above and a straight line connecting the following geographical positions:

(20)	53°34′.22 N,	000°17′.59 E	(South Haile)
(34)	53°36′.72 N,	000°21′.20 E	(Mid New Sand)
(37)	53°38′.35 N,	000°22′.49 E	(North New Sand)

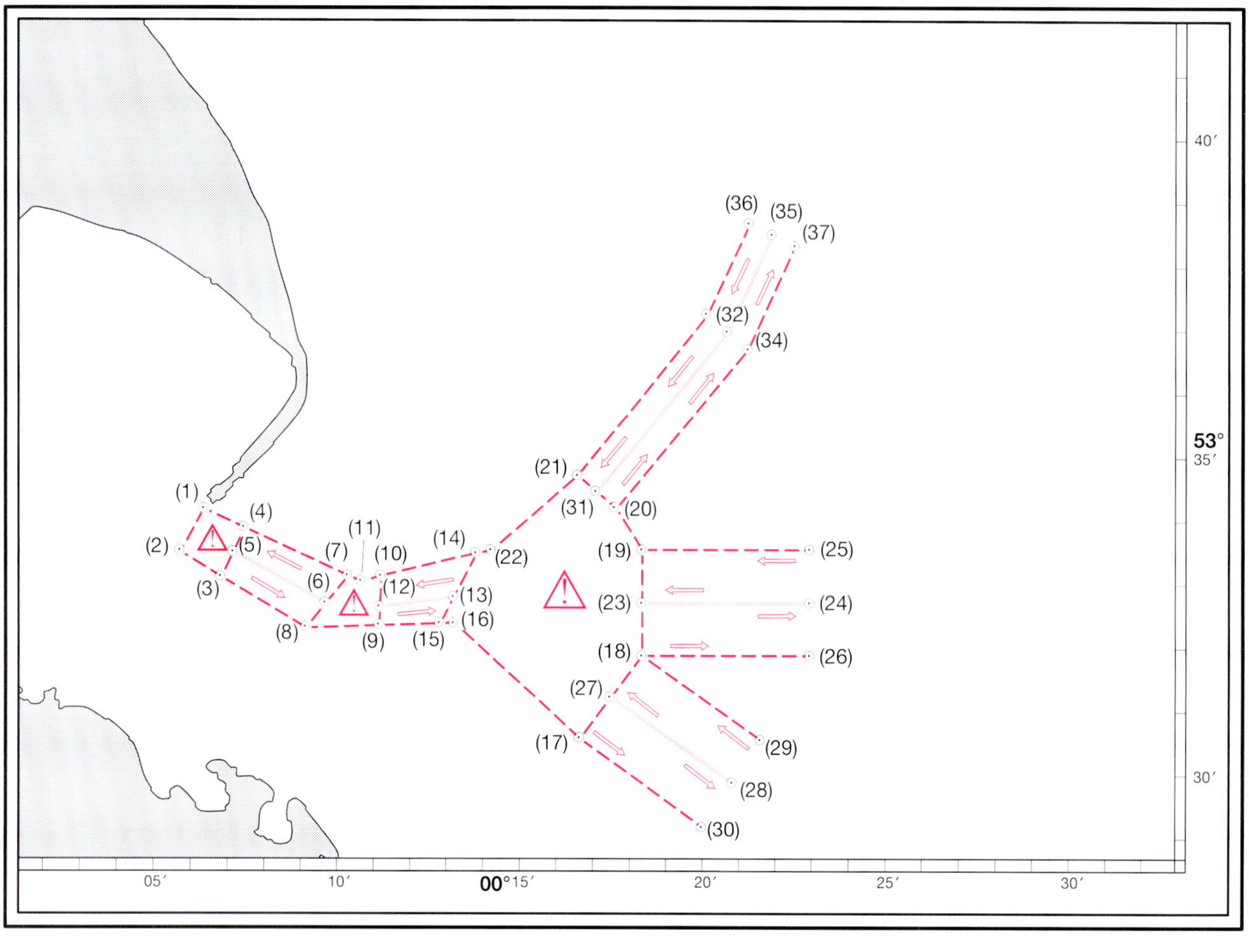

IN THE APPROACHES TO THE RIVER HUMBER

OFF THE COAST OF SOUTHERN NORWAY*

Note: See "Recommended routes joining the traffic separation schemes off the coast of southern Norway" in part E.

(Reference charts: Norwegian 305 (INT 1300) and 306 published by the Norwegian Hydrographic Service.
Note: These charts are based on European Datum 1950 (ED 50). The geographical positions, (1) to (55), listed below are based on World Geodetic System 1984 datum (WGS 84).)

Categories of ships to which the traffic separation schemes apply

(a) tankers as defined in Annex I of the International Convention for the Prevention of Pollution from Ships, 1973, as modified by the Protocol of 1978 (MARPOL 73/78);

(b) chemical tankers carrying noxious liquid substances in bulk assessed or provisionally assessed as Category X or Y in Annex II to MARPOL 73/78;

(c) ships of 5000 gross tonnage and upwards, in transit or on international voyages to or from Norwegian ports; and

(d) the routeing schemes **do not apply** to any size or category of ship in domestic traffic with passengers and/or goods between Norwegian ports.

International voyages to or from ports in Norway

Ships of above categories on international voyages, to or from ports in Norway, should follow the ships' routeing system until a course to port can be clearly set. This also applies to ships calling at Norwegian ports for supplies or service.

Description of the traffic separation schemes

I Off Egersund

(a) A separation zone is bounded by a line connecting the following geographical positions:

(1)	58°21′.00 N,	005°15′.23 E	(4)	58°18′.33 N,	005°26′.02 E
(2)	58°18′.78 N,	005°19′.20 E	(5)	58°20′.22 N,	005°21′.80 E
(3)	58°16′.82 N,	005°23′.58 E	(6)	58°22′.37 N,	005°18′.00 E

(b) A traffic lane for eastbound traffic is established between the separation zone described in paragraph (a) and a line connecting the following geographical positions:

(7)	58°18′.95 N,	005°11′.08 E	(9)	58°14′.53 N,	005°19′.90 E
(8)	58°16′.60 N,	005°15′.27 E			

(c) A traffic lane for westbound traffic is established between the separation zone described in paragraph (a) and a line connecting the following geographical positions:

(10)	58°24′.40 N,	005°22′.17 E	(12)	58°20′.63 N,	005°29′.70 E
(11)	58°22′.40 N,	005°25′.75 E			

II Off Farsund

(d) A separation zone is bounded by a line connecting the following geographical positions:

(13)	57°46′.62 N,	006°30′.43 E	(16)	57°46′.30 N,	006°41′.62 E
(14)	57°44′.43 N,	006°35′.20 E	(17)	57°46′.40 N,	006°36′.63 E
(15)	57°44′.30 N,	006°41′.48 E	(18)	57°48′.12 N,	006°32′.87 E

(e) A traffic lane for eastbound traffic is established between the separation zone described in paragraph (d) and a line connecting the following geographical positions:

(19)	57°44′.33 N,	006°26′.80 E	(21)	57°41′.32 N,	006°41′.25 E
(20)	57°41′.48 N,	006°33′.03 E			

* Date of implementation of new schemes: 0000 hours UTC on 1 June 2011.

(f) A traffic lane for westbound traffic is established between the separation zone described in paragraph (d) and a line connecting the following geographical positions:

(22)	57°50′.40 N,	006°36′.52 E	(24)	57°49′.28 N,	006°41′.85 E
(23)	57°49′.35 N,	006°38′.80 E			

B

III Off Ryvingen

(g) A separation zone is bounded by a line connecting the following geographical positions:

(25)	57°42′.80 N,	007°41′.87 E	(28)	57°44′.55 N,	007°50′.77 E
(26)	57°42′.55 N,	007°51′.72 E	(29)	57°44′.78 N,	007°42′.10 E
(27)	57°44′.87 N,	007°59′.92 E			

(h) A traffic lane for eastbound traffic is established between the separation zone described in paragraph (g) and a line connecting the following geographical positions:

(30)	57°39′.85 N,	007°41′.72 E	(32)	57°39′.92 N,	008°00′.25 E
(31)	57°39′.58 N,	007°52′.97 E			

(i) A traffic lane for westbound traffic is established between the separation zone described in paragraph (g) and a line connecting the following geographical positions:

(33)	57°47′.75 N,	007°42′.55 E	(35)	57°49′.40 N,	007°56′.00 E
(34)	57°47′.58 N,	007°49′.68 E			

IV Off Lillesand

(j) A separation zone is bounded by a line connecting the following geographical positions:

(36)	57°58′.25 N,	008°46′.92 E	(39)	58°03′.47 N,	008°53′.38 E
(37)	57°59′.75 N,	008°52′.25 E	(40)	58°01′.35 N,	008°49′.88 E
(38)	58°02′.17 N,	008°56′.22 E	(41)	58°00′.02 N,	008°45′.15 E

(k) A traffic lane for eastbound traffic is established between the separation zone described in paragraph (j) and a line connecting the following geographical positions:

(42)	57°55′.60 N,	008°49′.55 E	(44)	58°00′.18 N,	009°00′.47 E
(43)	57°57′.37 N,	008°55′.82 E			

(l) A traffic lane for westbound traffic is established between the separation zone described in paragraph (j) and a line connecting the following geographical positions:

(45)	58°02′.67 N,	008°42′.50 E	(47)	58°05′.45 N,	008°49′.13 E
(46)	58°03′.73 N,	008°46′.32 E			

V Off Risør

(m) A separation zone is bounded by a line connecting the following geographical positions:

(48)	58°26′.27 N,	009°36′.28 E	(50)	58°31′.33 N,	009°39′.67 E
(49)	58°30′.03 N,	009°42′.53 E	(51)	58°27′.57 N,	009°33′.42 E

(n) A traffic lane for eastbound traffic is established between the separation zone described in paragraph (m) and a line connecting the following geographical positions:

(52)	58°24′.30 N,	009°40′.60 E	(53)	58°28′.07 N,	009°46′.85 E

(o) A traffic lane for westbound traffic is established between the separation zone described in paragraph (m) and a line connecting the following geographical positions:

(54)	58°29′.53 N,	009°29′.08 E	(55)	58°33′.30 N,	009°35′.33 E

Description of recommended routes

The recommended routes between the traffic separation schemes are described in part E.

Note:

Chart number	Title	Scale	Datum
306	Skagerrak, vestre blad	1:350 000	ED 50
305 (INT 1300)	Skagerrak	1:350 000	WGS 84

Typical shifts of position co-ordinates referred to the WGS 84 datum to the ED 50 datum are:

From datum	To datum	Approximate latitude in the area	Datum shift
WGS 84	ED 50	62°30′ N	99 m (NE-diagonal)
WGS 84	ED 50	59°00′ N	109 m (NE-diagonal)

(chartlets overleaf)

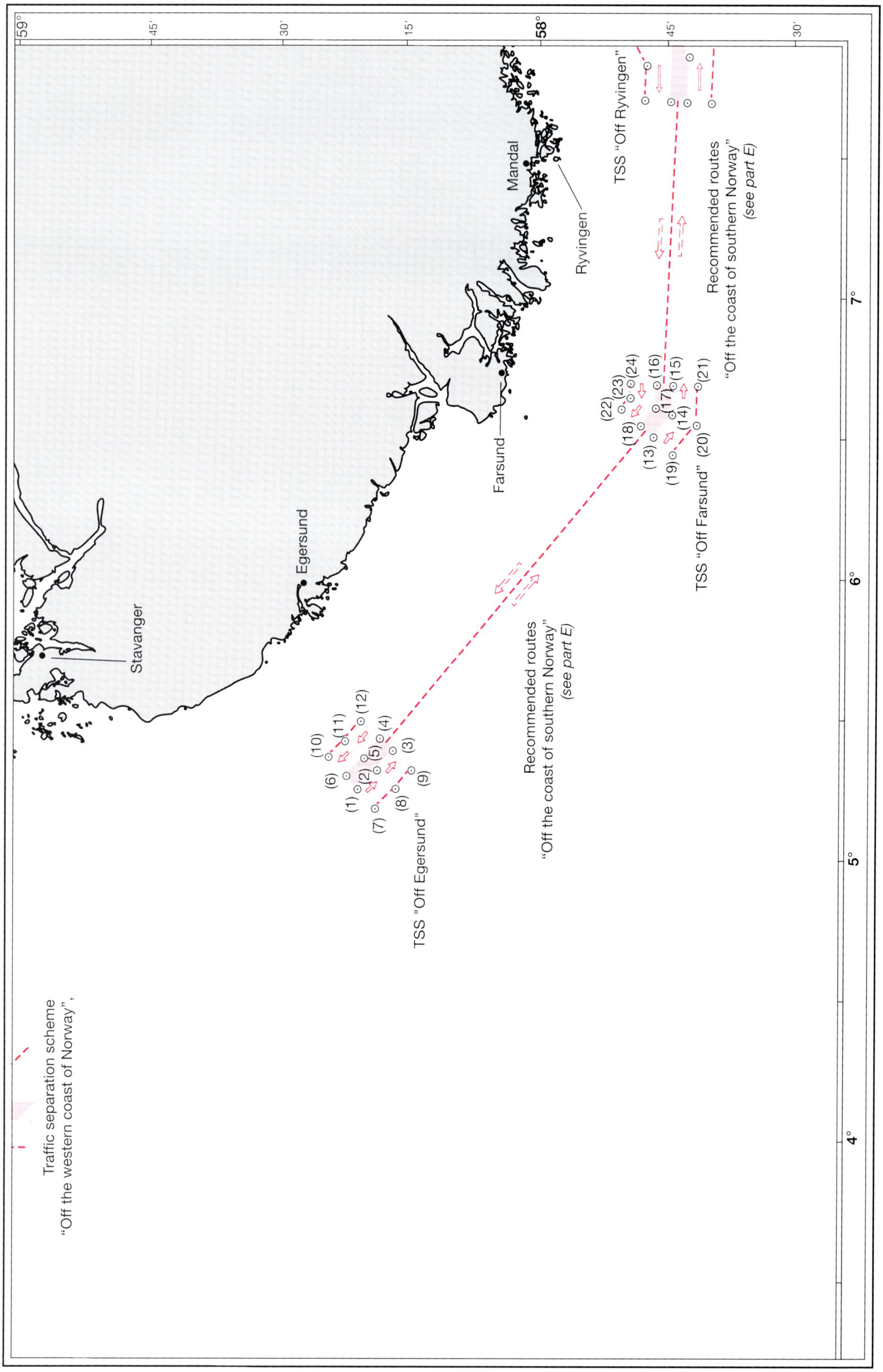

OFF THE COAST OF SOUTHERN NORWAY – WEST

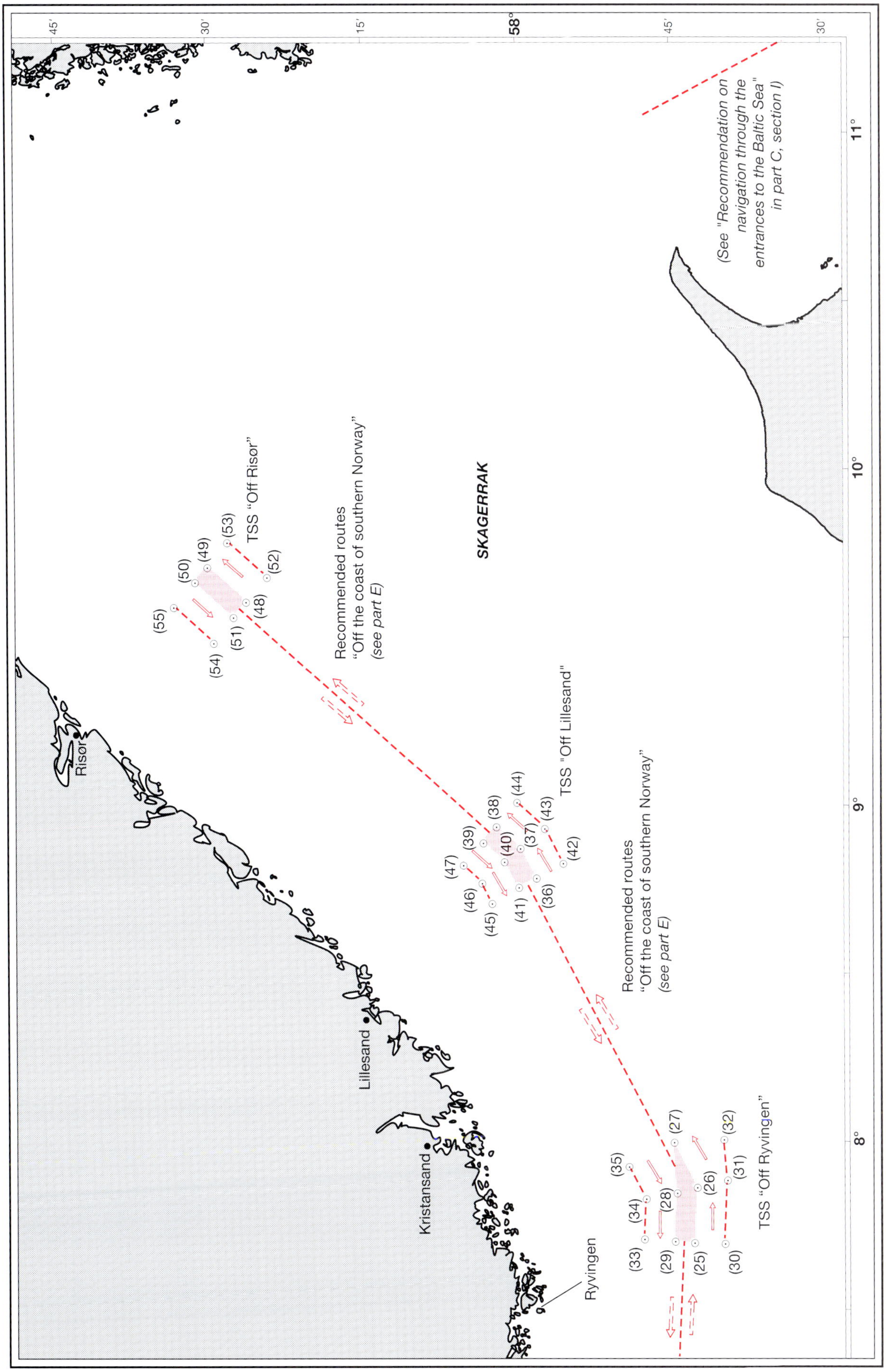

OFF THE COAST OF SOUTHERN NORWAY – EAST

OFF FEISTEIN [revoked]

The traffic separation scheme "Off Feistein" has been revoked from 0000 hours UTC on 1 June 2011.

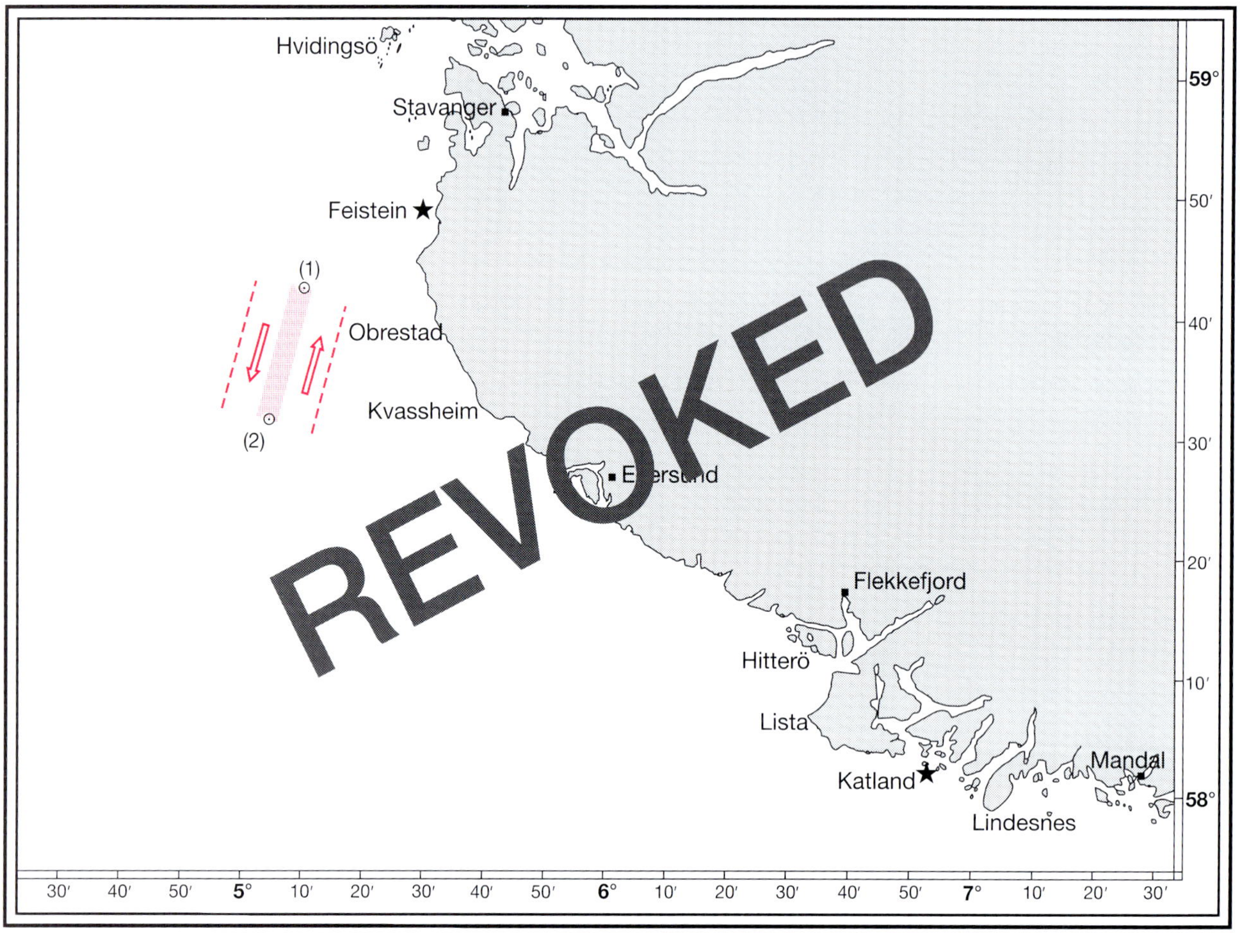

OFF FEISTEIN

OFF THE WESTERN COAST OF NORWAY*

Note: See "Recommended routes joining the traffic separation schemes off the western coast of Norway" in part E.

(Reference charts: Norwegian 306, 307 and 308 published by the Norwegian Hydrographic Service.
Note: These charts are based on European Datum 1950 (ED 50). The geographical positions, (1) to (37), listed below are based on World Geodetic System 1984 datum (WGS 84).)

Categories of ships to which the traffic separation schemes apply

(a) tankers as defined in Annex I of the International Convention for the Prevention of Pollution from Ships, 1973, as modified by the Protocol of 1978 (MARPOL 73/78);

(b) chemical tankers carrying noxious liquid substances in bulk assessed or provisionally assessed as Category X or Y in Annex II to MARPOL 73/78;

(c) ships of 5000 gross tonnage and upwards, in transit or on international voyages to or from Norwegian ports; and

(d) the routeing schemes **do not apply** to any size or category of ship in domestic traffic with passengers and/or goods between Norwegian ports.

International voyages to or from ports in Norway

Ships of above categories on international voyages, to or from ports in Norway, should follow the ships' routeing system until a course to port can be clearly set. This also applies to ships calling at Norwegian ports for supplies or service.

Description of the traffic separation schemes

I Off Runde

(a) A separation zone is bounded by a line connecting the following geographical positions:

(1)	62°59′.95 N,	004°08′.40 E	(4)	62°49′.98 N,	004°08′.43 E
(2)	62°55′.17 N,	004°04′.07 E	(5)	62°54′.78 N,	004°08′.43 E
(3)	62°49′.98 N,	004°04′.07 E	(6)	62°59′.18 N,	004°12′.45 E

(b) A traffic lane for southbound traffic is established between the separation zone described in paragraph (a) and a line connecting the following geographical positions:

(7)	63°01′.12 N,	004°02′.32 E	(9)	62°50′.00 N,	003°57′.52 E
(8)	62°55′.78 N,	003°57′.50 E			

(c) A traffic lane for northbound traffic is established between the separation zone described in paragraph (a) and a line connecting the following geographical positions:

(10)	62°58′.05 N,	004°18′.52 E	(12)	62°50′.00 N,	004°14′.97 E
(11)	62°54′.20 N,	004°15′.00 E			

II Off Stad

(d) A separation zone is bounded by a line connecting the following geographical positions:

(13)	61°59′.00 N,	004°04′.13 E	(15)	61°54′.00 N,	004°08′.37 E
(14)	61°54′.00 N,	004°04′.13 E	(16)	61°59′.00 N,	004°08′.37 E

(e) A traffic lane for southbound traffic is established between the separation zone described in paragraph (d) and a line connecting the following geographical positions:

(17)	61°59′.00 N,	003°57′.78 E	(18)	61°54′.00 N,	003°57′.80 E

(f) A traffic lane for northbound traffic is established between the separation zone described in paragraph (d) and a line connecting the following geographical positions:

(19)	61°59′.00 N,	004°14′.72 E	(20)	61°54′.00 N,	004°14′.70 E

* Date of implementation of new schemes: 0000 hours UTC on 1 June 2011.

B

III Off Sotra

(g) A separation zone is bounded by a line connecting the following geographical positions:

(21)	60°20′.00 N,	004°04′.23 E	(23)	60°15′.00 N,	004°08′.25 E
(22)	60°15′.00 N,	004°04′.25 E	(24)	60°20′.00 N,	004°08′.27 E

(h) A traffic lane for southbound traffic is established between the separation zone described in paragraph (g) and a line connecting the following geographical positions:

(25)	60°20′.00 N,	003°58′.20 E	(26)	60°15′.00 N,	003°58′.23 E

(i) A traffic lane for northbound traffic is established between the separation zone described in paragraph (g) and a line connecting the following geographical positions:

(27)	60°20′.00 N,	004°14′.30 E	(28)	60°15′.00 N,	004°14′.27 E

IV Off Utsira

(j) A separation zone is bounded by a line connecting the following geographical positions:

(29)	59°05′.00 N,	004°04′.32 E	(31)	58°57′.72 N,	004°08′.20 E
(30)	58°59′.83 N,	004°04′.32 E	(32)	59°05′.00 N,	004°08′.20 E

(k) A traffic lane for southbound traffic is established between the separation zone described in paragraph (j) and a line connecting the following geographical positions:

(33)	59°05′.00 N,	003°58′.47 E	(34)	58°58′.50 N,	003°58′.47 E

(l) A traffic lane for northbound traffic is established between the separation zone described in paragraph (j) and a line connecting the following geographical positions:

(35) 59°05′.00 N, 004°14′.03 E
(36) 59°01′.73 N, 004°14′.03 E
(37) 58°58′.50 N, 004°19′.95 E

Description of recommended routes

The recommended routes between the traffic separation schemes are described in part E.

Note:

Chart number	Title	Scale	Datum
306	Skagerrak, vestre blad	1:350 000	ED 50
307	Stavanger–Florø	1:350 000	ED 50
308	Florø–Smøla	1:350 000	ED 50

Typical shift of position co-ordinates referred to the WGS 84 datum to the ED 50 datum are:

From datum	To datum	Approximate latitude in the area	Datum shift
WGS 84	ED 50	62°30′ N	99 m (NE-diagonal)
WGS 84	ED 50	59°00′ N	109 m (NE-diagonal)

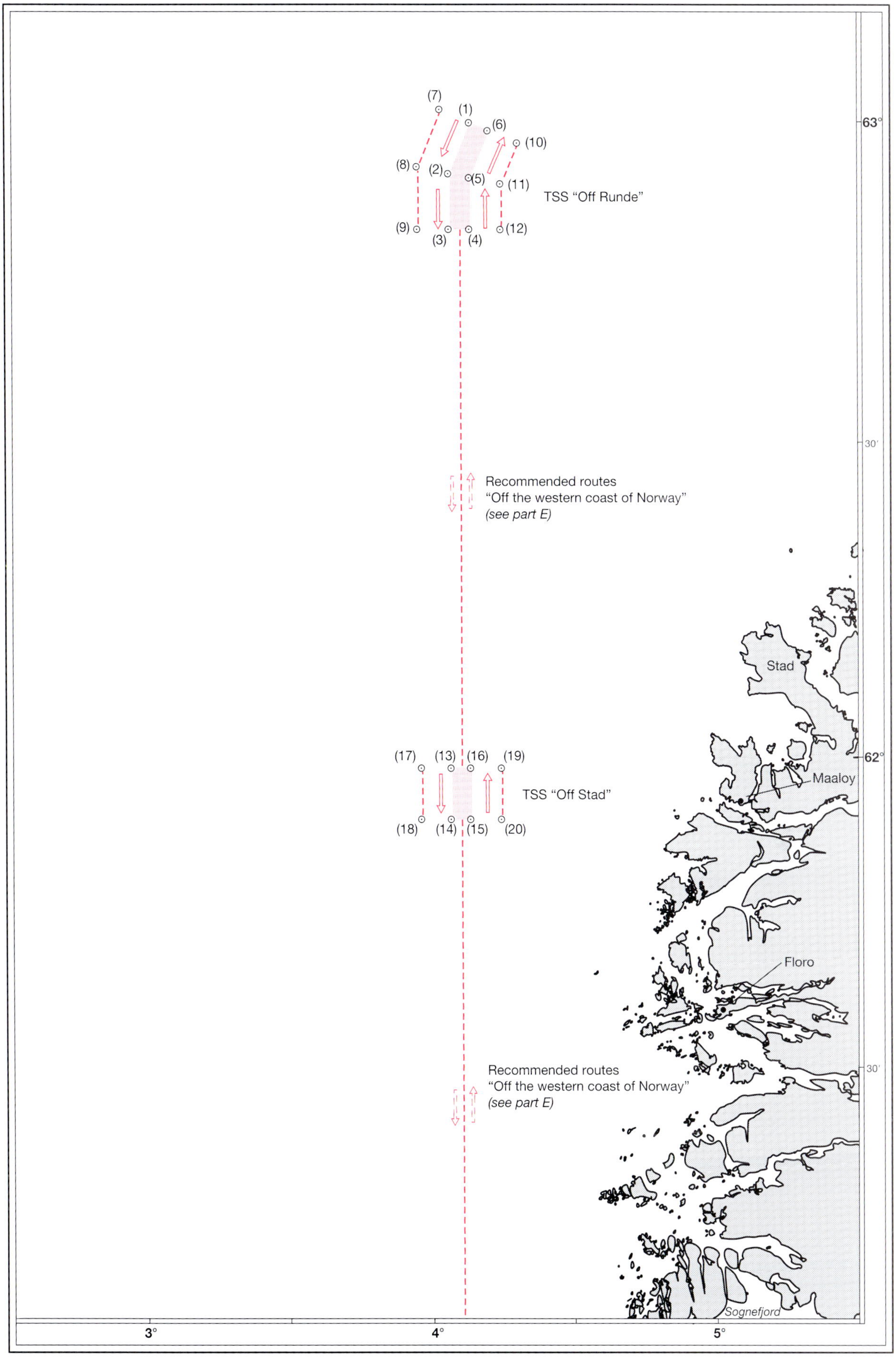

OFF THE WESTERN COAST OF NORWAY – NORTH

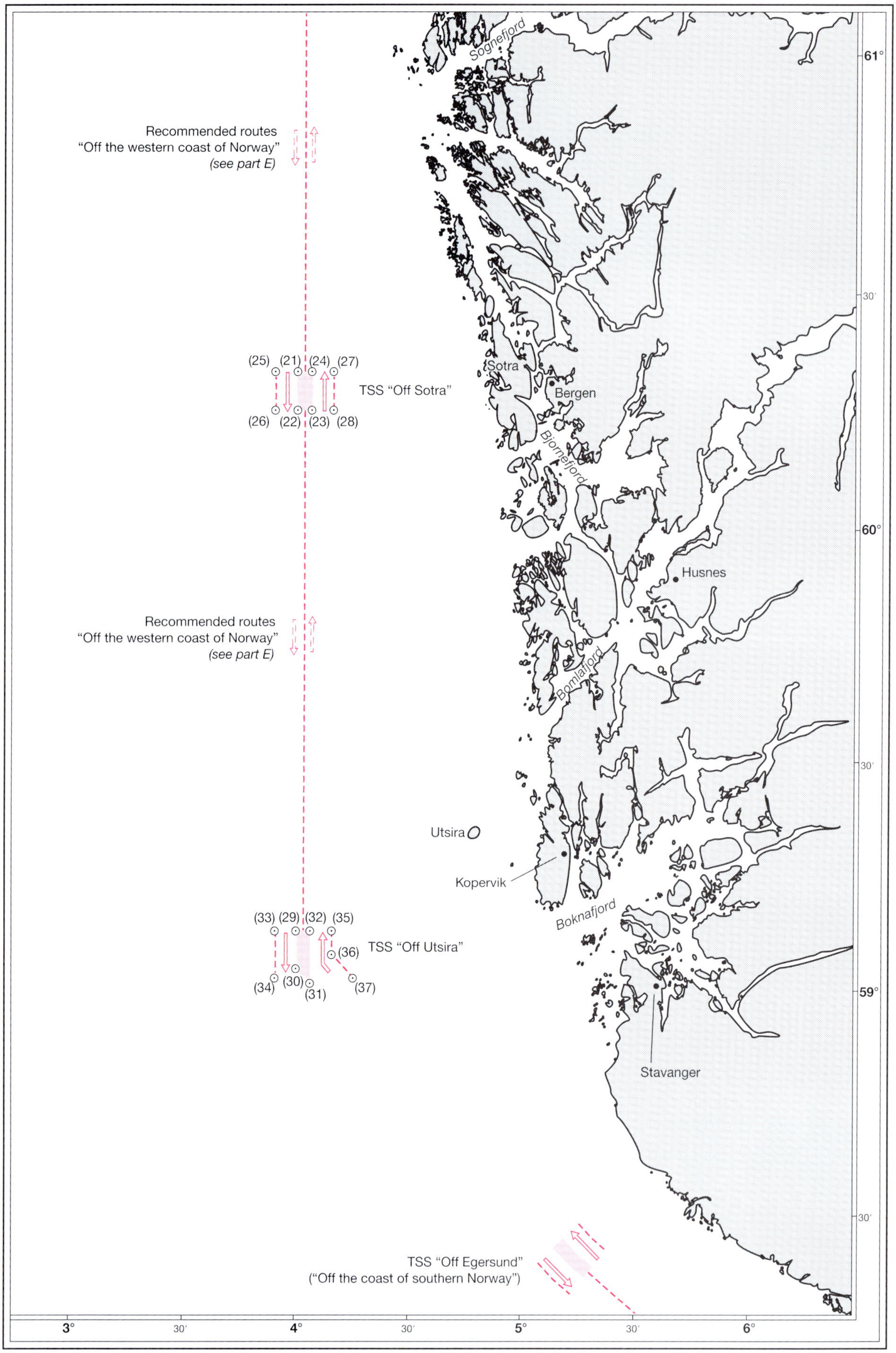

OFF THE WESTERN COAST OF NORWAY – SOUTH

OFF THE COAST OF NORWAY FROM VARDØ TO RØST

Note: See mandatory ship reporting system "In the Barents area" in part G, section I.

(Reference charts: Norwegian Hydrographic Service Fisheries Chart Series 551, 1963 edition; 552, 1964 edition; 557, 1966 edition. These charts are based on European datum 1950 (ED 50).
Note: The geographical positions (1)–(84) listed below are given in the WGS 84 datum.)

Categories of ships to which the traffic separation schemes apply

Tankers of all sizes, including gas and chemical tankers, and all other cargo ships of 5000 gross tonnage and upwards engaged on international voyages should follow the routeing system consisting of a series of traffic separation schemes joined by recommended routes off the coast of Norway from Vardø to Røst.

International voyages to or from ports in Norway from Vardø to Røst

Ships on international voyages to or from ports in Norway from Vardø to Røst should follow the ship's routeing systems until a course to port can be clearly set. This also applies to ships calling at Norwegian ports for supplies or service.

Description of the traffic separation schemes

I Off Vardø

(a) A separation zone is bounded by a line connecting the following geographical positions:

(1)	70°44′.55 N,	031°49′.52 E	(3)	70°51′.05 N,	031°33′.87 E
(2)	70°49′.44 N,	031°30′.08 E	(4)	70°46′.20 N,	031°53′.31 E

(b) A traffic lane for westbound traffic is established between the separation zone described in paragraph (a) and a line connecting the following geographical positions:

(5)	70°48′.59 N,	031°58′.90 E	(6)	70°53′.40 N,	031°39′.19 E

(c) A traffic lane for eastbound traffic is established between the separation zone described in paragraph (a) and a line connecting the following geographical positions:

(7)	70°42′.22 N,	031°44′.20 E	(8)	70°47′.08 N,	031°24′.76 E

II Off Slettnes

(d) A separation zone is bounded by a line connecting the following geographical positions:

(9)	71°23′.01 N,	029°11′.08 E	(12)	71°29′.21 N,	028°44′.33 E
(10)	71°26′.11 N,	028°58′.61 E	(13)	71°27′.86 N,	029°01′.25 E
(11)	71°27′.26 N,	028°42′.95 E	(14)	71°24′.63 N,	029°14′.78 E

(e) A traffic lane for westbound traffic is established between the separation zone described in paragraph (d) and a line connecting the following geographical positions:

(15)	71°27′.06 N,	029°20′.38 E	(17)	71°32′.13 N,	028°46′.76 E
(16)	71°30′.60 N,	029°05′.28 E			

(f) A traffic lane for eastbound traffic is established between the separation zone described in paragraph (d) and a line connecting the following geographical positions:

(18)	71°20′.58 N,	029°05′.48 E	(20)	71°24′.39 N,	028°40′.62 E
(19)	71°23′.35 N,	028°54′.38 E			

III Off North Cape

(g) A separation zone is bounded by a line connecting the following geographical positions:

(21)	71°40′.27 N,	026°08′.73 E	(24)	71°42′.53 N,	025°26′.58 E
(22)	71°41′.78 N,	025°49′.27 E	(25)	71°43′.72 N,	025°49′.45 E
(23)	71°40′.61 N,	025°27′.86 E	(26)	71°42′.19 N,	026°10′.46 E

(h) A traffic lane for westbound traffic is established between the separation zone described in paragraph (g) and a line connecting the following geographical positions:

(27) 71°45′.05 N,	026°13′.20 E	(29) 71°45′.39 N,	025°24′.48 E
(28) 71°47′.03 N,	025°49′.12 E		

(i) A traffic lane for eastbound traffic is established between the separation zone described in paragraph (g) and a line connecting the following geographical positions:

(30) 71°37′.34 N,	026°06′.36 E	(32) 71°37′.60 N,	025°29′.77 E
(31) 71°38′.80 N,	025°48′.40 E		

IV Off Sørøya

(j) A separation zone is bounded by a line connecting the following geographical positions:

(33) 71°30′.11 N,	022°39′.50 E	(36) 71°28′.08 N,	021°59′.45 E
(34) 71°28′.95 N,	022°20′.05 E	(37) 71°30′.73 N,	022°18′.35 E
(35) 71°26′.29 N,	022°01′.90 E	(38) 71°32′.06 N,	022°38′.23 E

(k) A traffic lane for westbound traffic is established between the separation zone described in paragraph (j) and a line connecting the following geographical positions:

(39) 71°35′.00 N,	022°36′.42 E	(41) 71°30′.85 N,	021°55′.63 E
(40) 71°33′.65 N,	022°15′.39 E		

(l) A traffic lane for eastbound traffic is established between the separation zone described in paragraph (j) and a line connecting the following geographical positions:

(42) 71°27′.17 N,	022°41′.31 E	(44) 71°23′.55 N,	022°05′.83 E
(43) 71°26′.00 N,	022°23′.00 E		

V Off Torsvåg

(m) A separation zone is bounded by a line connecting the following geographical positions:

(45) 71°02′.07 N,	019°13′.93 E	(48) 70°56′.51 N,	018°36′.45 E
(46) 70°59′.63 N,	018°55′.90 E	(49) 71°01′.26 N,	018°52′.77 E
(47) 70°55′.07 N,	018°40′.45 E	(50) 71°03′.97 N,	019°11′.40 E

(n) A traffic lane for westbound traffic is established between the separation zone described in paragraph (m) and a line connecting the following geographical positions:

(51) 71°06′.72 N,	019°07′.81 E	(53) 70°58′.73 N,	018°30′.34 E
(52) 71°03′.77 N,	018°47′.82 E		

(o) A traffic lane for eastbound traffic is established between the separation zone described in paragraph (m) and a line connecting the following geographical positions:

(54) 70°59′.40 N,	019°17′.65 E	(56) 70°52′.80 N,	018°46′.70 E
(55) 70°56′.97 N,	019°00′.60 E		

VI Off Andenes

(p) A separation zone is bounded by a line connecting the following geographical positions:

(57) 69°48′.74 N,	015°06′.86 E	(59) 69°44′.77 N,	014°46′.12 E
(58) 69°43′.32 N,	014°50′.07 E	(60) 69°50′.22 N,	015°03′.14 E

(q) A traffic lane for westbound traffic is established between the separation zone described in paragraph (p) and a line connecting the following geographical positions:

(61) 69°52′.41 N,	014°57′.25 E	(62) 69°47′.00 N,	014°40′.38 E

(r) A traffic lane for eastbound traffic is established between the separation zone described in paragraph (p) and a line connecting the following geographical positions:

(63) 69°46′.52 N,	015°12′.75 E	(64) 69°41′.09 N,	014°55′.85 E

IN THE SUNK AREA AND IN THE NORTHERN APPROACHES TO THE THAMES ESTUARY*

Note: See mandatory ship reporting system "West European Tanker Reporting System" in part G, section I.

(Reference chart: British Admiralty 1610, 2012 edition.
Note: This chart is based on World Geodetic System 1984 datum (WGS 84).)

An integrated traffic routeing scheme for the SUNK area consists of several elements comprising:

.1 One two-way route (Long Sand Head);

.2 Two traffic lanes 1.9 miles wide in two parts (SUNK North and South TSS);

.3 Two traffic lanes 1.0 mile wide in one part (SUNK East TSS);

.4 An inner precautionary area, named SUNK Inner precautionary area;

.5 A precautionary area, adjacent to the SUNK Inner precautionary area, named SUNK Outer precautionary area;

.6 A 1 nautical mile diameter area to be avoided in the SUNK Outer precautionary area; and

.7 A recommended route ("Galloper" recommended route) (see part E).

Part I:
Description of the two-way route

Long Sand Head two-way route is established. (Note that entry is restricted to piloted vessels, vessels operated under pilotage exemption certificate (PEC), and vessels exempt from pilotage under the destination port's pilotage directions.)

(a) A boundary line connecting the following geographical positions:

(1)	51°38′.09 N,	001°40′.43 E	(3)	51°47′.77 N,	001°38′.16 E
(2)	51°47′.90 N,	001°39′.42 E			

(b) A separation zone bounded by a line connecting the following geographical positions:

(4)	51°38′.31 N,	001°43′.60 E	(10)	51°49′.49 N,	001°40′.06 E
(5)	51°38′.33 N,	001°43′.89 E	(11)	51°49′.30 N,	001°38′.16 E
(6)	51°42′.16 N,	001°43′.20 E	(12)	51°49′.11 N,	001°38′.16 E
(7)	51°48′.29 N,	001°42′.08 E	(13)	51°49′.30 N,	001°40′.01 E
(8)	51°48′.98 N,	001°41′.64 E	(14)	51°48′.84 N,	001°41′.40 E
(9)	51°49′.28 N,	001°40′.72 E	(15)	51°48′.24 N,	001°41′.79 E

(c) A two-way route bounded by the boundary line described in (a) above and the separation zone described in (b) above.

Part II:
Description of the traffic separation schemes

SUNK South traffic separation scheme

(d) A separation zone bounded by a line connecting the following geographical positions:

(16)	51°38′.54 N,	001°46′.87 E	(18)	51°42′.44 N,	001°47′.16 E
(17)	51°38′.61 N,	001°47′.85 E	(19)	51°42′.37 N,	001°46′.18 E

(e) A traffic lane for northbound traffic between the separation zone described in (d) above and a line connecting the following geographical positions:

(20)	51°38′.82 N,	001°50′.83 E	(21)	51°42′.65 N,	001°50′.14 E

(f) A traffic lane for southbound traffic between the separation zone described in (d) above and that portion of the separation zone described in (b) above connecting the following geographical positions:

(5)	51°38′.33 N,	001°43′.89 E	(6)	51°42′.16 N,	001°43′.20 E

* Date of implementation of amended scheme: 0000 hours UTC on 1 December 2012.

B

SUNK East traffic separation scheme

(g) A separation zone bounded by a line connecting the following geographical positions:

(22)	51°53′.07 N,	002°07′.46 E	(24)	51°48′.84 N,	001°51′.86 E
(23)	51°53′.39 N,	002°07′.55 E	(25)	51°48′.54 N,	001°51′.85 E

(h) A separation zone bounded by a line connecting the following geographical positions:

(26)	51°54′.59 N,	002°07′.93 E	(31)	51°55′.59 N,	001°51′.73 E
(27)	51°49′.92 N,	001°51′.89 E	(32)	51°52′.31 N,	001°50′.68 E
(28)	51°52′.06 N,	001°49′.37 E	(33)	51°50′.99 N,	001°52′.27 E
(29)	51°53′.90 N,	001°49′.96 E	(34)	51°55′.63 N,	002°08′.24 E
(30)	51°55′.72 N,	001°50′.54 E			

(i) A traffic lane for eastbound traffic between the separation zone described in (g) above and a line connecting the following geographical positions:

(35)	51°47′.45 N,	001°51′.82 E	(36)	51°51′.89 N,	002°07′.08 E

(j) A traffic lane for westbound traffic between the separation zone described in (g) above and that portion of the separation zone described in (h) above connecting the following geographical positions:

(26)	51°54′.59 N,	002°07′.93 E,	(27)	51°49′.92 N,	001°51′.89 E

SUNK North traffic separation scheme

(k) A separation zone bounded by a line connecting the following geographical positions:

(37)	51°56′.06 N,	001°47′.40 E	(39)	51°54′.34 N,	001°45′.87 E
(38)	51°56′.16 N,	001°46′.45 E	(40)	51°54′.24 N,	001°46′.81 E

(l) A traffic lane for northbound traffic between the separation zone described in (k) above and that portion of the separation zone described in (h) above connecting the following geographical positions:

(29)	51°53′.90 N,	001°49′.96 E	(30)	51°55′.72 N,	001°50′.54 E

(m) A traffic lane for southbound traffic between the separation zone described in (k) above and a line connecting the following geographical positions:

(41)	51°56′.50 N,	001°43′.31 E	(42)	51°54′.68 N,	001°42′.72 E

SUNK Inner precautionary area

(n) A precautionary area is established by a line connecting the following geographical positions:

(12)	51°49′.11 N,	001°38′.16 E	(47)	51°52′.46 N,	001°32′.35 E
(11)	51°49′.30 N,	001°38′.16 E	(48)	51°51′.59 N,	001°31′.32 E
(10)	51°49′.49 N,	001°40′.06 E	(49)	51°49′.61 N,	001°31′.32 E
(9)	51°49′.28 N,	001°40′.72 E	(50)	51°48′.51 N,	001°29′.50 E
(43)	51°52′.61 N,	001°41′.12 E	(51)	51°46′.07 N,	001°33′.42 E
(44)	51°53′.03 N,	001°39′.03 E	(52)	51°47′.50 N,	001°35′.64 E
(45)	51°52′.73 N,	001°34′.26 E	(3)	51°47′.77 N,	001°38′.16 E
(46)	51°52′.46 N,	001°33′.20 E			

SUNK Outer precautionary area

(o) A precautionary area is established by a line connecting the following geographical positions:

(43)	51°52′.61 N,	001°41′.12 E	(35)	51°47′.45 N,	001°51′.82 E
(9)	51°49′.28 N,	001°40′.72 E	(27)	51°49′.92 N,	001°51′.89 E
(8)	51°48′.98 N,	001°41′.64 E	(28)	51°52′.06 N,	001°49′.37 E
(7)	51°48′.29 N,	001°42′.08 E	(29)	51°53′.90 N,	001°49′.96 E
(6)	51°42′.16 N,	001°43′.20 E	(42)	51°54′.68 N,	001°42′.72 E
(21)	51°42′.65 N,	001°50′.14 E			

Area to be avoided

(p) An area to be avoided, 1 nautical mile in diameter, is centred upon the following geographical position:

(53) 51°50′.10 N, 001°46′.02 E

Note: The flow of traffic around the ATBA is counter-clockwise, as indicated by the recommended directions of traffic flow in the precautionary area. All ships should avoid the area within a circle of radius 0.5 miles, centred upon the following geographical position: 51°50′.10 N, 001°46′.02 E.
This area is established to avoid hazard to a navigational aid which is established at the geographical position listed above, and which is considered vital to the safety of navigation.

Part III:
Recommended route

See part E for the description of the "Galloper" recommended route.

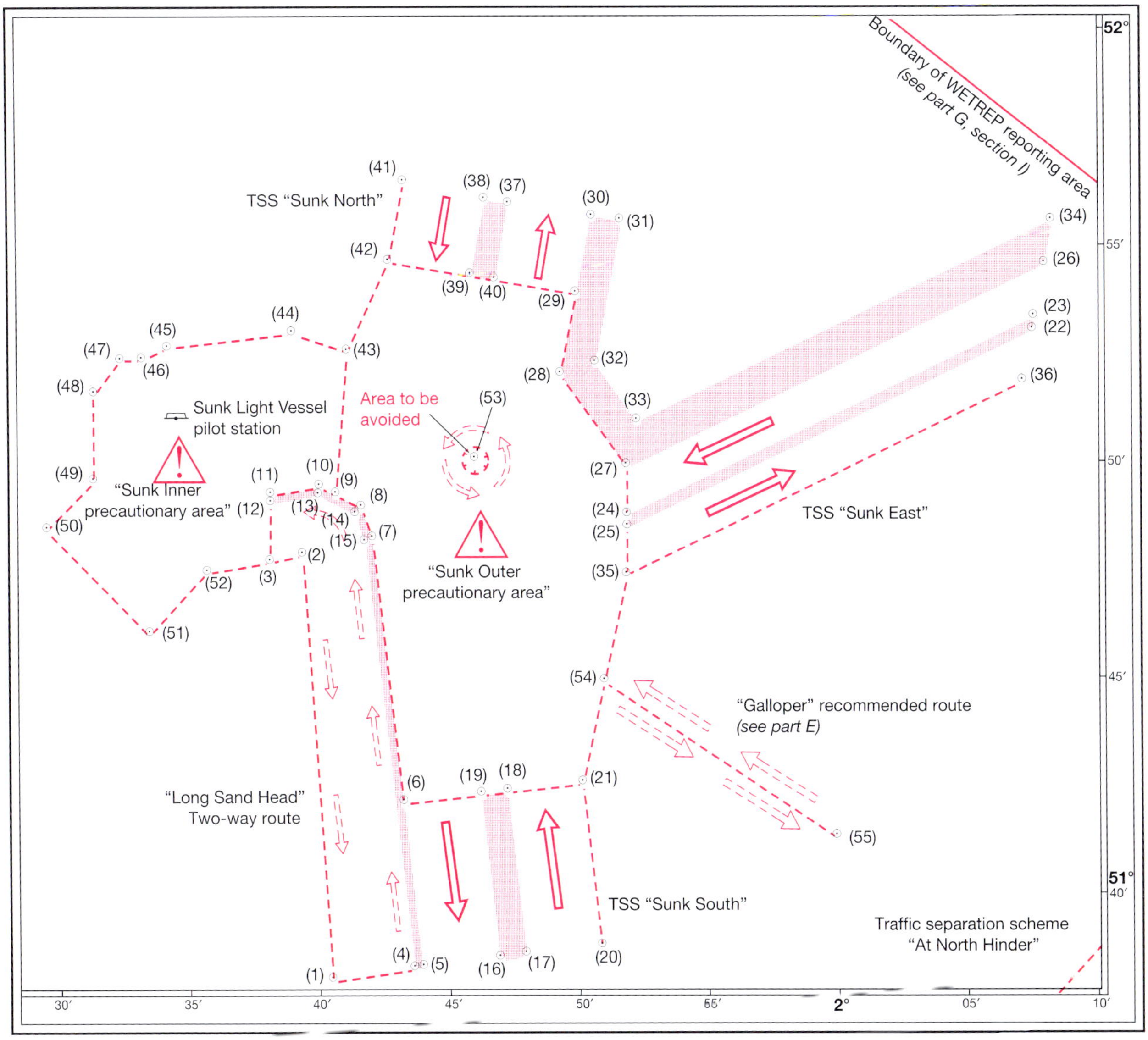

IN THE SUNK AREA AND IN THE NORTHERN APPROACHES TO THE THAMES ESTUARY

OFF FRIESLAND

(Reference charts: British Admiralty 1405, 1978 edition; 1406, 1988 edition; 1408, 1988 edition; 1505 and 2182A, 1978 edition; Netherlands Hydrographic Office INT 1419, 1990 edition; INT 1420, 1990 edition, 1014 (INT 1043), 1988 edition; 1035 (INT 1046), 1988 edition; 1037 (INT 1045), 1989 edition; German Hydrographic Office 50 (INT 1045), 1986 edition; 53, 1984 edition.

Note: These charts are based on European datum. Co-ordinates of the amendments to the scheme are from British Admiralty chart 1632, 2005 edition, which is based on the World Geodetic System 1984 datum (WGS 84); these are shown in colour.)

The following traffic separation schemes form part of the routeing system "Off Friesland".

Description of the traffic separation scheme

(a) Geographical positions (1) to (6) form the deep-water route "From North Hinder to traffic separation scheme 'Off Brown Ridge'" (see "Deep-water routes forming parts of routeing system 'Off Friesland'" in part C, section II).

Off Brown Ridge scheme

(b) A separation zone is bounded by a line connecting the following geographical positions:

(7)	53°03′.14 N,	003°21′.85 E	(9)	52°54′.81 N,	003°18′.87 E
(8)	52°55′.11 N,	003°17′.38 E	(10)	53°02′.84 N,	003°23′.34 E

(c) A traffic lane for northbound traffic is established between the separation zone in paragraph (b) above and a line connecting the following geographical positions:

(6)	52°54′.17 N,	003°22′.00 E	(11)	53°02′.20 N,	003°26′.48 E

(d) A traffic lane for southbound traffic is established between the separation zone in paragraph (b) above and a line connecting the following geographical positions:

(12)	53°03′.78 N,	003°18′.71 E	(1)	52°55′.75 N,	003°14′.25 E

(e) Geographical positions (11) to (14) form the deep-water route "From traffic separation scheme 'Off Brown Ridge' to traffic separation scheme 'West Friesland'" (see "Deep-water routes forming parts of routeing system 'Off Friesland" in part C, section II).

West Friesland scheme

(f) A separation zone is bounded by a line connecting the following geographical positions:

(15)	53°42′.99 N,	003°42′.12 E	(19)	53°46′.73 N,	004°20′.00 E
(16)	53°22′.12 N,	003°31′.47 E	(20)	53°56′.69 N,	004°36′.00 E
(17)	53°20′.67 N,	003°36′.85 E	(21)	53°59′.22 N,	004°36′.00 E
(18)	53°31′.12 N,	003°44′.72 E	(22)	53°57′.60 N,	004°15′.17 E

(g) A traffic lane for north-eastbound traffic is established between the separation zone in paragraph (f) above and a line connecting the following geographical positions:

(14)	53°19′.89 N,	003°39′.74 E	(24)	53°45′.90 N,	004°23′.32 E
(23)	53°30′.00 N,	003°47′.37 E	(25)	54°00′.00 N,	004°46′.00 E

(h) A traffic lane for south-westbound traffic is established between the separation zone in paragraph (f) above and a line connecting the following geographical positions:

(26)	53°57′.20 N,	004°10′.02 E	(13)	53°22′.94 N,	003°28′.40 E
(27)	53°43′.39 N,	003°38′.81 E			

Friesland Junction precautionary area

(i) A precautionary area is established directly to the north of the "West Friesland" traffic separation scheme. The area is bounded by a line connecting the following geographical positions:

(26)	53°57′.20 N,	004°10′.02 E	(29)	54°05′.59 N,	004°59′.32 E
(25)	54°00′.00 N,	004°46′.00 E	(30)	54°02′.57 N,	004°20′.92 E
(28)	54°01′.14 N,	005°00′.34 E	(31)	54°01′.91 N,	004°08′.96 E

East Friesland scheme

(j) A separation zone is bounded by a line connecting the following geographical positions:

(32)	54°02′.62 N,	005°00′.00 E	(35)	54°08′.97 N,	006°01′.33 E
(33)	54°04′.21 N,	005°20′.00 E	(36)	54°05′.69 N,	005°19′.66 E
(34)	54°08′.00 N,	006°01′.90 E	(37)	54°04′.11 N,	004°59′.66 E

(k) A traffic lane for eastbound traffic is established between the separation zone in paragraph (j) above and a line connecting the following geographical positions:

(28)	54°01′.14 N,	005°00′.34 E	(38)	54°06′.10 N,	006°03′.00 E

(l) A traffic lane for westbound traffic is established between the separation zone in paragraph (j) above and a line connecting the following geographical positions:

(39)	54°10′.90 N,	006°00′.20 E	(29)	54°05′.59 N,	004°59′.32 E
(40)	54°07′.17 N,	005°19′.32 E			

Note: The positions (38), (34), (35) and (39) coincide with the positions (15), (11), (8) and (14) of the "German Bight western approach" traffic separation scheme.

(m) Geographical positions (26), (41), (42) and (31) form the deep-water route "From traffic separation scheme 'Off Botney Ground' to precautionary area 'Friesland Junction' "(see "Deep-water routes forming parts of routeing system 'Off Friesland'" in part C, section II).

Off Botney Ground scheme

(n) A separation zone is bounded by a line connecting the following geographical positions:

(43)	53°57′.19 N,	003°44′.18 E	(49)	53°21′.38 N,	002°49′.20 E
(44)	53°55′.10 N,	003°27′.47 E	(50)	53°36′.22 N,	002°58′.80 E
(45)	53°41′.57 N,	003°08′.91 E	(50)	53°36′.28 N,	002°58′.85 E
(46)	53°35′.30 N,	003°03′.12 E	(51)	53°43′.71 N,	003°03′.66 E
(46)	53°35′.25 N,	003°03′.05 E	(52)	53°56′.66 N,	003°18′.18 E
(47)	53°29′.82 N,	002°58′.05 E	(53)	53°58′.50 N,	003°43′.71 E
(48)	53°20′.69 N,	002°52′.13 E			

(o) A traffic lane for west-/south-west- and south-bound traffic is established between the separation zone in paragraph (n) above and a line connecting the following geographical positions:

(42)	54°00′.46 N,	003°43′.01 E	(56)	53°36′.81 N,	002°56′.50 E
(54)	53°58′.61 N,	003°17′.32 E	(56)	53°36′.70 N,	002°56′.40 E
(55)	53°44′.40 N,	003°01′.40 E	(57)	53°21′.88 N,	002°46′.88 E

(p) A traffic lane for north-/north-east- and east-bound traffic is established between the separation zone in paragraph (n) above and a line connecting the following geographical positions:

(58)	53°20′.15 N,	002°54′.48 E	(61)	53°40′.71 N,	003°11′.00 E
(59)	53°29′.40 N,	003°00′.60 E	(62)	53°53′.13 N,	003°28′.02 E
(60)	53°34′.66 N,	003°05′.40 E	(41)	53°55′.24 N,	003°44′.88 E
(60)	53°34′.76 N,	003°05′.49 E			

(q) Geographical positions (56), (57), (63), (64), (3), (4), (65), (66), (58), (59) and (60) form the deep-water route "From North Hinder to Indefatigable Bank via DR1 lightbuoy" (see "Deep-water routes forming parts of routeing system 'Off Friesland'" in part C, section II).

(chartlet overleaf)

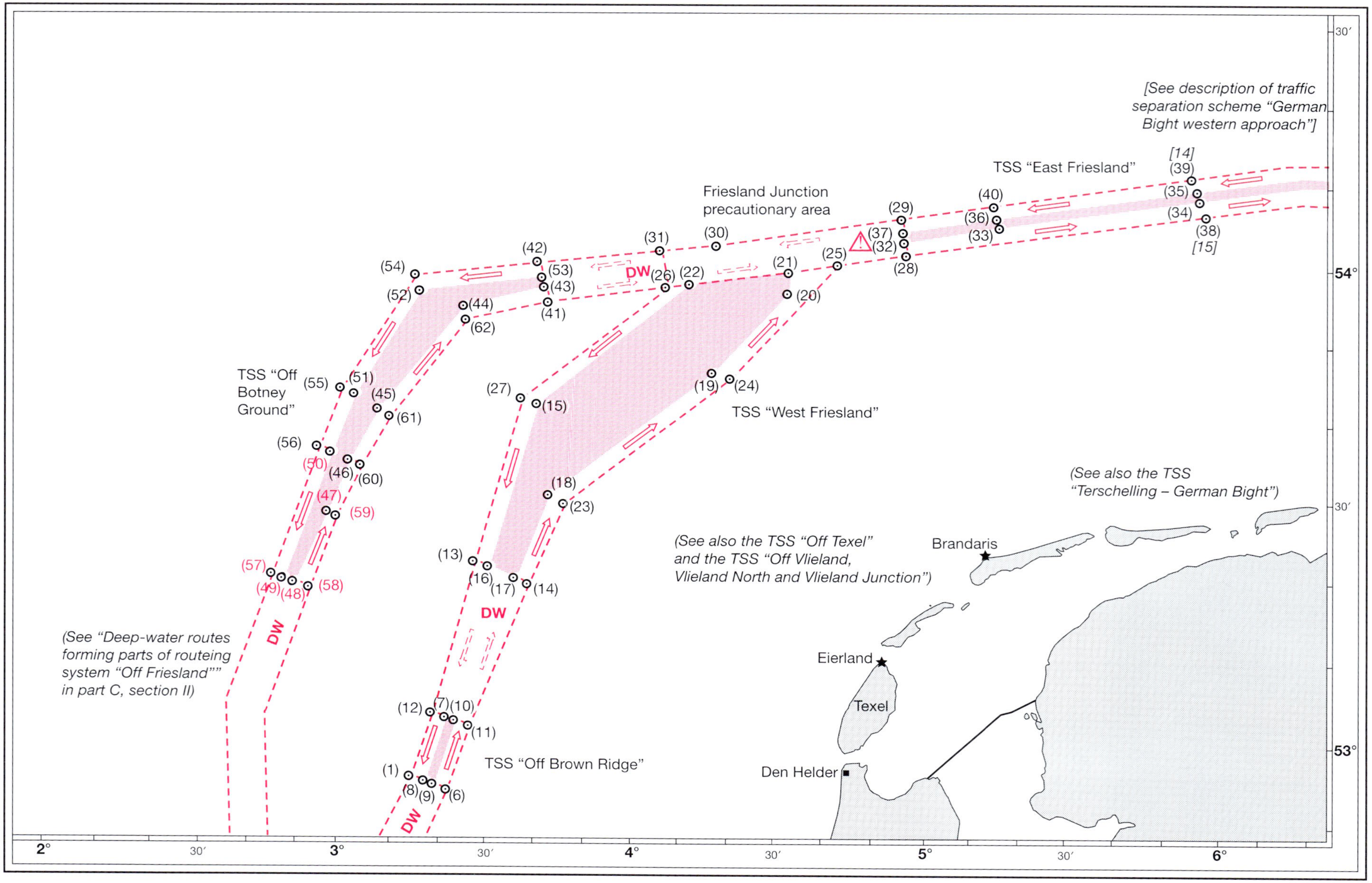

OFF FRIESLAND

IN THE APPROACHES TO HOOK OF HOLLAND AND AT NORTH HINDER*

Note: See "Deep-water route leading to Europoort" in part C, section II and area to be avoided "At Maas North" in part D, section I and precautionary areas "In the approaches to Hook of Holland and at North Hinder" in part E.

(Reference chart: Netherlands 1630 (INT 1416), edition 4/2010.
Note: This chart is based on World Geodetic System 1984 datum (WGS 84).)

Maas North traffic separation scheme

(a) A separation zone is bounded by a line connecting the following geographical positions:

(1)	52°22′.21 N,	003°51′.38 E	(4)	52°07′.14 N,	003°47′.10 E
(2)	52°19′.17 N,	003°50′.38 E	(5)	52°17′.07 N,	003°47′.69 E
(3)	52°07′.17 N,	003°54′.08 E	(6)	52°22′.45 N,	003°49′.51 E

(b) A traffic lane for northbound traffic is established between the separation zone in paragraph (a) above and a line connecting the following geographical positions:

(7)	52°21′.97 N,	003°53′.28 E	(9)	52°07′.18 N,	003°55′.95 E
(8)	52°19′.03 N,	003°52′.34 E			

(c) A traffic lane for southbound traffic is established between the separation zone in paragraph (a) above and a line connecting the following geographical positions:

(10)	52°22′.68 N,	003°47′.73 E	(12)	52°07′.13 N,	003°44′.66 E
(11)	52°14′.02 N,	003°44′.96 E			

Maas North-west traffic separation scheme

(a) A separation zone is bounded by a line connecting the following geographical positions:

(15)	52°07′.98 N,	003°31′.54 E	(17)	52°05′.96 N,	003°36′.27 E
(16)	52°06′.17 N,	003°36′.64 E	(18)	52°07′.72 N,	003°31′.29 E

(b) A traffic lane for north-westbound traffic is established between the separation zone in paragraph (a) above and a line connecting the following geographical positions:

(13)	52°07′.09 N,	003°38′.25 E	(14)	52°09′.08 N,	003°32′.64 E

(c) A traffic lane for south-eastbound traffic is established between the separation zone in paragraph (a) above and a line connecting the following geographical positions:

(19)	52°06′.62 N,	003°30′.19 E	(20)	52°05′.04 N,	003°34′.66 E

Maas West Inner traffic separation scheme

(a) A separation zone to the north of the deep-water route leading to Europoort is outwardly bounded by a line connecting the following geographical positions:

(24)	52°02′.12 N,	003°25′.73 E	(26)	52°00′.57 N,	003°35′.17 E
(25)	52°02′.56 N,	003°34′.94 E	(27)	51°59′.75 N,	003°25′.29 E

and inwardly bounded by a line connecting the following geographical positions:

(39)	52°02′.15 N,	003°33′.36 E	(41)	52°00′.03 N,	003°27′.01 E
(40)	52°01′.89 N,	003°27′.31 E	(42)	52°00′.57 N,	003°33′.51 E

Note: The inside of the area in the separation zone to the north of the deep-water route leading to Europoort, bounded by a line connecting the geographical positions (39), (40), (41) and (42), is designated as an anchorage area.

(b) A separation zone to the south of the deep-water route is outwardly bounded by a line connecting the following geographical positions:

(28)	51°59′.92 N,	003°35′.24 E	(32)	51°59′.09 N,	003°25′.17 E
(29)	51°59′.89 N,	003°34′.87 E	(33)	51°56′.90 N,	003°24′.78 E
(30)	51°58′.86 N,	003°33′.51 E	(34)	51°58′.25 N,	003°35′.44 E
(31)	51°59′.47 N,	003°29′.78 E			

* Date of implementation of amended scheme: 0000 hours UTC on 1 August 2013.

B

Positions (29) and (30) are connected by a circular arc centred on point (35). Radius of the arc = 0.729 miles.

(35) 51°59′.56 N, 003°33′.82 E

(c) A traffic lane for westbound traffic is established between the separation zone in paragraph (a) above and a line connecting the following geographical positions:

(21) 52°04′.74 N, 003°34′.69 E (23) 52°04′.63 N, 003°26′.20 E

(d) A traffic lane for eastbound traffic is established between the separation zone in paragraph (b) above and a line connecting the following geographical positions:

(36) 51°54′.10 N, 003°24′.29 E (37) 51°56′.26 N, 003°35′.66 E

(e) A separation zone between the westbound traffic lane of TSS Maas West Inner and the south-eastbound traffic lane of TSS Maas North-west is bounded by a line connecting the following geographical positions:

(19) 52°06′.62 N, 003°30′.19 E (21) 52°04′.74 N, 003°34′.69 E
(20) 52°05′.04 N, 003°34′.66 E (22) 52°04′.66 N, 003°28′.25 E

Inshore traffic zone

An inshore traffic zone south of the Maas West Inner TSS and the Maas Centre precautionary area is established between the coast and a line connecting the following geographical positions:

(70) 51°34′.00 N, 003°30′.00 E (66) 51°58′.12 N, 003°57′.86 E
(36) 51°54′.10 N, 003°24′.29 E (67) 51°59′.14 N, 004°02′.49 E
(38) 51°57′.11 N, 003°40′.05 E

Maas West Outer traffic separation scheme

(a) A separation zone to the north of the deep-water route leading to Europoort is outwardly bounded by a line connecting the following geographical positions:

(45) 52°01′.26 N, 003°08′.37 E (48) 51°58′.79 N, 003°13′.86 E
(46) 52°01′.77 N, 003°18′.81 E (49) 51°59′.49 N, 003°12′.47 E
(47) 51°59′.15 N, 003°18′.13 E (50) 51°59′.13 N, 003°08′.26 E

Positions (48) and (49) are connected by a circular arc centred on point (51). Radius of the arc = 0.729 miles.

(51) 51°58′.77 N, 003°12′.66 E

and inwardly bounded by a line connecting the following geographical positions:

(52) 51°59′.88 N, 003°13′.89 E (54) 52°01′.05 N, 003°08′.36 E
(53) 52°01′.26 N, 003°12′.56 E (55) 51°59′.40 N, 003°08′.28 E

Thus the created inside area in the separation zone is designated as an anchorage area.

(b) A separation zone to the south of the deep-water route leading to Europoort is outwardly bounded by a line connecting the following geographical positions:

(56) 51°58′.49 N, 003°17′.96 E (58) 51°54′.77 N, 003°07′.49 E
(57) 51°57′.64 N, 003°08′.00 E (59) 51°55′.99 N, 003°17′.31 E

and inwardly bounded by a line connecting the following geographical positions:

(62) 51°55′.64 N, 003°12′.25 E (64) 51°56′.89 N, 003°07′.87 E
(63) 51°57′.37 N, 003°13′.55 E (65) 51°55′.06 N, 003°07′.54 E

The area thus created inside the separation zone is designated as an anchorage area.

(c) A traffic lane for westbound traffic is established between the separation zone in paragraph (a) above and a line connecting the following geographical positions:

(43) 52°04′.54 N, 003°19′.53 E (44) 52°04′.37 N, 003°08′.52 E

(d) A traffic lane for eastbound traffic is established between the separation zone in paragraph (b) above and a line connecting the following geographical positions:

(60) 51°52′.59 N, 003°16′.43 E (61) 51°50′.72 N, 003°06′.78 E

Note: The inside of the area in the separation zone to the north of the Eurochannel, bounded by a line connecting the geographical positions (52), (53), (54) and (55), and the inside of the area in the separation zone to the south of the Eurochannel, bounded by a line connecting the geographical positions (62), (63), (64) and (65), are designated as anchorage areas.

North Hinder North traffic separation scheme

(a) A separation zone is bounded by a line connecting the following geographical positions:

(71)	52°07′.29 N,	003°03′.08 E	(73)	52°11′.51 N,	003°02′.62 E
(72)	52°09′.38 N,	003°06′.60 E	(74)	52°09′.03 N,	002°59′.83 E

(b) A traffic lane for south-westbound traffic is established between the separation zone in paragraph (a) above and a line connecting the following geographical positions:

(75)	52°13′.42 N,	002°59′.03 E	(76)	52°10′.99 N,	002°56′.16 E

(c) A traffic lane for north-eastbound traffic is established between the separation zone in paragraph (a) above and a line connecting the following geographical positions:

(77)	52°05′.55 N,	003°06′.32 E	(78)	52°07′.72 N,	003°09′.70 E

North Hinder South traffic separation scheme

Note: See mandatory ship reporting system "West European Tanker Reporting System" in part G, section I.

(a) A separation zone is bounded by a line connecting the following geographical positions:

(79)	51°31′.07 N,	002°07′.90 E	(81)	51°47′.88 N,	002°35′.27 E
(80)	51°29′.84 N,	002°10′.62 E	(82)	51°48′.53 N,	002°34′.04 E

(b) A traffic lane for north-eastbound traffic is established between the separation zone in paragraph (a) above and a line connecting the following geographical positions:

(83)	51°26′.97 N,	002°16′.95 E	(85)	51°45′.42 N,	002°39′.92 E
(84)	51°36′.20 N,	002°27′.25 E			

(c) A traffic lane for south-westbound traffic is established between the separation zone in paragraph (a) above and a line connecting the following geographical positions:

(86)	51°33′.66 N, 002°02′.17 E	(87)	51°51′.35 N, 002°28′.70 E

Notes:
Cautions

1 (Maas Junction precautionary area between "Maas West Outer" traffic separation scheme and "Maas West Inner" traffic separation scheme)
Mariners are warned that, in this precautionary area, ships on routes to and from the traffic separation scheme "Off Texel", the River Scheldt and Europoort are merging or crossing.

2 (Off the seaward entrances to the "Maas West Inner", the "Maas North-west" and the "Maas North" traffic separation schemes)
The precautionary area "Maas Centre" in the approaches to Hook of Holland should be avoided by passing traffic which is not entering or leaving the adjacent ports.

3 (Near the deep-water route in the North Hinder Junction precautionary area and near the "deep-water route leading to Europoort" between the "Maas West Outer" and the "Maas West Inner" traffic separation schemes)
For ships that have to cross the deep-water route, attention is drawn to rule 18(d)(i) of the 1972 Collision Regulations. Mariners are, however, reminded that, when risk of collision is deemed to exist, the 1972 Collision Regulations fully apply and, in particular, the rules of part B, sections II and III are of specific relevance to the crossing situation.

(chartlets overleaf)

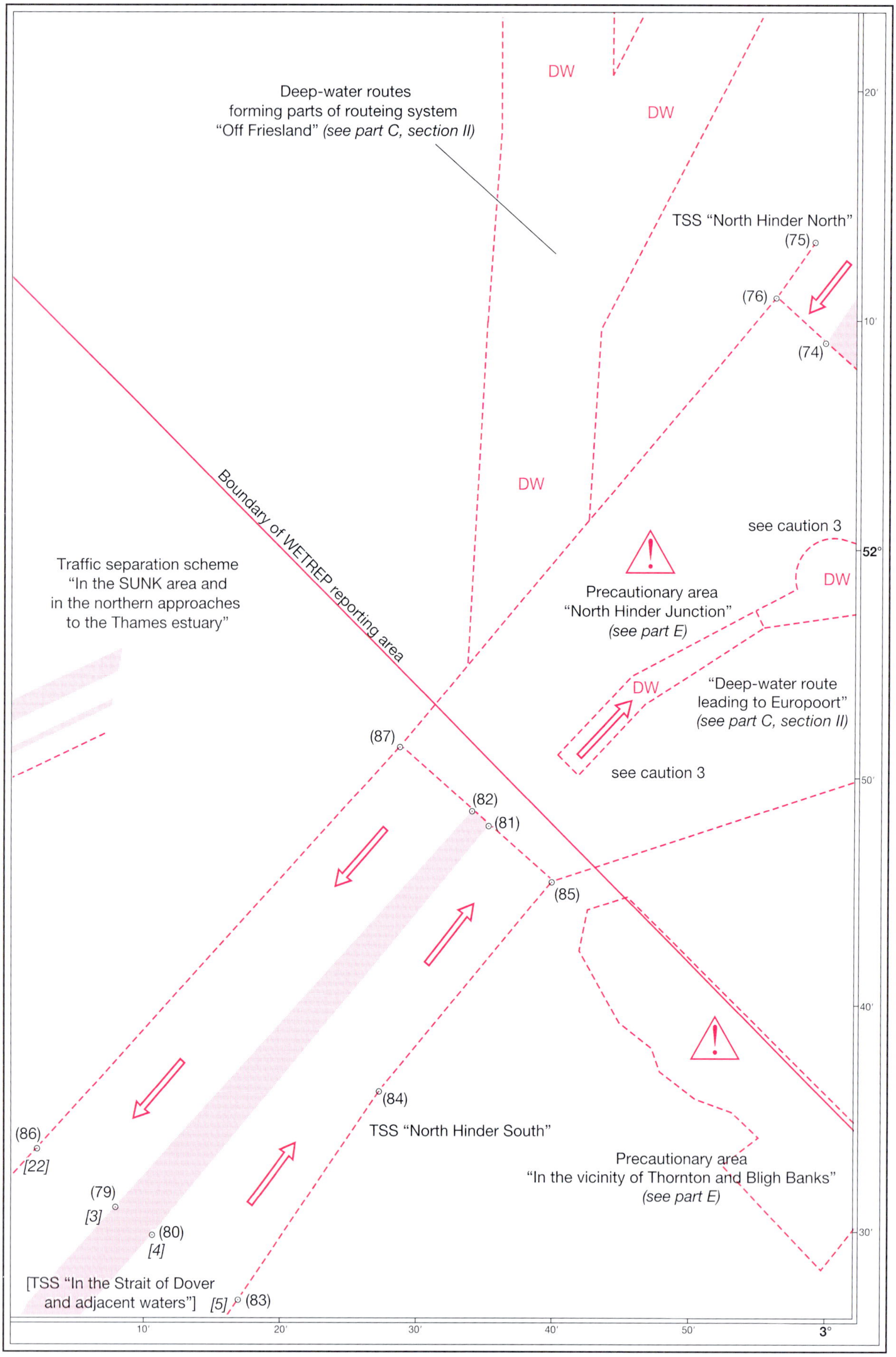

IN THE APPROACHES TO HOOK OF HOLLAND AND AT NORTH HINDER – WEST

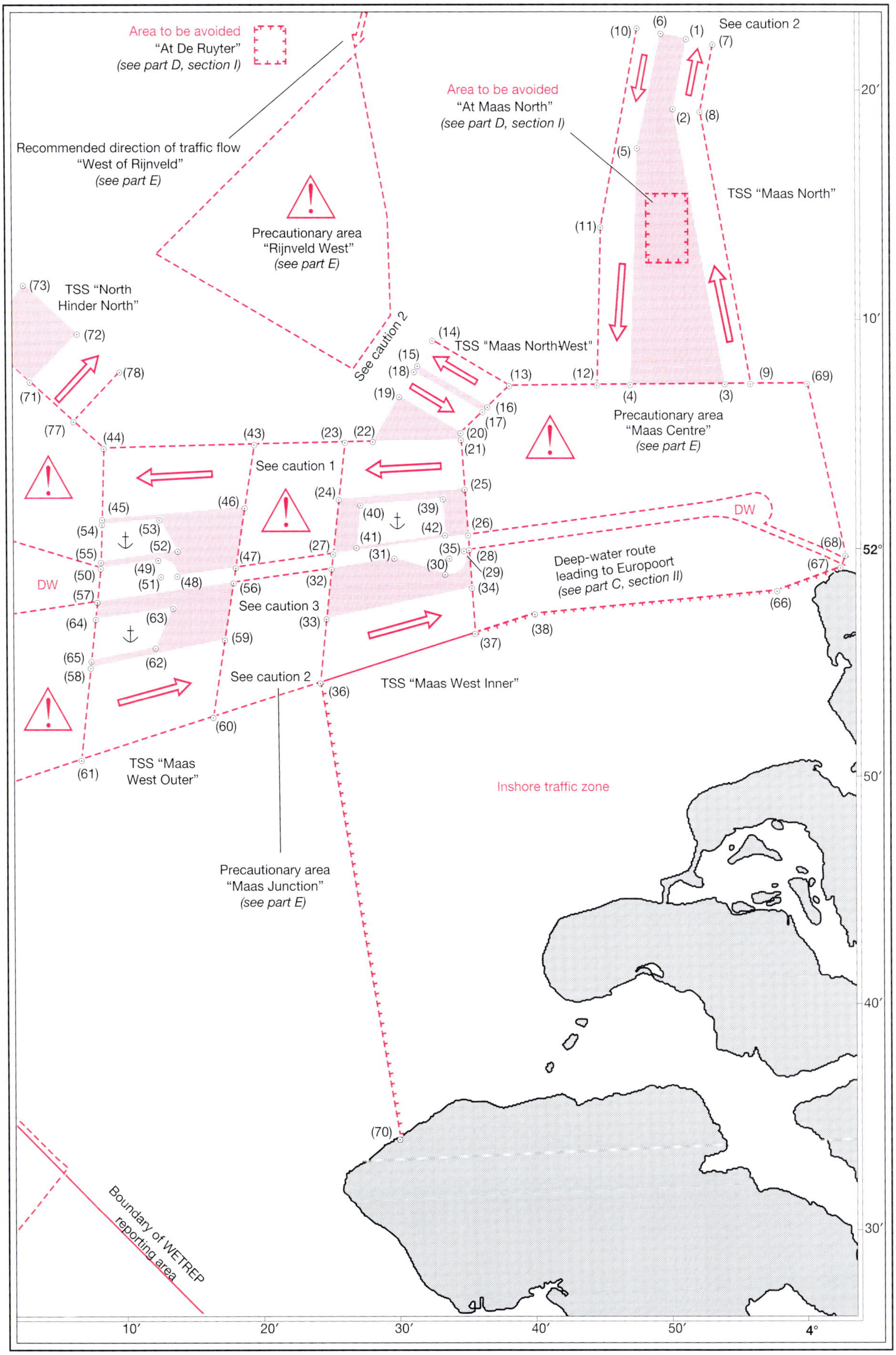

IN THE APPROACHES TO HOOK OF HOLLAND AND AT NORTH HINDER – EAST

IN THE APPROACHES TO IJMUIDEN*

Note: See "Deep-water route leading to IJmuiden" in part C, section II and area to be avoided "By IJmuiden northern approaches" in part D, section I and precautionary areas "In the approaches to IJmuiden" in part E.

(Reference chart: Netherlands 1631 (INT 1418, edition 3).
Note: This chart is based on World Geodetic System 1984 datum (WGS 84).)

B

IJmuiden West Inner traffic separation scheme

(a) A separation zone to the north of the IJmuiden-geul is bounded by a line connecting the following geographical positions:

(1)	52°29′.47 N,	004°20′.03 E	(4)	52°30′.90 N,	004°08′.55 E
(2)	52°29′.76 N,	004°20′.12 E	(5)	52°30′.36 N,	004°08′.93 E
(3)	52°30′.90 N,	004°10′.17 E	(6)	52°30′.38 N,	004°11′.84 E

(b) A triangular separation zone north of the IJmuiden-geul is bounded by a line connecting the following geographical positions:

(7)	52°31′.50 N,	004°10′.60 E	(9)	52°32′.73 N,	004°07′.26 E
(8)	52°31′.50 N,	004°08′.13 E			

(c) A traffic lane for westbound traffic is established between the separation zones in paragraphs (a) and (b) above and a line connecting the following geographical positions:

(16)	52°30′.52 N,	004°20′.35 E	(17)	52°31′.35 N,	004°13′.25 E

(d) A separation zone to the south of the IJmuiden-geul is bounded by a line connecting the following geographical positions:

(11)	52°28′.70 N,	004°19′.80 E	(14)	52°30′.04 N,	004°09′.16 E
(12)	52°29′.23 N,	004°19′.96 E	(15)	52°29′.87 N,	004°09′.28 E
(13)	52°30′.06 N,	004°12′.50 E			

(e) A traffic lane for eastbound traffic is established between the separation zone in paragraph (d) above and a line connecting the following geographical positions:

(20)	52°27′.62 N,	004°19′.48 E	(21)	52°28′.58 N,	004°10′.85 E

IJmuiden North traffic separation scheme

(a) A separation line extending north-north-west from the small triangular separation zone in the IJmuiden West Inner traffic separation scheme is established between the following geographical positions:

(9)	52°32′.73 N,	004°07′.26 E	(10)	52°35′.72 N,	004°05′.15 E

(b) A traffic lane for north-north-westbound traffic is established between the separation line in paragraph (a) and the small triangular separation zone in paragraph (b) of the IJmuiden West Inner traffic separation scheme and a line connecting the following geographical positions:

(17)	52°31′.35 N,	004°13′.25 E	(19)	52°36′.04 N,	004°06′.36 E
(18)	52°33′.28 N,	004°08′.30 E			

(c) A traffic lane for south-south-eastbound traffic is established between the separation line in paragraph (a) and the triangular separation zone in paragraph (b) of the IJmuiden West Inner traffic separation scheme and a line connecting the following geographical positions:

(31)	52°35′.40 N,	004°03′.95 E,	(32)	52°31′.50 N,	004°06′.70 E

IJmuiden West Outer traffic separation scheme

(a) A separation zone to the north of the IJmuiden-geul is bounded by a line connecting the following geographical positions:

(23)	52°30′.36 N,	004°07′.51 E	(25)	52°30′.91 N,	003°56′.18 E
(24)	52°30′.91 N,	004°07′.12 E	(26)	52°30′.27 N,	003°55′.98 E

* Date of implementation of new scheme: 0000 hours UTC on 1 August 2013.

(b) A separation zone to the south of the IJmuiden-geul is bounded by a line connecting the following geographical positions:

(27)	52°29′.22 N,	004°08′.31 E	(29)	52°29′.95 N,	003°55′.87 E
(28)	52°30′.03 N,	004°07′.74 E	(30)	52°27′.60 N,	003°55′.10 E

(c) A traffic lane for westbound traffic is established between the separation zone in paragraph (a) above and a line connecting the following geographical positions:

(32)	52°31′.50 N,	004°06′.70 E	(33)	52°31′.50 N,	003°56′.38 E

(d) A traffic lane for eastbound traffic is established between the separation zone in paragraph (b) above and a line connecting the following geographical positions:

(22)	52°28′.29 N,	004°08′.97 E	(35)	52°25′.53 N,	003°54′.43 E
(34)	52°26′.55 N,	003°57′.50 E			

(chartlet overleaf)

IN THE APPROACHES TO IJMUIDEN

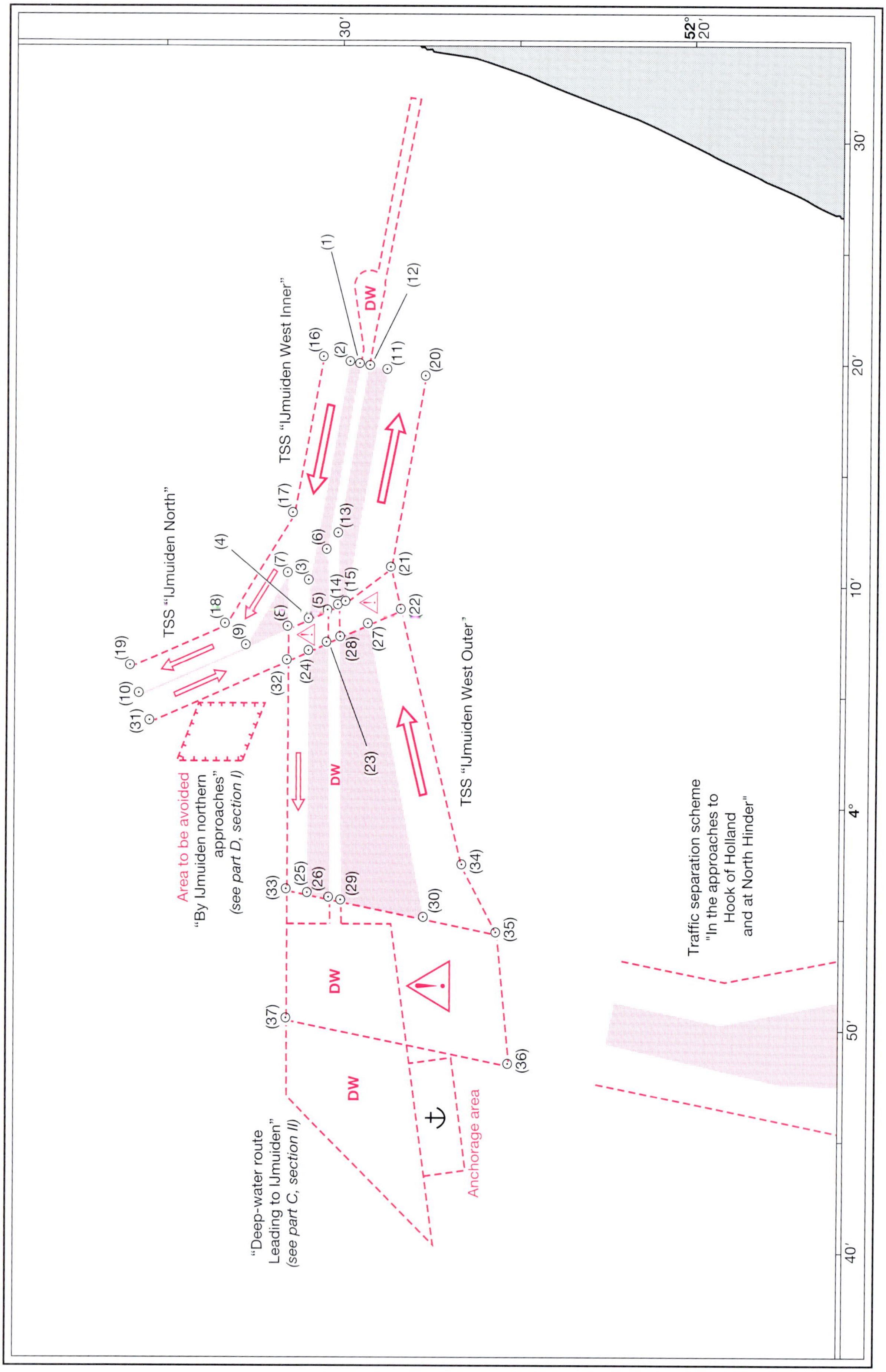

OFF TEXEL*

(Reference chart: Netherlands 1631 (INT 1418, edition 3).
Note: This chart is based on World Geodetic System 1984 datum (WGS 84).)

Description of the traffic separation scheme

(a) A separation zone is bounded by a line connecting the following geographical positions:

(1)	53°05′.42 N,	004°23′.60 E	(5)	52°49′.59 N,	003°58′.56 E
(2)	52°59′.95 N,	004°17′.89 E	(6)	52°56′.53 N,	004°00′.92 E
(3)	52°51′.85 N,	004°12′.64 E	(7)	53°06′.48 N,	004°20′.79 E
(4)	52°45′.85 N,	004°05′.04 E			

(b) A traffic lane for north-eastbound traffic is established between the separation zone in paragraph (a) and a line connecting the following geographical positions:

(8)	53°03′.82 N,	004°27′.80 E	11)	52°44′.60 N,	004°09′.90 E
(9)	52°58′.60 N,	004°22′.34 E	(12)	52°43′.48 N,	004°09′.14 E
(10)	52°50′.38 N,	004°17′.01 E			

(c) A traffic lane for south-westbound traffic is established between the separation zone in paragraph (a) and a line connecting the following geographical positions:

(15)	52°56′.67 N,	003°53′.44 E	(16)	53°08′.17 N,	004°16′.35 E

(d) A separation zone west of the separation zone in paragraph (a) is bounded by the following geographical positions:

(17)	52°50′.60 N,	003°56′.80 E	(19)	52°54′.31 N,	003°56′.67 E
(18)	52°55′.22 N,	003°58′.32 E	(20)	52°52′.31 N,	003°53′.83 E

(e) A southbound traffic lane branching off from the main south-westbound traffic lane is established between the separation zones in paragraphs (a) and (d), and the boundaries of the south-westbound traffic lane are extended, as described in paragraphs (f) and (g).

(f) The north-western boundary of the extended south-westbound traffic lane is formed by a line connecting the following geographical positions:

(14)	52°35′.71 N,	003°25′.56 E	(15)	52°56′.67 N,	003°53′.44 E

(g) The south-eastern boundary of the extended south-westbound traffic lane is formed by a line connecting the following geographical positions:

(20)	52°52′.31 N,	003°53′.83 E	(21)	52°36′.04 N,	003°31′.02 E

(h) A separation zone at the south-western end of the south-westbound traffic lane is bounded by the following geographical positions:

(23)	52°34′.34 N,	003°28′.65 E	(25)	52°31′.94 N,	003°28′.01 E
(24)	52°32′.35 N,	003°26′.36 E			

(i) A traffic lane for south-westbound traffic is established between the separation zone in paragraph (h) and a line connecting the following geographical positions:

(13)	52°33′.71 N,	003°23′.17 E	(14)	52°35′.71 N,	003°25′.56 E

(j) A southbound traffic lane branching off from the main south-westbound traffic lane is established between the separation zone in paragraph (h) and a line connecting the following geographical positions:

(21)	52°36′.04 N,	003°31′.02 E	(22)	52°31′.76 N,	003°29′.87 E

Note: The following classes of ships are referred to the provisions being part of the description of the "Mandatory route for tankers from North Hinder to the German Bight and vice versa" (see part G, section II):

(a) tankers of 10,000 tons gross tonnage and upwards, carrying oil as defined under Annex I to the International Convention for the Prevention of Pollution from Ships, 1973, as modified by the Protocol of 1978 relating thereto (MARPOL 73/78);

* Date of implementation of amended scheme: 0000 hours UTC on 1 August 2013.

(b) chemical tankers of 5000 tons gross tonnage and upwards, carrying noxious liquid substances in bulk assessed or provisionally assessed as Category X or Y of Annex II to the International Convention for the Prevention of Pollution from Ships, 1973, as modified by the Protocol of 1978 relating thereto (MARPOL 73/78);

(c) chemical tankers and NLS tankers of 10,000 tons gross tonnage and upwards, carrying noxious liquid substances in bulk assessed or provisionally assessed as Category Z of Annex II to the International Convention for the Prevention of Pollution from Ships, 1973, as modified by the Protocol of 1978 relating thereto (MARPOL 73/78);

(d) ships of 10,000 tons gross tonnage and upwards, carrying liquefied gases in bulk.

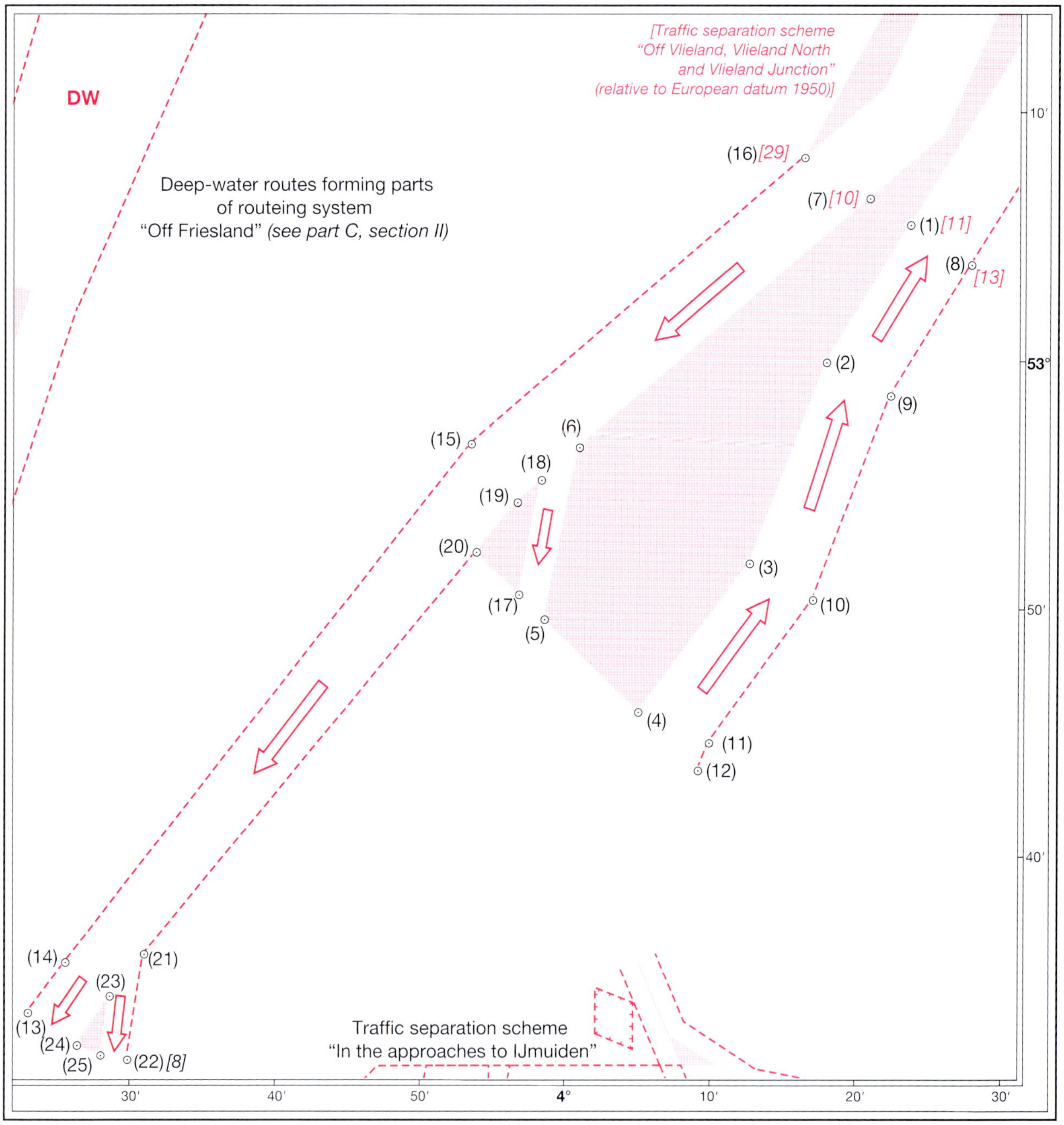

OFF TEXEL

OFF VLIELAND, VLIELAND NORTH AND VLIELAND JUNCTION

(Reference charts: German Hydrographic Office 84; Netherlands Hydrographic Office 1352 (INT 1414), 1988 edition.
Note: These charts are based on European datum.)

A Description of the traffic separation scheme "Off Vlieland"

(a) A separation zone is bounded by a line connecting the following geographical positions:

(1)	53°34′.30 N,	005°08′.60 E	(4)	53°30′.97 N,	005°02′.21 E
(2)	53°29′.07 N,	004°46′.66 E	(5)	53°32′.37 N,	005°09′.70 E
(3)	53°26′.35 N,	004°44′.68 E			

(b) A separation zone is bounded by a line connecting the following geographical positions:

(6)	53°28′.02 N,	004°42′.25 E	(10)	53°06′.53 N,	004°20′.87 E
(7)	53°27′.03 N,	004°38′.10 E	(11)	53°05′.47 N,	004°23′.68 E
(8)	53°17′.27 N,	004°32′.28 E	(12)	53°12′.40 N,	004°30′.97 E
(9)	53°09′.13 N,	004°26′.08 E			

(c) A traffic lane for northbound and eastbound traffic is established between the separation zones described in paragraphs (a) and (b) above, the southern boundary of the precautionary area Vlieland Junction described below, and the following line and separation zone:

(i) a line connecting the following geographical positions:

(13)	53°03′.87 N,	004°27′.88 E	(14)	53°11′.00 N,	004°35′.39 E

(ii) a separation zone bounded by lines connecting the following geographical positions:

(14)	53°11′.00 N,	004°35′.39 E	(18)	53°29′.07 N,	005°11′.38 E
(15)	53°22′.90 N,	004°44′.00 E	(19)	53°27′.70 N,	005°04′.30 E
(16)	53°28′.16 N,	005°04′.00 E	(20)	53°25′.99 N,	004°57′.80 E
(17)	53°29′.57 N,	005°11′.28 E	(21)	53°15′.00 N,	004°39′.60 E

(d) A traffic lane for westbound traffic is established between the separation zone described in paragraph (a) above and a separation zone bounded by lines connecting the following geographical positions:

(22)	53°37′.13 N,	005°07′.00 E	(24)	53°36′.32 N,	004°51′.93 E
(23)	53°32′.97 N,	004°49′.49 E			

(e) A traffic lane for westbound and southbound traffic is established between the separation zone described in paragraph (b) above, the western boundary of the precautionary area Vlieland Junction described below, and the following lines and separation zone:

(i) an uncharted line representing the junction of the scheme with the adjacent scheme "Vlieland North" and connecting the following geographical positions:

(25)	53°29′.21 N,	004°33′.69 E	(30)	53°31′.92 N,	004°45′.07 E

(ii) a line connecting the following geographical positions:

(25)	53°29′.21 N,	004°33′.69 E	(26)	53°22′.62 N,	004°30′.00 E

(iii) a separation zone bounded by a line connecting the following geographical positions:

(26)	53°22′.62 N,	004°30′.00 E	(28)	53°11′.00 N,	004°22′.02 E
(27)	53°18′.37 N,	004°27′.63 E	(29)	53°08′.22 N,	004°16′.43 E

Inshore traffic zone

The area between the landward boundary of the traffic separation scheme and the coast between an uncharted line drawn from position (18) [53°29′.07 N, 005°11′.38 E] to Brandaris lighthouse (53°21′.66 N, 005°12′.93 E) and a line drawn from position (14) [53°11′.00 N, 004°35′.39 E] to Eierland lighthouse (53°10′.97 N, 004°51′.39 E) is designated as an inshore traffic zone.

Note: The following classes of ships are referred to the provisions being part of the description of the Mandatory route for tankers from North Hinder to the German Bight and vice versa (see part G, section II):

(a) tankers of 10,000 tons gross tonnage and upwards, carrying oil as defined under Annex I to the International Convention for the Prevention of Pollution from Ships, 1973, as modified by the Protocol of 1978 relating thereto (MARPOL 73/78);

B

(b) chemical tankers of 5000 tons gross tonnage and upwards, carrying noxious liquid substances in bulk assessed or provisionally assessed as Category X or Y of Annex II to the International Convention for the Prevention of Pollution from Ships, 1973, as modified by the Protocol of 1978 relating thereto (MARPOL 73/78);

(c) chemical tankers and NLS tankers of 10,000 tons gross tonnage and upwards, carrying noxious liquid substances in bulk assessed or provisionally assessed as Category Z of Annex II to the International Convention for the Prevention of Pollution from Ships, 1973, as modified by the Protocol of 1978 relating thereto (MARPOL 73/78);

(d) ships of 10,000 tons gross tonnage and upwards, carrying liquefied gases in bulk.

Precautionary area "Vlieland Junction"

A precautionary area is established off Vlieland. The area is bounded by a line connecting the following geographical positions:

(2)	53°29′.07 N,	004°46′.66 E	(30)	53°31′.92 N,	004°45′.07 E
(6)	53°28′.02 N,	004°42′.25 E	(23)	53°32′.97 N,	004°49′.49 E

B Description of the traffic separation scheme "Vlieland North"

(a) A separation zone is bounded by a line connecting the following geographical positions:

(30)	53°31′.92 N,	004°45′.07 E	(32)	53°35′.69 N,	004°40′.16 E
(31)	53°29′.99 N,	004°36′.96 E	(33)	53°36′.11 N,	004°48′.12 E

(b) A traffic lane for northbound traffic is established between the separation zone described in paragraph (a) above and a line (coinciding with the western boundary of the separation zone described in section A, paragraph (d)) connecting the following geographical positions:

(23)	53°32′.97 N,	004°49′.49 E	(24)	53°36′.32 N,	004°51′.93 E

(c) A traffic lane for southbound traffic is established between the separation zone described in paragraph (a) above and a line connecting the following geographical positions:

(25)	53°29′.21 N,	004°33′.69 E	(34)	53°35′.53 N,	004°37′.24 E

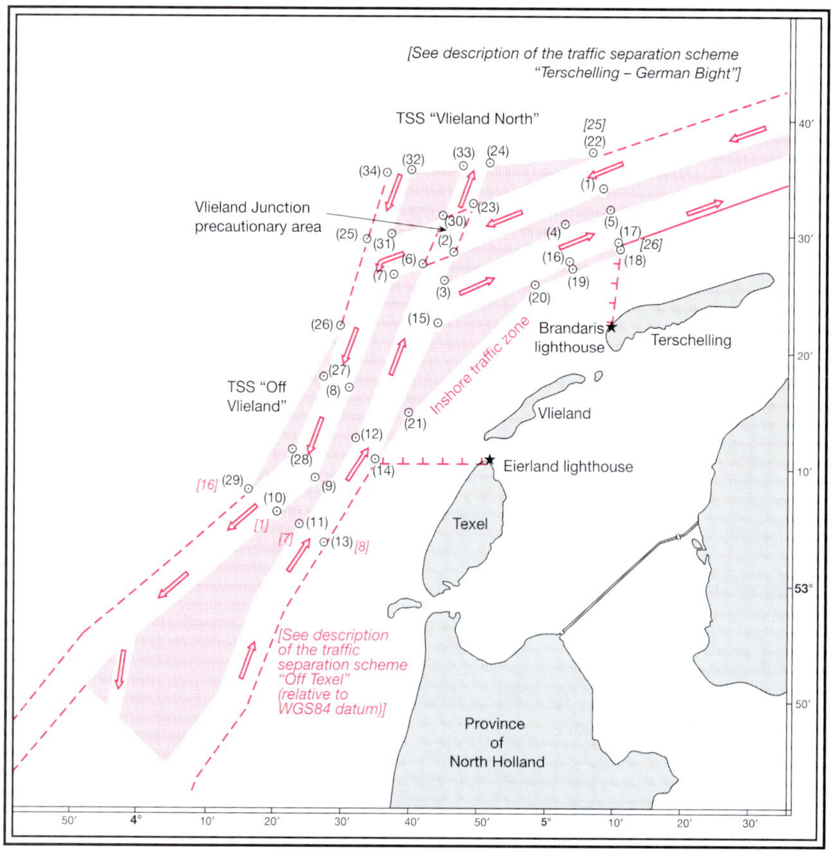

OFF VLIELAND, VLIELAND NORTH AND VLIELAND JUNCTION

VII Off Røst (1)

(s) A separation zone is bounded by a line connecting the following geographical positions:

(65)	68°12′.89 N,	010°16′.07 E	(68)	68°03′.57 N,	009°50′.12 E
(66)	68°08′.36 N,	010°02′.92 E	(69)	68°09′.41 N,	009°58′.73 E
(67)	68°02′.64 N,	009°54′.93 E	(70)	68°14′.26 N,	010°12′.03 E

(t) A traffic lane for westbound traffic is established between the separation zone described in paragraph (s) and a line connecting the following geographical positions:

(71)	68°16′.38 N,	010°06′.20 E	(73)	68°04′.83 N,	009°43′.01 E
(72)	68°11′.32 N,	009°52′.34 E			

(u) A traffic lane for eastbound traffic is established between the separation zone described in paragraph (s) and a line connecting the following geographical positions:

(74)	68°10′.82 N,	010°21′.89 E	(76)	68°01′.24 N,	010°02′.10 E
(75)	68°06′.71 N,	010°09′.50 E			

VIII Off Røst (2)

(v) A separation zone is bounded by a line connecting the following geographical positions:

(77)	67°37′.66 N,	009°21′.34 E	(79)	67°31′.31 N,	009°07′.29 E
(78)	67°30′.42 N,	009°12′.05 E	(80)	67°38′.55 N,	009°16′.66 E

(w) A traffic lane for westbound traffic is established between the separation zone described in paragraph (v) and a line connecting the following geographical positions:

(81)	67°40′.00 N,	009°09′.73 E	(82)	67°32′.64 N,	009°00′.28 E

(x) A traffic lane for eastbound traffic is established between the separation zone described in paragraph (v) and a line connecting the following geographical positions:

(83)	67°36′.29 N,	009°28′.33 E	(84)	67°29′.06 N,	009°18′.88 E

Descriptions of the recommended routes

The recommended routes between the traffic separation schemes are described in part E.

(chartlets overleaf)

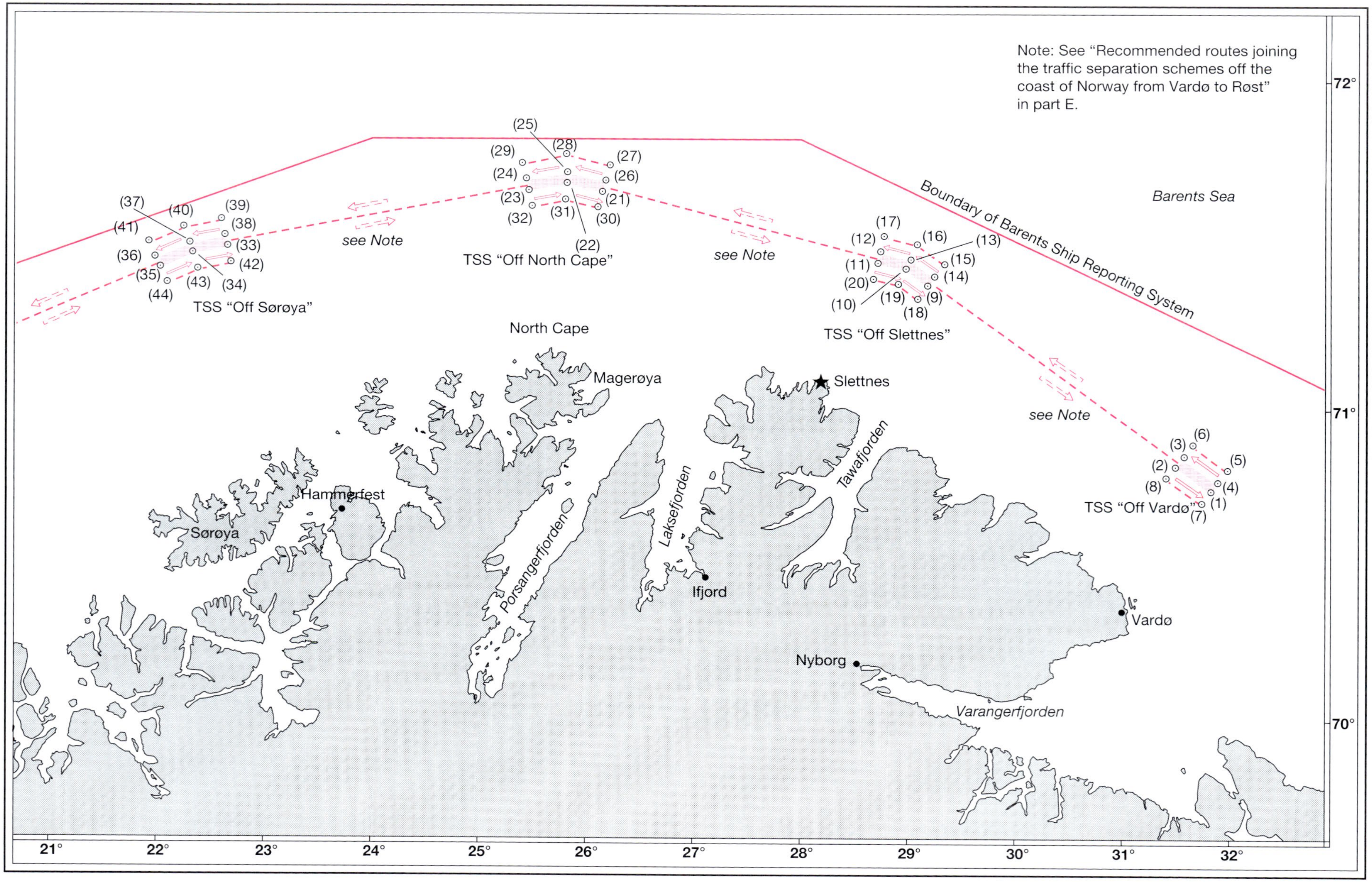

OFF THE COAST OF NORWAY FROM VARDØ TO RØST – Off Vardø to Off Sørøya

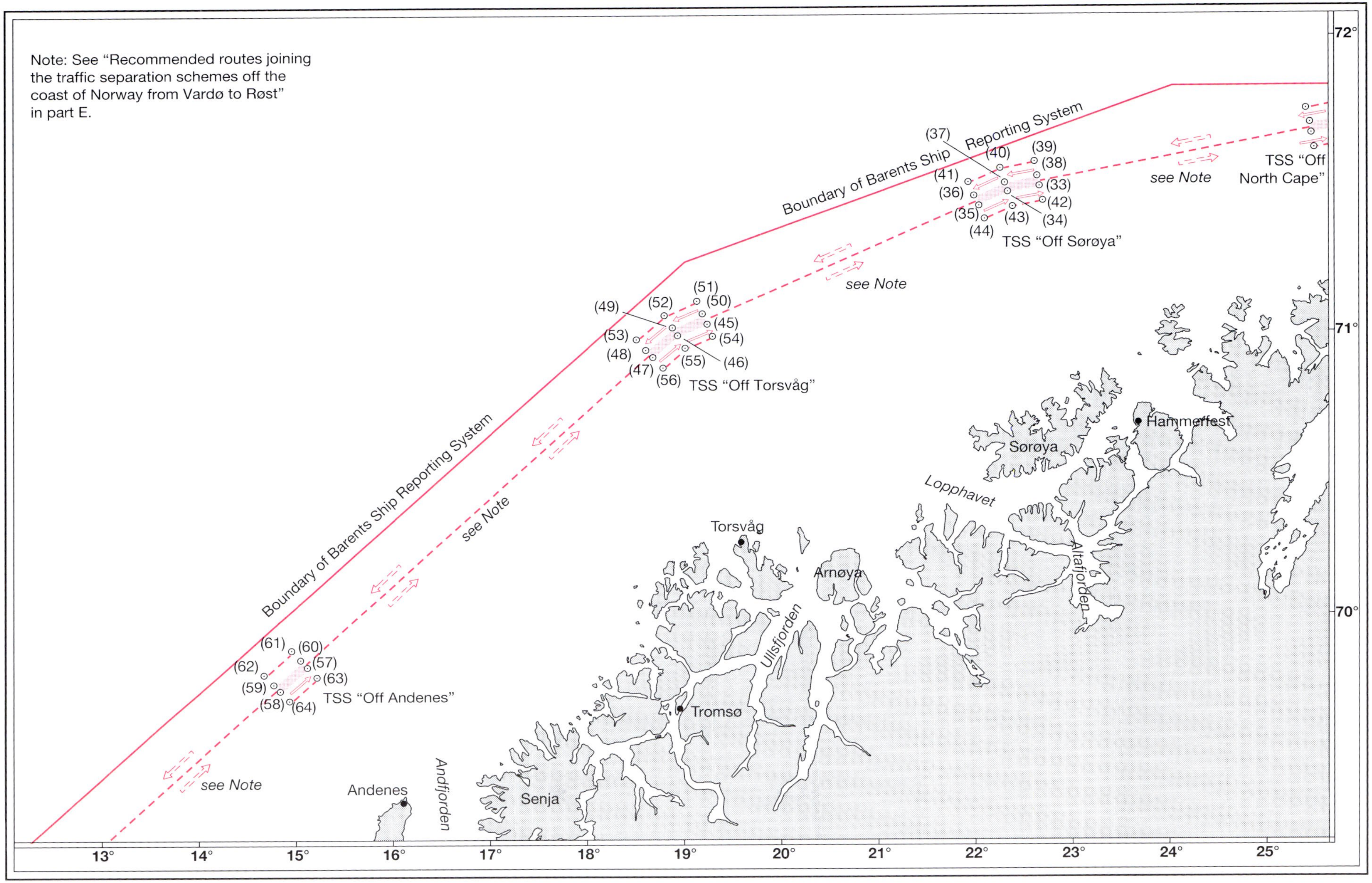

OFF THE COAST OF NORWAY FROM VARDØ TO RØST – Off North Cape to Off Andenes

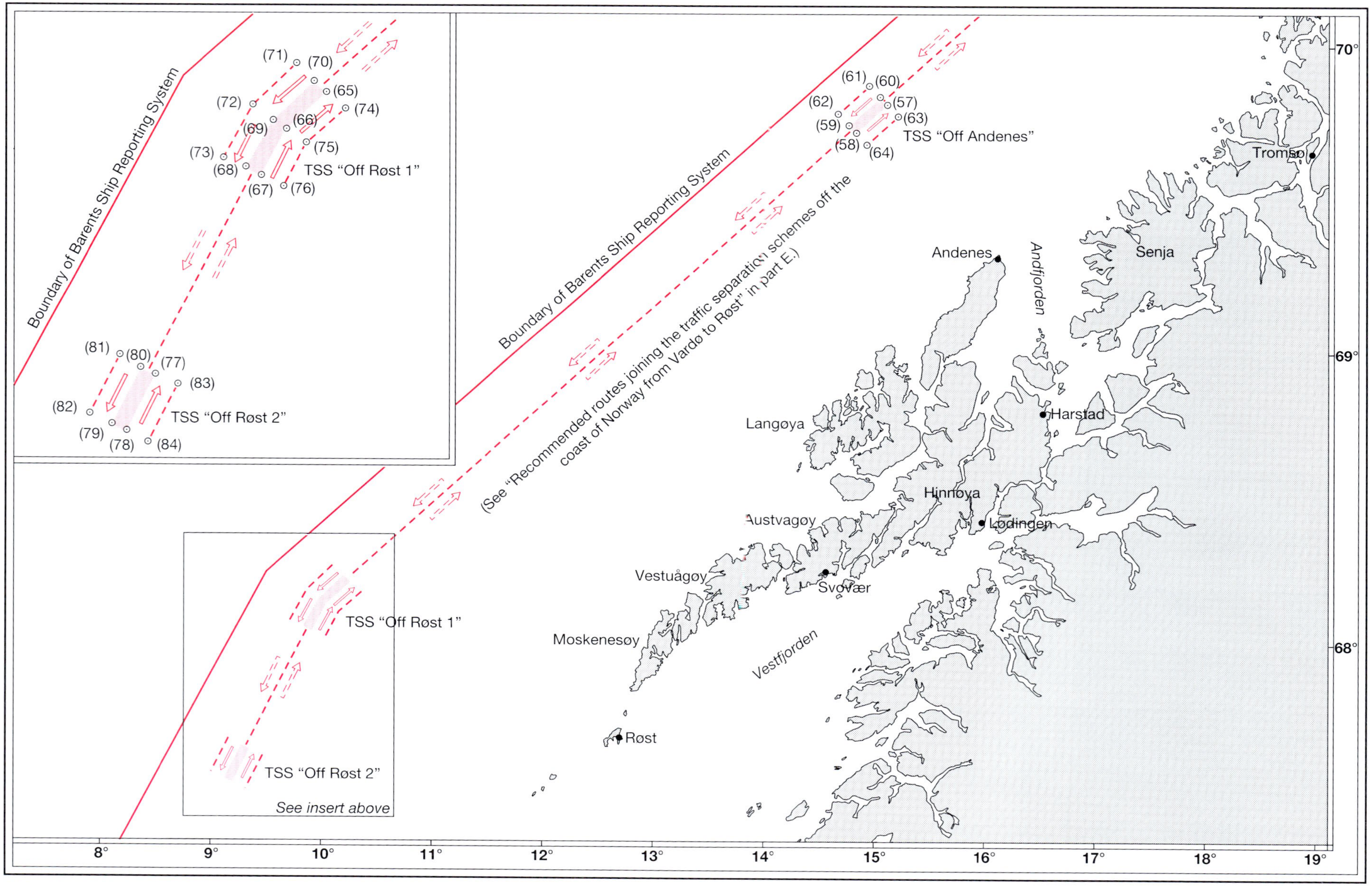

OFF THE COAST OF NORWAY FROM VARDØ TO RØST – Off Andenes to Off Røst (2)

B

OFF FASTNET ROCK

Note: See mandatory ship reporting system "West European Tanker Reporting System" in part G, section I.

(Reference chart: British Admiralty 2424, 1981 edition.
Note: This chart is based on Ordnance Survey of Ireland datum.)

Description of the traffic separation scheme

(a) A separation zone, two miles wide, is centred upon the following geographical positions:

(1)	51°20′.00 N,	009°25′.80 W	(2)	51°18′.20 N,	009°35′.20 W

(b) A traffic lane, two miles wide, is established on each side of the separation zone.

Inshore traffic zone

The area between the landward boundary of the traffic separation scheme and lines connecting Fastnet Rock lighthouse (51°23′.30 N, 009°36′.20 W) and the following geographical positions is designated an inshore traffic zone:

(3)	51°22′.90 N,	009°27′.30 W	(easterly corner of the scheme)
(4)	51°21′.10 N,	009°36′.60 W	(westerly corner of the scheme)

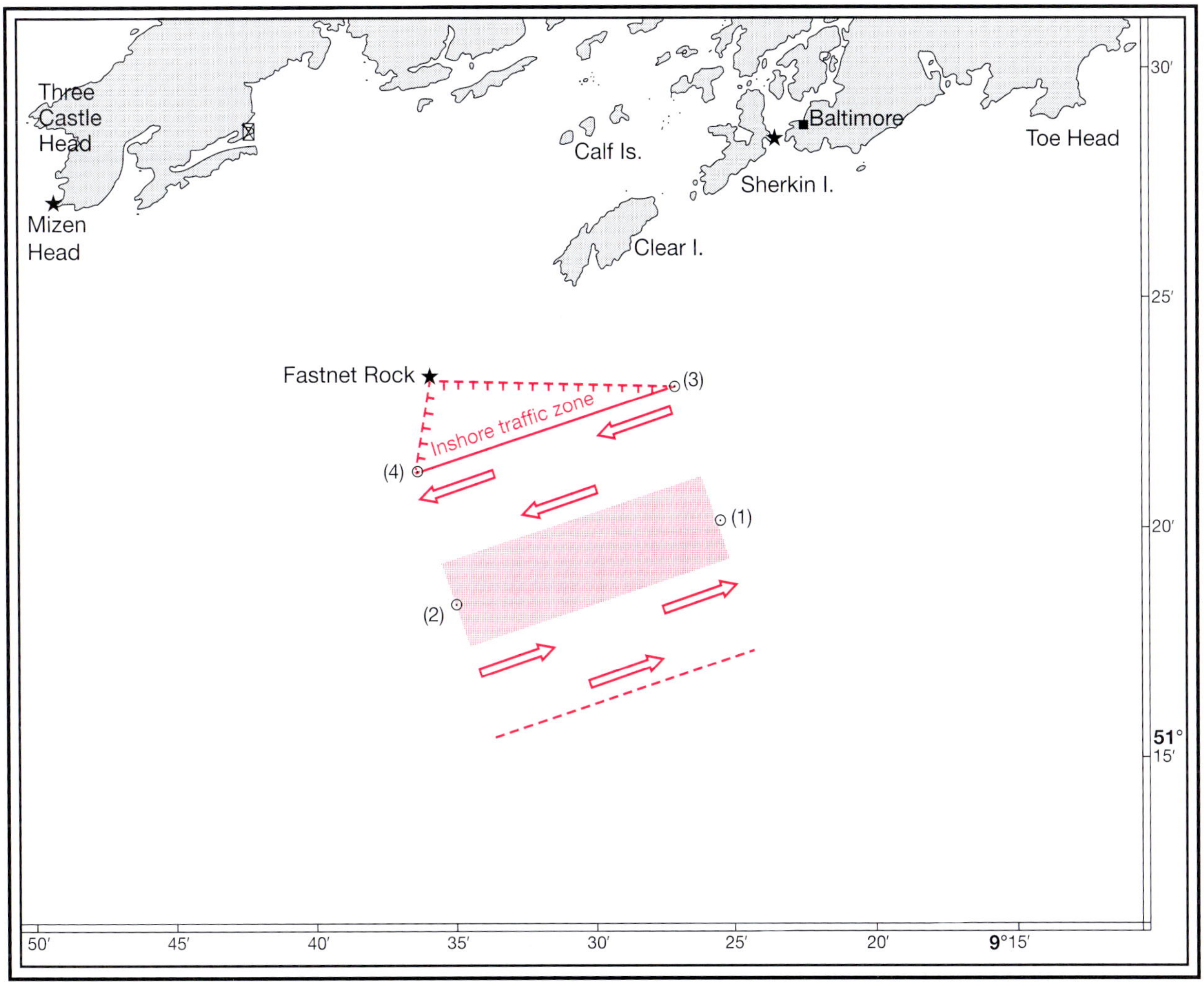

OFF FASTNET ROCK

OFF SMALLS

Note: See mandatory ship reporting system "West European Tanker Reporting System" in part G, section I and "Recommendations on navigation around the United Kingdom coast" in part E.

(Reference chart: British Admiralty 1478, 1988 edition.
Note: This chart is based on Ordnance Survey of Great Britain 1936 datum.)

Description of the traffic separation scheme

(a) A separation zone, two miles wide, is bounded by lines connecting the following geographical positions:

(1)	51°51′.60 N,	005°51′.60 W	(3)	51°40′.00 N,	005°53′.40 W
(2)	51°51′.00 N,	005°48′.30 W	(4)	51°40′.00 N,	005°56′.90 W

(b) A traffic lane for north-eastbound traffic, three miles wide, is established between the separation zone and a line connecting the following geographical positions:

(5)	51°50′.20 N,	005°43′.70 W	(6)	51°40′.00 N,	005°48′.40 W

(c) A traffic lane for south-westbound traffic, three miles wide, is established between the separation zone and a line connecting the following geographical positions:

(7)	51°52′.40 N,	005°56′.20 W	(8)	51°40′.00 N,	006°01′.90 W

Note:
Laden tankers should avoid the area between the traffic separation scheme and The Smalls.

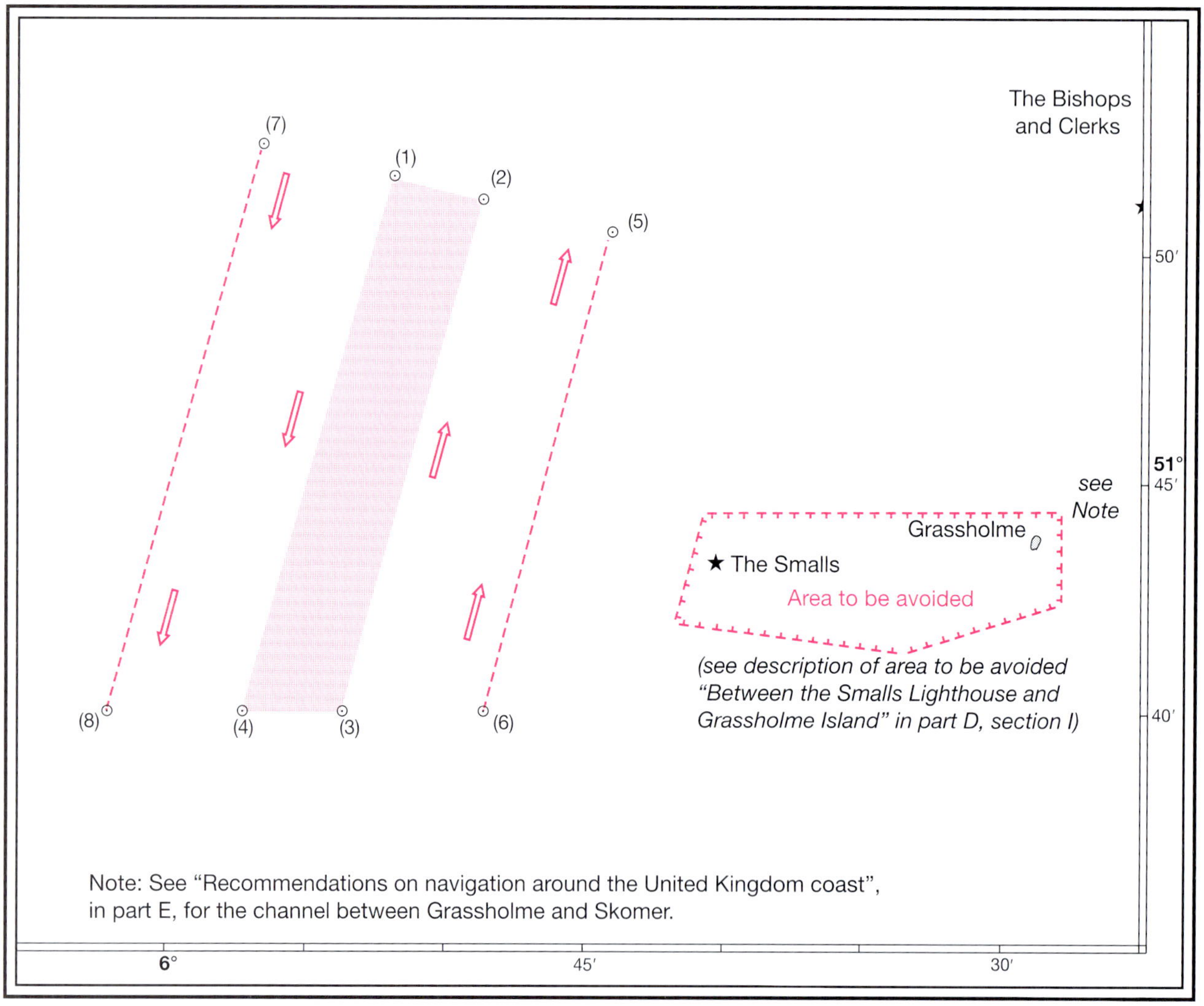

OFF SMALLS

OFF TUSKAR ROCK

Note: See mandatory ship reporting system "West European Tanker Reporting System" in part G, section I.

(Reference chart: British Admiralty 1787, 1984 edition.
Note: This chart is based on Ordnance Survey of Ireland datum.)

Description of the traffic separation scheme

(a) A separation zone, two miles wide, is centred upon the following geographical positions:

(1)	52°14′.00 N,	006°00′.80 W	(3)	52°04′.70 N,	006°11′.50 W
(2)	52°08′.50 N,	006°03′.80 W			

(b) A traffic lane, three miles wide, is established on each side of the separation zone.

Inshore traffic zone

The area bounded between the landward boundary of the traffic separation scheme and lines connecting Tuskar Rock lighthouse (52°12′.20 N, 006°12′.40 W) and the following geographical positions is designated an inshore traffic zone:

(4)	52°15′.20 N,	006°07′.00 W	(northerly corner of the scheme)
(5)	52°07′.80 N,	006°15′.60 W	(westerly corner of the scheme)

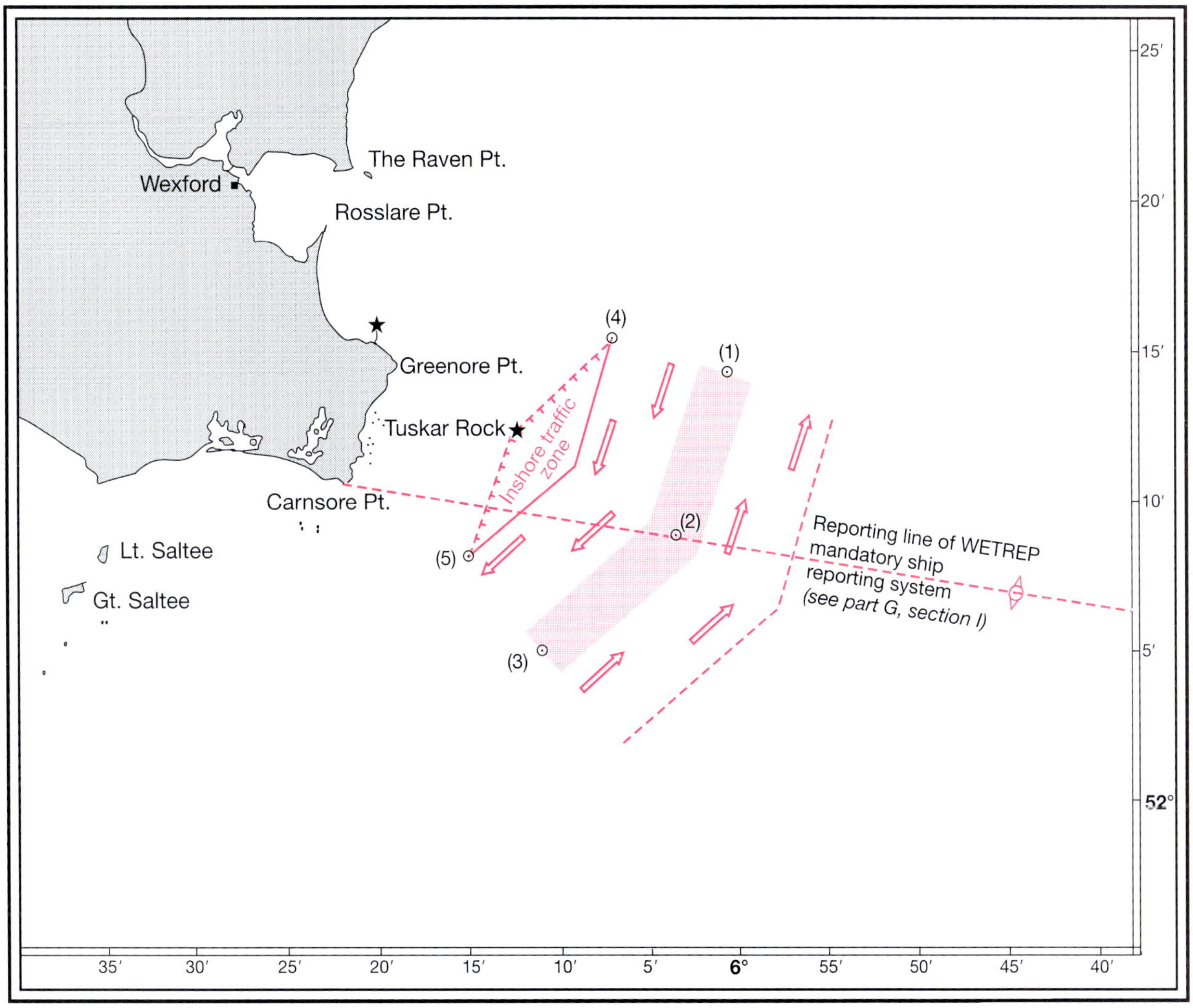

OFF TUSKAR ROCK

B

OFF SKERRIES

Note: See mandatory ship reporting system "West European Tanker Reporting System" in part G, section I.

(Reference chart: British Admiralty 1977, 1986 edition.
Note: This chart is based on Ordnance Survey of Great Britain 1936 datum.)

Description of the traffic separation scheme

(a) A separation zone, two miles wide, is centred upon the following geographical positions:

(1)	53°22′.80 N,	004°52′.00 W	(3)	53°32′.10 N,	004°31′.60 W
(2)	53°31′.30 N,	004°41′.70 W			

(b) A traffic lane, two miles wide, is established on each side of the separation zone.

Note:
Laden tankers should avoid the area between the south-eastern boundary of the scheme and the coast.

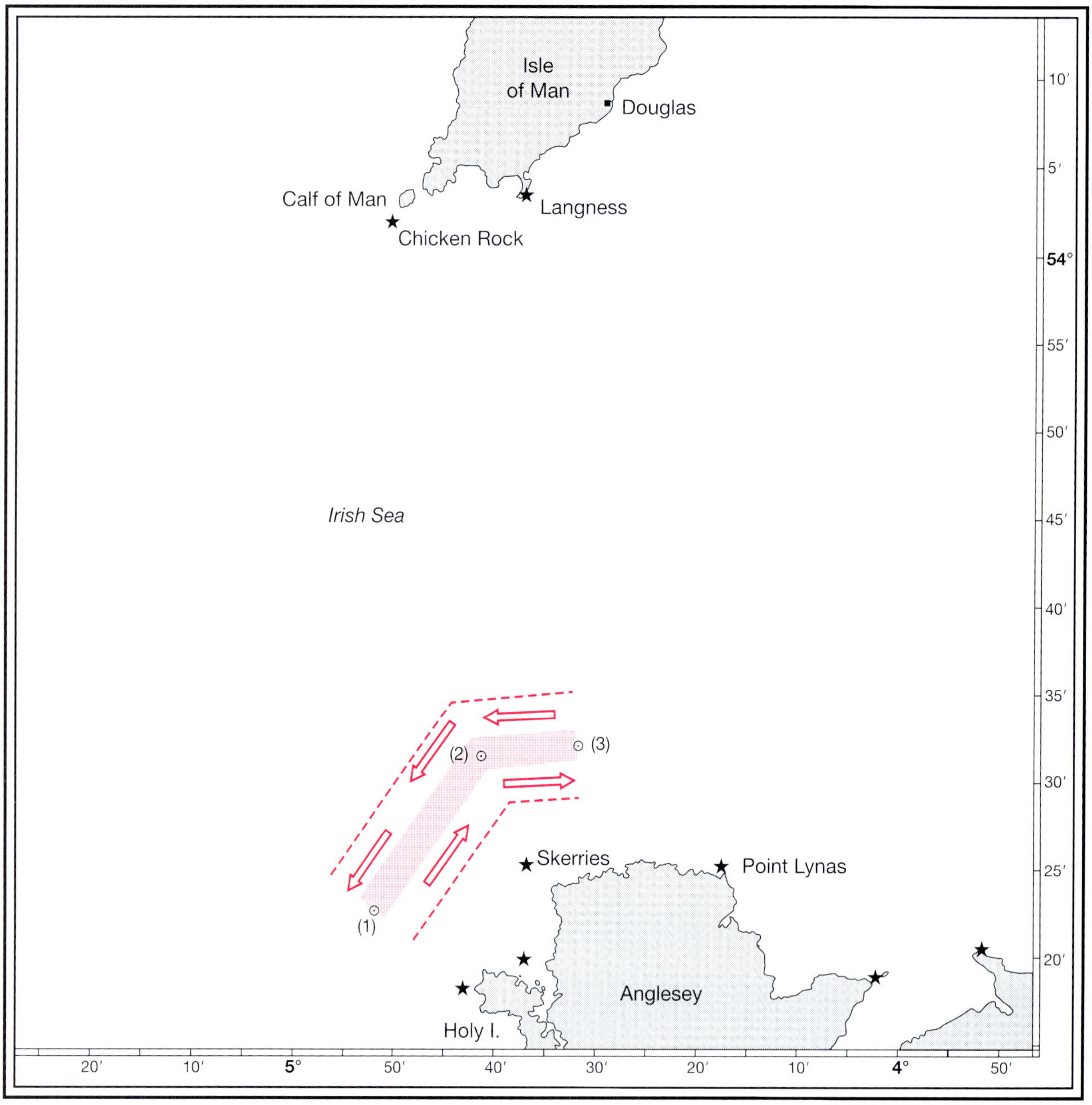

OFF SKERRIES

IN LIVERPOOL BAY

Note: See area to be avoided "In Liverpool Bay" in part D, section I.

(Reference chart: British Admiralty 1978, 2007 edition.
Note: This chart is based on World Geodetic System 1984 datum (WGS 84).)

Description of the traffic separation scheme

(a) A separation zone (east of the "Douglas Oil Field" platform), 1.0 nautical mile wide, is bounded by lines connecting the following geographical positions:

(1)	53°32′.76 N,	003°32′.18 W	(3)	53°31′.74 N,	003°33′.80 W
(2)	53°32′.74 N,	003°33′.83 W	(4)	53°31′.76 N,	003°32′.15 W

(b) A separation zone (west of the "Douglas Oil Field" platform), 1.0 nautical mile wide, is bounded by lines connecting the following geographical positions:

(5)	53°32′.72 N,	003°35′.51 W	(7)	53°31′.64 N,	003°41′.27 W
(6)	53°32′.64 N,	003°41′.30 W	(8)	53°31′.72 N,	003°35′.48 W

(c) A traffic lane for eastbound traffic, 1.8 nautical miles wide, is established between the separation zones and a separation line connecting the following geographical positions:

(9)	53°29′.96 N,	003°32′.10 W	(10)	53°29′.84 N,	003°41′.21 W

(d) A traffic lane for westbound traffic, 1.8 nautical miles wide, is established between the separation zones and a separation line connecting the following geographical positions:

(11)	53°34′.56 N,	003°32′.24 W	(12)	53°34′.44 N,	003°41′.36 W

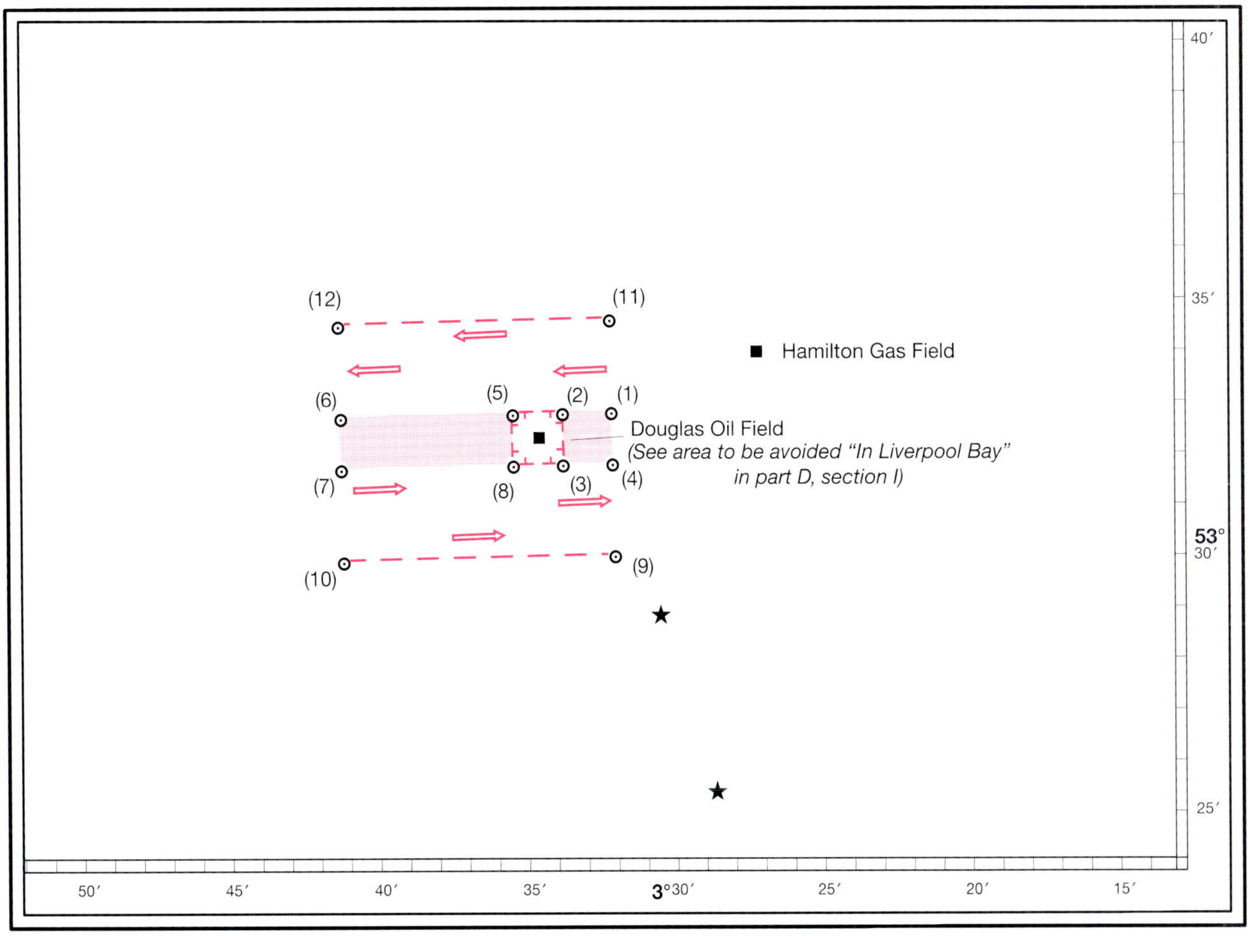

IN LIVERPOOL BAY

B

IN THE NORTH CHANNEL

Note: See mandatory ship reporting system "West European Tanker Reporting System" in part G, section I and "Recommendations on navigation around the United Kingdom coast" in part E.

(Reference chart: British Admiralty 2798, 1988 edition.
Note: This chart is based on Ordnance Survey of Ireland datum and Ordnance Survey of Great Britain 1936 datum.)

Description of the traffic separation scheme

(a) A separation zone, two miles wide, is centred upon the following geographical positions:

(1)	55°15′.30 N,	005°55′.40 W	(3)	55°24′.00 N,	006°15′.00 W
(2)	55°22′.80 N,	006°04′.60 W			

(b) A traffic lane, two miles wide, is established on each side of the separation zone.

Note:
Laden tankers of over 10,000 gross tonnage should avoid the areas between the traffic separation scheme and the Mull of Kintyre and between the traffic separation scheme and Rathlin Island.

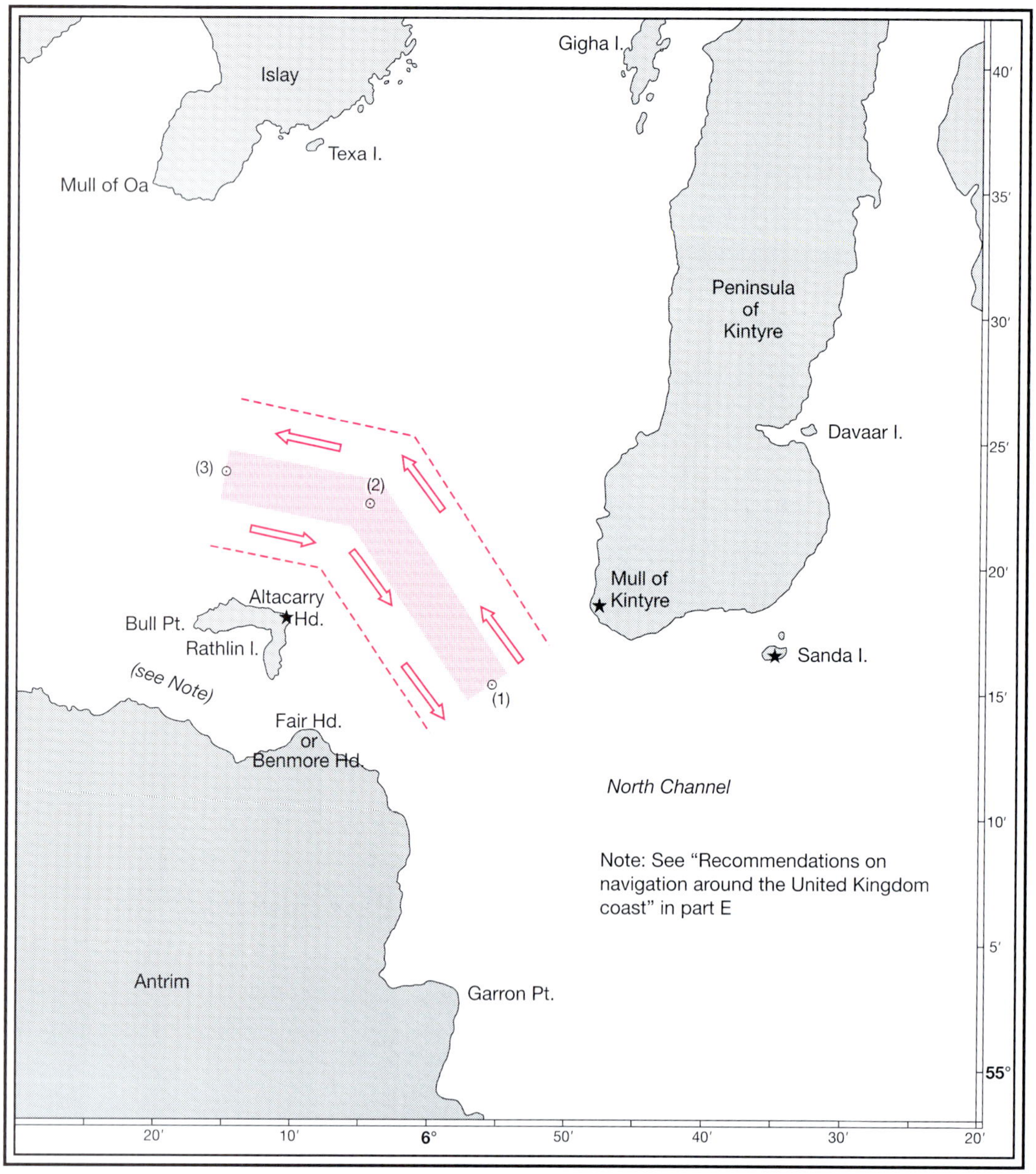

IN THE NORTH CHANNEL

OFF NEIST POINT IN THE MINCHES

Note: See "Recommendations on navigation around the United Kingdom coast" in part E and mandatory ship reporting system "West European Tanker Reporting System" in part G, section I.

(Reference charts: British Admiralty 2635, 1794, 1795.
Note: These charts are based on the Ordnance Survey of Great Britain, 1936 datum (OSGB 36). Position co-ordinates in colour are based on World Geodetic System 1984 datum (WGS 84).)

Description of the traffic separation scheme

Little Minches traffic separation scheme

(a) A separation zone bounded by a line connecting the following geographical positions:

(1)	57°23′.90 N,	006°53′.40 W	(4)	57°28′.20 N,	006°53′.06 W
(2)	57°26′.20 N,	006°52′.80 W	(5)	57°26′.50 N,	006°54′.40 W
(3)	57°27′.90 N,	006°51′.60 W	(6)	57°24′.06 N,	006°55′.10 W

(1)	57°23′.84 N,	006°53′.33 W	(4)	57°28′.37 N,	006°52′.96 W
(2)	57°26′.16 N,	006°52′.88 W	(5)	57°26′.39 N,	006°54′.52 W
(3)	57°28′.02 N,	006°51′.42 W	(6)	57°23′.93 N,	006°54′.99 W

(b) A traffic lane for northbound traffic between the separation zone and a line connecting the following geographical positions:

(7)	57°23′.70 N,	006°50′.50 W	(9)	57°27′.44 N,	006°48′.86 W
(8)	57°25′.80 N,	006°50′.10 W			

(7)	57°23′.68 N,	006°50′.56 W	(9)	57°27′.44 N,	006°48′.86 W
(8)	57°25′.78 N,	006°50′.16 W			

(c) A traffic lane for southbound traffic between the separation zone and a line connecting the following geographical positions:

(10)	57°24′.26 N,	006°57′.60 W	(12)	57°28′.70 N,	006°55′.55 W
(11)	57°26′.94 N,	006°57′.08 W			

(10)	57°24′.08 N,	006°57′.75 W	(12)	57°28′.96 N,	006°55′.52 W
(11)	57°26′.76 N,	006°57′.24 W			

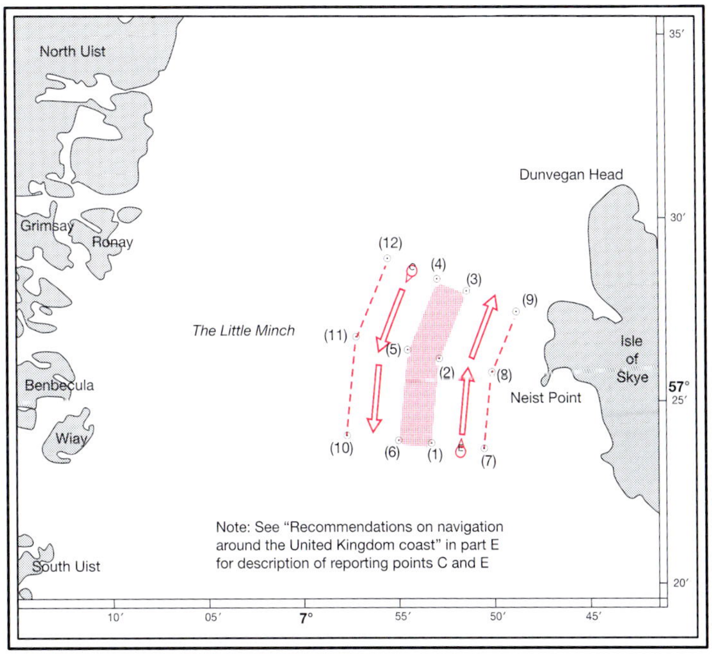

OFF NEIST POINT IN THE MINCHES

B

OFF THE SOUTH-WEST COAST OF ICELAND*

(Reference chart: Icelandic 31 (INT 1103) Dyrhólaey – Snæfellsnes (May 2008 edition).
Note: The chart is based on World Geodetic System 1984 datum (WGS 84).)

Description of the traffic separation schemes

Part I
The routeing measures consist of a traffic separation scheme north-west of Garðskagi Point with attached two-way routes at both ends.

Description of the traffic separation scheme north-west of Garðskagi Point

A separation zone is established bounded by a line connecting the following geographical positions:

(1)	64°09′.02 N,	022°41′.40 W	(4)	64°06′.65 N,	022°52′.14 W
(2)	64°09′.02 N,	022°49′.60 W	(5)	64°08′.40 N,	022°48′.92 W
(3)	64°07′.03 N,	022°53′.25 W	(6)	64°08′.40 N,	022°41′.40 W

A traffic lane for north-eastbound/eastbound traffic is established between the separation zone and a line connecting the following geographical positions:

(7)	64°05′.91 N,	022°50′.06 W	(9)	64°07′.20 N,	022°41′.40 W
(8)	64°07′.20 N,	022°47′.51 W			

A traffic lane for westbound/south-westbound traffic is established between the separation zone and a line connecting the following geographical positions:

(10)	64°10′.26 N,	022°41′.40 W	(12)	64°07′.80 N,	022°55′.46 W
(11)	64°10′.26 N,	022°50′.94 W			

Description of the two-way routes

A two-way route for eastbound/westbound traffic north of Garðskagi Point is established by lines connecting the following geographical positions:

(9)	64°07′.20 N,	022°41′.40 W	(13)	64°10′.26 N,	022°33′.26 W
(10)	64°10′.26 N,	022°41′.40 W	(14)	64°07′.20 N,	022°33′.26 W

A two-way route for north-eastbound/south-westbound traffic west of Garðskagi Point is established by lines connecting the following geographical positions:

(15)	64°05′.63 N,	022°59′.45 W	(16)	64°03′.54 N,	022°54′.70 W
(12)	64°07′.80 N,	022°55′.46 W	(7)	64°05′.91 N,	022°50′.06 W

Part II
The routeing measures consist of a traffic separation scheme south-west of the Reykjanes Peninsula, with an attached two-way route.

Description of the traffic separation scheme south-west of the Reykjanes Peninsula

A separation zone is established bounded by a line connecting the following geographical positions:

(30)	63°31′.75 N,	023°32′.28 W	(32)	63°33′.69 N,	023°35′.26 W
(31)	63°33′.90 N,	023°33′.92 W	(33)	63°31′.55 N,	023°33′.62 W

A traffic lane for north-north-westbound traffic is established between the separation zone and a line connecting the following geographical positions:

(29)	63°32′.00 N,	023°29′.50 W	(34)	63°34′.30 N,	023°31′.23 W

A traffic lane for south-south-eastbound traffic is established between the separation zone and a line connecting the following geographical positions:

(35)	63°30′.82 N,	023°36′.06 W
(36)	63°33′.37 N,	023°38′.00 W

* Date of implementation of amended scheme: 0000 hours UTC on 1 June 2011.

Description of the two-way route

A two-way route (the outer route) west of the Reykjanes Peninsula, located off the south-west corner of the western area to be avoided, is established by lines connecting the following geographical positions:

(34)	63°34′.30 N,	023°31′.23 W	(28)	63°42′.00 N,	023°37′.00 W
(36)	63°33′.37 N,	023°38′.00 W	(37)	63°41′.00 N,	023°43′.69 W

Notes:

1.1 All ships of over 5000 gross tonnage in size and all ships carrying dangerous or noxious cargoes in bulk or cargo tanks should navigate the outer route, south-west of the Reykjanes Peninsula, unless they are permitted to navigate the inner route, Hullið Passage, according to the provisions of paragraphs 1.2 to 1.5 below.

1.2 Ships of up to 5000 gross tonnage not carrying dangerous or noxious cargoes in bulk or cargo tanks may transit the inner route.

1.3 Ships of up to 20,000 gross tonnage may transit the inner route provided that:

.1 the ship does not carry any dangerous or noxious cargoes in bulk or cargo tanks; and

.2 the master of the ship has attended a course held by Icelandic authorities and achieved a transit permit. In order to be eligible to attend the course, the master must have been involved in six passages without any incidents and/or remarks to Faxaflói Bay ports as master or chief mate in the preceding 18 months. The master's transit permit expires if the master has not navigated a ship to Faxaflói Bay port in 24 months.

1.4 Tankers with a cargo capacity of up to 5000 gross tonnage may navigate the inner route carrying gas cargoes or petroleum products with a maximum kinematic viscosity of 11.0 cSt at 40°C*. The master shall fulfil the conditions as provided for in paragraph 1.3.2 above.

1.5 Passenger ships of unlimited size may only navigate the Inner Route (Húllið Passage) during the period from 1 May to 1 October.

2 Mariners should be aware that fishing vessels may be encountered in the area and should navigate accordingly.

3 Exceptions applying to the routeing measures are in accordance with SOLAS chapter V, regulation 1.1. Exempt are warships, naval auxiliaries and other ships owned or operated by a contracting Government and used only on Government non-commercial service. The exceptions do not apply to the traffic separation scheme.

(chartlets overleaf)

* According to ISO 8217:2005.

B

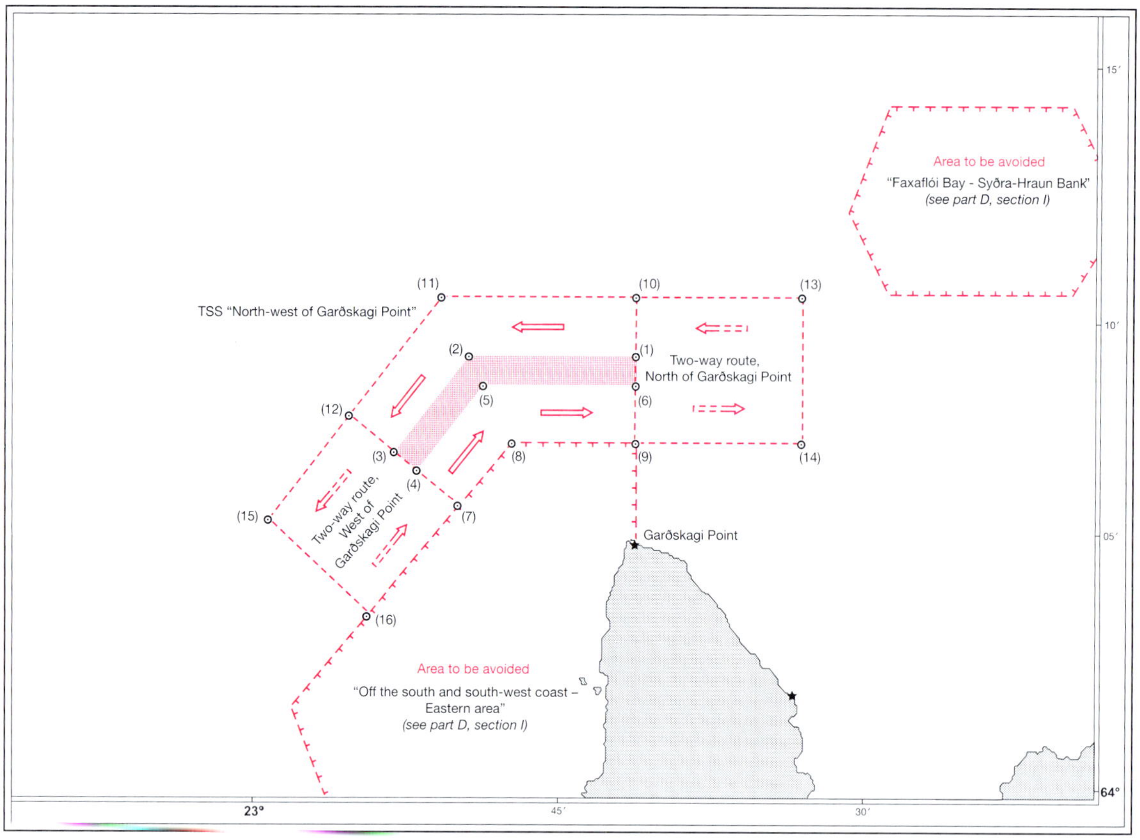

OFF THE SOUTH-WEST COAST OF ICELAND: NORTH-WEST OF GARÐSKAGI POINT + TWO-WAY ROUTES

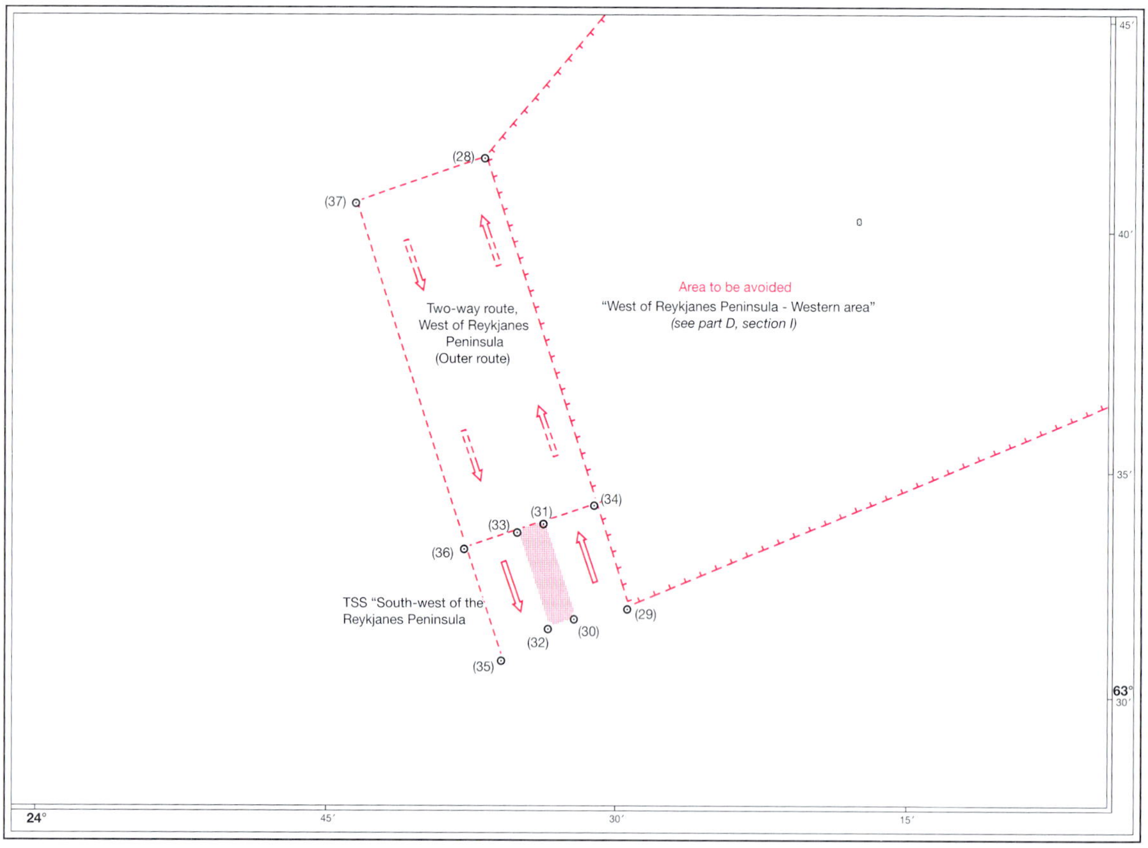

OFF THE SOUTH-WEST COAST OF ICELAND: SOUTH-WEST OF THE REYKJANES PENINSULA + TWO-WAY ROUTE

OFF FINISTERRE

Note: See mandatory ship reporting systems "West European Tanker Reporting System" and "Off Finisterre" in part G, section I.

(Reference chart: Spanish Hydrographic Institute 41, 1978 edition.
Note: This chart is based on European datum (Potsdam).)

Description of the traffic separation scheme

(a) A separation zone is bounded by a line connecting the following geographical positions:

(1)	42°52′.90 N,	009°44′.00 W	(4)	43°21′.50 N,	009°37′.70 W
(2)	43°10′.50 N,	009°44′.00 W	(5)	43°11′.00 N,	009°45′.20 W
(3)	43°21′.00 N,	009°36′.40 W	(6)	42°52′.90 N,	009°45′.20 W

(b) A separation zone is bounded by a line connecting the following geographical positions:

(7)	42°52′.90 N,	009°49′.40 W	(10)	43°25′.00 N,	009°47′.00 W
(8)	43°12′.20 N,	009°49′.40 W	(11)	43°13′.70 N,	009°54′.80 W
(9)	43°23′.00 N,	009°41′.90 W	(12)	42°52′.90 N,	009°54′.80 W

(c) A traffic lane for northbound traffic is established between the separation zones described in paragraphs (a) and (b).

(d) A traffic lane for northbound traffic is established between the separation zones described in paragraphs (b) and (e).

(e) A separation zone, at the outside limit of the existing scheme, is bounded by lines connecting the following geographical positions:

(13)	42°52′.90 N,	009°59′.00 W	(16)	43°28′.20 N,	009°56′.00 W
(14)	43°14′.70 N,	009°59′.00 W	(17)	43°16′.45 N,	010°04′.25 W
(15)	43°26′.40 N,	009°50′.90 W	(18)	42°52′.90 N,	010°04′.25 W

(f) A traffic separation zone is bounded by lines connecting the following geographical positions:

(19)	42°52′.90 N,	010°08′.30 W	(22)	43°30′.00 N,	010°01′.20 W
(20)	43°17′.40 N,	010°08′.30 W	(23)	43°17′.75 N,	010°09′.75 W
(21)	43°29′.30 N,	010°00′.00 W	(24)	42°52′.90 N,	010°09′.75 W

(g) A traffic lane for southbound traffic is established between the separation zones described in paragraphs (e) and (f).

(h) A traffic lane for southbound traffic is established between the traffic separation zone described in paragraph (f) and a line connecting the following geographical positions:

(25)	42°52′.90 N,	010°13′.70 W	(27)	43°31′.40 N,	010°05′.15 W
(26)	43°19′.00 N,	010°13′.70 W			

Inshore traffic zone

The area between the landward boundary of the traffic separation scheme and the Spanish coast and lying between a line drawn from position 43°06′.70 N, 009°13′.40 W to position (3) [43°21′.00 N, 009°36′.40 W] (northern limit) and a line drawn from position 42°52′.90 N, 009°16′.20 W to position (1) [42°52′.90 N, 009°44′.00 W] (southern limit) is designated as an inshore traffic zone.

Notes:

1 The traffic lane described in paragraph (c) should be used by northbound ships not carrying dangerous cargoes in bulk.

2 The traffic lane described in paragraph (d) should be used by northbound ships carrying dangerous cargoes in bulk.*

3 The traffic lane described in paragraph (g) should be used by southbound ships not carrying dangerous cargoes in bulk.

4 The traffic lane described in paragraph (h) should be used by southbound ships carrying dangerous cargoes in bulk.

* "Dangerous cargoes in bulk" refers to the IMDG Code and Annexes I and II of MARPOL 73/78.

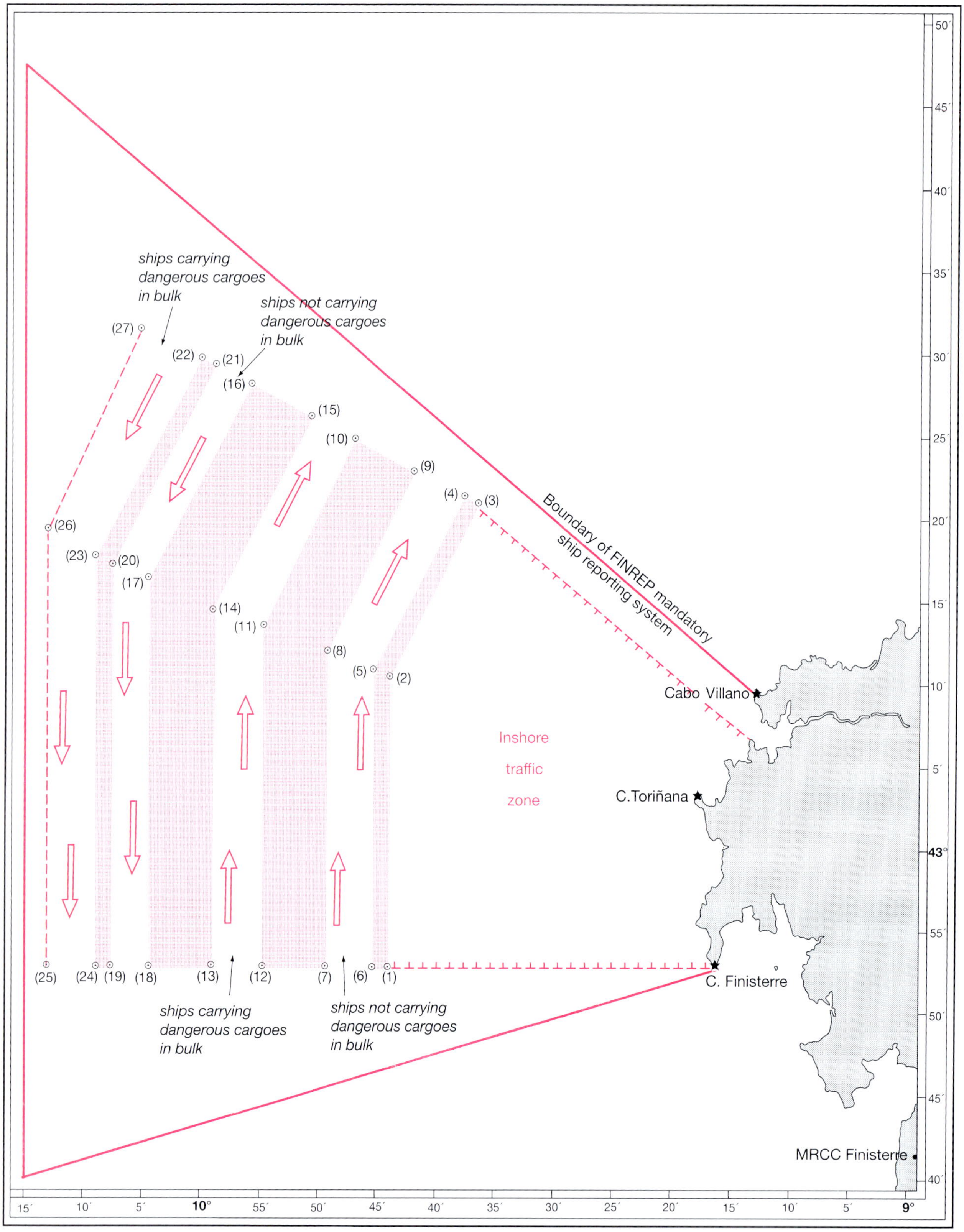

OFF FINISTERRE

OFF CAPE ROCA

Note: See mandatory ship reporting systems "West European Tanker Reporting System" and "Off the coast of Portugal" in part G, section I.

(Reference chart: Portuguese Hydrographic Office 21101 (INT 1081), 4th impression, April 2002.
Note: All positions are given in World Geodetic System 1984 datum (WGS 84).)

B

Description of the traffic separation scheme

(a) A separation zone bounded by lines connecting the following geographical positions:

(1)	38°39′.17 N,	009°43′.12 W	(4)	38°43′.20 N,	009°49′.48 W
(2)	38°51′.91 N,	009°44′.43 W	(5)	38°38′.27 N,	009°48′.02 W
(3)	38°51′.91 N,	009°49′.48 W			

(b) A northbound traffic lane between the separation zone described in (a) and a separation zone bounded by lines connecting the following geographical positions, for ships not carrying dangerous or pollutant cargoes in bulk:

(6)	38°37′.56 N,	009°51′.86 W	(9)	38°51′.91 N,	009°54′.88 W
(7)	38°42′.85 N,	009°53′.43 W	(10)	38°42′.71 N,	009°54′.88 W
(8)	38°51′.91 N,	009°53′.43 W	(11)	38°37′.30 N,	009°53′.28 W

(c) A northbound traffic lane between the separation zone described in (b) and a central separation zone bounded by lines connecting the following geographical positions, for ships carrying dangerous or pollutant cargoes in bulk *(see note)*:

(12)	38°36′.55 N,	009°57′.37 W	(15)	38°51′.91 N,	010°04′.33 W
(13)	38°42′.31 N,	009°59′.08 W	(16)	38°41′.83 N,	010°04′.33 W
(14)	38°51′.91 N,	009°59′.08 W	(17)	38°35′.61 N,	010°02′.49 W

(d) A southbound traffic lane between the separation zone described in (c) and a separation zone bounded by lines connecting the following geographical positions, for ships not carrying dangerous or pollutant cargoes in bulk:

(18)	38°34′.88 N,	010°06′.43 W	(21)	38°51′.91 N,	010°09′.83 W
(19)	38°41′.45 N,	010°08′.38 W	(22)	38°41′.32 N,	010°09′.83 W
(20)	38°51′.91 N,	010°08′.38 W	(23)	38°34′.62 N,	010°07′.84 W

(e) A southbound traffic lane between the separation zone described in (d) and a line connecting the following geographical positions, for ships carrying dangerous or pollutant cargoes in bulk *(see note)*:

(24)	38°33′.92 N,	010°11′.69 W	(26)	38°51′.91 N,	010°13′.78 W
(25)	38°40′.96 N,	010°13′.77 W			

(f) A two-way traffic route, 2 miles wide, established between the separation zone described in (a) and a separation zone bounded by the lines connecting the following geographical positions, for ships sailing between ports situated between Cape Finisterre and Punta del Perro and southbound ships bound to the port of Lisbon or northbound ships leaving the port of Lisbon, except for ships carrying oils listed in appendix I of Annex I of the International Convention for the Prevention of Pollution from Ships, 1973, as modified by the Protocol of 1978 (MARPOL 73/78) and ships carrying in bulk the substances listed in categories X and Y in appendices I and II of Annex II of that same Convention:

(27)	38°39′.63 N,	009°40′.63 W	(29)	38°51′.91 N,	009°41′.23 W
(28)	38°51′.91 N,	009°41′.87 W	(30)	38°39′.74 N,	009°39′.99 W

(g) The area between the separation zone described in paragraph (f) and the Portuguese coast, bounded on the north by the parallel of 38°51′.91 N and on the south by the line connecting point with position 38°39′.74 N, 009°39′.99 W and Cape Raso lighthouse (38°42′.56 N, 009°29′.14 W), is designated as an inshore traffic zone.

Note: "Dangerous cargoes in bulk" refers to the IMDG Code and Annexes I and II of MARPOL 73/78.

(chartlet overleaf)

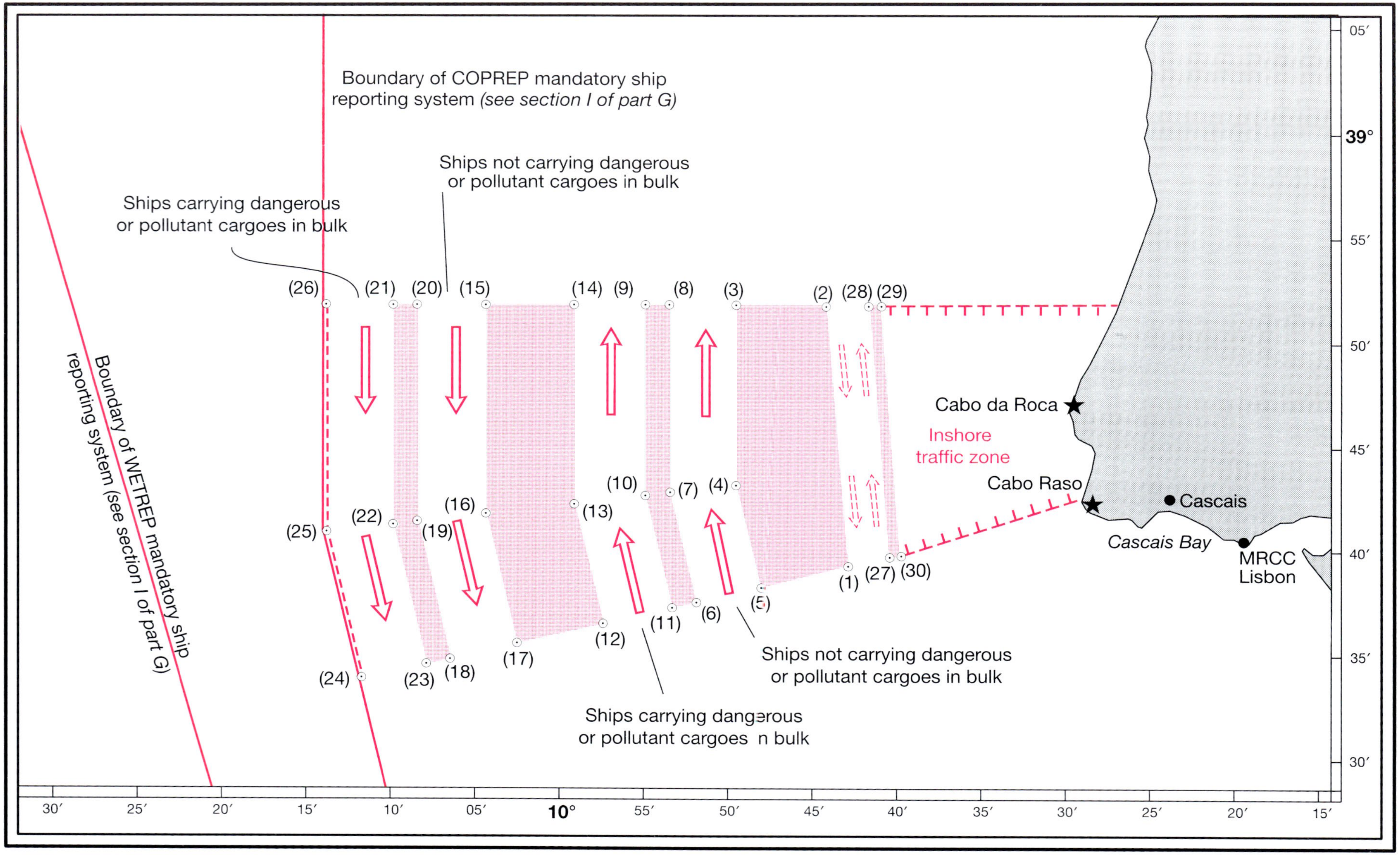

OFF CAPE ROCA

OFF CAPE S. VICENTE

Note: See mandatory ship reporting systems "West European Tanker Reporting System" and "Off the coast of Portugal" in part G, section I.

(Reference chart: Portuguese Hydrographic Office 21101 (INT 1081), 4th impression, April 2002)
Note: All positions are given in World Geodetic System 1984 datum (WGS 84)

B

Description of the traffic separation scheme

(a) A separation zone bounded by lines connecting the following geographical positions:

(1)	36°47′.73 N,	008°58′.09 W	(5)	37°01′.06 N,	009°19′.56 W
(2)	36°49′.36 N,	009°05′.96 W	(6)	36°53′.79 N,	009°17′.46 W
(3)	36°55′.58 N,	009°13′.12 W	(7)	36°45′.98 N,	009°08′.40 W
(4)	37°01′.94 N,	009°14′.78 W	(8)	36°43′.96 N,	008°59′.40 W

(b) A northbound traffic lane between the separation zone described in (a) and a separation zone bounded by lines connecting the following geographical positions, for ships not carrying dangerous or pollutant cargoes in bulk:

(9)	36°40′.89 N,	009°00′.47 W	(13)	37°00′.08 N,	009°24′.82 W
(10)	36°43′.16 N,	009°10′.53 W	(14)	36°51′.68 N,	009°22′.40 W
(11)	36°52′.25 N,	009°21′.07 W	(15)	36°42′.13 N,	009°11′.32 W
(12)	37°00′.34 N,	009°23′.41 W	(16)	36°39′.77 N,	009°00′.86 W

(c) A northbound traffic lane between the separation zone described in (b) and a central separation zone bounded by lines connecting the following geographical positions, for ships carrying dangerous or pollutant cargoes in bulk *(see note)*:

(17)	36°36′.49 N,	009°02′.00 W	(21)	36°58′.35 N,	009°34′.07 W
(18)	36°39′.11 N,	009°13′.60 W	(22)	36°47′.98 N,	009°31′.07 W
(19)	36°50′.04 N,	009°26′.26 W	(23)	36°35′.34 N,	009°16′.44 W
(20)	36°59′.31 N,	009°28′.94 W	(24)	36°32′.40 N,	009°03′.41 W

(d) A southbound traffic lane between the separation zone described in (c) and a separation zone bounded by lines connecting the following geographical positions, for ships not carrying dangerous or pollutant cargoes in bulk:

(25)	36°29′.28 N,	009°04′.49 W	(29)	36°57′.36 N,	009°39′.40 W
(26)	36°32′.47 N,	009°18′.61 W	(30)	36°45′.83 N,	009°36′.07 W
(27)	36°46′.40 N,	009°34′.74 W	(31)	36°31′.42 N,	009°19′.40 W
(28)	36°57′.62 N,	009°37′.98 W	(32)	36°28′.14 N,	009°04′.88 W

(e) A southbound traffic lane between the separation zone described in (d) and a line connecting the following geographical positions, for ships carrying dangerous or pollutant cargoes in bulk *(see note)*:

(33)	36°25′.07 N,	009°05′.95 W	(35)	36°44′.29 N,	009°39′.67 W
(34)	36°28′.60 N,	009°21′.53 W	(36)	36°56′.64 N,	009°43′.24 W

(f) A one-way traffic route, 2 miles wide, established between the separation zone described in (a) and a separation zone bounded by the lines connecting the following geographical positions, for southbound ships sailing between ports situated between Cape Finisterre and Punta del Perro and southbound ships bound to the port of Portimão, except for ships carrying oils listed in appendix I of Annex I of the International Convention for the Prevention of Pollution from Ships, 1973, as modified by the Protocol of 1978 (MARPOL 73/78) and ships carrying in bulk the substances listed in categories X and Y in appendices I and II of Annex II of that same Convention:

(37)	36°49′.65 N,	008°57′.43 W	(41)	37°02′.50 N,	009°11′.72 W
(38)	36°51′.05 N,	009°04′.68 W	(42)	36°56′.74 N,	009°10′.36 W
(39)	36°56′.51 N,	009°10′.91 W	(43)	36°51′.51 N,	009°04′.34 W
(40)	37°02′.39 N,	009°12′.34 W	(44)	36°50′.14 N,	008°57′.25 W

(g) The area between the separation zone described in paragraph (f) and the Portuguese coast, bounded on the north by the line connecting point with position 37°02′.50 N, 009°11′.72 W and Cape S. Vicente lighthouse (37°01′.37 N, 008°59′.79 W) and on the east by the line connecting point with position 36°50′.14 N, 008°57′.25 W and Ponta de Sagres lighthouse (36°59′.67 N, 008°56′.95 W), is designated as an inshore traffic zone.

Note: "Dangerous cargoes in bulk" refers to the IMDG Code and Annexes I and II of MARPOL 73/78.

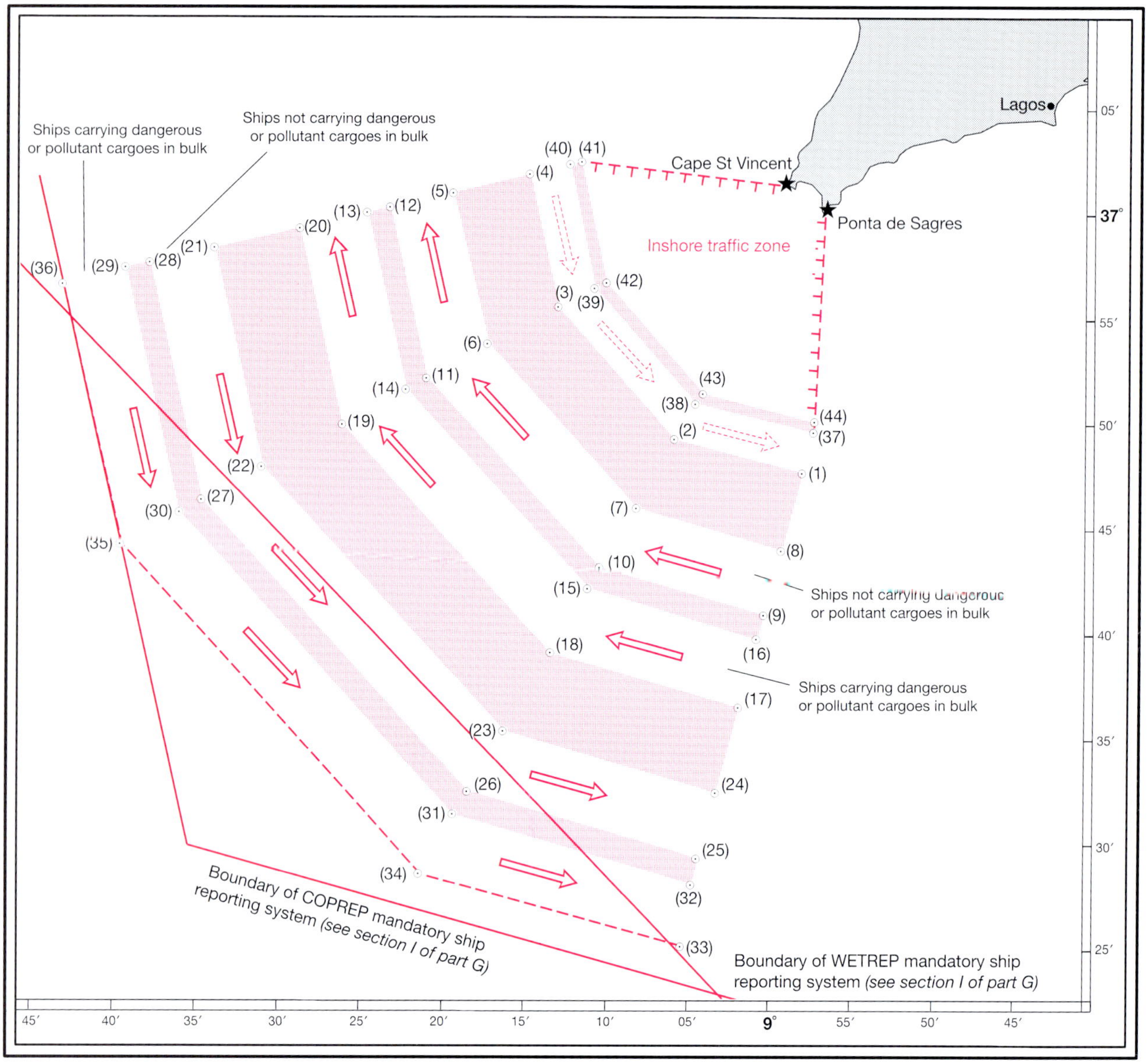

OFF CAPE S. VICENTE

AT BANCO DEL HOYO

(Reference charts: British Admiralty 142; Spanish Hydrographic Office 105.
Note: These charts are based on European datum. For older charts based on Madrid datum, 0′.29 should be subtracted from the latitudes and 0′.1 should be added to the longitudes.)

Description of the traffic separation scheme

(a) A separation zone, two miles wide, is centred upon the following geographical positions:

(1) 35°55′.79 N, 006°05′.90 W (2) 35°55′.79 N, 006°11′.90 W

(b) A traffic lane for westbound traffic is established between the separation zone and a line connecting the following geographical positions:

(3) 35°58′.49 N, 006°05′.90 W (4) 35°58′.49 N, 006°11′.90 W

(c) A traffic lane for eastbound traffic is established between the separation zone and a line connecting the following geographical positions:

(5) 35°52′.59 N, 006°05′.90 W (6) 35°52′.59 N, 006°11′.90 W

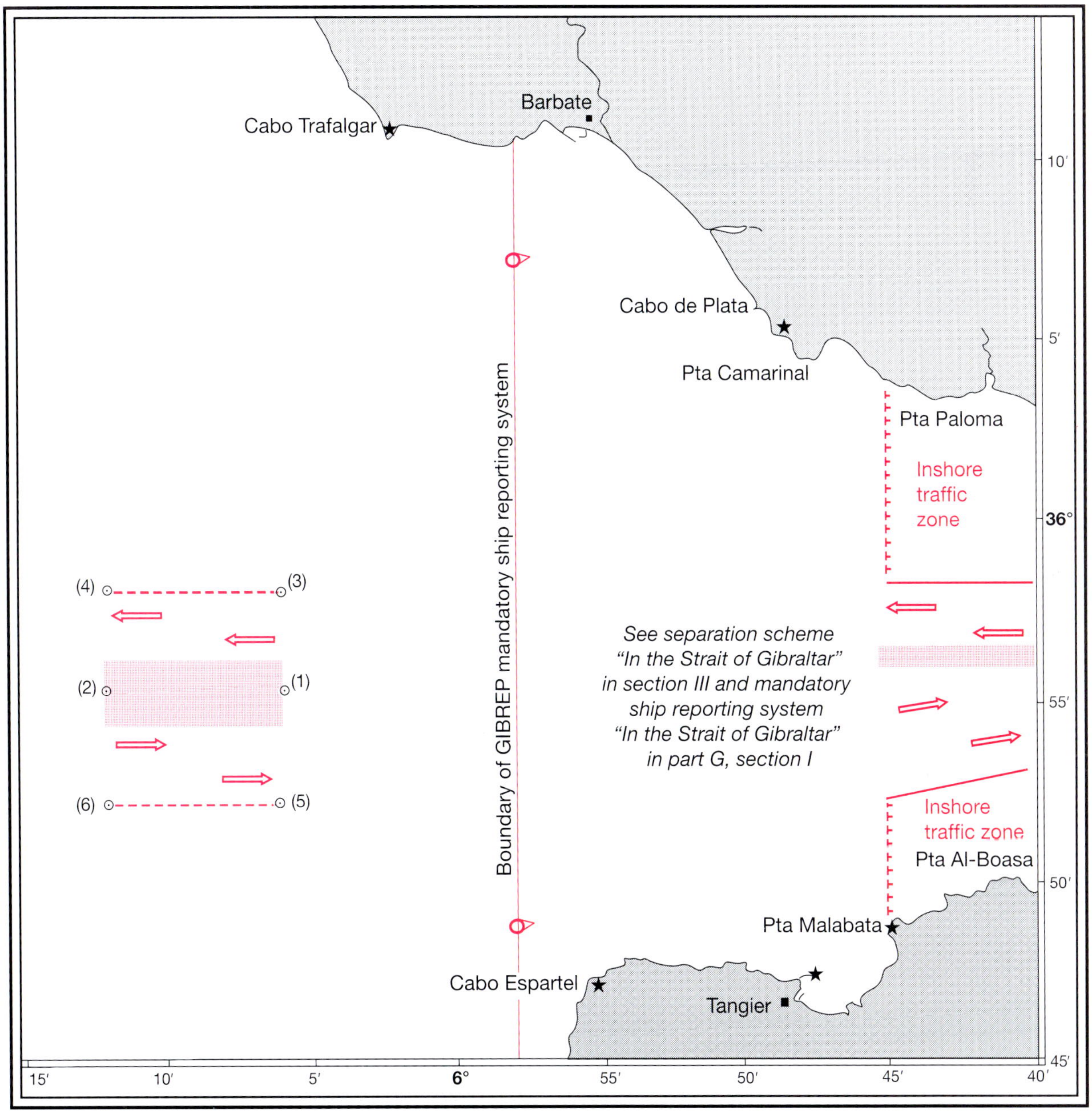

AT BANCO DEL HOYO

B

Section III

Mediterranean Sea and Black Sea

Caution: The chartlets are for illustrative purposes only and must not be used for navigation. Mariners should consult the appropriate nautical publications and charts for up-to-date details on aids to navigation and other relevant information.

Warning: The geographical positions given in the descriptions of the routeing systems are only correct for charts using the same geodetic datum as the reference charts indicated under each scheme. Charts published by other hydrographic offices may use a different geodetic datum, as may new editions of the reference charts published after the adoption of the routeing system. Where amendments to existing systems are not based on the same geodetic datum as the original system, this is emphasized by the use of different colours for definitions of positions.

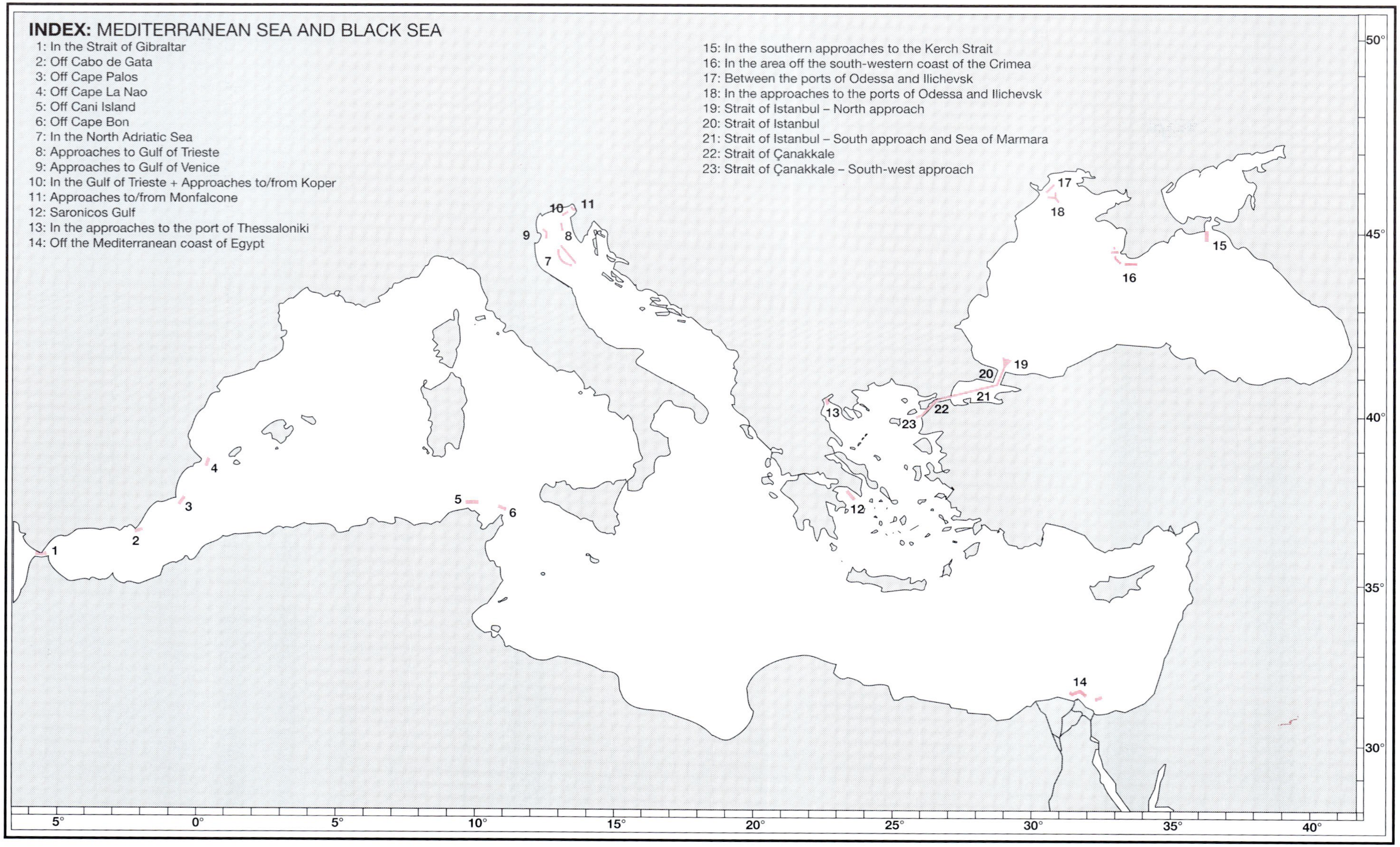
INDEX: MEDITERRANEAN SEA AND BLACK SEA
1: In the Strait of Gibraltar
2: Off Cabo de Gata
3: Off Cape Palos
4: Off Cape La Nao
5: Off Cani Island
6: Off Cape Bon
7: In the North Adriatic Sea
8: Approaches to Gulf of Trieste
9: Approaches to Gulf of Venice
10: In the Gulf of Trieste + Approaches to/from Koper
11: Approaches to/from Monfalcone
12: Saronicos Gulf
13: In the approaches to the port of Thessaloniki
14: Off the Mediterranean coast of Egypt
15: In the southern approaches to the Kerch Strait
16: In the area off the south-western coast of the Crimea
17: Between the ports of Odessa and Ilichevsk
18: In the approaches to the ports of Odessa and Ilichevsk
19: Strait of Istanbul – North approach
20: Strait of Istanbul
21: Strait of Istanbul – South approach and Sea of Marmara
22: Strait of Çanakkale
23: Strait of Çanakkale – South-west approach
50°
45°
40°
35°
30°
5°
0°
5°
10°
15°
20°
25°
30°
35°
40°

IN THE STRAIT OF GIBRALTAR

Note: See mandatory ship reporting system "In the Strait of Gibraltar" in part G, section I.

(Reference chart: Spanish Hydrographic Institute 445, 3rd edition, December 2003.
Note: This chart is based on World Geodetic System 1984 datum (WGS 84).)

Description of the traffic separation scheme

(a) A separation zone, half a mile wide, is centred upon the following geographical positions:

(1)	35°59′.01 N,	005°25′.68 W	(2)	35°58′.36 N,	005°28′.19 W

(b) A separation zone, half a mile wide, is centred upon the following geographical positions:

(3)	35°57′.08 N,	005°33′.08 W	(5)	35°56′.21 N,	005°44′.98 W
(4)	35°56′.21 N,	005°36′.48 W			

(c) A traffic lane for westbound traffic is established between the separation zone described in paragraph (a) and a line connecting the following geographical positions:

(7)	36°01′.21 N,	005°25′.68 W	(8)	36°00′.35 N,	005°28′.98 W

(d) A traffic lane for westbound traffic is established between the separation zone described in paragraph (b) and a line connecting the following geographical positions:

(9)	35°59′.07 N,	005°33′.87 W	(11)	35°58′.41 N,	005°44′.98 W
(10)	35°58′.41 N,	005°36′.48 W			

(e) A traffic lane for eastbound traffic is established between the separation zone described in paragraph (b) and a line connecting the following geographical positions:

(12)	35°52′.51 N,	005°44′.98 W	(14)	35°54′.97 N,	005°32′.25 W
(13)	35°53′.81 N,	005°36′.48 W			

(f) A traffic lane for eastbound traffic is established between the separation zone described in paragraph (a) and a line connecting the following geographical positions:

(15)	35°56′.35 N,	005°27′.40 W	(16)	35°56′.84 N,	005°25′.68 W

(g) A precautionary area is established on the eastern side of the Gibraltar TSS by the lines connecting the following geographical positions:

(6)	36°02′.80 N,	005°19′.68 W	(16)	35°56′.84 N,	005°25′.68 W
(7)	36°01′.21 N,	005°25′.68 W	(17)	35°58′.78 N,	005°18′.55 W

(h) A precautionary area with recommended directions of traffic flow is established off the Moroccan port of Tanger-Med in the Gibraltar TSS formed by the lines connecting the following geographical positions:

(8)	36°00′.35 N,	005°28′.98 W	(14)	35°54′.97 N,	005°32′.25 W
(9)	35°59′.07 N,	005°33′.87 W	(15)	35°56′.35 N,	005°27′.40 W

Inshore traffic zones

Description of the northern inshore traffic zone

(a) The area between the northern boundary of the scheme formed by the continuing line that links points (7), (8), (9), (10) and (11) and the Spanish coast, and lying between the following limits, is designated as an inshore traffic zone:

(1) *Eastern limit:* That part of the meridian 005°25′.68 W (23) between the northern boundary of the westbound traffic lane (latitude 36°01′.21 N, corresponding to point (7) on the attached chartlet) and the Spanish coast.

(2) *Western limit:* That part of the meridian 005°44′.98 W (22) between the northern boundary of the westbound traffic lane (latitude 35°58′.41 N, corresponding to point (11) on the attached chartlet) and the Spanish coast.

Description of the south-eastern and the south-western inshore traffic zones

(b) The southern inshore traffic zone is divided into two inshore traffic zones to east and west, with a free navigational area between them, located between the southern limit of the TSS and the coast of Morocco; these are bounded by eight geographical positions.

(1) *South-eastern zone:* a traffic zone within the inshore zone formed by the coast of Morocco, the external limit of the traffic lane for the traffic heading towards the eastern area of the scheme and the lines connecting the following geographical positions:

(18) 35°54′.45 N, 005°25′.68 W
(16) 35°56′.84 N, 005°25′.68 W

and

(15) 35°56′.35 N, 005°27′.40 W
(19) 35°54′.88 N, 005°27′.40 W

(2) *South-western zone:* a traffic zone within the inshore zone formed by the coast of Morocco, the external limit of the traffic lane for the traffic heading towards the eastern area of the scheme and the lines connecting the following geographical positions:

(20) 35°51′.33 N, 005°32′.25 W
(14) 35°54′.97 N, 005°32′.25 W

and

(12) 35°52′.51 N, 005°44′.98 W
(21) 35°49′.09 N, 005°44′.98 W

Notes:

1 Within this zone are arranged three areas serving the port of Tanger-Med as anchoring areas. These areas are configured as three circles centred on the following co-ordinates and having a radius of 0.4 miles:

First anchoring area (A): 35°51′.05 N, 005°40′.34 W
Second anchoring area (B): 35°52′.03 N, 005°34′.65 W
Third anchoring area (C): 35°52′.03 N, 005°33′.49 W

2 Ships heading for the anchorages indicated in the south-western inshore traffic zone must sail through that zone if coming from the Atlantic Ocean or from the port of Tanger or if proceeding from these areas to anchorages at Tanger-Med or vice versa.

3 Given the absence of ports or any type of facility in the south-eastern inshore traffic zone, ships entering or leaving the port of Tanger-Med must sail along the corresponding traffic lanes.

4 Ships sailing from the Atlantic Ocean or the Mediterranean Sea towards the port of Tanger-Med, or departing from it for the Atlantic Ocean or the Mediterranean Sea, must sail along the corresponding traffic lanes.

5 Ships heading from the Atlantic Ocean to the anchoring areas of the south-western inshore traffic zone must sail, in accordance with rule 10 of the 1972 COLREGs, through that same inshore traffic zone.

6 Ships heading from the port of Tanger-Med to the anchoring areas of the south-western inshore traffic zone must sail, in accordance with rule 10 of the 1972 COLREGs, through that same inshore traffic zone.

7 Ships heading from the anchoring areas of the south-western inshore traffic zone towards the Atlantic Ocean must sail, in accordance with rule 10 of the 1972 COLREGs, through that same inshore traffic zone.

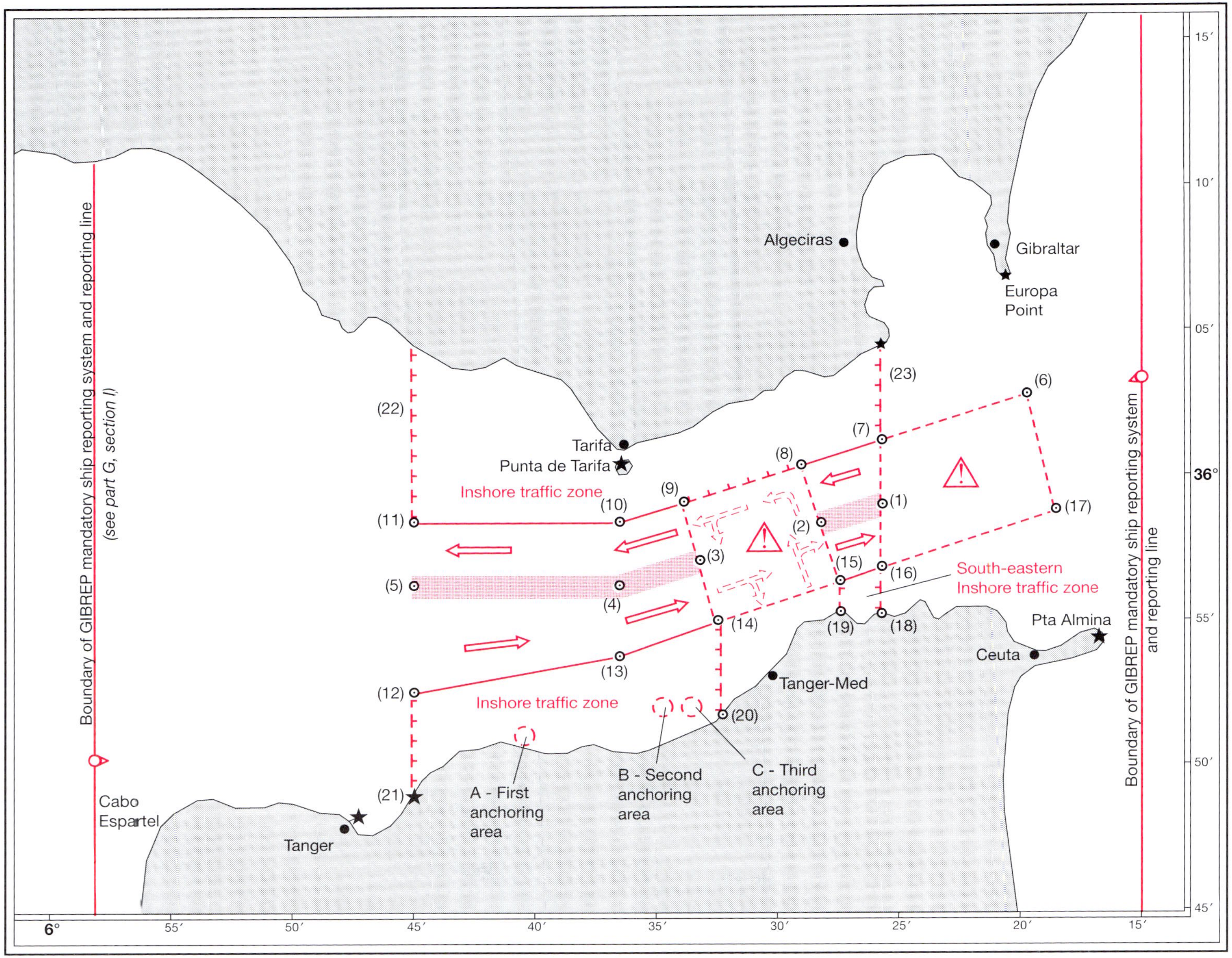

IN THE STRAIT OF GIBRALTAR

B

OFF CABO DE GATA

(Reference chart: Spanish Hydrographic Institute 45B, March 2001 edition.
Note: This chart is based on European datum (Potsdam).)

Description of the traffic separation scheme

(a) A separation line connecting the following geographical positions:

(1)	36°26′.89 N,	002°15′.23 W	(3)	36°28′.13 N,	002°09′.65 W
(2)	36°26′.89 N,	002°11′.47 W			

(b) An intermediate separation zone bounded by a line connecting the following geographical positions:

(4)	36°25′.70 N,	002°09′.37 W	(7)	36°22′.45 N,	002°16′.24 W
(5)	36°24′.27 N,	002°11′.47 W	(8)	36°23′.06 N,	002°11′.47 W
(6)	36°23′.70 N,	002°15′.96 W	(9)	36°24′.55 N,	002°09′.23 W

(c) A traffic lane for south-westbound traffic is established between the separation line and the separation zone described in paragraphs (a) and (b) above.

(d) An outer separation zone bounded by a line connecting the following geographical positions:

(10)	36°21′.36 N,	002°08′.85 W	(12)	36°19′.84 N,	002°16′.84 W
(11)	36°20′.36 N,	002°16′.72 W	(13)	36°20′.87 N,	002°08′.80 W

(e) A traffic lane for north-eastbound traffic is established between the separation zones described in paragraphs (b) and (d) above.

Precautionary area

(f) A precautionary area bounded by a line connecting the following geographical positions:

(1)	36°26′.89 N,	002°15′.23 W	(14)	36°19′.84 N,	002°20′.00 W
(12)	36°19′.84 N,	002°16′.84 W	(15)	36°26′.89 N,	002°20′.00 W

Inshore traffic zone

(g) An inshore traffic zone contained between the coast of Cabo de Gata and a line connecting the following geographical positions:

(16) Ermita de la Virgen del Mar (36°49′.60 N, 002°17′.80 W)
(1) 36°26′.89 N, 002°15′.23 W
(2) 36°26′.89 N, 002°11′.47 W
(3) 36°28′.13 N, 002°09′.65 W
(17) Punta de la Polacra lighthouse (36°50′.60 N, 002°00′.10 W)

Note: Ships that so wish may give voluntary notification of entry to and departure from the traffic separation scheme, via the Almería MRCC, using VHF channel 16.

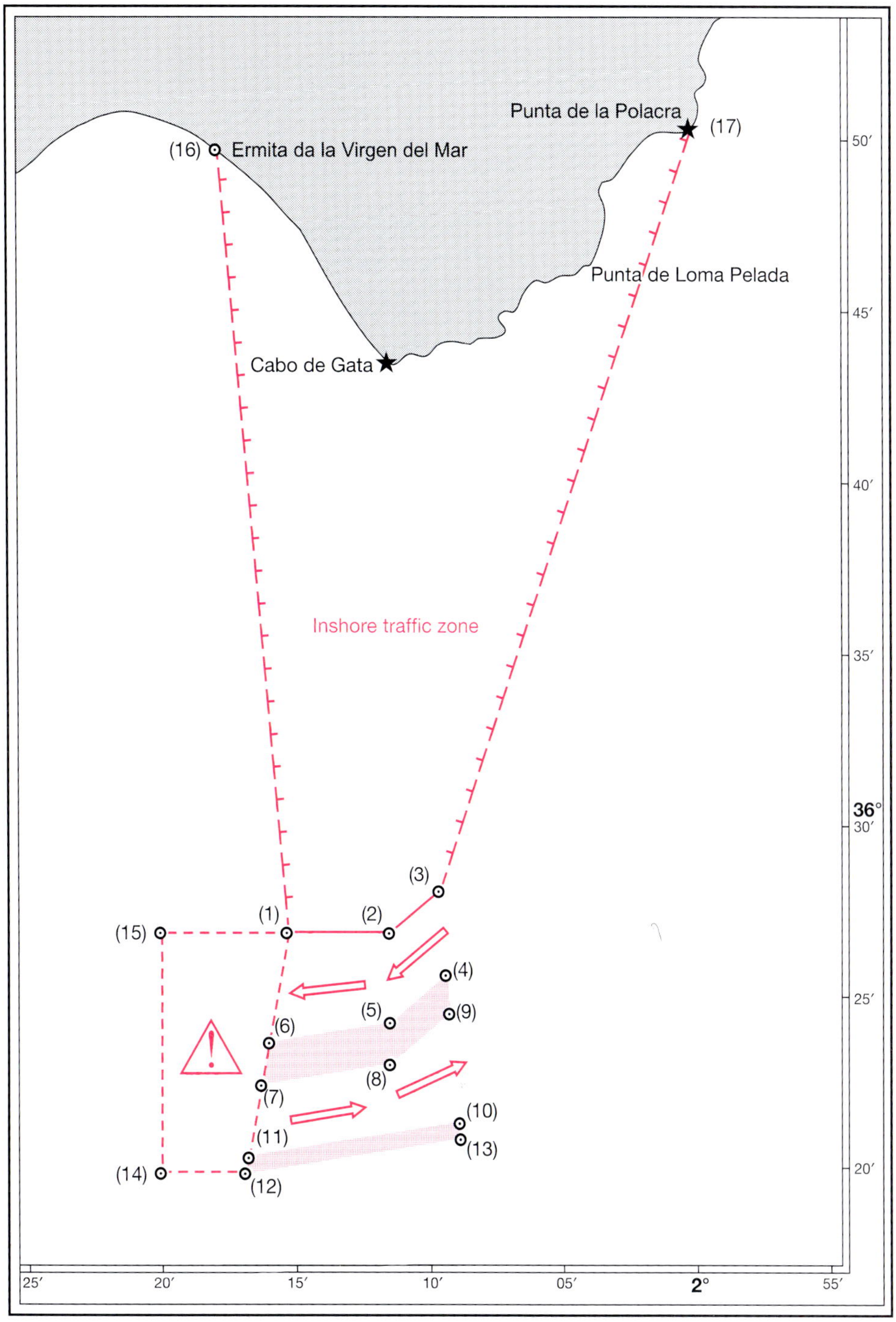

OFF CABO DE GATA

B

OFF CAPE PALOS

(Reference chart: Spanish Hydrographic Institute 47, 1995 edition.
Note: This chart is based on European datum.)

Description of the traffic separation scheme

(a) A separation line for northbound traffic delimited by a line connecting the following geographical positions:

(1)	37°34′.30 N,	000°28′.70 W	(3)	37°31′.20 N,	000°32′.30 W
(2)	37°32′.50 N,	000°30′.00 W			

(b) A separation zone delimited by a line connecting the following geographical positions:

(4)	37°32′.00 N,	000°33′.50 W	(7)	37°35′.20 N,	000°31′.40 W
(5)	37°33′.50 N,	000°31′.40 W	(8)	37°34′.40 N,	000°32′.20 W
(6)	37°34′.85 N,	000°30′.30 W	(9)	37°32′.80 N,	000°34′.60 W

(c) An inshore traffic zone situated between the coast and a line which passes through the following geographical positions:

(10)	37°33′.75 N,	000°35′.75 W	(12)	37°35′.70 N,	000°33′.40 W
(11)	37°35′.00 N,	000°33′.80 W			

and a line which joins the geographical position (10) and Cape Agua

and a line which joins the geographical position (12) and Cape Roig.

(d) A northbound traffic lane leading north-east situated between the separation line/zone described in (a) and (b).

(e) A southbound traffic lane leading south-west situated between the separation zone described in (b) and the inshore traffic zone described in (c).

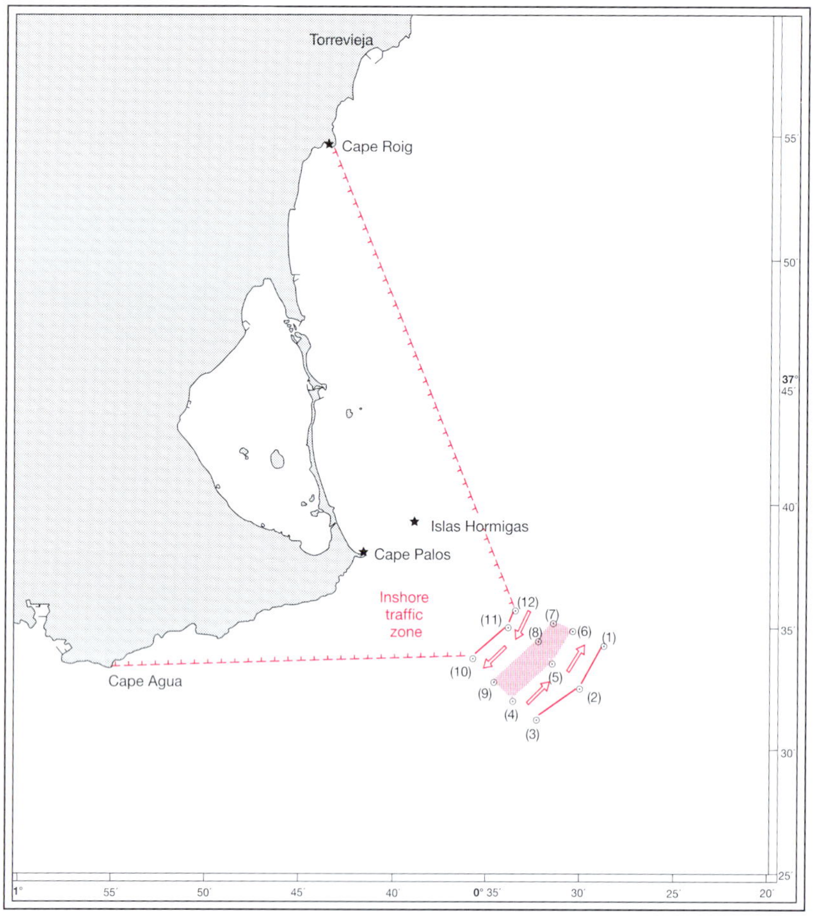

OFF CAPE PALOS

OFF CAPE LA NAO

(Reference chart: Spanish Hydrographic Institute 47, 1995 edition.
Note: This chart is based on European datum.)

Description of the traffic separation scheme

(a) Northbound traffic separation line bounded by a line connecting the following geographical positions:

(1)	38°41′.40 N,	000°28′.80 E	(2)	38°37′.70 N,	000°26′.00 E

(b) Intermediate traffic separation zone bounded by a line connecting the following geographical positions:

(3)	38°37′.90 N,	000°23′.10 E	(5)	38°43′.00 N,	000°25′.00 E
(4)	38°42′.20 N,	000°26′.80 E	(6)	38°37′.90 N,	000°20′.60 E

(c) Associated inshore traffic zone established between the coast and a line passing through the following geographical positions:

(7)	38°37′.90 N,	000°13′.50 E	(9)	38°44′.00 N,	000°22′.60 E
(8)	38°41′.00 N,	000°20′.20 E			

and the connection of point (7) with the Ifach Headland

and the connection of point (9) with the Cape San Antonio lighthouse.

(d) A northbound traffic lane for north-eastbound shipping established between the separation line/zone described in (a) and (b).

(e) A southbound traffic lane for south-westbound shipping established between the traffic separation zone described in (b) and the associated inshore traffic zone described in (c).

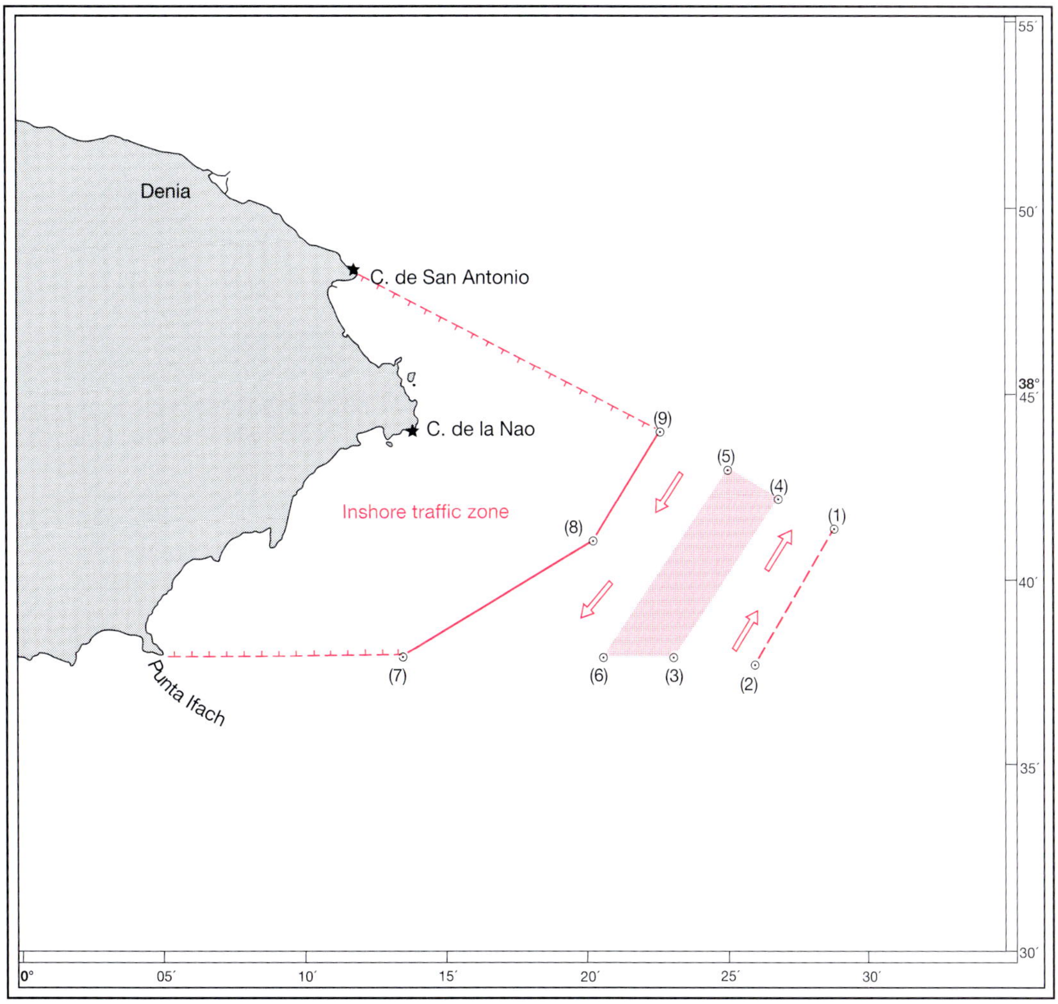

OFF CAPE LA NAO

OFF CANI ISLAND

(Reference chart: Tunisian Hydrographic and Oceanographic Service 150-DST, 2006 edition.
Note: this chart is based on World Geodetic System 1984 datum (WGS 84).)

Description of the traffic separation scheme

(a) A separation zone is established between the inshore traffic zone and the eastbound traffic lane, bounded by the following geographical positions:

(1)	37°31′.41 N,	010°02′.44 E	(3)	37°32′.41 N,	010°13′.36 E
(2)	37°31′.41 N,	010°13′.36 E	(4)	37°32′.41 N,	010°02′.44 E

(b) A separation zone is established between the eastbound and westbound traffic lanes, bounded by the following geographical positions:

(5)	37°35′.41 N,	010°02′.44 E	(7)	37°37′.41 N,	010°13′.36 E
(6)	37°35′.41 N,	010°13′.36 E	(8)	37°37′.41 N,	010°02′.44 E

(c) A separation line is established between the westbound traffic lane and the open sea, bounded by the following geographical positions:

(9)	37°40′.41 N,	010°02′.44 E	(10)	37°40′.41 N,	010°13′.36 E

Inshore traffic zone

The inshore traffic zone to the south of the traffic separation scheme forms a triangle whose base is a line joining the following geographical positions:

(1)	37°31′.41 N,	010°02′.44 E	(2)	37°31′.41 N,	010°13′.36 E

and whose apex is represented on chart 150-DST by the Cani Island light, with the co-ordinates 37°21′.31 N, 010°07′.54 E.

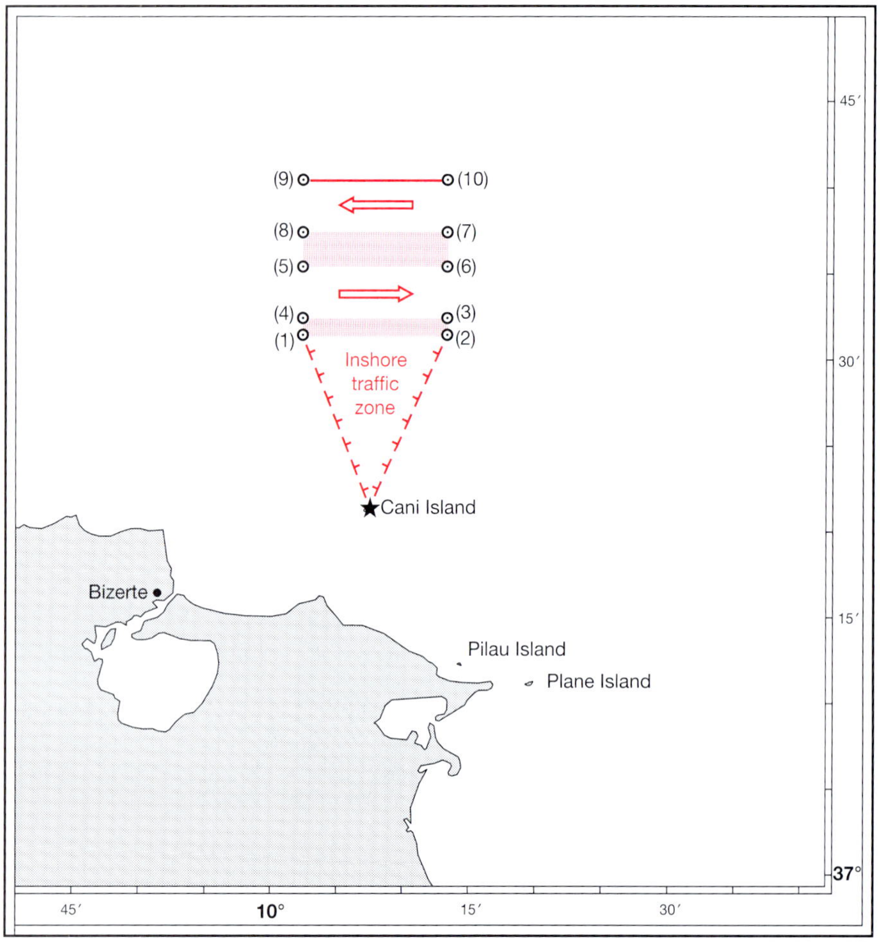

OFF CANI ISLAND

OFF CAPE BON

(Reference chart: Tunisian Hydrographic and Oceanographic Service 150-DST, 2006 edition.
Note: this chart is based on World Geodetic System 1984 datum (WGS 84).)

Description of the traffic separation scheme

(a) A separation zone is established between the inshore traffic zone and the eastbound traffic lane, bounded by the following geographical positions:

(1)	37°21′.06 N,	011°06′.51 E	(3)	37°17′.68 N,	011°16′.38 E
(2)	37°16′.76 N,	011°15′.71 E	(4)	37°21′.93 N,	011°07′.13 E

(b) A separation zone is established between the eastbound and westbound traffic lanes, bounded by the following geographical positions:

(5)	37°24′.53 N,	011°09′.01 E	(7)	37°22′.01 N,	011°19′.46 E
(6)	37°20′.26 N,	011°18′.29 E	(8)	37°26′.26 N,	011°10′.26 E

(c) A separation line is established between the westbound traffic lane and the open sea, bounded by the following geographical positions:

(9)	37°28′.93 N,	011°12′.16 E	(10)	37°24′.61 N,	011°21′.39 E

Inshore traffic zone

The inshore traffic zone to the south of the traffic separation scheme forms a triangle whose base is a line joining the following geographical positions:

(1)	37°21′.06 N,	011°06′.51 E	(2)	37°16′.76 N,	011°15′.71 E

and whose apex is represented on chart 150-DST by the Cape Bon light, with the co-ordinates 37°04′.72 N, 011°02′.56 E.

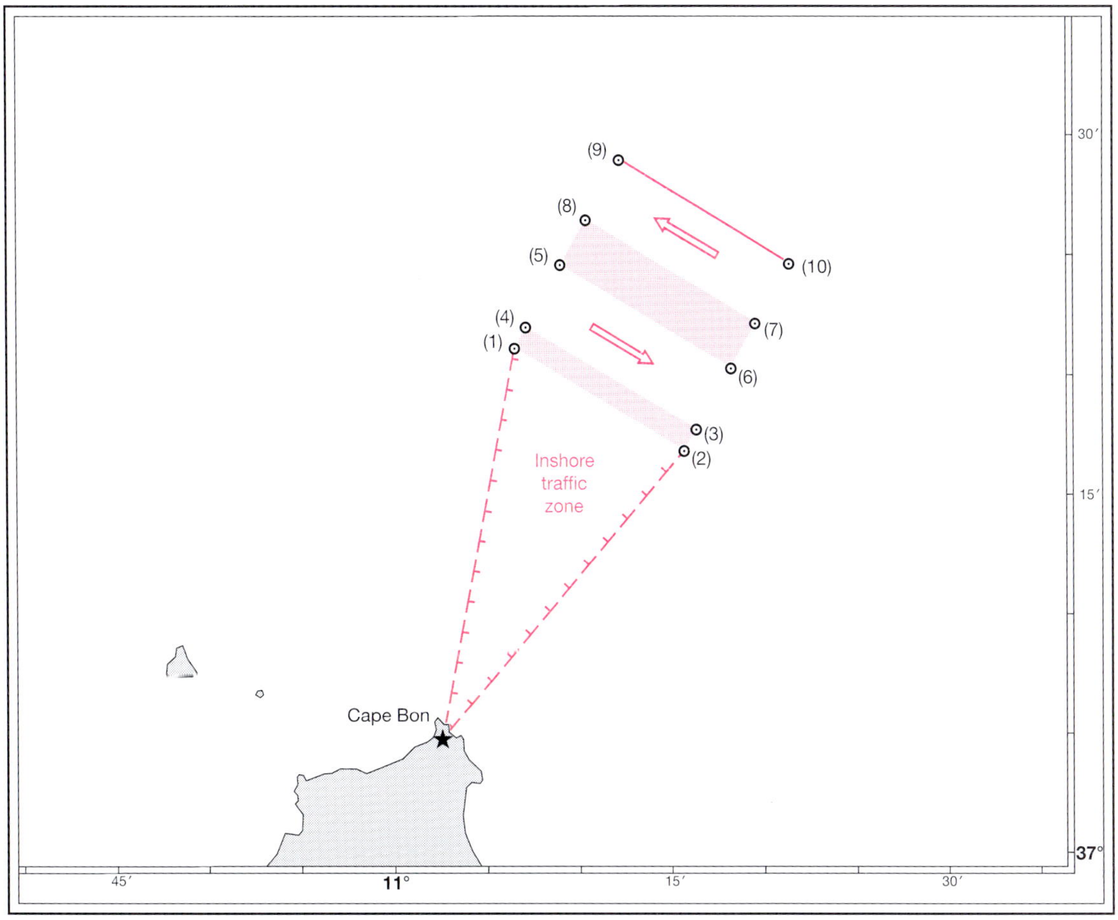

OFF CAPE BON

B

IN THE ADRIATIC SEA: IN THE NORTH ADRIATIC SEA

Note: See mandatory ship reporting system "In the Adriatic Sea" in part G, section I.

(Reference charts: Italian Navy Hydrographical Institute 435, 1993 edition (ED 50 datum); Hydrographical Institute of the Republic of Croatia 101, 1998 edition (Hermannskögel datum, Bessel ellipsoid).
Note: The co-ordinates listed below are in World Geodetic System 1984 datum (WGS 84)).

Description of the traffic separation scheme

Eastern part

(a) A separation zone is bounded by a line connecting the following geographical positions:

(1)	44°05′.90 N,	014°03′.97 E	(3)	44°55′.30 N,	013°21′.17 E
(2)	44°06′.70 N,	014°05′.77 E	(4)	44°54′.80 N,	013°19′.57 E

(b) A traffic lane for northbound traffic is established between the separation zone and a line connecting the following geographical positions:

(5)	44°08′.20 N,	014°08′.77 E	(6)	44°56′.90 N,	013°24′.67 E

(c) A traffic lane for southbound traffic is established between the separation zone and a line connecting the following geographical positions:

(7)	44°04′.40 N,	014°00′.97 E	(8)	44°53′.20 N,	013°16′.17 E

Western part

(d) A separation zone is bounded by a line connecting the following geographical positions:

(9)	43°54′.90 N,	013°49′.20 E	(12)	44°45′.50 N,	013°00′.00 E
(10)	43°56′.40 N,	013°50′.50 E	(13)	44°45′.40 N,	012°59′.40 E
(11)	44°17′.20 N,	013°12′.80 E	(14)	44°12′.10 N,	013°14′.50 E

(e) A traffic lane for northbound traffic is established between the separation zone and a line connecting the following geographical positions:

(15)	43°58′.40 N,	013°52′.70 E	(17)	44°46′.10 N,	013°03′.45 E
(16)	44°18′.80 N,	013°15′.90 E			

(f) A traffic lane for southbound traffic is established between the separation zone and a line connecting the following geographical positions:

(18)	43°53′.00 N,	013°47′.40 E	(20)	44°44′.70 N,	012°55′.80 E
(19)	44°10′.50 N,	013°11′.20 E			

Precautionary area

A precautionary area is established by a line connecting the following geographical positions:

(21)	43°47′.50 N,	013°58′.20 E	(7)	44°04′.40 N,	014°00′.97 E
(22)	43°59′.85 N,	014°16′.61 E	(15)	43°58′.40 N,	013°52′.70 E
(5)	44°08′.20 N,	014°08′.77 E	(18)	43°53′.00 N,	013°47′.40 E

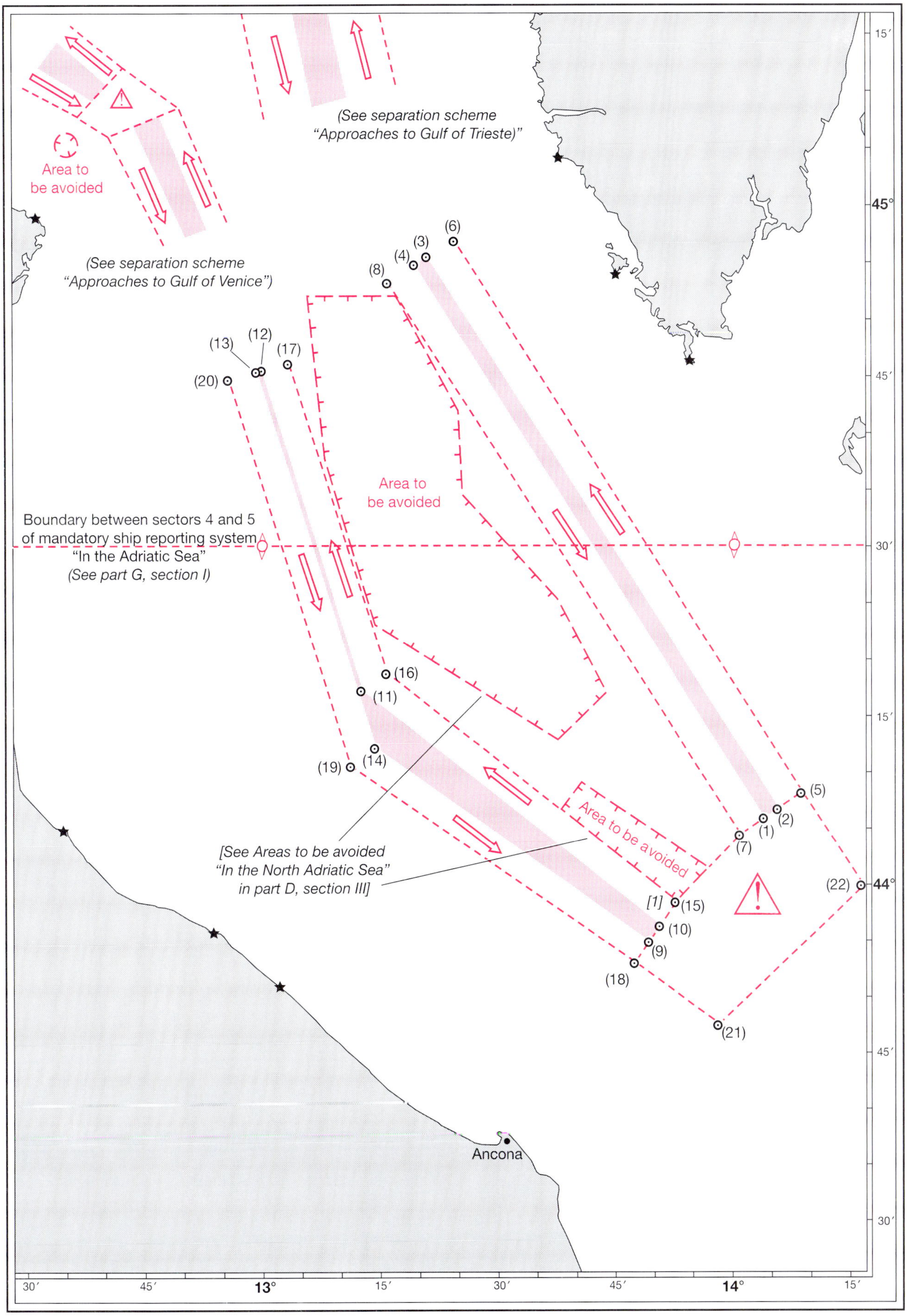

IN THE NORTH ADRIATIC SEA

B

IN THE ADRIATIC SEA: APPROACHES TO GULF OF TRIESTE

Note: See mandatory ship reporting system "In the Adriatic Sea" in part G, section I.

(Reference charts: Italian Navy Hydrographical Institute 435, 1993 edition (ED 50 datum); Hydrographical Institute of the Republic of Croatia 101, 1998 edition (Hermannskögel datum, Bessel ellipsoid).
Note: The co-ordinates listed below are in World Geodetic System 1984 datum (WGS 84).)

Description of the traffic separation scheme

(a) A separation zone is bounded by a line connecting the following geographical positions:

(1)	45°08′.60 N,	013°06′.47 E	(3)	45°23′.20 N,	013°06′.47 E
(2)	45°09′.40 N,	013°10′.97 E	(4)	45°21′.50 N,	013°02′.57 E

(b) A traffic lane for northbound traffic is established between the separation zone and a line connecting the following geographical positions:

(5)	45°10′.50 N,	013°17′.17 E	(6)	45°22′.50 N,	013°13′.27 E

(c) A traffic lane for southbound traffic is established between the separation zone and a line connecting the following geographical positions:

(7)	45°07′.50 N,	013°00′.37 E	(8)	45°19′.00 N,	012°56′.87 E

IN THE ADRIATIC SEA: APPROACHES TO GULF OF VENICE

Note: See mandatory ship reporting system "In the Adriatic Sea" in part G, section I.

(Reference charts: Italian Navy Hydrographical Institute 435, 1993 edition (ED 50 datum); Hydrographical Institute of the Republic of Croatia 101, 1998 edition (Hermannskögel datum, Bessel ellipsoid).
Note: The co-ordinates listed below are in World Geodetic System 1984 datum (WGS 84).)

Description of the traffic separation scheme

Northern part

(a) A separation zone is bounded by a line connecting the following geographical positions:

(1)	45°09′.10 N,	012°38′.50 E	(3)	45°14′.30 N,	012°34′.00 E
(2)	45°10′.50 N,	012°40′.40 E	(4)	45°12′.00 N,	012°31′.50 E

(b) A traffic lane for northbound traffic is established between the separation zone and a line connecting the following geographical positions:

(5)	45°12′.00 N,	012°42′.40 E	(6)	45°15′.70 N,	012°35′.70 E

(c) A traffic lane for southbound traffic is established between the separation zone and a line connecting the following geographical positions:

(7)	45°07′.70 N,	012°36′.50 E	(8)	45°10′.30 N,	012°29′.50 E

Southern part

(d) A separation zone is bounded by a line connecting the following geographical positions:

(9)	44°57′.20 N,	012°50′.30 E	(11)	45°07′.80 N,	012°47′.10 E
(10)	44°57′.90 N,	012°53′.00 E	(12)	45°06′.80 N,	012°43′.80 E

(e) A traffic lane for northbound traffic is established between the separation zone and a line connecting the following geographical positions:

(13)	44°58′.50 N,	012°55′.60 E	(14)	45°08′.50 N,	012°49′.50 E

(f) A traffic lane for southbound traffic is established between the separation zone and a line connecting the following geographical positions:

(15)	44°56′.50 N,	012°47′.60 E	(16)	45°06′.00 N,	012°40′.50 E

Precautionary area

(g) A precautionary area is established by a line connecting the following geographical positions:

(16)	45°06′.00 N,	012°40′.50 E	(5)	45°12′.00 N,	012°42′.40 E
(7)	45°07′.70 N,	012°36′.50 E	(14)	45°08′.50 N,	012°49′.50 E

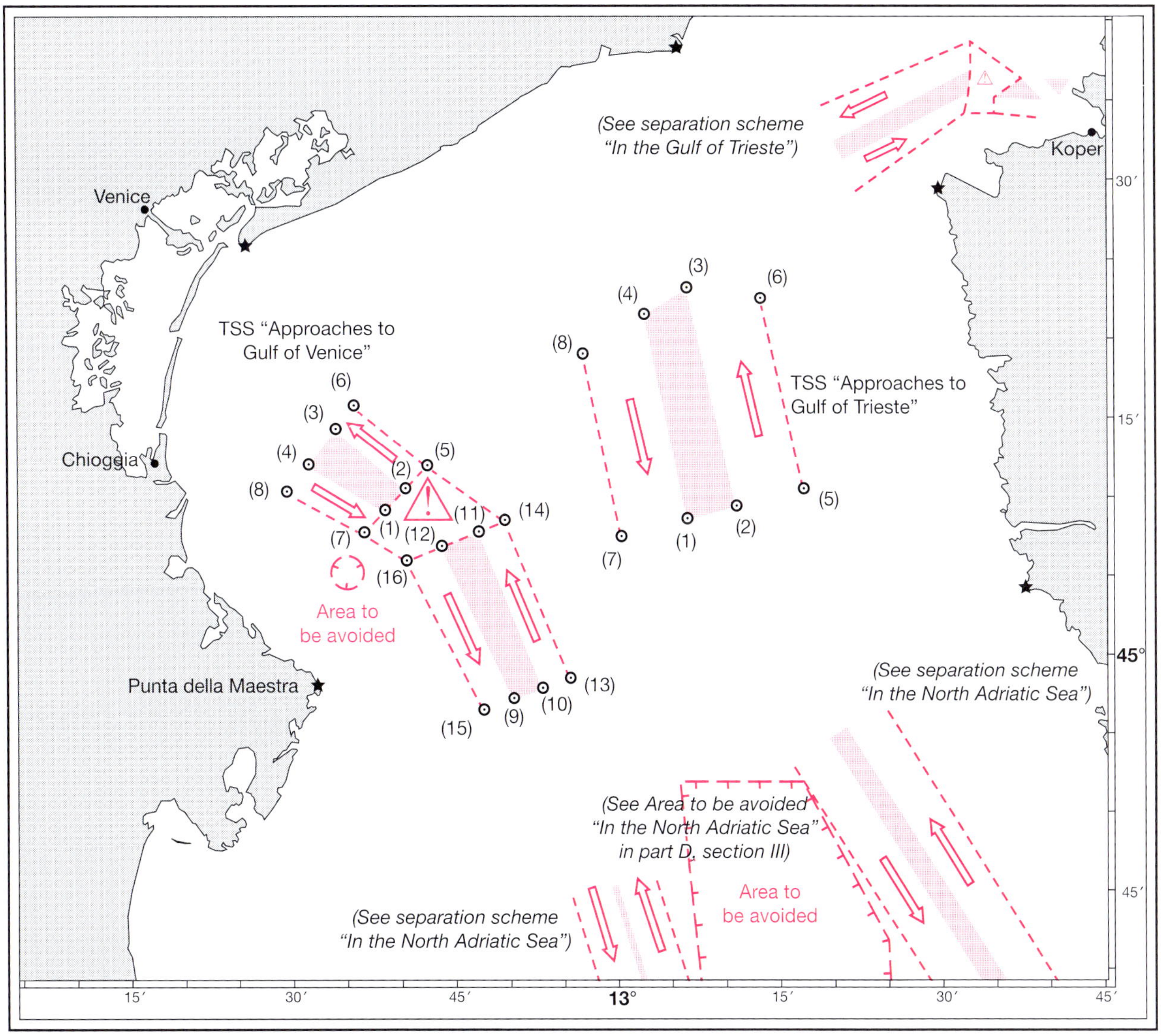

APPROACHES TO GULF OF TRIESTE + APPROACHES TO GULF OF VENICE

IN THE ADRIATIC SEA: IN THE GULF OF TRIESTE

Note: See mandatory ship reporting system "In the Adriatic Sea" in part G, section I.

(Reference charts: Italian Navy Hydrographical Institute 39, 2004 edition (Roma 40 datum); Hydrographical Institute of the Republic of Croatia 100-15, 1998 edition (Hermannskögel datum, Bessel ellipsoid).
Note: The co-ordinates listed below are in World Geodetic System 1984 datum (WGS 84).)

Description of the traffic separation scheme

(a) A separation zone is bounded by a line connecting the following geographical positions:

(1)	45°31′.34 N,	013°20′.90 E	(3)	45°36′.97 N,	013°32′.83 E
(2)	45°35′.48 N,	013°32′.62 E	(4)	45°32′.84 N,	013°20′.00 E

(b) A traffic lane for north-eastbound traffic is established between the separation zone and a line connecting the following geographical positions:

(5)	45°29′.30 N,	013°22′.10 E	(6)	45°34′.24 N,	013°32′.20 E

(c) A traffic lane for south-westbound traffic is established between the separation zone and a line connecting the following geographical positions:

(7)	45°34′.74 N,	013°18′.90 E	(8)	45°38′.74 N,	013°32′.80 E

IN THE ADRIATIC SEA: APPROACHES TO/FROM KOPER

Description of the traffic separation scheme

(a) A separation zone is bounded by a line connecting the following geographical positions:

(9)	45°35′.24 N,	013°35′.00 E	(11)	45°36′.44 N,	013°37′.50 E
(10)	45°35′.04 N,	013°39′.50 E			

(b) A traffic lane for eastbound traffic is established between the separation zone and a line connecting the following geographical positions:

(12)	45°34′.24 N,	013°35′.00 E	(13)	45°33′.94 N,	013°39′.40 E

(c) A traffic lane for north-westbound traffic is established between the separation zone as defined in paragraph (a) and a separation zone bounded by a line connecting the following geographical positions:

(14)	45°36′.34 N,	013°39′.70 E	(16)	45°36′.34 N,	013°41′.80 E
(15)	45°35′.44 N,	013°41′.00 E			

Precautionary area

A precautionary area is established by a line connecting the following geographical positions:

(6)	45°34′.24 N,	013°32′.20 E	(11)	45°36′.44 N,	013°37′.50 E
(2)	45°35′.48 N,	013°32′.62 E	(9)	45°35′.24 N,	013°35′.00 E
(3)	45°36′.97 N,	013°32′.83 E	(12)	45°34′.24 N,	013°35′.00 E
(8)	45°38′.74 N,	013°32′.80 E			

IN THE ADRIATIC SEA: APPROACHES TO/FROM MONFALCONE

Note: See mandatory ship reporting system "In the Adriatic Sea" in part G, section I.

(Reference charts: Italian Navy Hydrographical Institute 39, 2004 edition (Roma 40 datum); Hydrographical Institute of the Republic of Croatia 100-15, 1998 edition (Hermannskögel datum, Bessel ellipsoid).
Note: The co-ordinates listed below are in World Geodetic System 1984 datum (WGS 84).)

Description of the traffic separation scheme

(a) A separation zone is bounded by a line connecting the following geographical positions:

(1)	45°40′.34 N,	013°38′.00 E	(3)	45°42′.74 N,	013°37′.30 E
(2)	45°40′.34 N,	013°37′.30 E	(4)	45°42′.74 N,	013°38′.00 E

(b) A traffic lane for northbound traffic is established between the separation zone and a line connecting the following geographical positions:

(5)	45°40′.34 N,	013°38′.65 E	(6)	45°42′.74 N,	013°38′.65 E

(c) A traffic lane for southbound traffic is established between the separation zone and a line connecting the following geographical positions:

(7)	45°42′.74 N,	013°36′.50 E	(8)	45°40′.34 N,	013°36′.50 E

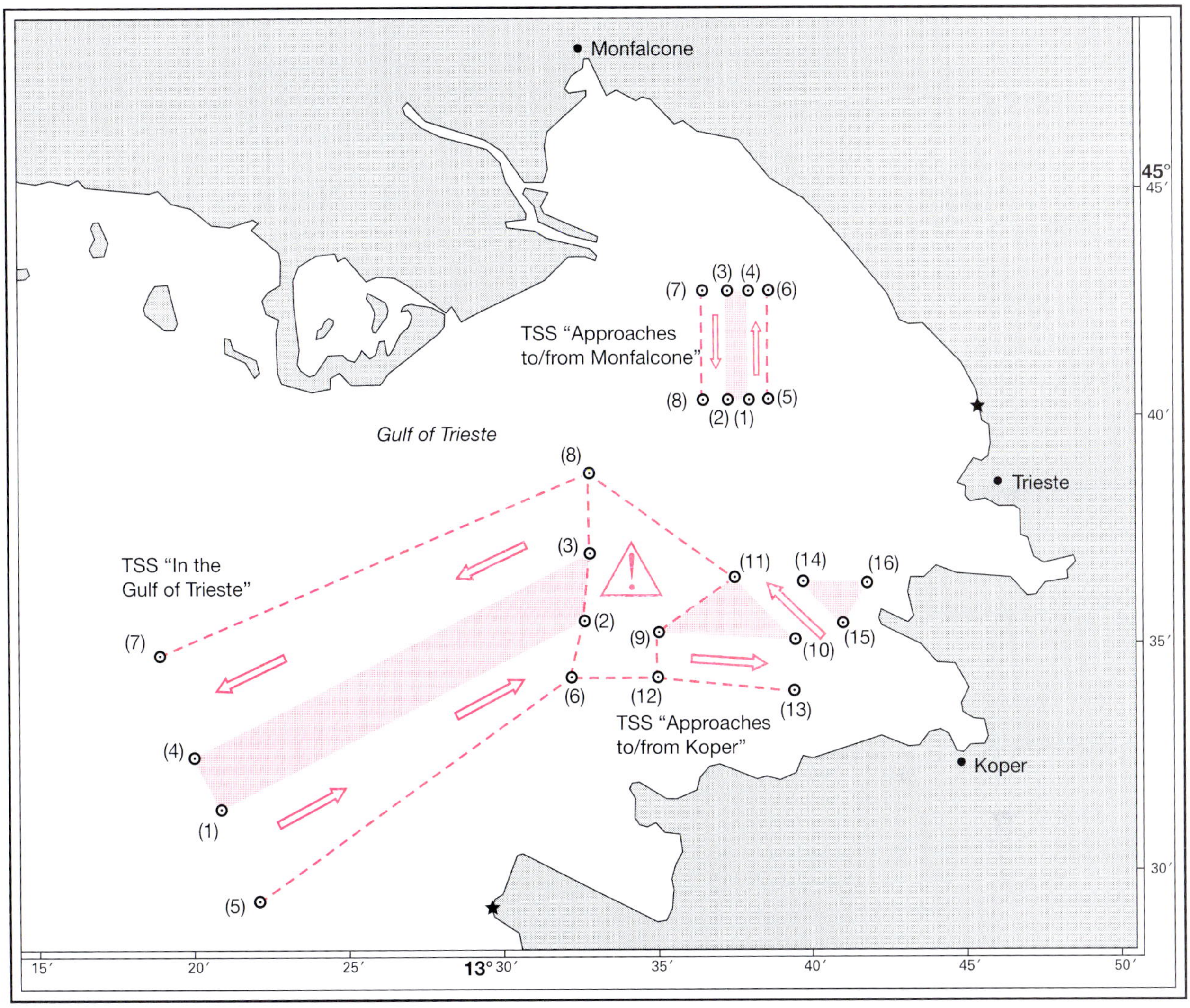

IN THE GULF OF TRIESTE + APPROACHES TO/FROM KOPER + APPROACHES TO/FROM MONFALCONE

SARONICOS GULF (in the approaches to Piraeus Harbour)

(Reference charts: British Admiralty 1657; Greek Hydrographic Office 413, 1986 edition.
Note: These charts are based on European datum.)

Description of the traffic separation scheme

(a) A separation zone, one and a half miles wide, is centred upon the following geographical positions:

(1) 37°40′.00 N, 023°44′.00 E (2) 37°50′.00 N, 023°38′.00 E

(b) A traffic lane, one mile wide, is established on each side of the separation zone.

Notes:

1 Ships in the area between the northern boundaries of the scheme and the adjacent coast of the mainland and Salamis Island should proceed with caution, as heavy traffic, especially of small ships, fishing boats and pleasure craft, from all directions may be encountered.

2 Large ships bound to Piraeus and Salamis Strait should reduce speed to bare steerage way before entering the appropriate lane of the scheme.

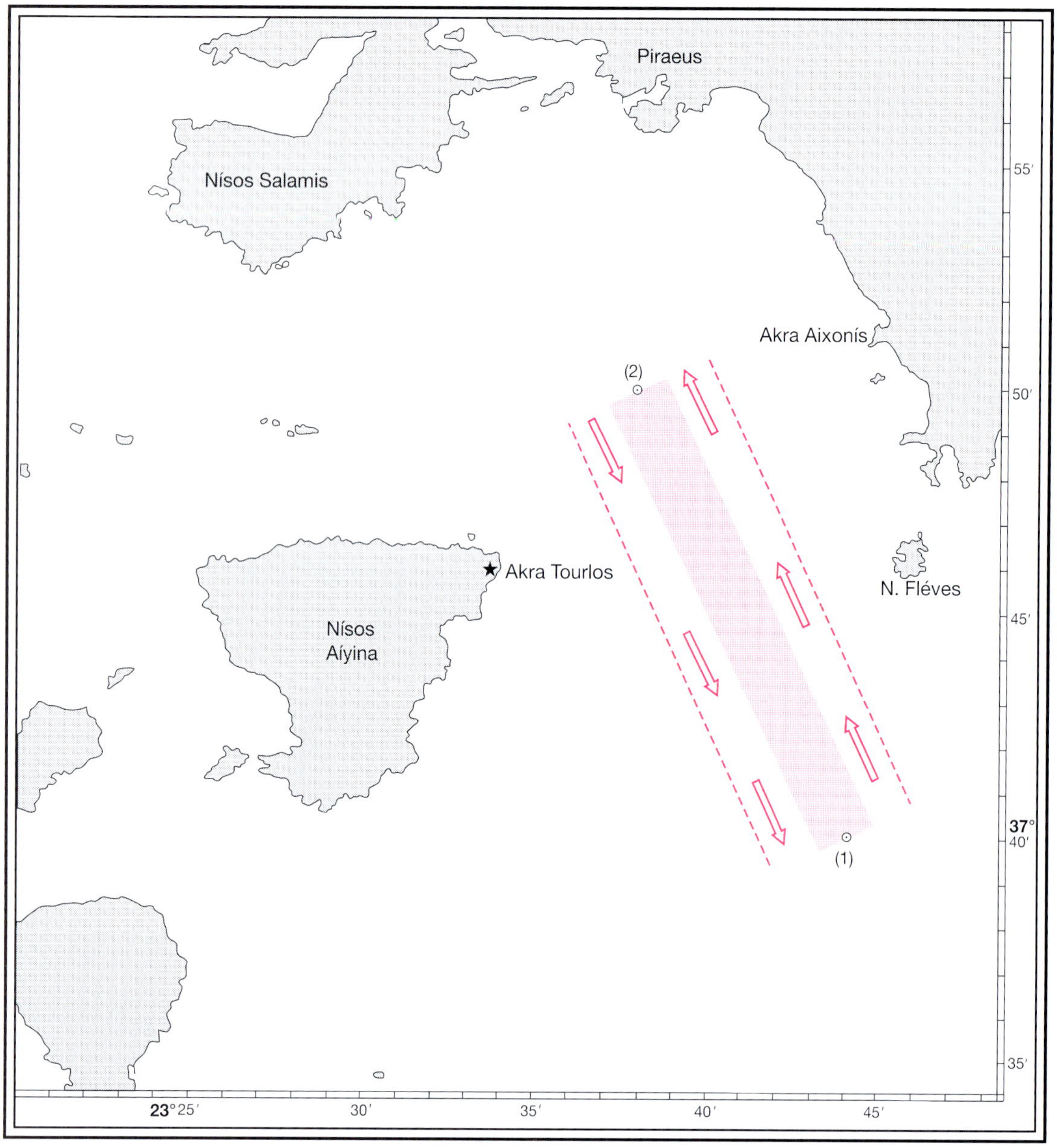

SARONICOS GULF (IN THE APPROACHES TO PIRAEUS HARBOUR)

IN THE APPROACHES TO THE PORT OF THESSALONIKI

(Reference chart: Hellenic Navy Hydrographic Service 255, edition of May 1979, as updated.
Note: This chart is based on European Datum 1950 (ED 50); however, the positions mentioned below are in accordance with World Geodetic System 1984 datum (WGS 84).)

Description of the traffic separation scheme

The routeing measures consist of a traffic separation scheme south-west of the Akra Mikro Emvolon.

(a) A separation line connects the following geographical positions:

(4)	40°33′.39 N,	022°51′.96 E	(5)	40°29′.94 N,	022°46′.66 E

(b) A separation zone is bounded by a line connecting the following geographical positions:

(5)	40°29′.94 N,	022°46′.66 E	(7)	40°27′.24 N,	022°45′.18 E
(6)	40°27′.24 N,	022°46′.11 E			

(c) A traffic lane for northbound traffic is established between the separation line and the separation zone and a line connecting the following geographical positions:

(1)	40°27′.24 N,	022°47′.21 E	(3)	40°33′.06 N,	022°52′.36 E
(2)	40°29′.94 N,	022°47′.46 E			

(d) A traffic lane for southbound traffic is established between the separation line and the separation zone and a line connecting the following geographical positions:

(8)	40°27′.24 N,	022°43′.86 E	(10)	40°33′.69 N,	022°51′.61 E
(9)	40°30′.12 N,	022°46′.11 E			

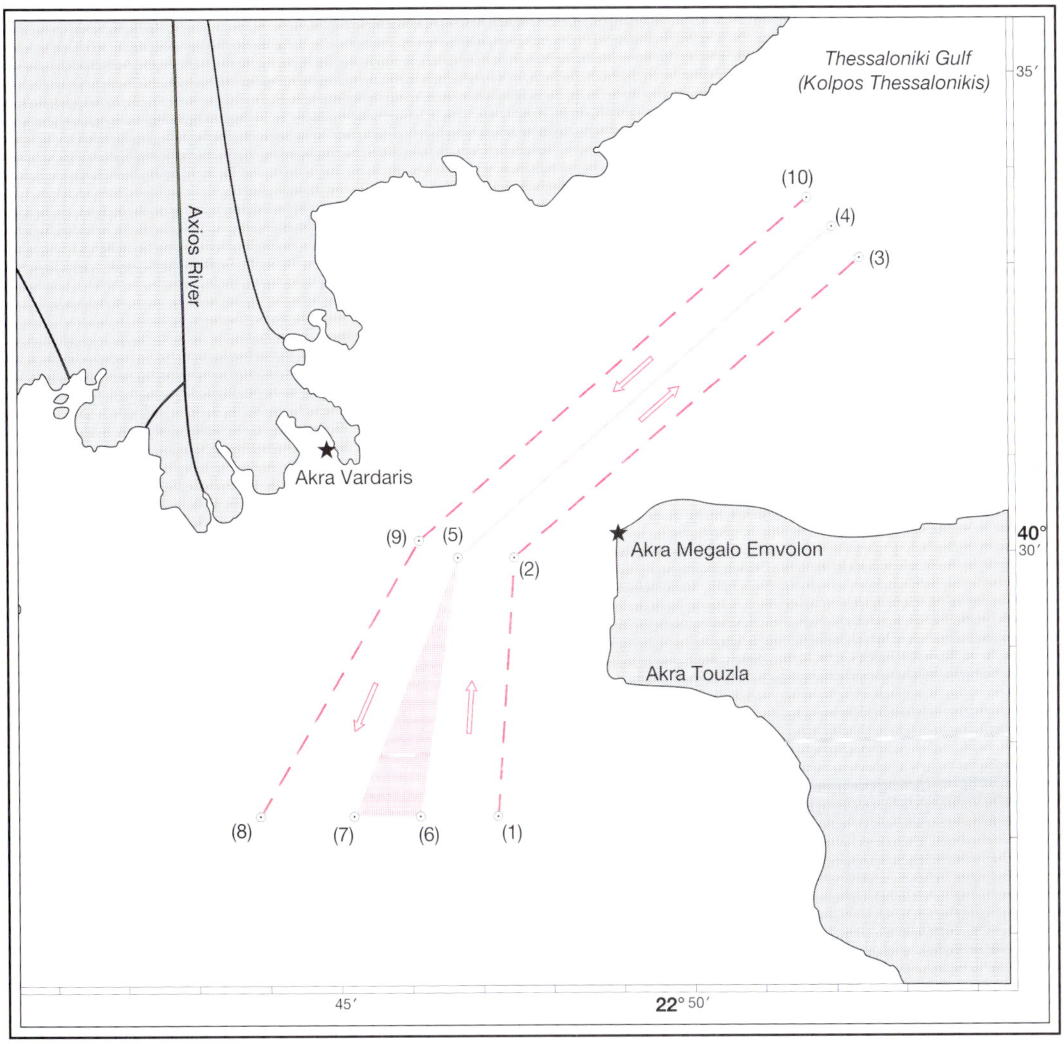

IN THE APPROACHES TO THE PORT OF THESSALONIKI

OFF THE MEDITERRANEAN COAST OF EGYPT

(Reference charts: British Admiralty 2573, 2574 and 2578.
Note: All positions are referred to World Geodetic System 1984 datum (WGS 84).)

Description of the traffic separation schemes

Western approach to Mina Dumyat

(a) A separation line connects the following geographical positions:

(1) 31°38′.60 N, 031°47′.15 E (2) 31°45′.10 N, 031°41′.50 E

(b) A traffic lane for northbound traffic is established between the separation line and a separation line connecting the following geographical positions:

(3) 31°39′.00 N, 031°47′.80 E (4) 31°45′.10 N, 031°42′.40 E

(c) A traffic lane for southbound traffic is established between the separation line and a separation line connecting the following geographical positions:

(5) 31°37′.75 N, 031°47′.00 E (6) 31°45′.10 N, 031°40′.50 E

Precautionary area

(d) A precautionary area north of Dumyat is established by a line connecting the following geographical positions:

(5) 31°37′.75 N, 031°47′.00 E
(1) 31°38′.60 N, 031°47′.15 E
(3) 31°39′.00 N, 031°47′.80 E
(7) 31°38′.45 N, 031°48′.25 E
(9) 31°37′.50 N, 031°48′.00 E

Eastern approaches to Mina Dumyat

(a) A separation line connects the following geographical positions:

(7) 31°38′.45 N, 031°48′.25 E (8) 31°44′.05 N, 031°57′.55 E

(b) A traffic lane for northbound traffic is established between the separation line and a separation line connecting the following geographical positions:

(9) 31°37′.50 N, 031°48′.00 E (10) 31°43′.55 N, 031°58′.10 E

(c) A traffic lane for southbound traffic is established between the separation line and a separation line connecting the following geographical positions:

(11) 31°39′.00 N, 031°47′.80 E (12) 31°44′.50 N, 031°57′.00 E

Western approaches to Bur Said

(a) A separation zone half a mile wide has the following geographical positions:

(13) 31°44′.25 N, 031°59′.30 E
(14) 31°44′.00 N, 031°58′.85 E
(15) 31°31′.85 N, 032°12′.95 E
(16) 31°32′.20 N, 032°13′.40 E

(b) A traffic lane for northbound traffic is established between the separation zone and a separation line connecting the following geographical positions (one mile wide):

(17) 31°32′.70 N, 032°14′.00 E (18) 31°44′.70 N, 032°00′.05 E

(c) A traffic lane for southbound traffic is established between the separation zone and a line connecting the following geographical positions (one mile wide):

(19) 31°31′.30 N, 032°12′.35 E (20) 31°43′.55 N, 031°58′.10 E

Eastern approach to Bur Said

(a) A separation zone half a mile wide has the following geographical positions:

(21)	31°35′.45 N,	032°22′.95 E	(23)	31°42′.55 N,	032°35′.65 E
(22)	31°35′.85 N,	032°22′.65 E	(24)	31°42′.15 N,	032°35′.95 E

(b) A traffic lane for northbound traffic is established between the separation zone and a line connecting the following geographical positions (one mile wide):

(25)	31°34′.80 N,	032°23′.40 E	(26)	31°46′.00 N,	032°45′.30 E

(c) A traffic lane for southbound traffic is established between the separation zone and a line connecting the following geographical positions (one mile wide):

(27)	31°46′.00 N,	032°35′.20 E	(29)	31°35′.80 N,	032°20′.80 E
(28)	31°43′.20 N,	032°35′.20 E			

Precautionary area

(d) A precautionary area north west of Bur Said is established by a line connecting the following geographical positions:

	31°45′.40 N,	031°55′.95 E	(18)	31°44′.70 N,	032°00′.05 E
(10)	31°43′.55 N,	031°58′.10 E		31°45′.40 N,	031°59′.52 E

(chartlet overleaf)

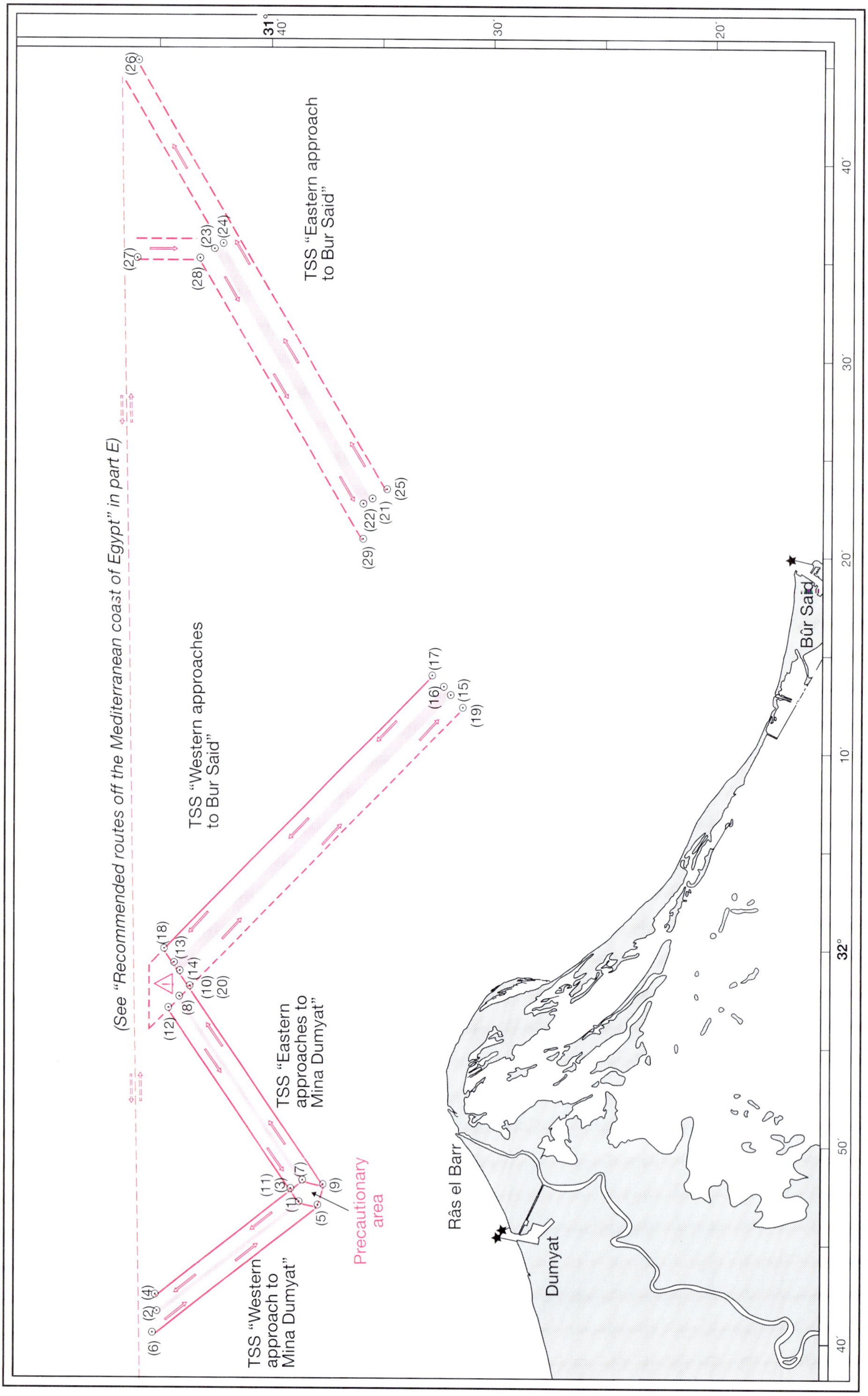

OFF THE MEDITERRANEAN COAST OF EGYPT

IN THE SOUTHERN APPROACHES TO THE KERCH STRAIT

(Reference chart: USSR 514, 1989 edition.
Note: This chart is based on the single geodetic datum for Soviet nautical charts.)

Description of the traffic separation scheme

(a) A separation zone is bounded by a line connecting the following geographical positions:

(1)	44°49′.70 N,	036°29′.00 E	(3)	44°49′.70 N,	036°31′.00 E
(2)	45°02′.30 N,	036°30′.00 E			

(b) A separation line connects the following geographical positions:

(2)	45°02′.30 N,	036°30′.00 E	(4)	45°06′.80 N,	036°30′.00 E

(c) A traffic lane for northbound traffic is established between the separation zone/line and a line connecting the following geographical positions:

(5)	44°49′.70 N,	036°33′.20 E	(6)	45°06′.80 N,	036°30′.30 E

(d) A traffic lane for southbound traffic is established between the separation zone/line and a line connecting the following geographical positions:

(7)	45°06′.80 N,	036°29′.70 E	(8)	44°49′.70 N,	036°26′.80 E

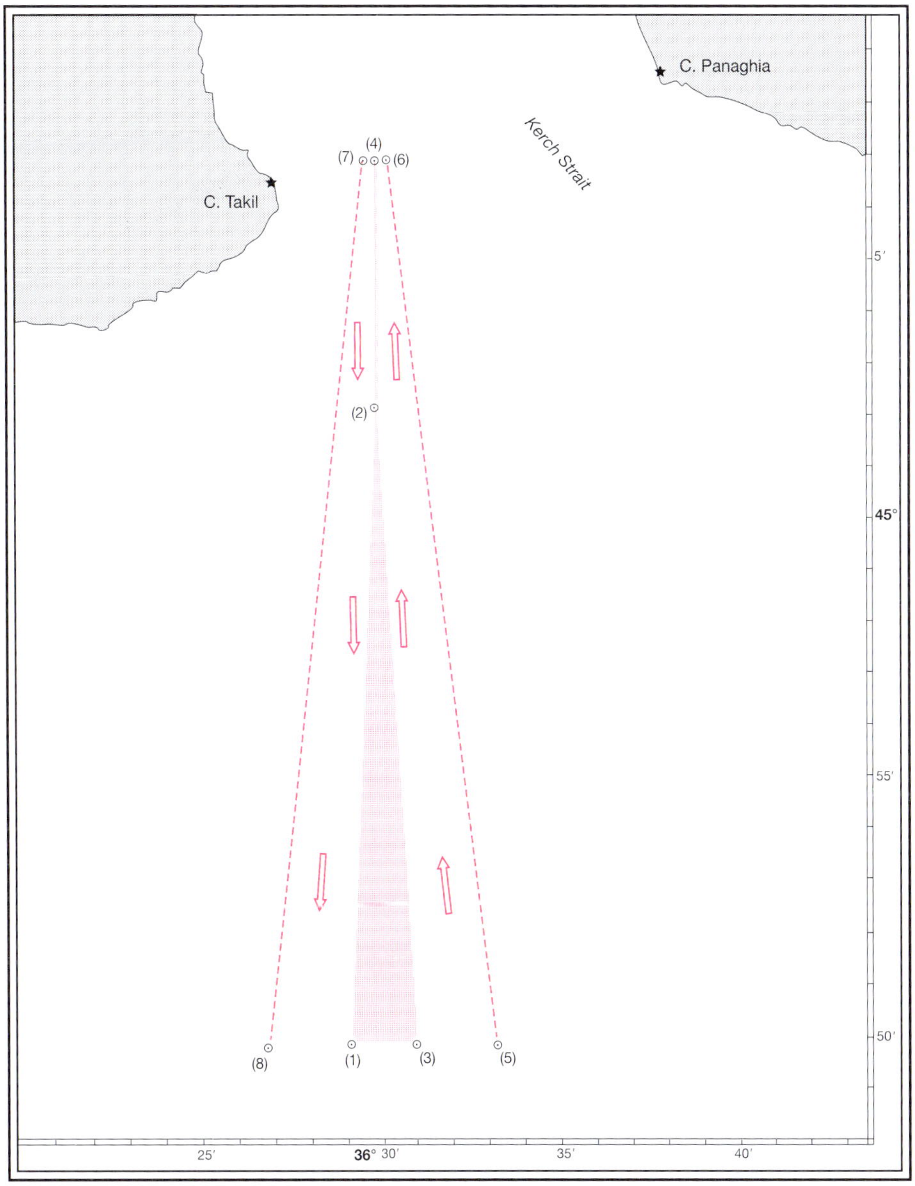

IN THE SOUTHERN APPROACHES TO THE KERCH STRAIT

IN THE AREA OFF THE SOUTH-WESTERN COAST OF THE CRIMEA

(Reference chart: State Hydrographic Service of Ukraine 3301 (published 03/2009).
Note: This chart is based on World Geodetic System 1984 datum (WGS 84).)

Description of the traffic separation scheme

The traffic separation scheme consists of two parts:

Part one, Routeing System No. 9 "Sevastopol Harbour Approach"; and

Part two, Routeing System No. 3 "From Cape Khersones to Cape Aitodor".

Note: All geographical positions are referred to WGS 84 datum.

Part one, Routeing System No. 9 "Sevastopol Harbour Approach"

The system consists of five elements.

Element I (Western) for entering (leaving) the roundabout area, which includes two traffic lanes and a traffic separation zone limited by lines connecting the following geographical positions:

(1)	44°40′.44 N,	033°08′.91 E	(3)	44°38′.59 N,	033°13′.31 E
(2)	44°39′.79 N,	033°13′.31 E	(4)	44°38′.84 N,	033°08′.91 E

The outer limit of the traffic lane for entering the roundabout area passes through the following geographical positions:

(5)	44°38′.04 N,	033°08′.91 E	(6)	44°37′.79 N,	033°13′.31 E

The established direction of the traffic flow is 094.5°.

The outer limit of the traffic lane for leaving the roundabout area passes through the following geographical positions:

(7)	44°40′.44 N,	033°13′.31 E	(8)	44°41′.09 N,	033°08′.91 E

The established direction of the traffic flow is 281°.

Element II (Northern) for entering (leaving) the roundabout area includes two traffic lanes and a traffic separation zone limited by lines connecting the following geographical positions:

(9)	44°43′.34 N,	033°14′.71 E	(12)	44°40′.19 N,	033°15′.21 E
(10)	44°40′.29 N,	033°16′.71 E	(13)	44°40′.89 N,	033°14′.71 E
(11)	44°40′.11 N,	033°15′.87 E			

The outer limit of the traffic lane for entering the roundabout area passes through the following geographical positions:

(14)	44°43′.34 N,	033°13′.31 E	(7)	44°40′.44 N,	033°13′.31 E

The established direction of the traffic flow is 180°.

The outer limit of the traffic lane for leaving the roundabout area passes through the following geographical positions:

(15)	44°40′.11 N,	033°17′.83 E	(16)	44°43′.34 N,	033°15′.73 E

The established direction of the traffic flow is 335°.

Element III (Southern) for entering (leaving) the roundabout area includes two traffic lanes and a traffic separation zone limited by lines connecting the following geographical positions:

(17)	44°37′.55 N,	033°15′.41 E	(19)	44°30′.73 N,	033°13′.29 E
(18)	44°37′.28 N,	033°16′.81 E	(20)	44°31′.64 N,	033°12′.19 E

The outer limit of the traffic lane for entering the roundabout area passes through the following geographical positions:

(21)	44°30′.09 N,	033°14′.06 E	(22)	44°37′.59 N,	033°18′.13 E

The established direction of the traffic flow is 021°.

The outer limit of the traffic lane for leaving the roundabout area passes through the following geographical positions:

(6)	44°37′.79 N,	033°13′.31 E	(23)	44°32′.84 N,	033°10′.63 E

The established direction of the traffic flow is 201°.

Element IV (roundabout area) includes the circular separation zone of the routeing system, with a radius of 5 cables, for which the centre is situated in the geographical position 44°38′.8 N, 033°16′.9 E, and a circular traffic lane 1.0 mile wide.

The established direction of the traffic flow is counter-clockwise around the circular separation zone.

Element V (Eastern) includes four traffic lanes and two traffic separation zones.

Separation zones are limited by lines connecting the following geographical positions:

A	(24)	44°38′.26 N,	033°18′.88 E	(26)	44°38′.69 N,	033°21′.41 E
	(25)	44°38′.99 N,	033°18′.96 E	(27)	44°38′.12 N,	033°21′.41 E
B	(28)	44°37′.97 N,	033°23′.91 E	(30)	44°37′.99 N,	033°25′.91 E
	(29)	44°38′.29 N,	033°23′.91 E	(31)	44°37′.89 N,	033°25′.91 E

The outer limits of the traffic lane for entering Sevastopol's'ka Bay pass through the following geographical positions:

(32)	44°37′.79 N,	033°18′.44 E	(33)	44°37′.63 N,	033°21′.41 E
and					
(34)	44°37′.49 N,	033°23′.93 E	(35)	44°37′.29 N,	033°27′.71 E

The established direction of the traffic flow is 094.5° (Inkermans'kyi leading line).

The outer limits of the traffic lane for leaving Sevastopol's'ka Bay pass through the following geographical positions:

(36)	44°38′.47 N,	033°27′.71 E	(37)	44°38′.99 N,	033°23′.93 E
and					
(38)	44°39′.34 N,	033°21′.41 E	(39)	44°39′.72 N,	033°18′.52 E

The established direction of the traffic flow is 280.9° (Kostiantynivs'kyi leading line).

Crossing northbound and southbound traffic should follow appropriate lanes on either side of a separation line which passes through the following geographical positions:

(40)	44°38′.52 N,	033°22′.91 E	(41)	44°38′.04 N,	033°22′.91 E

Lanes on both sides of the line are limited by separation zones. The established directions of the traffic flow are 000° (eastward of the separation line) and 180° (westward of the separation line).

Notes:

1 In the centre of the circular separation zone of the routeing system (44°38′.8 N, 033°16′.9 E) a special light buoy is positioned, light-yellow, flashing, 5s 5M (Y Fl 5s 5M).

2 Going out on Kostiantynivs'kyi leading lights should be followed:

- for all vessels: from geographical position 44°37′.44 N, 033°29′.61 E (crossing Inkermans'kyi and Lukul's'kyi leading lines);
- for vessels with actual draught over 10 metres: from geographical position 44°37′.49 N, 033°28′.56 E.

3 Separation of traffic at the crossing for northbound and southbound traffic is established for vessels following to/from Kozacha, Komysheva and Kruhla Bays and also vessels using anchorage point No. 386 and the degaussing range near Khersones Cape may enter/leave the system and cross Part V of the system.

4 Between meridians 33°26′.0 E and 033°28′.4 E, vessels following to/from Striletz'ka Bay and also vessels using anchorage points No. 384 and No. 386 and degaussing ranges northward from Kruhla Bay may enter/leave the system and cross Part V of the system.

Part two, Routeing System No. 3 "From Cape Khersones to Cape Aitodor"

The system consists of two elements.

Element I (North-western) includes a junction area, where the traffic separation scheme and local routes merge, associated separation zones, and two traffic lanes, limited by lines connecting the following geographical positions:

Route junction and separation of traffic at crossing:

A	(42)	44°30′.62 N,	033°11′.64 E	(44)	44°28′.72 N,	033°12′.21 E
	(43)	44°29′.73 N,	033°12′.75 E	(45)	44°29′.61 N,	033°11′.08 E

with the associated route junction border line passing through the following geographical positions:

(51)	44°28′.59 N,	033°10′.55 E	(52)	44°27′.74 N,	033°11′.63 E

Separation zone:

B	(46)	44°29′.12 N,	033°13′.52 E	(48)	44°17′.99 N,	033°25′.46 E
	(47)	44°17′.99 N,	033°27′.21 E	(49)	44°28′.09 N,	033°12′.99 E

The north-eastern border of the north-westbound traffic lane is limited by the line passing through the following geographical positions:

(50)	44°17′.99 N,	033°29′.11 E	(21)	44°30′.09 N,	033°14′.06 E

The established direction of the traffic flow is 318°.

The south-western border of the south-eastbound traffic lane is limited by the line passing through the following geographical positions:

A	(53)	44°27′.09 N,	033°12′.46 E	(54)	44°17′.99 N,	033°23′.71 E

The established direction of the traffic flow is 138°.

Element II (Eastern) includes a junction area, where the traffic separation scheme and local routes merge, associated separation zones and four traffic lanes limited by lines connecting the following geographical positions:

(53)	44°16′.99 N,	033°26′.71 E	(55)	44°15′.99 N,	033°29′.81 E
(54)	44°16′.99 N,	033°28′.51 E	(56)	44°15′.99 N,	033°28′.01 E

with the associated route junction border lines passing through the following geographical positions:

South-western

(55)	44°16′.99 N,	033°24′.91 E	(56)	44°15′.99 N,	033°26′.21 E

Southern

(72)	44°14′.99 N,	033°29′.31 E	(73)	44°14′.99 N,	033°31′.11 E

Two separation zones:

B	(61)	44°16′.99 N,	033°30′.31 E	(63)	44°15′.99 N,	034°03′.11 E
	(62)	44°16′.99 N,	034°03′.61 E	(64)	44°15′.99 N,	033°31′.61 E
C	(65)	44°16′.99 N,	034°06′.81 E	(67)	44°15′.99 N,	034°14′.91 E
	(66)	44°16′.99 N,	034°14′.91 E	(68)	44°15′.99 N,	034°06′.31 E

Traffic lanes

The northern borders of the westbound traffic lane are limited by lines passing through the following geographical positions:

A	(69)	44°17′.99 N,	034°14′.91 E	(70)	44°17′.99 N,	034°07′.31 E
B	(71)	44°17′.99 N,	034°04′.11 E	(50)	44°17′.99 N,	033°29′.11 E

The established direction of the traffic flow is 270°.

The southern borders of the eastbound traffic lane are limited by lines passing through the following geographical positions:

C	(74) 44°14′.99 N,	033°32′.91 E	(75)	44°14′.99 N,	034°02′.61 E
D	(76) 44°14′.99 N,	034°05′.81 E	(77)	44°14′.99 N,	034°14′.91 E

The established direction of the traffic flow is 090°.

Crossing north-eastbound and south-westbound traffic should follow appropriate lanes on either side of a line which passes through the following geographical positions:

(78) 44°16′.99 N, 034°05′.21 E (79) 44°15′.99 N, 034°04′.71 E

Lanes on both sides of the line are limited by the separation zones.

The established directions of the traffic flow are 020° (eastward of the separation line) and 200° (westward of the separation line).

Notes:

1 Traffic lanes alongside the traffic separation line are used by vessels following from the south to the port of Yalta and in the opposite direction.

2 While proceeding from Routeing System No. 3 to the port of Yalta and in the opposite direction, it is necessary to follow the recommended track No. 8.

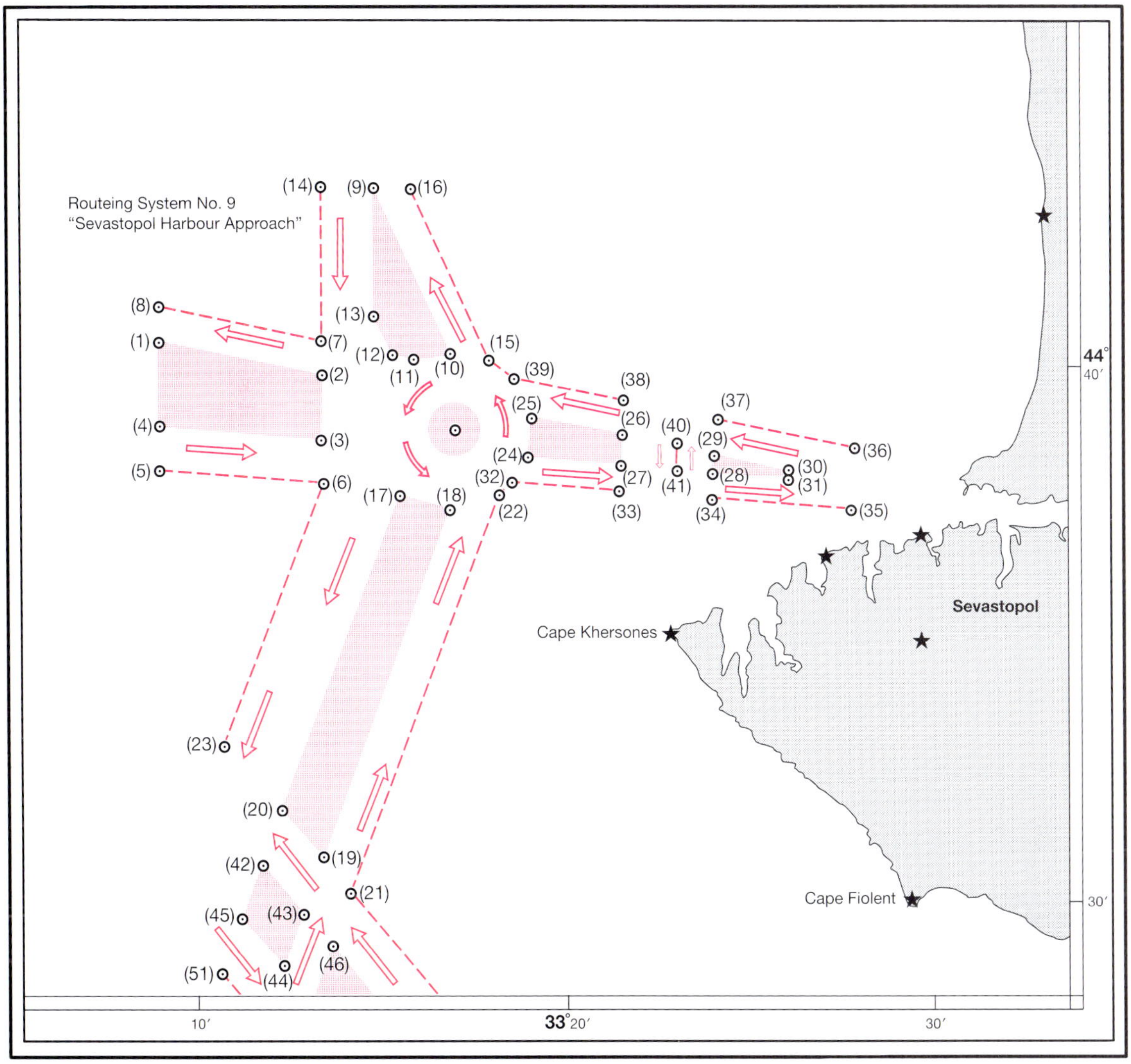

IN THE AREA OFF THE SOUTH-WESTERN COAST OF THE CRIMEA: SEVASTOPOL HARBOUR APPROACH

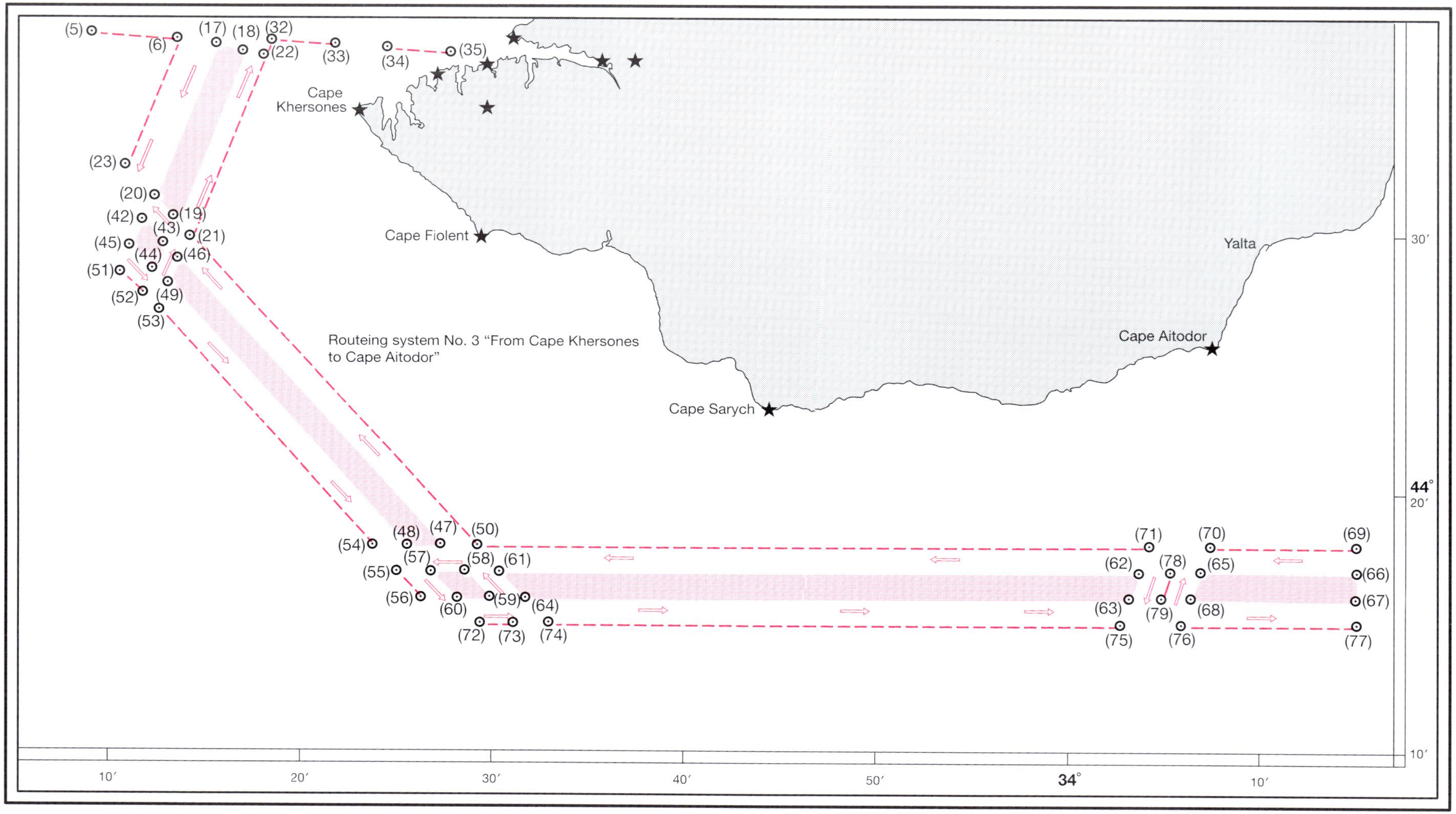

IN THE AREA OFF THE SOUTH-WESTERN COAST OF THE CRIMEA:
FROM CAPE KHERSONES TO CAPE AITODOR

BETWEEN THE PORTS OF ODESSA AND ILICHEVSK

(Reference chart: USSR 508, November 1974 edition.
Note: This chart is based on the system of co-ordinates used in Soviet marine navigational charts.)

Description of the traffic separation scheme

(a) A separation line connects the following geographical positions:

(1)	46°27′.30 N,	030°48′.50 E	(3)	46°19′.10 N,	030°44′.80 E
(2)	46°21′.90 N,	030°47′.40 E			

(b) A traffic lane, one quarter of a mile wide, is established on each side of the separation line.

IN THE APPROACHES TO THE PORTS OF ODESSA AND ILICHEVSK

(Reference chart: USSR 508, November 1974 edition.
Note: This chart is based on the system of co-ordinates used in Soviet marine navigational charts.)

Description of the traffic separation scheme

The traffic separation scheme consists of four parts:

Part I:

(a) A separation zone, two miles wide, is centred upon the following geographical positions:

(1)	46°08′.20 N,	031°06′.10 E	(2)	46°13′.00 N,	030°59′.60 E

(b) An outside boundary of an inbound traffic lane connects the following geographical positions:

(3)	46°09′.60 N,	031°08′.10 E	(4)	46°14′.70 N,	031°01′.00 E

(c) An outside boundary of an outbound traffic lane connects the following geographical positions:

(5)	46°06′.90 N,	031°04′.10 E	(6)	46°12′.10 N,	030°57′.10 E

Part II:

(a) A roundabout consists of a circular separation zone of two miles in diameter with its centre at the point:

(7) 46°15′.60 N, 030°56′.10 E

and a circular traffic lane, two and a half miles wide, around the zone indicated.

CAUTION:
The roundabout may be entered and left by ships going from the arm of Prorva to the Bugsko–Dneprovsko–Limanskiy Channel and back.

Part III:
Approaches to the Port of Odessa

(a) A separation zone, half a mile wide, is centred upon the following geographical positions:

(8)	46°18′.50 N,	030°53′.50 E	(9)	46°27′.50 N,	030°50′.40 E

(b) An outside boundary of the inbound traffic lane connects the following geographical positions:

(10)	46°18′.90 N,	030°54′.60 E	(11)	46°27′.70 N,	030°51′.60 E

(c) An outside boundary of the outbound traffic lane connects the following geographical positions:

(12)	46°27′.50 N,	030°49′.20 E	(13)	46°18′.00 N,	030°52′.50 E

Part IV:
Approaches to the Port of Ilichevsk

(a) A separation zone, half a mile wide, is centred upon the following geographical positions:

(14)	46°16′.70 N,	030°51′.40 E	(15)	46°18′.00 N,	030°45′.80 E

(b) An outside boundary of the inbound traffic lane connects the following geographical positions:

(16)	46°17′.50 N,	030°51′.80 E	(17)	46°18′.80 N,	030°46′.40 E

(c) An outside boundary of the outbound traffic lane connects the following geographical positions:

(18)	46°15′.90 N,	030°51′.05 E	(19)	46°17′.20 N,	030°45′.30 E

(chartlet overleaf)

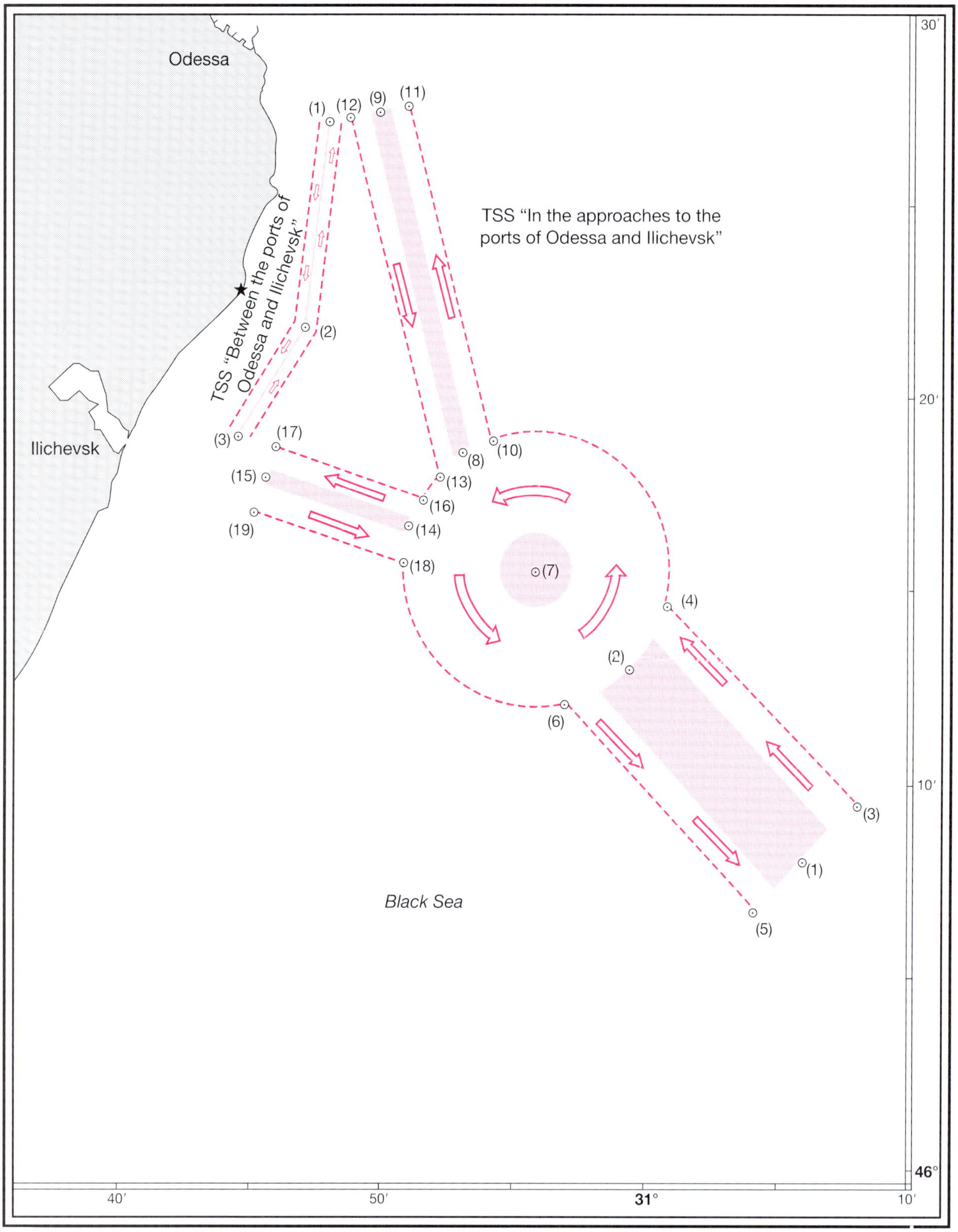

BETWEEN THE PORTS OF ODESSA AND ILICHEVSK +
IN THE APPROACHES TO THE PORTS OF ODESSA AND ILICHEVSK

B

STRAIT OF ISTANBUL – NORTH APPROACH

Note: See "Rules and recommendations on navigation through the Strait of Istanbul, the Strait of Çanakkale and the Marmara Sea" in part F.

(Reference chart: Turkish 1811 (INT 3758), 1993 edition.
Note: This chart is based on European datum.)

Description of the traffic separation scheme

(a) A separation zone is bounded by a line connecting the following geographical positions:

(1)	41°20′.50 N,	029°09′.90 E	(3)	41°13′.60 N,	029°07′.98 E
(2)	41°20′.00 N,	029°12′.50 E			

(b) A traffic lane for north-eastbound traffic is established between the separation zone and the line connecting the following geographical positions:

(4)	41°15′.80 N,	029°16′.90 E	(6)	41°13′.36 N,	029°08′.55 E
(5)	41°14′.10 N,	029°10′.00 E			

(c) A traffic lane for southbound and south-westbound traffic is established between the separation zone and the line connecting the following geographical positions:

(7)	41°19′.40 N,	029°02′.00 E	(9)	41°13′.80 N,	029°07′.50 E
(8)	41°14′.70 N,	029°07′.20 E			

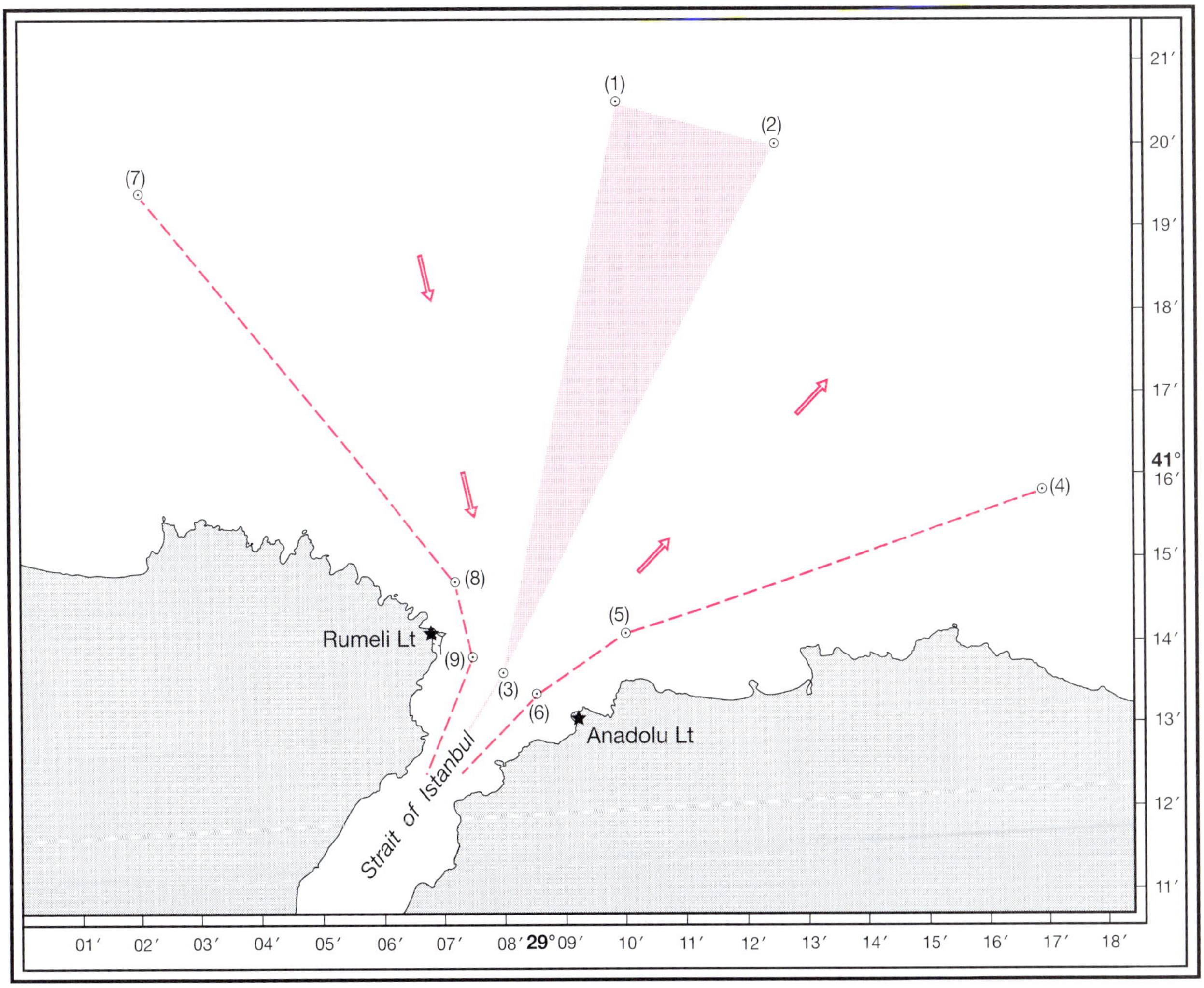

STRAIT OF ISTANBUL – NORTH APPROACH

B

STRAIT OF ISTANBUL

Note: See "Rules and recommendations on navigation through the Strait of Istanbul, the Strait of Çanakkale and the Marmara Sea" in part F.

(Reference charts: Turkish 2921 (INT 3756), 1993 edition; 2921A, 1992 edition and 2921B, 1992 edition.
Note: These charts are based on European datum.)

Description of the traffic separation scheme

The traffic lanes encompass the area defined by the line joining the Anadolu lighthouse and Rumeli lighthouse in the north, the line joining the Ahirkapi lighthouse and Kadiköy Cape Inci breakwater lighthouse in the south and the outer boundaries of the lanes whose co-ordinates are given below:

(a) A separation line connects the following geographical positions:

(3)	41°13′.60 N,	029°07′.98 E	(17)	41°06′.00 N,	029°03′.67 E
(10)	41°12′.18 N,	029°06′.83 E	(18)	41°04′.98 N,	029°03′.65 E
(11)	41°10′.88 N,	029°05′.08 E	(19)	41°04′.53 N,	029°03′.17 E
(12)	41°09′.38 N,	029°03′.53 E	(20)	41°03′.10 N,	029°02′.60 E
(13)	41°08′.92 N,	029°03′.53 E	(21)	41°01′.55 N,	028°59′.91 E
(14)	41°07′.38 N,	029°05′.00 E	(22)	41°01′.40 N,	028°59′.80 E
(15)	41°07′.21 N,	029°05′.00 E	(23)	41°00′.15 N,	028°59′.75 E
(16)	41°06′.38 N,	029°03′.81 E			

(b) A traffic lane for northbound traffic is established between the separation line and the following geographical positions:

(24)	41°00′.00 N,	029°00′.06 E	(32)	41°07′.20 N,	029°05′.40 E
(25)	41°01′.10 N,	029°00′.07 E	(33)	41°07′.40 N,	029°05′.35 E
(26)	41°01′.50 N,	029°00′.20 E	(34)	41°08′.85 N,	029°03′.89 E
(27)	41°03′.10 N,	029°02′.96 E	(35)	41°09′.48 N,	029°03′.84 E
(28)	41°04′.50 N,	029°03′.33 E	(36)	41°10′.80 N,	029°05′.20 E
(29)	41°04′.97 N,	029°03′.92 E	(37)	41°11′.67 N,	029°06′.78 E
(30)	41°06′.05 N,	029°03′.85 E	(38)	41°12′.30 N,	029°07′.20 E
(31)	41°06′.35 N,	029°04′.00 E	(6)	41°13′.36 N,	029°08′.55 E

(c) A traffic lane for southbound traffic is established between the separation line and the following geographical positions:

(9)	41°13′.80 N,	029°07′.50 E	(46)	41°05′.13 N,	029°03′.53 E
(39)	41°12′.30 N,	029°06′.63 E	(47)	41°04′.92 N,	029°03′.40 E
(40)	41°12′.00 N,	029°06′.00 E	(48)	41°04′.57 N,	029°02′.94 E
(41)	41°10′.51 N,	029°04′.50 E	(49)	41°04′.13 N,	029°02′.85 E
(42)	41°09′.52 N,	029°03′.29 E	(50)	41°02′.97 N,	029°02′.07 E
(43)	41°09′.03 N,	029°03′.27 E	(51)	41°01′.73 N,	028°59′.73 E
(44)	41°07′.48 N,	029°04′.62 E	(52)	41°01′.29 N,	028°59′.45 E
(45)	41°06′.25 N,	029°03′.50 E	(53)	41°00′.30 N,	028°59′.42 E

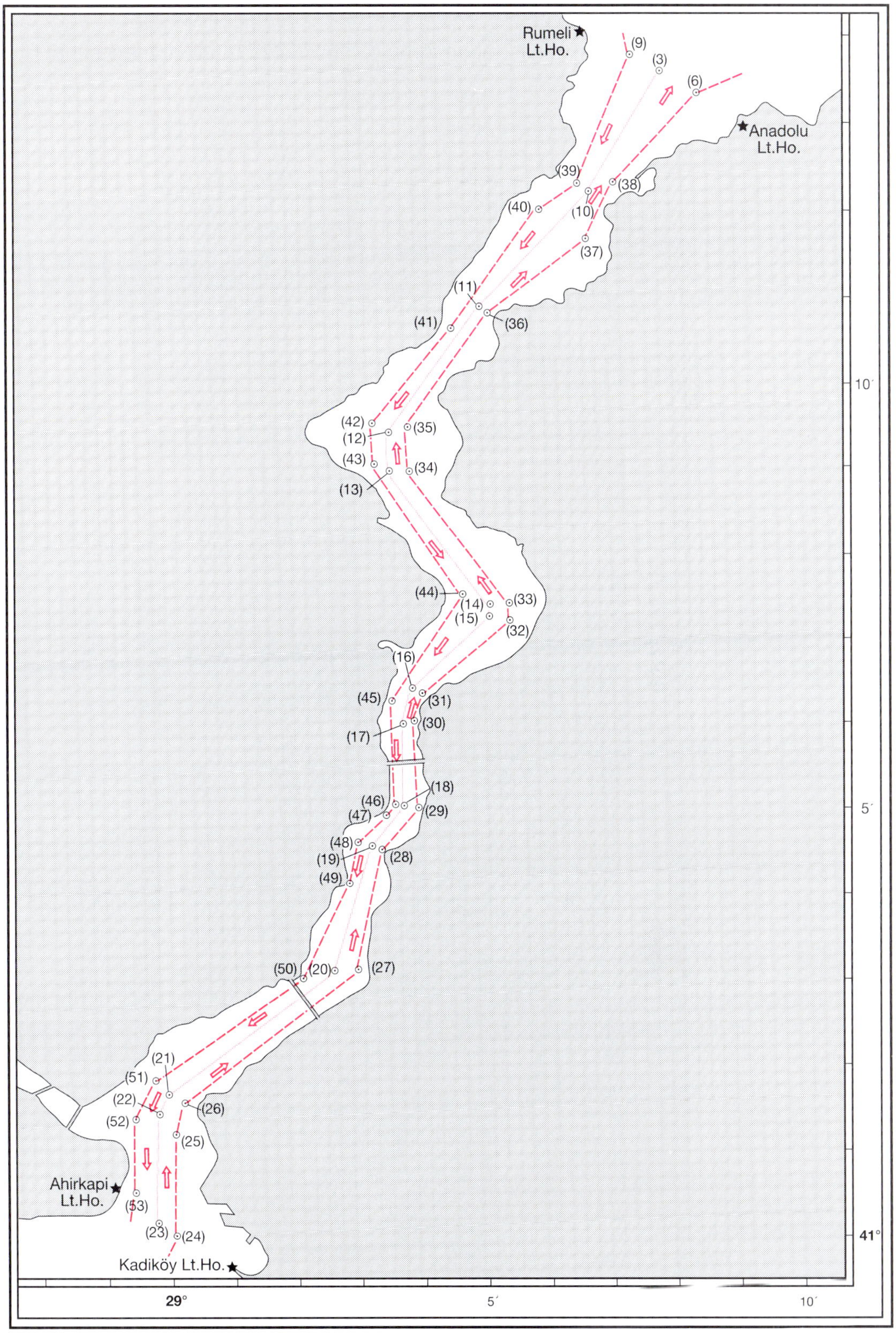

STRAIT OF ISTANBUL

STRAIT OF ISTANBUL – SOUTH APPROACH AND SEA OF MARMARA

Note: See "Rules and recommendations on navigation through the Strait of Istanbul, the Strait of Çanakkale and the Marmara Sea" in part F.

(Reference charts: Turkish 2923 (INT 3754), 1991 edition; 293, 1990 edition; 295 (INT 3752), 1988 edition. **Note:** These charts are based on European datum.)

Description of the traffic separation scheme

(a) A separation line connects the following geographical positions:

(22)	41°01′.40 N,	028°59′.80 E	(54)	40°59′.53 N,	028°59′.73 E
(23)	41°00′.15 N,	028°59′.75 E	(55)	40°58′.80 N,	028°59′.44 E

(b) A separation zone is bounded by a line joining the following geographical positions:

(55)	40°58′.80 N,	028°59′.44 E	(57)	40°57′.78 N,	028°58′.11 E
(56)	40°57′.53 N,	028°58′.63 E			

(c) A precautionary area is established bounded by a line joining the following geographical positions:

(71)	40°58′.21 N,	028°57′.22 E	(68)	40°53′.78 N,	028°57′.15 E
(57)	40°57′.78 N,	028°58′.11 E	(78)	40°52′.90 N,	028°55′.92 E
(56)	40°57′.53 N,	028°58′.63 E	(59)	40°54′.30 N,	028°55′.40 E
(81A)	40°56′.83 N,	029°00′.06 E	(65)	40°55′.58 N,	028°54′.82 E
(81)	40°55′.00 N,	029°00′.06 E	(71A)	40°56′.83 N,	028°54′.23 E
(67)	40°54′.70 N,	028°58′.55 E			

(d) The focal point of the precautionary area is located at the following geographical position:

(58) 40°56′.10 N, 028°57′.00 E

A circular area to be avoided with a 0.15 mile radius is established around position (58).

(e) A separation zone is bounded by a line joining the following geographical positions:

(59)	40°54′.30 N,	028°55′.40 E	(63)	40°45′.42 N,	027°38′.09 E
(60)	40°52′.40 N,	028°52′.10 E	(64)	40°53′.90 N,	028°52′.10 E
(61)	40°44′.20 N,	027°38′.09 E	(65)	40°55′.58 N,	028°54′.82 E
(62)	40°26′.00 N,	026°45′.25 E			

(f) A separation zone is bounded by a line connecting the following geographical positions:

(66)	40°51′.50 N,	029°00′.31 E	(68)	40°53′.78 N,	028°57′.15 E
(67)	40°54′.70 N,	028°58′.55 E	(69)	40°51′.95 N,	028°58′.00 E

(g) A traffic lane for traffic bound for the Çanakkale Strait is established in the Sea of Marmara between the separation zones/lines in paragraphs (a), (b), (c), (d) and (e) above and a line connecting the following geographical positions:

(53)	41°00′.30 N,	028°59′.42 E	(72)	40°55′.89 N,	028°52′.09 E
(70)	40°59′.50 N,	028°59′.39 E	(73)	40°47′.40 N,	027°38′.09 E
(71)	40°58′.21 N,	028°57′.22 E	(74)	40°26′.50 N,	026°45′.25 E

(h) A traffic lane for traffic bound for the Strait of Istanbul is established in the Sea of Marmara between the separation zones/lines in paragraphs (e), (d), (c), (b) and (a) above and a line connecting the following geographical positions:

(75)	40°25′.50 N,	026°45′.25 E	(77)	40°50′.39 N,	028°52′.07 E
(76)	40°42′.20 N,	027°38′.09 E	(78)	40°52′.90 N,	028°55′.92 E

(i) A traffic lane for traffic from the Strait of Istanbul headed for the Gulf of Izmit is established between the traffic lane/separation zones in paragraphs (c), (e), (f) and (g) above and a line connecting the following geographical positions:

(78)	40°52′.90 N,	028°55′.92 E	(79)	40°51′.50 N,	028°56′.57 E

(j) A traffic lane for traffic from the south and south-east of the Sea of Marmara and the Gulf of Izmit sailing toward the Strait of Istanbul is established between the traffic separation zone in paragraph (f) and a line connecting the following geographical positions:

(80)	40°52′.00 N,	029°01′.73 E	(24)	41°00′.00 N,	029°00′.06 E
(81)	40°55′.00 N,	029°00′.06 E			

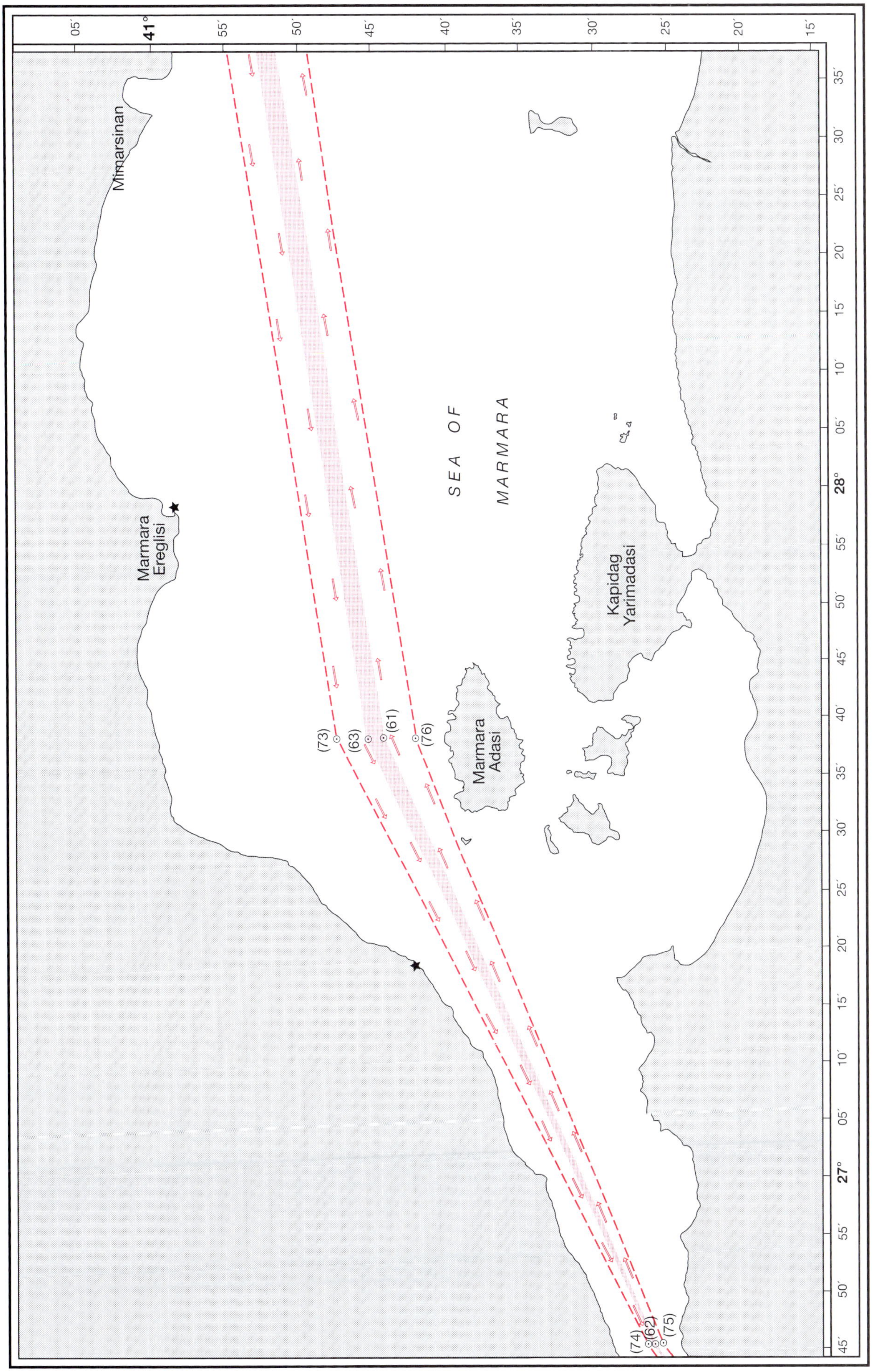

STRAIT OF ISTANBUL – SOUTH APPROACH AND SEA OF MARMARA (WEST)

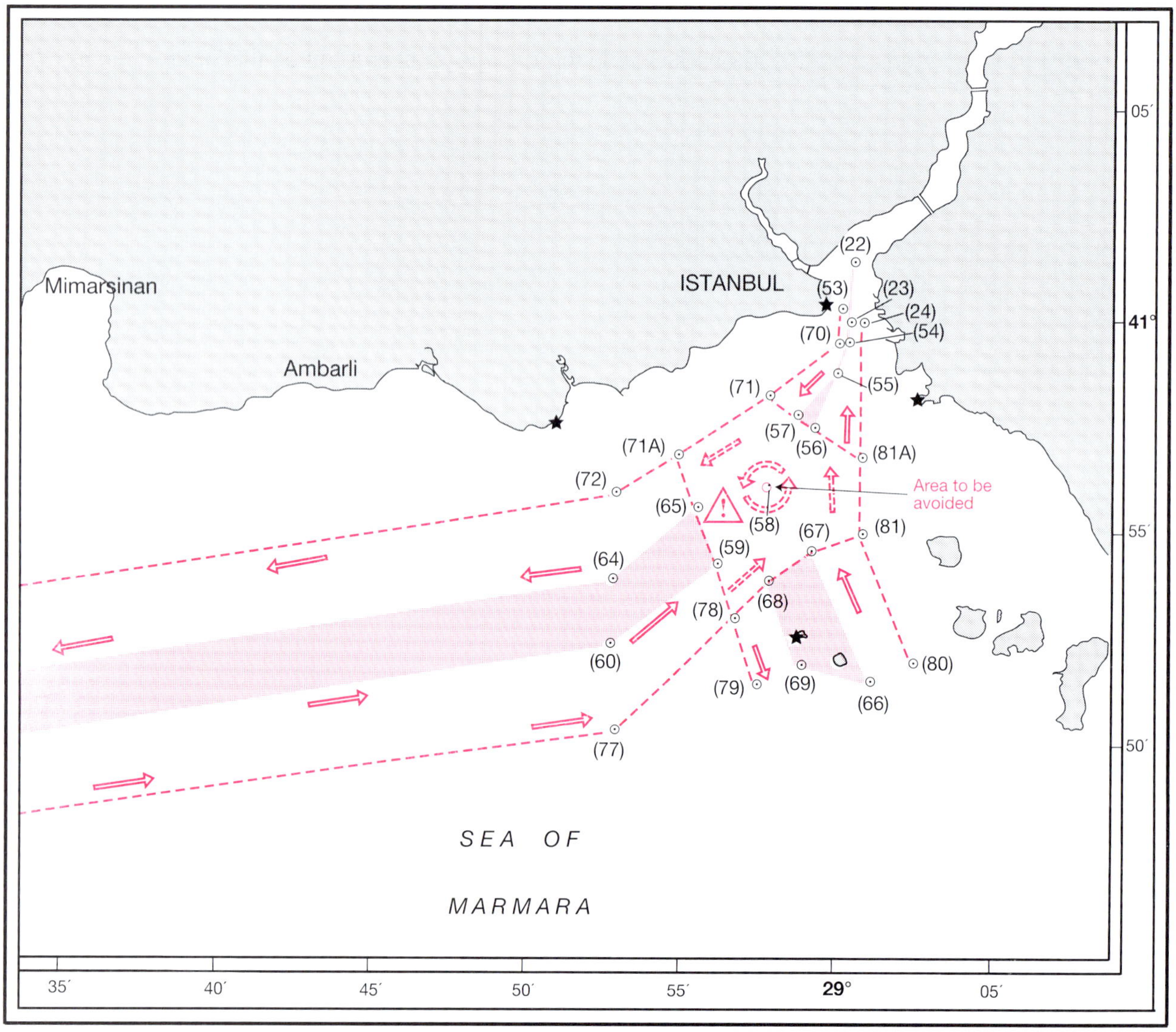

STRAIT OF ISTANBUL – SOUTH APPROACH AND SEA OF MARMARA (EAST)

B

STRAIT OF ÇANAKKALE

Note: See "Rules and recommendations on navigation through the Strait of Istanbul, the Strait of Çanakkale and the Marmara Sea" in part F.

(Reference chart: Turkish 212 (INT 3750), 1991 edition.
Note: This chart is based on European datum.)

Description of the traffic separation scheme

The Strait of Çanakkale traffic lane is the area between the line joining Cape Mehmetcik lighthouse and Cape Kumkale lighthouse in the south-west, the line joining the Gelibolu lighthouse to the Cardak lighthouse in the north-east, and the outer boundaries of the Strait of Çanakkale traffic lane whose co-ordinates are given below:

(a) A separation line connects the following geographical positions:

(62)	40°26′.00 N,	026°45′.25 E	(88)	40°11′.63 N,	026°22′.95 E
(82)	40°24′.05 N,	026°41′.65 E	(89)	40°09′.00 N,	026°23′.40 E
(83)	40°22′.83 N,	026°40′.21 E	(90)	40°08′.55 N,	026°23′.31 E
(84)	40°20′.90 N,	026°38′.55 E	(91)	40°08′.15 N,	026°23′.09 E
(85)	40°18′.62 N,	026°35′.88 E	(92)	40°04′.25 N,	026°18′.54 E
(86)	40°13′.40 N,	026°27′.80 E	(93)	40°02′.59 N,	026°15′.44 E
(87)	40°12′.11 N,	026°23′.50 E			

(b) A separation zone is bounded by a line connecting the following geographical positions:

(93)	40°02′.59 N,	026°15′.45 E	(125)	40°01′.28 N,	026°11′.41 E
(120)	40°01′.52 N,	026°11′.18 E	(126)	40°01′.90 N,	026°14′.32 E

(c) A traffic lane for north-eastbound traffic is established between the separation zone/line in paragraphs (b) and (a) above and a line connecting the following geographical positions:

(94)	40°00′.99 N,	026°11′.70 E	(101)	40°13′.10 N,	026°28′.90 E
(95)	40°01′.10 N,	026°15′.01 E	(102)	40°16′.90 N,	026°34′.35 E
(96)	40°01′.90 N,	026°17′.22 E	(103)	40°18′.10 N,	026°36′.30 E
(97)	40°07′.70 N,	026°23′.48 E	(104)	40°20′.50 N,	026°39′.18 E
(98)	40°08′.90 N,	026°23′.70 E	(105)	40°23′.65 N,	026°42′.04 E
(99)	40°09′.50 N,	026°23′.95 E	(75)	40°25′.50 N,	026°45′.25 E
(100)	40°11′.84 N,	026°23′.62 E			

(d) A traffic lane for south-westbound traffic is established between the separation zone/line in paragraphs (b) and (a) above and a line connecting the following geographical positions:

(74)	40°26′.50 N,	026°45′.25 E	(113)	40°12′.02 N,	026°22′.50 E
(106)	40°24′.45 N,	026°41′.20 E	(114)	40°11′.39 N,	026°22′.19 E
(107)	40°23′.20 N,	026°39′.25 E	(115)	40°08′.73 N,	026°23′.10 E
(108)	40°21′.30 N,	026°37′.82 E	(116)	40°08′.42 N,	026°22′.91 E
(109)	40°19′.10 N,	026°35′.45 E	(117)	40°05′.60 N,	026°18′.95 E
(110)	40°14′.50 N,	026°27′.88 E	(118)	40°02′.67 N,	026°13′.24 E
(111)	40°13′.12 N,	026°25′.55 E	(119)	40°02′.00 N,	026°11′.03 E
(112)	40°12′.46 N,	026°23′.31 E			

(chartlet overleaf)

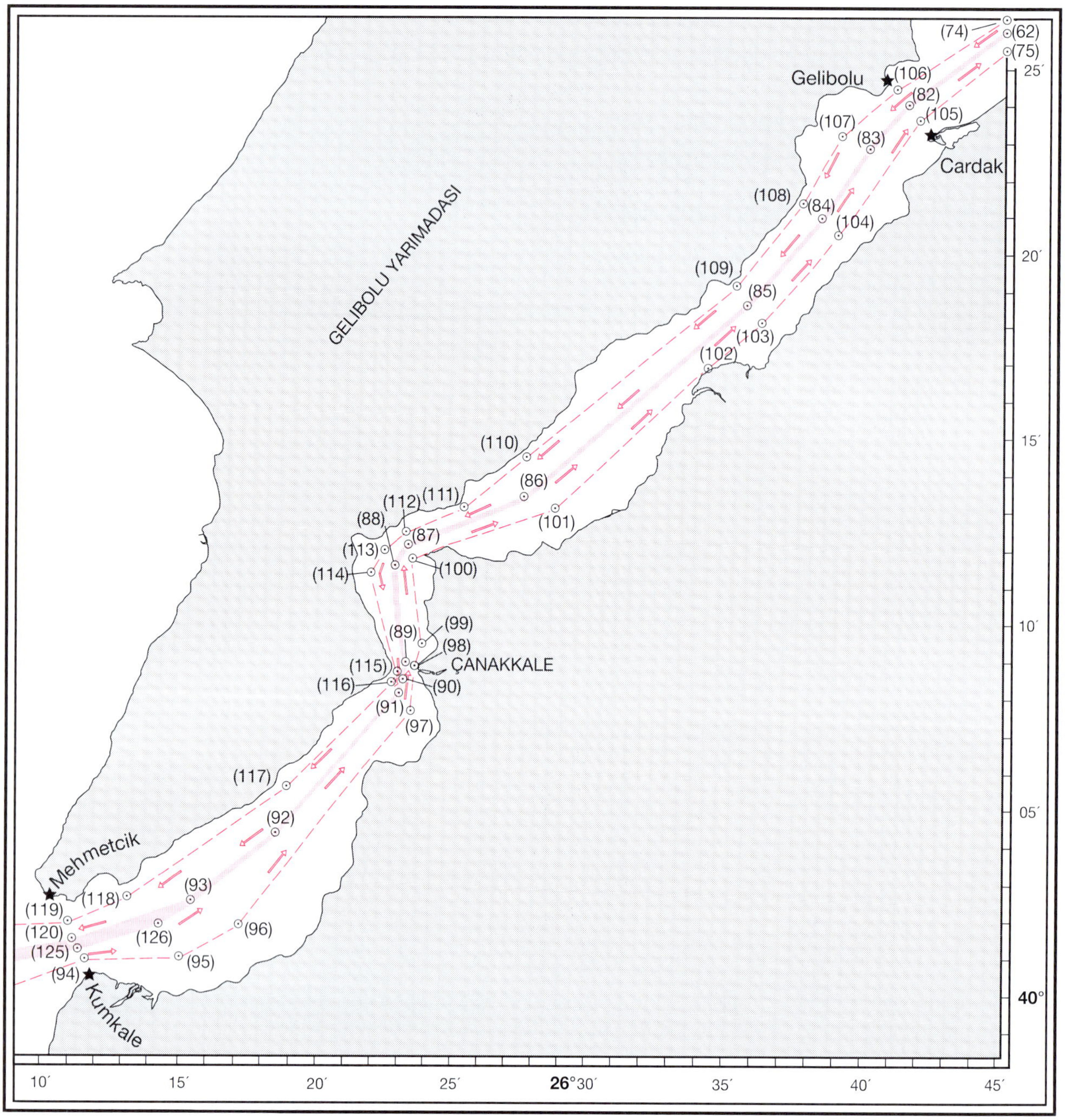

STRAIT OF ÇANAKKALE

STRAIT OF ÇANAKKALE – SOUTH-WEST APPROACH

Note: See "Rules and recommendations on navigation through the Strait of Istanbul, the Strait of Çanakkale and the Marmara Sea" in part F.

(Reference charts: Turkish 2134, 1992 edition; 213, 1993 edition.
Note: These charts are based on European datum.)

Description of the traffic separation scheme

(a) A separation zone is bounded by a line connecting the following geographical positions:

(120)	40°01′.52 N,	026°11′.18 E	(123) 39°57′.20 N,	025°57′.70 E
(121)	40°00′.20 N,	025°59′.70 E	(124) 39°59′.70 N,	026°00′.40 E
(122)	39°58′.80 N,	025°57′.70 E	(125) 40°01′.28 N,	026°11′.41 E

(b) A traffic lane for westbound traffic is established between the separation zone and a line connecting the following geographical positions:

(119)	40°02′.00 N,	026°11′.03 E	(127) 40°01′.55 N,	025°57′.70 E

(c) A traffic lane for north-eastbound traffic is established between the separation zone and a line connecting the following geographical positions:

(94)	40°00′.99 N,	026°11′.70 E	(129) 39°55′.00 N,	025°57′.70 E
(128)	39°58′.29 N,	026°01′.60 E		

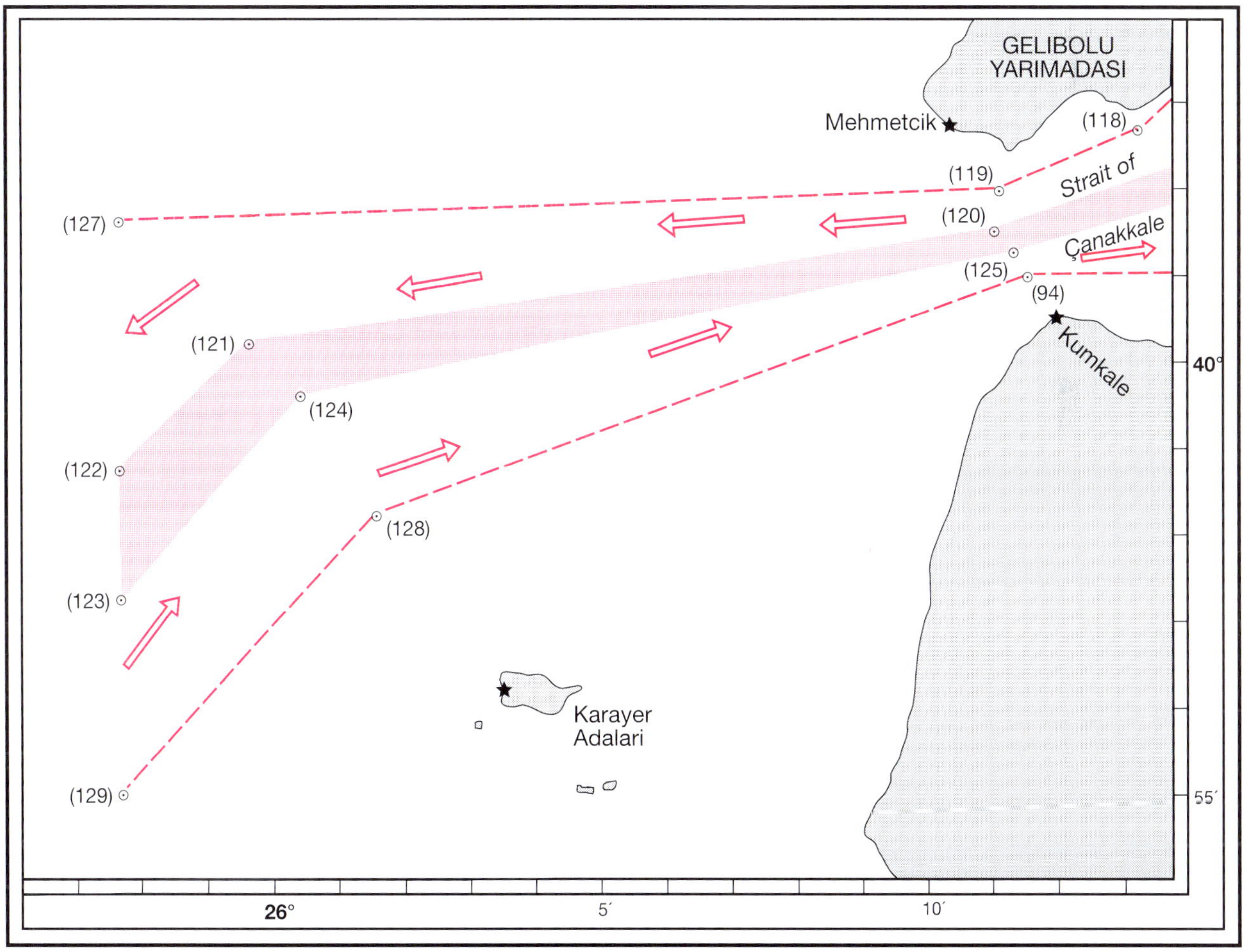

STRAIT OF ÇANAKKALE – SOUTH-WEST APPROACH

Section IV

Indian Ocean and adjacent waters

Caution: The chartlets are for illustrative purposes only and must not be used for navigation. Mariners should consult the appropriate nautical publications and charts for up-to-date details on aids to navigation and other relevant information.

Warning: The geographical positions given in the descriptions of the routeing systems are only correct for charts using the same geodetic datum as the reference charts indicated under each scheme. Charts published by other hydrographic offices may use a different geodetic datum, as may new editions of the reference charts published after the adoption of the routeing system. Where amendments to existing systems are not based on the same geodetic datum as the original system, this is emphasized by the use of different colours for definitions of positions.

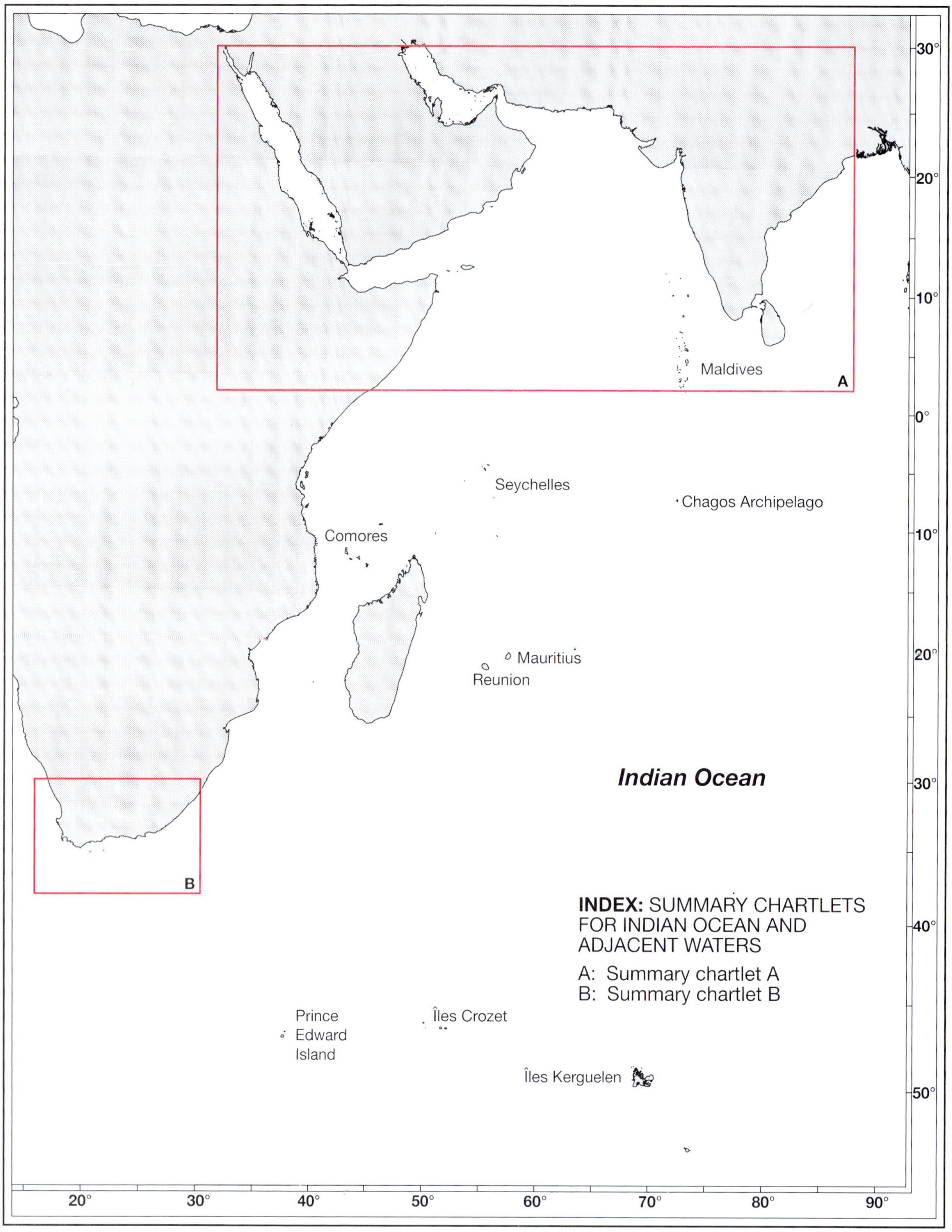
30°
20°
10°
0°
10°
20°
30°
40°
50°
20°
30°
40°
50°
60°
70°
80°
90°
A
B
Maldives
Seychelles
Chagos Archipelago
Comores
Mauritius
Reunion
Indian Ocean
Prince Edward Island
Îles Crozet
Îles Kerguelen
INDEX: SUMMARY CHARTLETS FOR INDIAN OCEAN AND ADJACENT WATERS
A: Summary chartlet A
B: Summary chartlet B

SUMMARY CHARTLET A

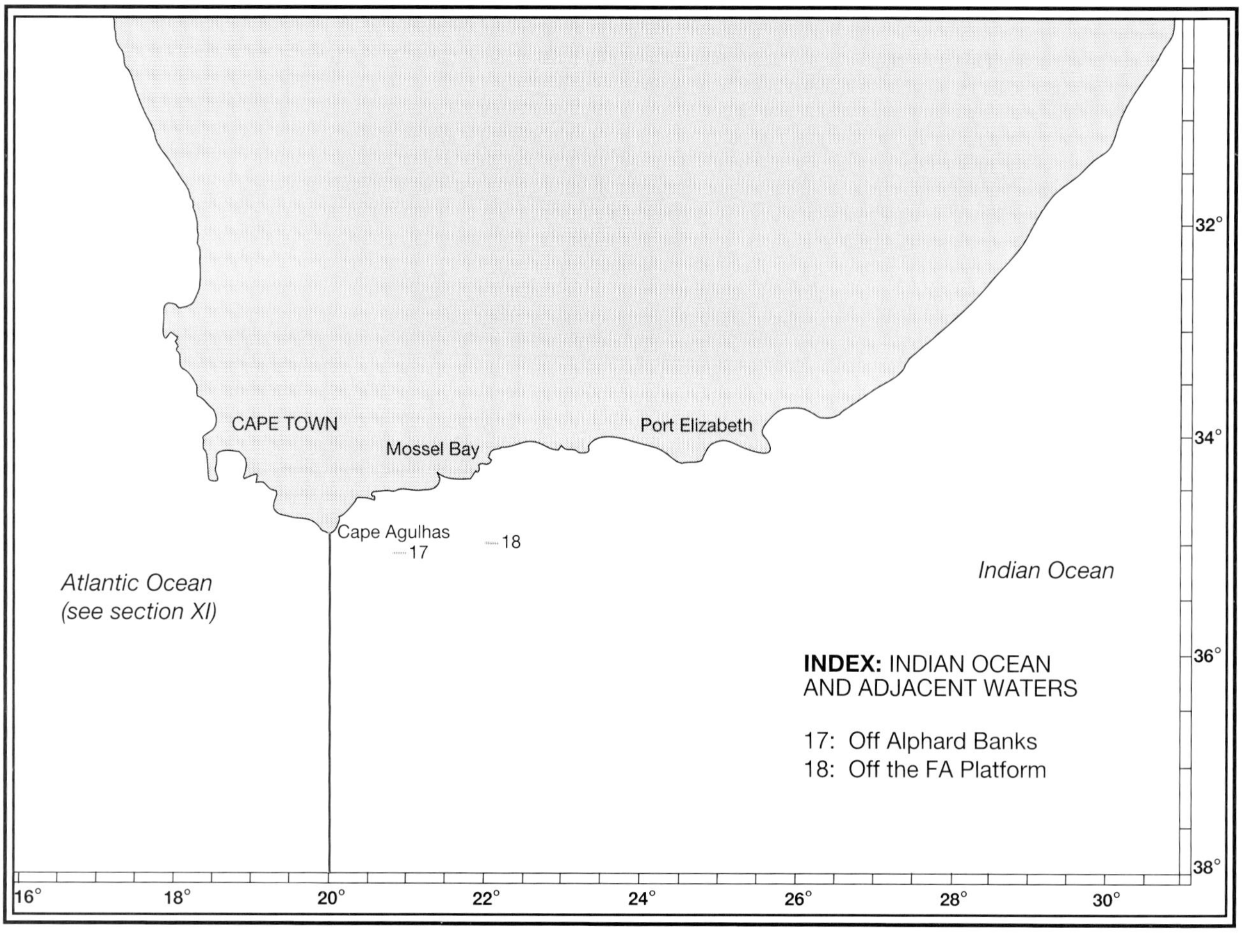

SUMMARY CHARTLET B

IN THE GULF OF SUEZ

Note: See "Rules for ships navigating in the Gulf of Suez" in part F and "Recommended directions of traffic flow off Ras Shukheir" in part E.

(Reference charts: British Admiralty 2373, 1997 edition; 2374, 1997 edition; 2375, 1997 edition; 2090, 1997 edition; 2098, 1997 edition.
Note: These charts are based on World Geodetic System 1984 datum (WGS 84).)

Description of the traffic separation scheme

Part A:
Northern scheme

(a) A separation zone is bounded by a line connecting the following geographical positions:

(1)	29°46′.60 N,	032°31′.80 E	(3)	29°38′.00 N,	032°32′.90 E
(2)	29°37′.89 N,	032°32′.10 E	(4)	29°46′.60 N,	032°32′.25 E

(b) A separation line connects the following geographical positions:

(5)	29°37′.97 N,	032°32′.50 E	(6)	29°35′.55 N,	032°32′.90 E

(c) A separation zone is bounded by a line connecting the following geographical positions:

(7)	29°35′.56 N,	032°32′.60 E	(9)	29°28′.68 N,	032°36′.50 E
(8)	29°29′.10 N,	032°35′.60 E	(10)	29°35′.53 N,	032°33′.25 E

(d) A separation line connects the following geographical positions:

(11)	29°28′.90 N,	032°36′.05 E	(12)	29°25′.20 N,	032°37′.80 E

(e) A separation zone is bounded by a line connecting the following geographical positions:

(13)	29°25′.50 N,	032°37′.30 E	(18)	28°11′.25 N,	033°19′.70 E
(14)	29°09′.00 N,	032°45′.80 E,	(19)	28°36′.00 N,	033°02′.40 E
(15)	28°45′.70 N,	032°54′.90 E	(20)	29°09′.20 N,	032°46′.50 E
(16)	28°15′.25 N,	033°14′.40 E	(21)	29°24′.90 N,	032°38′.20 E
(17)	28°10′.55 N,	033°18′.40 E			

(f) A traffic lane for southbound traffic is established between:

(i) The separation zone and a line connecting the following geographical positions:

(22)	29°46′.60 N,	032°30′.80 E	(23)	29°37′.58 N,	032°30′.10 E

(ii) The separation line and a line connecting the following geographical positions:

(24)	29°37′.58 N,	032°30′.10 E	(25)	29°35′.68 N,	032°29′.95 E

(iii) The separation zone and a line connecting the following geographical positions:

(26)	29°35′.68 N,	032°29′.95 E	(27)	29°30′.60 N,	032°32′.35 E

(iv) The separation line and a line connecting the following geographical positions:

(28)	29°30′.60 N,	032°32′.35 E	(29)	29°27′.60 N,	032°33′.90 E

(v) The separation zone and a line connecting the following geographical positions:

(30)	29°27′.60 N,	032°33′.90 E	(33)	28°15′.00 N,	033°12′.60 E
(31)	29°08′.20 N,	032°43′.80 E	(34)	28°09′.80 N,	033°17′.00 E
(32)	28°45′.80 N,	032°52′.70 E			

(g) A traffic lane for northbound traffic is established between the separation zone/line and a line connecting the following geographical positions:

(35)	28°11′.95 N,	033°20′.90 E	(38)	29°22′.80 N,	032°41′.50 E
(36)	28°36′.00 N,	033°04′.80 E	(39)	29°35′.45 N,	032°35′.40 E
(37)	29°10′.00 N,	032°48′.40 E	(40)	29°46′.60 N,	032°33′.40 E

B

Part B:
Southern scheme

(h) A separation zone is bounded by a line connecting the following geographical positions:

(41)	28°08′.15 N,	033°21′.70 E	(46)	27°44′.20 N,	033°50′.35 E
(42)	27°49′.65 N,	033°44′.10 E	(47)	27°50′.20 N,	033°44′.50 E
(43)	27°43′.60 N,	033°50′.00 E	(48)	27°53′.00 N,	033°41′.40 E
(44)	27°30′.20 N,	034°05′.45 E	(49)	27°54′.60 N,	033°38′.85 E
(45)	27°31′.05 N,	034°06′.40 E	(50)	28°08′.55 N,	033°22′.30 E

(i) A traffic lane for southbound traffic is established between the separation zone and a line connecting the following geographical positions:

(51)	28°07′.40 N,	033°20′.40 E	(53)	27°42′.45 N,	033°49′.40 E
(52)	27°48′.70 N,	033°43′.40 E	(54)	27°28′.65 N,	034°03′.90 E

(j) A traffic lane for northbound traffic is established between the separation zone and a line connecting the following geographical positions:

(55)	27°33′.15 N,	034°08′.60 E	(58)	27°53′.75 N,	033°42′.65 E
(56)	27°45′.20 N,	033°50′.95 E	(59)	27°56′.35 N,	033°38′.40 E
(57)	27°51′.35 N,	033°45′.35 E	(60)	28°09′.30 N,	033°23′.60 E

Part C:
Junction scheme off Ain Sukhna

(k) A separation zone is bounded by a line connecting the following geographical positions:

(61)	29°32′.27 N,	032°28′.80 E	(63)	29°35′.68 N,	032°29′.95 E
(62)	29°30′.60 N,	032°32′.35 E	(64)	29°35′.80 N,	032°27′.50 E

(l) A traffic lane for south-eastbound traffic is established between the separation zone and a line connecting the following geographical positions:

(65)	29°30′.50 N,	032°29′.35 E	(66)	29°27′.60 N,	032°33′.90 E

(m) A traffic lane for westbound traffic is established between the separation zone and a line connecting the following geographical positions:

(67)	29°37′.58 N,	032°30′.10 E	(68)	29°37′.11 N,	032°27′.00 E

Part D:
Precautionary area off Ras Shukheir

(n) A precautionary area is established by a line connecting the following geographical positions:

(69)	28°09′.80 N,	033°17′.00 E	(71)	28°09′.30 N,	033°23′.60 E
(70)	28°06′.80 N,	033°19′.40 E	(72)	28°12′.20 N,	033°21′.40 E

Note: Recommended directions of traffic flow off Ras Shukheir:
Recommended directions of traffic flow are established in the approaches to Ras Shukheir Oil Terminal, July, Ramadan and Morgan oilfields.

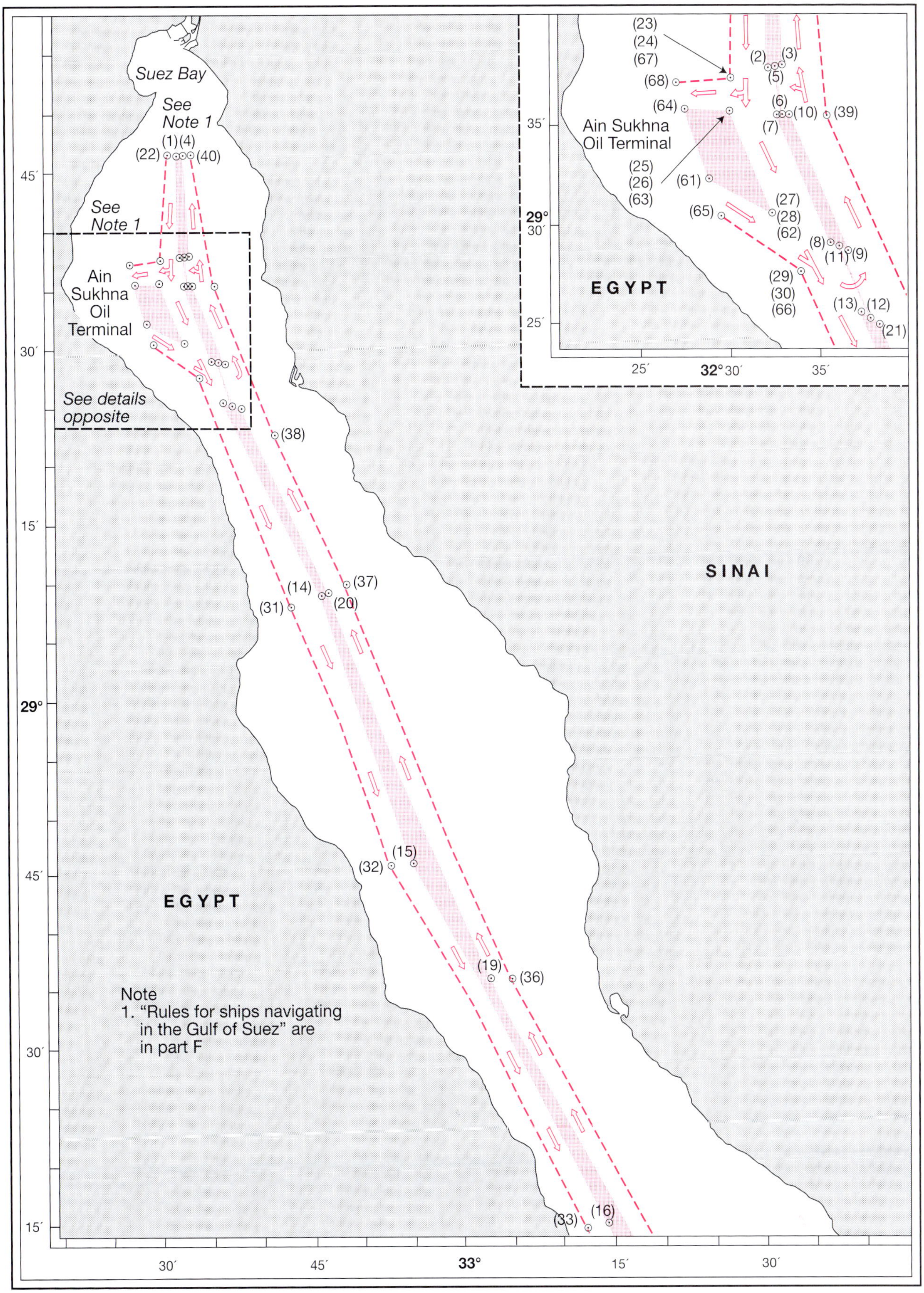

IN THE GULF OF SUEZ (NORTH)

B

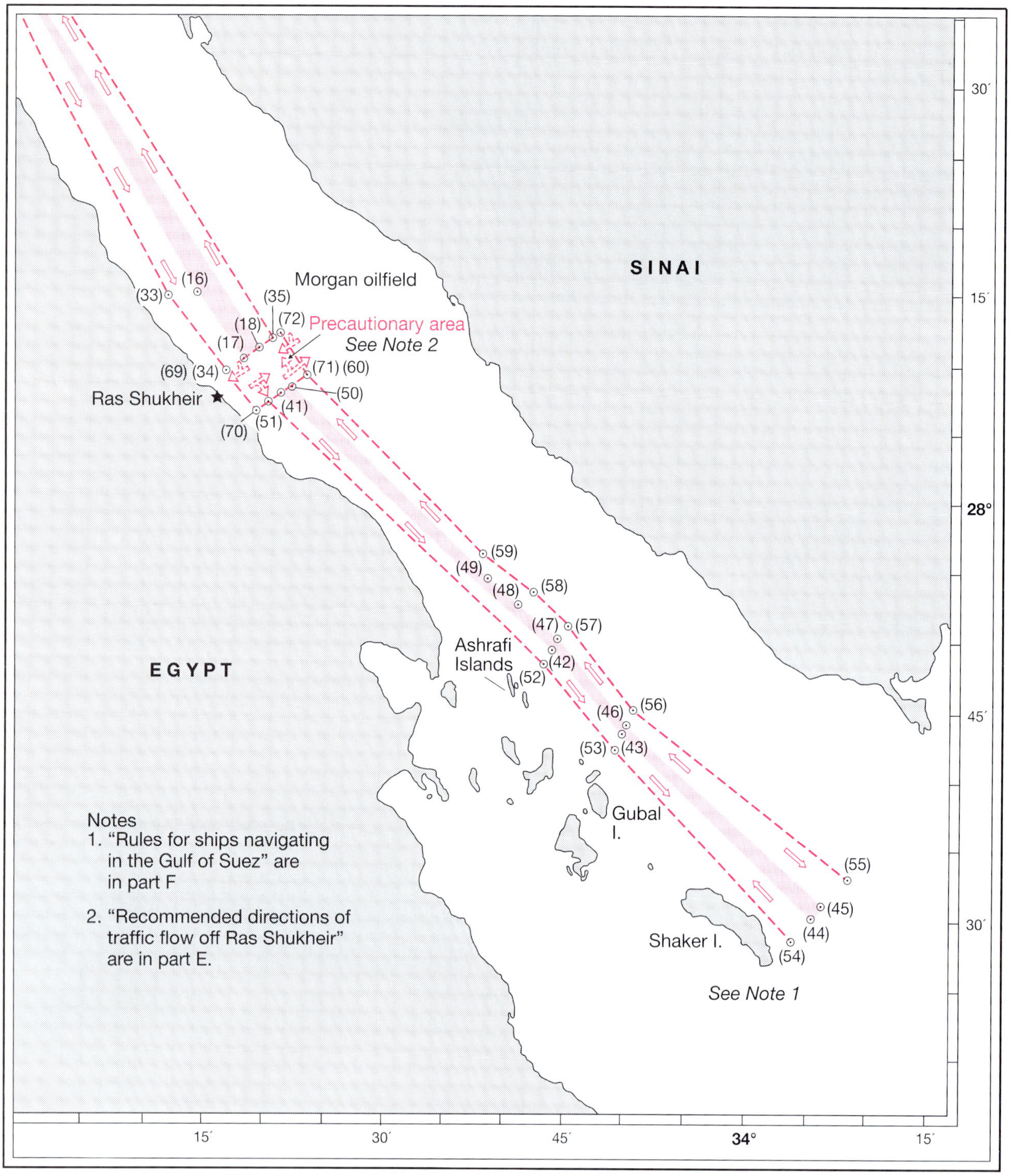

IN THE GULF OF SUEZ (SOUTH)

IN THE ENTRANCE TO THE GULF OF AQABA

(Reference chart: British Admiralty 3595, 1986 edition.
Note: This chart is based on European datum.)

Description of the traffic separation scheme

(a) A separation zone is bounded by a line connecting the following geographical positions:

(1) 28°01′.00 N, 034°27′.38 E
(2) 27°57′.00 N, 034°26′.45 E
(3) 27°57′.00 N, 034°27′.75 E
(4) 28°01′.00 N, 034°28′.69 E

(b) A traffic lane for southbound traffic is established between the separation zone and a line joining the following geographical positions:

(5) 28°01′.00 N, 034°26′.81 E
(6) 27°57′.00 N, 034°25′.88 E

(c) A traffic lane for northbound traffic is established between the separation zone and a line joining the following geographical positions:

(7) 27°57′.00 N, 034°28′.22 E
(8) 28°01′.00 N, 034°29′.15 E

Aids to navigation for entrance to the Gulf of Aqaba

	Station	Co-ordinates		Light characteristics		Range (N M) (T=0.74)	Racon/ Radio mon.	Tower – Daymark
		Lat. (N)	Long. (E)	Colour	Rhythm			
Northbound channel	Chisholm Point	27°57′.00	34°30′.20	White	Fl(2+1).20 s	9	Racon (Morse C) +Rad. mon.	10 m GRP – Pigmented white
Northbound channel	Reef west of Johnson Point	28°00′.00	34°29′.02	Green	Fl.10 s	5	Rad. mon.	5 m GRP – Pigmented green
Northbound channel	Reef north-west of Johnson Point	28°00′.94	34°29′.20	Green	Fl(2).20 s	5	Rad. mon.	5 m GRP – Pigmented: upper half green, lower white
Northbound channel	Jackson Reef (east)	28°00′.58	34°28′.55	Red	Fl.10 s	5	Rad. mon.	5 m GRP – Pigmented red. Synchronized with W. Johnson
Southbound channel	Ras Nusrani	27°58′.89	34°26′.16	White Green	Fl.10 s Occ.7 s	15 5	Racon (Morse Y) +Rad. mon	10 m GRP – Pigmented green
Southbound channel	Gordon Reef (west)	27°59′.25	34°26′.99	Red	Occ.7 s	5	Racon (Morse G) +Rad. mon.	10 m GRP – Pigmented red over white. Light synchronized with green light of Ras Nusrani

(chartlet overleaf)

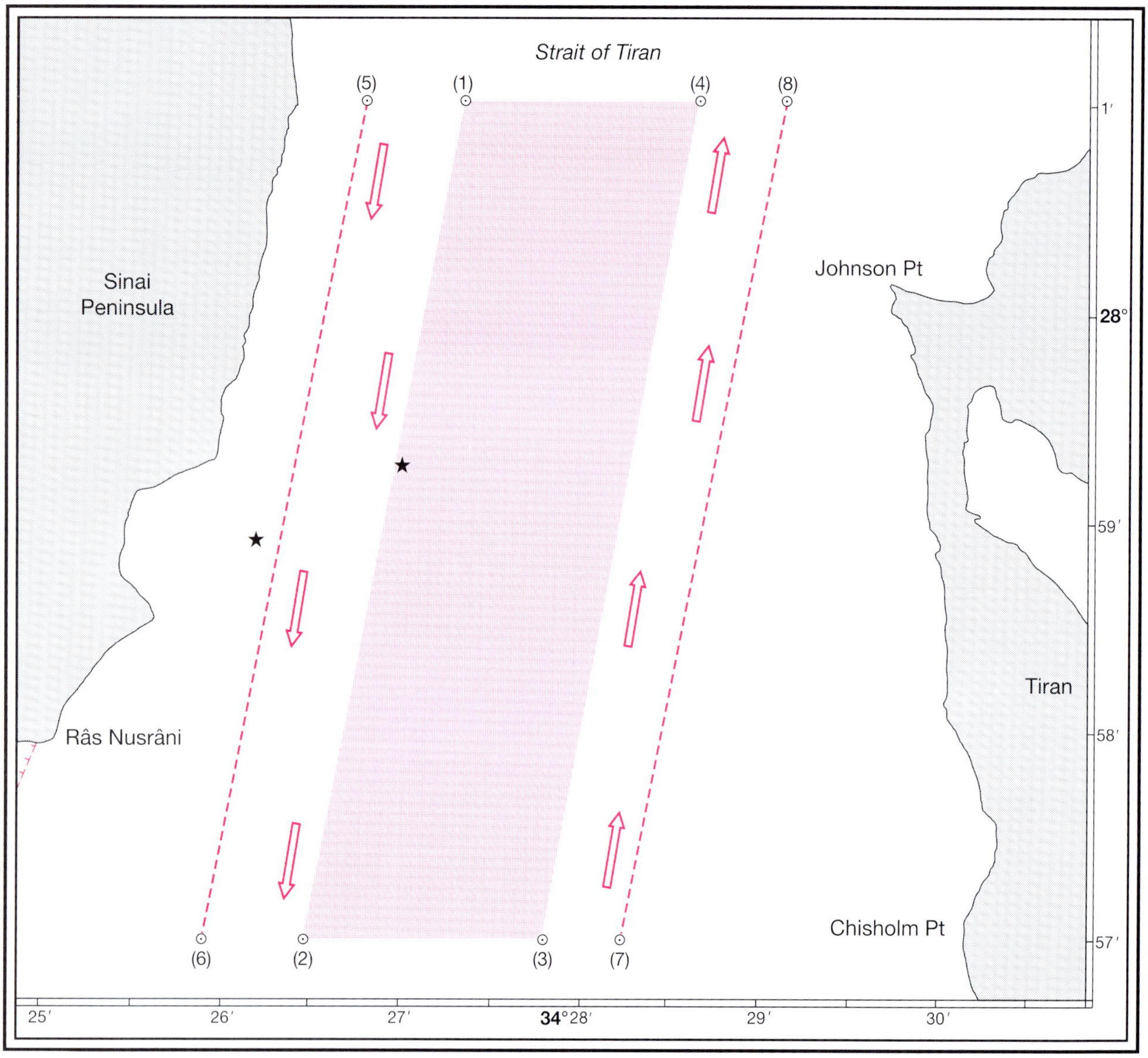

IN THE ENTRANCE TO THE GULF OF AQABA

NEAR THE DEEP-WATER ROUTE LEADING TO JAZAN ECONOMIC CITY PORT

(Reference chart: British Admiralty 15, edition 2, 22 June 2000.
Note: This chart is based on World Geodetic System 1984 datum (WGS 84).)

Description of the traffic separation scheme

(a) A separation zone is bounded by the lines connecting the following geographical positions:

(1)	16°56′.48 N,	041°17′.16 E	(3)	17°01′.87 N,	041°20′.98 E
(2)	16°56′.13 N,	041°17′.70 E	(4)	17°02′.20 N,	041°20′.49 E

Thence back to the point of origin (1)

(b) A traffic lane for northbound traffic is established between the separation zone (a) and a line connecting the following geographical positions:

(5)	16°55′.72 N,	041°18′.42 E	(6)	17°01′.52 N,	041°21′.63 E

(c) A traffic lane for southbound traffic is established between the separation zone (a) and a line connecting the following geographical positions:

(7)	17°02′.48 N,	041°19′.90 E	(8)	16°56′.74 N,	041°16′.59 E

B

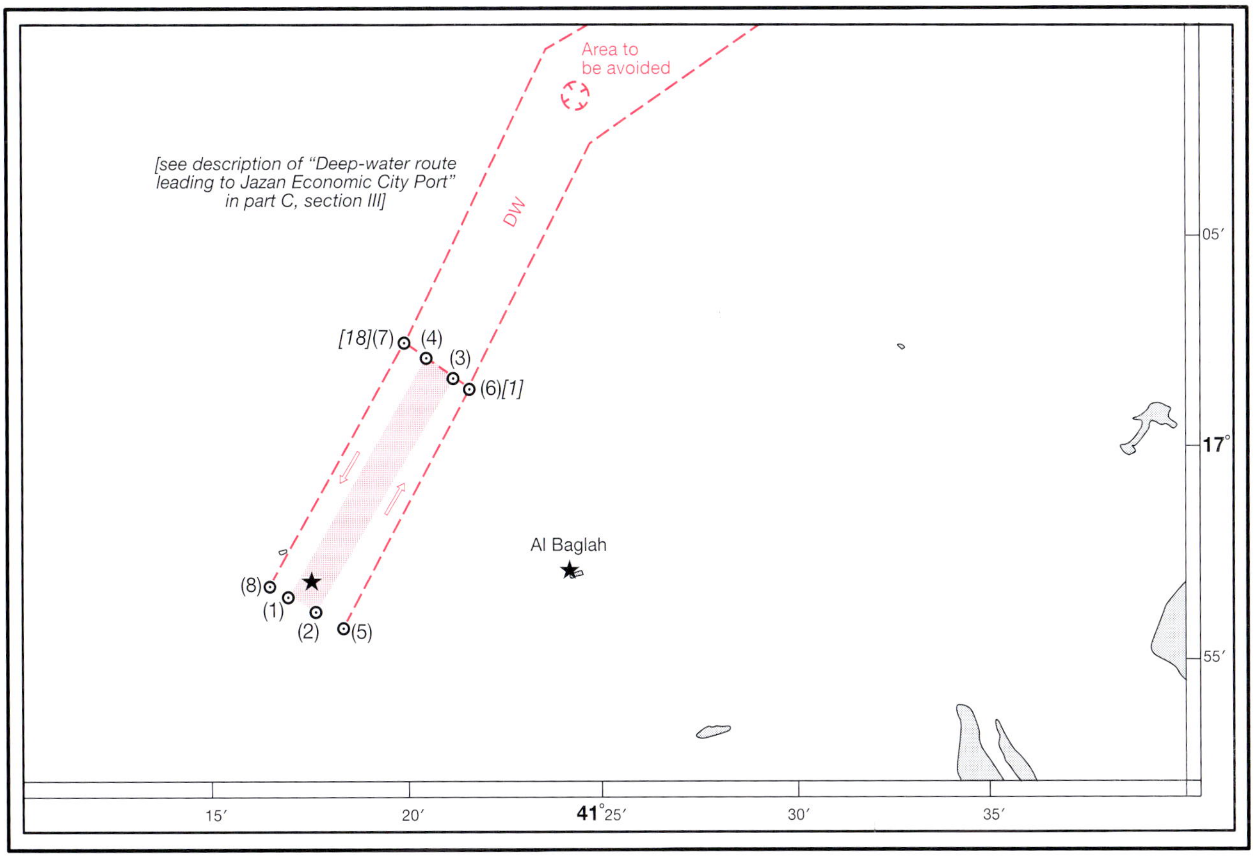

NEAR THE DEEP-WATER ROUTE LEADING TO JAZAN ECONOMIC CITY PORT

IN THE SOUTHERN RED SEA – WEST AND SOUTH OF HANISH AL KUBRA

(Reference charts: British Admiralty 452, 2002 edition; 453, 2002 edition.
Note: These charts are based on World Geodetic System 1984 datum (WGS 84).)

Description of the traffic separation scheme

(a) A separation zone bounded by a line connecting the following geographical positions:

(1)	13°38′.33 N,	042°31′.78 E	(4)	13°29′.12 N,	042°44′.22 E
(2)	13°30′.95 N,	042°35′.60 E	(5)	13°33′.20 N,	042°39′.08 E
(3)	13°26′.61 N,	042°42′.18 E	(6)	13°40′.15 N,	042°35′.50 E

(b) A traffic lane for southbound traffic between the separation zone and a line connecting the following geographical positions:

(7)	13°37′.40 N,	042°29′.93 E	(9)	13°25′.22 N,	042°41′.05 E
(8)	13°29′.82 N,	042°33′.88 E			

(c) A traffic lane for northbound traffic between the separation zone and a line connecting the following geographical positions:

(10)	13°40′.82 N,	042°36′.90 E	(12)	13°30′.25 N,	042°45′.18 E
(11)	13°34′.06 N,	042°40′.38 E			

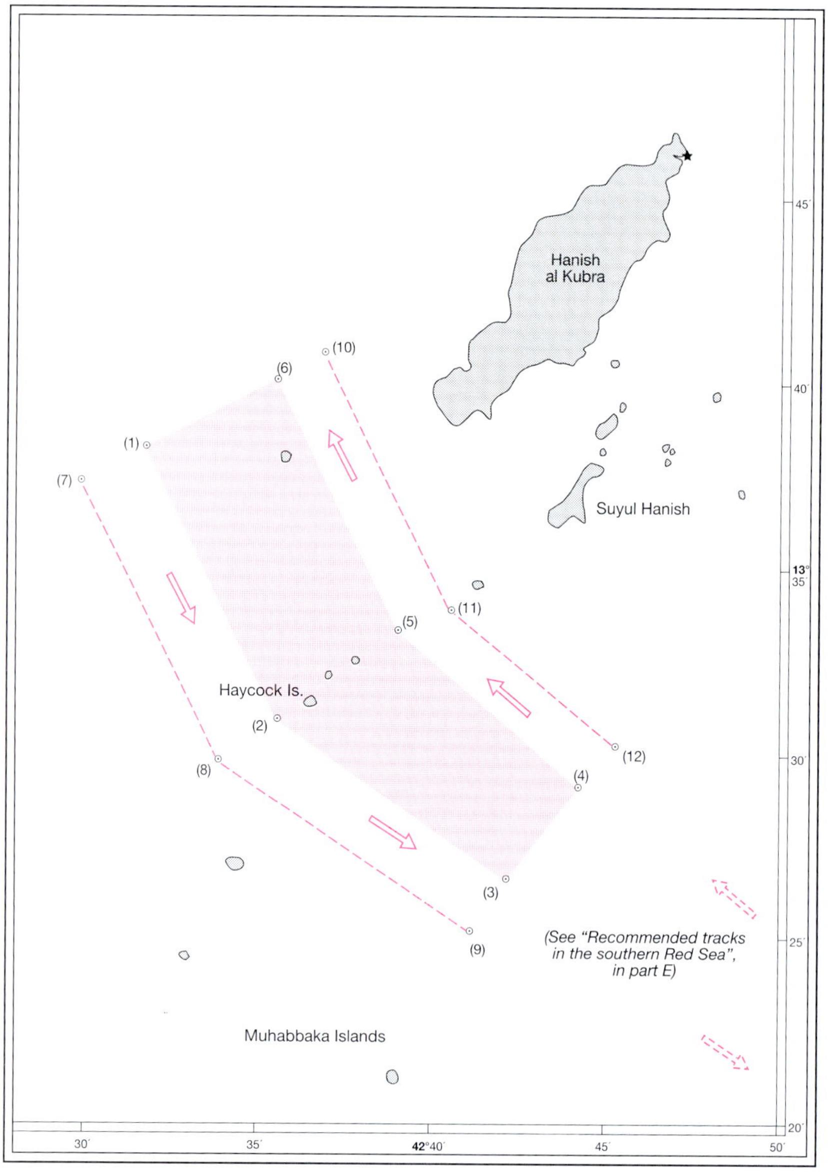

IN THE SOUTHERN RED SEA – WEST AND SOUTH OF HANISH AL KUBRA

IN THE SOUTHERN RED SEA – EAST OF JABAL ZUQAR ISLAND

(Reference charts: British Admiralty 452, 2002 edition; 453, 2002 edition.
Note: These charts are based on World Geodetic System 1984 datum (WGS 84).)

Description of the traffic separation scheme

(a) A separation zone bounded by a line connecting the following geographical positions:

(1)	14°07′.28 N,	042°45′.96 E	(4)	13°58′.55 N,	042°52′.30 E
(2)	14°02′.76 N,	042°49′.85 E	(5)	14°03′.76 N,	042°51′.00 E
(3)	13°58′.21 N,	042°51′.00 E	(6)	14°08′.27 N,	042°47′.10 E

(b) A traffic lane for southbound traffic between the separation zone and a line connecting the following geographical positions:

(7)	14°06′.49 N,	042°44′.98 E	(9)	13°57′.97 N,	042°49′.95 E
(8)	14°01′.93 N,	042°48′.94 E			

(c) A traffic lane for northbound traffic between the separation zone and a line connecting the following geographical positions:

(10)	14°09′.40 N,	042°48′.42 E	(12)	13°58′.94 N,	042°53′.83 E
(11)	14°04′.88 N,	042°52′.35 E			

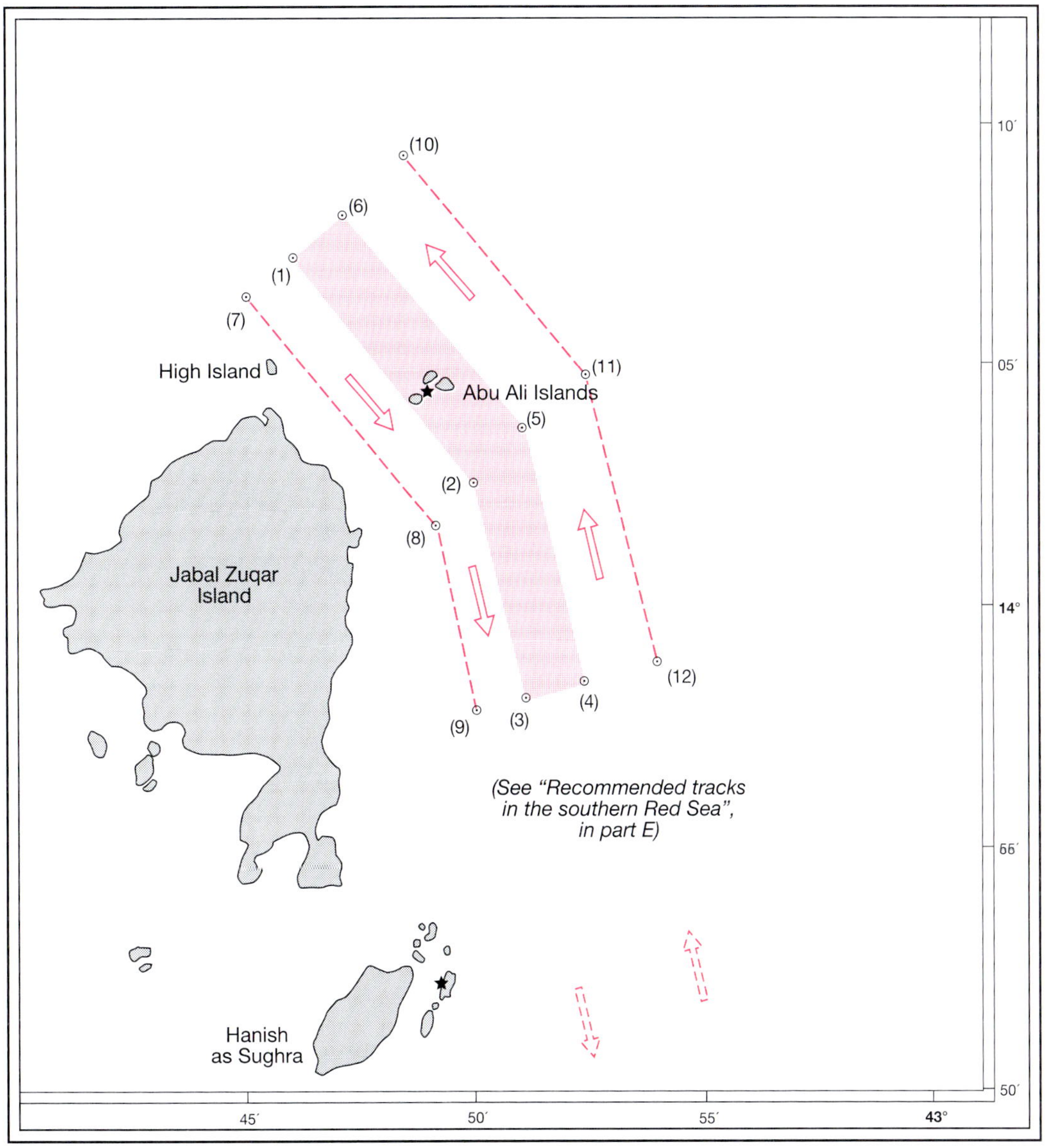

IN THE SOUTHERN RED SEA – EAST OF JABAL ZUQAR ISLAND

IN THE STRAIT OF BAB EL MANDEB

(Reference chart: British Admiralty 452, 2002 edition; 453, 2002 edition.
Note: These charts are based on World Geodetic System 1984 datum (WGS 84).)

Description of the traffic separation scheme

(a) A separation zone is bounded by a line connecting the following geographical positions:

(1)	13°13′.07 N,	043°02′.87 E	(4)	12°33′.37 N,	043°28′.30 E
(2)	12°36′.82 N,	043°20′.22 E	(5)	12°37′.50 N,	043°21′.00 E
(3)	12°32′.53 N,	043°27′.79 E	(6)	13°13′.83 N,	043°03′.60 E

(b) A traffic lane for southbound traffic between the separation zone and a line connecting the following geographical positions:

(7)	13°11′.94 N,	043°01′.72 E	(9)	12°31′.25 N,	043°27′.04 E
(8)	12°35′.78 N,	043°18′.98 E			

(c) A traffic lane for northbound traffic between the separation zone and a line connecting the following geographical positions:

(10)	13°15′.00 N,	043°04′.70 E	(12)	12°34′.69 N,	043°29′.03 E
(11)	12°38′.50 N,	043°22′.21 E			

Note: In the passage between Mayyun (Perim) Island and the mainland, coastal traffic may be proceeding in both directions.

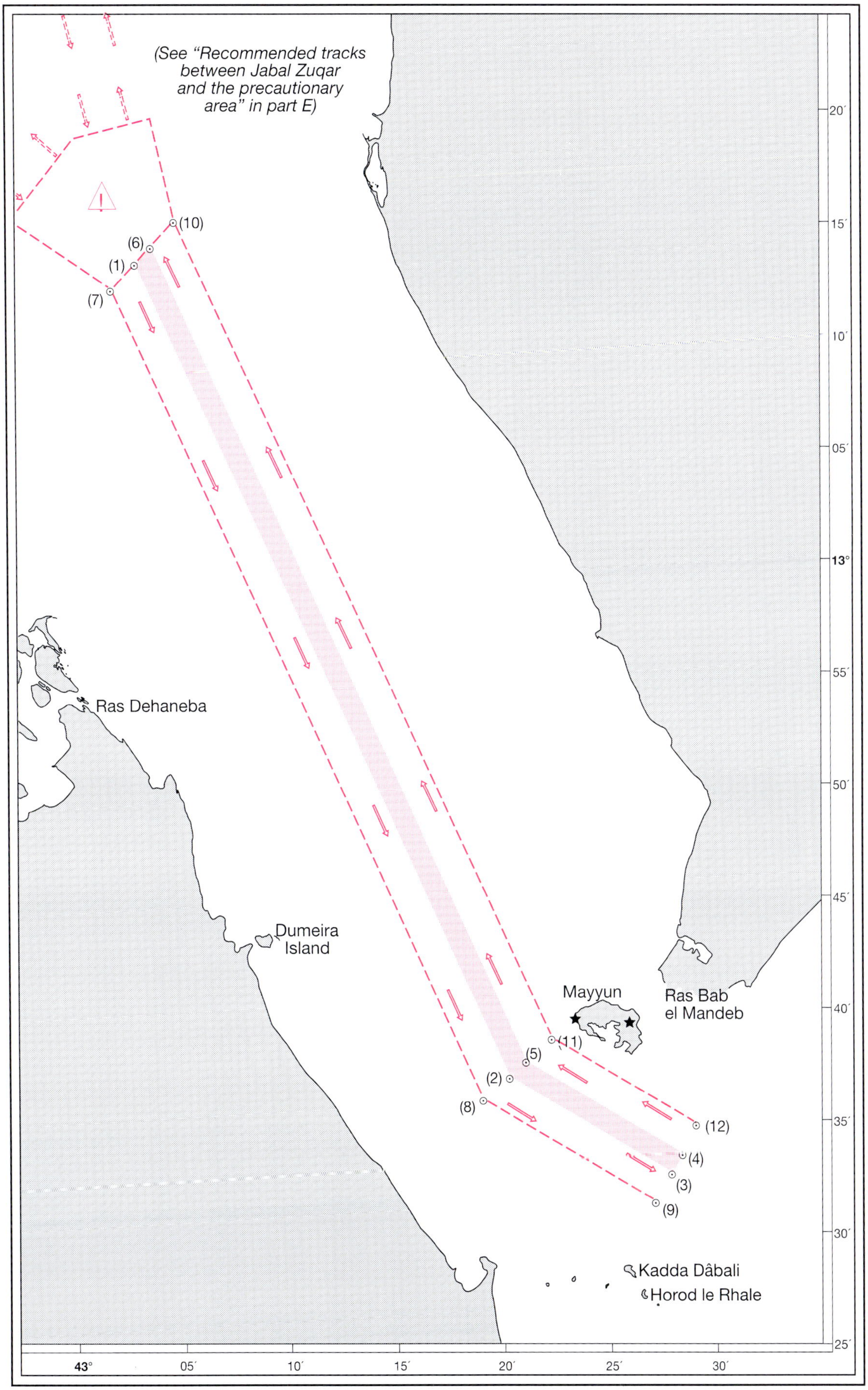

IN THE STRAIT OF BAB EL MANDEB

OFF RAS AL HADD

(Reference chart: British Admiralty 2851, 1983 edition.
Note: This chart is based on World Geodetic System 1972 datum.)

Description of the traffic separation scheme

(a) A separation zone, three nautical miles wide, is centred upon the following geographical positions:

(1)	22°39′.00 N,	059°56′.70 E	(3)	22°25′.40 N,	060°02′.00 E
(2)	22°33′.30 N,	060°02′.00 E			

(b) A traffic lane for southbound traffic, two nautical miles wide, is established between the separation zone and a separation line connecting the following geographical positions:

(4)	22°36′.50 N,	059°54′.00 E	(6)	22°25′.40 N,	059°58′.20 E
(5)	22°32′.00 N,	059°58′.20 E			

(c) A traffic lane for northbound traffic, four nautical miles wide, is established between the separation zone and a line connecting the following geographical positions:

(7)	22°25′.40 N,	060°08′.20 E	(9)	22°43′.00 N,	060°01′.00 E
(8)	22°35′.20 N,	060°08′.20 E			

Inshore traffic zone

The area between the coast and the landward boundary of the traffic separation scheme, and lying between a line connecting the following geographical positions:

(4) 22°36′.50 N, 059°54′.00 E to Ras al Hadd, position (10) 22°32′.00 N, 059°47′.93 E and a line drawn from position (6) 22°25′.40 N, 059°58′.20 E to Ras al Junaiz, position (11) 22°25′.40 N, 059°50′.00 E

is designated as an inshore traffic zone.

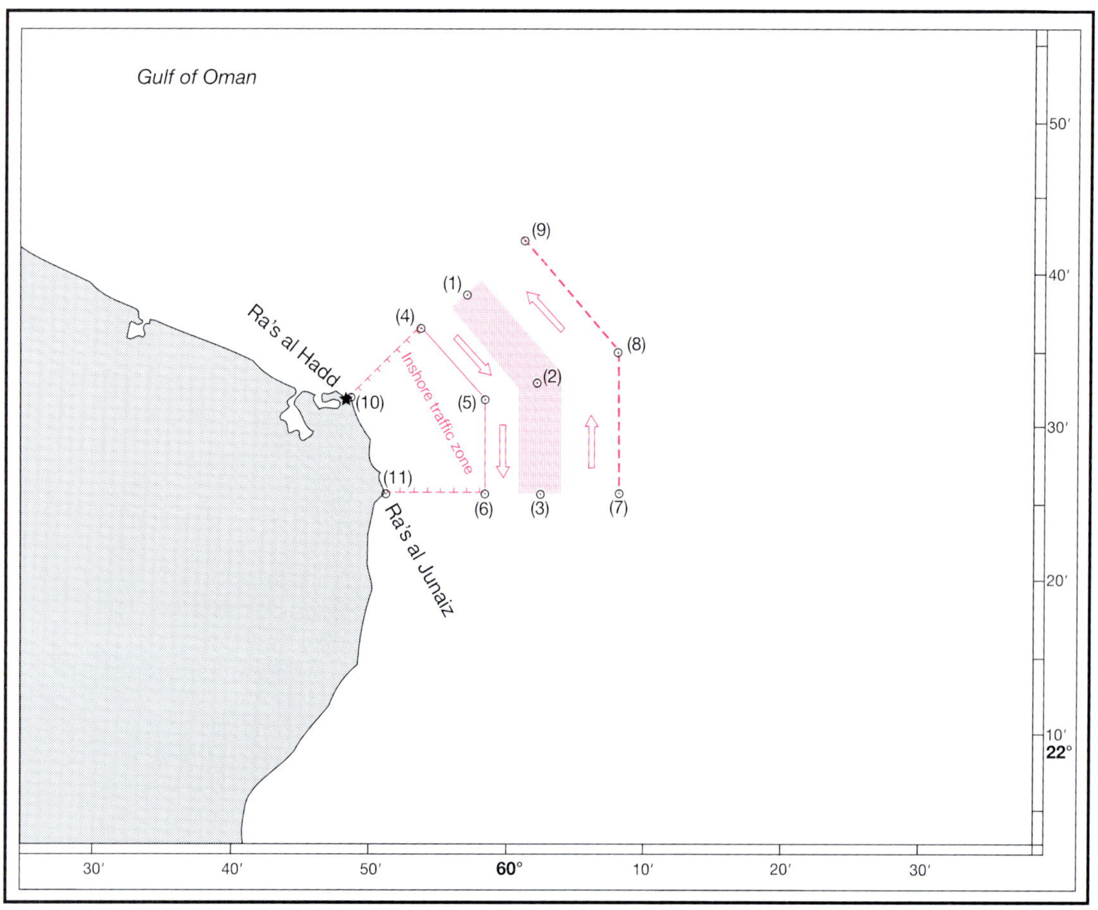

OFF RAS AL HADD

OFF RA'S AL KUH

(Reference chart: British Admiralty 2851.
Note: This chart is based on World Geodetic System 1984 datum (WGS 84).)

Description of the traffic separation scheme

(a) Outer traffic separation line connecting the following geographical positions:

(1)	25°45′.50 N,	057°03′.30 E	(3)	25°34′.05 N,	057°12′.00 E
(2)	25°39′.60 N,	057°07′.10 E			

(b) Traffic separation zone bounded by a line connecting the following geographical positions:

(4)	25°47′.50 N,	057°07′.20 E	(7)	25°35′.30 N,	057°13′.80 E
(5)	25°42′.25 N,	057°10′.55 E	(8)	25°40′.90 N,	057°08′.80 E
(6)	25°36′.65 N,	057°15′.55 E	(9)	25°46′.50 N,	057°05′.30 E

(c) The limits of the inshore traffic zone along the coastline lie between the following geographical positions:

(13)	25°52′.50 N,	057°17′.30 E	(12)	25°39′.30 N,	057°19′.10 E
(10)	25°48′.45 N,	057°09′.15 E	(14)	25°45′.30 N,	057°26′.70 E
(11)	25°43′.55 N,	057°12′.25 E			

(d) An outer traffic lane for south-eastbound shipping established between the separation zones described in (a) and (b).

(e) An inner traffic lane for north-westbound shipping established between the traffic separation zone described in (b) and the associated inshore traffic zone described in (c).

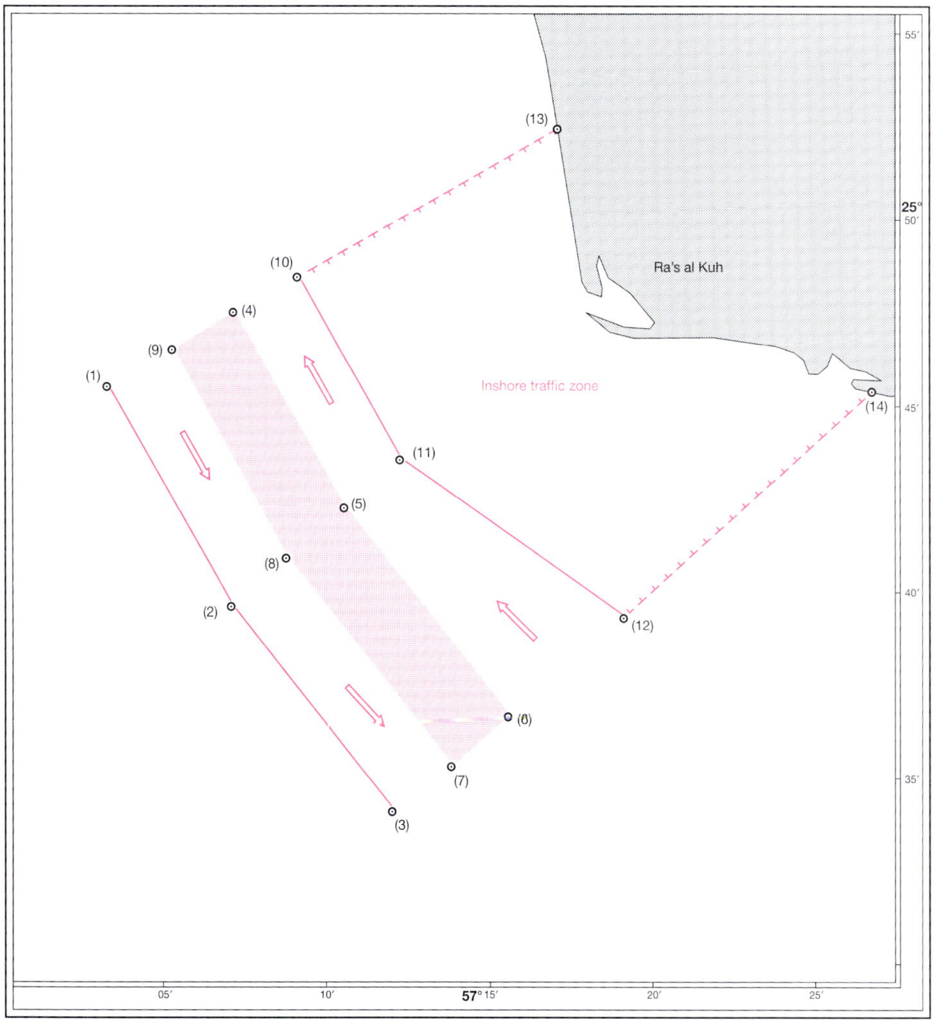

OFF RA'S AL KUH

IN THE STRAIT OF HORMUZ

(Reference chart: British Admiralty 3172, 1994 edition.
Note: This chart is based on World Geodetic System 1984 datum (WGS 84).)

Description of the traffic separation scheme

(a) A separation zone is bounded by a line connecting the following geographical positions:

(1)	26°34′.80 N,	056°21′.05 E	(5)	26°28′.60 N,	056°37′.55 E
(2)	26°36′.50 N,	056°28′.05 E	(6)	26°34′.50 N,	056°33′.60 E
(3)	26°36′.50 N,	056°34′.90 E	(7)	26°34′.50 N,	056°28′.55 E
(4)	26°29′.65 N,	056°39′.45 E	(8)	26°32′.00 N,	056°22′.40 E

(b) A traffic lane for eastbound traffic is established between the separation zone and a separation line connecting the following geographical positions:

(9)	26°30′.20 N,	056°23′.25 E	(11)	26°32′.50 N,	056°32′.35 E
(10)	26°32′.50 N,	056°28′.95 E	(12)	26°27′.60 N,	056°35′.65 E

(c) A traffic lane for westbound traffic is established between the separation zone and a line connecting the following geographical positions:

(13)	26°30′.70 N,	056°41′.35 E	(15)	26°38′.50 N,	056°27′.70 E
(14)	26°38′.50 N,	056°36′.15 E	(16)	26°36′.70 N,	056°20′.15 E

Inshore traffic zone

The area between the Musandam Peninsula coast and landward boundary of the traffic separation scheme bounded by a line connecting the following geographical positions:

	26°15′.35 N,	056°12′.92 E,
(9)	26°30′.20 N,	056°23′.25 E,
(10)	26°32′.50 N,	056°28′.95 E,
(11)	26°32′.50 N,	056°32′.35 E,
(12)	26°27′.60 N,	056°35′.65 E, and
	26°19′.05 N,	056°31′.25 E,

is designated as an inshore traffic zone.

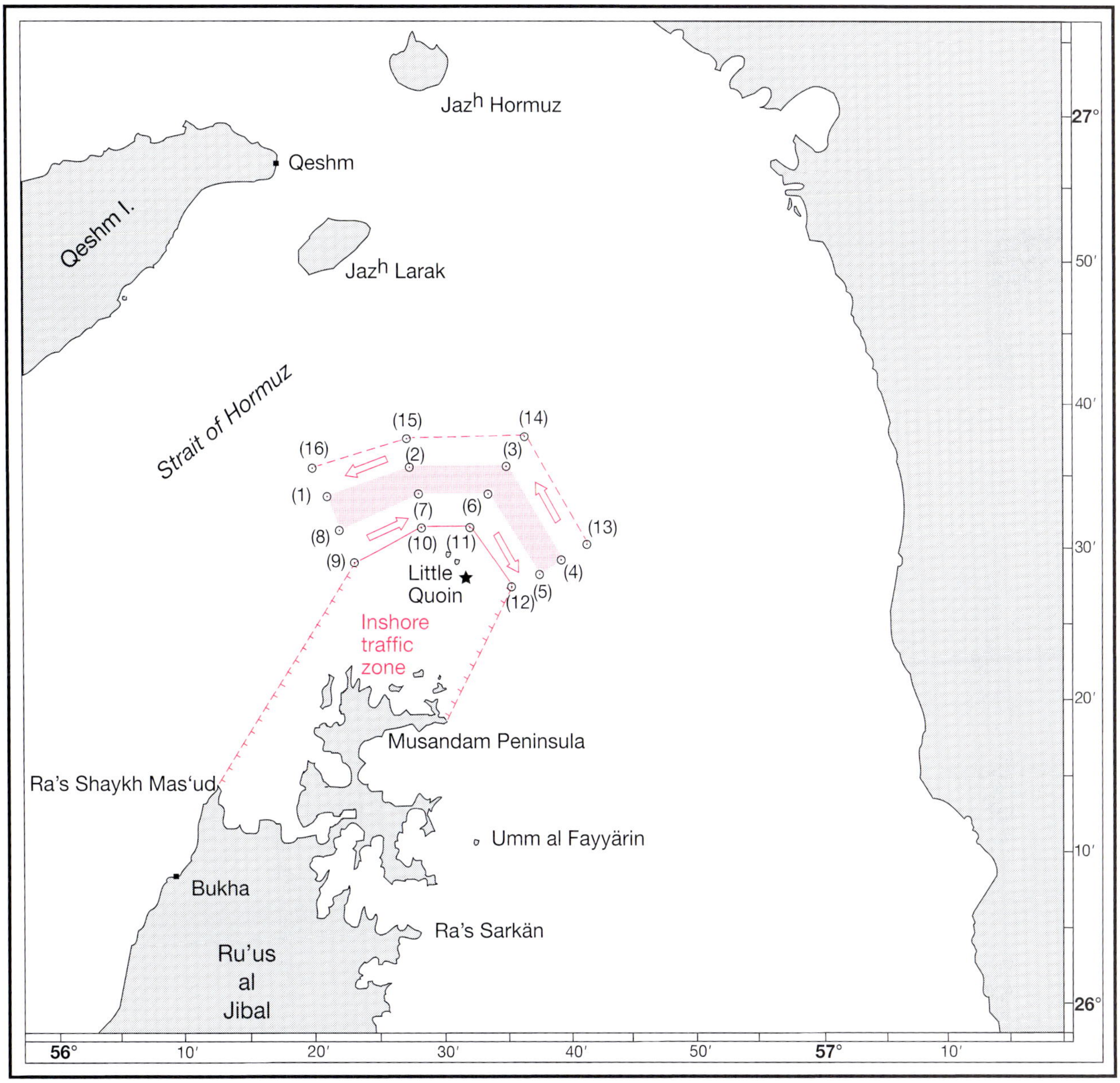

IN THE STRAIT OF HORMUZ

TUNB–FARUR

(Reference chart: British Admiralty 2837, 1989 edition.
Note: This chart is based on revised Nahrwan datum.)

Description of the traffic separation scheme

Separation of traffic in this area is achieved by establishing separate traffic lanes.

(a) A traffic lane for westbound traffic is established between a line connecting the following geographical positions:

(1)	26°22′.70 N,	055°30′.00 E	(3)	26°23′.00 N,	054°30′.00 E
(2)	26°18′.70 N,	055°07′.70 E			

and a line connecting the following geographical positions:

(4)	26°20′.60 N,	055°30′.00 E	(6)	26°21′.00 N,	054°30′.00 E
(5)	26°16′.60 N,	055°08′.00 E			

(b) A traffic lane for eastbound traffic is established between a line connecting the following geographical positions:

(7)	26°13′.00 N,	054°30′.00 E	(9)	26°11′.80 N,	055°30′.00 E
(8)	26°08′.00 N,	055°17′.50 E			

and a line connecting the following geographical positions:

(10)	26°10′.00 N,	054°30′.00 E	(12)	26°08′.80 N,	055°30′.00 E
(11)	26°05′.00 N,	055°17′.50 E			

Note: Westbound traffic which has passed Quoin Islands should proceed so as to keep Jazt. Tunb and Jazh-e Farur on the port side.
Eastbound traffic should proceed so as to keep Jazh-e Farur and Jazt. Tunb on the port side in order to get into the appropriate traffic lane in the Strait of Hormuz traffic separation scheme.

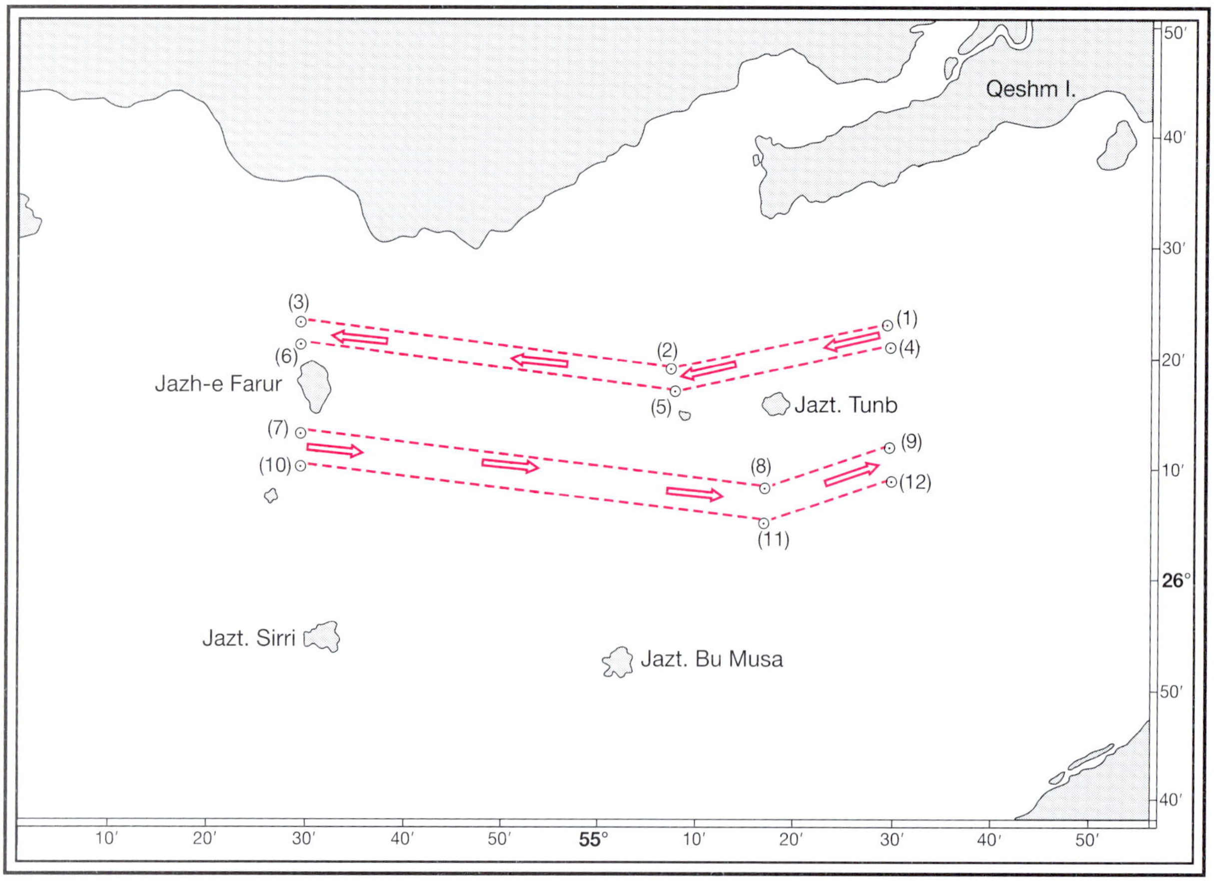

TUNB–FARUR

BETWEEN ZAQQUM AND UMM SHAIF

(Reference chart: British Admiralty 3733, 1987 edition.
Note: This chart is based on revised Nahrwan datum.)

Description of the traffic separation scheme

(a) A separation zone, 0.75 nautical miles wide, is bounded by a line connecting the following geographical positions:

(1)	25°07′.00 N,	053°24′.90 E	(4)	24°56′.30 N,	053°00′.10 E
(2)	25°02′.77 N,	053°19′.36 E	(5)	25°02′.10 N,	053°19′.78 E
(3)	24°56′.90 N,	052°59′.45 E	(6)	25°06′.40 N,	053°25′.41 E

(b) A traffic lane for westbound traffic, 1.25 nautical miles wide, is established between the separation zone and a line connecting the following geographical positions:

(7)	25°07′.95 N,	053°24′.01 E	(9)	24°57′.90 N,	052°58′.40 E
(8)	25°03′.89 N,	053°18′.70 E			

(c) A traffic lane for eastbound traffic, 1.25 nautical miles wide, is established between the separation zone and a line connecting the following geographical positions:

(10)	24°55′.28 N,	053°01′.15 E	(12)	25°05′.44 N,	053°26′.30 E
(11)	25°00′.97 N,	053°20′.46 E			

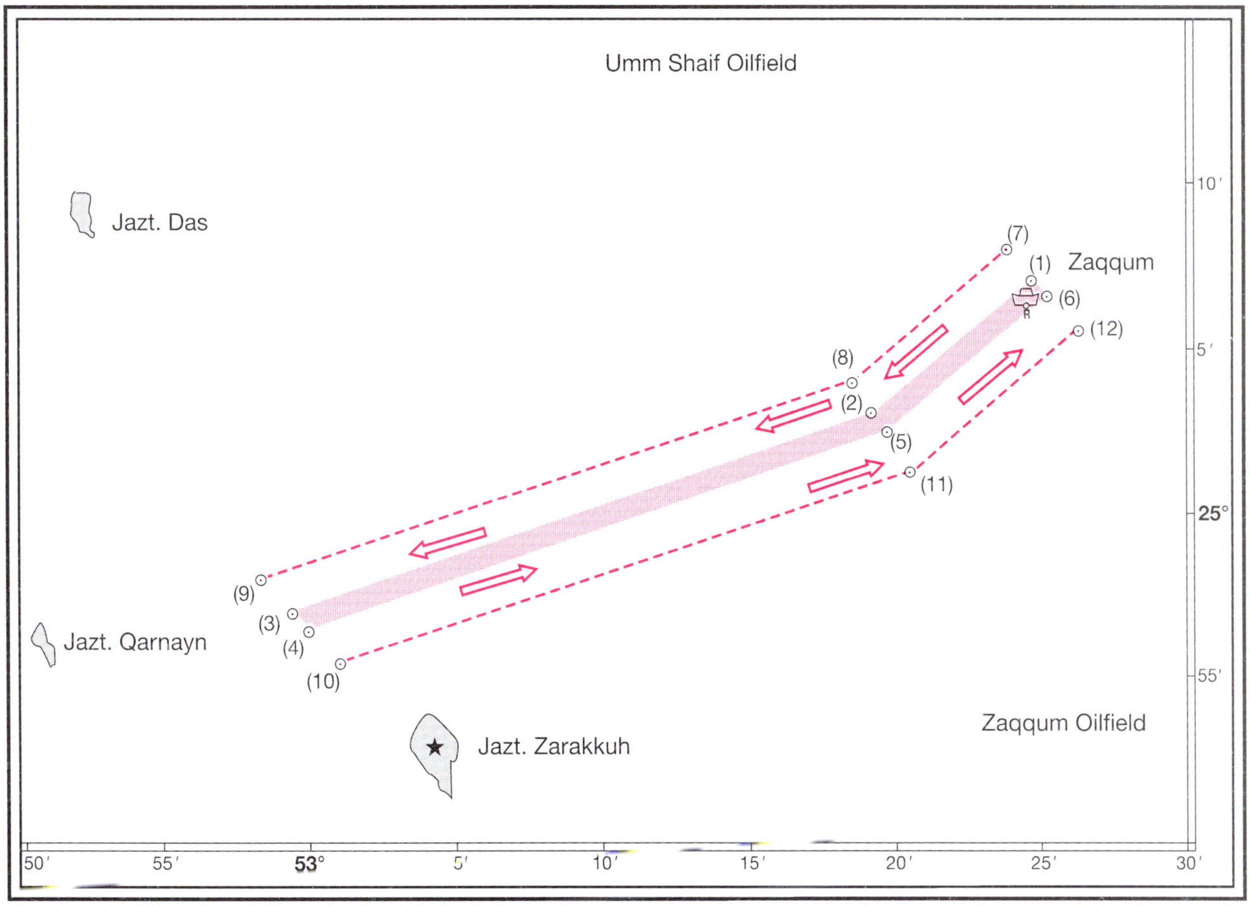

BETWEEN ZAQQUM AND UMM SHAIF

IN THE APPROACHES TO RAS TANURA AND JU'AYMAH

(Reference charts: British Admiralty 3788, 1986 edition; United States Naval Oceanographic Office 62415. **Note:** These charts are based on Nahrwan datum.)

Description of the traffic separation scheme

Part I:
Ras Tanura approach

(a) A separation zone is bounded by a line connecting the following geographical positions:

(1)	27°06′.83 N,	050°42′.00 E	(4)	26°57′.50 N,	050°14′.60 E
(2)	27°06′.10 N,	050°23′.30 E	(5)	27°05′.27 N,	050°23′.50 E
(3)	26°58′.00 N,	050°14′.00 E	(6)	27°06′.13 N,	050°42′.08 E

(b) A separation line connects the following geographical positions:

(7)	26°57′.75 N,	050°14′.20 E	(8)	26°56′.20 N,	050°12′.60 E

(c) A separation zone is bounded by a line connecting the following geographical positions:

(9)	26°56′.47 N,	050°12′.30 E	(12)	26°51′.15 N,	050°11′.28 E
(10)	26°56′.00 N,	050°11′.85 E	(13)	26°55′.55 N,	050°12′.38 E
(11)	26°49′.30 N,	050°10′.43 E	(14)	26°55′.93 N,	050°12′.87 E

(d) A separation line connects the following geographical positions:

(15)	26°49′.30 N,	050°10′.43 E	(19)	26°43′.00 N,	050°11′.88 E
(16)	26°48′.32 N,	050°10′.25 E	(20)	26°41′.93 N,	050°12′.23 E
(17)	26°45′.20 N,	050°11′.15 E	(21)	26°41′.02 N,	050°12′.13 E
(18)	26°44′.43 N,	050°11′.47 E	(22)	26°40′.87 N,	050°12′.10 E

(e) A traffic lane for traffic bound for Ras Tanura is established between the separation zones/lines and a line connecting the following geographical positions:

(23)	27°07′.27 N,	050°42′.00 E	(27)	26°48′.03 N,	050°09′.87 E
(24)	27°06′.47 N,	050°23′.00 E	(28)	26°42′.03 N,	050°11′.70 E
(25)	26°56′.35 N,	050°11′.48 E	(29)	26°40′.87 N,	050°11′.73 E
(26)	26°49′.53 N,	050°09′.83 E			

(f) A traffic lane for traffic departing from Ras Tanura is established between the separation zones/lines and a line connecting the following geographical positions:

(30)	26°40′.87 N,	050°12′.27 E	(37)	26°49′.27 N,	050°10′.70 E
(31)	26°41′.00 N,	050°12′.30 E	(38)	26°50′.90 N,	050°11′.60 E
(32)	26°41′.95 N,	050°12′.40 E	(39)	26°55′.12 N,	050°13′.03 E
(33)	26°42′.42 N,	050°12′.37 E	(40)	26°55′.53 N,	050°13′.13 E
(34)	26°43′.12 N,	050°12′.12 E	(41)	27°04′.85 N,	050°23′.87 E
(35)	26°44′.28 N,	050°11′.70 E	(42)	27°05′.57 N,	050°42′.10 E
(36)	26°47′.38 N,	050°10′.95 E			

Part II:
Ju'aymah approach

(g) A traffic lane, two miles wide, for traffic bound for Ju'aymah is centred upon the following geographical positions:

(43)	26°57′.60 N,	050°12′.80 E	(44)	26°59′.00 N,	050°11′.30 E

Part III:
Ju'aymah departure

(h) A traffic lane, two miles wide, for traffic departing from Ju'aymah is centred upon the following geographical positions:

(45)	27°01′.40 N,	050°09′.20 E	(47)	27°11′.50 N,	050°36′.00 E
(46)	27°11′.50 N,	050°11′.75 E			

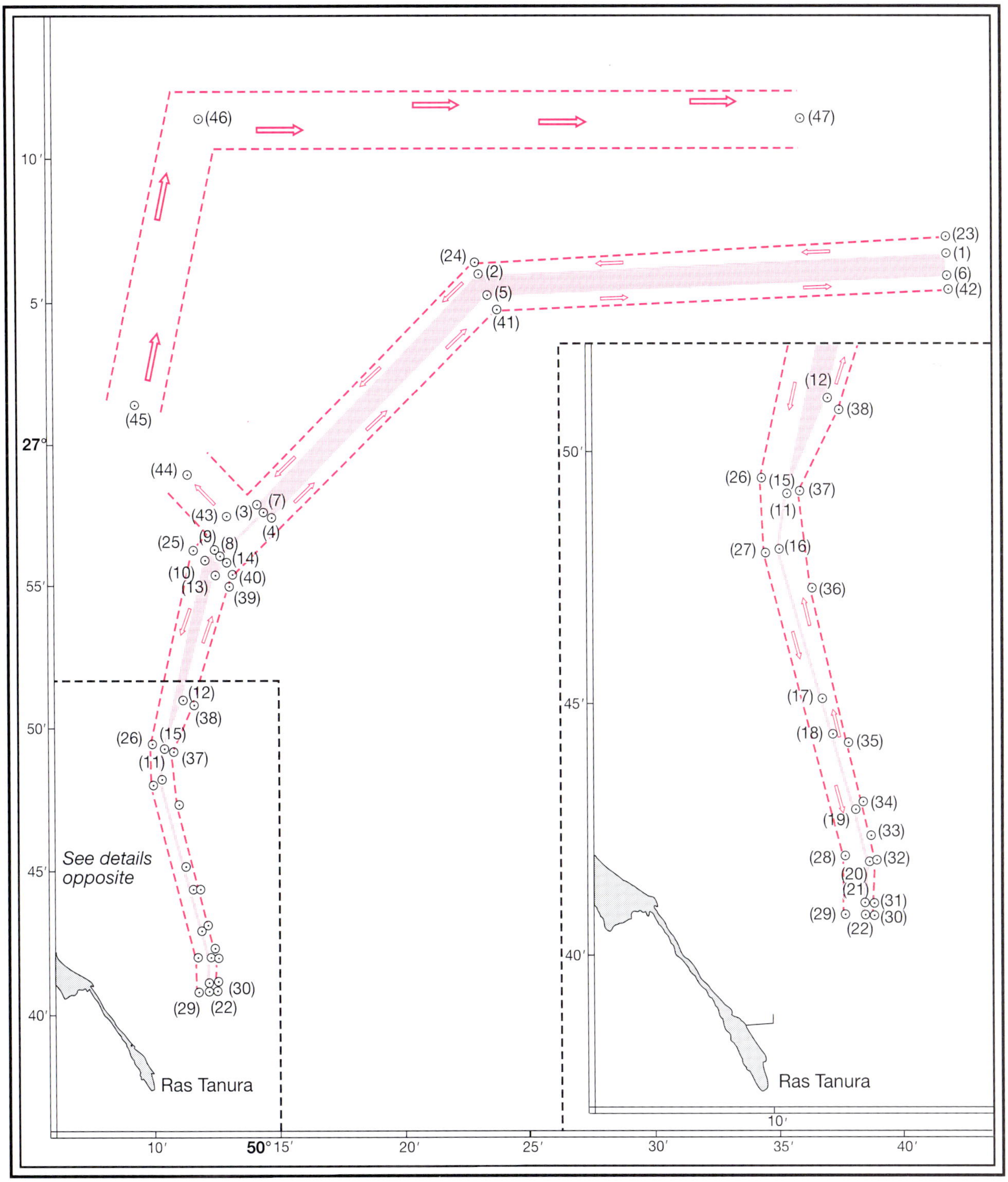

IN THE APPROACHES TO RAS TANURA AND JU'AYMAH

MARJAN/ZULUF

(Reference chart: British Admiralty 3774, 1991 edition.
Note: This chart is based on World Geodetic System 1984 datum (WGS 84).)

Description of the traffic separation scheme

(a) A separation zone of 0.54 nautical miles (1000 metres) wide is centred upon the following geographical positions:

(1)	28°14′.98 N,	049°18′.60 E	(4)	28°24′.33 N,	049°27′.80 E
(2)	28°16′.76 N,	049°18′.58 E	(5)	28°30′.11 N,	049°30′.04 E
(3)	28°18′.41 N,	049°19′.24 E	(6)	28°32′.04 N,	049°30′.15 E

(b) A traffic lane for southbound traffic is established between the separation zone and a line connecting the following geographical positions:

(7)	28°14′.94 N,	049°17′.19 E	(10)	28°25′.16 N,	049°26′.60 E
(8)	28°17′.00 N,	049°17′.13 E	(11)	28°30′.36 N,	049°28′.61 E
(9)	28°19′.28 N,	049°18′.09 E	(12)	28°32′.05 N,	049°28′.70 E

(c) A traffic lane for northbound traffic is established between the separation zone and a line connecting the following geographical positions:

(13)	28°15′.00 N,	049°20′.01 E	(16)	28°23′.63 N,	049°29′.06 E
(14)	28°16′.55 N,	049°19′.97 E	(17)	28°29′.87 N,	049°31′.47 E
(15)	28°17′.69 N,	049°20′.45 E	(18)	28°32′.03 N,	049°31′.59 E

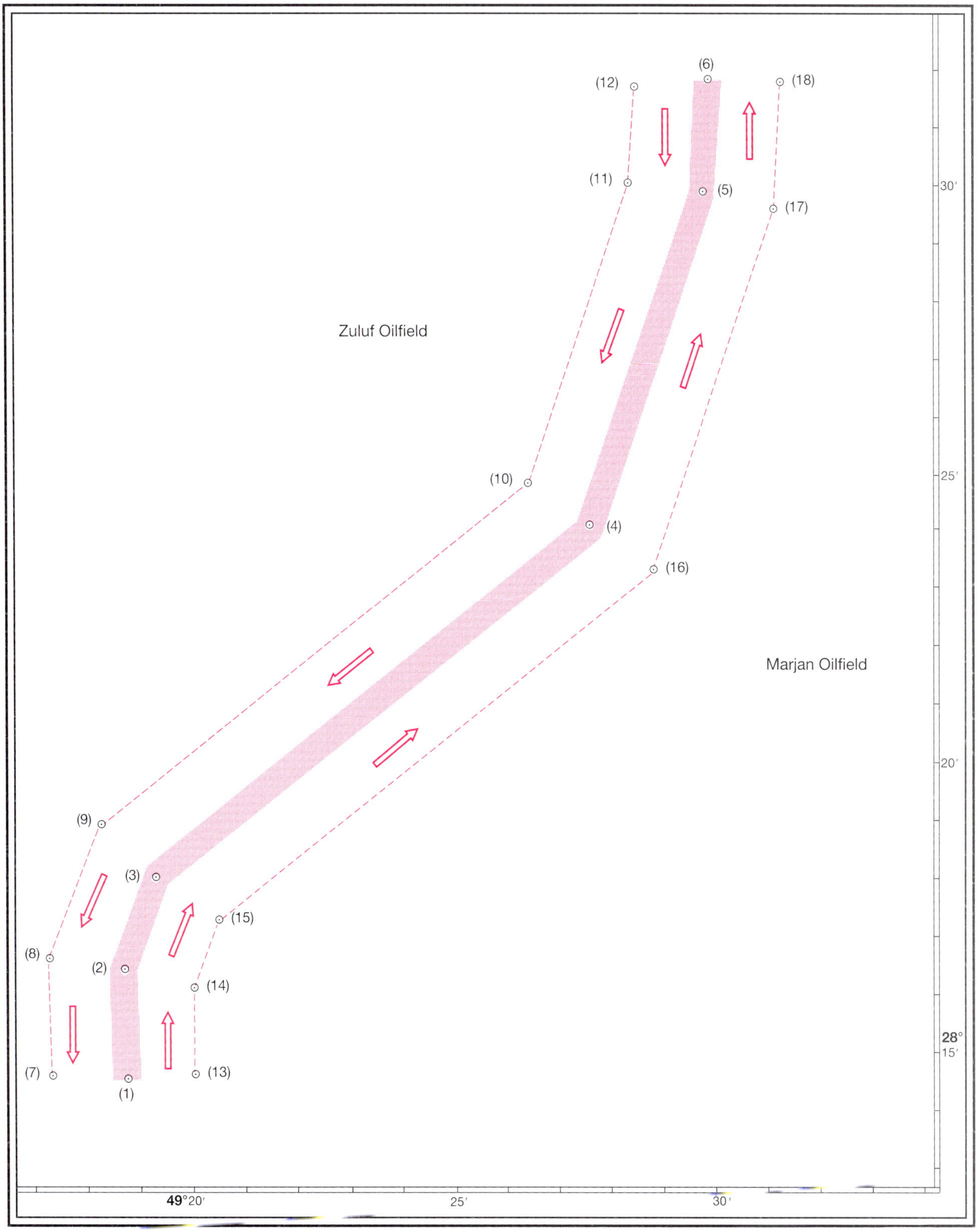

MARJAN/ZULUF

APPROACHES TO THE PORT OF RA'S AL KHAFJI

(Reference chart: British Admiralty 3774, 1999 edition.
Note: This chart is based on World Geodetic System 1984 datum (WGS 84).)

Description of the traffic separation scheme

(a) A separation zone bounded by a line connecting the following geographical positions:

(1)	28°38′.40 N,	049°07′.00 E	(4)	28°30′.07 N,	048°41′.12 E
(2)	28°38′.40 N,	048°45′.83 E	(5)	28°38′.20 N,	048°46′.30 E
(3)	28°30′.30 N,	048°40′.66 E	(6)	28°38′.20 N,	049°07′.00 E

(b) A traffic lane for inbound traffic between the separation zone and the following geographical positions:

(7)	28°39′.40 N,	049°07′.00 E	(9)	28°30′.82 N,	048°39′.58 E
(8)	28°39′.40 N,	048°45′.03 E			

(c) A traffic lane for outbound traffic between the separation zone and the following geographical positions:

(10)	28°29′.60 N,	048°42′.05 E	(12)	28°36′.10 N,	049°07′.00 E
(11)	28°37′.17 N,	048°46′.90 E			

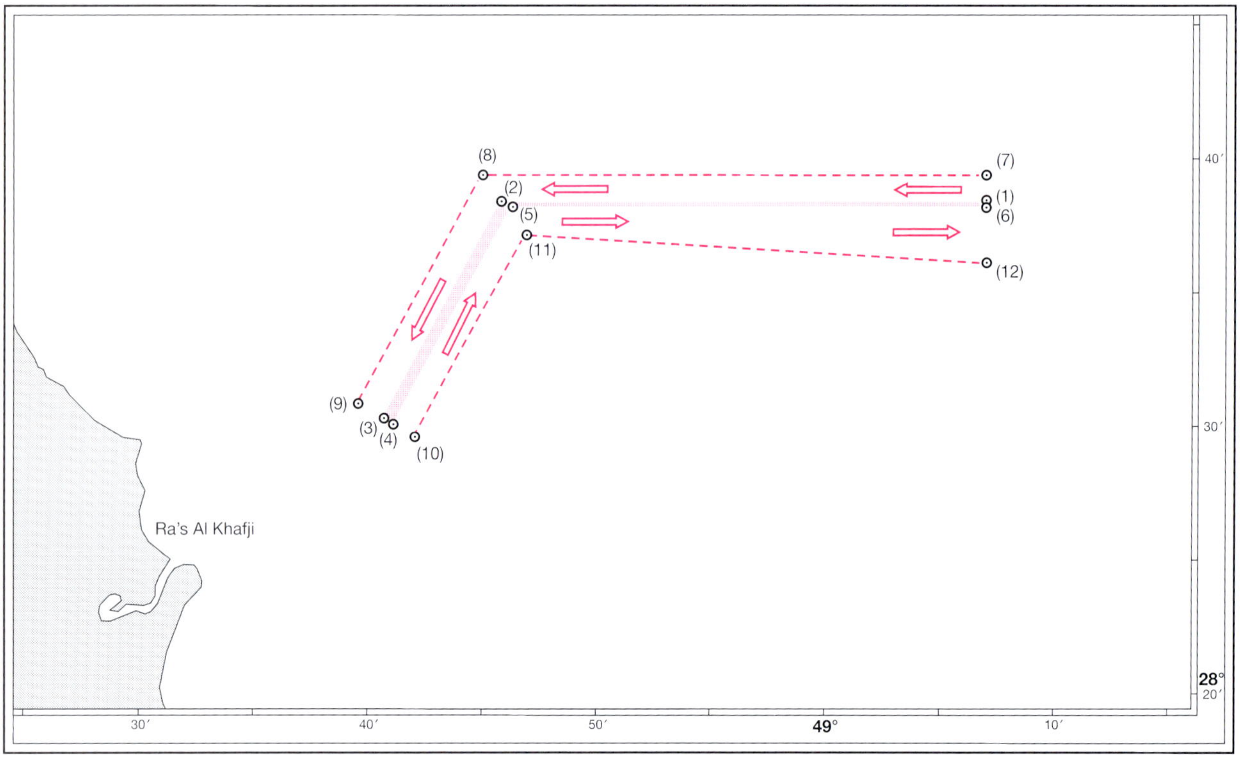

APPROACHES TO THE PORT OF RA'S AL KHAFJI

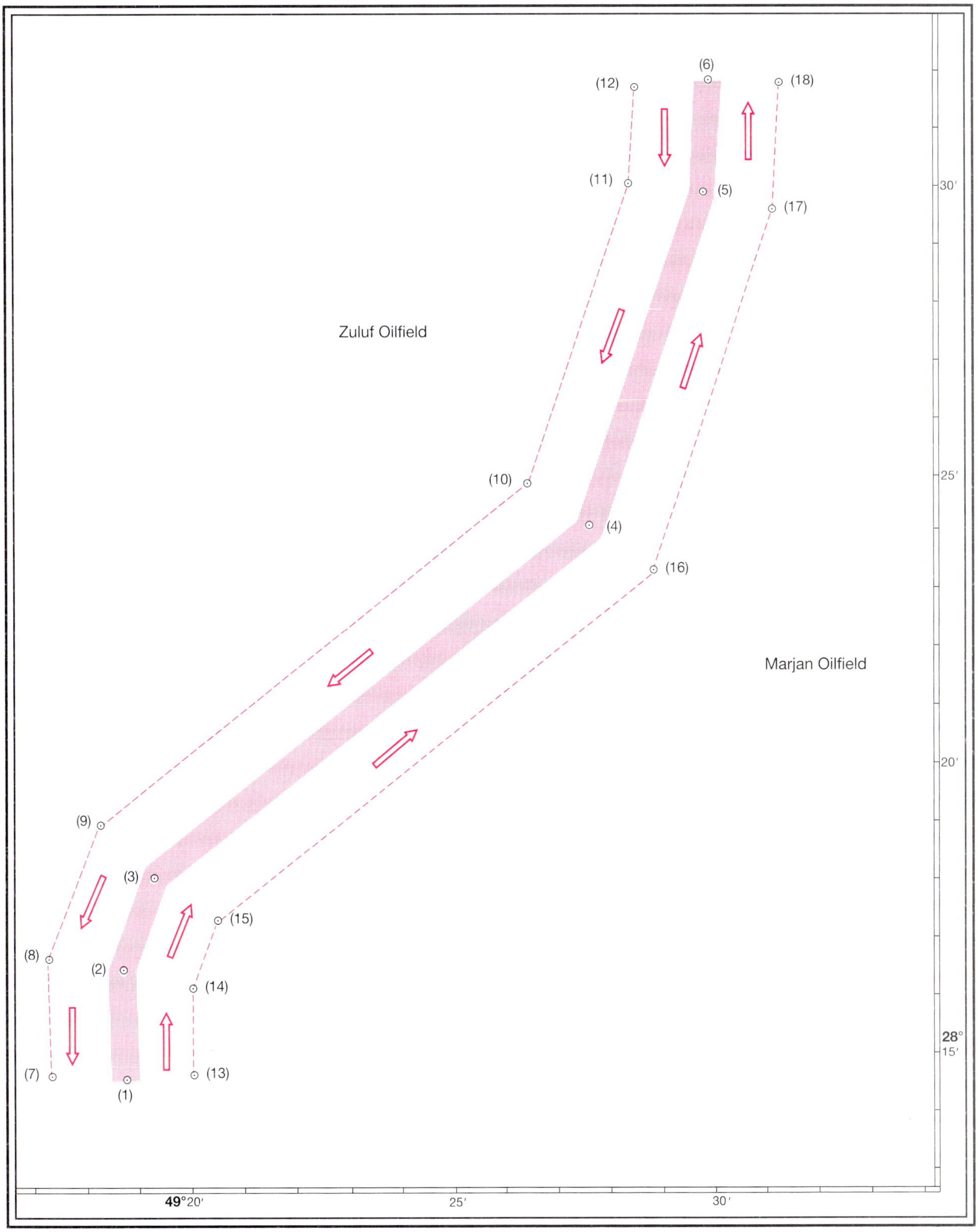

MARJAN/ZULUF

APPROACHES TO THE PORT OF RA'S AL KHAFJI

(Reference chart: British Admiralty 3774, 1999 edition.
Note: This chart is based on World Geodetic System 1984 datum (WGS 84).)

Description of the traffic separation scheme

(a) A separation zone bounded by a line connecting the following geographical positions:

(1)	28°38′.40 N,	049°07′.00 E	(4)	28°30′.07 N,	048°41′.12 E
(2)	28°38′.40 N,	048°45′.83 E	(5)	28°38′.20 N,	048°46′.30 E
(3)	28°30′.30 N,	048°40′.66 E	(6)	28°38′.20 N,	049°07′.00 E

(b) A traffic lane for inbound traffic between the separation zone and the following geographical positions:

(7)	28°39′.40 N,	049°07′.00 E	(9)	28°30′.82 N,	048°39′.58 E
(8)	28°39′.40 N,	048°45′.03 E			

(c) A traffic lane for outbound traffic between the separation zone and the following geographical positions:

(10)	28°29′.60 N,	048°42′.05 E	(12)	28°36′.10 N,	049°07′.00 E
(11)	28°37′.17 N,	048°46′.90 E			

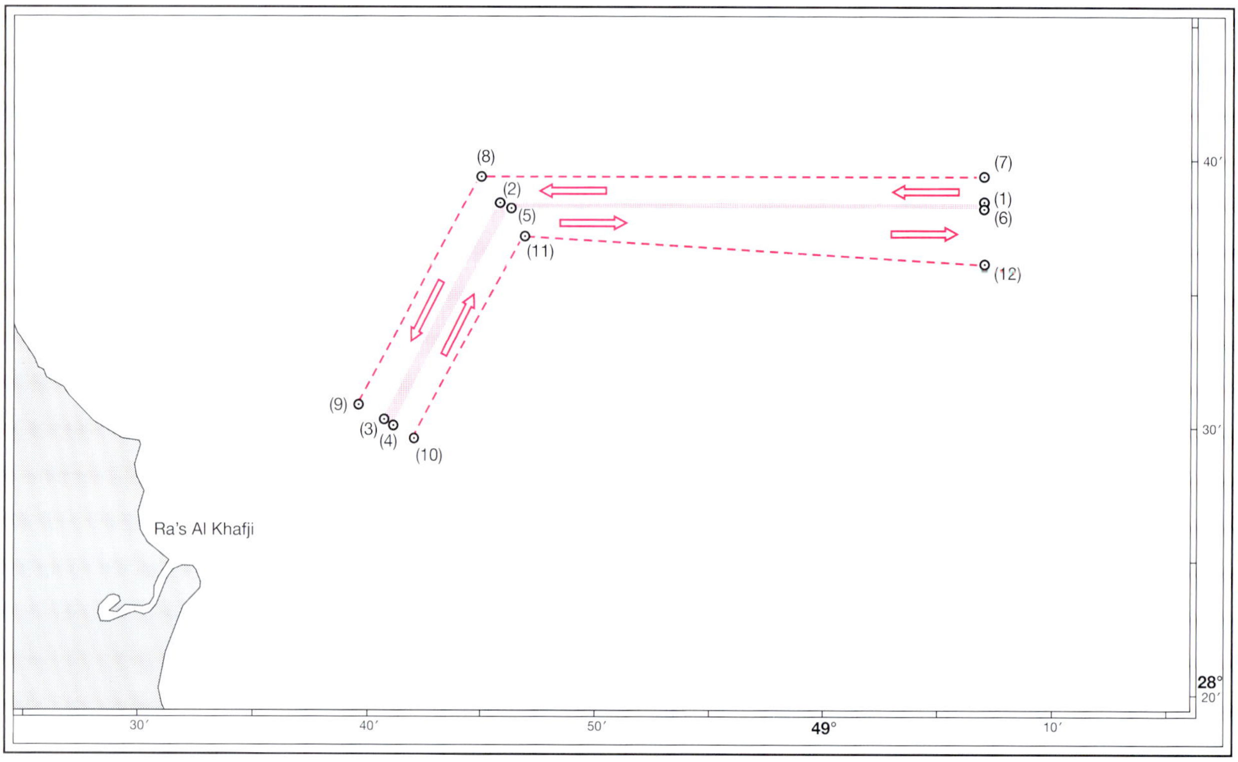

APPROACHES TO THE PORT OF RA'S AL KHAFJI

B

OFF MINA AL-AHMADI

(Reference charts: British Admiralty 3773, edition No. 4 dated 06/12/2001; 1223, edition No. 4 dated 16/5/2002.
Note: All positions are referred to World Geodetic System 1984 datum (WGS 84).).

Description of the traffic separation schemes

North scheme I

(a) A separation zone for the North scheme No. I bounded by a line joining the following geographical positions:

(1) 29°03′.40 N, 048°45′.00 E
(2) 29°05′.85 N, 048°30′.00 E
(3) 29°06′.97 N, 048°27′.57 E
(4) 29°05′.80 N, 048°26′.00 E
(5) 29°03′.35 N, 048°28′.10 E
(6) 29°03′.40 N, 048°34′.50 E
(7) 29°01′.40 N, 048°45′.00 E

(b) A traffic line for inbound traffic is established between the separation zone in (a) and the line joining the following geographical positions:

(8) 29°04′.50 N, 048°45′.00 E
(9) 29°06′.85 N, 048°30′.00 E
(10) 29°07′.60 N, 048°28′.40 E

(c) A traffic line for outbound traffic is established between the separation zone in (a) and the line joining the following geographical positions:

(11) 29°05′.28 N, 048°25′.22 E
(12) 29°02′.40 N, 048°27′.80 E
(13) 29°02′.55 N, 048°34′.50 E
(14) 29°00′.50 N, 048°45′.00 E

North scheme II

(d) A separation zone for the North scheme No. II bounded by a line joining the following geographical positions:

(15) 29°07′.94 N, 048°25′.75 E
(16) 29°07′.40 N, 048°24′.77 E
(17) 29°09′.20 N, 048°23′.00 E

(e) A separation line joins the co-ordinates of (17) to the following geographical position:

(18) 29°12′.30 N, 048°15′.00 E

(f) A traffic lane for inbound traffic is established between the separation zone in (d) and the separation line in (e) and the line joining the following geographical positions:

(19) 29°08′.40 N, 048°26′.62 E
(20) 29°10′.05 N, 048°23′.40 E
(21) 29°13′.20 N, 048°15′.00 E

(g) A traffic lane for outbound traffic is established between the separation zone in (d) and the separation line in (e) and the line joining the following geographical positions:

(22) 29°11′.45 N, 048°15′.00 E
(23) 29°08′.70 N, 048°22′.20 E
(24) 29°06′.85 N, 048°23′.82 E

(h) A junction buoy "A" is laid in position (17):

(17) 29°09′.20 N, 048°23′.00 E – special mark yellow.

(i) A first precautionary area is bounded by a line joining the following geographical positions:

(21) 29°13′.20 N, 048°15′.00 E
(22) 29°11′.45 N, 048°15′.00 E
(25) 29°11′.45 N, 048°11′.60 E
(26) 29°15′.00 N, 048°09′.60 E
(27) 29°15′.00 N, 048°13′.40 E

(j) A second precautionary area is bounded by a line joining the following geographical positions:

(10) 29°07′.60 N, 048°28′.40 E
(11) 29°05′.28 N, 048°25′.22 E
(24) 29°06′.85 N, 048°23′.82 E
(19) 29°08′.40 N, 048°26′.62 E

The South scheme

(a) A separation zone for the South scheme bounded by a line joining the following geographical positions:

(28)	28°57′.70 N,	048°26′.95 E
(29)	28°57′.00 N,	048°26′.00 E
(30)	29°00′.40 N,	048°22′.96 E

(b) A separation line joining the co-ordinates of position (30) to the following geographical position:

(31)	29°02′.60 N,	048°17′.65 E

(c) A traffic lane for inbound traffic is established between the separation zone in (a) and the separation line in (b) and the line joining the following geographical positions:

(32)	28°58′.40 N,	048°27′.60 E
(33)	29°01′.15 N,	048°23′.50 E
(34)	29°03′.30 N,	048°18′.40 E

(d) A traffic lane for outbound traffic is established between the separation zone in (a) and the separation line in (b) and the line joining the following geographical positions:

(35)	29°01′.90 N,	048°17′.00 E
(36)	28°59′.80 N,	048°22′.00 E
(37)	28°56′.30 N,	048°25′.10 E

(e) A junction buoy "B" is laid in position (30):

(30) 29°00′.40 N, 048°22′.96 E – special mark yellow.

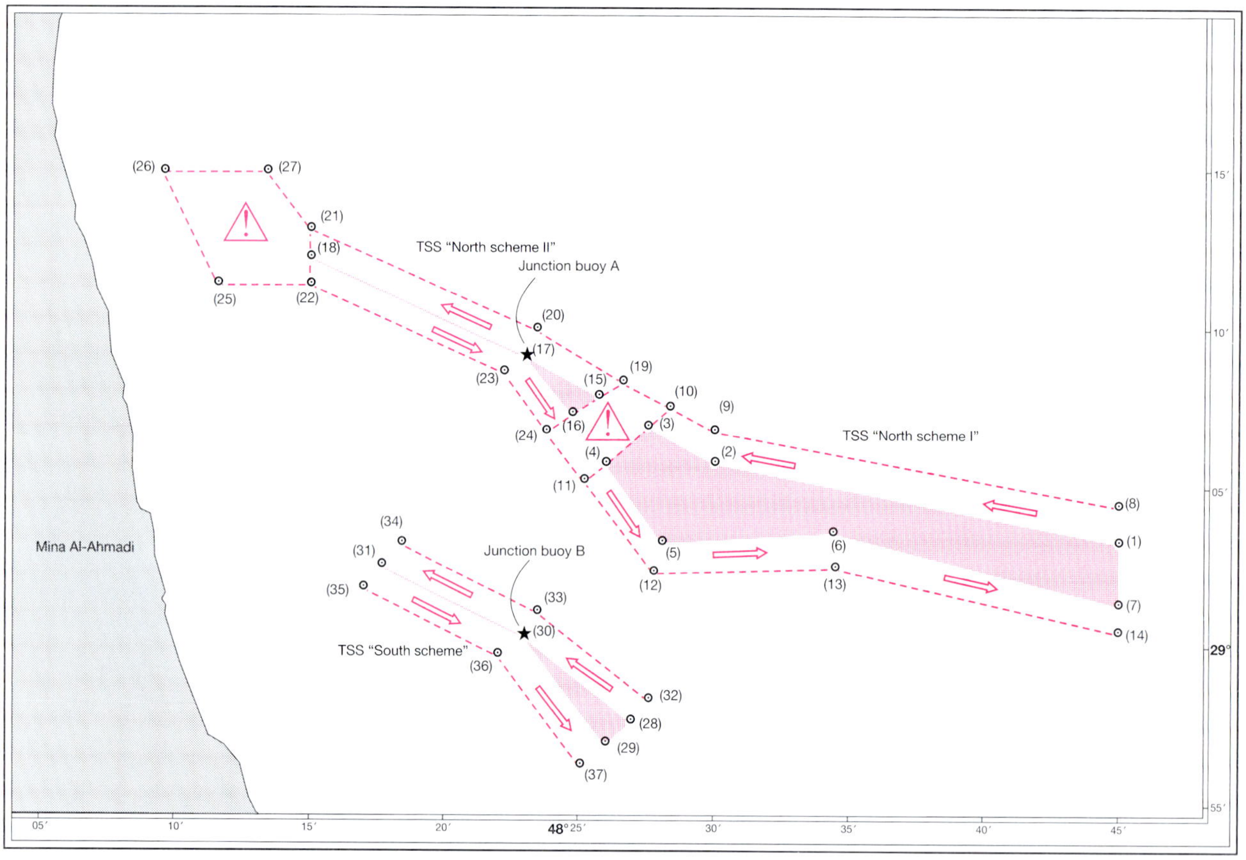

OFF MINA AL-AHMADI

OFF DONDRA HEAD

(Reference chart: British Admiralty 3265, 1981 edition.
Note: This chart is based on Ceylon 1933 datum.)

Description of the traffic separation scheme

(a) A separation zone, two miles wide, is centred upon the following geographical positions:

(1)	05°51′.20 N,	080°32′.38 E	(2)	05°51′.20 N,	080°38′.54 E

(b) A separation zone, three miles wide, is centred upon the following geographical positions:

(3)	05°45′.70 N,	080°32′.38 E	(4)	05°45′.70 N,	080°38′.54 E

(c) A traffic lane for westbound ships, three miles wide, is established between the separation zones described in paragraphs (a) and (b) above.

(d) A traffic lane for eastbound ships, three miles wide, is established to the seaward side of the separation zone described in paragraph (b) above.

Inshore traffic zone

The area between the coast and the landward boundary of the traffic separation scheme is designated as an inshore traffic zone.

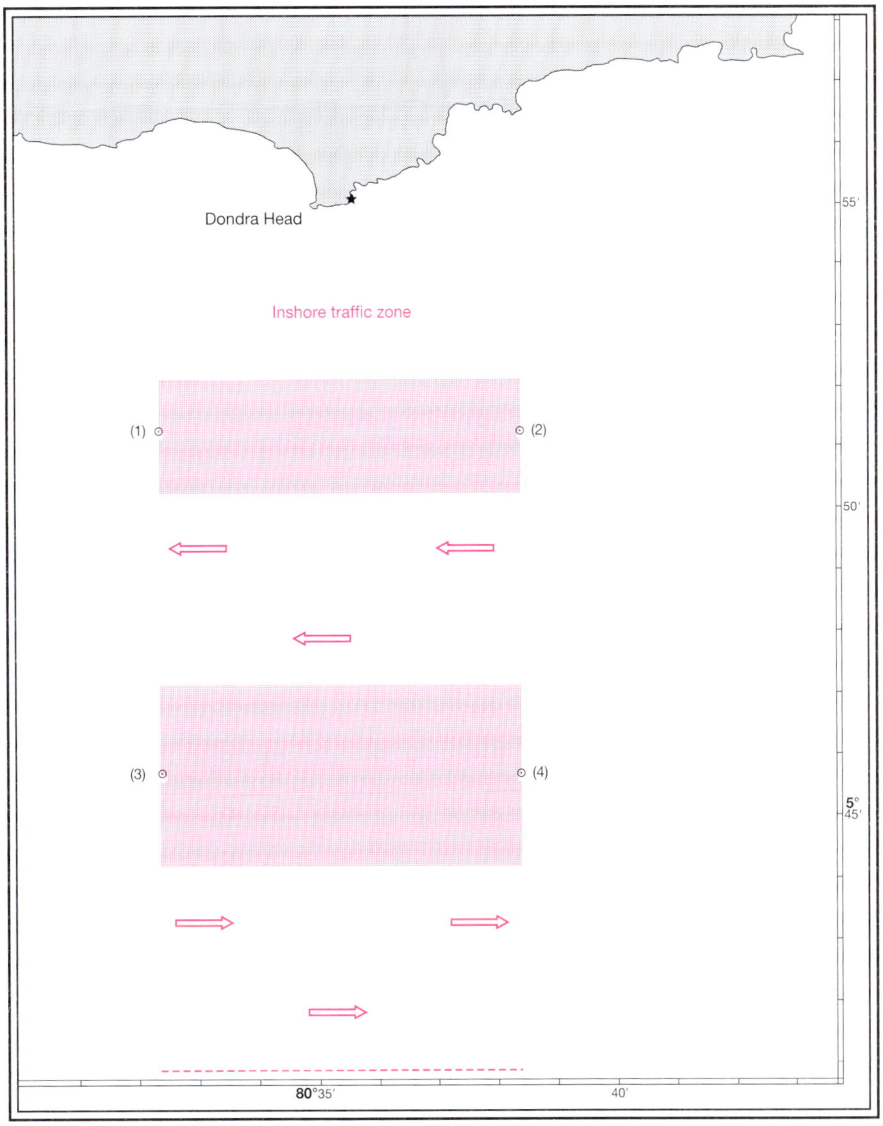

OFF DONDRA HEAD

B

OFF ALPHARD BANKS 34 MILES SOUTH OF CAPE INFANTA

Note: See "Rules for navigation of laden tankers off the South African coast" in part F.*

(Reference charts: South African Navy SAN 57, 121; British Admiralty 2083, 2084.
Note: The SAN charts are based on Cape datum (Clarke 1880 Modified ellipsoid).)

Description of the traffic separation scheme

(a) A separation zone is bounded by a line connecting the following geographical positions:

(1)	34°58′.79 S,	020°45′.00 E	(3)	35°08′.10 S,	021°05′.00 E
(2)	34°56′.48 S,	021°05′.00 E	(4)	35°09′.54 S,	020°45′.00 E

(b) A traffic lane for westbound traffic is established between the separation zone and the line connecting the following geographical positions:

(5)	34°55′.76 S,	020°45′.00 E	(6)	34°53′.45 S,	021°05′.00 E

(c) A traffic lane for eastbound traffic is established between the traffic separation zone and the line connecting the following geographical positions:

(7)	35°12′.55 S,	020°45′.00 E	(8)	35°11′.11 S,	021°05′.00 E

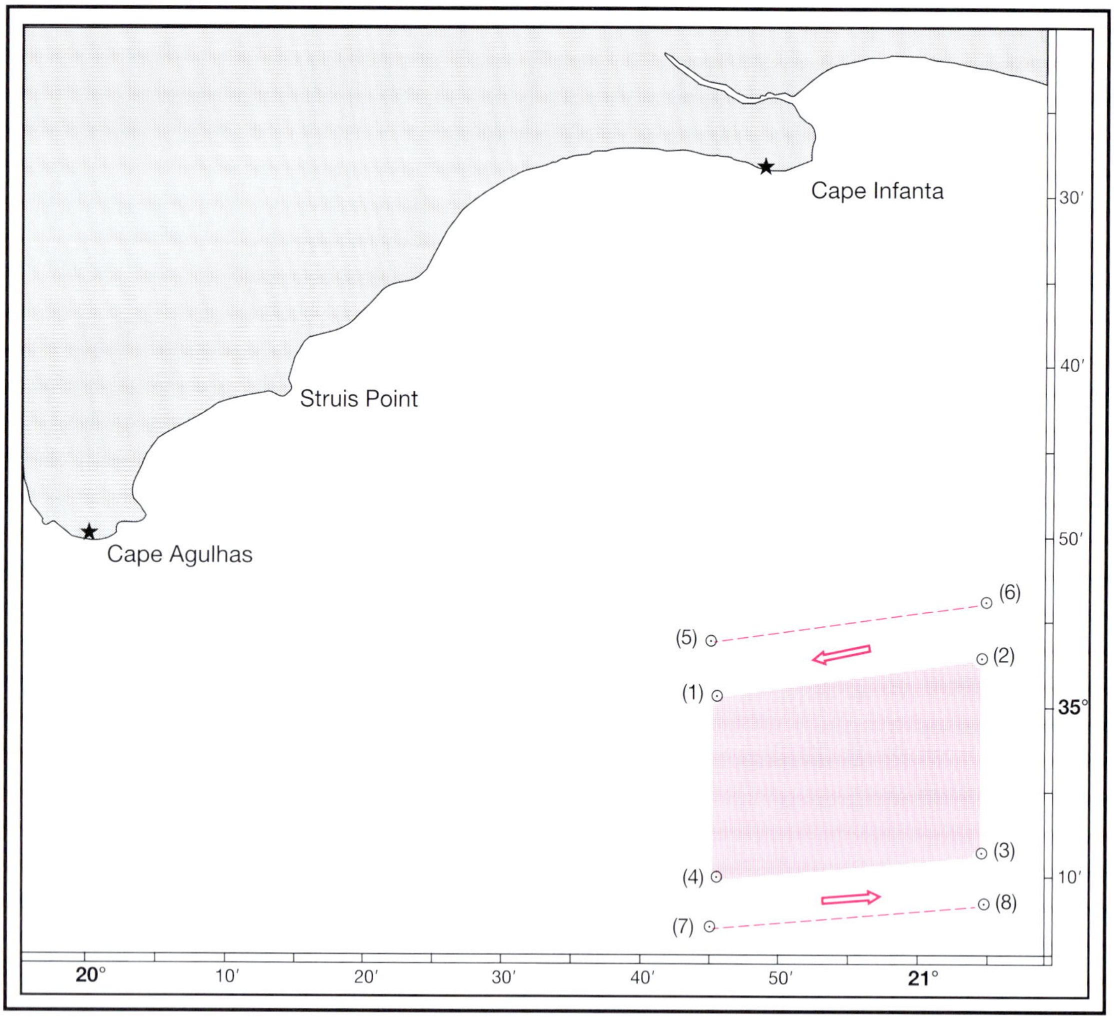

OFF ALPHARD BANKS

* The chartlet has been updated following the repositioning of the northern boundary of the Southern Winter Seasonal Zone of the International Convention on Load Lines, 1966, as amended in December 2012.

OFF THE FA PLATFORM 47 MILES SOUTH OF MOSSEL BAY

Note: See "Rules for navigation of laden tankers off the South African coast" in part F.*

(Reference charts: South African Navy SAN 57, 122; British Admiralty 2083, 2084.
Note: The SAN charts are based on Cape datum (Clarke 1880 Modified ellipsoid).)

Description of the traffic separation scheme

(a) A separation zone is bounded by a line connecting the following geographical positions:

(1)	34°50′.11 S,	022°00′.00 E	(4)	35°03′.37 S,	022°10′.86 E
(2)	34°47′.39 S,	022°20′.00 E	(5)	35°04′.06 S,	022°00′.00 E
(3)	35°01′.77 S,	022°20′.00 E			

(b) A traffic lane for eastbound traffic is established between the separation zone and the line connecting the following geographical positions:

(6)	35°07′.16 S,	022°00′.00 E	(8)	35°04′.81 S,	022°20′.00 E
(7)	35°06′.35 S,	022°11′.18 E			

(c) A traffic lane for westbound traffic is established between the traffic separation zone and the line connecting the following geographical positions:

(9)	34°47′.07 S,	022°00′.00 E	(10)	34°44′.75 S,	022°20′.00 E

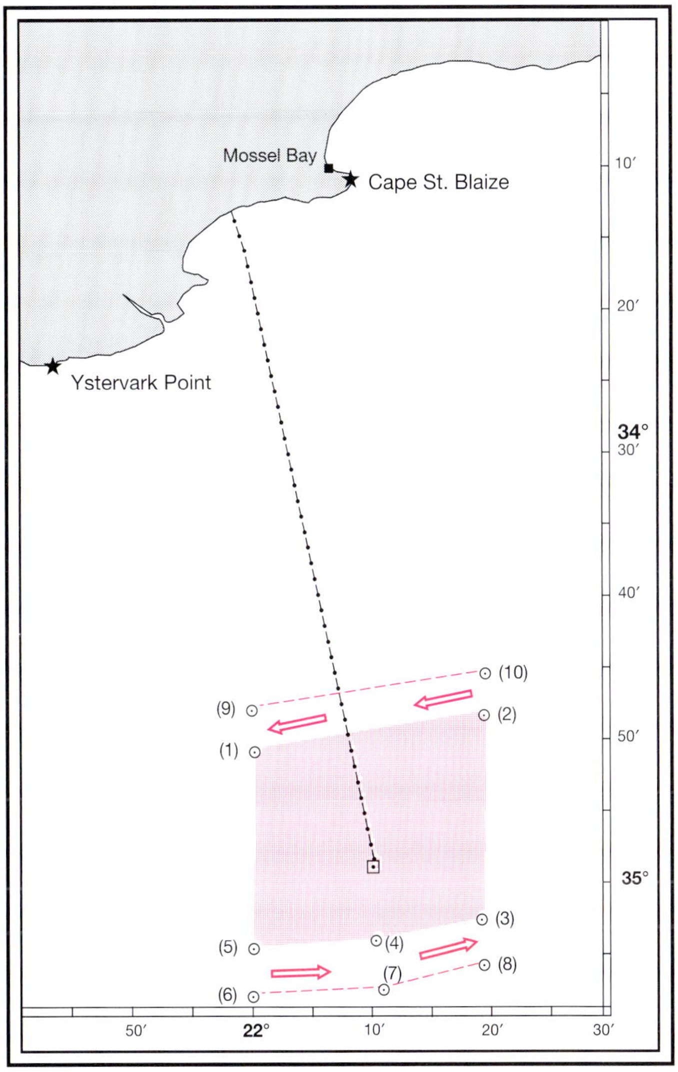

OFF THE FA PLATFORM

* The chartlet has been updated following the repositioning of the northern boundary of the Southern Winter Seasonal Zone of the International Convention on Load Lines, 1966, as amended in December 2012.

B

Section V

South-East Asia

Caution: The chartlets are for illustrative purposes only and must not be used for navigation. Mariners should consult the appropriate nautical publications and charts for up-to-date details on aids to navigation and other relevant information.

Warning: The geographical positions given in the descriptions of the routeing systems are only correct for charts using the same geodetic datum as the reference charts indicated under each scheme. Charts published by other hydrographic offices may use a different geodetic datum, as may new editions of the reference charts published after the adoption of the routeing system. Where amendments to existing systems are not based on the same geodetic datum as the original system, this is emphasized by the use of different colours for definitions of positions.

B

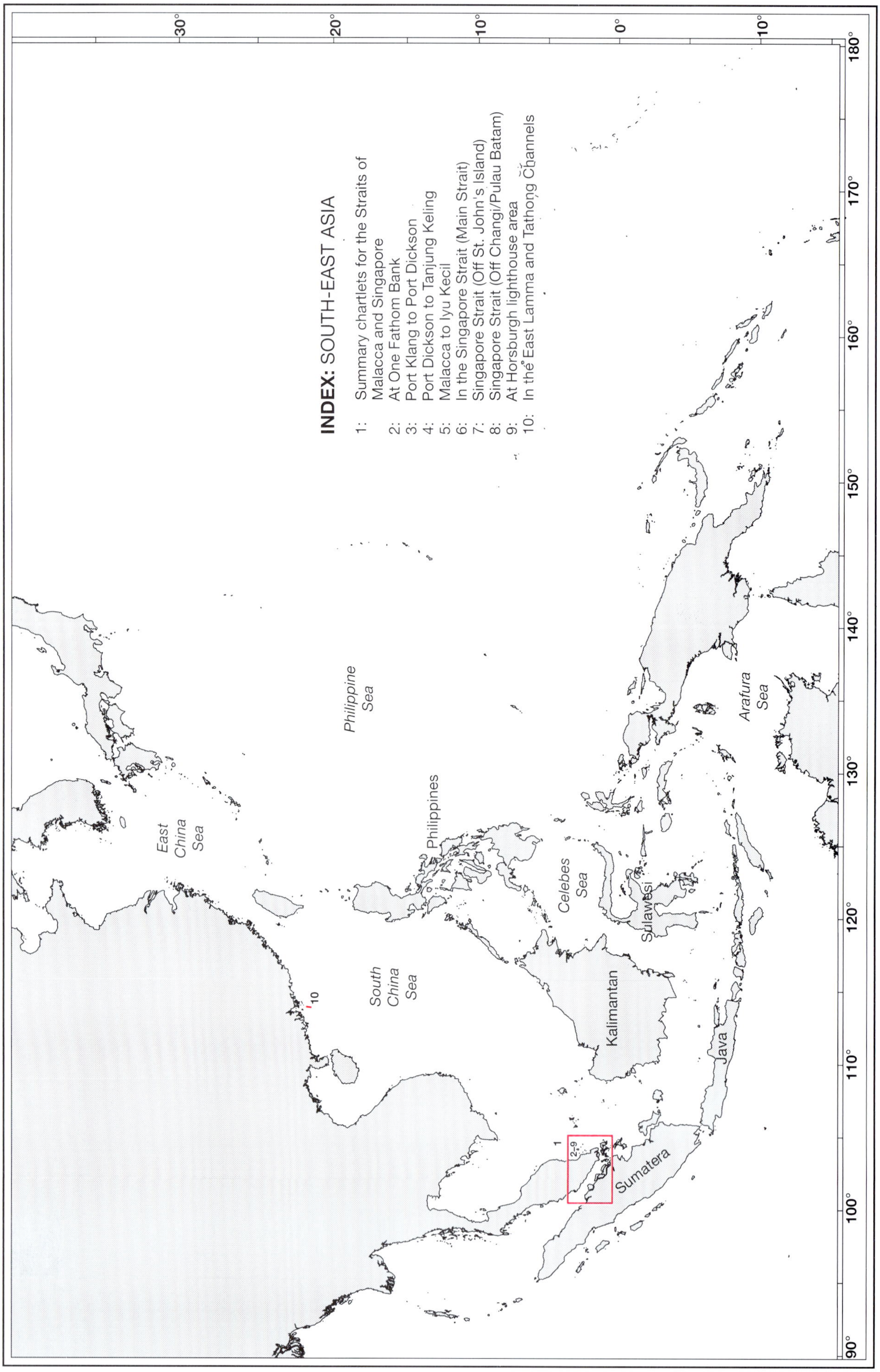
INDEX: SOUTH-EAST ASIA
1: Summary chartlets for the Straits of Malacca and Singapore
2: At One Fathom Bank
3: Port Klang to Port Dickson
4: Port Dickson to Tanjung Keling
5: Malacca to Iyu Kecil
6: In the Singapore Strait (Main Strait)
7: Singapore Strait (Off St. John's Island)
8: Singapore Strait (Off Changi/Pulau Batam)
9: At Horsburgh lighthouse area
10: In the East Lamma and Tathong Channels
East China Sea
Philippine Sea
Philippines
South China Sea
Celebes Sea
Sulawesi
Kalimantan
Java
Sumatera
Arafura Sea
1
2-9
10
30°
20°
10°
0°
10°
90°
100°
110°
120°
130°
140°
150°
160°
170°
180°

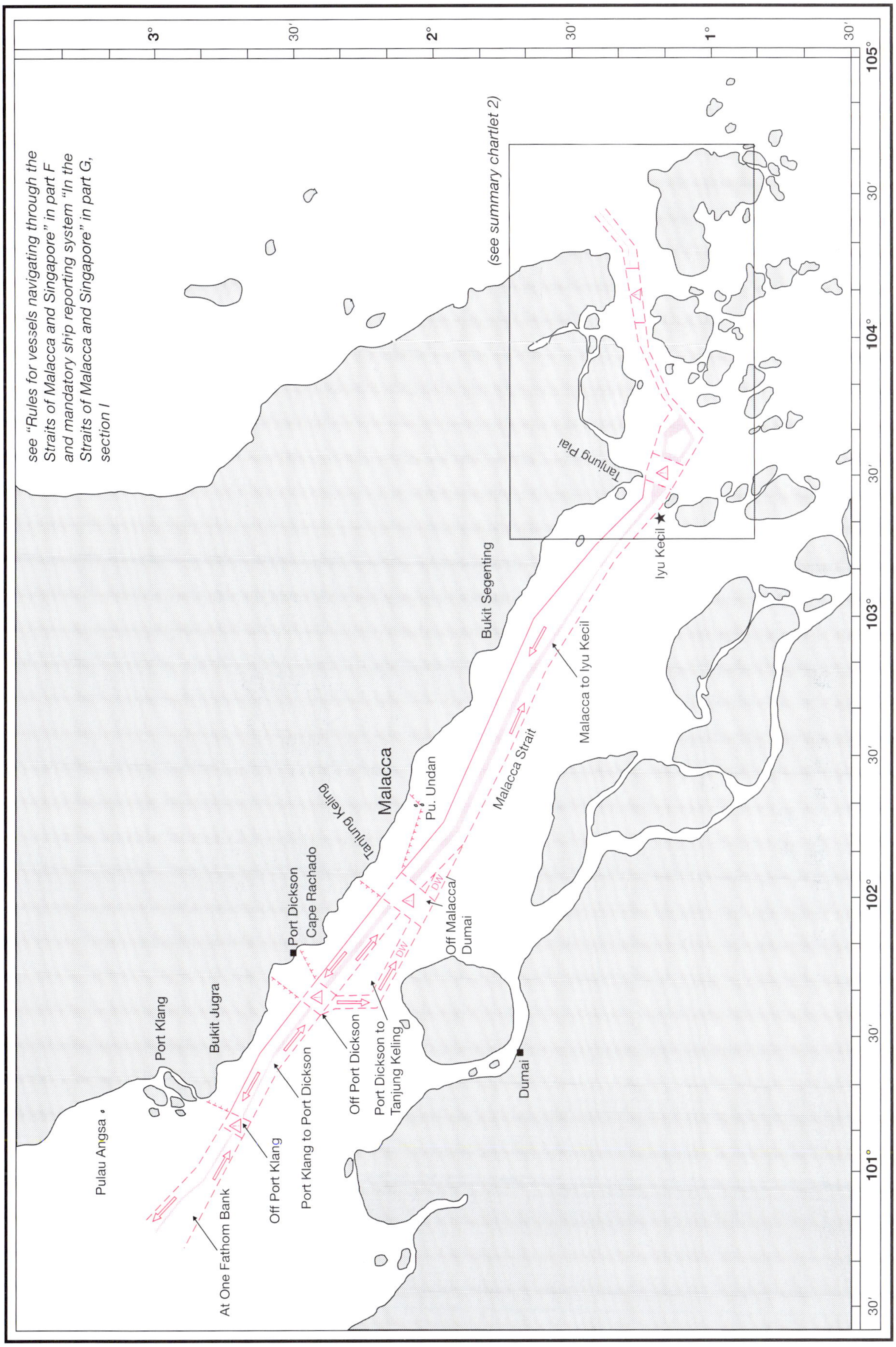

STRAITS OF MALACCA AND SINGAPORE: SUMMARY CHARTLET 1

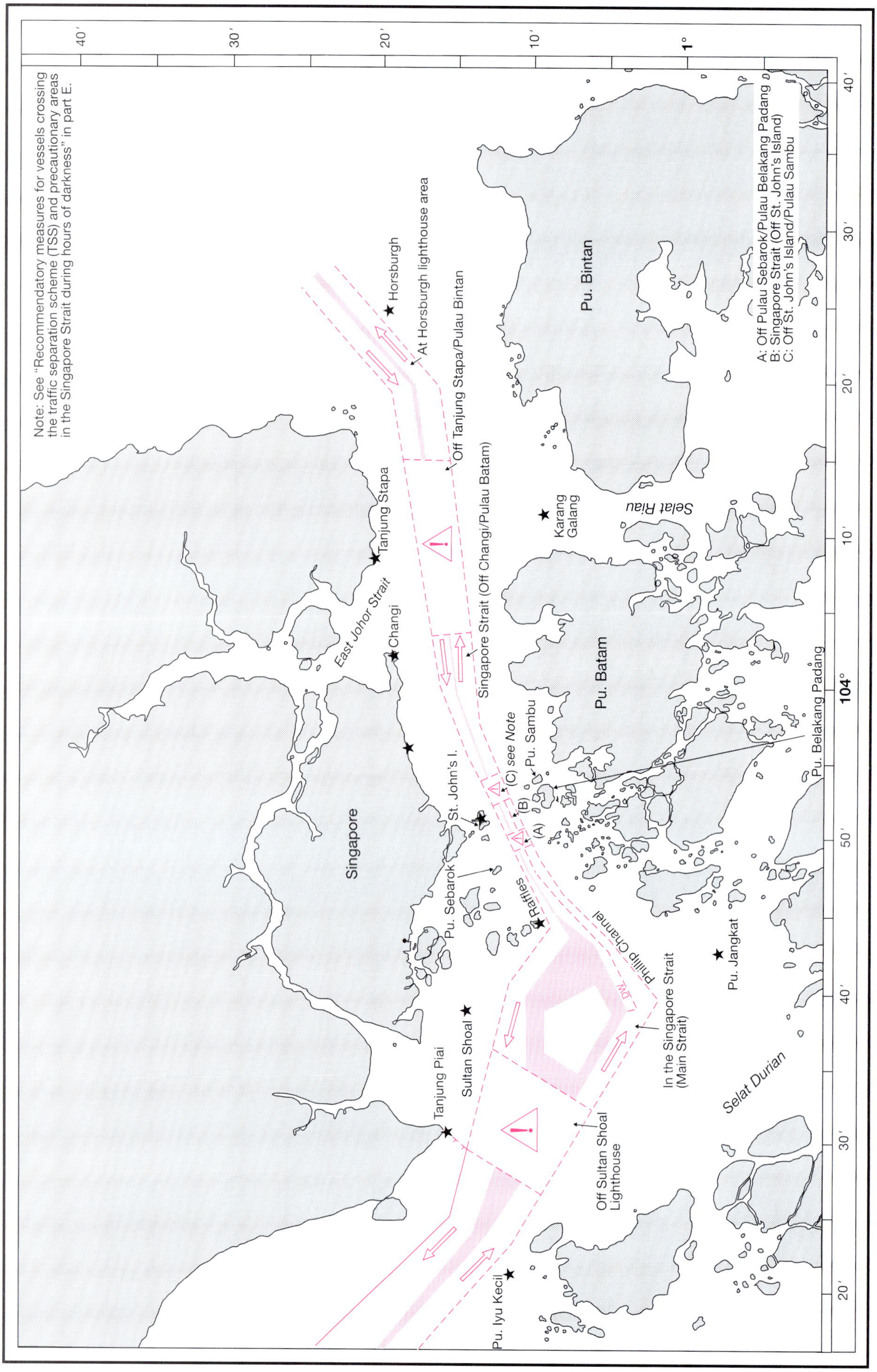

STRAITS OF MALACCA AND SINGAPORE: SUMMARY CHARTLET 2

AT ONE FATHOM BANK

Note: See "Rules for vessels navigating through the Straits of Malacca and Singapore" in part F and mandatory ship reporting system "In the Straits of Malacca and Singapore" in part G, section I.

(Reference chart: British Admiralty 3946, 1996 edition.
Note: This chart is based on revised Kertau datum.)

Description of the traffic separation scheme

(a) A separation zone is bounded by a line connecting the following geographical positions:

(1)	03°00′.70 N,	100°47′.40 E	(5)	02°43′.40 N,	101°10′.00 E
(2)	02°53′.70 N,	100°55′.80 E	(6)	02°49′.00 N,	100°59′.50 E
(3)	02°49′.50 N,	100°59′.50 E	(7)	02°53′.40 N,	100°55′.40 E
(4)	02°43′.90 N,	101°10′.30 E	(8)	03°00′.30 N,	100°47′.10 E

(b) A traffic lane for north-westbound traffic is established between the separation zone and a line connecting the following geographical positions:

(9)	03°02′.70 N,	100°48′.80 E	(11)	02°46′.30 N,	101°11′.50 E
(10)	02°52′.50 N,	101°00′.00 E			

(c) A traffic lane for south-eastbound traffic is established between the separation zone and a line connecting the following geographical positions:

(12)	02°54′.70 N,	100°43′.10 E	(13)	02°41′.20 N,	101°08′.80 E

OFF PORT KLANG

(Reference chart: British Admiralty 3946, 1996 edition.
Note: This chart is based on revised Kertau datum.)

Description of the precautionary area

A precautionary area is established by a line connecting the following geographical positions:

(14)	02°46′.30 N,	101°11′.50 E	(16)	02°39′.40 N,	101°12′.40 E
(15)	02°44′.30 N,	101°15′.00 E	(17)	02°41′.20 N,	101°08′.80 E

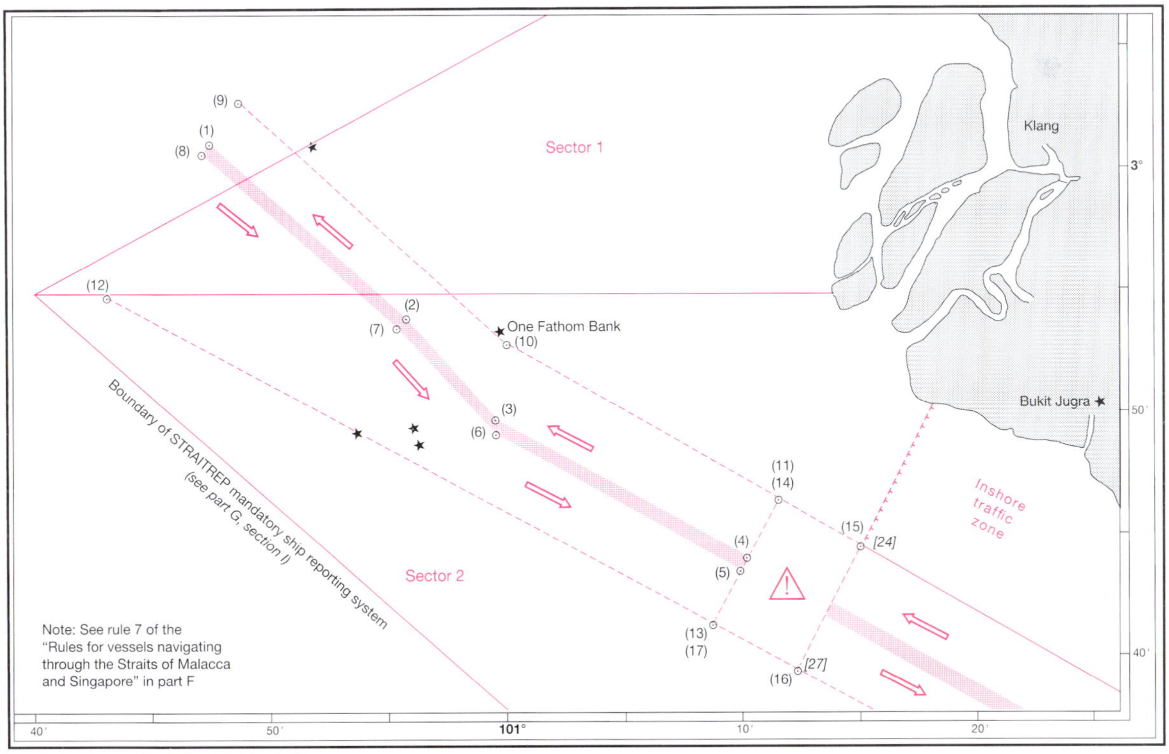

AT ONE FATHOM BANK + OFF PORT KLANG

PORT KLANG TO PORT DICKSON

Note: See "Rules for vessels navigating through the Straits of Malacca and Singapore" in part F and mandatory ship reporting system "In the Straits of Malacca and Singapore" in part G, section I.

(Reference chart: British Admiralty 3946, 1996 edition.
Note: This chart is based on revised Kertau datum.)

Description of the traffic separation scheme

(a) A separation zone is bounded by a line connecting the following geographical positions:

(18)	02°42′.00 N,	101°13′.80 E	(21)	02°26′.50 N,	101°36′.80 E
(19)	02°35′.00 N,	101°27′.10 E	(22)	02°35′.20 N,	101°25′.80 E
(20)	02°27′.10 N,	101°37′.30 E	(23)	02°41′.60 N,	101°13′.60 E

(b) A traffic lane for north-westbound traffic is established between the separation zone and a separation line connecting the following geographical positions:

(24)	02°44′.30 N,	101°15′.00 E	(26)	02°29′.00 N,	101°38′.80 E
(25)	02°37′.40 N,	101°28′.00 E			

(c) A traffic lane for south-eastbound traffic is established between the separation zone and a line connecting the following geographical positions:

(27)	02°39′.40 N,	101°12′.40 E	(29)	02°24′.60 N,	101°35′.30 E
(28)	02°34′.00 N,	101°23′.30 E			

Inshore traffic zone

The area between the landward boundary of the traffic separation scheme and the Malaysian coast between a line drawn from position (24) [02°44′.30 N, 101°15′.00 E] in a direction of 027° to meet the coast and a line drawn from position (26) [02°29′.00 N, 01°38′.80 E] in a direction of 034° to meet the Malaysian coast.

OFF PORT DICKSON

(Reference charts: British Admiralty 3946, 1996 edition; 3947, 1997 edition.
Note: These charts are based on revised Kertau datum.)

Description of the precautionary area

A precautionary area is established by a line connecting the following geographical positions:

(30)	02°29′.00 N,	101°38′.80 E	(32)	02°21′.40 N,	101°39′.40 E
(31)	02°25′.80 N,	101°42′.90 E	(33)	02°24′.60 N,	101°35′.30 E

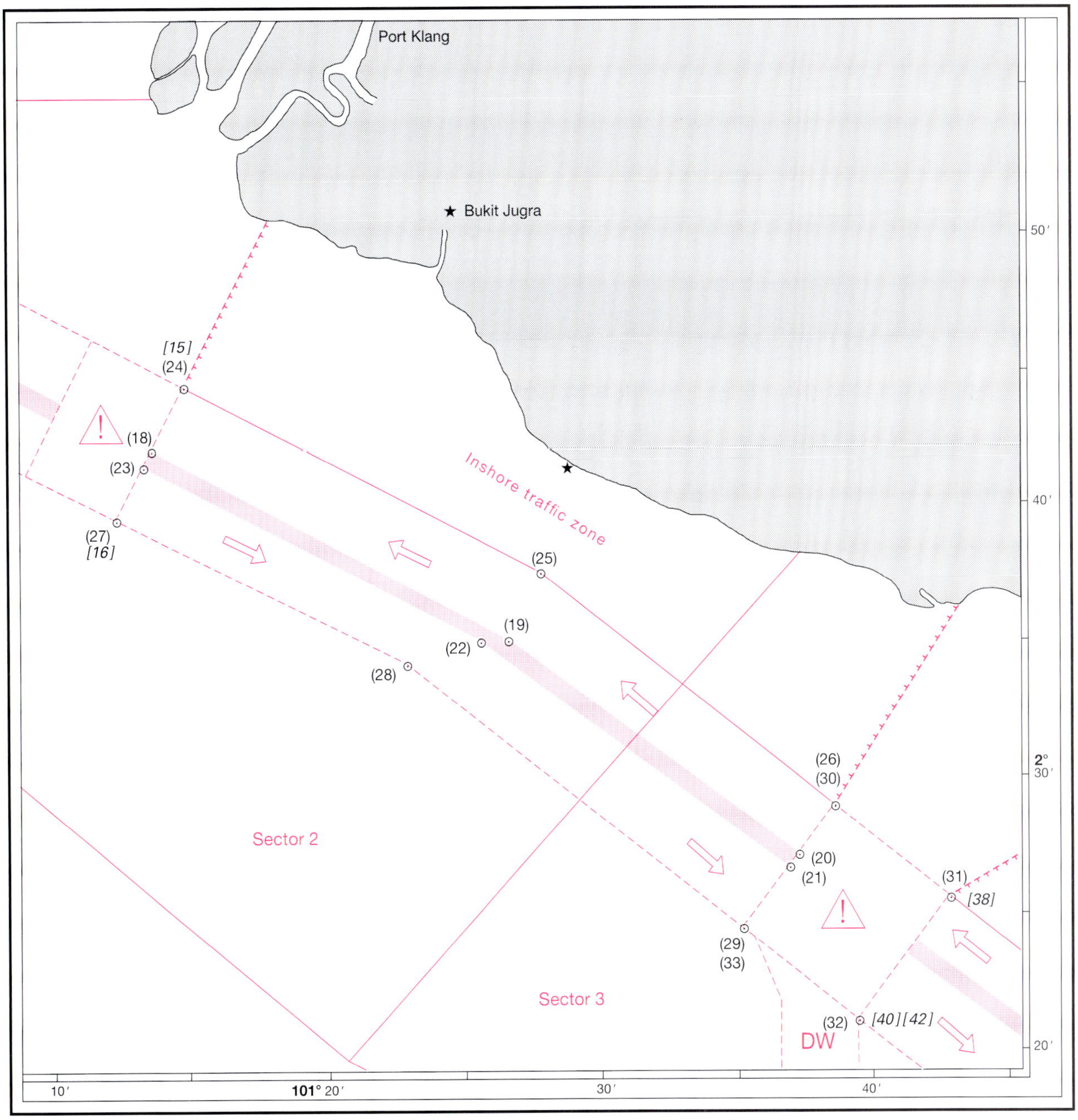

PORT KLANG TO PORT DICKSON + OFF PORT DICKSON

PORT DICKSON TO TANJUNG KELING

Note: See "Rules for vessels navigating through the Straits of Malacca and Singapore" in part F and mandatory ship reporting system "In the Straits of Malacca and Singapore" in part G, section I.

(Reference charts: British Admiralty 3946, 1996 edition; 3947, 1997 edition.
Note: These charts are based on revised Kertau datum.)

Description of the traffic separation scheme

(a) A separation zone is bounded by a line connecting the following geographical positions:

(34)	02°23′.90 N,	101°41′.40 E	(36)	02°09′.00 N,	101°59′.00 E
(35)	02°09′.70 N,	101°59′.60 E	(37)	02°23′.20 N,	101°40′.90 E

(b) A traffic lane for north-westbound traffic is established between the separation zone and a separation line connecting the following geographical positions:

(38)	02°25′.80 N,	101°42′.90 E	(39)	02°11′.60 N,	102°01′.00 E

(c) A traffic lane for south-eastbound traffic is established between the separation zone and a line connecting the following geographical positions:

(40)	02°21′.40 N,	101°39′.40 E	(41)	02°07′.10 N,	101°57′.50 E

(d) A deep-water route for south-eastbound traffic is established by connecting the following geographical positions:

(42)	02°21′.40 N,	101°39′.40 E	(46)	02°12′.30 N,	101°36′.80 E
(43)	02°13′.80 N,	101°39′.30 E	(47)	02°22′.20 N,	101°36′.80 E
(44)	02°05′.10 N,	101°55′.90 E	(48)	02°24′.00 N,	101°36′.10 E
(45)	02°03′.00 N,	101°54′.20 E			

Inshore traffic zone

The area between the landward boundary of the traffic separation scheme and the Malaysian coast between a line drawn from position (38) [02°25′.80 N, 101°42′.90 E] in a direction of 059° to meet the Malaysian coast and a line drawn from position (39) [02°11′.60 N, 102°01′.00 E] in a direction of 034° to meet the Malaysian coast.

OFF MALACCA/DUMAI

(Reference charts: British Admiralty 3947, 1997 edition; 3833, 1988 edition; 2403, 1983 edition.
Note: These charts are based on revised Kertau datum.)

Description of the precautionary area

A precautionary area is established by a line connecting the following geographical positions:

(49)	02°11′.60 N,	102°01′.00 E	(51)	02°00′.00 N,	101°59′.80 E
(50)	02°07′.20 N,	102°06′.20 E	(52)	02°03′.00 N,	101°54′.20 E

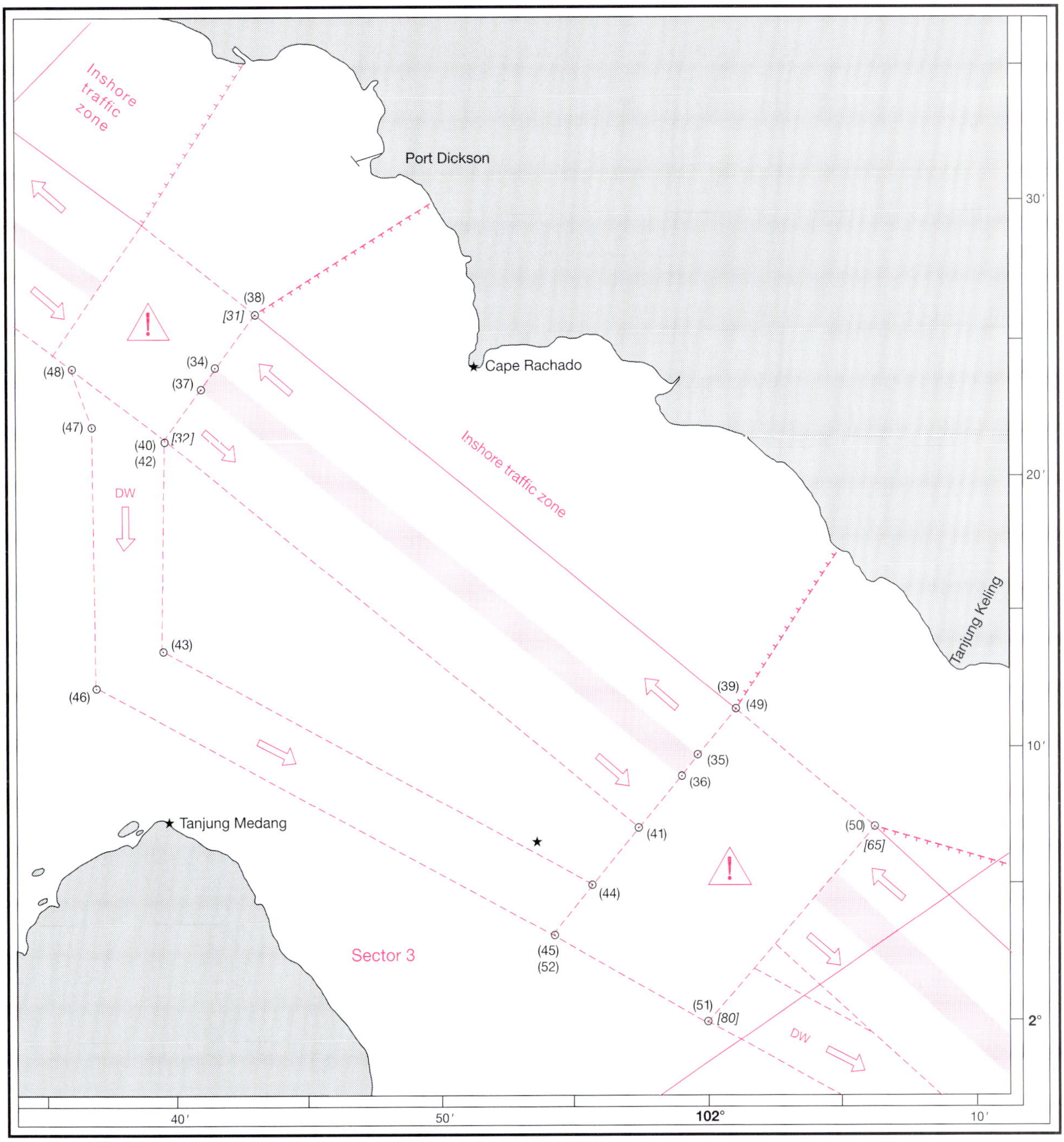

PORT DICKSON TO TANJUNG KELING + OFF MALACCA/DUMAI

B

MALACCA TO IYU KECIL

Note: See "Rules for vessels navigating through the Straits of Malacca and Singapore" in part F and mandatory ship reporting system "In the Straits of Malacca and Singapore" in part G, section I.

(Reference charts: British Admiralty 3947, 1997 edition; 3833, 1988 edition; 2403, 1983 edition.
Note: These charts are based on revised Kertau datum.)

Description of the traffic separation scheme

(a) A separation zone is bounded by a line connecting the following geographical positions:

(53)	02°05′.40 N,	102°04′.60 E	(59)	01°10′.50 N,	103°27′.50 E
(54)	01°55′.70 N,	102°15′.40 E	(60)	01°13′.20 N,	103°23′.40 E
(55)	01°40′.00 N,	102°48′.30 E	(61)	01°23′.20 N,	103°12′.40 E
(56)	01°23′.20 N,	103°12′.40 E	(62)	01°39′.10 N,	102°48′.00 E
(57)	01°13′.80 N,	103°24′.00 E	(63)	01°54′.80 N,	102°14′.80 E
(58)	01°12′.20 N,	103°28′.50 E	(64)	02°04′.60 N,	102°03′.80 E

(b) A traffic lane for north-westbound traffic is established between the separation zone and a separation line connecting the following geographical positions:

(65)	02°07′.20 N,	102°06′.20 E	(68)	01°25′.50 N,	103°15′.00 E
(66)	01°57′.90 N,	102°16′.60 E	(69)	01°15′.20 N,	103°25′.30 E
(67)	01°38′.40 N,	103°00′.00 E	(70)	01°14′.30 N,	103°29′.70 E

(c) A traffic lane for south-eastbound traffic is established between the separation zone and a line connecting the following geographical positions:

(71)	02°02′.80 N,	102°02′.20 E	(74)	01°22′.00 N,	103°11′.10 E
(72)	01°52′.60 N,	102°13′.30 E	(75)	01°11′.60 N,	103°22′.80 E
(73)	01°36′.80 N,	102°46′.90 E	(76)	01°09′.20 N,	103°26′.80 E

(d) A deep-water route for south-eastbound traffic is established by connecting the following geographical positions:

(77)	02°01′.90 N,	102°01′.50 E	(79)	01°52′.60 N,	102°13′.30 E
(78)	01°59′.70 N,	102°05′.60 E	(80)	02°00′.00 N,	101°59′.80 E

Inshore traffic zone

The area between the landward boundary of the traffic separation scheme and the Malaysian coast between a line drawn from position (65) [02°07′.20 N, 102°06′.20 E] to Pulau Undan lighthouse [02°02′.90 N, 102°20′.10 E], then in a direction of 040° to meet the Malaysian coast and a line drawn from position (70) [01°14′.30 N, 103°29′.70 E] in a direction of 038° to meet the Malaysian coast.

OFF SULTAN SHOAL LIGHTHOUSE

(Reference charts: British Admiralty 2598, 1990 edition; 2556, 1994 edition; 3833, 1988 edition; 2403, 1983 edition.
Note: These charts are based on revised Kertau datum.)

Description of the precautionary area

A precautionary area is established by a line connecting the following geographical positions:

(81)	01°14′.28 N,	103°29′.73 E	(83)	01°05′.94 N,	103°32′.30 E
(82)	01°12′.62 N,	103°36′.24 E	(84)	01°09′.23 N,	103°26′.76 E

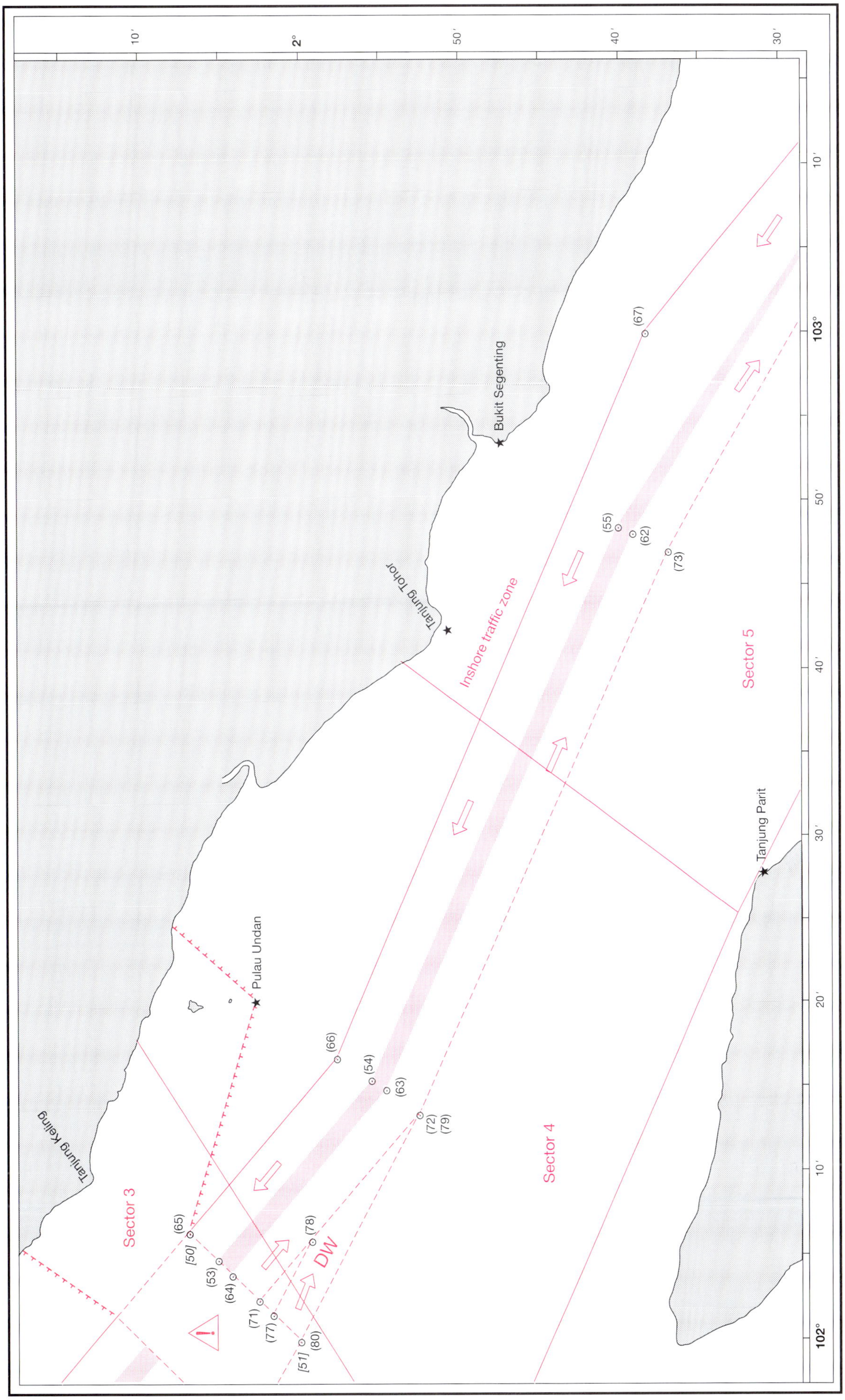

MALACCA TO IYU KECIL (WEST)

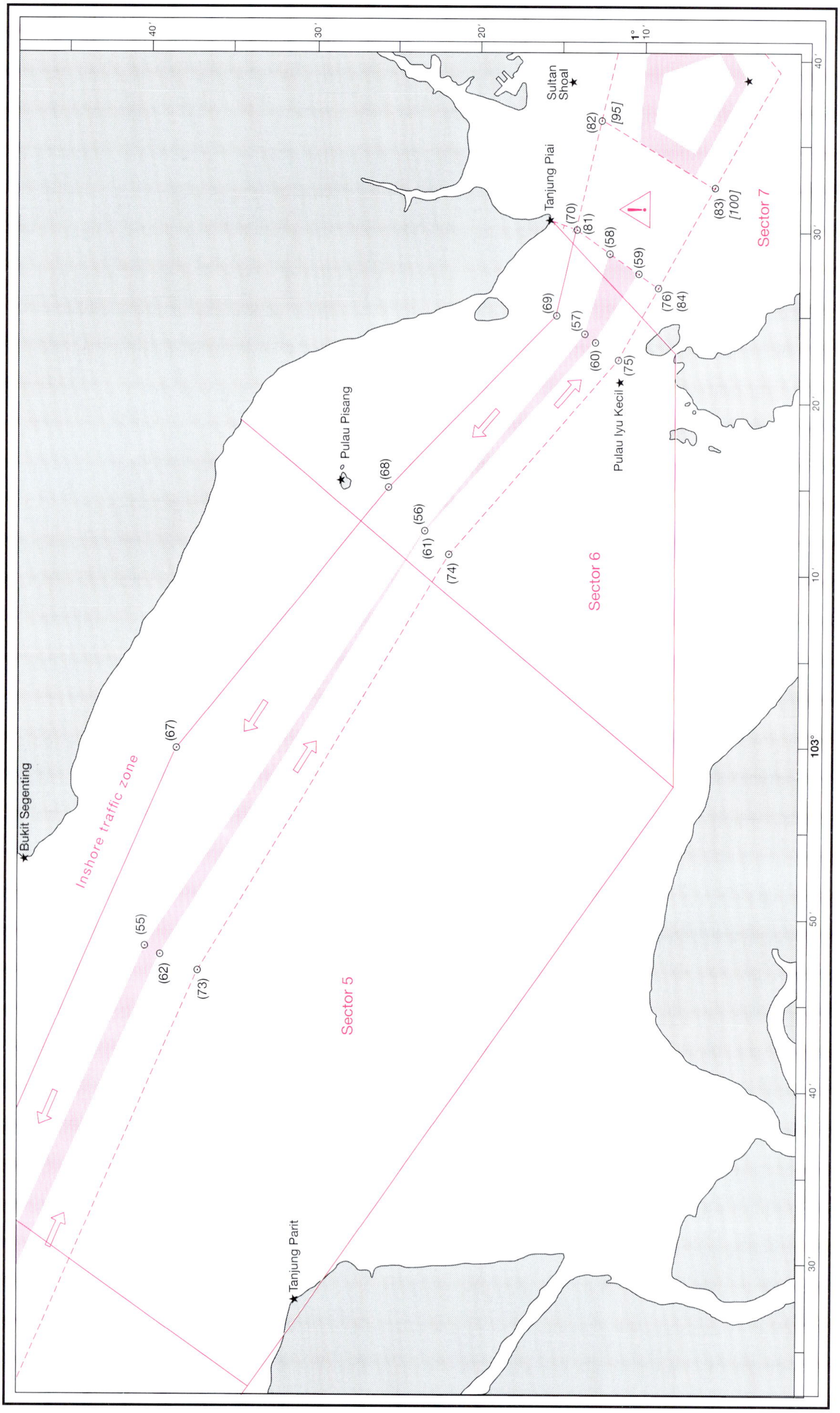

MALACCA TO IYU KECIL (EAST) + OFF SULTAN SHOAL LIGHTHOUSE

IN THE SINGAPORE STRAIT (MAIN STRAIT)

Note: See "Recommendatory measure for vessels crossing the traffic separation scheme (TSS) and precautionary areas in the Singapore Strait during hours of darkness" in part E, "Rules for vessels navigating through the Straits of Malacca and Singapore" in part F and mandatory ship reporting system "In the Straits of Malacca and Singapore" in part G, section I.

(Reference charts: British Admiralty 2598, 1990 edition; 2556, 1994 edition; 3833, 1988 edition; 2403, 1983 edition.
Note: These charts are based on revised Kertau datum.
Indonesian 40, November 1977 edition.
Note: This chart is based on World Geodetic System 1984 datum (WGS 84).)

Description of the traffic separation scheme

(a) A separation zone is bounded by a line connecting the following geographical positions (relative to WGS 84 datum):

(85)	01°10′.35 N,	103°34′.90 E	(89)	01°05′.90 N,	103°43′.38 E
(86)	01°10′.35 N,	103°39′.85 E	(90)	01°03′.60 N,	103°38′.98 E
(87)	01°07′.50 N,	103°43′.72 E	(91)	01°07′.06 N,	103°32′.96 E
(88)	01°08′.60 N,	103°45′.43 E			

(b) An anchorage area is established within the separation zone described in paragraph (a) that is bounded by a line connecting the following geographical positions (relative to WGS 84 datum):

(85a)	01°09′.40 N,	103°36′.60 E	(90a)	01°04′.50 N,	103°38′.90 E
(86a)	01°09′.10 N,	103°38′.60 E	(91a)	01°06′.80 N,	103°35′.00 E
(89a)	01°05′.50 N,	103°40′.80 E			

(c) A separation line connects the following geographical positions (relative to Kertau datum):

(92)	01°08′.60 N,	103°45′.43 E	(94)	01°10′.81 N,	103°49′.30 E
(93)	01°10′.26 N,	103°47′.91 E			

(d) A traffic lane for westbound traffic is established between the separation zone/line and a line connecting the following geographical positions (relative to Kertau datum):

(95)	01°12′.62 N,	103°36′.24 E	(98)	01°10′.45 N,	103°47′.50 E
(96)	01°11′.50 N,	103°40′.55 E	(99)	01°11′.13 N,	103°49′.18 E
(97)	01°08′.65 N,	103°44′.40 E			

(e) A traffic lane for eastbound traffic is established between the separation zone/line and a line connecting the following geographical positions (relative to Kertau datum):

(100)	01°05′.94 N,	103°32′.30 E	(103)	01°07′.80 N,	103°46′.25 E
(101)	01°01′.60 N,	103°39′.65 E	(104)	01°09′.47 N,	103°48′.70 E
(102)	01°05′.00 N,	103°43′.67 E	(105)	01°09′.92 N,	103°49′.65 E

(f) A deep-water route is established within the eastbound lane described in paragraph (e). The deep-water route is bounded by a line connecting the following geographical positions (relative to Kertau datum):

(i)	01°03′.60 N,	103°38′.95 E	(vi)	01°10′.45 N,	103°49′.45 E
(ii)	01°05′.90 N,	103°43′.38 E	(vii)	01°09′.95 N,	103°48′.28 E
(iii)	01°08′.61 N,	103°45′.44 E	(viii)	01°08′.90 N,	103°46′.82 E
(iv)	01°10′.26 N,	103°47′.91 E	(ix)	01°04′.95 N,	103°42′.87 E
(v)	01°10′.81 N,	103°49′.30 E	(x)	01°02′.97 N,	103°39′.10 E

SINGAPORE STRAIT (OFF PULAU SEBAROK/PULAU BELAKANG PADANG)

Note: See "Recommendatory measure for vessels crossing the traffic separation scheme (TSS) and precautionary areas in the Singapore Strait during hours of darkness" in part E, "Rules for vessels navigating through the Straits of Malacca and Singapore" in part F and mandatory ship reporting system "In the Straits of Malacca and Singapore" in part G, section I.

(Reference charts: British Admiralty 2598, 1990 edition; 2556, 1994 edition; 3833, 1988 edition; 2403, 1983 edition.
Note: These charts are based on revised Kertau datum.)

Description of the precautionary area

A precautionary area is established by a line connecting the following geographical positions:

(106)	01°11′.13 N,	103°49′.18 E	(108)	01°10′.45 N,	103°50′.75 E
(107)	01°11′.59 N,	103°50′.31 E	(109)	01°09′.92 N,	103°49′.65 E

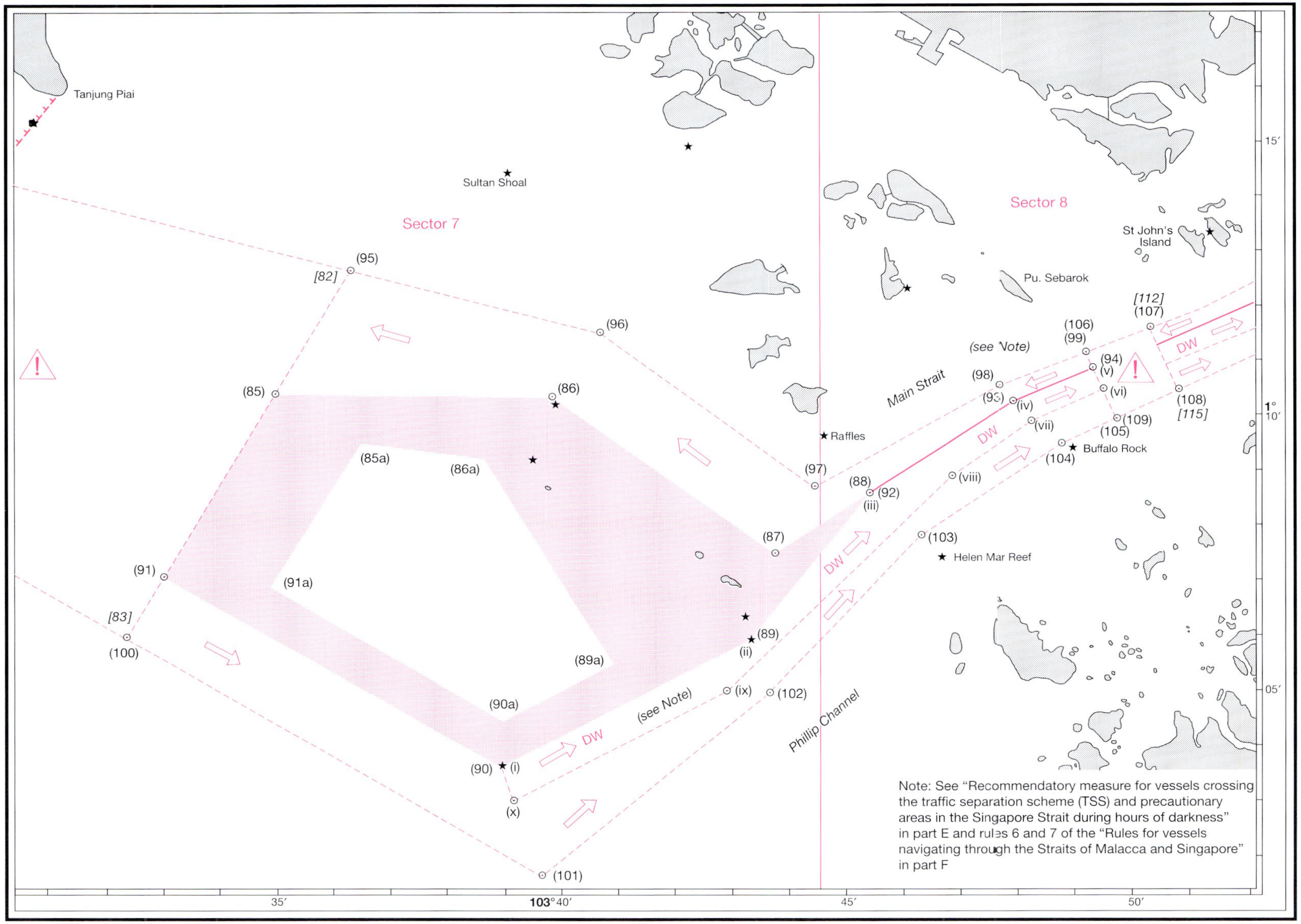

IN THE SINGAPORE STRAIT (MAIN STRAIT) +
SINGAPORE STRAIT (OFF PULAU SEBAROK/PULAU BELAKANG PADANG)

SINGAPORE STRAIT (OFF ST. JOHN'S ISLAND)

Note: See "Recommendatory measure for vessels crossing the traffic separation scheme (TSS) and precautionary areas in the Singapore Strait during hours of darkness" in part E, "Rules for vessels navigating through the Straits of Malacca and Singapore" in part F and mandatory ship reporting system "In the Straits of Malacca and Singapore" in part G, section I.

(Reference charts: British Admiralty 2556, 1994 edition; 3833, 1988 edition; 2403, 1983 edition.
Note: These charts are based on revised Kertau datum.)

Description of the traffic separation scheme

(a) A separation line connects the following geographical positions:

(110)	01°11′.27 N,	103°50′.43 E	(111)	01°12′.21 N,	103°52′.40 E

(b) A traffic lane for westbound traffic is established between the separation line and a line connecting the following geographical positions:

(112)	01°11′.59 N,	103°50′.31 E	(114)	01°12′.51 N,	103°52′.25 E
(113)	01°11′.96 N,	103°51′.21 E			

(c) A traffic lane for eastbound traffic is established between the separation line and a line connecting the following geographical positions:

(115)	01°10′.45 N,	103°50′.75 E	(116)	01°11′.41 N,	103°52′.76 E

(d) A deep-water route is established within the eastbound lane described in paragraph (c). The deep-water route is bounded by a line connecting the following geographical positions:

(xi)	01°11′.27 N,	103°50′.43 E	(xiii)	01°11′.78 N,	103°52′.58 E
(xii)	01°12′.21 N,	103°52′.40 E	(xiv)	01°10′.92 N,	103°50′.57 E

SINGAPORE STRAIT (OFF ST. JOHN'S ISLAND/PULAU SAMBU)

Note: See "Recommendatory measure for vessels crossing the traffic separation scheme (TSS) and precautionary areas in the Singapore Strait during hours of darkness" in part E, "Rules for vessels navigating through the Straits of Malacca and Singapore" in part F and mandatory ship reporting system "In the Straits of Malacca and Singapore" in part G, section I.

(Reference charts: British Admiralty 2556, 1994 edition; 3833, 1988 edition; 2403, 1983 edition.
Note: These charts are based on revised Kertau datum.)

Description of the precautionary area

(a) A precautionary area is established by a line connecting the following geographical positions:

(117)	01°12′.51 N,	103°52′.25 E	(119)	01°12′.11 N,	103°54′.40 E
(118)	01°13′.38 N,	103°53′.85 E	(120)	01°11′.41 N,	103°52′.76 E

(b) The focal point of the precautionary area is located at the following geographical position:

(121)	01°12′.60 N,	103°53′.20 E

Description of the area to be avoided

A circular area to be avoided with a diameter of one cable is established around position (121).

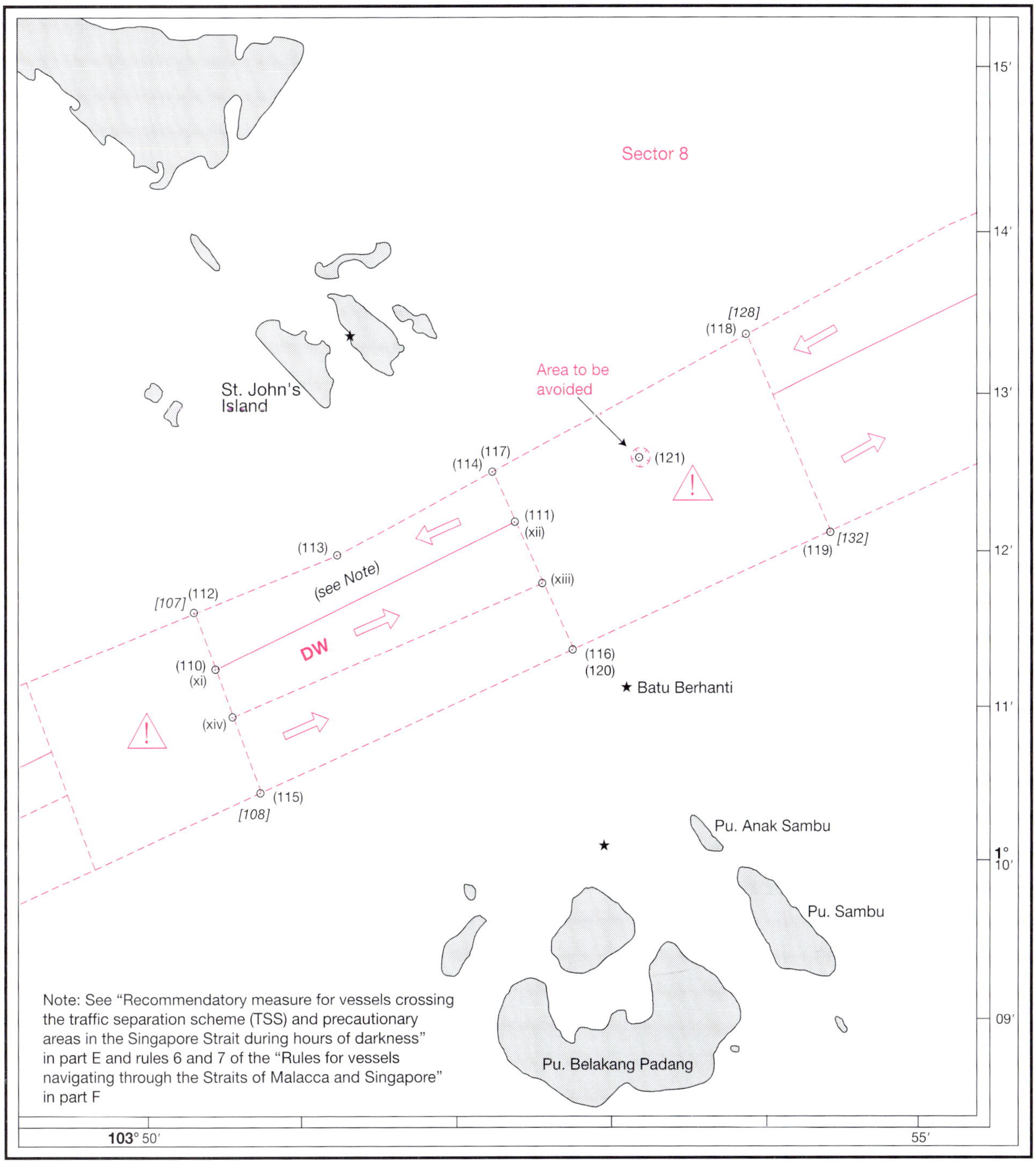

SINGAPORE STRAIT (OFF ST. JOHN'S ISLAND)
+ SINGAPORE STRAIT (OFF ST. JOHN'S ISLAND/PULAU SAMBU)

SINGAPORE STRAIT (OFF CHANGI/PULAU BATAM)

Note: See "Recommendatory measure for vessels crossing the traffic separation scheme (TSS) and precautionary areas in the Singapore Strait during hours of darkness" in part E, "Rules for vessels navigating through the Straits of Malacca and Singapore" in part F and mandatory ship reporting system "In the Straits of Malacca and Singapore" in part G, section I.

(Reference charts: British Admiralty 2569, 1990 edition; 3833, 1988 edition; 3831, 1988 edition; 2403, 1983 edition.
Note: These charts are based on revised Kertau datum.)

Description of the traffic separation scheme

(a) A separation line connects the following geographical positions:

(122)	01°12′.97 N,	103°54′.03 E	(124)	01°14′.89 N,	103°59′.01 E
(123)	01°13′.57 N,	103°55′.40 E			

(b) A separation zone is bounded by a line connecting the following geographical positions:

(125)	01°14′.89 N,	103°59′.01 E	(127)	01°15′.42 N,	104°03′.45 E
(126)	01°15′.67 N,	104°03′.40 E			

(c) A traffic lane for westbound traffic is established between the separation zone/line and a line connecting the following geographical positions:

(128)	01°13′.38 N,	103°53′.85 E	(130)	01°16′.02 N,	104°00′.00 E
(129)	01°14′.07 N,	103°55′.18 E	(131)	01°16′.60 N,	104°03′.32 E

(d) A traffic lane for eastbound traffic is established between the separation zone/line and a line connecting the following geographical positions:

(132)	01°12′.11 N,	103°54′.40 E	(134)	01°14′.05 N,	104°03′.58 E
(133)	01°13′.50 N,	103°57′.67 E			

SINGAPORE STRAIT (OFF TANJUNG STAPA/PULAU BINTAN)

Note: See "Recommendatory measure for vessels crossing the traffic separation scheme (TSS) and precautionary areas in the Singapore Strait during hours of darkness" in part E, "Rules for vessels navigating through the Straits of Malacca and Singapore" in part F and mandatory ship reporting system "In the Straits of Malacca and Singapore" in part G, section I.

(Reference charts: British Admiralty 2569, 1990 edition; 3833, 1988 edition; 3831, 1988 edition; 2403, 1983 edition.
Note: These charts are based on revised Kertau datum.)

Description of the precautionary area

A precautionary area is established by a line connecting the following geographical positions:

(135)	01°16′.60 N,	104°03′.32 E	(137)	01°15′.40 N,	104°15′.00 E
(136)	01°18′.63 N,	104°15′.00 E	(138)	01°14′.05 N,	104°03′.58 E

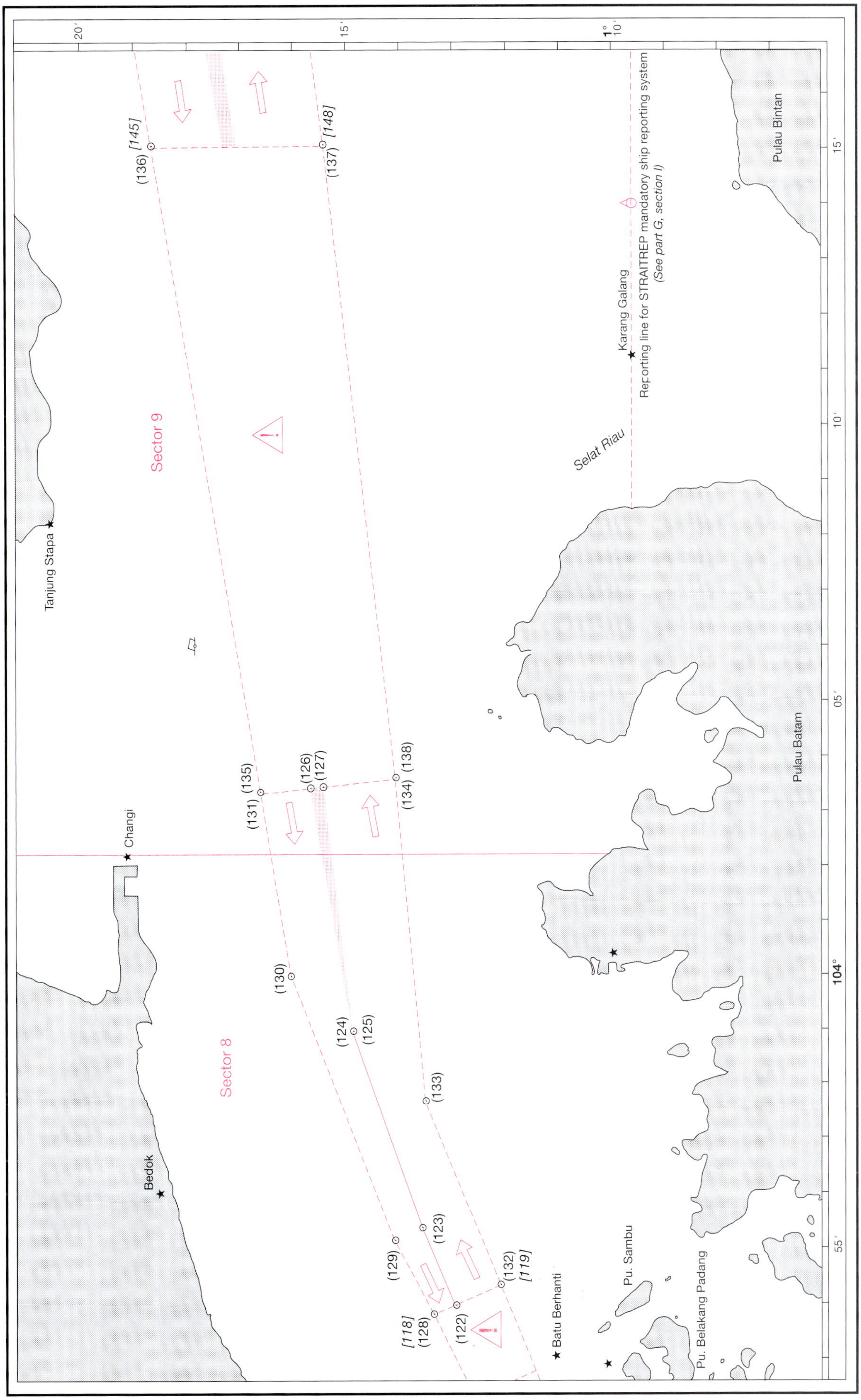

SINGAPORE STRAIT (OFF CHANGI/PULAU BATAM) +
SINGAPORE STRAIT (OFF TANJUNG STAPA/PULAU BINTAN)

AT HORSBURGH LIGHTHOUSE AREA

Note: See "Rules for vessels navigating through the Straits of Malacca and Singapore" in part F and mandatory ship reporting system "In the Straits of Malacca and Singapore" in part G, section I.

(Reference charts: British Admiralty 3831, 1988 edition; 2403, 1983 edition.
Note: These charts are based on revised Kertau datum.)

Description of the traffic separation scheme

(a) A separation zone is bounded by a line connecting the following geographical positions:

(139)	01°17′.32 N,	104°15′.00 E	(142)	01°24′.30 N,	104°27′.25 E
(140)	01°18′.00 N,	104°19′.70 E	(143)	01°17′.80 N,	104°19′.85 E
(141)	01°24′.55 N,	104°27′.05 E	(144)	01°17′.10 N,	104°15′.00 E

(b) A traffic lane for south-westbound traffic is established between the separation zone and a line connecting the following geographical positions:

(145)	01°18′.63 N,	104°15′.00 E	(147)	01°25′.40 N,	104°26′.32 E
(146)	01°19′.40 N,	104°19′.50 E			

(c) A traffic lane for north-eastbound traffic is established between the separation zone and a line connecting the following geographical positions:

(148)	01°15′.40 N,	104°15′.00 E	(150)	01°23′.40 N,	104°27′.95 E
(149)	01°16′.30 N,	104°19′.85 E			

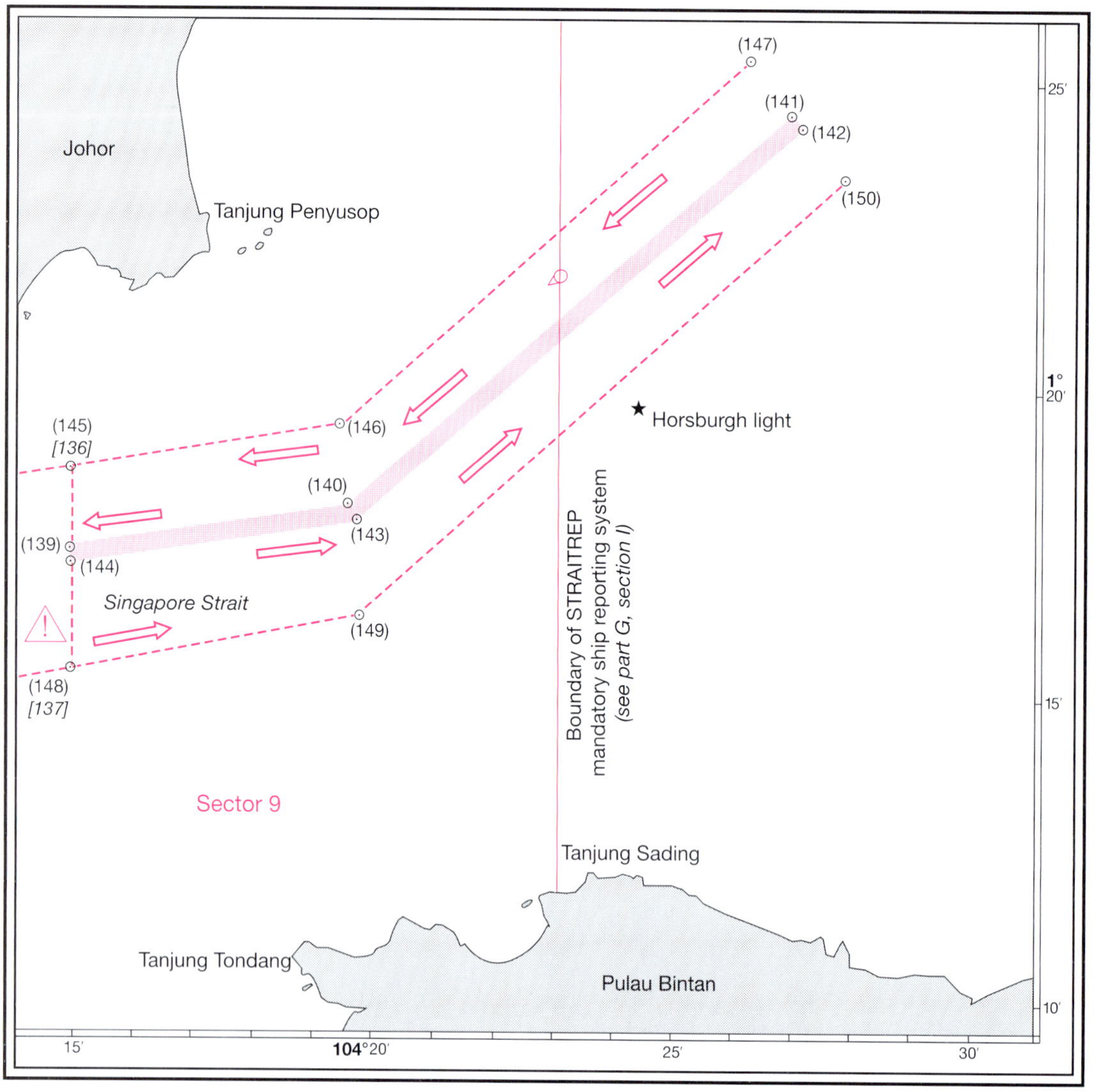

AT HORSBURGH LIGHTHOUSE AREA

IN THE EAST LAMMA AND TATHONG CHANNELS

(Reference charts: British Admiralty 937, 1989 edition; 1917, 1988 edition; 1918, 1988 edition.
Note: These charts are based on Hong Kong 1963 datum.)

Description of the traffic separation schemes

The traffic separation schemes in the approaches to Hong Kong consist of two parts:

Part I:
Eastern approaches to Victoria Port (Tathong Channel)

(a) A separation zone is bounded by lines connecting the following geographical positions:

(1)	22°13′.42 N,	114°20′.00 E	(3)	22°13′.25 N,	114°17′.47 E
(2)	22°13′.07 N,	114°20′.00 E	(4)	22°13′.42 N,	114°20′.00 E

(b) A separation line connects the following geographical positions:

(5)	22°13′.25 N,	114°17′.47 E	(7)	22°16′.33 N,	114°15′.50 E
(6)	22°14′.12 N,	114°16′.42 E	(8)	22°17′.05 N,	114°14′.33 E

(c) A traffic lane for inbound traffic is established between the separation zone/line and a line connecting the following geographical positions:

(9)	22°14′.08 N,	114°20′.00 E	(12)	22°16′.38 N,	114°15′.78 E
(10)	22°13′.93 N,	114°17′.27 E	(13)	22°17′.15 N,	114°14′.40 E
(11)	22°14′.23 N,	114°16′.67 E			

(d) A traffic lane for outbound traffic is established between the separation zone/line and a line connecting the following geographical positions:

(14)	22°12′.30 N,	114°20′.00 E	(17)	22°16′.30 N,	114°15′.22 E
(15)	22°12′.47 N,	114°17′.67 E	(18)	22°16′.97 N,	114°14′.27 E
(16)	22°14′.02 N,	114°16′.13 E			

Inshore traffic zones

The area enclosed by the outer limit of the inbound traffic lane and the adjacent coast, and a line drawn from position (13) [22°17′.15 N, 114°14′.40 E] in the direction 034° true to the shore, and a line drawn from position 22°13′.95 N, 114°17′.75 E in the direction 360° true to the shore, is designated as an inshore traffic zone.

The area enclosed by the outer limit of the outbound traffic lane and the adjacent coast, and a line drawn from position (18) [22°16′.97 N, 114°14′.27 E] in the direction 214° true to the shore, and a line drawn from position (15) [22°12′.47 N, 114°17′.67 E] in the direction 270° true to the shore, is designated as an inshore traffic zone.

Part II:
Western approaches to Victoria Port (East Lamma Channel)

The traffic separation scheme for the western approaches to Victoria Port (East Lamma Channel) comprises:

(a) A separation line connecting the following geographical positions:

(1)	22°09′.43 N,	114°12′.58 E	(2)	22°10′.35 N,	114°11′.92 E

(b) A traffic lane for inbound traffic established between the separation line specified in (a) and a straight line connecting the following geographical positions:

(3)	22°09′.83 N,	114°13′.22 E	(4)	22°10′.68 N,	114°12′.43 E

(c) A traffic lane for outbound traffic established between the separation line specified in (a) and a straight line connecting the following geographical positions:

(5)	22°09′.00 N,	114°11′.88 E	(6)	22°10′.00 N,	114°11′.37 E

(d) A precautionary area established by a line connecting the following geographical positions:

(7)	22°10′.68 N,	114°12′.43 E	
(8)	22°11′.30 N,	114°11′.87 E	(Chesterman)
(9)	22°10′.73 N,	114°10′.97 E	
(10)	22°10′.00 N,	114°11′.37 E	

B

(e) A separation line connecting the following geographical positions:

(11) 22°11′.02 N, 114°11′.42 E
(12) 22°12′.65 N, 114°10′.23 E (LCS 1)
(13) 22°14′.92 N, 114°07′.18 E (Lamma Patch)
(14) 22°16′.37 N, 114°06′.43 E (LCS 2)

(f) A traffic lane for inbound traffic established between the separation line specified in (e) and straight lines connecting the following geographical positions:

(15) 22°11′.30 N, 114°11′.87 E (Chesterman)
(16) 22°12′.87 N, 114°10′.42 E (LCS 1 NE)
(17) 22°15′.10 N, 114°07′.43 E (Lamma Patch NE)
(18) 22°16′.47 N, 114°06′.67 E (LCS 2 NE)

(g) A traffic lane for outbound traffic established between the separation line specified in (e) and straight lines connecting the following geographical positions:

(19) 22°10′.73 N, 114°10′.97 E
(20) 22°12′.45 N, 114°10′.07 E (LCS 1 SW)
(21) 22°14′.73 N, 114°06′.97 E (Lamma Patch SW)
(22) 22°16′.23 N, 114°06′.13 E (LCS 2 SW)

Inshore traffic zones

(h) A designated inshore traffic zone on the landward side of the inbound traffic lane is established as follows:

The area between the outer boundary of the inbound traffic lane specified in (f) and a straight line drawn from the position (15) in the direction 056° true to the shore and a straight line drawn from position (18) in the direction 063° true to the shore.

(i) A designated inshore traffic zone on the landward side of the outbound traffic lane as follows:

The area between the outer boundary of a part of the outbound traffic lane specified in (g) and the adjacent coast, and a straight line drawn from position (20) in the direction 218.5° true to the shore, and a straight line drawn from position (21) in the direction 231° true to the shore.

Remarks:

A Safe Water Mark LCS 1 is to be laid in position (1) with the characteristics of Lfl 10 s in conjunction with the amended traffic separation scheme "Western approaches to Victoria Port (East Lamma Channel)". The existing LCS 1 and LCS 2 will be renamed LCS 2 and LCS 3 respectively; their type and characteristics will remain unchanged.

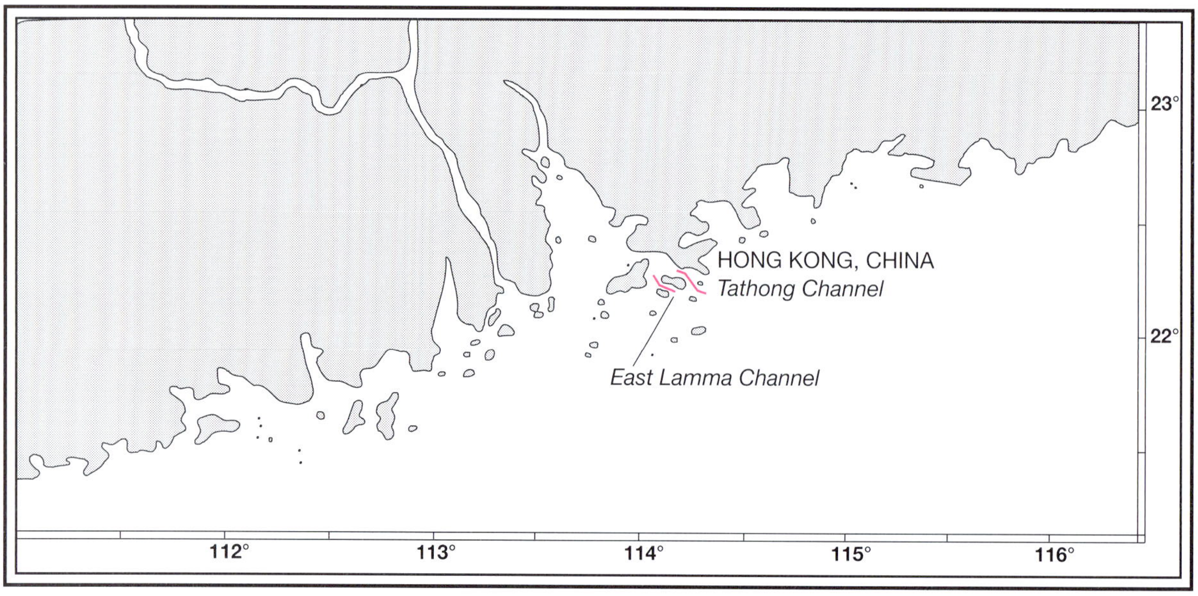

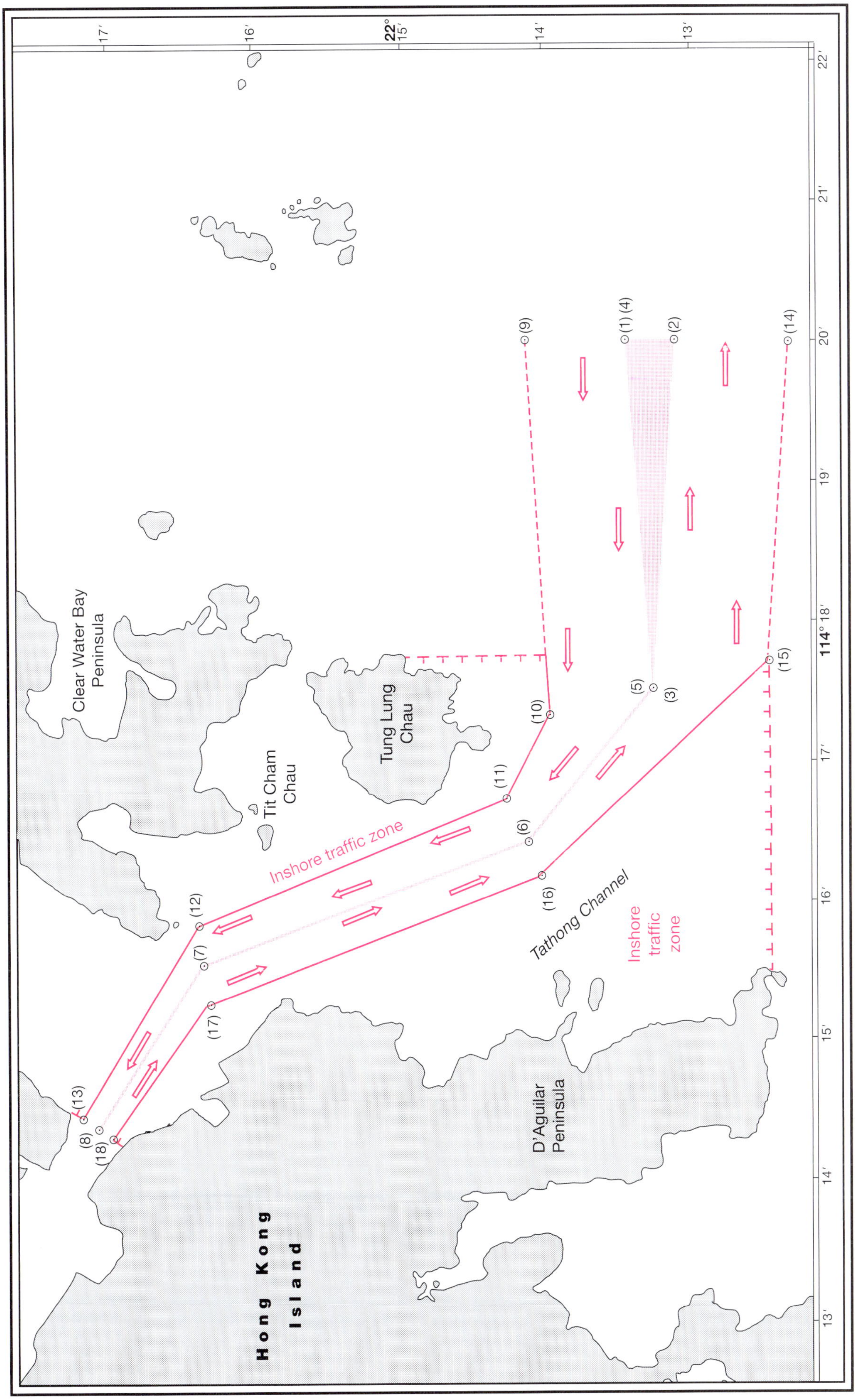

IN THE TATHONG CHANNEL

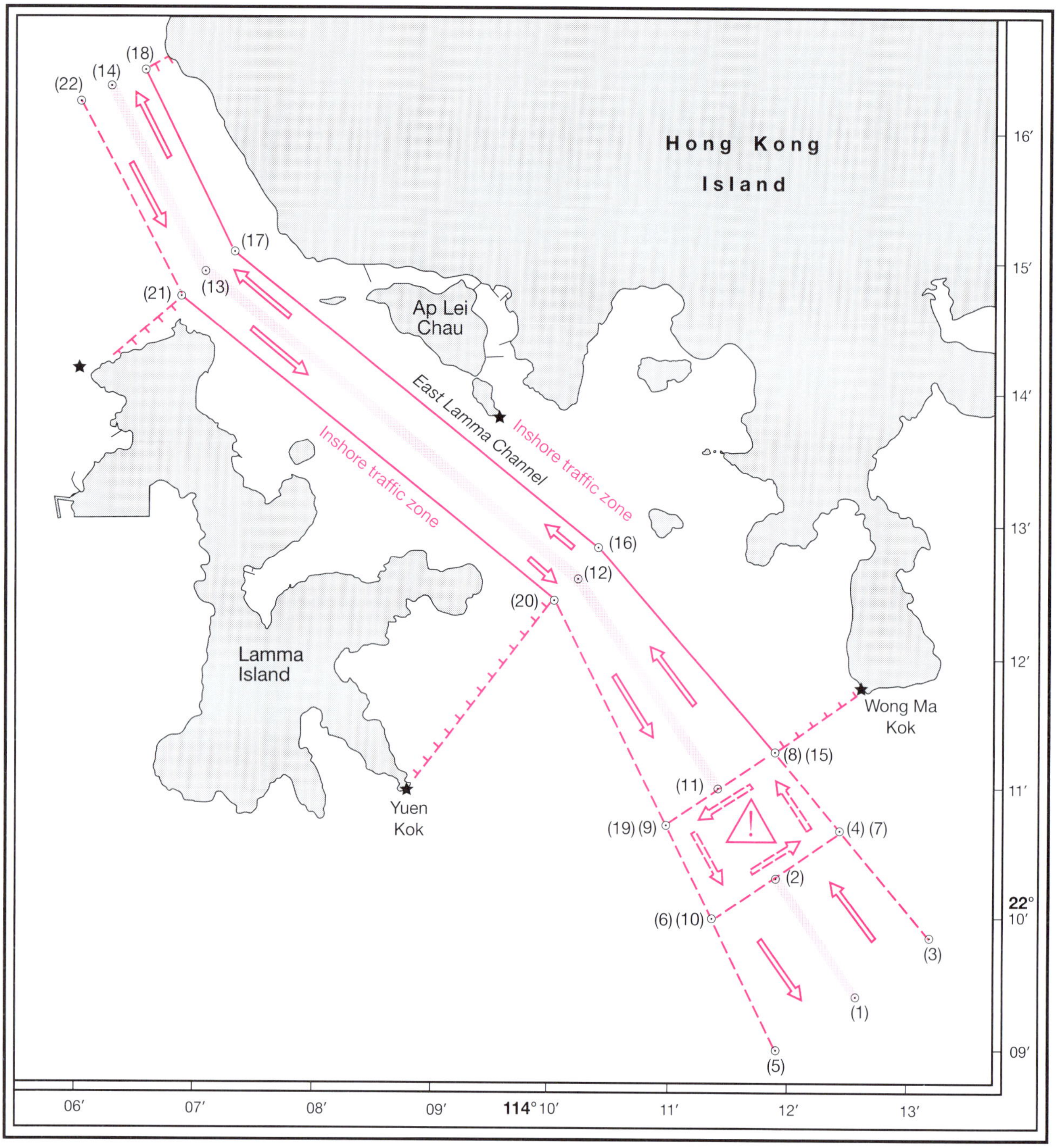

IN THE EAST LAMMA CHANNEL

Section VI

Australasia

Caution: The chartlets are for illustrative purposes only and must not be used for navigation. Mariners should consult the appropriate nautical publications and charts for up-to-date details on aids to navigation and other relevant information.

Warning: The geographical positions given in the descriptions of the routeing systems are only correct for charts using the same geodetic datum as the reference charts indicated under each scheme. Charts published by other hydrographic offices may use a different geodetic datum, as may new editions of the reference charts published after the adoption of the routeing system. Where amendments to existing systems are not based on the same geodetic datum as the original system, this is emphasized by the use of different colours for definitions of positions.

B

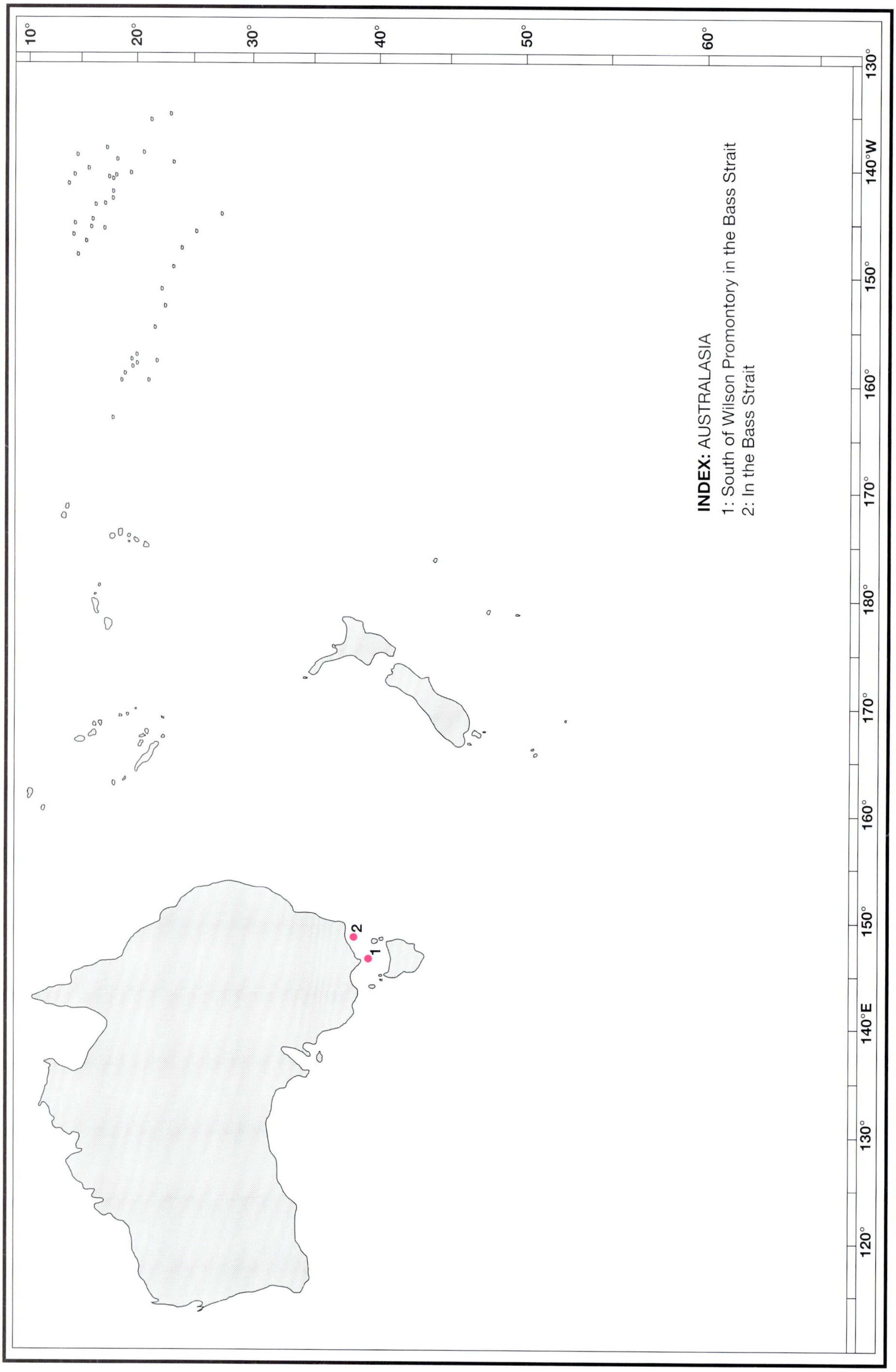
INDEX: AUSTRALASIA
1: South of Wilson Promontory in the Bass Strait
2: In the Bass Strait
10°
20°
30°
40°
50°
60°
120°
130°
140°E
150°
160°
170°
180°
170°
160°
150°
140°W
130°
1
2

SOUTH OF WILSON PROMONTORY IN THE BASS STRAIT

(Reference charts: British Admiralty 1695A; Australian AUS 801, 1975 edition; AUS 350, 1971 edition.
Note: These charts are based on Australian Geodetic datum 1966.)

Description of the traffic separation scheme

(a) A separation zone is bounded by a line connecting the following geographical positions:

(1)	39°11′.00 S,	146°45′.00 E	(3)	39°15′.00 S,	146°15′.00 E
(2)	39°15′.00 S,	146°33′.00 E	(4)	39°12′.00 S,	146°25′.00 E

(b) A traffic lane for westbound traffic is established between the separation zone and a separation line connecting the following geographical positions:

(5)	39°02′.00 S,	146°45′.00 E	(7)	39°10′.80 S,	146°19′.20 E
(6)	39°09′.00 S,	146°26′.00 E	(8)	39°10′.80 S,	146°15′.00 E

(c) A traffic lane for eastbound traffic is established between the separation zone and a line connecting the following geographical positions:

(9)	39°19′.00 S,	146°15′.00 E	(10)	39°19′.00 S,	146°45′.00 E

Inshore traffic zone

The area between Wilson Promontory and the landward boundary of the traffic separation scheme and lying between a line drawn from position 39°02′.00 S, 146°45′.00 E to position 39°04′.10 S, 146°28′.70 E (Cape Wellington) (South Head) (north-eastern limit) and a line drawn from position 39°10′.80 S, 146°15′.00 E to position 39°04′.80 S, 146°19′.20 E (Oberon Point) (western limit) is designated as an inshore traffic zone.

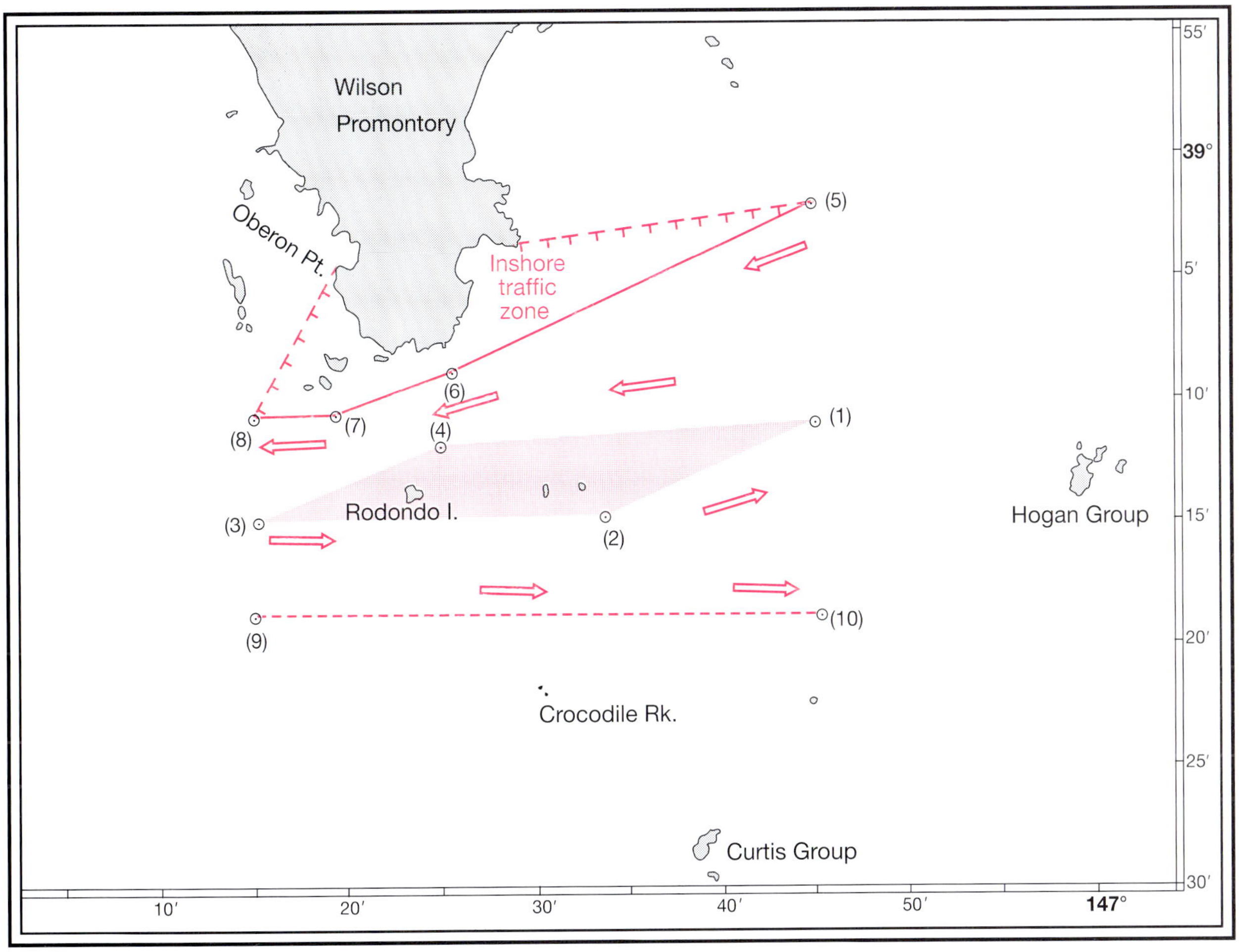

SOUTH OF WILSON PROMONTORY IN THE BASS STRAIT

B

IN THE BASS STRAIT

(Reference charts: Australian AUS 422, 1971 edition; AUS 357A, 1983 edition.
Note: These charts are based on Australian Geodetic datum 1966.)

Description of the traffic separation scheme

(a) A separation zone 1.5 miles wide is centred on the following geographical positions:

(1)	38°41′.50 S,	148°20′.20 E	(3)	38°46′.30 S,	148°09′.00 E
(2)	38°44′.50 S,	148°14′.90 E			

(b) A traffic lane for westbound traffic is established between the separation zone and a line connecting the following geographical positions:

(4)	38°38′.50 S,	148°17′.50 E	(6)	38°42′.80 S,	148°07′.30 E
(5)	38°41′.00 S,	148°13′.20 E			

(c) A traffic lane for eastbound traffic is established between the separation zone and a line connecting the following geographical positions:

(7)	38°49′.80 S,	148°10′.80 E	(9)	38°44′.60 S,	148°23′.00 E
(8)	38°48′.00 S,	148°16′.70 E			

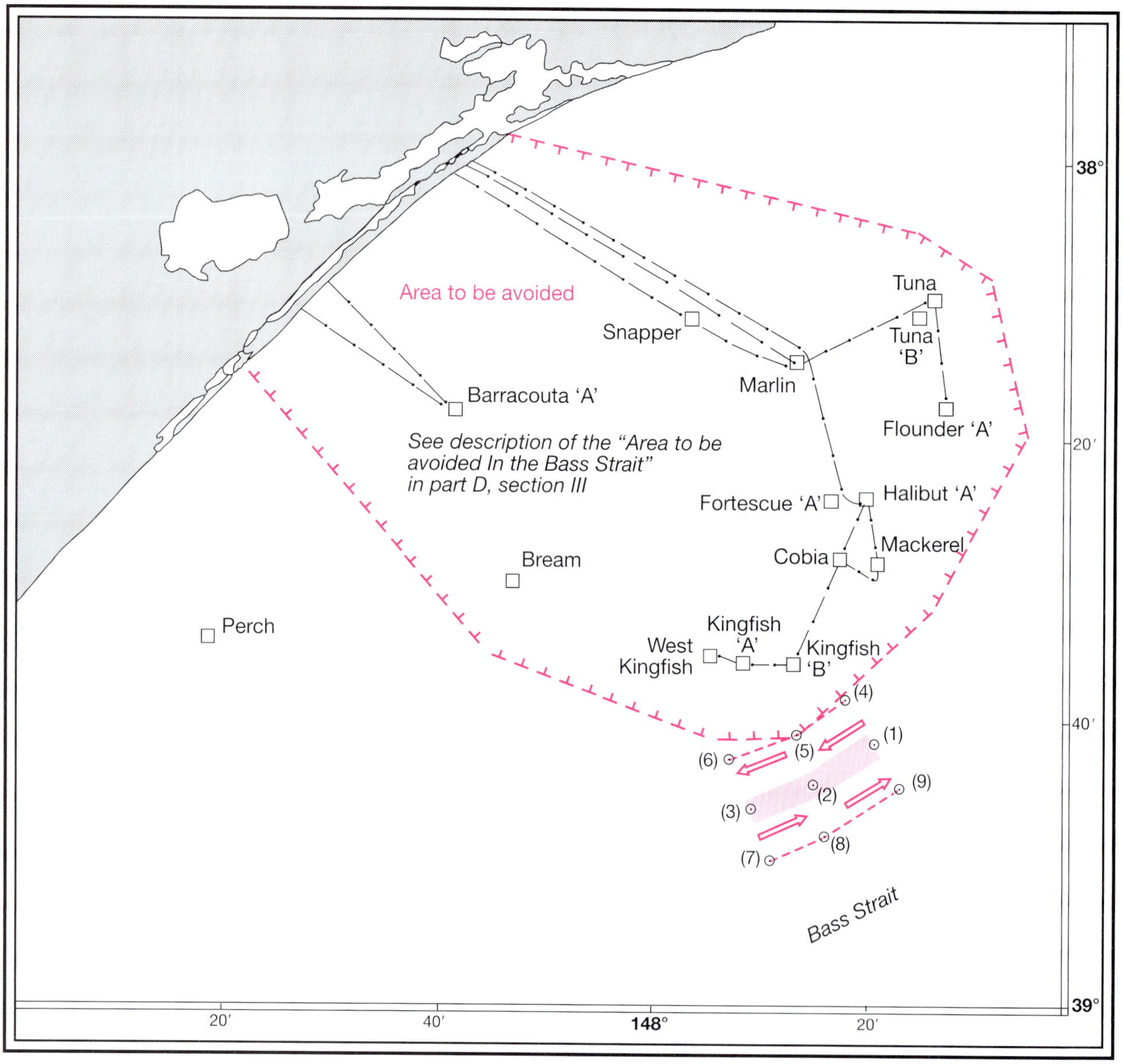

IN THE BASS STRAIT

B

Section VII

North America, Pacific coast

Caution: The chartlets are for illustrative purposes only and must not be used for navigation. Mariners should consult the appropriate nautical publications and charts for up-to-date details on aids to navigation and other relevant information.

Warning: The geographical positions given in the descriptions of the routeing systems are only correct for charts using the same geodetic datum as the reference charts indicated under each scheme. Charts published by other hydrographic offices may use a different geodetic datum, as may new editions of the reference charts published after the adoption of the routeing system. Where amendments to existing systems are not based on the same geodetic datum as the original system, this is emphasized by the use of different colours for definitions of positions.

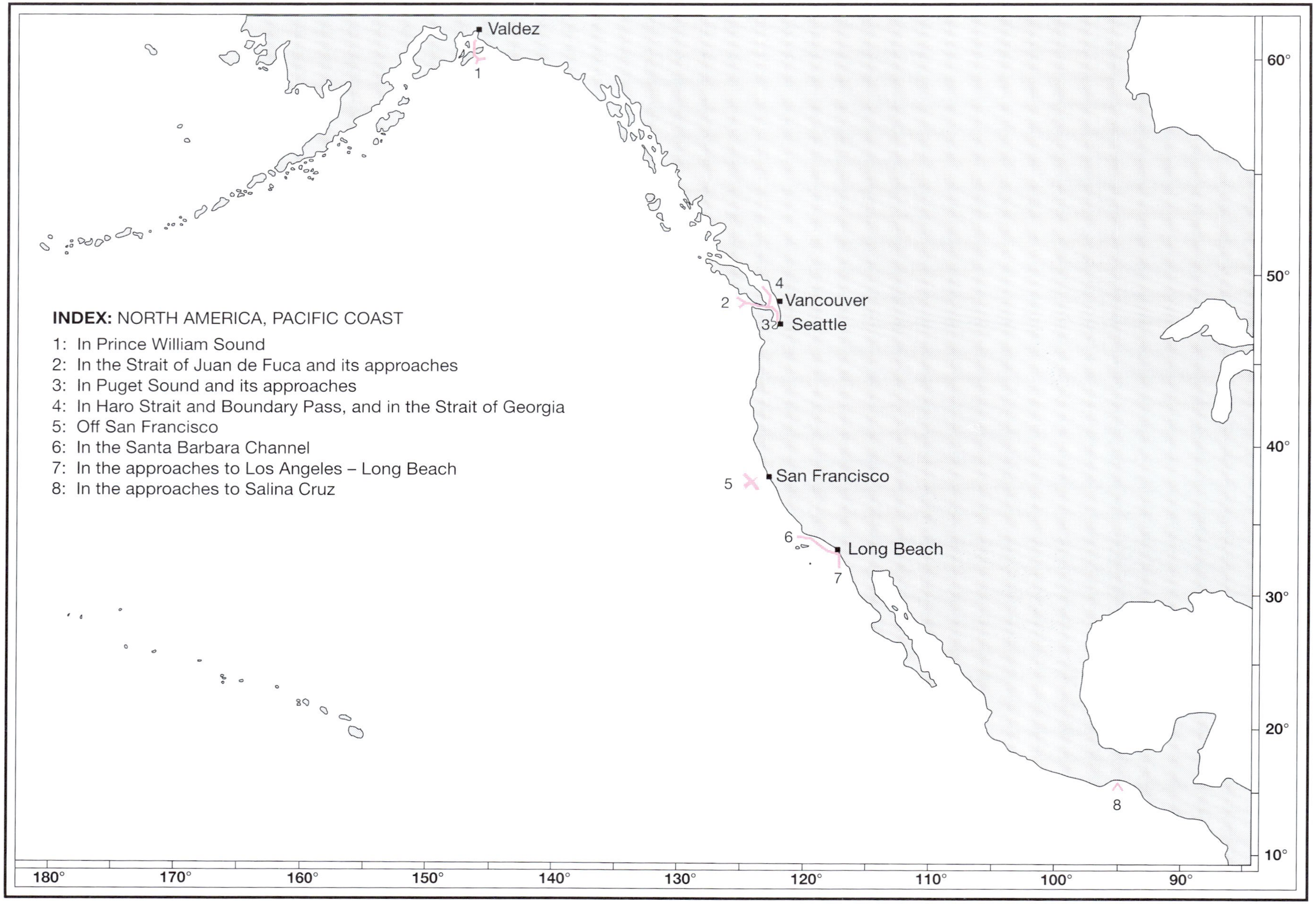
INDEX: NORTH AMERICA, PACIFIC COAST
1: In Prince William Sound
2: In the Strait of Juan de Fuca and its approaches
3: In Puget Sound and its approaches
4: In Haro Strait and Boundary Pass, and in the Strait of Georgia
5: Off San Francisco
6: In the Santa Barbara Channel
7: In the approaches to Los Angeles – Long Beach
8: In the approaches to Salina Cruz
Valdez
Vancouver
Seattle
San Francisco
Long Beach
1
2
3
4
5
6
7
8
60°
50°
40°
30°
20°
10°
180°
170°
160°
150°
140°
130°
120°
110°
100°
90°

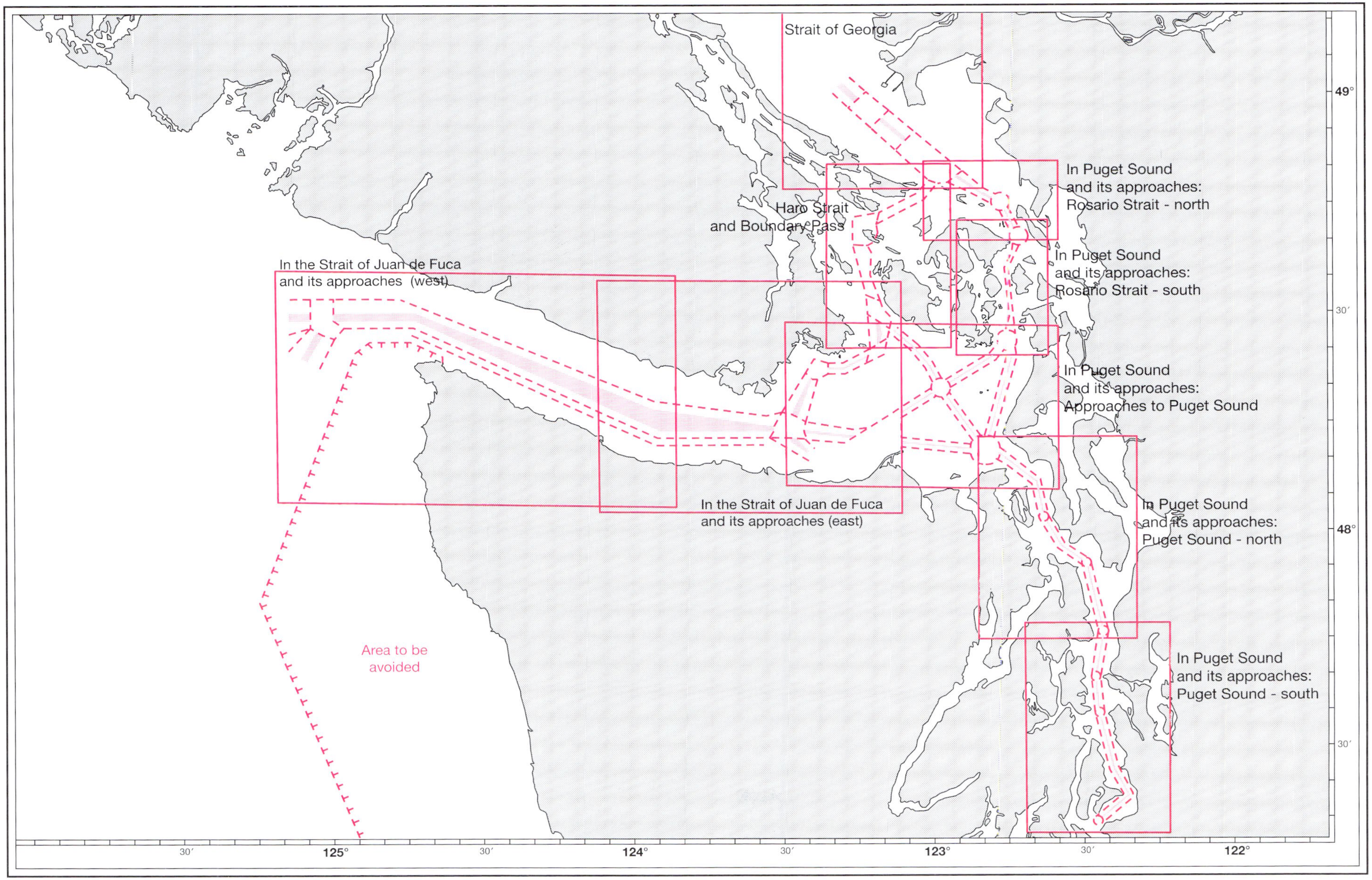

SUMMARY OF CHARTLETS FOR AREA AROUND VANCOUVER AND SEATTLE

B

IN PRINCE WILLIAM SOUND

(Reference chart: United States 16700, 1998 edition.
Note: This chart is based on North American 1983 geodetic datum.)

Description of the traffic separation scheme

The traffic separation scheme "In Prince William Sound" consists of two parts:

Part I:
Prince William Sound

(a) A separation zone is bounded by a line connecting the following geographic positions:

(1)	60°20′.77 N,	146°52′.31 W	(3)	60°48′.29 N,	146°59′.77 W
(2)	60°48′.12 N,	147°01′.78 W	(4)	60°20′.93 N,	146°50′.32 W

(b) A traffic lane for northbound traffic is established between the separation zone and a line connecting the following geographic positions:

(5)	60°20′.59 N,	146°48′.18 W	(6)	60°49′.49 N,	146°58′.19 W

(c) A traffic lane for southbound traffic is established between the separation zone and a line connecting the following geographic positions:

(7)	60°49′.10 N,	147°04′.19 W	(8)	60°20′.60 N,	146°54′.31 W

Part II:
Valdez Arm

(a) A separation zone is bounded by a line connecting the following geographic positions:

(9)	60°51′.08 N,	147°00′.33 W	(11)	60°58′.30 N,	146°47′.10 W
(10)	60°58′.60 N,	146°48′.10 W	(12)	60°50′.45 N,	146°58′.75 W

(b) A traffic lane for northbound traffic is established between the separation zone and a line connecting the following geographic positions:

(6)	60°49′.49 N,	146°58′.19 W	(13)	60°58′.04 N,	146°46′.52 W

(c) A traffic lane for southbound traffic is established between the separation zone and a line connecting the following geographic positions:

(14)	60°58′.93 N,	146°48′.86 W	(15)	60°50′.61 N,	147°03′.60 W

Precautionary areas

Cape Hinchinbrook: A precautionary area is established, bounded by a line connecting the following geographical positions:

(5)	60°20′.59 N,	146°48′.18 W	(21)	59°51′.80 N,	146°37′.51 W
(16)	60°12′.67 N,	146°40′.43 W	(22)	59°53′.52 N,	146°46′.84 W
(17)	60°11′.01 N,	146°28′.65 W	(23)	60°07′.76 N,	146°36′.24 W
(18)	60°05′.47 N,	146°00′.01 W	(24)	60°11′.51 N,	146°46′.64 W
(19)	60°00′.81 N,	146°03′.53 W	(8)	60°20′.60 N,	146°54′.31 W
(20)	60°05′.44 N,	146°27′.58 W			

Bligh Reef: A precautionary area of radius 1.5 miles is centred upon geographical position:
60°49′.63 N, 147°01′.33 W

Note: A pilot boarding area is located near the centre of the Bligh Reef precautionary area. Due to heavy vessel traffic, mariners are advised not to anchor or linger in this precautionary area except to pick up or disembark a pilot.

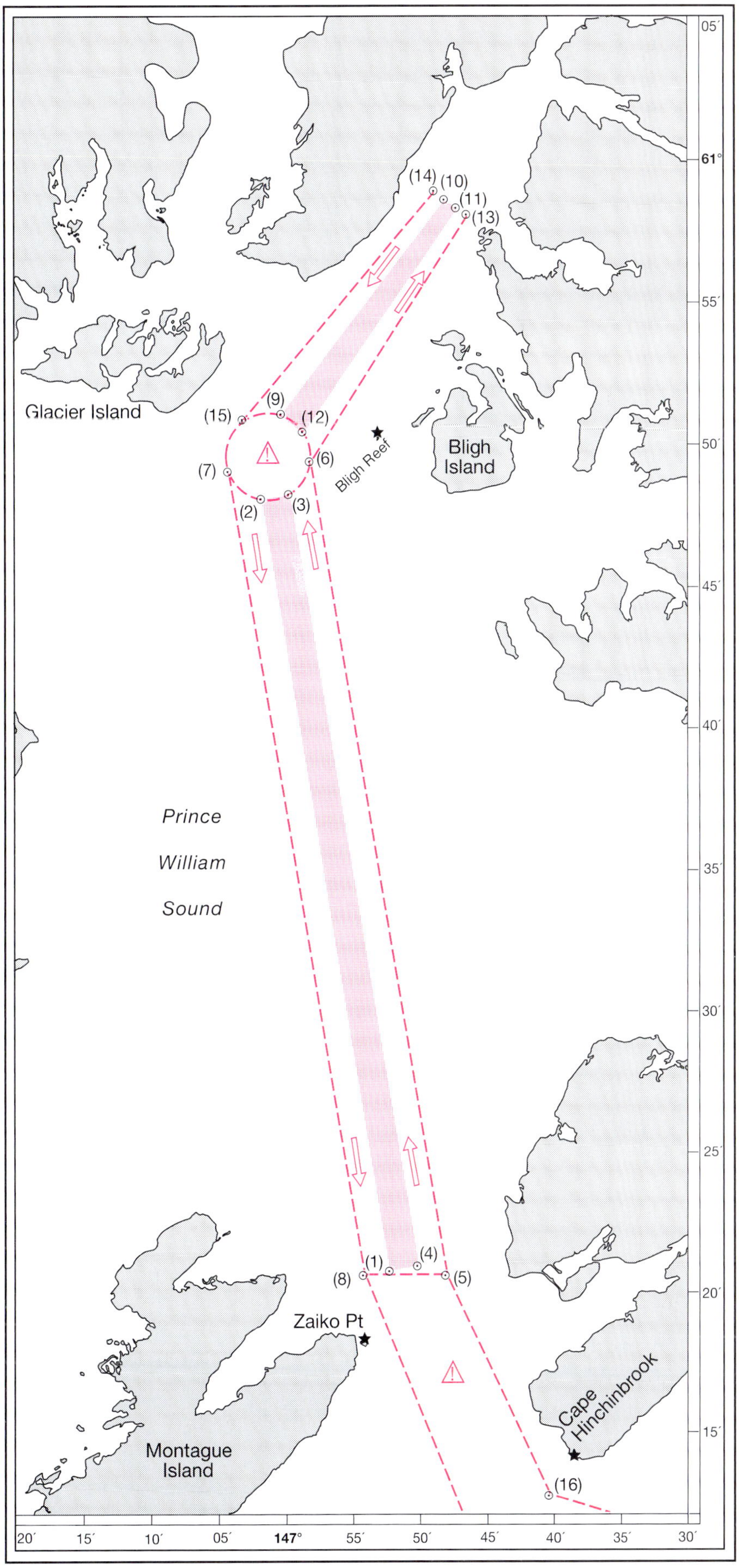

IN PRINCE WILLIAM SOUND (NORTH)

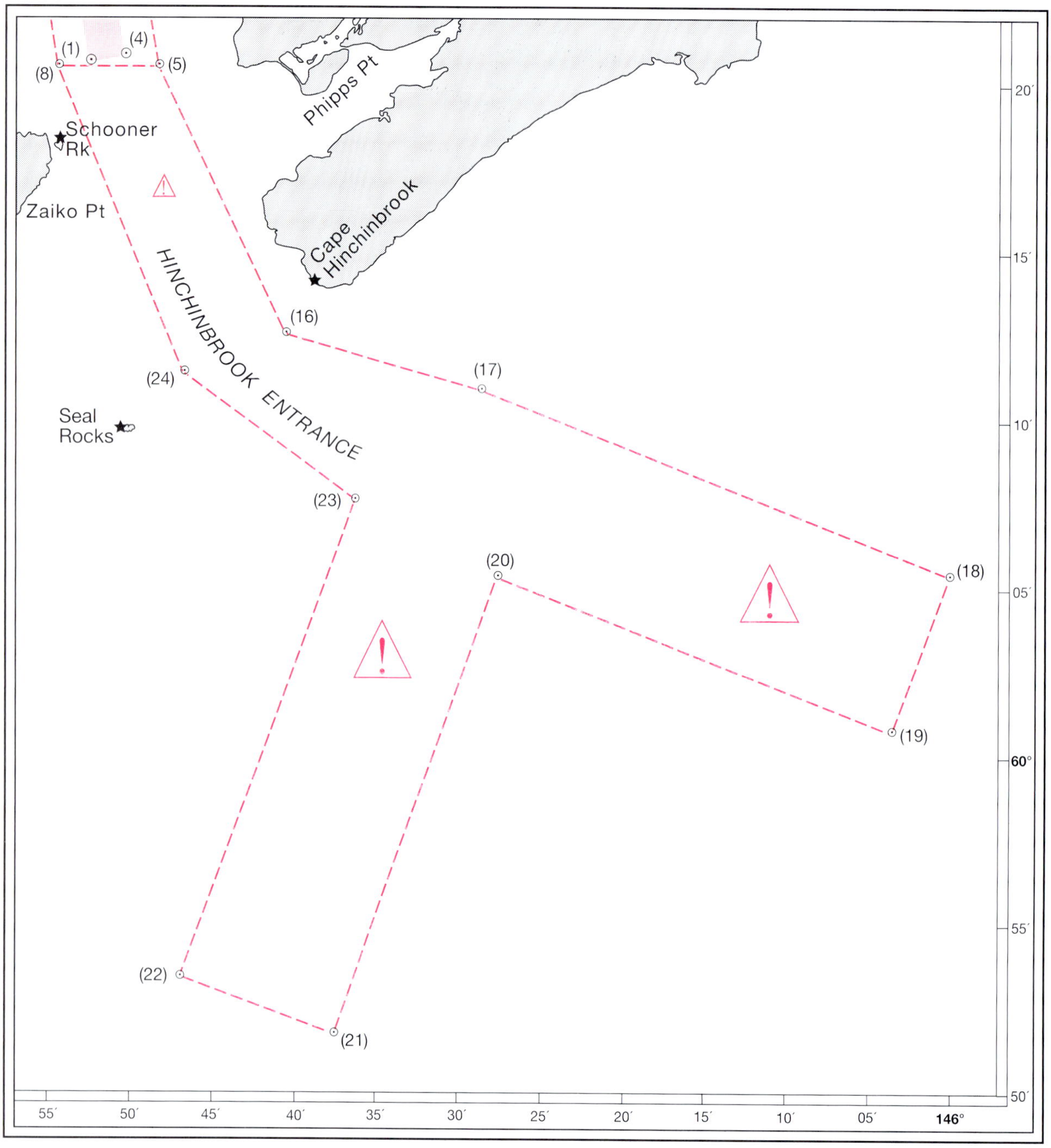

IN PRINCE WILLIAM SOUND (SOUTH)

IN THE STRAIT OF JUAN DE FUCA AND ITS APPROACHES

(Reference charts: Canadian Hydrographic Service 3440, 1998 edition; 3602, 2002 edition; 3481, 2000 edition; 3526, 2001 edition; United States 18400, 2000 edition; 18421, 2000 edition; 18440, 2000 edition; 18460, 1998 edition; 18465, 1995 edition; 18480, 1999 edition; 18485, 1998 edition. **Note:** These charts are based on World Geodetic System 1984 datum (WGS 84).)

Description of the traffic separation schemes

Part I

In the approaches to the Strait of Juan de Fuca there are two traffic separation schemes and one precautionary area:

Western approach

(a) A separation zone is bounded by a line connecting the following geographical positions:

(1)	48°30′.10 N,	125°09′.00 W	(3)	48°29′.11 N,	125°04′.67 W
(2)	48°30′.10 N,	125°04′.67 W	(4)	48°29′.11 N,	125°09′.00 W

(b) A traffic lane for westbound traffic is established between the separation zone and a line connecting the following geographical positions:

(5)	48°32′.09 N,	125°04′.67 W	(6)	48°32′.09 N,	125°08′.98 W

(c) A traffic lane for eastbound traffic is established between the separation zone and a line connecting the following geographical positions:

(7)	48°27′.31 N,	125°09′.00 W	(8)	48°28′.13 N,	125°04′.67 W

South-western approach

(a) A separation zone is bounded by a line connecting the following geographical positions:

(10)	48°23′.99 N,	125°06′.54 W	(12)	48°27′.14 N,	125°02′.08 W
(11)	48°27′.63 N,	125°03′.38 W	(13)	48°23′.50 N,	125°05′.26 W

(b) A traffic lane for north-eastbound traffic is established between the separation zone and a line connecting the following geographical positions:

(14)	48°22′.55 N,	125°02′.80 W	(15)	48°26′.64 N,	125°00′.81 W

(c) A traffic lane for south-westbound traffic is established between the separation zone and a line connecting the following geographical positions:

(8)	48°28′.13 N,	125°04′.67 W	(9)	48°24′.94 N,	125°09′.00 W

Precautionary area "JF"

A precautionary area "JF" is bounded by a line connecting the following geographical positions:

(5)	48°32′.09 N,	125°04′.67 W	(15)	48°26′.64 N,	125°00′.81 W
(2)	48°30′.10 N,	125°04′.67 W	(16)	48°28′.13 N,	124°57′.90 W
(3)	48°29′.11 N,	125°04′.67 W	(18)	48°29′.11 N,	125°00′.00 W
(8)	48°28′.13 N,	125°04′.67 W	(25)	48°30′.10 N,	125°00′.00 W
(11)	48°27′.63 N,	125°03′.38 W	(17)	48°32′.09 N,	125°00′.00 W
(12)	48°27′.14 N,	125°02′.08 W			

thence back to the point of origin at (5).

Part II

Within part II there are four traffic separation schemes and one precautionary area in the Strait of Juan de Fuca:

Western lanes

(a) A separation zone is bounded by a line connecting the following geographical positions:

(18)	48°29′.11 N,	125°00′.00 W	(22)	48°14′.49 N,	123°31′.98 W
(19)	48°29′.11 N,	124°43′.78 W	(23)	48°17′.02 N,	123°56′.46 W
(20)	48°13′.89 N,	123°54′.84 W	(24)	48°30′.10 N,	124°43′.50 W
(21)	48°13′.89 N,	123°31′.98 W	(25)	48°30′.10 N,	125°00′.00 W

(b) A traffic lane for north-westbound traffic is established between the separation zone and a line connecting the following geographical positions:

(26)	48°16′.45 N,	123°30′.42 W	(29)	48°32′.00 N,	124°46′.57 W
(27)	48°15′.97 N,	123°33′.54 W	(30)	48°32′.09 N,	124°49′.90 W
(28)	48°18′.00 N,	123°56′.07 W	(17)	48°32′.09 N,	125°00′.00 W

Traffic may exit the lane between points (29) and (30) or may remain in the lane between points (30) and (17) *en route* to the precautionary area.

B

(c) A traffic lane for south-eastbound traffic is established between the separation zone and a line connecting the following geographical positions:

(16)	48°28′.13 N,	124°57′.90 W	(32)	48°12′.90 N,	123°55′.24 W
(31)	48°28′.13 N,	124°44′.07 W	(33)	48°12′.94 N,	123°32′.89 W

Southern lanes

(a) A separation zone is bounded by a line connecting the following geographical positions:

(34)	48°10′.82 N,	123°25′.44 W	(37)	48°12′.84 N,	123°27′.46 W
(35)	48°12′.38 N,	123°28′.68 W	(38)	48°10′.99 N,	123°24′.84 W
(36)	48°12′.90 N,	123°28′.68 W			

(b) A traffic lane for northbound traffic is established between the separation zone and a line connecting the following geographical positions:

(39)	48°11′.24 N,	123°23′.82 W	(40)	48°12′.72 N,	123°25′.34 W

(c) A traffic lane for southbound traffic is established between the separation zone and a line connecting the following geographical positions:

(33)	48°12′.94 N,	123°32′.89 W	(41)	48°09′.42 N,	123°24′.24 W

Northern lanes

(a) A separation zone is bounded by a line connecting the following geographical positions:

(42)	48°21′.15 N,	123°24′.83 W	(44)	48°15′.77 N,	123°27′.18 W
(43)	48°16′.16 N,	123°28′.50 W	(45)	48°20′.93 N,	123°24′.26 W

(b) A traffic lane for southbound traffic is established between the separation zone and a line connecting the following geographical positions:

(46)	48°21′.83 N,	123°25′.56 W	(26)	48°16′.45 N,	123°30′.42 W

(c) A traffic lane for northbound traffic is established between the separation zone and a line connecting the following geographical positions:

(47)	48°20′.93 N,	123°23′.22 W	(48)	48°15′.13 N,	123°25′.62 W

Eastern lanes

(a) A separation zone is established bounded by a line connecting the following geographical positions:

(49)	48°13′.22 N,	123°15′.91 W	(51)	48°13′.54 N,	123°25′.86 W
(50)	48°14′.03 N,	123°25′.98 W	(52)	48°12′.89 N,	123°16′.69 W

(b) A traffic lane for westbound traffic is established between the separation zone and a line connecting the following geographical positions:

(54)	48°14′.27 N,	123°13′.41 W	(48)	48°15′.13 N,	123°25′.62 W
(55)	48°14′.05 N,	123°16′.08 W			

(c) A traffic lane for eastbound traffic is established between the separation zone and a line connecting the following geographical positions:

(40)	48°12′.72 N,	123°25′.34 W	(53)	48°12′.34 N,	123°18′.01 W

Precautionary area "PA"

A precautionary area "PA" is bounded by a line connecting the following geographical positions:

(33)	48°12′.94 N,	123°32′.89 W	(48)	48°15′.13 N,	123°25′.62 W
(21)	48°13′.89 N,	123°31′.98 W	(50)	48°14′.03 N,	123°25′.98 W
(22)	48°14′.49 N,	123°31′.98 W	(51)	48°13′.54 N,	123°25′.86 W
(26)	48°16′.45 N,	123°30′.42 W	(40)	48°12′.72 N,	123°25′.34 W
(43)	48°16′.16 N,	123°28′.50 W	(37)	48°12′.84 N,	123°27′.46 W
(44)	48°15′.77 N,	123°27′.18 W	(36)	48°12′.90 N,	123°28′.68 W

thence back to the point of origin at (33).

(chartlets overleaf)

B

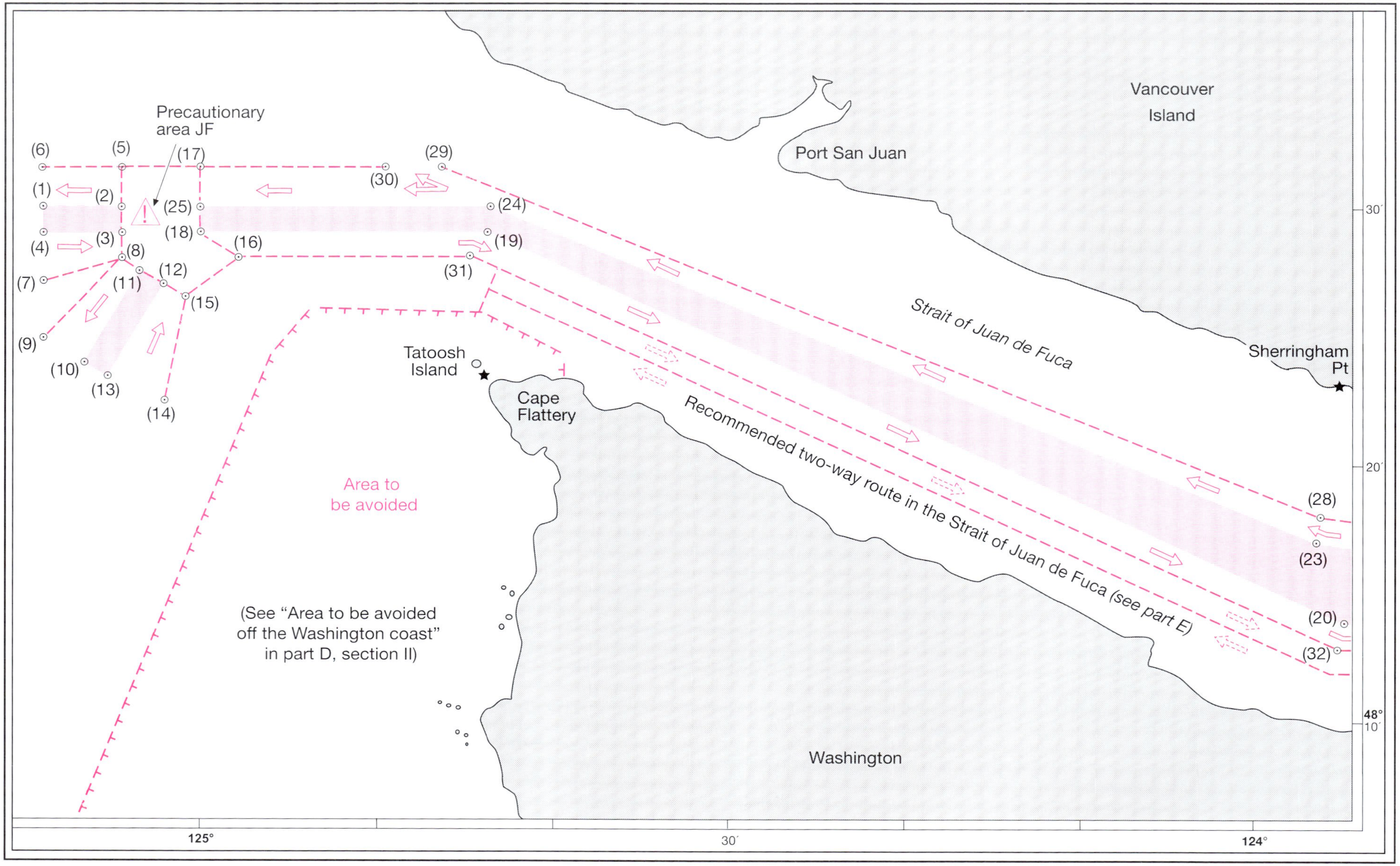

IN THE STRAIT OF JUAN DE FUCA AND ITS APPROACHES (WEST)

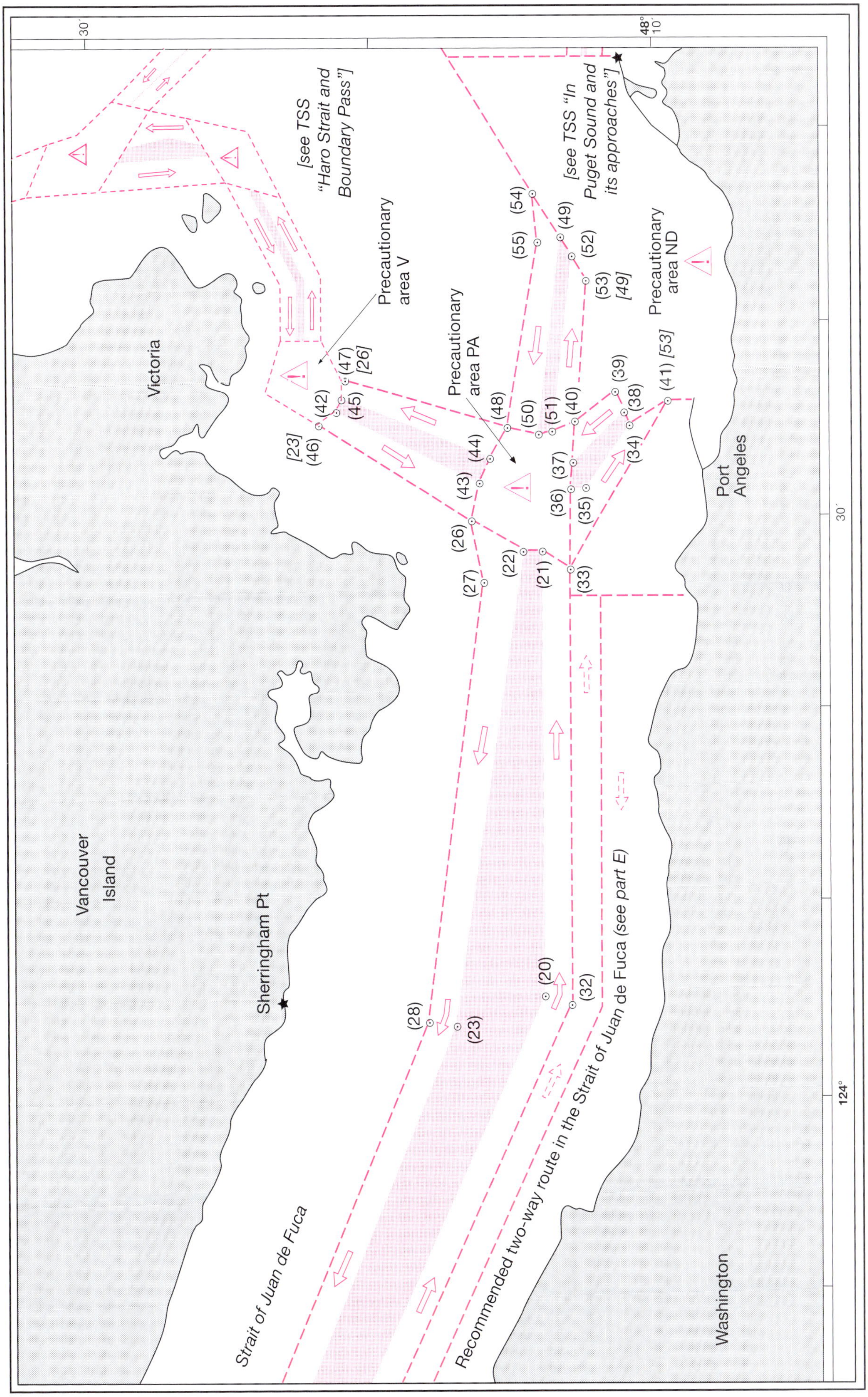

IN THE STRAIT OF JUAN DE FUCA AND ITS APPROACHES (EAST)

IN PUGET SOUND AND ITS APPROACHES

(Reference charts: United States 18421, 2000 edition; 18429, 1999 edition; 18430, 1996 edition; 18440, 2000 edition.
Note: These charts are based on North American 1983 geodetic datum.)

Description of the traffic separation scheme

The traffic separation scheme "In Puget Sound and its approaches" consists of a series of traffic separation schemes and precautionary areas broken into three geographic designations as follows:

Part I: Rosario Strait
Part II: Approaches to Puget Sound
Part III: Puget Sound

Part I
Rosario Strait

(a) A separation zone is bounded by a line connecting the following geographical positions:

(1)	48°48′.98 N,	122°55′.20 W	(4)	48°45′.56 N,	122°48′.36 W
(2)	48°46′.76 N,	122°50′.43 W	(5)	48°46′.39 N,	122°50′.76 W
(3)	48°45′.97 N,	122°48′.12 W	(6)	48°48′.73 N,	122°55′.68 W

(b) A traffic lane for northbound traffic is established between the separation zone and a line connecting the following geographical positions:

(7)	48°49′.49 N,	122°54′.24 W	(9)	48°46′.35 N,	122°47′.50 W
(8)	48°47′.14 N,	122°50′.10 W			

(c) A traffic lane for southbound traffic is established between the separation zone and a line connecting the following geographical positions:

(10)	48°44′.95 N,	122°48′.28 W	(12)	48°47′.93 N,	122°57′.12 W
(11)	48°46′.76 N,	122°53′.10 W			

(d) Connecting with precautionary area "CA", the waters contained within a circle of radius 1.24 miles centred at geographical position 48°45′.30 N, 122°46′.50 W.

(e) A separation zone is bounded by a line connecting the following geographical positions:

(13)	48°44′.27 N,	122°45′.53 W	(15)	48°41′.60 N,	122°43′.82 W
(14)	48°41′.72 N,	122°43′.50 W	(16)	48°44′.17 N,	122°45′.87 W

(f) A traffic lane for northbound traffic is established between the separation zone and a line connecting the following geographical positions:

(17)	48°44′.62 N,	122°44′.96 W	(18)	48°41′.80 N,	122°42′.70 W

(g) A traffic lane for southbound traffic is established between the separation zone and a line connecting the following geographical positions:

(19)	48°44′.08 N,	122°46′.65 W	(20)	48°41′.25 N,	122°44′.37 W

(h) Connecting with precautionary area "C", the waters contained within a circle of radius 1.24 miles centred at geographical position 48°40′.55 N, 122°42′.80 W.

(i) A two-way route is established between the following geographical positions:

(21)	48°39′.33 N,	122°42′.73 W	(25)	48°29′.48 N,	122°44′.77 W
(22)	48°36′.08 N,	122°45′.00 W	(26)	48°36′.13 N,	122°45′.80 W
(23)	48°26′.82 N,	122°43′.53 W	(27)	48°38′.38 N,	122°44′.20 W
(24)	48°27′.62 N,	122°45′.53 W	(28)	48°39′.63 N,	122°44′.03 W

(j) Connecting with precautionary area "RB", bounded to the north by the arc of a circle of radius 1.24 miles centred on geographical position 48°26′.38 N, 122°45′.27 W and connecting the following geographical positions:

(42)	48°25′.97 N,	122°47′.03 W	(83)	48°25′.55 N,	122°43′.93 W

and bounded to the south by a line connecting the following geographical positions:

(42)	48°25′.97 N,	122°47′.03 W	(86)	48°25′.17 N,	122°45′.62 W
(43)	48°24′.62 N,	122°48′.68 W	(87)	48°24′.15 N,	122°45′.27 W
(38)	48°23′.75 N,	122°47′.47 W	(84)	48°24′.08 N,	122°43′.38 W
(37)	48°25′.20 N,	122°45′.73 W	(83)	48°25′.55 N,	122°43′.93 W

Part II

Approaches to Puget Sound

The traffic separation scheme in the approaches to Puget Sound consists of a north-east/south-west approach, a north-west/south-east approach, a north/south approach and an east/west approach connecting with precautionary areas as follows:

North-east/south-west approach

(a) A separation zone is bounded by a line connecting the following geographical positions:

(29)	48°24′.13 N,	122°47′.97 W	(31)	48°20′.53 N,	122°57′.22 W
(30)	48°20′.32 N,	122°57′.02 W	(32)	48°24′.32 N,	122°48′.22 W

connecting with precautionary area "RA", the waters contained within a circle of radius 1.24 miles centred at 48°19′.77 N, 122°58′.57 W, and thence to:

(33)	48°16′.25 N,	123°06′.58 W	(35)	48°19′.20 N,	123°00′.35 W
(34)	48°16′.57 N,	123°06′.58 W	(36)	48°19′.00 N,	123°00′.17 W

(b) A traffic lane for northbound traffic is established between the separation zone and a line connecting the following geographical positions:

(38)	48°23′.75 N,	122°47′.47 W	(39)	48°19′.80 N,	122°56′.83 W

connecting with precautionary area "RA", and thence to:

(40)	48°15′.70 N,	123°06′.58 W	(41)	48°18′.67 N,	122°59′.57 W

(c) A traffic lane for southbound traffic is established between the separation zone and a line connecting the following geographical positions:

(43)	48°24′.62 N,	122°48′.68 W	(44)	48°20′.85 N,	122°57′.80 W

connecting with precautionary area "RA", and thence to:

(45)	48°19′.70 N,	123°00′.53 W	(46)	48°17′.15 N,	123°06′.57 W

(d) Connecting with precautionary area "ND", which is bounded by a line connecting the following geographical positions:

(47)	48°11′.00 N,	123°06′.58 W	(51)	48°11′.24 N,	123°23′.82 W
(46)	48°17′.15 N,	123°06′.57 W	(52)	48°10′.82 N,	123°25′.44 W
(48)	48°14′.27 N,	123°13′.41 W	(53)	48°09′.42 N,	123°24′.24 W
(49)	48°12′.34 N,	123°18′.01 W	(54)	48°08′.39 N,	123°24′.24 W
(50)	48°12′.72 N,	123°25′.34 W			

thence along the shoreline to the point of beginning (47).

North-west/south-east approach

(e) A separation zone is bounded by a line connecting the following geographical positions:

(55)	48°28′.72 N,	123°08′.53 W	(59)	48°20′.82 N,	122°59′.62 W
(56)	48°25′.43 N,	123°03′.88 W	(60)	48°22′.72 N,	123°01′.12 W
(57)	48°22′.88 N,	123°00′.82 W	(61)	48°25′.32 N,	123°04′.30 W
(58)	48°20′.93 N,	122°59′.30 W	(62)	48°28′.39 N,	123°08′.64 W

connecting with precautionary area "RA", and thence to:

(63)	48°18′.83 N,	122°57′.48 W	(65)	48°13′.00 N,	122°51′.62 W
(64)	48°13′.15 N,	122°51′.33 W	(66)	48°18′.70 N,	122°57′.77 W

(f) A traffic lane for northbound traffic is established between the separation zone and a line connecting the following geographical positions:

(67)	48°29′.28 N,	123°08′.35 W	(69)	48°23′.20 N,	123°00′.20 W
(68)	48°25′.60 N,	123°03′.13 W	(70)	48°21′.00 N,	122°58′.50 W

connecting with precautionary area "RA", and thence to:

(71)	48°19′.20 N,	122°57′.03 W	(72)	48°13′.35 N,	122°50′.63 W

(g) A traffic lane for southbound traffic is established between the separation zone and a line connecting the following geographical positions:

(73)	48°27′.86 N,	123°08′.81 W	(75)	48°22′.48 N,	123°01′.73 W
(74)	48°25′.17 N,	123°04′.98 W	(76)	48°20′.47 N,	123°00′.20 W

connecting with precautionary area "RA", and thence to:

(77)	48°18′.52 N,	122°58′.50 W	(78)	48°12′.63 N,	122°52′.15 W

(h) Connecting with precautionary area "SA", the waters contained within a circle of radius 2 miles centred at geographical position 48°11′.45 N, 122°49′.78 W.

North/south approach (between precautionary areas "RB" and "SA")

(i) A separation zone is bounded by a line connecting the following geographical positions:

(79)	48°24′.15 N,	122°44′.08 W	(81)	48°13′.38 N,	122°49′.15 W
(80)	48°13′.33 N,	122°48′.78 W	(82)	48°24′.17 N,	122°44′.48 W

(j) A traffic lane for northbound traffic is established between the separation zone and a line connecting the following geographical positions:

(84)	48°24′.08 N,	122°43′.38 W	(85)	48°13′.10 N,	122°48′.12 W

(k) A traffic lane for southbound traffic is established between the separation zone and a line connecting the following geographical positions:

(87)	48°24′.15 N,	122°45′.27 W	(88)	48°13′.43 N,	122°49′.90 W

East/west approach (between precautionary areas "ND" and "SA")

(l) A separation zone is bounded by a line connecting the following geographical positions:

(89)	48°11′.50 N,	122°52′.73 W	(91)	48°12′.48 N,	123°06′.58 W
(90)	48°11′.73 N,	122°52′.70 W	(92)	48°12′.23 N,	123°06′.58 W

(m) A traffic lane for westbound traffic is established between the separation zone and a line connecting the following geographical positions:

(93)	48°12′.22 N,	122°52′.52 W	(94)	48°12′.98 N,	123°06′.58 W

(n) A traffic lane for eastbound traffic is established between the separation zone and a line connecting the following geographical positions:

(95)	48°11′.73 N,	123°06′.58 W	(96)	48°10′.98 N,	122°52′.65 W

Part III

Puget Sound

The traffic separation scheme in Puget Sound consists of a series of traffic lanes with separation zones connecting with precautionary areas.

(a) A separation zone is bounded by a line connecting the following geographical positions:

(97)	48°11′.08 N,	122°46′.88 W	(100)	48°02′.43 N,	122°38′.52 W
(98)	48°06′.85 N,	122°39′.52 W	(101)	48°06′.72 N,	122°39′.83 W
(99)	48°02′.48 N,	122°38′.17 W	(102)	48°10′.82 N,	122°46′.98 W

connecting with precautionary area "SC", the waters contained within a circle of radius 0.62 miles centred at geographical position 48°01′.85 N, 122°38′.15 W,, and thence to:

(103)	48°01′.40 N,	122°37′.57 W	(106)	47°55′.67 N,	122°30′.40 W
(104)	47°57′.95 N,	122°34′.67 W	(107)	47°57′.78 N,	122°34′.92 W
(105)	47°55′.85 N,	122°30′.22 W	(108)	48°01′.28 N,	122°37′.87 W

connecting with precautionary area "SE", the waters contained within a circle of radius 0.62 miles centred at geographical position 47°55′.40 N, 122°29′.55 W, and thence to:

(109)	47°54′.85 N,	122°29′.18 W	(111)	47°46′.47 N,	122°26′.62 W
(110)	47°46′.52 N,	122°26′.30 W	(112)	47°54′.80 N,	122°29′.53 W

connecting with precautionary area "SF", the waters contained within a circle of radius 0.62 miles centred at geographical position 47°45′.90 N, 122°26′.25 W, and thence to:

(113)	47°45′.20 N,	122°26′.25 W	(115)	47°40′.30 N,	122°27′.88 W
(114)	47°40′.27 N,	122°27′.55 W	(116)	47°45′.33 N,	122°26′.60 W

connecting with precautionary area "SG", the waters contained within a circle of radius 0.62 miles centred at geographical position 47°39′.68 N, 122°27′.87 W, and thence to:

(117)	47°39′.12 N,	122°27′.62 W	(119)	47°35′.17 N,	122°27′.35 W
(118)	47°35′.18 N,	122°27′.08 W	(120)	47°39′.08 N,	122°27′.97 W

connecting with precautionary area "T", the waters contained within a circle of radius 0.62 miles centred at geographical position 47°34′.55 N, 122°27′.07 W, and thence to:

(121)	47°34′.02 N,	122°26′.70 W	(125)	47°19′.98 N,	122°26′.83 W
(122)	47°26′.92 N,	122°24′.10 W	(126)	47°23′.15 N,	122°21′.45 W
(123)	47°23′.07 N,	122°20′.98 W	(127)	47°26′.85 N,	122°24′.45 W
(124)	47°19′.78 N,	122°26′.58 W	(128)	47°33′.95 N,	122°27′.03 W

connecting with precautionary area "TC", the waters contained within a circle of radius 0.62 miles centred at geographical position 47°19′.48 N, 122°27′.38 W.

(b) A traffic lane for northbound traffic is established between the separation zone and a line connecting the following geographical positions:

(129)	48°11′.72 N,	122°46′.83 W	(135)	47°39′.68 N,	122°26′.95 W
(130)	48°07′.13 N,	122°38′.83 W	(136)	47°34′.65 N,	122°26′.18 W
(131)	48°02′.10 N,	122°37′.32 W	(137)	47°27′.13 N,	122°23′.40 W
(132)	47°58′.23 N,	122°34′.07 W	(138)	47°23′.33 N,	122°20′.37 W
(133)	47°55′.83 N,	122°28′.80 W	(139)	47°22′.67 N,	122°20′.53 W
(134)	47°45′.92 N,	122°25′.33 W	(140)	47°19′.07 N,	122°26′.75 W

(c) A traffic lane for southbound traffic is established between the separation zone and a line connecting the following geographical positions:

(141)	48°10′.15 N,	122°47′.58 W	(147)	47°45′.90 N,	122°27′.18 W
(142)	48°09′.35 N,	122°45′.55 W	(148)	47°39′.70 N,	122°28′.78 W
(143)	48°06′.45 N,	122°40′.52 W	(149)	47°34′.47 N,	122°27′.98 W
(144)	48°01′.65 N,	122°39′.03 W	(150)	47°26′.63 N,	122°25′.12 W
(145)	47°57′.47 N,	122°35′.45 W	(151)	47°23′.25 N,	122°22′.42 W
(146)	47°55′.07 N,	122°30′.35 W	(152)	47°20′.00 N,	122°27′.90 W

(chartlets overleaf)

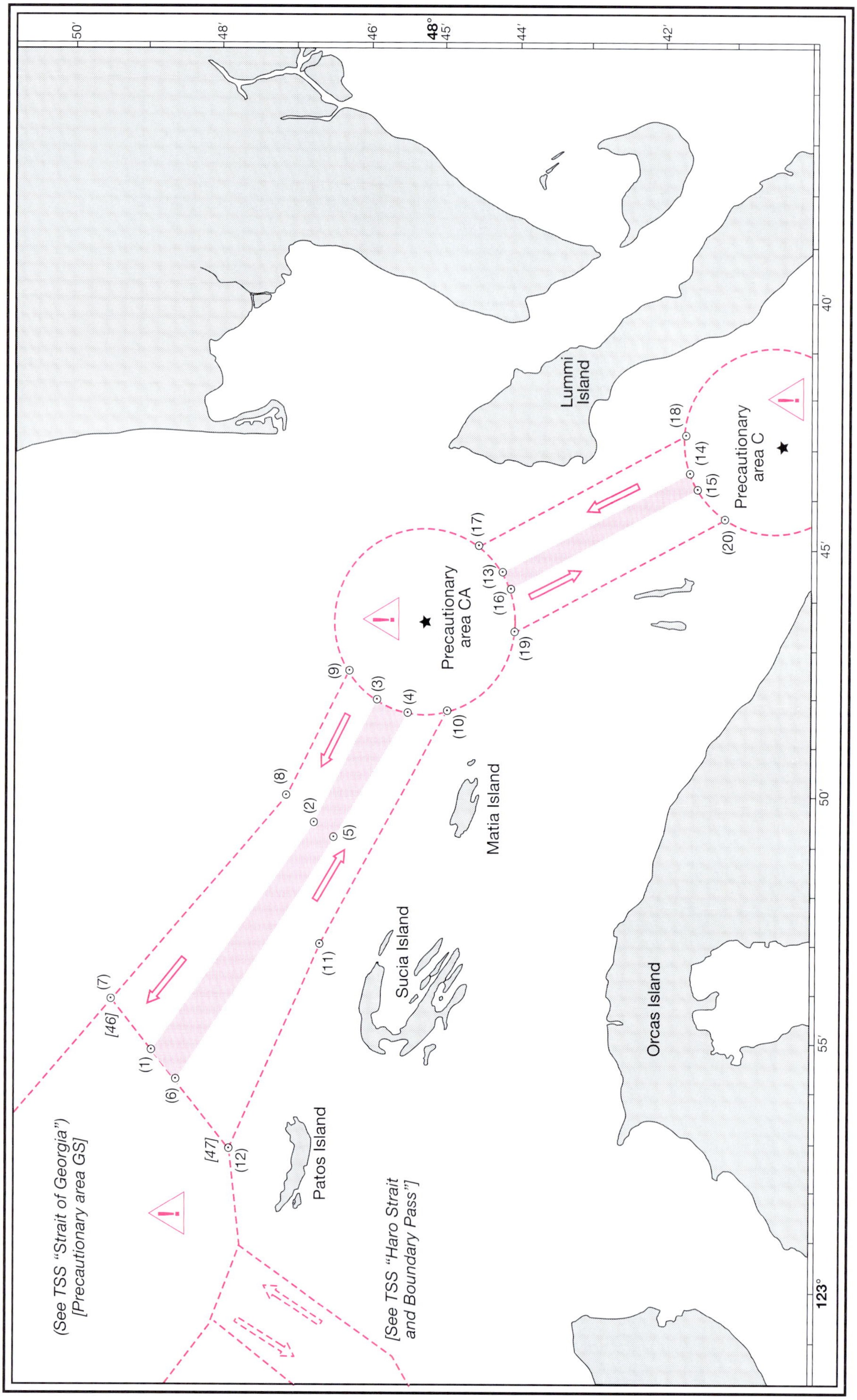

IN PUGET SOUND AND ITS APPROACHES: ROSARIO STRAIT – NORTH

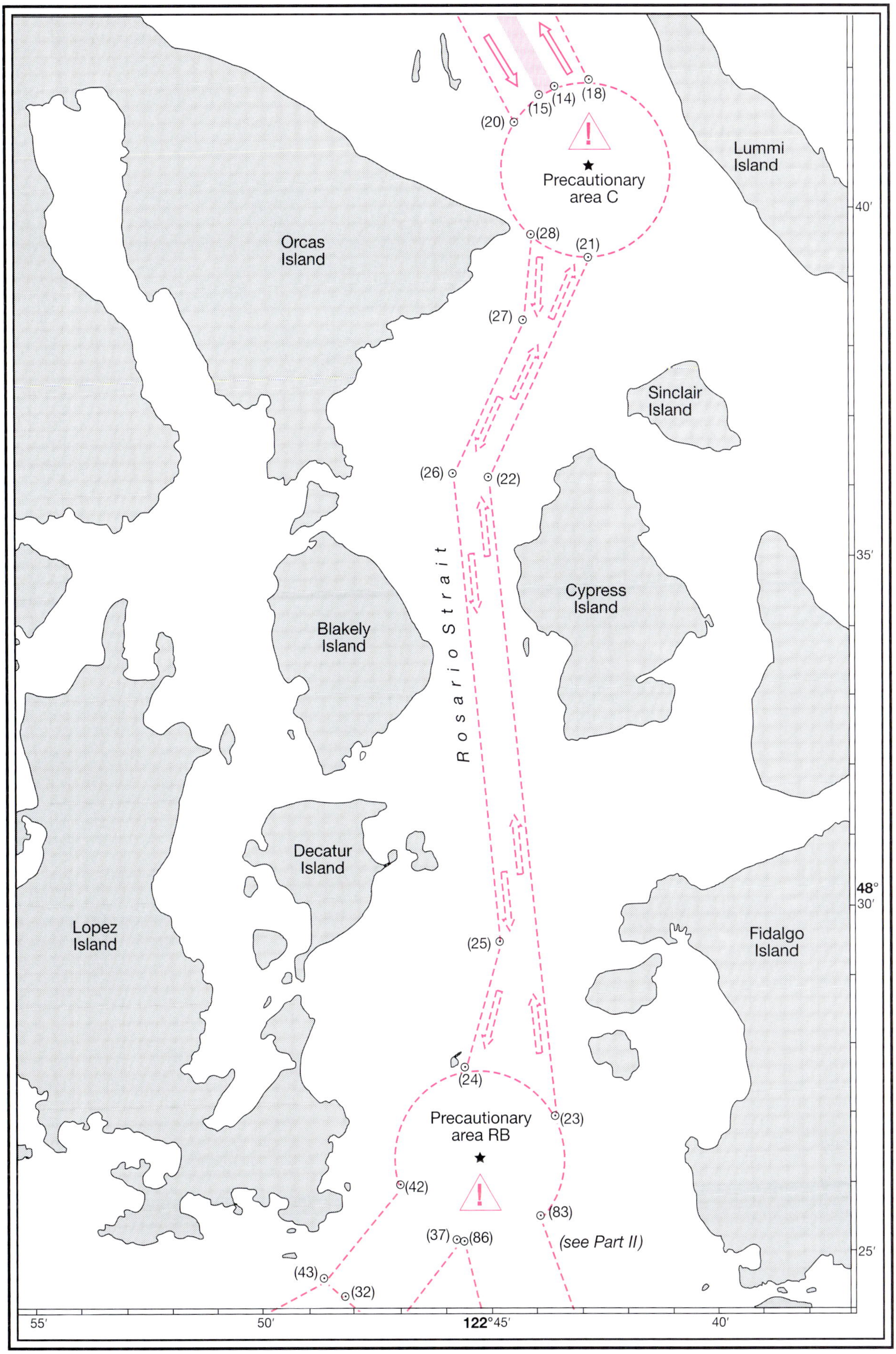

IN PUGET SOUND AND ITS APPROACHES: ROSARIO STRAIT – SOUTH

B

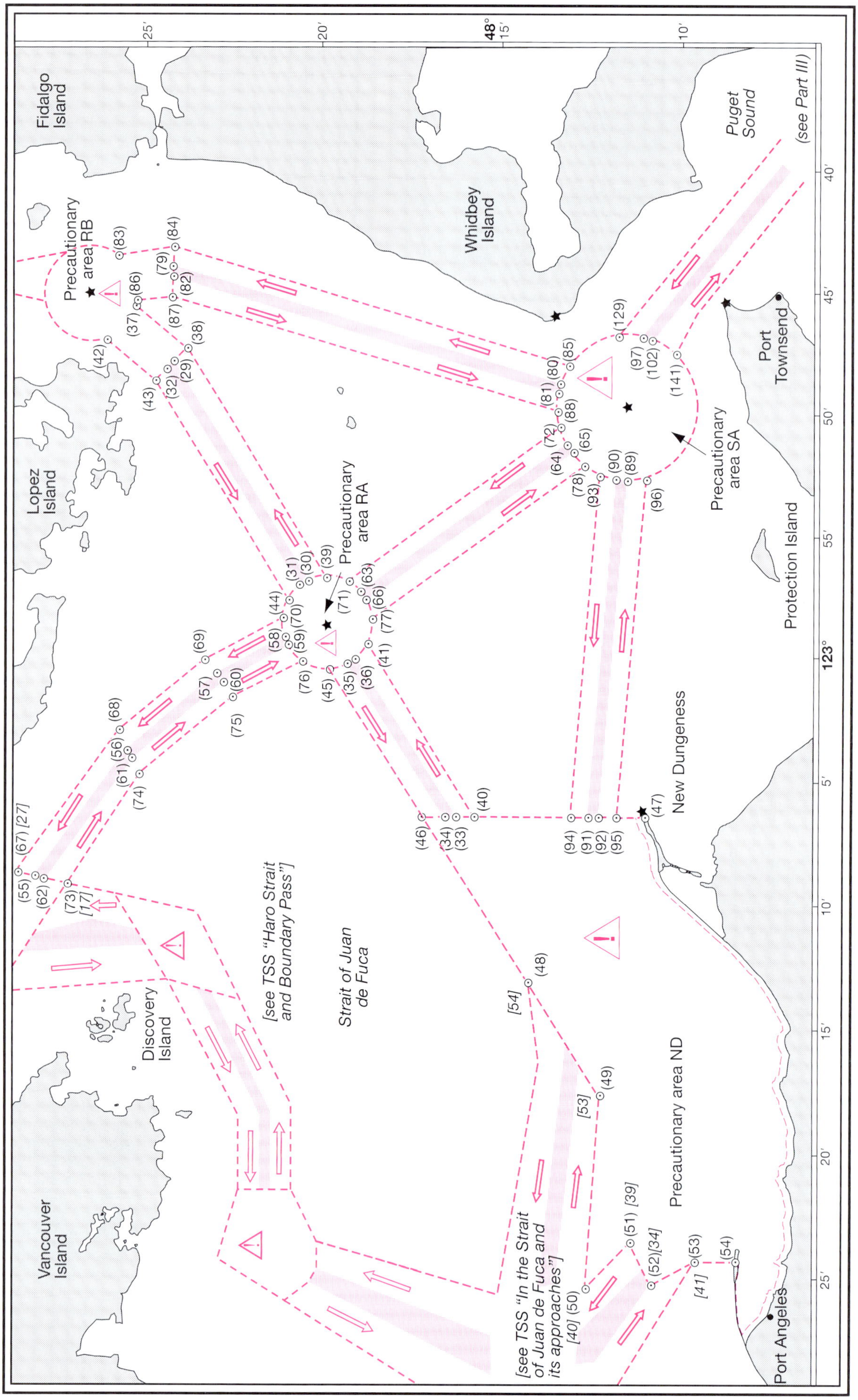

IN PUGET SOUND AND ITS APPROACHES: APPROACHES TO PUGET SOUND

(r) A separation zone is established, bounded by a line connecting the following geographical positions:

(56) 49°01′.39 N, 123°17′.53 W (58) 49°03′.24 N, 123°22′.41 W
(57) 49°03′.84 N, 123°21′.30 W (59) 49°00′.75 N, 123°18′.52 W

thence back to point of origin (56).

(s) A traffic lane for north-westbound traffic is established between the separation zone and a line connecting the following geographical positions:

(54) 49°02′.20 N, 123°16′.28 W (61) 49°04′.52 N, 123°20′.04 W

(t) A traffic lane for south-eastbound traffic is established between the separation zone and a line connecting the following geographical positions:

(60) 49°02′.51 N, 123°23′.76 W (55) 49°00′.00 N, 123°19′.69 W

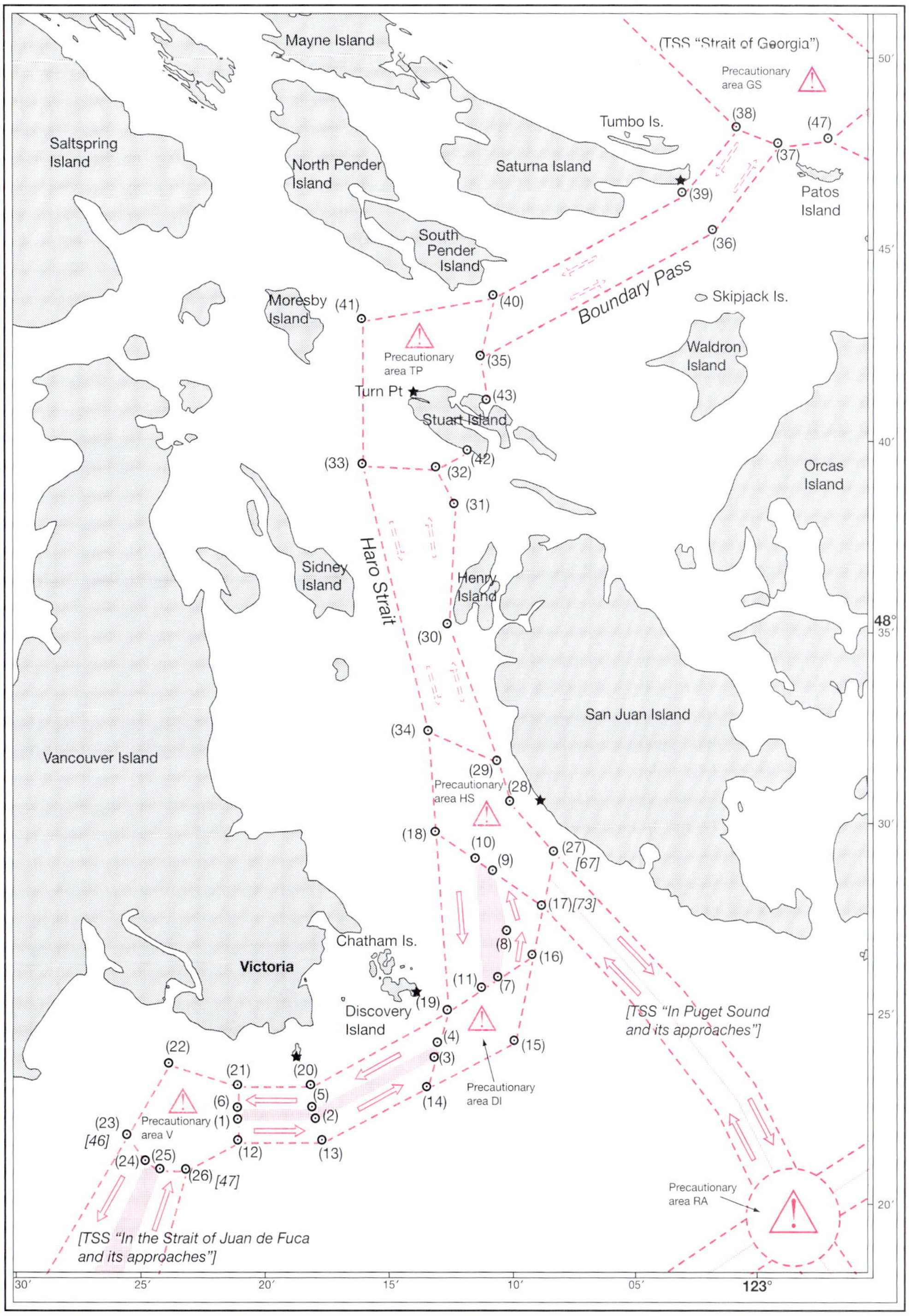

HARO STRAIT AND BOUNDARY PASS

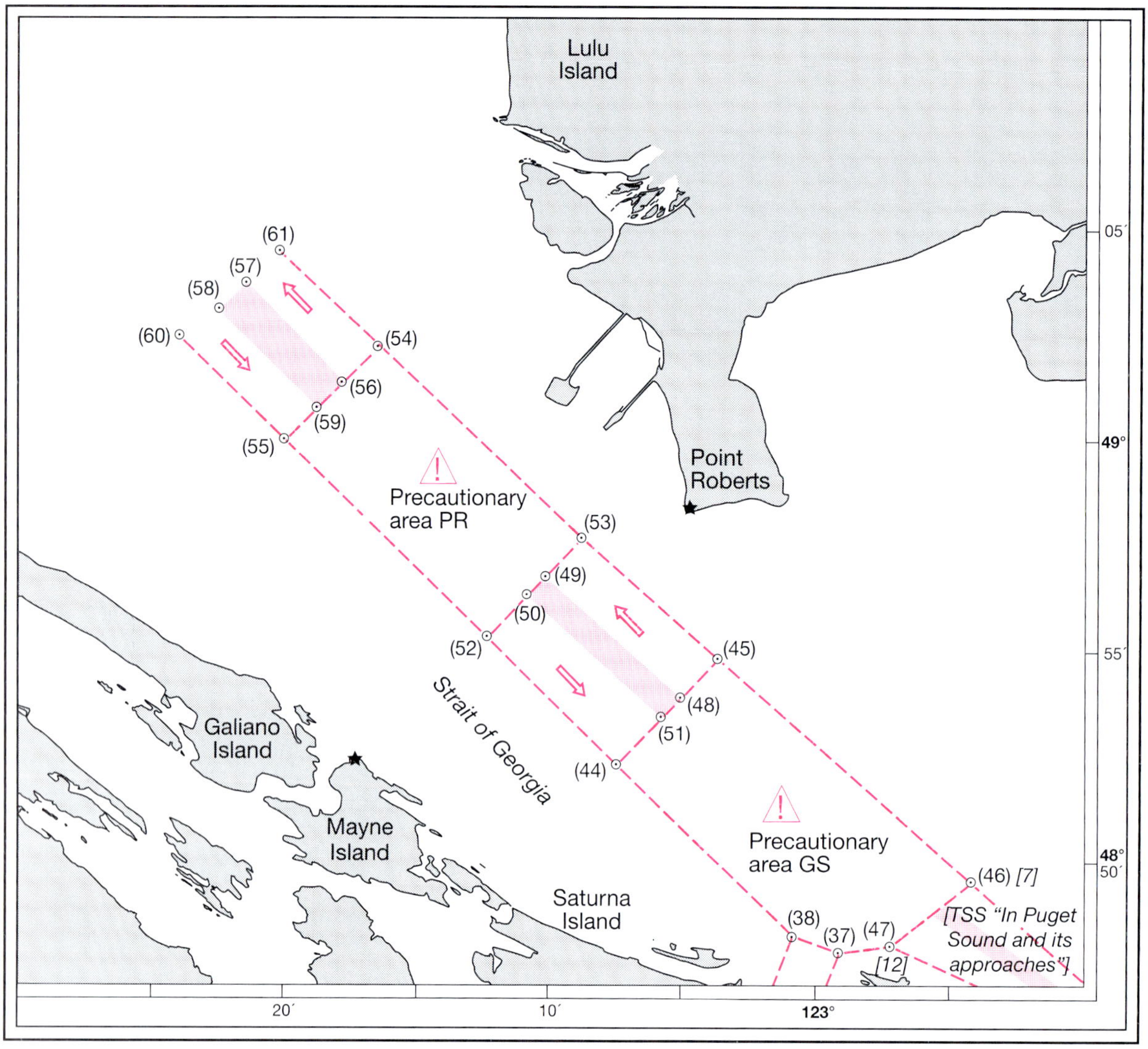

STRAIT OF GEORGIA

IN HARO STRAIT AND BOUNDARY PASS, AND IN THE STRAIT OF GEORGIA

(Reference charts: Canadian Hydrographic Service 3461, 2002 edition; 3462, 2002 edition; 3463, 2002 edition.
United States 18421, 2003 edition; 18423, 2003 edition; 18431, 2002 edition; 18432, 2003 edition; 18433, 2002 edition.
Note: The charts are based on North American 1983 datum.)

Description of the traffic separation schemes

The traffic separation schemes "In Haro Strait and Boundary Pass" and "In the Strait of Georgia" consist of a series of traffic separation schemes, two-way routes, and precautionary areas broken into two geographic designations as follows:
Part I: Haro Strait and Boundary Pass
Part II: Strait of Georgia

Part I
Haro Strait and Boundary Pass

(a) A separation zone is established, bounded by a line connecting the following geographical positions:

(1)	48°22′.25 N,	123°21′.12 W	(4)	48°24′.30 N,	123°13′.00 W
(2)	48°22′.25 N,	123°17′.95 W	(5)	48°22′.55 N,	123°18′.05 W
(3)	48°23′.88 N,	123°13′.18 W	(6)	48°22′.55 N,	123°21′.12 W

thence back to point of origin (1).

(b) A traffic lane for eastbound traffic is established between the separation zone and a line connecting the following geographical positions:

(12)	48°21′.67 N,	123°21′.12 W	(14)	48°23′.10 N,	123°13′.50 W
(13)	48°21′.67 N,	123°17′.70 W			

(c) A traffic lane for westbound traffic is established between the separation zone and a line connecting the following geographical positions:

(19)	48°25′.10 N,	123°12′.67 W	(21)	48°23′.15 N,	123°21′.12 W
(20)	48°23′.15 N,	123°18′.30 W			

(d) A precautionary area "V" is established, bounded by a line connecting the following geographical positions:

(21)	48°23′.15 N,	123°21′.12 W	(25)	48°20′.93 N,	123°24′.26 W
(22)	48°23′.71 N,	123°23′.88 W	(26)	48°20′.93 N,	123°23′.22 W
(23)	48°21′.83 N,	123°25′.56 W	(12)	48°21′.67 N,	123°21′.12 W
(24)	48°21′.15 N,	123°24′.83 W			

thence back to point of origin (21).

(e) A separation zone is established, bounded by a line connecting the following geographical positions:

(7)	48°25′.96 N,	123°10′.65 W	(10)	48°29′.10 N,	123°11′.59 W
(8)	48°27′.16 N,	123°10′.25 W	(11)	48°25′.69 N,	123°11′.28 W
(9)	48°28′.77 N,	123°10′.84 W			

thence back to point of origin (7).

(f) A traffic lane for northbound traffic is established between the separation zone and a line connecting the following geographical positions:

(16)	48°26′.57 N,	123°09′.22 W	(17)	48°27′.86 N,	123°08′.81 W

(g) A traffic lane for southbound traffic is established between the separation zone and a line connecting the following geographical positions:

(18)	48°29′.80 N,	123°13′.15 W	(19)	48°25′.10 N,	123°12′.67 W

(h) A precautionary area "DI" is established, bounded by a line connecting the following geographical positions:

(14)	48°23′.10 N,	123°13′.50 W	(16)	48°26′.57 N,	123°09′.22 W
(15)	48°24′.30 N,	123°09′.95 W	(19)	48°25′.10 N,	123°12′.67 W

thence back to point of origin (14).

(i) A two-way route is established between the following geographical positions:

(29)	48°31′.60 N,	123°10′.65 W	(32)	48°39′.32 N,	123°13′.14 W
(30)	48°35′.21 N,	123°12′.61 W	(33)	48°39′.41 N,	123°16′.06 W
(31)	48°38′.37 N,	123°12′.36 W	(34)	48°32′.83 N,	123°13′.45 W

thence back to point of origin (29).

(j) A precautionary area "HS" is established, bounded by a line connecting the following geographical positions:

(17)	48°27′.86 N,	123°08′.81 W	(29)	48°31′.60 N,	123°10′.65 W
(27)	48°29′.28 N,	123°08′.35 W	(34)	48°32′.83 N,	123°13′.45 W
(28)	48°30′.55 N,	123°10′.12 W	(18)	48°29′.80 N,	123°13′.15 W

thence back to point of origin (17).

(k) A two-way route is established between the following geographical positions:

(35)	48°42′.23 N,	123°11′.35 W	(38)	48°48′.19 N,	123°00′.84 W
(36)	48°45′.51 N,	123°01′.82 W	(39)	48°46′.43 N,	123°03′.12 W
(37)	48°47′.78 N,	122°59′.12 W	(40)	48°43′.80 N,	123°10′.77 W

thence back to point of origin (35).

(l) A precautionary area "TP" is established, bounded by a line connecting the following geographical positions:

(43)	48°41′.06 N,	123°11′.04 W	(33)	48°39′.41 N,	123°16′.06 W
(35)	48°42′.23 N,	123°11′.35 W	(32)	48°39′.32 N,	123°13′.14 W
(40)	48°43′.80 N,	123°10′.77 W	(42)	48°39′.76 N,	123°11′.84 W
(41)	48°43′.20 N,	123°16′.06 W			

Part II

Strait of Georgia

(m) A precautionary area "GS" is established, bounded by a line connecting the following geographical positions:

(44)	48°52′.30 N,	123°07′.44 W	(47)	48°47′.93 N,	122°57′.12 W
(45)	48°54′.81 N,	123°03′.66 W	(37)	48°47′.78 N,	122°59′.12 W
(46)	48°49′.49 N,	122°54′.24 W	(38)	48°48′.19 N,	123°00′.84 W

thence to the point of origin (44).

(n) A separation zone is established, bounded by a line connecting the following geographical positions:

(48)	48°53′.89 N,	123°05′.04 W	(50)	48°56′.30 N,	123°10′.80 W
(49)	48°56′.82 N,	123°10′.08 W	(51)	48°53′.39 N,	123°05′.70 W

(o) A traffic lane for north-westbound traffic is established between the separation zone and a line connecting the following geographical positions:

(45)	48°54′.81 N,	123°03′.66 W	(53)	48°57′.68 N,	123°08′.76 W

(p) A traffic lane for south-eastbound traffic is established between the separation zone and a line connecting the following geographical positions:

(52)	48°55′.34 N,	123°12′.30 W	(44)	48°52′.30 N,	123°07′.44 W

(q) A precautionary area "PR" is established, bounded by a line connecting the following geographical positions:

(52)	48°55′.34 N,	123°12′.30 W	(54)	49°02′.20 N,	123°16′.28 W
(53)	48°57′.68 N,	123°08′.76 W	(55)	49°00′.00 N,	123°19′.69 W

thence back to point of origin (52).

OFF SAN FRANCISCO*

(Reference charts: United States 18680, 2005 edition; 18645, 2008 edition.
Note: These charts are based on North American 1983 datum, which is equivalent to WGS 1984 datum.)

Description of the traffic separation scheme

The traffic separation scheme Off San Francisco consists of four parts:

Part I
Northern approach

(a) A separation zone is bounded by a line connecting the following geographical positions:

(1)	37°48′.52 N,	122°47′.63 W	(38)	38°08′.03 N,	123°21′.34 W
(2)	37°58′.45 N,	123°09′.49 W	(3)	37°57′.67 N,	123°10′.31 W
(37)	38°09′.09 N,	123°20′.82 W	(4)	37°47′.66 N,	122°48′.29 W

(b) A traffic lane for north-westbound traffic is established between the separation zone and a line connecting the following geographical positions:

(5)	37°49′.29 N,	122°46′.79 W	(36)	38°10′.14 N,	123°20′.29 W
(6)	37°59′.22 N,	123°08′.66 W			

(c) A traffic lane for south-eastbound traffic is established between the separation zone and a line connecting the following geographical positions:

(39)	38°06′.92 N,	123°21′.82 W	(8)	37°46′.72 N,	122°48′.76 W
(7)	37°56′.89 N,	123°11′.14 W			

Part II
Southern approach

(a) A separation zone is bounded by a line connecting the following geographical positions:

(9)	37°39′.07 N,	122°40′.40 W	(11)	37°18′.71 N,	122°43′.00 W
(10)	37°18′.45 N,	122°40′.40 W	(12)	37°39′.12 N,	122°43′.00 W

(b) A traffic lane for northbound traffic is established between the separation zone and a line connecting the following geographical positions:

(13)	37°39′.30 N,	122°39′.14 W	(14)	37°18′.36 N,	122°39′.14 W

(c) A traffic lane for southbound traffic is established between the separation zone and a line connecting the following geographical positions:

(15)	37°18′.89 N,	122°44′.26 W	(16)	37°39′.41 N,	122°44′.26 W

Part III
Western approach

(a) A separation zone is bounded by a line connecting the following geographical positions:

(17)	37°41′.90 N,	122°47′.99 W	(19)	37°32′.70 N,	123°03′.10 W
(18)	37°33′.54 N,	123°03′.79 W	(20)	37°41′.09 N,	122°47′.25 W

(b) A traffic lane for south-westbound traffic is established between the separation zone and a line connecting the following geographical positions:

(21)	37°42′.81 N,	122°48′.55 W	(22)	37°34′.37 N,	123°04′.49 W

(c) A traffic lane for north-eastbound traffic is established between the separation zone and a line connecting the following geographical positions:

(23)	37°31′.87 N,	123°02′.40 W	(24)	37°40′.38 N,	122°46′.33 W

Part IV
Main ship channel

(a) A separation line connects the following geographical positions:

(25)	37°45′.90 N,	122°38′.00 W	(27)	37°48′.10 N,	122°31′.00 W
(26)	37°47′.00 N,	122°34′.30 W			

* Date of implementation of amended scheme: 0000 hours UTC on 1 June 2013.

(b) A traffic lane for eastbound traffic is established between the separation line and a line connecting the following geographical positions:

(28)	37°45′.80 N,	122°37′.70 W	(29)	37°47′.80 N,	122°30′.80 W

(c) A traffic lane for westbound traffic is established between the separation line and a line connecting the following geographical positions:

(30)	37°46′.20 N,	122°37′.90 W	(32)	37°48′.50 N,	122°31′.30 W
(31)	37°46′.90 N,	122°35′.30 W			

Area to be avoided

A circular area to be avoided, of radius half a mile, is centred upon geographical position:

(33) 37°45′.00 N, 122°41′.50 W

Precautionary area

A precautionary area is established bounded to the west by an arc of a circle of radius 6 miles centring upon geographic position (33) 37°45′.00 N, 122°41′.50 W and connecting with the following geographical positions:

(34)	37°42′.70 N,	122°34′.60 W	(35)	37°50′.30 N,	122°38′.00 W

The precautionary area is bounded to the east by a line connecting the following geographical positions:

(34)	37°42′.70 N,	122°34′.60 W	(35)	37°50′.30 N,	122°38′.00 W
(25)	37°45′.90 N,	122°38′.00 W			

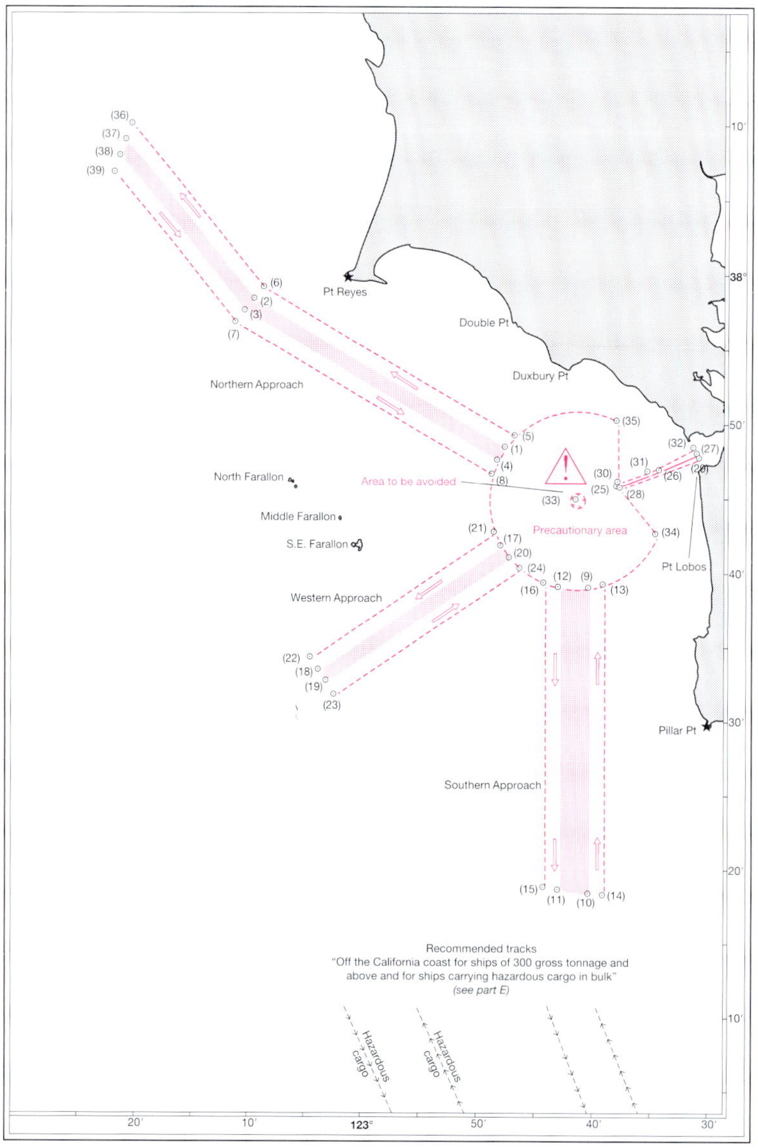

OFF SAN FRANCISCO

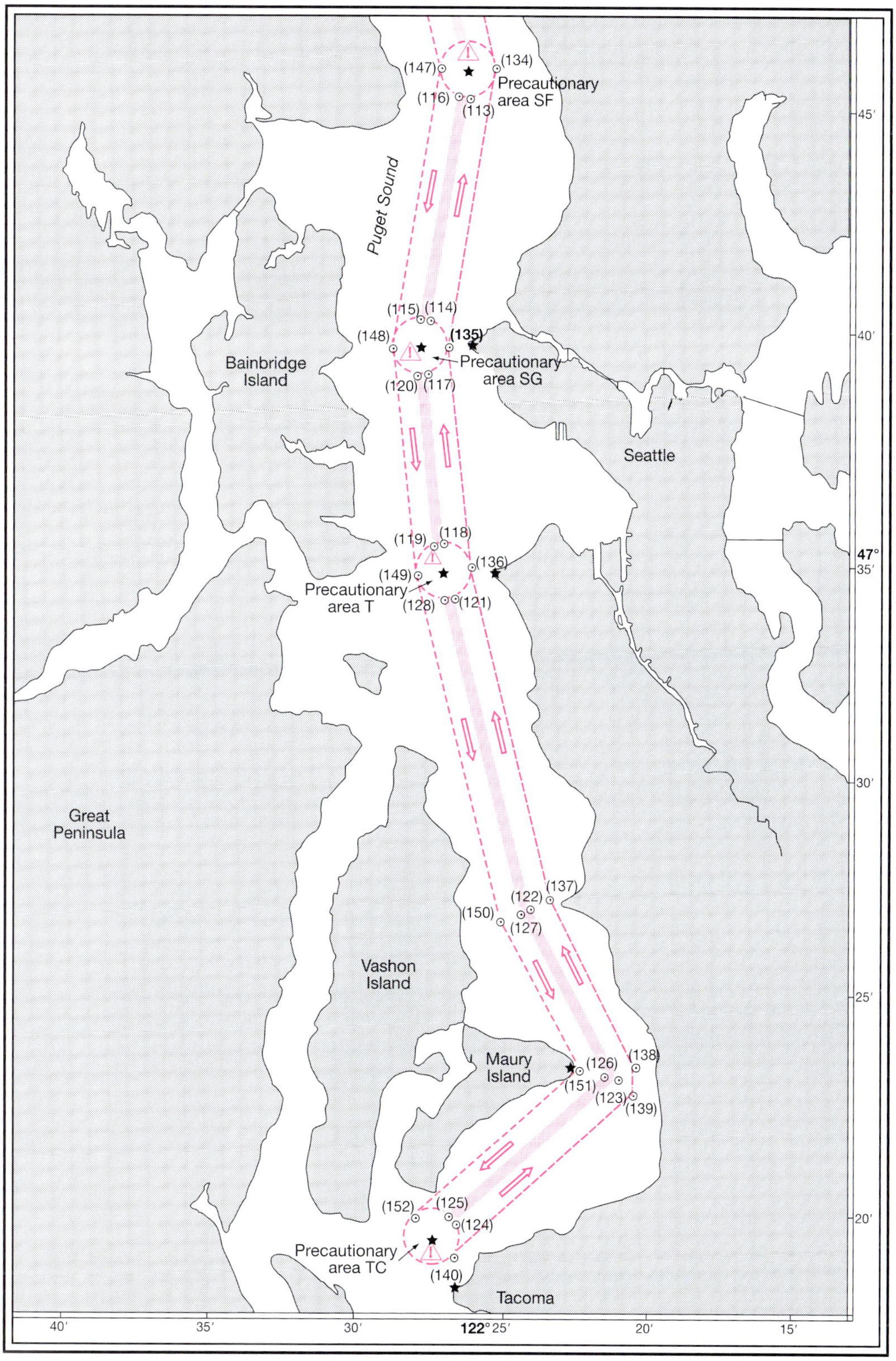

IN PUGET SOUND AND ITS APPROACHES: PUGET SOUND – SOUTH

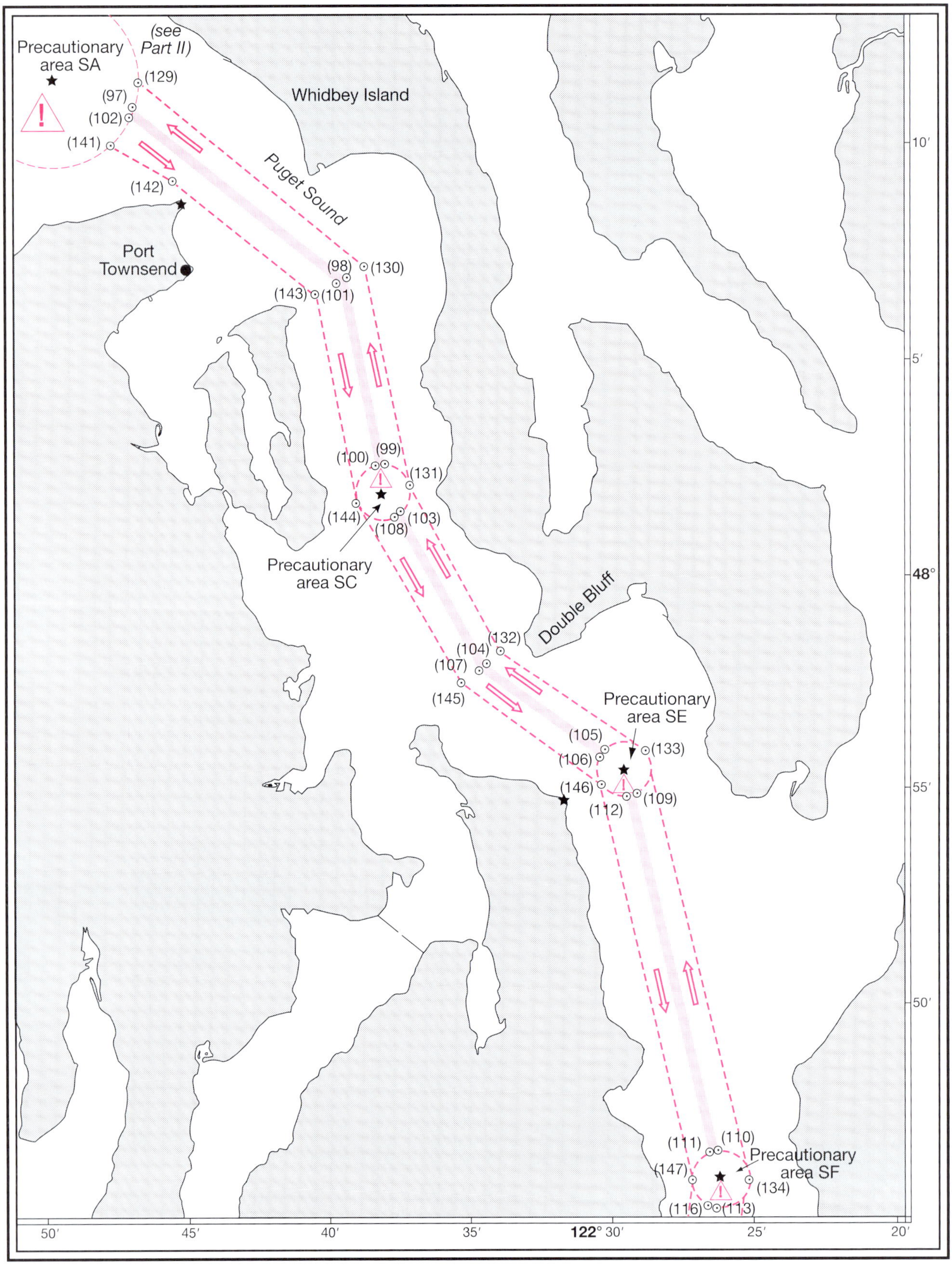

IN PUGET SOUND AND ITS APPROACHES: PUGET SOUND – NORTH

IN THE SANTA BARBARA CHANNEL*

(Reference charts: United States 18700, 2003 edition; 18720, 2008 edition.
Note: These charts are based on North American 1983 datum, which is equivalent to WGS 1984 datum.)

Description of the traffic separation scheme

The traffic separation scheme in the Santa Barbara Channel consists of two parts:

Part I
Between Point Vicente and Point Conception

(a) A separation zone is bounded by a line connecting the following geographical positions:

(1)	34°20′.84 N,	120°30′.28 W	(4)	33°44′.06 N,	118°36′.34 W
(2)	34°03′.87 N,	119°15′.63 W	(5)	34°02′.94 N,	119°16′.09 W
(3)	33°44′.93 N,	118°35′.75 W	(6)	34°19′.88 N,	120°30′.59 W

(b) A traffic lane for north-westbound traffic is established between the separation zone and a line connecting the following geographical positions:

(7)	34°21′.80 N.	120°29′.96 W	(9)	33°45′.80 N,	118°35′.15 W
(8)	34°04′.80 N,	119°15′.16 W			

(c) A traffic lane for south-eastbound traffic is established between the separation zone and a line connecting the following geographical positions:

(10)	33°43′.18 N,	118°36′.94 W	(12)	34°18′.92 N,	120°30′.91 W
(11)	34°02′.01 N,	119°16′.56 W			

Note:
Port Hueneme Fairway
A safety fairway is established in the approach to Port Hueneme.

Part II
Between Point Conception and Point Arguello

(a) A separation zone is bounded by a line connecting the following geographical positions:

(1)	34°20′.84 N,	120°30′.28 W	(13)	34°24′.76 N,	120°52′.10 W
(6)	34°19′.88 N,	120°30′.59 W	(14)	34°25′.72 N,	120°51′.78 W

(b) A traffic lane for westbound traffic is established between the separation zone and a line connecting the following geographical positions:

(7)	34°21′.80 N,	120°29′.96 W	(15)	34°26′.68 N,	120°51′.46 W

(c) A traffic lane for eastbound traffic is established between the separation zone and a line connecting the following geographical positions:

(12)	34°18′.92 N,	120°30′.91 W	(16)	34°23′.80 N,	120°52′.42 W

(chartlet overleaf)

* Date of implementation of amended scheme: 0000 hours UTC on 1 June 2013.

B

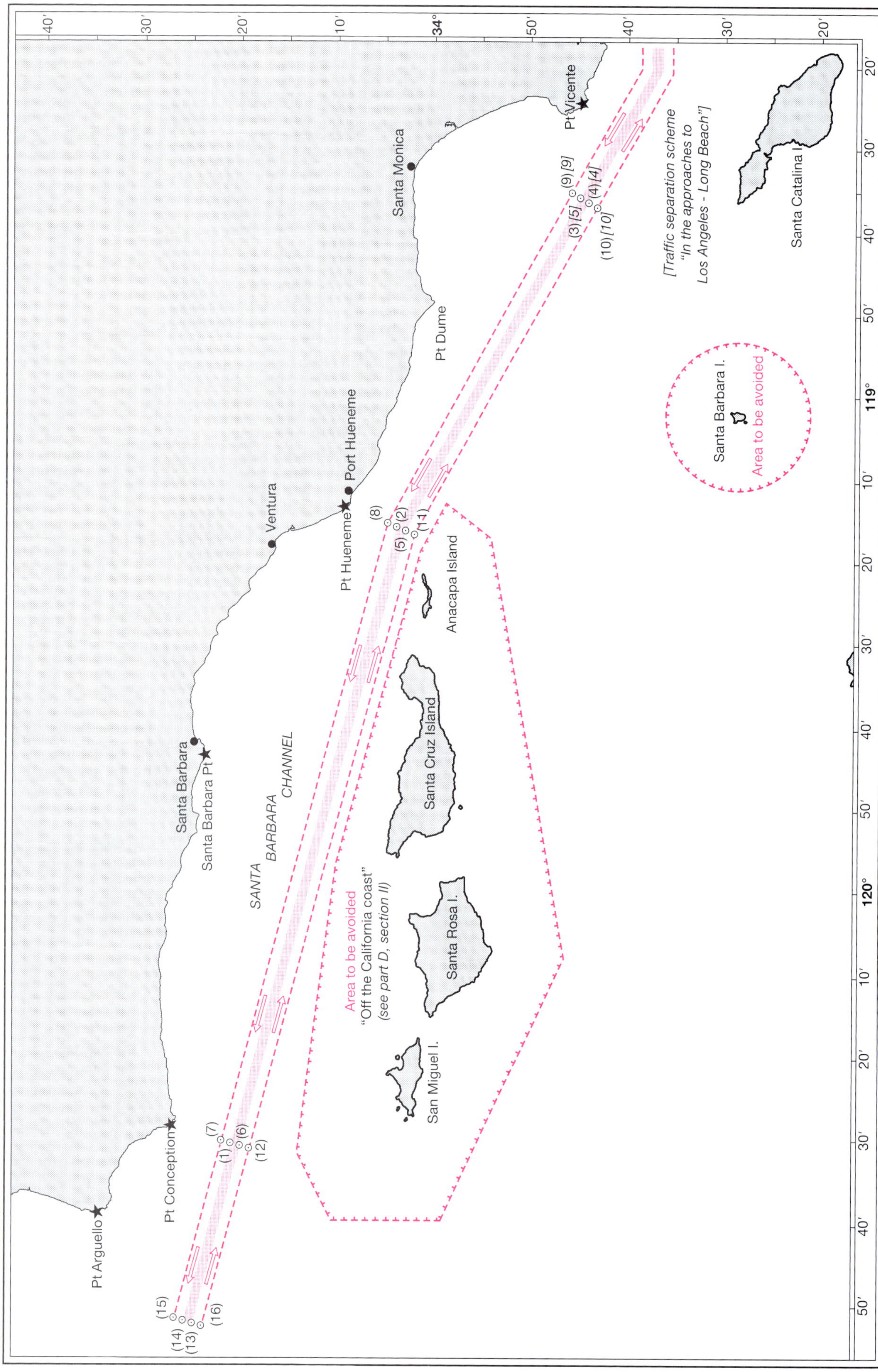

IN THE SANTA BARBARA CHANNEL

IN THE APPROACHES TO LOS ANGELES – LONG BEACH*

(A continuation of the Santa Barbara Channel scheme)
(Reference chart: United States 18746, 2009 edition.
Note: This chart is based on North American 1983 datum, which is equivalent to WGS 1984 datum.)

Description of the traffic separation scheme

The traffic separation scheme "In the Approaches to Los Angeles – Long Beach" consists of three parts:

Western approach

(a) A separation zone is bounded by a line connecting the following geographical positions:

(1)	33°37′.70 N,	118°17′.60 W	(4)	33°44′.06 N,	118°36′.34 W
(2)	33°36′.50 N,	118°17′.60 W	(5)	33°44′.93 N,	118°35′.75 W
(3)	33°36′.50 N,	118°20′.48 W	(6)	33°37′.70 N,	118°20′.57 W

(b) A traffic lane for northbound coastwise traffic is established between the separation zone and a line connecting the following geographical positions:

(7)	33°38′.70 N,	118°17′.60 W	(9)	33°45′.80 N,	118°35′.15 W
(8)	33°38′.70 N,	118°20′.24 W			

(c) A traffic lane for southbound coastwise traffic is established between the separation zone and a line connecting the following geographical positions:

(10)	33°35′.50 N,	118°17′.60 W	(12)	33°43′.18 N,	118°36′.94 W
(11)	33°35′.50 N,	118°20′.81 W			

Southern approach

(a) A separation zone is established bounded by a line connecting the following geographic positions:

(13)	33°35′.50 N,	118°10′.30 W	(15)	33°19′.00 N,	118°05′.60 W
(14)	33°35′.50 N,	118°12′.75 W	(16)	33°19′.70 N,	118°03′.50 W

(b) A traffic lane for northbound traffic is established between the separation zone and a line connecting the following geographical positions:

(17)	33°35′.50 N,	118°09′.00 W	(18)	33°20′.00 N,	118°02′.30 W

(c) A traffic lane for southbound traffic is established between the separation zone and a line connecting the following geographical positions:

(19)	33°35′.50 N,	118°14′.00 W	(20)	33°18′.70 N,	118°06′.75 W

Precautionary area

(a) The precautionary area consists of the water area enclosed by the Los Angeles – Long Beach breakwater and a line connecting Point Fermin light, at 33°42′.30 N, 118°17′.60 W, with the following geographical positions:

(10)	33°35′.50 N,	118°17′.60 W	(21)	33°37′.70 N,	118°06′.50 W
(17)	33°35′.50 N,	118°09′.00 W	(22)	33°43′.40 N,	118°10′.80 W

Note:

Pilot boarding areas are located in the precautionary area. Due to heavy vessel traffic, mariners are advised not to anchor or linger in this precautionary area except to pick up or disembark a pilot.

(chartlet overleaf)

* Date of implementation of amended scheme: 0000 hours UTC on 1 June 2013.

B

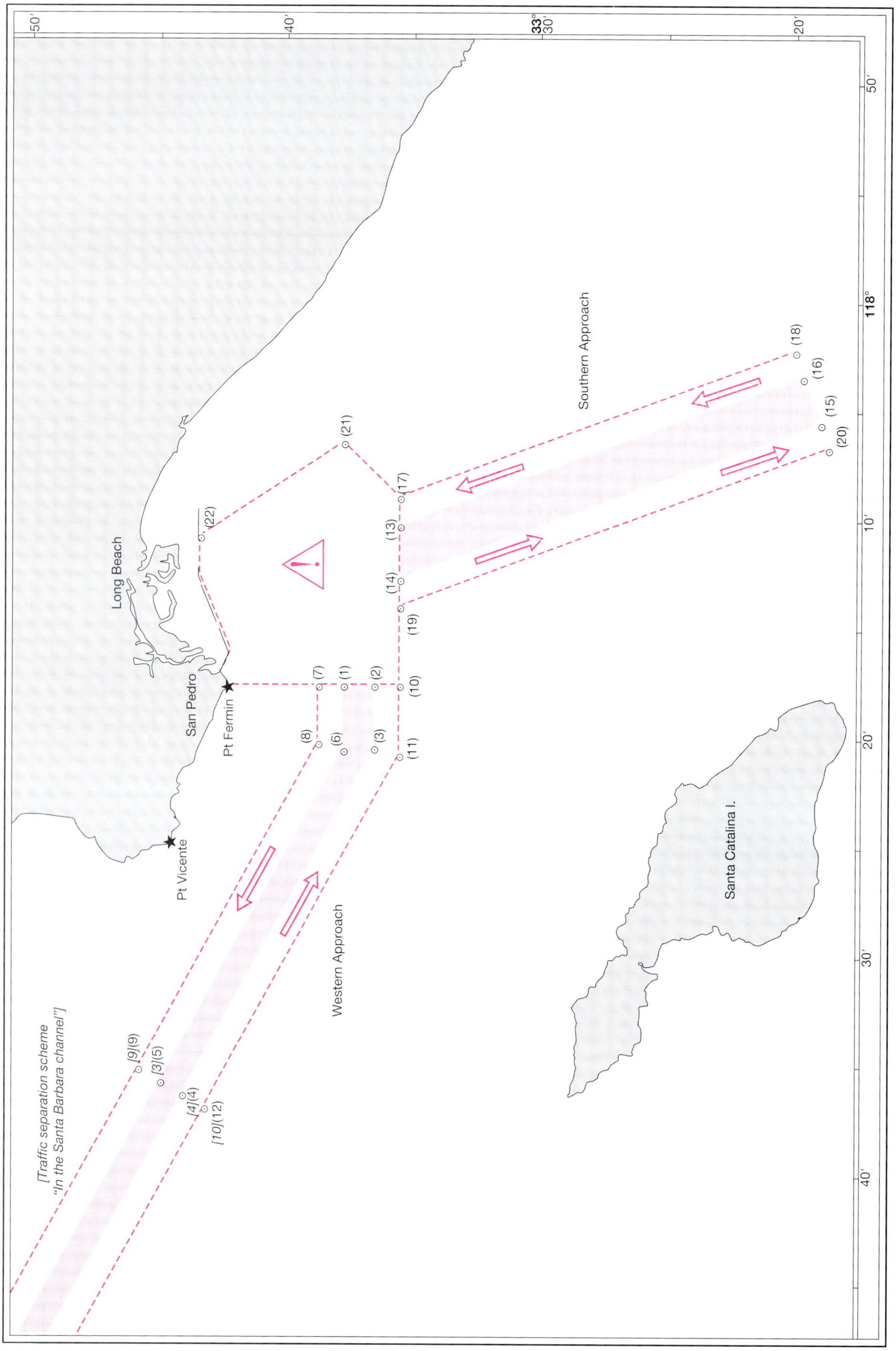

IN THE APPROACHES TO LOS ANGELES – LONG BEACH

IN THE APPROACHES TO SALINA CRUZ

(Reference chart: United States 21441, 1986 edition.
Note: This chart is based on the World Geodetic System 1972 datum.)

Description of the traffic separation scheme

The traffic separation scheme is composed of two parts:

Part I

South-western approach: recommended for oil tankers proceeding to or coming from the three single-point moorings or the oil terminal.

(a) A separation zone is bounded by a line connecting the following geographical positions:

(1)	16°06′.23 N,	095°14′.27 W	(3)	15°57′.70 N,	095°17′.47 W
(2)	15°58′.43 N,	095°19′.00 W	(4)	16°06′.00 N,	095°13′.83 W

(b) A traffic lane for south-westbound traffic is established between the separation zone and a line connecting the following geographical positions:

(5)	16°06′.50 N,	095°14′.70 W	(6)	15°59′.35 N,	095°20′.43 W

(c) A traffic lane for north-eastbound traffic is established between the separation zone and a line connecting the following geographical positions:

(7)	15°57′.15 N,	095°15′.85 W	(8)	16°05′.85 N,	095°13′.35 W

Part II

Southern approach: recommended for ships of over 500 gross tonnes arriving at or leaving the port of Salina Cruz, Oaxaca.

(a) A separation zone is bounded by a line connecting the following geographical positions:

(9)	16°05′.75 N,	095°11′.70 W	(11)	15°56′.70 N,	095°11′.03 W
(10)	15°56′.70 N,	095°11′.70 W	(12)	16°05′.75 N,	095°11′.03 W

(b) A traffic lane for southbound traffic is established between the separation zone and a line connecting the following geographical positions:

(13)	16°05′.75 N,	095°12′.73 W	(14)	15°56′.70 N,	095°12′.73 W

(c) A traffic lane for northbound traffic is established between the separation zone and a line connecting the following geographical positions:

(15)	15°56′.70 N,	095°10′.00 W	(16)	16°05′.75 N,	095°10′.00 W

Notes:

1 Ship movement in the port area is supervised by a Port Vessel Traffic Supervisor on a 24-hour basis. Any ship intending to use any traffic separation scheme is requested to contact the Salina Cruz, Oaxaca, Port Vessel Traffic Supervisor on channel 6 VHF and follow his advice while transiting the scheme.

2 The master of any ship with appropriate equipment may obtain continuous and precise information on his ship's position in the traffic lane by using the racon identified by the letter Z, located at geographical position:

(23) 16°09′.75 N, 095°12′.31 W

(chartlet overleaf)

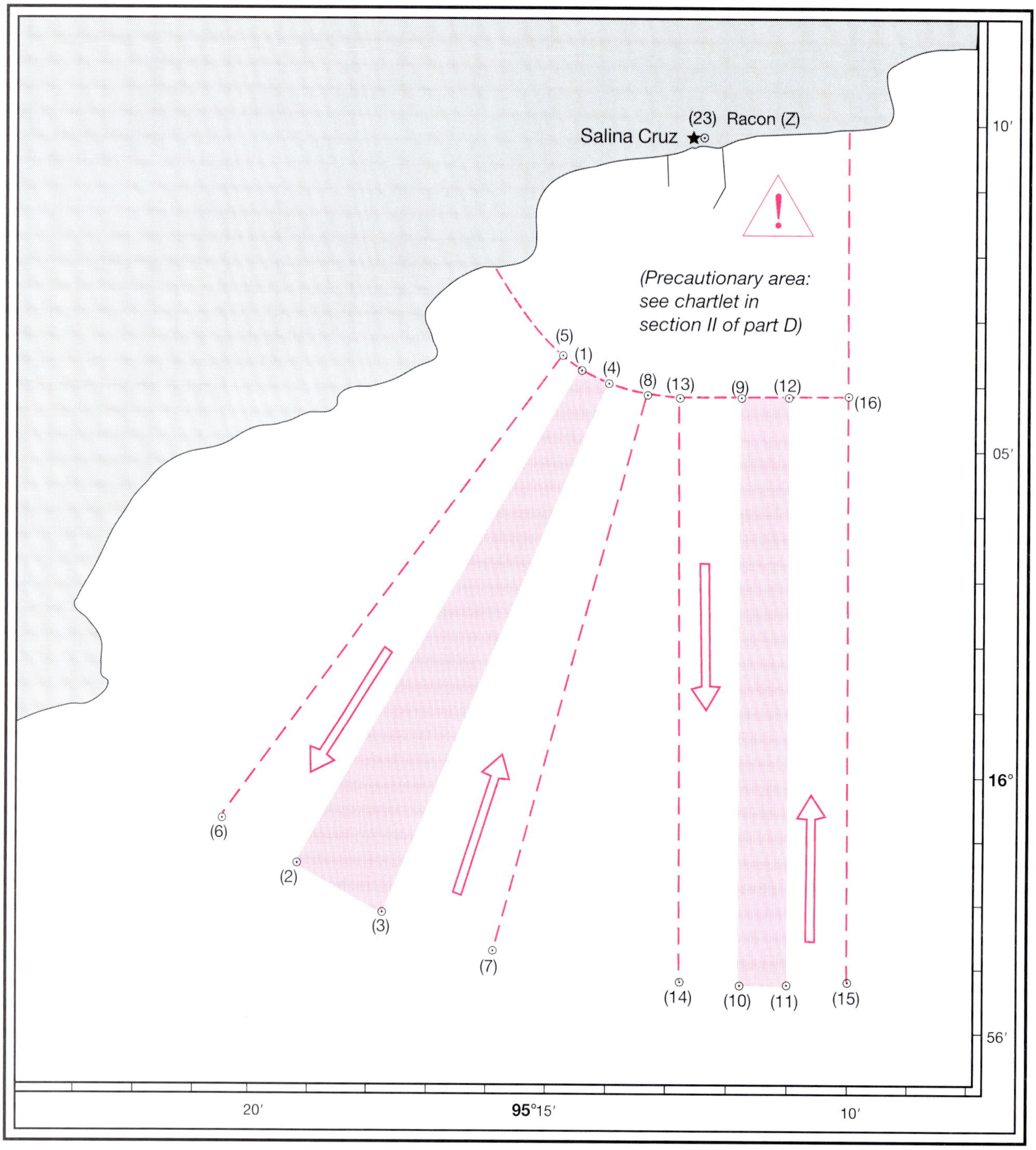

IN THE APPROACHES TO SALINA CRUZ

Section VIII

South America, Pacific coast

Caution: The chartlets are for illustrative purposes only and must not be used for navigation. Mariners should consult the appropriate nautical publications and charts for up-to-date details on aids to navigation and other relevant information.

Warning: The geographical positions given in the descriptions of the routeing systems are only correct for charts using the same geodetic datum as the reference charts indicated under each scheme. Charts published by other hydrographic offices may use a different geodetic datum, as may new editions of the reference charts published after the adoption of the routeing system. Where amendments to existing systems are not based on the same geodetic datum as the original system, this is emphasized by the use of different colours for definitions of positions.

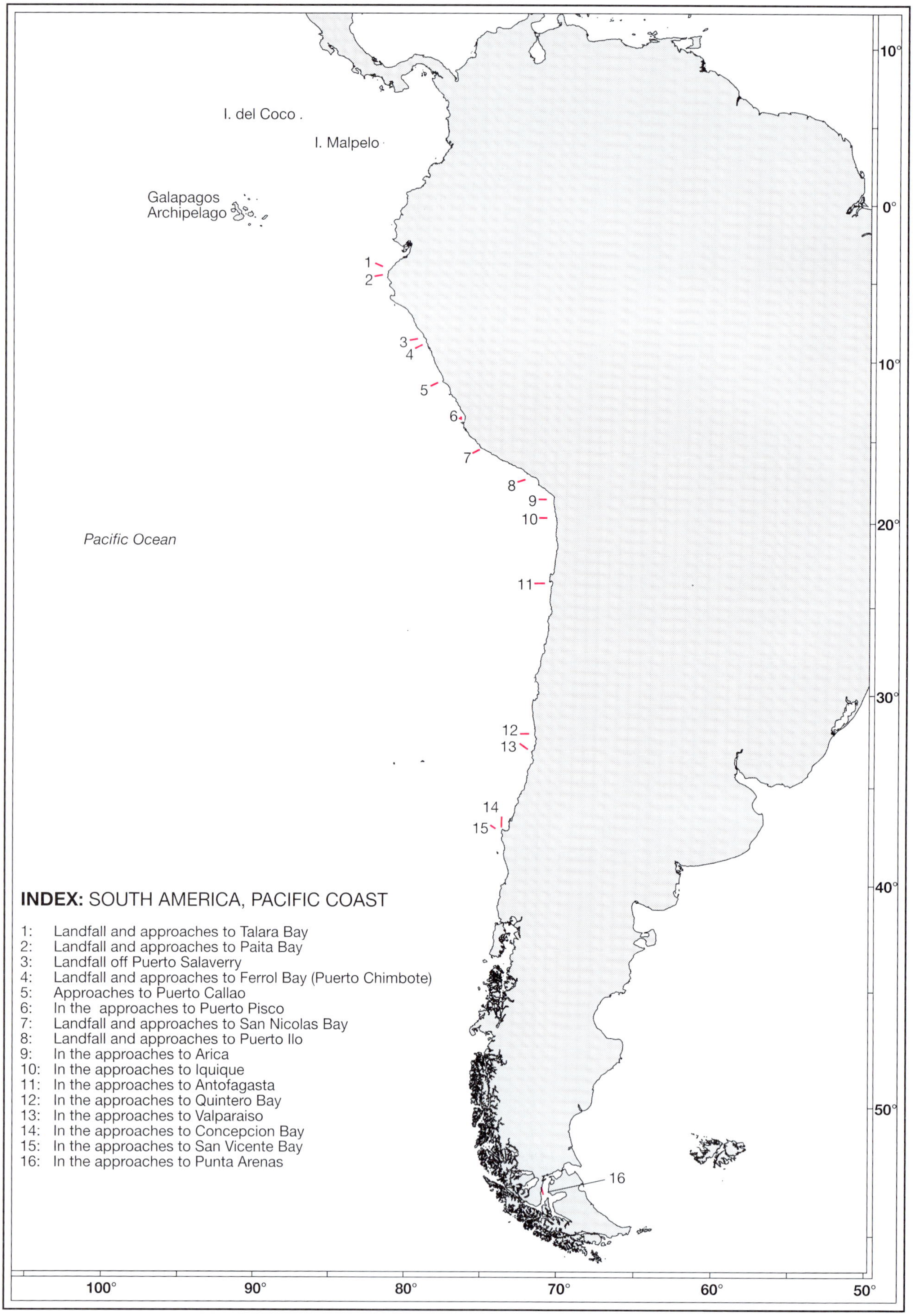

I. del Coco
I. Malpelo
Galapagos Archipelago
Pacific Ocean
1
2
3
4
5
6
7
8
9
10
11
12
13
14
15
16
10°
0°
10°
20°
30°
40°
50°
100°
90°
80°
70°
60°
50°
INDEX: SOUTH AMERICA, PACIFIC COAST
1: Landfall and approaches to Talara Bay
2: Landfall and approaches to Paita Bay
3: Landfall off Puerto Salaverry
4: Landfall and approaches to Ferrol Bay (Puerto Chimbote)
5: Approaches to Puerto Callao
6: In the approaches to Puerto Pisco
7: Landfall and approaches to San Nicolas Bay
8: Landfall and approaches to Puerto Ilo
9: In the approaches to Arica
10: In the approaches to Iquique
11: In the approaches to Antofagasta
12: In the approaches to Quintero Bay
13: In the approaches to Valparaiso
14: In the approaches to Concepcion Bay
15: In the approaches to San Vicente Bay
16: In the approaches to Punta Arenas

LANDFALL AND APPROACHES TO TALARA BAY

(Reference charts: PERU HIDRONAV 1126, 1984 edition (revised 1998); 1150, 1999 edition.
Note: these charts are based on the World Geodetic System 1984 datum (WGS 84).)

Description of the traffic separation scheme

The traffic separation scheme for the landfall and approaches to Talara Bay consists of the following:

(a) A separation zone bounded by a line connecting the following geographical points:

(1)	04°33′.10 S,	081°19′.13 W	(3)	04°33′.90 S,	081°22′.13 W
(2)	04°32′.90 S,	081°22′.13 W	(4)	04°33′.70 S,	081°19′.13 W

(b) A traffic lane for westbound traffic, between the separation zone and a line connecting the following geographical points:

(5)	04°32′.40 S,	081°19′.13 W	(6)	04°31′.10 S,	081°22′.13 W

(c) A traffic lane for eastbound traffic, between the separation zone and a line connecting the following geographical points:

(7)	04°35′.70 S,	081°22′.13 W	(8)	04°34′.60 S,	081°19′.13 W

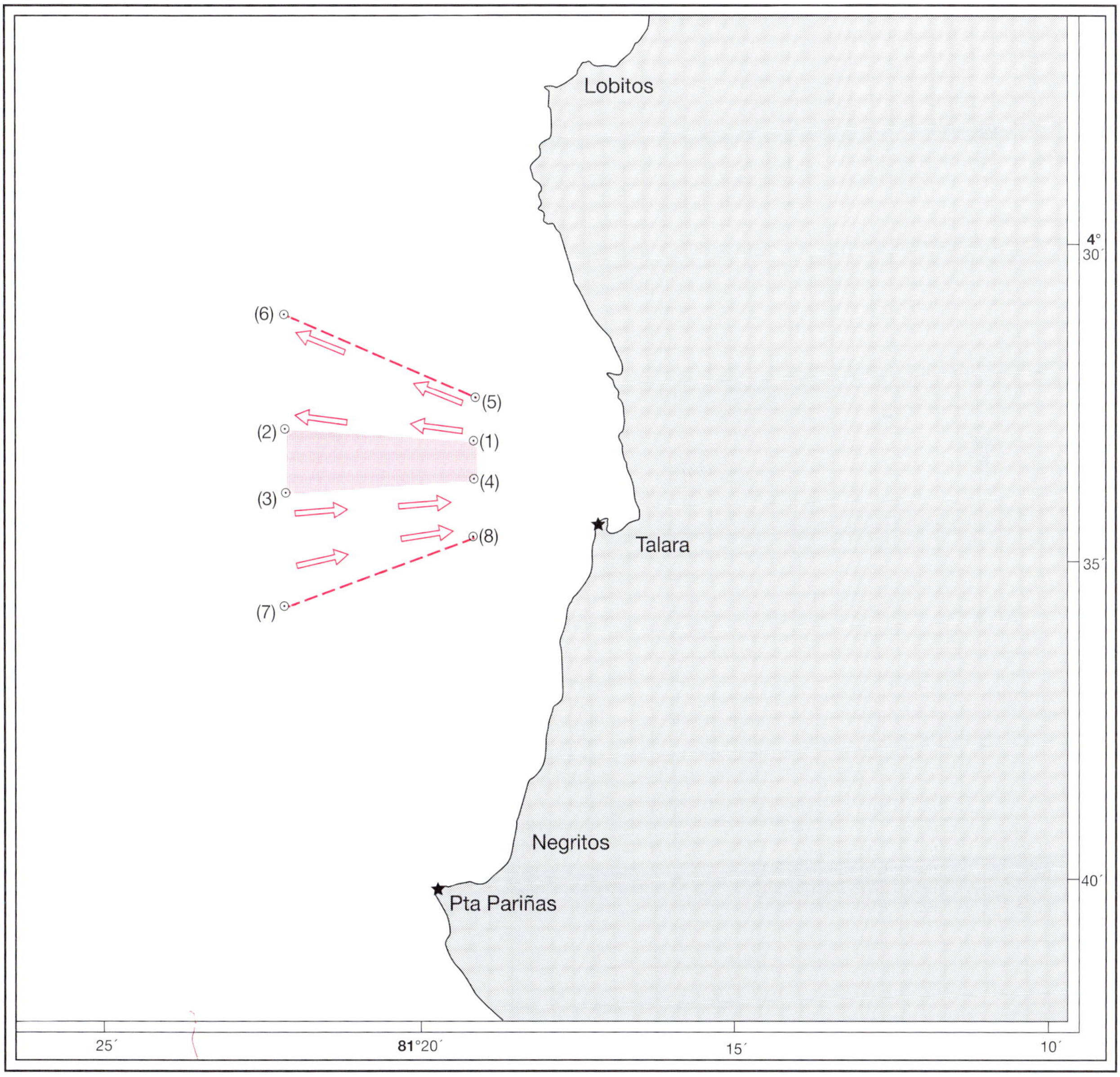

LANDFALL AND APPROACHES TO TALARA BAY

LANDFALL AND APPROACHES TO PAITA BAY

(Reference charts: PERU HIDRONAV 1133, 1997 edition (revised 1998); 1150, 1987 edition (revised 1997).
Note: these charts are based on World Geodetic System 1984 datum (WGS 84).)

Description of the traffic separation scheme

The traffic separation scheme for the approaches to Paita Bay consists of the following:

(a) A separation zone bounded by a line connecting the following geographical points:

(1)	05°02′.06 S,	081°08′.95 W	(3)	05°02′.77 S,	081°13′.14 W
(2)	05°01′.80 S,	081°13′.14 W	(4)	05°02′.52 S,	081°08′.95 W

(b) A traffic lane for westbound traffic, between the separation zone and a line connecting the following geographical points:

(5)	05°00′.93 S,	081°08′.95 W	(6)	04°59′.63 S,	081°13′.14 W

(c) A traffic lane for eastbound traffic, between the separation zone and a line connecting the following geographical points:

(7)	05°04′.96 S,	081°13′.14 W	(8)	05°03′.65 S,	081°08′.95 W

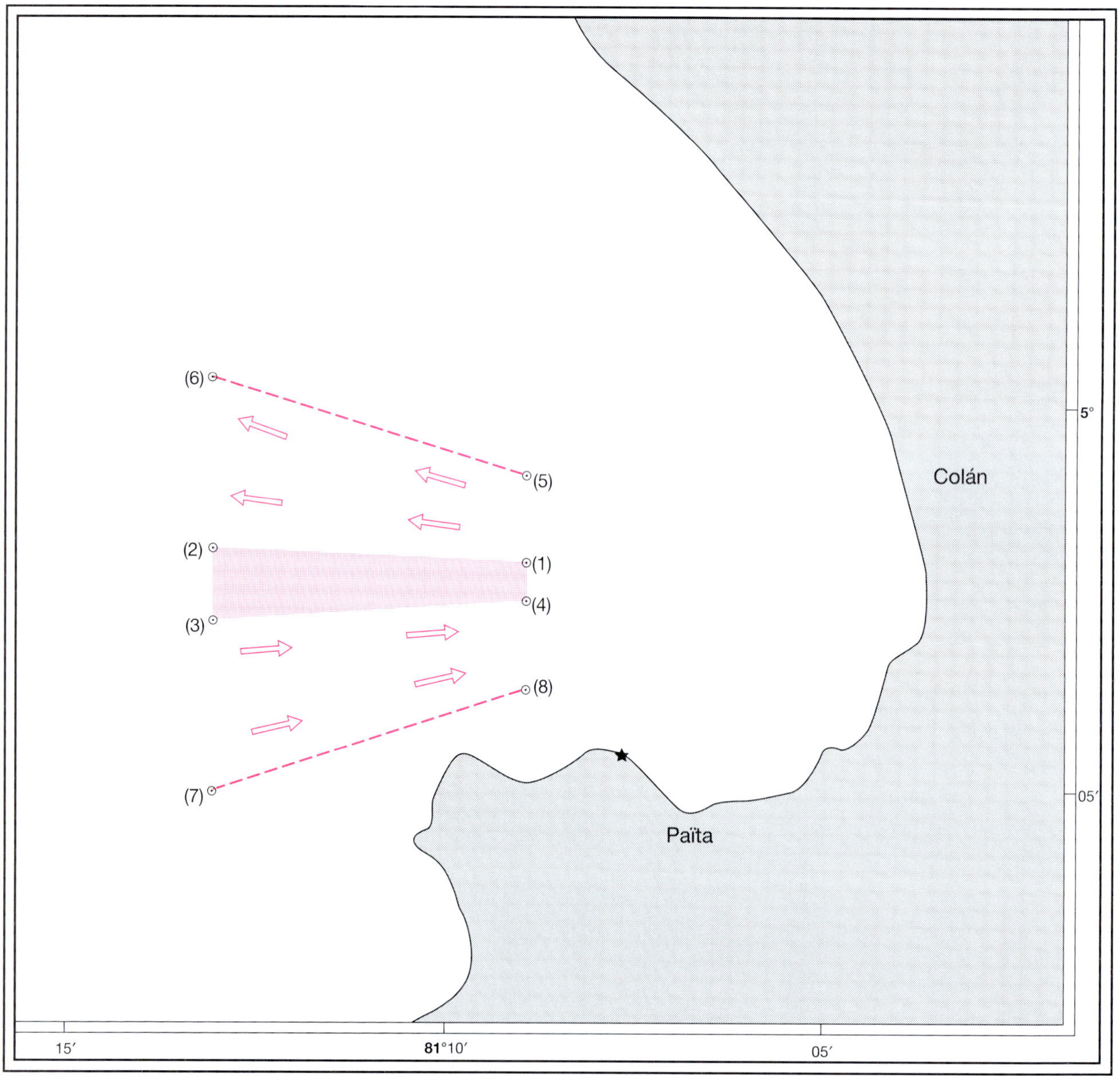

LANDFALL AND APPROACHES TO PAITA BAY

LANDFALL OFF PUERTO SALAVERRY

(Reference charts: PERU HIDRONAV 1270, 1988 edition (revised 1998); 2111, 1987 edition (revised 1994).
Note: these charts are based on the World Geodetic System 1984 datum (WGS 84).)

Description of the traffic separation scheme

The traffic separation scheme for the landfall off Puerto Salaverry consists of the following:

(a) A separation zone bounded by a line connecting the following geographical points:

(1)	08°12′.65 S,	079°02′.23 W	(3)	08°13′.30 S,	079°04′.63 W
(2)	08°12′.65 S,	079°04′.63 W	(4)	08°13′.30 S,	079°02′.23 W

(b) A traffic lane for westbound traffic, between the separation zone and a line connecting the following geographical points:

(5)	08°11′.96 S,	079°02′.23 W	(6)	08°11′.10 S,	079°04′.63 W

(c) A traffic lane for eastbound traffic, between the separation zone and a line connecting the following geographical points:

(7)	08°14′.80 S,	079°04′.63 W	(8)	08°14′.00 S,	079°02′.23 W

LANDFALL OFF PUERTO SALAVERRY

B

LANDFALL AND APPROACHES TO FERROL BAY (PUERTO CHIMBOTE)

(Reference charts: PERU HIDRONAV 1310, 1993 edition (revised 1997); 2123, 1980 edition (revised 1998).
Note: these charts are based on the World Geodetic System 1984 datum (WGS 84).)

Description of the traffic separation scheme

The traffic separation scheme for the landfall and approaches to Ferrol Bay (Puerto Chimbote) consists of the following:

(a) A separation zone bounded by a line connecting the following geographical points:

(1)	09°07′.20 S,	078°37′.83 W	(3)	09°07′.80 S,	078°40′.33 W
(2)	09°07′.20 S,	078°40′.33 W	(4)	09°07′.80 S,	078°37′.83 W

(b) A traffic lane for westbound traffic, between the separation zone and a line connecting the following geographical points:

(5)	09°06′.70 S,	078°37′.83 W	(6)	09°05′.80 S,	078°40′.33 W

(c) A traffic lane for eastbound traffic, between the separation zone and a line connecting the following geographical points:

(7)	09°09′.40 S,	078°40′.33 W	(8)	09°08′.40 S,	078°37′.83 W

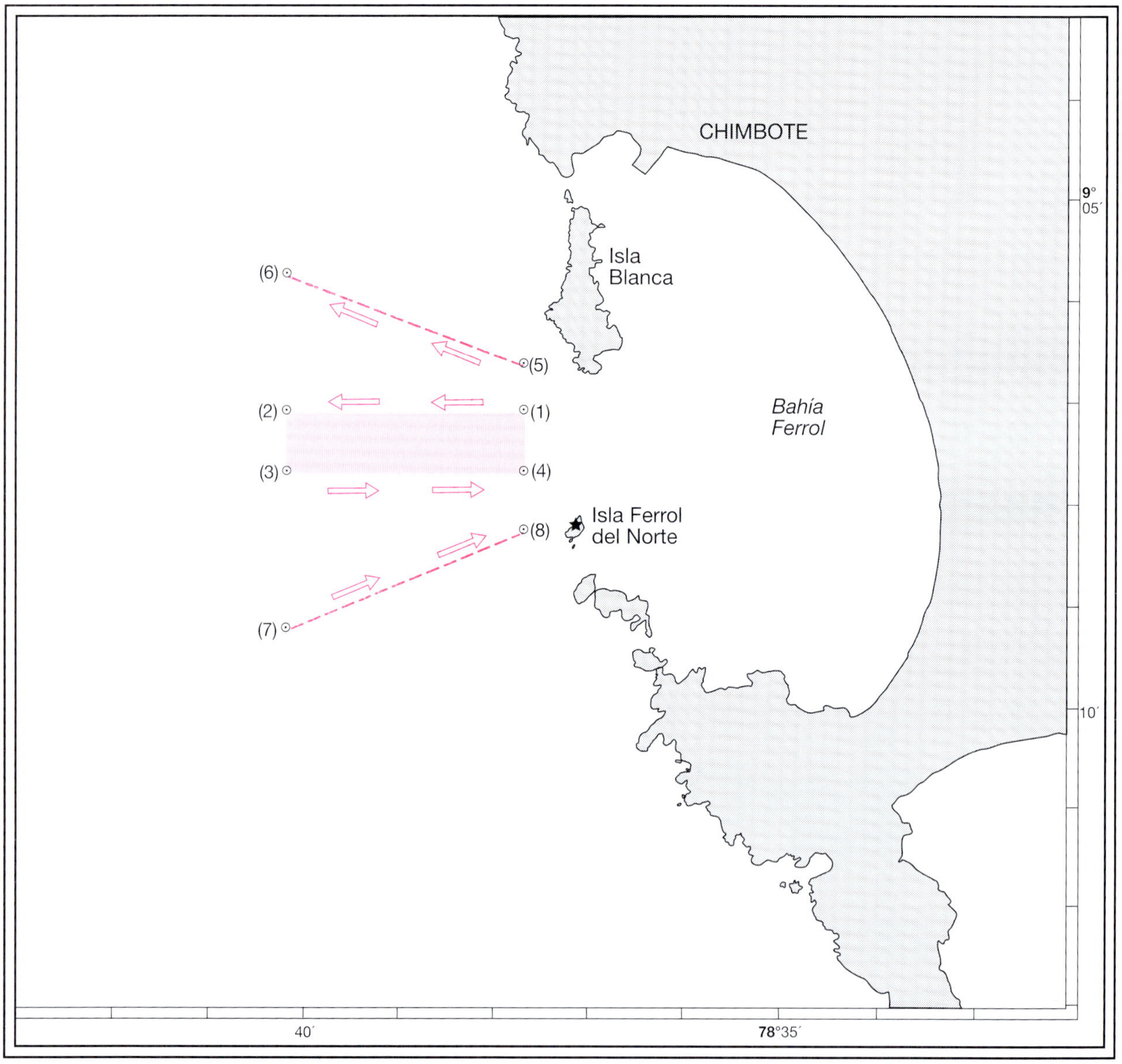

LANDFALL AND APPROACHES TO FERROL BAY (PUERTO CHIMBOTE)

APPROACHES TO PUERTO CALLAO

(Reference charts: PERU HIDRONAV 1396, 1984 edition (revised 1996).
Note: this chart is based on World Geodetic System 1984 datum (WGS 84).)

Description of the traffic separation scheme

The traffic separation scheme for the approaches to Puerto Callao consists of three parts:

Part I
North-west approaches

(a) A separation zone bounded by a line connecting the following geographical points:

(1)	12°01′.14 S,	077°15′.06 W	(3)	12°00′.07 S,	077°16′.57 W
(2)	11°59′.86 S,	077°16′.36 W	(4)	12°01′.31 S,	077°15′.31 W

(b) A traffic lane for north-westbound traffic, between the separation zone and a line connecting the following geographical points:

(5)	12°01′.01 S,	077°14′.28 W	(6)	11°59′.26 S,	077°15′.70 W

(c) A traffic lane for south-eastbound traffic, between the separation zone and a line connecting the following geographical points:

(7)	12°00′.70 S,	077°17′.21 W	(8)	12°01′.78 S,	077°15′.61 W

Part II
South-west approaches

(a) A separation zone bounded by a line connecting the following geographical points:

(9)	12°02′.50 S,	077°15′.56 W	(11)	12°03′.72 S,	077°16′.89 W
(10)	12°03′.50 S,	077°17′.08 W	(12)	12°02′.78 S,	077°15′.40 W

(b) A traffic lane for south-westbound traffic, between the separation zone and a line connecting the following geographical points:

(13)	12°01′.92 S,	077°15′.65 W	(14)	12°02′.80 S,	077°17′.81 W

(c) A traffic lane for north-eastbound traffic, between the separation zone and a line connecting the following geographical points:

(15)	12°04′.40 S,	077°16′.20 W	(16)	12°03′.00 S,	077°14′.87 W

Part III
Main shipping channel

(a) A separation zone bounded by a line connecting the following geographical points:

(17)	12°02′.62 S,	077°11′.00 W	(19)	12°02′.28 S,	077°13′.65 W
(18)	12°02′.16 S,	077°13′.63 W			

(b) A traffic lane for eastbound traffic, between the separation zone and a line connecting the following geographical points:

(20)	12°02′.44 S,	077°13′.71 W	(21)	12°02′.78 S,	077°11′.00 W

(c) A traffic lane for westbound traffic, between the separation zone and a line connecting the following geographical points:

(22)	12°02′.47 S,	077°11′.00 W	(23)	12°02′.00 S,	077°13′.63 W

Precautionary area

A precautionary area of 1 mile in radius, centred on the following geographical position:

(24) 12°02′.05 S, 077°14′.64 W

Area to be avoided

There is a circular area to be avoided of 0.11 miles radius (200 metres, 1.1 cables) at the following geographical position:

(24) 12°02′.05 S, 077°14′.64 W

(chartlet overleaf)

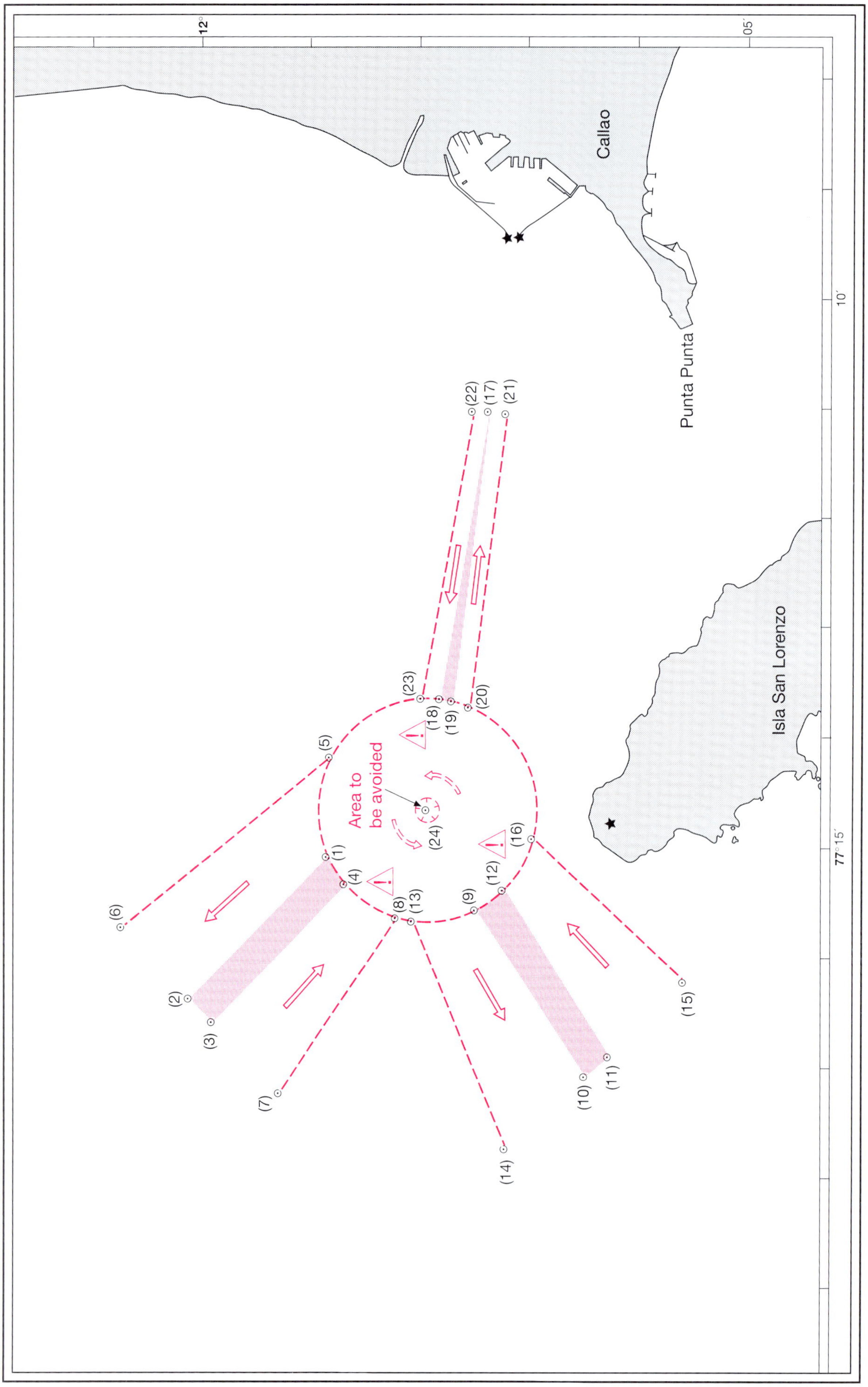

APPROACHES TO PUERTO CALLAO

IN THE APPROACHES TO PUERTO PISCO

(Reference charts: PERU HIDRONAV 226, 2262 and 2263.
Note: these charts are based on World Geodetic System 1984 datum (WGS 84).)

Description of the traffic separation scheme

The traffic separation scheme "In the approaches to Puerto Pisco" consists of two parts:

Part I
Northern approaches

(a) Two separation zones bounded by lines connecting the following geographical points:

(1)	13°36′.59 S,	076°18′.86 W	(3)	13°41′.24 S,	076°18′.03 W
(2)	13°41′.23 S,	076°18′.25 W	(4)	13°36′.59 S,	076°18′.64 W

and

(5)	13°42′.11 S,	076°18′.13 W	(7)	13°44′.74 S,	076°17′.57 W
(6)	13°44′.74 S,	076°17′.80 W	(8)	13°42′.12 S,	076°17′.91 W

(b) A traffic lane for northbound traffic, between the separation zones and a line connecting the following geographical points:

(9)	13°36′.59 S,	076°18′.32 W	(10)	13°44′.74 S,	076°17′.25 W,

(c) A traffic lane for southbound traffic, between the separation zones and the lines connecting the following geographical points:

(11)	13°44′.74 S,	076°18′.13 W	(12)	13°42′.08 S,	076°18′.46 W

and

(13)	13°41′.20 S,	076°18′.58 W	(14)	13°36′.59 S,	076°19′.18 W

Part II
Western approaches

(a) A separation zone bounded by a line connecting the following geographical points:

(15)	13°41′.53 S,	076°18′.53 W	(17)	13°41′.28 S,	076°24′.99 W
(16)	13°41′.75 S,	076°18′.50 W	(18)	13°41′.06 S,	076°24′.99 W

(b) A traffic lane for westbound traffic, between the separation zone and a line connecting the following geographical points:

(19)	13°41′.20 S,	076°18′.58 W	(20)	13°40′.73 S,	076°24′.99 W

(c) A traffic lane for eastbound traffic, between the separation zones and a line connecting the following geographical points:

(21)	13°42′.08 S,	076°18′.46 W	(22)	13°41′.60 S,	076°24′.99 W

Precautionary area

A precautionary area is established bounded by a line connecting the following geographical points and the east line of the traffic separation scheme:

(3)	13°41′.24 S,	076°18′.03 W
(19)	13°41′.20 S,	076°18′.58 W
(21)	13°42′.08 S,	076°18′.46 W
(8)	13°42′.12 S,	076°17′.91 W

and

(9)	13°36′.59 S,	076°18′.32 W
(10)	13°44′.74 S,	076°17′.25 W

Area to be avoided

There is a circular area to be avoided of 200 metres radius centred on the following geographical position:

(23) 13°41′.68 S, 076°18′.11 W

This area is to be avoided by all ships.

B

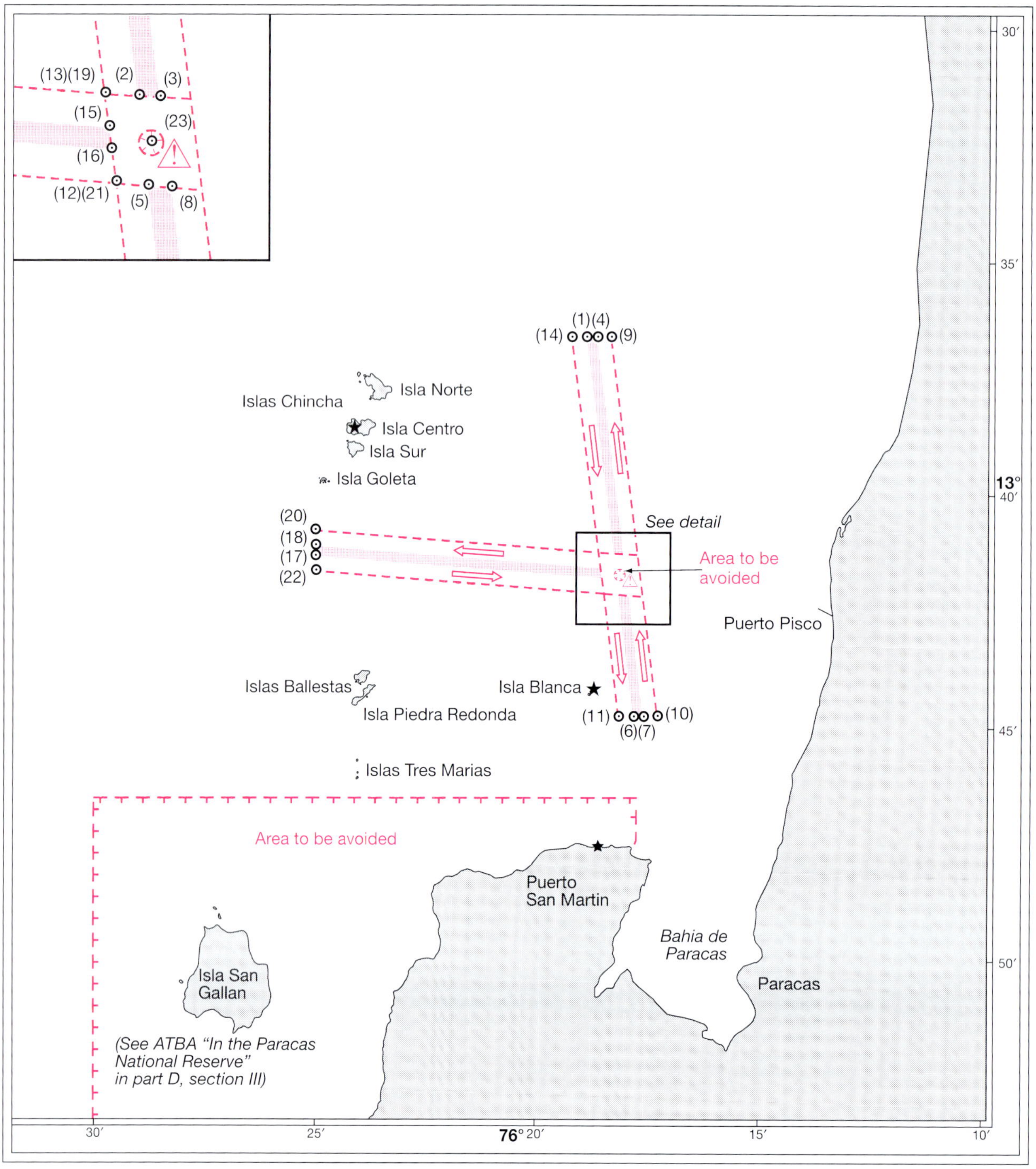

IN THE APPROACHES TO PUERTO PISCO

LANDFALL AND APPROACHES TO SAN NICOLAS BAY

(Reference charts: PERU HIDRONAV 312, 1999 edition; 3122, 1999 edition.
Note: these charts are based on the World Geodetic System 1984 datum (WGS 84).)

Description of the traffic separation scheme

The traffic separation scheme for the landfall and approaches to San Nicolas Bay consists of the following:

(a) A separation zone bounded by a line connecting the following geographical points:

(1)	15°13′.10 S,	075°16′.13 W	(3)	15°13′.85 S,	075°18′.77 W
(2)	15°13′.10 S,	075°18′.77 W	(4)	15°13′.85 S,	075°16′.13 W

(b) A traffic lane for westbound traffic, between the separation zone and a line connecting the following geographical points:

(5)	15°12′.54 S,	075°16′.13 W	(6)	15°11′.70 S,	075°18′.77 W

(c) A traffic lane for eastbound traffic, between the separation zone and a line between the following geographical points:

(7)	15°15′.40 S,	075°18′.77 W	(8)	15°14′.45 S,	075°16′.13 W

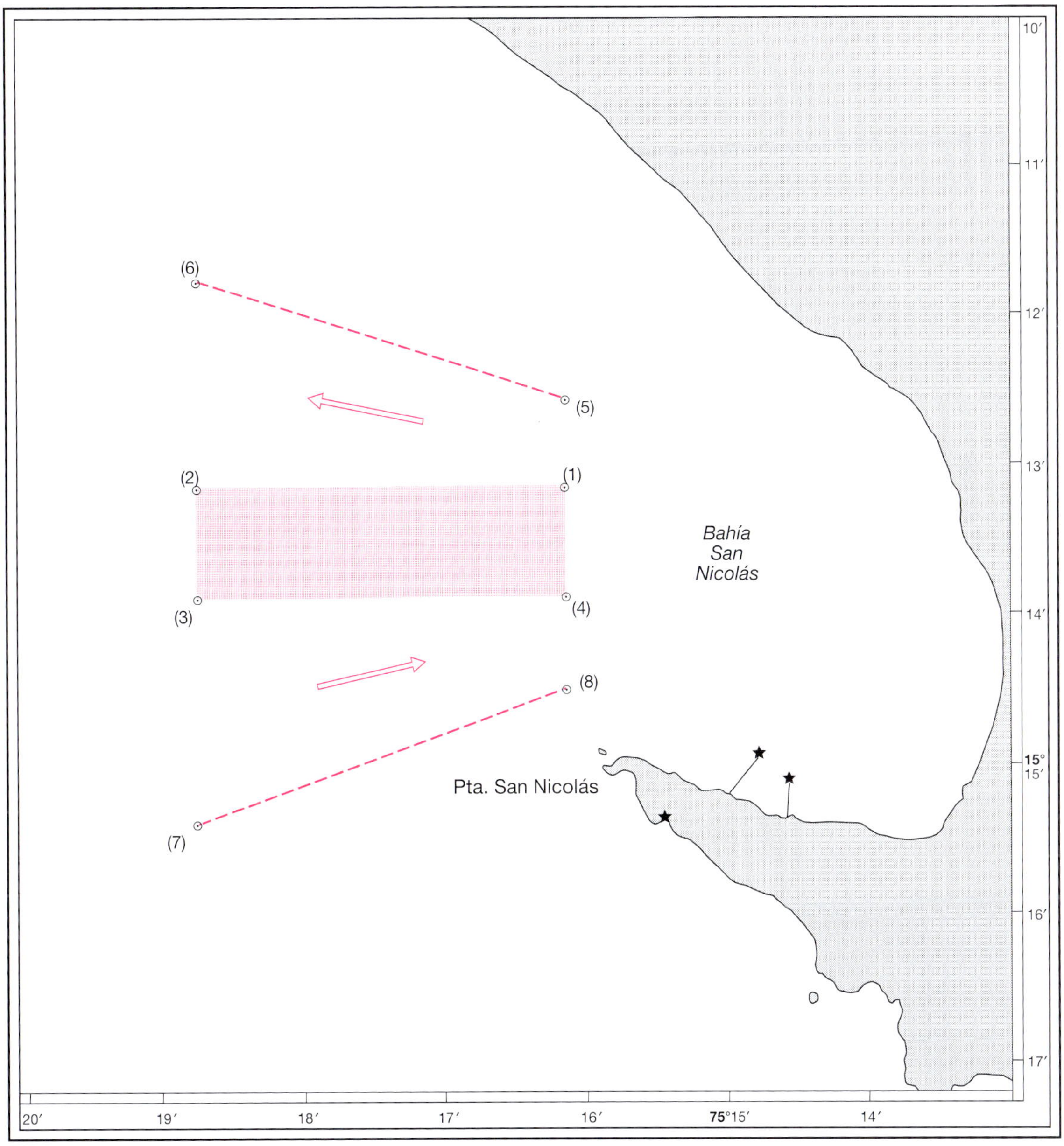

LANDFALL AND APPROACHES TO SAN NICOLAS BAY

LANDFALL AND APPROACHES TO PUERTO ILO

(Reference charts: PERU HIDRONAV 2350, 1980 edition (revised 1991); 3245, 1995 edition (revised 1997).
Note: these charts are based on World Geodetic System 1984 datum (WGS 84).)

Description of the traffic separation scheme

The traffic separation scheme for the landfall and approaches to Puerto Ilo consists of the following:

(a) A separation zone bounded by a line connecting the following geographical points:

(1)	17°38′.20 S,	071°24′.10 W	(3)	17°39′.20 S,	071°27′.00 W
(2)	17°38′.20 S,	071°27′.00 W	(4)	17°39′.20 S,	071°24′.10 W

(b) A traffic lane for westbound traffic, between the separation zone and a line connecting the following geographical points:

(5)	17°37′.40 S,	071°24′.10 W	(6)	17°36′.20 S,	071°27′.00 W

(c) A traffic lane for eastbound traffic, between the separation zone and a line connecting the following geographical points:

(7)	17°41′.35 S,	071°27′.00 W	(8)	17°40′.00 S,	071°24′.10 W

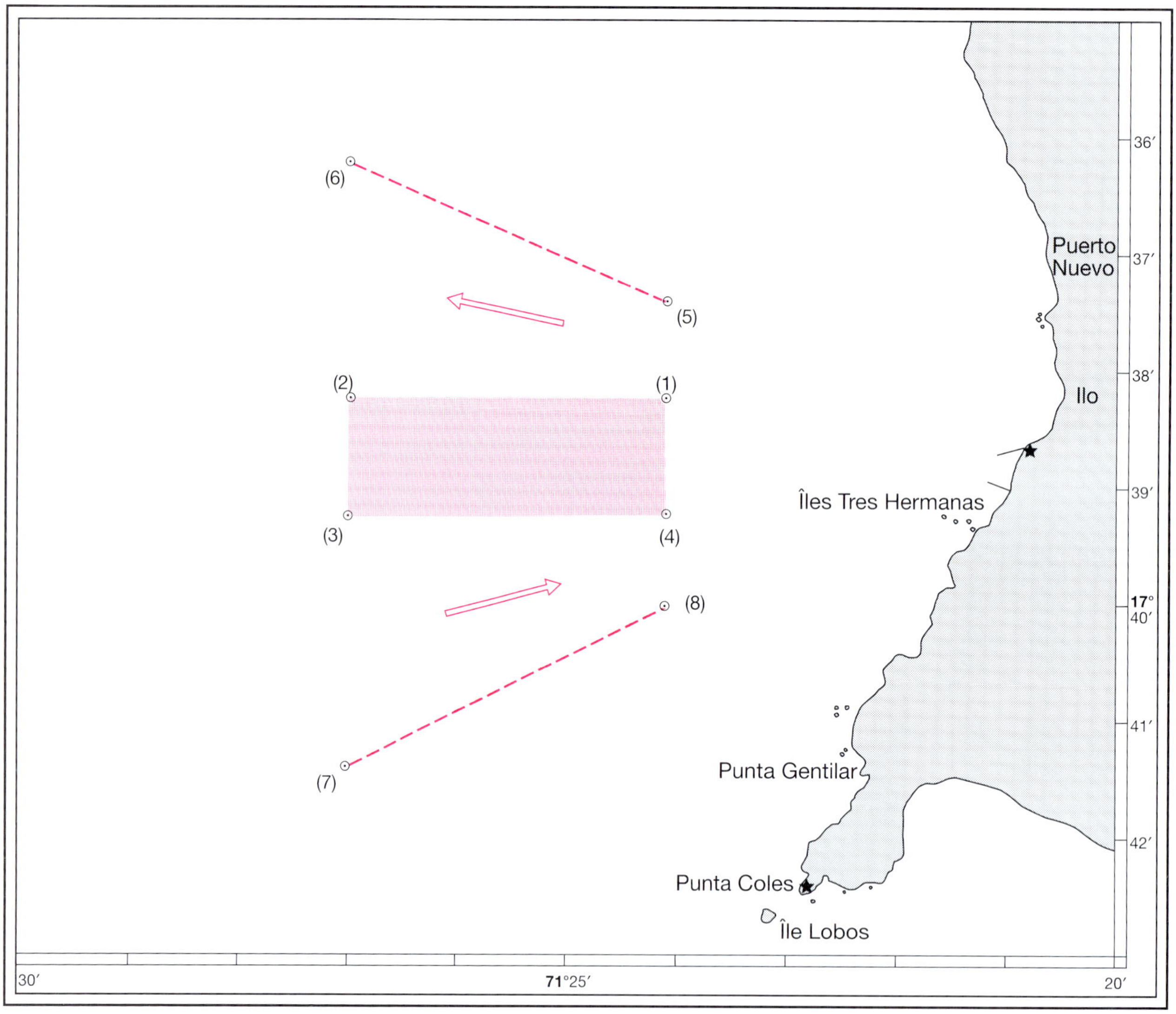

LANDFALL AND APPROACHES TO PUERTO ILO

IN THE APPROACHES TO ARICA

(Reference chart: Chilean Hydrographic Office 101, 1989 edition.
Note: This chart is based on South American 1969 datum.)

Description of the traffic separation scheme

(a) A separation zone, half a mile wide, is centred upon the following geographical positions:

(1)	18°27′.74 S,	070°21′.07 W	(2)	18°27′.74 S,	070°25′.49 W

(b) A traffic lane for westbound traffic is established between the separation zone and a line connecting the following geographical positions:

(3)	18°26′.99 S,	070°21′.07 W	(4)	18°25′.49 S,	070°25′.49 W

(c) A traffic lane for eastbound traffic is established between the separation zone and a line connecting the following geographical positions:

(5)	18°28′.49 S,	070°21′.07 W	(6)	18°29′.99 S,	070°25′.49 W

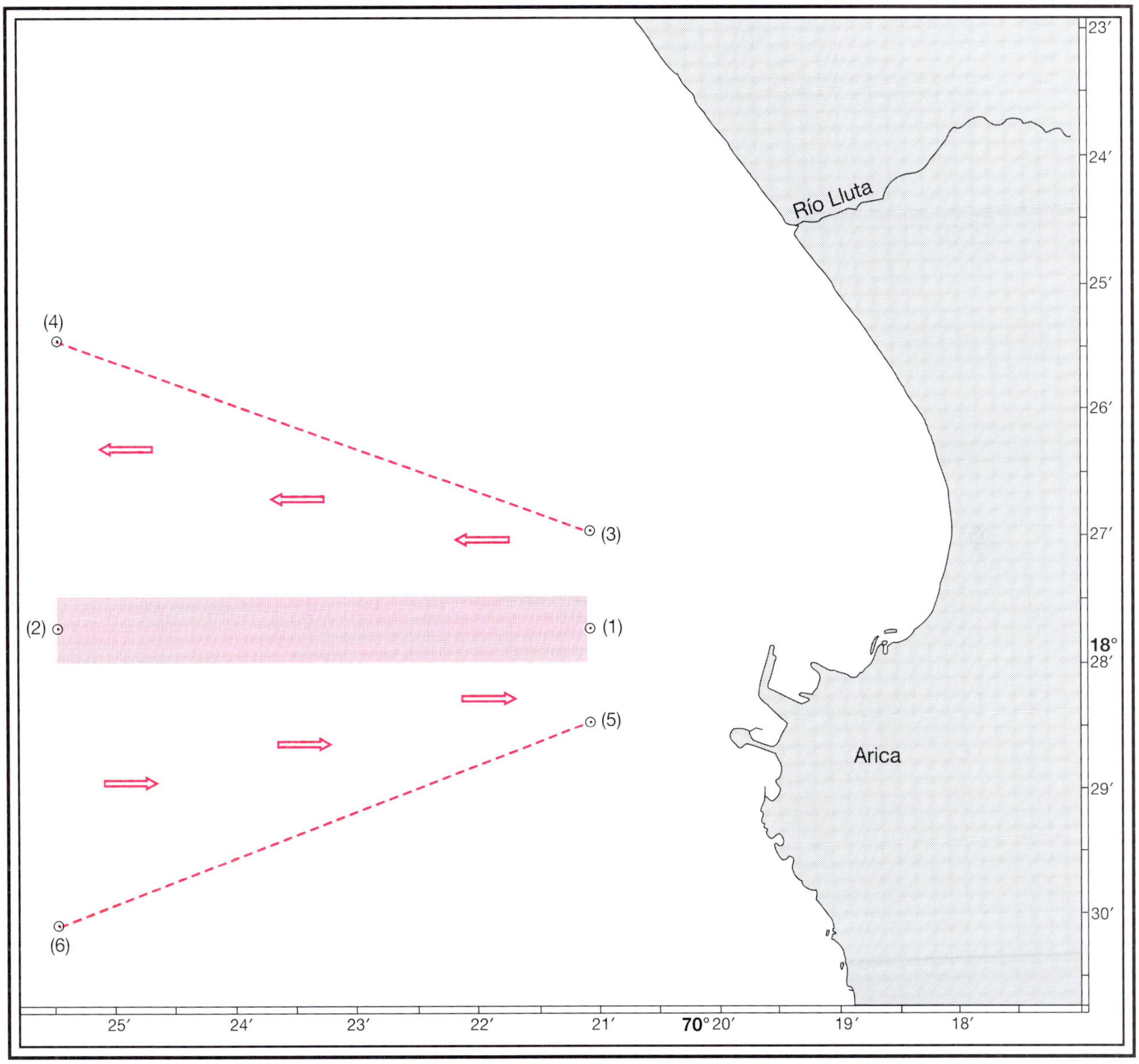

IN THE APPROACHES TO ARICA

IN THE APPROACHES TO IQUIQUE

(Reference chart: Chilean Hydrographic Office 104, 1988 edition.
Note: This chart is based on South American 1969 datum.)

Description of the traffic separation scheme

(a) Northern limit, consisting of a line connecting the following geographical positions:

(1)	20°10′.40 S,	070°10′.80 W	(2)	20°11′.10 S,	070°10′.18 W

(b) Southern limit, consisting of a line connecting the following geographical positions:

(3)	20°12′.60 S,	070°10′.95 W	(4)	20°11′.87 S,	070°10′.17 W

(c) Traffic separation zones, consisting of the following:

– The area within a line connecting the following geographical positions:

(5)	20°10′.72 S,	070°11′.22 W	(7)	20°11′.28 S,	070°10′.33 W
(6)	20°11′.22 S,	070°10′.30 W	(8)	20°10′.88 S,	070°11′.32 W

– The area within a line connecting the following geographical positions:

(9)	20°11′.38 S,	070°11′.45 W	(11)	20°11′.52 S,	070°10′.38 W
(10)	20°11′.45 S,	070°10′.38 W	(12)	20°11′.60 S,	070°11′.45 W

– The area within a line connecting the following geographical positions:

(13)	20°12′.10 S,	070°11′.30 W	(15)	20°11′.73 S,	070°10′.30 W
(14)	20°11′.68 S,	070°10′.33 W	(16)	20°12′.28 S,	070°11′.18 W

(d) Traffic lanes for entry to the port, at the following positions:

Direction east:

(17) 20°11′.25 S, 070°10′.85 W

Direction north-east:

(18) 20°12′.10 S, 070°10′.68 W

(e) Traffic lanes for exit from the port, at the following positions:

Direction north-west:

(19) 20°10′.87 S, 070°10′.60 W

Direction west:

(20) 20°11′.72 S, 070°10′.80 W

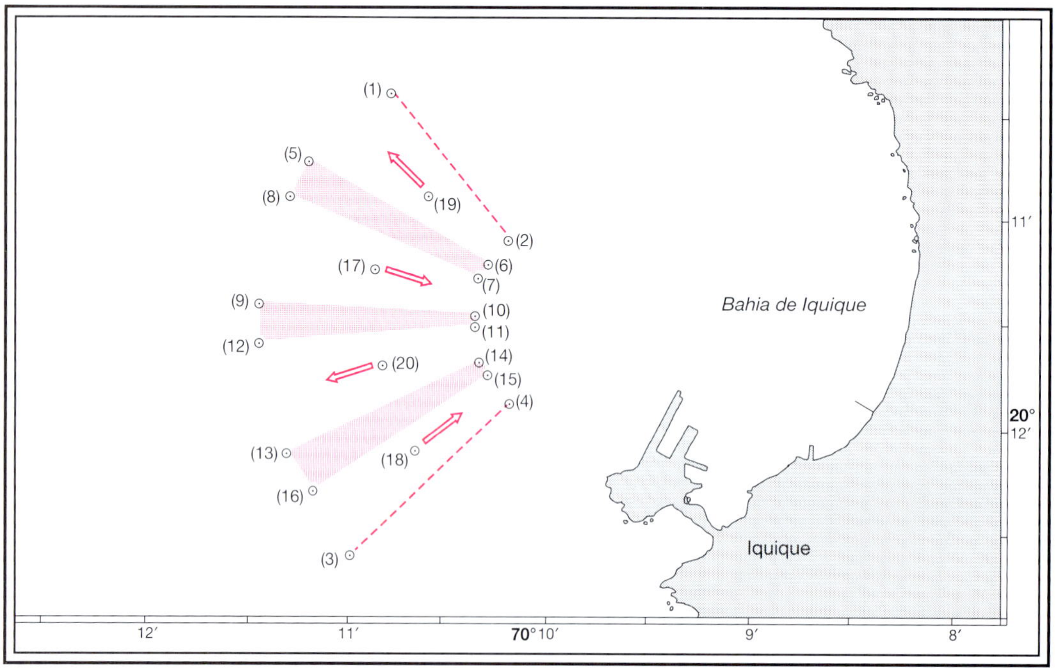

IN THE APPROACHES TO IQUIQUE

IN THE APPROACHES TO ANTOFAGASTA

(Reference chart: Chilean Hydrographic Office 212, 1982 edition.
Note: This chart is based on Provisional South American 1956 datum.)

Description of the traffic separation scheme

(a) A separation zone, one mile wide, is centred upon the following geographical positions:

(1)	23°38′.53 S,	070°25′.52 W	(2)	23°38′.53 S,	070°29′.60 W

(b) A traffic lane for westbound traffic is established between the separation zone and a line connecting the following geographical positions:

(3)	23°37′.03 S,	070°25′.52 W	(4)	23°36′.03 S,	070°29′.60 W

(c) A traffic lane for eastbound traffic is established between the separation zone and a line connecting the following geographical positions:

(5)	23°40′.03 S,	070°25′.52 W	(6)	23°41′.03 S,	070°29′.60 W

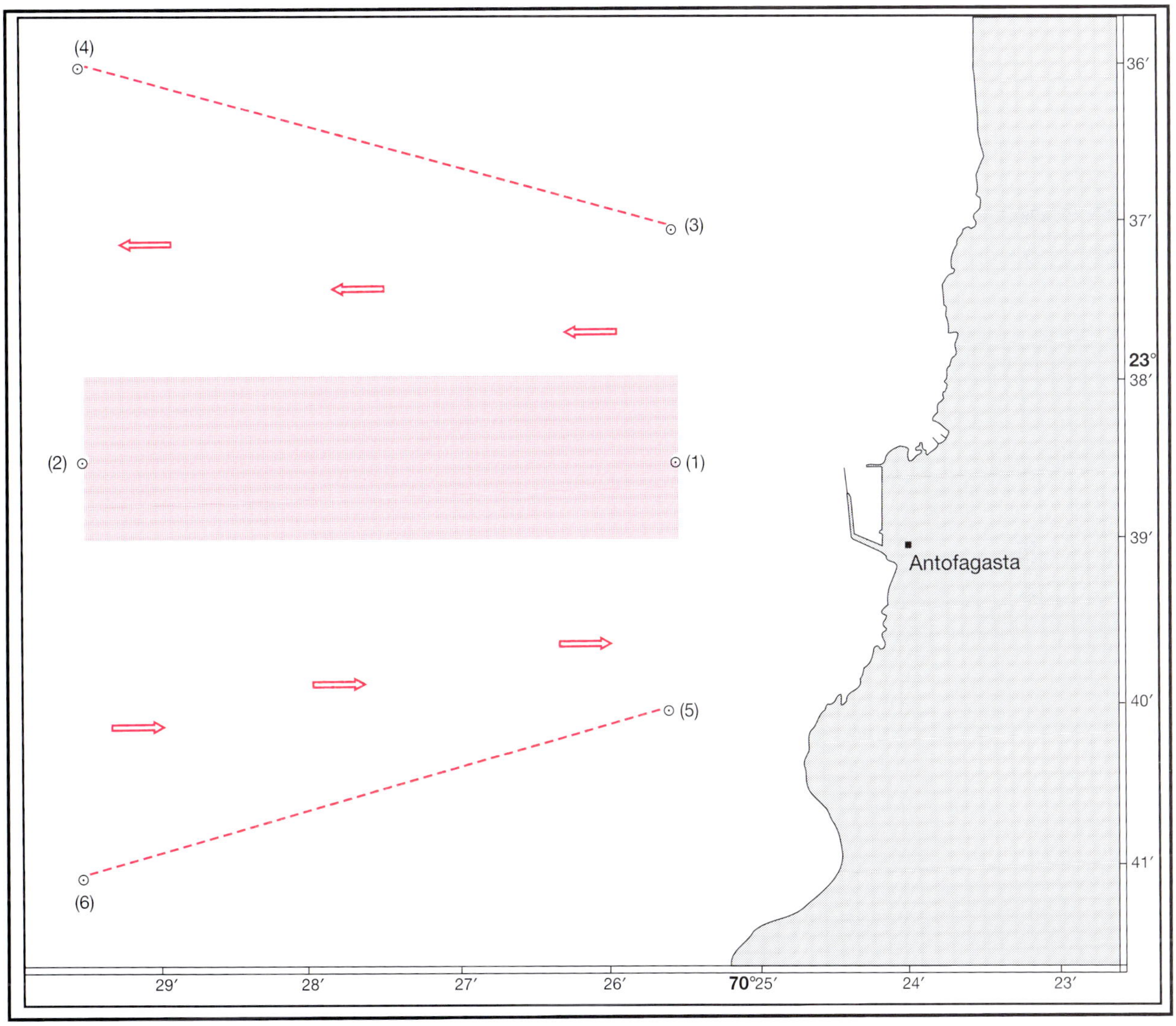

IN THE APPROACHES TO ANTOFAGASTA

IN THE APPROACHES TO QUINTERO BAY

(Reference chart: Chilean Hydrographic Office 424, 1983 edition.
Note: This chart is based on Provisional South American 1956 datum.)

Description of the traffic separation scheme

(a) A separation zone, half a mile wide, is centred upon the following geographical positions:

(1)	32°44′.43 S,	071°32′.00 W	(2)	32°44′.43 S,	071°36′.43 W

(b) A traffic lane for westbound traffic is established between the separation zone and a line connecting the following geographical positions:

(3)	32°43′.43 S,	071°32′.00 W	(4)	32°42′.93 S,	071°36′.43 W

(c) A traffic lane for eastbound traffic is established between the separation zone and a line connecting the following geographical positions:

(5)	32°45′.43 S,	071°32′.00 W	(6)	32°45′.93 S,	071°36′.43 W

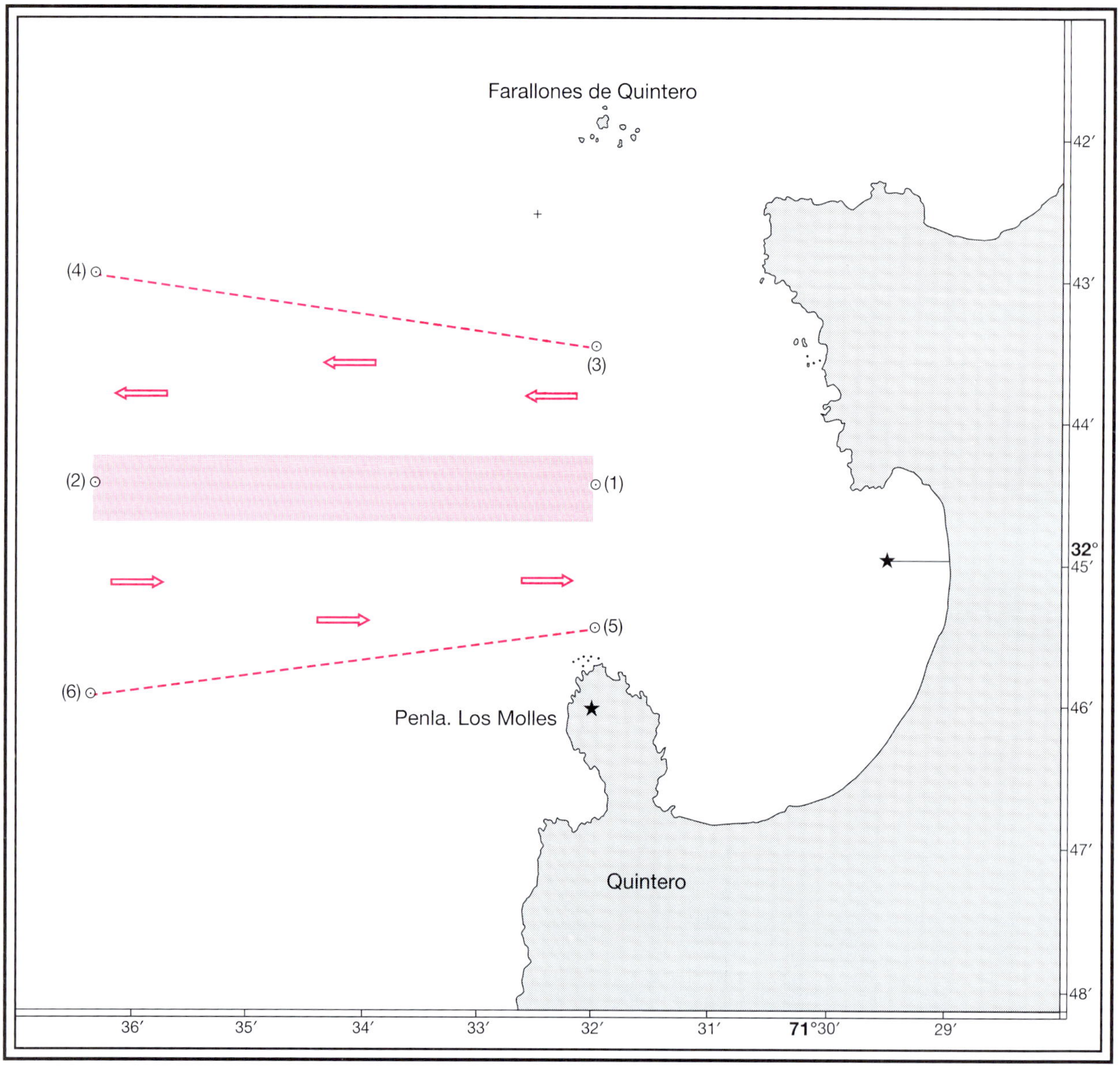

IN THE APPROACHES TO QUINTERO BAY

IN THE APPROACHES TO VALPARAISO

(Reference chart: Chilean Hydrographic Office 511, 1985 edition.
Note: This chart is based on Provisional South American 1956 datum.)

Description of the traffic separation scheme

(a) A separation zone, half a mile wide, is centred upon the following geographical positions:

(1)	32°57′.62 S,	071°37′.27 W	(2)	33°00′.53 S,	071°36′.52 W

(b) A traffic lane for traffic sailing towards Valparaiso is established between the separation zone and a line connecting the following geographical positions:

(3)	32°57′.87 S,	071°38′.70 W	(4)	33°00′.70 S,	071°37′.38 W

(c) A traffic lane for traffic sailing from Valparaiso is established between the separation zone and a line connecting the following geographical positions:

(5)	32°57′.33 S,	071°35′.82 W	(6)	33°00′.35 S,	071°35′.65 W

Inshore traffic zone

The area between the coast and the landward boundary of the traffic separation scheme is designated as an inshore traffic zone.

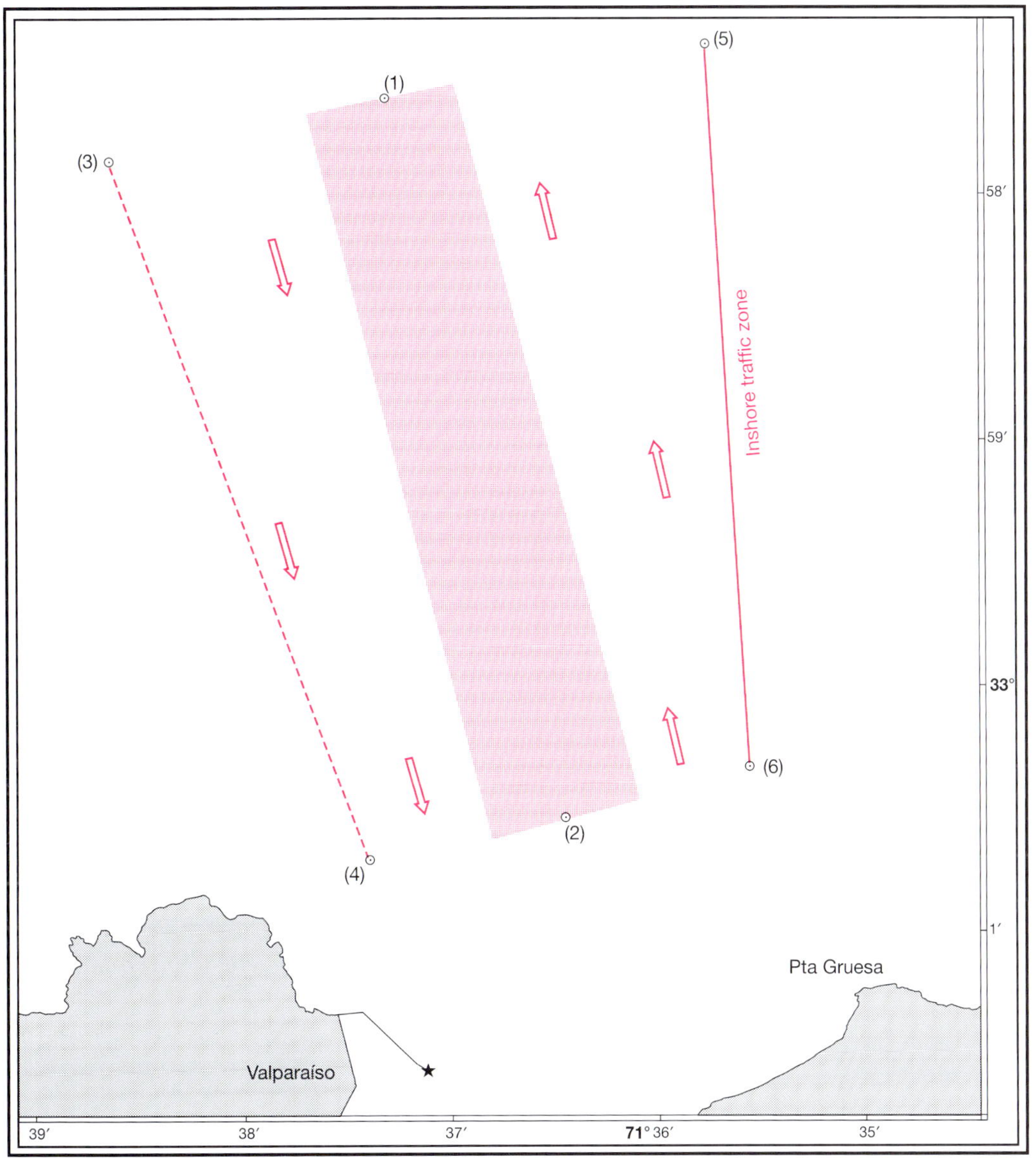

IN THE APPROACHES TO VALPARAISO

IN THE APPROACHES TO CONCEPCION BAY

(Reference chart: Chilean Hydrographic Office 611, 1985 edition.
Note: This chart is based on Provisional South American 1956 datum.)

Description of the traffic separation scheme

(a) A separation zone, a quarter of a mile wide, is centred upon the following geographical positions:

(1)	36°33′.85 S,	073°01′.95 W	(3)	36°38′.27 S,	073°01′.55 W
(2)	36°35′.87 S,	073°01′.55 W			

(b) A traffic lane, half a mile wide, is established on each side of the separation zone.

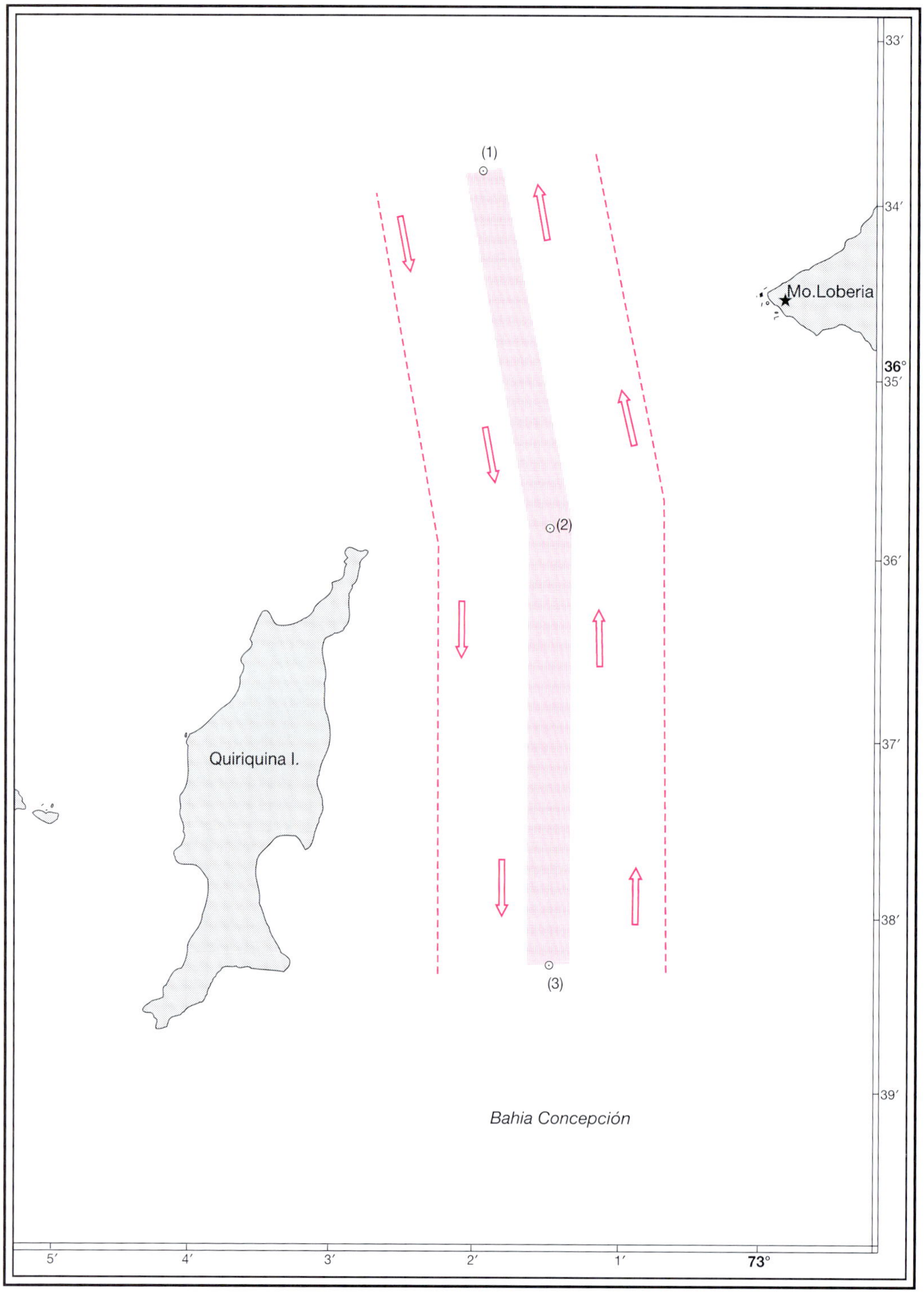

IN THE APPROACHES TO CONCEPCION BAY

IN THE APPROACHES TO SAN VICENTE BAY

(Reference chart: Chilean Hydrographic Office 613, 1984 edition.
Note: This chart is based on Provisional South American 1956 datum.)

Description of the traffic separation scheme

(a) A separation zone is bounded by a line connecting the following geographical positions:

(1)	36°40′.78 S,	073°13′.44 W	(3)	36°43′.68 S,	073°10′.02 W
(2)	36°43′.78 S,	073°10′.14 W	(4)	36°40′.47 S,	073°12′.98 W

(b) A traffic lane for southbound traffic is established between the separation zone and a line connecting the following geographical positions:

(5)	36°41′.65 S,	073°14′.73 W	(6)	36°44′.05 S,	073°10′.54 W

(c) A traffic lane for northbound traffic is established between the separation zone and a line connecting the following geographical positions:

(7)	36°39′.72 S,	073°11′.86 W	(8)	36°43′.40 S,	073°09′.57 W

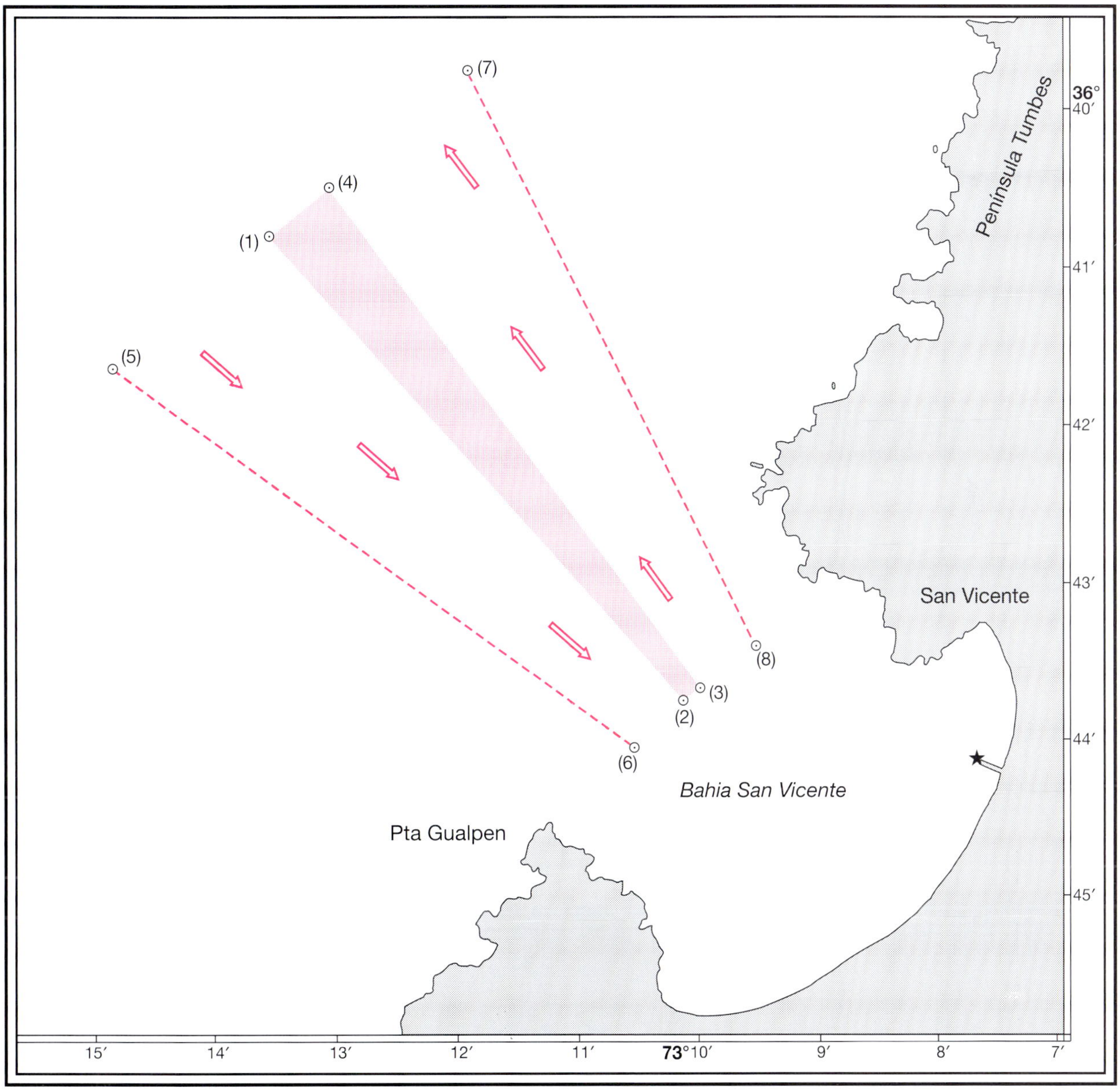

IN THE APPROACHES TO SAN VICENTE BAY

IN THE APPROACHES TO PUNTA ARENAS

(Reference chart: Chilean Hydrographic Office 11410, 1991 edition.
Note: This chart is based on South American 1969 datum.)

Description of the traffic separation scheme

(a) Northern limit, consisting of a line connecting the following geographical positions:

(1)	53°10′.25 S,	070°49′.90 W	(2)	53°10′.90 S,	070°46′.65 W

(b) Southern limit, consisting of a line connecting the following geographical positions:

(3)	53°11′.42 S,	070°51′.07 W	(4)	53°12′.80 S,	070°48′.70 W

(c) Traffic separation zone, the area within a line connecting the following geographical positions:

(5)	53°10′.65 S,	070°50′.30 W	(7)	53°12′.03 S,	070°47′.85 W
(6)	53°11′.72 S,	070°47′.50 W	(8)	53°11′.02 S,	070°50′.67 W

(d) Traffic lanes for entry to the port, at the following position:

(9) 53°11′.00 S, 070°48′.30 W

(e) Traffic lanes for exit from the port, at the following position:

(10) 53°11′.80 S, 070°49′.60 W

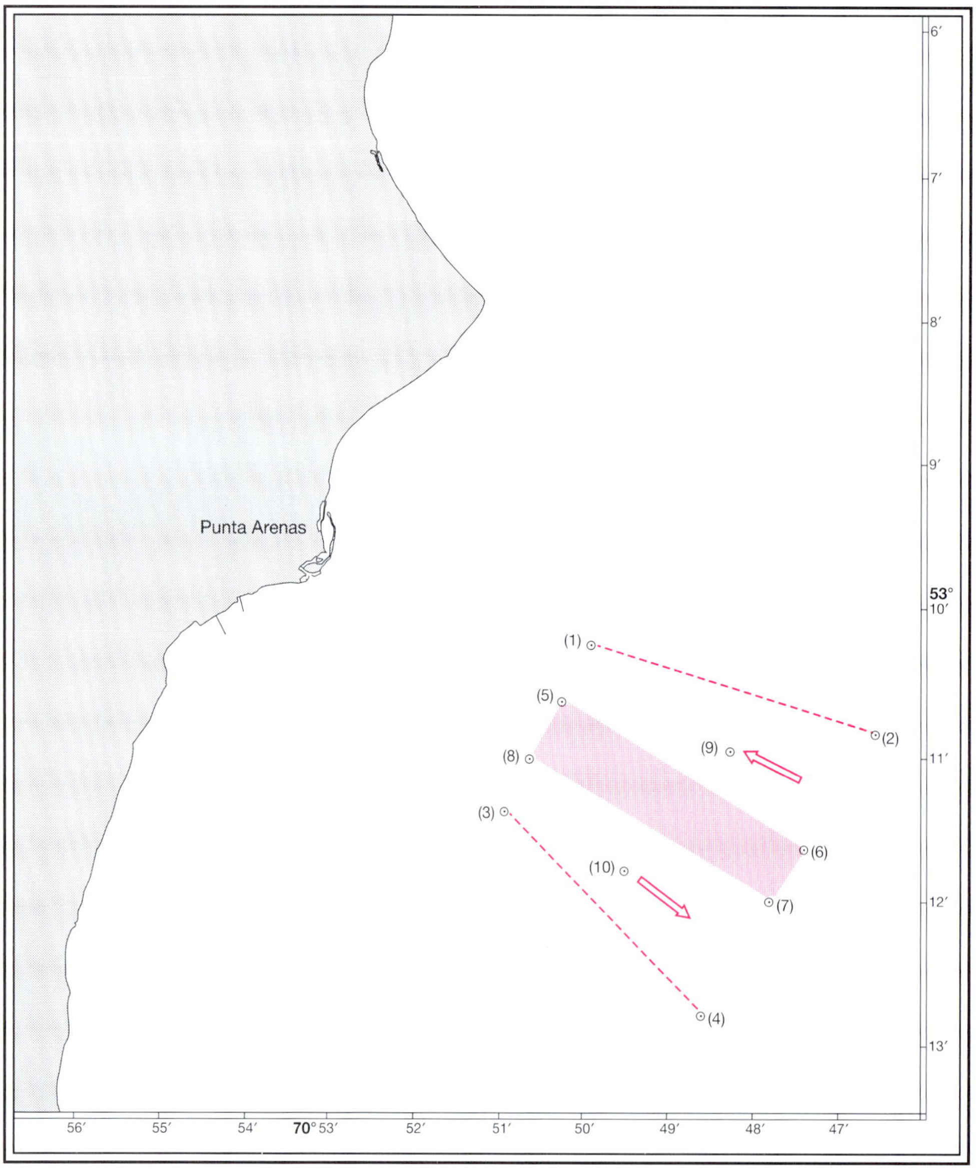

IN THE APPROACHES TO PUNTA ARENAS

Section IX

Western North Atlantic Ocean, Gulf of Mexico and Caribbean Sea

Caution: The chartlets are for illustrative purposes only and must not be used for navigation. Mariners should consult the appropriate nautical publications and charts for up-to-date details on aids to navigation and other relevant information.

Warning: The geographical positions given in the descriptions of the routeing systems are only correct for charts using the same geodetic datum as the reference charts indicated under each scheme. Charts published by other hydrographic offices may use a different geodetic datum, as may new editions of the reference charts published after the adoption of the routeing system. Where amendments to existing systems are not based on the same geodetic datum as the original system, this is emphasized by the use of different colours for definitions of positions.

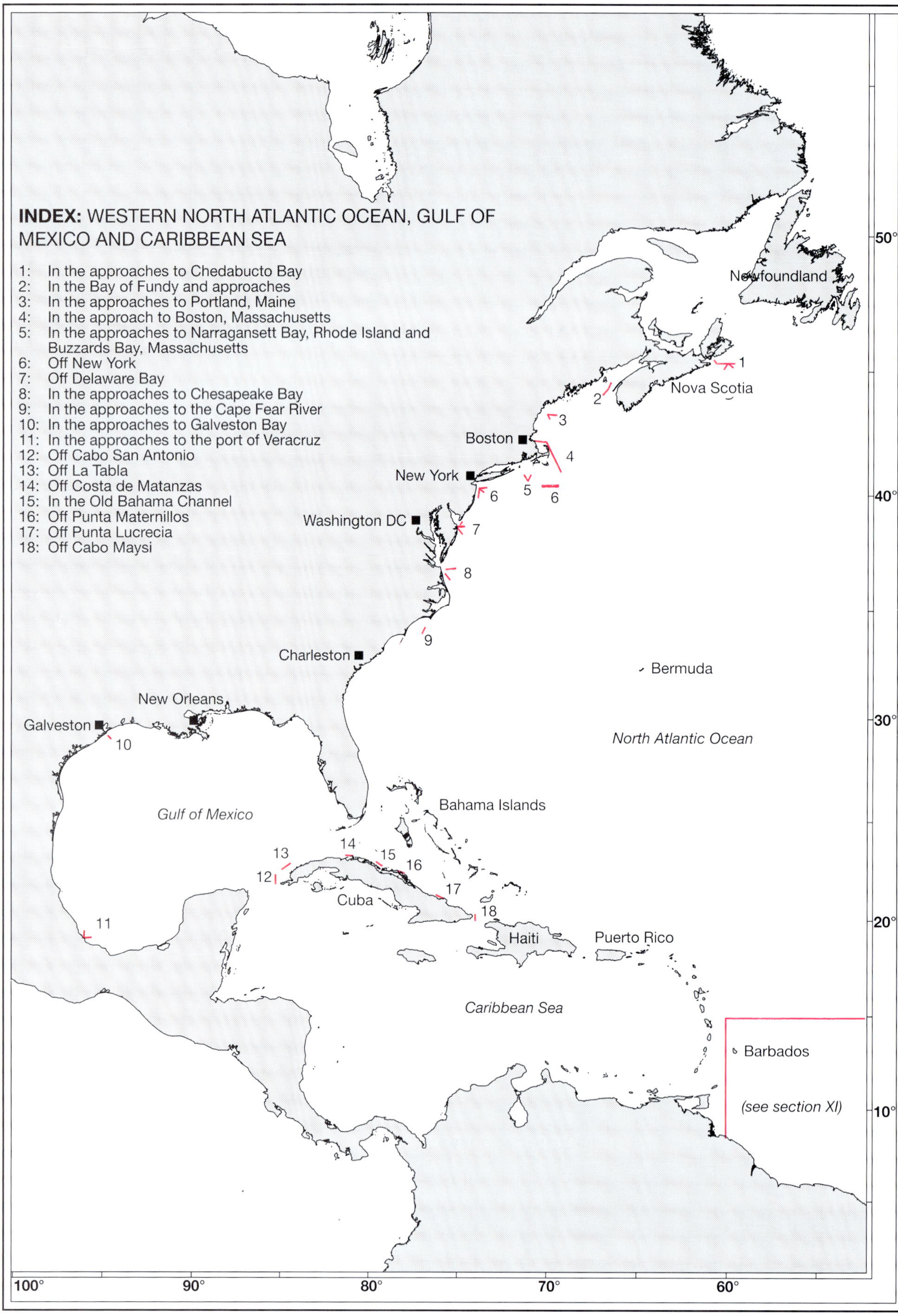
INDEX: WESTERN NORTH ATLANTIC OCEAN, GULF OF MEXICO AND CARIBBEAN SEA
1: In the approaches to Chedabucto Bay
2: In the Bay of Fundy and approaches
3: In the approaches to Portland, Maine
4: In the approach to Boston, Massachusetts
5: In the approaches to Narragansett Bay, Rhode Island and Buzzards Bay, Massachusetts
6: Off New York
7: Off Delaware Bay
8: In the approaches to Chesapeake Bay
9: In the approaches to the Cape Fear River
10: In the approaches to Galveston Bay
11: In the approaches to the port of Veracruz
12: Off Cabo San Antonio
13: Off La Tabla
14: Off Costa de Matanzas
15: In the Old Bahama Channel
16: Off Punta Maternillos
17: Off Punta Lucrecia
18: Off Cabo Maysi
Newfoundland
Nova Scotia
Boston
New York
Washington DC
Charleston
Bermuda
New Orleans
Galveston
North Atlantic Ocean
Gulf of Mexico
Bahama Islands
Cuba
Haiti
Puerto Rico
Caribbean Sea
Barbados
(see section XI)
50°
40°
30°
20°
10°
100°
90°
80°
70°
60°

IN THE APPROACHES TO CHEDABUCTO BAY

(Reference charts: Canadian Hydrographic Service 4013, 2002 edition; 4307, 2002 edition; 4335, 1998 edition.
Note: These charts are based on North American 1983 geodetic datum, which is equivalent to WGS 84.)

Description of the traffic separation scheme

The traffic separation scheme "In the approaches to Chedabucto Bay" consists of three parts:

Part I

(a) A separation zone is bounded by a line connecting the following geographical positions:

(1)	45°24′.00 N,	060°36′.70 W	(3)	45°23′.70 N,	060°28′.20 W
(2)	45°24′.20 N,	060°27′.17 W	(4)	45°23′.82 N,	060°36′.48 W

(b) A traffic lane for westbound traffic is established between the separation zone and a line connecting the following geographical positions:

(5)	45°26′.00 N,	060°23′.20 W	(6)	45°25′.43 N,	060°41′.70 W

(c) A traffic lane for eastbound traffic is established between the separation zone and a line connecting the following geographical positions:

(7)	45°22′.30 N,	060°34′.50 W	(8)	45°22′.15 N,	060°31′.60 W

Part II

(a) A separation zone is bounded by a line connecting the following geographical positions:

(9)	45°22′.57 N,	060°40′.00 W	(11)	45°19′.30 N,	060°37′.80 W
(10)	45°19′.88 N,	060°36′.50 W	(12)	45°22′.68 N,	060°42′.17 W

(b) A traffic lane for north-westbound traffic is established between the separation zone and a line connecting the following geographical positions:

(13)	45°21′.35 N,	060°33′.30 W	(14)	45°22′.30 N,	060°34′.50 W

(c) A traffic lane for southbound traffic is established between the separation zone and a line connecting the following geographical positions:

(15)	45°22′.90 N,	060°46′.50 W	(17)	45°14′.47 N,	060°48′.38 W
(16)	45°21′.28 N,	060°44′.40 W			

Part III

(a) A separation zone is bounded by a line connecting the following geographical positions:

(18)	45°24′.00 N,	060°41′.70 W	(22)	45°28′.45 N,	061°10′.33 W
(19)	45°23′.82 N,	060°41′.50 W	(23)	45°24′.92 N,	061°06′.07 W
(20)	45°23′.82 N,	061°05′.00 W	(24)	45°24′.00 N,	061°02′.65 W
(21)	45°28′.36 N,	061°10′.46 W			

(b) A traffic lane for west inbound traffic is established between the separation zone and a line connecting the following geographical positions:

(25)	45°25′.43 N,	060°41′.70 W	(27)	45°25′.63 N,	061°06′.29 W
(26)	45°24′.77 N,	061°03′.26 W	(28)	45°28′.70 N,	061°09′.94 W

(c) A traffic lane for east outbound traffic is established between the separation zone and a line connecting the following geographical positions:

(29)	45°22′.90 N,	060°46′.50 W	(31)	45°28′.12 N,	061°10′.83 W
(30)	45°22′.89 N,	061°04′.52 W			

(chartlet overleaf)

B

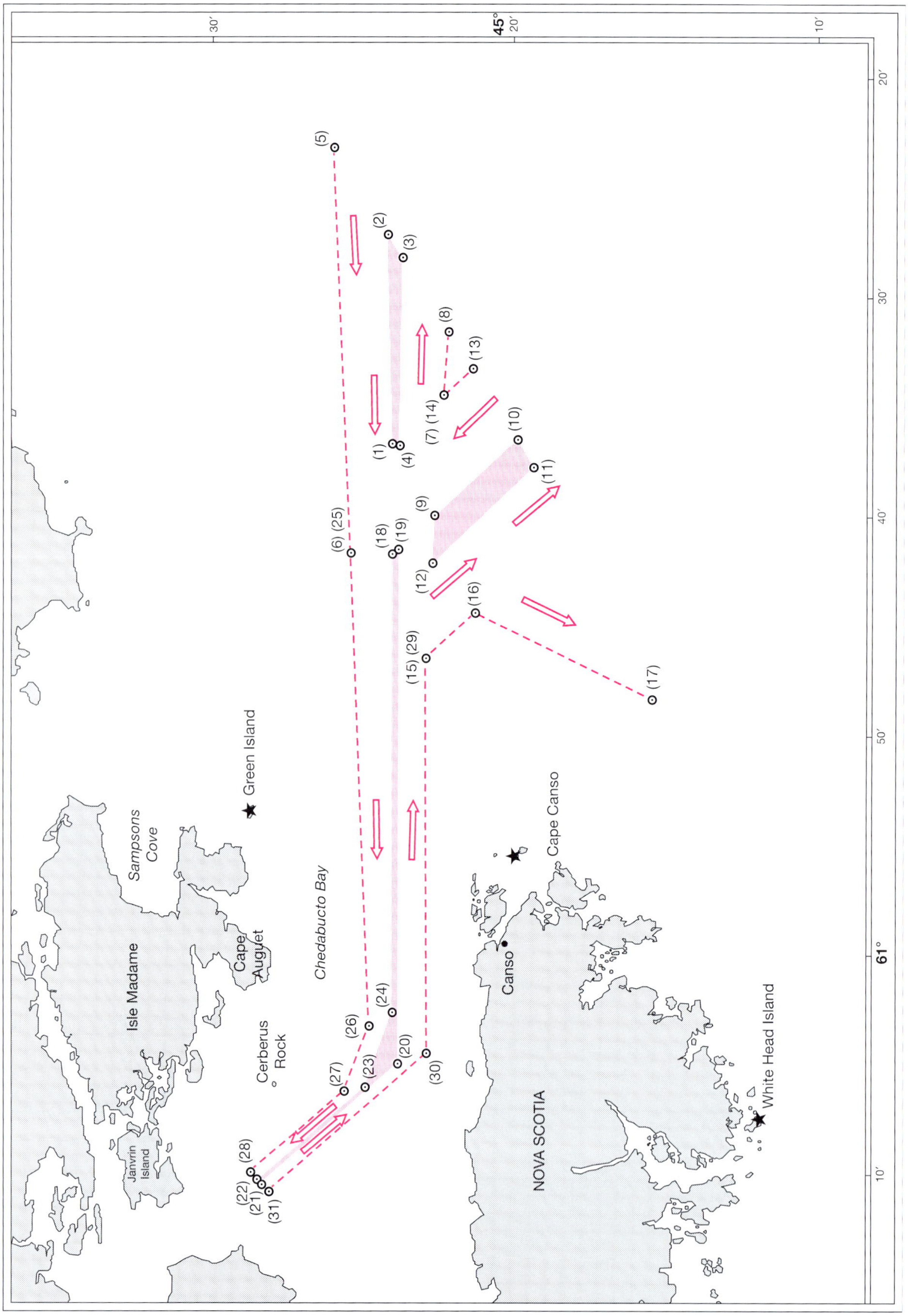

IN THE APPROACHES TO CHEDABUCTO BAY

IN THE BAY OF FUNDY AND APPROACHES

(Reference chart: Canadian Hydrographic Service L/C-4011, 1997 edition.
Note: This chart is based on North American 1983 geodetic datum, which is equivalent at this scale to North American 1927 geodetic datum.)

Description of the traffic separation scheme

The amended traffic separation scheme "In the Bay of Fundy and Approaches" consists of two parts. (Positions are in North American 1927 geodetic datum co-ordinates.)

Part I

(a) Three separation zones bounded by lines connecting the following geographical positions:

	(i)	(1)	44°46′.40 N,	066°14′.39 W	(4)	44°11′.83 N,	066°49′.55 W
		(2)	44°31′.85 N,	066°19′.60 W	(5)	44°30′.70 N,	066°17′.20 W
		(3)	44°14′.95 N,	066°52′.70 W	(6)	44°45′.90 N,	066°11′.68 W
	(ii)	(7)	44°48′.32 N,	066°13′.65 W	(9)	44°46′.88 N,	066°11′.30 W
		(8)	44°47′.33 N,	066°14′.00 W	(10)	44°47′.86 N,	066°10′.95 W
and	(iii)	(11)	45°02′.50 N,	066°08′.25 W	(13)	44°48′.80 N,	066°10′.58 W
		(12)	44°49′.30 N,	066°13′.30 W	(14)	45°02′.00 N,	066°05′.55 W

(b) A traffic lane for north-eastbound traffic is established between the separation zones and a line connecting the following geographical positions:

(15)	44°09′.50 N,	066°47′.05 W	(17)	45°01′.50 N,	066°02′.80 W
(16)	44°29′.60 N,	066°14′.75 W			

(c) A traffic lane for south-westbound traffic is established between the separation zones and lines connecting the following geographical positions:

	(i)	(18)	45°03′.00 N,	066°11′.00 W	(19)	44°49′.80 N,	066°15′.98 W
and	(ii)	(20)	44°46′.90 N,	066°17′.00 W	(22)	44°17′.35 N,	066°55′.17 W
		(21)	44°33′.00 N,	066°22′.00 W			

Part II

(d) A separation zone bounded by a line connecting the following geographical positions:

(23)	44°48′.60 N,	066°20′.72 W	(25)	44°48′.88 N,	066°16′.35 W
(24)	44°47′.90 N,	066°16′.70 W	(26)	44°49′.58 N,	066°20′.40 W

(e) A traffic lane for north-westbound traffic is established between the separation zone and a line connecting the following geographical positions:

(27)	44°49′.80 N,	066°15′.98 W	(28)	44°50′.58 N,	066°20′.05 W

(f) A traffic lane for south-eastbound traffic is established between the separation zone and a line connecting the following geographical positions:

(29)	44°47′.65 N,	066°21′.10 W	(30)	44°46′.90 N,	066°17′.00 W

(chartlet overleaf)

B

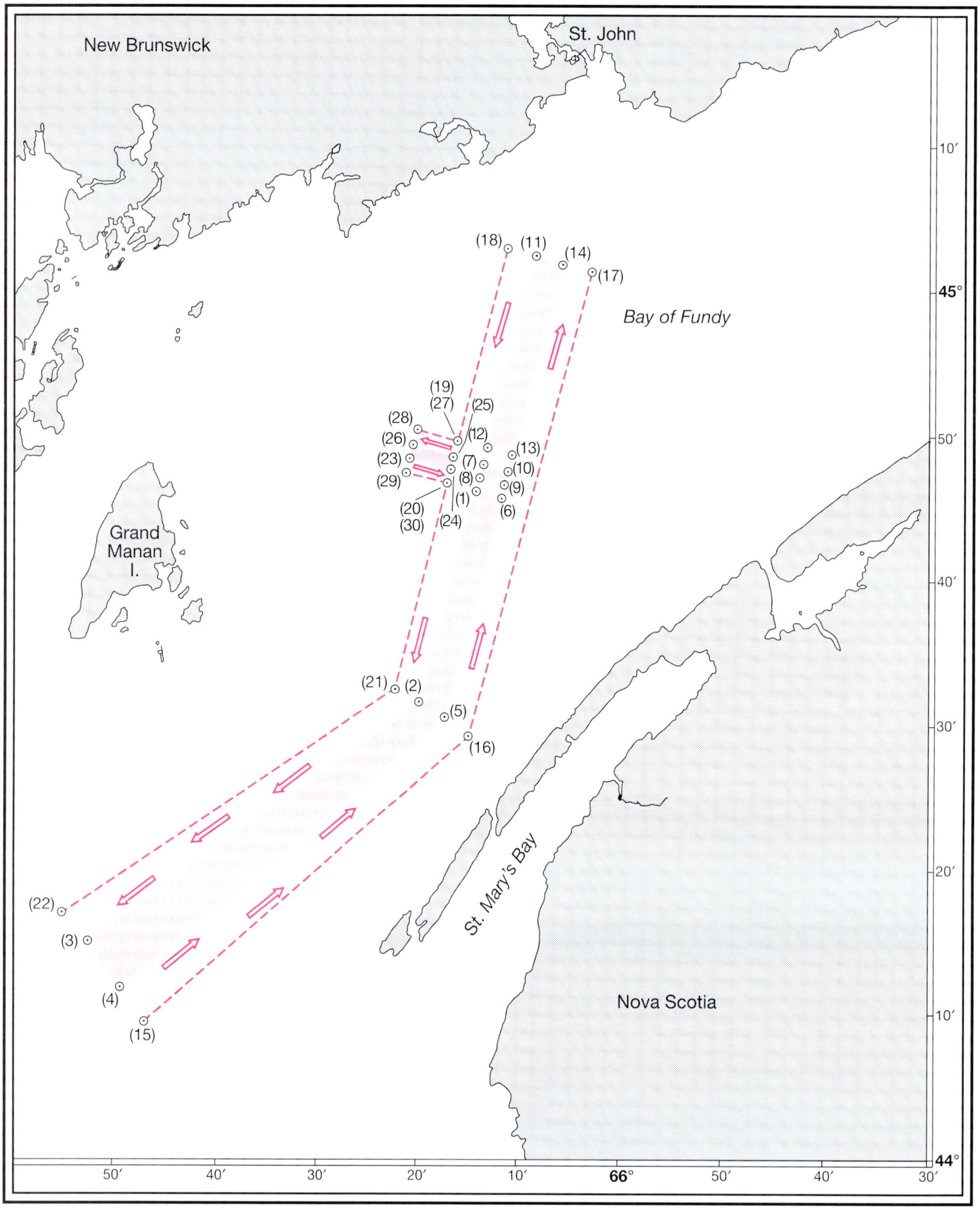

IN THE BAY OF FUNDY AND APPROACHES

IN THE APPROACHES TO PORTLAND, MAINE

(Reference charts: United States 13006, 1982 edition; 13009, 1985 edition; 13260, 1986 edition; 13286, 1985 edition; 13288, 1985 edition; 13290, 1987 edition.
Note: These charts are based on North American 1927 geodetic datum.)

Description of the traffic separation scheme

The traffic separation scheme "In the approaches to Portland, Maine" consists of three parts:

Part I
Precautionary area

(a) A precautionary area of radius 5.45 miles is centred upon geographical position 43°31′.60 N, 070°05′.53 W, the areas within separation zones and traffic lanes excluded.

Part II
Eastern approach

(a) A separation zone, one mile wide, is centred upon the following geographical positions:

(1) 43°30′.18 N, 069°59′.17 W (2) 43°24′.28 N, 069°32′.70 W

(b) A traffic lane, one and a half miles wide, is established on each side of the separation zone.

Part III
Southern approach

(a) A separation zone, one mile wide, is centred upon the following geographical positions:

(3) 43°27′.00 N, 070°03′.48 W (4) 43°07′.82 N, 069°54′.95 W

(b) A traffic lane, one and a half miles wide, is established on each side of the separation zone.

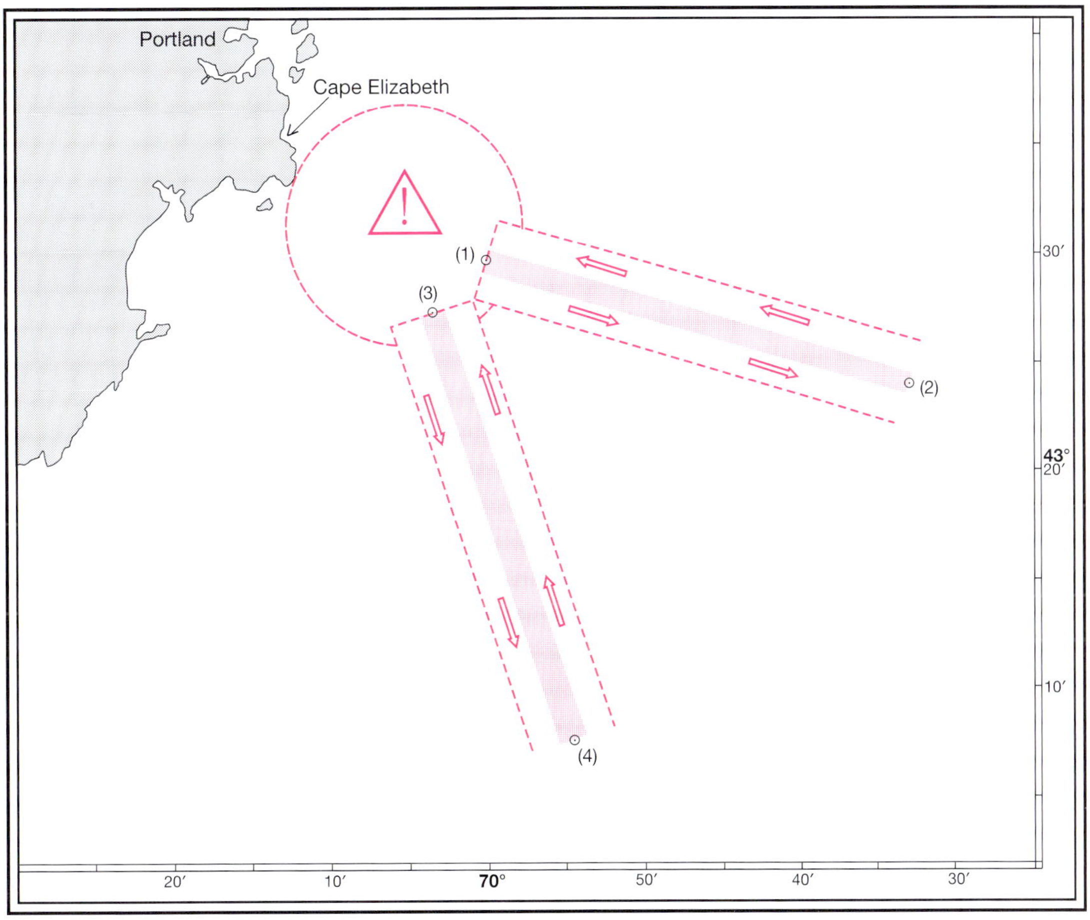

IN THE APPROACHES TO PORTLAND, MAINE

IN THE APPROACH TO BOSTON, MASSACHUSETTS

(Reference charts: United States 13009, 2007 edition; 13200, 2007 edition.
Note: These charts are based on North American 1983 datum, which is equivalent to World Geodetic System 1984 datum (WGS 84).)

Description of the traffic separation scheme

(a) A separation zone, one mile wide, is centred upon the following geographical positions:

(1)	42°20′.73 N,	070°39′.06 W	(3)	40°49′.25 N,	069°00′.81 W
(2)	42°18′.28 N,	070°01′.14 W			

(b) A traffic lane for northbound traffic is established between the separation zone and a line connecting the following geographical positions:

(4)	40°50′.47 N,	068°58′.67 W	(6)	42°22′.71 N,	070°38′.62 W
(5)	42°20′.17 N,	069°59′.40 W			

(c) A traffic lane for southbound traffic is established between the separation zone and a line connecting the following geographical positions:

(7)	42°18′.82 N,	070°40′.49 W	(9)	40°48′.03 N,	069°02′.96 W
(8)	42°16′.39 N,	070°02′.88 W			

Precautionary areas

(a) A precautionary area of radius 6.17 miles is centred upon geographical position:

(12) 42°22′.71 N, 070°46′.97 W

(b) A precautionary area is bounded to the east by a circle of radius 15.5 nautical miles, centred upon geographical position (13) 40°35′.01 N, 068°59′.97 W, intersected by the traffic separation schemes "In the approach to Boston, Massachusetts" and "Eastern Approach, Off Nantucket" (part II of the traffic separation scheme "Off New York") at the following geographical positions:

(4)	40°50′.47 N,	068°58′.67 W	(11)	40°23′.75 N,	069°13′.95 W

The precautionary area is bounded to the west by a line connecting the two traffic separation schemes between the following geographical positions:

(9)	40°48′.03 N,	069°02′.96 W	(10)	40°36′.76 N,	069°15′.13 W

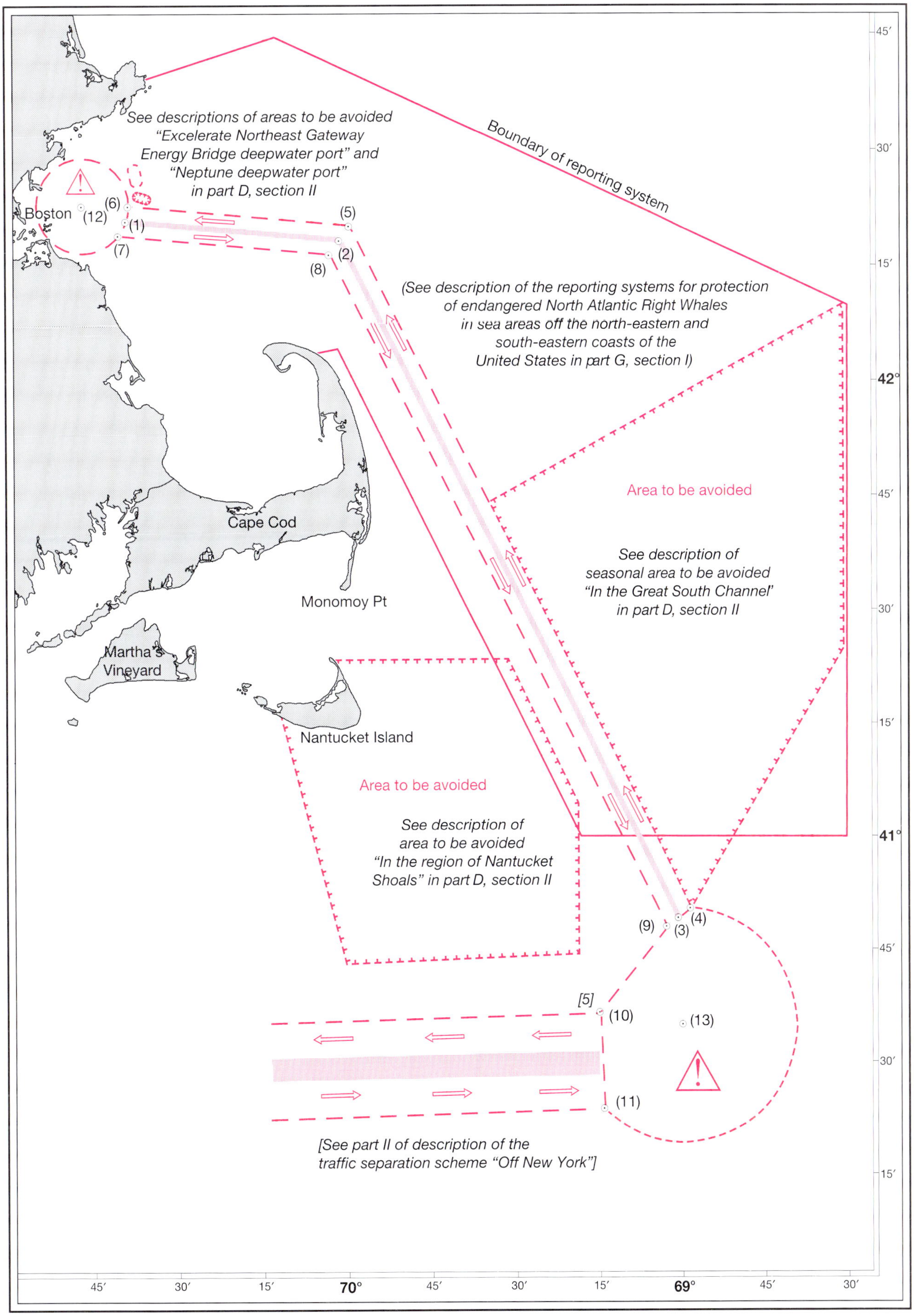

IN THE APPROACH TO BOSTON, MASSACHUSETTS

IN THE APPROACHES TO NARRAGANSETT BAY, RHODE ISLAND, AND BUZZARDS BAY, MASSACHUSETTS

(Reference chart: United States 13218, 1987 edition.
Note: This chart is based on North American 1983 geodetic datum.)

Description of the traffic separation scheme

The traffic separation scheme "In the approaches to Narragansett Bay, Rhode Island, and Buzzards Bay, Massachusetts" consists of two parts:

Part I
Narragansett Bay approach

(a) A separation zone, two miles wide, is centred upon the following geographical positions:

(1) 41°22′.70 N, 071°23′.30 W (2) 41°11′.10 N, 071°23′.30 W

(b) A traffic lane, one mile wide, is established on each side of the separation zone.

Part II
Buzzards Bay approach

(a) A separation zone, one mile wide, is centred upon the following geographical positions:

(3) 41°10′.20 N, 071°19′.10 W (4) 41°21′.80 N, 071°07′.10 W

(b) A traffic lane, one mile wide, is established on each side of the separation zone.

Precautionary areas

A precautionary area of radius 5.4 miles is centred upon geographical position 41°06′.00 N, 071°23′.30 W.
A precautionary area of radius 3.55 miles is centred upon geographical position 41°25′.60 N, 071°23′.30 W.

Restricted area

Note: A restricted area, two miles wide, extending from the southern limit of the Narragansett Bay approach traffic separation zone to latitude 41°24′.70 N, has been established.

The restricted area will only be closed to ship traffic by the Naval Underwater System Center during periods of daylight and optimum weather conditions for torpedo range usage. The closing of the restricted area will be indicated by the activation of a white strobe light mounted on Brenton Reef Light and controlled by a naval ship supporting the torpedo range activities. There would be no ship restrictions expected during inclement weather or when the torpedo range is not in use.

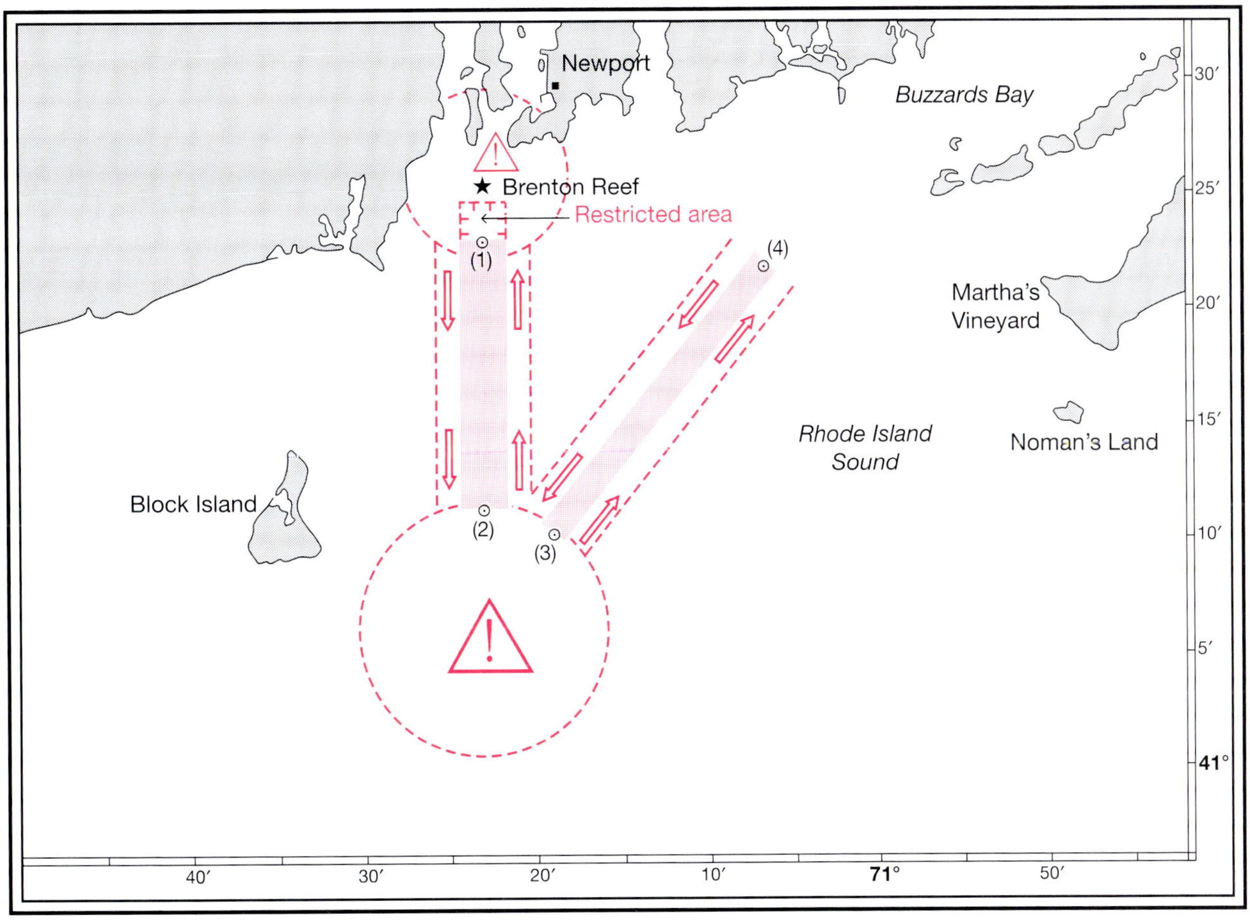

IN THE APPROACHES TO NARRAGANSETT BAY, RHODE ISLAND, AND BUZZARDS BAY, MASSACHUSETTS

OFF NEW YORK

(Reference charts: United States 12300, 1985 edition; 12326, 1986 edition.
Note: These charts are based on North American 1927 geodetic datum.)

Description of the traffic separation scheme

B

The traffic separation scheme "Off New York" consists of five parts:

Part I
Precautionary areas

(a) A precautionary area of radius seven miles is centred upon Ambrose Light in geographical position 40°27′.50 N, 073°49′.90 W.

(b) A precautionary area is located between part II of this traffic separation scheme (Eastern approach, off Nantucket) and the traffic separation scheme "In the approach to Boston, Massachusetts". Details of the precautionary area are contained in paragraph (b) of the description of the precautionary areas in the amended traffic separation scheme "In the approach to Boston, Massachusetts".

Part II
Eastern approach, off Nantucket

(a) A separation zone is bounded by a line connecting the following geographical positions:

(1)	40°28′.75 N,	069°14′.83 W	(3)	40°30′.62 N,	070°14′.00 W
(2)	40°27′.62 N,	070°13′.77 W	(4)	40°31′.75 N,	069°14′.97 W

(b) A traffic lane for westbound traffic is established between the separation zone and a line connecting the following geographical positions:

(5)	40°36′.75 N,	069°15′.17 W	(6)	40°35′.62 N,	070°14′.15 W

(c) A traffic lane for eastbound traffic is established between the separation zone and a line connecting the following geographical positions:

(7)	40°22′.62 N,	070°13′.60 W	(8)	40°23′.75 N,	069°14′.63 W

Part III
Eastern approach, off Ambrose Light

(a) A separation zone is bounded by a line connecting the following geographical positions:

(9)	40°24′.33 N,	073°04′.97 W	(12)	40°27′.00 N,	073°40′.75 W
(10)	40°24′.20 N,	073°11′.50 W	(13)	40°27′.20 N,	073°11′.50 W
(11)	40°26′.00 N,	073°40′.93 W	(14)	40°27′.33 N,	073°04′.95 W

(b) A traffic lane for westbound traffic is established between the separation zone and a line connecting the following geographical positions:

(15)	40°32′.33 N,	073°04′.95 W	(17)	40°28′.00 N,	073°40′.73 W
(16)	40°32′.20 N,	073°11′.50 W			

(c) A traffic lane for eastbound traffic is established between the separation zone and a line connecting the following geographical positions:

(18)	40°25′.05 N,	073°41′.32 W	(20)	40°19′.33 N,	073°04′.97 W
(19)	40°19′.20 N,	073°11′.50 W			

Part IV
South-eastern approach

(a) A separation zone is bounded by a line connecting the following geographical positions:

(21)	40°03′.10 N,	073°17′.93 W	(24)	40°23′.20 N,	073°42′.70 W
(22)	40°06′.50 N,	073°22′.73 W	(25)	40°08′.72 N,	073°20′.10 W
(23)	40°22′.45 N,	073°43′.55 W	(26)	40°05′.32 N,	073°15′.28 W

(b) A traffic lane for north-westbound traffic is established between the separation zone and a line connecting the following geographical positions:

(27)	40°08′.98 N,	073°10′.87 W	(29)	40°24′.02 N,	073°41′.97 W
(28)	40°12′.42 N,	073°15′.67 W			

(c) A traffic lane for south-eastbound traffic is established between the separation zone and a line connecting the following geographical positions:

(30)	40°21′.82 N,	073°44′.55 W	(32)	39°59′.43 N,	073°22′.35 W
(31)	40°02′.80 N,	073°27′.15 W			

Part V

Southern approach

(a) A separation zone is bounded by a line connecting the following geographical positions:

(33)	39°45′.70 N,	073°48′.00 W	(35)	40°20′.87 N,	073°47′.07 W
(34)	40°20′.63 N,	073°48′.33 W	(36)	39°45′.70 N,	073°44′.00 W

(b) A traffic lane for northbound traffic is established between the separation zone and a line connecting the following geographical positions:

(37)	39°45′.70 N,	073°37′.70 W	(38)	40°21′.25 N,	073°45′.85 W

(c) A traffic lane for southbound traffic is established between the separation zone and a line connecting the following geographical positions:

(39)	40°20′.53 N,	073°49′.65 W	(40)	39°45′.70 N,	073°54′.40 W

Note: Use of LORAN-C enables masters of appropriately equipped ships to be informed highly accurately and continuously about the ship's position in the area covered by this scheme.

(chartlet overleaf)

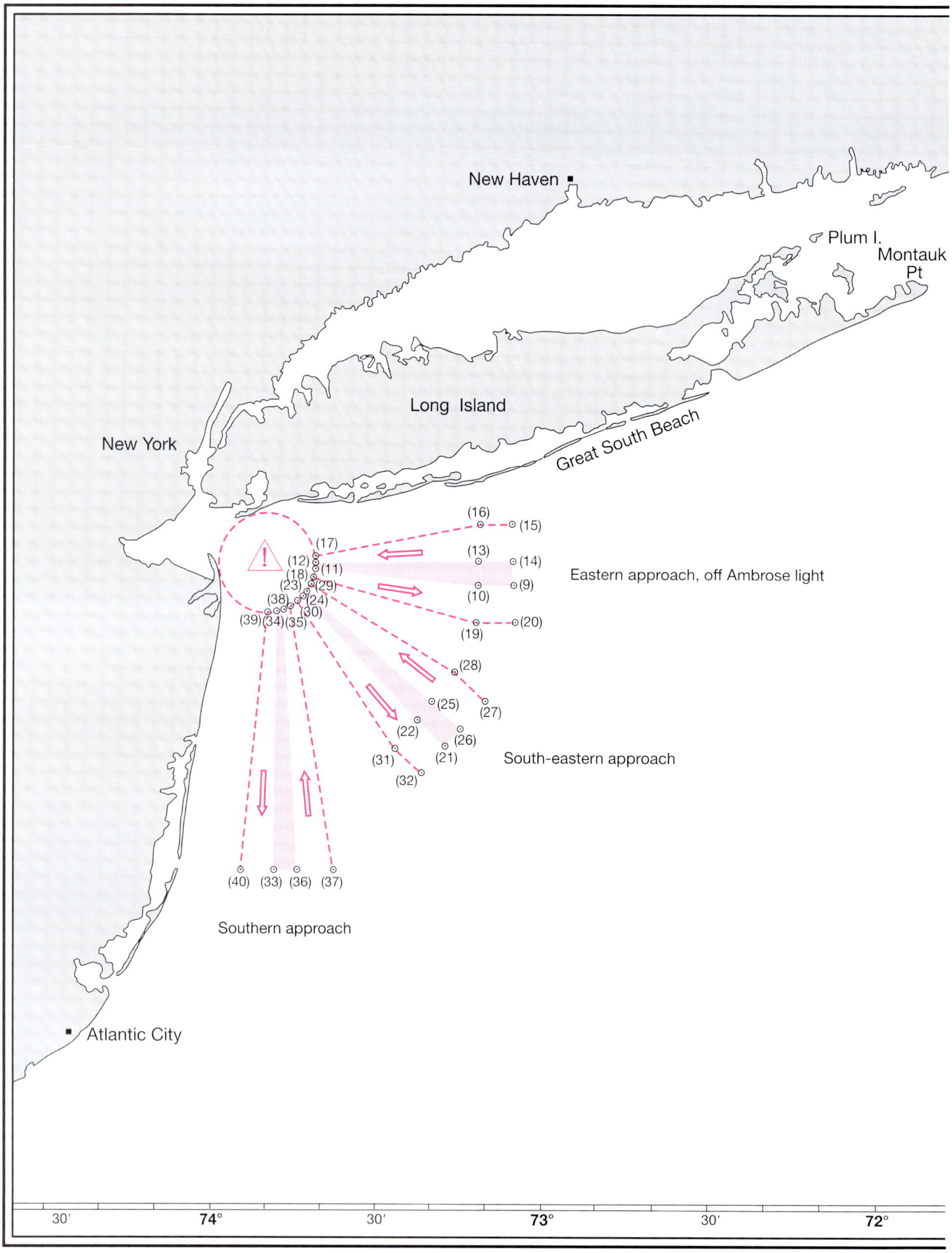

New Haven
Plum I.
Montauk Pt
Long Island
New York
Great South Beach
(16)
(15)
(17)
(12)
(11)
(13)
(14)
(18)
(23)
(29)
(9)
(10)
(38)
(24)
(39)
(34)
(35)
(30)
(20)
(19)
(28)
(25)
(27)
(22)
(26)
(21)
(31)
(32)
Eastern approach, off Ambrose light
South-eastern approach
(40)
(33)
(36)
(37)
Southern approach
Atlantic City
30′
74°
30′
73°
30′
72°

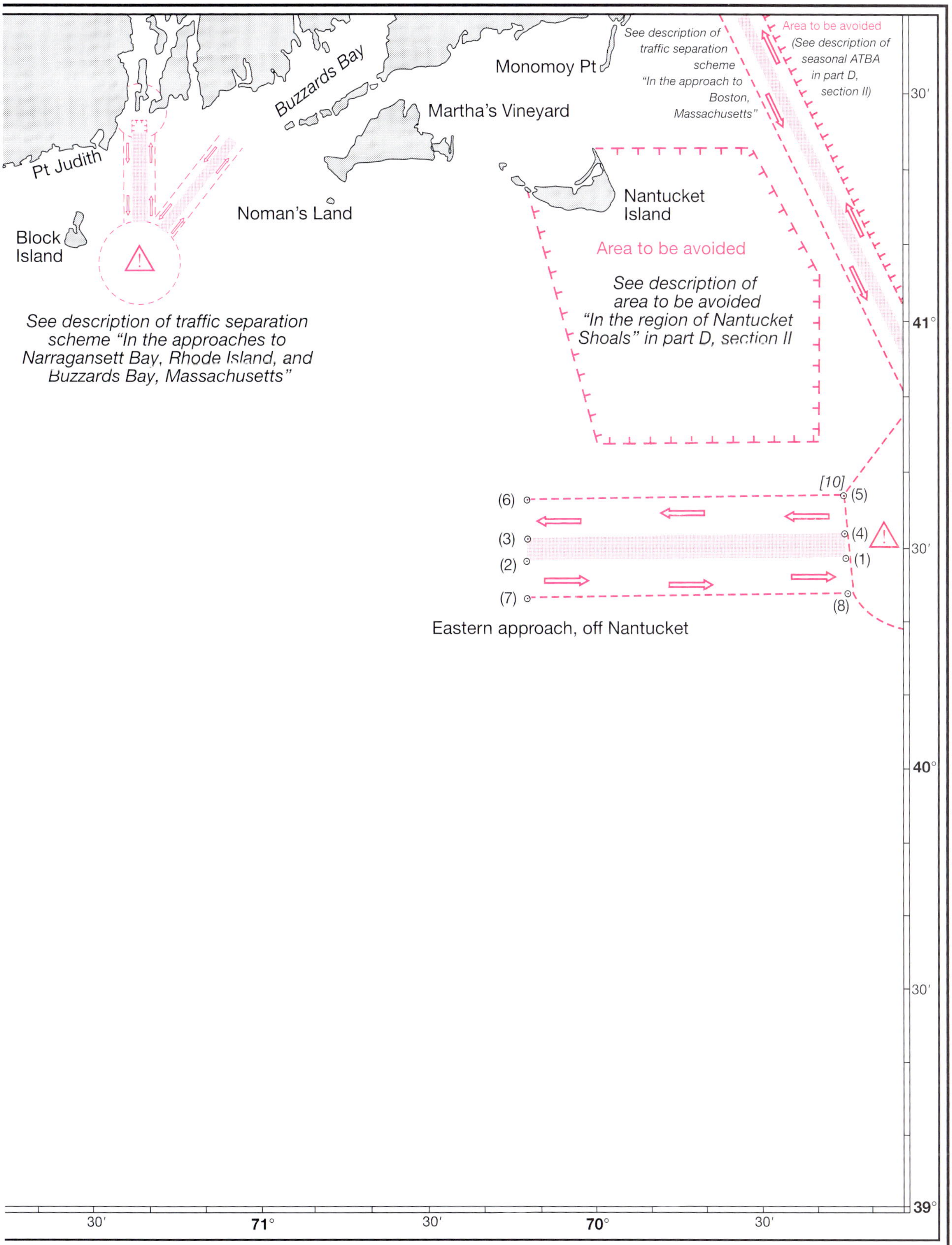
Buzzards Bay
Monomoy Pt
See description of traffic separation scheme "In the approach to Boston, Massachusetts"
Area to be avoided
(See description of seasonal ATBA in part D, section II)
Martha's Vineyard
Pt Judith
Noman's Land
Nantucket Island
Block Island
Area to be avoided
See description of area to be avoided "In the region of Nantucket Shoals" in part D, section II
See description of traffic separation scheme "In the approaches to Narragansett Bay, Rhode Island, and Buzzards Bay, Massachusetts"
[10]
(6)
(5)
(3)
(4)
(2)
(1)
(7)
(8)
Eastern approach, off Nantucket
30′
41°
30′
40°
30′
39°
30′
71°
30′
70°
30′

OFF NEW YORK

OFF DELAWARE BAY

(Reference chart: United States 12214, 1994 edition.
Note: This chart is based on North American datum 1983.)

Description of the traffic separation scheme

Part I
Eastern approach

(a) A separation zone is bounded by a line connecting the following geographical positions:

(1)	38°46′.30 N,	074°34′.45 W	(3)	38°47′.45 N,	074°55′.40 W
(2)	38°46′.33 N,	074°55′.75 W	(4)	38°47′.35 N,	074°34′.50 W

(b) A traffic lane for westbound traffic is established between the separation zone and a line connecting the following geographical positions:

(5)	38°48′.32 N,	074°55′.30 W	(6)	38°49′.80 N,	074°34′.60 W

(c) A traffic lane for eastbound traffic is established between the separation zone and a line connecting the following geographical positions:

(7)	38°45′.45 N,	074°56′.20 W	(8)	38°44′.45 N,	074°34′.35 W

Part II
South-eastern approach

(a) A separation zone is bounded by a line connecting the following geographical positions:

(9)	38°27′.00 N,	074°42′.30 W	(11)	38°44′.20 N,	074°57′.20 W
(10)	38°43′.40 N,	074°58′.00 W	(12)	38°27′.60 N,	074°41′.30 W

(b) A traffic lane for north-westbound traffic is established between the separation zone and a line connecting the following geographical positions:

(13)	38°28′.80 N,	074°39′.30 W	(14)	38°45′.10 N,	074°56′.60 W

(c) A traffic lane for south-eastbound traffic is established between the separation zone and a line connecting the following geographical positions:

(15)	38°42′.80 N,	074°58′.90 W	(16)	38°27′.00 N,	074°45′.40 W

Precautionary area

A precautionary area is established as follows: from 38°42′.80 N, 074°58′.90 W,; thence northerly by an arc of 8 nautical miles centred at 38°48′.90 N, 075°05′.60 W to 38°48′.32 N, 074°55′.30 W; thence westerly to 38°47′.50 N, 075°01′.80 W; thence northerly to 38°50′.75 N, 075°03′.40 W; thence north-easterly to 38°51′.27 N, 075°02′.83 W; thence northerly to 38°54′.80 N, 075°01′.60 W; thence westerly by an arc of radius 6.7 nautical miles centred at 38°48′.90 N, 075°05′.60 W to 38°55′.53 N, 075°05′.87 W; thence south-westerly to 38°54′.00 N, 075°08′.00 W; thence southerly to 38°46′.60 N, 075°03′.55 W; thence south-easterly to 38°42′.80 N, 074°58′.90 W.

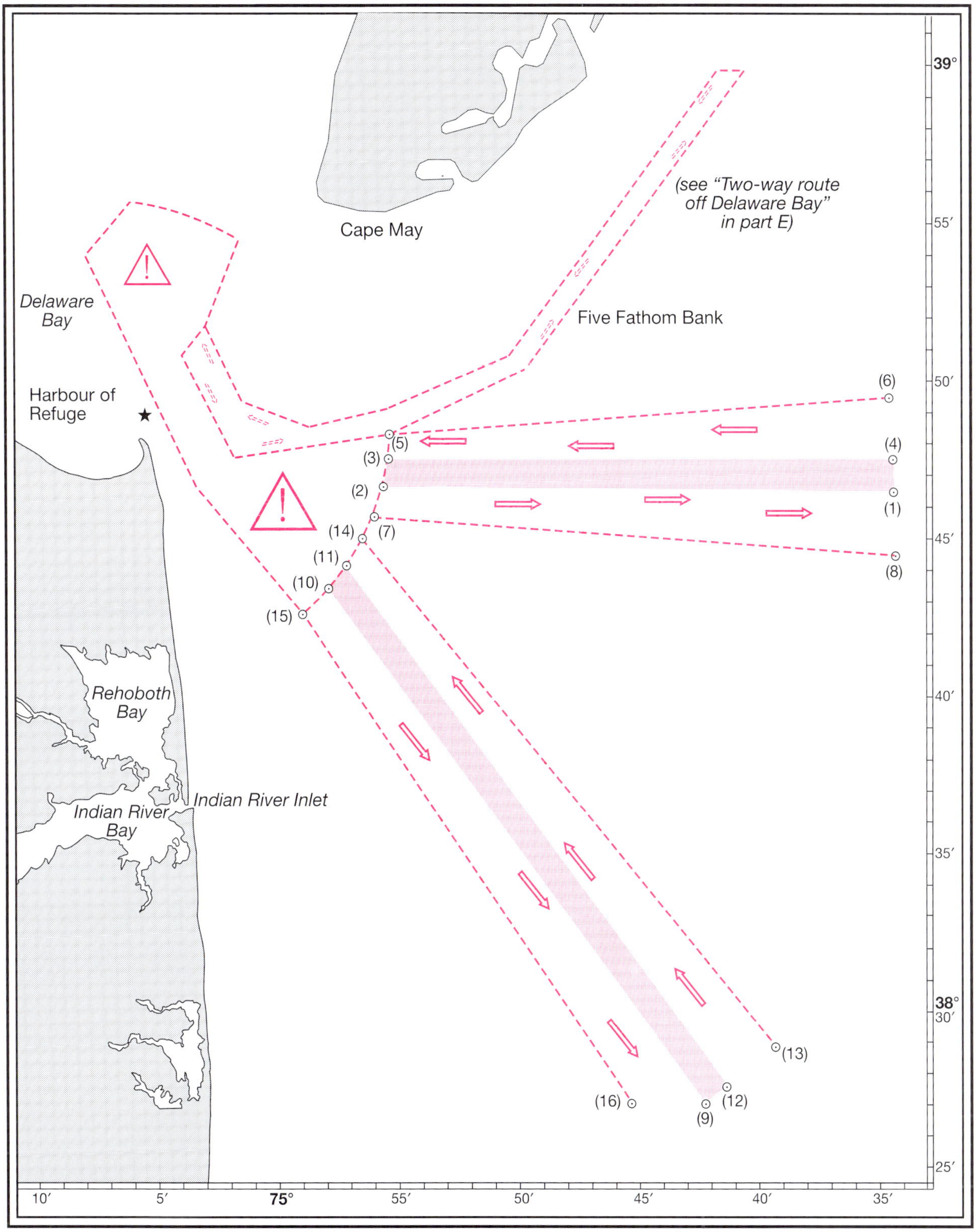

OFF DELAWARE BAY

IN THE APPROACHES TO CHESAPEAKE BAY

(Reference charts: United States 12200, 2002 edition; 12207, 1998 edition; 12221, 2003 edition.
Note: These charts are based on North American 1983 datum.)

Description of the traffic separation scheme

The traffic separation scheme "In the approaches to Chesapeake Bay" consists of three parts:

Part I
Precautionary area

(a) A precautionary area of radius two miles is centred upon geographical position 36°56′.13 N, 075°57′.45 W.

Part II
Eastern approach

(a) A separation line connects the following geographical positions:

(1)	36°57′.50 N,	075°48′.21 W	(3)	36°56′.40 N,	075°54′.95 W
(2)	36°56′.40 N,	075°52′.40 W			

(b) A traffic lane for westbound traffic is established between the separation line and a line connecting the following geographical positions:

(4)	36°57′.94 N,	075°48′.41 W	(6)	36°56′.90 N,	075°55′.14 W
(5)	36°56′.90 N,	075°52′.40 W			

(c) A traffic lane for eastbound traffic is established between the separation line and a line connecting the following geographical positions:

(7)	36°57′.04 N,	075°48′.01 W	(9)	36°55′.88 N,	075°54′.95 W
(8)	36°55′.88 N,	075°52′.40 W			

Part III
Southern approach

(a) A separation line connects the following geographical positions:

(10)	36°50′.33 N,	075°46′.29 W	(12)	36°55′.96 N,	075°54′.97 W
(11)	36°52′.90 N,	075°51′.52 W			

(b) A separation line connects the following geographical positions:

(13)	36°55′.11 N,	075°55′.23 W	(15)	36°49′.70 N,	075°46′.80 W
(14)	36°52′.35 N,	075°52′.12 W			

(c) A separation line connects the following geographical positions:

(16)	36°49′.52 N,	075°46′.94 W	(18)	36°54′.97 N,	075°55′.43 W
(17)	36°52′.18 N,	075°52′.29 W			

(d) A separation line connects the following geographical positions:

(19)	36°54′.44 N,	075°56′.09 W	(21)	36°48′.87 N,	075°47′.42 W
(20)	36°51′.59 N,	075°52′.92 W			

(e) A traffic lane for inbound traffic is established between the separation lines described in paragraphs (a) and (b).

(f) A traffic lane for outbound traffic is established between the separation lines described in paragraphs (c) and (d).

(g) A deep-water route is established between the separation lines described in paragraphs (b) and (c). The types of ships which are recommended to use the deep-water route are given in the description of the deep-water route (see part C, section IV). All other ships using the southern approach traffic separation scheme should use the appropriate inbound or outbound traffic lane.

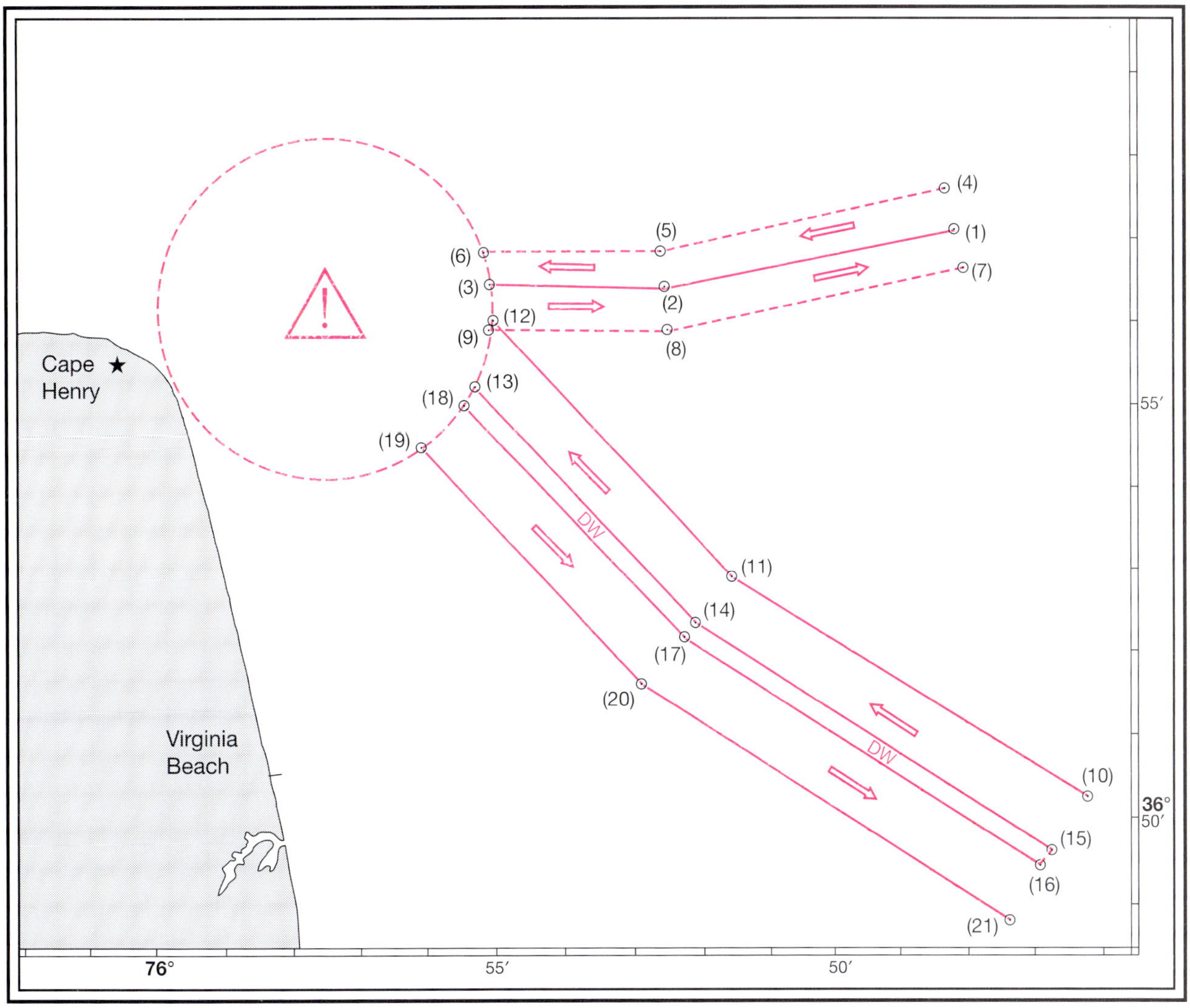

IN THE APPROACHES TO CHESAPEAKE BAY

IN THE APPROACHES TO THE CAPE FEAR RIVER

(Reference charts: United States 11536, 2003 edition; 11537, 2004 edition.
Note: These charts are based on North American 1983 datum.)

Description of the traffic separation scheme

(a) A traffic separation zone is bounded by a line connecting the following geographical positions:

(1)	33°44′.94 N,	078°04′.81 W	(3)	33°34′.50 N,	078°14′.70 W
(2)	33°32′.75 N,	078°09′.66 W	(4)	33°45′.11 N,	078°04′.98 W

(b) A traffic lane for northbound traffic is established between the separation zone and a line connecting the following geographic positions:

(5)	33°32′.75 N,	078°05′.99 W	(6)	33°44′.38 N,	078°03′.77 W

(c) A traffic lane for southbound traffic is established between the separation zone and a line connecting the following geographic positions:

(7)	33°36′.22 N,	078°18′.00 W	(8)	33°46′.03 N,	078°05′.41 W

Precautionary area

(a) A precautionary area is established bounded by a line connecting the following geographical positions:

from	(9)	33°47′.65 N,	078°04′.78 W, to
	(10)	33°48′.50 N,	078°04′.27 W, to
	(11)	33°49′.53 N,	078°03′.10 W, to
	(12)	33°48′.00 N,	078°01′.00 W, to
	(13)	33°41′.00 N,	078°01′.00 W, to
	(14)	33°41′.00 N,	078°04′.00 W, to
	(15)	33°44′.28 N,	078°03′.02 W

thence by an arc of 2 nautical miles radius, centred at (16) 33°46′.28 N, 078°03′.03 W
thence to the point of origin at (9).

Note: A pilot boarding area is located inside the precautionary area. Due to heavy ship traffic, mariners are advised not to anchor or linger in the precautionary area except to pick up or disembark a pilot.

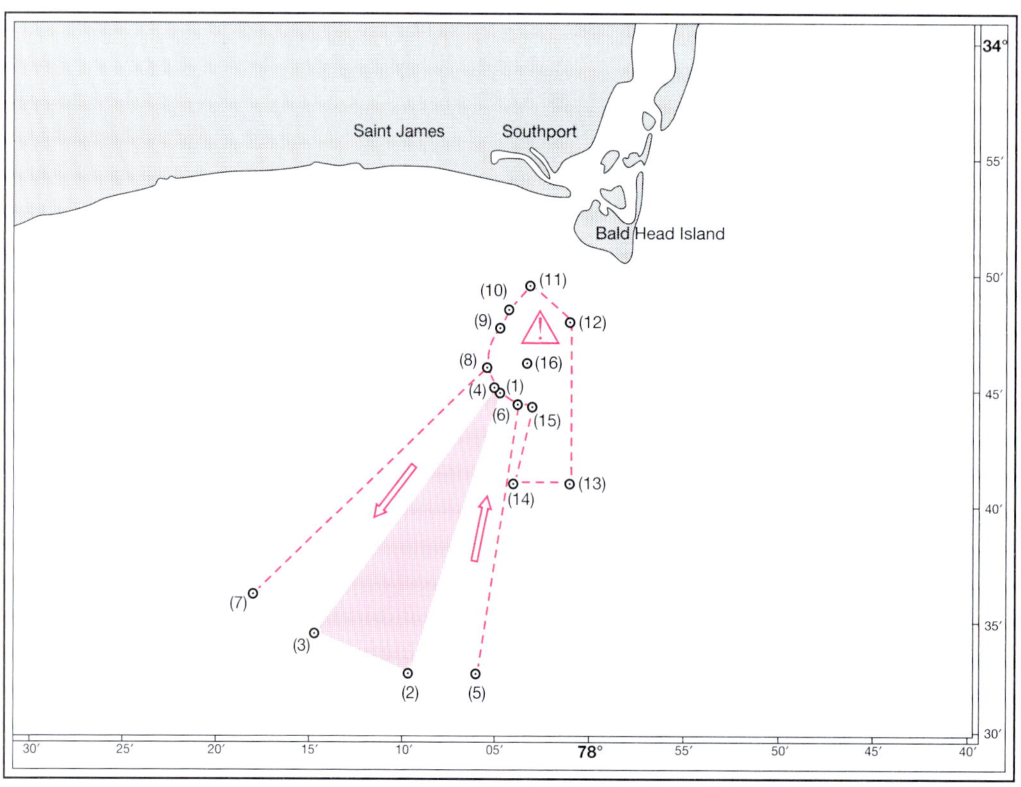

IN THE APPROACHES TO THE CAPE FEAR RIVER

IN THE APPROACHES TO GALVESTON BAY

(Reference charts: United States National Ocean Survey 11323, 1986 edition; 11332, 1987 edition.
Note: These charts are based on North American 1927 geodetic datum.)

Description of the traffic separation scheme

(a) A traffic separation zone is bounded by a line connecting the following geographical positions:

(1)	29°17′.15 N,	094°35′.80 W	(3)	29°09′.05 N,	094°26′.36 W
(2)	29°09′.20 N,	094°26′.23 W	(4)	29°17′.04 N,	094°35′.93 W

(b) A traffic lane for north-westbound traffic is established between the separation zone and a line connecting the following geographical positions:

(5)	29°18′.00 N,	094°34′.90 W	(6)	29°11′.20 N,	094°24′.00 W

(c) A traffic lane for south-eastbound traffic is established between the separation zone and a line connecting the following geographical positions:

(7)	29°16′.10 N,	094°37′.00 W	(8)	29°07′.70 N,	094°27′.80 W

Precautionary areas

(a) An inshore precautionary area is established, bounded by a line connecting the following geographical positions:

(7)	29°16′.10 N,	094°37′.00 W	(10)	29°19′.80 N,	094°38′.10 W
(5)	29°18′.00 N,	094°34′.90 W	(11)	29°18′.10 N,	094°39′.20 W
(9)	29°19′.40 N,	094°37′.10 W			

(b) An offshore precautionary area is established, bounded by a line connecting the following geographical positions:

(6)	29°11′.20 N,	094°24′.00 W	(13)	29°06′.40 N,	094°23′.90 W
(8)	29°07′.70 N,	094°27′.80 W	(14)	29°09′.10 N,	094°20′.60 W
(12)	29°06′.40 N,	094°26′.20 W			

Note: A pilot boarding area is located near the centre of the inshore precautionary area. Due to heavy ship traffic, mariners are advised not to anchor or linger in this precautionary area except to pick up or disembark a pilot.

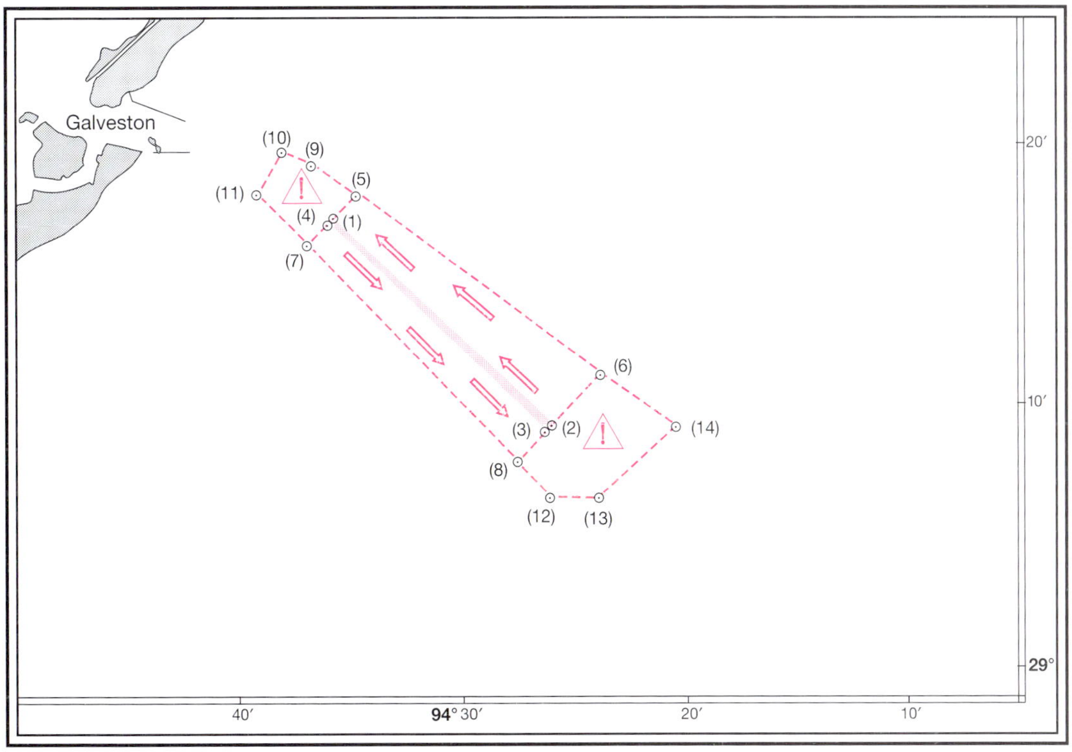

IN THE APPROACHES TO GALVESTON BAY

B

IN THE APPROACHES TO THE PORT OF VERACRUZ

(Reference chart: United States 28302, 1991 edition.
Note: This chart is based on World Geodetic System 1984 datum.)

Description of the traffic separation scheme

The traffic separation scheme in the approaches to Veracruz, Mexico consists of two parts:

Part I
East approach: Recommended for vessels entering or leaving the port of Veracruz

(a) A separation zone bounded by a line connecting the following geographical positions:

(1)	19°14′.00 N,	095°45′.00 W	(3)	19°12′.50 N,	095°53′.43 W
(2)	19°14′.00 N,	095°53′.43 W	(4)	19°12′.50 N,	095°45′.00 W

(b) A separation zone bounded by a line connecting the following geographical positions:

(5)	19°11′.50 N,	095°45′.00 W	(7)	19°10′.90 N,	095°53′.43 W
(6)	19°11′.50 N,	095°53′.43 W	(8)	19°10′.90 N,	095°46′.60 W

(c) A traffic lane for westbound traffic is established between separation zone (a) and a line connecting the following geographical positions:

(9)	19°15′.00 N,	095°45′.00 W	(10)	19°15′.00 N,	095°53′.43 W

(d) A traffic lane for eastbound traffic is established between separation zone (a) and separation zone (b).

Part II
North approach: Recommended for vessels entering or leaving the port of Veracruz

(a) A separation zone bounded by a line connecting the following geographical positions:

(11)	19°19′.00 N,	095°59′.62 W	(13)	19°15′.00 N,	095°58′.05 W
(12)	19°15′.00 N,	095°59′.62 W	(14)	19°19′.00 N,	095°58′.05 W

(b) A traffic lane for southbound traffic is established between the separation zone and a line connecting the following geographical positions:

(15)	19°19′.00 N,	096°00′.65 W	(16)	19°15′.00 N,	096°00′.65 W

(c) A traffic lane for northbound traffic is established between the separation zone and a line connecting the following geographical positions:

(17)	19°15′.00 N,	095°57′.00 W	(18)	19°19′.00 N,	095°57′.00 W

Precautionary area

A precautionary area is established bounded by a line connecting the following geographical positions:

(10)	19°15′.00 N,	095°53′.43 W
(17)	19°15′.00 N,	095°57′.00 W
(16)	19°15′.00 N,	096°00′.65 W
(21)	19°12′.07 N,	096°01′.77 W
(23)	19°07′.65 N,	095°58′.92 W
(7)	19°10′.90 N,	095°53′.43 W

back to position (10).

Note: Masters of all appropriately equipped ships should have continual access to highly accurate information on the position of their ships in the traffic lane, using the radar beacons of:

– Sacrificios Island, identified on the radar by Morse letter "Z" and located in geographical position:
(28) 19°10′.49 N, 096°05′.53 W.

– Santiaguillo Island, identified on the radar by Morse letter "O" and located in geographical position:
(29) 19°08′.52 N, 095°48′.47 W.

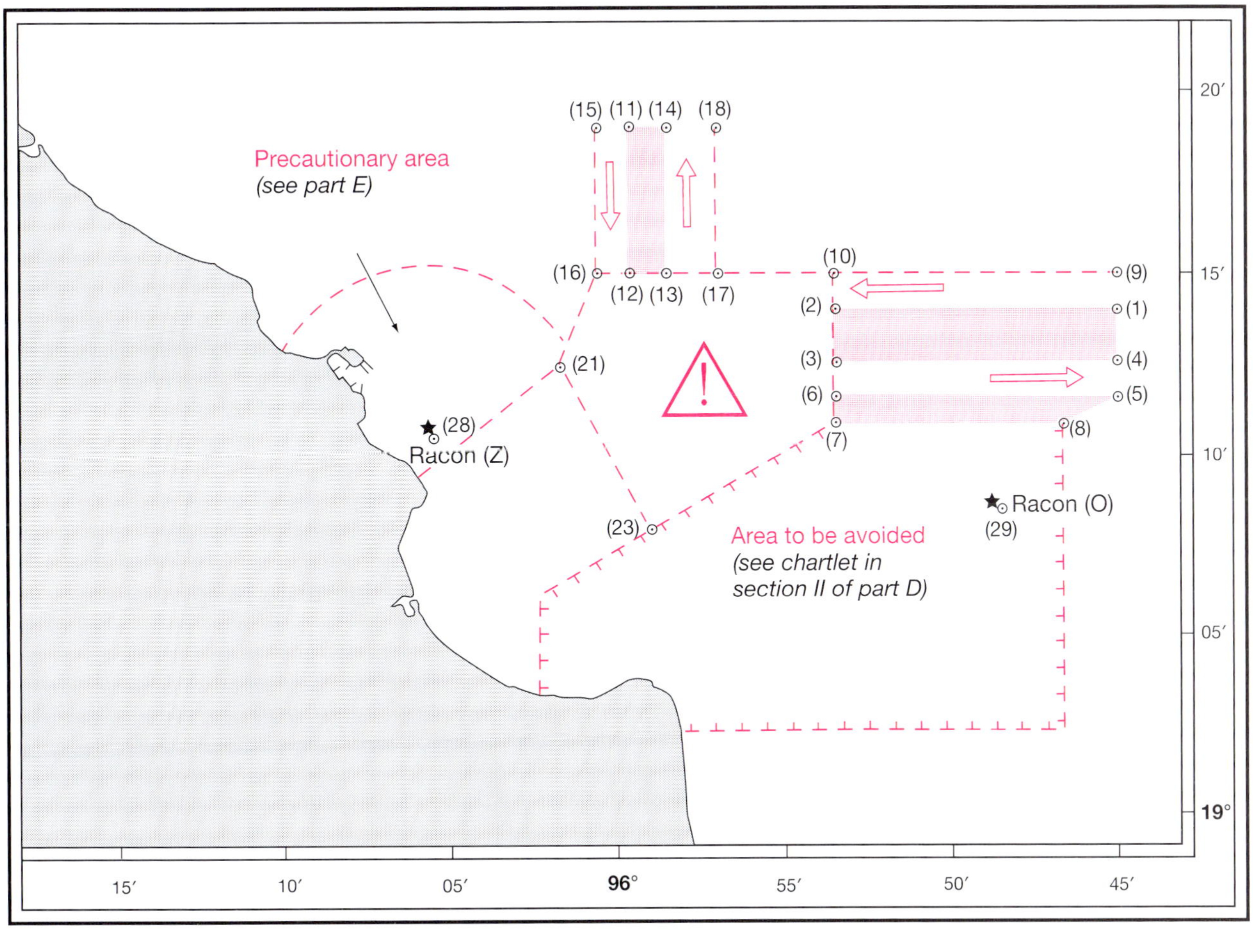

IN THE APPROACHES TO THE PORT OF VERACRUZ

B

OFF CABO SAN ANTONIO

(Reference charts: Instituto Cubano de Hidrografia 1001, 1101 and 1122.
Note: These charts are based on North American 1927 geodetic datum.
British Admiralty 1220, 1977 edition; 2579, 1934 edition; 3867, 1980 edition.)

Description of the traffic separation scheme

(a) A separation zone, two miles wide, is centred upon the following geographical positions:
(1) 21°43′.90 N, 085°07′.20 W (2) 22°01′.00 N, 085°07′.20 W

(b) A traffic lane, three miles wide, for southbound traffic is established between the separation zone and a line connecting the following geographical positions:
(3) 21°42′.70 N, 085°11′.50 W (4) 22°01′.00 N, 085°11′.50 W

(c) A traffic lane, three miles wide, for northbound traffic is established between the separation zone and a line connecting the following geographical positions:
(5) 21°45′.00 N, 085°03′.00 W (6) 22°01′.00 N, 085°03′.00 W

Inshore traffic zone

The area within the lines bounded by the following geographical positions:

Punta del Holandes (21°48′.60 N, 084°48′.20 W), positions (5) and (6) of the "Off Cabo San Antonio" traffic separation scheme and a point on the coast marked by the co-ordinates 22°00′.00 N, 084°34′.50 W

is designated as an inshore traffic zone.

OFF LA TABLA

(Reference charts: Instituto Cubano de Hidrografia 1001, 1101 and 1122.
Note: These charts are based on North American 1927 geodetic datum.
British Admiralty 1220, 1977 edition; 2579, 1934 edition; 3867, 1980 edition.)

Description of the traffic separation scheme

(a) A separation zone, one mile wide, is centred upon the following geographical positions:
(1) 22°27′.90 N, 084°42′.10 W (2) 22°19′.70 N, 084°49′.90 W

(b) A traffic lane, two miles wide, for south-westbound traffic is established between the separation zone and a line connecting the following geographical positions:
(3) 22°21′.40 N, 084°51′.90 W (4) 22°29′.80 N, 084°44′.20 W

(c) A traffic lane, two miles wide, for north-eastbound traffic is established between the separation zone and a line connecting the following geographical positions:
(5) 22°18′.00 N, 084°47′.80 W (6) 22°26′.40 N, 084°40′.20 W

Inshore traffic zone

The area within the lines bounded by the following geographical positions:

Punta Plumaies (22°02′.80 N, 084°29′.30 W), positions (5) and (6) of the traffic separation scheme "Off La Tabla", and the point on the coast marked by the co-ordinates 22°14′.00 N, 084°25′.00 W

is designated as an inshore traffic zone.

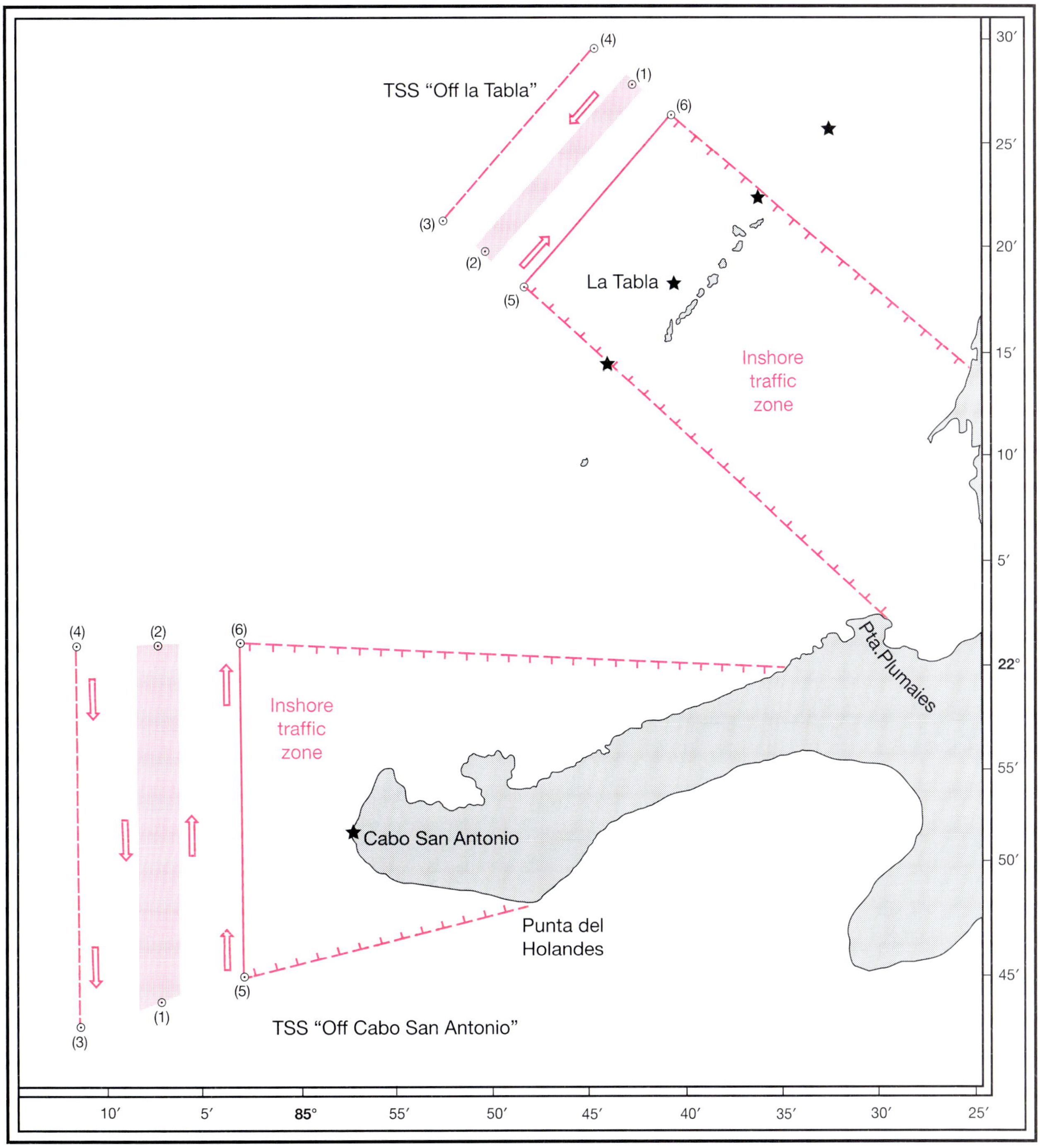

OFF CABO SAN ANTONIO + OFF LA TABLA

B

OFF COSTA DE MATANZAS

(Reference charts: Instituto Cubano de Hidrografia 1001, 1101, 1102, 1126, 1127, 2001, 3001, 4001, 4002 and 4101.
Note: These charts are based on North American 1927 geodetic datum.
British Admiralty 1220, 1977 edition; 2579, 1934 edition; 3867, 1980 edition.)

Description of the traffic separation scheme

(a) A separation zone, one mile wide, is centred upon the following geographical positions:

(1)	23°23′.50 N,	081°08′.00 W	(3)	23°23′.00 N,	080°28′.00 W
(2)	23°25′.00 N,	080°53′.80 W			

(b) A traffic lane, two miles wide, for westbound traffic is established between the separation zone and a line connecting the following geographical positions:

(4)	23°26′.00 N,	081°08′.30 W	(6)	23°25′.50 N,	080°27′.60 W
(5)	23°27′.50 N,	080°54′.00 W			

(c) A traffic lane, two miles wide, for eastbound traffic is established between the separation zone and a line connecting the following geographical positions:

(7)	23°21′.10 N,	081°07′.80 W	(9)	23°20′.50 N,	080°28′.00 W
(8)	23°22′.50 N,	080°54′.00 W			

Inshore traffic zone

The area within the lines bounded by the following geographical positions:

Punta de Molas (23°11′.50 N, 081°07′.15 W), positions (7), (8) and (9) of the traffic separation scheme "Off Costa de Matanzas", and Cayo Bahía de Cádiz lighthouse (23°12′.30 N, 080°28′.90 W)

is designated as an inshore traffic zone.

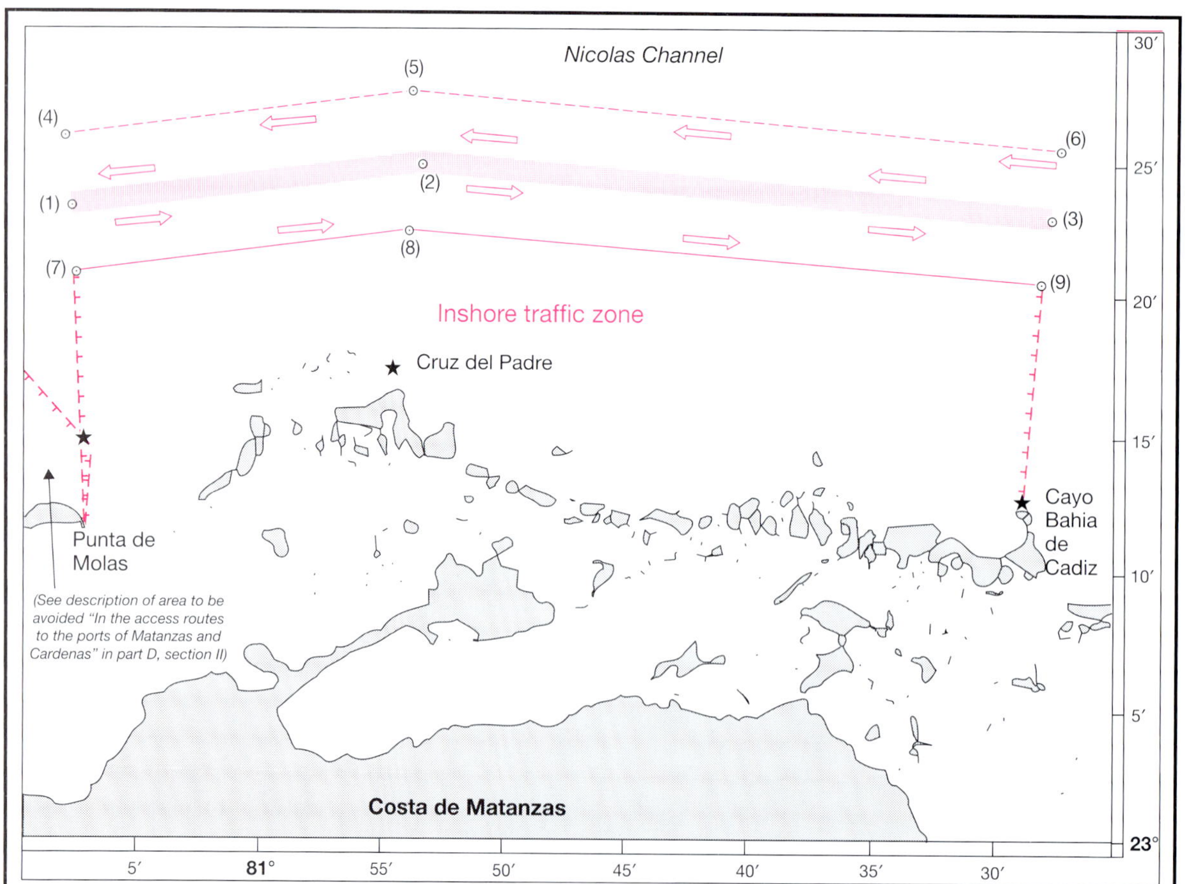

OFF COSTA DE MATANZAS

IN THE OLD BAHAMA CHANNEL

(Reference charts: Instituto Cubano de Hidrografia 1001, 1102, 1103, 1129, 1130, 3001, 4001, 4002 and 4104.
Note: These charts are based on North American 1927 geodetic datum.
British Admiralty 1220, 1977 edition; 2579, 1934 edition; 3867, 1980 edition.)

Description of the traffic separation scheme

(a) A separation zone, half a mile wide, is centred upon the following geographical positions:

(1)	22°48′.40 N,	078°45′.00 W	(3)	22°18′.90 N,	077°39′.40 W
(2)	22°35′.20 N,	078°06′.40 W	(4)	22°09′.00 N,	077°27′.80 W

(b) A traffic lane, two miles wide, for north-westbound traffic is established between the separation zone and a line connecting the following geographical positions:

(5)	22°50′.20 N,	078°43′.30 W	(7)	22°20′.80 N,	077°38′.10 W
(6)	22°37′.30 N,	078°05′.40 W	(8)	22°10′.70 N,	077°26′.30 W

(c) A traffic lane, two miles wide, for south-eastbound traffic is established between the separation zone and a line connecting the following geographical positions:

(9)	22°46′.70 N,	078°47′.00 W	(11)	22°17′.20 N,	077°41′.00 W
(10)	22°33′.20 N,	078°07′.70 W	(12)	22°07′.30 N,	077°29′.60 W

Inshore traffic zone

The area within the lines bounded by the following geographical positions:

> the point on the coast marked by the co-ordinates 22°30′.40 N, 078°53′.30 W, positions (9), (10), (11) and (12) of the traffic separation scheme "In the Old Bahama Channel", and Point Mangle (21°59′.80 N, 077°37′.40 W)

is designated as an inshore traffic zone.

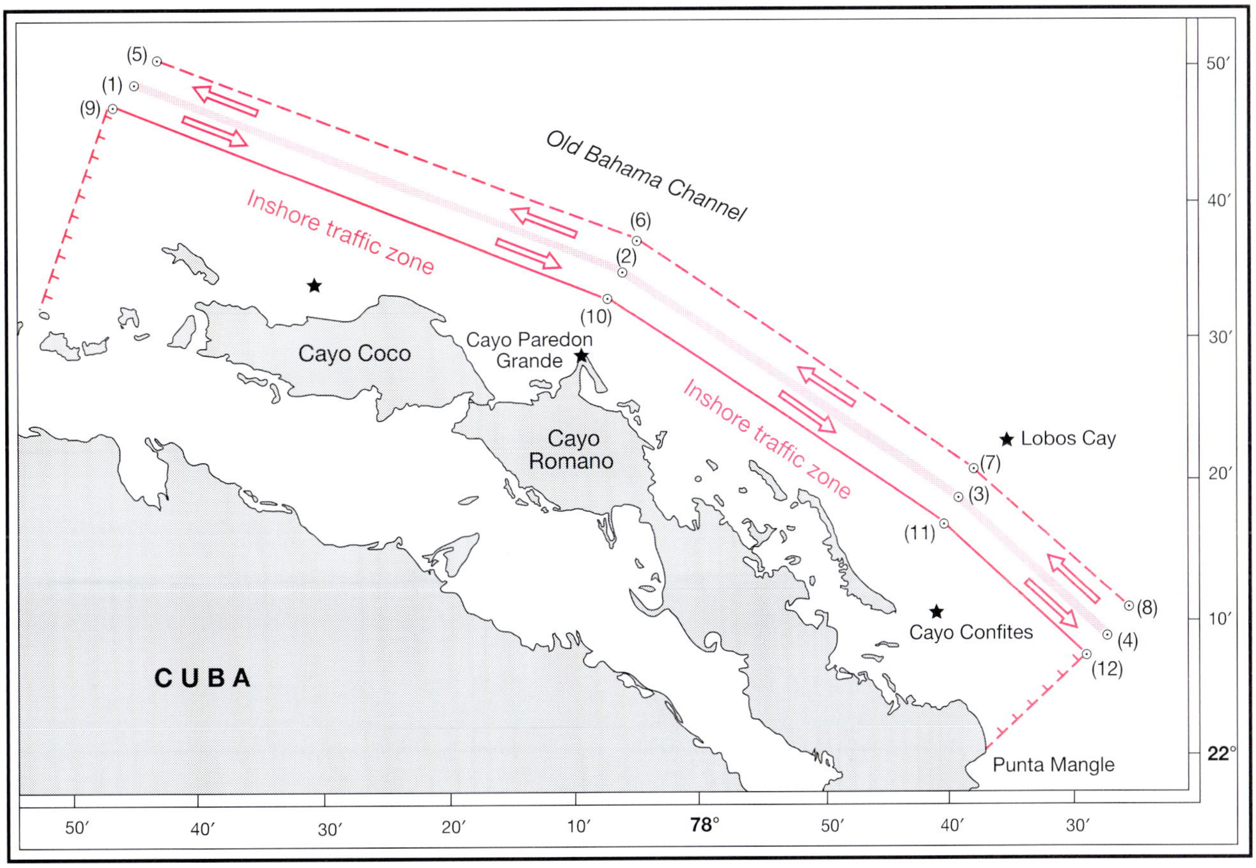

IN THE OLD BAHAMA CHANNEL

OFF PUNTA MATERNILLOS

(Reference charts: Instituto Cubano de Hidrografia 1001, 1103, 1130, 3001, 4001 and 4002.
Note: These charts are based on North American 1927 geodetic datum.
British Admiralty 1220, 1977 edition; 2579, 1934 edition; 3867, 1980 edition.)

Description of the traffic separation scheme

(a) A separation zone, one mile wide, is centred upon the following geographical positions:

(1)	21°51′.20 N,	077°06′.80 W	(3)	21°44′.20 N,	076°54′.00 W
(2)	21°47′.80 N,	077°02′.80 W			

(b) A traffic lane, two miles wide, for north-westbound traffic is established between the separation zone and a line connecting the following geographical positions:

(4)	21°53′.10 N,	077°04′.90 W	(6)	21°46′.50 N,	076°53′.00 W
(5)	21°49′.80 N,	077°01′.20 W			

(c) A traffic lane, two miles wide, for south-eastbound traffic is established between the separation zone and a line connecting the following geographical positions:

(7)	21°49′.50 N,	077°08′.80 W	(9)	21°42′.00 N,	076°55′.00 W
(8)	21°45′.70 N,	077°04′.20 W			

Inshore traffic zone

The area within the lines bounded by the following geographical positions:

> Punta Central (21°40′.80 N, 077°12′.60 W), positions (7), (8) and (9) of the traffic separation scheme "Off Punta Maternillos", and Punta Ganado (21°31′.25 N, 076°59′.75 W)

is designated as an inshore traffic zone.

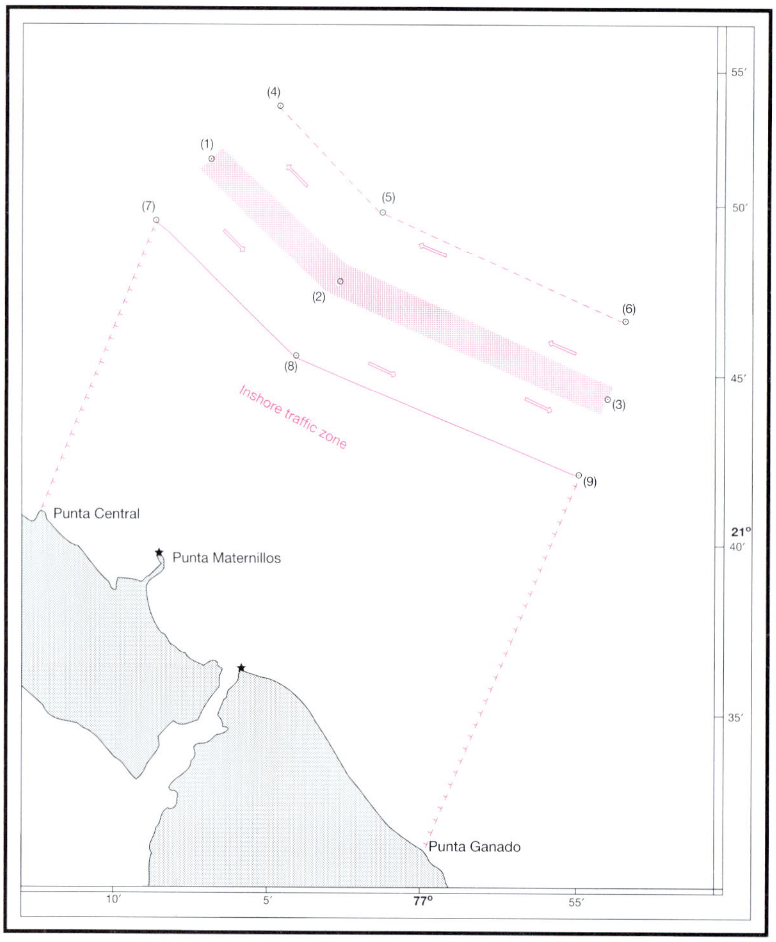

OFF PUNTA MATERNILLOS

OFF PUNTA LUCRECIA

(Reference charts: Instituto Cubano de Hidrografia 1001, 1103, 1131, 1132, 3001, 3002, 4001, 4002 and 4104.
Note: These charts are based on North American 1927 geodetic datum.
British Admiralty 1220, 1977 edition; 2579, 1934 edition; 3867, 1980 edition.)

Description of the traffic separation scheme

(a) A separation zone, one mile wide, is centred upon the following geographical positions:

(1)	21°15′.00 N,	075°42′.20 W	(3)	21°07′.00 N,	075°25′.00 W
(2)	21°11′.40 N,	075°33′.40 W			

(b) A traffic lane, two miles wide, for north-westbound traffic is established between the separation zone and a line connecting the following geographical positions:

(4)	21°17′.30 N,	075°41′.20 W	(6)	21°09′.20 N,	075°23′.70 W
(5)	21°13′.70 N,	075°32′.30 W			

(c) A traffic lane, two miles wide, for south-eastbound traffic is established between the separation zone and a line connecting the following geographical positions:

(7)	21°12′.80 N,	075°43′.20 W	(9)	21°04′.90 N,	075°26′.20 W
(8)	21°09′.20 N,	075°34′.50 W			

Inshore traffic zone

The area within the lines bounded by the following geographical positions:

Bahia de Sama lighthouse (21°07′.30 N, 075°46′.40 W), positions (7), (8) and (9) of the traffic separation scheme "Off Punta Lucrecia", and Punta Morales (20°55′.10 N, 075°36′.80 W)

is designated as an inshore traffic zone.

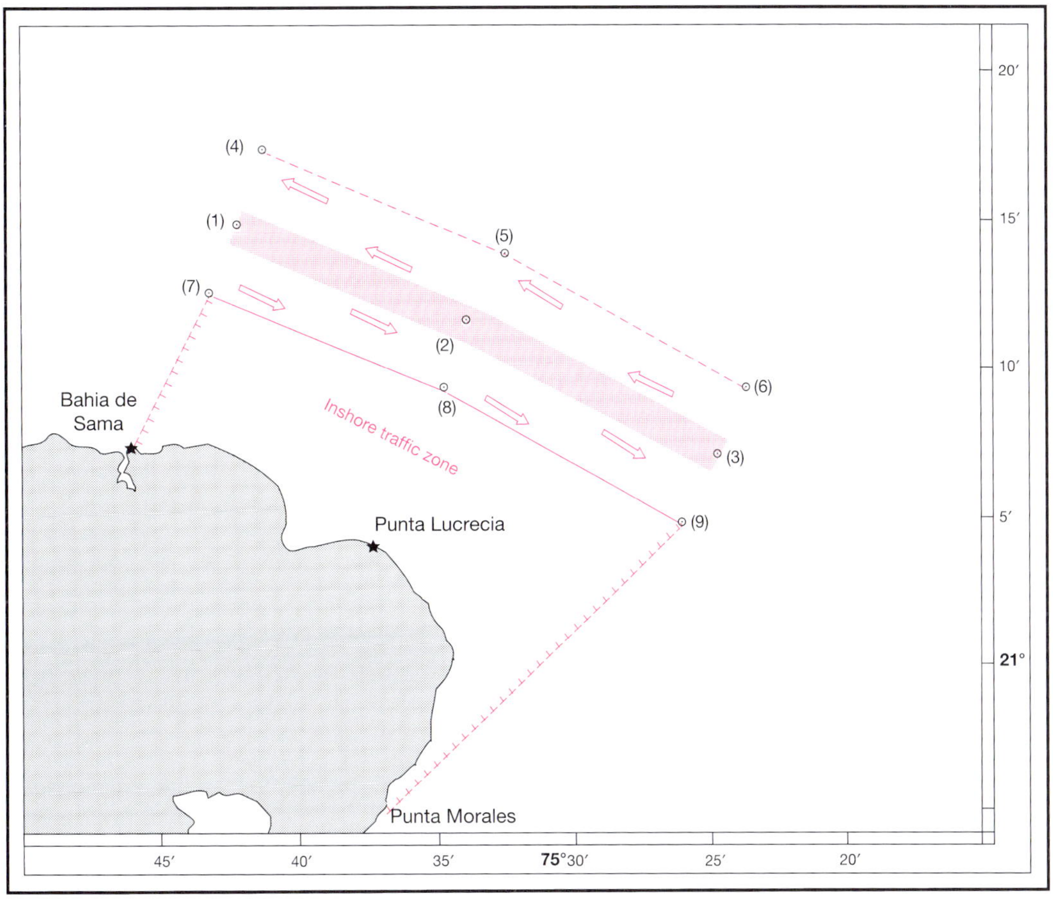

OFF PUNTA LUCRECIA

B

OFF CABO MAYSI

(Reference charts: Instituto Cubano de Hidrografia 1001, 1103, 1133, 1134, 3001, 3002, 3103, 4001, 4002, 4104 and 4106.
Note: These charts are based on North American 1927 geodetic datum.
British Admiralty 1220, 1977 edition; 2579, 1934 edition; 3867, 1980 edition.)

Description of the traffic separation scheme

(a) A separation zone, two miles wide, is centred upon the following geographical positions:

(1) 20°22′.80 N, 073°58′.80 W (2) 20°05′.00 N, 073°58′.80 W

(b) A traffic lane, two and a half miles wide, for northbound traffic is established between the separation zone and a line connecting the following geographical positions:

(3) 20°23′.70 N, 073°55′.00 W (4) 20°05′.00 N, 073°55′.00 W

(c) A traffic lane, two and a half miles wide, for southbound traffic is established between the separation zone and a line connecting the following geographical positions:

(5) 20°21′.80 N, 074°02′.60 W (6) 20°05′.00 N, 074°02′.60 W

Inshore traffic zone

The area within the lines bounded by the following geographical positions:

Punta Fraile (20°19′.10 N, 074°13′.75 W), positions (5) and (6) of the traffic separation scheme "Off Cabo Maysi", and Punta Negra (20°05′.55 N, 074°14′.10 W)

is designated as an inshore traffic zone.

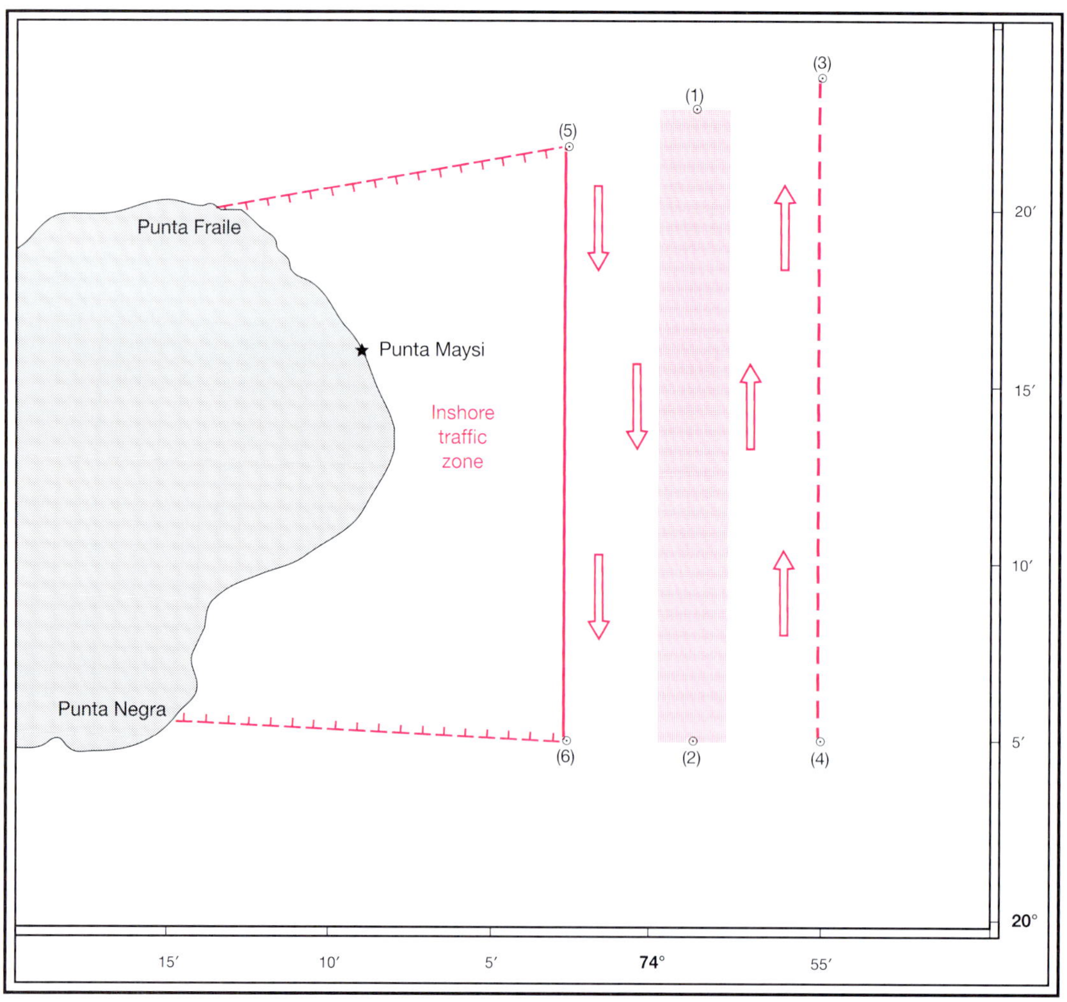

OFF CABO MAYSI

Section X

Asia, Pacific coast

Caution: The chartlets are for illustrative purposes only and must not be used for navigation. Mariners should consult the appropriate nautical publications and charts for up-to-date details on aids to navigation and other relevant information.

Warning: The geographical positions given in the descriptions of the routeing systems are only correct for charts using the same geodetic datum as the reference charts indicated under each scheme. Charts published by other hydrographic offices may use a different geodetic datum, as may new editions of the reference charts published after the adoption of the routeing system. Where amendments to existing systems are not based on the same geodetic datum as the original system, this is emphasized by the use of different colours for definitions of positions.

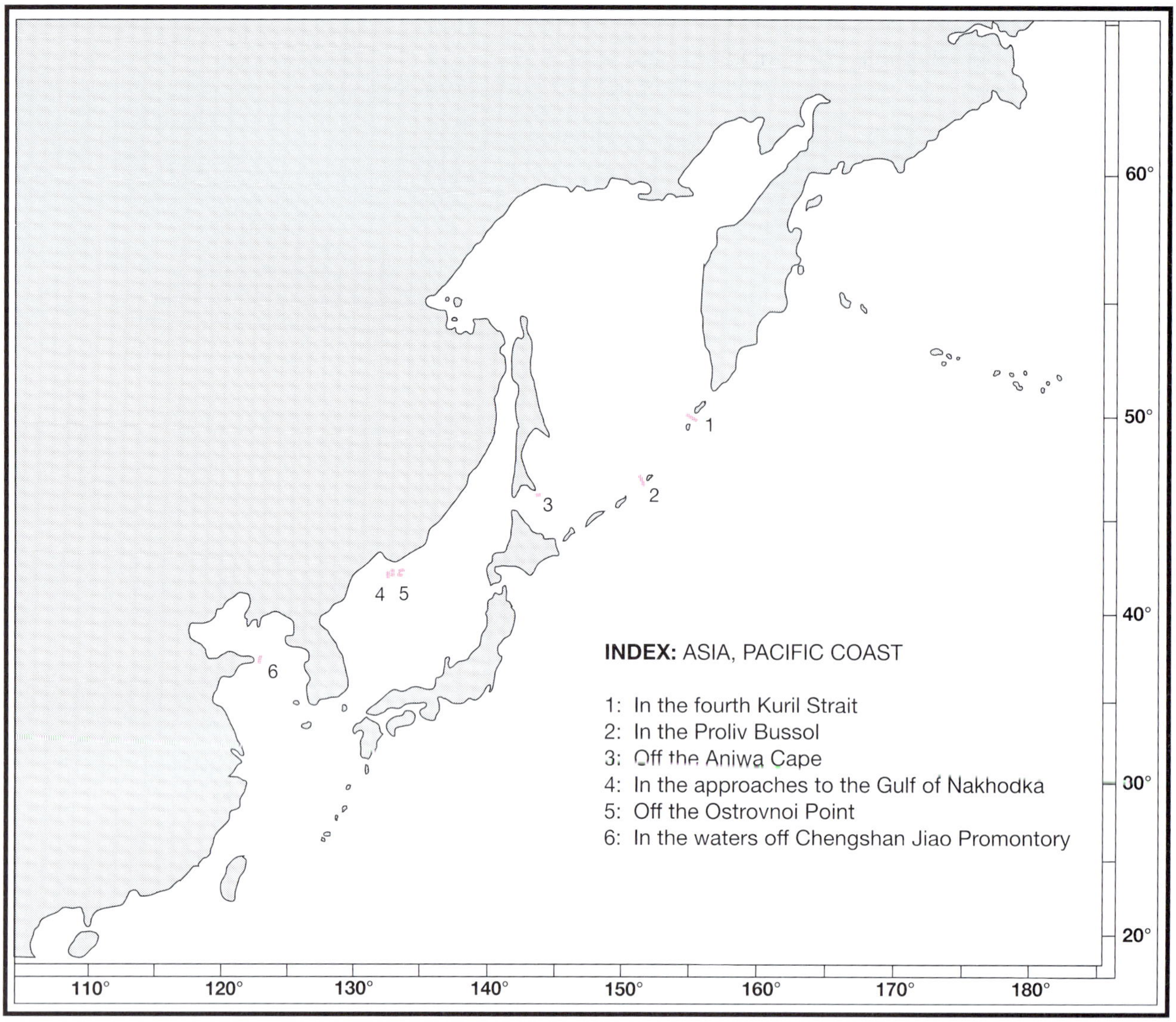

INDEX: ASIA, PACIFIC COAST

1: In the fourth Kuril Strait
2: In the Proliv Bussol
3: Off the Aniwa Cape
4: In the approaches to the Gulf of Nakhodka
5: Off the Ostrovnoi Point
6: In the waters off Chengshan Jiao Promontory

IN THE FOURTH KURIL STRAIT

(Reference chart: USSR 1083, 1989 edition.
Note: This chart is based on the single geodetic datum for Soviet nautical charts.)

Description of the traffic separation scheme

A separation zone is bounded by a line connecting the following geographical positions:

(1)	50°05′.30 N,	154°34′.00 E	(3)	49°43′.80 N,	155°14′.20 E
(2)	49°45′.50 N,	155°16′.10 E	(4)	50°03′.70 N,	154°32′.10 E

A traffic lane, two miles wide, is established on each side of the separation zone.

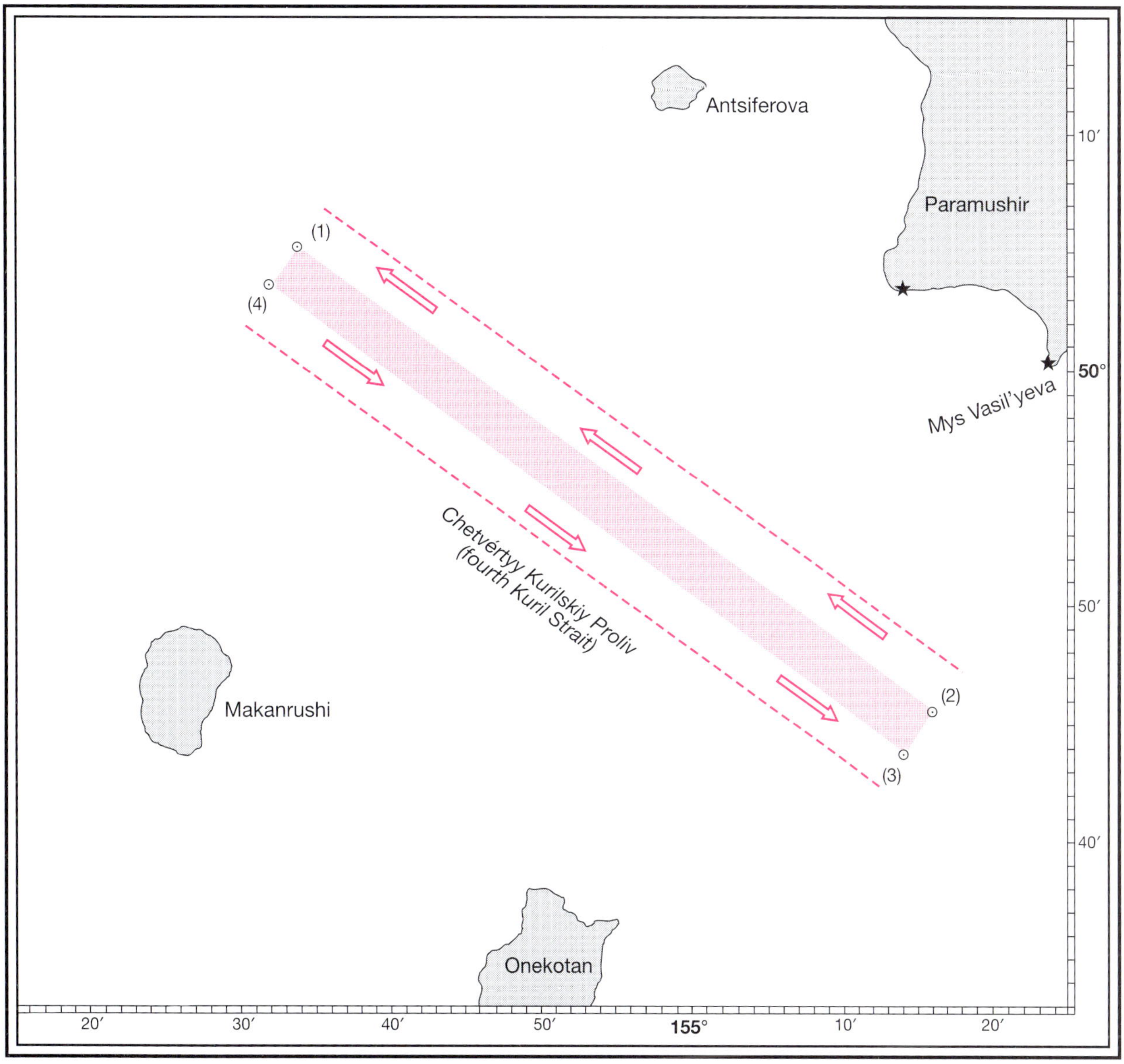

IN THE FOURTH KURIL STRAIT

IN THE PROLIV BUSSOL

(Reference chart: USSR 1075, 1989 edition.
Note: This chart is based on the single geodetic datum for Soviet nautical charts.)

Description of the traffic separation scheme

A separation zone is bounded by a line connecting the following geographical positions:

(1)	47°02′.20 N,	151°03′.90 E	(3)	46°25′.00 N,	151°28′.50 E
(2)	46°27′.00 N,	151°33′.50 E	(4)	47°00′.30 N,	150°58′.80 E

A traffic lane, four miles wide, is established on each side of the separation zone.

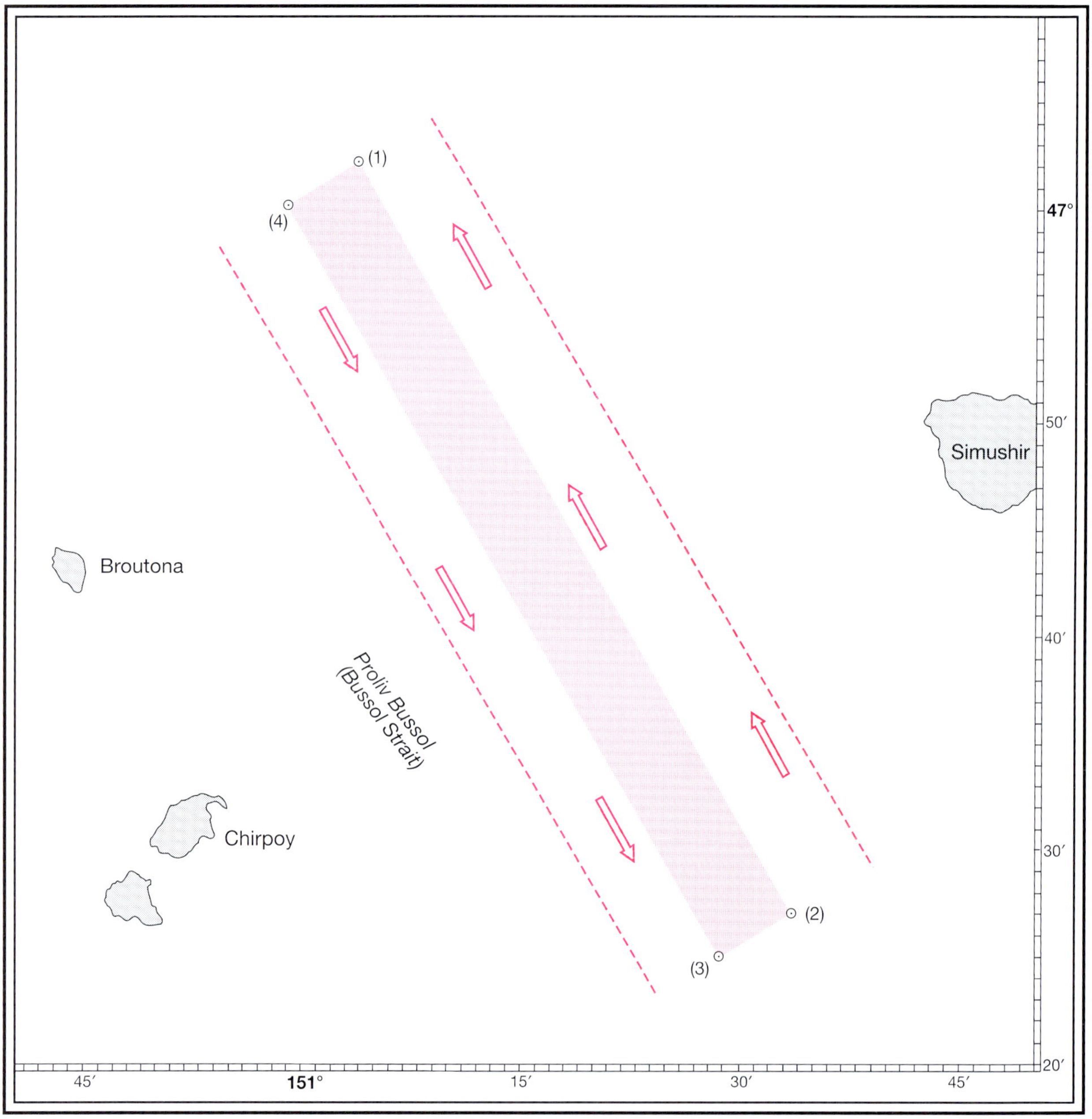

IN THE PROLIV BUSSOL

OFF THE ANIWA CAPE

(Reference chart: USSR 702, 1981 edition.
Note: This chart is based on the single geodetic datum for Soviet nautical charts.)

Description of the traffic separation scheme

(a) A separation zone, four miles wide, is centred upon the following geographical positions:

(1)	45°54′.00 N,	143°20′.00 E	(3)	45°58′.80 N,	143°40′.00 E
(2)	45°54′.90 N,	143°30′.00 E			

(b) A traffic lane, two miles wide, is established south of the separation zone.

(c) An outside boundary of the traffic lane north of the separation zone connects the following geographical positions:

(4)	45°59′.00 N,	143°20′.00 E	(6)	46°05′.20 N,	143°35′.20 E
(5)	45°58′.50 N,	143°25′.50 E			

Inshore traffic zone

The area between the landward boundary of the traffic separation scheme and Sakhalin Island and lying between a line drawn from position 46°03′.50 N, 143°24′.30 E to position 45°59′.00 N, 143°20′.00 E (western limit) and a line drawn from position 46°03′.20 N, 143°32′.00 E to position 46°06′.00 N, 143°28′.00 E (eastern limit) is designated as an inshore traffic zone.

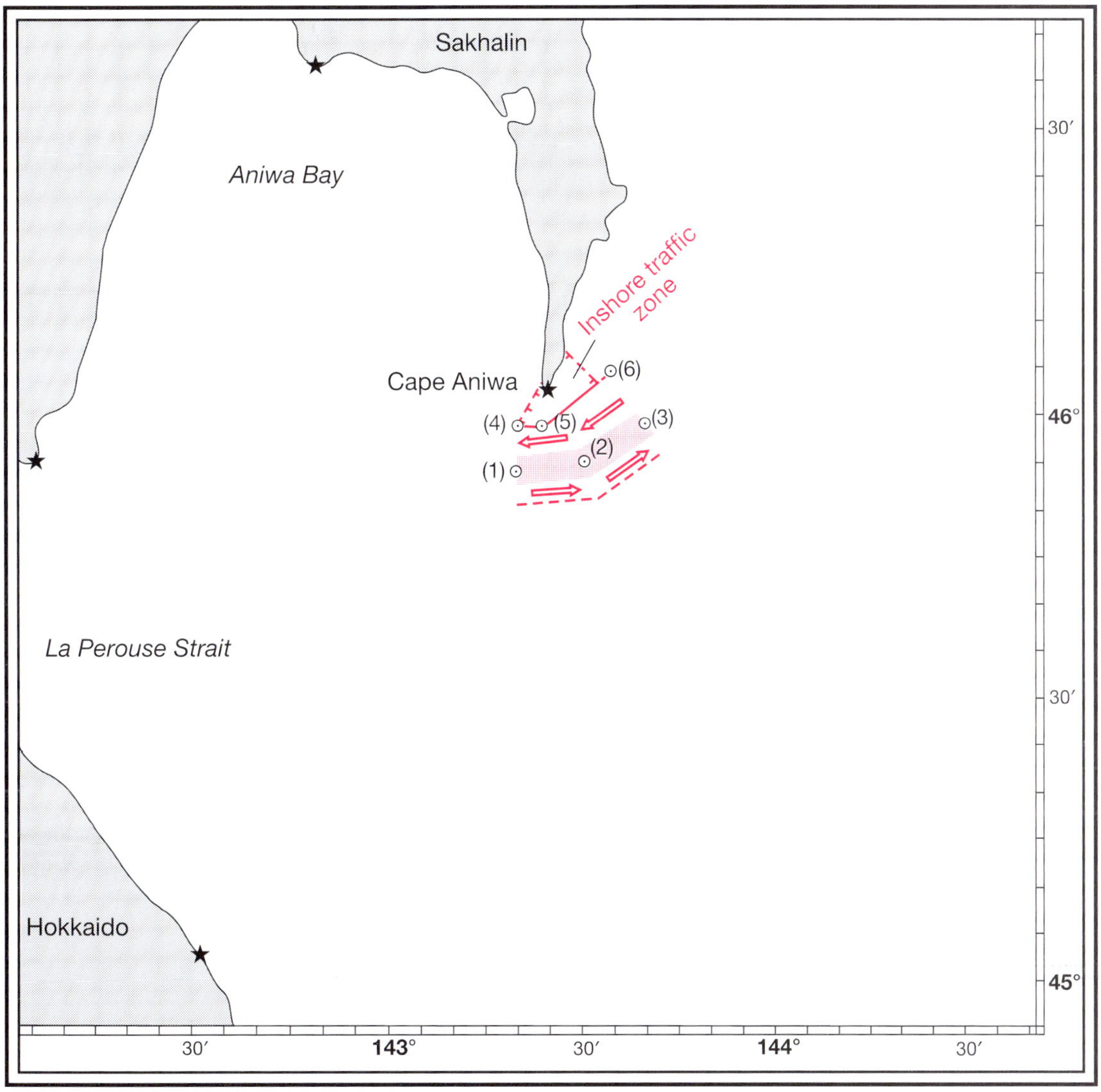

OFF THE ANIWA CAPE

IN THE APPROACHES TO THE GULF OF NAKHODKA

(Reference charts: USSR 700, 1978 edition; 1063, 1989 edition.
Note: These charts are based on the single geodetic datum for Soviet nautical charts.)

Description of the traffic separation scheme

The traffic separation scheme consists of two parts:

Part I

(a) A roundabout consists of a circular traffic separation zone, two miles in diameter, centred upon the following geographical position:

42°38′.30 N, 132°56′.20 E

and a circular traffic lane two miles wide.

(b) A separation line connects the following geographical positions:

(1)	42°34′.80 N,	132°56′.30 E	(2)	42°27′.00 N,	132°56′.30 E

(c) A traffic lane, one mile wide, is established on each side of the separation line.

(d) A separation zone is bounded by lines connecting the following geographical positions:

(2)	42°27′.00 N,	132°56′.30 E	(4)	42°10′.00 N,	132°59′.40 E
(3)	42°10′.00 N,	132°52′.80 E			

(e) An outside boundary of the traffic lane east of the separation zone connects the following geographical positions:

(5)	42°10′.00 N,	133°02′.20 E	(6)	42°27′.00 N,	132°57′.60 E

(f) An outside boundary of the traffic lane west of the separation zone connects the following geographical positions:

(7)	42°27′.00 N,	132°55′.00 E	(8)	42°10′.00 N,	132°50′.20 E

Part II

(a) A separation zone, one mile wide, is centred upon the following geographical positions:

(9)	42°36′.20 N,	132°58′.90 E	(11)	42°33′.50 N,	133°07′.30 E
(10)	42°33′.50 N,	133°02′.90 E			

(b) A traffic lane, one and a half miles wide, is established south of the separation zone.

(c) An outside boundary of the traffic lane north of the separation zone connects the following geographical positions:

(12)	42°35′.50 N,	133°07′.30 E	(14)	42°37′.40 N,	133°00′.20 E
(13)	42°35′.50 N,	133°03′.00 E			

(d) A separation zone is bounded by lines connecting the following geographical positions:

(12)	42°35′.50 N,	133°07′.30 E	(15)	42°39′.00 N,	133°00′.40 E
(13)	42°35′.50 N,	133°03′.00 E	(16)	42°39′.00 N,	133°07′.30 E
(14)	42°37′.40 N,	133°00′.20 E			

Inshore traffic zone

The area between the north-eastern landward boundary of the roundabout and the northern boundary of the separation zone and the Russian Federation coast, and lying between a line drawn from position 42°41′.30 N, 133°07′.30 E, to position 42°39′.00 N, 133°07′.30 E (eastern limit) and a line drawn from position 42°40′.80 N, 132°58′.50 E to position 42°43′.50 N, 132°57′.20 E and then to position 42°42′.80 N, 132°59′.90 E (north-western limit), is designated as an inshore traffic zone.

CAUTION:

While navigating within the traffic separation scheme, ships should strictly keep within traffic-lane boundaries.

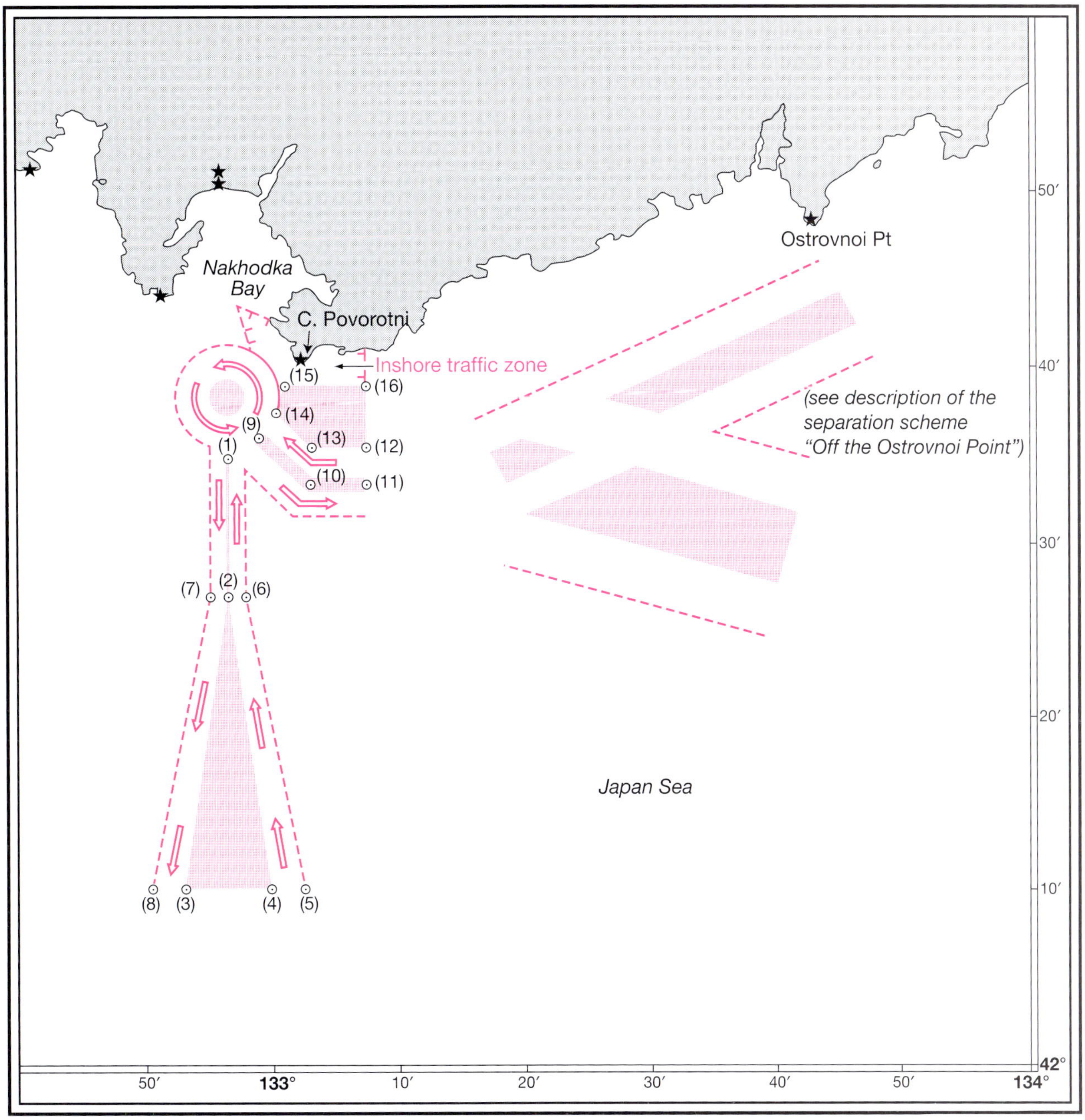

IN THE APPROACHES TO THE GULF OF NAKHODKA

OFF THE OSTROVNOI POINT

(Reference chart: USSR 700, 1975 edition.
Note: This chart is based on the single geodetic datum for Soviet nautical charts.)

Description of the traffic separation scheme

The traffic separation scheme consists of two parts:

Part I

(a) Two separation zones are bounded by lines connecting the following geographical positions:

(i)	(1) 42°35′.20 N,	133°17′.50 E	(3)	42°35′.20 N,	133°24′.40 E
	(2) 42°36′.00 N,	133°20′.00 E	(4)	42°33′.40 N,	133°18′.50 E
and (ii)	(5) 42°38′.30 N,	133°26′.50 E	(7)	42°42′.80 N,	133°46′.80 E
	(6) 42°44′.60 N,	133°45′.70 E	(8)	42°37′.40 N,	133°30′.80 E

(b) A traffic lane, two miles wide, is established on each side of the separation zones.

Part II

(a) A separation zone is bounded by lines connecting the following geographical positions:

(9)	42°31′.50 N,	133°20′.00 E	(11)	42°32′.10 N,	133°42′.00 E
(10)	42°34′.50 N,	133°28′.60 E	(12)	42°27′.80 N,	133°40′.40 E

(b) A traffic lane, three miles wide, is established on each side of the separation zone.

CAUTION:

The traffic lane north of the separation zone (lane between points (5) and (6)) in part I is designated for the navigation of Soviet ships only.

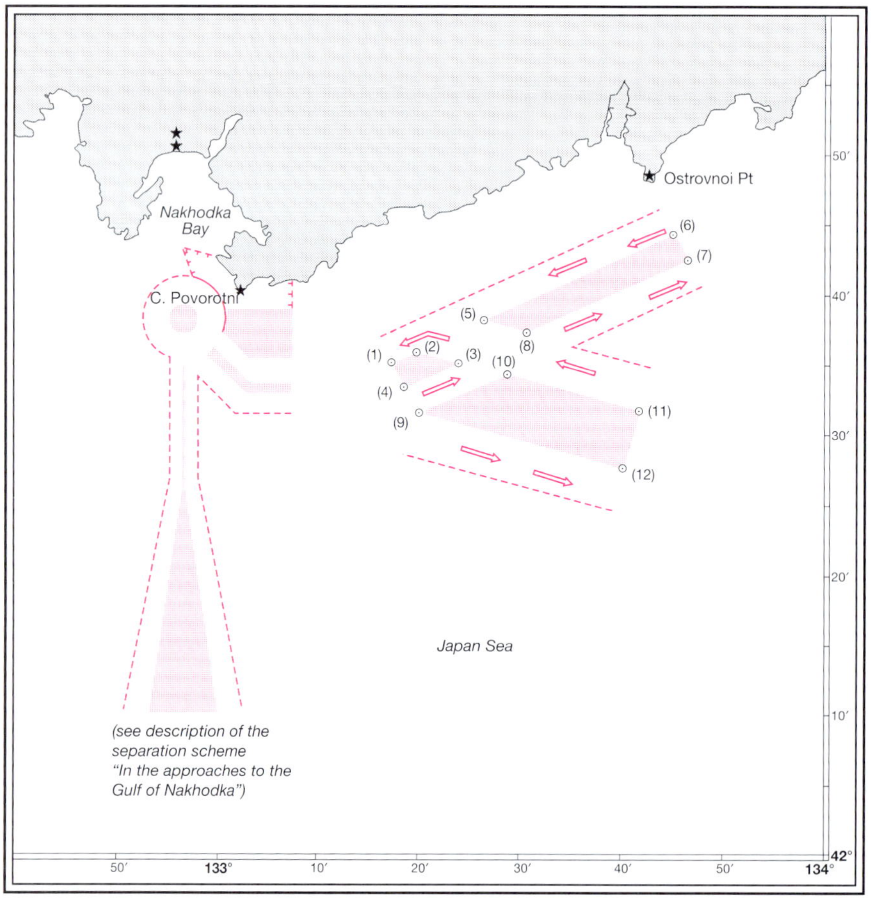

OFF THE OSTROVNOI POINT

IN THE WATERS OFF CHENGSHAN JIAO PROMONTORY

Note: see mandatory ship reporting system "Off Chengshan Jiao Promontory" in part G, section I.

(Reference charts: Chinese charts 9701, 9304, and 9305.
Note: These charts are based on World Geodetic System 1984 datum (WGS 84).)

The ships' routeing system in the waters off Chengshan Jiao promontory consists of the traffic separation scheme, the inshore traffic zone and the precautionary area.

Description of the traffic separation scheme

(a) The separation zone, two nautical miles wide, is centred upon the line connecting the following geographical positions:

(1)	37°31′.18 N,	122°45′.40 E	(3)	37°11′.60 N,	122°49′.68 E
(2)	37°25′.29 N,	122°49′.68 E			

(b) The inner limit of the traffic separation scheme is the line connecting the following geographical positions:

(4)	37°29′.69 N,	122°42′.13 E	(6)	37°11′.60 N,	122°45′.91 E
(5)	37°24′.49 N,	122°45′.91 E			

(c) The outer limit of the traffic separation scheme is the line connecting the following geographical positions:

(7)	37°32′.69 N,	122°48′.68 E	(9)	37°11′.60 N,	122°53′.46 E
(8)	37°26′.09 N,	122°53′.46 E			

(d) The traffic lane for northbound traffic, two miles wide, is established between the separation zone and the outer limit of the traffic separation scheme.

(e) The traffic lane for southbound traffic, two miles wide, is established between the separation zone and the inner limit of the traffic separation scheme.

Inshore traffic zone

The inshore traffic zone is the waters between the inner limit of the traffic separation scheme and the adjacent coast.

Precautionary area

The precautionary area is the area with the geographical position 37°34′.65 N, 122°42′.88 E as the centre and 5 miles as the radius.

(chartlet overleaf)

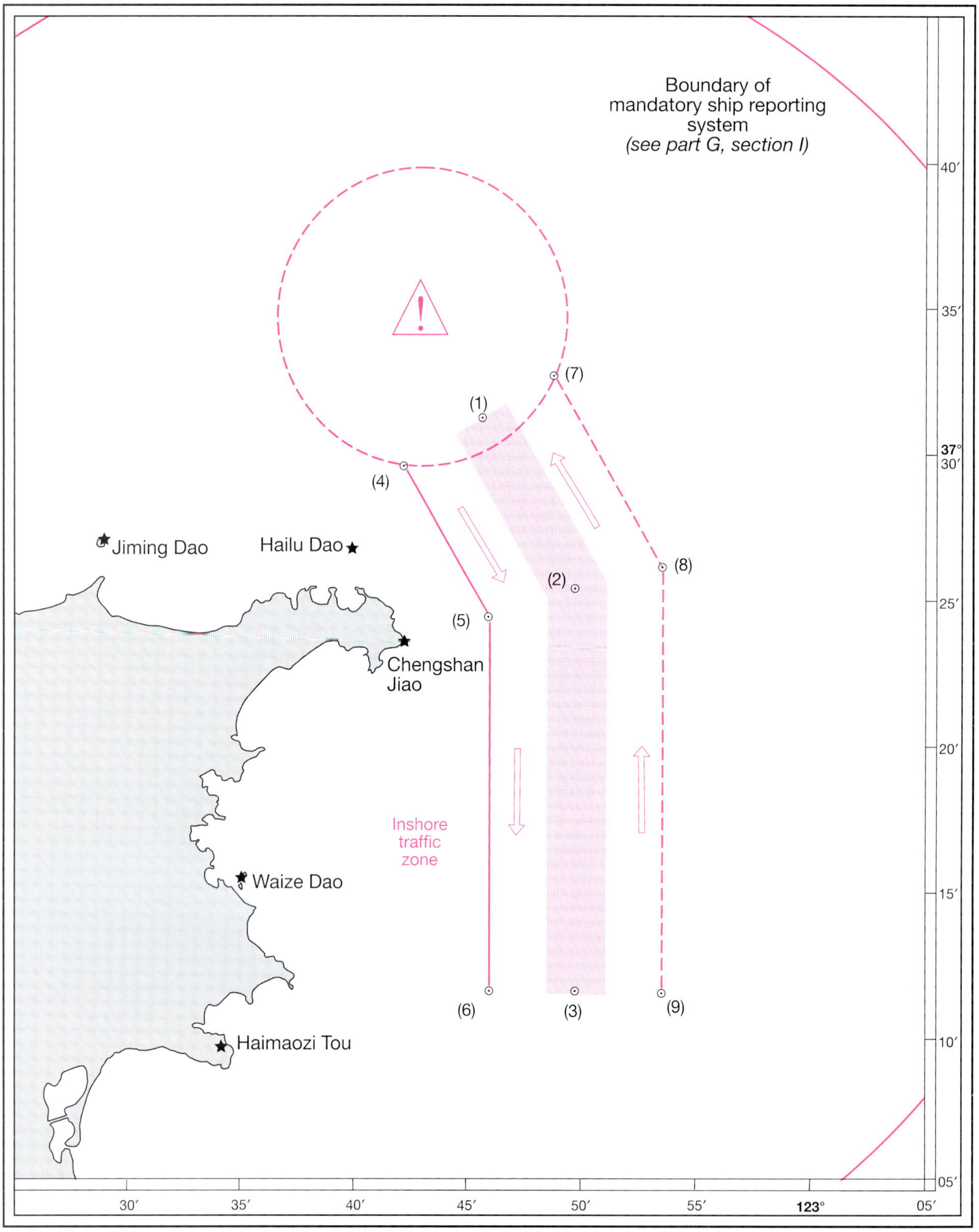

IN THE WATERS OFF CHENGSHAN JIAO PROMONTORY

B

Section XI

Eastern North Atlantic and South Atlantic Oceans

Caution: The chartlets are for illustrative purposes only and must not be used for navigation. Mariners should consult the appropriate nautical publications and charts for up-to-date details on aids to navigation and other relevant information.

Warning: The geographical positions given in the descriptions of the routeing systems are only correct for charts using the same geodetic datum as the reference charts indicated under each scheme. Charts published by other hydrographic offices may use a different geodetic datum, as may new editions of the reference charts published after the adoption of the routeing system. Where amendments to existing systems are not based on the same geodetic datum as the original system, this is emphasized by the use of different colours for definitions of positions.

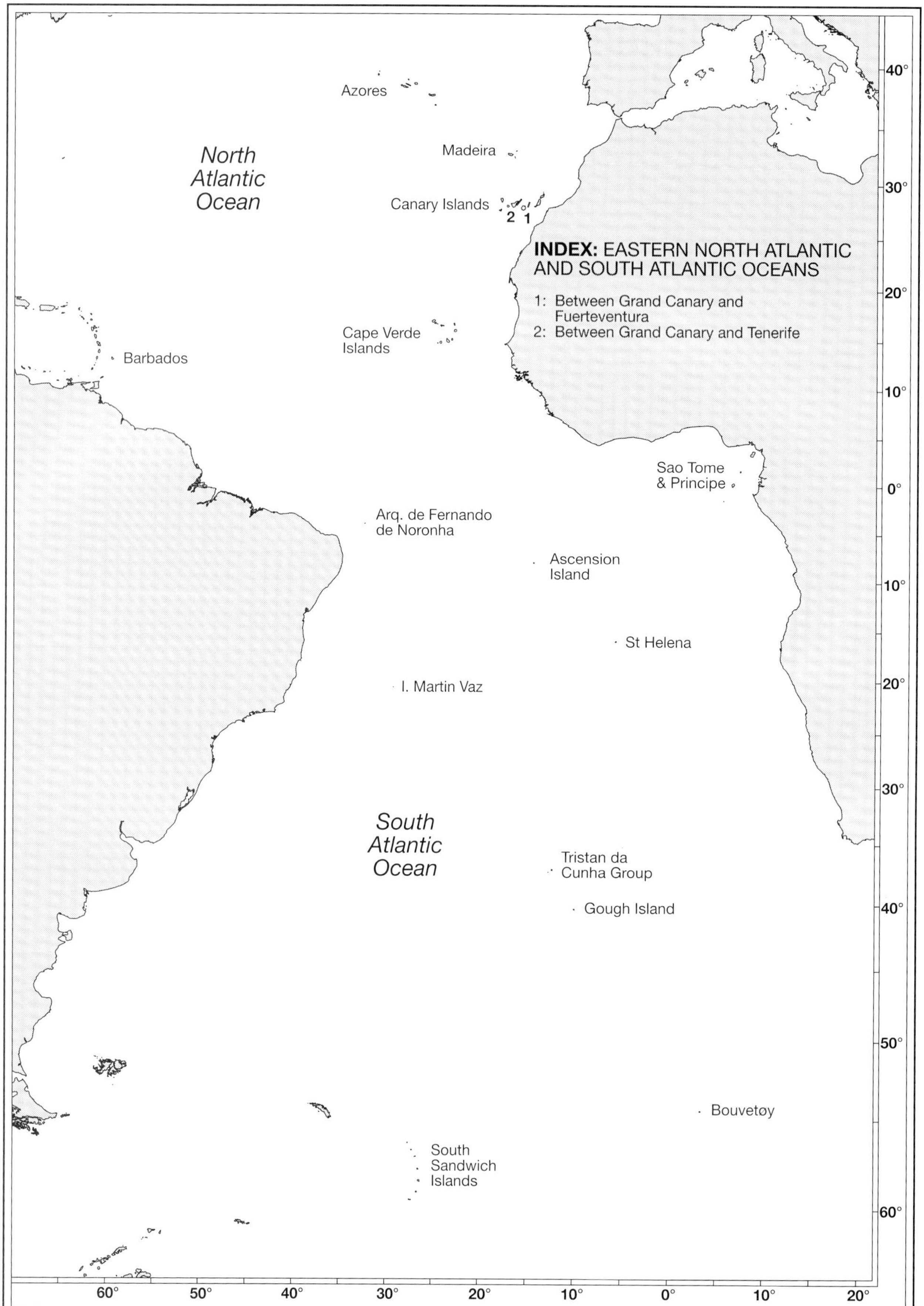
INDEX: EASTERN NORTH ATLANTIC AND SOUTH ATLANTIC OCEANS
1: Between Grand Canary and Fuerteventura
2: Between Grand Canary and Tenerife
North Atlantic Ocean
South Atlantic Ocean
Azores
Madeira
Canary Islands
2 1
Barbados
Cape Verde Islands
Sao Tome & Principe
Arq. de Fernando de Noronha
Ascension Island
St Helena
I. Martin Vaz
Tristan da Cunha Group
Gough Island
Bouvetøy
South Sandwich Islands
40°
30°
20°
10°
0°
10°
20°
30°
40°
50°
60°
60°
50°
40°
30°
20°
10°
0°
10°
20°

BETWEEN GRAND CANARY AND FUERTEVENTURA

Note: See mandatory ship reporting system "The Canary Islands" in part G, section I.

(Reference chart: Spanish Navy Hydrographical Institute 209, second edition (12th impression of September 2003).
Note: This chart is based on World Geodetic System 1984 datum (WGS 84).)

Description of the traffic separation scheme

(a) A separation line connecting the following geographical positions:

(3)	28°20′.47 N,	014°56′.91 W	(5)	28°02′.90 N,	015°04′.17 W
(4)	28°12′.30 N,	015°00′.29 W	(6)	27°51′.62 N,	015°08′.81 W

(b) An intermediate traffic separation zone bounded by the lines connecting the following geographical positions:

	(8)	27°50′.60 N,	015°05′.63 W	(12)	28°01′.26 N,	014°58′.91 W
	(9)	28°01′.87 N,	015°00′.98 W	(13)	27°49′.99 N,	015°03′.55 W
and	(10)	28°11′.27 N,	014°57′.10 W	(14)	28°20′.06 N,	014°51′.15 W
	(11)	28°20′.20 N,	014°53′.41 W	(15)	28°10′.66 N,	014°55′.03 W

(c) A traffic lane for southbound traffic on a 200° (T) course is established between the separation line/zone described in paragraphs (a) and (b) above.

(d) A line of separation from the inshore traffic zone, connecting the following geographical positions:

(16)	27°48′.96 N,	015°00′.36 W	(18)	28°09′.63 N,	014°51′.84 W
(17)	28°00′.24 N,	014°55′.72 W	(19)	28°19′.78 N,	014°47′.76 W

(e) A traffic lane for northbound traffic on a 020° (T) course is established between the separation line/zone described in paragraphs (b) and (d) above.

Precautionary area

(f) A precautionary area bounded by a line connecting the geographical positions (4), (5), (17) and (18).

Inshore traffic zones

(g) An inshore traffic zone between the east coast of Grand Canary island and a line joining the following geographical positions:

(1) La Isleta light (28°10′.40 N, 015°25′.00 W)
(2) 28°22′.00 N, 015°19′.00 W
(3) 28°20′.47 N, 014°56′.91 W
(4) 28°12′.30 N, 015°00′.29 W
(5) 28°02′.90 N, 015°04′.17 W
(6) 27°51′.62 N, 015°08′.81 W
(7) Punta Arinaga light (27°51′.70 N, 015°23′.00 W)

(h) An inshore traffic zone bounded by a line joining the following geographical positions:

(16) 27°48′.96 N, 015°00′.36 W
(17) 28°00′.24 N, 014°55′.72 W
(18) 28°09′.63 N, 014°51′.84 W
(19) 28°19′.78 N, 014°47′.76 W
(20) 28°19′.00 N, 014°36′.00 W
(21) Punta Jandia light (28°03′.80 N, 014°30′.30 W)
(22) 27°45′.00 N, 014°44′.00 W
(16) 27°48′.96 N, 015°00′.36 W

Note: Ships that so wish may give voluntary notification of entry to and departure from the traffic separation scheme via the Las Palmas Regional MRCC, using VHF channel 16.

(chartlet overleaf)

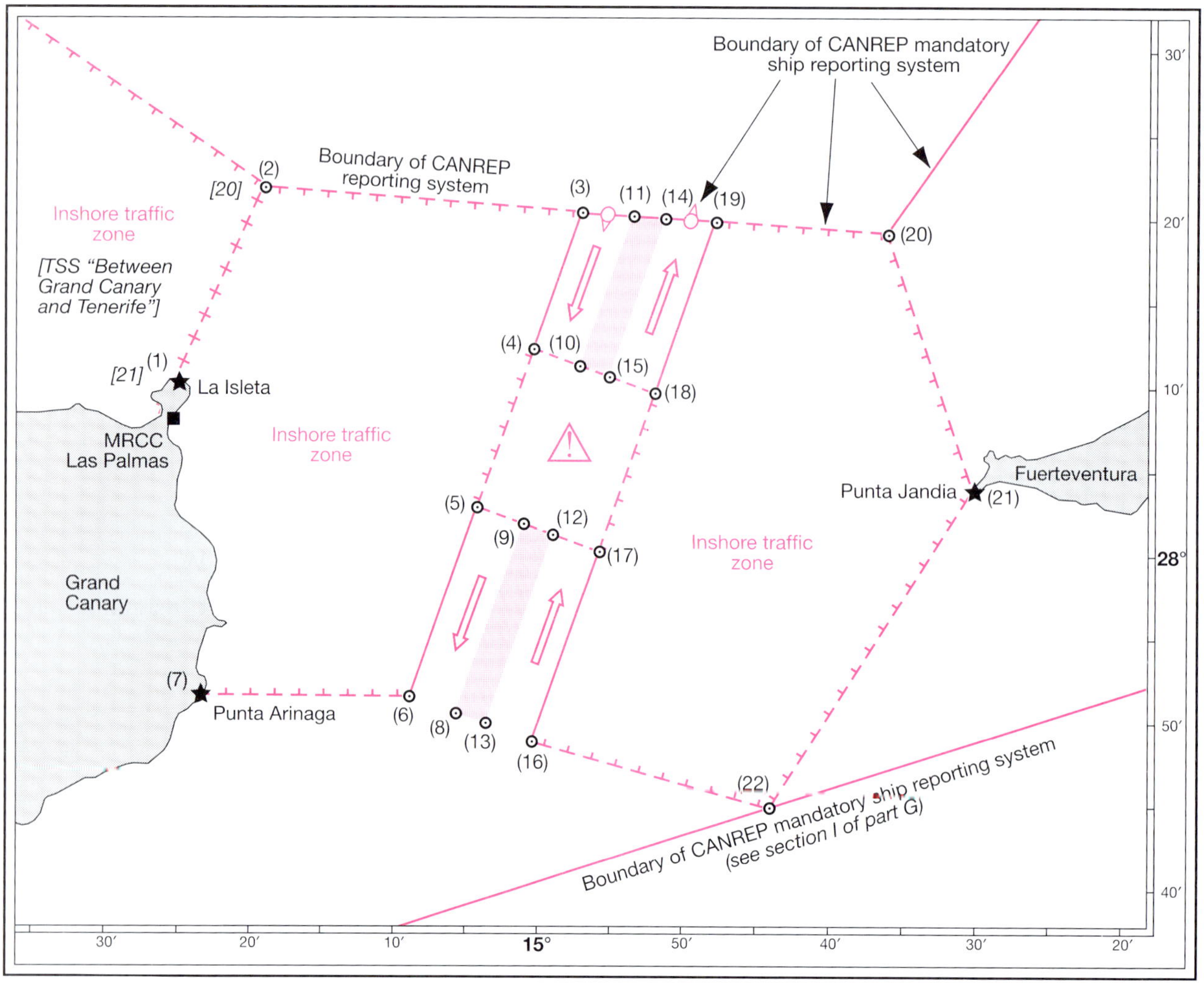

BETWEEN GRAND CANARY AND FUERTEVENTURA

BETWEEN GRAND CANARY AND TENERIFE

Note: See mandatory ship reporting system "The Canary Islands" in part G, section I.

(Reference chart: Spanish Navy Hydrographical Institute 209, second edition (12th impression of September 2003).
Note: This chart is based on World Geodetic System 1984 datum (WGS 84).)

Description of the traffic separation scheme

(a) A separation line, connecting the following geographical positions:

(3)	28°38′.01 N,	015°46′.66 W	(5)	28°18′.86 N,	016°04′.94 W
(4)	28°27′.28 N,	015°56′.90 W	(6)	28°03′.54 N,	016°19′.52 W

(b) An intermediate traffic separation zone bounded by the lines connecting the following geographical positions:

(8)	28°01′.61 N,	016°16′.92 W	(12)	28°15′.83 N,	016°01′.00 W
(9)	28°16′.93 N,	016°02′.34 W	(13)	28°00′.51 N,	016°15′.58 W

and

(10)	28°25′.36 N,	015°54′.30 W	(14)	28°35′.44 N,	015°42′.33 W
(11)	28°36′.33 N,	015°43′.84 W	(15)	28°24′.26 N,	015°52′.97 W

(c) A traffic lane for southbound traffic on a 220° (T) course is established between the separation line/zones described in paragraphs (a) and (b) above.

(d) A line of separation from the inshore traffic zone, connecting the following geographical positions:

(16)	27°58′.58 N,	016°12′.96 W	(18)	28°22′.33 N,	015°50′.37 W
(17)	28°13′.90 N,	015°58′.40 W	(19)	28°33′.81 N,	015°39′.43 W

(e) A traffic lane for northbound traffic on a 040° (T) course is established between the separation line/zone described in paragraphs (b) and (d) above.

Precautionary area

(f) A precautionary area bounded by the line connecting the geographical positions (4), (5), (17) and (18).

Inshore traffic zones

(g) An inshore traffic zone between the east coast of Santa Cruz de Tenerife island and a line connecting the following geographical positions:

(1) Punta Anaga light (28°34′.80 N, 016°08′.30 W)
(2) 28°48′.00 N, 016°04′.00 W
(3) 28°38′.01 N, 015°46′.66 W
(4) 28°27′.28 N, 015°56′.90 W
(5) 28°18′.86 N, 016°04′.94 W
(6) 28°03′.54 N, 016°19′.52 W
(7) Punta Roja (28°01′.48 N, 016°32′.88 W)

(h) An inshore traffic zone between the west coast of Grand Canary island and a line connecting the following geographical positions:

(16) 27°58′.58 N, 016°12′.98 W
(17) 28°13′.90 N, 015°58′.40 W
(18) 28°22′.33 N, 015°50′.37 W
(19) 28°33′.81 N, 015°39′.43 W
(20) 28°22′.00 N, 015°19′.00 W
(21) La Isleta light (28°10′.40 N, 015°25′.00 W)
(22) 28°00′.00 N, 015°49′.18 W
(23) 28°00′.00 N, 016°00′.00 W
(24) 27°44′.00 N, 016°00′.00 W

Note: Ships that so wish may give voluntary notification of entry to and departure from the traffic separation scheme via Tenerife MRCC, using VHF channel 16.

(chartlet overleaf)

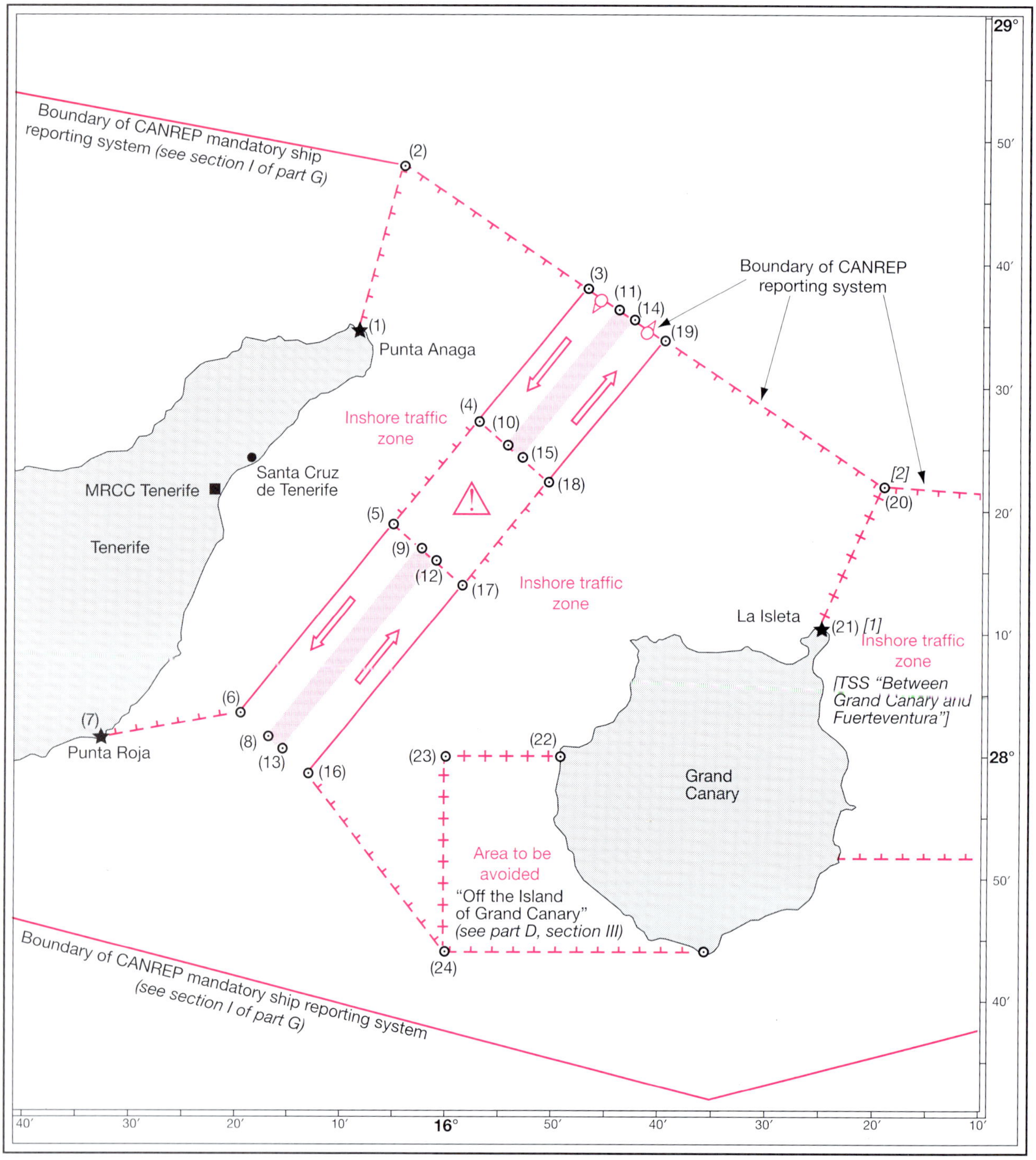

BETWEEN GRAND CANARY AND TENERIFE

Part C

Deep-water routes

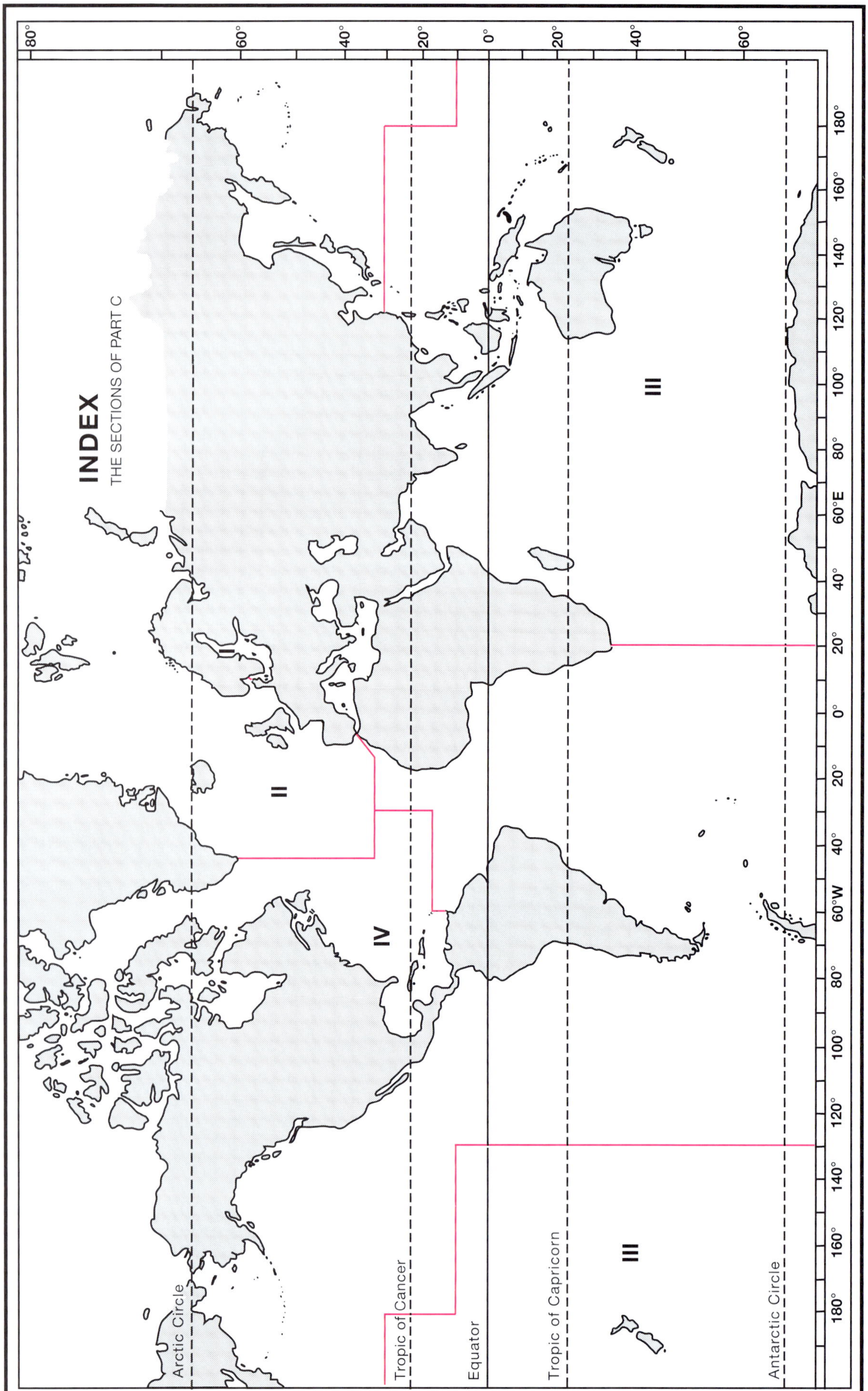
INDEX
THE SECTIONS OF PART C
Arctic Circle
Tropic of Cancer
Equator
Tropic of Capricorn
Antarctic Circle
I
II
III
IV
III
80°
60°
40°
20°
0°
20°
40°
60°
180°
160°
140°
120°
100°
80°
60°W
40°
20°
0°
20°
40°
60°E
80°
100°
120°
140°
160°
180°

C

Section I

Baltic Sea and adjacent waters

Caution: The chartlets are for illustrative purposes only and must not be used for navigation. Mariners should consult the appropriate nautical publications and charts for up-to-date details on aids to navigation and other relevant information.

Warning: The geographical positions given in the descriptions of the deep-water routes are only correct for charts using the same geodetic datum as the reference charts indicated under each scheme. Charts published by other hydrographic offices may use a different geodetic datum, as may new editions of the reference charts published after the adoption of the routes. Where amendments to existing routes are not based on the same geodetic datum as the original route or where positions are defined relative to two geodetic datums, this is emphasized by the use of different colours for definitions of positions.

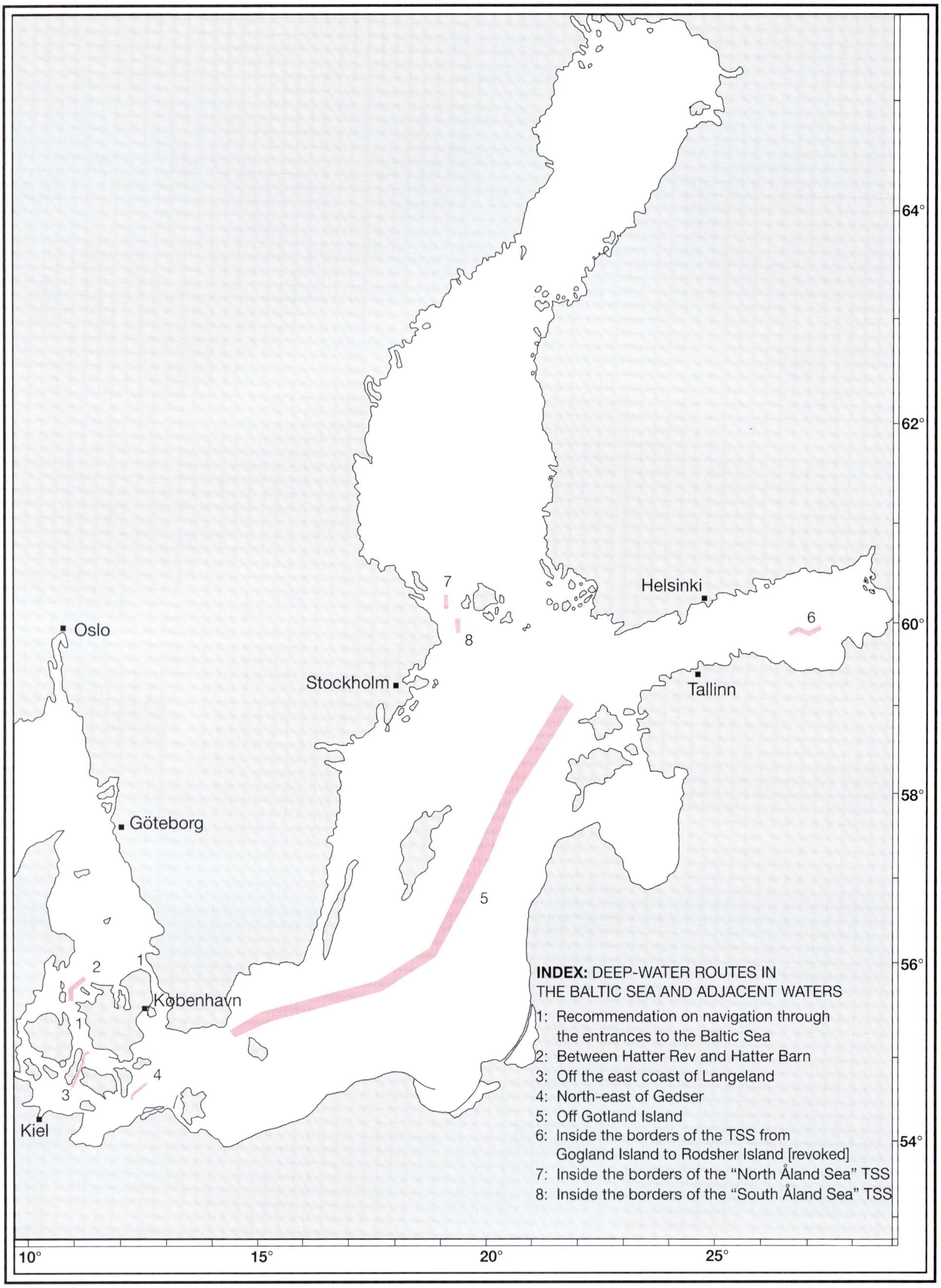
64°
62°
60°
58°
56°
54°
10°
15°
20°
25°
Oslo
Göteborg
Stockholm
Helsinki
Tallinn
København
Kiel
1
2
3
4
5
6
7
8
INDEX: DEEP-WATER ROUTES IN THE BALTIC SEA AND ADJACENT WATERS
1: Recommendation on navigation through the entrances to the Baltic Sea
2: Between Hatter Rev and Hatter Barn
3: Off the east coast of Langeland
4: North-east of Gedser
5: Off Gotland Island
6: Inside the borders of the TSS from Gogland Island to Rodsher Island [revoked]
7: Inside the borders of the "North Åland Sea" TSS
8: Inside the borders of the "South Åland Sea" TSS

RECOMMENDATION ON NAVIGATION THROUGH THE ENTRANCES TO THE BALTIC SEA

Route T

1 When passing through the entrances to the Baltic Sea, ships should note that the maximum obtainable depth in most parts of Route T is 17 metres. However, in some areas the maximum obtainable depth is to some extent permanently reduced due to sand migration.

2 The effect of sea level variations caused by a combination of tide and meteorological conditions together with unknown obstructions on the sea bottom and sand migration could decrease the depth by as much as 2 metres. Bearing these facts in mind, ships should:

.1 not pass the area unless they have a draught with which it is safe to navigate, taking into account draught-increasing effects such as squat effect and the effect of a course alteration, etc.;

.2 exhibit the signal prescribed in rule 28 of the International Regulations for Preventing Collisions at Sea, 1972, as amended, in certain areas in the Storebælt (Great Belt), Hatter Rev, Vengeancegrund and in the narrow route east of Langeland, when constrained by their draught.

3 Ships with a draught of 11 metres or more should, furthermore:

.1 use for the passage the pilotage services locally established by the coastal States; and

.2 be aware that anchoring may be necessary owing to the weather and sea conditions in relation to the size and draught of the ship and the sea level and, in this respect, take special account of the information available from the pilot and from radio navigation information services in the area.

4 Ships, irrespective of size or draught, carrying a shipment of irradiated nuclear fuel, plutonium or high-level radioactive wastes (INF Code materials) should:

.1 use for the passage the pilotage services locally established by the coastal States.

5 Shipowners and masters should consider the full potential of new and improved navigation equipment required in SOLAS chapter V, including Electronic Chart Display and Information Systems (ECDIS), when navigating these narrow waters.

Note: See mandatory ship reporting system "In the Storebælt (Great Belt) Traffic area" in part G, section I.

The Sound

1 Loaded oil tankers with a draught of 7 metres or more, loaded chemical tankers and gas carriers, irrespective of size, and ships carrying a shipment of irradiated nuclear fuel, plutonium or high-level radioactive wastes (INF Code materials), when navigating The Sound between a line connecting Svinbådan lighthouse and Hornbæk Harbour and a line connecting Skanör Harbour and Aflandshage (the southernmost point of Amager Island), should:

.1 use the pilotage services established by the Governments of Denmark and Sweden;

.2 be aware that anchoring may be necessary owing to the weather and sea conditions in relation to the size and draught of the ship and the sea level and, in this respect, take special account of the information available from the pilot and from radio navigation information services in the area.

2 Shipowners and masters should consider the full potential of new and improved navigation equipment required in SOLAS chapter V, including Electronic Chart Display and Information Systems (ECDIS), when navigating these narrow waters.

Note: See mandatory ship reporting system "In the Sound between Denmark and Sweden" in part G, section I.

(chartlets overleaf)

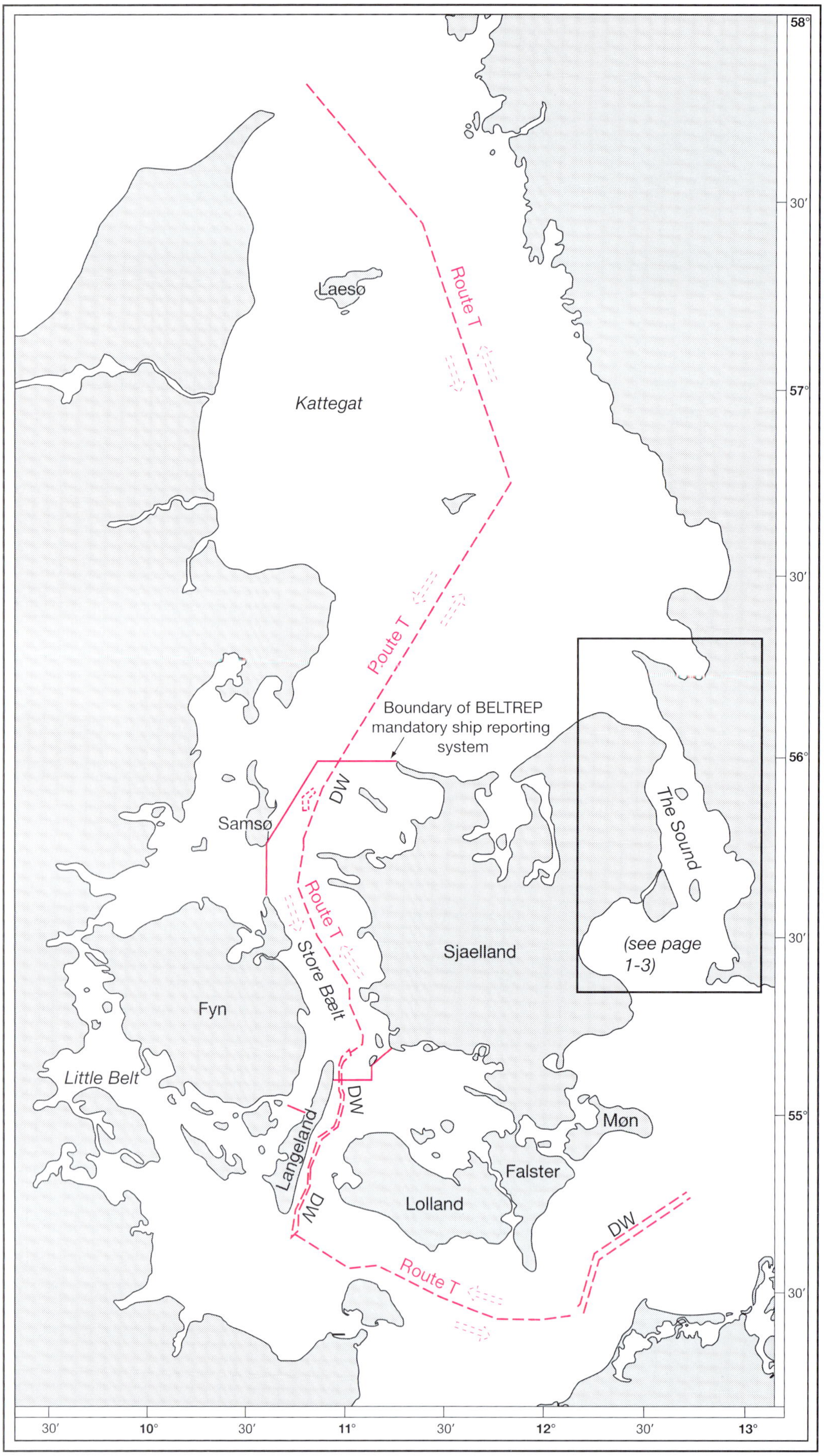

58°
30′
57°
30′
56°
30′
55°
30′
30′
10°
30′
11°
30′
12°
30′
13°
Laeso
Kattegat
Route T
Route T
Boundary of BELTREP mandatory ship reporting system
DW
Samsø
Route T
Store Bælt
Sjaelland
The Sound
(see page 1-3)
Fyn
Little Belt
DW
Langeland
DW
Møn
Falster
Lolland
DW
Route T

ROUTE T

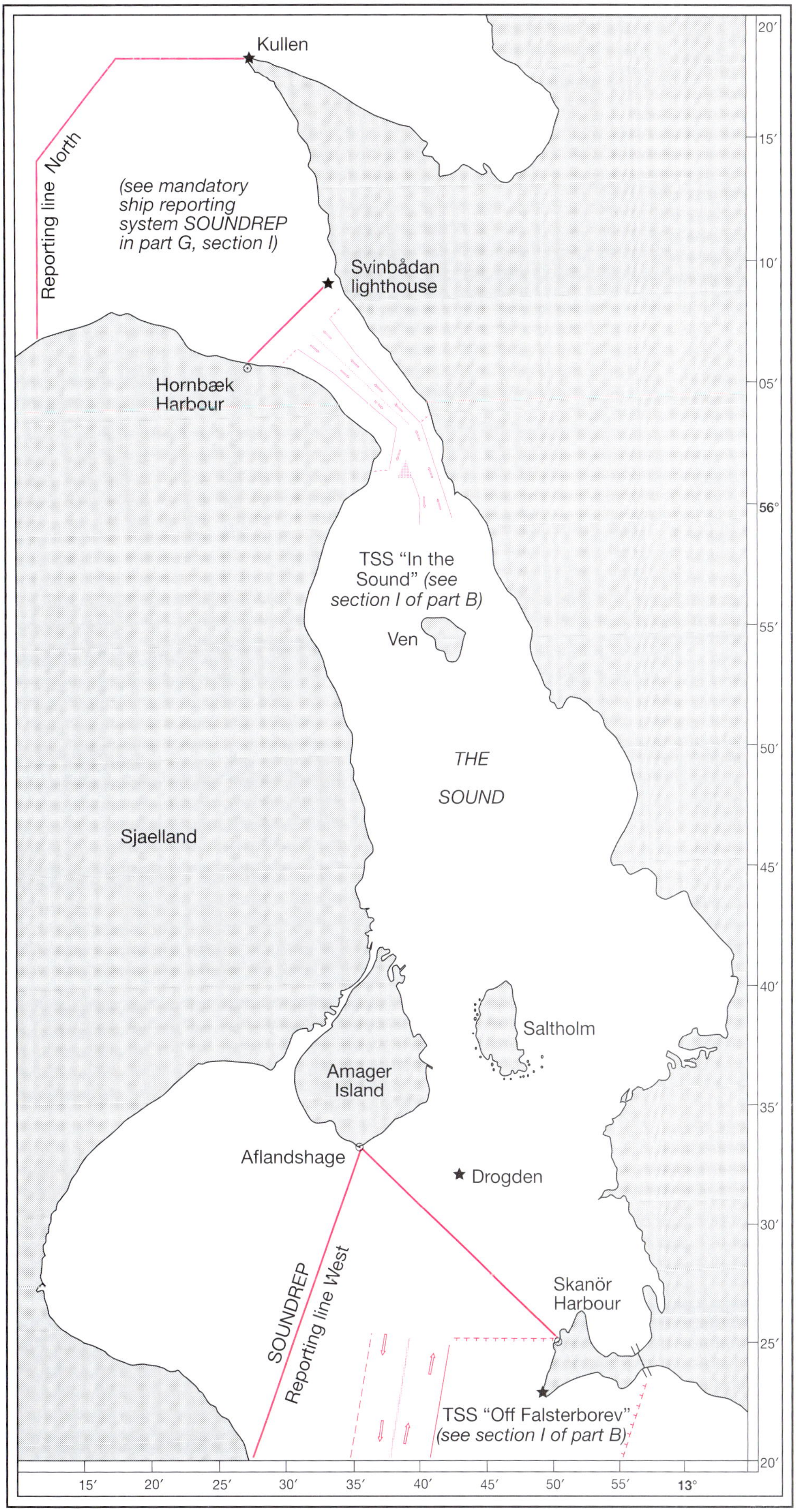
Kullen
Reporting line North
(see mandatory ship reporting system SOUNDREP in part G, section I)
Svinbådan lighthouse
Hornbæk Harbour
TSS "In the Sound" (see section I of part B)
Ven
THE SOUND
Sjaelland
Saltholm
Amager Island
Aflandshage
Drogden
SOUNDREP Reporting line West
Skanör Harbour
TSS "Off Falsterborev" (see section I of part B)
20′
15′
10′
05′
56°
55′
50′
45′
40′
35′
30′
25′
20′
15′
20′
25′
30′
35′
40′
45′
50′
55′
13°

THE SOUND

DEEP-WATER ROUTE BETWEEN HATTER REV AND HATTER BARN

Note: See mandatory ship reporting system "In the Storebælt (Great Belt) Traffic area" in part G, section I and "Recommendation on navigation through the entrances to the Baltic Sea".

(Reference chart: Danish 128, 1985 edition.
Note: This chart is based on European datum.)

Description of the deep-water route

A deep-water route with a minimum depth of water below mean sea level of 19 metres is bounded by lines connecting the following geographical positions:

(i)	55°55′.52 N,	010°56′.68 E	(v)	55°50′.58 N,	010°49′.42 E
(ii)	55°54′.15 N,	010°51′.78 E	(vi)	55°53′.20 N,	010°49′.60 E
(iii)	55°53′.40 N,	010°48′.30 E	(vii)	55°54′.65 N,	010°55′.39 E
(iv)	55°50′.61 N,	010°48′.07 E			

Note: Ships which are not obliged by reason of their draught (13 metres or less) to use the deep-water route should use the traffic separation scheme which lies east of that route and where there is a minimum depth of water below mean sea level of 15 metres.

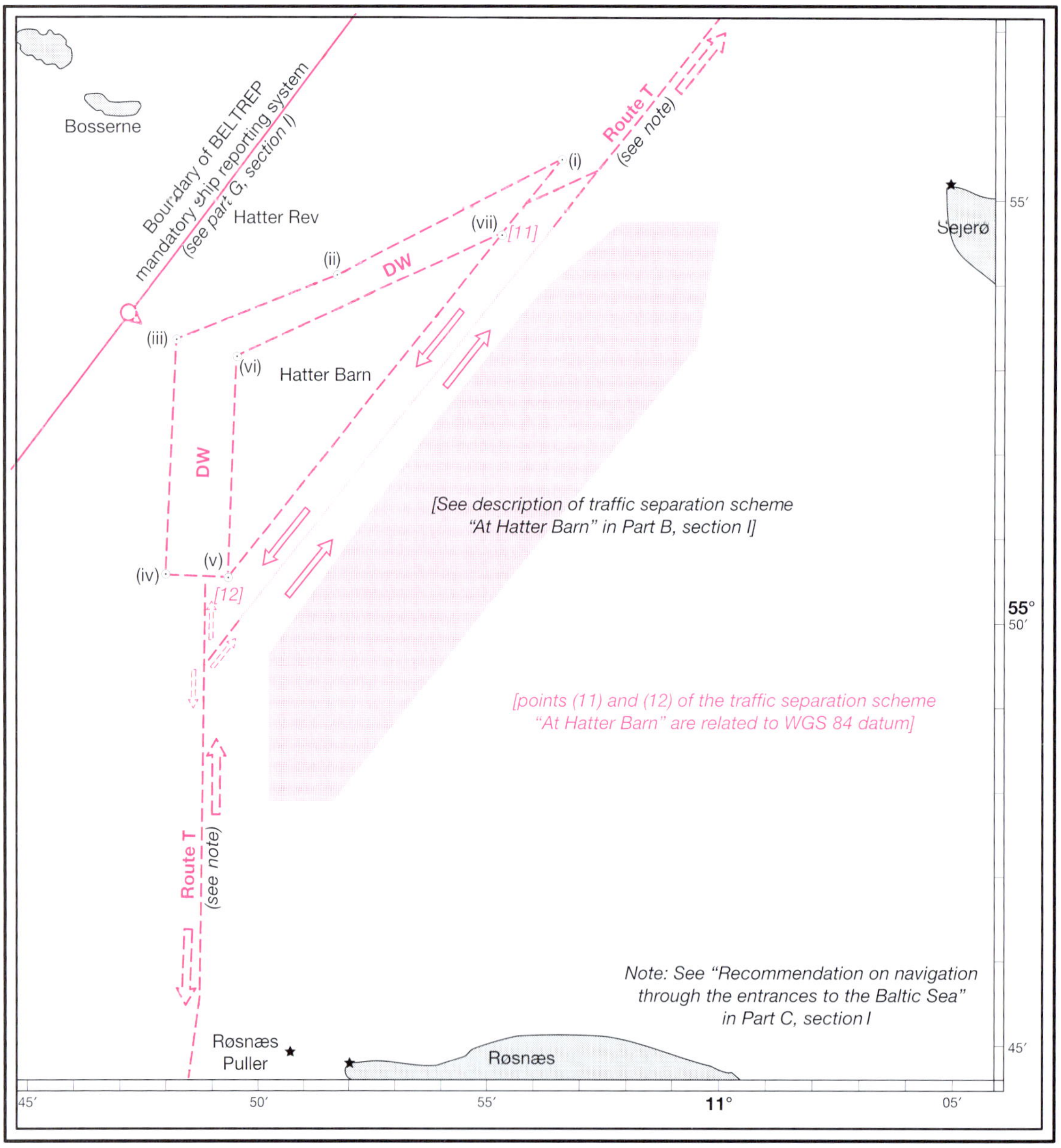

DEEP-WATER ROUTE BETWEEN HATTER REV AND HATTER BARN

DEEP-WATER ROUTE OFF THE EAST COAST OF LANGELAND*

Note: See mandatory ship reporting system "In the Storebælt (Great Belt) Traffic area" in part G, section I and "Recommendation on navigation through the entrances to the Baltic Sea" in part C, section I.

(Reference charts: Danish 142, 1985 edition; 196, 1989 edition.
Note: These charts are based on European datum.)

Description of the deep-water route

A deep-water route with a minimum depth of water below mean sea level of 19 metres is bounded by a line connecting the following geographical positions:

(1)	55°11′.30 N,	011°02′.10 E	(14)	54°41′.20 N,	010°47′.10 E
(2)	55°10′.30 N,	011°00′.00 E	(15)	54°44′.10 N,	010°47′.30 E
(3)	55°08′.90 N,	010°59′.10 E	(16)	54°48′.30 N,	010°50′.30 E
(4)	55°04′.40 N,	010°59′.00 E	(17)	54°52′.50 N,	010°50′.60 E
(5)	55°03′.90 N,	010°59′.50 E	(18)	54°56′.30 N,	010°53′.80 E
(6)	55°02′.40 N,	010°59′.60 E	(19)	54°58′.40 N,	010°58′.60 E
(7)	54°59′.20 N,	010°58′.10 E	(20)	55°01′.80 N,	011°00′.20 E
(8)	54°58′.40 N,	010°57′.40 E	(21)	55°04′.00 N,	011°00′.50 E
(9)	54°56′.60 N,	010°52′.60 E	(22)	55°04′.80 N,	010°59′.80 E
(10)	54°52′.70 N,	010°50′.20 E	(23)	55°08′.60 N,	010°59′.90 E
(11)	54°48′.20 N,	010°49′.80 E	(24)	55°09′.40 N,	011°00′.50 E
(12)	54°44′.30 N,	010°46′.40 E	(25)	55°10′.40 N,	011°02′.70 E
(13)	54°40′.20 N,	010°45′.30 E			

Note: The deep-water route is intended for use by ships which, because of their draught, are unable to navigate safely in areas outside the deep-water route.
Ships with a draught of 10 metres or less should use the nationally recommended Route H, which lies to the east. The recommended Route H has a minimum depth of water below mean sea level of 12 metres.
Ship masters should take into account the information given in *Recommendation on navigation through the entrances to the Baltic Sea* in part C, section I.

(chartlet overleaf)

* Date of implementation of amended measure: 0000 hours UTC on 1 December 2012.

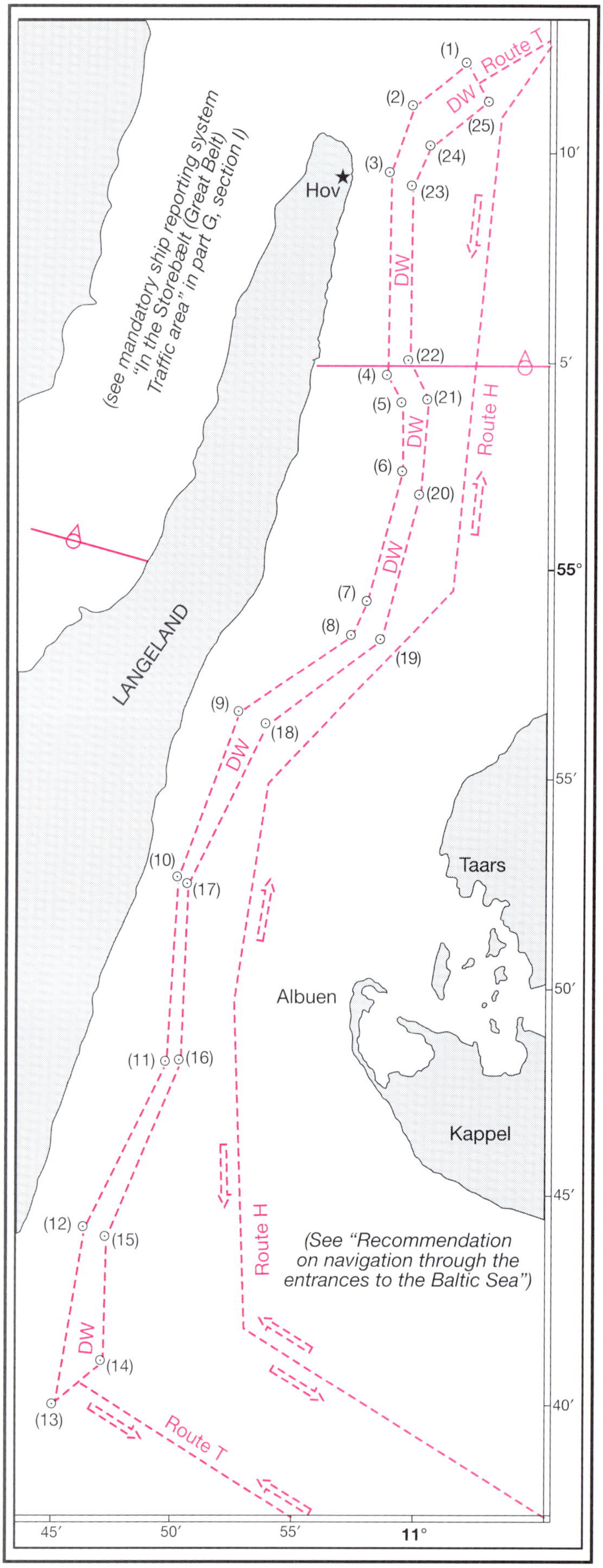

DEEP-WATER ROUTE OFF THE EAST COAST OF LANGELAND

DEEP-WATER ROUTE NORTH-EAST OF GEDSER

Note: See "Recommendation on navigation through the entrances to the Baltic Sea".

(Reference charts: Danish 197, April 2006 edition; German 163 (INT 1351), 2006 edition.
Note: These charts are based on World Geodetic System 1984 datum (WGS 84).)

Description of the deep-water route

A deep-water route with a minimum depth of water below mean sea level of 16.5 metres is bounded by a line connecting the following geographical positions:

(1)	54°27′.10 N,	012°10′.50 E	(6)	54°46′.06 N,	012°44′.03 E
(2)	54°27′.73 N,	012°11′.30 E	(7)	54°35′.36 N,	012°16′.93 E
(3)	54°31′.30 N,	012°12′.80 E	(8)	54°31′.00 N,	012°15′.20 E
(4)	54°36′.46 N,	012°15′.83 E	(9)	54°27′.40 N,	012°13′.10 E
(5)	54°46′.86 N,	012°43′.23 E	(10)	54°26′.57 N,	012°11′.90 E

Note: Ships, other than ships which must use the deep-water route due to their draught, are recommended to use the areas to the north and south of this route, in such manner that eastbound ships proceed on the south side of the deep-water route and westbound ships on the north side.

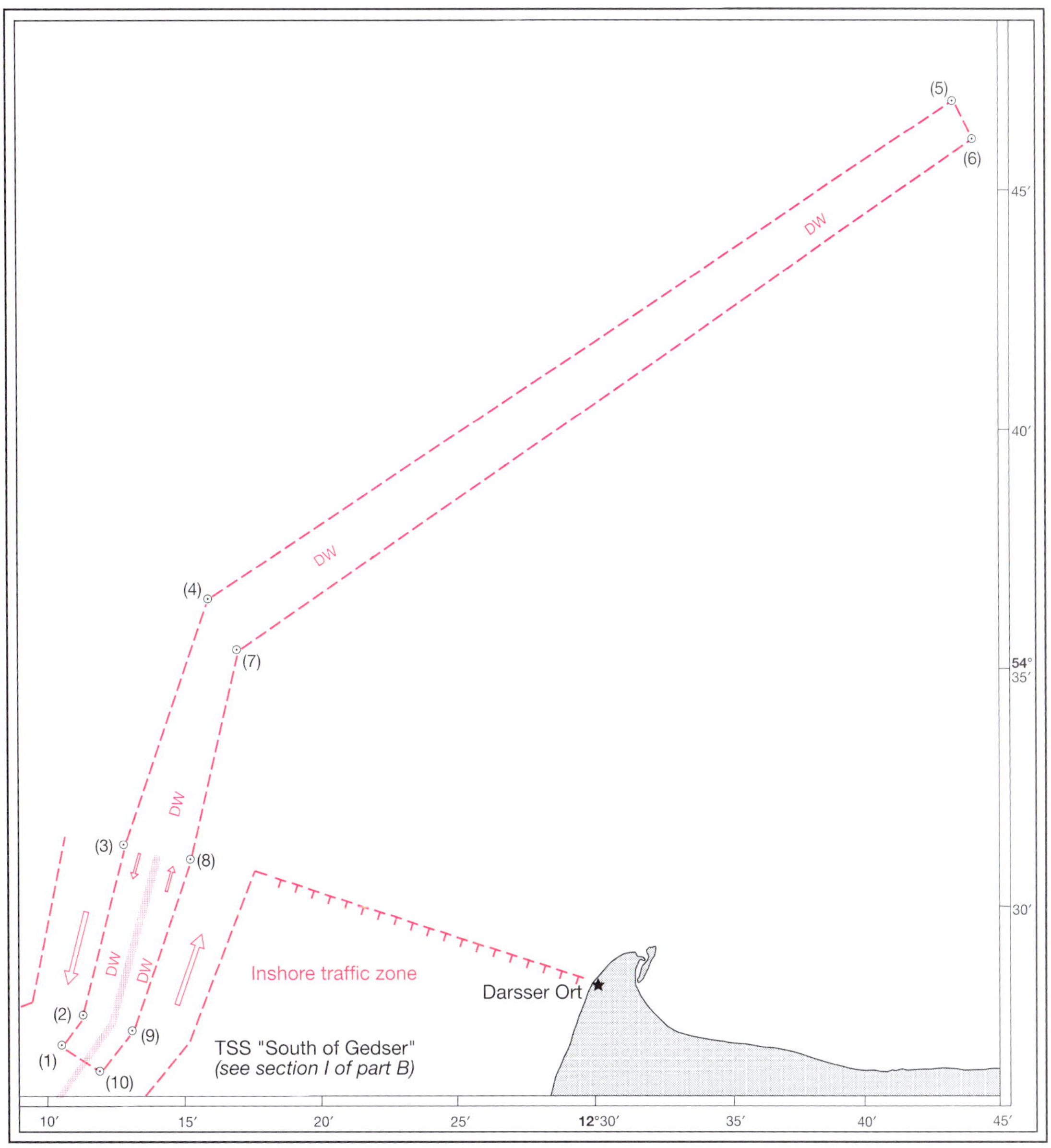

DEEP-WATER ROUTE NORTH-EAST OF GEDSER

DEEP-WATER ROUTE OFF GOTLAND ISLAND

(Reference charts: Swedish 7 and 8, 2001 edition.
Note: These charts are based on World Geodetic System 1984 datum (WGS 84).)

Description of the deep-water route

A deep-water route is established between the existing TSS "Off Köpu Peninsula" and the TSS "In Bornholmsgat" and south of the ATBAs "Hoburgs Bank" and "Norra Midsjöbanken" situated south of the island of Gotland, and is bounded by a line connecting the following geographical positions:

(1)	59°05′.85 N,	021°27′.88 E	(8)	55°22′.34 N,	014°40′.28 E
(2)	58°12′.54 N,	020°22′.54 E	(9)	55°35′.18 N,	015°29′.98 E
(3)	57°22′.16 N,	019°41′.73 E	(10)	55°53′.85 N,	017°43′.75 E
(4)	56°22′.64 N,	018°42′.82 E	(11)	56°17′.23 N,	018°51′.80 E
(5)	56°00′.30 N,	017°40′.04 E	(12)	57°18′.89 N,	019°52′.95 E
(6)	55°39′.32 N,	015°11′.61 E	(13)	57°58′.27 N,	020°24′.41 E
(7)	55°27′.55 N,	014°33′.62 E	(14)	58°59′.78 N,	021°42′.94 E

Notes:

1 The depths in the deep-water route, bounded by the line connecting positions (2)–(6) and (9)–(13) and approximately 6 miles wide, are confirmed by detailed hydrographic surveys in accordance with IHO standard S-44 in the Swedish area of responsibility. The depths are nowhere less than 25 metres.

2 The areas bounded by the line connecting positions (1), (2), (13) and (6)–(9) are not yet surveyed in accordance with IHO standard S-44. The survey will be carried out not later than 2008.

3 All ships passing east and south of the island of Gotland bound to or from the north-eastern part of the Baltic Sea, with a draught exceeding 12 metres, are recommended to use the deep-water route.

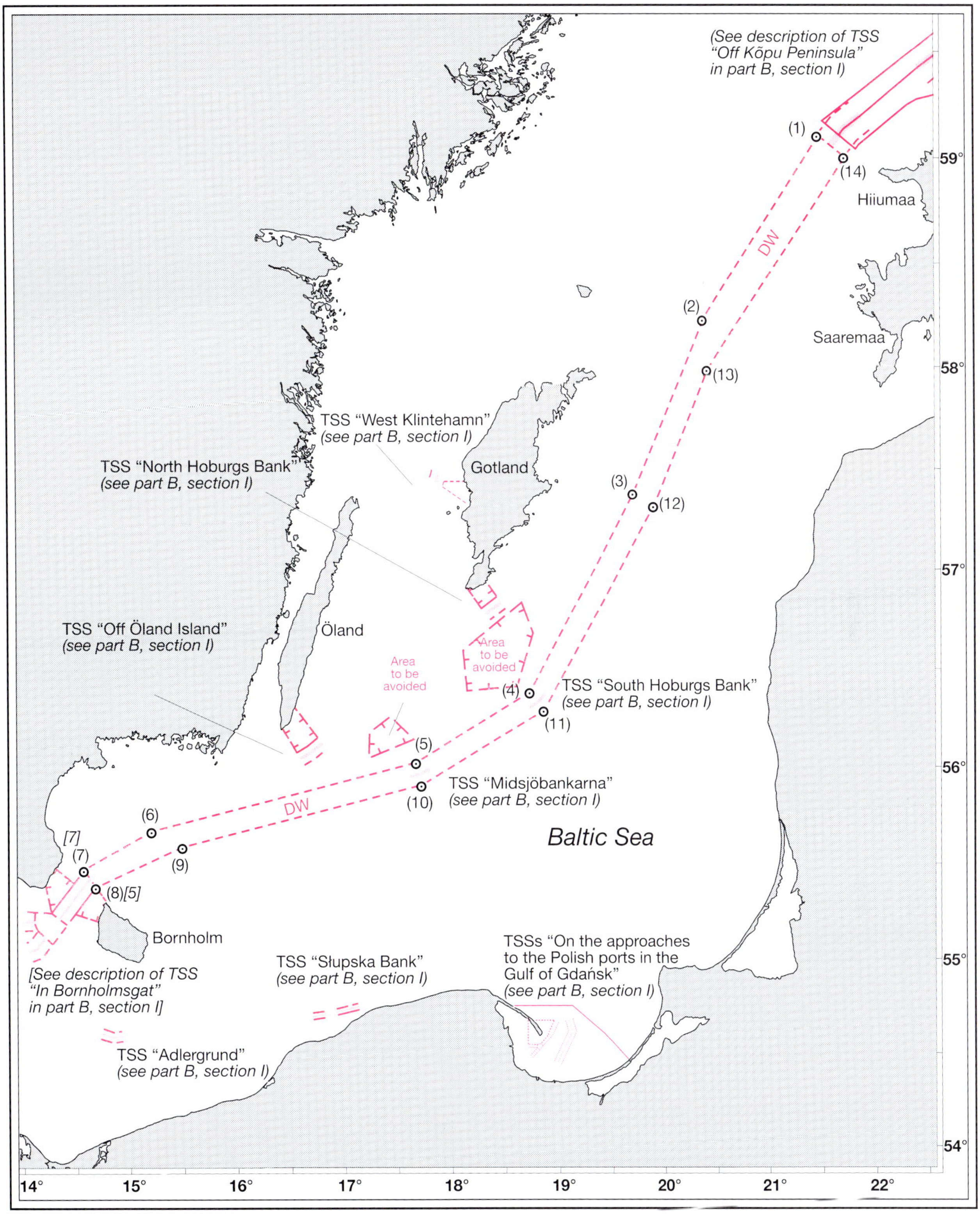

DEEP-WATER ROUTE OFF GOTLAND ISLAND

DEEP-WATER ROUTE INSIDE THE BORDERS OF THE TRAFFIC SEPARATION SCHEME FROM GOGLAND ISLAND TO RODSHER ISLAND [revoked]*

Note: See "Recommended tracks and traffic separation line between the traffic separation schemes "Off Rodsher Island" and "Off Gogland Island"" in part E.

The deep water route with established direction of traffic flow within the borders of the traffic separation scheme from Gogland Island to Rodsher Island, intended for the passage of ships with a draught up to 15 metres, is revoked.

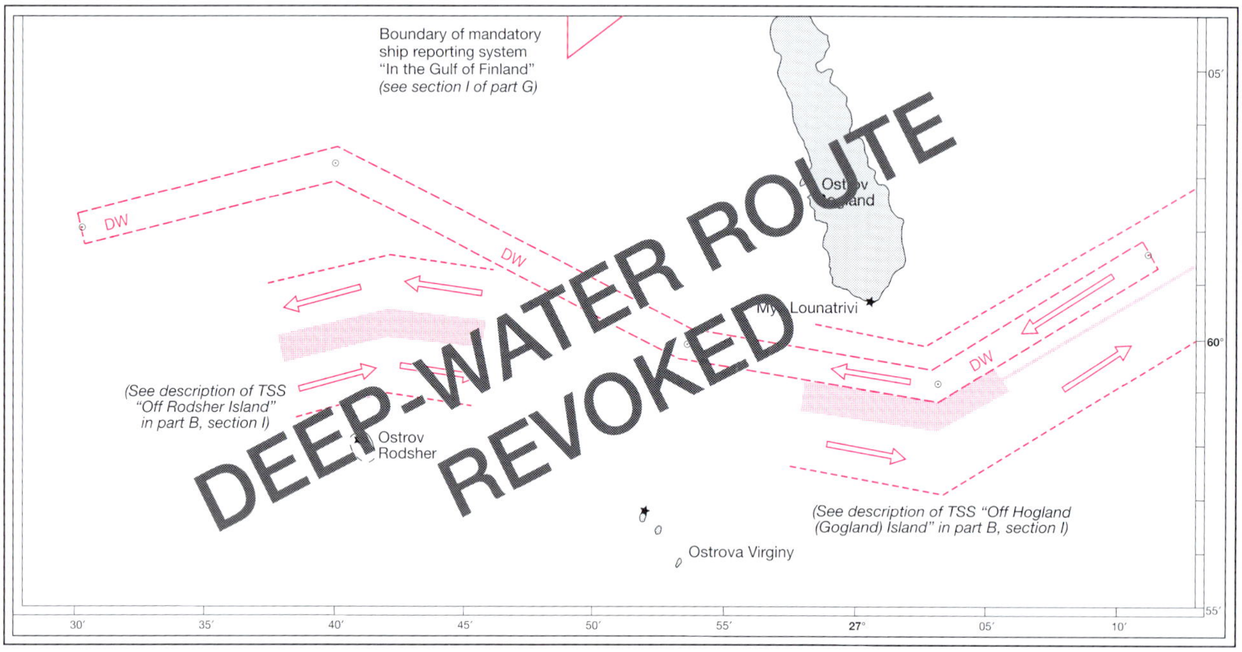

DEEP-WATER ROUTE INSIDE THE BORDERS OF THE TRAFFIC SEPARATION SCHEME FROM GOGLAND ISLAND TO RODSHER ISLAND

* Date of implementation of revocation of deep-water route: 0000 hours UTC on 1 June 2013.

DEEP-WATER ROUTES LEADING TO THE ÅLAND SEA

Note: See traffic separation scheme "The Åland Sea" in part B, section I.

(Reference charts: Finnish 953, edition 2007 V, and Swedish SE61 (INT1205), edition 21/2-2008.
Note: These charts are based on the World Geodetic System 1984 datum (WGS 84).)

Description of the deep-water routes

Inside the borders of the "North Åland Sea" traffic separation scheme

A deep-water route forming part of the "North Åland Sea" traffic separation scheme is established between the lines connecting the following geographical positions:

(i)	60°29′.54 N,	018°56′.36 E	(iv)	60°15′.26 N,	019°03′.50 E
(ii)	60°18′.87 N,	018°59′.16 E	(v)	60°18′.47 N,	019°01′.68 E
(iii)	60°15′.28 N,	018°58′.08 E	(vi)	60°29′.51 N,	019°04′.56 E

Inside the borders of the "South Åland Sea" traffic separation scheme

A deep-water route forming part of the "South Åland Sea" traffic separation scheme is established between the lines connecting the following geographical positions:

(vii)	59°42′.26 N,	019°51′.55 E	(xi)	59°30′.27 N,	020°06′.51 E
(viii)	59°39′.70 N,	019°55′.19 E	(xii)	59°33′.75 N,	020°06′.51 E
(ix)	59°34′.26 N,	020°08′.40 E	(xiii)	59°39′.44 N,	019°54′.13 E
(x)	59°30′.27 N,	020°08′.40 E	(xiv)	59°41′.91 N,	019°50′.60 E

(chartlet overleaf)

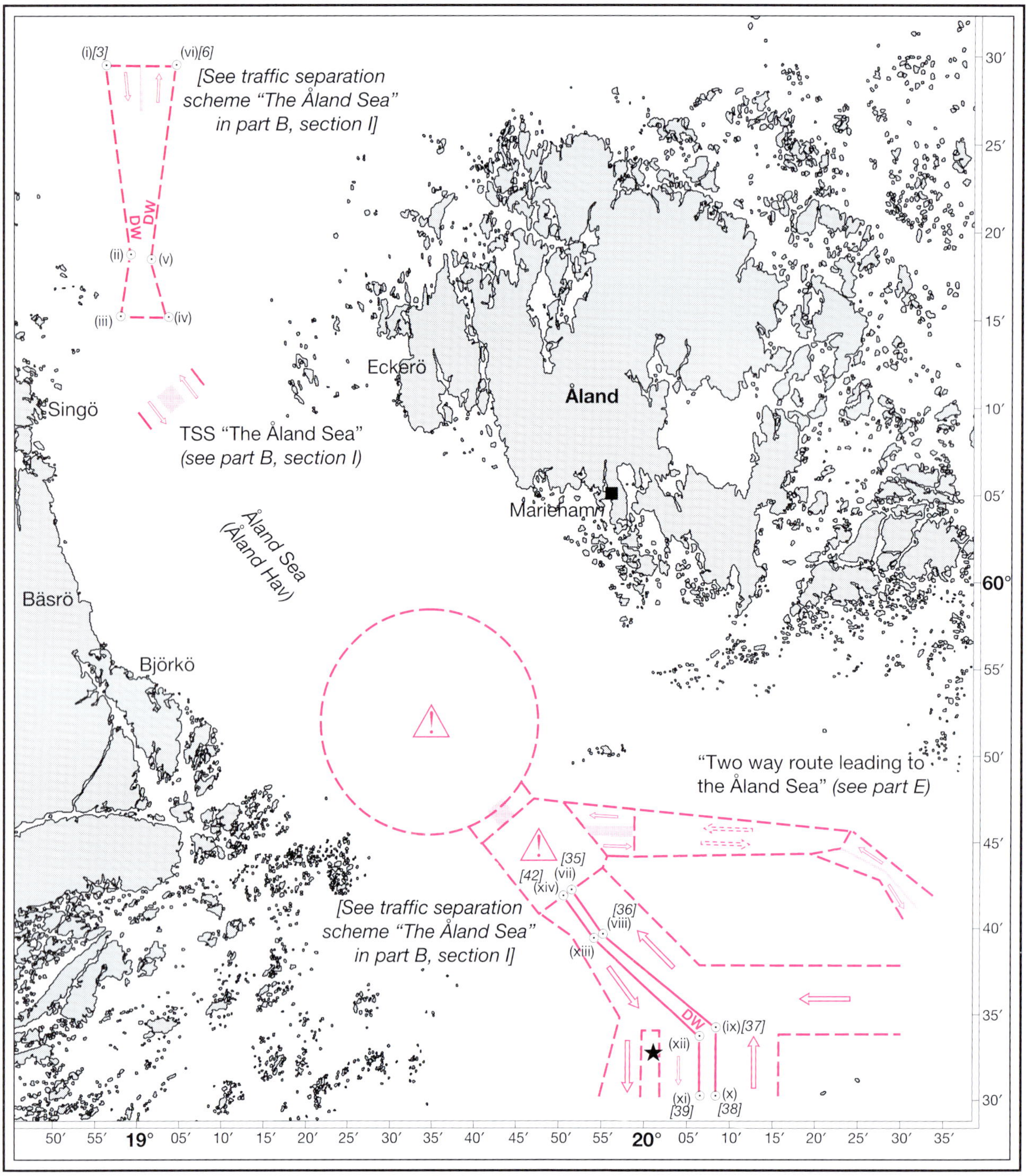

DEEP-WATER ROUTES LEADING TO THE ÅLAND SEA

Section II

Western European waters

Caution: The chartlets are for illustrative purposes only and must not be used for navigation. Mariners should consult the appropriate nautical publications and charts for up-to-date details on aids to navigation and other relevant information.

Warning: The geographical positions given in the descriptions of the deep-water routes are only correct for charts using the same geodetic datum as the reference charts indicated under each scheme. Charts published by other hydrographic offices may use a different geodetic datum, as may new editions of the reference charts published after the adoption of the routes. Where amendments to existing routes are not based on the same geodetic datum as the original route or where positions are defined relative to two geodetic datums, this is emphasized by the use of different colours for definitions of positions.

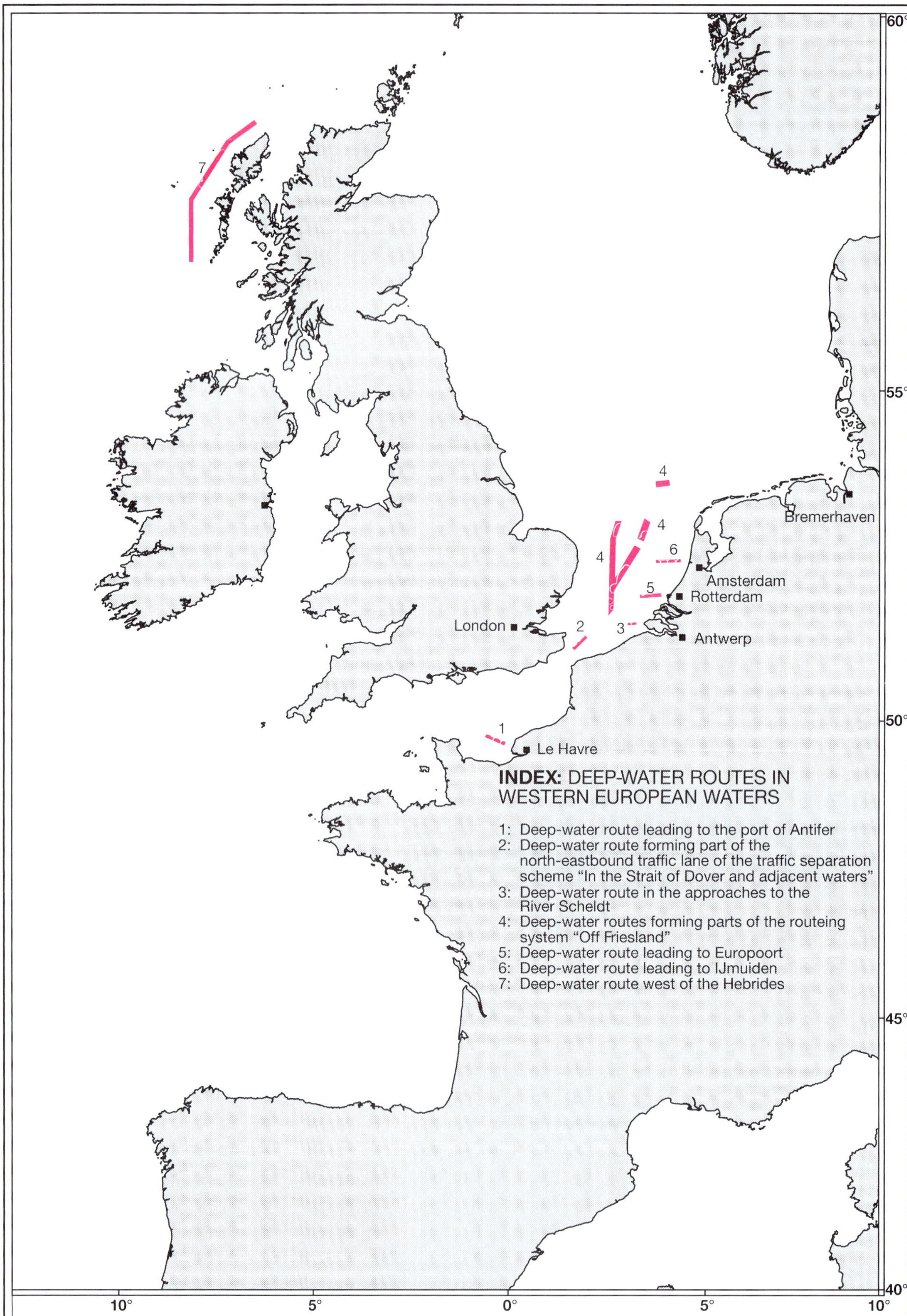

60°
55°
50°
45°
40°
10°
5°
0°
5°
10°
7
4
4
4
6
5
3
2
1
Bremerhaven
Amsterdam
Rotterdam
London
Antwerp
Le Havre
INDEX: DEEP-WATER ROUTES IN WESTERN EUROPEAN WATERS
1: Deep-water route leading to the port of Antifer
2: Deep-water route forming part of the north-eastbound traffic lane of the traffic separation scheme "In the Strait of Dover and adjacent waters"
3: Deep-water route in the approaches to the River Scheldt
4: Deep-water routes forming parts of the routeing system "Off Friesland"
5: Deep-water route leading to Europoort
6: Deep-water route leading to IJmuiden
7: Deep-water route west of the Hebrides

DEEP-WATER ROUTE LEADING TO THE PORT OF ANTIFER

(Reference charts: 6614-T, 6614-D by Service hydrographique et océanographique de la Marine, France)

Description of the deep-water route

The deep-water route is bounded by a line connecting the following geographical positions:

(1)	49°55′.30 N,	000°40′.70 W	(4)	49°45′.10 N,	000°06′.50 W
(2)	49°44′.80 N,	000°10′.80 W	(5)	49°47′.40 N,	000°08′.50 W
(3)	49°44′.70 N,	000°06′.80 W	(6)	49°58′.20 N,	000°39′.20 W

Note: This deep-water route is a continuation of the buoyed fairway leading from Antifer harbour.

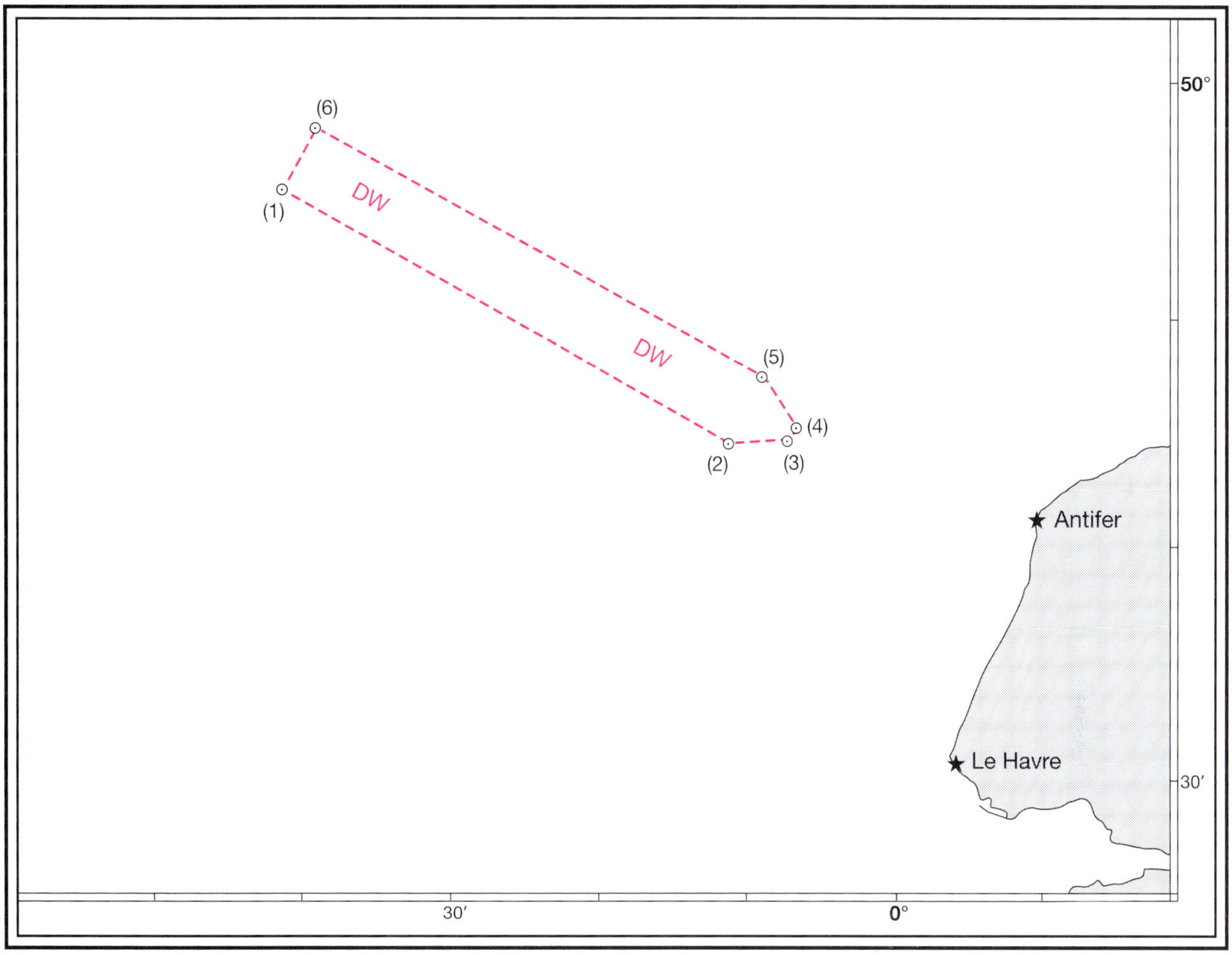

DEEP-WATER ROUTE LEADING TO ANTIFER

DEEP-WATER ROUTE FORMING PART OF THE NORTH-EASTBOUND TRAFFIC LANE OF THE TRAFFIC SEPARATION SCHEME "IN THE STRAIT OF DOVER AND ADJACENT WATERS"*

Note: See "Recommendations on navigation through the English Channel and the Dover Strait" in part F and mandatory ship reporting system "In the Dover Strait/Pas de Calais" in part G, section I.

(Reference chart: British Admiralty 2449, June 2007 edition.
Note: This chart is based on World Geodetic System 1984 datum (WGS 84).)

Description of the deep-water route

The deep-water route forming part of the north-eastbound traffic lane between the separation zone described in paragraph (i) and the separation zone/line described in paragraphs (c) and (e) of the separation scheme "In the Strait of Dover and adjacent waters" has been established between a line connecting the following geographical positions:

(i)	51°09′.75 N,	001°45′.61 E	(ii)	51°10′.26 N,	001°43′.74 E

and a line connecting:

(iii)	51°22′.03 N,	001°58′.39 E	(iv)	51°18′.43 N,	002°04′.69 E

Notes:

WARNING
The main traffic lane for north-eastbound traffic lies to the south-east of the Sandettie Bank and should be followed by all such ships as can safely navigate therein having regard to their draught.

In the area of the deep-water route east of the separation line, ships are recommended to avoid overtaking where traffic and navigation do not allow sufficient sea room and passing distance. If overtaking is performed then a safe distance must be maintained and COLREG Rule 13 observed.

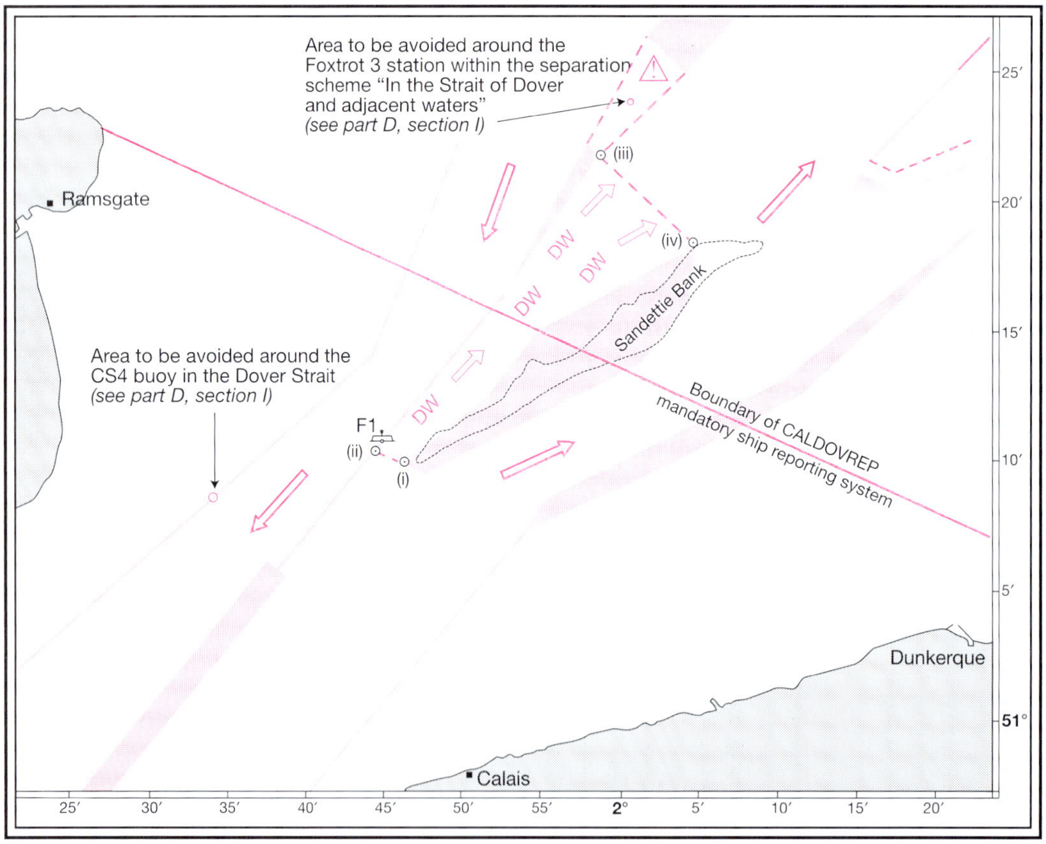

DEEP-WATER ROUTE FORMING PART OF THE NORTH-EASTBOUND TRAFFIC LANE OF THE TRAFFIC SEPARATION SCHEME "IN THE STRAIT OF DOVER AND ADJACENT WATERS"

* Date of implementation of amended deep-water route: 0000 hours UTC on 1 June 2011.

DEEP-WATER ROUTE IN THE APPROACHES TO THE RIVER SCHELDT*

(Reference charts: D11 and 102 (INT 1480) published by the Agency of Maritime and Coastal Services, Flemish Hydrography.
Note: These charts are based on World Geodetic System 1984 datum (WGS 84).)

Description of the deep-water route

A deep-water route for ships with a draught of more than 13.1 metres is bounded by a line connecting the following geographical positions:

(1)	51° 24′.25 N,	002° 44′.52 E	GZ buoy
(2)	51° 25′.95 N,	002° 48′.12 E	VG2 buoy
(3)	51° 25′.50 N,	002° 52′.92 E	VG4 buoy
(4)	51° 25′.07 N,	002° 57′.92 E	VG6 buoy
(5)	51° 25′.03 N,	003° 02′.85 E	S4 buoy
(6)	51° 24′.53 N,	002° 59′.92 E	VG7 buoy
(7)	51° 24′.63 N,	002° 57′.92 E	VG5 buoy
(8)	51° 25′.05 N,	002° 52′.92 E	VG3 buoy
(9)	51° 25′.03 N,	002° 49′.05 E	VG1 buoy
(10)	51° 23′.38 N,	002° 46′.21 E	VG buoy

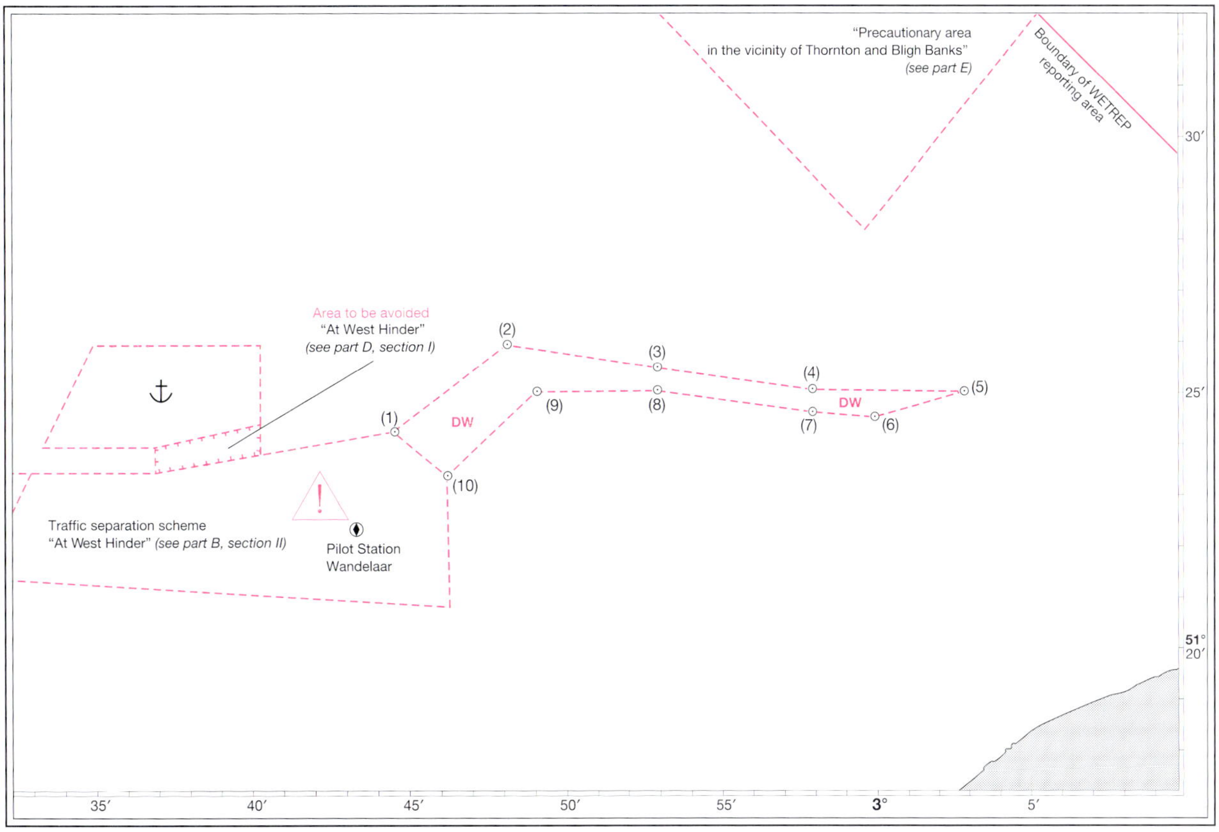

DEEP-WATER ROUTE IN THE APPROACHES TO THE RIVER SCHELDT

* Date of implementation of new deep-water route: 0000 hours UTC on 1 December 2012.

DEEP-WATER ROUTES FORMING PARTS OF ROUTEING SYSTEM "OFF FRIESLAND"

Note: See "Off Friesland" in part B, section II and "Mandatory route for tankers from North Hinder to the German Bight and vice versa" in part G, section II.

(Reference charts: British Admiralty 1405, 1978 edition; 1406, 1988 edition; 1408, 1988 edition; 1505 and 2182A, 1978 edition; Netherlands Hydrographic Office 1014 (INT 1043), 1988 edition; 1035 (INT 1046), 1988 edition; 1037 (INT 1045), 1989 edition; German Hydrographic Office 50 (INT 1045), 1986 edition; 53, 1984 edition.

Note: These charts are based on European datum (1950). Co-ordinates of amendments to the route are from British Admiralty 1632, 2005 edition, which is based on World Geodetic System 1984 datum (WGS 84); these are shown in colour.)

Description of the deep-water routes

Deep-water route from North Hinder to traffic separation scheme "Off Brown Ridge"

(a) The deep-water route is bounded by a line connecting the following geographical positions:

(1)	52°55′.75 N,	003°14′.25 E	(4)	52°01′.23 N,	002°42′.47 E
(2)	52°09′.92 N,	002°35′.00 E	(5)	52°09′.58 N,	002°43′.33 E
(3)	51°54′.88 N,	002°33′.60 E	(6)	52°54′.17 N,	003°22′.00 E

(b) Geographical positions (1) and (6) to (12) form the traffic separation scheme "Off Brown Ridge" (see "Off Friesland", paragraphs (b), (c) and (d), in section II of part B).

Deep-water route from traffic separation scheme "Off Brown Ridge" to traffic separation scheme "West Friesland"

(c) The deep-water route is bounded by a line connecting the following geographical positions:

(11)	53°02′.20 N,	003°26′.48 E	(13)	53°22′.94 N,	003°28′.40 E
(12)	53°03′.78 N,	003°18′.71 E	(14)	53°19′.89 N,	003°39′.74 E

(d) Geographical positions (13) to (27) form the traffic separation scheme "West Friesland" (see "Off Friesland", paragraphs (f), (g) and (h), in section II of part B).

"Friesland Junction" precautionary area

(e) The "Friesland Junction" precautionary area is bounded by a line connecting the following geographical positions:

(26)	53°57′.20 N,	004°10′.02 E	(29)	54°05′.59 N,	004°59′.32 E
(25)	54°00′.00 N,	004°46′.00 E	(30)	54°02′.57 N,	004°20′.92 E
(28)	54°01′.14 N,	005°00′.34 E	(31)	54°01′.91 N,	004°08′.96 E

(f) Geographical positions (28), (29) and (32) to (40) form the traffic separation scheme "East Friesland" (see "Off Friesland", paragraphs (j), (k) and (l), in section II of part B).

Deep-water route from the traffic separation scheme "Off Botney Ground" to the precautionary area "Friesland Junction"

(g) The deep-water route is bounded by a line connecting the following geographical positions:

(26)	53°57′.20 N,	004°10′.02 E	(42)	54°00′.46 N,	003°43′.01 E
(41)	53°55′.24 N,	003°44′.88 E	(31)	54°01′.91 N,	004°08′.96 E

(h) Geographical positions (41) to (62) form the traffic separation scheme "Off Botney Ground" (see "Off Friesland", paragraphs (n), (o) and (p), in section II of part B).

Deep-water route from North Hinder to Indefatigable Bank via DR1 lightbuoy

(i) The deep-water route is bounded by a line connecting the following geographical positions:

(56)	53°36′.70 N,	002°56′.40 E	(65)	52°18′.20 N,	002°44′.00 E
(57)	53°21′.88 N,	002°46′.88 E	(66)	53°04′.00 N,	002°44′.00 E
(63)	53°04′.80 N,	002°36′.00 E	(58)	53°20′.15 N,	002°54′.48 E
(64)	52°18′.20 N,	002°36′.00 E	(59)	53°29′.40 N,	003°00′.60 E
(3)	51°54′.88 N,	002°33′.60 E	(60)	53°34′.66 N,	003°05′.40 E
(4)	52°01′.23 N,	002°42′.47 E			

Notes:

1 *Least water depths*

The deep-water routes from North Hinder to the traffic separation scheme "Off Brown Ridge" and from the traffic separation scheme "Off Brown Ridge" to the traffic separation scheme "West Friesland", and the traffic lanes of the traffic separation schemes "Off Brown Ridge" and "West Friesland" were closely surveyed in the period 1981 to 1986. The least water depth found in these areas was more than 23 metres at LLWS except for one wreck in geographical position 52°46′.17 N, 003°13′.83 E. The least water depth over that wreck found by wire-sweeping was 20.0 metres at LLWS.

See also the note pertaining to the traffic separation scheme "German Bight western approach".

2 *Least water depths*

The deep-water routes from the traffic separation scheme "Off Botney Ground" to precautionary area "Friesland Junction" and "From North Hinder to Indefatigable Bank via DR1 lightbuoy", the traffic lanes of the traffic separation scheme "Off Botney Ground", the precautionary area "Friesland Junction", and the traffic separation scheme "East Friesland" were closely surveyed in the period 1981 to 1986. The least water depth found in these areas was more than 29 metres at LLWS except for a few patches just north of the parallel 52° N, which have a depth of 26.5 metres at LLWS.

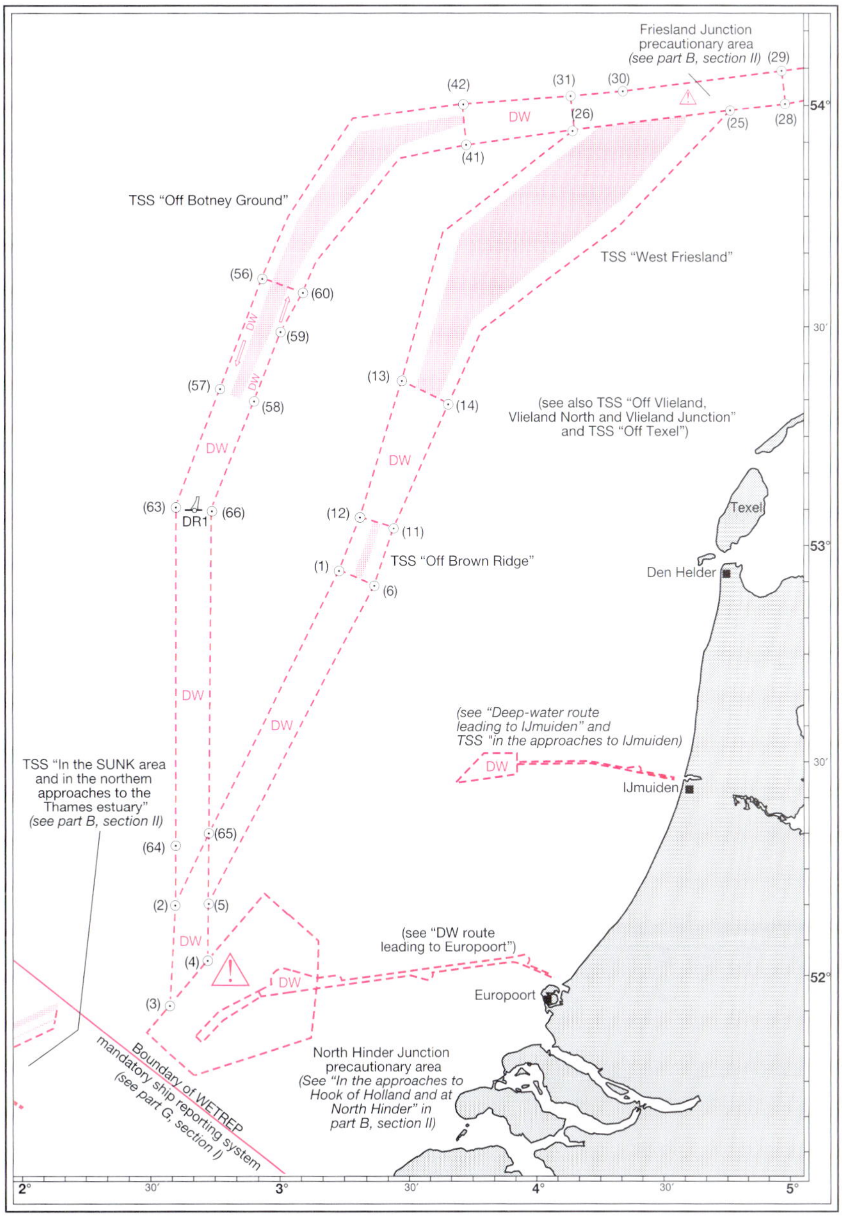

DEEP-WATER ROUTES FORMING PARTS OF ROUTEING SYSTEM "OFF FRIESLAND"

C

DEEP-WATER ROUTE LEADING TO EUROPOORT*

Note: See traffic separation scheme "In the approaches to Hook of Holland and at North Hinder" in part B, section II and area to be avoided "At Maas North" in part D, section I and precautionary areas "In the approaches to Hook of Holland and at North Hinder" in part E.

(Reference chart: Netherlands 1630 (INT 1416), edition 4/2010.
Note: This chart is based on World Geodetic System 1984 datum (WGS 84).)

Description of the deep-water route

The deep-water route is bounded by a line connecting the following geographical positions:

(1)	51° 59′.52 N,	004° 02′.74 E	(14)	51° 57′.28 N,	002° 54′.68 E
(2)	51° 59′.94 N,	004° 01′.32 E	(19)	51° 56′.53 N,	002° 55′.29 E
(3)†	52° 01′.03 N,	003° 56′.91 E	(20)	51° 57′.64 N,	003° 08′.00 E
(4)†	52° 02′.33 N,	003° 55′.89 E	(21)	51° 58′.49 N,	003° 17′.96 E
(5)	52° 02′.00 N,	003° 53′.00 E	(22)	51° 59′.09 N,	003° 25′.17 E
(6)	52° 00′.57 N,	003° 35′.17 E	(23)	51° 59′.47 N,	003° 29′.78 E
(7)	51° 59′.75 N,	003° 25′.29 E	(24)†	51° 58′.86 N,	003° 33′.51 E
(8)	51° 59′.15 N,	003° 18′.13 E	(25)†	51° 59′.89 N,	003° 34′.87 E
(9)†	51° 58′.79 N,	003° 13′.86 E	(26)†	52° 01′.35 N,	003° 52′.98 E
(10)†	51° 59′.47 N,	003° 12′.28 E	(27)†	52° 01′.16 N,	003° 55′.07 E
(11)	51° 59′.13 N,	003° 08′.26 E	(28)	51° 59′.66 N,	004° 01′.12 E
(12)†	52° 00′.37 N,	003° 01′.29 E	(29)	51° 59′.26 N,	004° 02′.57 E
(13)†	51° 58′.24 N,	002° 57′.73 E			

The mandatory one-way deep-water approach route to Eurogeul for inbound vessels with the draught over 17.4 metres from the south is bounded by a line connecting the following geographical positions:

(14)	51° 57′.28 N,	002° 54′.68 E	(17)	51° 50′.04 N,	002° 41′.75 E
(15)	51° 54′.41 N,	002° 45′.65 E	(18)	51° 53′.17 N,	002° 46′.62 E
(16)	51° 50′.94 N,	002° 40′.25 E	(19)	51° 56′.53 N,	002° 55′.29 E

Notes:

1 *Least water depths*

The limiting depths in the route should be ascertained by reference to the latest large-scale navigation charts of the area, noting that the charted depths are checked and maintained by frequent surveys and dredging.

2 *Electronic navigational aids*

(i) Uninterrupted differential GPS coverage is normally available in this area, so masters of deep-draught ships equipped with GPS navigational systems can be informed continuously and highly accurately about the ship's deviation from and progress along the axis of the route.

(ii) Those ships which, because of their draught, are confined to the mid-channel zone are strongly advised to make use of the above equipment.

---

* Date of implementation of amended deep-water route: 0000 hours UTC on 1 August 2013.

† These positions are connected by circular arcs centred about the following points:

Ref.	Latitude	Longitude	Radius in NM	Arc between points
(a)	52° 01′.65 N	003° 56′.28 E	0.729	(3) & (4)
(b)	51° 58′.77 N	003° 12′.66 E	0.729	(9) & (10)
(c)	51° 58′.73 N	003° 00′.42 E	1.728	(12) & (13)
(d)	51° 59′.56 N	003° 33′.82 E	0.729	(24) & (25)
(e)	51° 58′.59 N	003° 53′.40 E	2.775	(26) & (27)

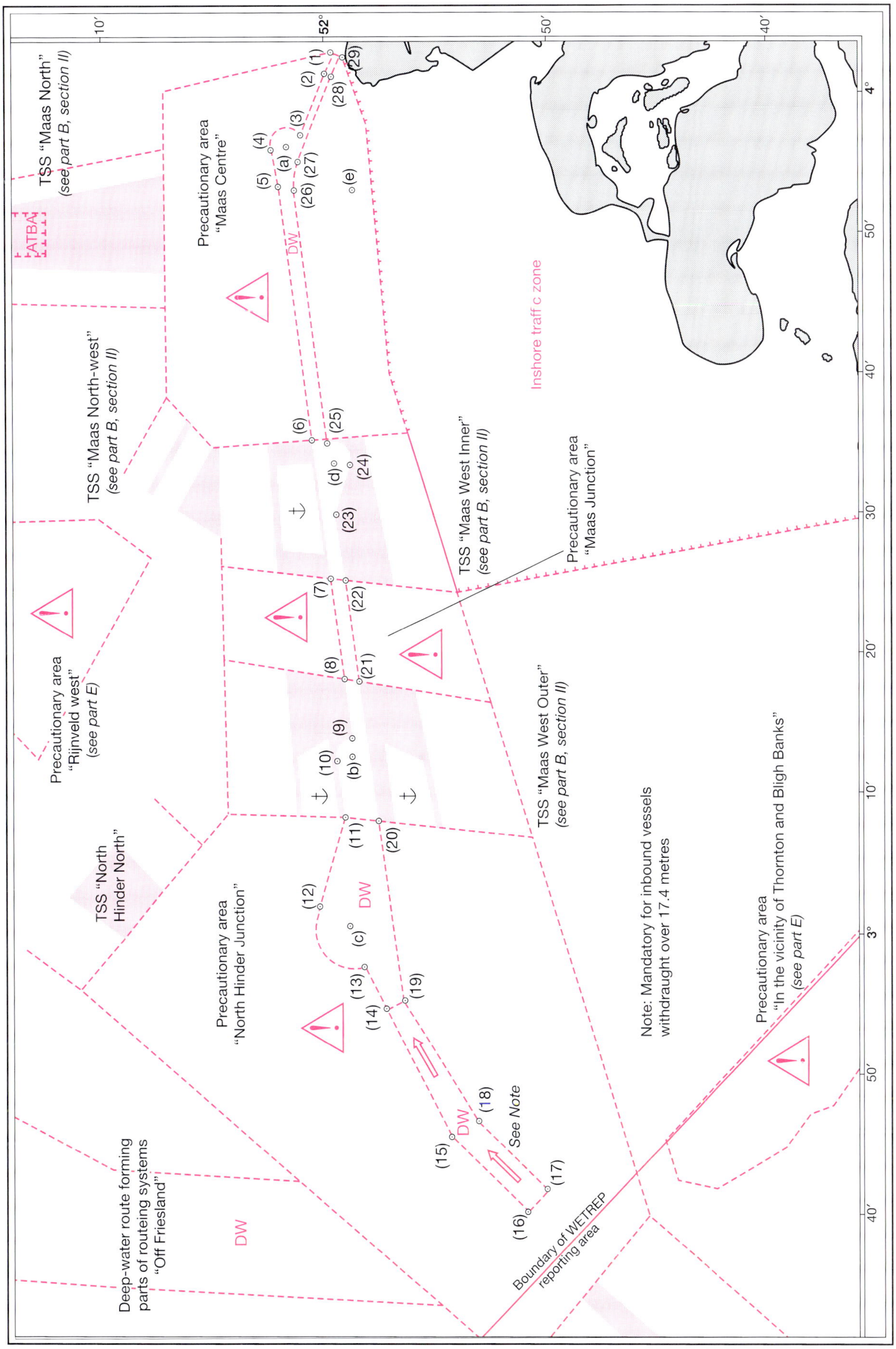

DEEP-WATER ROUTE LEADING TO EUROPOORT

DEEP-WATER ROUTE LEADING TO IJMUIDEN*

Note: See traffic separation schemes "In the approaches to IJmuiden" in part B, section II and area to be avoided "By IJmuiden northern approaches" in part D, section I and precautionary areas "In the approaches to IJmuiden" in part E.

(Reference chart: Netherlands 1631 (INT 1418, edition 3).
Note: This chart is based on World Geodetic System 1984 datum (WGS 84).)

Description of the deep-water route

The deep-water route consists of a deep-water channel (IJ-geul) and a deep-water approach area (IJ-geul approach area).

The deep-water channel (IJ-geul)

(a) The specific deep-water channel is bounded by a line connecting the following geographical positions:

(1)	52° 28′.10 N,	004° 32′.02 E	(16)	52° 29′.94 N,	003° 54′.91 E
(2)†	52° 29′.00 N,	004° 24′.16 E	(17)	52° 29′.95 N,	003° 55′.87 E
(3)†	52° 29′.65 N,	004° 23′.45 E	(18)	52° 30′.03 N,	004° 07′.74 E
(4)	52° 29′.39 N,	004° 20′.73 E	(19)	52° 30′.04 N,	004° 09′.16 E
(5)	52° 30′.38 N,	004° 11′.84 E	(20)	52° 30′.06 N,	004° 12′.50 E
(6)	52° 30′.36 N,	004° 08′.93 E	(21)	52° 29′.03 N,	004° 21′.70 E
(7)	52° 30′.36 N,	004° 07′.51 E	(22)†	52° 28′.80 N,	004° 23′.41 E
(8)	52° 30′.27 N,	003° 55′.98 E	(23)†	52° 28′.80 N,	004° 23′.72 E
(9)	52° 30′.26 N,	003° 54′.91 E	(24)	52° 27′.81 N,	004° 31′.95 E

The deep-water approach area (IJ-geul approach area)

(b) The specific deep-water approach area is bounded by a line connecting the following geographical positions:

(9)	52° 30′.26 N,	003° 54′.91 E	(13)	52° 27′.31 N,	003° 40′.51 E
(10)	52° 31′.50 N,	003° 54′.91 E	(14)	52° 28′.07 N,	003° 49′.47 E
(11)	52° 31′.50 N,	003° 50′.57 E	(15)	52° 28′.54 N,	003° 54′.91 E
(12)	52° 31′.49 N,	003° 47′.17 E	(16)	52° 29′.94 N,	003° 54′.91 E

Notes:

1 *Least water depths*
Limiting depths in the route should be ascertained by reference to the latest large-scale navigational charts of the area, noting that the charted depths are checked and maintained by frequent surveys and dredging.

2 Admission policy for the "Deep-water channel leading to IJmuiden":

.1 Maximum allowed draught for entering IJmuiden is 17.80 metres;

.2 Vessels with a draught of more than 14.10 metres and up to the maximum allowed draught of 17.80 metres are provided with a mandatory tidal window;

.3 Channel-bound vessels must, if necessary, make use of the deep-water anchorage on the south-western side of the deep-water approach area; and

.4 Channel-bound vessels must wait for pilotage in the deep-water approach area (IJ-geul approach area) west of the IJM buoy.

3 *Traffic Centre IJmuiden*
Traffic Centre IJmuiden can be reached on VHF channel 07. Traffic Centre IJmuiden will provide tidal windows for vessels with a draught of more than 14.10 metres.

---

* Date of implementation of amended deep-water route: 0000 hours UTC on 1 August 2013.

† Geographical positions (2) and (3) and positions (22) and (23) are connected by arcs of a circle with a radius of 0.432 miles centred at geographical position (x) 52° 29′.22 N, 004° 23′.56 E.

4 The deep-water anchorage is bounded by a line connecting the following geographical positions:

(25) 52°27′.57 N, 003°43′.53 E

(26) 52°26′.38 N, 003°43′.80 E

(27) 52°26′.81 N, 003°48′.89 E

(28) 52°28′.00 N, 003°48′.62 E

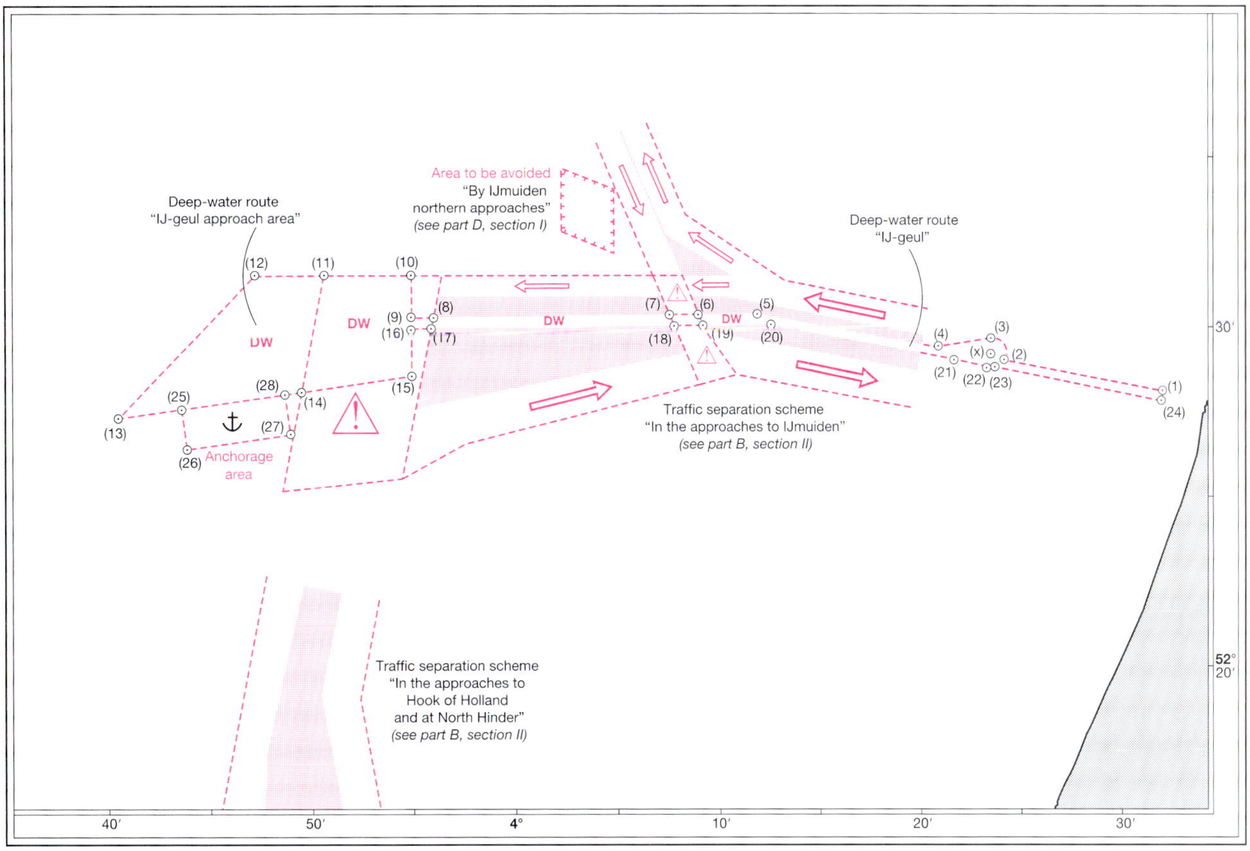

DEEP-WATER ROUTE LEADING TO IJMUIDEN

DEEP-WATER ROUTE WEST OF THE HEBRIDES

Note: See mandatory ship reporting system "West European Tanker Reporting System" in part G, section I.

(Reference chart: British Admiralty 2635, 1996 edition.
Note: This chart is based on Ordnance Survey of Great Britain 1936 datum. Co-ordinates relative to World Geodetic System 1984 datum are also shown, in colour)

Description of the deep-water route

(1)	56°46′.75 N,	008°03′.00 W	(1)	56°46′.74 N,	008°03′.05 W
(2)	57°36′.80 N,	008°03′.00 W	(2)	57°36′.78 N,	008°03′.05 W
(3)	58°21′.40 N,	007°08′.00 W	(3)	58°21′.37 N,	007°08′.06 W
(4)	58°37′.40 N,	006°26′.00 W,	(4)	58°37′.37 N,	006°26′.07 W
(5)	58°40′.54 N,	006°30′.76 W,	(5)	58°40′.51 N,	006°30′.83 W
(6)	58°24′.23 N,	007°13′.58 W,	(6)	58°24′.20 N,	007°13′.64 W
(7)	57°37′.97 N,	008°10′.50 W	(7)	57°37′.94 N,	008°10′.55 W
(8)	56°46′.75 N,	008°10′.29 W	(8)	56°46′.74 N,	008°10′.34 W

C

Notes:

1 The depths in the route, as confirmed by detailed hydrographic surveys, are nowhere less than 28.5 metres.

2 Laden tankers of over 10,000 gross tonnage are recommended, weather conditions permitting, to use this route in preference to sailing through the restricted waters of The Minches.

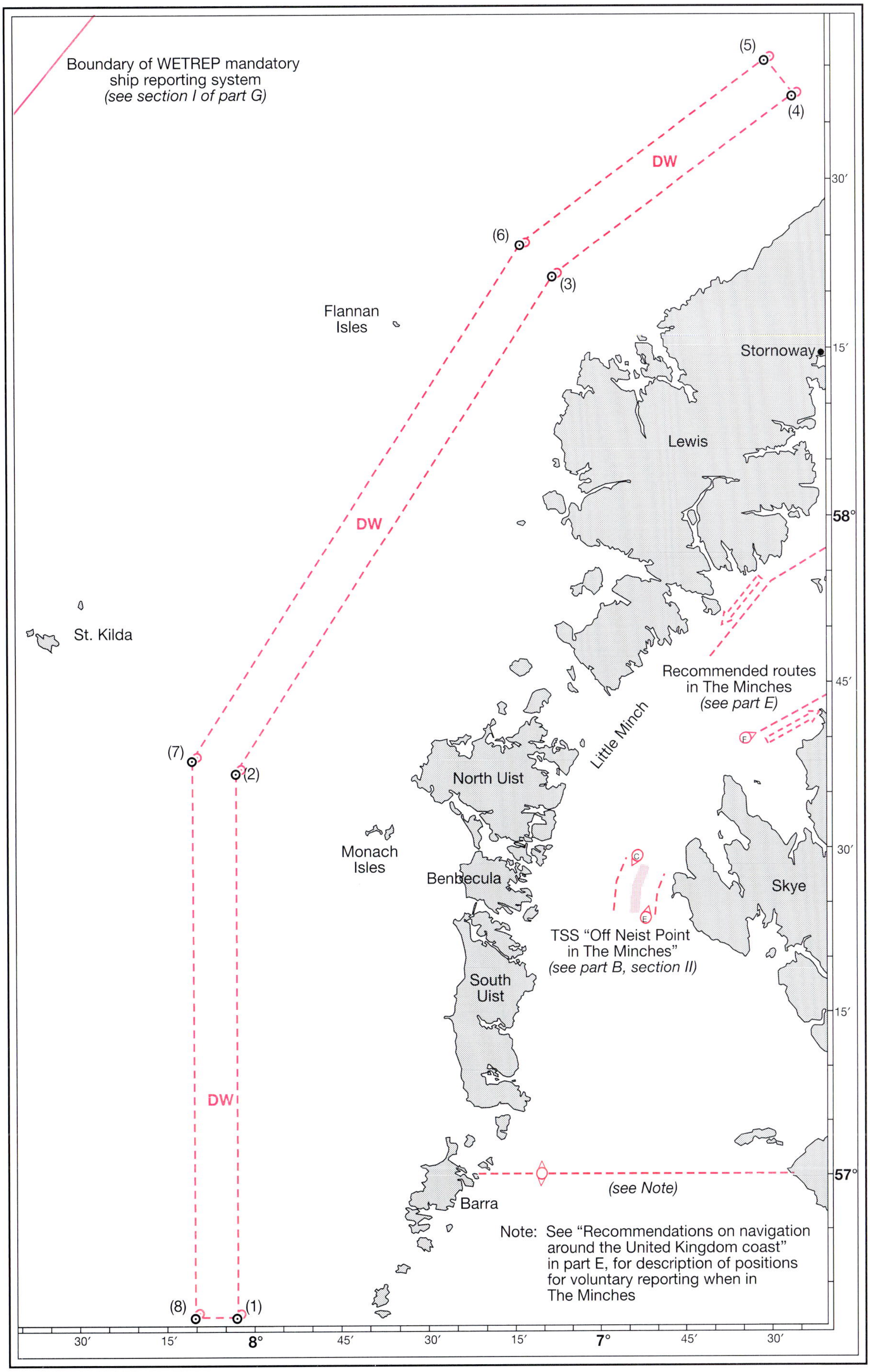

DEEP-WATER ROUTE WEST OF THE HEBRIDES

C

Section III

Indian Ocean and adjacent waters, South-East Asia and Australasia

Caution: The chartlets are for illustrative purposes only and must not be used for navigation. Mariners should consult the appropriate nautical publications and charts for up-to-date details on aids to navigation and other relevant information.

Warning: The geographical positions given in the descriptions of the deep-water routes are only correct for charts using the same geodetic datum as the reference charts indicated under each scheme. Charts published by other hydrographic offices may use a different geodetic datum, as may new editions of the reference charts published after the adoption of the routes. Where amendments to existing routes are not based on the same geodetic datum as the original route or where positions are defined relative to two geodetic datums, this is emphasized by the use of different colours for definitions of positions.

INDEX: DEEP-WATER ROUTES IN INDIAN OCEAN AND ADJACENT WATERS, SOUTH-EAST ASIA AND AUSTRALASIA

1: Deep-water route leading to King Abdullah Port
2: Deep-water route leading to Jazan Economic City Port
A: Summary chartlet A

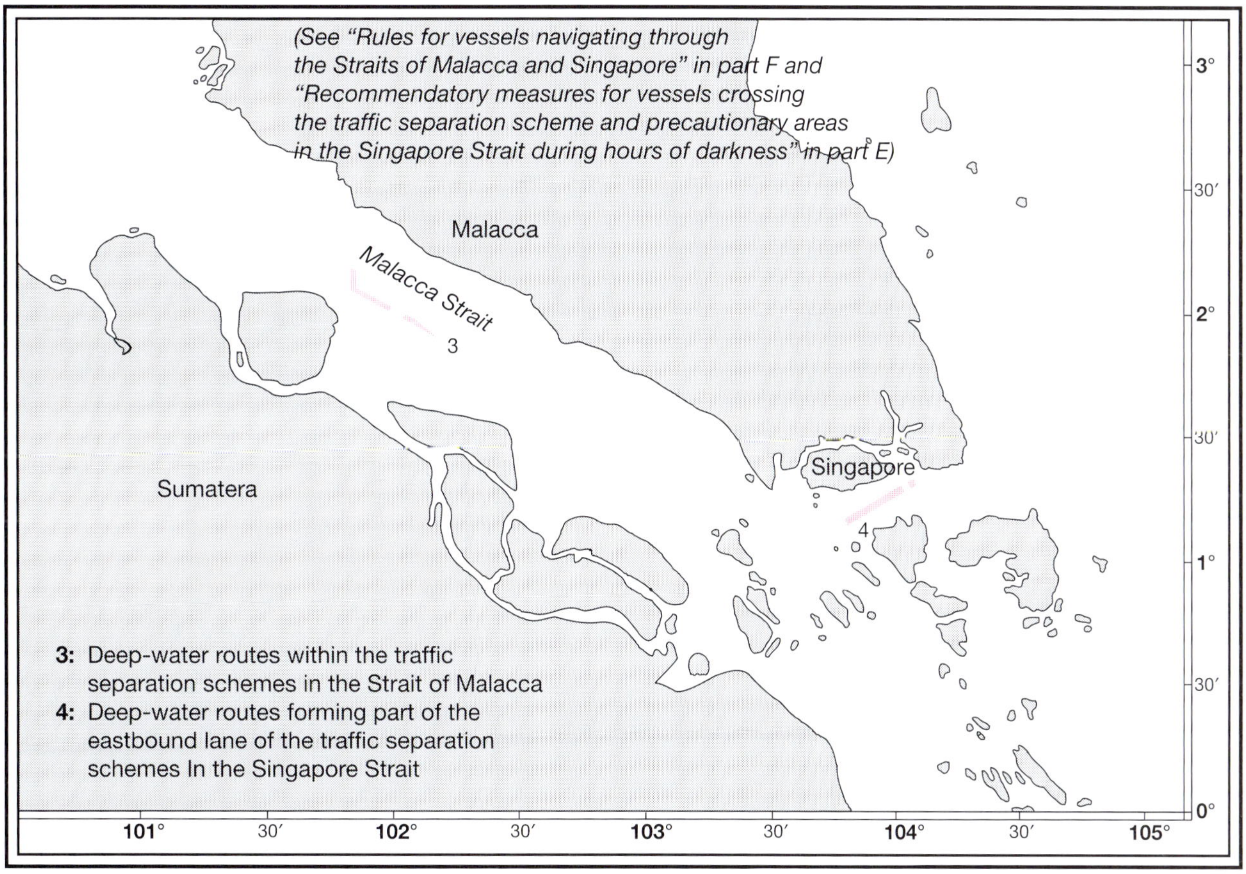

SUMMARY CHARTLET A

DEEP-WATER ROUTE IN THE APPROACHES TO THE NEW PORT OF KING ABDULLAH PORT (KAP PORT) IN THE NORTHERN RED SEA*

Note: See also "Precautionary area in the approaches to the new port of King Abdullah Port (KAP) in the northern Red Sea" in part E.

(Reference chart: British Admiralty (BA) 2659, 4 May 1990.
Note: This chart is not based on World Geodetic System 1984 datum (WGS 84). The geographical positions, (1) to (11), listed in item (a) below are referenced to BA 2659.)

Description of the deep-water route

(a) The deep-water route is bounded by a line drawn connecting the following geographical positions:

(1)	22°17′.24 N,	038°52′.93 E	(7)	22°29′.58 N,	039°03′.61 E
(2)	22°18′.61 N,	038°53′.60 E	(8)	22°26′.69 N,	038°59′.42 E
(3)	22°20′.57 N,	038°54′.64 E	(9)	22°21′.25 N,	038°56′.61 E
(4)	22°25′.94 N,	038°57′.47 E	(10)	22°19′.24 N,	038°55′.58 E
(5)	22°29′.00 N,	038°58′.98 E	(11)	22°15′.90 N,	038°53′.91 E
(6)	22°31′.75 N,	039°03′.01 E			

Notes:

Geographical positions referenced to WGS 84:

(1)	22°17′.24 N,	038°52′.94 E	(7)	22°29′.58 N,	039°03′.62 E
(2)	22°18′.61 N,	038°53′.61 E	(8)	22°26′.70 N,	038°59′.43 E
(3)	22°20′.57 N,	038°54′.65 E	(9)	22°21′.25 N,	038°56′.62 E
(4)	22°25′.94 N,	038°57′.48 E	(10)	22°19′.24 N,	038°55′.59 E
(5)	22°29′.00 N,	038°58′.99 E	(11)	22°15′.90 N,	038°53′.91 E
(6)	22°31′.75 N,	039°03′.02 E			

* Date of implementation of new deep-water route: 0000 hours UTC on 31 August 2011.

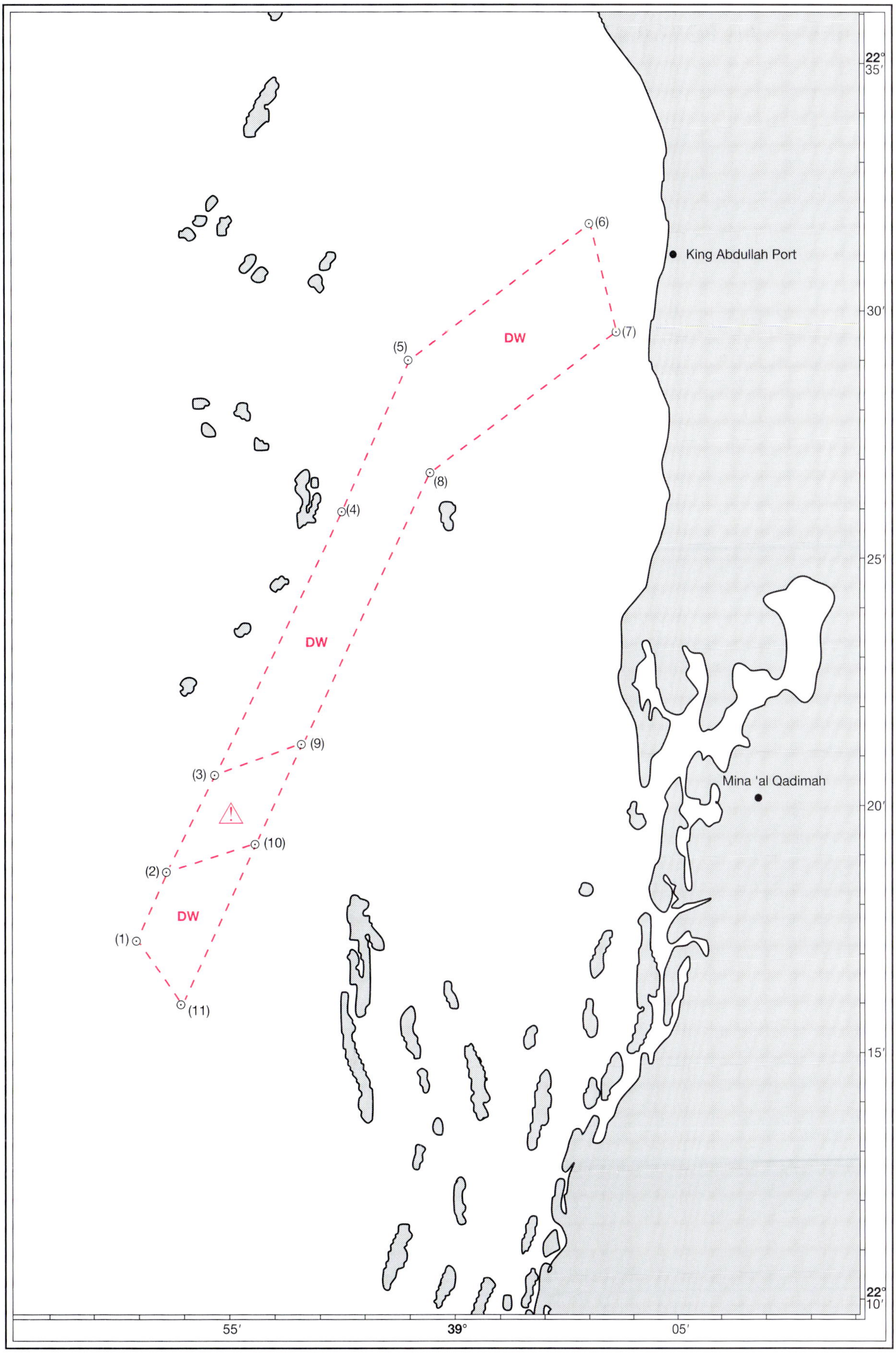

DEEP-WATER ROUTE IN THE APPROACHES TO THE NEW PORT OF KING ABDULLAH PORT (KAP PORT) IN THE NORTHERN RED SEA

DEEP-WATER ROUTE LEADING TO JAZAN ECONOMIC CITY PORT

(Reference chart: British Admiralty 15, edition 2, 22 June 2000).
Note: This chart is based on World Geodetic System 1984 datum (WGS 84).)

Description of the deep-water route

(a) A deep-water route is established bounded by a line connecting the following positions:

(1)	17°01′.52 N,	041°21′.63 E	(10)	17°15′.27 N,	042°14′.28 E
(2)	17°07′.24 N,	041°24′.67 E	(11)	17°15′.18 N,	042°11′.80 E
(3)	17°13′.45 N,	041°34′.19 E	(12)	17°10′.50 N,	042°13′.44 E
(4)	17°17′.30 N,	041°43′.11 E	(13)	17°04′.00 N,	042°07′.50 E
(5)	17°16′.34 N,	041°43′.83 E	(14)	17°05′.55 N,	042°03′.97 E
(6)	17°02′.35 N,	042°02′.07 E	(15)	17°19′.25 N,	041°43′.99 E
(7)	17°00′.50 N,	042°07′.93 E	(16)	17°14′.60 N,	041°33′.23 E
(8)	17°03′.34 N,	042°08′.88 E	(17)	17°09′.45 N,	041°23′.59 E
(9)	17°10′.50 N,	042°15′.44 E	(18)	17°02′.48 N,	041°19′.90 E

Thence back to the point of origin (1)

Note: The controlling depth for the deep-water route has been set at 27 metres.

Description of a precautionary area

(b) A precautionary area is established bounded by a line connecting the following positions:

(6)	17°02′.35 N,	042°02′.07 E	(13)	17°04′.00 N,	042°07′.50 E
(7)	17°00′.50 N,	042°07′.93 E	(14)	17°05′.55 N,	042°03′.97 E
(8)	17°03′.34 N,	042°08′.88 E			

Thence back to the point of origin (6)

Description of areas to be avoided

(c) An area to be avoided, 650 metres in radius, is centred upon the following geographical position:
(19) 17°08′.34 N, 041°24′.34 E

(d) An area to be avoided, 650 metres in radius, is centred upon the following geographical position:
(20) 17°10′.38 N, 041°53′.96 E

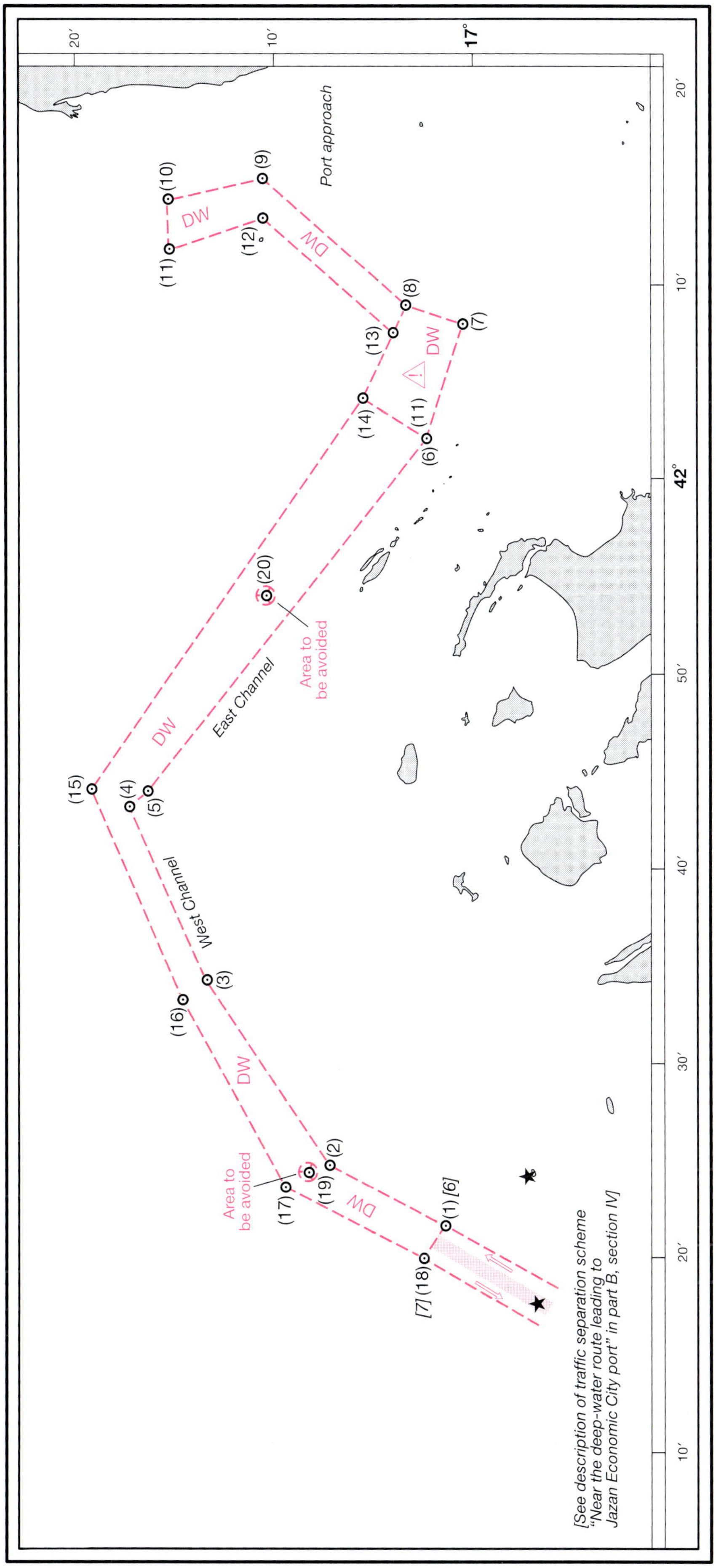

DEEP-WATER ROUTE LEADING TO JAZAN ECONOMIC CITY PORT

C

DEEP-WATER ROUTES WITHIN THE TRAFFIC SEPARATION SCHEMES IN THE STRAIT OF MALACCA

Note: See "Rules for vessels navigating through the Straits of Malacca and Singapore" in part F and mandatory ship reporting system "In the Straits of Malacca and Singapore" in part G, section I.

(Reference charts: British Admiralty 3946, 1996 edition; 3947, 1997 edition.
Note: These charts are based on revised Kertau datum.)

Description of the deep-water routes

(a) A deep-water route for south-eastbound traffic is bounded by a line connecting the following geographical positions of the traffic separation scheme "Port Dickson to Tanjung Keling":

(42)	02°21′.40 N,	101°39′.40 E	(46)	02°12′.30 N,	101°36′.80 E
(43)	02°13′.80 N,	101°39′.30 E	(47)	02°22′.20 N,	101°36′.80 E
(44)	02°05′.10 N,	101°55′.90 E	(48)	02°24′.00 N,	101°36′.10 E
(45)	02°03′.00 N,	101°54′.20 E			

(b) A deep-water route for south-eastbound traffic is bounded by a line connecting the following geographical positions of the traffic separation scheme "Malacca to Iyu Kecil":

(77)	02°01′.90 N,	102°01′.50 E	(79)	01°52′.60 N,	102°13′.30 E
(78)	01°59′.70 N,	102°05′.60 E	(80)	02°00′.00 N,	101°59′.80 E

Note: See "Rules for vessels navigating through the Straits of Malacca and Singapore" in part F.

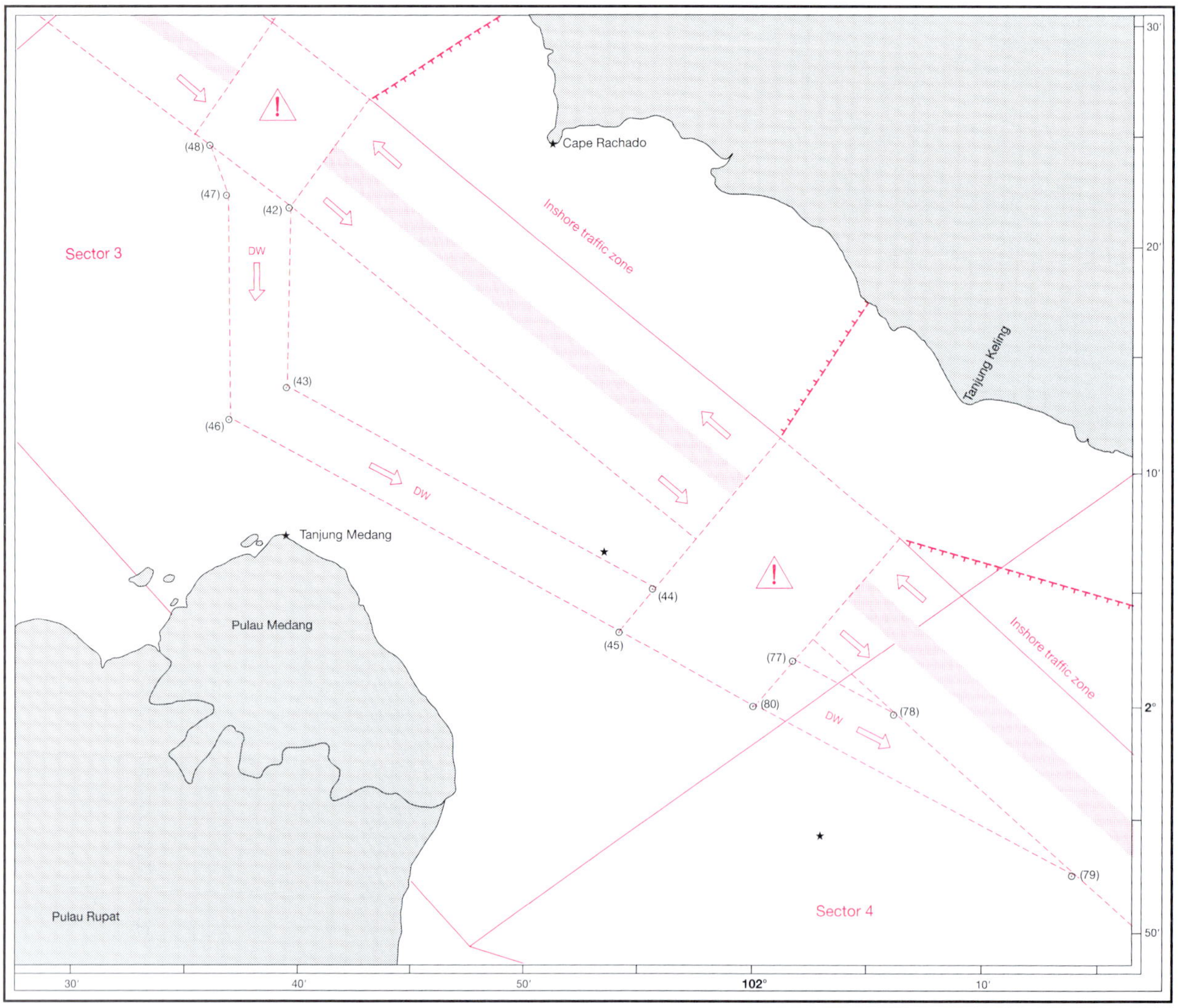

DEEP-WATER ROUTES WITHIN THE TRAFFIC SEPARATION SCHEMES
IN THE STRAIT OF MALACCA

DEEP-WATER ROUTES FORMING PART OF THE EASTBOUND TRAFFIC LANE OF TRAFFIC SEPARATION SCHEMES IN THE SINGAPORE STRAIT

Note: See "Rules for vessels navigating through the Straits of Malacca and Singapore" in part F and mandatory ship reporting system "In the Straits of Malacca and Singapore" in part G, section I and "Recommendatory measures for vessels crossing the traffic separation scheme and precautionary areas in the Singapore Strait during hours of darkness" in part E.

(Reference charts: British Admiralty 2556, 1994 edition; 3833, 1988 edition; 2403, 1983 edition.
Note: These charts are based on revised Kertau datum.)

Description of the deep-water routes

(a) The deep-water route is established within the eastbound lane described in paragraph (d) of the traffic separation scheme "In the Singapore Strait (Main Strait)". The deep-water route is bounded by a line connecting the following geographical positions:

(i)	01°03′.60 N,	103°38′.95 E	(vi)	01°10′.45 N,	103°49′.45 E
(ii)	01°05′.90 N,	103°43′.38 E	(vii)	01°09′.95 N,	103°48′.28 E
(iii)	01°08′.61 N,	103°45′.44 E	(viii)	01°08′.90 N,	103°46′.82 E
(iv)	01°10′.26 N,	103°47′.91 E	(ix)	01°04′.95 N,	103°42′.87 E
(v)	01°10′.81 N,	103°49′.30 E	(x)	01°02′.97 N,	103°39′.10 E

Note: Reference is made to rule 1 of the Rules for vessels navigating through the Straits of Malacca and Singapore (see part F).

(b) The deep-water route is established within the eastbound lane described in paragraph (c) of the traffic separation scheme "Singapore Strait (off St. John's Island)". The deep-water route is bounded by a line connecting the following geographical positions:

(xi)	01°11′.27 N,	103°50′.43 E	(xiii)	01°11′.78 N,	103°52′.58 E
(xii)	01°12′.21 N,	103°52′.40 E	(xiv)	01°10′.92 N,	103°50′.57 E

Note: Attention is drawn to the Rules for vessels navigating through the Straits of Malacca and Singapore (see part F).

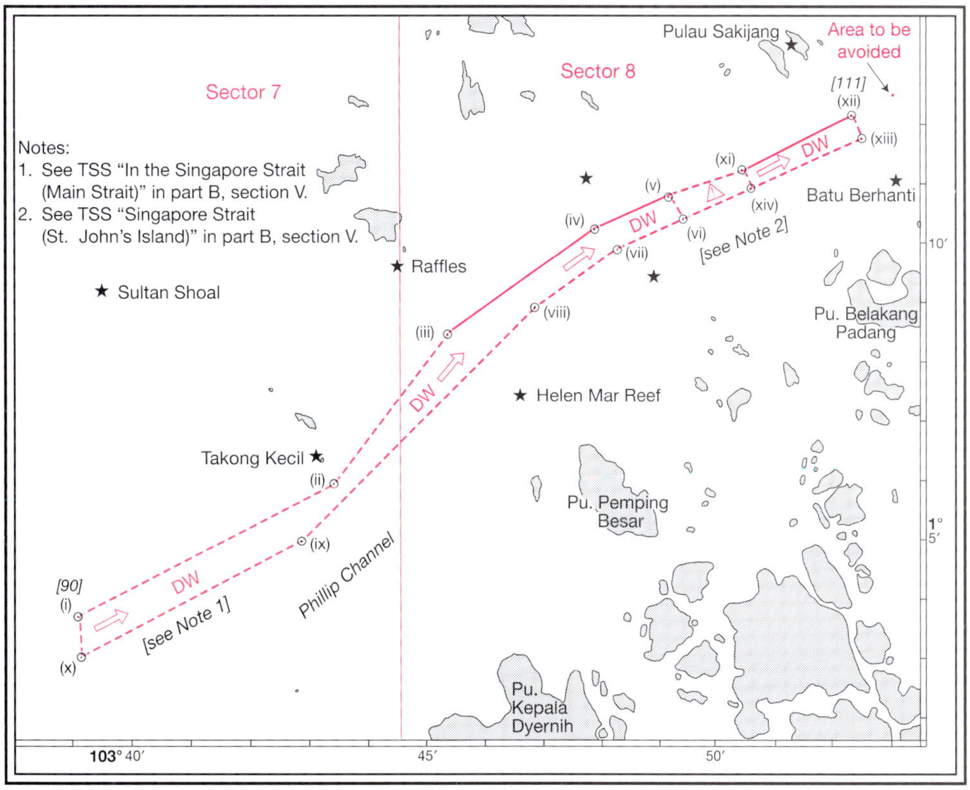

DEEP-WATER ROUTES FORMING PART OF THE EASTBOUND TRAFFIC LANE OF TRAFFIC SEPARATION SCHEMES IN THE SINGAPORE STRAIT

Section IV

Western North Atlantic Ocean, Gulf of Mexico and Caribbean Sea

Caution: The chartlets are for illustrative purposes only and must not be used for navigation. Mariners should consult the appropriate nautical publications and charts for up-to-date details on aids to navigation and other relevant information.

Warning: The geographical positions given in the descriptions of the deep-water routes are only correct for charts using the same geodetic datum as the reference charts indicated under each scheme. Charts published by other hydrographic offices may use a different geodetic datum, as may new editions of the reference charts published after the adoption of the routes.

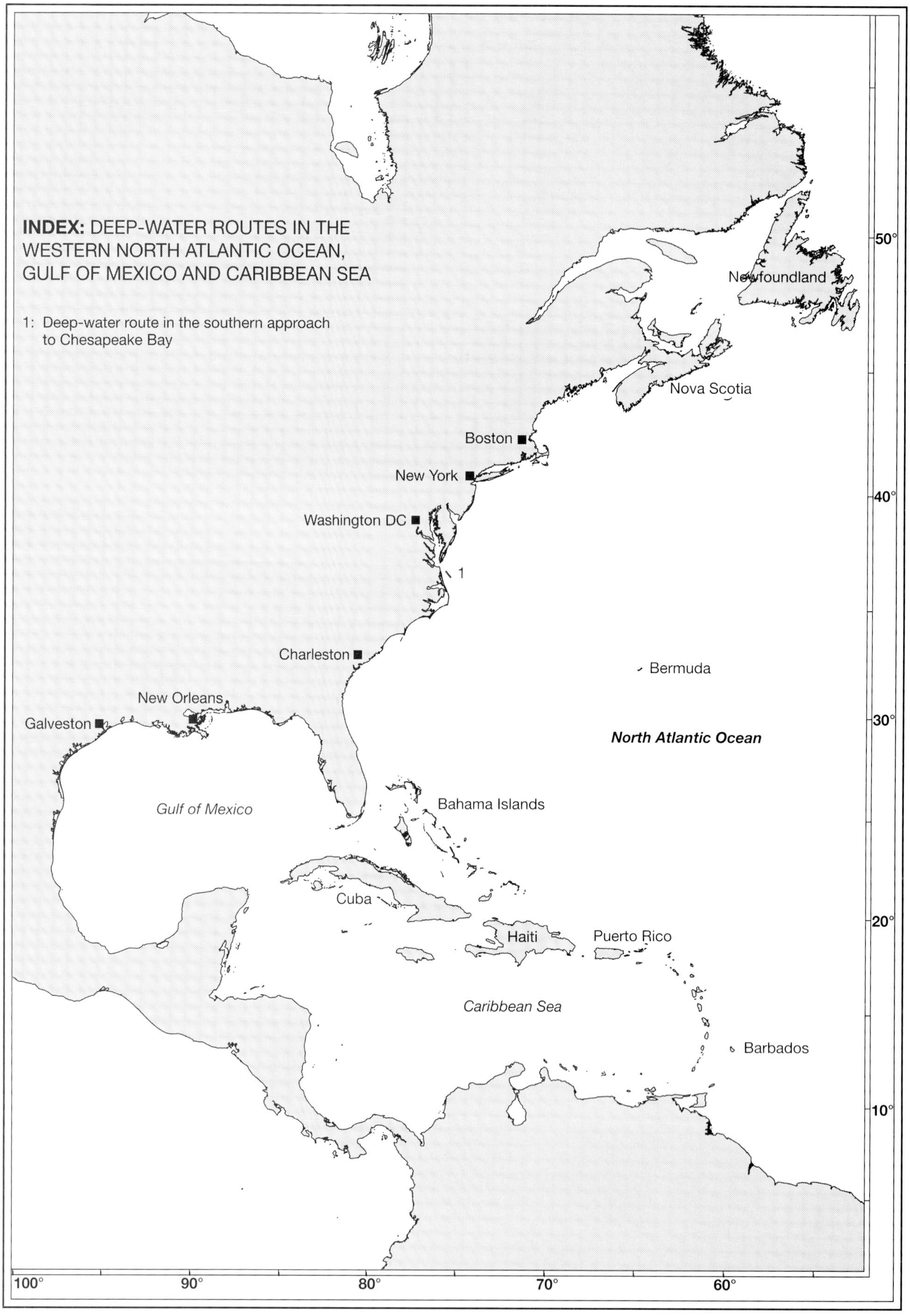
INDEX: DEEP-WATER ROUTES IN THE WESTERN NORTH ATLANTIC OCEAN, GULF OF MEXICO AND CARIBBEAN SEA
1: Deep-water route in the southern approach to Chesapeake Bay
Newfoundland
Nova Scotia
Boston
New York
Washington DC
1
Charleston
Bermuda
New Orleans
Galveston
North Atlantic Ocean
Bahama Islands
Gulf of Mexico
Cuba
Haiti
Puerto Rico
Caribbean Sea
Barbados
50°
40°
30°
20°
10°
100°
90°
80°
70°
60°

DEEP-WATER ROUTE IN THE SOUTHERN APPROACH TO CHESAPEAKE BAY

(Reference chart: United States 12221, 2003 edition.
Note: This chart is based on North American 1983 datum.)

Description of the deep-water route

A deep-water route is established in the southern approach of the traffic separation scheme "In the approaches to Chesapeake Bay" between the separation lines which connect the following geographical positions of the traffic separation scheme (see part B, section IX):

(13)	36°55′.11 N,	075°55′.23 W	(16)	36°49′.52 N,	075°46′.94 W
(14)	36°52′.35 N,	075°52′.12 W	(17)	36°52′.18 N,	075°52′.29 W
(15)	36°49′.70 N,	075°46′.80 W	(18)	36°54′.97 N,	075°55′.43 W

Notes:

1 It is recommended that the following ships use the deep-water route when bound for Chesapeake Bay from sea or to sea from Chesapeake Bay:

deep-draught ships, draughts defined as 12.8 m/42 ft or greater in fresh water, and naval aircraft carriers. Ships drawing less than 12.8 m/42 ft may use the deep-water route when, in their master's judgement, the effects of ship characteristics, its speed, and prevailing environmental conditions may cause the draught of the ship to equal or exceed 12.8 m/42 ft.

2 It is recommended that a ship using the deep-water route:

.1 announce its intention on VHF-FM channel 16 as it approaches Chesapeake Bay Southern Approach Lighted Whistle Buoy CB on the south end, or Chesapeake Bay Lighted Buoy CH, on the north end of the route;

.2 avoid, as far as practicable, overtaking other ships operating in the deep-water route;

.3 keep as near to the outer limit of the route which lies on the starboard side as is safe and practicable.

3 All other ships approaching the Chesapeake Bay traffic separation scheme should use the appropriate inbound or outbound traffic lane of the traffic separation scheme "In the approaches to Chesapeake Bay".

(chartlet overleaf)

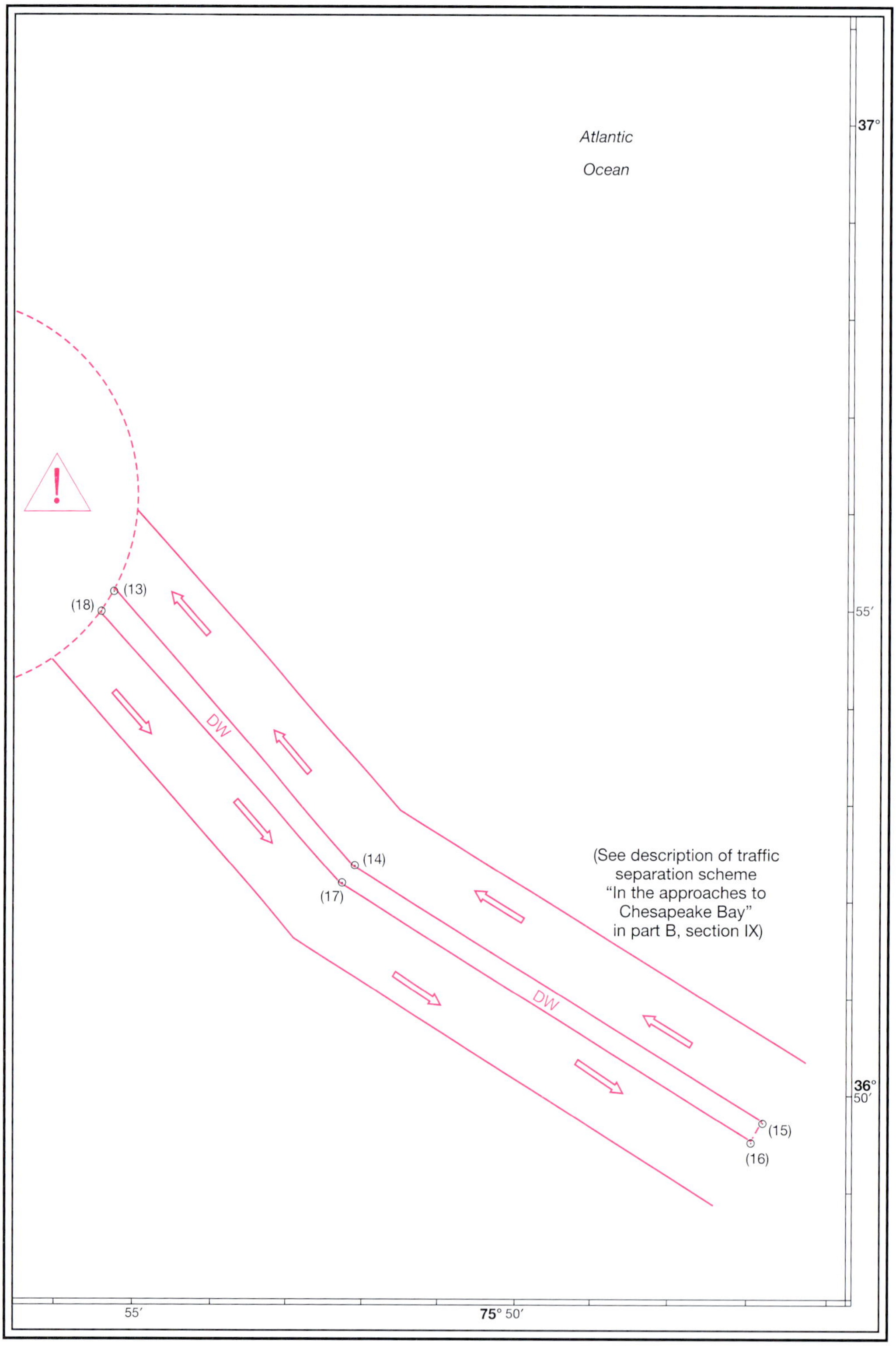

DEEP-WATER ROUTE IN THE SOUTHERN APPROACH TO CHESAPEAKE BAY

Part D

Areas to be avoided

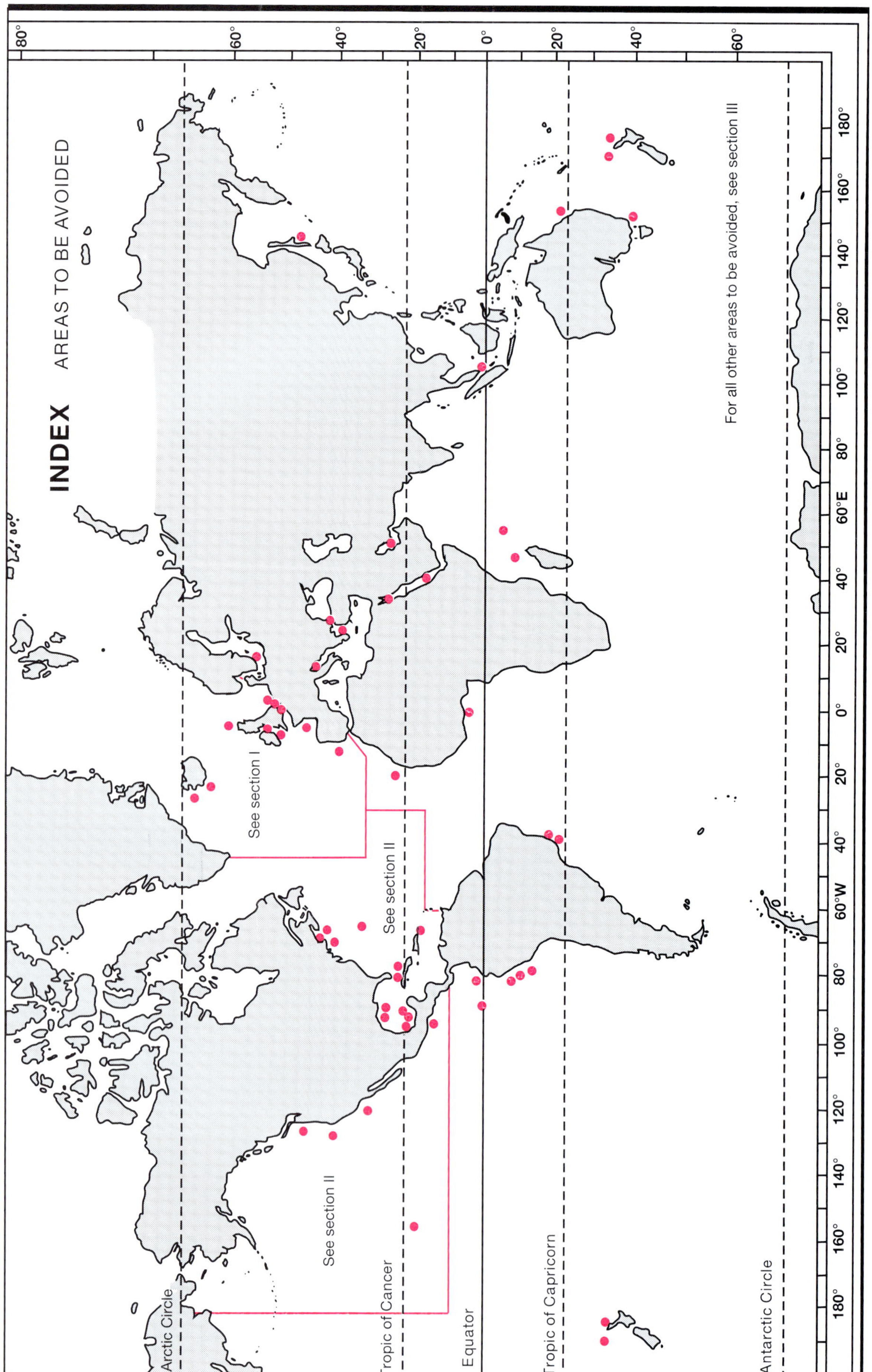
INDEX
AREAS TO BE AVOIDED
See section I
See section II
See section II
For all other areas to be avoided, see section III
Arctic Circle
Tropic of Cancer
Equator
Tropic of Capricorn
Antarctic Circle
80°
60°
40°
20°
0°
20°
40°
60°
180°
160°
140°
120°
100°
80°
60°W
40°
20°
0°
20°
40°
60°E
80°
100°
120°
140°
160°
180°

D

Section I

North-western European waters

Caution: The chartlets are for illustrative purposes only and must not be used for navigation. Mariners should consult the appropriate nautical publications and charts for up-to-date details on aids to navigation and other relevant information.

Warning: The geographical positions given in the descriptions of the areas to be avoided are only correct for charts using the same geodetic datum as the reference charts indicated under each description. Charts published by other hydrographic offices may use a different geodetic datum, as may new editions of the reference charts published after the adoption of the areas.

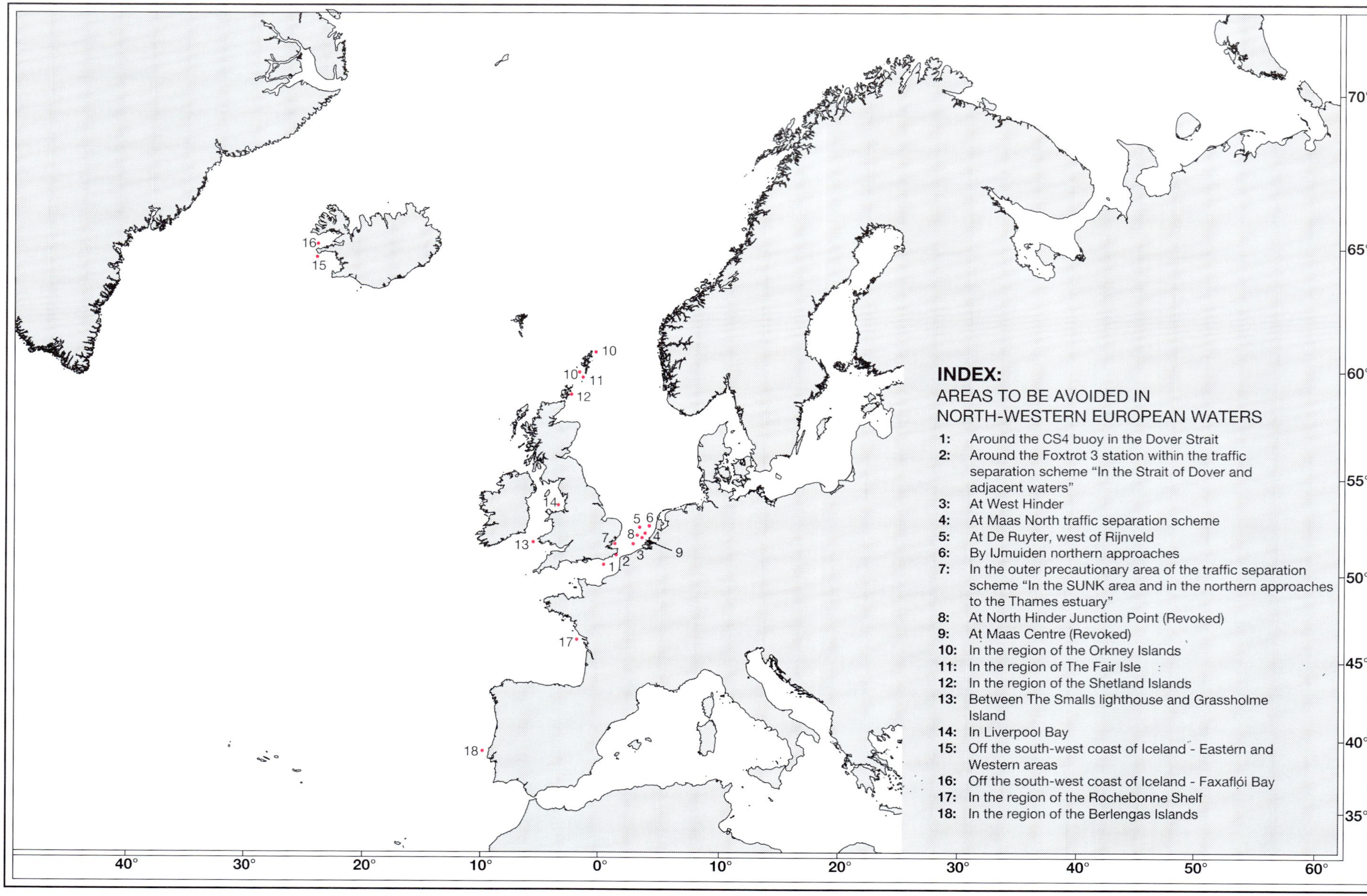

INDEX:

AREAS TO BE AVOIDED IN
NORTH-WESTERN EUROPEAN WATERS

1: Around the CS4 buoy in the Dover Strait
2: Around the Foxtrot 3 station within the traffic separation scheme "In the Strait of Dover and adjacent waters"
3: At West Hinder
4: At Maas North traffic separation scheme
5: At De Ruyter, west of Rijnveld
6: By IJmuiden northern approaches
7: In the outer precautionary area of the traffic separation scheme "In the SUNK area and in the northern approaches to the Thames estuary"
8: At North Hinder Junction Point (Revoked)
9: At Maas Centre (Revoked)
10: In the region of the Orkney Islands
11: In the region of The Fair Isle
12: In the region of the Shetland Islands
13: Between The Smalls lighthouse and Grassholme Island
14: In Liverpool Bay
15: Off the south-west coast of Iceland - Eastern and Western areas
16: Off the south-west coast of Iceland - Faxaflói Bay
17: In the region of the Rochebonne Shelf
18: In the region of the Berlengas Islands

AROUND THE CS4 BUOY IN THE DOVER STRAIT

(Reference charts: British Admiralty 1610, 2001 edition; 1828, 2002 edition.
Note: These charts are based on World Geodetic System 1984 datum (WGS 84).)

Description of the area to be avoided

All ships should avoid the area within a circle of radius 0.3 miles centred upon the following geographical position:

51°08′.67 N, 001°34′.02 E

This area is established to avoid hazard to the navigational aid which is established at the above geographical position, and which is considered vital to the safety of navigation.

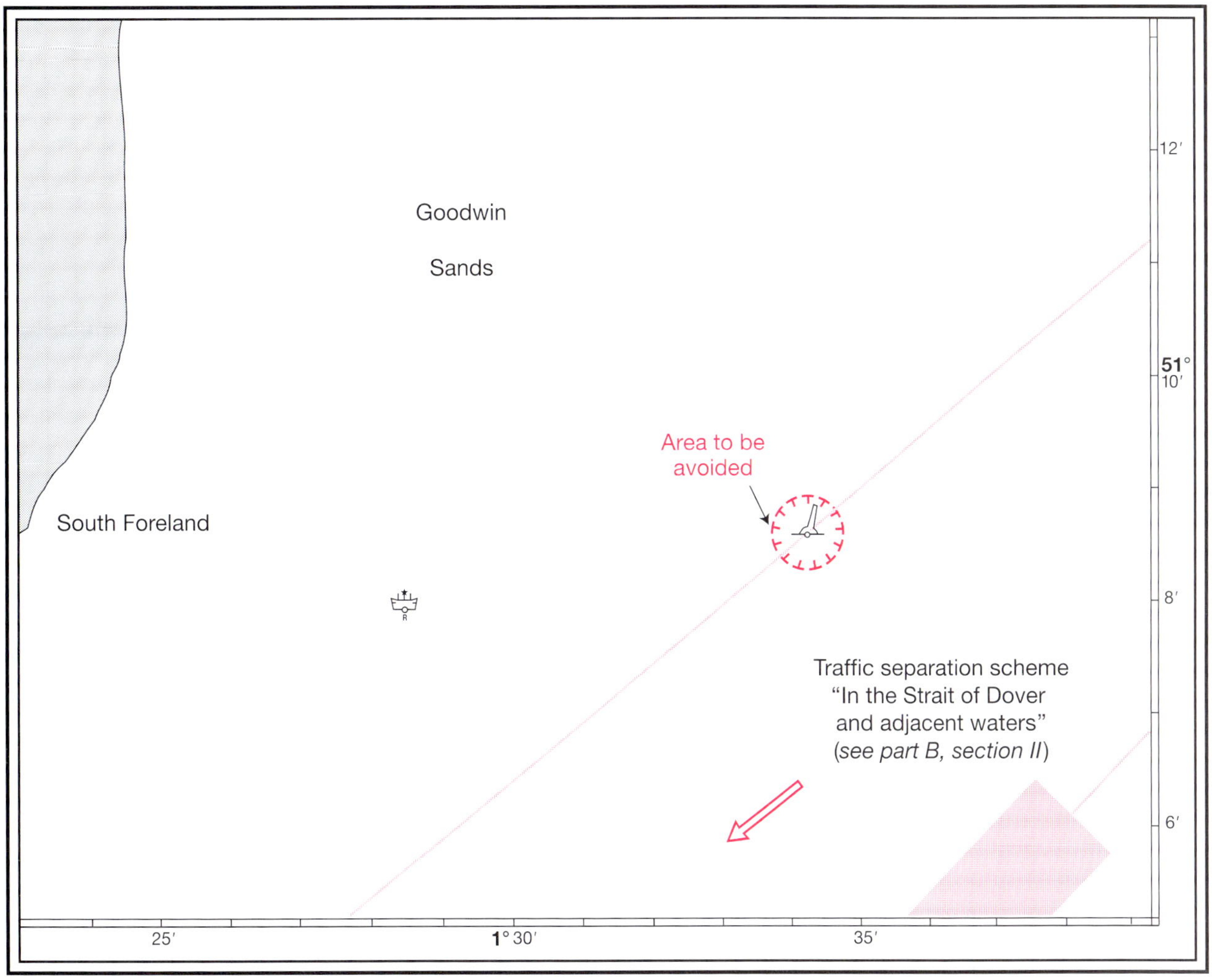

AROUND THE CS4 BUOY IN THE DOVER STRAIT

AROUND THE FOXTROT 3 STATION WITHIN THE TRAFFIC SEPARATION SCHEME "IN THE STRAIT OF DOVER AND ADJACENT WATERS"

(Reference chart: British Admiralty 2449, June 2007 edition.
Note: This chart is based on World Geodetic System 1984 datum (WGS 84).)

Description of the area to be avoided by all ships

The Foxtrot 3 station is in an area of heavy crossing traffic with some 11,000 crossing movements per annum and has suffered damage on several occasions. Therefore, with the aim of preventing further damage, an "area to be avoided" has been established centred on the Foxtrot 3 station.

The area to be avoided, by all ships, with a radius of 500 metres, is centred on the following geographical position:

51°24′.15 N, 002°00′.38 E

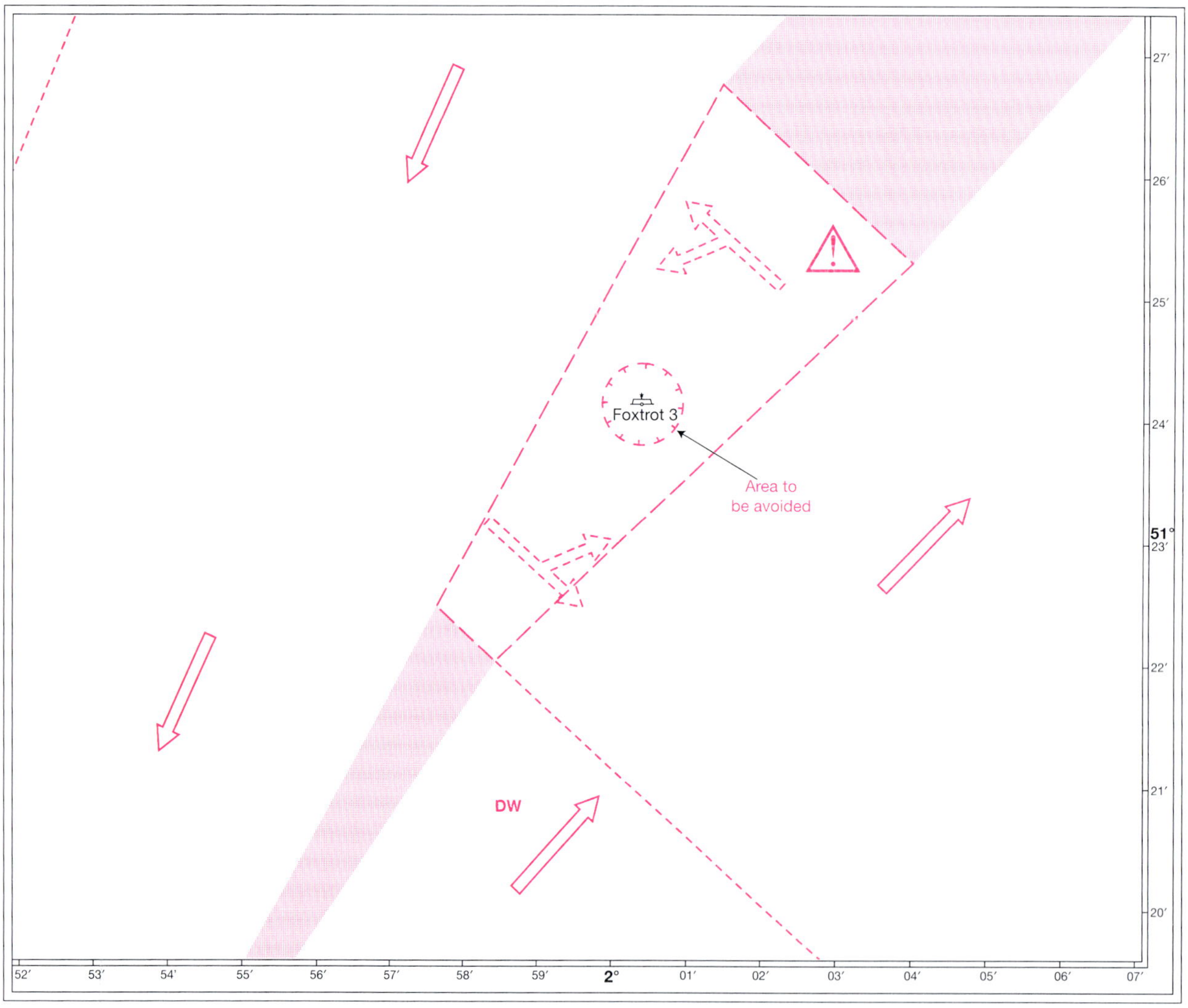

AROUND THE FOXTROT 3 STATION WITHIN THE TRAFFIC SEPARATION SCHEME "IN THE STRAIT OF DOVER AND ADJACENT WATERS"

AT WEST HINDER*

Note: See traffic separation scheme "At West Hinder" in part B, section II and mandatory ship reporting systems "In the Dover Strait/Pas de Calais" and "West European Tanker Reporting System" in part G, section I.

(Reference charts: D11 and 102 (INT 1480) published by the Agency of Maritime and Coastal Services, Flemish Hydrography.
Note: These charts are based on World Geodetic System 1984 datum (WGS 84).)

Description of the area to be avoided

An area to be avoided is established bounded by a line connecting the following geographical positions:

(1)	51° 23′.45 N,	002° 36′.92 E	AN buoy
(2)	51° 23′.95 N,	002° 36′.90 E	
(3)	51° 24′.40 N,	002° 40′.30 E	
(4)	51° 23′.81 N,	002° 40′.30 E	

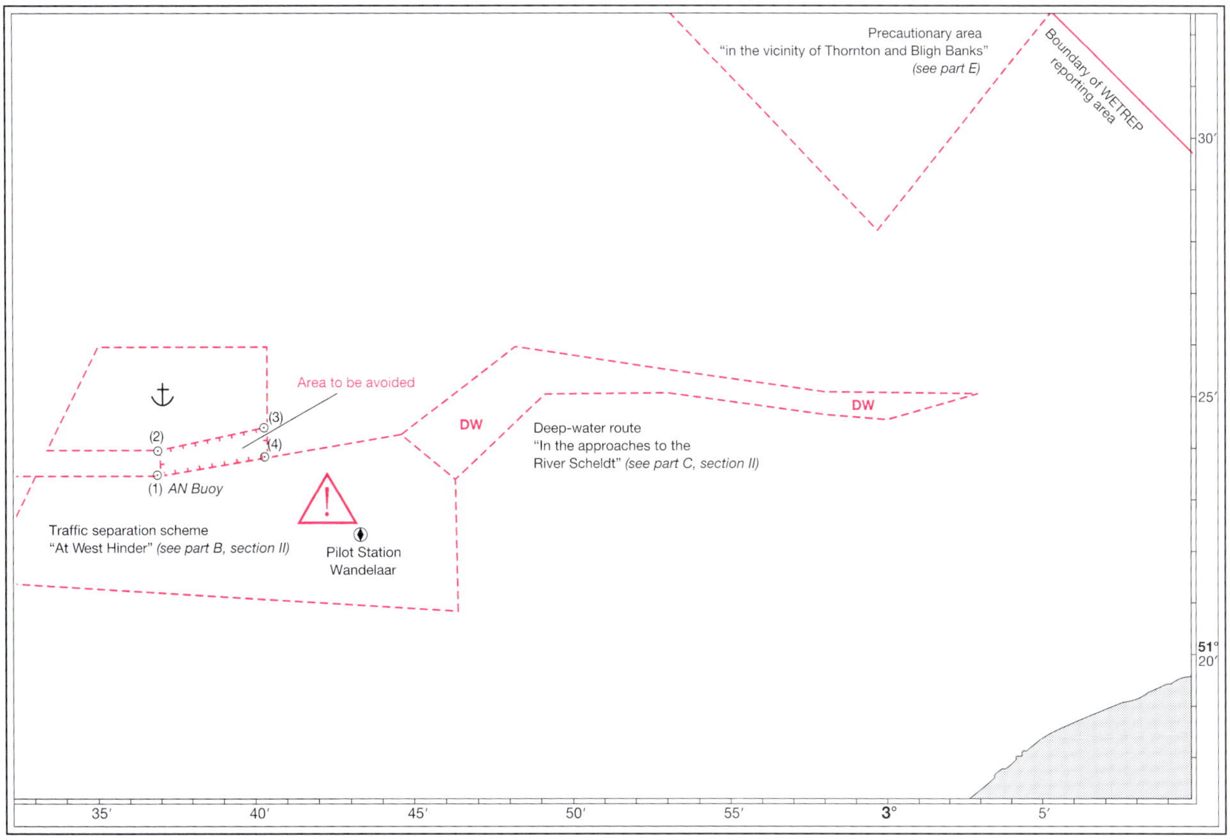

AT WEST HINDER

* Date of implementation of new area to be avoided: 0000 hours UTC on 1 December 2012.

AT MAAS NORTH TRAFFIC SEPARATION SCHEME*

Note: See traffic separation schemes "In the approaches to Hook of Holland and at North Hinder" in part B, section II and "Precautionary areas in the approaches to Hook of Holland and at North Hinder" in part E.

(Reference chart: Netherlands 1630 (INT 1416), edition 4/2010.
Note: This chart is based on World Geodetic System 1984 datum (WGS 84).)

Description of the area to be avoided

An area to be avoided for all ships is established within the separation zone of the Maas North traffic separation scheme and is bounded by a line connecting the following geographical positions:

(i)	52° 15′.45 N,	003° 51′.42 E	(iii)	52° 12′.45 N,	003° 48′.32 E
(ii)	52° 12′.45 N,	003° 51′.42 E	(iv)	52° 15′.45 N,	003° 48′.32 E

Note:
CAUTION
(In the Maas North separation zone, below the area to be avoided)

The area to be avoided within the Maas North separation zone encloses two ammunition dumps. Mariners are warned not to enter this area and, in particular, not to anchor in it, even in an emergency.

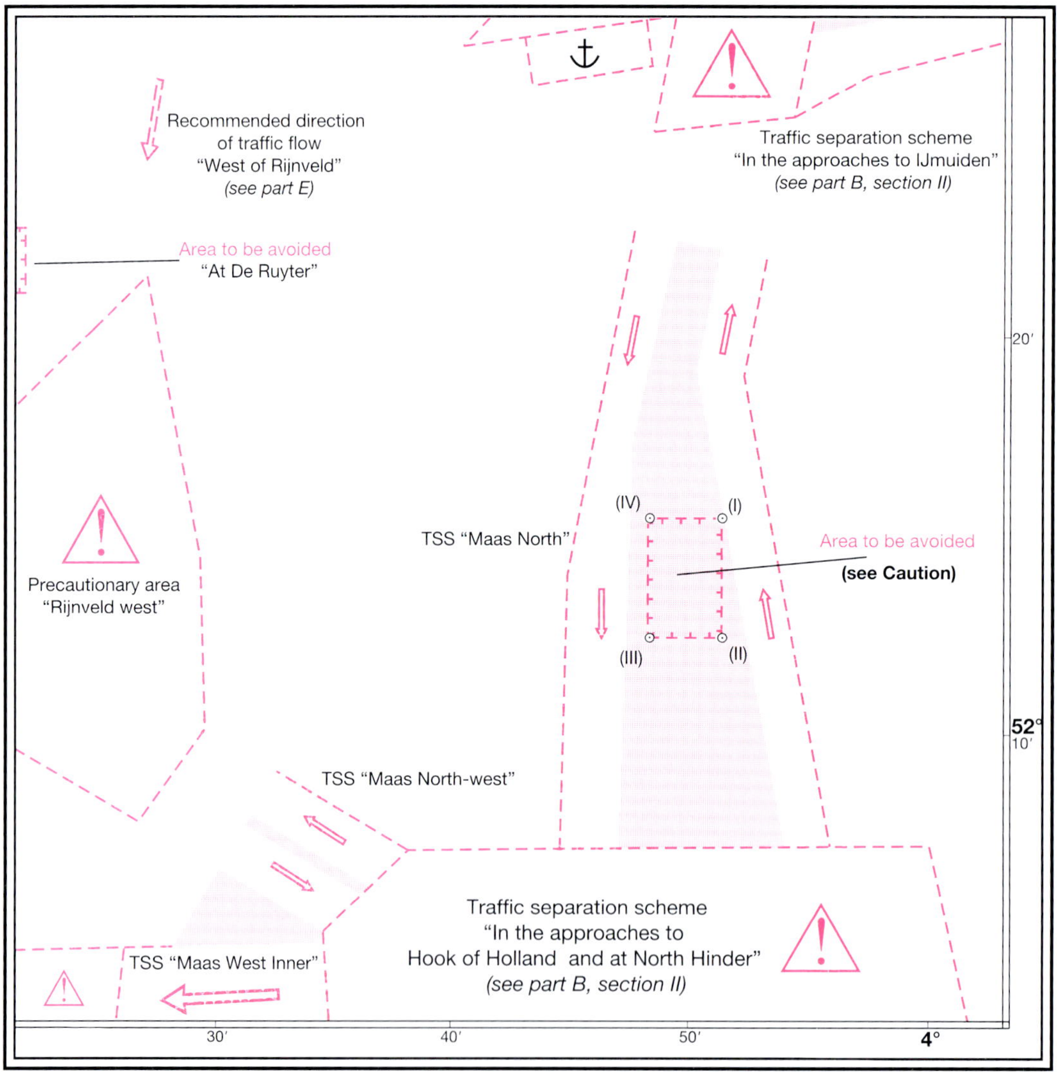

AT MAAS NORTH TRAFFIC SEPARATION SCHEME

* Date of implementation of new area to be avoided: 0000 hours UTC on 1 August 2013.

AT DE RUYTER, WEST OF RIJNVELD*

(Reference charts: Netherlands 1630 (INT 1416), edition 4/2010 and 1631 (INT 1418), edition 3.
Note: These charts are based on World Geodetic System 1984 datum (WGS 84).)

Description of the area to be avoided

An area to be avoided for all ships, except authorized, around the De Ruyter offshore oil and gas installation is established and bounded by a line connecting the following geographical positions:

(i)	52° 21′.12 N,	003° 19′.73 E	(iii)	52° 22′.75 N,	003° 22′.00 E
(ii)	52° 22′.75 N,	003° 19′.73 E	(iv)	52° 21′.12 N,	003° 22′.00 E

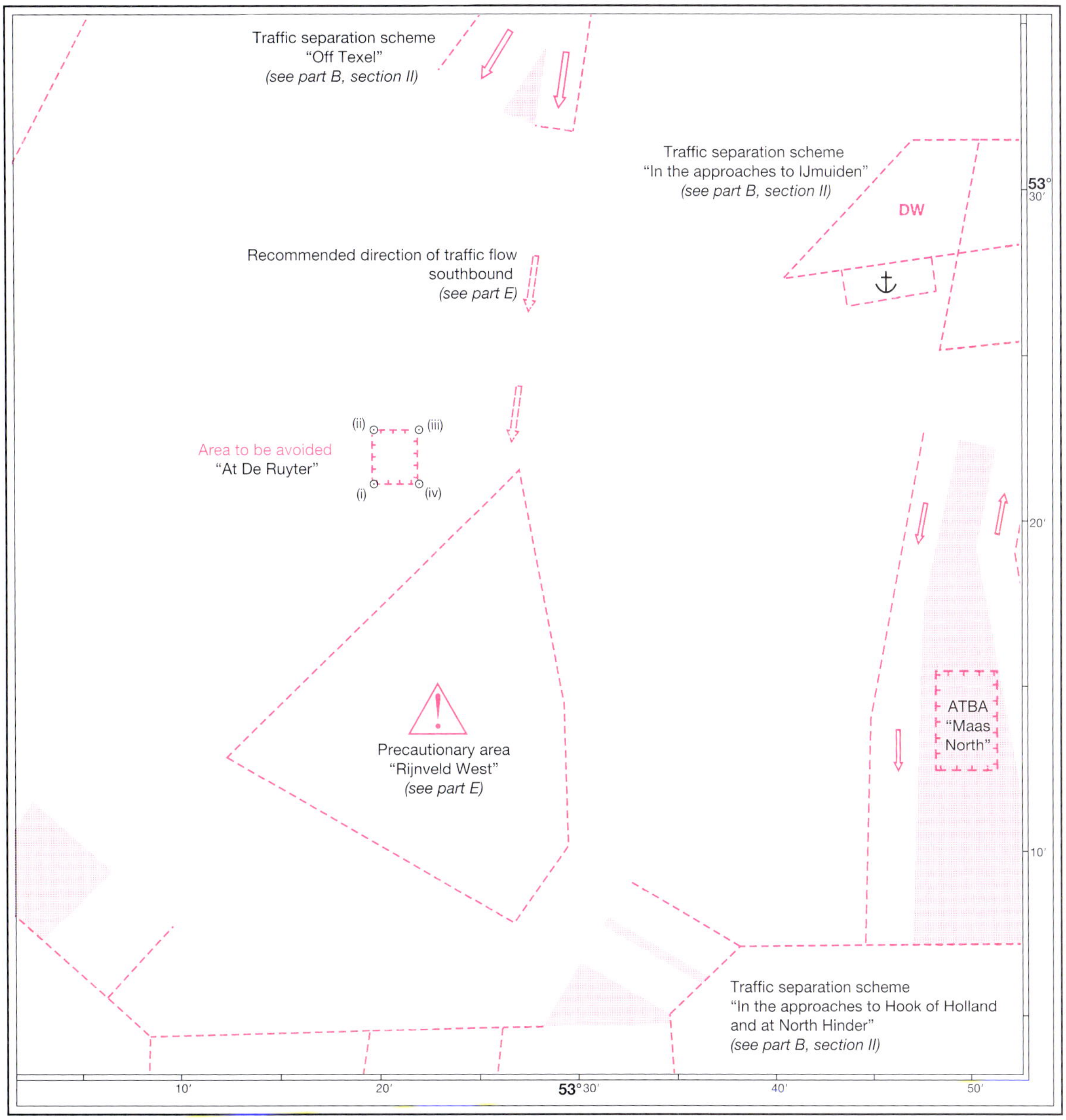

AT DE RUYTER, WEST OF RIJNVELD

* Date of implementation of new area to be avoided: 0000 hours UTC on 1 August 2013.

BY IJMUIDEN NORTHERN APPROACHES*

Note: See traffic separation scheme "In the approaches to IJmuiden" in part B, section II and "Deep-water route leading to IJmuiden" in part C, section II and "Precautionary areas in the approaches to IJmuiden" in part E.

(Reference chart: Netherlands 1631 (INT 1418), edition 3.
Note: This chart is based on World Geodetic System 1984 datum (WGS 84).)

Description of the area to be avoided

(a) An area to be avoided for all ships is bounded by a line connecting the following geographical positions:

(i)	52°32′.15 N, 004°04′.82 E	(iii)	52°34′.65 N, 004°02′.22 E
(ii)	52°34′.04 N, 004°04′.82 E	(iv)	52°32′.79 N, 004°02′.22 E

(b) The area to be avoided in paragraph (a) above is to be labelled *"Amm. Dumps"* on charts.

Note:
CAUTION

(By the entrance of the south-south-eastbound traffic lane of the IJmuiden North traffic separation scheme)

The area to be avoided on the western boundary of the IJmuiden North traffic separation scheme's south-south-eastbound lane encloses an ammunition dump dating from the end of the Second World War. Mariners are warned not to enter this area and, in particular, not to anchor in it, even in an emergency.

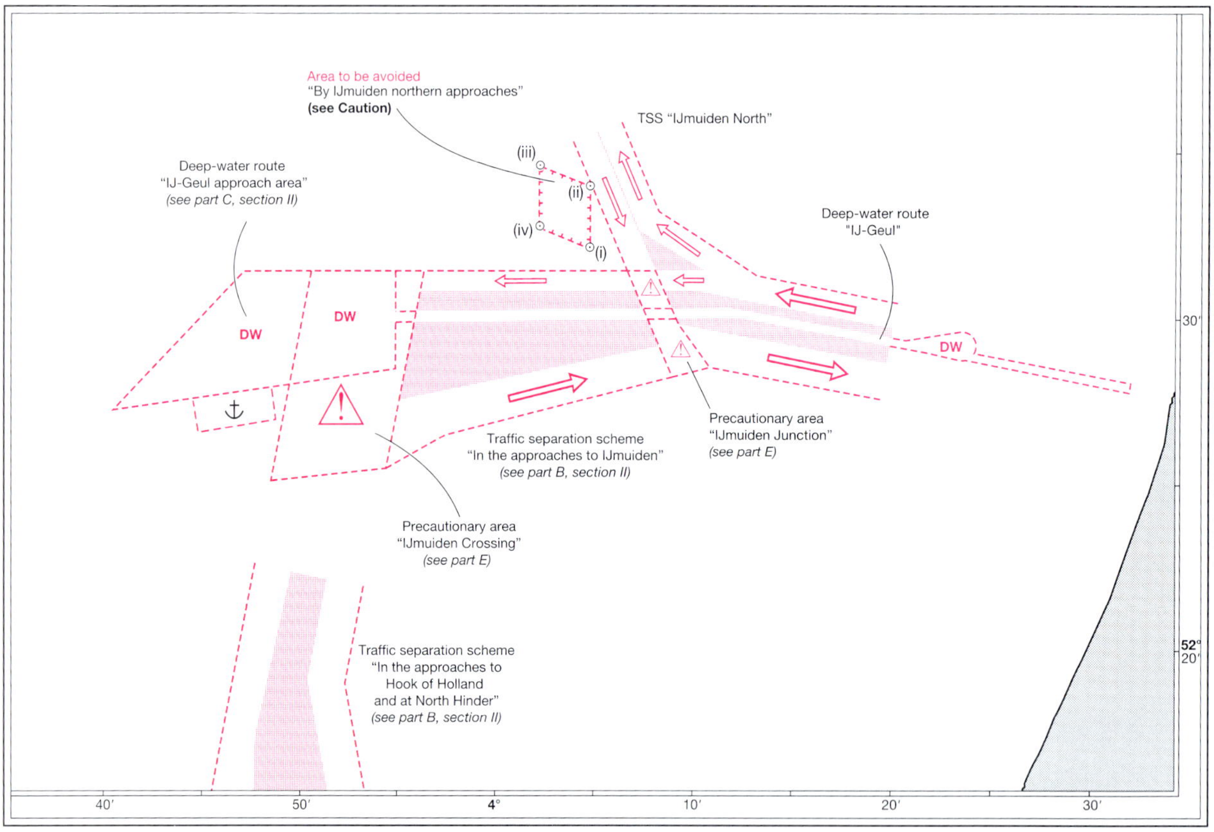

BY IJMUIDEN NORTHERN APPROACHES

* Date of implementation of new area to be avoided: 0000 hours UTC on 1 August 2013.

IN THE OUTER PRECAUTIONARY AREA OF THE TRAFFIC SEPARATION SCHEME "IN THE SUNK AREA AND IN THE NORTHERN APPROACHES TO THE THAMES ESTUARY"

Note: See mandatory ship reporting system "West European Tanker Reporting System" in part G, section I.

(Reference chart: British Admiralty 1183, 2005 edition.
Note: This chart is based on World Geodetic System 1984 datum (WGS 84).)

Description of the area to be avoided

An area to be avoided, 1 nautical mile in diameter, is centred upon the following geographical position:
51°50′.10 N, 001°46′.02 E

Note: The flow of traffic around the ATBA is counter-clockwise, as indicated by the recommended directions of traffic flow in the precautionary area.

All ships should avoid the area within a circle of radius 0.5 miles, centred upon the following geographical position:
51°50′.10 N, 001°46′.02 E.

This area is established to avoid hazard to a navigational aid which is established at the geographical position listed above, and which is considered vital to the safety of navigation.

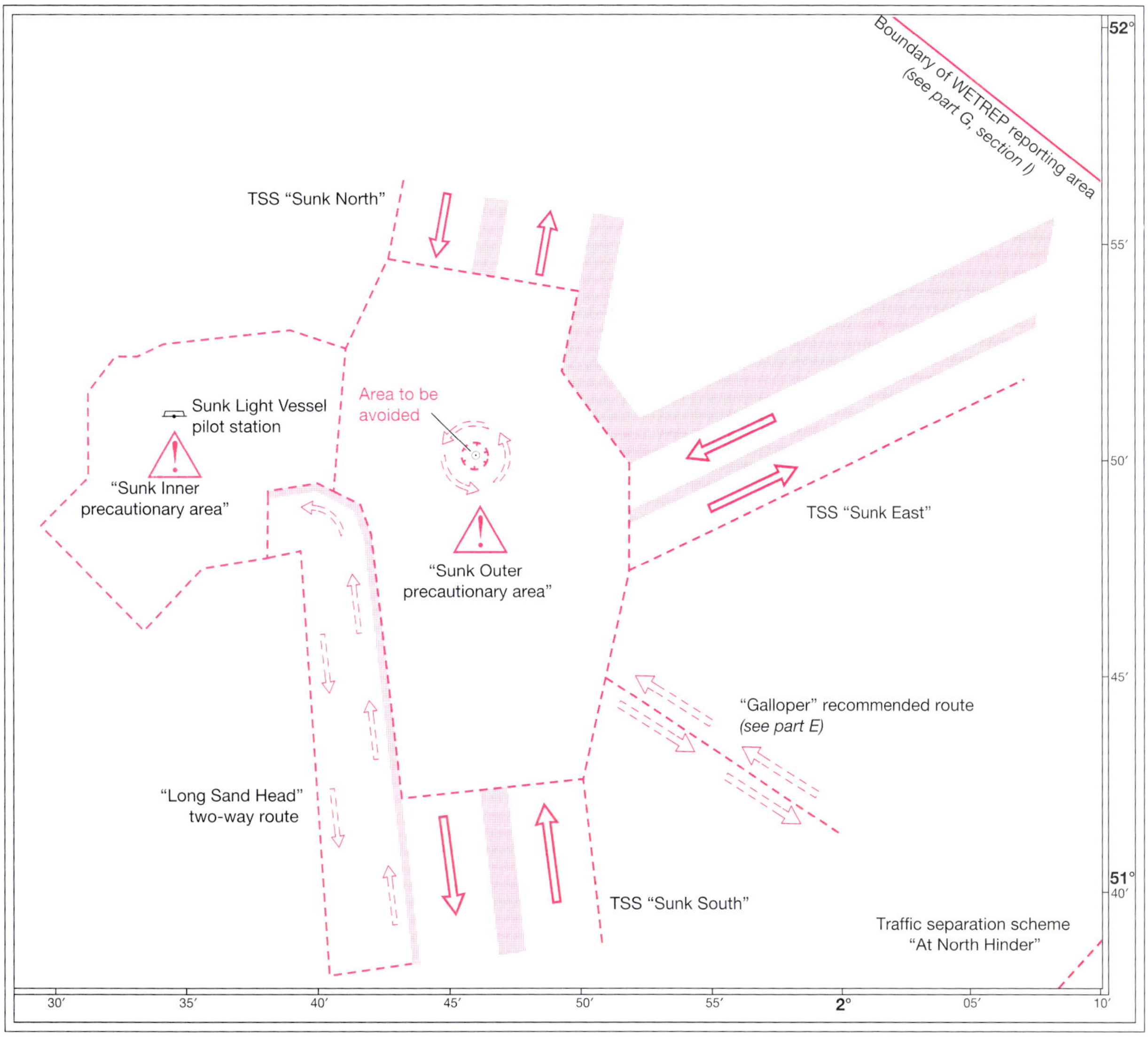

IN THE SUNK OUTER PRECAUTIONARY AREA

AT NORTH HINDER JUNCTION POINT [Revoked]*

The area to be avoided by all ships within the precautionary area off North Hinder, bounded by a circle of radius 0.5 miles centred upon the geographical position 52°00′.09 N, 002°51′.09 E is revoked.

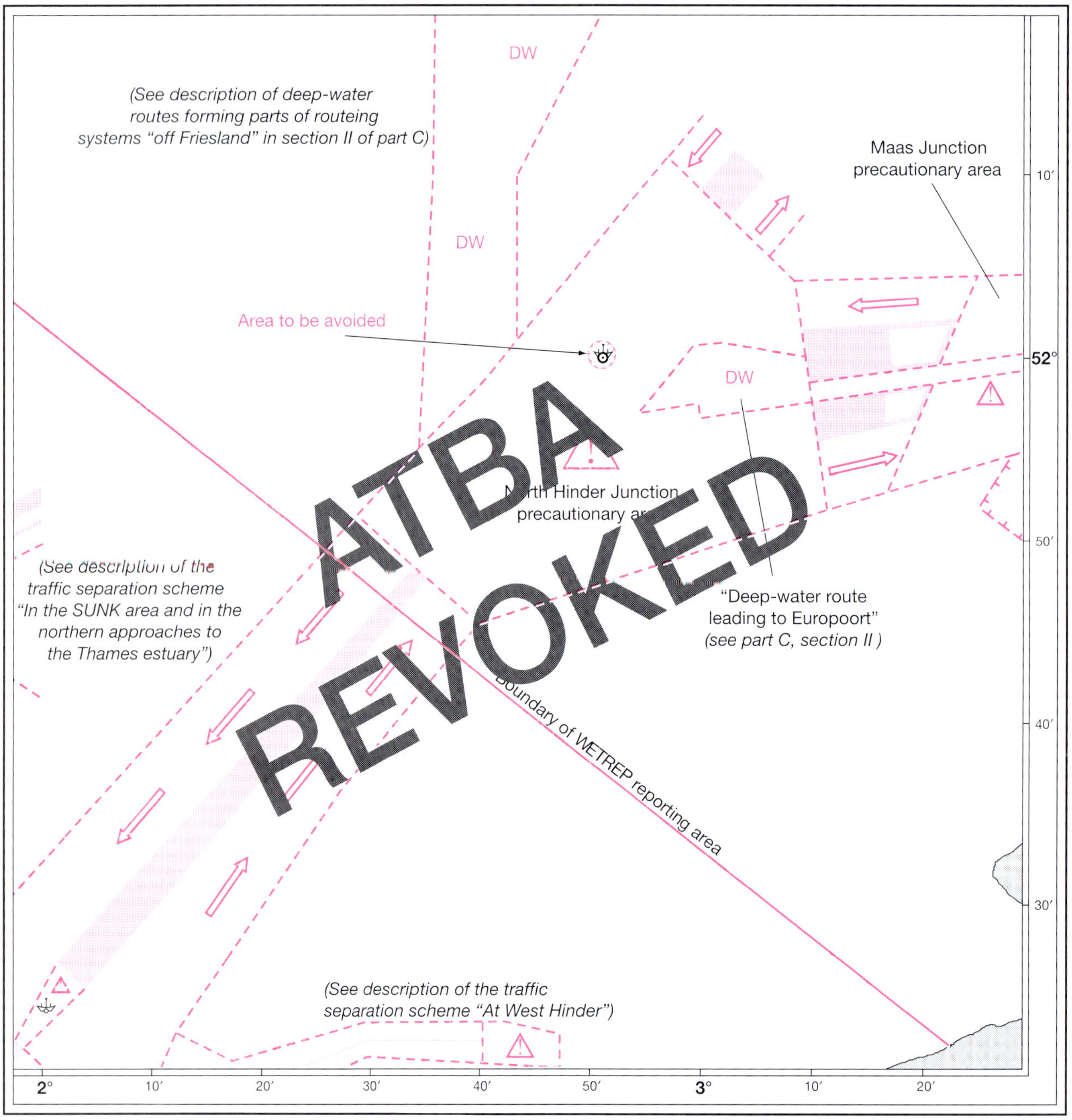

AT NORTH HINDER JUNCTION POINT

* Date of implementation of revocation of area to be avoided: 0000 hours UTC on 1 August 2013.

AT MAAS CENTRE [Revoked]*

The area to be avoided by all ships not compelled to adhere to the deep-water route off the entrance to the Rotterdam Waterway, bounded by a circle of radius 0.6 miles centred upon the geographical position 52°01′.68 N, 003°53′.11 E, is revoked.

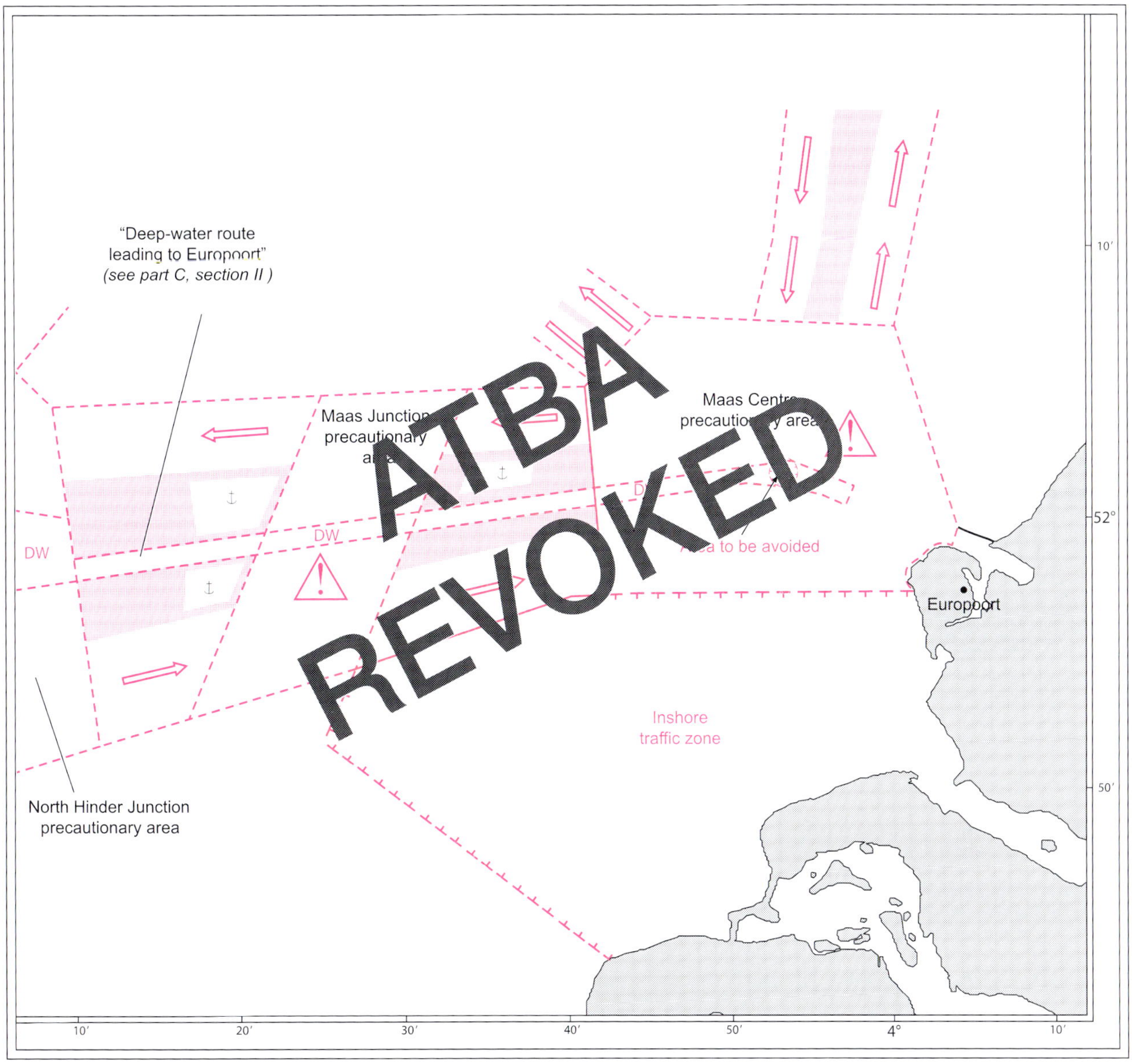

AT MAAS CENTRE

---

* Date of implementation of revocation of area to be avoided: 0000 hours UTC on 1 August 2013.

IN THE REGION OF THE ORKNEY ISLANDS

Note: See "Recommended routes in the Fair Isle Channel" in part E and mandatory ship reporting system "West European Tanker Reporting System" in part G, section I.

(Reference charts: British Admiralty 1954, 1988 edition; 1942, 1988 edition.
Note: These charts are based on Ordnance Survey of Great Britain 1936 datum.)

Description of the area to be avoided

In order to avoid the risk of oil pollution and severe damage to the environment of Orkney, ships of more than 5000 gross tonnage carrying oil or other hazardous cargoes in bulk should avoid the area bounded by lines connecting the following geographical positions:

(1)	58°46′.73 N,	003°17′.69 W	(Tor Ness)
(2)	58°55′.00 N,	003°50′.00 W	
(3)	59°17′.00 N,	003°50′.00 W	
(4)	59°28′.00 N,	003°15′.00 W	
(5)	59°28′.00 N,	002°19′.00 W	
(6)	59°24′.00 N,	002°09′.00 W	
(7)	59°05′.00 N,	002°09′.00 W	
(8)	58°50′.00 N,	002°35′.00 W	
(9)	58°44′.15 N,	002°54′.90 W	(Old Head)

Then around the coast of South Ronaldsay and Mainland to:

(10)	58°57′.84 N,	003°21′.11 W
(11)	58°55′.97 N,	003°21′.11 W

Thence along the coast of Hoy to (1).

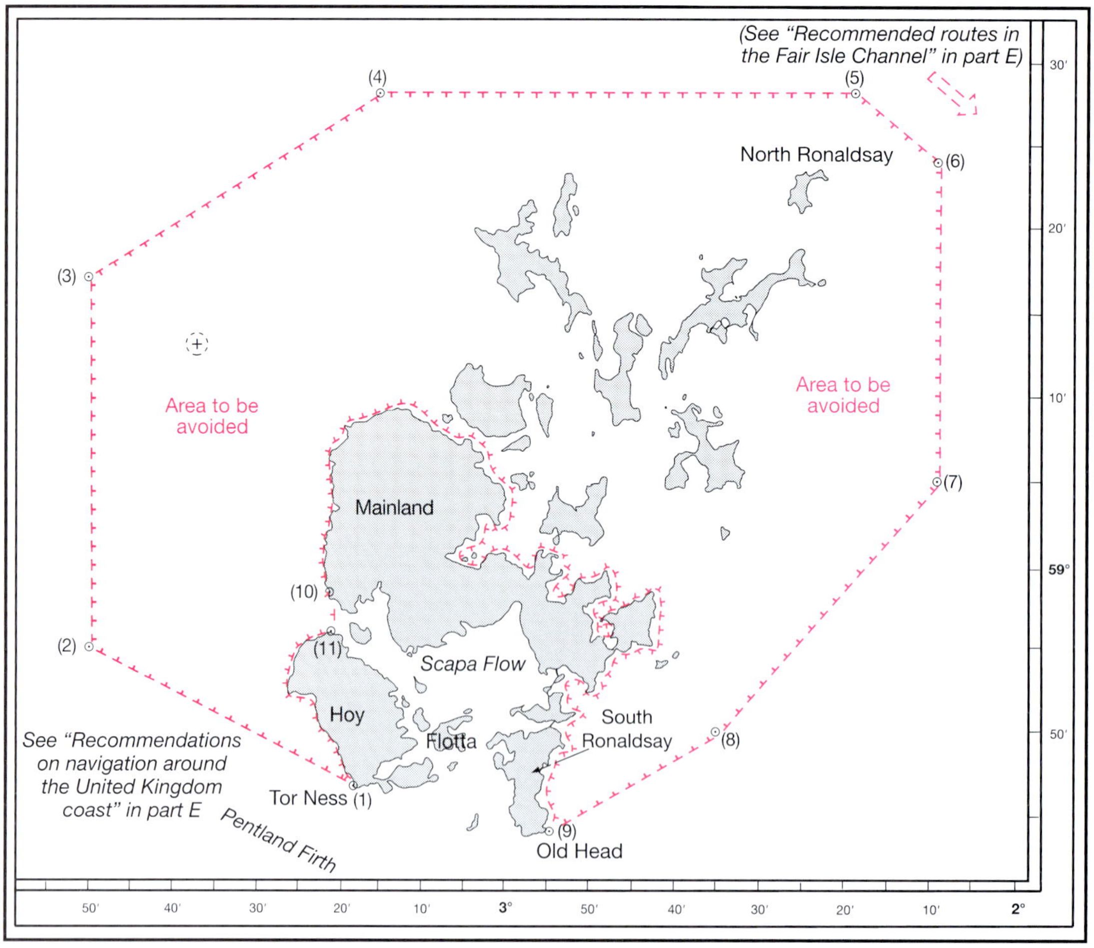

IN THE REGION OF THE ORKNEY ISLANDS

IN THE REGION OF THE FAIR ISLE

Note: See "Recommended routes in the Fair Isle Channel" in part E and mandatory ship reporting system "West European Tanker Reporting System" in part G, section I.

(Reference charts: British Admiralty 1119, 1989 edition
Note: This chart is based on Ordnance Survey of Great Britain 1936 datum.)

Description of the area to be avoided

In order to avoid the risk of oil pollution and severe damage to the environment of Fair Isle, ships of more than 5000 gross tonnage carrying oil or other hazardous cargoes in bulk should avoid the area contained within a circle of radius 6.5 miles centred upon geographical position 59°32′.00 N, 001°38′.00 W.

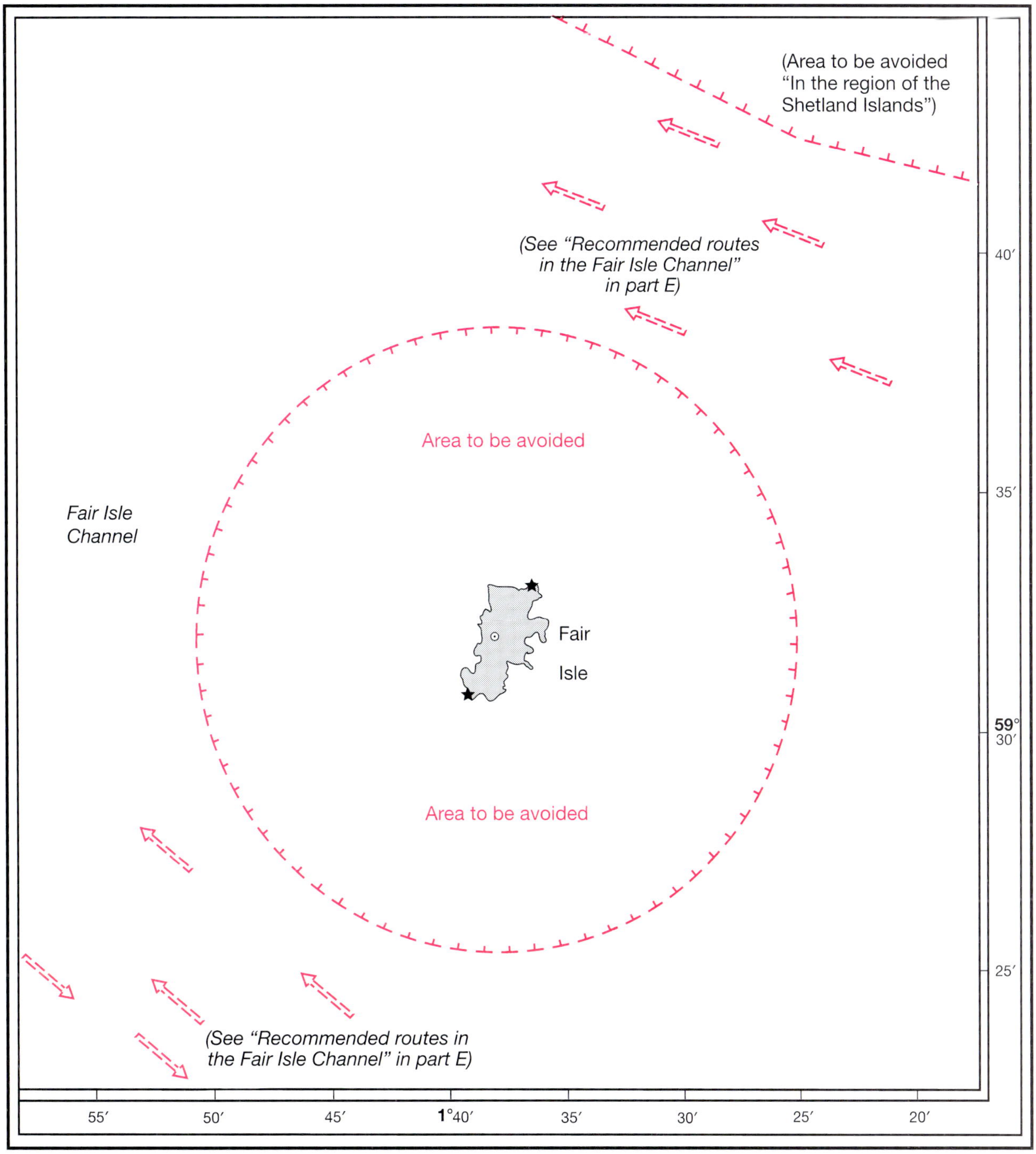

IN THE REGION OF THE FAIR ISLE

IN THE REGION OF THE SHETLAND ISLANDS

Note: See "Recommended routes in the Fair Isle Channel" in part E and mandatory ship reporting system "West European Tanker Reporting System" in part G, section I.

(Reference charts: British Admiralty 1119, 1989 edition; 1233, 1989 edition; 3292, 1986 edition.
Note: These charts are based on Ordnance Survey of Great Britain 1936 datum.)

Description of the areas to be avoided and precautionary areas

(a) **North of Shetland**

To avoid the risk of pollution and severe damage to the environment and economy of Shetland, all vessels over 5000 gross tonnage carrying, or capable of carrying, oil or other liquid hazardous cargoes in bulk should avoid the area bounded by lines connecting the following geographical positions:

(1) 60°39′.50 N, 001°09′.30 W
(2) 61°04′.30 N, 001°09′.30 W
(3) 61°04′.30 N, 000°29′.70 W
(4) 60°38′.40 N, 000°12′.20 W
(5) 60°34′.20 N, 000°48′.00 W (Funzie Ness)
(6) 60°33′.80 N, 000°53′.50 W (Rams Ness)
Thence up the eastern side of Colgrave Sound to:
(7) 60°35′.80 N, 000°55′.40 W
(8) 60°36′.80 N, 000°58′.00 W
(9) 60°38′.40 N, 000°58′.80 W
Thence along the coastline to position (1)

(b) **West and south of Shetland**

To avoid the risk of pollution and severe damage to the environment and economy of Shetland, all vessels over 5000 gross tonnage carrying, or capable of carrying, oil or other liquid hazardous cargoes in bulk should avoid the area bounded by lines connecting the following geographical positions:

(10) 60°02′.50 N, 001°10′.20 W (Helli Ness)
(11) 59°59′.87 N, 001°09′.37 W (Perie Bard light)
(12) 59°41′.00 N, 001°12′.00 W
(13) 59°42′.70 N, 001°26′.00 W
(14) 60°02′.00 N, 002°48′.00 W
(15) 60°15′.00 N, 002°48′.00 W
(16) 60°42′.50 N, 002°09′.00 W
(17) 60°42′.50 N, 001°22′.00 W
(18) 60°40′.00 N, 001°17′.00 W
(19) 60°37′.30 N, 001°17′.90 W
Thence along the west coastline to position (10)

(c) **Precautionary area in the northern approaches to Yell Sound**

A precautionary area is established in the northern approaches to Yell Sound. The area is bounded by a line connecting the following geographical positions:

(20) 61°04′.30 N, 001°09′.30 W
(21) 60°39′.50 N, 001°09′.30 W
(22) 60°40′.00 N, 001°17′.00 W
(23) 60°42′.50 N, 001°22′.00 W
(24) 60°42′.50 N, 002°09′.00 W

(d) **Precautionary area in the south-eastern approaches to Yell Sound**

A precautionary area is established in the south-eastern approaches to Yell Sound. The area is bounded by a line connecting the following geographical positions:

(25) 60°27′.40 N, 001°02′.40 W
(26) 60°24′.00 N, 000°02′.50 W
(27) 60°38′.40 N, 000°12′.20 W
(28) 60°34′.20 N, 000°48′.00 W
(29) 60°33′.80 N, 000°53′.50 W
Thence up the eastern side of Colgrave Sound to:
(30) 60°35′.80 N, 000°55′.40 W
(31) 60°36′.80 N, 000°58′.00 W

(e) **Precautionary area in the approaches to Lerwick**

A precautionary area is established in the approaches to Lerwick. The area is bounded by a line connecting the following geographical positions:

(25) 60°27′.40 N, 001°02′.40 W
(26) 60°24′.00 N, 000°02′.50 W
(12) 59°41′.00 N, 001°12′.00 W
(11) 59°59′.87 N, 001°09′.37 W (Perie Bard)
(10) 60°02′.50 N, 001°10′.20 W (Helli Ness)

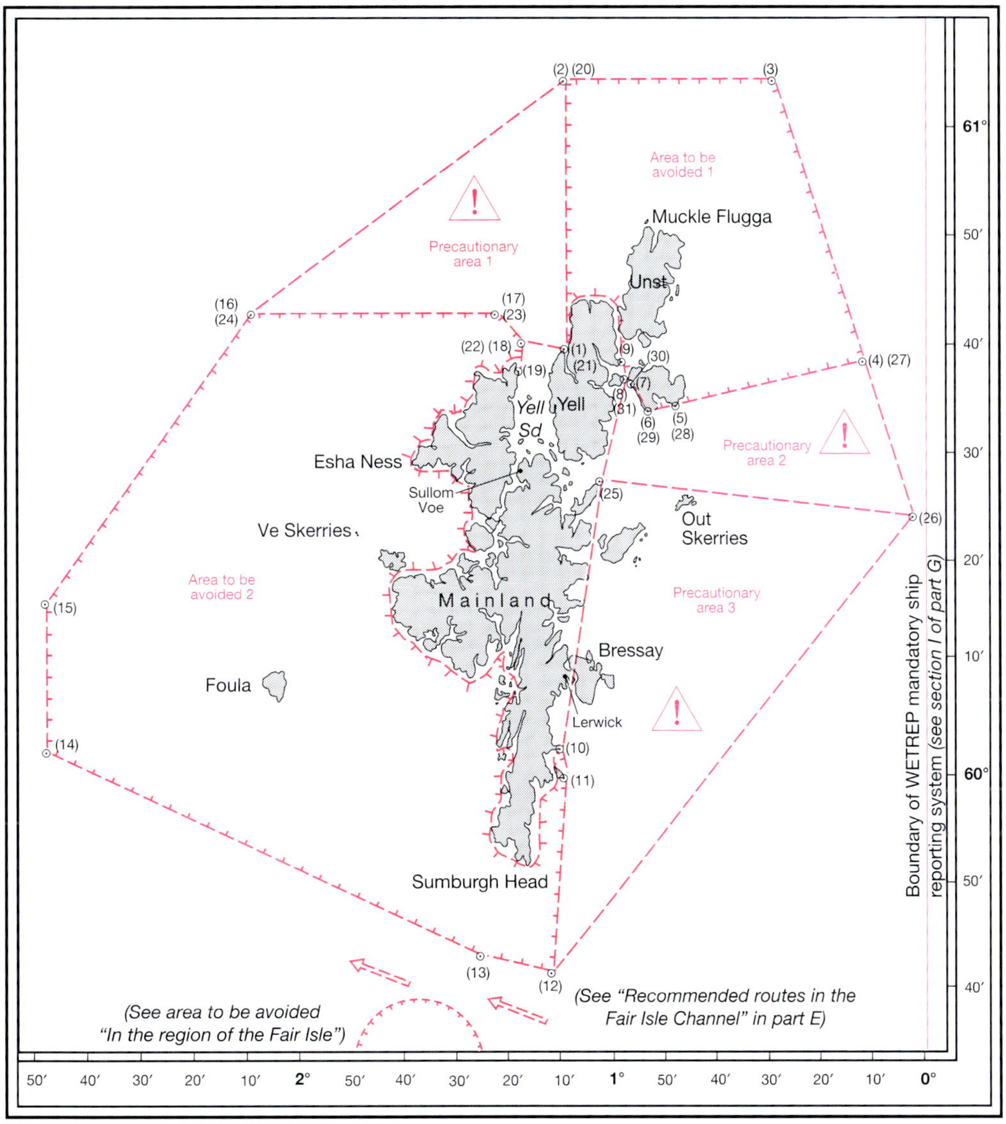

IN THE REGION OF THE SHETLAND ISLANDS

BETWEEN THE SMALLS LIGHTHOUSE AND GRASSHOLME ISLAND

Note: See mandatory ship reporting system "West European Tanker Reporting System" in part G, section I.

(Reference chart: British Admiralty 1478, 1988 edition.
Note: This chart is based on Ordnance Survey of Great Britain 1936 datum.)

Description of the area to be avoided

In order to avoid the risk of pollution due to a stranding in this area, which is in the close vicinity of important breeding grounds for sea-bird populations, all tankers, gas carriers, chemical tankers carrying noxious liquid substances, and all other ships of 500 gross tons or over should avoid the area bounded by lines connecting the following geographical positions:

(1)	51°44′.50 N,	005°40′.25 W	(4)	51°41′.50 N,	005°33′.25 W
(2)	51°44′.50 N,	005°27′.50 W	(5)	51°42′.20 N,	005°41′.30 W
(3)	51°42′.50 N,	005°27′.50 W			

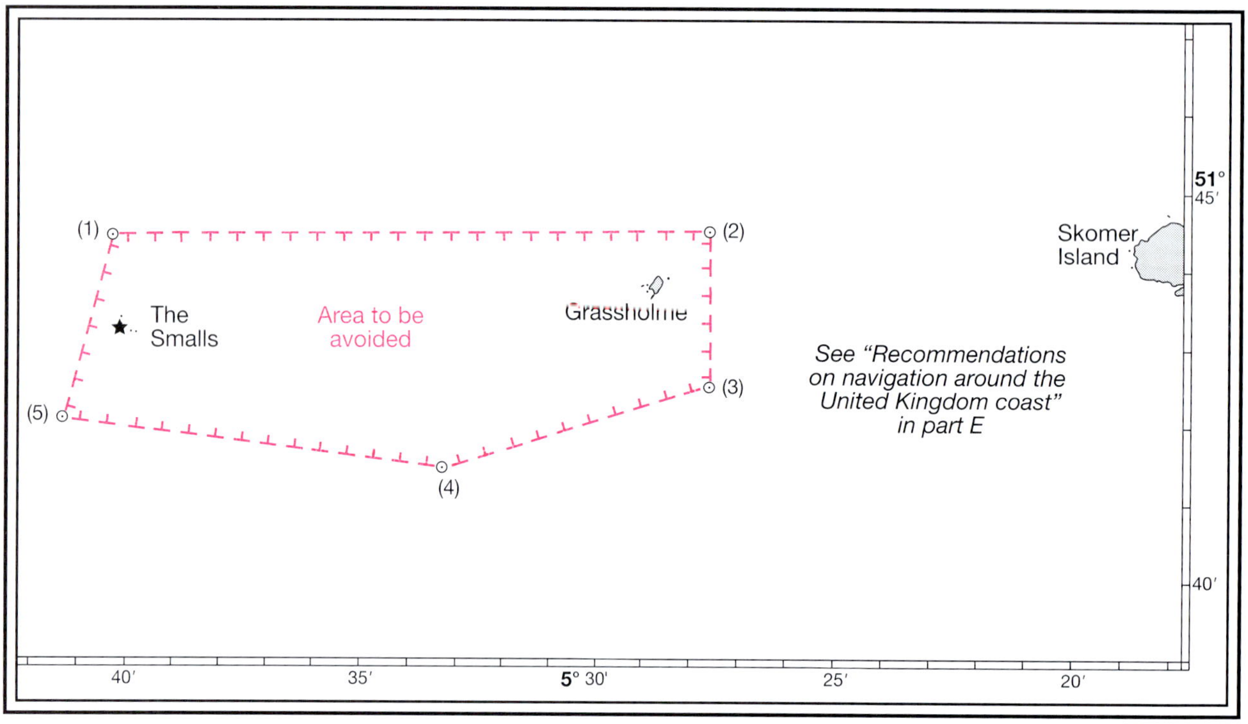

BETWEEN THE SMALLS LIGHTHOUSE AND GRASSHOLME ISLAND

IN LIVERPOOL BAY

Note: See the traffic separation scheme "In Liverpool Bay" in part B, section II.

(Reference chart: British Admiralty 1978, 2007 edition.
Note: This chart is based on World Geodetic System 1984 datum (WGS 84).)

Description of the area to be avoided

In order to provide access to the Douglas Oil Field platform, an area to be avoided of 1 nautical mile square, centred on the Douglas Field platform, has been established within the Liverpool Bay traffic separation scheme. The area is bounded by lines joining the following geographical positions:

(2)	53°32′.74 N,	003°33′.83 W
(3)	53°31′.74 N,	003°33′.80 W
(8)	53°31′.72 N,	003°35′.48 W
(5)	53°32′.72 N,	003°35′.51 W

Note: The area to be avoided should be avoided by all vessels, except in cases of emergency to avoid immediate danger, other than the following types (to the extent necessary to carry out their operations):

(a) a vessel restricted in her ability to manoeuvre when engaged in the laying, servicing or picking up of a navigation mark, submarine cable or pipeline;

(b) offshore supply, support, maintenance and Emergency Response and Rescue vessels attending the Douglas Field platform;

(c) vessels engaged in hydrographic survey operations; and

(d) vessels engaged in fishing.

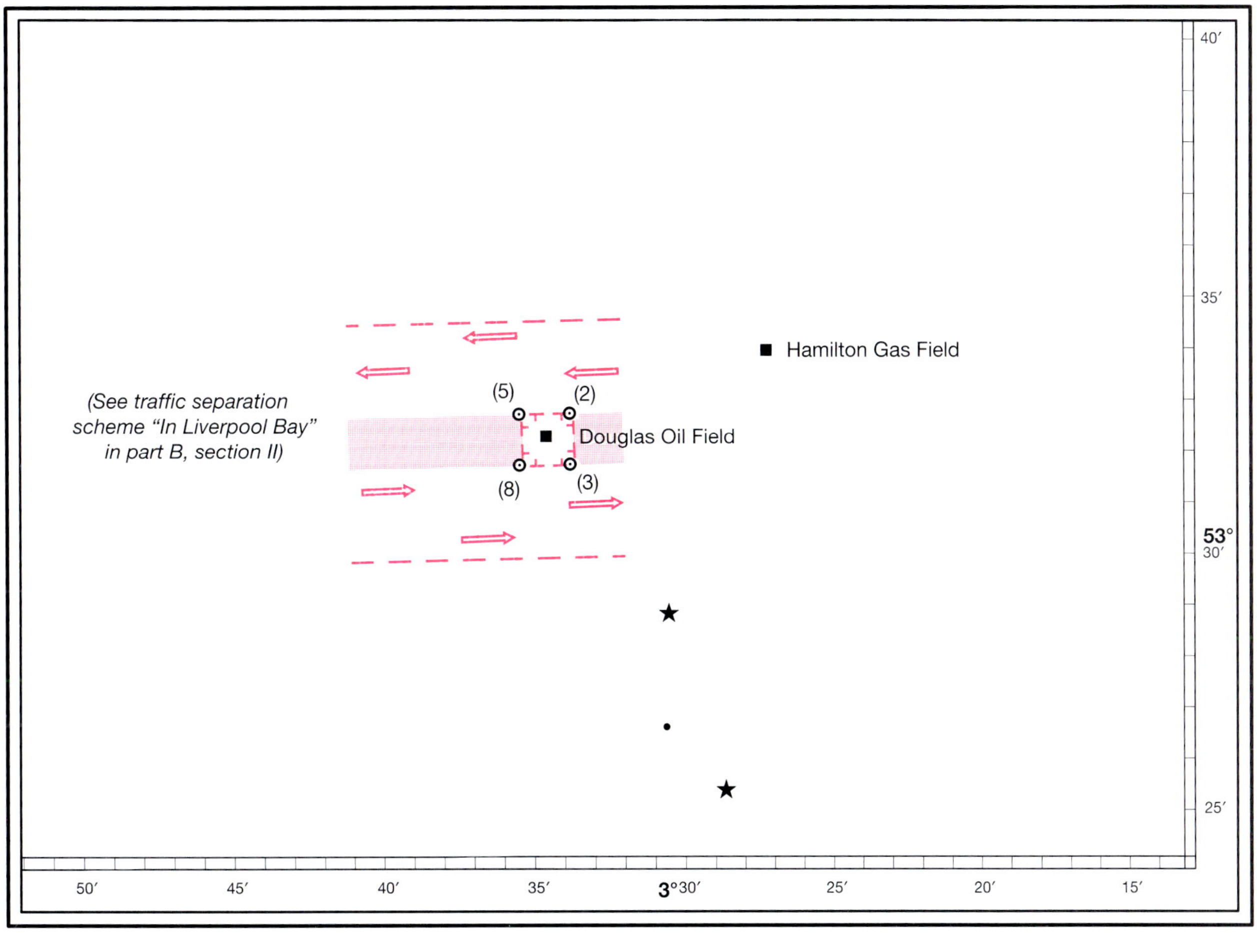

IN LIVERPOOL BAY

OFF THE SOUTH-WEST COAST OF ICELAND*

(Reference chart: Icelandic 31 (INT 1103) Dyrhólaey – Snæfellsnes (May 2008 edition).
Note: This chart is based on World Geodetic System 1984 datum (WGS 84).)

Description of the areas to be avoided

(a) **Off the south and south-west coast – Eastern area**

Note: See mandatory ship reporting system "Off the south-west coast of Iceland" in part G, section I.

The area to be avoided is bounded by lines connecting the following geographical positions:

(17)	64°04′.92 N,	022°41′.40 W	(21)	63°47′.00 N,	022°47′.60 W
(9)	64°07′.20 N,	022°41′.40 W	(22)	63°45′.80 N,	022°44′.40 W
(8)	64°07′.20 N,	022°47′.50 W	(23)	63°40′.90 N,	022°40′.20 W
(18)	64°01′.70 N,	022°58′.30 W	(24)	63°10′.00 N,	020°38′.00 W
(19)	63°49′.20 N,	022°47′.30 W	(25)	63°24′.13 N,	019°07′.83 W
(20)	63°48′.00 N,	022°48′.40 W			

(b) **West of Reykjanes Peninsula – Western area**

The area to be avoided is bounded by lines connecting the following geographical positions:

(26)	63°39′.70 N,	022°46′.70 W	(28)	63°42′.00 N,	023°37′.00 W
(27)	63°59′.10 N,	023°03′.50 W	(29)	63°32′.00 N,	023°29′.50 W

(c) **Faxaflói Bay – Syðra-Hraun Bank area**

The area to be avoided is bounded by lines connecting the following geographical positions:

(1)	64°10′.30 N,	022°29′.00 W	(4)	64°14′.20 N,	022°20′.00 W
(2)	64°10′.30 N,	022°20′.00 W	(5)	64°14′.20 N,	022°29′.00 W
(3)	64°12′.00 N,	022°17′.50 W	(6)	64°12′.00 N,	022°31′.00 W

Notes

1 The routeing measures are applicable to all SOLAS ships of 500 gross tonnage or more. The Eastern area may, however, be transited by ships as specified in paragraph 2 below.

2 Ships calling at ports located within the Eastern ATBA may navigate inside the area. Ships of less than 5000 gross tonnage engaged on voyages between Icelandic ports and not carrying dangerous or noxious cargoes in bulk or in cargo tanks may transit the area south of latitude 63°45′ N.

3 Ships of up to 20,000 gross tonnage, *en route* to or from Faxaflói Bay, which neither carry dangerous goods nor noxious materials in bulk or cargo tanks, may transit the Eastern area to be avoided south of latitude 63° 45′ N. When sailing such ships within this area, navigating officers should take utmost precaution and take special notice of weather and sea state forecasts in onshore wind conditions.

4 Passenger ships of unlimited size may only transit the area during the period 1 May to 1 October. When sailing such ships within this area, navigating officers should take utmost precaution and take special notice of weather and sea state forecasts in onshore wind conditions.

* Date of implementation of amended area to be avoided: 0000 hours UTC on 1 June 2011.

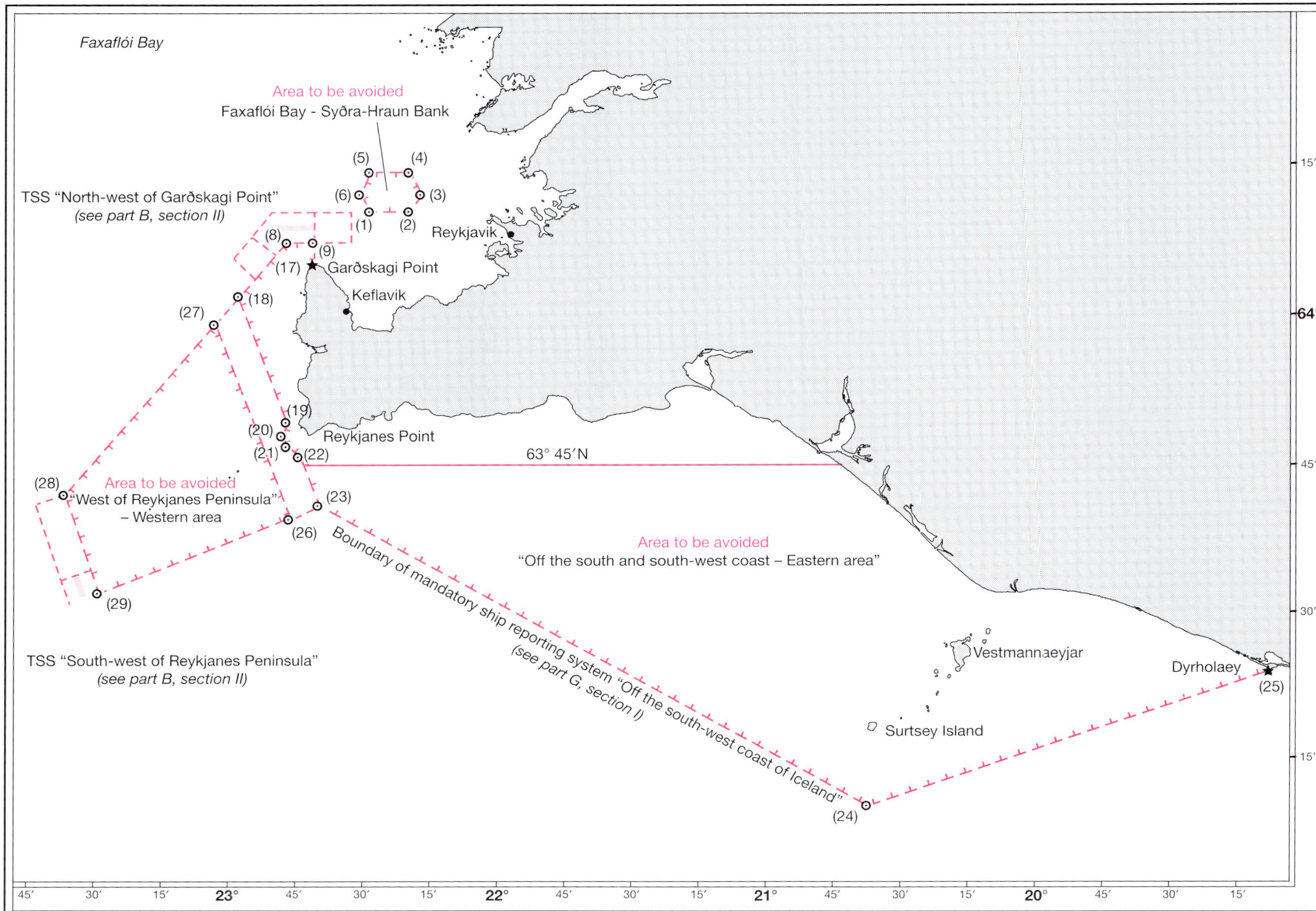

OFF THE SOUTH-WEST COAST OF ICELAND

IN THE REGION OF THE ROCHEBONNE SHELF

Note: See mandatory ship reporting system "West European Tanker Reporting System" in part G, section I.

(Reference chart: British Admiralty 2648)

Description of the area to be avoided

In order to avoid the risk of pollution due to an accident in the area, all tankers carrying oil should avoid the area contained within a circle of radius seven miles centred upon geographical position 46°10′.00 N, 002°26′.00 W. Local knowledge is essential for safe passage because of navigational hazards in the area.

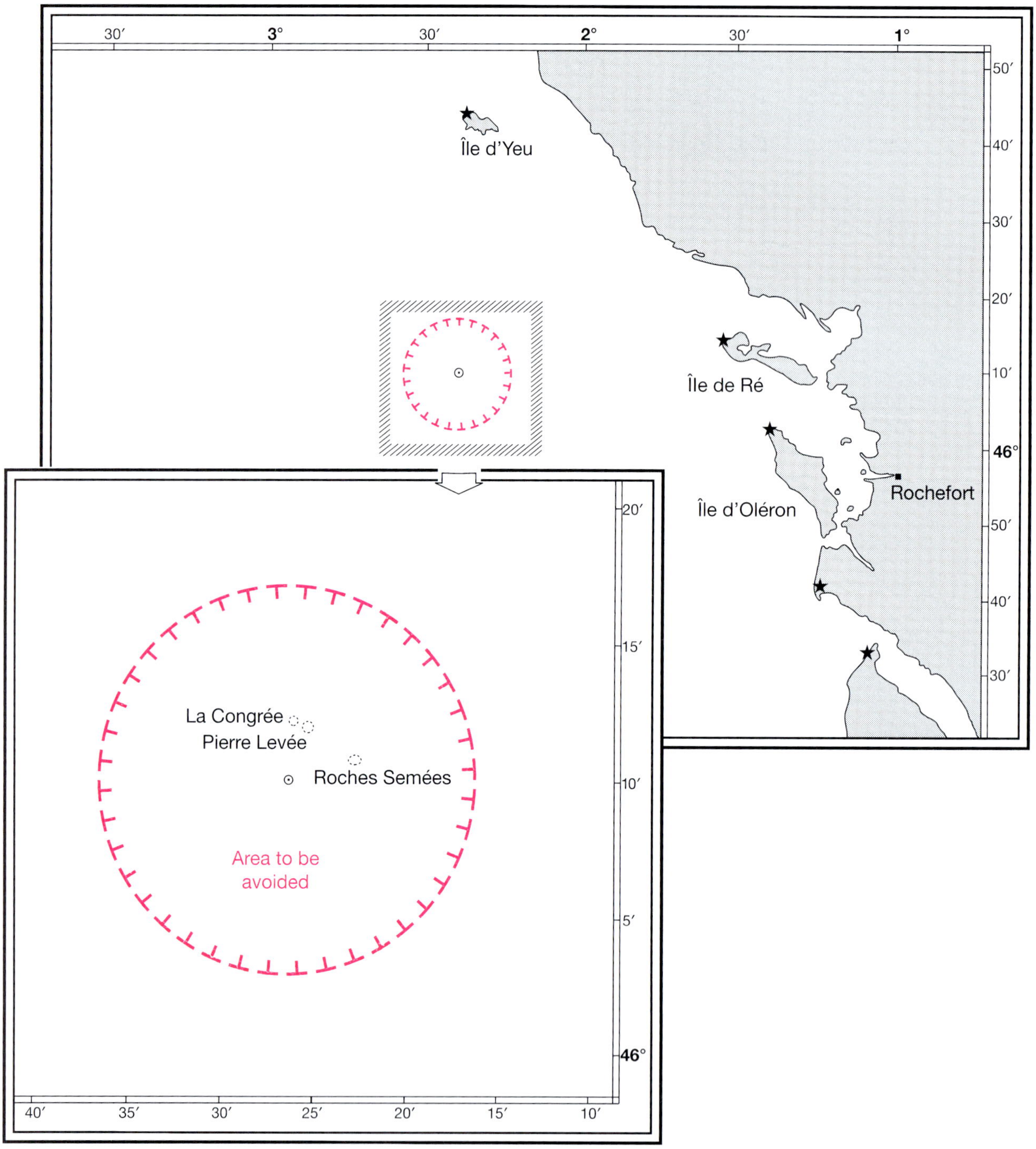

IN THE REGION OF THE ROCHEBONNE SHELF

IN THE REGION OF THE BERLENGAS ISLANDS

Note: See mandatory ship reporting systems "West European Tanker Reporting System" and "Off the coast of Portugal" in part G, section I.

(Reference chart: Portuguese Hydrographic Office 21101 (INT 1081), April 2002 edition.
Note: This chart is based on European datum 1950.)

Description of the area to be avoided

The ATBA applies to all vessels above 300 gross tonnage, except duly authorized ships navigating between Portuguese ports and not carrying dangerous cargoes or other harmful substances.

The area to be avoided consists of an area bounded on the north by the parallel of 39°30′.00 N, on the south by the parallel of 39°20′.00 N, on the west by the line connecting the geographical positions 39°20′.00 N, 009°42′.20 W and 39°30′.00 N, 009°42′.20 W, and on the east by the Portuguese coastline.

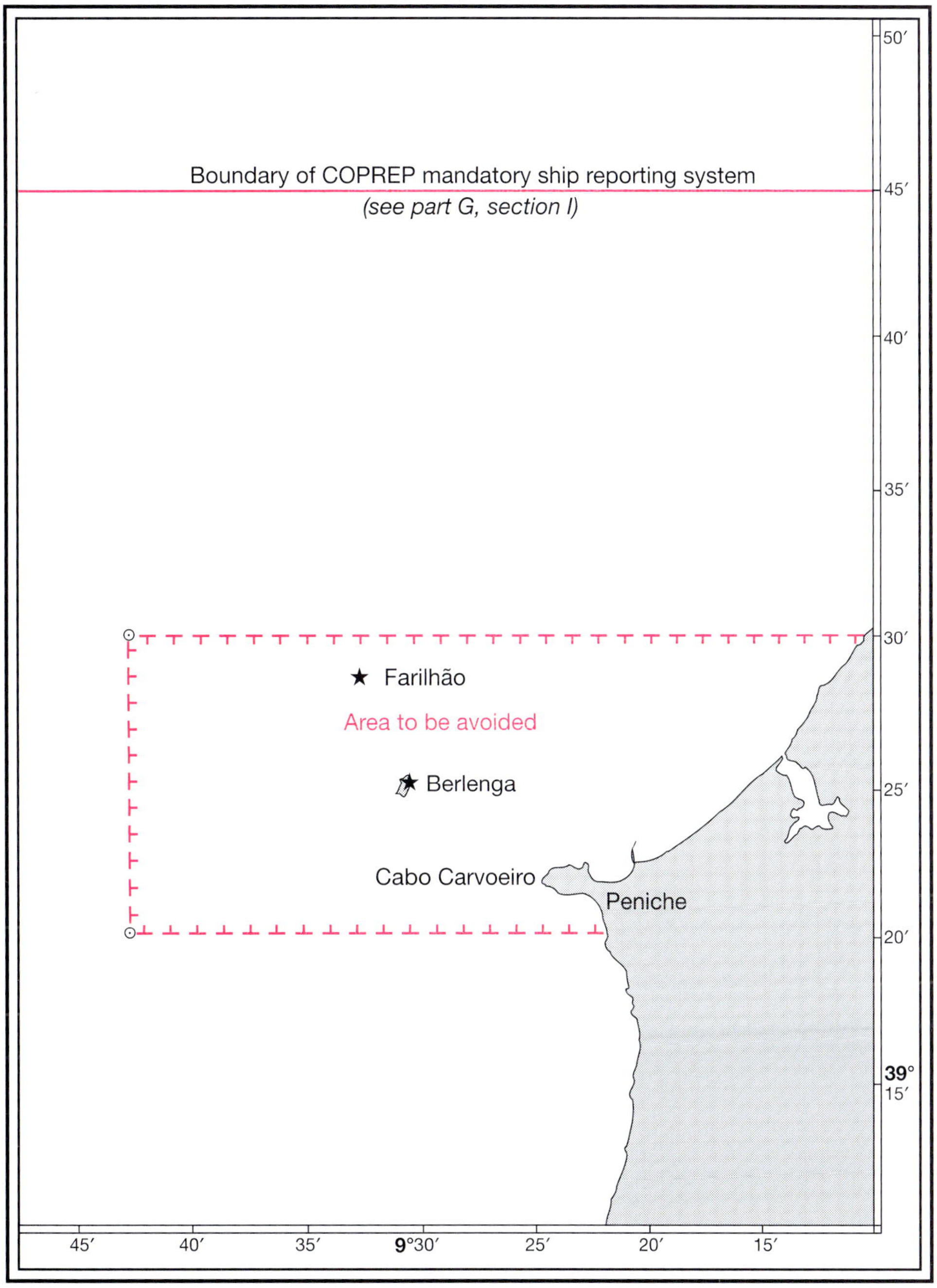

IN THE REGION OF THE BERLENGAS ISLANDS

Section II

North and Central American waters

Some small areas to be avoided, at the junction of traffic lanes of traffic separation schemes and to which no specified conditions of tonnage of vessels or of the cargoes that are carried apply, are not included in part D. One is described in the definition of this traffic separation scheme:

Off San Francisco (see section VII of part B)

Caution: The chartlets are for illustrative purposes only and must not be used for navigation. Mariners should consult the appropriate nautical publications and charts for up-to-date details on aids to navigation and other relevant information.

Warning: The geographical positions given in the descriptions of the areas to be avoided are only correct for charts using the same geodetic datum as the reference charts indicated under each description. Charts published by other hydrographic offices may use a different geodetic datum, as may new editions of the reference charts published after the adoption of the areas.

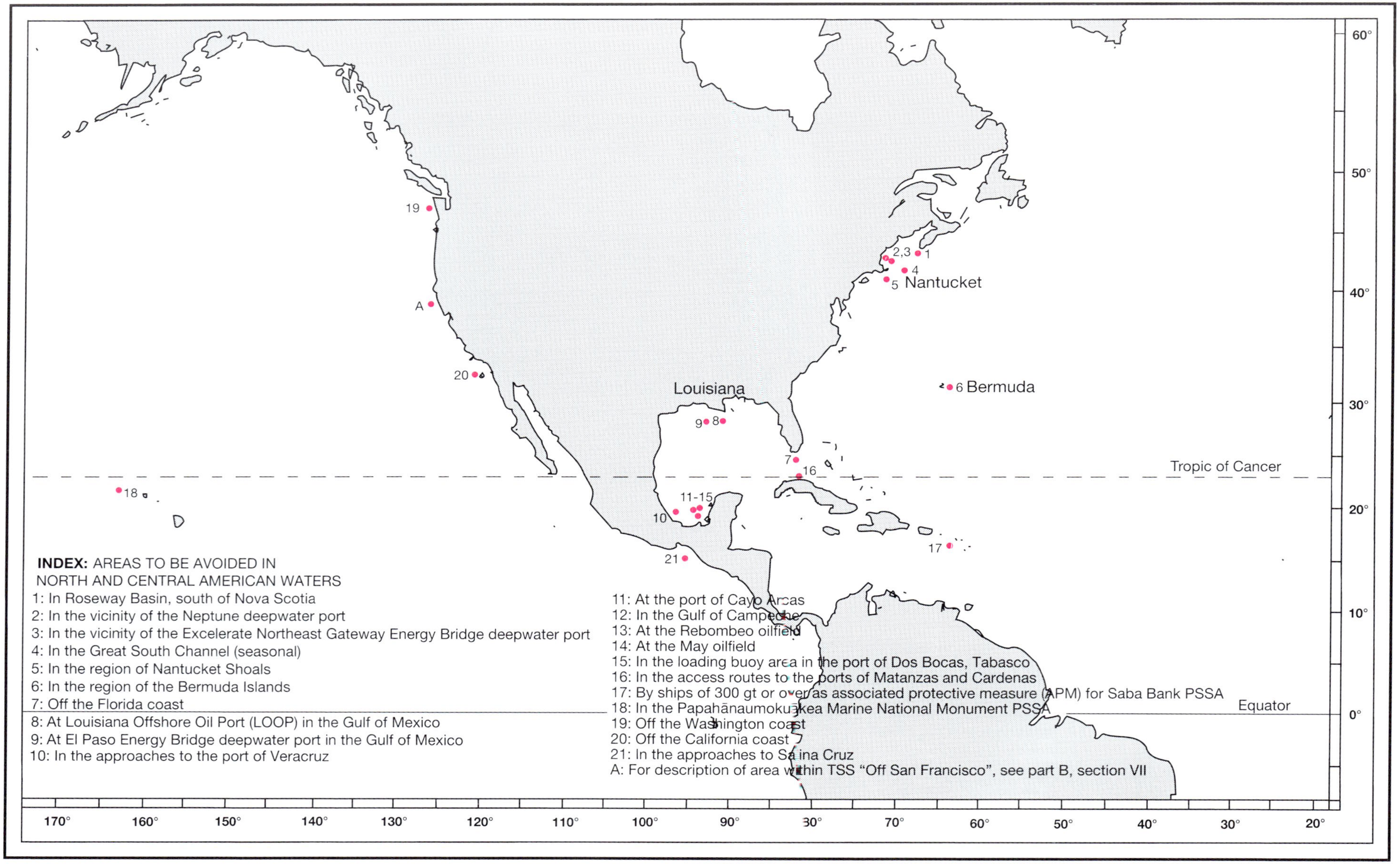

INDEX: AREAS TO BE AVOIDED IN NORTH AND CENTRAL AMERICAN WATERS

1: In Roseway Basin, south of Nova Scotia
2: In the vicinity of the Neptune deepwater port
3: In the vicinity of the Excelerate Northeast Gateway Energy Bridge deepwater port
4: In the Great South Channel (seasonal)
5: In the region of Nantucket Shoals
6: In the region of the Bermuda Islands
7: Off the Florida coast
8: At Louisiana Offshore Oil Port (LOOP) in the Gulf of Mexico
9: At El Paso Energy Bridge deepwater port in the Gulf of Mexico
10: In the approaches to the port of Veracruz
11: At the port of Cayo Arcas
12: In the Gulf of Campeche
13: At the Rebombeo oilfield
14: At the May oilfield
15: In the loading buoy area in the port of Dos Bocas, Tabasco
16: In the access routes to the ports of Matanzas and Cardenas
17: By ships of 300 gt or over as associated protective measure (APM) for Saba Bank PSSA
18: In the Papahānaumokuākea Marine National Monument PSSA
19: Off the Washington coast
20: Off the California coast
21: In the approaches to Salina Cruz
A: For description of area within TSS “Off San Francisco”, see part B, section VII

IN ROSEWAY BASIN, SOUTH OF NOVA SCOTIA

(Reference chart: Canadian Hydrographic Service 4003, 2003 edition.
Note: This chart is based on North American 1983 geodetic datum, which is equivalent to WGS 84 datum.)

Description of the recommended seasonal area to be avoided

In order to significantly reduce the risk of ship strikes of the highly endangered North Atlantic Right Whale, it is recommended that ships of 300 gross tonnage and upwards solely in transit **during the period of 1 June through 31 December** should avoid the area bounded by lines connecting the following geographical positions:

(1)	43°16′.00 N,	064°55′.00 W	(3)	42°39′.00 N,	065°31′.00 W
(2)	42°47′.00 N,	064°59′.00 W	(4)	42°52′.00 N,	066°05′.00 W

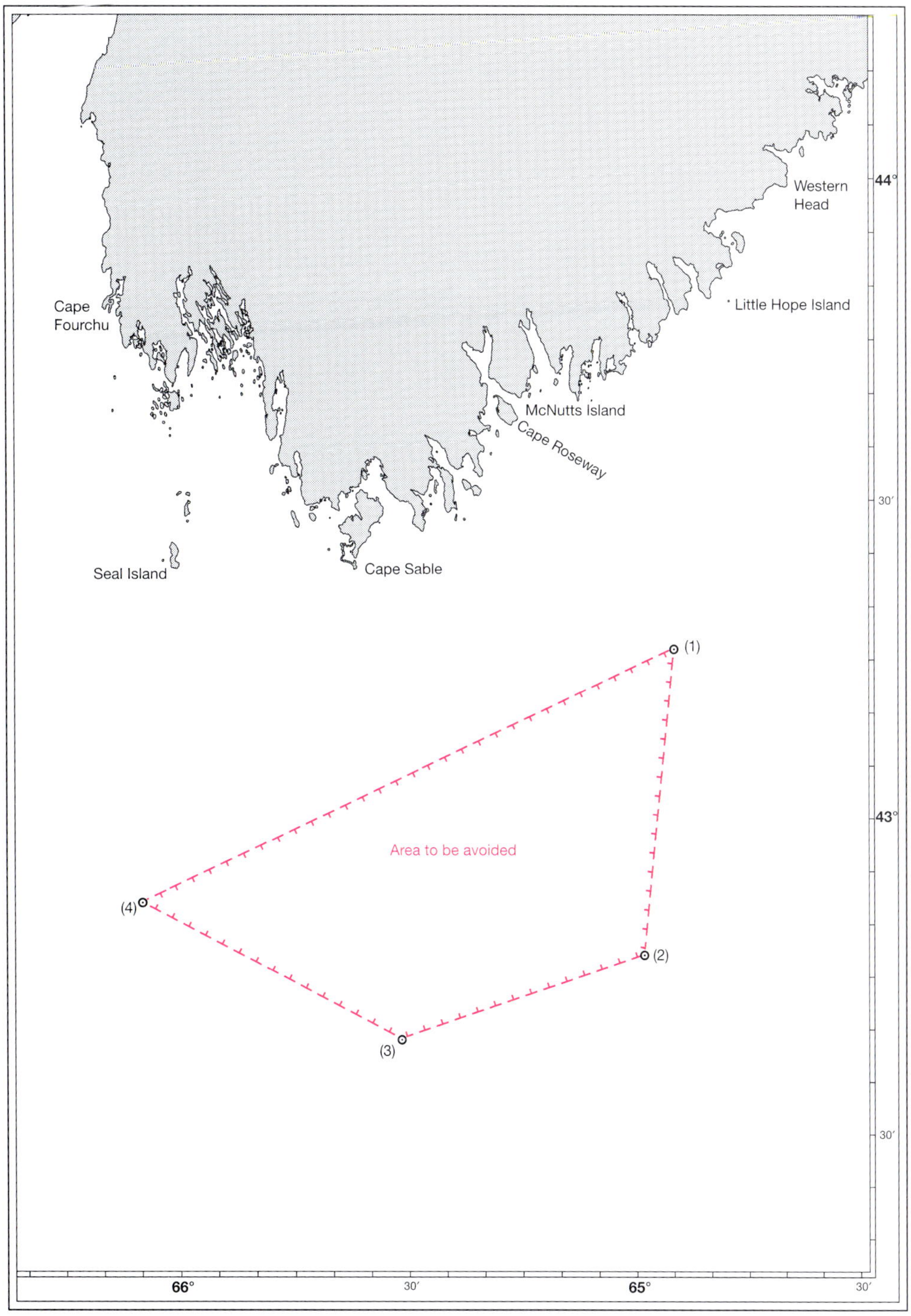

IN ROSEWAY BASIN, SOUTH OF NOVA SCOTIA

IN THE VICINITY OF THE NEPTUNE DEEPWATER PORT IN THE WESTERN NORTH ATLANTIC OCEAN

((Reference charts: United States 13009, 2007 edition; 13200, 2008 edition; 13260, 2007 edition; 13267, 2007 edition.)
Note: These charts are based on North American 1983 datum, which is equivalent to World Geodetic System 1984 datum (WGS 84).)

Description of the area to be avoided

An area of approximately 3.97 nautical square miles contained within an oval of radius 1250 metres vectored from the two centre positions for Neptune Buoys "A" and "B", respectively, an area to be avoided for all ships except authorized ships, is established in the area bounded as follows:

Starting at	(1)	42°27′.44 N,	070°35′.22 W
a rhumb line to	(2)	42°29′.31 N,	070°35′.59 W
then an arc with a 1250 m radius centred at	(3)	42°29′.21 N,	070°36′.50 W
to a point	(4)	42°29′.11 N,	070°37′.40 W
then a rhumb line to	(5)	42°27′.25 N,	070°37′.03 W
then an arc with a 1250 m radius centred at	(6)	42°27′.34 N,	070°36′.12 W
then to point	(1)	42°27′.44 N,	070°35′.22 W

IN THE VICINITY OF THE EXCELERATE NORTHEAST GATEWAY ENERGY BRIDGE DEEPWATER PORT IN THE ATLANTIC OCEAN

(Reference charts: United States 13009, 2007 edition; 13200, 2007 edition; 13246, 2006 edition; 13267, 2007 edition.
Note: These charts are based on North American 1983 datum, which is equivalent to World Geodetic System 1984 datum (WGS 84).)

Description of the area to be avoided

An area of approximately 2.86 nautical square miles contained within an oval of radius 1250 metres vectored from the two centre positions for STL Buoys "A" and "B", respectively (an area to be avoided for all ships except authorized ships) is established in the area bounded as follows:

Starting at	(1)	42°24′.29 N,	070°35′.27 W
a rhumb line to	(2)	42°24′.59 N,	070°36′.76 W
then an arc with a 1250 m radius centred at	(3)	42°23′.94 N,	070°37′.01 W
to a point	(4)	42°23′.29 N,	070°37′.25 W
then a rhumb line to	(5)	42°22′.99 N,	070°35′.76 W
then an arc with a 1250 m radius centred at	(6)	42°23′.64 N,	070°35′.52 W
then to point	(1)	42°24′.29 N,	070°35′.27 W

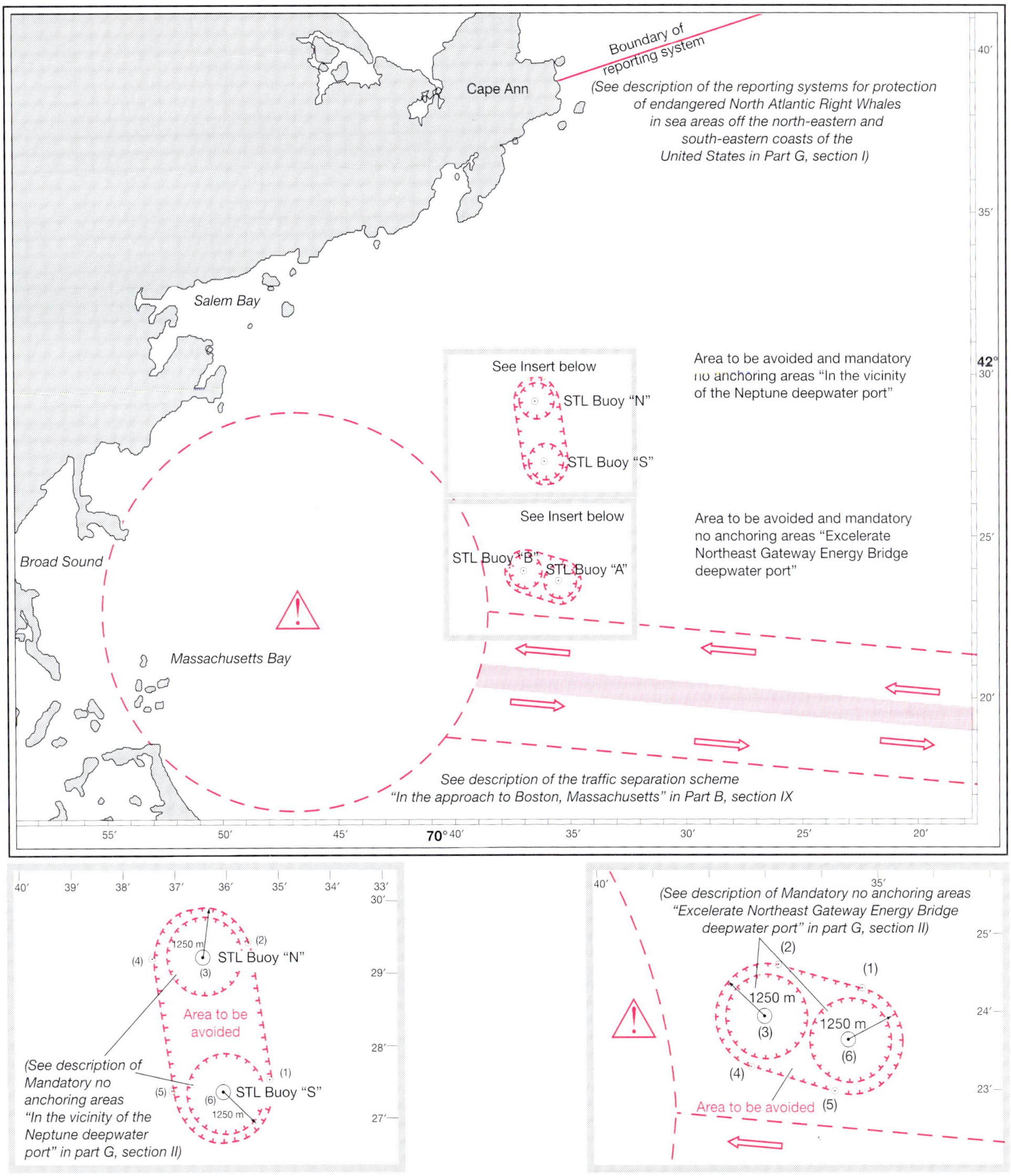

IN THE VICINITY OF THE NEPTUNE DEEPWATER PORT IN THE WESTERN NORTH ATLANTIC OCEAN + IN THE VICINITY OF THE EXCELERATE NORTHEAST GATEWAY ENERGY BRIDGE DEEPWATER PORT IN THE ATLANTIC OCEAN

RECOMMENDATORY SEASONAL AREA TO BE AVOIDED "IN THE GREAT SOUTH CHANNEL", OFF THE EAST COAST OF THE UNITED STATES

(Reference charts: United States 13009, 2007 edition; 13200, 2007 edition.
Note: These charts are based on North American 1983 datum, which is equivalent to World Geodetic System 1984 datum (WGS 84).)

Description of the area to be avoided

In order to significantly reduce ship strikes of the highly endangered North Atlantic Right Whale, ships of 300 gross tonnage and above – **during the period of April 1st through July 31st** – should avoid the area bounded by lines connecting the following geographical positions:

(1)	41°44′.14 N,	069°34′.83 W	(3)	41°24′.89 N,	068°31′.00 W
(2)	42°10′.00 N,	068°31′.00 W	(4)	40°50′.47 N,	068°58′.67 W

IN THE REGION OF NANTUCKET SHOALS

(Reference chart: United States 13009, 1985 edition.
Note: This chart is based on North American 1927 geodetic datum.)

Description of the area to be avoided

Because of the great danger of stranding and for reasons of environmental protection, all ships carrying cargoes of oil or hazardous materials and all other ships of more than 1000 gross tons should avoid the area bounded by a line connecting the following geographical positions:

(1)	41°16′.50 N,	070°12′.50 W	(4)	41°04′.50 N,	069°19′.00 W
(2)	40°43′.20 N,	070°00′.50 W	(5)	41°23′.50 N,	069°31′.50 W
(3)	40°44′.50 N,	069°19′.00 W	(6)	41°23′.40 N,	070°02′.80 W

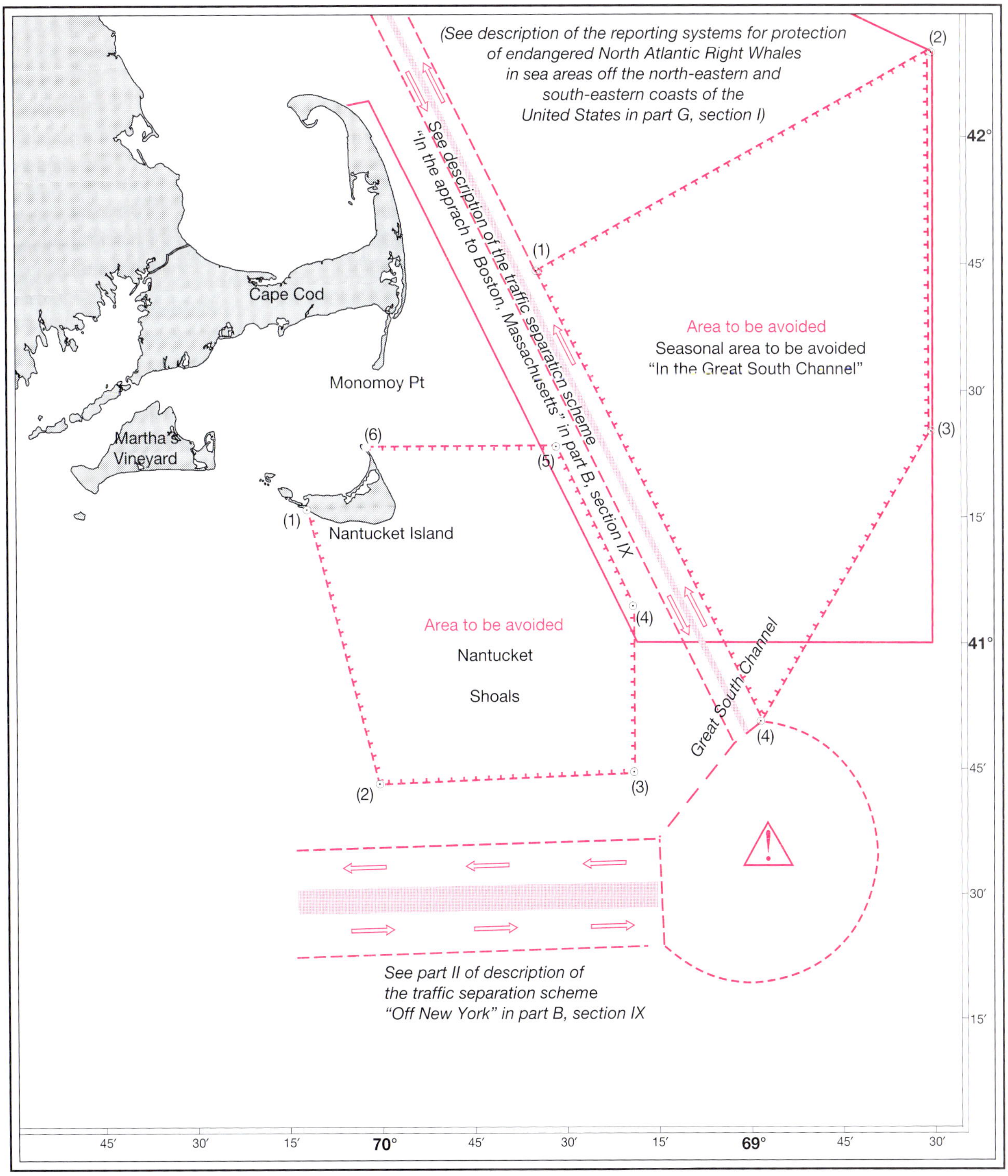

RECOMMENDATORY SEASONAL AREA TO BE AVOIDED "IN THE GREAT SOUTH CHANNEL" + IN THE REGION OF NANTUCKET SHOALS

IN THE REGION OF THE BERMUDA ISLANDS

(Reference chart: British Admiralty 360, 1983 edition.
Note: This chart is based on World Geodetic System 1972 datum.)

Description of the area to be avoided

Because of the great danger of stranding on the extensive reefs fringing Bermuda to the west, north and north-east of the islands, and for reasons of environmental protection, all ships carrying cargoes of oil or hazardous materials and all other ships of more than 1000 gross tons, whether or not bound for Bermuda ports, should avoid the area outside the reefs bounded by lines connecting the following geographical positions:

(1)	Gibb's Hill lighthouse	
	(32°15′.10 N,	064°50′.00 W)
(2)	32°08′.00 N,	064°53′.00 W
(3)	32°12′.00 N,	065°10′.00 W
(4)	32°24′.00 N,	065°10′.00 W
(5)	32°39′.00 N,	064°53′.00 W
(6)	32°39′.00 N,	064°38′.00 W
(7)	32°32′.00 N,	064°29′.00 W
(8)	St. David's lighthouse	
	(32°21′.80 N,	064°39′.00 W)

Note:

Mariners are warned to navigate with extreme care in the approaches to the Bermuda islands due to the extensive and dangerous fringing reefs. The only safe approach to the islands is from the south-east, preferably in daylight. The outer navigational aids may be unreliable.

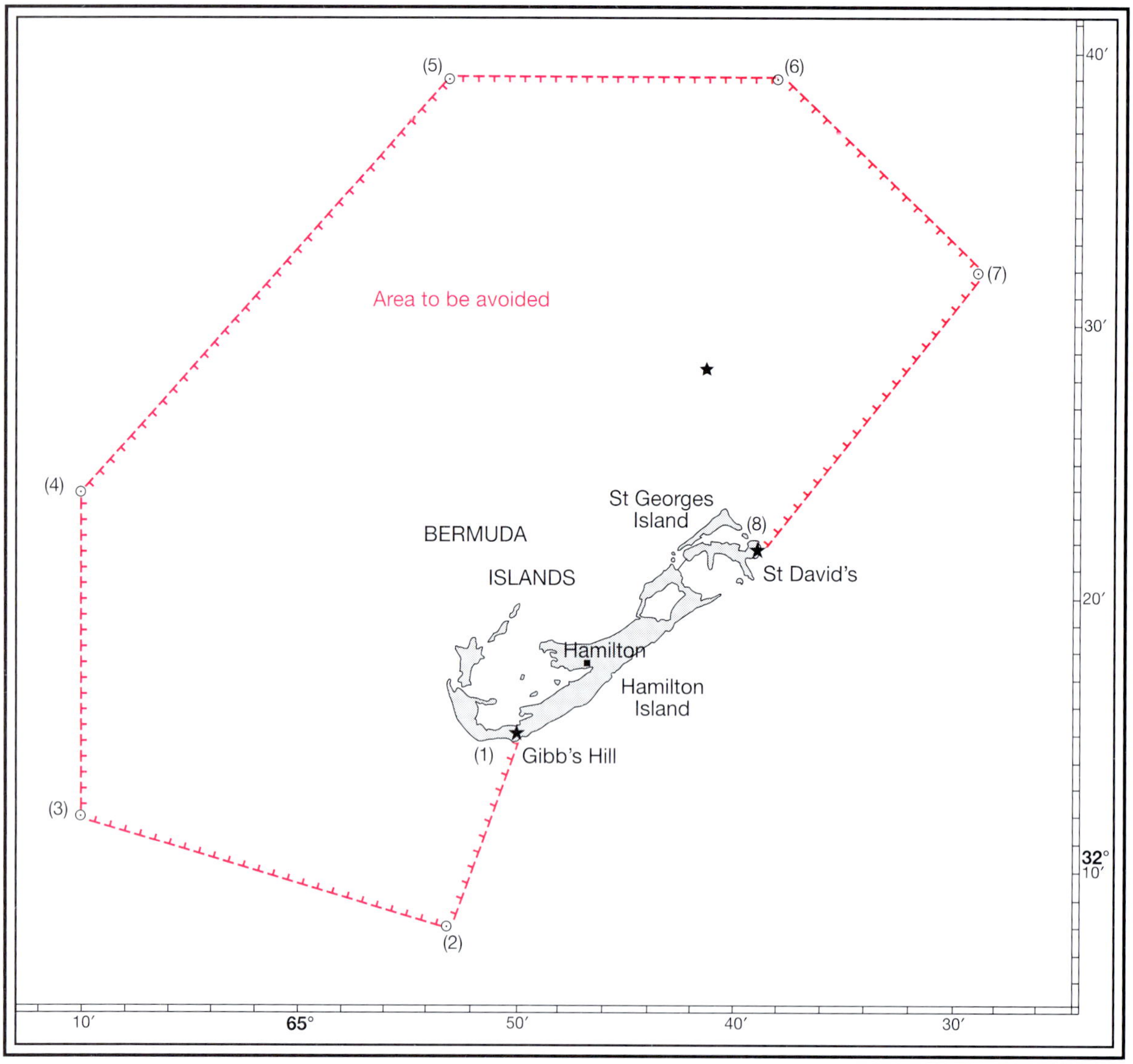

IN THE REGION OF THE BERMUDA ISLANDS

OFF THE FLORIDA COAST

(Reference charts: United States 11450, 1998 edition; 11460, 1999 edition; 11462, 1998 edition; 11463, 1997 edition.
Note: These charts are based on North American 1983 datum.)

Description of the areas to be avoided

In order to avoid risk of pollution and damage to the environment of these sensitive areas, all ships carrying cargoes of oil and hazardous materials and all other ships greater than 50 metres in length should avoid the following areas:

(a) **In the vicinity of the Florida Keys**

The area bounded by a line connecting the following geographical positions is designated as an area to be avoided:

(1)	25°45′.00 N,	080°06′.10 W	(13)	24°33′.60 N,	081°26′.00 W
(2)	25°38′.70 N,	080°02′.70 W	(14)	24°38′.20 N,	081°07′.00 W
(3)	25°22′.00 N,	080°03′.00 W	(15)	24°43′.20 N,	080°53′.20 W
(4)	25°06′.38 N,	080°10′.48 W	(16)	24°46′.10 N,	080°46′.15 W
(5)	24°56′.37 N,	080°19′.26 W	(17)	24°51′.10 N,	080°37′.10 W
(6)	24°37′.90 N,	080°47′.30 W	(18)	24°57′.50 N,	080°27′.50 W
(7)	24°29′.20 N,	081°17′.30 W	(19)	25°09′.90 N,	080°16′.20 W
(8)	24°22′.30 N,	081°43′.17 W	(20)	25°24′.00 N,	080°09′.10 W
(9)	24°28′.00 N,	081°43′.17 W	(21)	25°31′.50 N,	080°07′.00 W
(10)	24°28′.70 N,	081°43′.50 W	(22)	25°39′.70 N,	080°06′.85 W
(11)	24°29′.80 N,	081°43′.17 W	(1)	25°45′.00 N,	080°06′.10 W
(12)	24°33′.10 N,	081°35′.15 W			

(b) **In the vicinity of Key West Harbour**

The area bounded by a line connecting the following geographical positions is designated as an area to be avoided:

(23)	24°27′.95 N,	081°48′.65 W	(27)	24°29′.35 N,	081°53′.40 W
(24)	24°23′.00 N,	081°53′.50 W	(28)	24°29′.35 N,	081°50′.00 W
(25)	24°26′.60 N,	081°58′.50 W	(29)	24°27′.95 N,	081°48′.65 W
(26)	24°27′.75 N,	081°55′.70 W			

(c) **Surrounding the Marquesas Keys**

The area bounded by a line connecting the following geographical positions is designated as an area to be avoided:

(30)	24°26′.60 N,	081°59′.55 W	(37)	24°36′.15 N,	081°51′.78 W
(31)	24°23′.00 N,	082°03′.50 W	(38)	24°34′.40 N,	081°50′.60 W
(32)	24°23′.00 N,	082°27′.80 W	(39)	24°33′.44 N,	081°49′.73 W
(33)	24°34′.50 N,	082°37′.50 W	(40)	24°31′.20 N,	081°52′.10 W
(34)	24°43′.00 N,	082°26′.50 W	(41)	24°28′.70 N,	081°56′.80 W
(35)	24°38′.31 N,	081°54′.06 W	(42)	24°26′.60 N,	081°59′.55 W
(36)	24°37′.91 N,	081°53′.40 W			

(d) **Surrounding the Tortugas Islands**

The area bounded by a line connecting the following geographical positions is designated as an area to be avoided:

(43)	24°32′.00 N,	082°53′.50 W	(48)	24°42′.80 N,	082°43′.90 W
(44)	24°32′.00 N,	083°00′.05 W	(49)	24°39′.50 N,	082°43′.90 W
(45)	24°39′.70 N,	083°00′.05 W	(50)	24°35′.60 N,	082°46′.40 W
(46)	24°45′.60 N,	082°54′.40 W	(51)	24°32′.00 N,	082°53′.50 W
(47)	24°45′.60 N,	082°47′.20 W			

(chartlet overleaf)

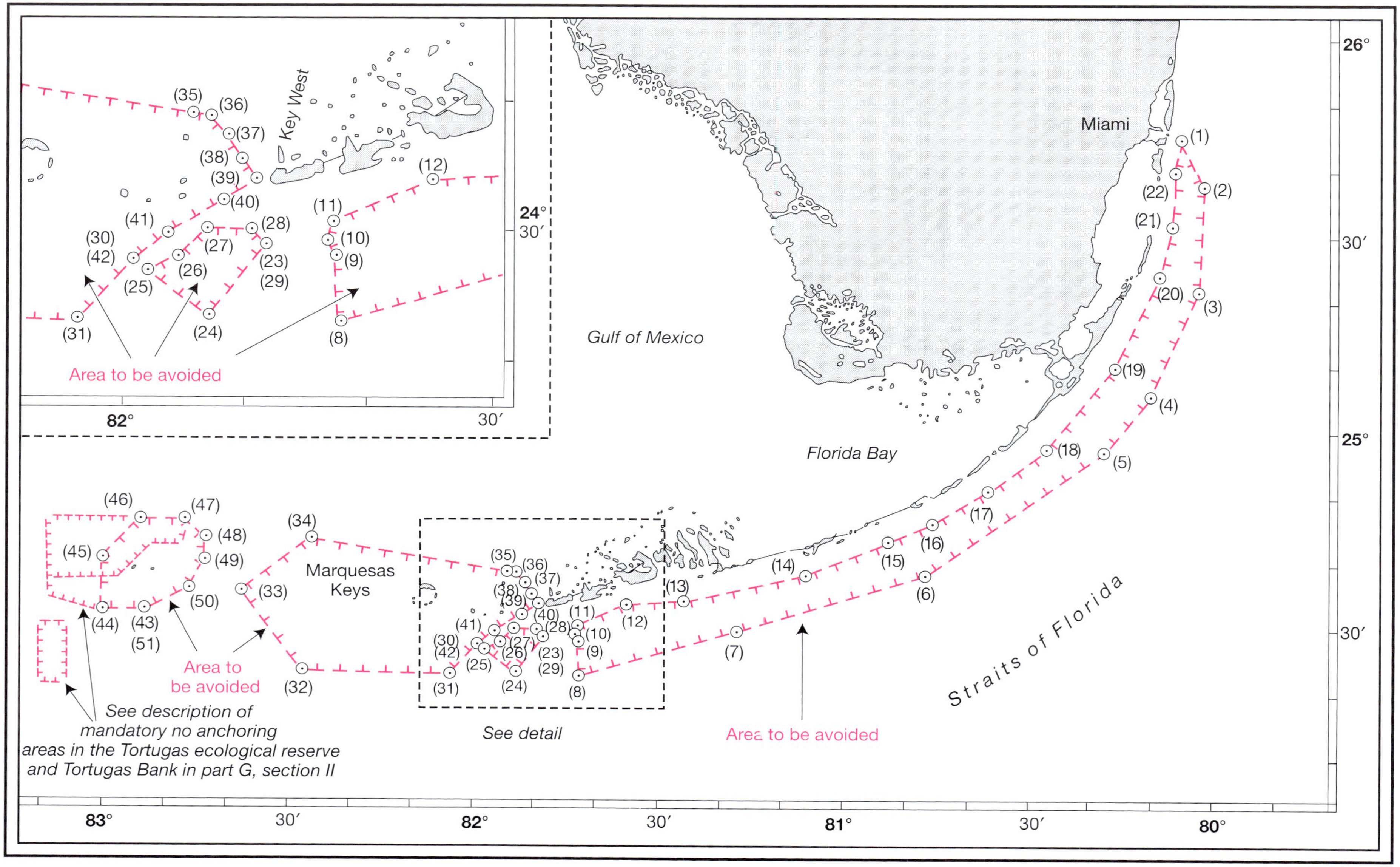

OFF THE FLORIDA COAST

AT LOUISIANA OFFSHORE OIL PORT (LOOP) IN THE GULF OF MEXICO

(Reference charts: United States 11340, 1988 edition; 11358, 1989 edition.
Note: These charts are based on North American 1927 geodetic datum.)

Description of a precautionary area and areas to be avoided

(a) **Precautionary area**

A precautionary area is established in the area bounded as follows:

starting at	(1)	28°55′.38 N,	090°00′.62 W
a rhumb line to	(2)	28°53′.83 N,	090°04′.12 W
then an arc with a 4465 m radius centred at	(3)	28°53′.10 N,	090°01′.50 W
to a point	(4)	28°51′.13 N,	089°59′.92 W
then a rhumb line to	(5)	28°48′.60 N,	089°55′.00 W
then a rhumb line to	(6)	28°52′.07 N,	089°52′.70 W
then a rhumb line to	(7)	28°54′.08 N,	089°56′.63 W
then a rhumb line to	(8)	28°52′.35 N,	089°57′.78 W
then a rhumb line to	(9)	28°52′.85 N,	089°58′.77 W
then an arc with a 4465 m radius centred at	(3)	28°53′.10 N,	090°01′.50 W
to a point	(1)	28°55′.38 N,	090°00′.62 W

(b) **Areas to be avoided**

The following areas to be avoided by all ships not calling at the deepwater port are established within the precautionary area:

an area to be avoided bounded by a circle of radius 600 m centred upon the following geographical position:

(3) 28°53′.10 N, 090°01′.50 W

and six areas to be avoided, each bounded by a circle of radius 500 m, centred upon the following geographical positions:

(10)	28°54′.20 N,	090°00′.62 W	(13)	28°51′.75 N,	090°01′.42 W
(11)	28°53′.27 N,	089°59′.98 W	(14)	28°52′.13 N,	090°02′.55 W
(12)	28°52′.25 N,	090°00′.32 W	(15)	28°53′.12 N,	090°03′.03 W

Note: Ship movement in the port area is monitored and supervised by a Port Vessel Traffic Supervisor on a 24-hour basis. Any ship planning to enter this precautionary area is requested to contact the LOOP Deepwater Port Vessel Traffic Supervisor on channel 10 VHF-FM and comply with his instructions while transiting the area.

(chartlet overleaf)

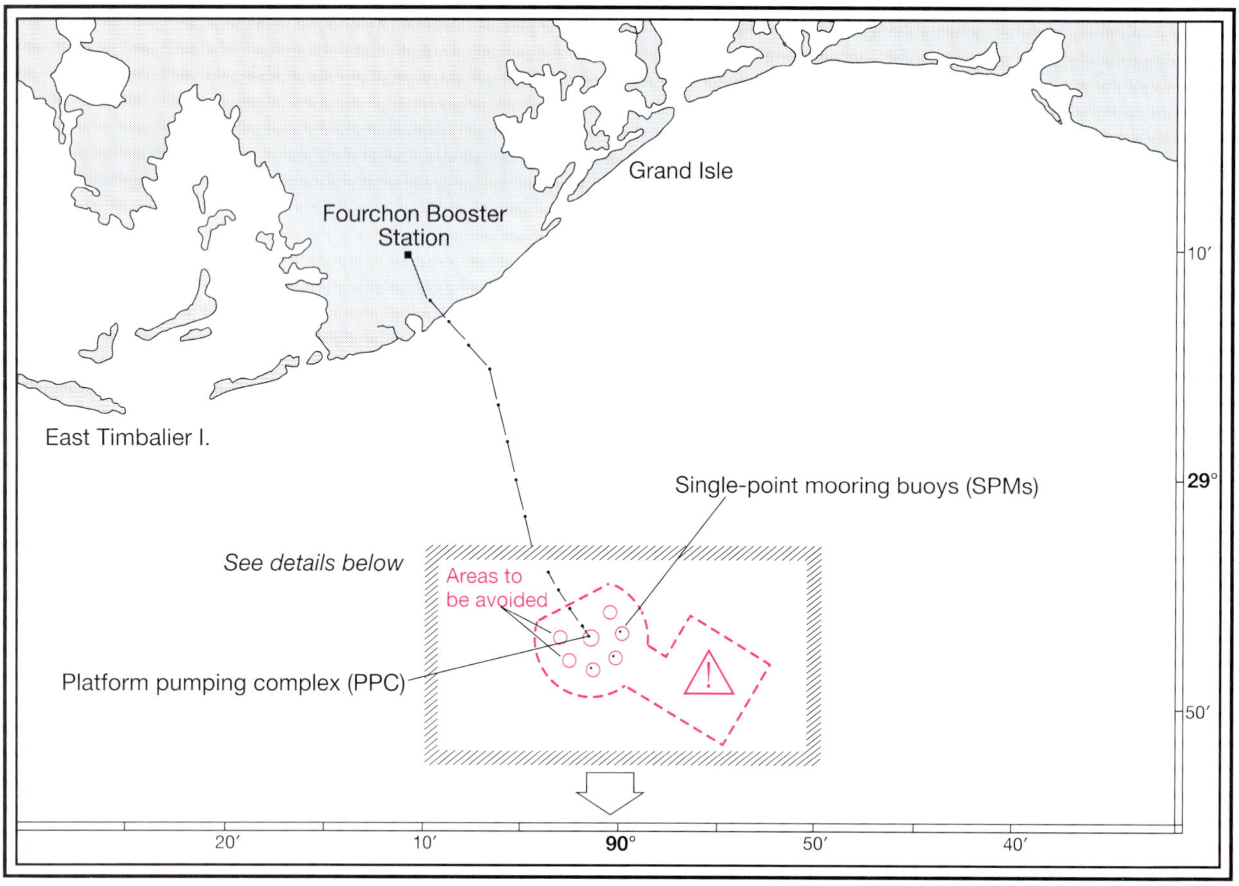

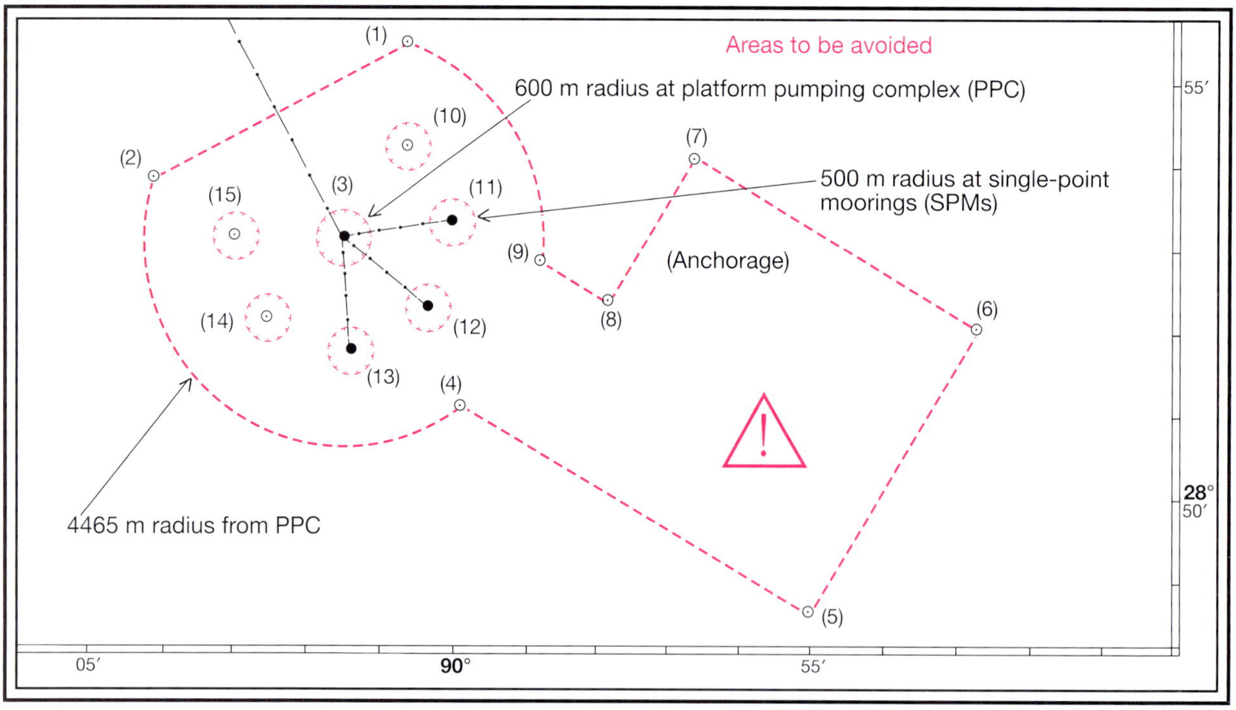

AT LOUISIANA OFFSHORE OIL PORT (LOOP)

AT EL PASO ENERGY BRIDGE DEEPWATER PORT IN THE GULF OF MEXICO

Note: See also "Mandatory no anchoring area at El Paso Energy Bridge deepwater port in the Gulf of Mexico" in part G, section II.

(Reference chart: United States 11340, 2003 edition.
Note: This chart is based on North American 1983 datum (WGS 84).)

Description of the area to be avoided

The area contained within a circle of radius 2000 metres centred on the following geographical position is designated as an area to be avoided:

28°05′.27 N, 093°03′.12 W

The area should be avoided by ships that are not going to carry out operations at the Deep Water Port.

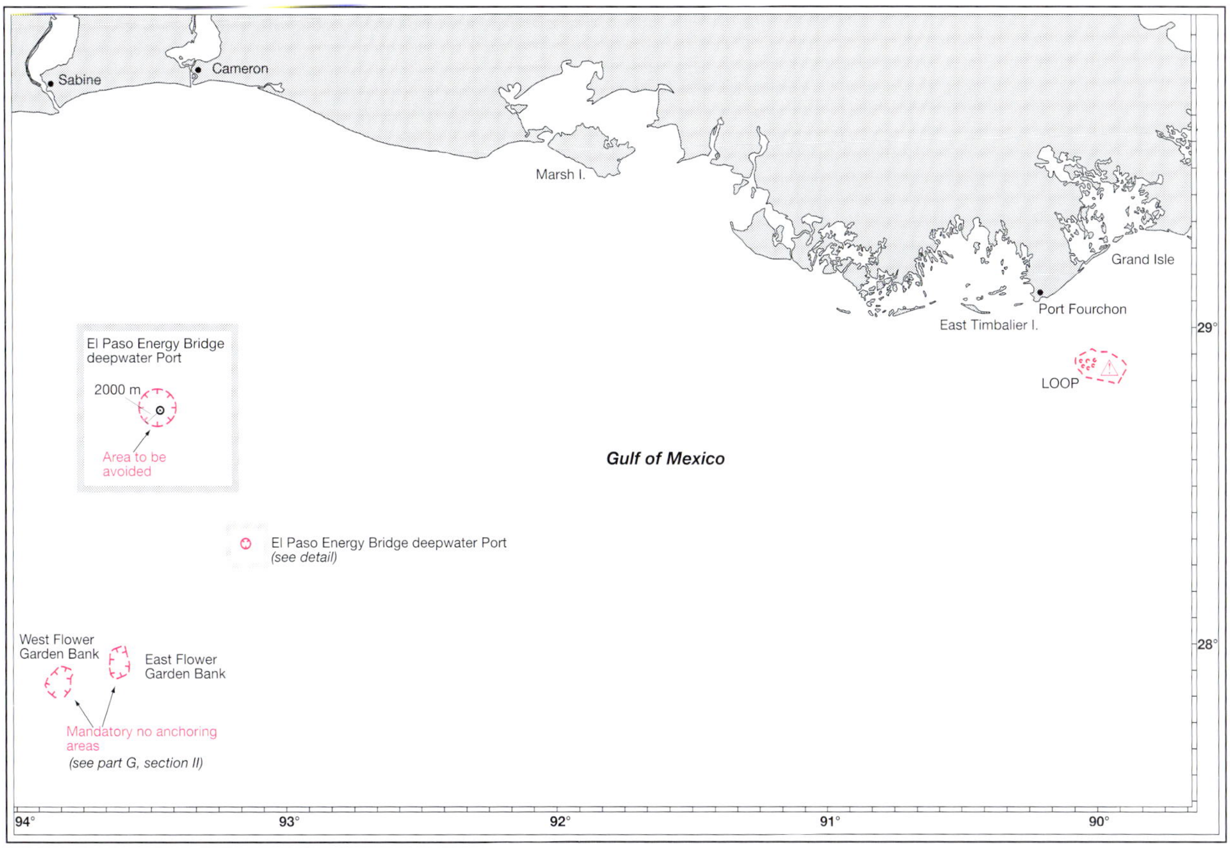

AT EL PASO ENERGY BRIDGE DEEPWATER PORT IN THE GULF OF MEXICO

D

IN THE APPROACHES TO THE PORT OF VERACRUZ

(Reference chart: United States 28302, 1991 edition.
Note: This chart is based on World Geodetic System 1984 datum (WGS 84).)

Description of the area to be avoided

With the aim of protecting the National Marine Park from the risk of pollution, which may be caused by the grounding of ships in the area, given the magnitude of the topographical obstacles which make navigation within the area hazardous, all ships of more than 500 gross tonnage and ships of less than 500 gross tonnage transporting oil, chemical, toxic or nuclear waste should avoid the area bounded by a line connecting the following geographical positions:

(24)	19°02′.20 N,	095°58′.10 W	(on the coast)
(25)	19°02′.20 N,	095°46′.60 W	
(8)	19°10′.90 N,	095°46′.60 W	
(7)	19°10′.90 N,	095°53′.43 W	
(26)	19°05′.80 N,	096°02′.04 W	
(27)	19°03′.40 N,	096°02′.04 W	(on the coast)

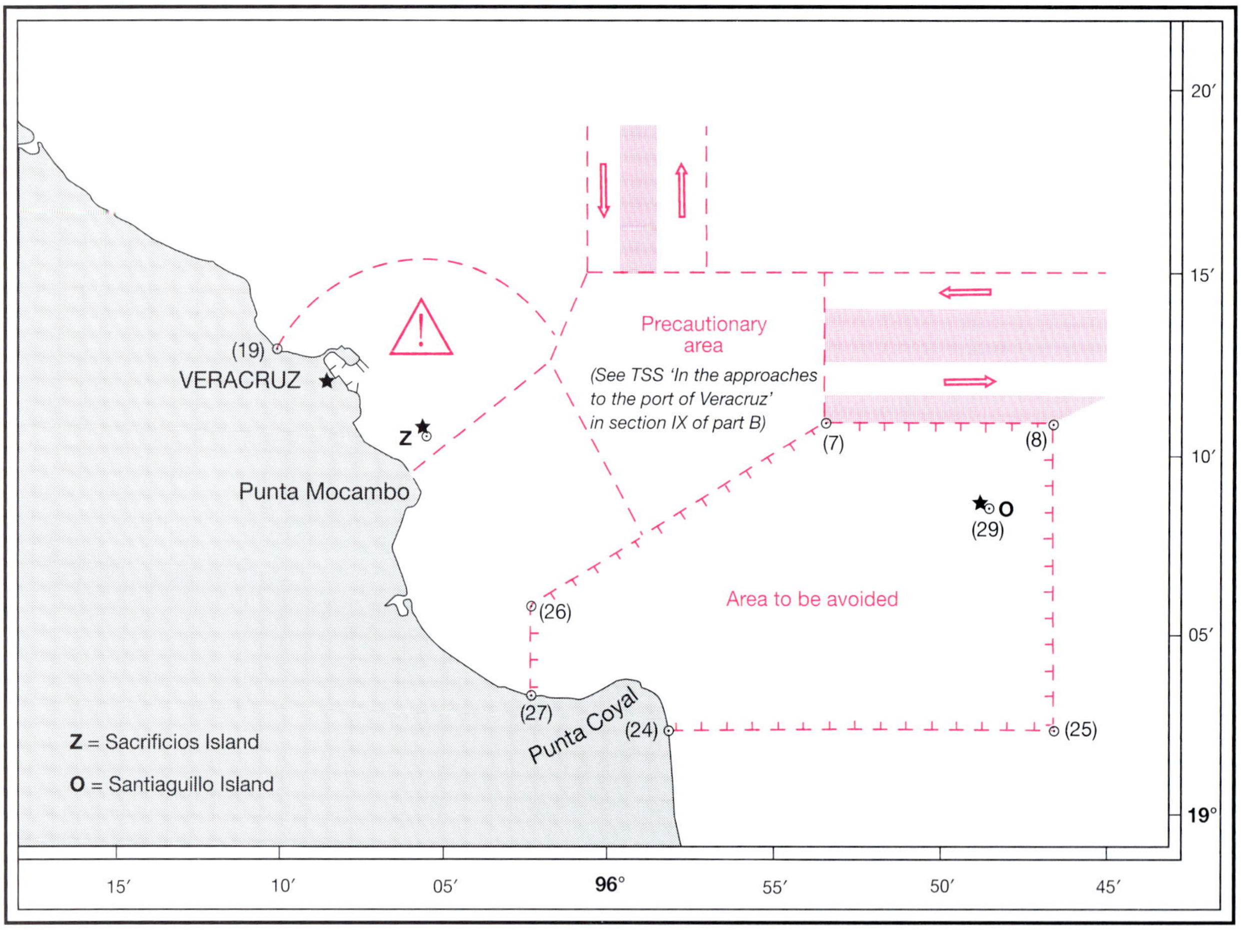

IN THE APPROACHES TO THE PORT OF VERACRUZ

IN THE GULF OF MEXICO (PORT AND OILFIELDS IN THE GULF OF CAMPECHE)*

AT THE PORT OF CAYO ARCAS (formerly "AT MARITIME OIL TERMINAL OFF CAYO ARCAS")*

Note: See "Recommended two-way routes and precautionary areas off the port of Cayo Arcas, FSO *Ta'kuntah* and FPSO *Yùum K'ak' Náab*" in part E.

(Reference chart: Chart of the Bay of Campeche, S.M. 840, Ministry of the Navy (fourth edition, October 2010).
Note: This chart is based on World Geodetic System 1984 datum (WGS 84).)

Description of the area to be avoided

The area to be avoided by ships not involved in oil-related activities in the port of Cayo Arcas is bounded by a line connecting the following geographical positions:

(51)	20°08′.54 N,	092°00′.58 W	(54)	20°12′.65 N,	091°59′.60 W
(52)	20°08′.54 N,	091°56′.67 W	(55)	20°12′.65 N,	092°00′.58 W
(53)	20°10′.24 N,	091°56′.67 W			

IN THE GULF OF CAMPECHE*

Note: See "Recommended two-way routes and precautionary areas to the north-west of the port of Isla del Carmen, Campeche" and "Recommended two-way routes to the north-east of the port of Dos Bocas, Tabasco" and "Recommended two-way routes and precautionary areas off the port of Cayo Arcas, FSO *Ta'kuntah* and FPSO *Yùum K'ak' Náab*" in part E.

(Reference chart: Chart of the Bay of Campeche, S.M. 840, Ministry of the Navy (fourth edition, October 2010).
Note: This chart is based on World Geodetic System 1984 datum (WGS 84).)

Description of the area to be avoided

The area to be avoided by ships not involved in oil-related activities in the Gulf of Campeche is bounded by a line connecting the following geographical positions:

(22)	19°05′.35 N,	092°23′.46 W	(61)	19°42′.20 N,	092°04′.00 W
(56)	19°08′.00 N,	092°12′.80 W	(62)	19°42′.20 N,	092°06′.20 W
(57)	19°12′.09 N,	092°03′.40 W	(63)	19°37′.50 N,	092°06′.20 W
(58)	19°17′.50 N,	091°56′.40 W	(64)	19°37′.50 N,	092°18′.65 W
(59)	19°30′.50 N,	091°56′.40 W	(65)	19°16′.20 N,	092°23′.95 W
(60)	19°36′.30 N,	092°04′.00 W	(23)	19°07′.09 N,	092°25′.02 W

AT THE REBOMBEO OILFIELD†

Note: See "Recommended two-way routes to the north-east of the port of Dos Bocas, Tabasco" and "Recommended two-way routes and precautionary areas to the north-west of the port of Isla del Carmen, Campeche" in part E.

(Reference chart: Chart of the Bay of Campeche, S.M. 840, Ministry of the Navy (fourth edition, October 2010).
Note: This chart is based on World Geodetic System 1984 datum (WGS 84).)

Description of the area to be avoided

The area to be avoided by ships not involved in oil-related activities in the Rebombeo oilfield is bounded by a line connecting the following geographical positions:

(66)	18°56′80 N,	092°43′.80 W	(11)	18°53′.09 N,	092°33′.27 W
(67)	18°51′.80 N,	092°37′.30 W	(68)	18°58′.80 N,	092°37′.60 W

* Date of implementation of amended area to be avoided: 0000 hours UTC on 1 December 2012.
† Date of implementation of new area to be avoided: 0000 hours UTC on 1 December 2012.

D

AT THE MAY OILFIELD†

Note: See "Recommended two-way routes and precautionary areas to the north-west of the port of Isla del Carmen, Campeche" in part E.

(Reference chart: Chart of the Bay of Campeche, S.M. 840, Ministry of the Navy (fourth edition, October 2010).
Note: This chart is based on World Geodetic System 1984 datum (WGS 84).)

Description of the area to be avoided

The area to be avoided by ships not involved in oil-related activities in the May oilfield is bounded by a line connecting the following geographical positions:

(69)	18°42′.60 N,	092°37′.10 W	(71)	18°42′.50 N,	092°33′.70 W
(70)	18°41′.85 N,	092°34′.10 W	(72)	18°44′.00 N,	092°36′.10 W

IN THE LOADING BUOY AREA IN THE PORT OF DOS BOCAS, TABASCO†

Note: See "Recommended two-way routes to the north-east of the port of Dos Bocas, Tabasco" in part E.

(Reference chart: Chart of the Bay of Campeche, S.M. 840, Ministry of the Navy (fourth edition, October 2010).
Note: This chart is based on World Geodetic System 1984 datum (WGS 84).)

Description of the area to be avoided

The area to be avoided by ships not involved in crude oil loading and loading operations for exportation in the loading buoy area in the port of Dos Bocas, Tabasco, is bounded by a line connecting the following geographical positions:

(73)	18°36′.50 N,	093°12′.10 W	(75)	18°38′.70 N,	093°08′.70 W
(74)	18°36′.50 N,	093°08′.70 W	(76)	18°38′.70 N,	093°12′.10 W

D

† Date of implementation of new area to be avoided: 0000 hours UTC on 1 December 2012.

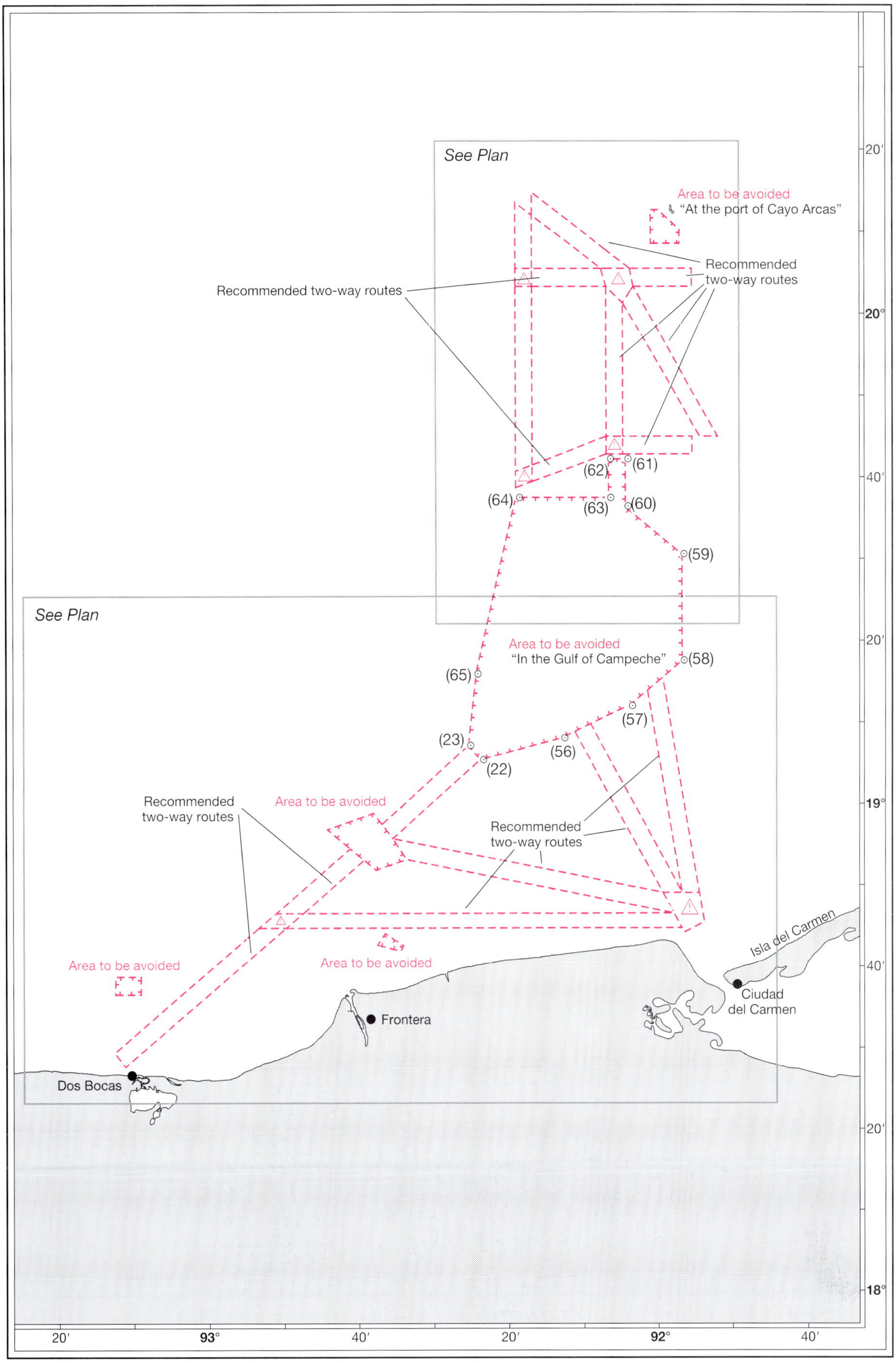

IN THE GULF OF MEXICO (PORT AND OILFIELDS IN THE GULF OF CAMPECHE)

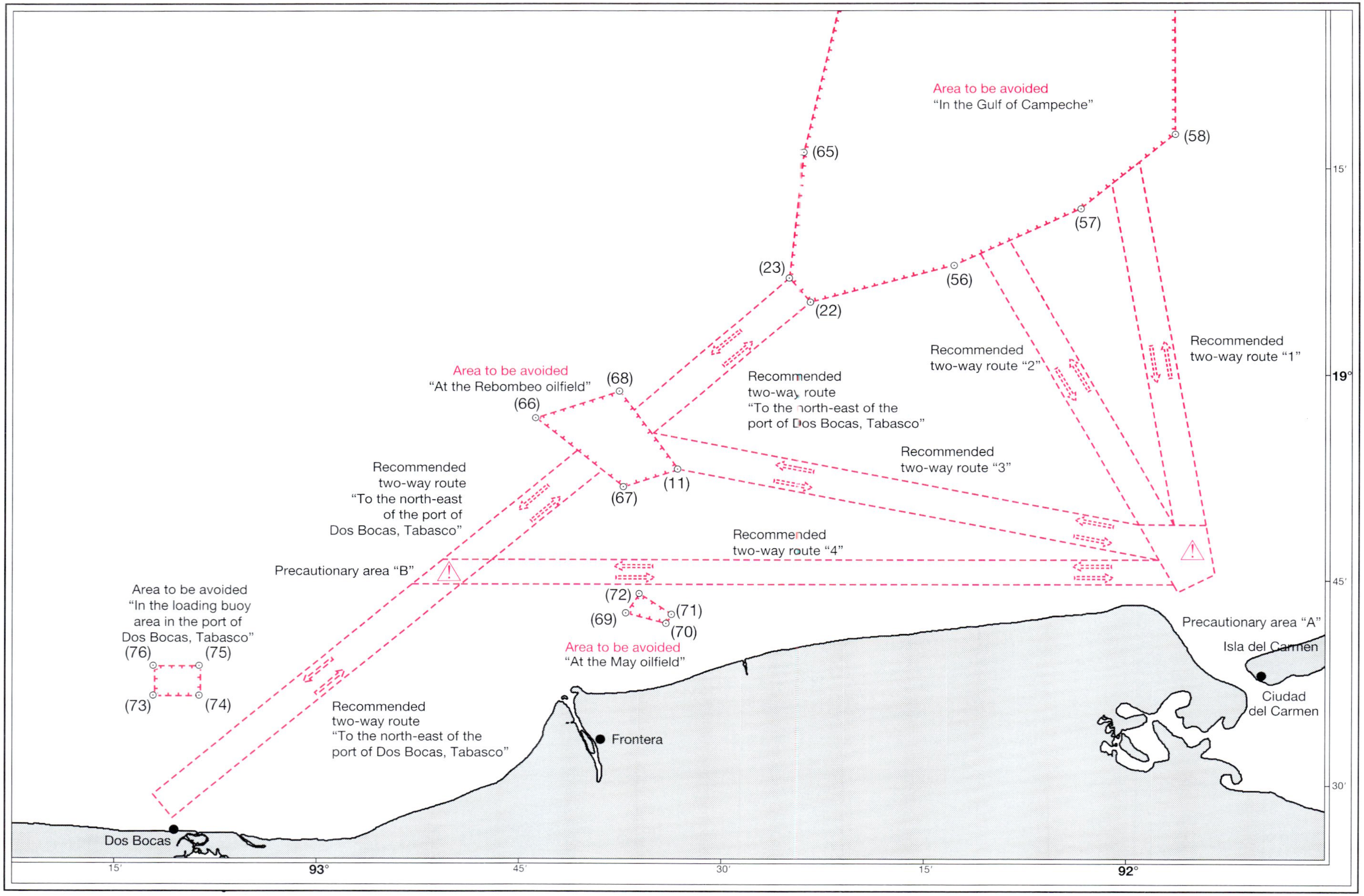

IN THE GULF OF MEXICO – AT THE REBOMBEO AND MAY OILFIELDS AND IN THE LOADING BUOY AREA OF DOS BOCAS

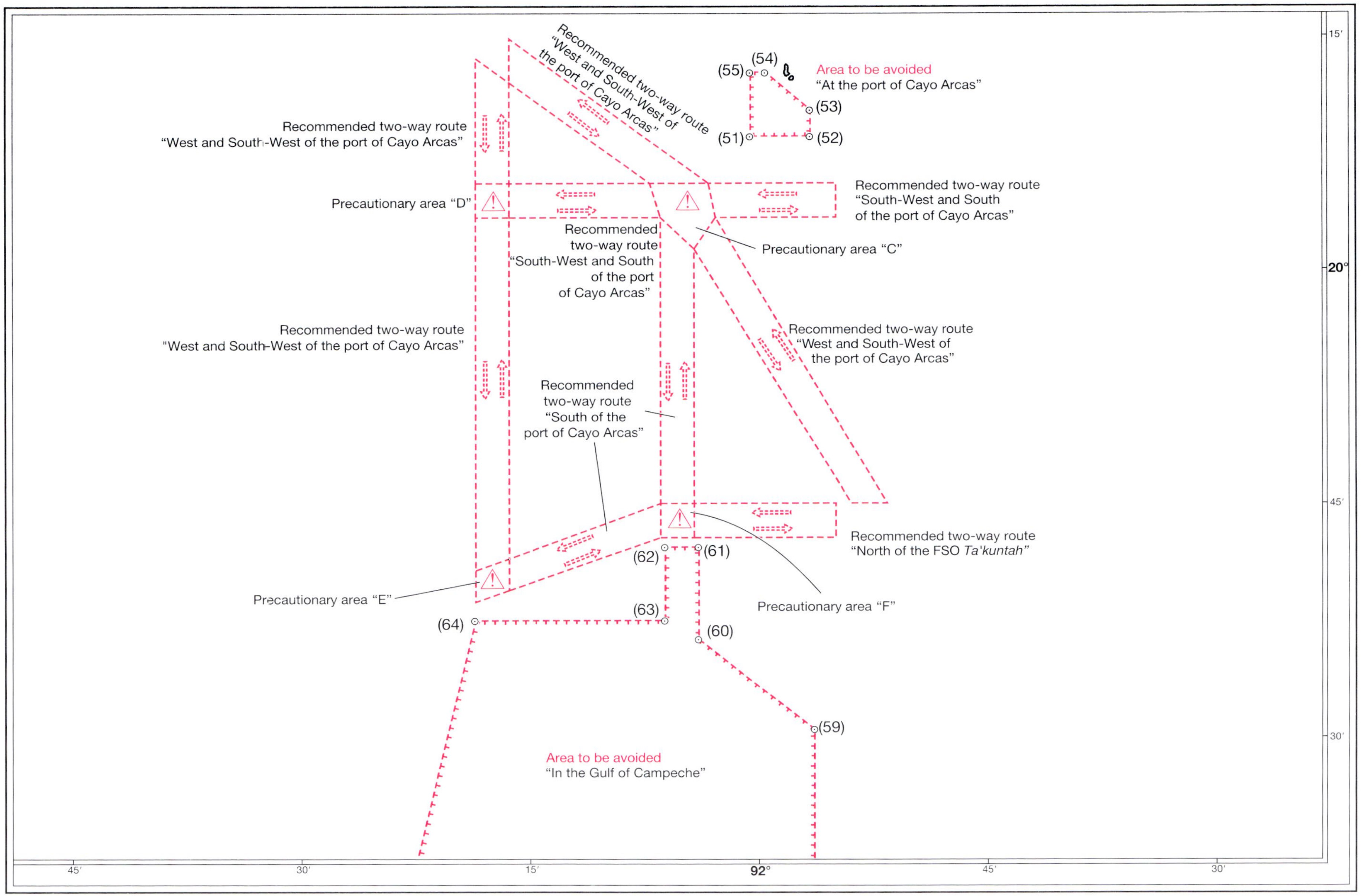

IN THE GULF OF MEXICO – AT THE PORT OF CAYO ARCAS

D

IN THE ACCESS ROUTES TO THE PORTS OF MATANZAS AND CARDENAS

(Reference chart: ICH 11425, 1998 edition.
Note: This chart is based on North American 1927 datum).

Description of the area to be avoided

The area described below should be avoided by all ships over 150 gross tonnage, for reasons of conservation of unique biodiversity, nature and beautiful scenery.

The area to be avoided lies within the coastline of the province of Matanzas and a line connecting the following geographical points:

(1)	23°05′.60 N,	081°28′.50 W	Punta Maya lighthouse
(2)	23°10′.60 N,	081°28′.50 W	
(3)	23°19′.50 N,	081°11′.50 W	
(4)	23°14′.60 N,	081°07′.20 W	Cayo Piedras del Norte
(5)	23°11′.50 N,	081°07′.20 W	Punta Las Morlas

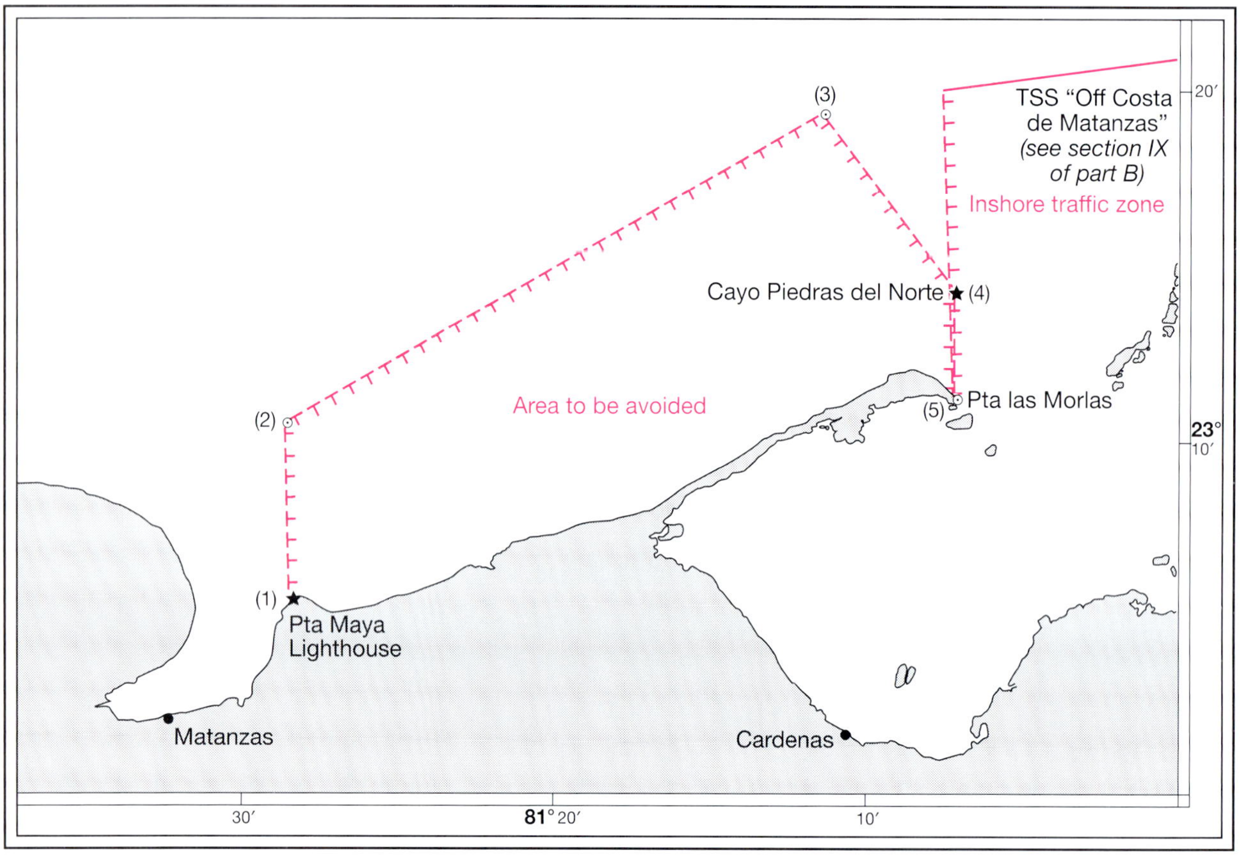

IN THE ACCESS ROUTES TO THE PORTS OF MATANZAS AND CARDENAS

BY SHIPS OF 300 GROSS TONNAGE OR OVER AS ASSOCIATED PROTECTIVE MEASURE (APM) FOR SABA BANK PSSA*

Note: See "Mandatory no anchoring area for all ships as associated protective measure (APM) for Saba Bank PSSA" in part G, section II.

(Reference chart: Netherlands 2020, November 2007 edition.
Note: This chart is based on World Geodetic System 1984 datum (WGS 84).)

Description of the area to be avoided

An area to be avoided by ships of 300 gross tonnage and over is established in the area designated as a Particularly Sensitive Sea Area and bounded by a line connecting the following geographical positions:

(1)	17°27′.06 N,	063°56′.14 W	(8)	17°30′.88 N,	063°10′.92 W
(2)	17°29′.00 N,	063°55′.09 W	(9)	17°23′.80 N,	063°11′.25 W
(3)	17°27′.94 N,	063°43′.32 W	(10)	17°16′.27 N,	063°15′.85 W
(4)	17°38′.03 N,	063°27′.41 W	(11)	17°13′.44 N,	063°26′.89 W
(5)	17°43′.35 N,	063°32′.74 W	(12)	17°10′.55 N,	063°41′.81 W
(6)	17°45′.98 N,	063°29′.98 W	(13)	17°20′.85 N,	063°49′.89 W
(7)	17°40′.34 N,	063°21′.10 W			

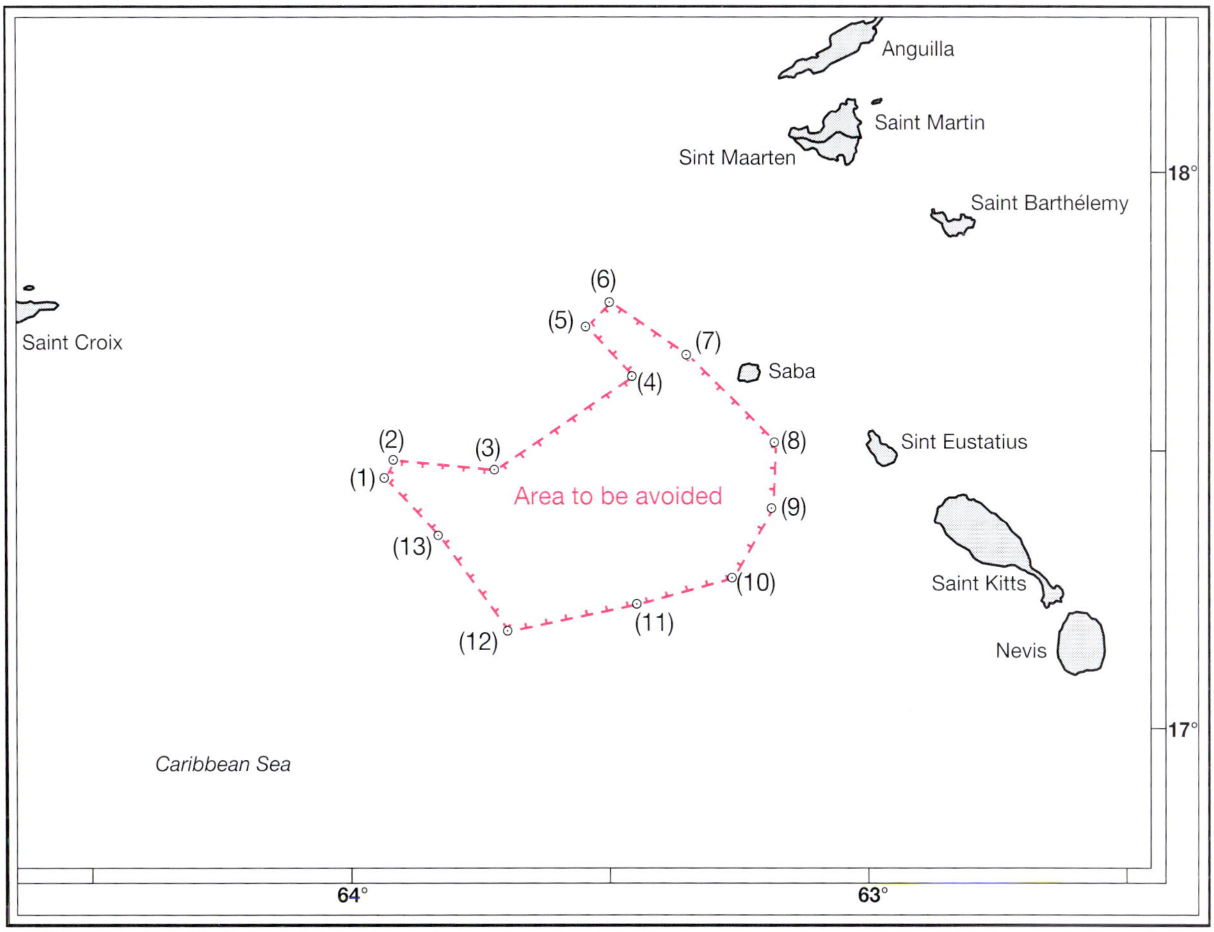

BY SHIPS OF 300 GROSS TONNAGE OR OVER AS ASSOCIATED PROTECTIVE MEASURE (APM) FOR SABA BANK PSSA

* Date of implementation of new area to be avoided: 0000 hours UTC on 1 June 2013.

IN THE PAPAHĀNAUMOKUĀKEA MARINE NATIONAL MONUMENT PARTICULARLY SENSITIVE SEA AREA

(Reference charts: United States 19016, 2007 edition; 19019, 2007 edition; 19022, 2007 edition.
Note: These charts are based on World Geodetic System 1984 datum (WGS 84) and astronomic datum.)

Description of the areas to be avoided

Given the magnitude of obstacles that make navigation in these areas hazardous, and in order to increase maritime safety, protection of the environment, preservation of cultural resources and areas of cultural importance significant to Native Hawaiians, and facilitate the ability to respond to developing maritime emergencies in the Papahānaumokuākea Marine National Monument, all ships solely in transit should avoid the following areas:

1 Those areas contained within a circle of radius of 50 nautical miles centred upon the following geographical positions:

(1) 28°25′.18 N, 178°19′.75 W (Kure Atoll)
(2) 28°14′.20 N, 177°22′.10 W (Midway Atoll)
(3) 27°50′.62 N, 175°50′.53 W (Pearl and Hermes Atoll)
(4) 26°03′.82 N, 173°58′.00 W (Lisianski Island)
(5) 25°46′.18 N, 171°43′.95 W (Laysan Island)
(6) 25°25′.45 N, 170°35′.32 W (Maro Reef)
(7) 25°19′.50 N, 170°00′.88 W (between Maro Reef and Raita Bank)
(8) 25°00′.00 N, 167°59′.92 W (Gardner Pinnacles)
(9) 23°45′.52 N, 166°14′.62 W (French Frigate Shoals)
(10) 23°34′.60 N, 164°42′.02 W (Necker Island)
(11) 23°03′.38 N, 161°55′.32 W (Nihoa Island)

2 The areas contained between the following geographical positions:

		Begin co-ordinates	End co-ordinates
Area 1	Lisianski Island (N) → Laysan Island	26°53′.22 N, 173°49′.64 W	26°35′.58 N, 171°35′.60 W
	Lisianski Island (S) → Laysan Island	25°14′.42 N, 174°06′.36 W	24°57′.63 N, 171°57′.07 W
Area 2	Gardner Pinnacles (N) → French Frigate Shoals	25°38′.90 N, 167°25′.31 W	24°24′.80 N, 165°40′.89 W
	Gardner Pinnacles (S) → French Frigate Shoals	24°14′.27 N, 168°22′.13 W	23°05′.84 N, 166°47′.81 W

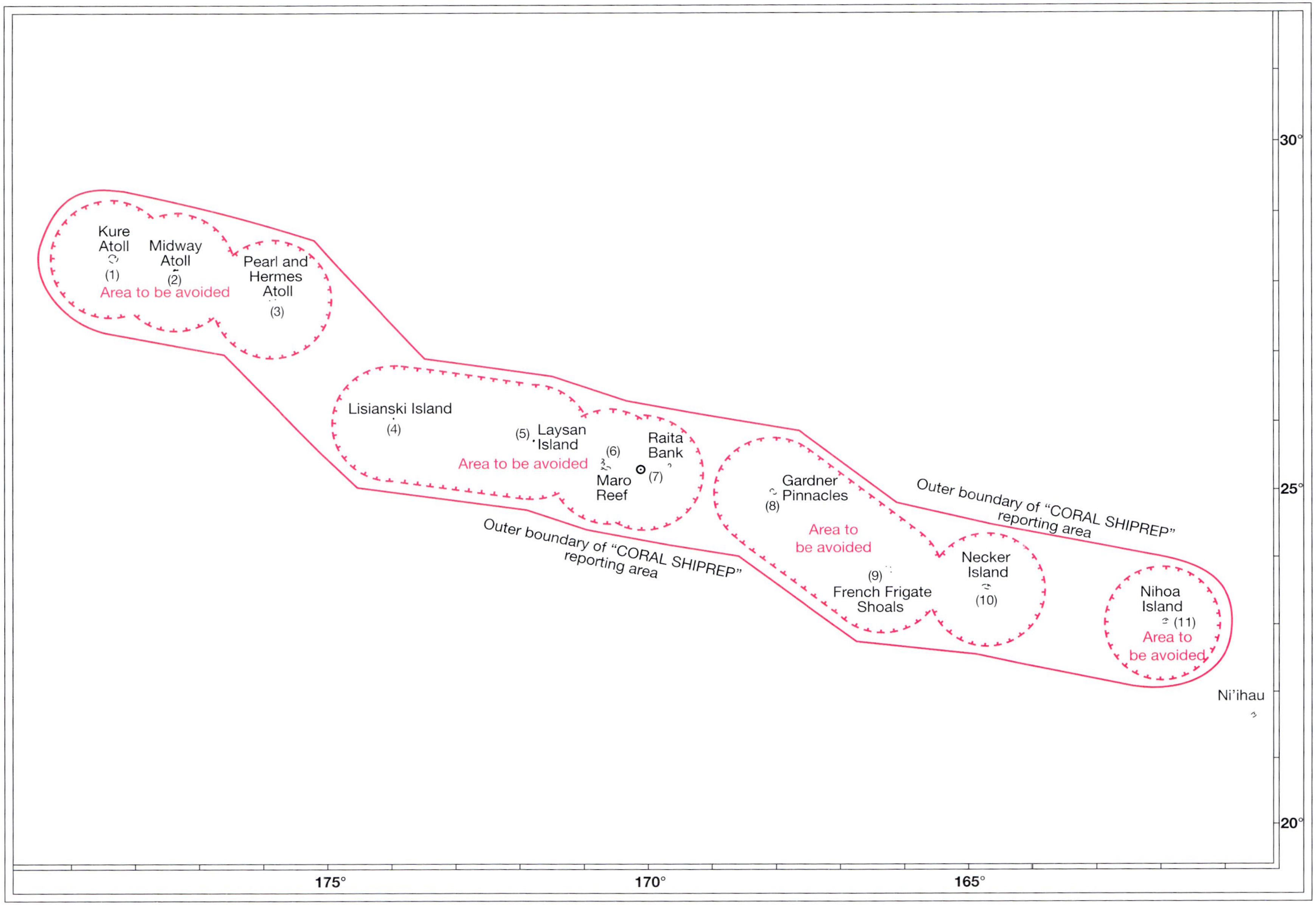

IN THE PAPAHĀNAUMOKUĀKEA MARINE NATIONAL MONUMENT PARTICULARLY SENSITIVE SEA AREA

D

OFF THE WASHINGTON COAST

(Reference charts: United States 18003, 2006 edition, 18500, 2008 edition, and 18480, 2006 edition.
Note: These charts are based on North American 1983 datum, which is equivalent to WGS 1984 datum)

Description of the area to be avoided

In order to reduce the risk of a marine casualty and resulting pollution and damage to the environment of the Olympic Coast National Marine Sanctuary, all ships and barges* that carry oil or hazardous materials in bulk as cargo or cargo residue and all ships 400 gross tonnage and above solely in transit should avoid the area bounded by a line connecting the following geographical positions:

(1)	48°23′.30 N,	124°38′.20 W	(5)	48°24′.67 N,	124°55′.71 W
(2)	48°24′.17 N,	124°38′.20 W	(6)	47°51′.70 N,	125°15′.50 W
(3)	48°26′.15 N,	124°44′.65 W	(7)	47°07′.70 N,	124°47′.50 W
(4)	48°26′.15 N,	124°52′.80 W	(8)	47°07′.70 N,	124°11′.00 W

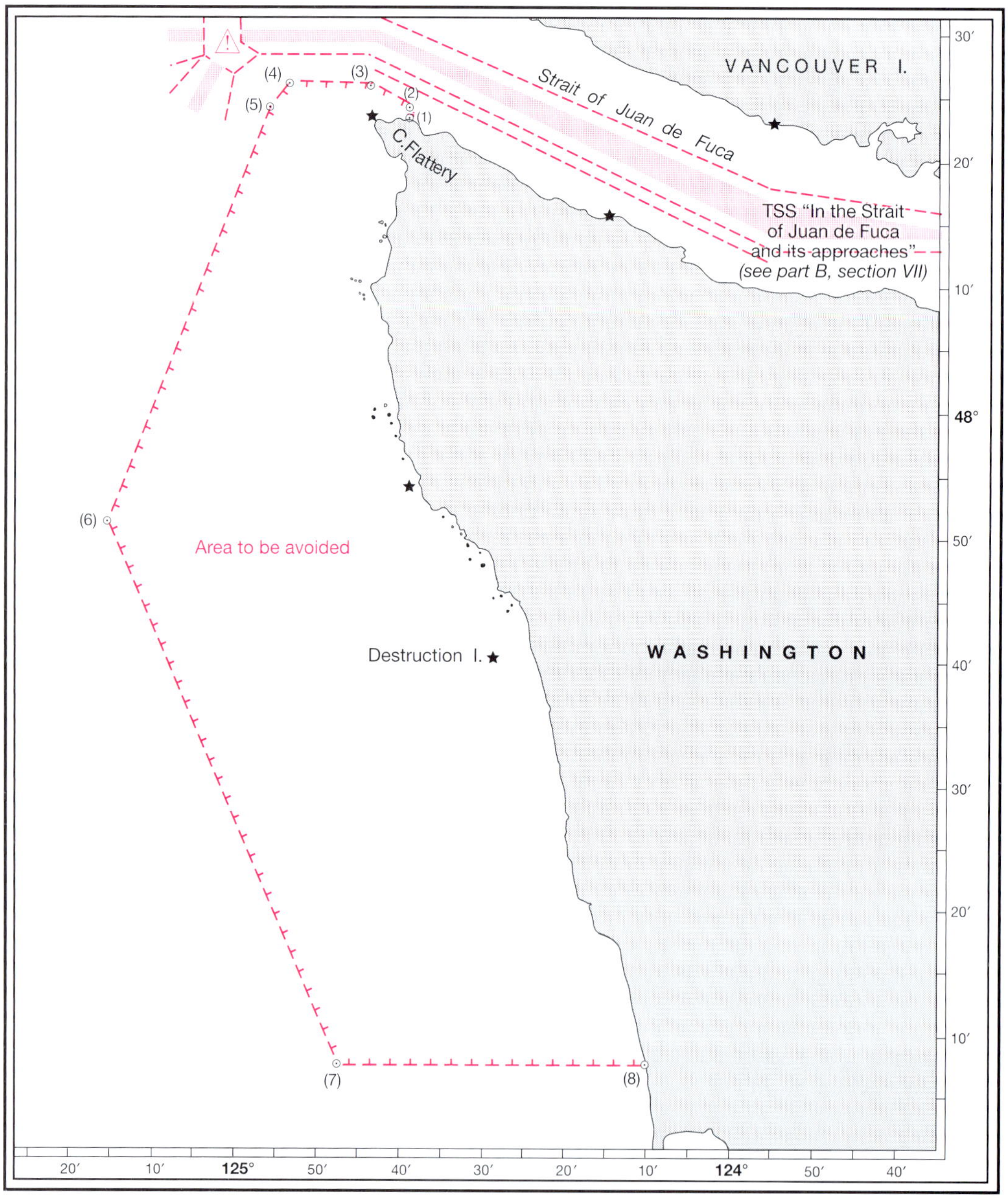

OFF THE WASHINGTON COAST

* This ATBA does not apply to any warship, naval auxiliary, barge (whether towed by a Government or commercial tug), or other ship owned or operated by a Contracting Government and used, for the time being, only on Government non-commercial service.

OFF THE CALIFORNIA COAST

(Reference chart: United States 18720, 1990 edition.
Note: This chart is based on North American 1983 datum.)

Description of the areas to be avoided

In order to avoid risk of pollution in the area designated as the Channel Islands National Marine Sanctuary, all ships, except those bound to and from ports on one of the islands within the area, engaged in the trade of carrying cargo, including but not limited to tankers and other bulk carriers and barges, should avoid the following areas:

(a) **In the region of San Miguel, Santa Rosa, Santa Cruz and Anacapa Islands off the coast of southern California**

The area bounded by a line connecting the following geographical positions is designated as an area to be avoided:

(1)	33°58′.70 N,	119°12′.80 W	(5)	34°10′.40 N,	120°39′.50 W
(2)	33°54′.00 N,	119°17′.00 W	(6)	34°14′.00 N,	120°31′.30 W
(3)	33°46′.30 N,	120°07′.80 W	(7)	34°10′.00 N,	119°56′.40 W
(4)	33°59′.00 N,	120°39′.50 W	(8)	34°01′.40 N,	119°18′.60 W

(b) **In the region of Santa Barbara Island off the coast of southern California**

The area contained within a circle of radius 7.5 nautical miles centred upon the following geographical position is designated as an area to be avoided:

(9) 33°28′.60 N, 119°02′.20 W

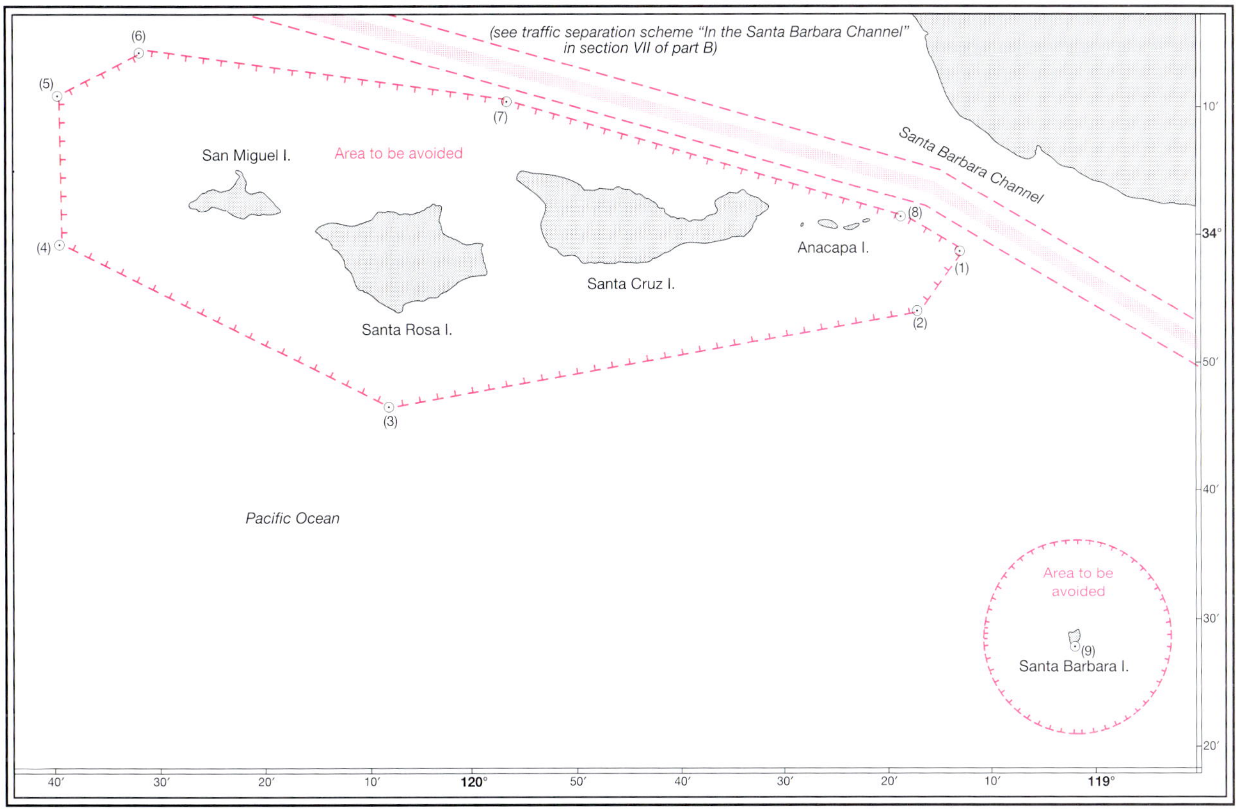

OFF THE CALIFORNIA COAST

IN THE APPROACHES TO SALINA CRUZ

(Reference chart: United States 21441, 1986 edition.
Note: This chart is based on the World Geodetic System 1972 datum.)

Description of a precautionary area and areas to be avoided

(a) **Precautionary area**

A precautionary area is established by an arc of a circle of 4 miles radius centred on the lighthouse of Salina Cruz, Oaxaca, Mexico, at geographical position:

(22) 16°09′.70 N, 095°12′.24 W

starting at the coastline at geographical position:

(17) 16°07′.85 N, 095°15′.90 W

as far as geographical position:

(13) 16°05′.75 N, 095°12′.73 W

continuing in a straight line as far as geographical position:

(16) 16°05′.75 N, 095°10′.00 W

and from geographical position (16) in a straight line as far as the coastline at geographical position:

(18) 16°09′.95 N, 095°10′.00 W

(b) **Areas to be avoided**

The following areas to be avoided by ships that are not going to carry out operations at the single-point moorings and the oil terminal at the port of Salina Cruz, Oaxaca, Mexico, are established within the precautionary area:

Three circular areas to be avoided, each bounded by a circle of 400 metres radius, centred respectively on the following geographical positions:

(19) 16°08′.63 N, 095°12′.94 W
(20) 16°08′.41 N, 095°13′.75 W
(21) 16°07′.11 N, 095°13′.28 W

Note:

Ship movement in the port area is monitored and supervised by a Port Vessel Traffic Supervisor on a 24-hour basis. Any ship planning to enter this precautionary area is requested to contact the Salina Cruz Port Vessel Traffic Supervisor on channel 6 VHF and follow his advice while transiting the areas.

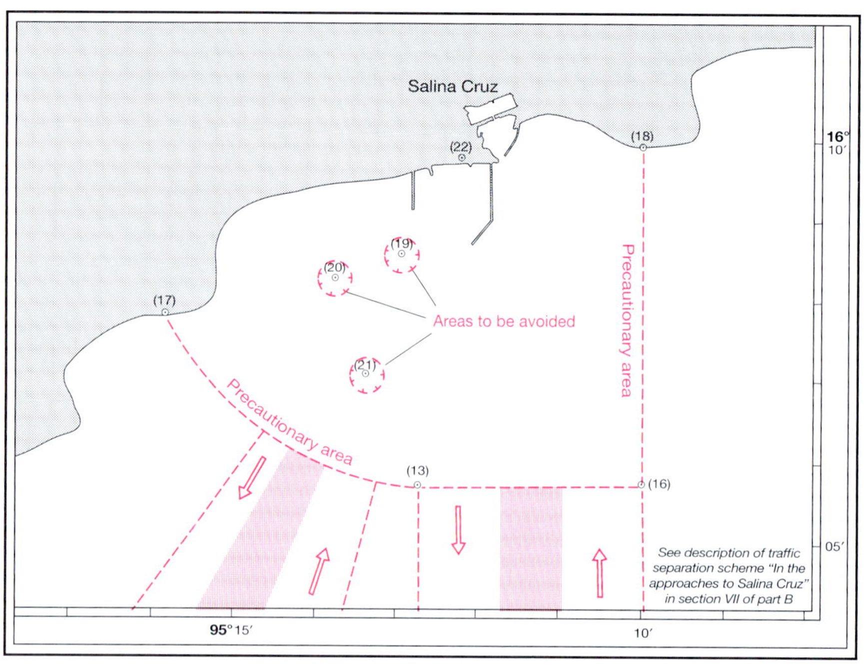

IN THE APPROACHES TO SALINA CRUZ

Section III

Other areas to be avoided

Some small areas to be avoided, at the junction of traffic lanes of traffic separation schemes and to which no specified conditions of tonnage of vessels or of the cargoes that are carried apply, are not included in part D. They are described in the definitions of these traffic separation schemes:

Strait of Istanbul – south approach and Sea of Marmara (see section III of part B)
Singapore Strait (Off St John's Island/Pulau Sambu) (see section V of part B)
Approaches to Puerto Callao (see section VIII of part B)
In the approaches to Puerto Pisco (see section VIII of part B)

and of this deep-water route:

In the approaches to Jazan Economic City Port (see section III of part C)

Caution: The chartlets are for illustrative purposes only and must not be used for navigation. Mariners should consult the appropriate nautical publications and charts for up-to-date details on aids to navigation and other relevant information.

Warning: The geographical positions given in the descriptions of the areas to be avoided are only correct for charts using the same geodetic datum as the reference charts indicated under each description. Charts published by other hydrographic offices may use a different geodetic datum, as may new editions of the reference charts published after the adoption of the areas.

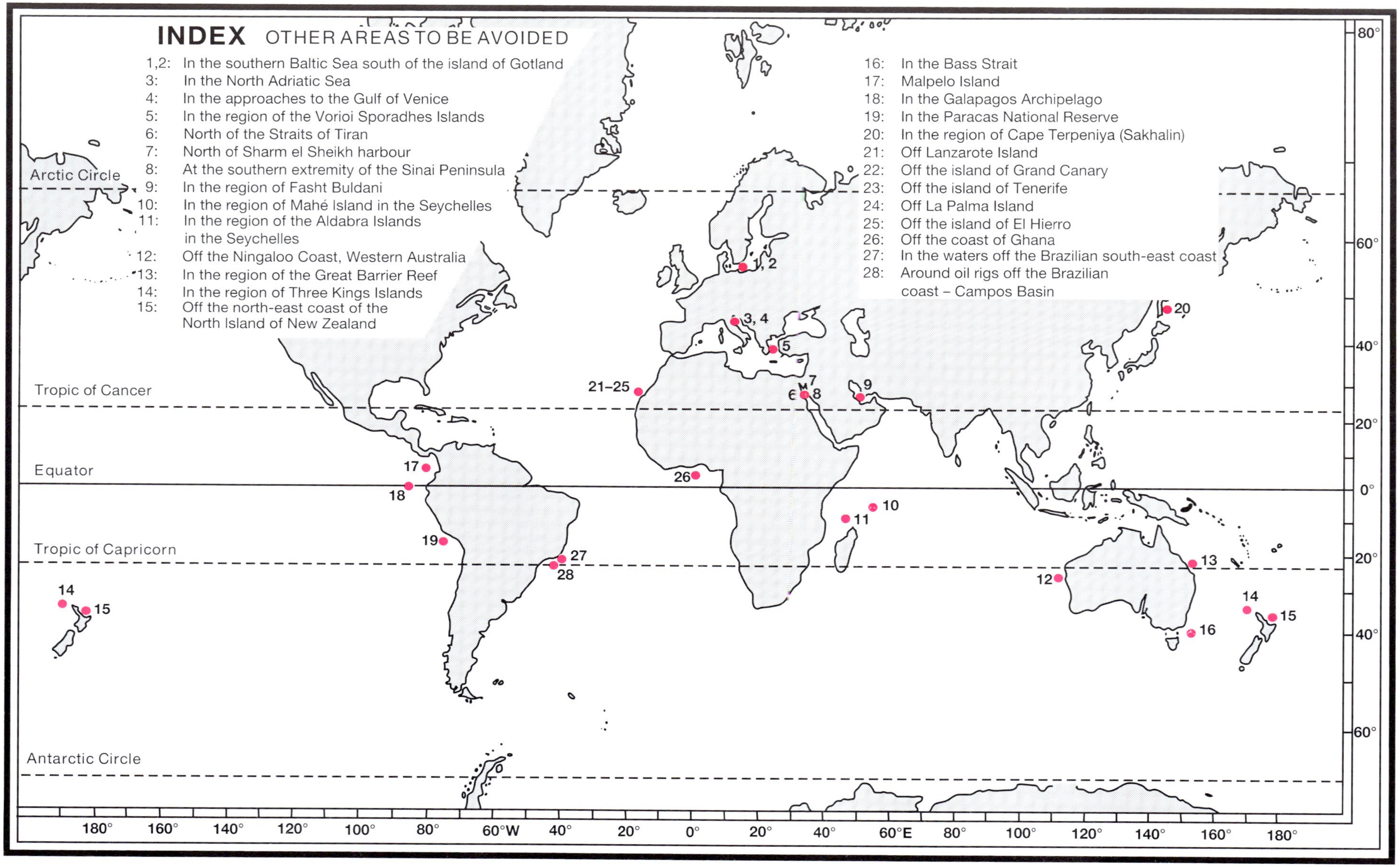
INDEX OTHER AREAS TO BE AVOIDED
1,2: In the southern Baltic Sea south of the island of Gotland
3: In the North Adriatic Sea
4: In the approaches to the Gulf of Venice
5: In the region of the Vorioi Sporadhes Islands
6: North of the Straits of Tiran
7: North of Sharm el Sheikh harbour
8: At the southern extremity of the Sinai Peninsula
9: In the region of Fasht Buldani
10: In the region of Mahé Island in the Seychelles
11: In the region of the Aldabra Islands in the Seychelles
12: Off the Ningaloo Coast, Western Australia
13: In the region of the Great Barrier Reef
14: In the region of Three Kings Islands
15: Off the north-east coast of the North Island of New Zealand
16: In the Bass Strait
17: Malpelo Island
18: In the Galapagos Archipelago
19: In the Paracas National Reserve
20: In the region of Cape Terpeniya (Sakhalin)
21: Off Lanzarote Island
22: Off the island of Grand Canary
23: Off the island of Tenerife
24: Off La Palma Island
25: Off the island of El Hierro
26: Off the coast of Ghana
27: In the waters off the Brazilian south-east coast
28: Around oil rigs off the Brazilian coast – Campos Basin
Arctic Circle
Tropic of Cancer
Equator
Tropic of Capricorn
Antarctic Circle
180° 160° 140° 120° 100° 80° 60°W 40° 20° 0° 20° 40° 60°E 80° 100° 120° 140° 160° 180°
80° 60° 40° 20° 0° 20° 40° 60°

IN THE SOUTHERN BALTIC SEA SOUTH OF THE ISLAND OF GOTLAND

(Reference chart: Swedish 8, 2001 edition.
Note: This chart is based on World Geodetic System 1984 datum (WGS 84).)

Description of the areas to be avoided

(a) **Hoburgs Bank**

The area bounded by a line connecting the following geographical positions is designated as an area to be avoided:

(1)	56°49′.52 N,	018°38′.77 E	(4)	56°22′.77 N,	018°08′.43 E
(2)	56°40′.23 N,	018°45′.08 E	(5)	56°34′.96 N,	018°06′.20 E
(3)	56°24′.06 N,	018°36′.20 E			

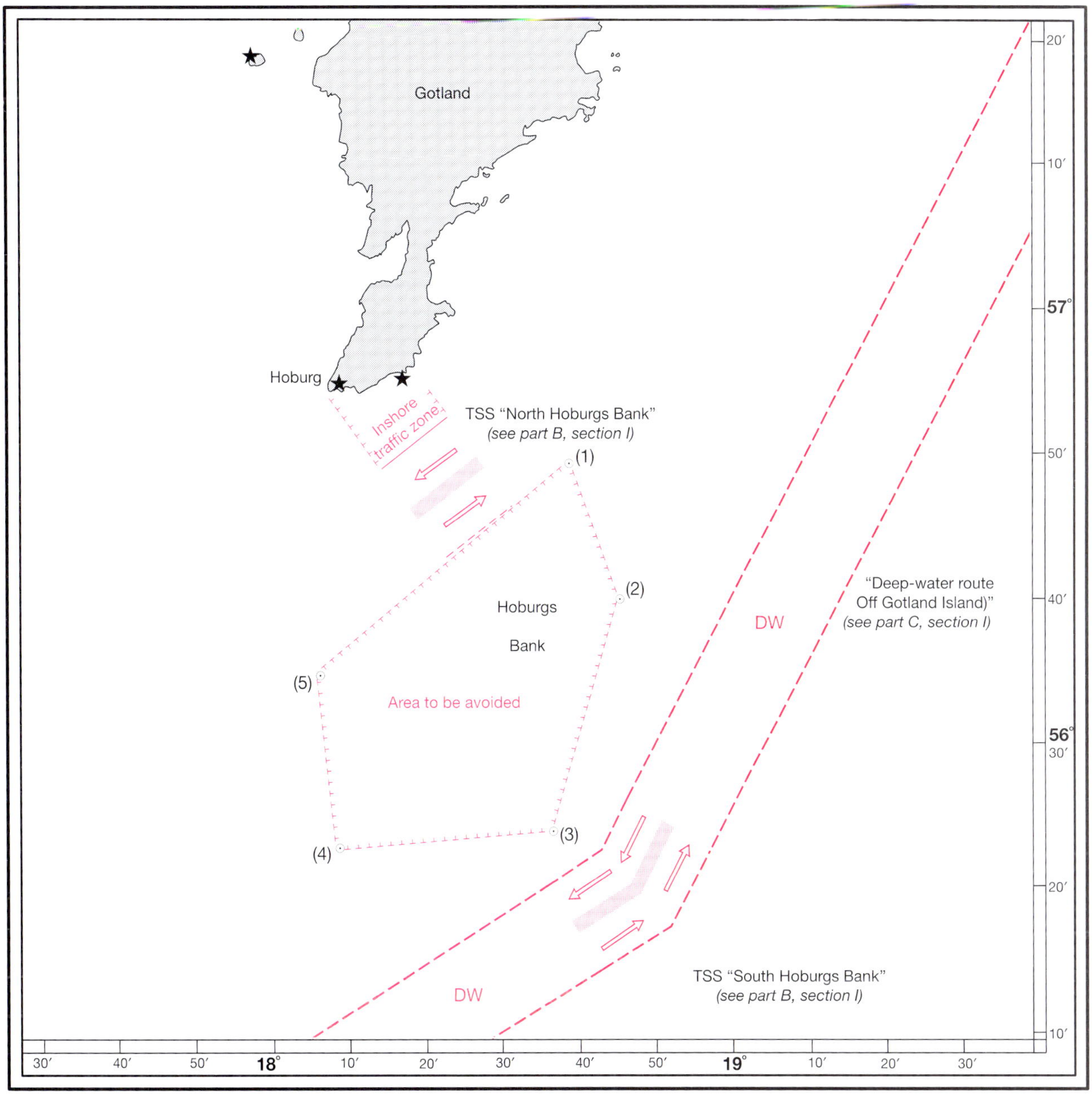

IN THE SOUTHERN BALTIC SEA SOUTH OF THE ISLAND OF GOTLAND: HOBURGS BANK

(b) **Norra Midsjöbanken**

The area bounded by a line connecting the following geographical positions is designated as an area to be avoided:

(1)	56°07′.87 N,	017°38′.41 E	(3)	56°10′.10 N,	017°13′.68 E
(2)	56°02′.17 N,	017°13′.17 E	(4)	56°15′.02 N,	017°25′.61 E

Note: All vessels with a gross tonnage of 500 or more should avoid the areas.

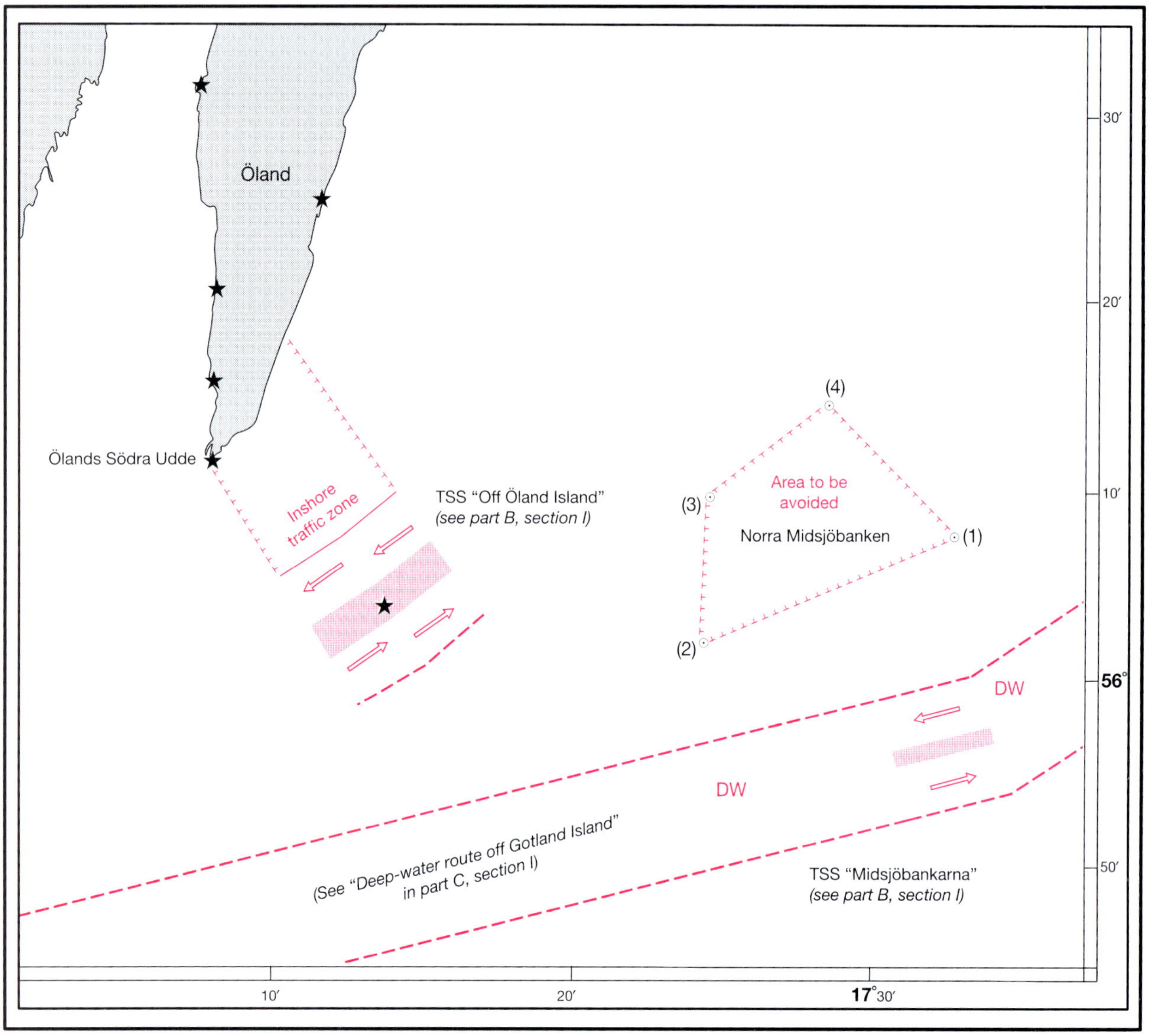

IN THE SOUTHERN BALTIC SEA SOUTH OF THE ISLAND OF GOTLAND: NORRA MIDSJÖBANKEN

IN THE NORTH ADRIATIC SEA

Note: See mandatory ship reporting system "In the Adriatic Sea" in part G, section I.

(Reference charts: Italian Navy Hydrographical Institute 435, 1993 edition (ED 50 datum); Hydrographical Institute of the Republic of Croatia 101, 1998 edition (Hermannskögel datum, Bessel ellipsoid).
Note: The co-ordinates listed below are in World Geodetic System 1984 datum (WGS 84).)

Northern part

Description of the area to be avoided

In order to avoid the risk of pollution due to damage of oil rigs, oil and gas pipelines in this area, the area described below should be avoided by ships of more than 200 gross tonnage.

The area to be avoided is bounded by a line connecting the following geographical positions:

(1)	44°12′.80 N,	013°37′.50 E	(6)	44°52′.00 N,	013°17′.07 E
(2)	44°17′.00 N,	013°43′.77 E	(7)	44°52′.00 N,	013°05′.77 E
(3)	44°25′.30 N,	013°37′.47 E	(8)	44°37′.70 N,	013°07′.90 E
(4)	44°34′.50 N,	013°25′.47 E	(9)	44°23′.00 N,	013°14′.30 E
(5)	44°41′.90 N,	013°24′.97 E			

Southern part

Description of the area to be avoided

In order to avoid the risk of pollution due to damage of oil rigs, oil and gas pipelines in this area, the area described below should be avoided by ships of more than 200 gross tonnage.

The area to be avoided is bounded by a line connecting the following geographical positions:

(1)	43°58′.40 N,	013°52′.70 E	(3)	44°09′.00 N,	013°40′.50 E
(2)	44°01′.40 N,	013°56′.80 E	(4)	44°06′.60 N,	013°37′.90 E

(chartlet overleaf)

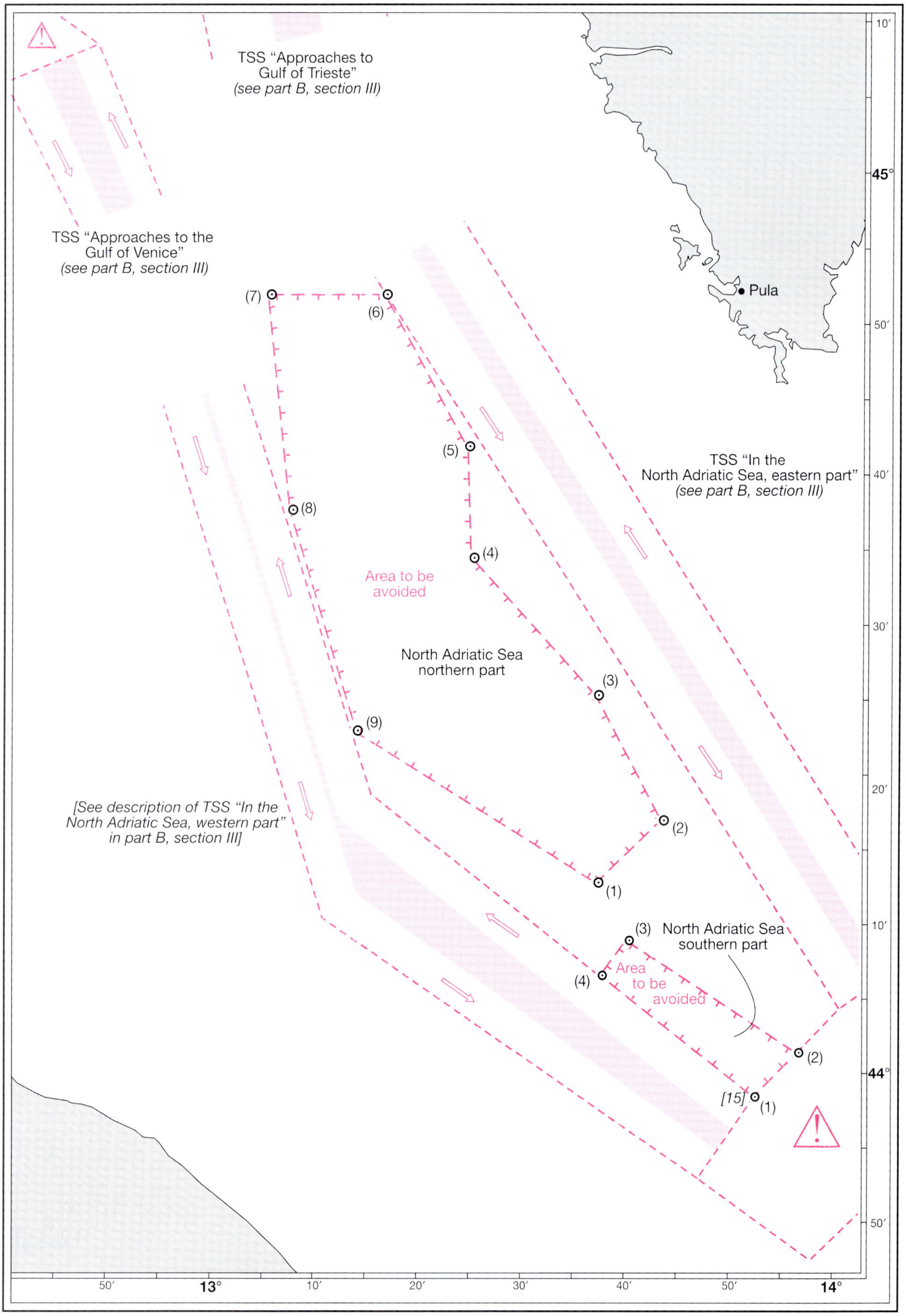

IN THE NORTH ADRIATIC SEA

IN THE APPROACHES TO THE GULF OF VENICE

Note: See mandatory ship reporting system "In the Adriatic Sea" in part G, section I and mandatory no anchoring area "In the approaches to the Gulf of Venice" in part G, section II.

(Reference chart: Italy 924, 2005 edition.
Note: This chart is based on Rome 1940 datum. The co-ordinates listed below are in World Geodetic System 1984 datum (WGS 84).)

Description of the area to be avoided

The area within the circle of 1.5 nautical miles radius centred on the following geographical position:

(1) 45°05′.30 N, 012°35′.10 E

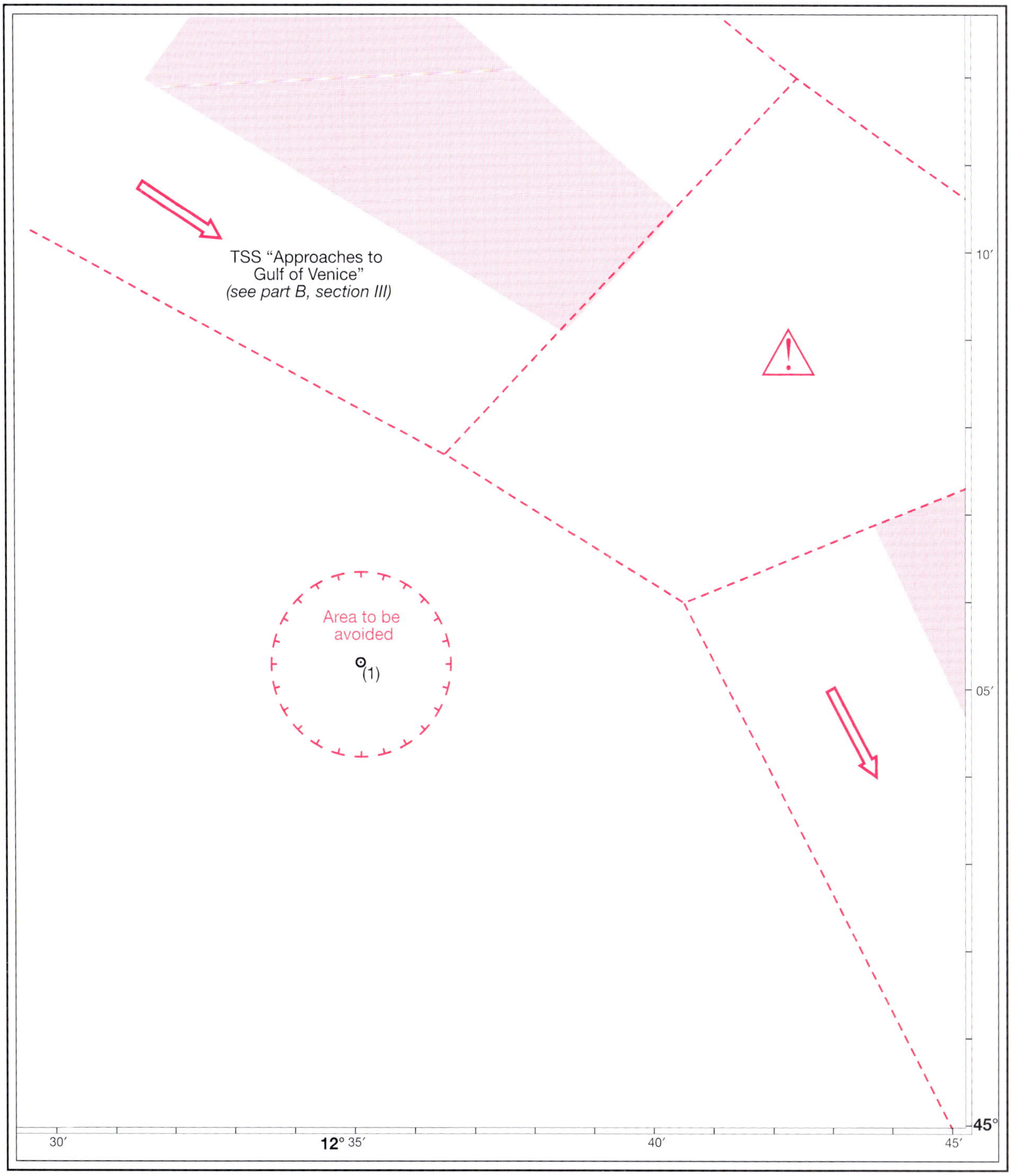

IN THE APPROACHES TO THE GULF OF VENICE

IN THE REGION OF THE VORIOI SPORADHES ISLANDS

(Reference chart: Greek Hydrographic Office 31 (INT 3704), 1987 edition.
Note: This chart is based on European datum.)

Description of the area to be avoided

In order to avoid risk of pollution and damage to the environment in the area surrounding the Vorioi (North) Sporadhes islands, designated to be a Marine Sanctuary, all ships carrying chemical, toxic or nuclear substances and tankers of more than 500 gross tonnage carrying oil should avoid the area bounded by a line connecting the following geographical positions:

(1)	39°34′.00 N,	024°10′.00 E	(5)	39°02′.00 N,	023°51′.00 E
(2)	39°20′.00 N,	024°25′.00 E	(6)	39°25′.00 N,	023°51′.00 E
(3)	39°00′.00 N,	024°10′.00 E	(7)	39°30′.00 N,	024°00′.00 E
(4)	39°00′.00 N,	024°00′.00 E			

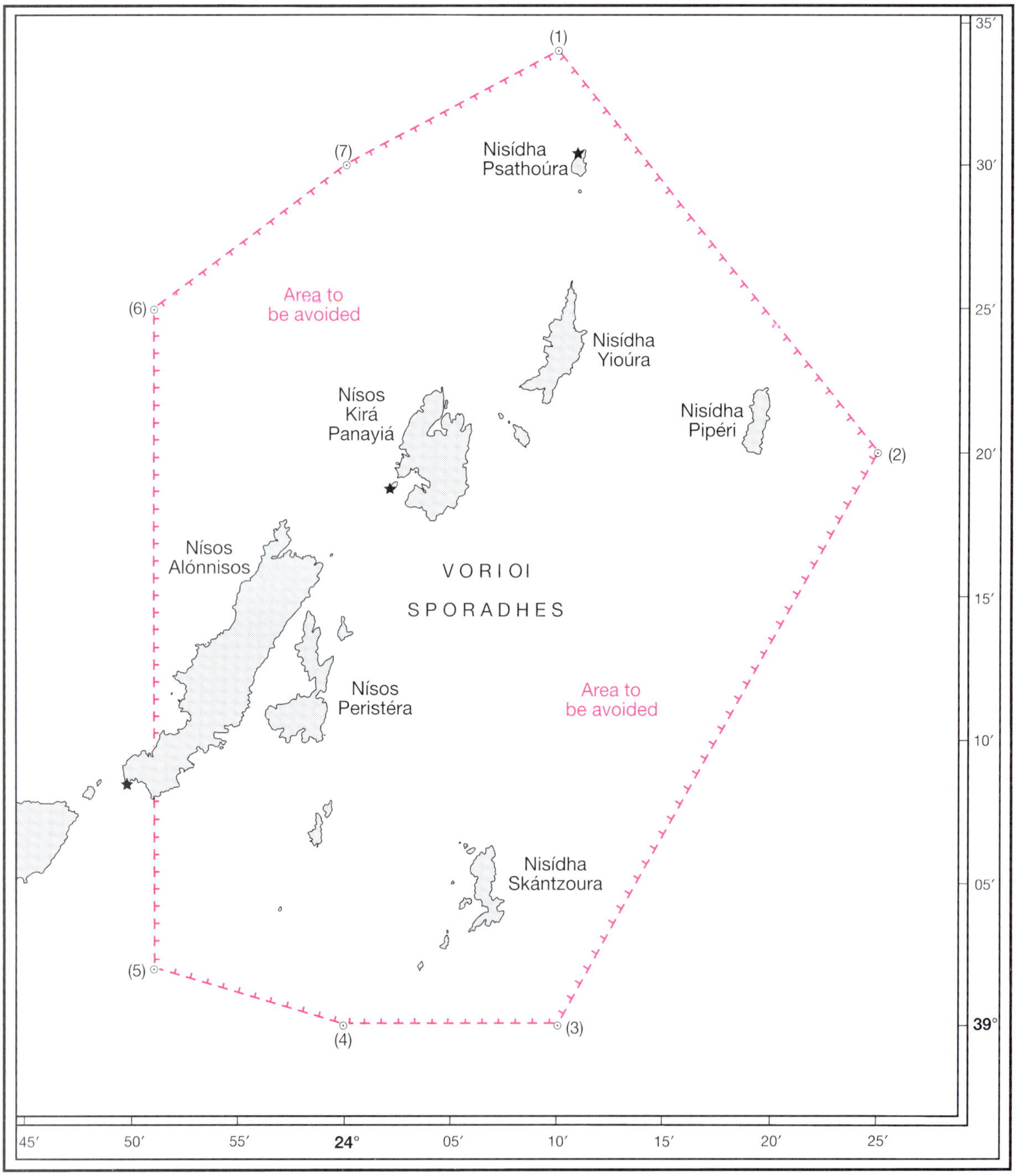

IN THE REGION OF THE VORIOI SPORADHES ISLANDS

NORTH OF THE STRAITS OF TIRAN

(Reference chart: British Admiralty 3595, 1986 edition.
Note: This chart is based on European datum 1950. To conform with a change from European datum 1950 to World Geodetic System 1984 datum (WGS 84), all locations are to be reduced by 0′.07 in latitude and by 0′.02 in longitude.)

Description of the area to be avoided

In order to avoid the risk of severe damage to critical ecosystems, the environment and the economy of the area, all ships carrying dangerous or toxic cargoes, or any other ship exceeding 500 gross tonnage, should avoid the area bounded by a line connecting the following geographical positions:

(1)	28°46′.00 N,	034°37′.50 E	(5)	28°11′.00 N,	034°29′.00 E
(2)	28°46′.00 N,	034°40′.00 E	(6)	28°06′.00 N,	034°28′.00 E
(3)	28°24′.00 N,	034°31′.00 E	(7)	28°01′.50 N,	034°26′.50 E
(4)	28°18′.00 N,	034°26′.00 E			

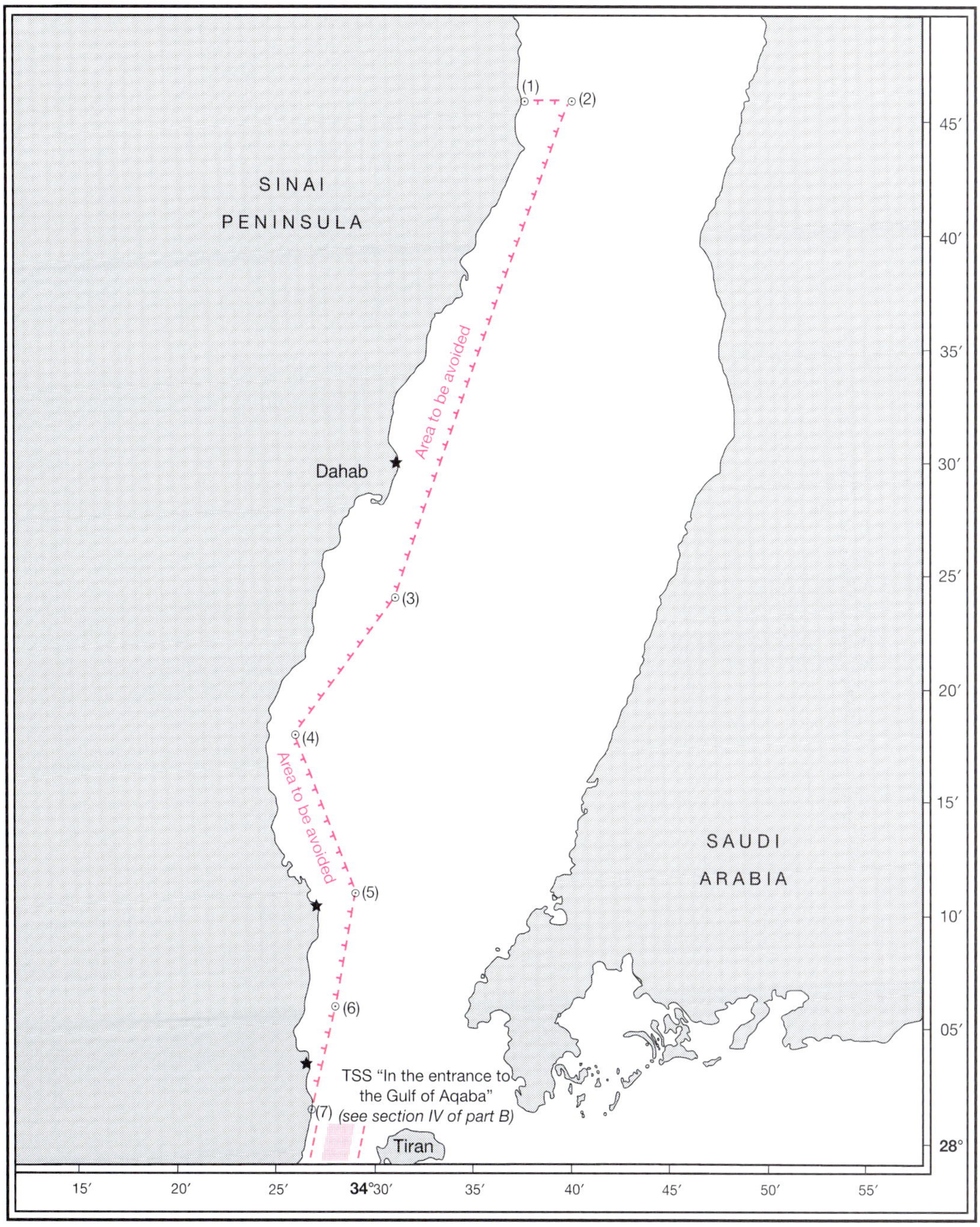

NORTH OF THE STRAITS OF TIRAN

NORTH OF SHARM EL SHEIKH HARBOUR

(Reference chart: British Admiralty 2375, 1988 edition
Note: This chart is based on European datum 1950. To conform with a change from European datum 1950 to World Geodetic System 1984 datum (WGS 84), all locations are to be reduced by 0′.07 in latitude and by 0′.02 in longitude.)

Description of the area to be avoided

In order to avoid the risk of severe damage to critical ecosystems, the environment and the economy of the area, all ships carrying dangerous or toxic cargoes, or any other ship exceeding 500 gross tonnage, should avoid the area bounded by a line connecting the following geographical positions:

(1) 27°58′.00 N, 034°25′.00 E
(2) 27°50′.50 N, 034°20′.60 E
(3) 27°51′.00 N, 034°17′.20 E

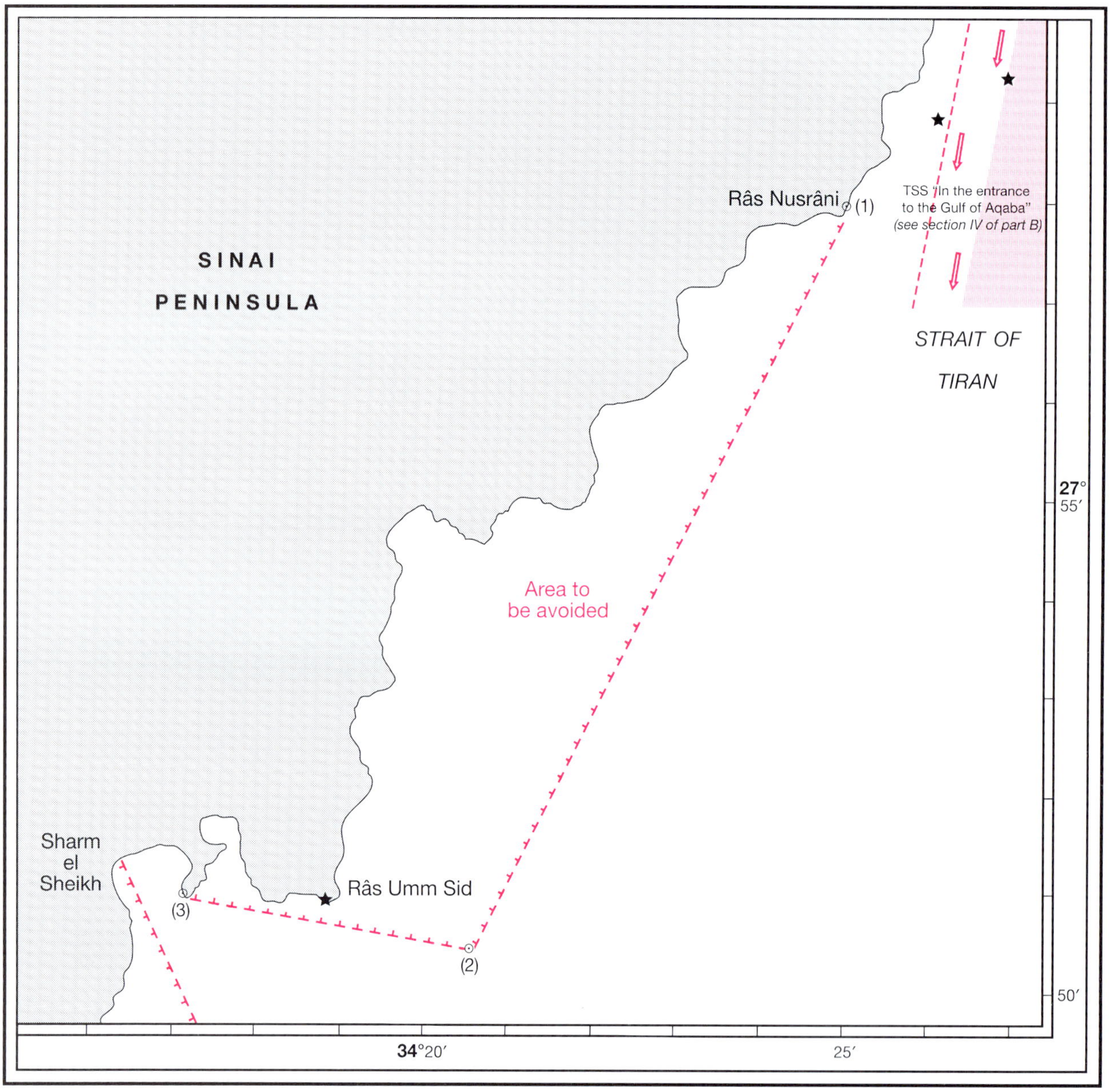

NORTH OF SHARM EL SHEIKH HARBOUR

AT THE SOUTHERN EXTREMITY OF THE SINAI PENINSULA

(Reference chart: British Admiralty 2375, 1988 edition.
Note: This chart is based on European datum 1950. To conform with a change from European datum 1950 to World Geodetic System 1984 datum (WGS 84), all locations are to be reduced by 0′.07 in latitude and by 0′.02 in longitude.)

Description of the area to be avoided

In order to avoid the risk of severe damage to critical ecosystems, the environment and natural resources contained within the declared boundaries of the Ras Muhammad National Park, all ships carrying dangerous or toxic cargoes, or any other ships exceeding 500 gross tonnage, should avoid the area bounded by a line connecting the following geographical positions:

(1)	27°51′.10 N,	034°16′.60 E	(4)	27°41′.00 N,	034°07′.00 E
(2)	27°47′.18 N,	034°19′.00 E	(5)	27°43′.00 N,	034°04′.00 E
(3)	27°42′.20 N,	034°17′.00 E	(6)	27°48′.30 N,	034°06′.00 E

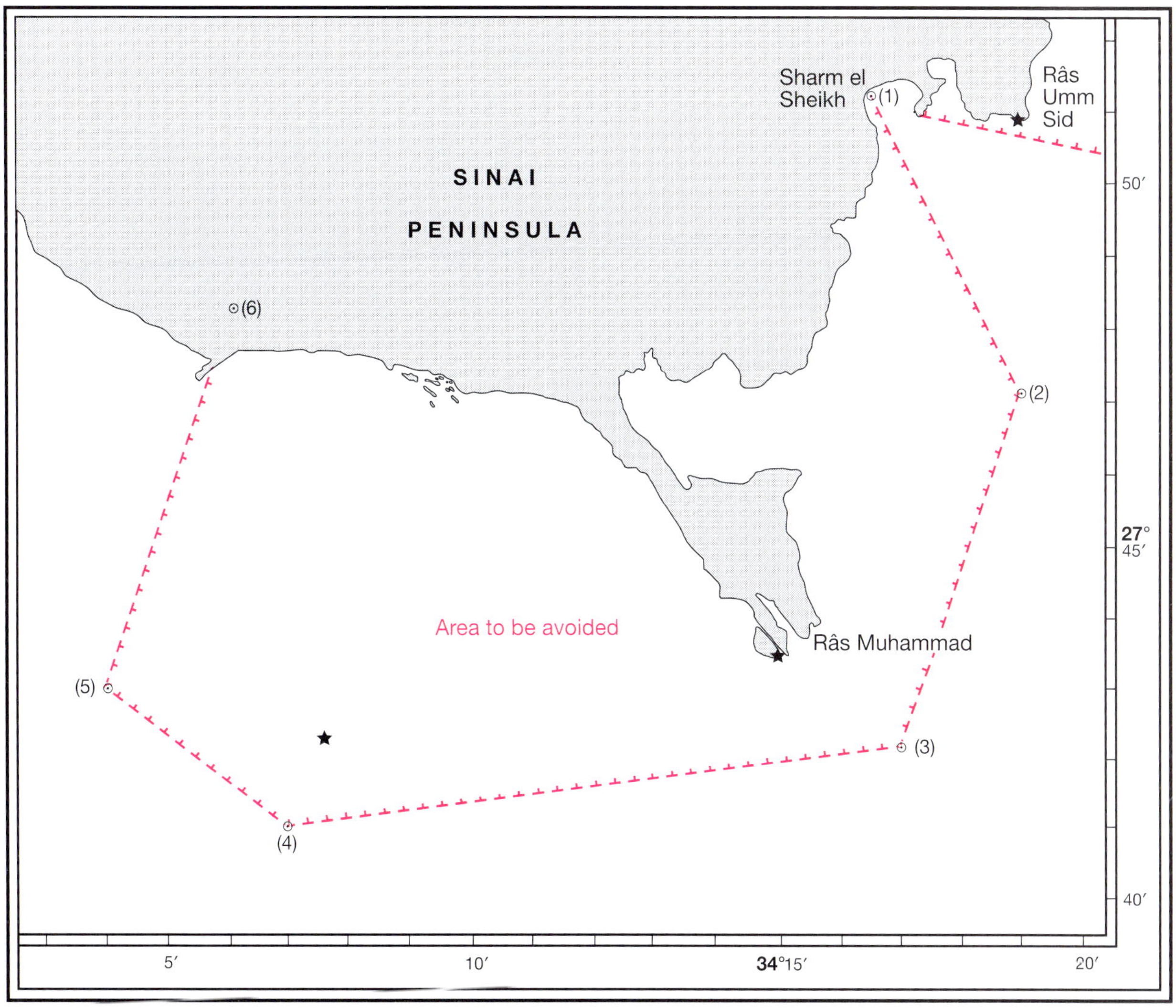

AT THE SOUTHERN EXTREMITY OF THE SINAI PENINSULA

IN THE REGION OF FASHT BULDANI

(Reference charts: British Admiralty 3774, 1986 edition; 3775, 1981 edition; 2882, 1987 edition.
Note: These charts are based on Nahrwan datum.)

Description of the area to be avoided

In order to avoid the risk of pollution due to stranding or of damage to major sub-sea oil and gas pipelines in this area, which is in the close vicinity of important seagrass banks and prawn breeding grounds, all tankers, gas carriers and chemical tankers carrying noxious liquid substances regardless of size, and all other vessels of more than 50,000 gross tonnage, should avoid the area bounded by a line connecting the following geographical positions:

(1)	28°13′.31 N,	048°55′.01 E	(5)	27°50′.90 N,	049°03′.50 E
(2)	28°18′.00 N,	049°08′.50 E	(6)	28°06′.39 N,	048°51′.78 E
(3)	28°08′.12 N,	049°18′.90 E	(7)	28°11′.10 N,	048°53′.21 E
(4)	27°53′.98 N,	049°20′.00 E			

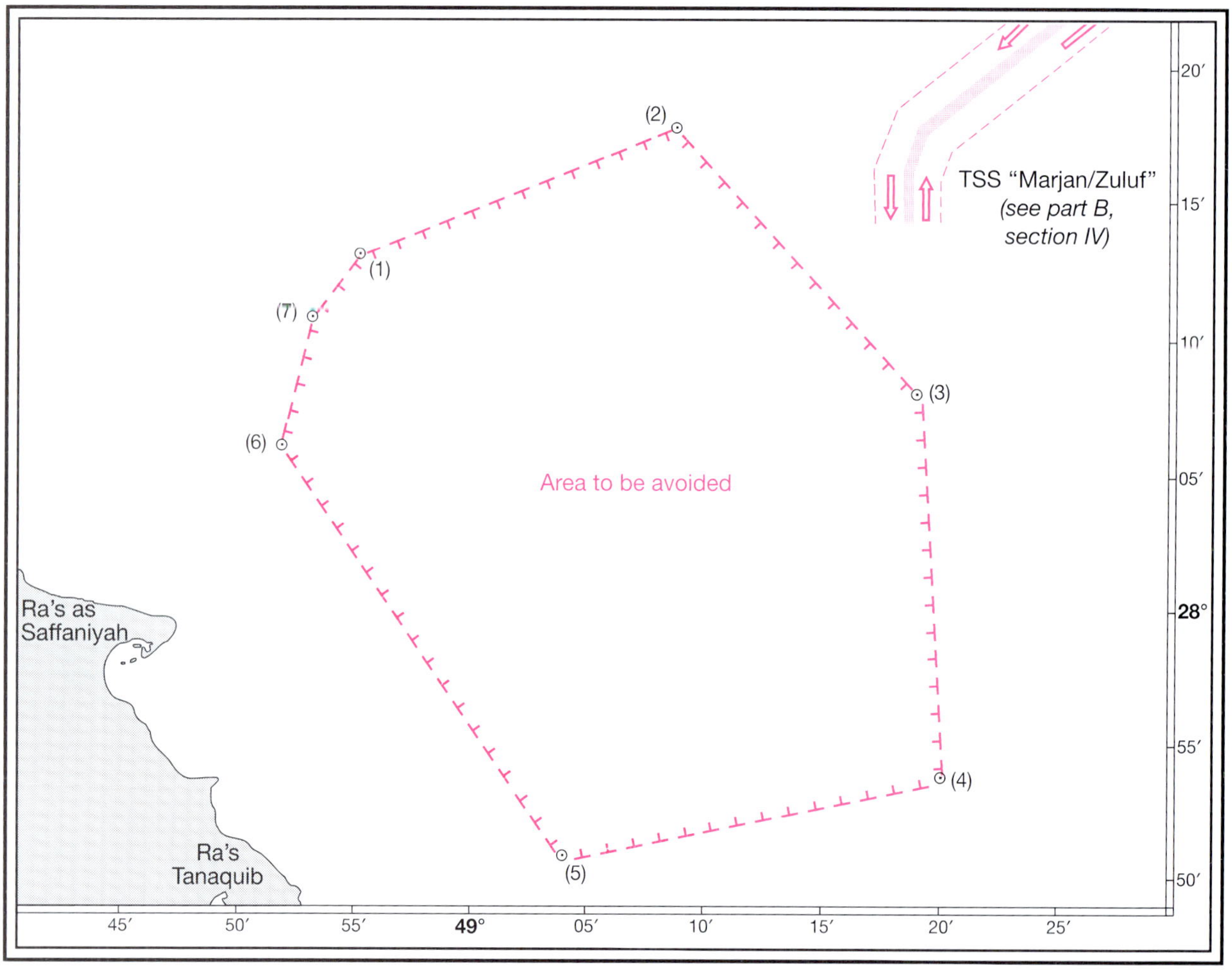

IN THE REGION OF FASHT BULDANI

IN THE REGION OF MAHÉ ISLAND IN THE SEYCHELLES

(Reference charts: British Admiralty 721, 1990 edition; 740, 1990 edition.
Note: These charts are based on South East Island datum.)

Description of the areas to be avoided

In order to avoid risk of pollution and damage to the environment, all ships of more than 200 gross tonnage, whether or not bound for ports in the Seychelles, should avoid the areas bounded by lines connecting the following geographical positions:

(a) **West of Mahé**

(1)	04°40′.80 S,	055°32′.20 E
(2)	04°49′.50 S,	055°34′.50 E
(3)	05°06′.80 S,	055°08′.50 E
(4)	04°42′.00 S,	053°52′.00 E
(5)	04°00′.00 S,	054°22′.00 E
(6)	03°40′.00 S,	054°58′.00 E
(7)	03°40′.00 S,	055°25′.00 E
(8)	04°33′.50 S,	055°25′.90 E

thence along the low water line on the west and south-east coasts of Mahé to the point of commencement; and

(b) **East of Mahé**

(1)	05°10′.00 S,	057°13′.00 E
(2)	05°50′.00 S,	057°00′.00 E
(3)	05°50′.00 S,	056°24′.00 E
(4)	05°12′.00 S,	055°36′.00 E
(5)	04°49′.00 S,	055°41′.50 E
(6)	04°31′.00 S,	055°40′.00 E
(7)	04°26′.00 S,	055°32′.00 E
(8)	03°42′.00 S,	055°38′.00 E
(9)	03°45′.00 S,	056°02′.00 E

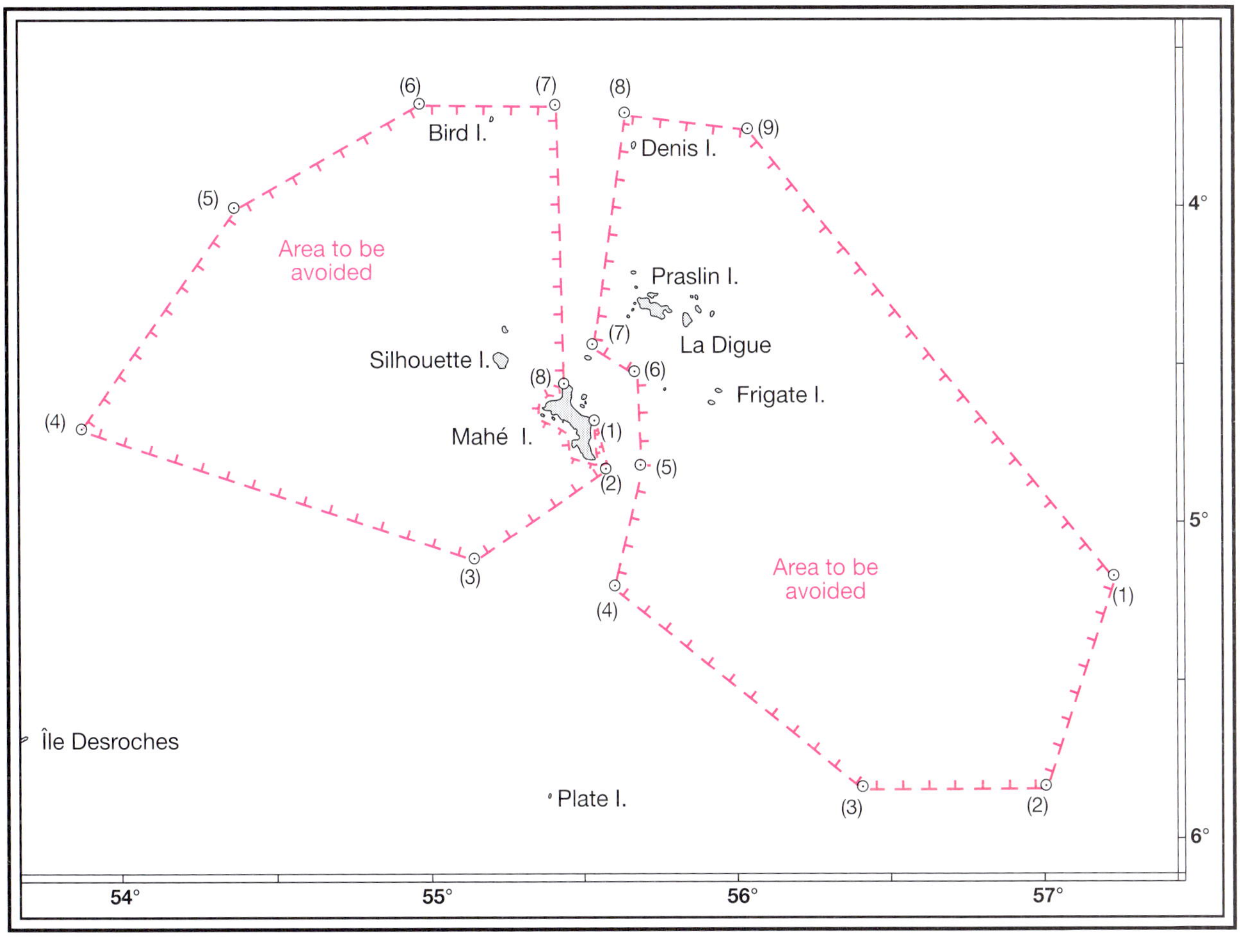

IN THE REGION OF MAHÉ ISLAND IN THE SEYCHELLES

IN THE REGION OF THE ALDABRA ISLANDS IN THE SEYCHELLES

(Reference chart: British Admiralty 758, 1965 edition.)

Description of the area to be avoided

In order to avoid risk of pollution and damage to the environment in this area of unique wildlife, all ships of more than 500 gross tons carrying cargoes of oil or hazardous materials should avoid the area contained within a circle of radius 30 nautical miles centred upon geographical position 09°36′ S, 046°21′ E.

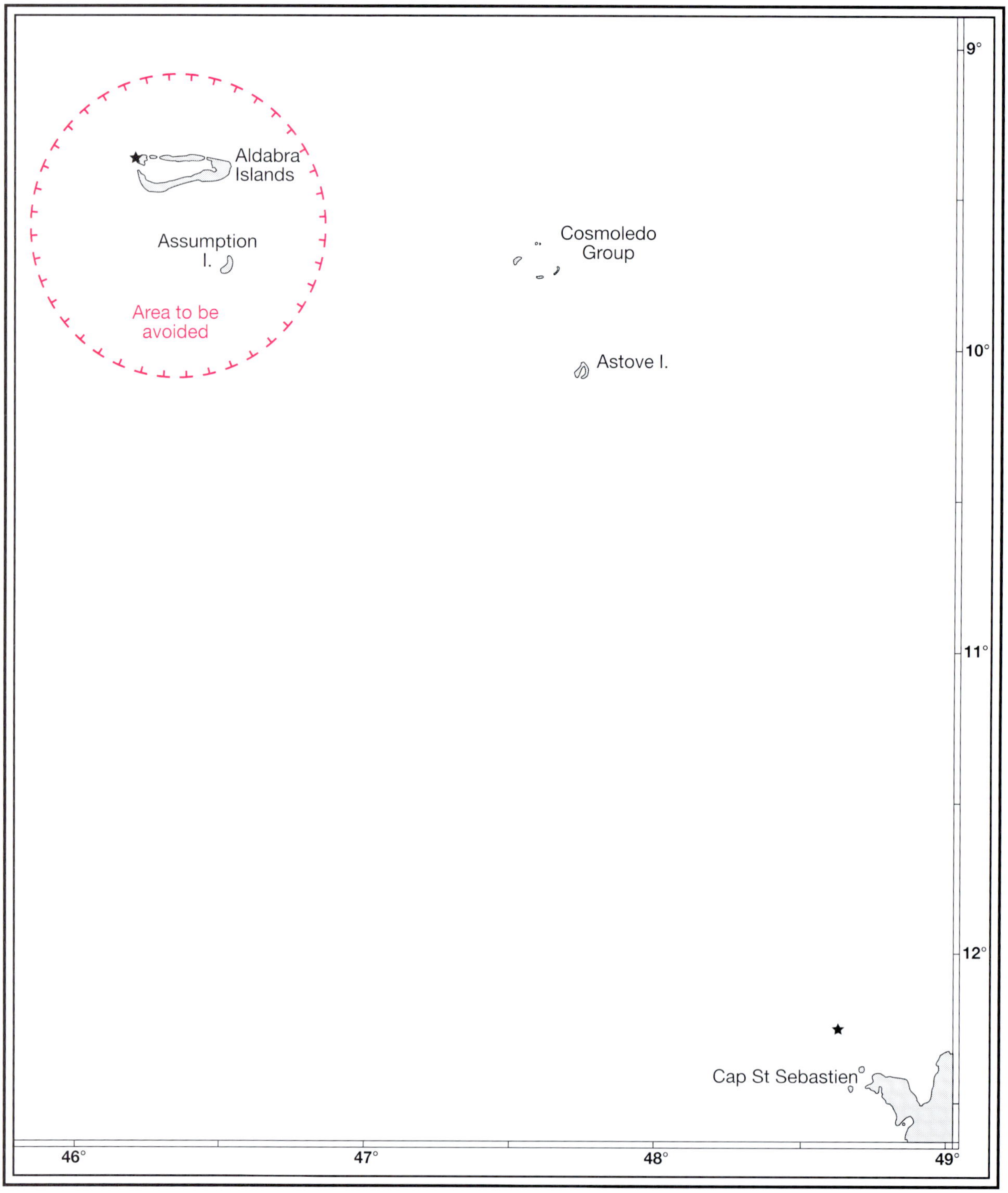

IN THE REGION OF THE ALDABRA ISLANDS IN THE SEYCHELLES

RECOMMENDATORY AREA TO BE AVOIDED OFF THE NINGALOO COAST, WESTERN AUSTRALIA*

(Reference charts: **Electronic Navigational Charts (ENC)** AU322113 (2008 edition), AU422114 (2008 edition), AU323113 (2008 edition), AU230110 (2010 edition); **Paper charts** AUS 72 (2011 edition), AUS 745 (1985 edition), AUS 744 (1984 edition), AUS 329 (1967 edition), AUS 328 (1985 edition), AUS 4725 (2010 edition), AX4723F (2011 edition) and AUS 4723 (2010 edition).
Note: These charts are based on World Geodetic System 1984 horizontal datum (WGS 84).)

Description of the area to be avoided

The area lies off the western Australian coast between latitudes 21° 47′.00 S and 22° 50′ S, extending between 3 and 12 nautical miles to seaward of the High Water Line.

In order to reduce the risk of a marine casualty and resulting pollution and damage to the sensitive marine environment off the Ningaloo Coast, all ships over 150 gross tonnage and ships engaged in towing operations, regardless of size, should avoid the area bounded by a line joining the geographical positions listed below:

(1) 21°47′.00 S, 114°09′.75 E
(2) 21°47′.00 S, 114°12′.50 E
(3) 21°44′.00 S, 114°12′.50 E
(4) 21°42′.00 S, 114°10′.50 E
(5) 21°42′.00 S, 114°00′.00 E
(6) 21°47′.00 S, 113°50′.00 E
(7) 22°40′.00 S, 113°29′.00 E
(8) 22°50′.00 S, 113°33′.80 E
(9) The coastline at 22°50′.00 S
(10) Then along the coastline to (1) above

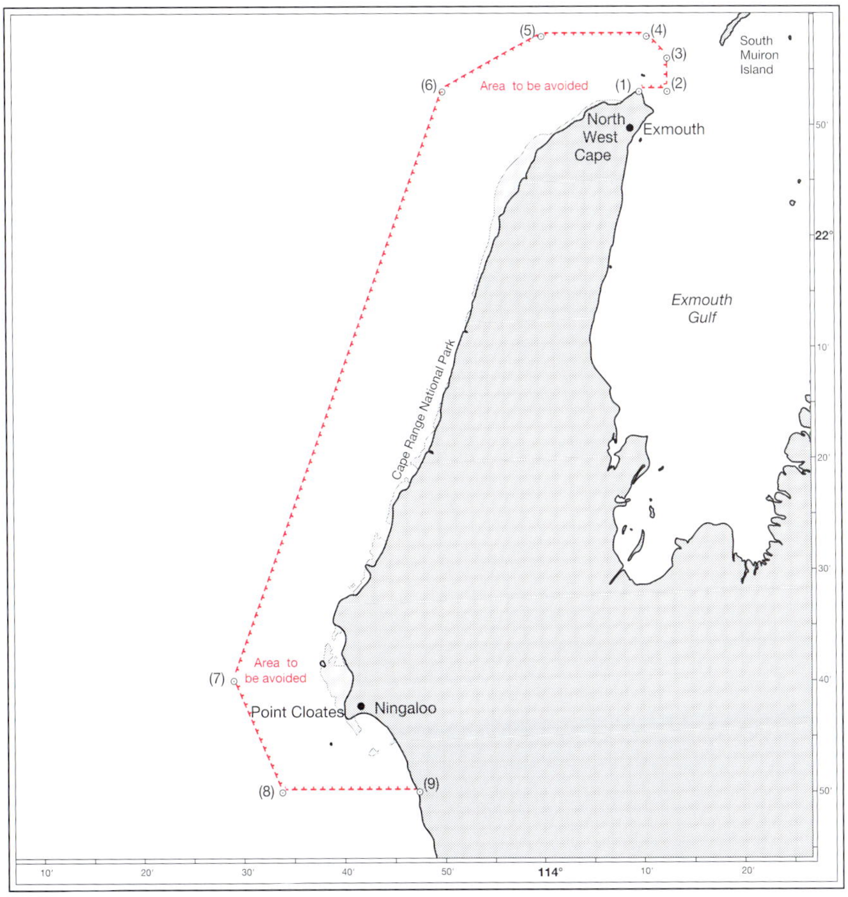

RECOMMENDATORY AREA TO BE AVOIDED OFF THE NINGALOO COAST, WESTERN AUSTRALIA

* Date of implementation of new recommendatory area to be avoided: 0000 hours UTC on 1 June 2013.

IN THE REGION OF THE GREAT BARRIER REEF

Note: See mandatory ship reporting system "In the Torres Strait region and the Inner Route of the Great Barrier Reef" in part G, section I.

(Reference chart: AUS 819, April 1978 edition.
Note: This chart is based on the Australian geodetic datum 1966.)

Description of the area to be avoided

In order to avoid the risk of pollution and damage to the environment in the Capricornia Section of the Great Barrier Reef Marine Park, all ships in excess of 500 gross tonnage should avoid the area bounded by a line connecting the following geographical positions:

(1)	23°10′.00 S,	151°56′.00 E	(8)	23°33′.00 S,	151°35′.00 E
(2)	23°53′.00 S,	152°28′.00 E	(9)	23°30′.00 S,	151°35′.00 E
(3)	23°55′.00 S,	152°28′.00 E	(10)	23°25′.00 S,	151°53′.00 E
(4)	23°57′.00 S,	152°26′.00 E	(11)	23°20′.00 S,	151°50′.00 E
(5)	23°57′.00 S,	152°24′.00 E	(12)	23°20′.00 S,	151°40′.00 E
(6)	23°32′.00 S,	151°55′.00 E	(13)	23°15′.00 S,	151°40′.00 E
(7)	23°36′.00 S,	151°39′.00 E	(14)	23°10′.00 S,	151°52′.00 E

thence to the point of commencement.

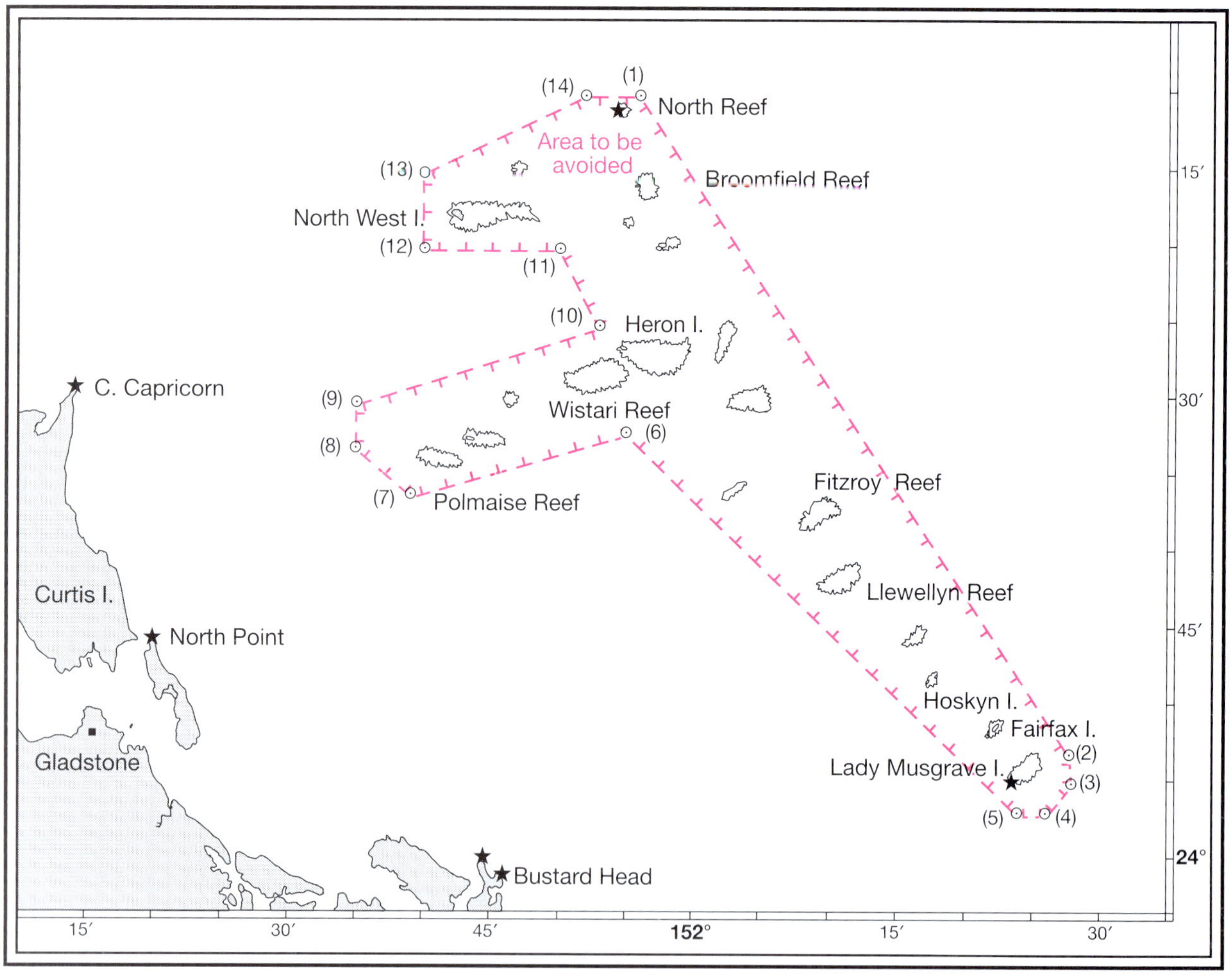

IN THE REGION OF THE GREAT BARRIER REEF

IN THE REGION OF THREE KINGS ISLANDS

(Reference charts: New Zealand 41, 1991 edition; 4111, 1992 edition.
Note: These charts are based on World Geodetic System 1972 datum.)

Description of the area to be avoided

In order to avoid risk of pollution and damage to the environment in the area around the Three Kings Islands, declared to be a Wildlife Sanctuary, ships of 500 gross tons or more should avoid the area bounded by a line connecting the following geographical positions:

(1)	34°06′.00 S,	172°00′.00 E	(3)	34°13′.50 S,	172°12′.50 E
(2)	34°06′.00 S,	172°12′.50 E	(4)	34°13′.50 S,	172°00′.00 E

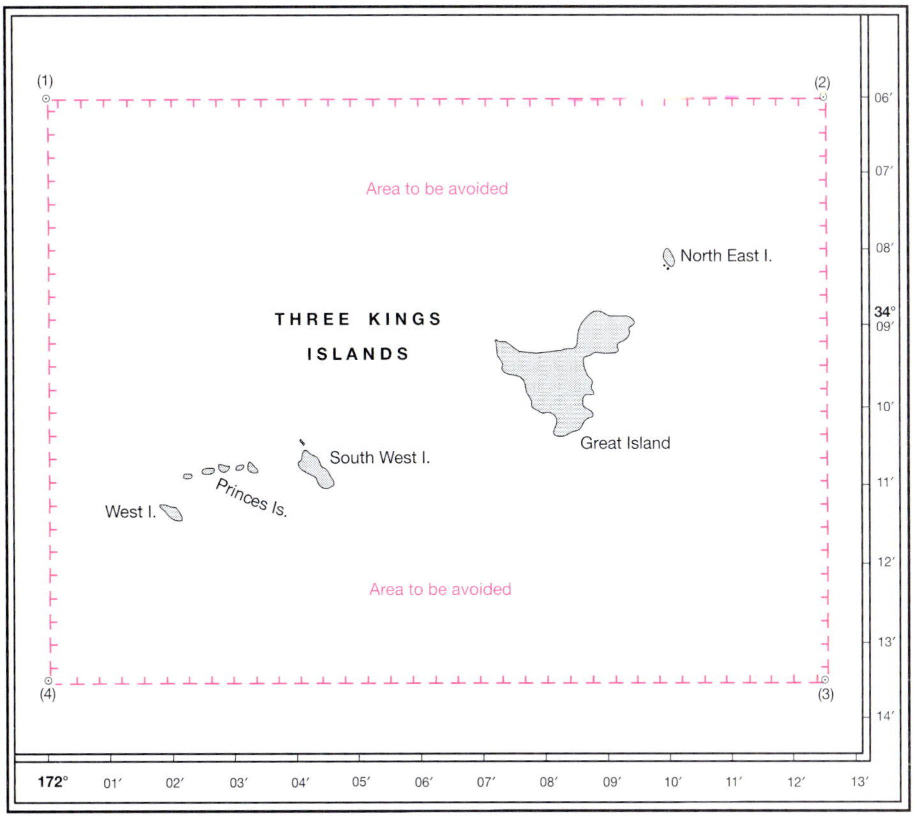

IN THE REGION OF THREE KINGS ISLANDS

OFF THE NORTH-EAST COAST OF THE NORTH ISLAND OF NEW ZEALAND

(Reference chart: New Zealand 521, January 1995 edition.
Note: This chart is based on World Geodetic System 1984 datum (WGS 84).)

Description of the mandatory area to be avoided

In order to avoid risk of pollution and damage to the environment of this sensitive area, all vessels greater than 45 metres in length (except as specified below) shall avoid the following area.

In the vicinity of the Poor Knights Islands

The area bounded by a line connecting the following geographical positions is designated as a mandatory area to be avoided, the westward boundary of which is delineated by Mean High Water Springs:

(1)	35°51′.30 S,	174°35′.50 E	(4)	35°24′.70 S,	174°50′.20 E
(2)	35°34′.55 S,	174°49′.20 E	(5)	35°10′.20 S,	174°20′.10 E
(3)	35°29′.60 S,	174°50′.80 E			

Exceptions: The following exemptions are granted in respect of vessels entering the mandatory area to be avoided:

- All vessels of the Royal New Zealand Navy. The exemption granted in respect of vessels of the Royal New Zealand Navy applies to "any warship, naval auxiliary, other vessels or aircraft owned or operated by a State and used, for the time being, only on government non-commercial service".
- All fishing vessels engaged in fishing operations.
- Barges under tow, provided the cargo is not oil or other harmful liquid substances as defined in Annexes I & II of MARPOL 73/78.

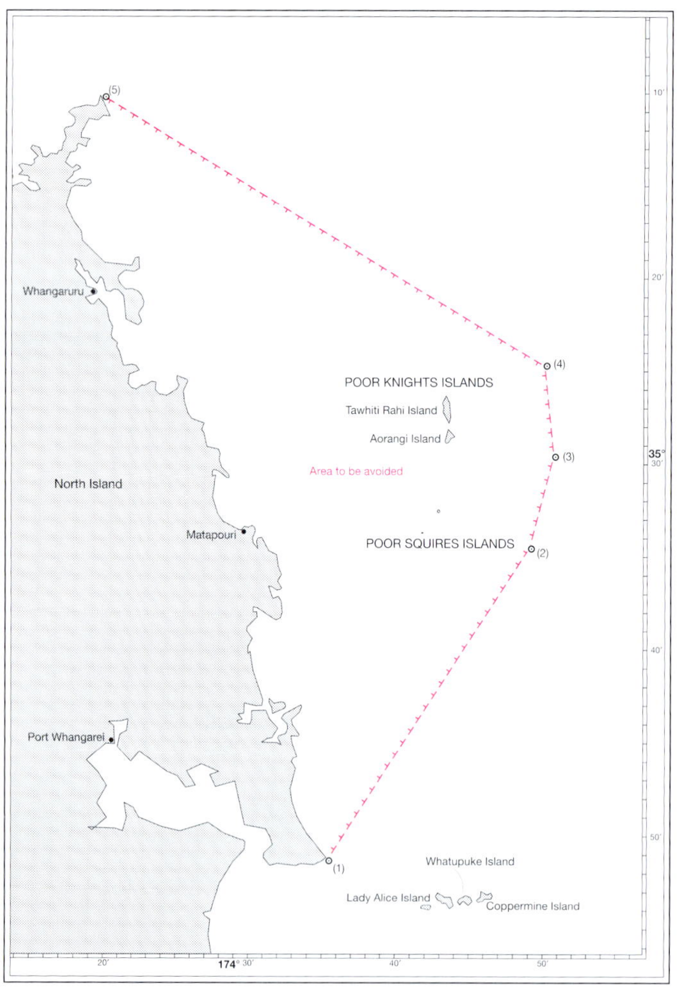

OFF THE NORTH-EAST COAST OF THE NORTH ISLAND OF NEW ZEALAND

IN THE BASS STRAIT

(Reference chart: Australian 422, April 1971 edition.
Note: This chart is based on the Australian geodetic datum 1966.)

Description of the area to be avoided

The area described below should be avoided by ships of more than 200 tons gross tonnage.
The area is bounded by lines joining the following points:

(1)	The low water line in latitude 38°15′.00 S,.	
(2)	38°35′.00 S,	147°44′.00 E
(3)	38°41′.00 S,	148°06′.00 E
(4)	38°41′.00 S,	148°13′.00 E
(5)	38°32′.00 S,	148°26′.00 E
(6)	38°19′.00 S,	148°35′.00 E
(7)	38°08′.00 S,	148°31′.00 E
(8)	38°05′.00 S,	148°24′.00 E
(9)	The low water line in latitude 37°58′.00 S	

Thence along the low water line to the point of commencement.

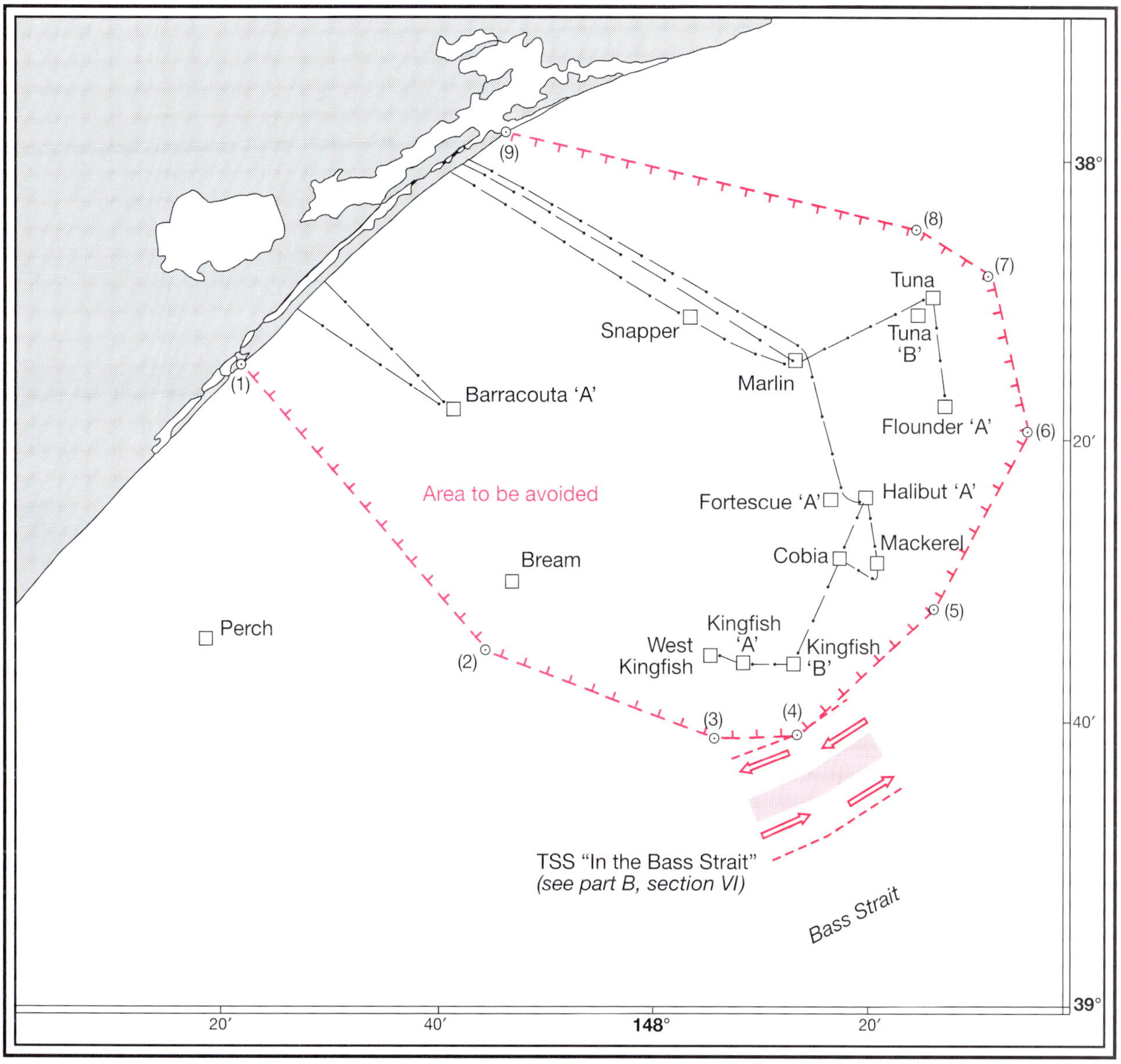

IN THE BASS STRAIT

MALPELO ISLAND

(Reference charts: INT 6105 and INT 6000).

Description of the area to be avoided

With a view to avoiding the risk of serious damage to important systems, to the environment, and to the economy of the area, all fishing vessels and all other ships in excess of 500 gross tonnage should avoid the area bounded by lines connecting the following geographical positions:

(1)	04°04′.80 N,	081°43′.30 W	(3)	03°52′.15 N,	081°28′.12 W
(2)	04°04′.80 N,	081°28′.12 W	(4)	03°52′.15 N,	081°43′.30 W

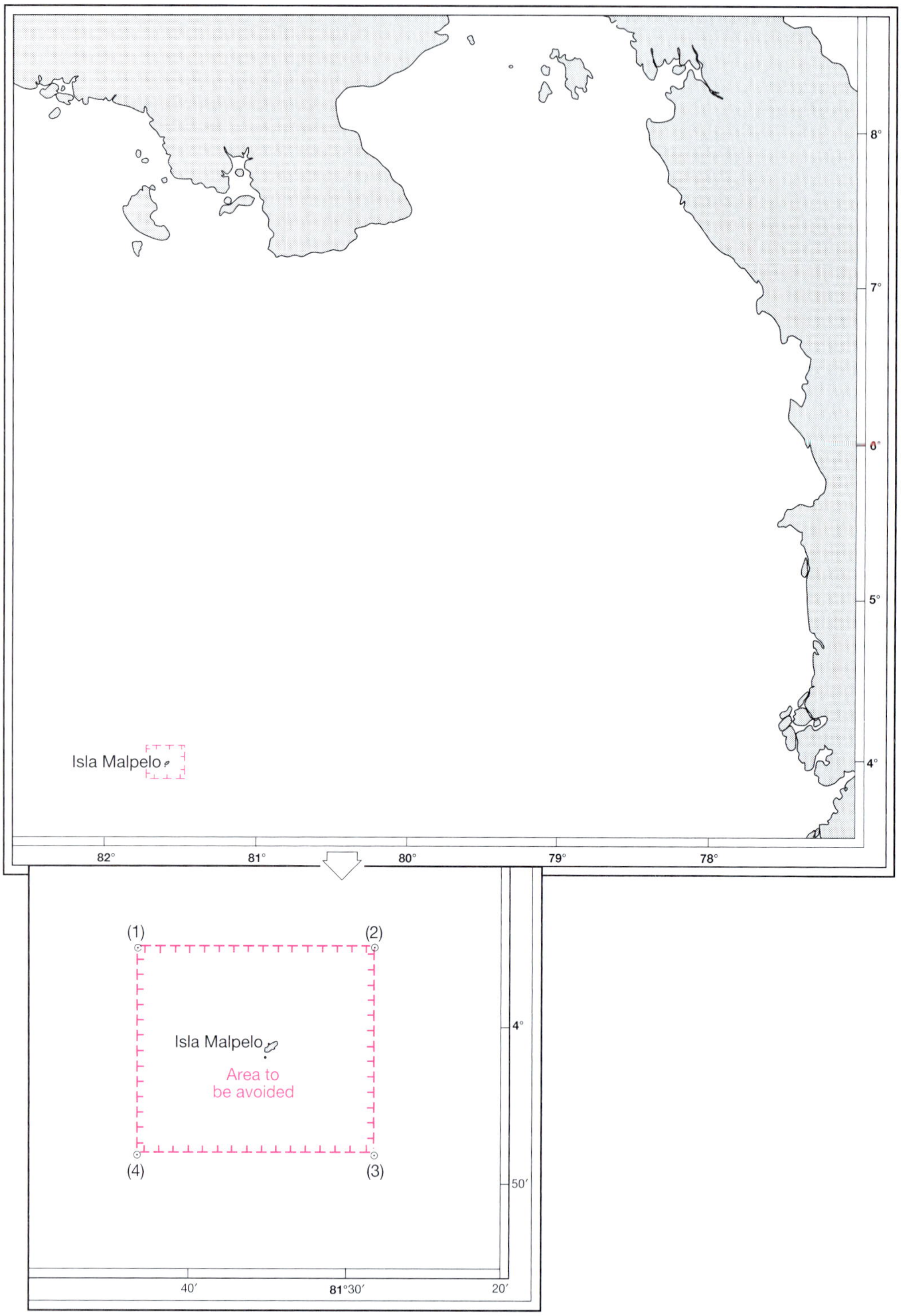

MALPELO ISLAND

IN THE GALAPAGOS ARCHIPELAGO

Note: See "Recommended tracks which are mandatory as a condition of port entry, through the Galapagos area to be avoided to enter the PSSA" in part E and mandatory ship reporting system "In the Galapagos Particularly Sensitive Sea Area" in part G, section I

(Reference chart: I.O.A. 20 (2nd edition, 1992).
Note: This chart is based on World Geodetic System 1984 datum (WGS 84).)

Description of the area to be avoided

All ships and barges carrying cargoes of oil or potentially hazardous material and all ships of 500 gross tonnage and above in transit should avoid the area bounded by a line connecting the following geographical positions:

(1)	02°29′.82 N,	092°21′.42 W	(7)	02°35′.07 S,	088°48′.30 W
(2)	01°25′.93 N,	089°03′.54 W	(8)	02°46′.20 S,	089°29′.69 W
(3)	00°00′.70 S,	088°05′.75 W	(9)	02°41′.99 S,	090°42′.21 W
(4)	00°11′.90 S,	088°00′.95 W	(10)	02°05′.20 S,	092°17′.68 W
(5)	00°34′.90 S,	087°54′.57 W	(11)	01°32′.02 S,	092°43′.92 W
(6)	01°02′.21 S,	087°52′.95 W	(12)	01°48′.67 N,	092°40′.51 W

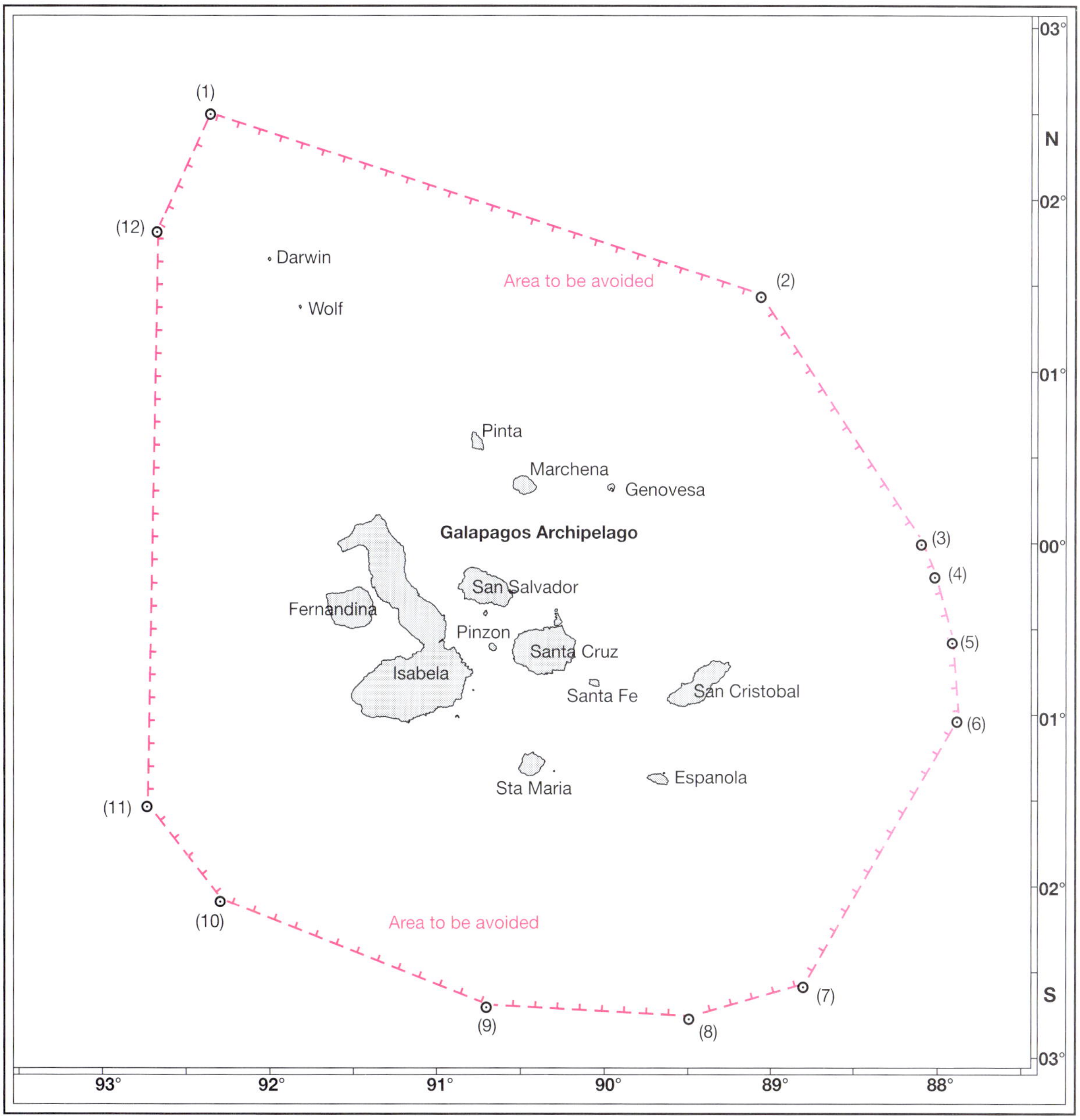

IN THE GALAPAGOS ARCHIPELAGO

IN THE PARACAS NATIONAL RESERVE

(Reference charts: PERU-HIDRONAV 226, 2nd edition, September 2000; 227, 1st edition, April 2002.
Note: These charts are based on World Geodetic System 1984 datum (WGS 84).)

Description of the area to be avoided

In order to avoid the risk of pollution and damage to the environment in the Peruvian Paracas National Reserve, ships of more than 200 gross tonnage carrying hydrocarbons and hazardous liquids in bulk should avoid the area bounded by a line connecting the following geographical positions and the coastal borderline:

(1)	13°47′.33 S,	076°17′.67 W	(4)	14°26′.70 S,	076°30′.00 W
(2)	13°46′.87 S,	076°17′.67 W	(5)	14°26′.70 S,	076°00′.00 W
(3)	13°46′.87 S,	076°30′.00 W			

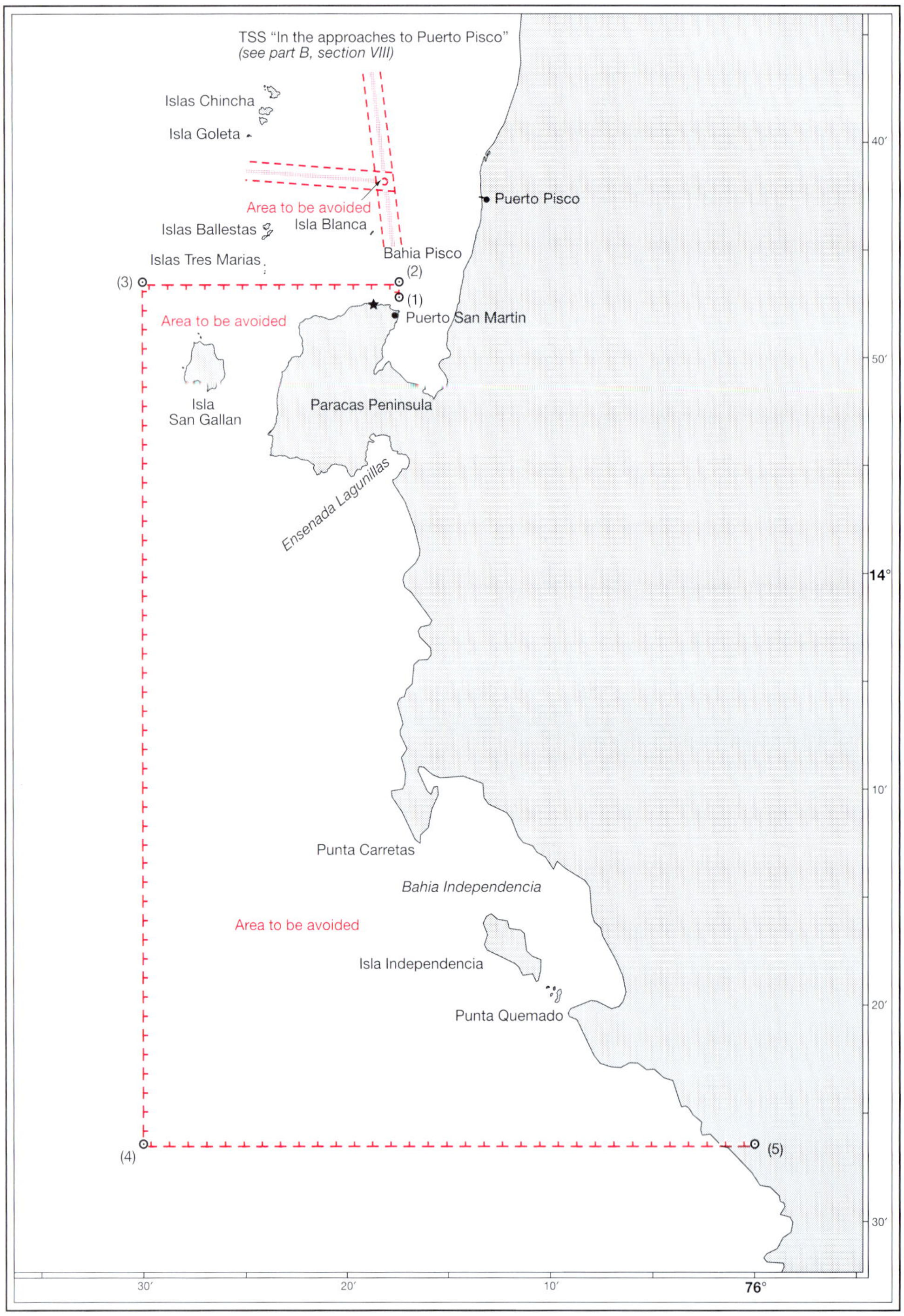

IN THE PARACAS NATIONAL RESERVE

IN THE REGION OF CAPE TERPENIYA (SAKHALIN)

(Reference chart: British Admiralty 2405)

Description of the area to be avoided

The area described below should be avoided by ships of more than 1000 gross tonnage carrying oil or hazardous cargoes, for reasons of conservation of unique wildlife in the area and of inadequate survey.

The area is bounded by a line passing through Cape Davydov and the points defined as follows:

(1) 21.8 miles at 100° from Terpeniya lighthouse
(2) 40.5 miles at 126° from Terpeniya lighthouse
(3) 41.6 miles at 146°.7 from Terpeniya lighthouse
(4) 20.2 miles at 208°.5 from Terpeniya lighthouse
(5) 12.0 miles at 307°.5 from Terpeniya lighthouse
and thence eastward to the coast.

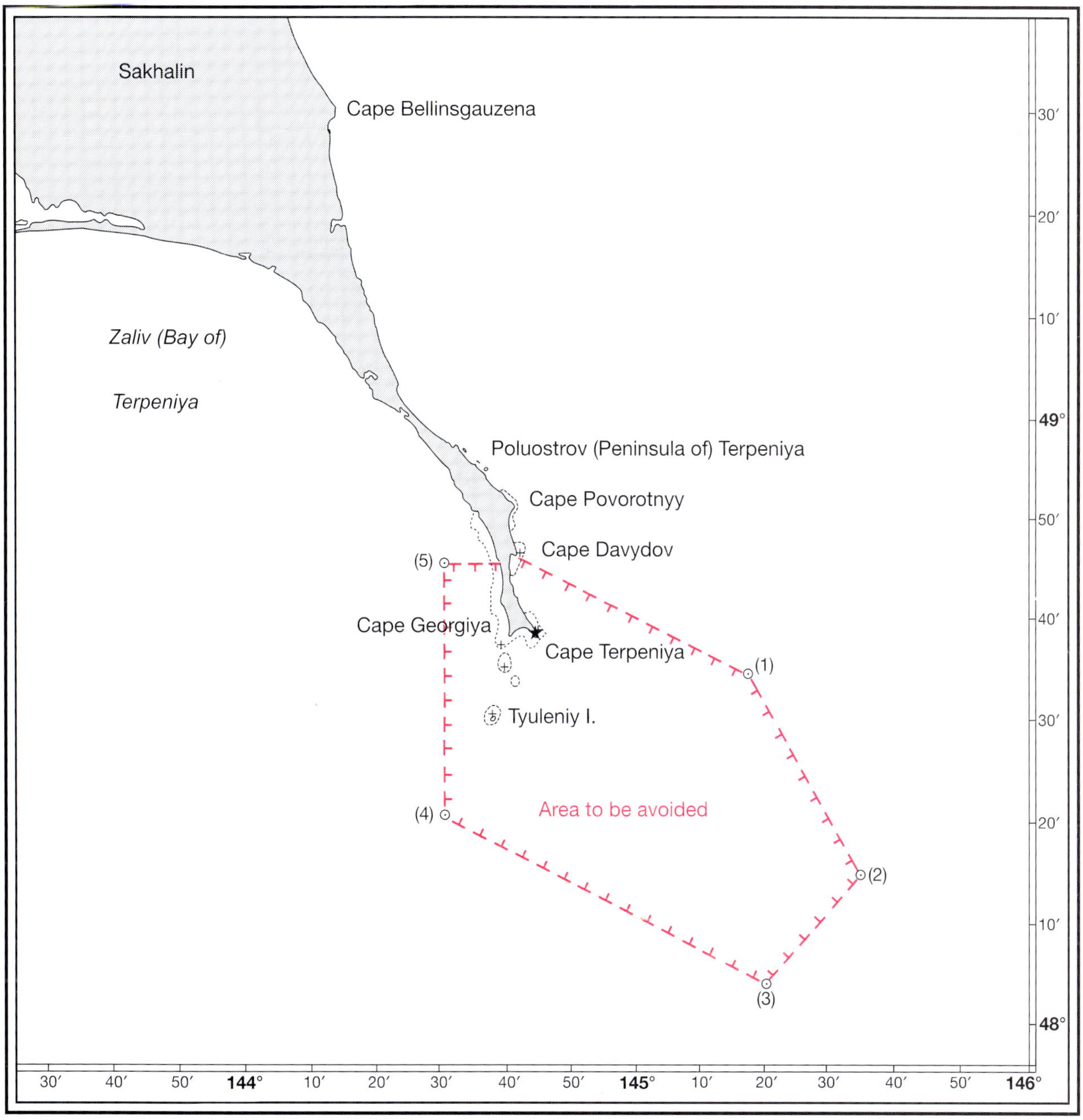

IN THE REGION OF CAPE TERPENIYA (SAKHALIN)

OFF LANZAROTE ISLAND

Note: See mandatory ship reporting system "The Canary Islands" in part G, section I.

(Reference chart: Spanish Navy Hydrographical Institute 209, second edition 1968, 12th impression 2003.
Note: This chart is based on World Geodetic System 1984 datum (WGS 84).)

Description of the area to be avoided

In order to prevent the risks of pollution and environmental damage in highly sensitive sea areas, all tankers and ships over 500 gross tonnage carrying oil or dangerous bulk cargo as cargo should avoid the following area:

An area contained between the meridians of longitude 013°15′.00 W and 013°39′.00 W and the parallels of latitude 29°07′.00 N and 29°30′.00 N.

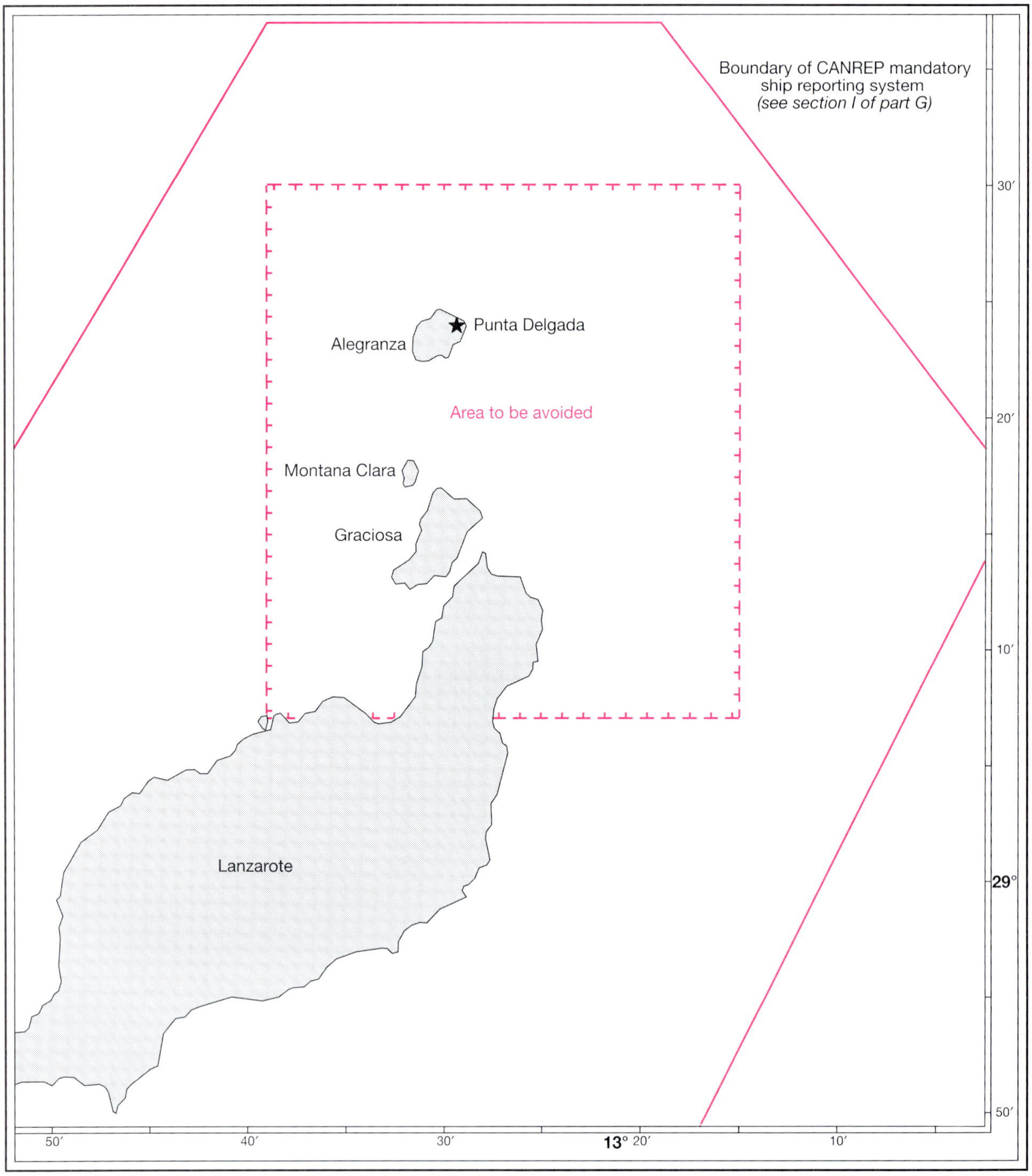

OFF LANZAROTE ISLAND

OFF THE ISLAND OF GRAND CANARY

Note: See mandatory ship reporting system "The Canary Islands" in part G, section I.

(Reference chart: Spanish Navy Hydrographical Institute 209, second edition 1968, 12th impression 2003.
Note: This chart is based on World Geodetic System 1984 datum (WGS 84).)

Description of the area to be avoided

In order to prevent the risks of pollution and environmental damage in highly sensitive sea areas, all tankers and ships over 500 gross tonnage carrying oil or dangerous bulk cargo as cargo should avoid the following area:

> An area contained between the meridian of longitude 016°00′.00 W and the coast and the parallels of latitude 27°44′.00 N and 28°00′.00 N.

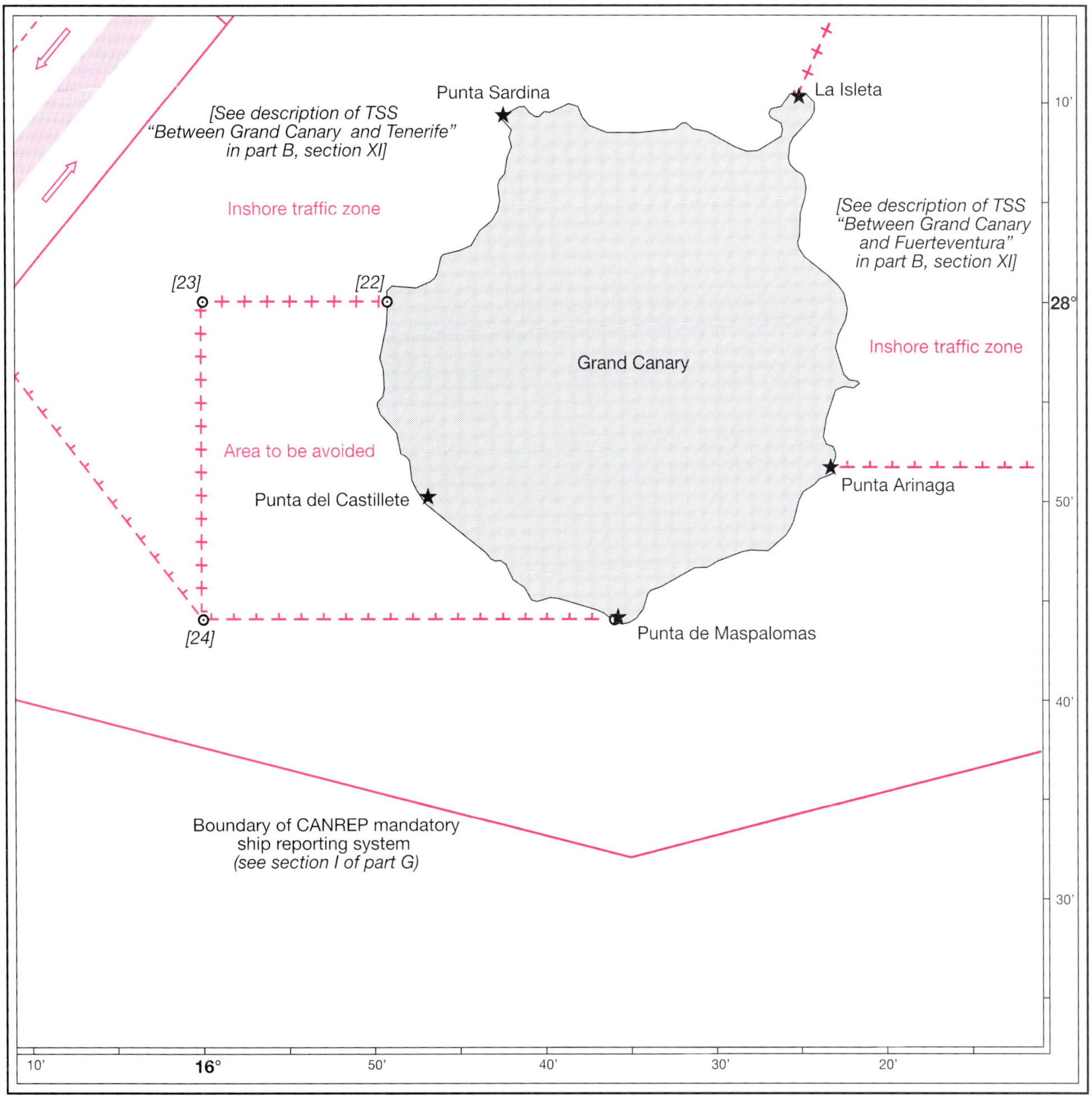

OFF THE ISLAND OF GRAND CANARY

OFF THE ISLAND OF TENERIFE

Note: See mandatory ship reporting system "The Canary Islands" in part G, section I.

(Reference chart: Spanish Navy Hydrographical Institute 209, second edition 1968, 12th impression 2003.
Note: This chart is based on World Geodetic System 1984 datum (WGS 84).)

Description of the area to be avoided

In order to prevent the risks of pollution and environmental damage in highly sensitive sea areas, all tankers and ships over 500 gross tonnage carrying oil or dangerous bulk cargo as cargo should avoid the following area:

> An area between the meridian of longitude 017°22′.00 W, and the south coast of the island and the parallels of latitude 28°00′.00 N and 28°21′.00 N.

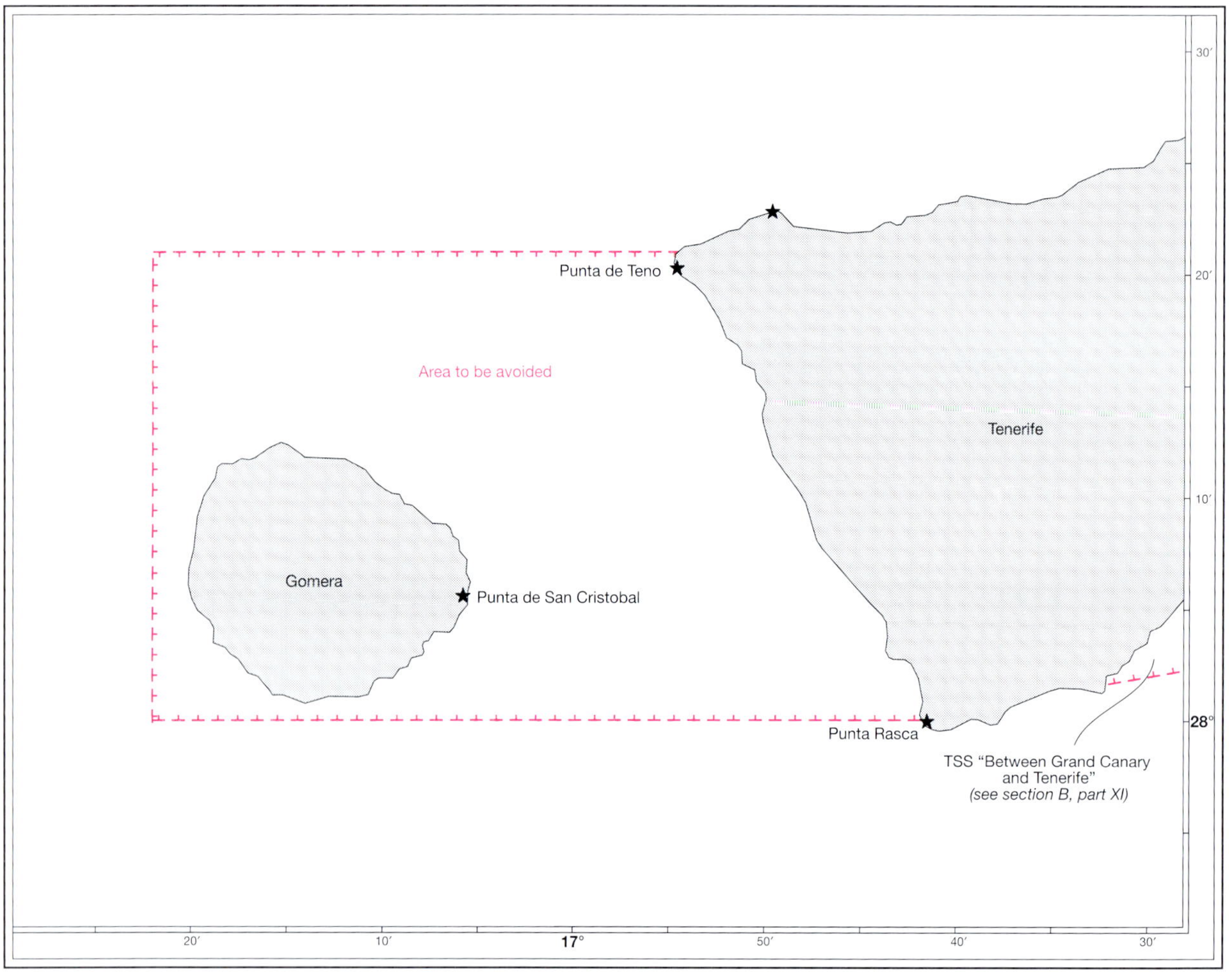

OFF THE ISLAND OF TENERIFE

OFF LA PALMA ISLAND

Note: See mandatory ship reporting system "The Canary Islands" in part G, section I.

(Reference chart: Spanish Navy Hydrographical Institute 209, second edition 1968, 12th impression 2003.
Note: This chart is based on World Geodetic System 1984 datum (WGS 84).)

Description of the area to be avoided

In order to prevent the risks of pollution and environmental damage in highly sensitive sea areas, all tankers and ships over 500 gross tonnage carrying oil or dangerous bulk cargo as cargo should avoid the following area:

An area contained between the meridians of longitude 017°35′.00 W and 018°00′.00 W and the parallels of latitude 28°17′.00 N and 29°00′.00 N.

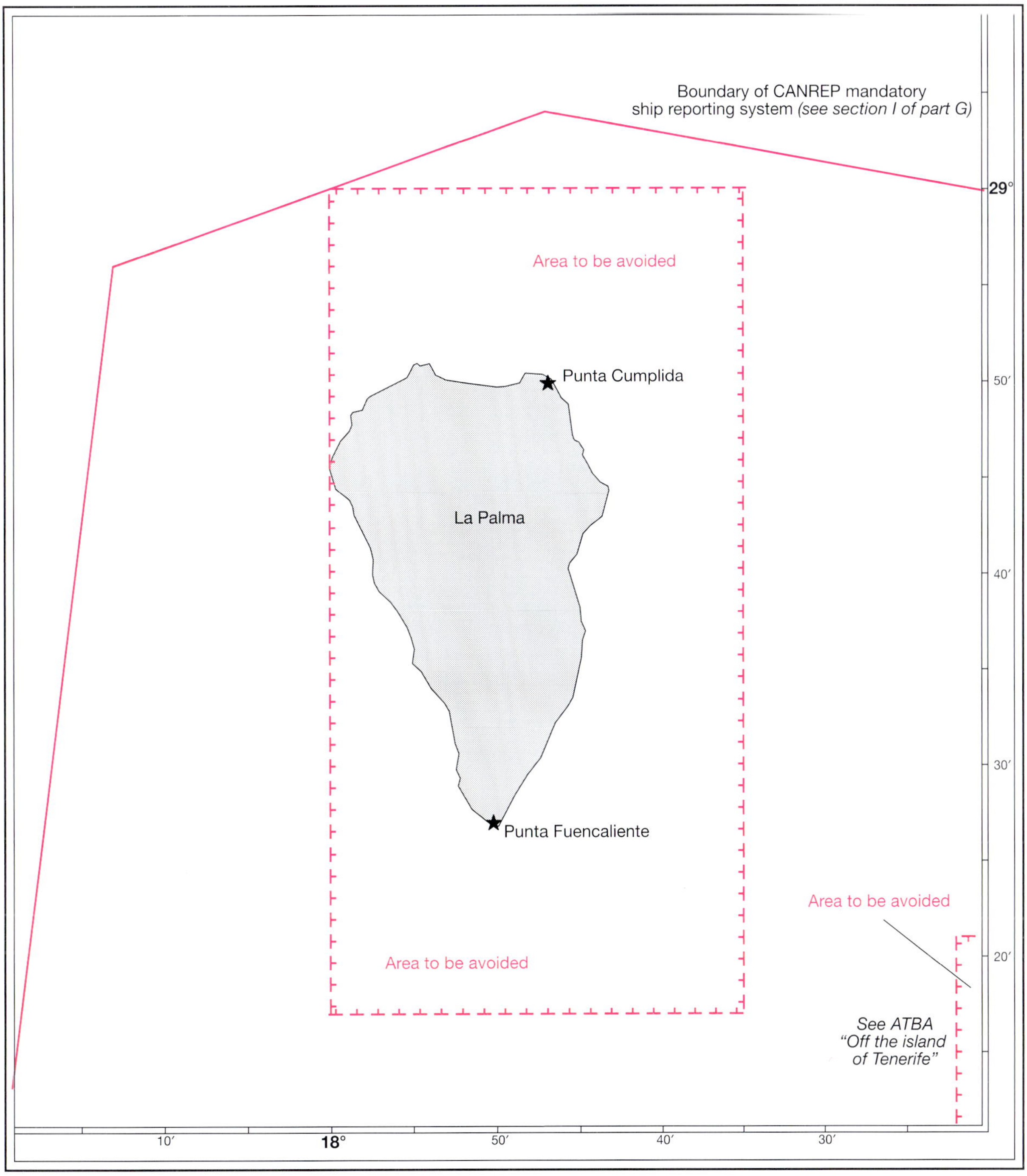

OFF LA PALMA ISLAND

OFF THE ISLAND OF EL HIERRO

Note: See mandatory ship reporting system "The Canary Islands" in part G, section I.

(Reference chart: Spanish Navy Hydrographical Institute 209, second edition 1968, 12th impression 2003.
Note: This chart is based on World Geodetic System 1984 datum (WGS 84).)

Description of the area to be avoided

In order to prevent the risks of pollution and environmental damage in highly sensitive sea areas, all tankers and ships over 500 gross tonnage carrying oil or dangerous bulk cargo as cargo should avoid the following area:

> An area contained between the parallel of latitude 28°00′.00 N, the meridians of longitude 017°42′.00 W and 018°21′.00 W and the geographical co-ordinates 27°31′.50 N, 017°42′.00 W; 27°23′.00 N, 017°58′.00 W; and 27°34′.00 N, 018°21′.00 W.

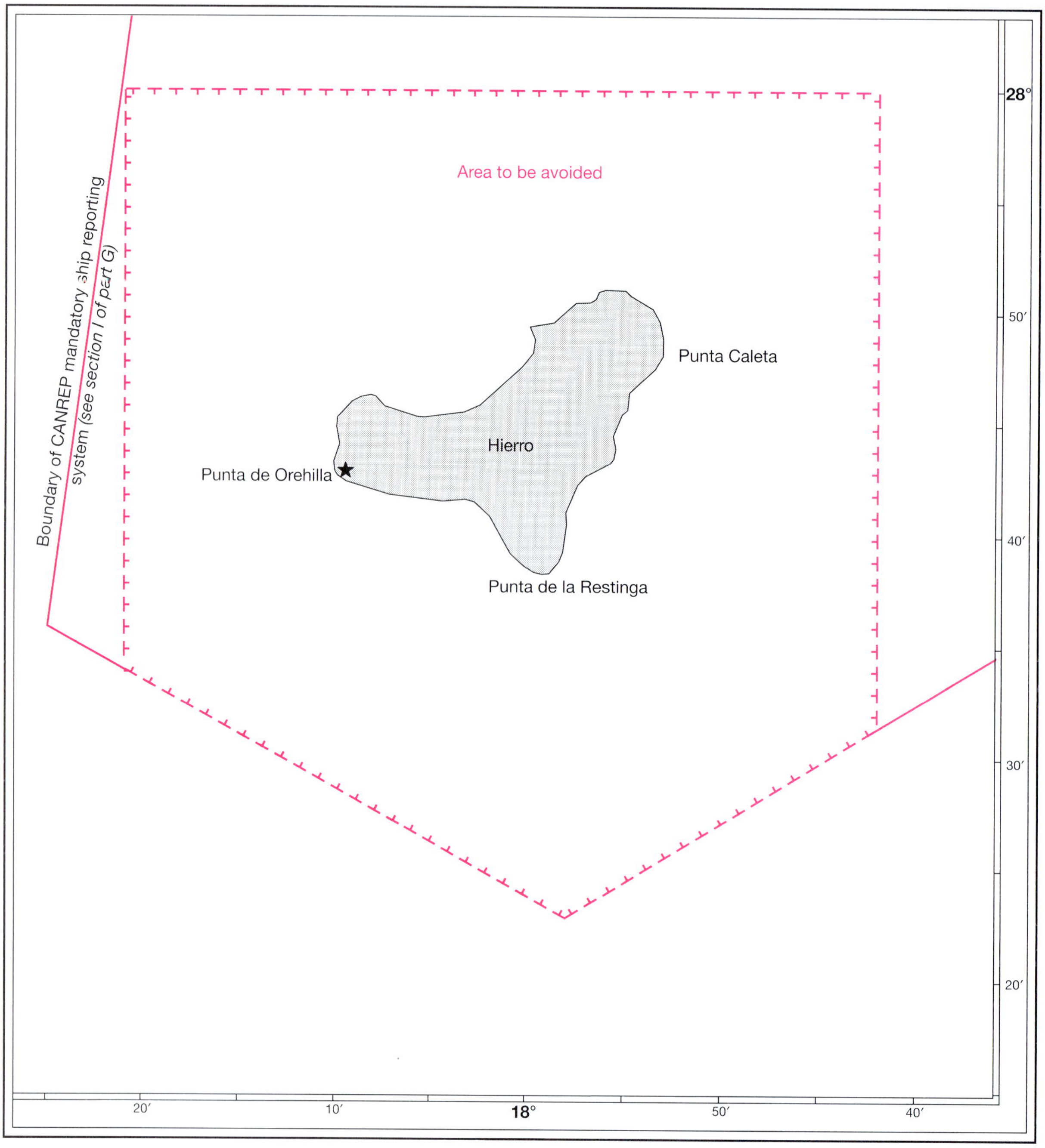

OFF THE ISLAND OF EL HIERRO

OFF THE COAST OF GHANA IN THE ATLANTIC OCEAN*

(Reference chart: British Admiralty 1383, 2009 edition.
Note: This chart is based on World Geodetic System 1984 datum (WGS 84).)

Description of the area to be avoided

Excepting ships authorized by the Ghana Maritime Authority, all ships should avoid the area within a radius of 5 nautical miles centred on the following geographical position:

04°32′.10 N, 002°54′.60 W (marked J-09).

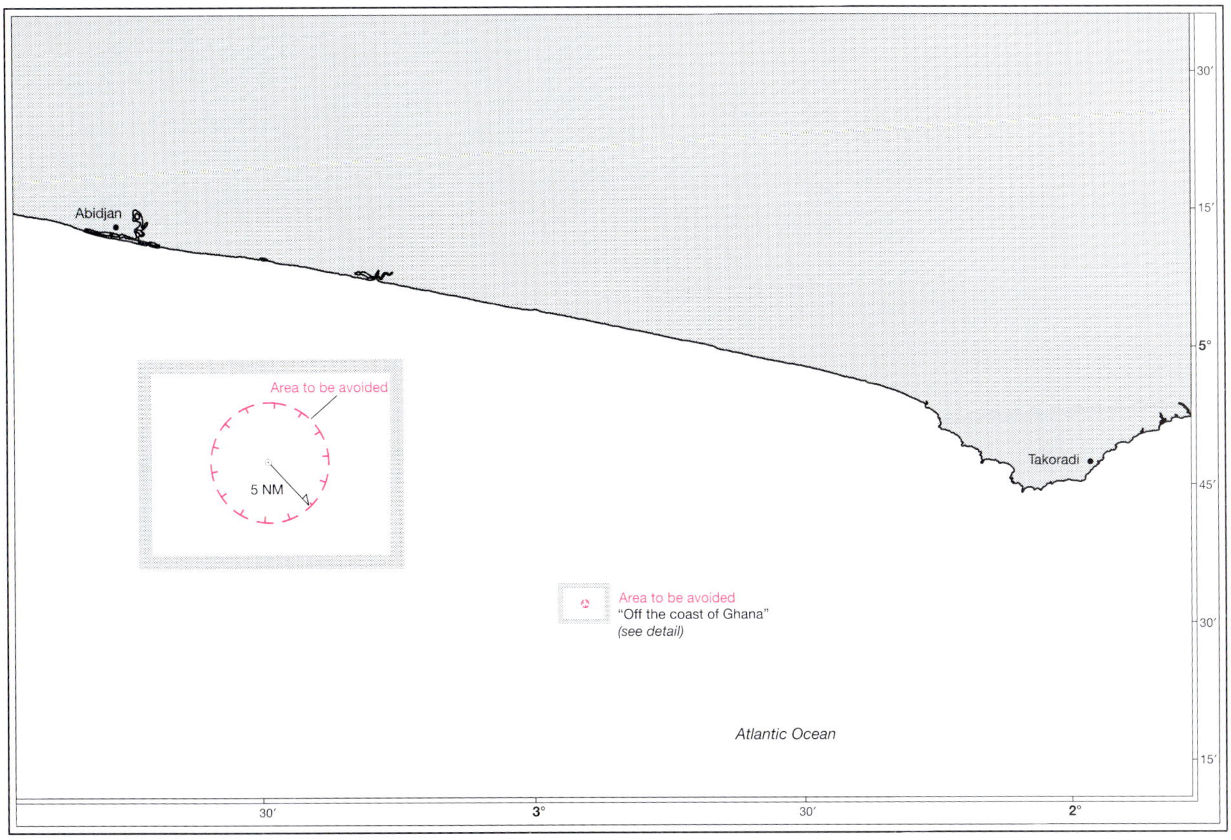

OFF THE COAST OF GHANA IN THE ATLANTIC OCEAN

* Date of implementation of new area to be avoided: 0000 hours UTC on 1 June 2011.

IN WATERS OFF THE BRAZILIAN SOUTH-EAST COAST*

(Reference charts: Brazil 22800, 2009 edition and Brazil 22900, 2008 edition.
Note: These charts are based on World Geodetic System 1984 datum (WGS 84).)

Description of the areas to be avoided

1 *Golfinho Field*

An area within the circle of 7 nautical miles radius centred on the following geographical position:
20° 00′ 10″ S, 039° 34′ 45″ W

2 *Jubarte Field*

An area within the circle of 7.5 nautical miles radius centred on the following geographical position:
21° 16′ 25″ S, 040° 01′ 54″ W

Note: All vessels not engaged in offshore activities are requested to avoid these areas.

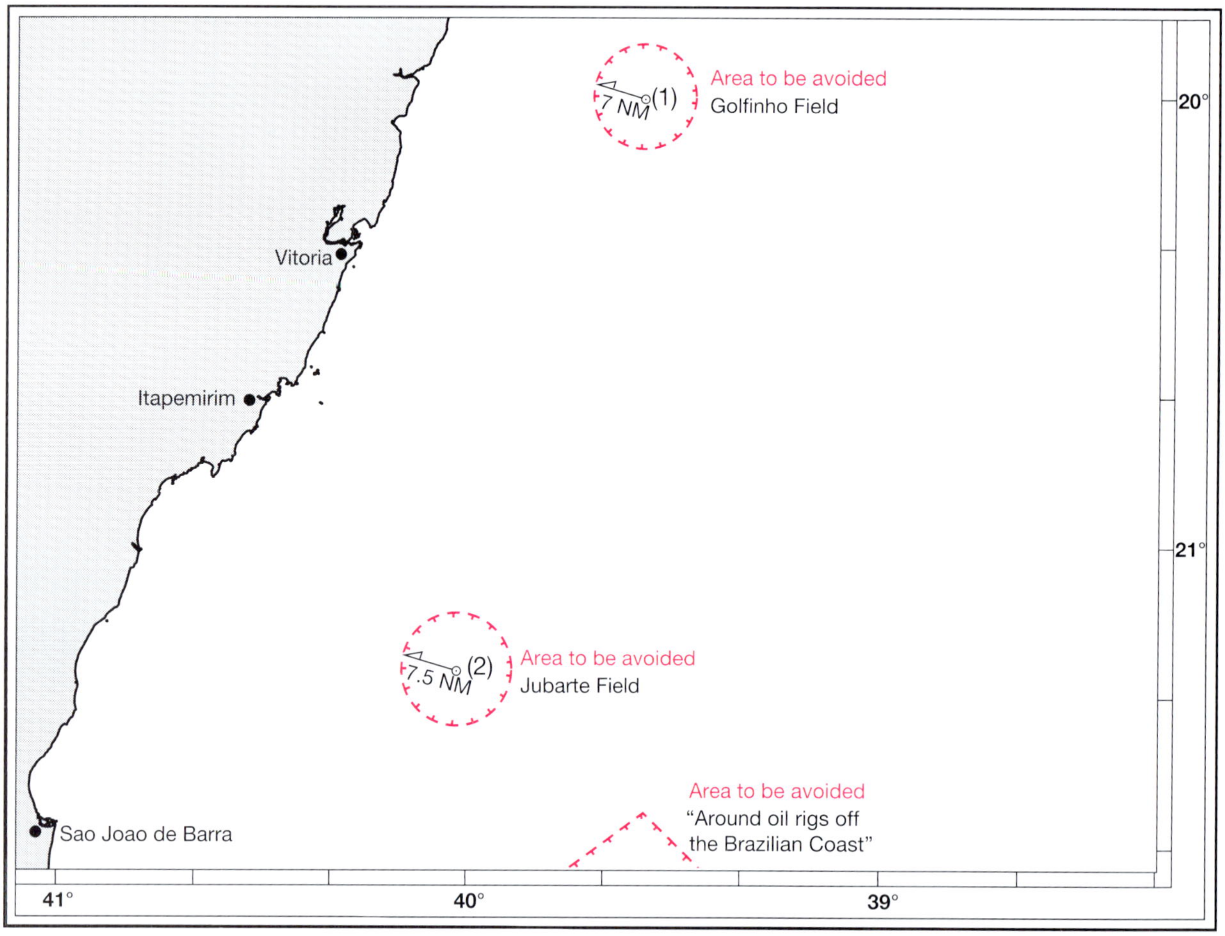

IN WATERS OFF THE BRAZILIAN SOUTH-EAST COAST

* Date of implementation of new areas to be avoided: 0000 hours UTC on 1 June 2013.

AROUND OIL RIGS OFF THE BRAZILIAN COAST – CAMPOS BASIN

(Reference chart: Brazilian Hydrographic Office 23000, October 2003 edition.
Note: This chart is based on World Geodetic System 1984 datum (WGS 84).)

Description of the area to be avoided

In order to avoid risks of collision, pollution and environmental damage in the area to be avoided with a high concentration of oil rigs, production systems and FPSOs, all ships, except those involved in support activities to oil and gas production and prospecting, should avoid the area bounded by a line connecting the following geographical positions:

(1)	23°02′.57 S,	041°03′.27 W	(4)	21°35′.50 S,	039°34′.50 W
(2)	22°41′.90 S,	040°56′.40 W	(5)	21°54′.57 S,	039°13′.43 W
(3)	22°07′.40 S,	040°22′.57 W	(6)	22°57′.23 S,	040°14′.30 W

Notes:

1 Oil and gas production rigs display night signalling lights, comprising a fixed red light at the top and a white rhythmical light, indicative letter "U" (··–) in Morse code – Mo(U)B. Non-authorized navigation inside safety zones around oil rigs is prohibited.

2 *Transit of supply vessels between the harbour of the town of Macaé and the area of oil drilling and production rigs (area to be avoided):* caution is advised in navigation when transiting the area of considerable volume of maritime traffic that crosses routes.

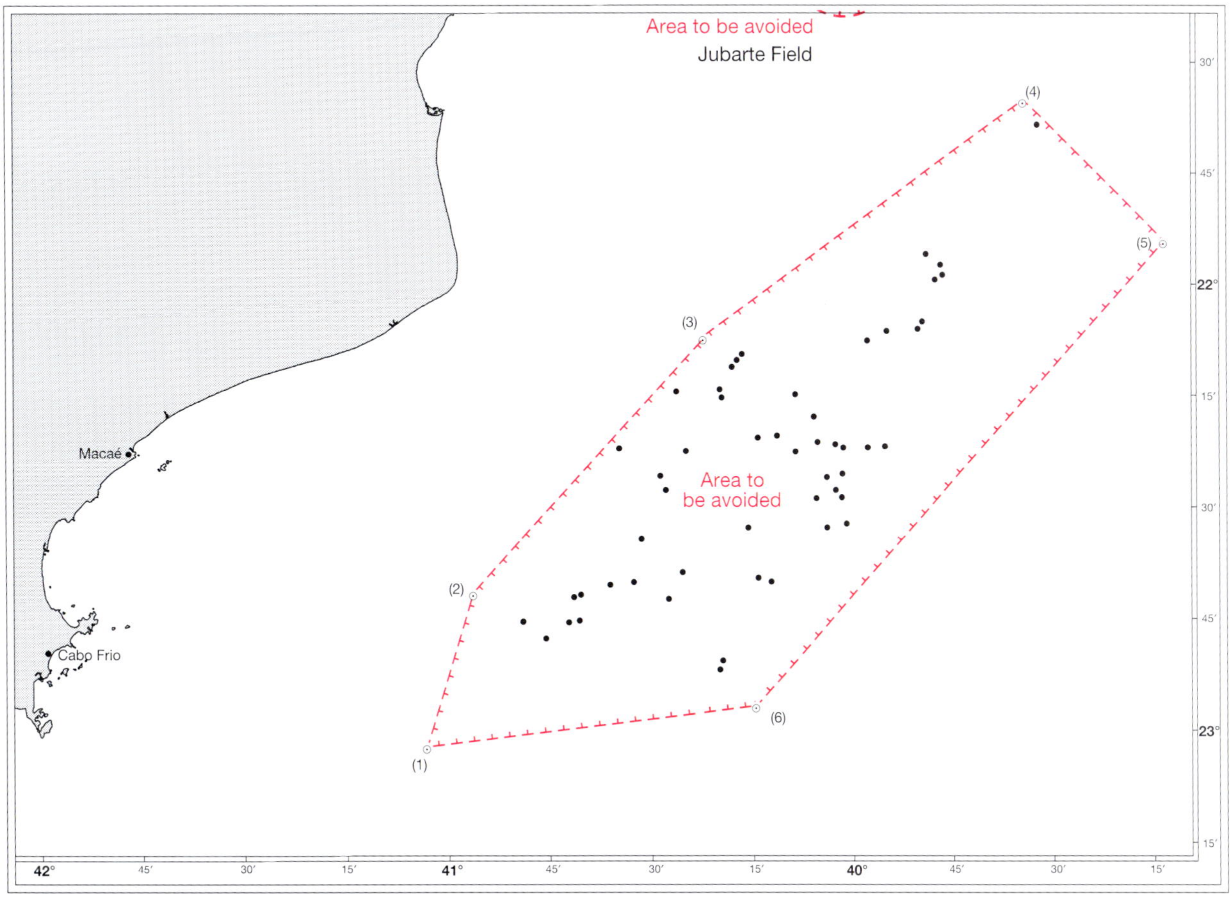

AROUND OIL RIGS OFF THE BRAZILIAN COAST – CAMPOS BASIN

Part E

Other routeing measures

Baltic Sea and adjacent waters

Western European waters

E

Mediterranean Sea and Black Sea

Indian Ocean and adjacent waters

Australasia

North America, Pacific coast

E

South America, Pacific coast

Western North Atlantic Ocean, Gulf of Mexico and Caribbean Sea

INDEX

OTHER ROUTEING MEASURES

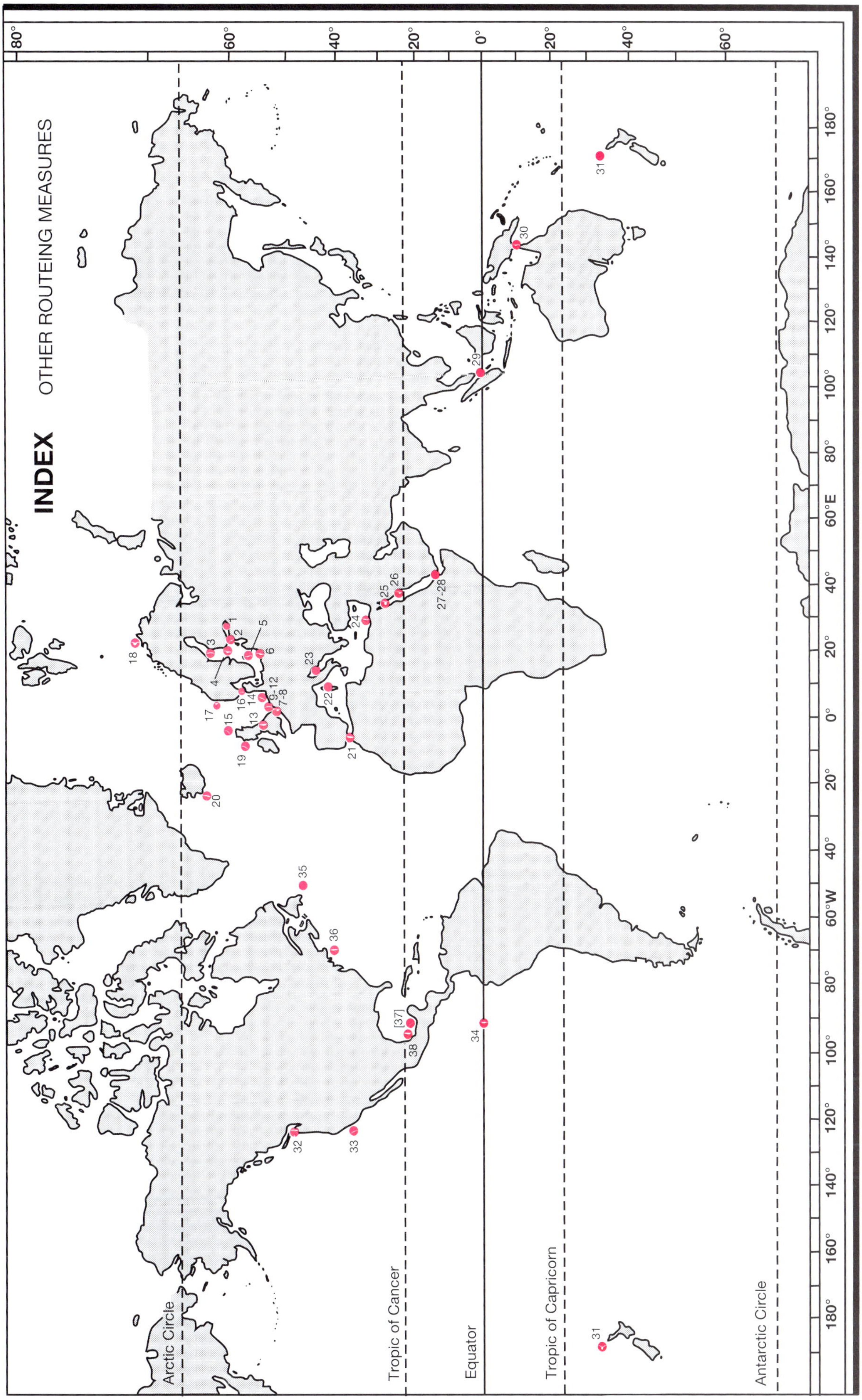

RECOMMENDED TRACKS AND TRAFFIC SEPARATION LINE BETWEEN THE TRAFFIC SEPARATION SCHEMES "OFF RODSHER ISLAND" AND "OFF GOGLAND ISLAND"*

Positions are based on World Geodetic System 1984 datum (WGS 84). The Russian Federation reference chart is 23004 (Pulkovo 1942). For obtaining position in WGS datum, charted positions should be moved 0′.14 (8″.3) westward.

Description of the recommended tracks and traffic separation line

Recommended tracks are eastbound and westbound traffic lanes separated by a traffic separation line connecting the following geographical positions:

(1) 60°00′.10 N, 026°44′.16 E (2) 59°59′.00 N, 026°57′.26 E

The traffic lanes are 1.25 miles wide.

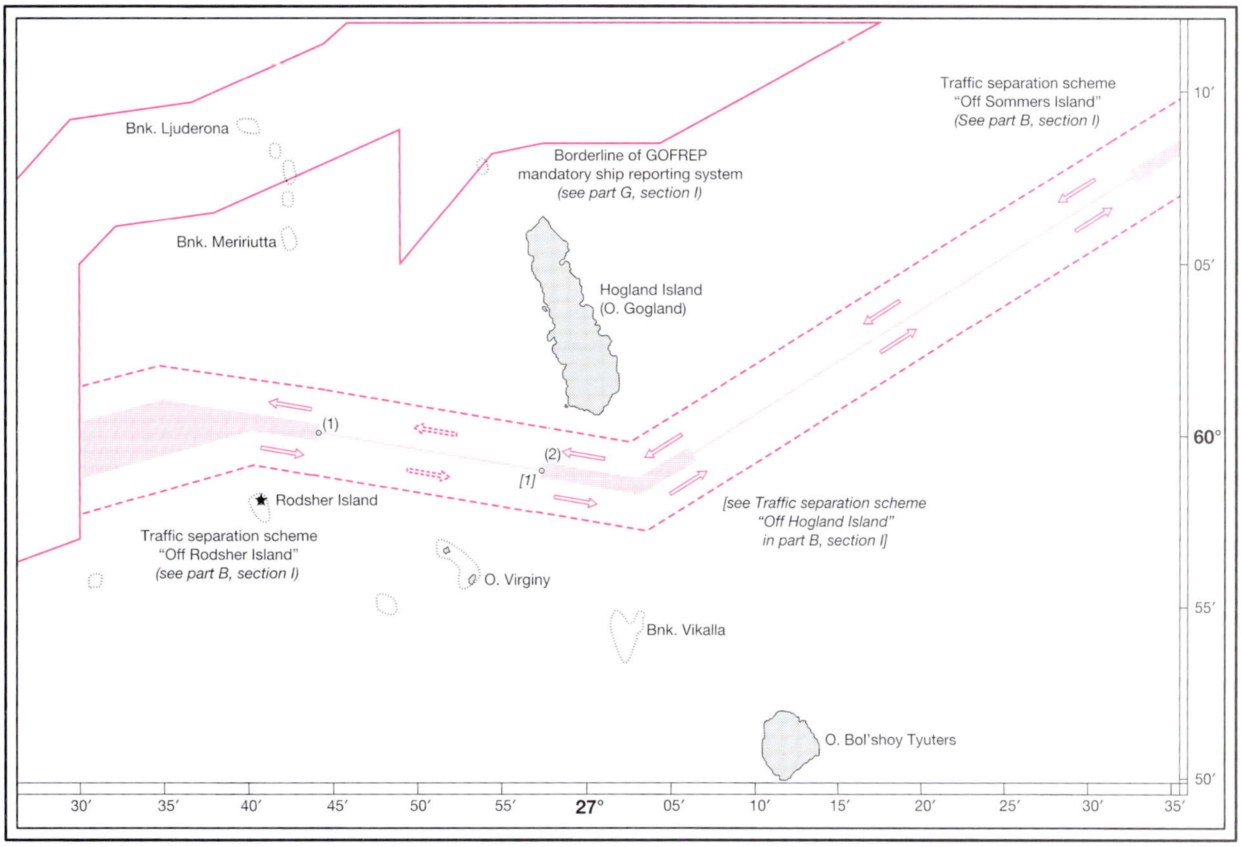

RECOMMENDED TRACKS AND TRAFFIC SEPARATION LINE BETWEEN TSS "OFF RODSHER ISLAND" AND TSS "OFF GOGLAND ISLAND"

E

* Date of implementation of new measures: 0000 hours UTC on 1 June 2013.

RECOMMENDED DIRECTIONS OF TRAFFIC FLOW WITHIN THE PRECAUTIONARY AREA OF THE SEPARATION SCHEME "OFF PORKKALA LIGHTHOUSE"

Note: See mandatory ship reporting system "In the Gulf of Finland" in part G, section I, and "Recommendations on navigation through the Gulf of Finland Traffic area" in part F.

(Reference charts: Estonian 300 (edition 2006-15-12) and 302 (edition 2004-24-11); Finnish 952 (edition 2008-11-10) and 953 (2008-06-10), and Russian 23068 (edition 2001).)
Note: Finnish and Estonian charts are based on World Geodetic System 1984 datum (WGS 84); Russian chart is based on Geodetic datum of the year 1942 (Pulkovo). For obtaining positions in WGS datum, such positions should be moved 0′.13 westward.

Description of the precautionary area

Note: All positions are referred to WGS 84 datum.

(a) A precautionary area with recommended direction of traffic flow is bounded by a line connecting the following geographical positions:

(15)	59°42′.98 N,	024°30′.50 E
(16)	59°43′.70 N,	024°36′.99 E
(24)	59°47′.18 N,	025°08′.10 E
(20)	59°49′.14 N,	025°07′.23 E
(23)	59°50′.80 N,	025°06′.50 E
(27)	59°52′.76 N,	025°05′.64 E
(17)	59°49′.29 N,	024°34′.53 E
(7)	59°47′.33 N,	024°35′.39 E
(12)	59°45′.67 N,	024°36′.13 E
(11)	59°45′.34 N,	024°33′.21 E
(3)	59°44′.94 N,	024°29′.64 E

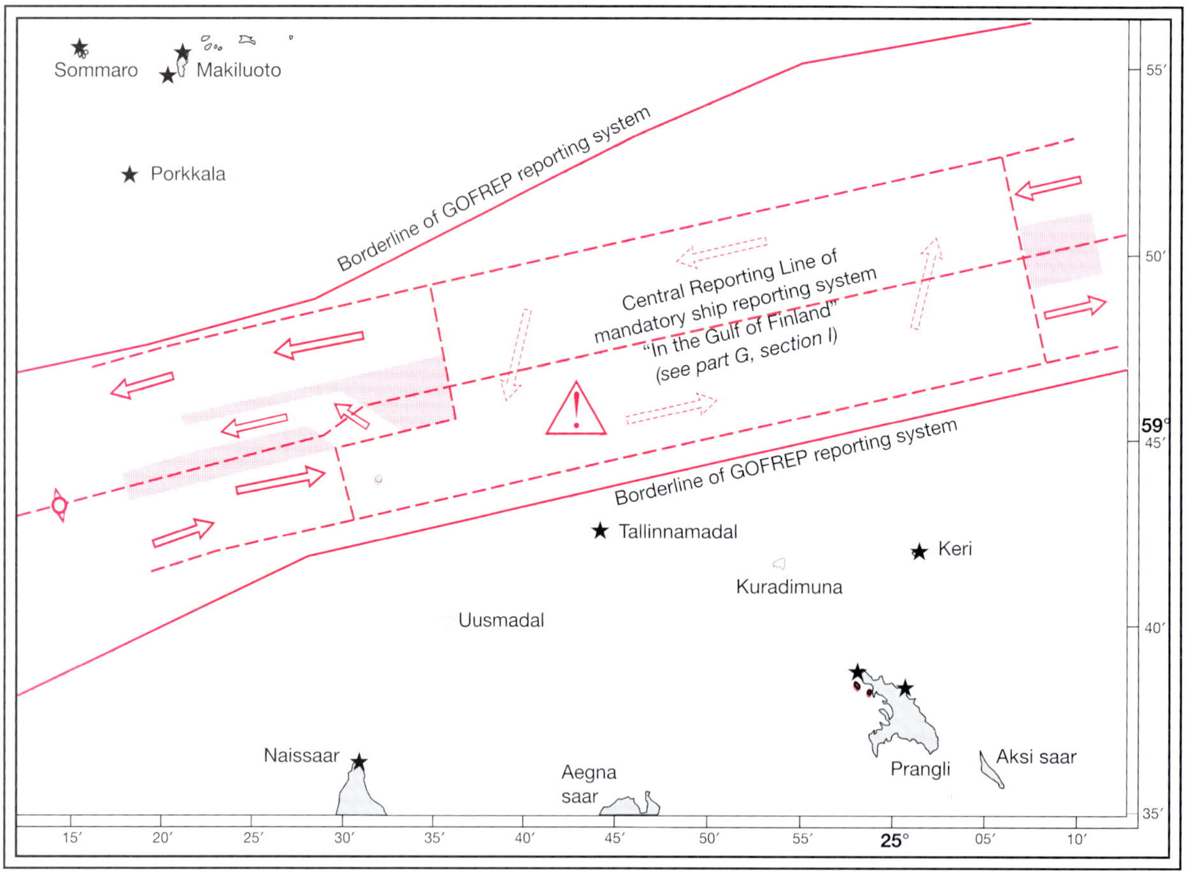

RECOMMENDED DIRECTIONS OF TRAFFIC FLOW WITHIN THE PRECAUTIONARY AREA OF THE SEPARATION SCHEME "OFF PORKKALA LIGHTHOUSE"

TWO-WAY ROUTES IN NORRA KVARKEN*

Note: See traffic separation schemes "In Norra Kvarken" in part B, section I.

(Reference chart: Finnish 47, edition 2005 V.
Note: this chart is based on World Geodetic System 1984 datum (WGS 84).)

Part I

(a) A two-way route is established bounded by a line connecting the following geographical positions:

(20)	63°25′.21 N,	020°35′.75 E
(6)	63°27′.42 N,	020°36′.84 E
(21)	63°25′.54 N,	020°33′.94 E
(3)	63°27′.03 N,	020°38′.32 E

Part II

(b) A two-way route is established bounded by a line connecting the following geographical positions:

(4)	63°27′.77 N,	020°39′.24 E
(13)	63°32′.23 N,	020°41′.09 E
(5)	63°28′.12 N,	020°37′.93 E
(10)	63°31′.19 N,	020°43′.77 E

Part III

(c) A two-way route is established bounded by a line connecting the following geographical positions:

(11)	63°32′.29 N,	020°46′.24 E
(23)	63°33′.49 N,	020°52′.35 E
(16)	63°34′.42 N,	021°01′.76 E
(12)	63°32′.71 N,	020°45′.40 E
(19)	63°35′.04 N,	021°01′.26 E
(22)	63°32′.90 N,	020°51′.03 E

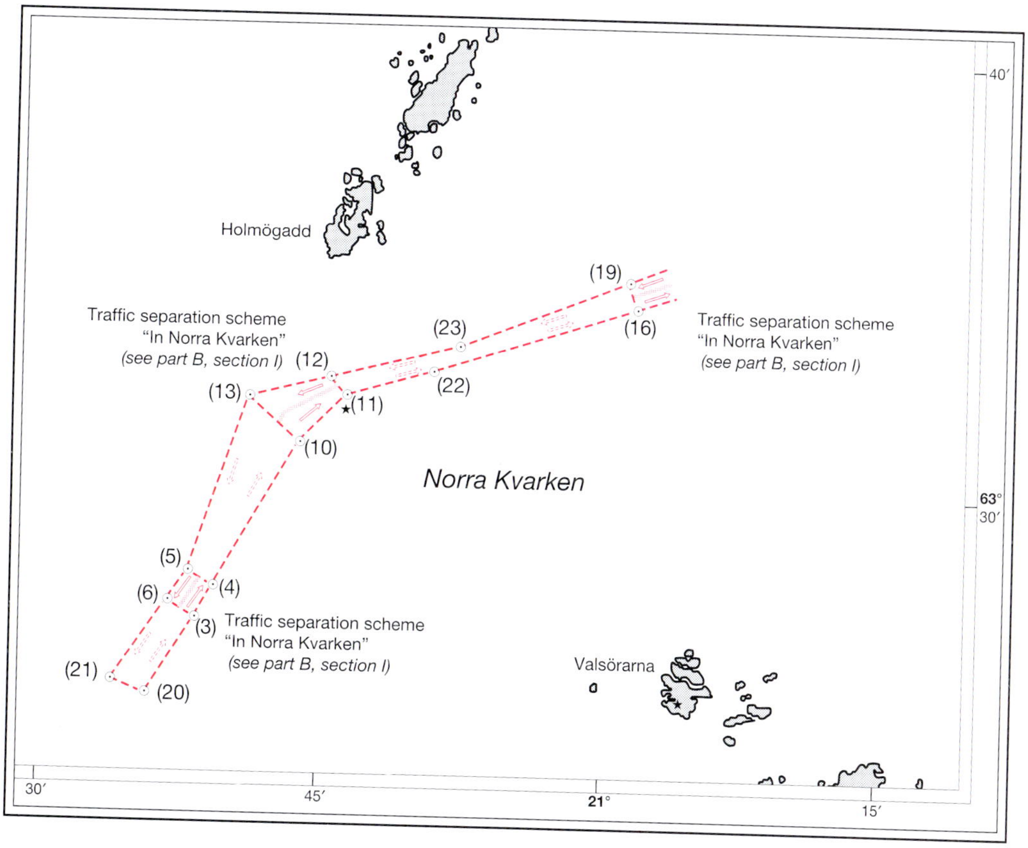

TWO-WAY ROUTES IN NORRA KVARKEN

* Date of implementation of new two-way routes: 0000 hours UTC on 1 May 2013.

RECOMMENDED TWO-WAY ROUTE LEADING TO THE ÅLAND SEA

Note: See traffic separation scheme "The Åland Sea" in part B, section I.

(Reference charts: Finnish 953, edition 2007 V, and Swedish SE61 (INT 1205), edition 21/2-2008.
Note: These charts are based on World Geodetic System 1984 datum (WGS 84).)

Description of the two-way route in the South Åland Sea

A recommended two-way route is established in the area defined by lines joining the following geographical positions:

(24)	59°44′.25 N,	019°58′.80 E,
(30)	59°44′.32 N,	020°19′.60 E,
(29)	59°44′.76 N,	020°23′.10 E,
(34)	59°45′.68 N,	020°24′.51 E,
(25)	59°46′.96 N,	019°58′.92 E

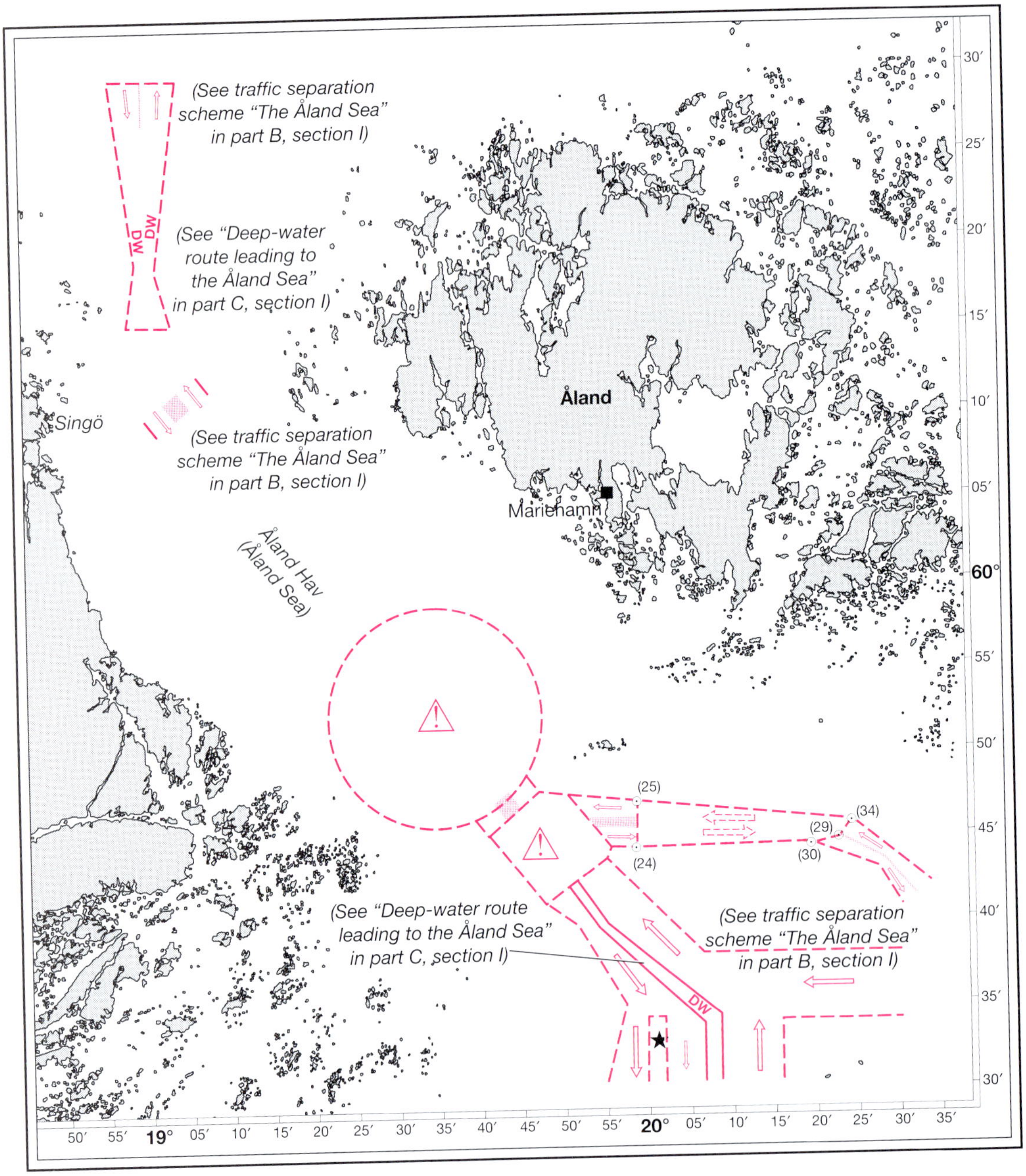

RECOMMENDED TWO-WAY ROUTE LEADING TO THE ÅLAND SEA

SALVOREV TWO-WAY ROUTE, NORTH OF GOTLAND ISLAND

(Reference chart: Swedish SE731 edition 11/3-2008.
Note: This chart is based on World Geodetic System 1984 datum (WGS 84).)

Description of the two-way route north of Gotland Island

Salvorev

A recommended two-way route is established within the following geographical positions:

(a) *Northern limit:*

(1) 57°57′.70 N, 018°27′.61 E (2) 58°08′.70 N, 019°18′.25 E

(b) *Southern limit:*

(3) 57°53′.97 N, 018°25′.44 E (4) 58°05′.92 N, 019°20′.36 E

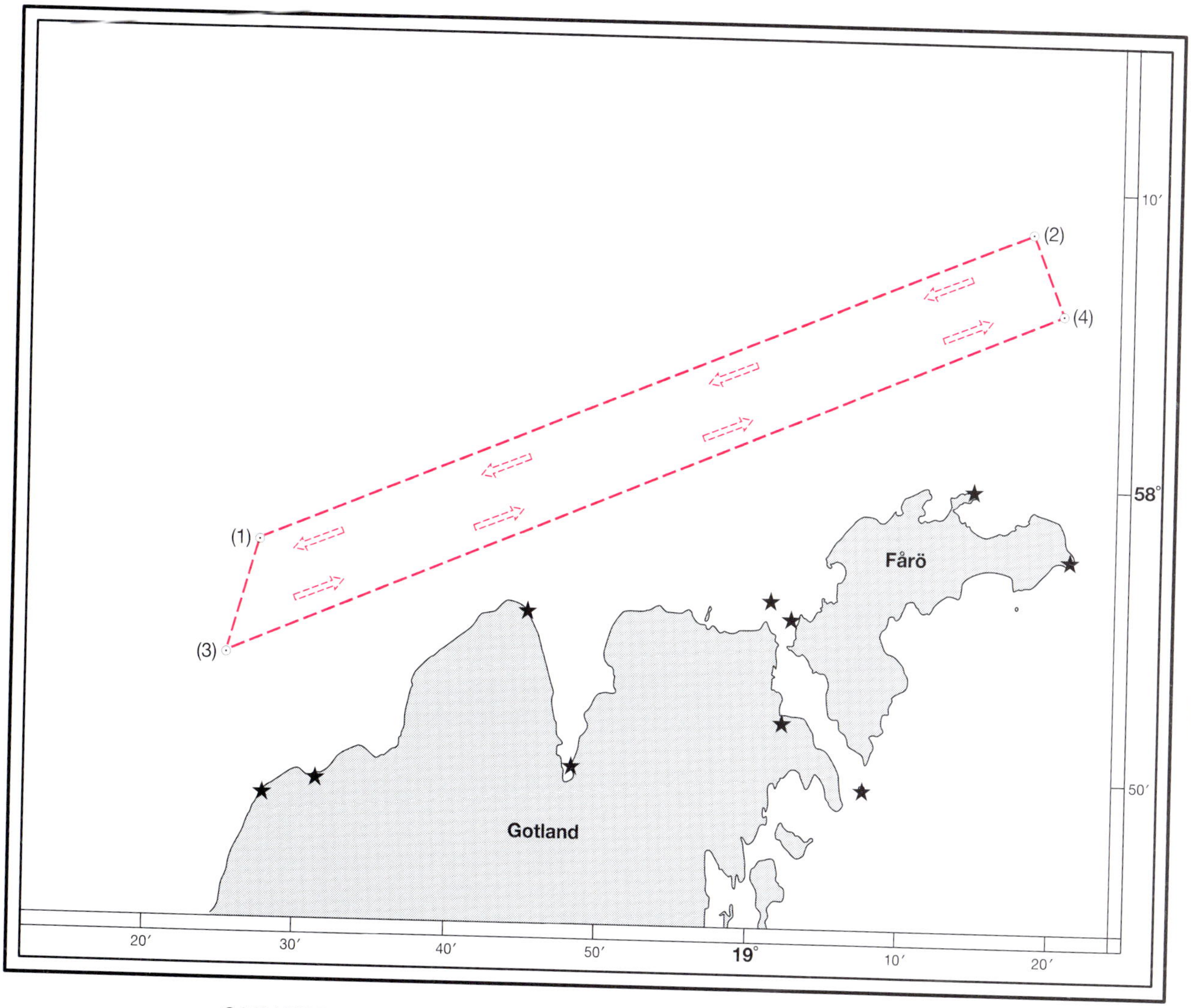

SALVOREV TWO-WAY ROUTE, NORTH OF GOTLAND ISLAND

E

RECOMMENDED TRACKS ON THE APPROACHES TO THE POLISH PORTS IN THE GULF OF GDAŃSK

Note: See mandatory ship reporting system "On the approaches to the Polish ports in the Gulf of Gdańsk" in part G, section I and "Recommendations on navigation to the Polish ports through the Gulf of Gdańsk Traffic area" in part F.

(Reference chart: Polish 73 (INT 1288), 2004 edition.
Note: This chart is based on World Geodetic System 1984 datum (WGS 84).)

Recommended track between GD and NP buoys

A recommended track is established between the following geographical positions:

(54)	54°32′.05 N,	018°39′.84 E	(buoy GD)
(55)	54°27′.90 N,	018°42′.05 E	(buoy NP)

The direction (T) of navigation is 163° – 343°.

Recommended track between GN and PP buoys

A recommended track is established between the following geographical positions:

(56)	54°31′.56 N,	018°48′.61 E	(vicinity of buoy GN)
(57)	54°28′.23 N,	018°54′.54 E	
(58)	54°25′.88 N,	018°54′.54 E	(vicinity of buoy PP)

The directions (T) of navigation are 134° – 314° and 000° – 180°.

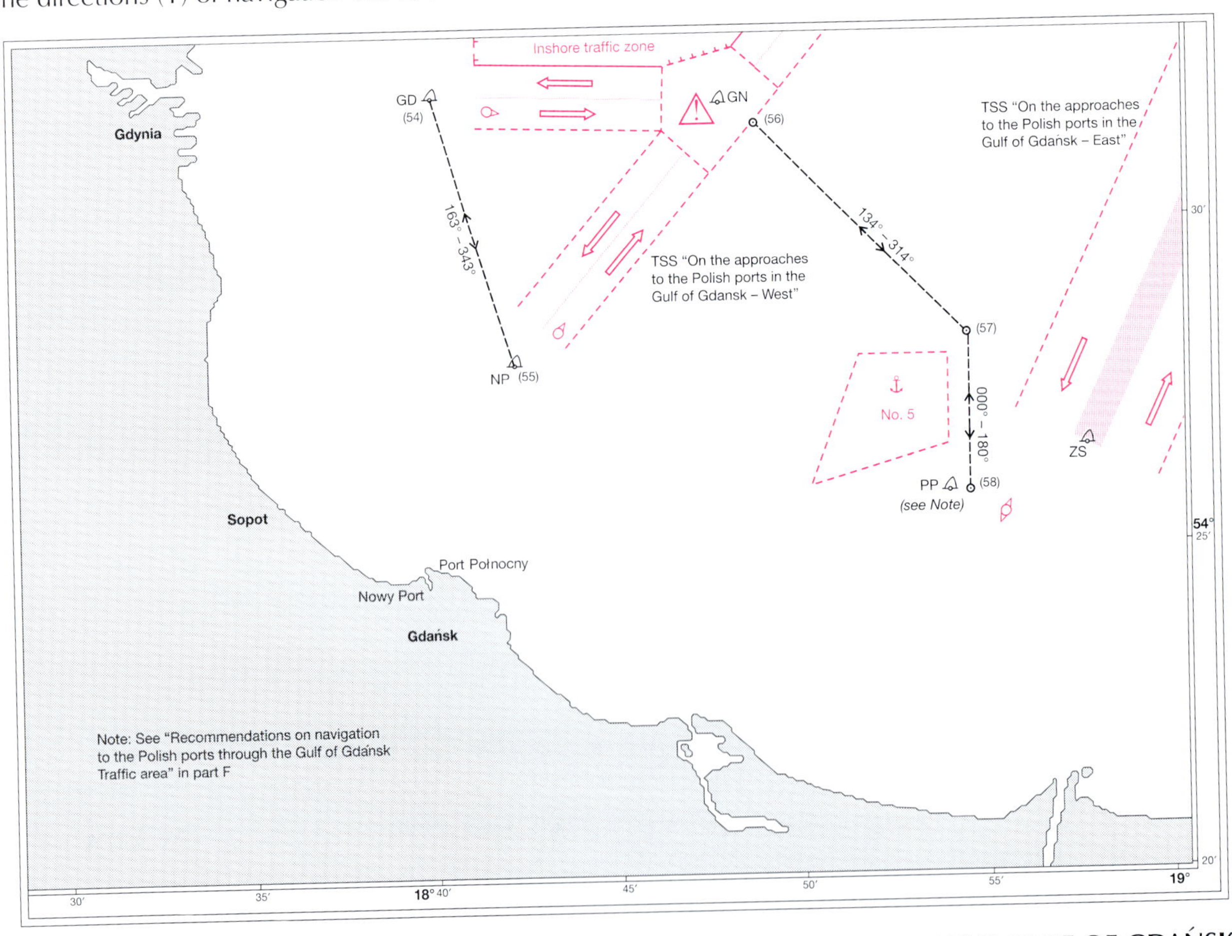

RECOMMENDED TRACKS ON THE APPROACHES TO THE POLISH PORTS IN THE GULF OF GDAŃSK

RECOMMENDED DIRECTIONS OF TRAFFIC FLOW WITHIN THE PRECAUTIONARY AREA SURROUNDING THE AREA TO BE AVOIDED AROUND THE FOXTROT 3 STATION, WITHIN THE SEPARATION SCHEME "IN THE STRAIT OF DOVER AND ADJACENT WATERS"

Note: See "Recommendations on navigation through the English Channel and the Dover Strait" in part F.

The geographical positions of the boundary for the precautionary area around the Foxtrot 3 station buoy are as follows (co-ordinates are based on World Geodetic System 1984 datum:

(1)	51°25′.31 N,	002°04′.03 E
(2)	51°26′.77 N,	002°01′.48 E
(8)	51°22′.49 N,	001°57′.61 E
(7)	51°22′.03 N,	001°58′.39 E

Recommended directions of traffic flow within the precautionary area around the area to be avoided surrounding the Foxtrot 3 station are shown in the chartlet below.

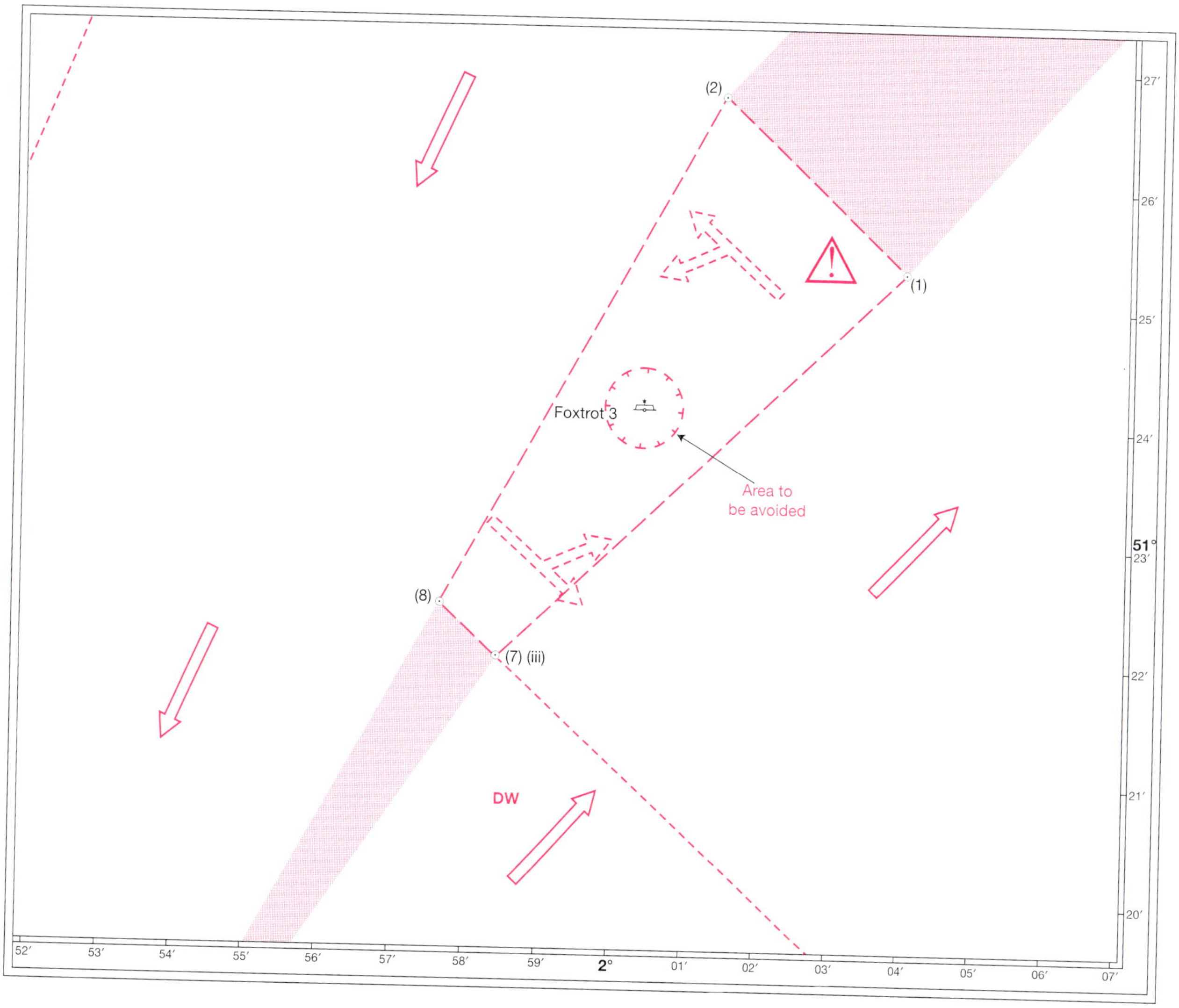

RECOMMENDED DIRECTIONS OF TRAFFIC FLOW WITHIN THE PRECAUTIONARY AREA SURROUNDING THE FOXTROT 3 STATION IN THE STRAIT OF DOVER

TWO-WAY ROUTE AND RECOMMENDED ROUTE IN THE SUNK AREA AND IN THE NORTHERN APPROACHES TO THE THAMES ESTUARY

Note: See mandatory ship reporting system "West European Tanker Reporting System" in part G, section I.

(Reference chart: British Admiralty 1183, 2005 edition.
Note: This chart is based on World Geodetic System 1984 datum (WGS 84).)

An integrated traffic routeing scheme for the SUNK area consists of several elements comprising:

Part I: One two-way route (Long Sand Head);

Part II: Three traffic separation schemes (SUNK North and South and East), two precautionary areas (SUNK Inner and SUNK Outer); see section II of part B; and an area to be avoided in the SUNK Outer precautionary area; see section II of part D; and

Part III: A recommended route (Galloper).

Part I:
Description of the two-way route

Long Sand Head two-way route is established. (Note that entry is restricted to piloted vessels, vessels operated under pilotage exemption certificate (PEC), and vessels exempt from pilotage under the destination port's pilotage directions.)

(a) A boundary line connecting the following geographical positions:

(1)	51°38′.09 N,	001°40′.43 E	(3)	51°47′.77 N,	001°38′.16 E
(2)	51°47′.90 N,	001°39′.42 E			

(b) A separation zone bounded by a line connecting the following geographical positions:

(4)	51°38′.31 N,	001°43′.60 E	(10)	51°49′.49 N,	001°40′.06 E
(5)	51°38′.33 N,	001°43′.89 E	(11)	51°49′.30 N,	001°38′.16 E
(6)	51°42′.16 N,	001°43′.20 E	(12)	51°49′.11 N,	001°38′.16 E
(7)	51°48′.29 N,	001°42′.08 E	(13)	51°49′.30 N,	001°40′.01 E
(8)	51°48′.98 N,	001°41′.64 E	(14)	51°48′.84 N,	001°41′.40 E
(9)	51°49′.28 N,	001°40′.72 E	(15)	51°48′.24 N,	001°41′.79 E

(c) A two-way route bounded by the boundary line described in (a) above and the separation zone described in (b) above.

Part III:
Description of the recommended route

(q) A recommended route ("Galloper" recommended route in the south-east sector of the scheme, to enable regular ferry traffic sailing to and from the port of Ostend to enter and leave the SUNK Outer precautionary area without deviating unnecessarily to use traffic separation lanes) connecting the following geographical positions:

(54)	51°44′.93 N,	001°50′.93 E	(55)	51°41′.33 N,	002°00′.03 E

E

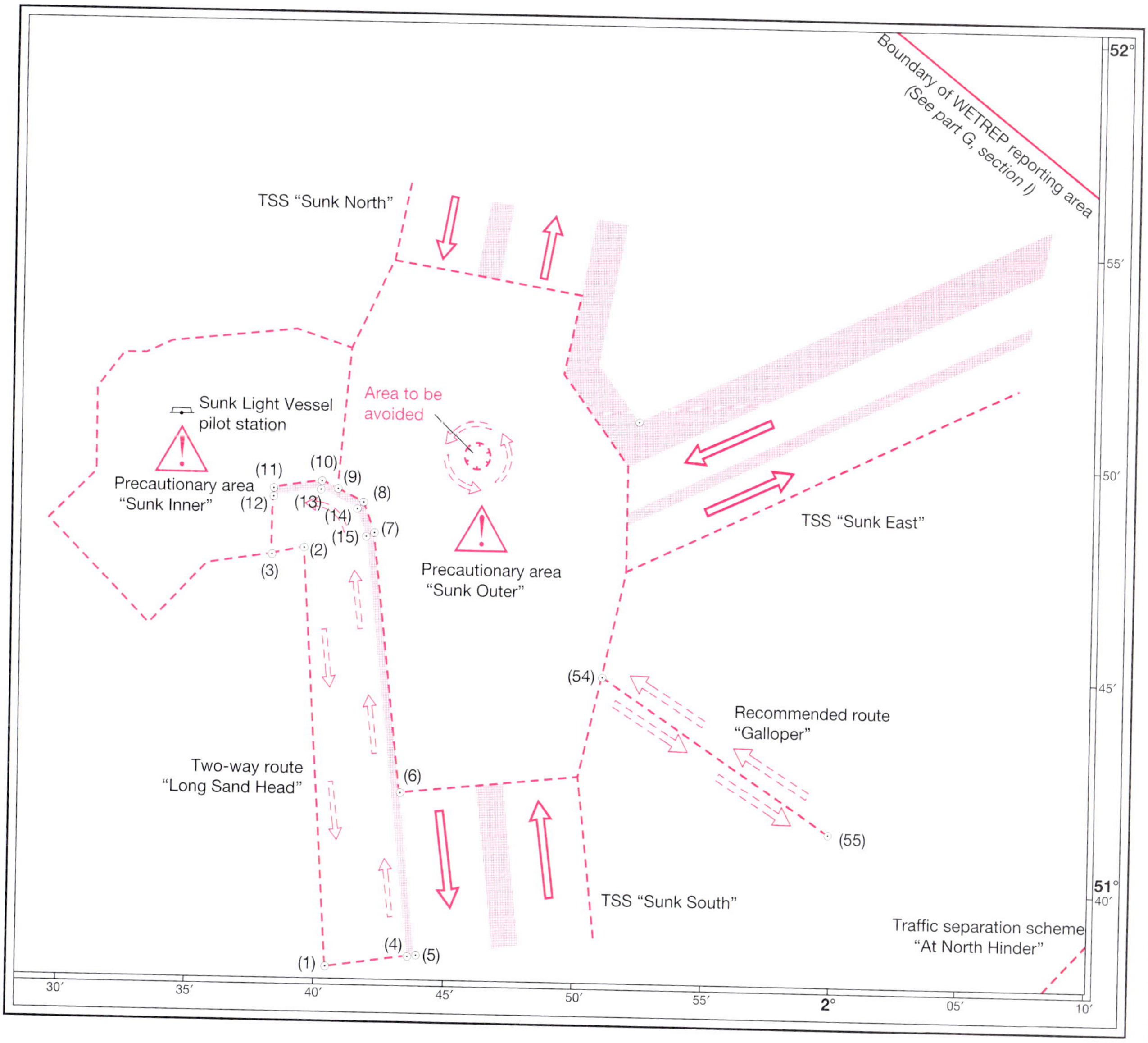

TWO-WAY ROUTE AND RECOMMENDED ROUTE IN THE SUNK AREA AND IN THE NORTHERN APPROACHES TO THE THAMES ESTUARY

PRECAUTIONARY AREA IN THE VICINITY OF THORNTON AND BLIGH BANKS*

Note: See mandatory ship reporting system "West European tanker reporting system" in part G, section I.

(Reference chart: 1630 (INT1416) published jointly by the Hydrographer of the Royal Netherlands Navy at Den Haag and by the United Kingdom National Hydrographer at Taunton.
Note: This chart is based on World Geodetic System 1984 datum (WGS 84).)

Description of the precautionary area

A new precautionary area is established bounded by a line joining the following geographical positions:

(1)	51°32′.66 N,	003°05′.56 E	(8)	51°36′.97 N,	002°47′.75 E
(2)	51°33′.05 N,	003°04′.81 E	(9)	51°35′.77 N,	002°50′.36 E
(3)	51°44′.69 N,	002°45′.36 E	(10)	51°35′.20 N,	002°53′.01 E
(4)	51°44′.11 N,	002°42′.45 E	(11)	51°34′.05 N,	002°55′.01 E
(5)	51°42′.31 N,	002°41′.85 E	(12)	51°32′.84 N,	002°52′.37 E
(6)	51°39′.13 N,	002°44′.78 E	(13)	51°28′.20 N,	002°59′.63 E
(7)	51°38′.02 N,	002°47′.15 E			

E

* Date of implementation of new precautionary area: 0000 hours UTC on 1 December 2012.

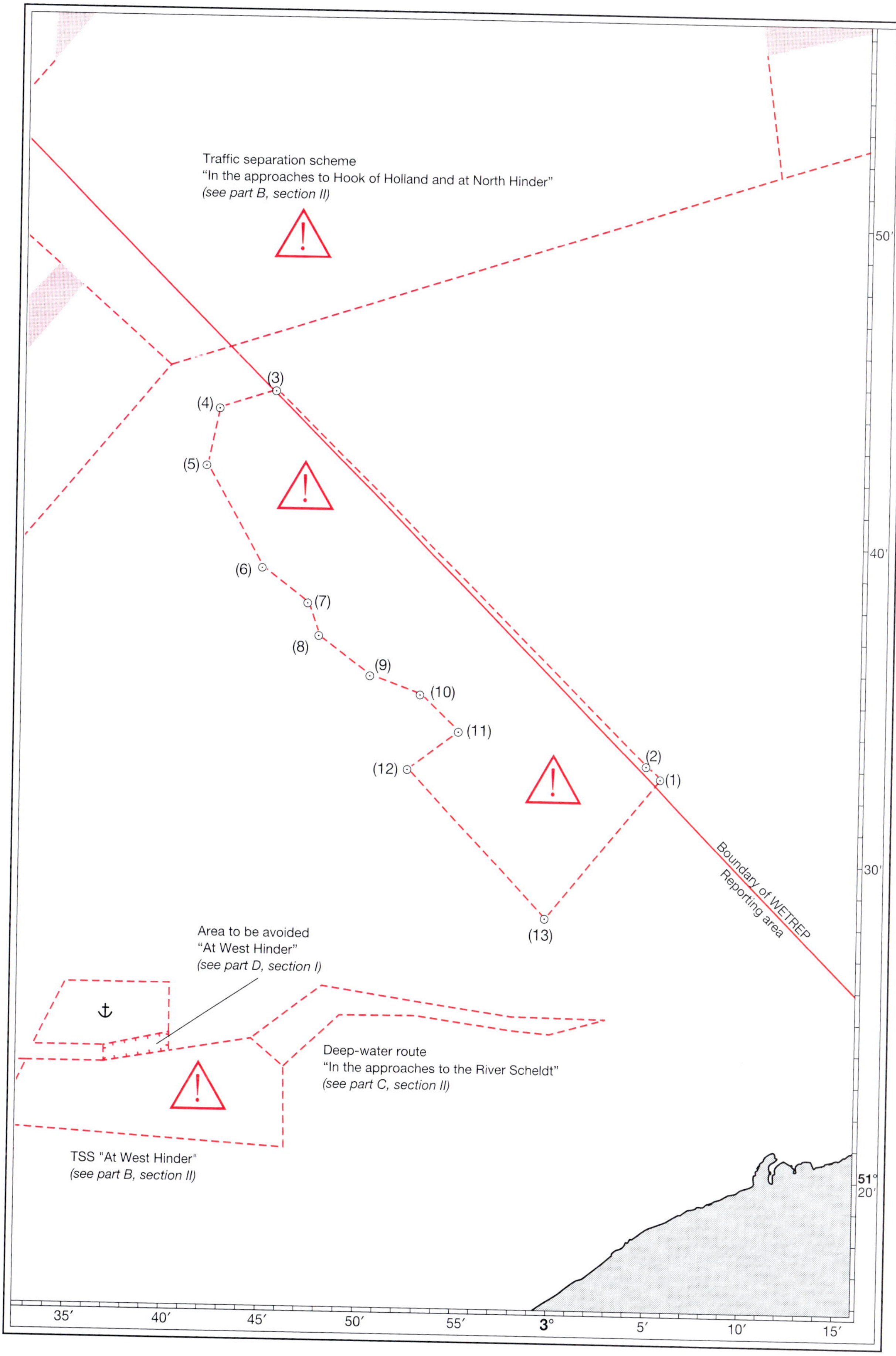

PRECAUTIONARY AREA IN THE VICINITY OF THORNTON AND BLIGH BANKS

E

PRECAUTIONARY AREAS IN THE APPROACHES TO HOOK OF HOLLAND AND AT NORTH HINDER*

Note: See traffic separation schemes "In the approaches to Hook of Holland and at North Hinder" in part B, section II, "Deep-water route leading to Europoort" in part C, section II and area to be avoided "At Maas North traffic separation scheme" in part D, section I.

(Reference chart: Netherlands 1630 (INT 1416), edition 4/2010.
Note: This chart is based on World Geodetic System 1984 datum (WGS 84).)

Maas Centre precautionary area

A precautionary area is established off the entrance to the Rotterdam Waterway. The area is bounded by a line connecting the following geographical positions:

(68)[1]	51°59′.67 N,	004°02′.84 E
(67)[1]	51°59′.14 N,	004°02′.49 E
(66)[2]	51°58′.12 N,	003°57′.86 E
(38)	51°57′.11 N,	003°40′.05 E
(37)	51°56′.26 N,	003°35′.66 E
(34)	51°58′.25 N,	003°35′.44 E
(28)	51°59′.92 N,	003°35′.24 E
(26)	52°00′.57 N,	003°35′.17 E
(25)	52°02′.56 N,	003°34′.94 E
(21)	52°04′.74 N,	003°34′.69 E
(20)	52°05′.04 N,	003°34′.66 E
(17)	52°05′.96 N,	003°36′.27 E
(16)	52°06′.17 N,	003°36′.64 E
(13)	52°07′.09 N,	003°38′.25 E
(12)	52°07′.13 N,	003°44′.66 E
(4)	52°07′.14 N,	003°47′.10 E
(3)	52°07′.17 N,	003°54′.08 E
(9)	52°07′.18 N,	003°55′.95 E
(69)	52°07′.19 N,	004°00′.08 E

[1] Position (68) is the North Mole Head light and position (67) is the South Mole Head light.
[2] The line between positions (67) and (66) follows the southern sea wall.

Maas Junction precautionary area

A precautionary area between the Maas West Inner and Maas West Outer traffic separation schemes is established by a line connecting the following geographical positions:

(23)	52°04′.63 N,	003°26′.20 E
(24)	52°02′.12 N,	003°25′.73 E
(27)	51°59′.75 N,	003°25′.29 E
(32)	51°59′.09 N,	003°25′.17 E
(33)	51°56′.90 N,	003°24′.78 E
(36)	51°54′.10 N,	003°24′.29 E
(60)	51°52′.59 N,	003°16′.43 E
(59)	51°55′.99 N,	003°17′.31 E
(56)	51°58′.49 N,	003°17′.96 E
(47)	51°59′.15 N,	003°18′.13 E
(46)	52°01′.77 N,	003°18′.81 E
(43)	52°04′.54 N,	003°19′.53 E

* Date of implementation of amended precautionary areas: 0000 hours UTC on 1 August 2013.

North Hinder Junction precautionary area

A precautionary area is established off North Hinder. The area is bounded by a line connecting the following geographical positions:

(85)	51°45′.42 N,	002°39′.92 E
(61)	51°50′.72 N,	003°06′.78 E
(58)	51°54′.77 N,	003°07′.49 E
(57)	51°57′.64 N,	003°08′.00 E
(50)	51°59′.13 N,	003°08′.26 E
(45)	52°01′.26 N,	003°08′.37 E
(44)	52°04′.37 N,	003°08′.52 E
(77)	52°05′.55 N,	003°06′.32 E
(71)	52°07′.29 N,	003°03′.08 E
(74)	52°09′.03 N,	002°59′.83 E
(76)	52°10′.99 N,	002°56′.16 E
(87)	51°51′.35 N,	002°28′.70 E
(82)	51°48′.53 N,	002°34′.04 E
(81)	51°47′.88 N,	002°35′.27 E

Notes:
CAUTIONS

1 (Maas Junction precautionary area between "Maas West Outer" traffic separation scheme and "Maas West Inner" traffic separation scheme)

Mariners are warned that, in this precautionary area, ships on routes to and from the traffic separation scheme "Off Texel", the River Scheldt and Europoort are merging or crossing.

2 (Off the seaward entrances to the "Maas West Inner", the "Maas North-west" and the "Maas North" traffic separation schemes)

The precautionary area "Maas Centre" in the approaches to Hook of Holland should be avoided by passing traffic which is not entering or leaving the adjacent ports.

3 (Near the deep-water route in the North Hinder Junction precautionary area and near the "Deep-water route leading to Europoort" between the "Maas West Outer" and the "Maas West Inner" traffic separation schemes)

For ships that have to cross the deep-water route, attention is drawn to rule 18(d)(i) of the 1972 Collision Regulations. Mariners are, however, reminded that, when risk of collision is deemed to exist, the 1972 Collision Regulations fully apply and, in particular, the rules of part B, sections II and III are of specific relevance to the crossing situation.

(chartlet overleaf)

E

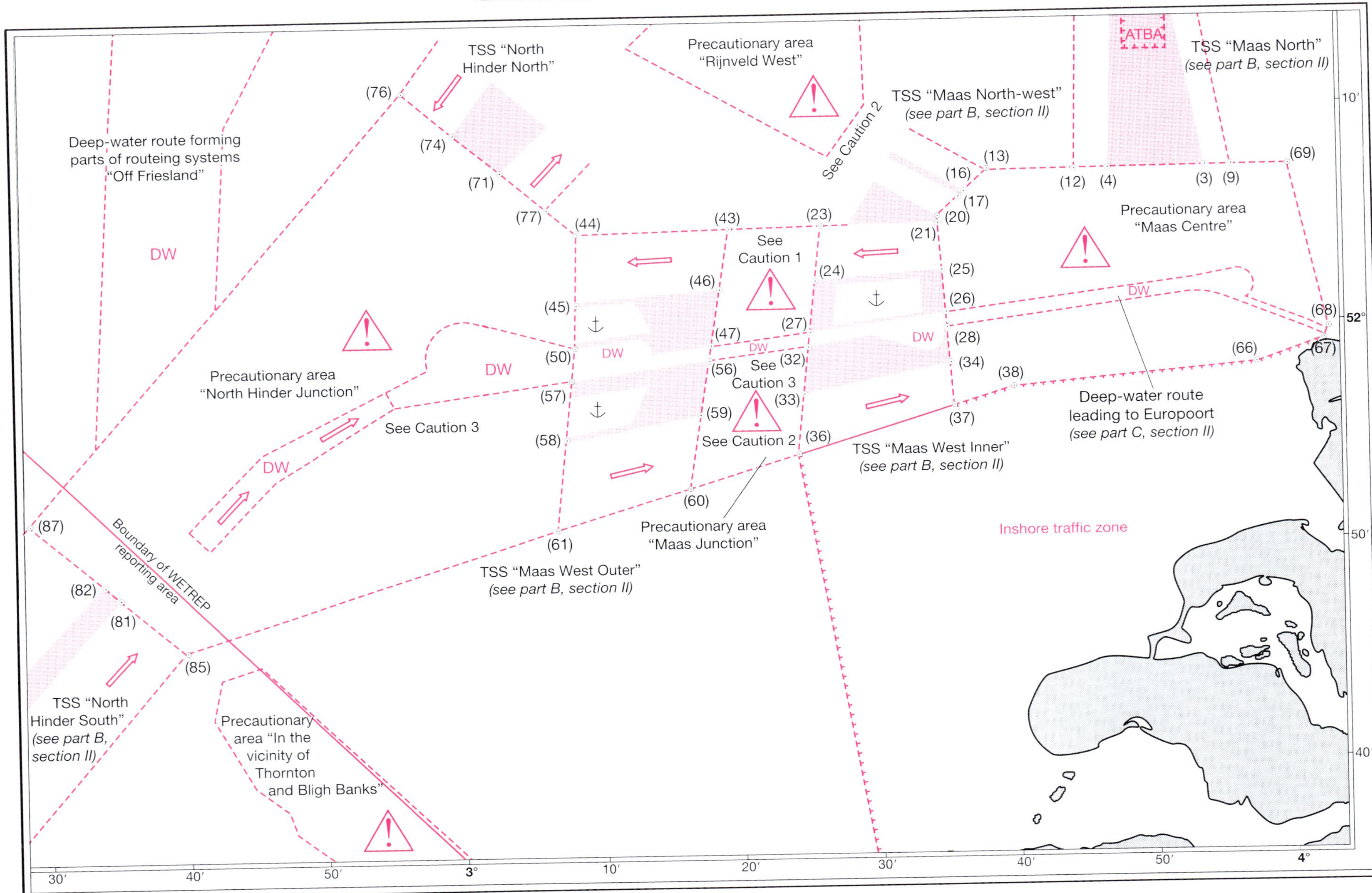

PRECAUTIONARY AREAS IN THE APPROACHES TO HOOK OF HOLLAND AND AT NORTH HINDER

PRECAUTIONARY AREA AND RECOMMENDED DIRECTION OF TRAFFIC FLOW IN THE AREA WEST OF RIJNVELD*

(Reference charts: Netherlands 1630 (INT 1416), edition 4/2010; 1631 (INT 1418), edition 3.
Note: These charts are based on World Geodetic System 1984 datum (WGS 84).)

"Rijnveld West" precautionary area

A precautionary area is established off the entrance to the Rotterdam Waterway. The area is bounded by a line connecting the following geographical positions:

(1)	52°21′.54 N,	003°27′.14 E	(4)	52°07′.81 N,	003°26′.80 E
(2)	52°14′.47 N,	003°29′.38 E	(5)	52°12′.85 N,	003°12′.42 E
(3)	52°10′.15 N,	003°29′.58 E	(6)	52°20′.22 N,	003°24′.90 E

Recommended direction of traffic flow southbound

A recommended direction of traffic flow southbound is established from the southern end of the southbound traffic lane branching from the south-westbound lane of the traffic separation scheme "Off Texel" to the north end of the Rijnveld West precautionary area. The direction is marked on charts by dashed outlined arrows which are placed in a direction of 189.2 degrees in between the following geographical positions:

(6)	52°20′.22 N,	003°24′.90 E	(8)	52°31′.76 N,	003°29′.87 E
(7)	52°31′.94 N,	003°28′.01 E	(1)	52°21′.54 N,	003°27′.14 E

Note:
CAUTION
(Rijnveld West precautionary area)

Mariners are warned that, in this precautionary area, ships on routes to and from the traffic separation scheme "Off Texel", the River Scheldt and Europoort are merging or crossing.

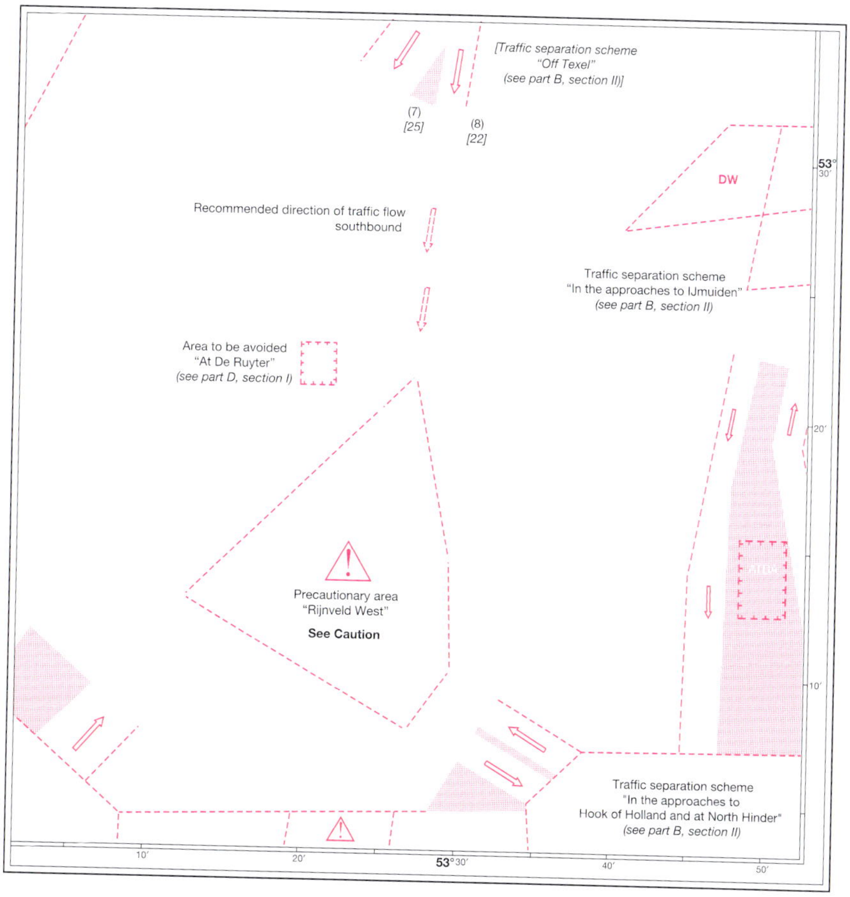

PRECAUTIONARY AREA AND RECOMMENDED DIRECTION OF TRAFFIC FLOW
IN THE AREA WEST OF RIJNVELD

* Date of implementation of new measures: 0000 hours UTC on 1 August 2013.

PRECAUTIONARY AREAS IN THE APPROACHES TO IJMUIDEN*

Note: See traffic separation schemes "In the approaches to IJmuiden" in part B, section II and "Deep-water route leading to IJmuiden" in part C, section II and area to be avoided "By IJmuiden northern approaches" in part D, section I.

(Reference chart: Netherlands 1631 (INT 1418, edition 3).
Note: This chart is based on World Geodetic System 1984 datum (WGS 84).)

IJmuiden Junction precautionary area

(a) A precautionary area between the IJmuiden West Inner and IJmuiden West Outer traffic separation schemes is bounded by a line connecting the following geographical positions:

(21)	52°28′.58 N,	004°10′.85 E	(8)	52°31′.50 N,	004°08′.13 E
(22)	52°28′.29 N,	004°08′.97 E	(15)	52°29′.87 N,	004°09′.28 E
(32)	52°31′.50 N,	004°06′.70 E			

IJmuiden Crossing precautionary area

(a) A precautionary area immediately west of the IJmuiden West Outer traffic separation scheme is established by a line connecting the following geographical positions:

(33)	52°31′.50 N,	003°56′.38 E	(36)	52°25′.16 N,	003°48′.53 E
(35)	52°25′.53 N,	003°54′.43 E	(37)	52°31′.50 N,	003°50′.57 E

Note:
CAUTION

(Near the buoyed deep-water channel route in the IJmuiden Junction and IJmuiden Crossing precautionary areas)
For ships that have to cross the deep-water route leading to IJmuiden, attention is drawn to rule 10(d)(i) of the 1972 Collision Regulations. Mariners are, however, reminded that, when risk of collision is deemed to exist, the 1972 Collision Regulations fully apply and, in particular, the rules of part B, sections II and III are of specific relevance to the crossing situation.

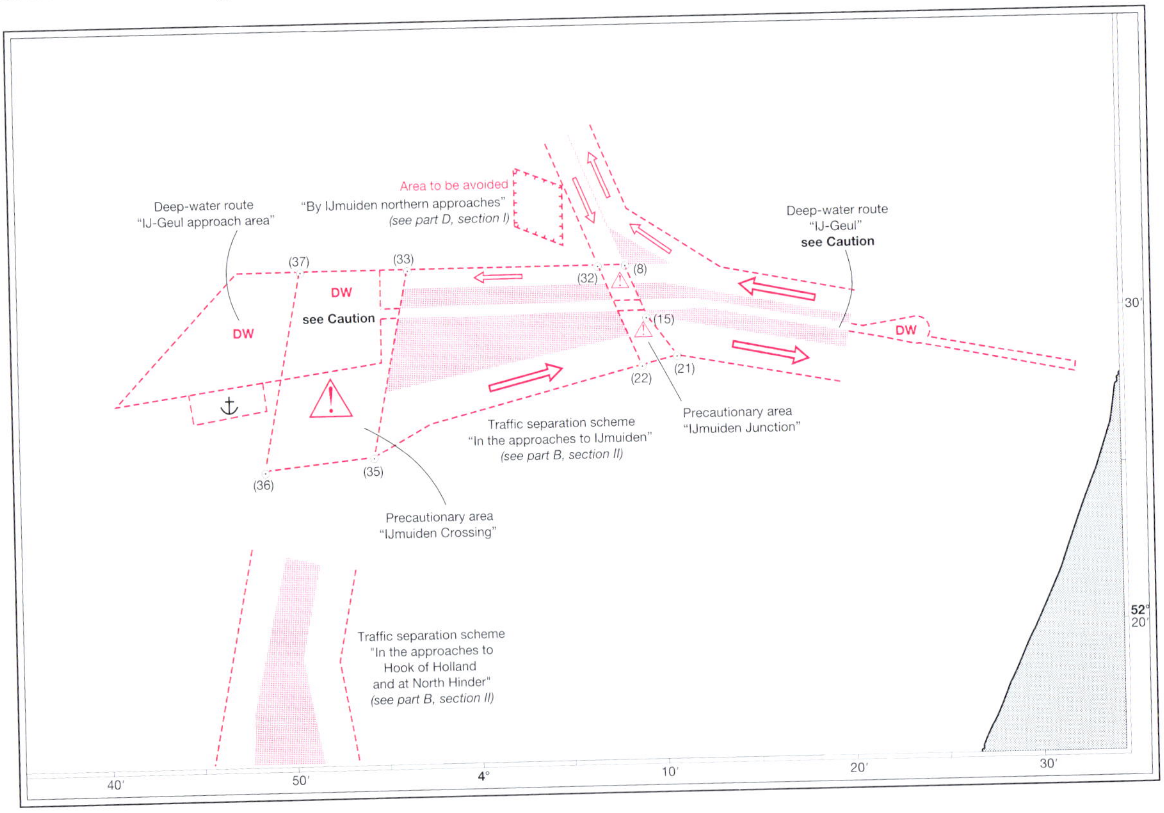

PRECAUTIONARY AREAS IN THE APPROACHES TO IJMUIDEN

* Date of implementation of new precautionary areas: 0000 hours UTC on 1 August 2013.

RECOMMENDATIONS ON NAVIGATION AROUND THE UNITED KINGDOM COAST

The following recommendations are made for specific locations around the coast of the United Kingdom:

.1 *In the Pentland Firth*

Mariners intending to use the Pentland Firth should be aware of very strong tidal streams and sets. Difficulties can be encountered when transiting either with or against the tide and masters should ensure that a close watch is kept at all times on the course, speed and position of their vessels.

Masters of laden tankers not bound to or from Flotta and Scapa Flow should not use the Pentland Firth in restricted visibility or adverse weather. At other times, there may be a case for transiting with the tide to reduce the time spent in the Firth, although masters should take account of the general navigational warning above.

.2 *Off the Isles of Scilly*

Laden tankers over 10,000 gross tonnage using the traffic separation scheme between Land's End and the Isles of Scilly should keep at least three miles to seaward of Wolf Rock, and should not use the scheme in restricted visibility or other adverse weather.

.3 *In The Minches*

Except due to stress of weather or any other case of *force majeure*, all laden tankers over 10,000 gross tonnage should not pass through The Minches.

.4 *In the North Channel*

The present requirements and recommendation as set out in *Ships' Routeing* continue to apply. In addition, no laden tanker should use the narrow passage through Rathlin Sound.

.5 *Off Smalls and Grassholme Channel*

Laden tankers over 10,000 gross tonnage should not use the channel between Grassholme Island and Skomer Island unless moving between the anchorage in St. Bride's Bay and Milford Haven.

.6 *In the Needles Channel*

Due to tidal problems and apparent movement of the sand banks in this channel, laden tankers over 10,000 gross tonnage should avoid this channel.

.7 *In the English Channel and Dover Strait*

All ships navigating in this area should have on board the latest edition of Chart 5500, Mariners Routeing Guide English Channel and Southern North Sea, or other equivalent guides.

.8 *In the Firth of Forth*

Laden tankers should avoid the area between Bass Rock and the coast.

E

Reporting requirements

The following recommendations are associated with the areas set out in the previous paragraph and in Recommended routes in the Fair Isle Channel.

Ships intending to use the following routes, when at least one hour from the Estimated Time of Arrival of entering the route, and on final departure, should report to Coastguard as described below.

Route	*Ship condition*	*Report to Coastguard*	*Report on VHF channel*
Fair Isle	laden	Shetland	16
Pentland Firth	laden	Pentland	16
The Minches	ALL ships over 300 gt	Stornoway*	16
Isles of Scilly	laden	Falmouth	16
Dover Strait TSS	**ALL SHIPS**	Dover or Cap Gris Nez	69
Casquets TSS	**ALL SHIPS**	Jobourg	69

* Voluntary reports can be made when passing the positions that are shown on the next page, which are relative to Ordnance Survey of Great Britain 1936 datum.

	Reporting reference	Latitude	Longitude
Southbound			
Initial Report	When passing	58°30′.00 N	
	B	57°58′.00 N	006°17′.00 W
	C	57°28′.50 N	006°54′.40 W
Final Report	When passing	57°00′.00 N	
Northbound			
Initial Report	When passing	57°00′.00 N	
	E	57°23′.80 N	006°51′.80 W
	F	57°40′.40 N	006°32′.00 W
Final Report	When passing	58°30′.00 N	

Format of reports

The reporting should be in accordance with IMO resolution A.648(16)* adopted on 19 October 1989 and should include the following:

ALFA	Name and call sign of the ship
BRAVO	Day of month (two figures) and time in hours and minutes (UT (GMT) in four figures)
CHARLIE	Latitude (4 figures + N or S) and longitude (5 figures + E or W)
DELTA	True bearing (first 3 figures) and distance in nautical miles from identified landmark
ECHO	True course in degrees (3 figures)
FOXTROT	Speed in knots and decimal of knots (3 figures)
GOLF	Last port of call
INDIA	Destination
MIKE	VHF Channels monitored
OSCAR	Deepest draught in metres and centimetres
PAPA	Type and quantity (tonnes) of cargo
QUEBEC	Brief details of damage/deficiency/other limitations.

E

* This has been revoked by resolution A.851(20).

RECOMMENDED DIRECTIONS OF TRAFFIC FLOW IN THE GERMAN BIGHT

Note: See the following traffic separation schemes in the German Bight: "Terschelling–German Bight", "Jade approach", "Elbe approach" and "German Bight western approach" (part B, section II).

Recommended directions of traffic flow are established between the traffic separation scheme "Elbe approach" and the eastern ends of the traffic separation schemes "Terschelling–German Bight" and "German Bight western approach" as shown in the chartlet below.

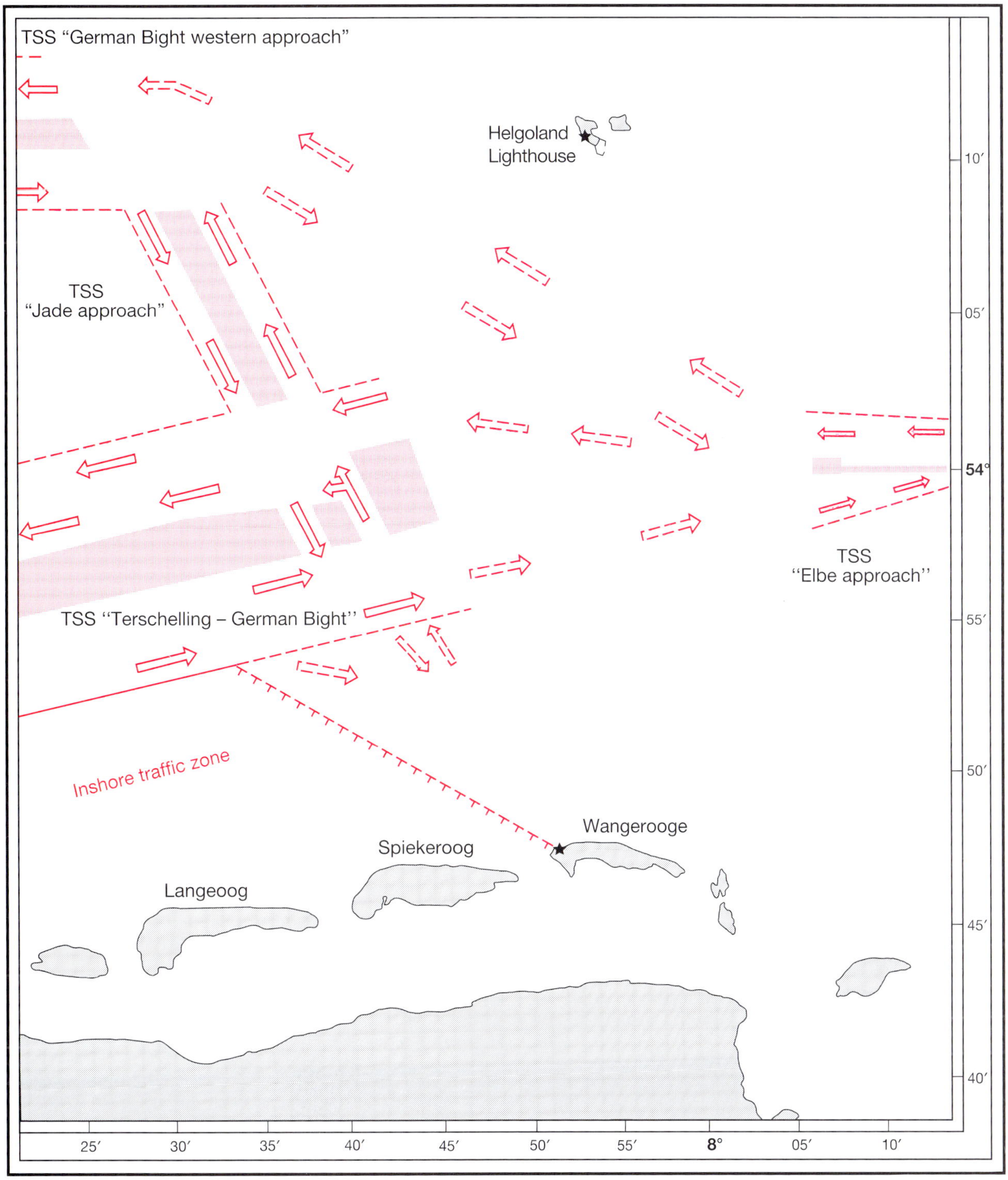

RECOMMENDED DIRECTIONS OF TRAFFIC FLOW IN THE GERMAN BIGHT

E

RECOMMENDED ROUTES IN THE FAIR ISLE CHANNEL

Note: See "Recommendations on navigation around the United Kingdom coast" and mandatory ship reporting system "West European Tanker Reporting System" in part G, section I.

Recommended directions of traffic flow are established in the Fair Isle Strait as follows:

(a) a single recommended route to the north of Fair Isle for use by westbound traffic; and

(b) separate recommended routes to the south-west of Fair Isle with eastbound traffic taking a route north-east of North Ronaldsay, and with westbound traffic taking a route to the south-west of Fair Isle.

These routes are recommended for use by all ships transiting the area.

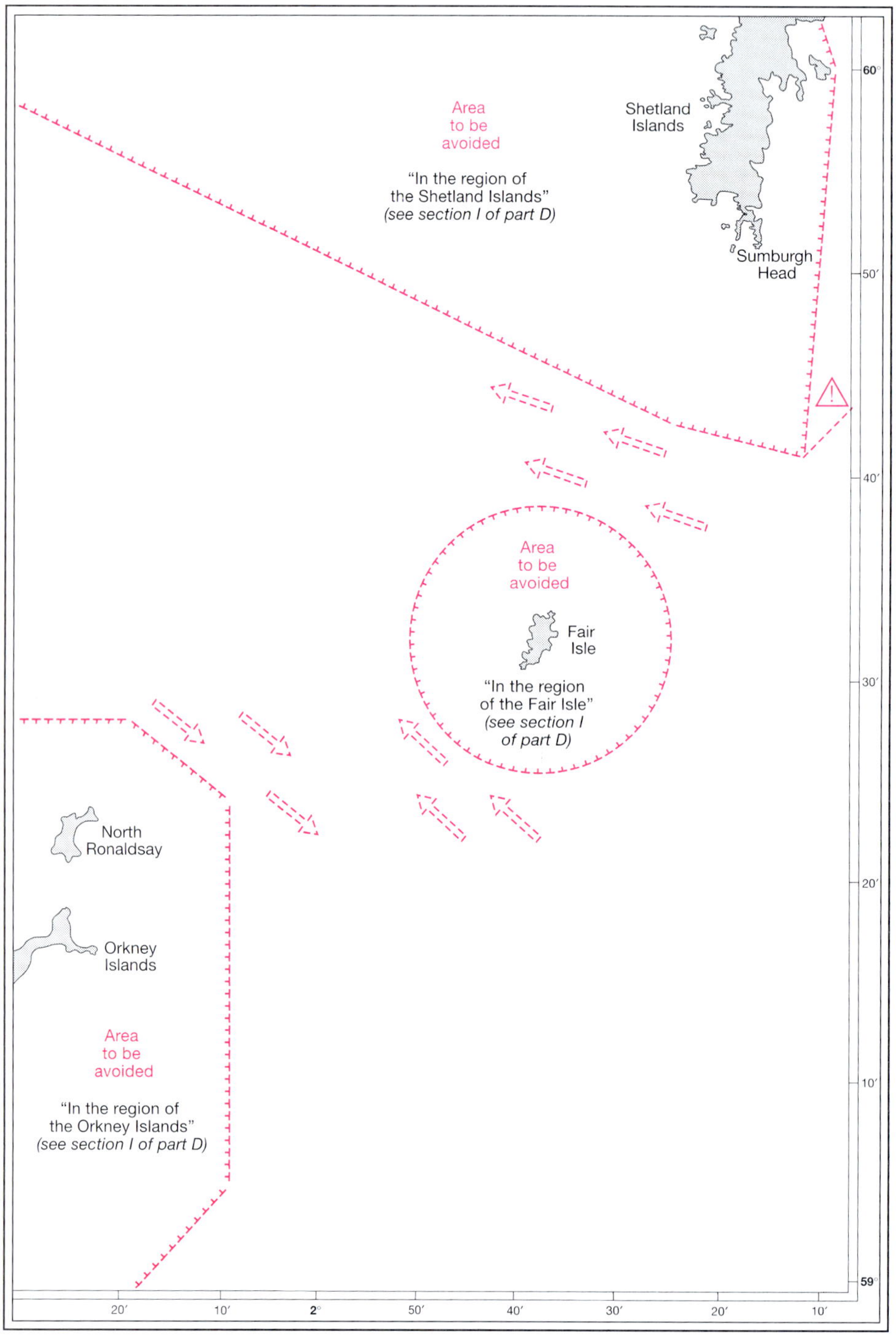

RECOMMENDED ROUTES IN THE FAIR ISLE CHANNEL

RECOMMENDED ROUTES JOINING THE TRAFFIC SEPARATION SCHEMES OFF THE COAST OF SOUTHERN NORWAY*

(Reference charts: Norwegian 305 (INT 1300) and 306 published by the Norwegian Hydrographic Service. **Note:** Chart 305 (INT 1300) is based on World Geodetic System 1984 datum (WGS 84) and chart 306 is based on European Datum 1950 (ED 50). The geographical positions, (56) to (63), listed below are based on World Geodetic System 1984 datum (WGS 84).)

Categories of ships to which the traffic separation schemes apply

(a) tankers as defined in Annex I of the International Convention for the Prevention of Pollution from Ships, 1973, as modified by the Protocol of 1978 (MARPOL 73/78);

(b) chemical tankers carrying noxious liquid substances in bulk assessed or provisionally assessed as Category X or Y in Annex II to MARPOL 73/78;

(c) ships of 5000 gross tonnage and upwards, in transit or on international voyages to or from Norwegian ports; and

(d) the routeing schemes **do not apply** to any size or category of ship in domestic traffic with passengers and/or goods between Norwegian ports.

International voyages to or from ports in Norway

Ships of above categories on international voyages, to or from ports in Norway, should follow the ships' routeing system until a course to port can be clearly set. This also applies to ships calling at Norwegian ports for supplies or service.

Description of the recommended routes

(p) A recommended route is established between the traffic separation schemes "Off Egersund" and "Off Farsund" with a central line between the following geographical positions:
(56) 58°17′.60 N, 005°24′.85 E (57) 57°47′.38 N, 006°31′.65 E

(q) A recommended route is established between the traffic separation schemes "Off Farsund" and "Off Ryvingen" with a central line between the following geographical positions:
(58) 57°45′.33 N, 006°41′.57 E (59) 57°43′.82 N, 007°41′.97 E

(r) A recommended route is established between the traffic separation schemes "Off Ryvingen" and "Off Lillesand" with a central line between the following geographical positions:
(60) 57°44′.70 N, 007°55′.23 E (61) 57°59′.17 N, 008°46′.03 E

(s) A recommended route is established between the traffic separation schemes "Off Lillesand" and "Off Risør" with a central line between the following geographical positions:
(62) 58°02′.78 N, 008°54′.80 E (63) 58°26′.95 N, 009°34′.78 E

Note: Typical shifts of position co-ordinates referred to the WGS 84 datum to the ED 50 datum are:

From datum	To datum	Approximate latitude in the area	Datum shift
WGS 84	ED 50	62° 30′ N	99 m (NE-diagonal)
WGS 84	ED 50	59° 00′ N	109 m (NE-diagonal)

(chartlets overleaf)

* Date of implementation of new routes: 0000 hours UTC on 1 June 2011.

E

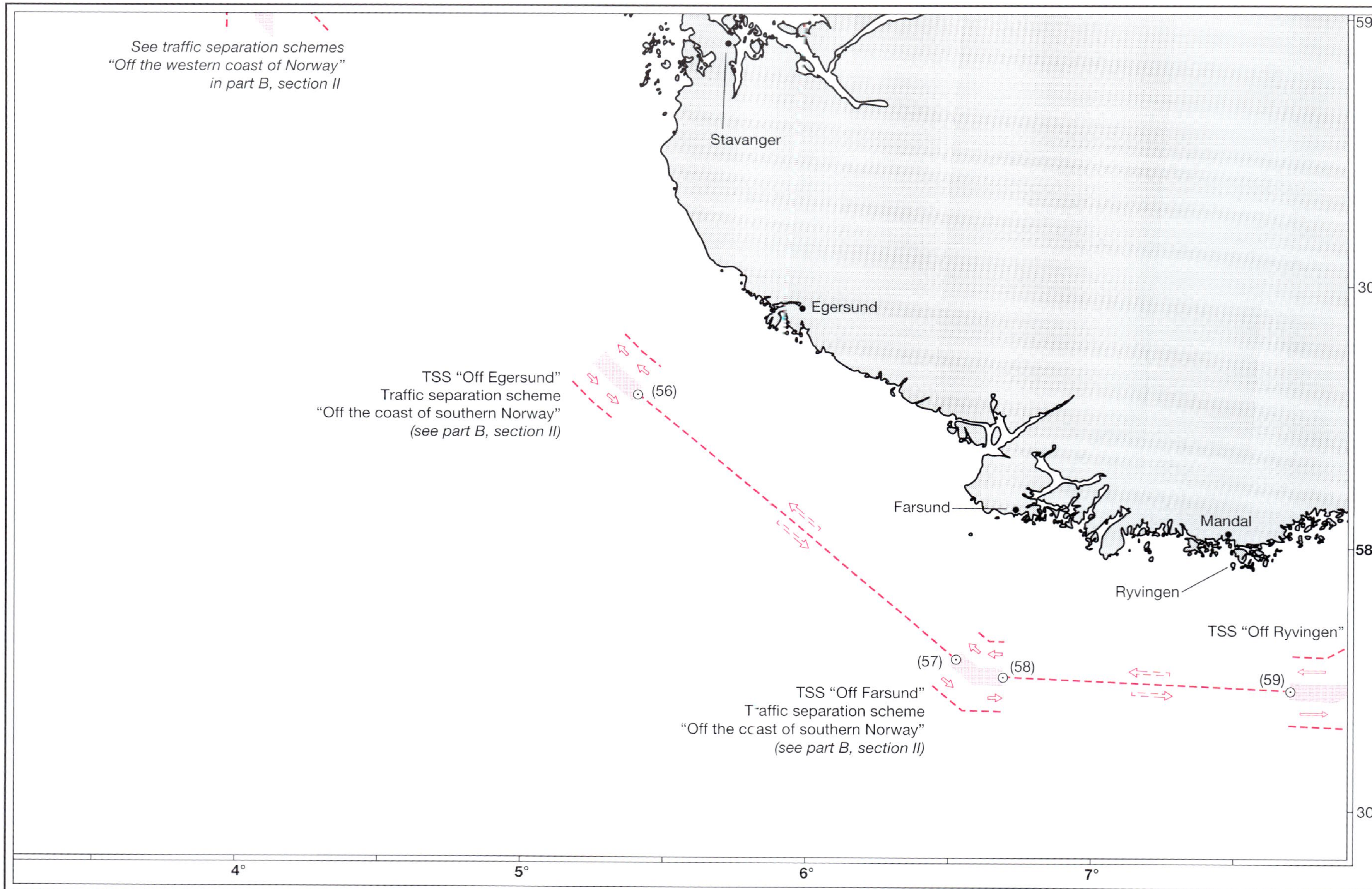

RECOMMENDED ROUTES JOINING THE TRAFFIC SEPARATION SCHEMES OFF THE COAST OF SOUTHERN NORWAY – WEST

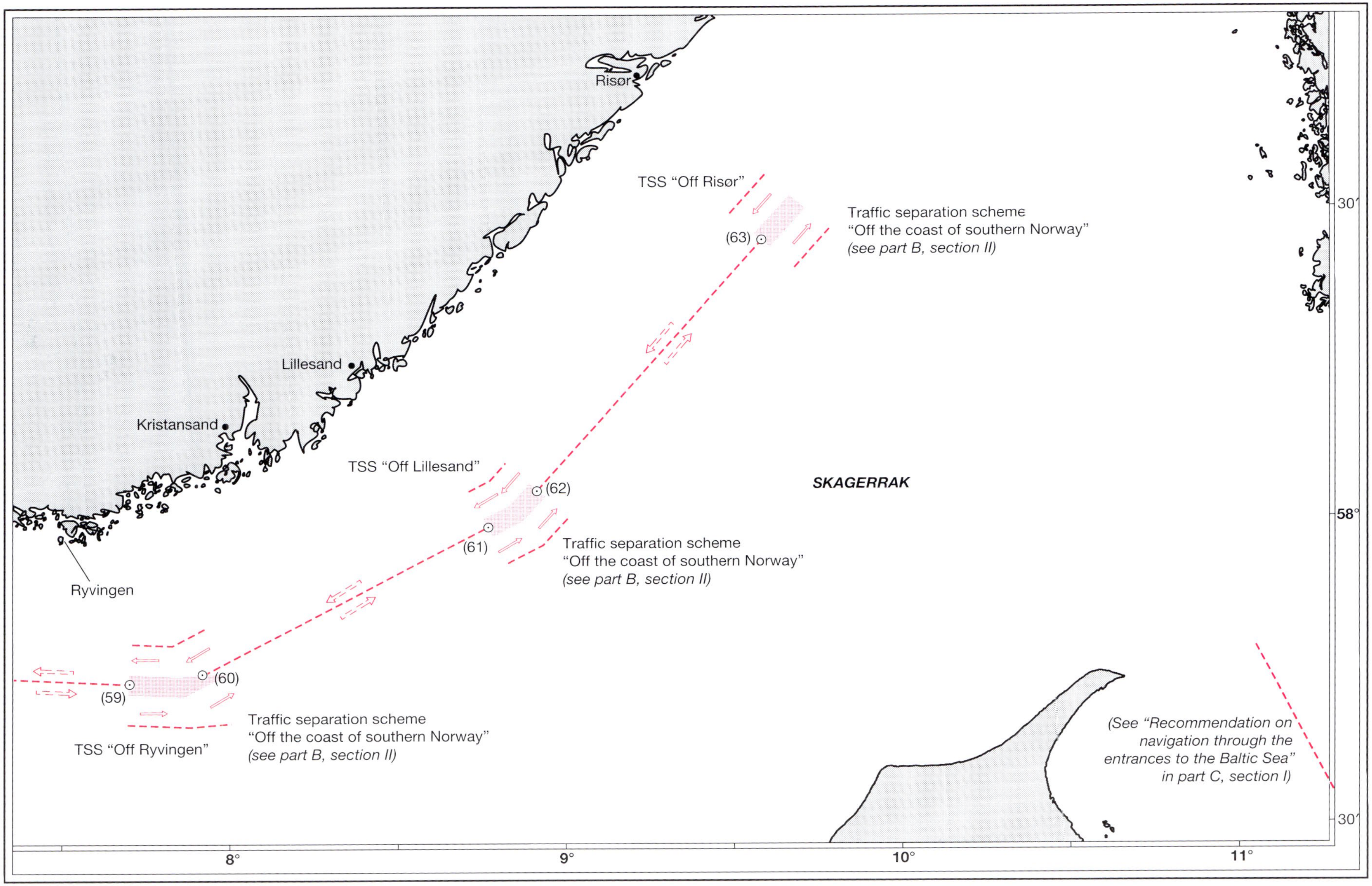

RECOMMENDED ROUTES JOINING THE TRAFFIC SEPARATION SCHEMES OFF THE COAST OF SOUTHERN NORWAY – EAST

E

RECOMMENDED ROUTES JOINING THE TRAFFIC SEPARATION SCHEMES OFF THE WESTERN COAST OF NORWAY*

(Reference charts: Norwegian 306, 307 and 308 published by the Norwegian Hydrographic Service.
Note: These charts are based on European Datum 1950 (ED 50). The geographical positions, (38) to (43), listed below are based on World Geodetic System 1984 datum (WGS 84).)

Categories of ships to which the traffic separation schemes apply

(a) tankers as defined in Annex I of the International Convention for the Prevention of Pollution from Ships, 1973, as modified by the Protocol of 1978 (MARPOL 73/78);

(b) chemical tankers carrying noxious liquid substances in bulk assessed or provisionally assessed as Category X or Y in Annex II to MARPOL 73/78;

(c) ships of 5000 gross tonnage and upwards, in transit or on international voyages to or from Norwegian ports; and

(d) the routeing schemes **do not apply** to any size or category of ship in domestic traffic with passengers and/or goods between Norwegian ports.

International voyages to or from ports in Norway

Ships of above categories on international voyages, to or from ports in Norway, should follow the ships' routeing system until a course to port can be clearly set. This also applies to ships calling at Norwegian ports for supplies or service.

Description of the recommended routes

(m) A recommended route is established between the traffic separation schemes "Off Runde" and "Off Stad" with a central line between the following geographical positions:

(38) 62°50′.00 N, 004°06′.25 E (39) 61°59′.00 N, 004°06′.25 E

(n) A recommended route is established between the traffic separation schemes "Off Stad" and "Off Sotra" with a central line between the following geographical positions:

(40) 61°54′.00 N, 004°06′.25 E (41) 60°20′.00 N, 004°06′.25 E

(o) A recommended route is established between the traffic separation schemes "Off Sotra" and "Off Utsira" with a central line between the following geographical positions:

(42) 60°15′.00 N, 004°06′.25 E (43) 59°05′.00 N, 004°06′.25 E

Note: Typical shifts of position co-ordinates referred to the WGS 84 datum to the ED 50 datum are:

From datum	To datum	Approximate latitude in the area	Datum shift
WGS 84	ED 50	62° 30′ N	99 m (NE-diagonal)
WGS 84	ED 50	59° 00′ N	109 m (NE-diagonal)

E

* Date of implementation of new routes: 0000 hours UTC on 1 June 2011.

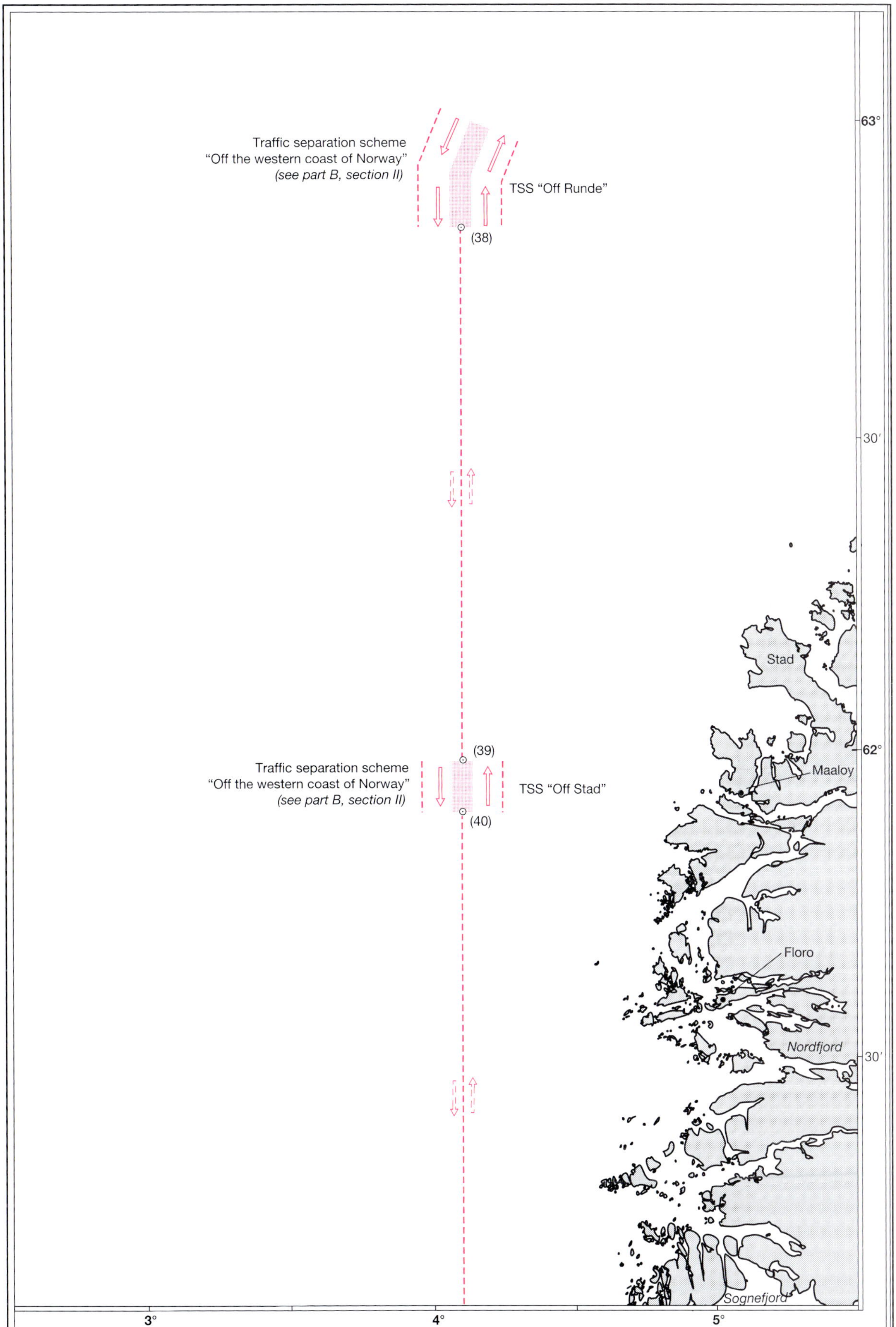

RECOMMENDED ROUTES JOINING THE TRAFFIC SEPARATION SCHEMES OFF THE WESTERN COAST OF NORWAY – NORTH

E

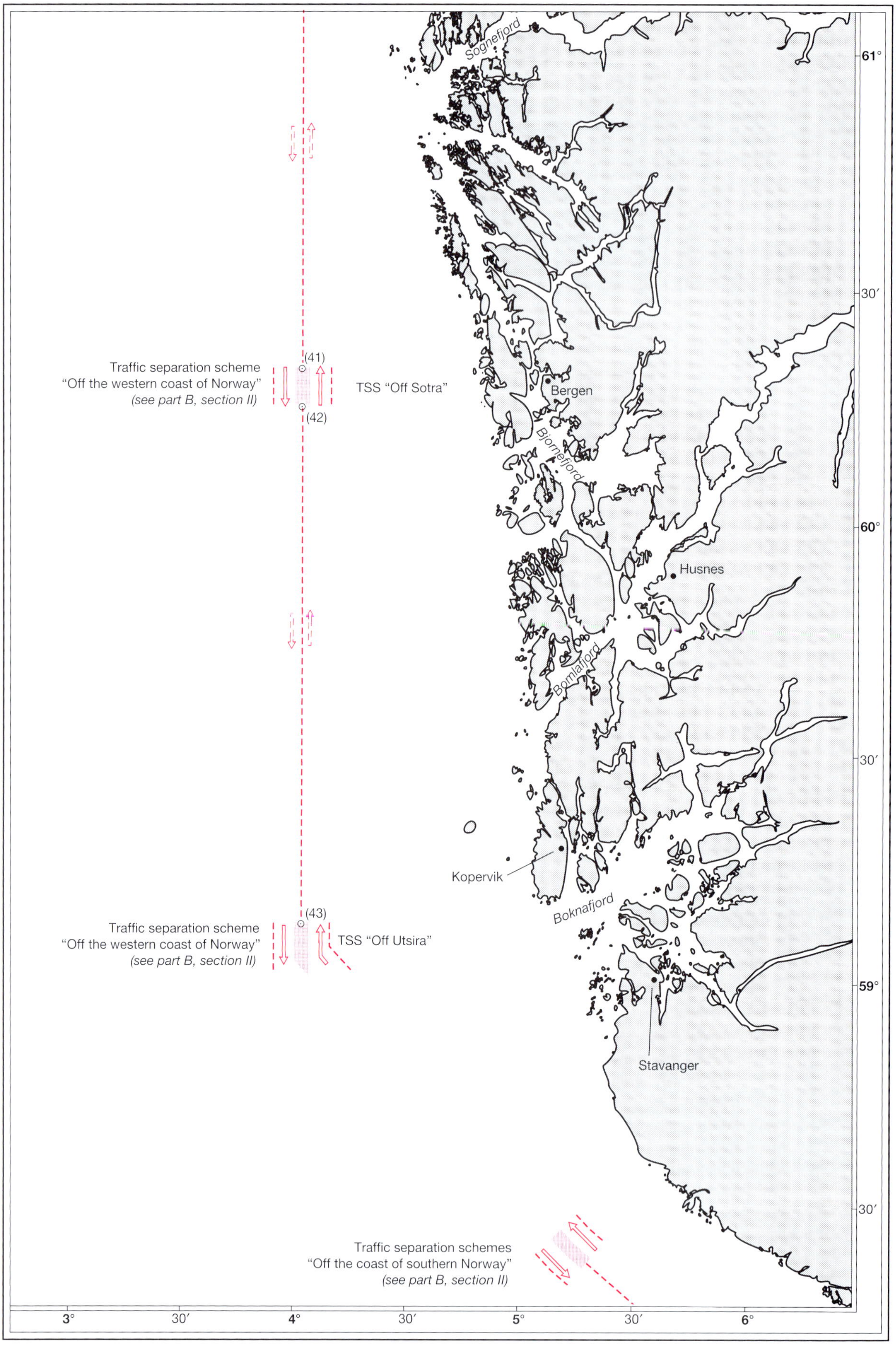

RECOMMENDED ROUTES JOINING THE TRAFFIC SEPARATION SCHEMES OFF THE WESTERN COAST OF NORWAY – SOUTH

RECOMMENDED ROUTES JOINING THE TRAFFIC SEPARATION SCHEMES OFF THE COAST OF NORWAY FROM VARDØ TO RØST

Note: See mandatory ship reporting system "In the Barents area" in part G, section I.

(Reference charts: Norwegian Hydrographic Service Fisheries Chart Series 551, 1963 edition; 552, 1964 edition; 557, 1966 edition. These charts are based on European datum 1950 (ED 50).
Note: The geographical positions (85)–(98) listed below are given in the WGS 84 datum.)

Categories of ships to which the traffic separation schemes apply

Tankers of all sizes, including gas and chemical tankers, and all other cargo ships of 5000 gross tonnage and upwards engaged on international voyages should follow the routeing system consisting of a series of traffic separation schemes joined by recommended routes off the coast of Norway from Vardø to Røst.

International voyages to or from ports in Norway from Vardø to Røst

Ships on international voyages to or from ports in Norway from Vardø to Røst should follow the ship's routeing systems until a course to port can be clearly set. This also applies to ships calling at Norwegian ports for supplies or service.

Description of the recommended routes

(y) A recommended route is established between the traffic separation schemes "Off Vardø" and "Off Slettnes" with a central line between the following geographical positions:

(85) 70°50′.43 N, 031°31′.22 E (86) 71°23′.64 N, 029°13′.67 E

(z) A recommended route is established between the traffic separation schemes "Off Slettnes" and "Off North Cape" with a central line between the following geographical positions:

(87) 71°28′.28 N, 028°42′.65 E (88) 71°41′.20 N, 026°10′.59 E

(aa) A recommended route is established between the traffic separation schemes "Off North Cape" and "Off Sørøya" with a central line between the following geographical positions:

(89) 71°41′.50 N, 025°26′.81 E (90) 71°31′.20 N, 022°39′.83 E

(bb) A recommended route is established between the traffic separation schemes "Off Sørøya" and "Off Torsvåg" with a central line between the following geographical positions:

(91) 71°27′.06 N, 022°00′.01 E (92) 71°03′.18 N, 019°13′.28 E

(cc) A recommended route is established between the traffic separation schemes "Off Torsvåg" and "Off Andenes" with a central line between the following geographical positions:

(93) 70°55′.68 N, 018°38′.05 E (94) 69°49′.78 N, 015°05′.38 E

(dd) A recommended route is established between the traffic separation schemes "Off Andenes" and "Off Røst (1)" with a central line between the following geographical positions:

(95) 69°43′.79 N, 014°47′.17 E (96) 68°13′.89 N, 010°15′.05 E

(ee) A recommended route is established between the traffic separation schemes "Off Røst (1)" and "Off Røst (2)" with a central line between the following geographical positions:

(97) 68°02′.84 N, 009°52′.08 E (98) 67°38′.34 N, 009°19′.26 E

(chartlets overleaf)

E

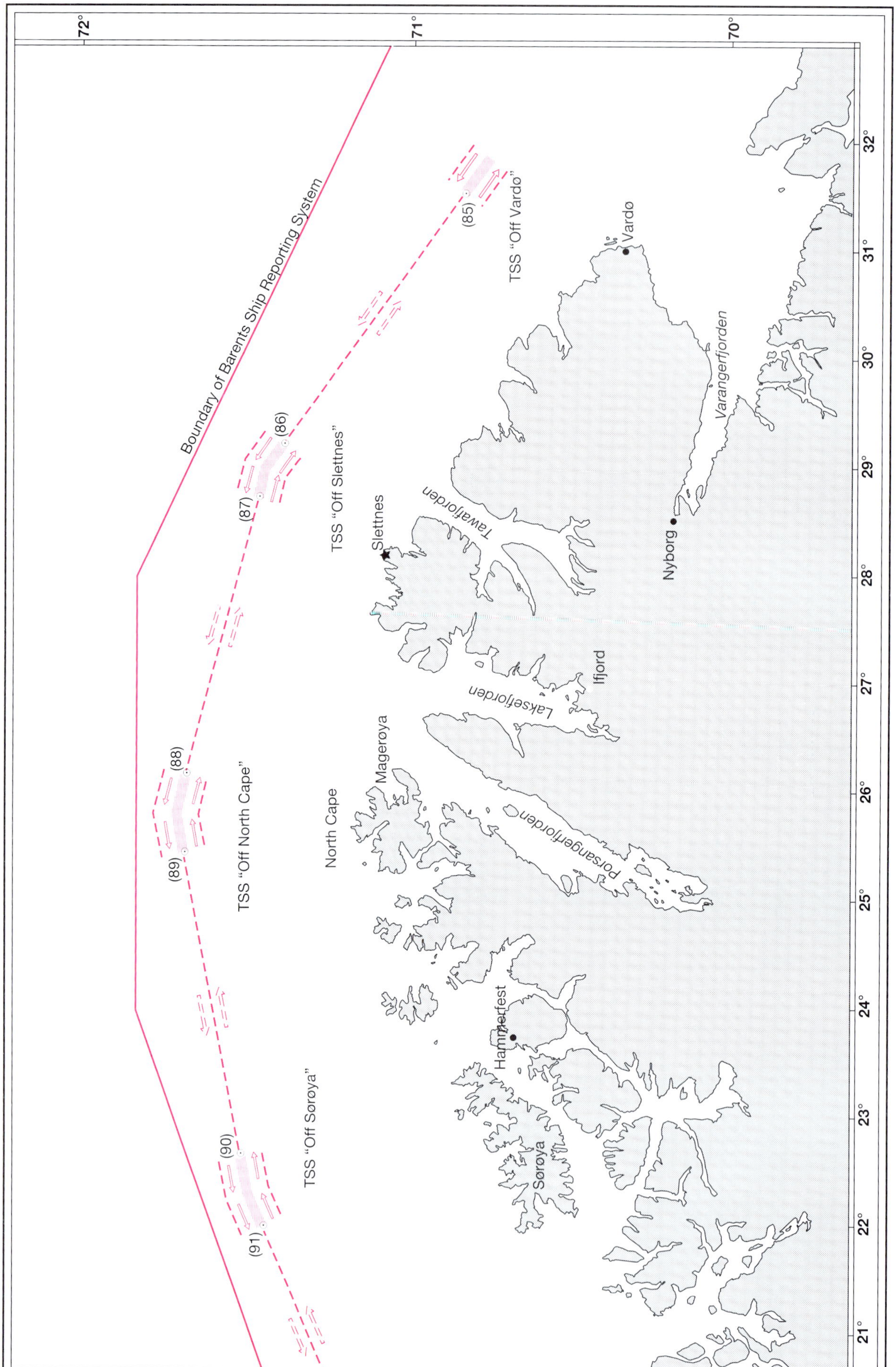

RECOMMENDED ROUTES OFF THE COAST OF NORWAY FROM VARDØ TO RØST – Off Vardø to Off Sørøya

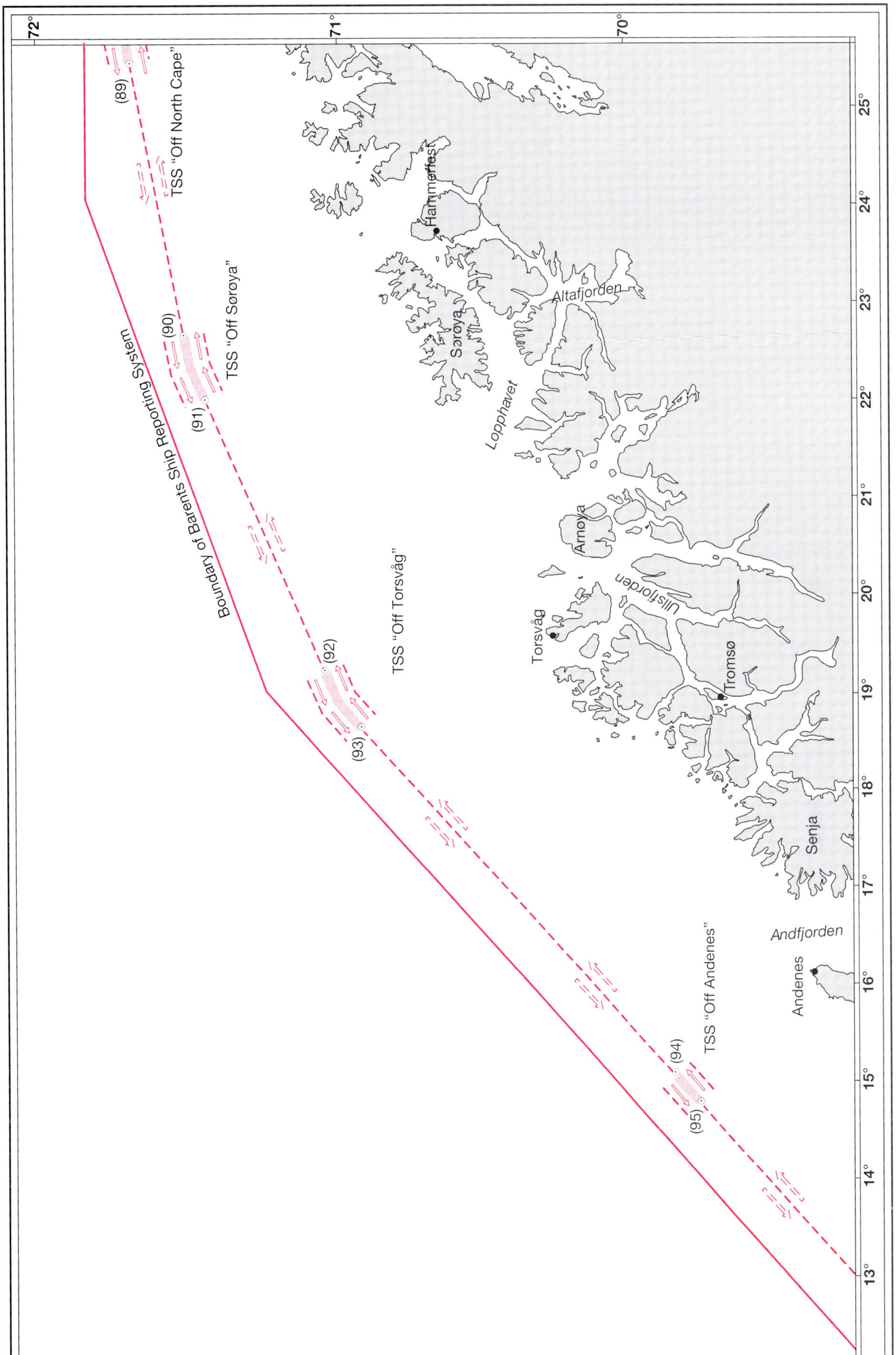

RECOMMENDED ROUTES OFF THE COAST OF NORWAY FROM VARDØ TO RØST – Off North Cape to Off Andenes

E

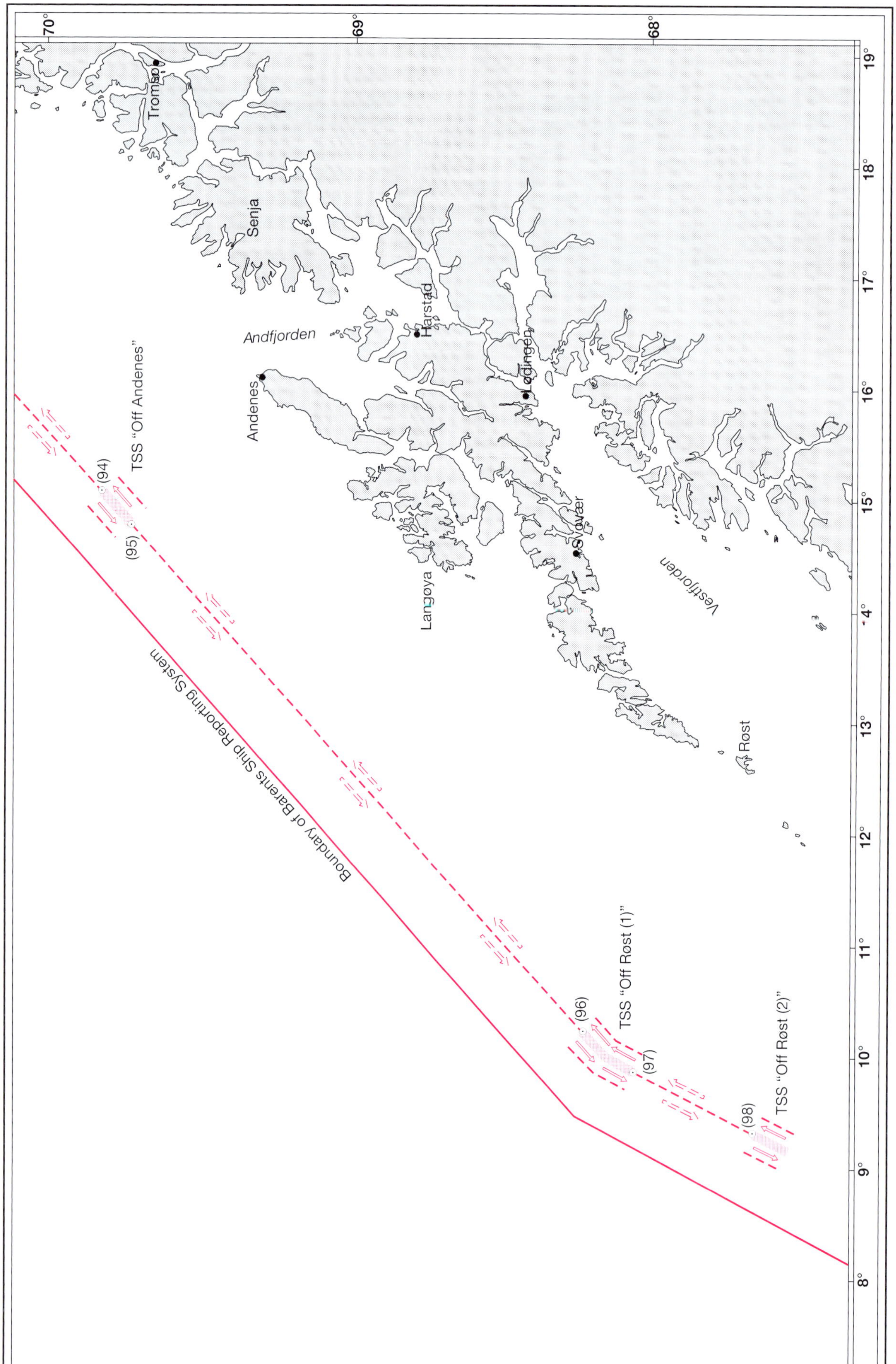

RECOMMENDED ROUTES OFF THE COAST OF NORWAY FROM VARDØ TO RØST – Off Andenes to Off Røst (2).

E

RECOMMENDED ROUTES IN THE MINCHES

Note: See "Recommendations on navigation around the United Kingdom coast" in part E and mandatory ship reporting system "West European Tanker Reporting System" in part G, section I.

(Reference charts: British Admiralty 2635, 1794, 1795.
Note: These charts are based on Ordnance Survey of Great Britain 1936 datum. Position co-ordinates in colour are based on World Geodetic System 1984 datum.)

Description of recommended routes

A recommended route for southbound traffic is defined by a line connecting the following geographical positions:

(1)	57°58′.00 N,	006°17′.00 W	(1)	57°57′.98 N,	006°17′.07 W
(2)	57°54′.00 N,	006°30′.00 W	(2)	57°53′.98 N,	006°30′.06 W
(3)	57°47′.00 N,	006°41′.00 W	(3)	57°46′.98 N,	006°41′.06 W

A recommended route for northbound traffic is defined by a line connecting the following geographical positions:

(4)	57°40′.00 N,	006°32′.14 W	(4)	57°40′.35 N,	006°32′.20 W
(5)	57°45′.00 N,	006°16′.00 W	(5)	57°44′.98 N,	006°16′.06 W
(6)	57°52′.00 N,	006°03′.00 W	(6)	57°51′.98 N,	006°03′.07 W

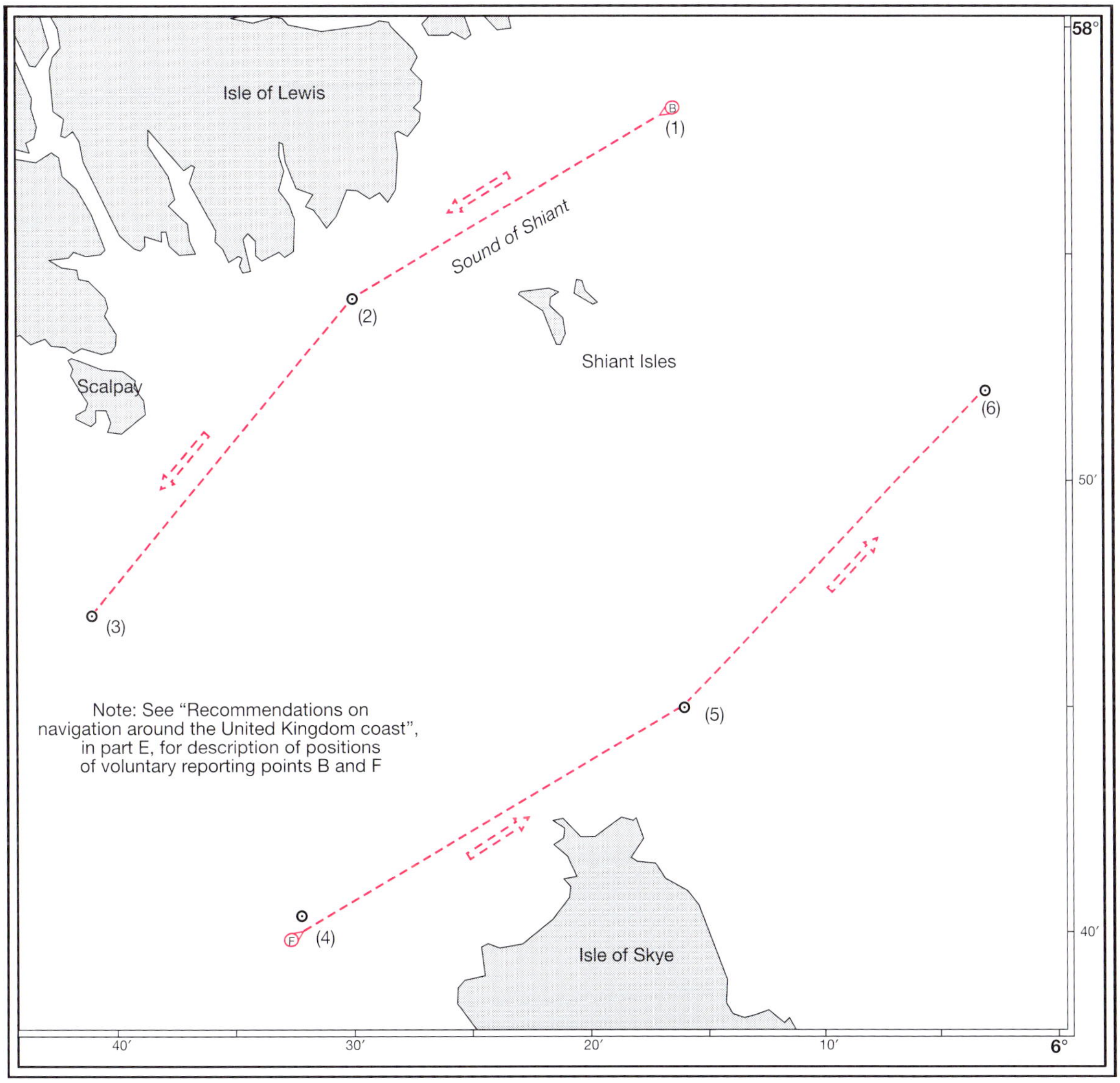

RECOMMENDED ROUTES IN THE MINCHES

TWO-WAY ROUTES OFF THE SOUTH-WEST COAST OF ICELAND

(Reference chart: Icelandic 31 (INT 1105), June 2004 edition.
Note: This chart is based on World Geodetic System 1984 datum (WGS 84).)

Description of the two-way route in the Hullið Passage

The routeing measure consists of a two-way route (the Inner Route) west of the Reykjanes Peninsula, located between the eastern and western areas to be avoided, established by lines connecting the following geographical positions:

(18)	64°01′.70 N,	022°58′.30 W	(22)	63°45′.80 N,	022°44′.40 W
(19)	63°49′.20 N,	022°47′.30 W	(23)	63°40′.90 N,	022°40′.20 W
(20)	63°48′.00 N,	022°48′.40 W	(26)	63°39′.70 N,	022°46′.70 W
(21)	63°47′.00 N,	022°47′.60 W	(27)	63°59′.10 N,	023°03′.50 W

There are also two-way routes attached to both ends of the traffic separation scheme north-west of Garðskagi Point and a two-way route attached to the northern end of the traffic separation scheme south-west of the Reykjanes Peninsula (see section II of part B).

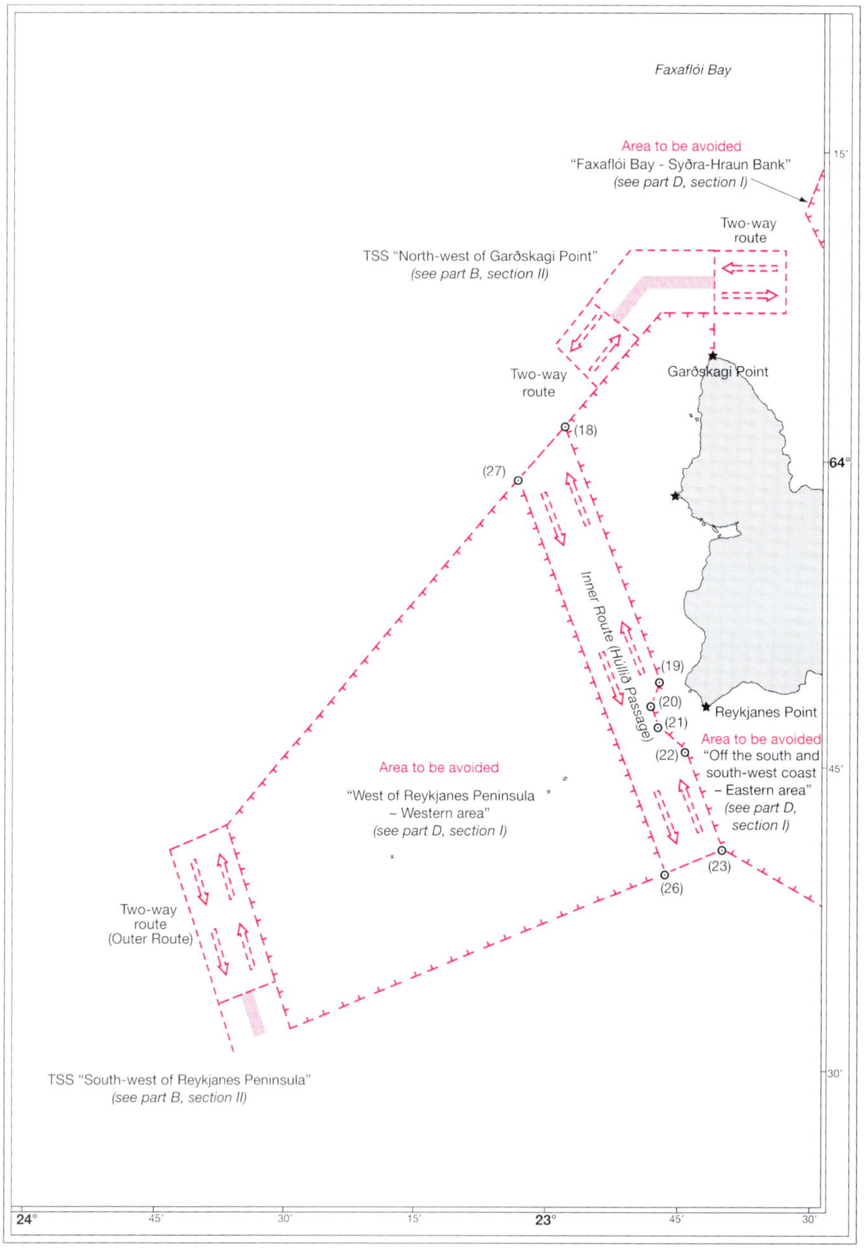

TWO-WAY ROUTES OFF THE SOUTH-WEST COAST OF ICELAND

RECOMMENDED DIRECTIONS OF TRAFFIC FLOW WITHIN THE PRECAUTIONARY AREA OFF TANGER-MED IN THE STRAIT OF GIBRALTAR

Note: See mandatory ship reporting system "In the Strait of Gibraltar" in part G, section I.

(Reference chart: Spanish 445, December 2003 edition.
Note: This chart is based on World Geodetic System 1984 datum (WGS 84).)

Description of the precautionary area off Tanger-Med

A precautionary area with recommended directions of traffic flow is established off the Moroccan port of Tanger-Med in the Gibraltar traffic separation scheme, formed by the lines connecting the following geographical positions:

(8)	36°00′.35 N,	005°28′.98 W	(14)	35°54′.97 N,	005°32′.25 W
(9)	35°59′.07 N,	005°33′.87 W	(15)	35°56′.35 N,	005°27′.40 W

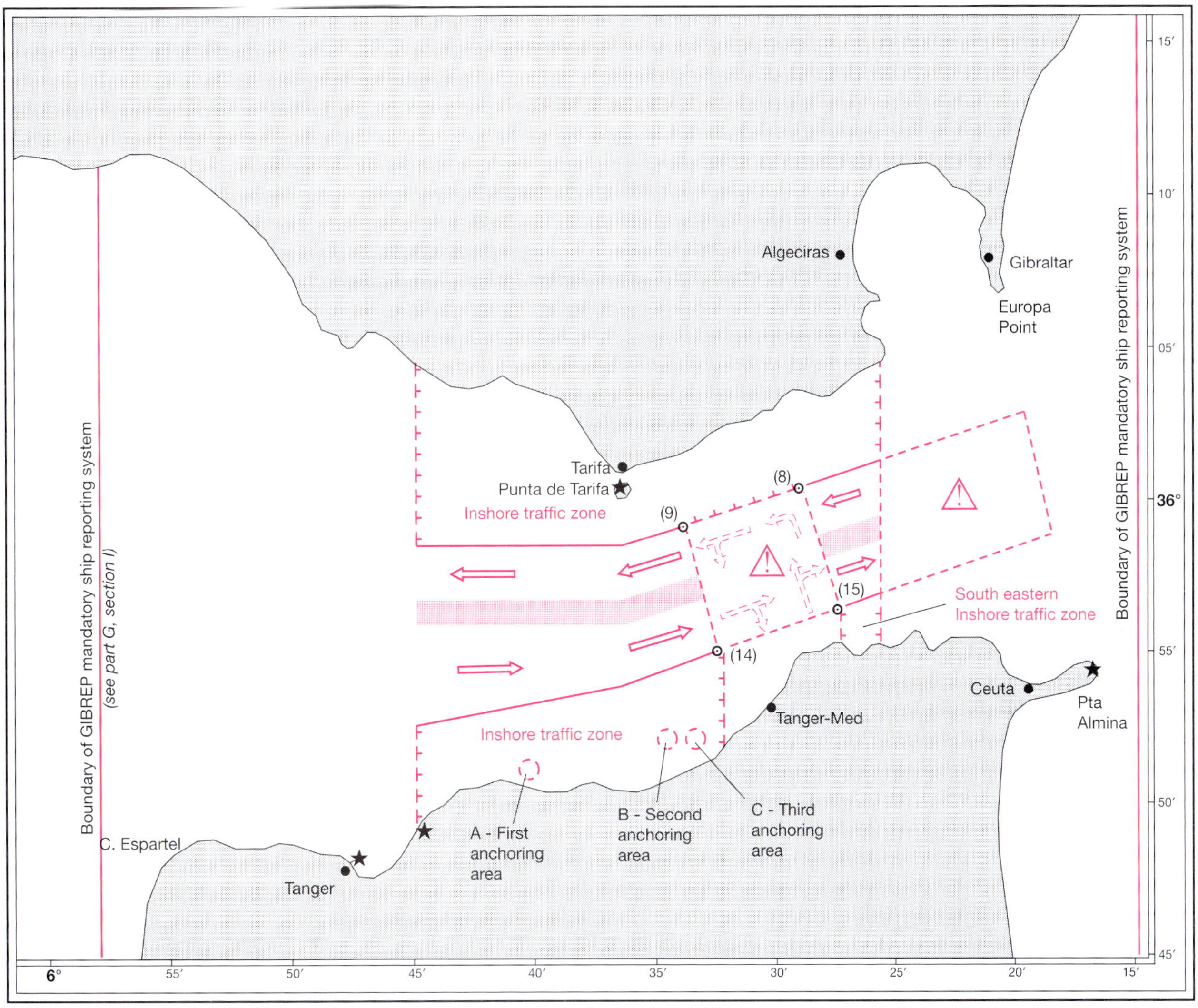

RECOMMENDED DIRECTIONS OF TRAFFIC FLOW WITHIN THE PRECAUTIONARY AREA OFF TANGER-MED IN THE STRAIT OF GIBRALTAR

ROUTEING MEASURES IN THE STRAIT OF BONIFACIO

Note: See "Recommendation on navigation through the Strait of Bonifacio" in part F and mandatory ship reporting system "In the Strait of Bonifacio" in part G, section I.

(Reference chart: French 7024 of the SHOM [Service hydrographique et océanographique de la Marine (Hydrographic and Oceanographic Service of the French Navy)] (INT 3350).
Note: This chart is based on European datum.)

1 Two-way route in the Strait of Bonifacio

1.1 *Categories of ships concerned*

All ships of more than 20 metres of overall length transiting through the Strait.

1.2 *Description*

Northern limit:

a line joining the geographical positions:

(1)	41°22′.55 N,	009°22′.38 E	(3)	41°19′.18 N,	009°06′.51 E
(2)	41°18′.00 N,	009°15′.25 E			

Southern limit:

a line joining the geographical positions:

(4)	41°21′.58 N,	009°23′.30 E	(6)	41°16′.75 N,	009°06′.18 E
(5)	41°16′.75 N,	009°15′.75 E			

2 Precautionary areas at the extremities of the two-way route

2.1 *Categories of ships concerned*

All ships.

2.2 *Eastern precautionary area*

A circular sector pointed on geographical position (7) [41°22′.05 N, 009°22′.85 E] with a radius of 5 nautical miles limited by lines joining geographical positions (1) (see above) and (8) [41°26′.90 N, 009°24′.50 E] and joining geographical positions (4) (see above) and (9) [41°19′.31 N, 009°28′.40 E].

2.3 *Western precautionary area*

A circular sector pointed on geographical position (10) [41°17′.96 N, 009°06′.33 E] with a radius of 5 nautical miles limited by lines joining geographical positions (3) (see above) and (11) [41°21′.37 N, 009°01′.47 E] and joining geographical positions (6) (see above) and (12) [41°13′.57 N, 009°03′.15 E].

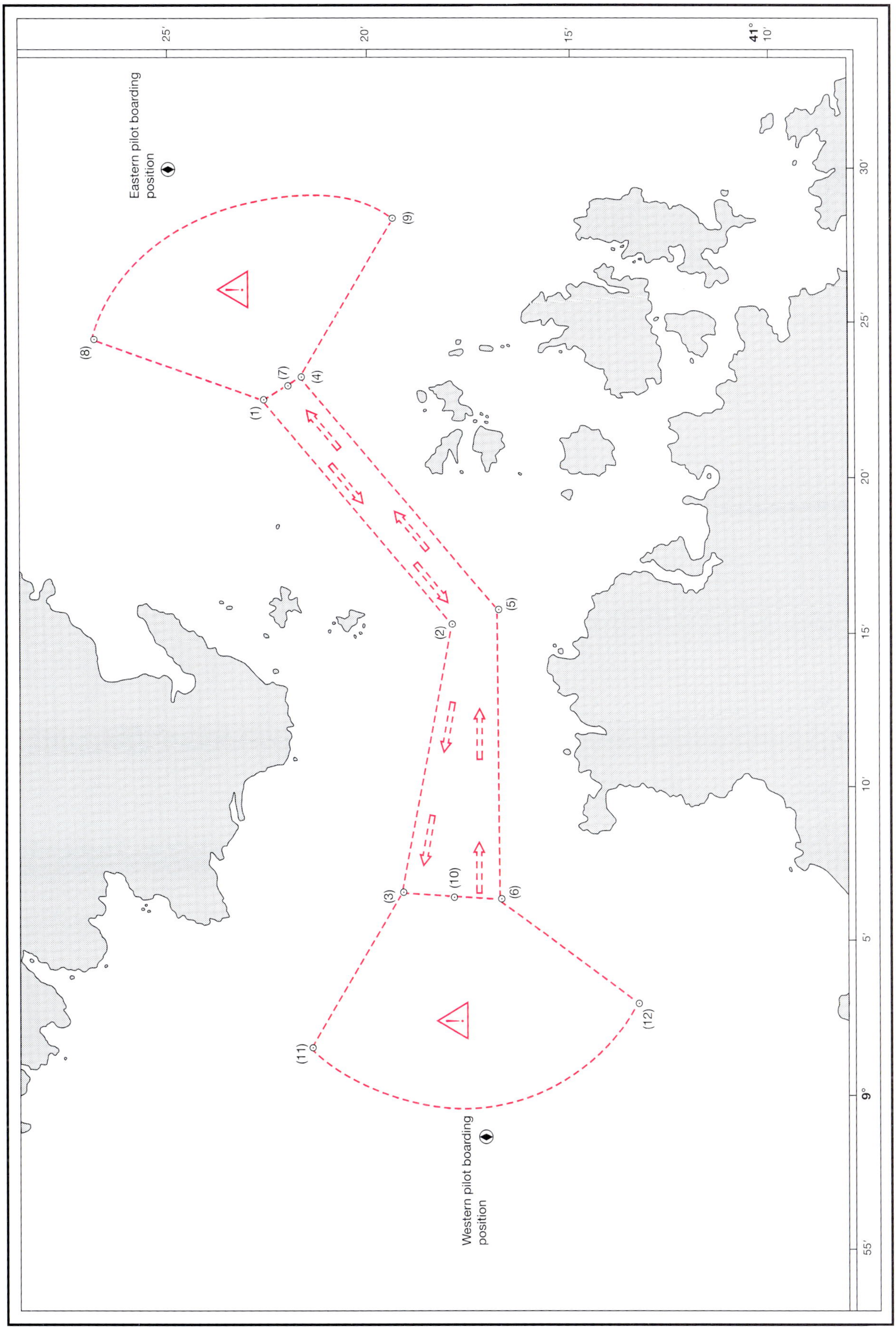

TWO-WAY ROUTE AND PRECAUTIONARY AREAS IN THE STRAIT OF BONIFACIO

E

RECOMMENDED DIRECTIONS OF TRAFFIC FLOW IN THE CHANNEL OF OTRANTO, SOUTHERN AND CENTRAL ADRIATIC SEA

Reference charts: Italian Navy Hydrographical Institute 435, 1993 edition (ED 50 datum); Hydrographical Institute of the Republic of Croatia 101, 1998 edition (Hermannskögel datum, Bessel ellipsoid).
Note: The co-ordinates listed below are in World Geodetic System 1984 datum (WGS 84).)

Description of the recommended directions of traffic flow

Recommended directions of traffic flow, which should remain as in the present, are established between the parallels of latitude 40°25′.00 N and 43°10′.01 N.

Recommended directions of traffic flow, which should be in accordance with the description as per chart below, are established between the parallel of latitude 43°10′.01 N and the precautionary area at the southern limits of the traffic separation schemes "In the North Adriatic Sea – eastern part" and "In the North Adriatic Sea – western part".

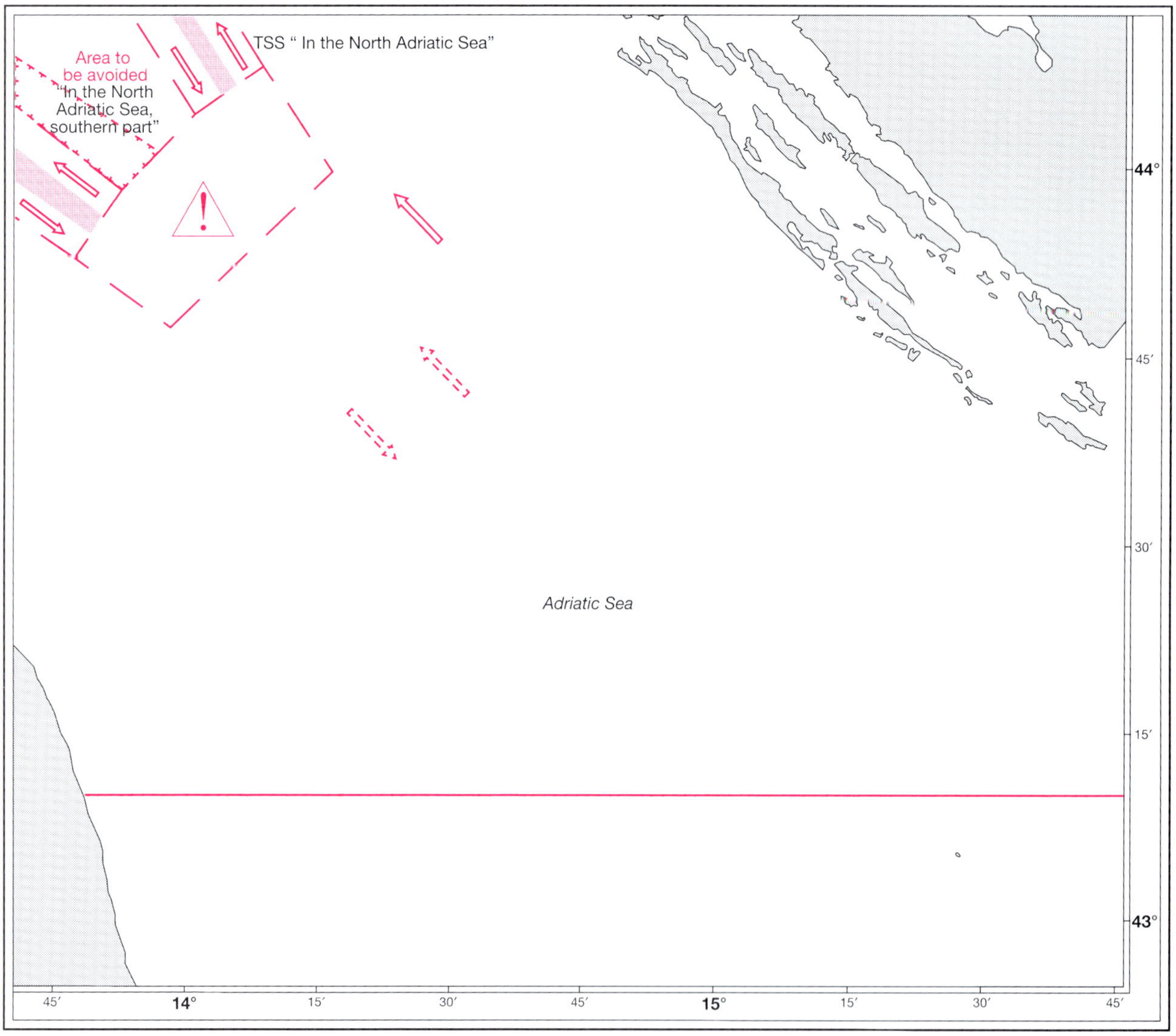

RECOMMENDED DIRECTIONS OF TRAFFIC FLOW BETWEEN 43°10′.01 N AND PRECAUTIONARY AREA IN THE NORTH ADRIATIC SEA

RECOMMENDED ROUTES OFF THE MEDITERRANEAN COAST OF EGYPT

(Reference charts: British Admiralty 3400, 2681, 2573 and 2574.
Note: These charts are based on World Geodetic System 1984 datum (WGS 84).)

Recommended routes

Recommended route between Sallum and Matrouh is defined by a line connecting the following geographical positions:

(1)	31°40′.60 N,	025°19′.50 E,	(3)	31°32′.50 N,	027°21′.10 E
(2)	31°51′.40 N,	025°54′.00 E			

Recommended route between Matrouh and El-Iskindaria is defined by a line connecting the following geographical positions:

(4)	31°32′.50 N,	027°21′.10 E	(5)	31°16′.30 N,	029°35′.20 E

Recommended route between El-Iskindaria and El-Arish is defined by a line connecting the following geographical positions:

(6)	31°12′.90 N,	029°47′.70 E	(9)	31°46′.80 N,	032°50′.70 E
(7)	31°39′.10 N,	030°18′.20 E	(10)	31°28′.30 N,	033°41′.50 E
(8)	31°45′.00 N,	031°02′.00 E	(11)	31°12′.00 N,	033°47′.00 E

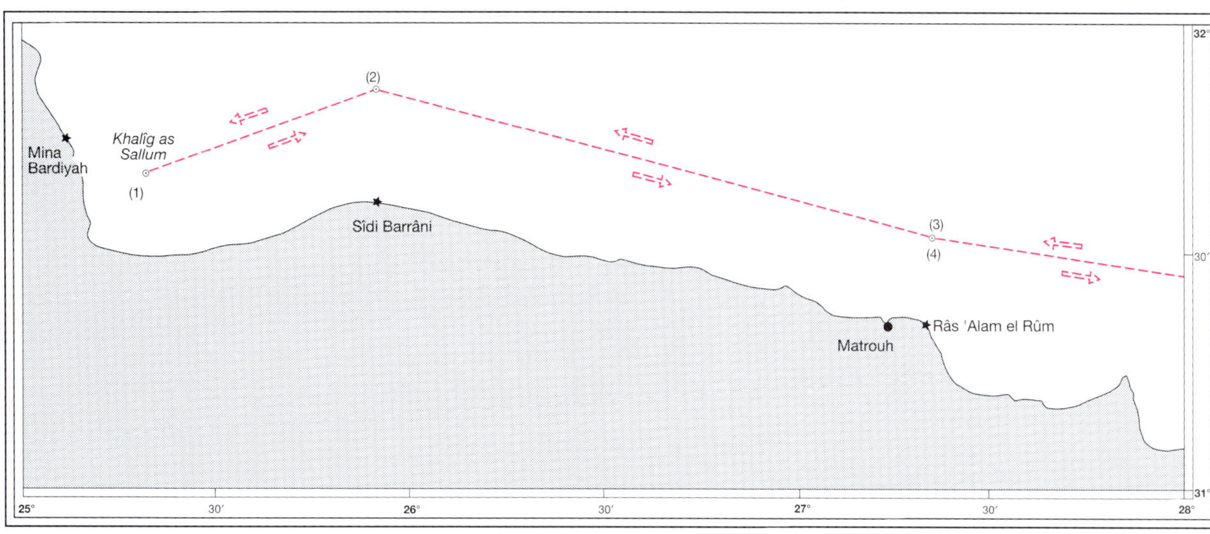

RECOMMENDED ROUTE BETWEEN SALLUM AND MATROUH

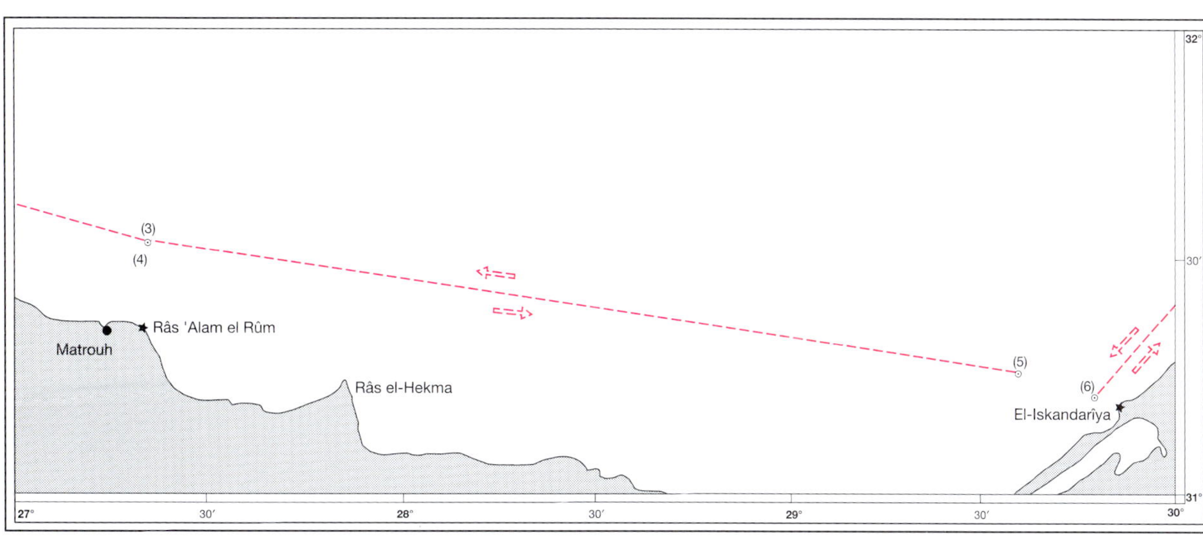

RECOMMENDED ROUTE BETWEEN MATROUH AND EL-ESKINDARIA

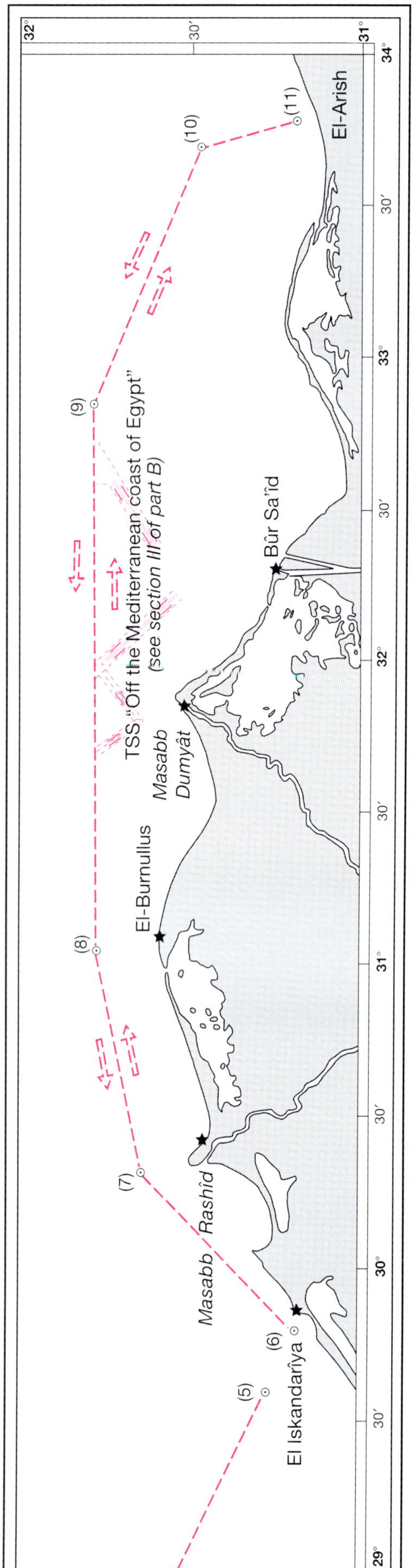

RECOMMENDED ROUTE BETWEEN EL-ESKINDARIA AND EL-ARISH

RECOMMENDED DIRECTIONS OF TRAFFIC FLOW OFF RAS SHUKHEIR

Note: See "Rules for ships navigating in the Gulf of Suez" in part F.

Recommended directions of traffic flow are established in the approaches to Ras Shukheir Oil Terminal, July, Ramadan and Morgan oilfields as shown in the chartlet below.

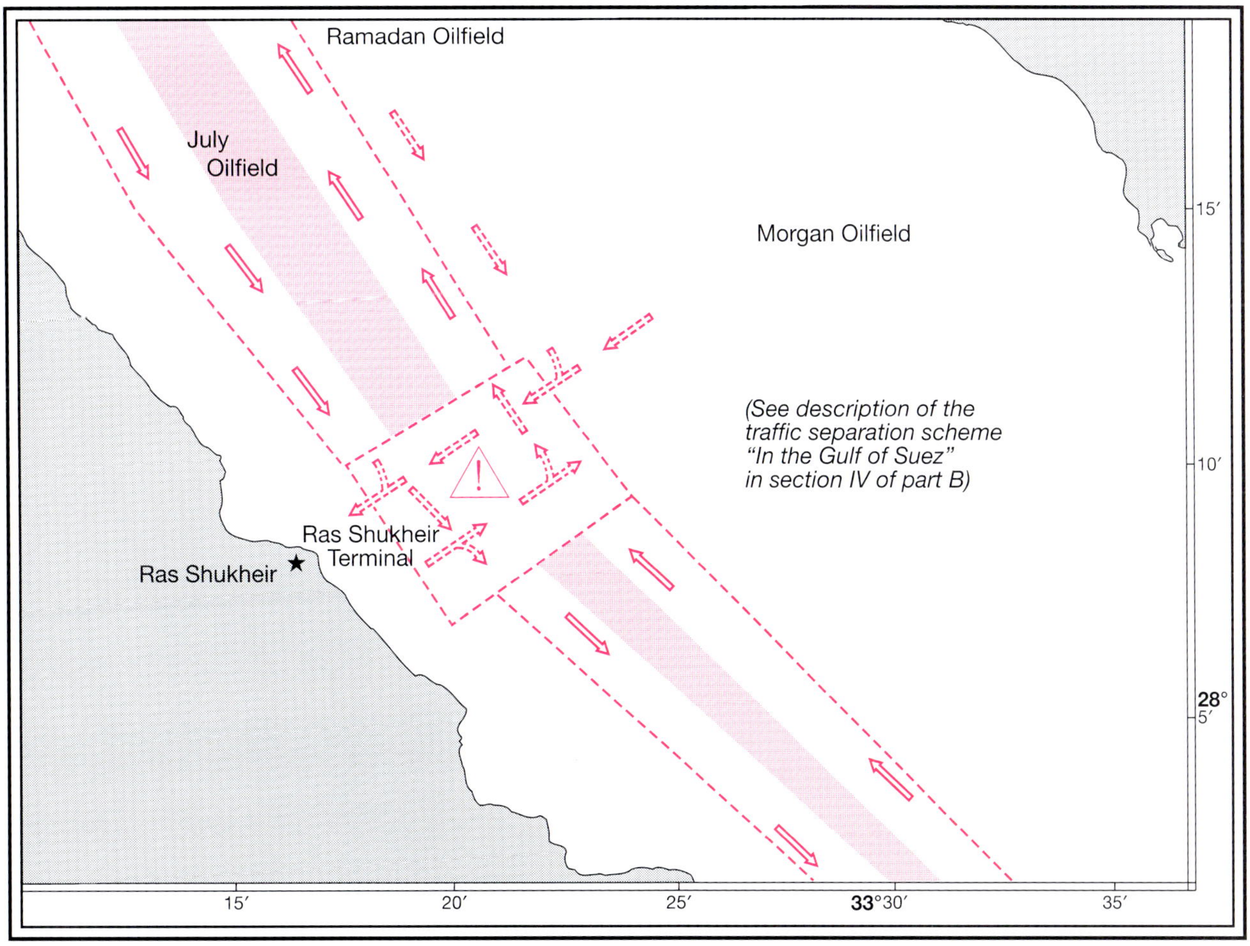

RECOMMENDED DIRECTIONS OF TRAFFIC FLOW OFF RAS SHUKHEIR

E

PRECAUTIONARY AREA IN THE APPROACHES TO THE NEW PORT OF KING ABDULLAH PORT (KAP) IN THE NORTHERN RED SEA*

(Reference chart: British Admiralty (BA) 2659, 4 May 1990.
Note: This chart is not based on World Geodetic System 1984 datum (WGS 84). The geographical positions listed in item (a) below are referenced to BA 2659.)

Description of the precautionary area

(a) The precautionary area is established bounded by a line connecting the following geographical positions:

(2)	22°18′.61 N,	038°53′.60 E	(9)	22°21′.25 N,	038°56′.61 E
(3)	22°20′.57 N,	038°54′.64 E	(10)	22°19′.24 N,	038°55′.58 E

Notes:

Geographical positions referenced to WGS 84:

(2)	22°18′.61 N,	038°53′.61 E	(9)	22°21′.25 N,	038°56′.62 E
(3)	22°20′.57 N,	038°54′.65 E	(10)	22°19′.24 N,	038°55′.59 E

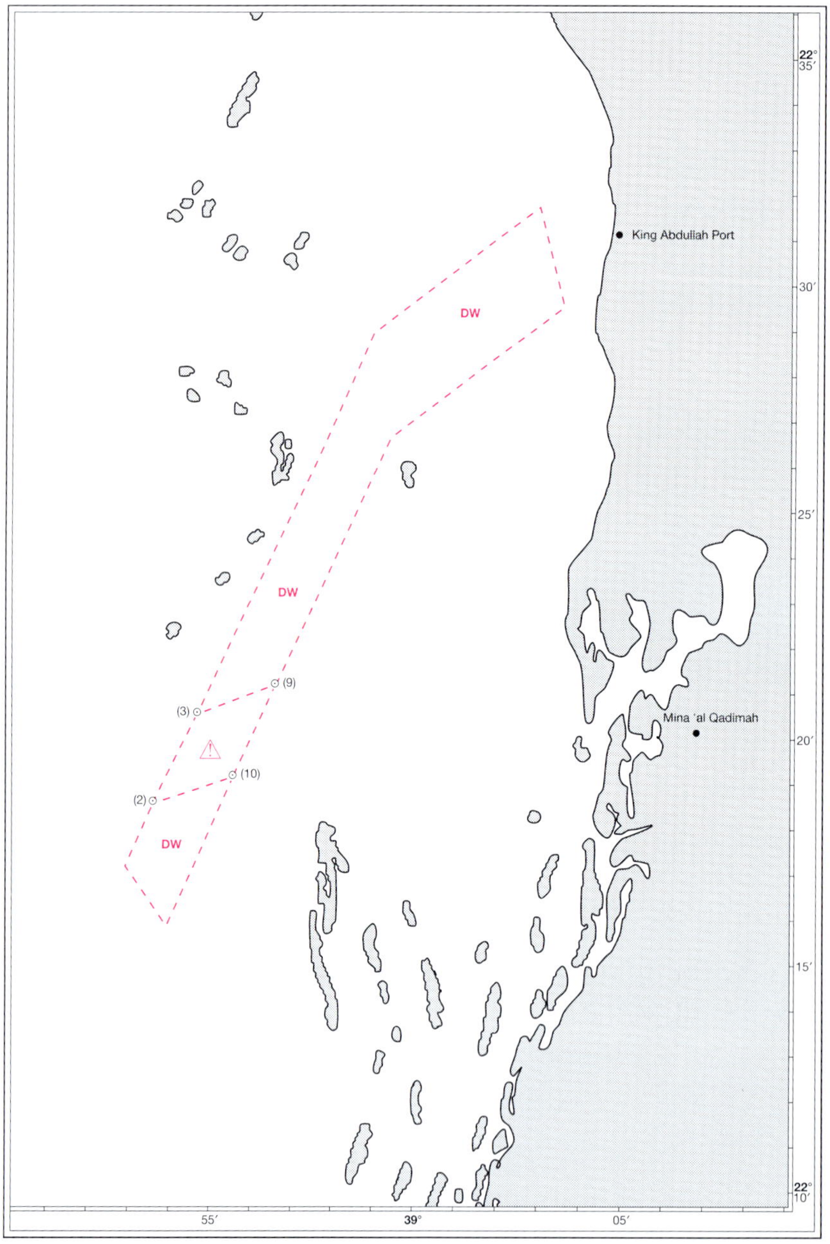

PRECAUTIONARY AREA IN THE APPROACHES TO KING ABDULLAH PORT

* Date of implementation of new precautionary area: 0000 hours UTC on 31 August 2011.

RECOMMENDED TRACKS AND A PRECAUTIONARY AREA FOR THE SOUTHERN RED SEA

(Reference charts: British Admiralty 452, 2002 edition; 453, 2002 edition.
Note: These charts are based on World Geodetic System 1984 datum (WGS 84).)

RECOMMENDED TRACKS BETWEEN JABAL ZUQAR AND THE PRECAUTIONARY AREA

The direction of navigation will be:

- a southbound traffic lane, 166°(T) from the southern limit of the traffic separation scheme "East of Jabal Zuqar Island" as far as the northern limit of the precautionary area lying north of the traffic separation scheme "In the Strait of Bab el Mandeb".
- a northbound traffic lane, 346°(T) from the northern limit of the precautionary area lying north of the traffic separation scheme "In the Strait of Bab el Mandeb" to the southern limit of the traffic separation scheme "East of Jabal Zuqar Island".

Description of the recommended tracks between the traffic separation schemes "East of Jabal Zuqar" and "In the Strait of Bab el Mandeb"

(a) Northern limit, consisting of a line connecting the following geographical positions:

(9)	(East of Jabal Zuqar)	13°57′.97 N,	042°49′.95 E
(12)	(East of Jabal Zuqar)	13°58′.94 N,	042°53′.83 E

(b) Southern limit, consisting of a line connecting the following geographical positions:

(X)	(precautionary area)	13°19′.52 N,	043°03′.60 E
(Y)	(precautionary area)	13°18′.64 N,	042°59′.95 E

RECOMMENDED TRACKS BETWEEN HANISH AL KUBRA AND THE PRECAUTIONARY AREA

The direction of navigation will be:

- a southbound traffic lane, 123°(T) from the south-eastern limit of the traffic separation scheme "West and south of Hanish al Kubra" as far as the north-western limit of the precautionary area lying north of the traffic separation scheme through Bab el Mandeb.
- a northbound traffic lane, 309°(T) from the north-western limit of the precautionary area lying north of the traffic separation scheme through Bab el Mandeb to the south-eastern limit of the traffic separation scheme "West and south of Hanish al Kubra".

Description of the recommended tracks between the traffic separation scheme "West and south of Hanish al Kubra" and the precautionary area

(a) North-western limit, consisting of a line connecting the following geographical positions:

(9)	(West and south of Hanish al Kubra)	13°25′.22 N,	042°41′.05 E
(12)	(West and south of Hanish al Kubra)	13°30′.25 N,	042°45′.18 E

(b) South-eastern limit, consisting of a line connecting the following geographical positions:

(Y)	(precautionary area)	13°18′.64 N,	042°59′.95 E
(Z)	(precautionary area)	13°15′.00 N,	042°56′.96 E

PRECAUTIONARY AREA NORTH OF THE TRAFFIC SEPARATION SCHEME "IN THE STRAIT OF BAB EL MANDEB"

A precautionary area is established by a line connecting the following geographical positions:

(10)	(North-west of Bab el Mandeb)	13°15′.00 N,	043°04′.70 E
(X)		13°19′.52 N,	043°03′.60 E
(Y)		13°18′.64 N,	042°59′.95 E
(Z)		13°15′.00 N,	042°56′.96 E
(7)	(North-west of Bab el Mandeb)	13°11′.94 N,	043°01′.72 E

(chartlet overleaf)

E

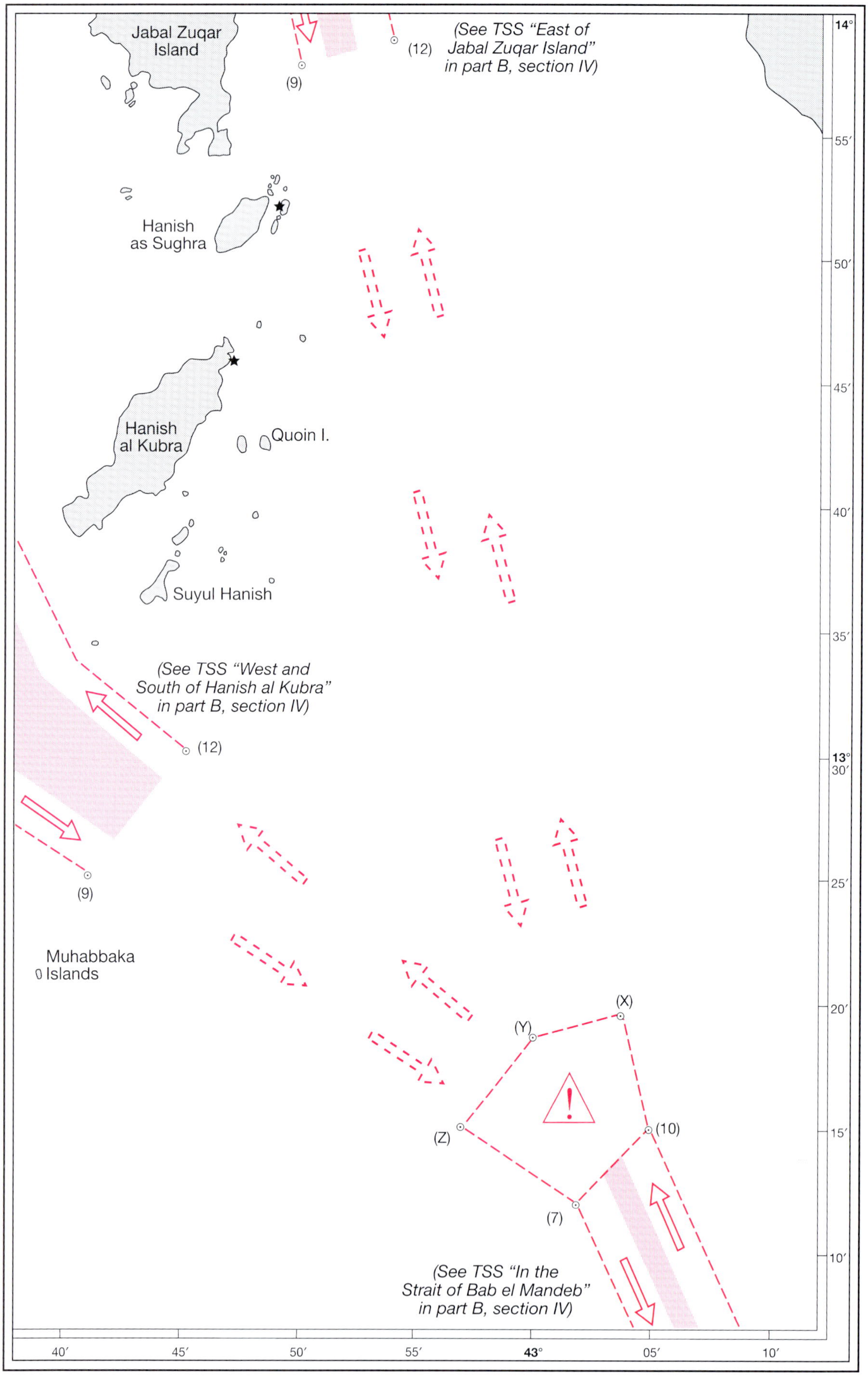

RECOMMENDED TRACKS AND A PRECAUTIONARY AREA FOR THE SOUTHERN RED SEA

RECOMMENDATORY MEASURES FOR VESSELS CROSSING THE TRAFFIC SEPARATION SCHEME (TSS) AND PRECAUTIONARY AREAS IN THE SINGAPORE STRAIT DURING HOURS OF DARKNESS*

1 Vessels are recommended to display, if carried, the night signals consisting of three all-round green lights† in a vertical line in the following situations:

(a) vessels departing from ports or anchorages when crossing the westbound or eastbound lane of the TSS or precautionary areas in the Singapore Strait to join the eastbound or westbound lane respectively; and

(b) eastbound or westbound vessels in the TSS or precautionary areas in the Singapore Strait crossing to proceed to ports or anchorages in the Singapore Strait.

2 The night signals are recommended to be displayed by:

(a) vessels of 300 gross tonnage and above;

(b) vessels of 50 metres or more in length; and

(c) vessels engaged in towing or pushing with a combined 300 gross tonnage and above, or with a combined length of 50 metres or more.

3 Vessels crossing the TSS and precautionary areas in the Singapore Strait to proceed to or from ports or anchorages should comply with the following procedures:

(a) a vessel in the Singapore Strait which intends to cross the eastbound or westbound traffic lanes in the TSS or precautionary areas, respectively, should comply with the following:

(i) report to the VTIS to indicate its intention in advance, allowing VTIS to alert ships in the vicinity of the crossing vessel;

(ii) display the signals consisting of three all-round green lights in a vertical line in ample time prior to crossing, in order for other vessels to note the intention to cross the TSS or precautionary areas;

(iii) when traffic conditions are favourable, make a large alteration of course, if necessary, so as to be readily apparent to other vessels in the vicinity observing visually or by radar, and cross the traffic lane on a heading as nearly as practicable at right angles to the general direction of traffic flow; and

(iv) report to VTIS and switch off the night signals when it has safely left/crossed or joined the appropriate traffic lane.

(b) displaying the night signals does not exempt the crossing vessel of its obligations to comply with the COLREG.

E

---

* Date of implementation of new measures: 0000 hours UTC on 1 June 2013.

† The technical specifications of the lights used in the "three green lights" signal should, if possible, comply closely with positioning and technical details of lights in annex I of COLREG.

TWO-WAY ROUTE IN THE GREAT NORTH-EAST CHANNEL, TORRES STRAIT

(Reference charts: AUS 376 (January 1984 edition), based on Australian geodetic datum 1966 (AGD 66); AUS 839 (August 1997 edition) and AUS 840 (August 1997 edition), based on World Geodetic System 1984 datum (WGS 84).)

The following geographical positions (based on WGS 84) define the two-way route:

(a) The northern limits are bounded by the line joining the following geographical positions:

(1)	10°29′.70 S,	142°22′.63 E	(7)	10°18′.14 S,	142°50′.82 E
(2)	10°29′.14 S,	142°25′.76 E	(8)	10°13′.38 S,	142°54′.96 E
(3)	10°27′.80 S,	142°28′.45 E	(9)	10°00′.50 S,	143°03′.42 E
(4)	10°26′.40 S,	142°31′.30 E	(10)	09°47′.73 S,	143°10′.40 E
(5)	10°21′.90 S,	142°41′.50 E	(11)	09°25′.80 S,	143°31′.07 E
(6)	10°19′.37 S,	142°47′.97 E	(12)	09°12′.47 S,	143°51′.34 E

(b) The southern limits are bounded by the line joining the following geographical positions:

(13)	10°30′.45 S,	142°24′.02 E	(19)	10°09′.78 S,	143°05′.55 E
(14)	10°28′.38 S,	142°28′.66 E	(20)	09°53′.97 S,	143°15′.61 E
(15)	10°27′.38 S,	142°31′.85 E	(21)	09°46′.02 S,	143°18′.48 E
(16)	10°22′.85 S,	142°41′.95 E	(22)	09°37′.96 S,	143°21′.97 E
(17)	10°19′.80 S,	142°48′.23 E	(23)	09°27′.60 S,	143°32′.15 E
(18)	10°17′.63 S,	142°53′.29 E	(24)	09°13′.95 S,	143°52′.62 E

(c) The centre polygon is defined by the following geographical positions:

(25)	10°16′.10 S,	142°53′.82 E	(29)	09°41′.04 S,	143°18′.87 E
(26)	10°13′.79 S,	142°55′.85 E	(30)	09°45′.72 S,	143°17′.51 E
(27)	10°01′.05 S,	143°04′.20 E	(31)	09°53′.84 S,	143°14′.50 E
(28)	09°48′.10 S,	143°11′.30 E	(32)	10°09′.15 S,	143°04′.70 E

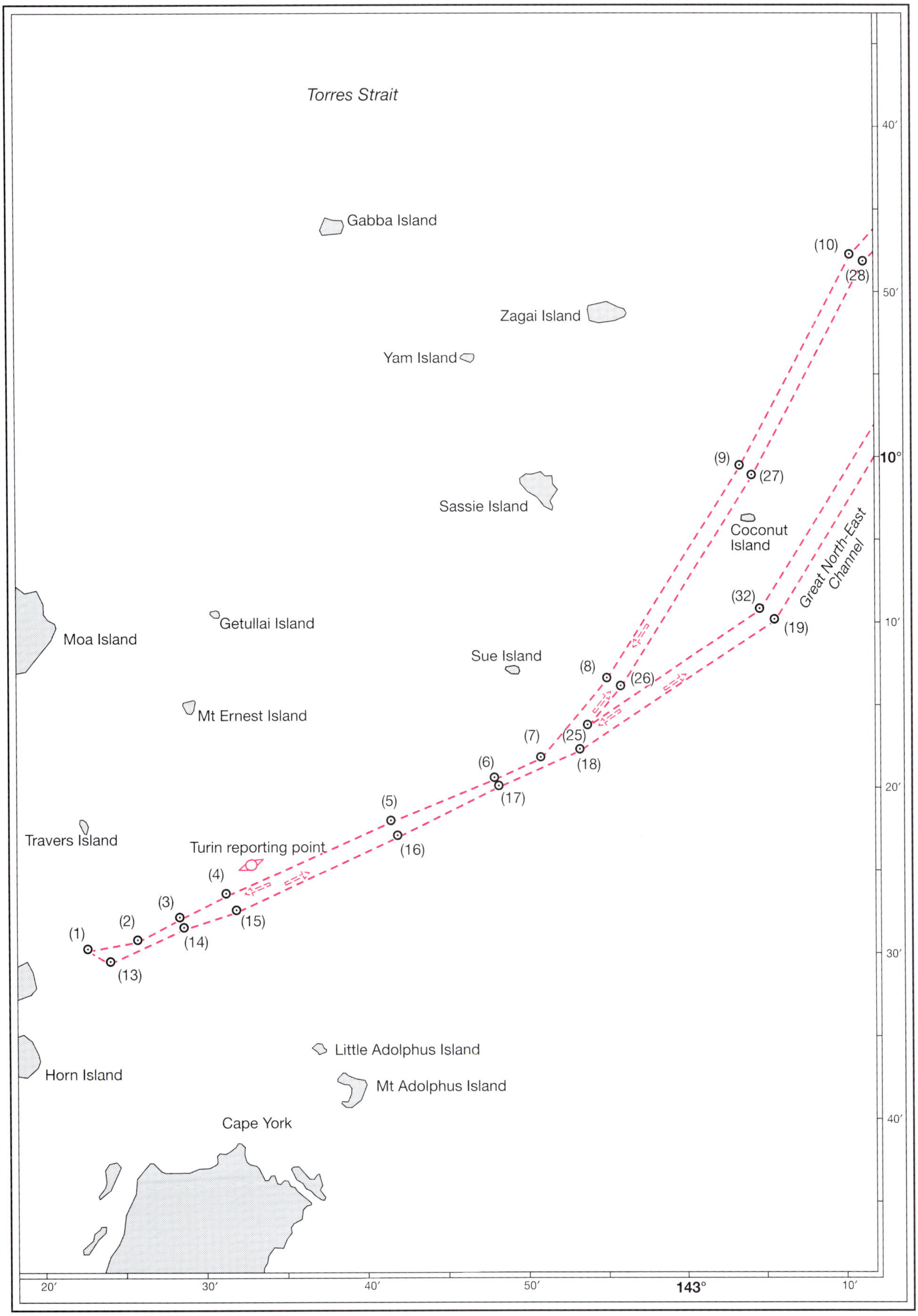

TWO-WAY ROUTE IN THE GREAT NORTH-EAST CHANNEL, TORRES STRAIT (WEST)

E

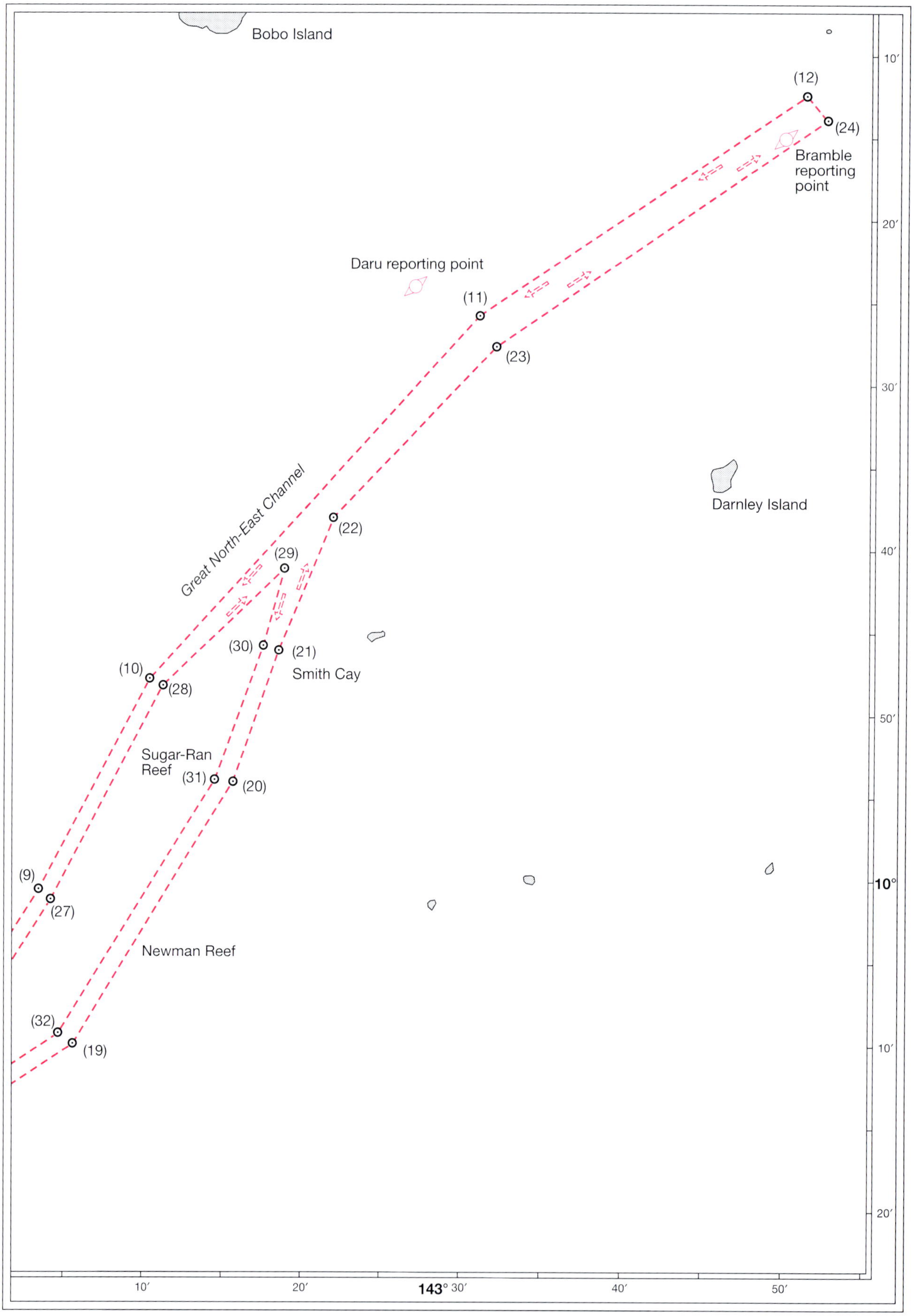

TWO-WAY ROUTE IN THE GREAT NORTH-EAST CHANNEL, TORRES STRAIT (EAST)

PRECAUTIONARY AREA OFF THE WEST COAST OF THE NORTH ISLAND OF NEW ZEALAND

(Reference charts: New Zealand NZ23, April 2005 edition; NZ48, April 2000 edition.
Note: these charts are based on World Geodetic System 1984 datum (WGS 84).)

Description of the precautionary area

The precautionary area is defined by a line connecting the following geographical positions, the landward extent of which is determined by Mean High Water Springs (MHWS):

(1) The charted line of MHWS at approximately 38°31′.00 S, 174°37′.80 E
(2) 39°18′.50 S, 173°05′.00 E
(3) 39°26′.00 S, 173°01′.00 E
(4) 40°03′.00 S, 173°04′.00 E
(5) 40°10′.00 S, 173°16′.00 E
(6) The charted line of MHWS at approximately 39°53′.50 S, 174°54′.50 E

Note: All ships should navigate with particular caution in order to reduce the risk of a maritime casualty and resulting marine pollution in the precautionary area.

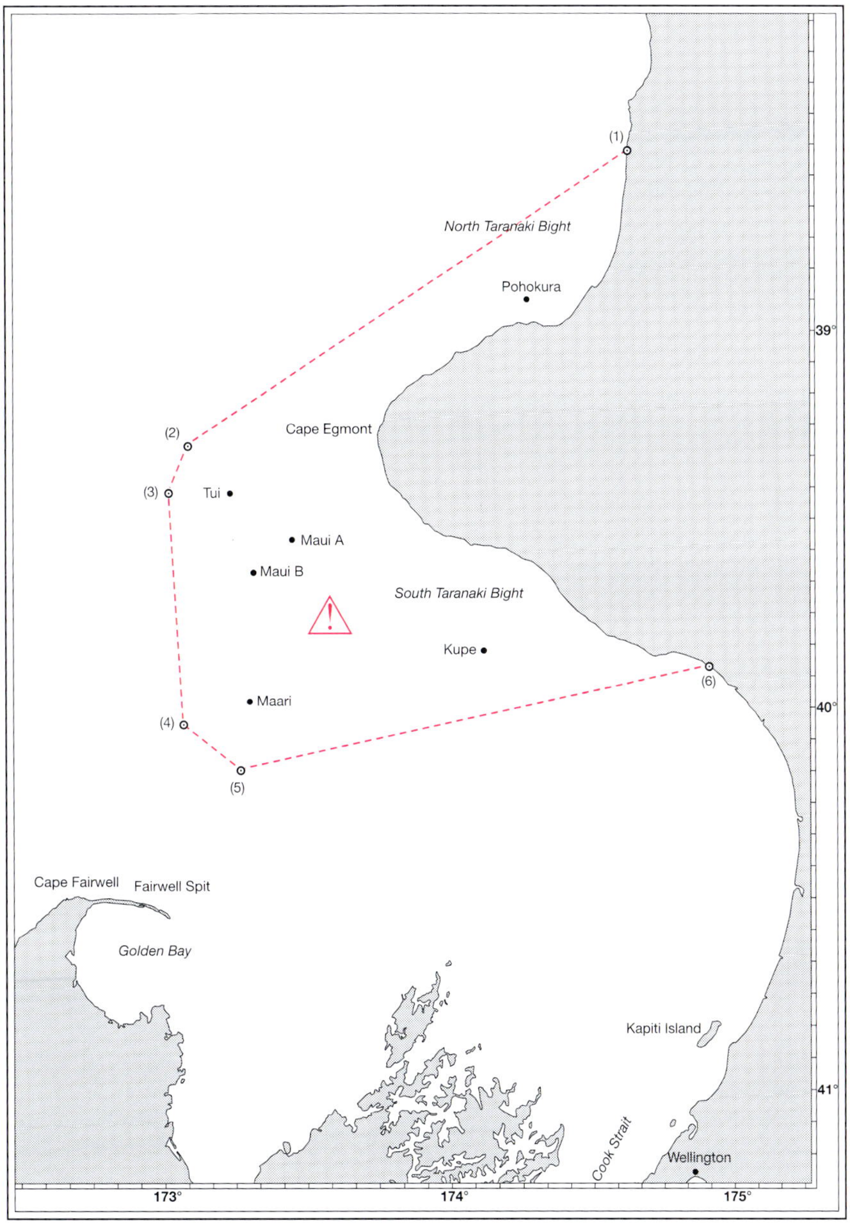

PRECAUTIONARY AREA OFF THE WEST COAST OF THE NORTH ISLAND OF NEW ZEALAND

E

RECOMMENDED TWO-WAY ROUTE IN THE STRAIT OF JUAN DE FUCA

(Reference charts: United States 18400, 2000 edition; 18460, 1998 edition; 18465, 1995 edition; 18480, 1999 edition.
Note: These charts are based on North American 1983 datum.)

Eastbound route

Slower moving traffic, such as tugs and barges and small fishing vessels, transiting eastbound should follow the route established south of the traffic separation scheme "In the Strait of Juan de Fuca" and north of the line created by the following geographical positions:

(1)	48°27′.14 N,	124°44′.36 W	
(2)	48°11′.90 N,	123°55′.57 W	
(3)	48°11′.94 N,	123°34′.00 W	

Westbound route

Slower moving traffic, such as tugs and barges and small fishing vessels, transiting westbound should follow the route established south of the line created by the following geographical positions:

(1)	48°27′.14 N,	124°44′.36 W	
(2)	48°11′.90 N,	123°55′.57 W	
(3)	48°11′.94 N,	123°34′.00 W	

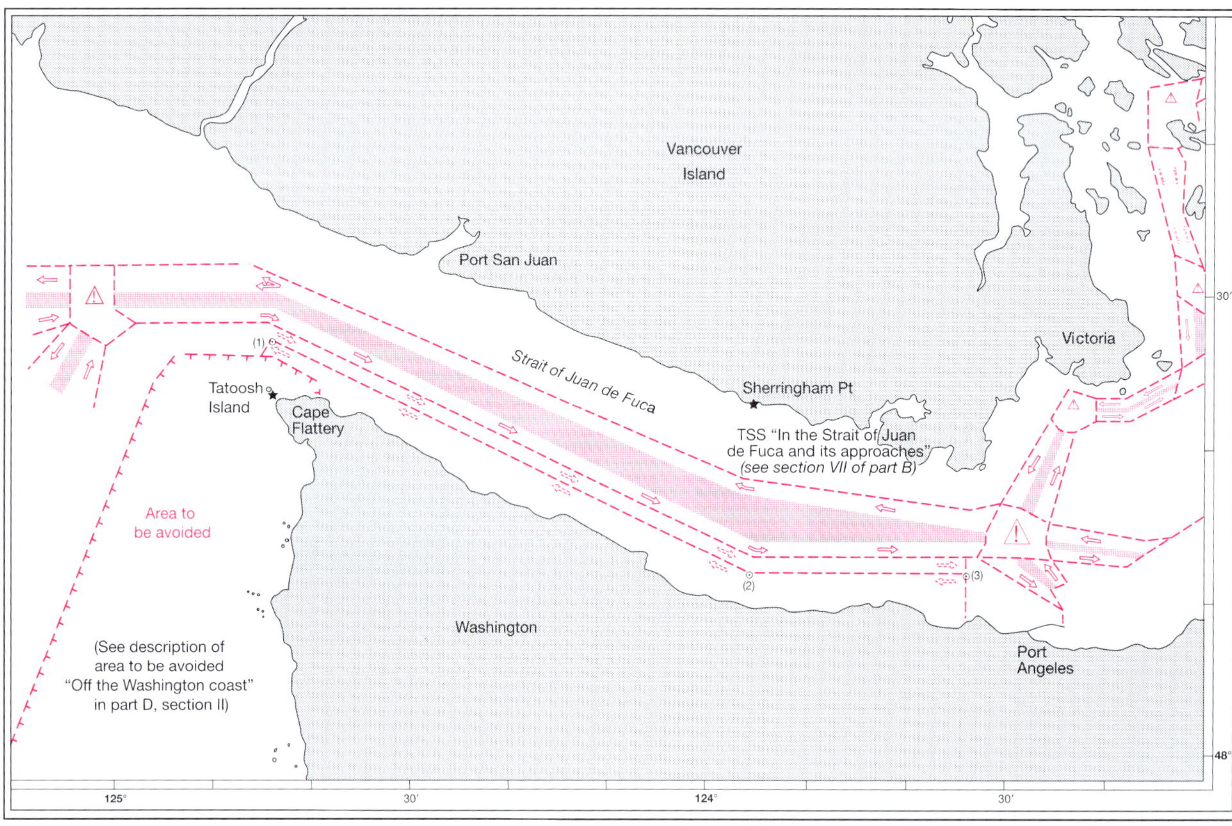

RECOMMENDED TWO-WAY ROUTE IN THE STRAIT OF JUAN DE FUCA

RECOMMENDED TRACKS OFF THE CALIFORNIA COAST FOR SHIPS OF 300 GROSS TONNAGE AND ABOVE AND FOR SHIPS CARRYING HAZARDOUS CARGO IN BULK

(Reference charts: NOAA 18022, 18680.
Note: These charts are based on World Geodetic System 1984 datum (WGS 84).)

1 Northbound ships of 300 gross tonnage and above (other than those described in paragraphs 3 and 4 below) should follow the route established by a recommended track between the following two points:

(1) 36°18′.31 N, 122°12′.79 W (15 miles off Point Sur); and
(2) 37°10′.86 N, 122°39′.74 W (12.7 miles off Pigeon Point).

2 Southbound ships of 300 gross tonnage and above (other than those described in paragraphs 3 and 4 below) should follow the route established by a recommended track between the following two points:

(3) 37°10′.85 N, 122°43′.87 W (16 miles off Pigeon Point); and
(4) 36°18′.29 N, 122°18′.98 W (20 miles off Point Sur).

3 Northbound ships carrying hazardous cargo in bulk should follow the route established by a recommended track between the following two points:

(5) 36°18′.27 N, 122°25′.16 W (25 miles off Point Sur); and
(6) 37°10′.81 N, 122°55′.14 W (25 miles off Pigeon Point).

4 Southbound ships carrying hazardous cargo in bulk should follow the route established by a recommended track between the following two points:

(7) 37°10′.78 N, 123°01′.39 W (30 miles off Pigeon Point); and
(8) 36°18′.24 N, 122°31′.35 W (30 miles off Point Sur).

Note: Ships carrying hazardous cargo in bulk when entering or leaving San Francisco should use the western approach of the traffic separation scheme.

(chartlet overleaf)

E

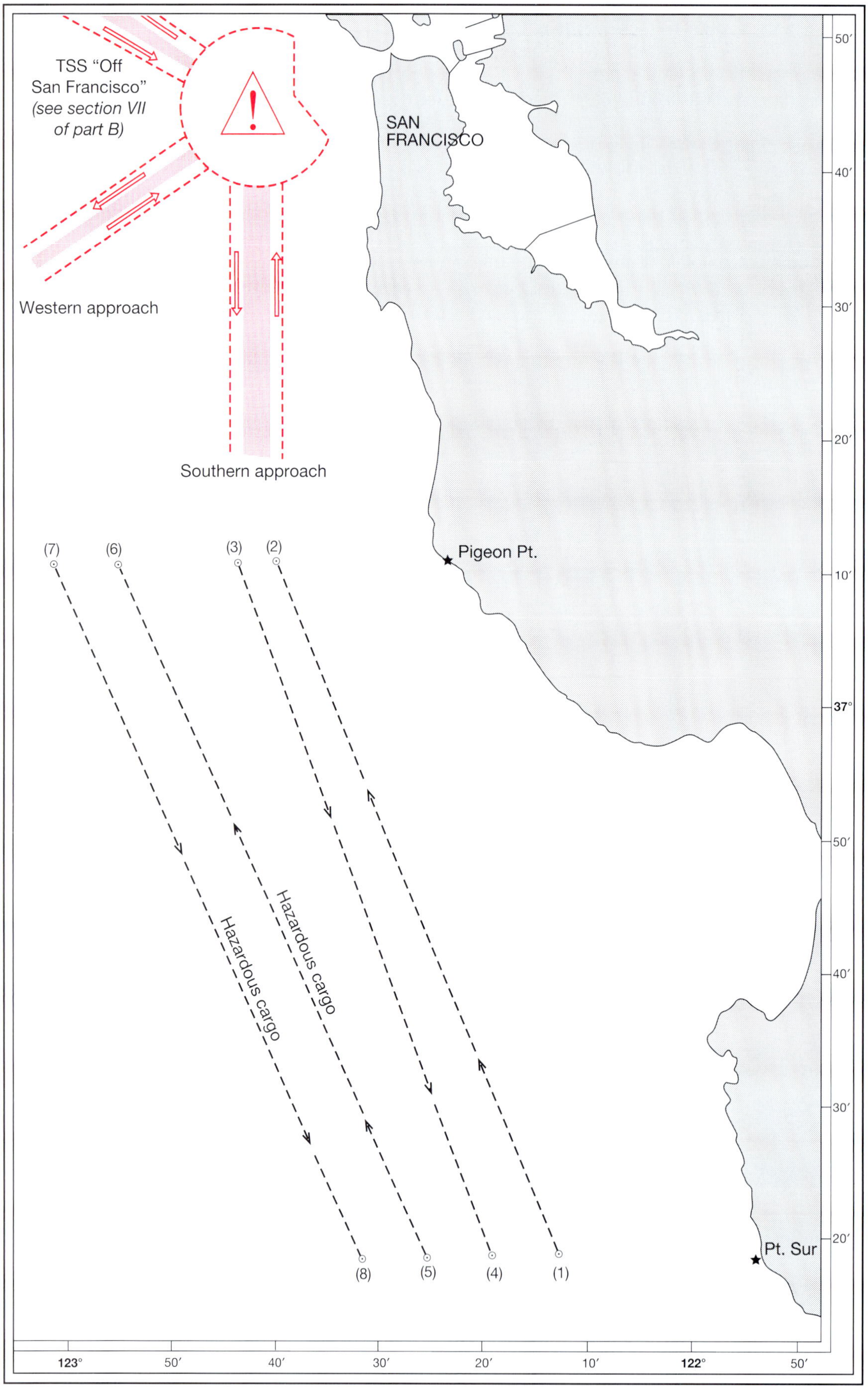

RECOMMENDED TRACKS OFF THE CALIFORNIA COAST FOR SHIPS OF 300 GROSS TONNAGE AND ABOVE AND FOR SHIPS CARRYING HAZARDOUS CARGO IN BULK

RECOMMENDED TRACKS, WHICH ARE MANDATORY AS A CONDITION OF PORT ENTRY, THROUGH THE GALAPAGOS AREA TO BE AVOIDED TO ENTER THE PARTICULARLY SENSITIVE SEA AREA (PSSA)

Note: See area to be avoided "In the Galapagos Archipelago" in part D, section III and mandatory ship reporting system "In the Galapagos Particularly Sensitive Sea Area" in part G, section I.

(Reference charts: I.O.A. 2, 1992 edition; I.O.A. 20, 1992 edition.
Note: These charts are based on World Geodetic System 1984 datum (WGS 84).)

All ships and barges carrying cargoes of oil or potentially hazardous material entering and departing any port in the Galapagos and all ships of 500 gross tonnage and above entering and departing any port in the Galapagos shall use the following routes:

1 On the eastern side of the area to be avoided, westbound ships shall follow the route established by a recommended track between the following two geographical positions:

(1)	01°05′.14 S,	087°54′.73 W	(2)	01°05′.14 S,	088°41′.32 W

2 On the eastern side of the area to be avoided, eastbound ships shall follow the route established by a recommended track between the following two geographical positions:

(3)	01°10′.16 S,	087°57′.71 W	(4)	01°10′.16 S,	088°44′.26 W

3 On the western side of the area to be avoided, westbound ships shall follow the route established by a recommended track between the following two geographical positions:

(5)	01°21′.08 S,	092°43′.73 W	(6)	01°14′.47 S,	092°06′.35 W

4 On the western side of the area to be avoided, eastbound ships shall follow the route established by a recommended track between the following two geographical positions:

(7)	01°26′.19 S,	092°43′.83 W	(8)	01°18′.94 S,	092°02′.81 W

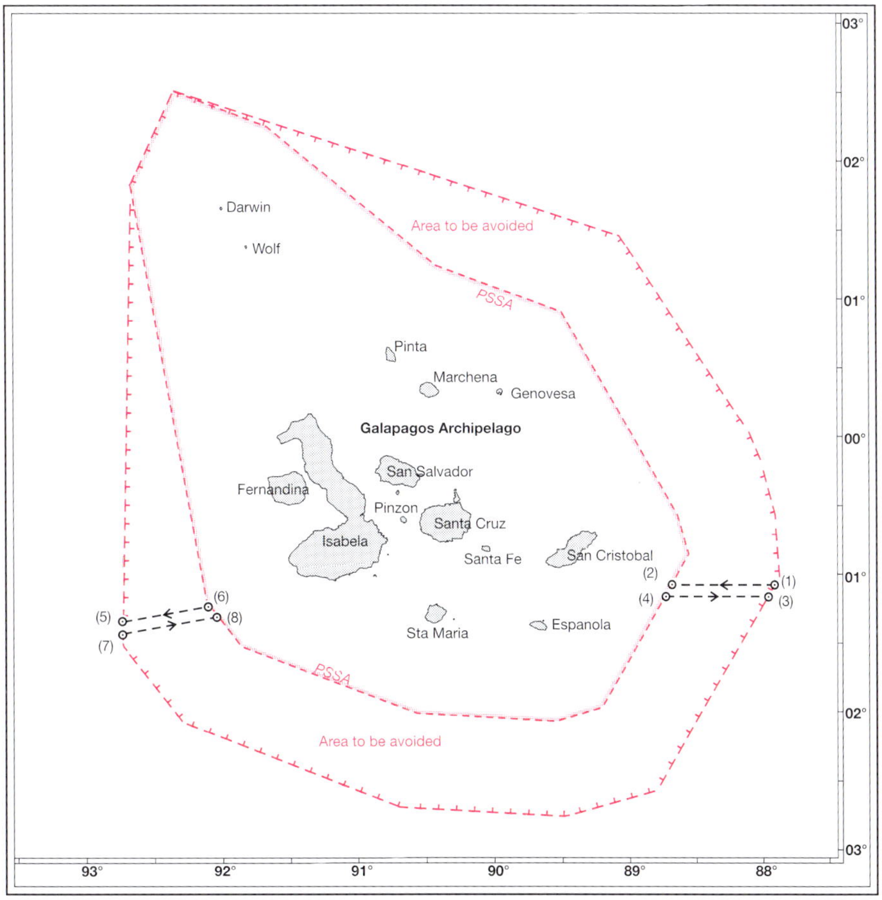

RECOMMENDED TRACKS THROUGH THE GALAPAGOS AREA TO BE AVOIDED TO ENTER THE PARTICULARLY SENSITIVE SEA AREA

PRECAUTIONARY AREA IN THE REGION OF THE GRAND BANKS OF NEWFOUNDLAND

(Reference charts: CHS 4001/INT 404, 1995 edition and CHS 4000, 1984 edition.
Note: These charts are based on North American 1983 datum and North American 1927 datum respectively.)

Description of the precautionary area

In order to reduce the risk of a marine casualty and resulting pollution and damage to the environment, all ships not involved in the oil-related activities being conducted within the area should navigate with particular caution in the area having a 10 NM radius centred on 46°28′.53 N, 048°28′.86 W. Ship movement in the area is monitored on a 24-hour basis. Any ship planning to transit the precautionary area is advised to contact the Terra Nova Floating Production Storage and Offloading Vessel (FPSO) on VHF channel 16 and to comply with the instructions given while transiting the area.

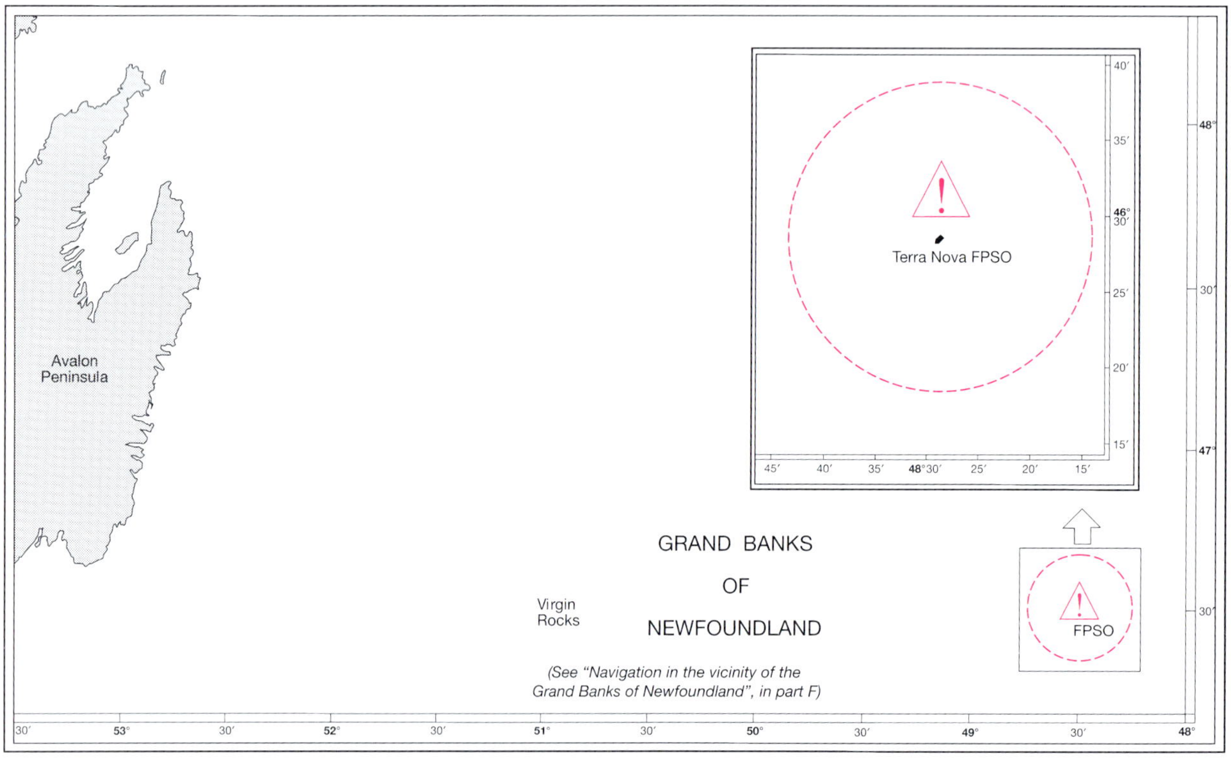

IN THE REGION OF THE GRAND BANKS OF NEWFOUNDLAND

E

TWO-WAY ROUTE OFF DELAWARE BAY

(Reference chart: United States 12214, 1994 edition.
Note: This chart is based on North American datum 1983.)

A two-way traffic route is bounded on the west and south by a line connecting the following geographical positions:

(1)	38°50′.75 N,	075°03′.40 W	(4)	38°50′.20 N,	074°49′.73 W
(2)	38°47′.50 N,	075°01′.80 W	(5)	39°00′.00 N,	074°40′.23 W
(3)	38°48′.32 N,	074°55′.30 W			

and is bounded on the east and north by a line connecting the following geographical positions:

(6)	39°00′.00 N,	074°41′.00 W	(9)	38°48′.33 N,	074°59′.30 W
(7)	38°50′.48 N,	074°50′.30 W	(10)	38°49′.10 N,	075°01′.65 W
(8)	38°48′.80 N,	074°55′.25 W	(11)	38°51′.27 N,	075°02′.83 W,

Note for the use of the two-way route:

This two-way route is recommended for use predominantly by tug and tow traffic transiting to and from the north-east in order to separate such traffic from large inbound vessel traffic.

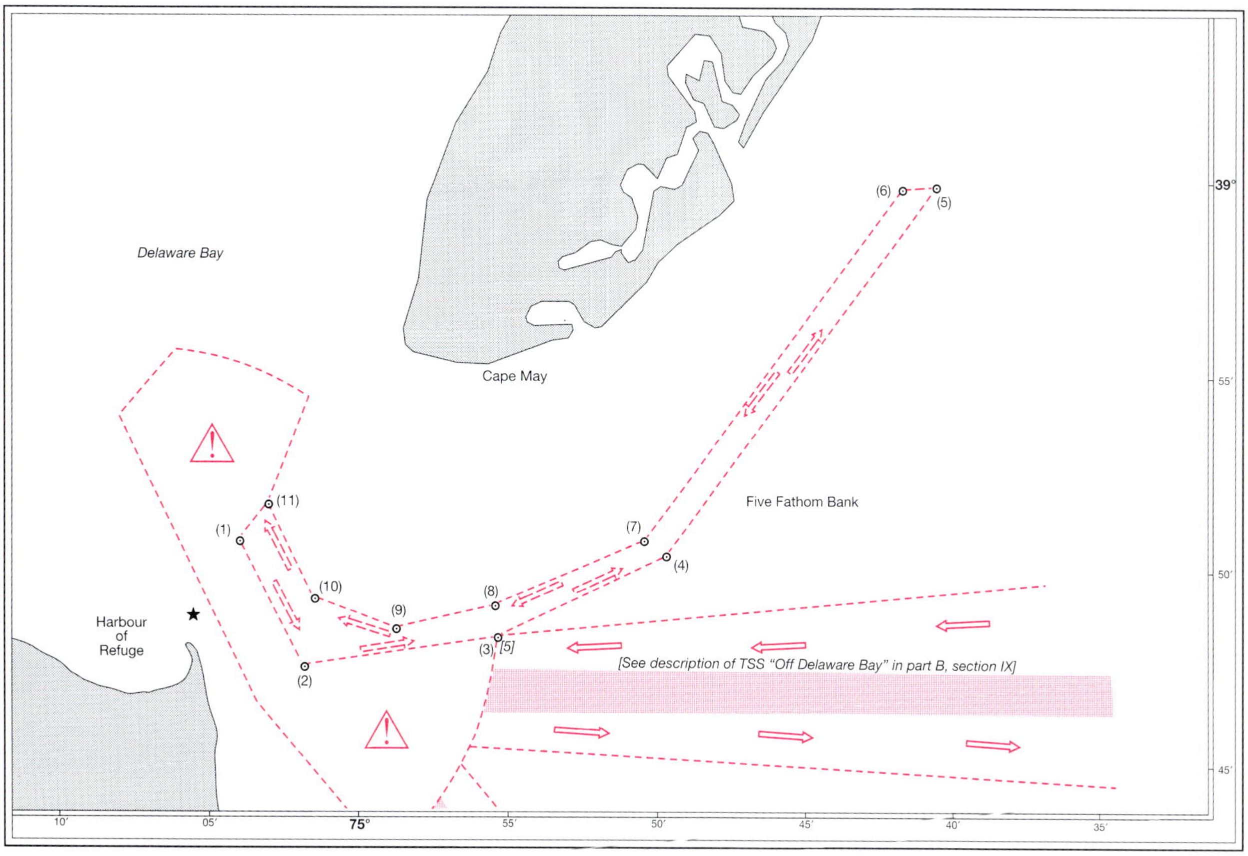

TWO-WAY ROUTE OFF DELAWARE BAY

RECOMMENDED TRACKS IN THE GULF OF CAMPECHE [Revoked]*

Existing recommended tracks and precautionary areas and their associated anchorages (adopted in 1983) in the Gulf of Campeche are revoked.

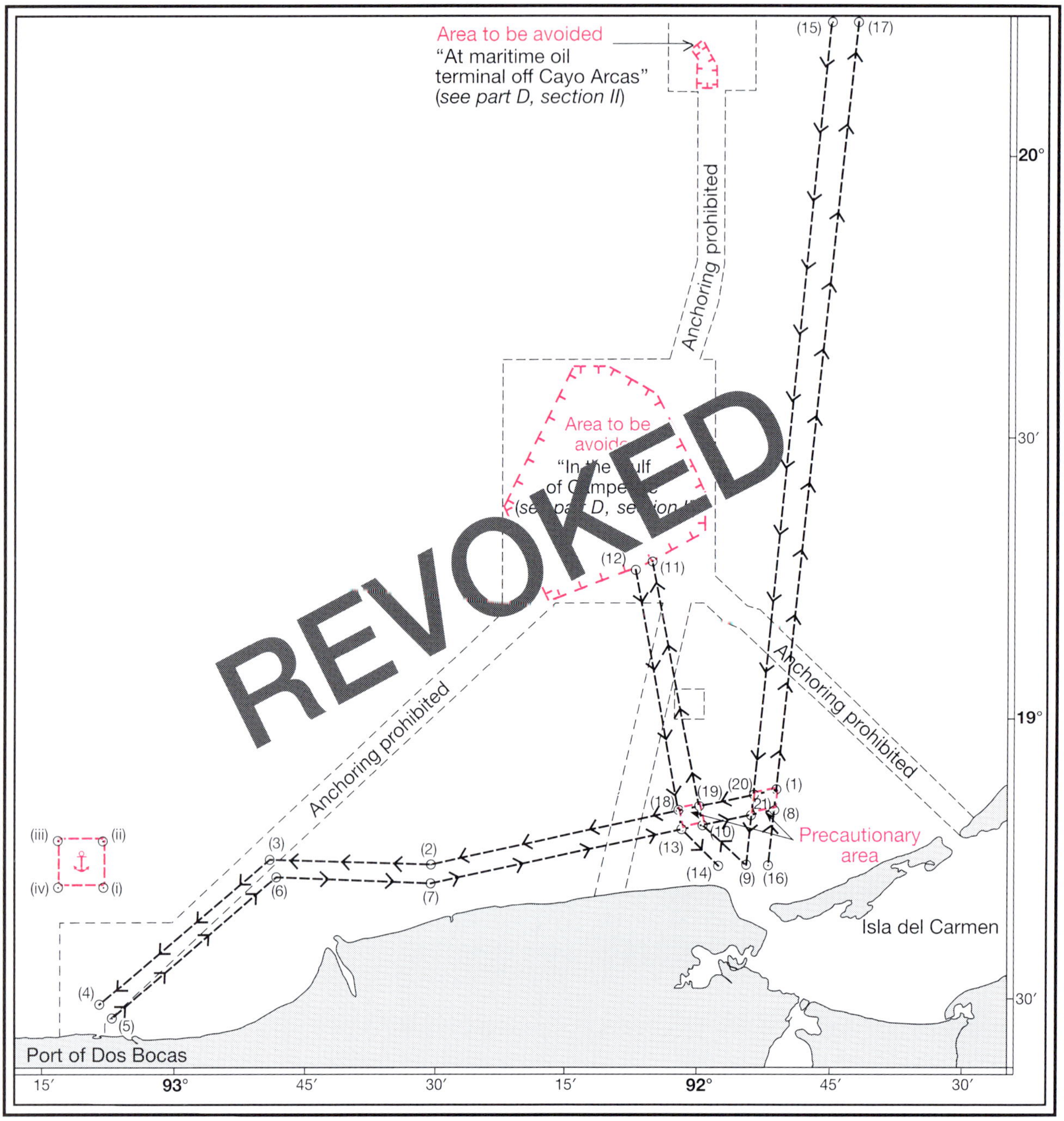

RECOMMENDED TRACKS IN THE GULF OF CAMPECHE

* Date of implementation of revocation: 0000 hours UTC on 1 December 2012.

RECOMMENDED TWO-WAY ROUTES AND PRECAUTIONARY AREAS TO THE NORTH-WEST OF THE PORT OF ISLA DEL CARMEN, CAMPECHE*

Note: See the areas to be avoided "In the Gulf of Campeche" and "At the Rebombeo oilfield" and "At the May oilfield" in part D, section II.

(Reference chart: Chart of the Bay of Campeche, S.M. 840, Ministry of the Navy (fourth edition, October 2010).
Note: This chart is based on World Geodetic System 1984 datum (WGS 84).)

Establishment of recommended routes and precautionary areas within the Gulf of Campeche oil exploration and production area

These recommended routes are primarily intended for oil exploration and production support vessels. Other vessels are strongly recommended to avoid the recommended system.

The ships' routeing measures from the port of Isla del Carmen, Campeche to the oil exploitation area of the Gulf of Campeche consist of the following:

- One precautionary area, labelled "A"
- Four two-way routes

Precautionary area "A"

All the recommended two-way routes lead to/away from the precautionary area labelled "A" located to the north-west of the port of Isla del Carmen, Campeche, with the direction of traffic flow indicated; it is bounded by a line connecting the following geographical positions:

(1)	18°45′.45 N,	091°53′.41 W	(3)	18°49′.03 N,	091°59′.04 W
(2)	18°49′.01 N,	091°54′.07 W	(4)	18°44′.14 N,	091°56′.15 W

Recommended two-way route 1

The following routes are only to be used for ships involved in oil-related activities.

Established at the north-north-west of the port of Isla del Carmen, Campeche:

(2)	18°49′.01 N,	091°54′.07 W	(6)	19°13′.88 N,	092°01′.09 W
(5)	19°15′.45 N,	091°59′.05 W	(7)	18°49′.02 N,	091°56′.44 W

Recommended two-way route 2

The following routes are only to be used for ships involved in oil-related activities.

Established at the north-west of the port of Isla del Carmen, Campeche:

(7)	18°49′.02 N,	091°56′.44 W	(9)	19°08′.83 N,	092°10′.84 W
(8)	19°09′.74 N,	092°08′.68 W	(3)	18°49′.03 N,	091°59′.04 W

Recommended two-way route 3

The following routes are only to be used for ships involved in oil-related activities.

Established at the west-north-west of the port of Isla del Carmen, Campeche:

(3)	18°49′.03 N,	091°59′.04 W	(11)	18°53′.09 N,	092°33′.27 W
(10)	18°55′.69 N,	092°35′.10 W	(12)	18°46′.50 N,	091°57′.55 W

* Date of implementation of new measures: 0000 hours UTC on 1 December 2012.

E

Recommended two-way route 4 with precautionary area "B"

The following routes are recommended for use by ships of 50 gross tonnage and upwards.

Established at the west of the port of Isla del Carmen, Campeche:

A junction, with a precautionary area labelled "B" bounded by a line connecting the following geographical positions:

(13)	18°46′.50 N,	092°47′.07 W	(15)	18°44′.70 N,	092°53′.00 W
(14)	18°46′.50 N,	092°50′.70 W	(16)	18°44′.70 N,	092°49′.37 W

A two-way route limited by the following geographical positions:

(12)	18°46′.50 N,	091°57′.55 W	(16)	18°44′.70 N,	092°49′.37 W
(13)	18°46′.50 N,	092°47′.07 W	(17)	18°44′.70 N,	091°56′.47 W

Note 1: An anchorage is established for vessels arriving at or manoeuvring north-east of the port of Isla del Carmen, Campeche, located north-west of the sea buoy.

Note 2: An anchorage is established for vessels arriving at or manoeuvring west to the port of Frontera, Tabasco.

(chartlet is on page 38-3/39-2)

E

RECOMMENDED TWO-WAY ROUTES TO THE NORTH-EAST OF THE PORT OF DOS BOCAS, TABASCO*

Note: See the areas to be avoided "In the Gulf of Campeche" and "At the Rebombeo oilfield" and "In the loading buoy area in the port of Dos Bocas, Tabasco" in part D, section II.

(Reference chart: Chart of the Bay of Campeche, S.M. 840, Ministry of the Navy (fourth edition, October 2010).
Note: This chart is based on World Geodetic System 1984 datum (WGS 84).)

The ships' routeing measures from the port of Dos Bocas, Tabasco to the oil exploitation area of the Gulf of Campeche consist of the following:

The following routes are only to be used for ships involved in oil-related activities.

Established at the north-east of the port of Dos Bocas, Tabasco:

Three two-way routes limited by the following geographical positions:

(18)	18°27′.63 N,	093°10′.78 W
(16)	18°44′.70 N,	092°49′.37 W
(15)	18°44′.70 N,	092°53′.00 W
(19)	18°29′.32 N,	093°12′.23 W

and

(13)	18°46′.50 N,	092°47′.07 W
(20)	18°53′.02 N,	092°38′.88 W
(21)	18°54′.43 N,	092°40′.74 W
(14)	18°46′.50 N,	092°50′.70 W

and

(10)	18°55′.69 N,	092°35′.10 W
(22)	19°05′.35 N,	092°23′.46 W
(23)	19°07′.09 N,	092°25′.02 W
(24)	18°57′.45 N,	092°36′.50 W

A junction, with a precautionary area labelled "B" as defined above.

Note 1: An anchorage is established for vessels other than tankers involved in cargo exportation activities, arriving at or manoeuvring north-west to the port of Dos Bocas, Tabasco.

Note 2: An anchorage is established for vessels involved in oil-related activities to the west of the Taratunich oil exploitation field.

Note 3: An anchorage is established for vessels involved in oil-related activities to the west of the oil exploitation area of the Rebombeo oilfield.

(chartlet is on page 38-3/39-2)

* Date of implementation of new measures: 0000 hours UTC on 1 December 2012.

E

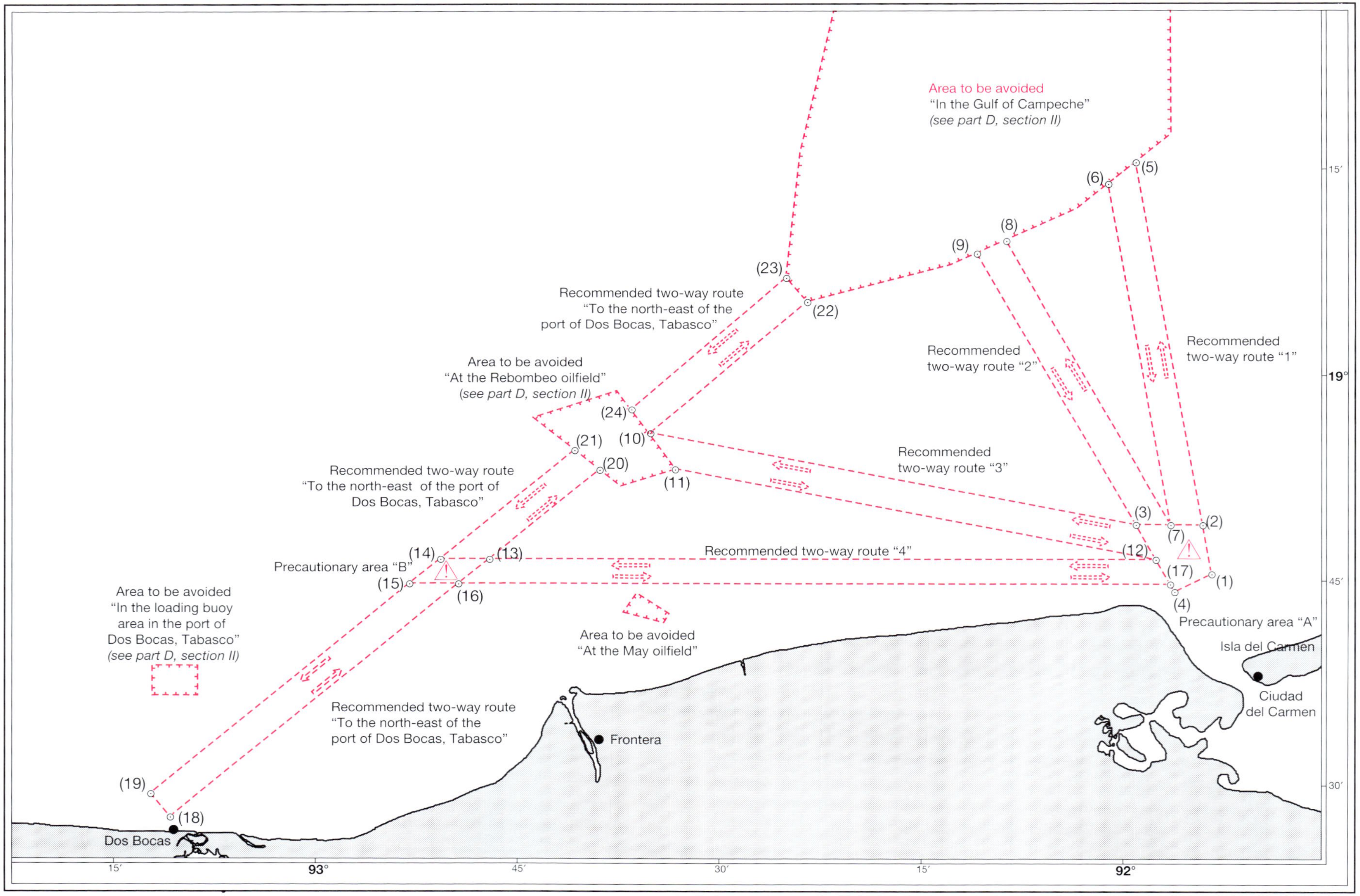

RECOMMENDED TWO-WAY ROUTES AND PRECAUTIONARY AREAS TO NORTH-WEST OF ISLA DEL CARMEN AND NORTH-EAST OF DOS BOCAS

RECOMMENDED TWO-WAY ROUTES AND PRECAUTIONARY AREAS OFF THE PORT OF CAYO ARCAS, FSO *TA'KUNTAH* AND FPSO *YÙUM K'AK' NÁAB*[*]

Note: See the areas to be avoided "At the port of Cayo Arcas" and "In the Gulf of Campeche" in part D, section II.

(Reference chart: Chart of the Bay of Campeche, S.M. 840, Ministry of the Navy (fourth edition, October 2010).
Note: This chart is based on World Geodetic System 1984 datum (WGS 84).)

The ships' routeing measures for tankers coming from abroad involved in loading crude oil for exportation and heading to the port of Cayo Arcas, FSO *Ta'kuntah* and FPSO *Yùum K'ak' Náab* in the Gulf of Mexico consist of the following elements:

- Four precautionary areas, labelled C, D, E and F
- Five two-way routes

The following routes are only to be used for oil tankers.

Routeing System I – Two two-way routes and a precautionary area

Established at the west and south-west of the port of Cayo Arcas for tankers arriving at the port or heading to the anchorage east of the FSO *Ta'kuntah* and vice versa:

Two-way route 1

(25)	20°12′.00 N,	092°16′.45 W	(27)	20°05′.50 N,	092°03′.36 W
(26)	20°05′.50 N,	092°07′.20 W	(28)	20°14′.80 N,	092°16′.45 W

A precautionary area labelled "C" bounded by a line connecting the following geographical positions:

(27)	20°05′.50 N,	092°03′.36 W	(30)	20°01′.30 N,	092°04′.30 W
(26)	20°05′.50 N,	092°07′.20 W	(31)	20°03′.30 N,	092°02′.90 W
(29)	20°03′.30 N,	092°06′.50 W			

Two-way route 2

(30)	20°01′.30 N,	092°04′.30 W	(33)	19°45′.00 N,	091°51′.20 W
(32)	19°45′.00 N,	091°53′.98 W	(31)	20°03′.30 N,	092°02′.90 W

Note: An anchorage for vessels involved in oil-related activities is established to the east of the Cantarell oilfield.

E

Routeing System II – Two two-way routes and a precautionary area

Established at the south-west and south of the port of Cayo Arcas with a two-way route for tankers arriving at the port or heading to the anchorage for this port:

Two-way route 1

(34)	20°03′.30 N,	092°16′.45 W	(26)	20°05′.50 N,	092°07′.20 W
(29)	20°03′.30 N,	092°06′.50 W	(35)	20°05′.50 N,	092°16′.45 W

A precautionary area labelled "D" is bounded by a line connecting the following geographical positions:

(35)	20°05′.50 N,	092°16′.45 W	(37)	20°03′.30 N,	092°18′.65 W
(36)	20°05′.50 N,	092°18′.65 W	(34)	20°03′.30 N,	092°16′.45 W

Two-way route 2

(31)	20°03′.30 N,	092°02′.90 W	(39)	20°05′.50 N,	091°55′.00 W
(38)	20°03′.30 N,	091°55′.00 W	(27)	20°05′.50 N,	092°03′.36 W

Note: An anchorage for tankers involved in loading operations in the port of Cayo Arcas is established to the south-east of the port of Cayo Arcas.

[*] Date of implementation of new measures: 0000 hours UTC on 1 December 2012.

Routeing System III – Two two-way routes and a precautionary area

Established at the west and south-west of the port of Cayo Arcas with a two-way route for tankers arriving at the FPSO *Yùum K'ak' Náab*:

Two-way route 1

(40)	20°13′.55 N,	092°18′.65 W	(35)	20°05′.50 N,	092°16′.45 W
(36)	20°05′.50 N,	092°18′.65 W	(25)	20°12′.00 N,	092°16′.45 W

A precautionary area labelled "D" as defined above.

Two-way route 2

(37)	20°03′.30 N,	092°18′.65 W	(42)	19°41′.65 N,	092°16′.45 W
(41)	19°40′.90 N,	092°18′.65 W	(34)	20°03′.30 N,	092°16′.45 W

A precautionary area labelled "E" is bounded by a line connecting the following geographical positions:

(41)	19°40′.90 N,	092°18′.65 W	(44)	19°39′.45 N,	092°16′.45 W
(43)	19°38′.70 N,	092°18′.65 W	(42)	19°41′.65 N,	092°16′.45 W

Routeing System IV – One two-way route and a precautionary area

Established at the south of the port of Cayo Arcas with a two-way route for tankers heading from the precautionary area labelled "C" to precautionary area labelled "F" and vice versa:

Two-way route

(29)	20°03′.30 N,	092°06′.50 W	(46)	19°45′.00 N,	092°04′.30 W
(45)	19°45′.00 N,	092°06′.50 W	(30)	20°01′.30 N,	092°04′.30 W

A precautionary area labelled "F" is bounded by a line connecting the following geographical positions:

(47)	19°42′.80 N,	092°06′.50 W	(46)	19°45′.00 N,	092°04′.30 W
(48)	19°42′.80 N,	092°04′.30 W	(45)	19°45′.00 N,	092°06′.50 W

E

Routeing System V – Two two-way routes

Established at the north of the FSO *Ta'kuntah* with a two-way route for tankers sailing from the anchorage to the east of this FSO and going on to handle cargo for the FSO *Ta'kuntah*, the FPSO *Yùum K'ak' Náab* and the port of Dos Bocas, Tabasco:

Two-way route 1

(49)	19°45′.00 N,	091°55′.00 W	(48)	19°42′.80 N,	092°04′.30 W
(46)	19°45′.00 N,	092°04′.30 W	(50)	19°42′.80 N,	091°55′.00 W

Precautionary areas labelled "E" and "F" as defined above.

Two-way route 2

(45)	19°45′.00 N,	092°06′.50 W	(44)	19°39′.45 N,	092°16′.45 W
(42)	19°41′.65 N,	092°16′.45 W	(47)	19°42′.80 N,	092°06′.50 W

Note: An anchorage is established for exportation tankers involved in loading operations at the FSO *Ta'kuntah* and the FPSO *Yùum K'ak' Náab*.

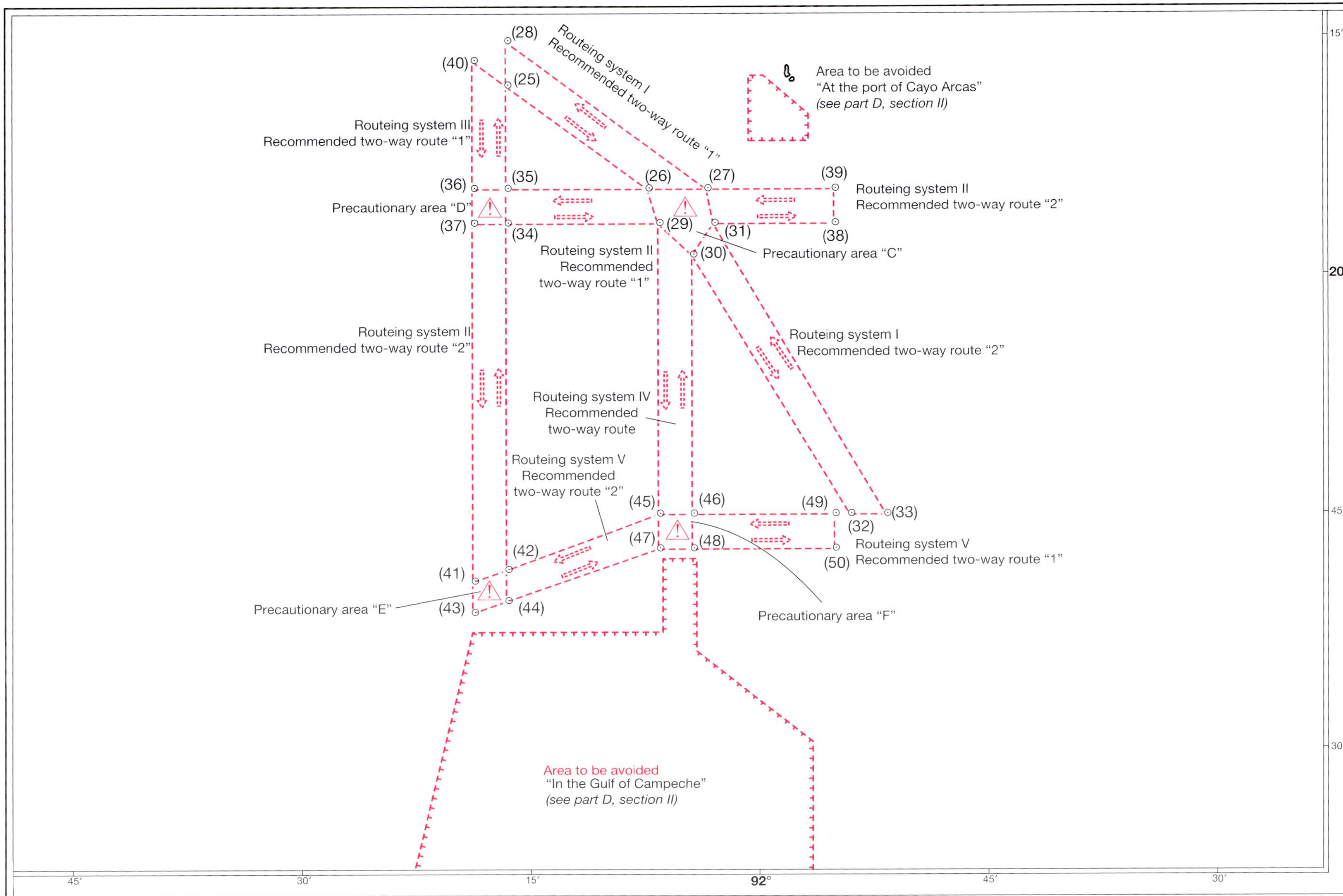

RECOMMENDED TWO-WAY ROUTES AND PRECAUTIONARY AREAS OFF CAYO ARCAS, FSO *TA'KUNTAH* AND FPSO *YÙUM K'AK' NÁAB*

E

PRECAUTIONARY AREA IN THE APPROACHES TO THE PORT OF VERACRUZ

(Reference chart: United States 28302, 1991 edition.
Note: This chart is based on World Geodetic System 1984 datum (WGS 84).)

Description of the precautionary area

A precautionary area is established comprising the islands and reefs where the approach channels to the port of Veracruz are situated. This area is bounded by an arc of a circle with a radius of 4.7 miles, centred on the lighthouse on the Island of Sacrificios, located in geographical position:

(28) 19°10′.49 N, 096°05′.53 W

starting on the coast in geographical position:

(19) 19°12′.93 N, 096°09′.70 W

to geographical position:

(20) 19°13′.03 N, 096°01′.39 W

thence bounded by a line connecting geographical position (20) and the following geographical positions:

(21) 19°12′.07 N, 096°01′.77 W
(22) 19°09′.57 N, 096°06′.00 W (on the coast)

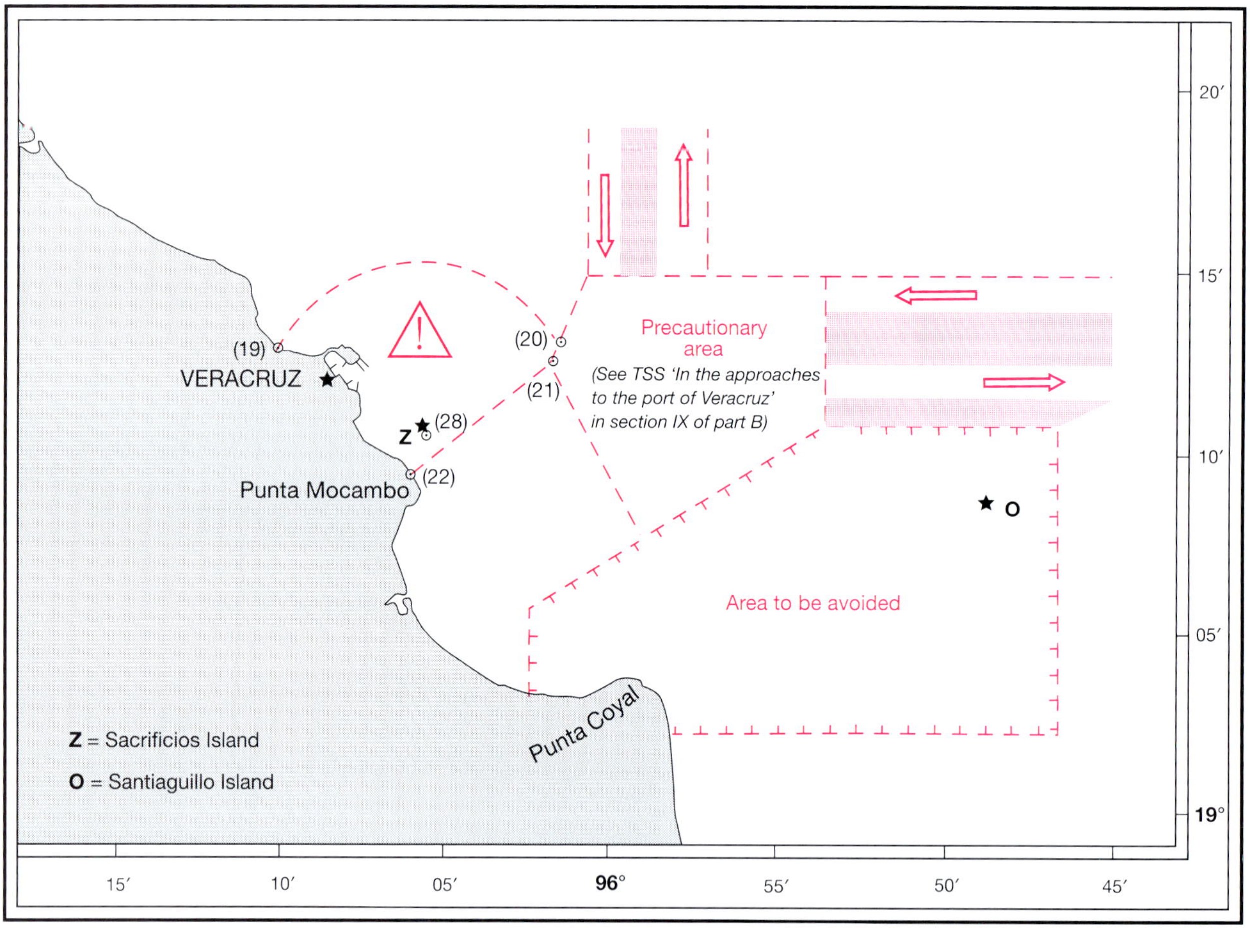

PRECAUTIONARY AREA IN THE APPROACHES TO THE PORT OF VERACRUZ

Part F

Associated Rules and Recommendations on navigation

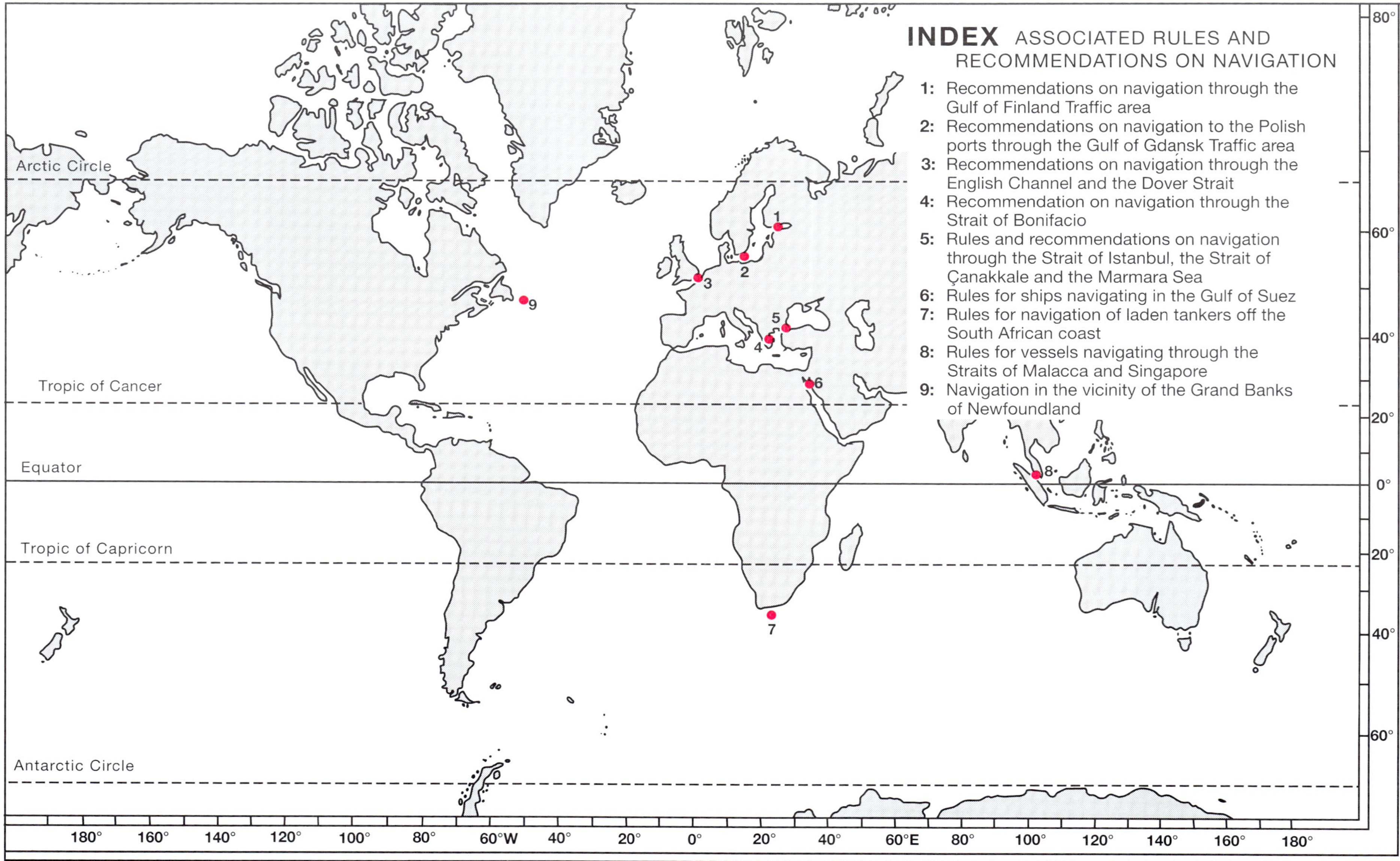

INDEX ASSOCIATED RULES AND RECOMMENDATIONS ON NAVIGATION

1: Recommendations on navigation through the Gulf of Finland Traffic area

2: Recommendations on navigation to the Polish ports through the Gulf of Gdańsk Traffic area

3: Recommendations on navigation through the English Channel and the Dover Strait

4: Recommendation on navigation through the Strait of Bonifacio

5: Rules and recommendations on navigation through the Strait of Istanbul, the Strait of Çanakkale and the Marmara Sea

6: Rules for ships navigating in the Gulf of Suez

7: Rules for navigation of laden tankers off the South African coast

8: Rules for vessels navigating through the Straits of Malacca and Singapore

9: Navigation in the vicinity of the Grand Banks of Newfoundland

RECOMMENDATIONS ON NAVIGATION THROUGH THE GULF OF FINLAND TRAFFIC AREA

1 Use of ships' routeing system

1.1 The traffic separation schemes in the Gulf of Finland have been adopted by IMO and rule 10 of the International Regulations for Preventing Collisions at Sea, 1972, as amended, applies. Subject to any factors that may adversely affect safe navigation, ships (especially oil and chemical tankers, ships carrying hazardous cargo and deep-draught ships) proceeding from the Baltic Sea to the Gulf of Finland and vice versa are strongly recommended to use the traffic separation schemes in the Gulf of Finland.

1.2 Ships crossing the east–westerly flow of traffic between the traffic separation schemes should cross as nearly as practicable at right angles to the traffic flow. Ships leaving or joining the east–westerly flow of traffic between the traffic separation schemes should do it at as small an angle as practicable to the recommended directions of traffic flow.

2 Crossing traffic

In the ice-free season there is heavy crossing traffic, consisting mainly of high-speed craft, between Helsinki and Tallinn. This increases the risk of collision in this area. Mariners are reminded that, when risk of collision is deemed to exist, the rules of the 1972 Collision Regulations fully apply and in particular the rules of part B, sections II and III, of which rules 15 and 19(d) are of specific relevance in a crossing situation.

3 Fishing and recreational sailing activities

Mariners should be aware that concentrations of recreational craft may be encountered between Porkkala, Helsinki and Tallinn in summer and should navigate with caution. Fishing vessels are reminded of the requirements of rule 10(i), and sailing vessels and all other vessels of less than 20 metres in length of the requirements of rule 10(j) of the 1972 Collision Regulations.

4 Pilotage

Under national laws, pilotage is mandatory in territorial waters.

5 Defects affecting safety

Ships having defects affecting operational safety should take appropriate measures to overcome these defects before entering the Gulf of Finland.

(chartlet overleaf)

F

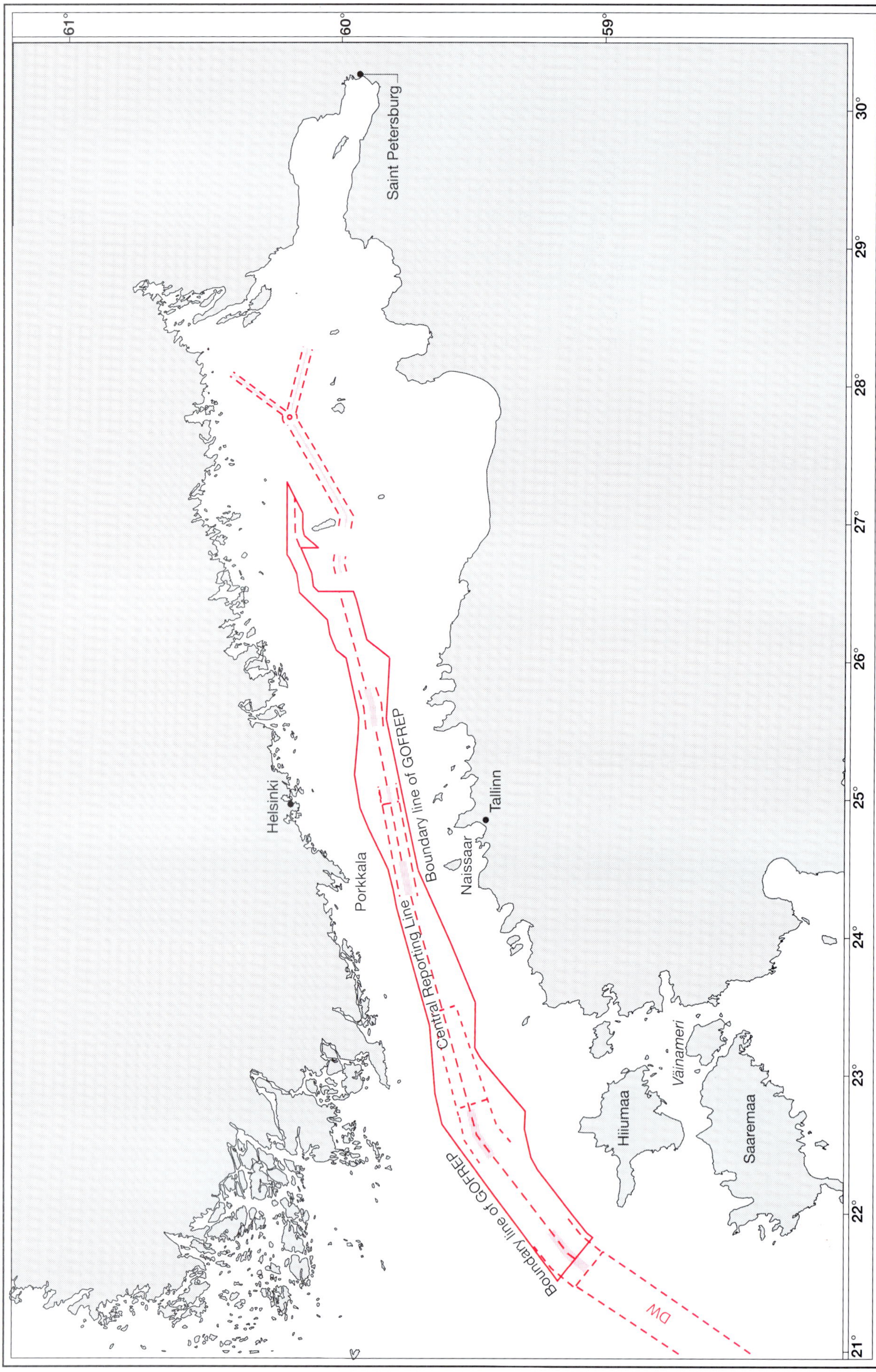

NAVIGATION THROUGH THE GULF OF FINLAND TRAFFIC AREA

RECOMMENDATIONS ON NAVIGATION TO THE POLISH PORTS THROUGH THE GULF OF GDAŃSK TRAFFIC AREA

1 Use of ships' routeing system

The traffic separation schemes for the approaches to the ports of Gdańsk and Gdynia in the Gulf of Gdańsk have been adopted by IMO and rule 10 of the International Regulations for Preventing Collisions at Sea, 1972, as amended, applies. Subject to any factors that may adversely affect safe navigation, ships proceeding from the Baltic Sea to the ports of Gdańsk and Gdynia and vice versa are strongly recommended to use the traffic separation schemes in the Gulf of Gdańsk.

1.1 Ships proceeding from the Baltic Sea to Gdańsk Northern Port (Port Północny) and vice versa are strongly recommended to use the traffic separation scheme "East".

1.2 Ships proceeding from the Baltic Sea to Gdańsk New Port (Nowy Port) and vice versa are strongly recommended to use the north-east part and south-west part of the traffic separation scheme "West".

1.3 Ships proceeding from the Baltic Sea to Gdynia and vice versa are strongly recommended to use the north-east part and the west part of the traffic separation scheme "West".

1.4 Ships approaching and navigating within the precautionary area should navigate with caution and should follow the recommended direction of traffic flow.

1.5 Ships engaged on international voyages proceeding between Gdańsk New Port (Nowy Port) (port, road) and Gdynia (port, road) are required* to proceed along the 163°–343° recommended track established between GD and NP buoys or transit along the proper one-way traffic lanes between GD, GN and NP buoys.

1.6 Ships engaged on international voyages proceeding from Gdańsk Northern Port (Port Północny) to Gdynia (port, road) or to Gdańsk New Port (Nowy Port) (port, road) are required*, after leaving pilot near the buoy PP, to proceed into north direction. After passing anchorage No. 5 for tankers they are required* to alter course to 314° and steer into direction of the buoy GN established in the precautionary area, alter course at this buoy and proceed further along the proper one-way traffic lane.

1.7 Ships engaged on international voyages proceeding from Gdańsk New Port (Nowy Port) (port, road) or from Gdynia (port, road) to Gdańsk Northern Port (Port Północny) (port, road) are required* to proceed along the proper one-way traffic lane to the precautionary area established around buoy GN, thence they are required* to alter course to 134° and proceed along the recommended track into direction of buoy ZS. After passing anchorage No. 5 for tankers they are required* to alter course to south and proceed into direction of the pilot embarkation position marked by the buoy PP.

2 Crossing traffic

There is a crossing traffic consisting mainly of recreational sailing vessels, fishing vessels and high-speed craft between Polish harbours situated in the Gulf of Gdańsk. This increases the risk of collision in this area. Mariners are reminded that, when risk of collision is deemed to exist, the rules of the 1972 Collision Regulations fully apply and in particular the rules of part B, sections II and III, of which rules 15 and 19(d) are of specific relevance in the crossing situation.

3 Fishing and recreational sailing activities

Mariners should be aware that concentrations of recreational craft may be encountered in the summer in the Gulf of Gdańsk between Gdynia, Sopot, Hel and Gdańsk and should navigate with caution. Fishing vessels are operating mainly from harbours situated in the Pucka Bay to fishing grounds in the Gulf of Gdańsk. Fishing vessels are reminded of the requirements of rule 10(i), and sailing vessels and all other vessels of less than 20 metres in length of the requirements of rule 10(j) of the 1972 Collision Regulations.

* Under the national law of Poland.

4 Pilotage

Under national laws, pilotage is mandatory in the roads and ports.

5 Defects affecting safety

Ships having defects affecting operational safety should take appropriate measures to overcome these defects before entering the Gulf of Gdańsk.

6 Ship reporting system and navigation information service

A mandatory ship reporting system (GDANREP) is established in the south-west part of the Gulf of Gdańsk in the territorial and internal waters of Poland. All ships navigating in the GDANREP ship reporting area are required to make use of the mandatory ship reporting system and information broadcasts made and operated by the Polish Maritime Administration through VTS "Gulf of Gdańsk", and to keep watch on VHF as appropriate.

Vessel Traffic Service "Gulf of Gdańsk" monitors compliance with the ships' routeing systems and mandatory ship reporting system adopted by the Organization.

7 Areas temporarily closed to navigation and fishing

Mariners are reminded that extensive areas that are temporarily closed to navigation and fishing are established in the waters of Gulf of Gdańsk.

F

RECOMMENDATIONS ON NAVIGATION THROUGH THE ENGLISH CHANNEL AND THE DOVER STRAIT

1 Use of ships' routeing system

1.1 Subject to any factors that may adversely affect safe navigation, ships proceeding from the western part of the English Channel to the Dover Strait and vice versa are strongly recommended to use the traffic separation scheme "Off Casquets".

1.2 Ships crossing or leaving or joining the easterly or westerly flow of traffic between the traffic separation schemes "Off Casquets" and "In the Dover Strait and adjacent waters" should cross as nearly as practicable at right angles or join or leave at as small an angle as practicable to the recommended directions of traffic flow.

1.3 Attention is drawn to the warnings relating to the use of the "Deep-water route forming part of the north-eastbound traffic lane of the Strait of Dover and adjacent waters traffic separation scheme".

1.4 Ships leaving the traffic separation scheme "At West Hinder" and intending to proceed through the Dover Strait should, when crossing the north-eastbound traffic lane of the traffic separation scheme "In the Strait of Dover and adjacent waters" and proceeding through the precautionary area in the vicinity of the Foxtrot 3 station (51°24′.15 N, 002°00′.38 E), maintain a course so as to leave the Foxtrot 3 station on their port side.

2 Crossing traffic

2.1 Heavy crossing traffic exists in parts of the English Channel and the Dover Strait, with increased risk of collision in these areas. Mariners are reminded that, when risk of collision is deemed to exist, the rules of the 1972 Collision Regulations fully apply and in particular the rules of part B, sections II and III, of which rules 15 and 19(d) are of specific relevance in the crossing situation.

3 Fishing and recreational sailing activities

3.1 Mariners should be aware that concentrations of fishing vessels and recreational craft may be encountered in the English Channel and the Dover Strait and should navigate with caution. Fishing vessels are reminded of the requirements of rule 10(i) and sailing vessels and all other vessels of less than 20 metres in length of the requirements of rule 10(j) of the 1972 Collision Regulations.

4 Pilotage

4.1 Masters of ships passing through the English Channel and the Dover Strait should take into account the possibility of availing themselves of the services of an adequately qualified deep-sea pilot* in connection with the requirements of safe navigation.

4.2 Masters of ships taking a deep-sea pilot in the North Sea are advised to embark the pilot prior to sailing.

4.3 Masters of ships approaching from the west are advised to embark their deep-sea pilot as far westward in the English Channel as practicable and make an early decision either to request helicopter delivery or to approach a pilot station (e.g. Brixham or Cherbourg).

4.4 Ships wishing to embark a Thames district pilot should proceed to the NE Spit or the Sunk pilot stations. Ships should not use the English inshore traffic zone as a route to these pilot stations if they can safely use the north-east traffic lane of the traffic separation scheme and make a judicious crossing of the south-west traffic lane in accordance with rule 10(c) of the 1972 Collision Regulations. Arrangements can also be made to embark district pilots in the western approaches to the English Channel (see paragraph 4.3).

5 Under-keel allowance for deep-draught ships

5.1 Masters of ships, when planning their passage through the Dover Strait and its approaches, should ensure that there is an adequate under-keel clearance at the time of passage. To achieve this, allowance must be made for the effects of squat at the passage speed, for uncertainties in charted depths and tide levels, and for the effects of waves and swell resulting from local and distant storms.

---

* Reference is made to the Recommendation on the use of adequately qualified deep-sea pilots in the North Sea, English Channel and Skagerrak (Assembly resolution A.486(XII)). This resolution may be revoked and replaced by one of similar title that is adopted by 28th session of IMO Assembly in 2013.

5.2 In assessing a safe under-keel allowance, masters of vessels constrained by their draught are strongly advised to consult the Sailing Directions, Mariners' Routeing Guides and Deep-Draught Planning Guides published for the area by hydrographic offices, and to be guided by the recommendations for under-keel allowance contained therein.

6 Tidal height predictions

6.1 When calculating the depth of water, mariners are reminded that the height of the tide in mid-Strait can be up to one metre less than that predicted for the adjacent standard port.

7 Mandatory and voluntary ship movement reporting schemes

7.1 A mandatory ship movement reporting scheme (CALDOVREP) has been jointly operated by the Governments of the United Kingdom and France in the English Channel and the Dover Strait since 1 July 1999. It is compulsory for all merchant ships of 300 gross tonnage and over to participate in the scheme.

7.2 Ships of less than 300 gross tonnage should continue to make reports under the existing voluntary MAREP scheme in circumstances where they:

- are "not under command" or at anchor in the traffic separation scheme or its inshore traffic zones;
- are "restricted in their ability to manoeuvre"; or
- have defective navigational aids.

The MAREP arrangements outside the coverage area remain unchanged.

8 Defects affecting safety

8.1 Ships having defects affecting operational safety, in addition to reporting such defects through the CALDOVREP scheme or by participating in the MAREP scheme, should take appropriate measures to overcome these defects before entering the Dover Strait.

9 Navigation information service

9.1 All ships navigating in the English Channel and the Dover Strait are recommended to make use of the information broadcasts made by the information services operated by the Governments of the United Kingdom and France, and to keep watch on VHF as appropriate, as set out in the CALDOVREP and MAREP schemes.

Note: See section II of part B, section II of part C, section I of part D and part E for description of traffic separation schemes, deep-water routes, areas to be avoided and recommended directions of traffic flow involved.

RECOMMENDATION ON NAVIGATION THROUGH THE STRAIT OF BONIFACIO*

Note: See "Routeing measures in the Strait of Bonifacio" in part E and mandatory ship reporting system "In the Strait of Bonifacio" in part G, section I.

1 Use of ships' routeing

Vessels navigating in the Strait shall exercise full diligence and regard for the requirements of the existing recommended two-way route in the Strait of Bonifacio. Due to the narrowness of the Strait, masters of vessels shall ensure that an appropriate monitoring of the ship's route is done on board in order to avoid groundings and collisions.

2 Ship reporting and navigation information

Ships of 300 gross tonnage and over entering the Strait shall participate in the mandatory ship reporting system (BONIFREP) established by the competent authorities as described in IMO's publication on Ships' Routeing (part G, section I).

3 Pilotage

Masters of vessels passing through the Strait are recommended to avail themselves of the services of a qualified pilot.

3.1 *Categories of ships concerned*

Ships for which the IMO Assembly recommends in its resolution A.766(18) of 4 November 1993 to Governments to prohibit or at least strongly discourage the transit in the Strait of Bonifacio:

> laden oil tankers and ships carrying dangerous chemicals or substances in bulk, as listed in the annex to resolution MEPC.49(31) adopted on 4 July 1991.

3.2 *Description of the applicable procedure for requesting a pilot*

Vessels wishing to order a Bonifacio Strait pilot should, as much as possible, send by e-mail or by fax the following information to the service named "Bonifacio Strait pilotage":

- Ship's name and call sign;
- type of vessel and gross tonnage;
- draught;
- destination port/name and address of the local agent;
- boarding position and ETA.

Twenty-four hours prior to arrival, vessels should inform or confirm their ETA to the head office of the Bonifacio Strait pilotage service.

Once on Bonifacio Strait road, vessels should confirm their ETA two hours prior to arrival, calling "Bonifacio Traffic" on VHF channel 10.

3.3 *Description of the pilotage service*

The pilotage area covers the Strait and its approaches. Usually the vessels entering the Strait board their pilots out of the "BONIFREP" zone.

The boarding positions are the following (WGS 84):

- Eastern boarding position: 41°24′.80 N, 009°30′.00 E;
- Western boarding position: 41°17′.28 N, 008°58′.50 E.

F

* Date of implementation of new recommendation: 0000 hours UTC on 1 July 2014.

RULES AND RECOMMENDATIONS ON NAVIGATION THROUGH THE STRAIT OF ISTANBUL, THE STRAIT OF ÇANAKKALE AND THE MARMARA SEA*

1 Use of ships' routeing

1.1 Vessels navigating in the Straits shall exercise full diligence and regard for the requirements of the traffic separation schemes (TSSs).

1.2 A vessel that is not able to comply with the requirements of the TSS shall inform the traffic control station well in advance. In such circumstances, the competent authority may temporarily suspend the particular TSS, or section(s) of it, and inform the vessels sailing in the area and advise them to comply with rule 9 of the International Regulations for Preventing Collisions at Sea, 1972.

1.3 In order to ensure safe transit of vessels which cannot comply with the TSS, the competent authority may temporarily suspend two-way traffic and regulate one-way traffic to maintain a safe distance between vessels.

2 Ship reporting and navigation information

2.1 All vessels entering the Straits are strongly recommended to participate in the reporting system (TUBRAP) established by the competent authority and concerning which the appropriate information has been promulgated by Notices to Mariners and other means.

2.2 For the purpose of efficient and expeditious traffic management, in the interest of safety of navigation and protection of the marine environment, vessels intending to pass through the Straits are strongly advised to give prior information on the size of the vessel, whether in ballast or loaded condition and whether carrying any hazardous and noxious cargo, as defined in relevant international conventions.

2.3 All vessels navigating in the Straits are recommended to make use of the information broadcasts made by the information services operated by the competent authority, and to keep watch on VHF as appropriate, in accordance with the TUBRAP scheme.

3 Pilotage

3.1 Masters of vessels passing through the Straits are strongly recommended to avail themselves of the services of a qualified pilot in order to comply with the requirements of safe navigation.

4 Daylight transit

Vessels having a maximum draught of 15 metres or more and vessels over 200 metres in overall length are advised to navigate the Straits in daylight.

5 Towing

Passage of a vessel under tow may only be carried out when using tugboat(s) or vessel(s) suitably equipped for the operation in order to ensure safe navigation.

6 Anchorage

When required, vessels may use the anchorages designated for this purpose.

* Hereinafter referred to as "the Straits".

RULES FOR SHIPS NAVIGATING IN THE GULF OF SUEZ

1 General provisions

1.1 Ships should take into account that crossing traffic may be encountered in the traffic junction eastward of Ain Sukhna and in the precautionary area off Ras Shukheir, and should be in a high state of readiness to manoeuvre in these areas.

1.2 Exceptional care is needed, when overtaking another ship within a lane, not to enter the separation zone or force the overtaken ship to do so.

1.3 Ships navigating in the Gulf of Suez are requested to keep continuous listening watch on the Suez Gulf Traffic Information Broadcasts and report to "SUZ" as from 1 January 1983 any aids to navigation which are malfunctioning or are out of position and which are not already included in the Suez Gulf Traffic Information Broadcasts.

2 Rules

2.1 All ocean ships should have their radar in effective use by day and night throughout the passage between Shaker Island and Suez Port as an aid to achieving maximum feasible lane conformity and avoiding risk of collision. Particular care is required for strict adherence to the confines of relevant traffic lanes.

2.2 Ships proceeding south from Suez should be alert for tankers heading for the SUMED oil terminal off Ain Sukhna.

2.3 Northbound tankers heading for the SUMED oil terminal should report their intention of using the traffic junction off Ain Sukhna on the appropriate frequencies.

2.4 All ships north- and south-bound, when navigating through the precautionary area off Ras Shukheir or in the vicinity of the July oilfield, should avoid overtaking in the traffic lanes in these areas.

2.5 All ships proceeding in and out of Ras Shukheir oil terminal, including service and supply craft serving the oil workings in July, Ramadan and Morgan oilfields, should only cross the south- and north-bound traffic flow through the precautionary area off Ras Shukheir. Within the precautionary area local rules relating to crossing traffic apply.

2.6 Tankers leaving the Ras Shukheir oil terminal and intending to join the northbound traffic lane should only do so when no through southbound traffic is in the vicinity and should always report their movements to other ships beforehand on VHF.

2.7 Ships anchored in the designated waiting area for Ras Shukheir should ensure that they are never less than 0.25 miles from the edge of the southbound traffic lane and should pay special regard to their correct light signals for ships at anchor. They should also show their deck lights.

(Adopted 1983)

RULES FOR NAVIGATION OF LADEN TANKERS OFF THE SOUTH AFRICAN COAST

1 Laden* tankers, when westbound, off the South African coast, should adhere to the following:

.1 Laden tankers should maintain a minimum distance of 20 nautical miles off the following landmarks:

.1 South Sand Bluff (International No. D4664)

.2 Bashee River (Mbashe Point) (D6438)

.3 Hood Point (D6420)

.4 Cape Receife (D6390).

.2 These tankers should then steer to pass through the westbound or northern lanes of the traffic separation schemes off the FA Platform and the Alphard Banks and then maintain a minimum distance of 20 nautical miles from the following landmarks:

.1 Cape Agulhas (D6370)

.2 Quoin Point (D6322)

.3 Cape Point (D6120)

.4 Slangkop Point (D6110)

.5 Cape Columbine (D5810).

2 Laden tankers, when eastbound off the South African coast, should similarly maintain a minimum distance of 25 nautical miles when passing the points listed in 1.1 and 1.2 and, when between Cape Agulhas and Cape Receife, steer a course to pass through the eastbound or southern lanes of the traffic separation schemes off the Alphard Banks and FA Platform.

Exemptions

3 The following exemptions to the laden tanker rules apply:

.1 Vessels calling at Cape Town (Table Bay) to rendezvous with service craft or helicopters should follow the recommended routes until, in the case of laden tankers when proceeding westbound, Cape Point light bears 000°(T) × 20 nautical miles, thence altering course to position Slangkop Point light 070°(T) × 20 nautical miles. From this position, course may be altered to the rendezvous area 5 nautical miles to the west of Green Point light (D5900) (replenishment area shown on chart SAN 1013).

.2 Laden tankers engaged on voyages solely between ports in the Republic of South Africa are exempted from the provisions in paragraphs 1 and 2 of these regulations and are to maintain a minimum distance of 10 nautical miles off salient points of the coast, subject to weather, sea and current conditions, when setting courses to their ports of loading and discharging.

.3 During the winter season (16 April to 15 October), westbound laden tankers should maintain the minimum distance of 20 nautical miles off the appropriate landmarks in paragraph 1.1. However, on approaching the winter zone, they may remain within the summer zone as close to the separation line as possible, and for the minimum period necessary, to ensure that they can remain on their Summer Load Line throughout. In the vicinity of the Alphard Banks and the FA Platform, they are to adjust their course to pass through the westbound traffic lanes.

F

* Definition: *laden tanker* means any tanker other than a tanker in ballast having in its cargo tanks residual cargo only.

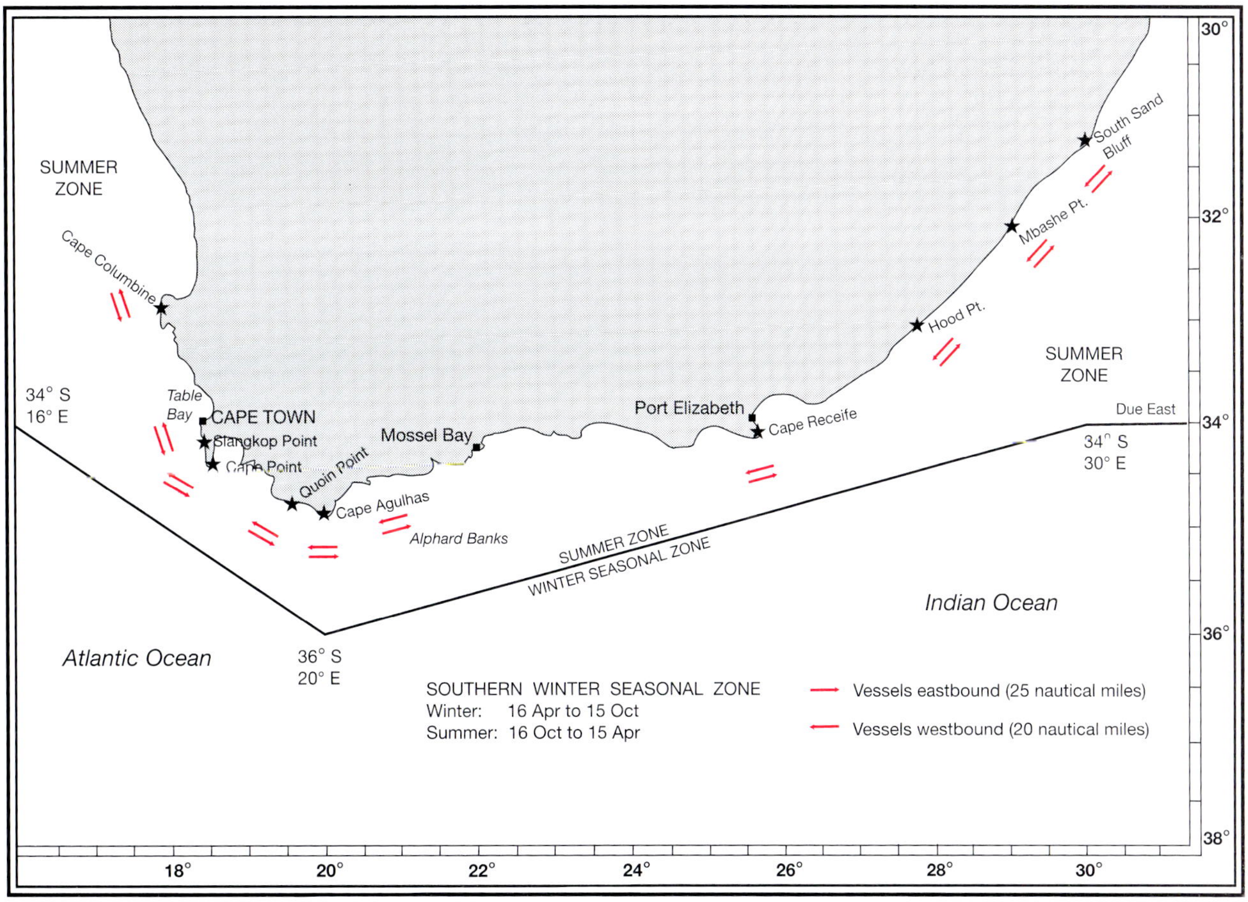

NAVIGATION OF LADEN TANKERS OFF THE SOUTH AFRICAN COAST

F

RULES FOR VESSELS NAVIGATING THROUGH THE STRAITS OF MALACCA AND SINGAPORE

Note: See also "Recommendatory measures for vessels crossing the traffic separation scheme and precautionary areas in the Singapore Strait during hours of darkness" in part E.

1 Definitions

For the purpose of these Rules the following definitions shall apply:

1 A vessel having a draught of 15 metres or more shall be deemed to be a deep-draught vessel.

2 A tanker of 150,000 dwt and above shall be deemed to be a very large crude carrier (VLCC).

Note: The above definitions do not prejudice the definition of "vessel constrained by her draught" described in rule 3(h) of the International Regulations for Preventing Collisions at Sea, 1972.

2 General provisions

1 Deep-draught vessels and VLCCs shall allow for an under-keel clearance of at least 3.5 metres at all times during the entire passage through the Straits of Malacca and Singapore and shall also take all necessary safety precautions, when navigating through the traffic separation schemes.

2 Masters of deep-draught vessels and VLCCs shall have particular regard to navigational constraints when planning their passage through the Straits.

3 All deep-draught vessels and VLCCs navigating within the traffic separation schemes are recommended to use the pilotage service of the respective countries when they become available.

4 Vessels shall take into account the precautionary areas where crossing traffic may be encountered and be in a maximum state of manoeuvring readiness in these areas.

3 Rules

Rule 1 Eastbound deep-draught vessels shall use the designated deep-water routes.

Rule 2 Eastbound deep-draught vessels navigating in the deep-water routes in Phillip Channel and Singapore Strait shall, as far as practicable, avoid overtaking.

Rule 3 All vessels navigating within the traffic separation scheme shall proceed in the appropriate traffic lane in the general direction of traffic flow for that lane and maintain as steady a course as possible, consistent with safe navigation.

Rule 4 All vessels having defects affecting operational safety shall take appropriate measures to overcome these defects before entering the Straits of Malacca and Singapore.

Rule 5 In the event of an emergency or breakdown of a vessel in the traffic lane the vessel shall, as far as practicable and safe, leave the lane by pulling out to the starboard side.

Rule 6 (a) Vessels proceeding in the westbound lane of the traffic separation scheme "In the Singapore Strait" when approaching Raffles lighthouse shall proceed with caution, taking note of the local warning system, and, in compliance with rule 18(d) of the International Regulations for Preventing Collisions at Sea, 1972, avoid impeding the safe passage of a vessel constrained by her draught which is exhibiting the signals required by rule 28 and which is obliged to cross the westbound lane of the scheme in order to approach the single-point mooring facility (in approximate position 01°11′.42 N, 103°47′.50 E) from Phillip Channel.

(b) Vessels proceeding in the traffic separation schemes, when approaching any of the precautionary areas, shall proceed with caution, taking note of the local warning system, and, in compliance with rule 18(d) of the International Regulations for Preventing Collisions at Sea, 1972, avoid impeding the safe passage of a vessel constrained by her draught which is exhibiting the signals required by rule 28 and which is obliged to cross that precautionary area.

F

(c) Information relating to the movement of ships constrained by their draught as referred to in paragraphs (a) and (b) above will be given by radio broadcasts. The particulars of such broadcasts are promulgated by Notices to Mariners. All vessels navigating in the area of the traffic separation scheme should monitor these radio broadcasts and take account of the information received.

Rule 7 VLCCs and deep-draught vessels navigating in the Straits of Malacca and Singapore shall, as far as it is safe and practicable, proceed at a speed of not more than 12 knots over the ground in the following areas:

(a) At One Fathom Bank traffic separation scheme;

(b) deep-water routes in the Phillip Channel and in Singapore Strait; and

(c) westbound lanes between positions 01°12′.51 N, 103°52′.25 E and 01°11′.59 N, 103°50′.31 E and between positions 01°11′.13 N, 103°49′.18 E and 01°08′.65 N, 103°44′.40 E.

Rule 8 All vessels navigating in the routeing system of the Straits of Malacca and Singapore shall maintain at all times a safe speed consistent with safe navigation, shall proceed with caution, and shall be in a maximum state of manoeuvring readiness.

Rule 9 (a) Vessels which are fitted with VHF radio communication are to participate in the ship reporting system adopted by the Organization.

(b) VLCCs and deep-draught vessels navigating in the Straits of Malacca and Singapore are advised to broadcast, eight hours before entering the traffic separation schemes, navigational information giving name, deadweight tonnage, draught, speed and times of passing One Fathom Bank lighthouse, Raffles lighthouse and Horsburgh lighthouse. Difficult and unwieldy tows are also advised to broadcast similar information.

Rule 10 All vessels navigating in the Straits of Malacca and Singapore are requested to report by radio to the nearest shore authority any damage to or malfunction of the aids to navigation in the Straits, or any aids out of position in the Straits.

Rule 11 Flag States, owners and operators should ensure that their vessels are adequately equipped in accordance with the appropriate international conventions/recommendations.

4 Warning

Mariners are warned that local traffic could be unaware of the internationally agreed regulations and practices of seafarers and may be encountered in or near the traffic separation schemes, and should take any precautions which may be required by the ordinary practice of seamen or by the special circumstances of the case.

NAVIGATION IN THE VICINITY OF THE GRAND BANKS OF NEWFOUNDLAND

All ships proceeding on voyages in the vicinity of the Grand Banks of Newfoundland shall avoid, as far as practicable, the fishing banks of Newfoundland north of latitude 43° N and pass outside regions known or believed to be endangered by ice.

F

Part G

Mandatory Ship Reporting Systems,
Mandatory Routeing Systems
and
Mandatory No Anchoring Areas

G

INTERNATIONAL CONVENTION FOR THE SAFETY OF LIFE AT SEA, 1974, AS AMENDED

Regulation V/11 – Ship reporting systems

1 Ship reporting systems contribute to safety of life at sea, safety and efficiency of navigation, and/or protection of the marine environment. A ship reporting system, when adopted and implemented in accordance with the guidelines and criteria developed by the Organization* pursuant to this regulation, shall be used by all ships, or certain categories of ships or ships carrying certain cargoes in accordance with the provisions of each system so adopted.

2 The Organization is recognized as the only international body for developing guidelines, criteria and regulations on an international level for ship reporting systems. Contracting Governments shall refer proposals for the adoption of ship reporting systems to the Organization.* The Organization will collate and disseminate to Contracting Governments all relevant information with regard to any adopted ship reporting system.

3 The initiation of action for establishing a ship reporting system is the responsibility of the Government or Governments concerned. In developing such systems, provisions of the guidelines and criteria developed by the Organization shall be taken into account.

4 Ship reporting systems not submitted to the Organization for adoption do not necessarily need to comply with this regulation. However, Governments implementing such systems are encouraged to follow, wherever possible, the guidelines and criteria developed by the Organization.* Contracting Governments may submit such systems to the Organization for recognition.

5 Where two or more Governments have a common interest in a particular area, they should formulate proposals for a co-ordinated ship reporting system on the basis of agreement between them. Before proceeding with a proposal for adoption of a ship reporting system, the Organization shall disseminate details of the proposal to those Governments which have a common interest in the area covered by the proposed system. Where a co-ordinated ship reporting system is adopted and established, it shall have uniform procedures and operations.

6 After adoption of a ship reporting system in accordance with this regulation, the Government or Governments concerned shall take all measures necessary for the promulgation of any information needed for the efficient and effective use of the system. Any adopted ship reporting system shall have the capability of interaction and the ability to assist ships with information when necessary. Such systems shall be operated in accordance with the guidelines and criteria developed by the Organization* pursuant to this regulation.

7 The master of a ship shall comply with the requirements of adopted ship reporting systems and report to the appropriate authority all information required in accordance with the provisions of each such system.

8 All adopted ship reporting systems and actions taken to enforce compliance with those systems shall be consistent with international law, including the relevant provisions of the United Nations Convention on the Law of the Sea.

9 Nothing in this regulation or its associated guidelines and criteria shall prejudice the rights and duties of Governments under international law or the legal regime of straits used for international navigation and archipelagic sea lanes.

10 The participation of ships in accordance with the provisions of adopted ship reporting systems shall be free of charge to the ships concerned.

11 The Organization shall ensure that adopted ship reporting systems are reviewed under the guidelines and criteria developed by the Organization.*

G

* Refer to the Guidelines and criteria for ship reporting systems, adopted by the Maritime Safety Committee of the Organization by resolution MSC.43(64) and amended by resolutions MSC.111(73) and MSC.189(79). Refer also to the General principles for ship reporting systems and ship reporting requirements, including guidelines for reporting incidents involving dangerous goods, harmful substances and/or marine pollutants, adopted by the Organization by resolution A.851(20).

Section I

Mandatory Ship Reporting Systems

Caution: The chartlets are for illustrative purposes only and must not be used for navigation. Mariners should consult the appropriate nautical publications and charts for up-to-date details on aids to navigation and other relevant information.

Warning: The geographical positions given in the descriptions of the reporting systems are only correct for charts using the same geodetic datum as the reference charts indicated under each description. Charts published by other hydrographic offices may use a different geodetic datum, as may new editions of the reference charts published after the adoption of the reporting system.

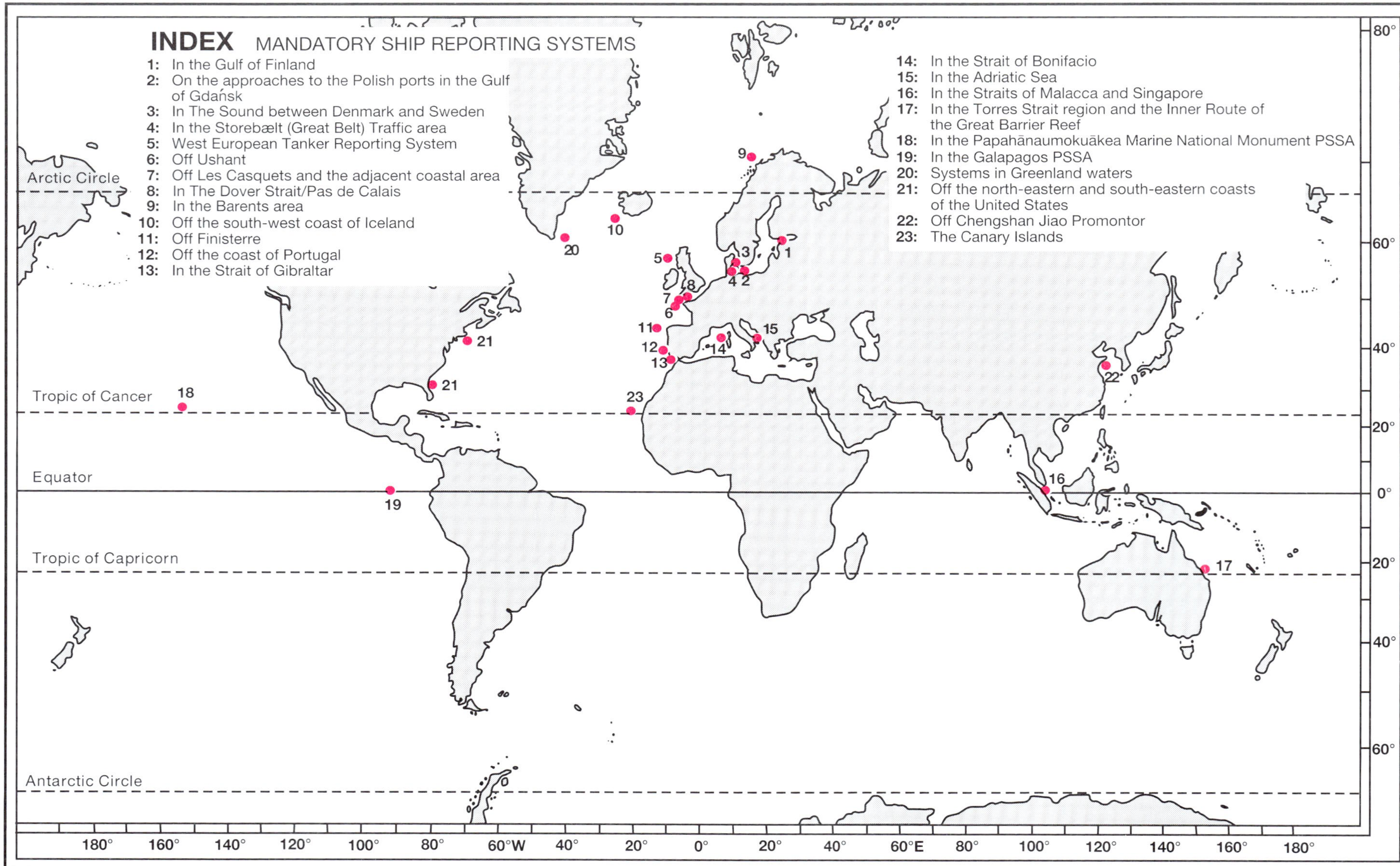
INDEX MANDATORY SHIP REPORTING SYSTEMS
1: In the Gulf of Finland
2: On the approaches to the Polish ports in the Gulf of Gdańsk
3: In The Sound between Denmark and Sweden
4: In the Storebælt (Great Belt) Traffic area
5: West European Tanker Reporting System
6: Off Ushant
7: Off Les Casquets and the adjacent coastal area
8: In The Dover Strait/Pas de Calais
9: In the Barents area
10: Off the south-west coast of Iceland
11: Off Finisterre
12: Off the coast of Portugal
13: In the Strait of Gibraltar
14: In the Strait of Bonifacio
15: In the Adriatic Sea
16: In the Straits of Malacca and Singapore
17: In the Torres Strait region and the Inner Route of the Great Barrier Reef
18: In the Papahānaumokuākea Marine National Monument PSSA
19: In the Galapagos PSSA
20: Systems in Greenland waters
21: Off the north-eastern and south-eastern coasts of the United States
22: Off Chengshan Jiao Promontor
23: The Canary Islands
Arctic Circle
Tropic of Cancer
Equator
Tropic of Capricorn
Antarctic Circle
180° 160° 140° 120° 100° 80° 60°W 40° 20° 0° 20° 40° 60°E 80° 100° 120° 140° 160° 180°
80° 60° 40° 20° 0° 20° 40° 60°

IN THE GULF OF FINLAND (GOFREP)

A ship reporting system is established in the Gulf of Finland on international waters.

1 Categories of ships required to participate in the system

1.1 Ships of 300 gross tonnage and over are required to participate in the mandatory ship reporting system. Ships under 300 gross tonnage should make reports in circumstances where they:

.1 are not under command or at anchor in the TSS;

.2 are restricted in their ability to manoeuvre; and

.3 have defective navigational aids.

2 Geographical coverage of the system and the number and edition of the reference chart used for the delineation of the system

2.1 The mandatory ship reporting system in the Gulf of Finland covers the international waters in the Gulf of Finland. In addition, Estonia and Finland have implemented mandatory ship reporting systems to their national water areas outside VTS areas. These reporting systems provide same services and make same requirements to shipping as the system operating in the international waters. The mandatory ship reporting system and the Estonian and Finnish national mandatory ship reporting systems are together referred as the GOFREP and their area of coverage respectively as the GOFREP area.

2.2 The reference charts are:

.1 Finnish Maritime Administration chart 901 (2006 edition, scale 1:200 000), Geodetic datum is the national geodetic chart co-ordinate system (KKJ). WGS 84 latitude correction is −0′.01 and the longitude correction +0′.19. Finnish Maritime Administration charts 952 (2004 edition, scale 1:250 000) and 953 (2004 edition, scale 1:250 000). Geodetic datum for charts 952 and 953 is WGS 84.

.2 Head Department of Navigation and Oceanography RF Ministry of Defence charts 22060-INT1213 (edition 2000, scale 1:250 000). Geodetic datum of year 1942 (Pulkovo). For obtaining position in WGS 84 datum such positions should be moved 0′.12 westward. 22061-INT1214 (edition 2002, scale 1:250 000). For obtaining position in WGS 84 datum such positions should be moved 0′.14 westward.

.3 Estonian Maritime Administration updated charts 502, 504, 507, 509, 511 (all charts in scale 1:100 000, WGS 84 datum).

Borderline point by point of the Gulf of Finland ship reporting area

(The co-ordinates below are in WGS 84 datum)

(1)	59°33′.30 N,	022°30′.00 E	(19)	60°09′.70 N,	026°36′.70 E
(2)	59°36′.50 N,	022°38′.10 E	(20)	60°11′.40 N,	026°44′.50 E
(3)	59°38′.10 N,	022°51′.40 E	(21)	60°12′.00 N,	026°45′.90 E
(4)	59°39′.40 N,	023°21′.10 E	(22)	60°12′.00 N,	027°13′.40 E
(5)	59°47′.00 N,	024°12′.40 E	(23)	60°12′.00 N,	027°17′.60 E
(6)	59°47′.80 N,	024°19′.90 E	(24)	60°10′.30 N,	027°10′.90 E
(7)	59°49′.00 N,	024°29′.30 E	(25)	60°08′.50 N,	027°04′.20 E
(8)	59°53′.50 N,	024°47′.10 E	(26)	60°08′.50 N,	026°57′.50 E
(9)	59°55′.30 N,	024°55′.80 E	(27)	60°08′.20 N,	026°54′.50 E
(10)	59°56′.60 N,	025°10′.20 E	(28)	60°05′.00 N,	026°49′.00 E
(11)	59°55′.90 N,	025°28′.30 E	(29)	60°08′.90 N,	026°49′.00 E
(12)	59°55′.70 N,	025°35′.00 E	(30)	60°06′.50 N,	026°38′.00 E
(13)	59°55′.90 N,	025°37′.20 E	(31)	60°06′.10 N,	026°32′.20 E
(14)	59°58′.60 N,	026°01′.00 E	(32)	60°05′.00 N,	026°30′.00 E
(15)	60°00′.80 N,	026°04′.50 E	(33)	59°57′.00 N,	026°30′.00 E
(16)	60°02′.30 N,	026°11′.30 E	(34)	59°56′.30 N,	026°26′.10 E
(17)	60°02′.80 N,	026°17′.70 E	(35)	59°54′.00 N,	026°09′.10 E
(18)	60°09′.20 N,	026°29′.50 E	(36)	59°48′.90 N,	026°01′.20 E

(37)	59°49′.60 N,	025°34′.60 E	(44)	59°17′.50 N,	022°43′.90 E
(38)	59°42′.20 N,	024°28′.80 E	(45)	59°17′.70 N,	022°36′.10 E
(39)	59°34′.60 N,	023°57′.10 E	(46)	59°16′.20 N,	022°23′.80 E
(40)	59°28′.90 N,	023°31′.20 E	(47)	59°14′.70 N,	022°18′.40 E
(41)	59°29′.00 N,	023°11′.40 E	(48)	59°03′.40 N,	021°50′.90 E
(42)	59°28′.20 N,	023°08′.50 E	(49)	59°02′.10 N,	021°49′.00 E
(43)	59°27′.40 N,	023°06′.40 E	(50)	59°10′.00 N,	021°30′.00 E

3 Format, content of reports, times and geographical positions for submitting reports, Authority to whom reports should be sent and available services

Short Report is always reported verbally on VHF. The short title for ship report is GOFREP. Vessels are urged to update their AIS information before entering the Gulf of Finland since they may fulfil the Full Report reporting requirements through the use of AIS. In cases where it is not possible to transmit the report fully with AIS, additional information may be reported by other means.

3.1 *Format*

3.1.1 The information given below is derived from the format-type given in paragraph 2 of the appendix to the annex to resolution A.851(20).

3.2 *Content*

3.2.1 A Short Report by voice from a ship to the shore-based Authorities should contain the following information:

A Vessel's name, call sign and IMO identification. MMSI may be reported.

C Geographical position by two six-digit groups; *or*

D Bearing and distance in nautical miles from a clearly identified landmark.

E True course in three-digit group.

3.2.2 A Full Report from a ship to the shore-based Authorities by voice or by non-verbal means should contain the following information:

A Vessel's name, call sign and IMO identification. MMSI may be reported.

C Geographical position by two six-digit groups; *or*

D Bearing and distance in nautical miles from a clearly identified landmark.

E True course in three-digit group.

F Speed in knots with one decimal.

H Time (UTC) and point of entry into the GOFREP area.

I Destination and ETA.

O Vessel's present draught in metres with one decimal.

P Dangerous goods on board, main classes and total quantity in metric tons with up to two decimals. The amount of classes 1 and 7, if any, shall be reported separately.*

Q Brief details of defects or restrictions of manoeuvrability.

R Description of pollution or dangerous goods lost overboard.

T Address for the communication of cargo information.

U Ship's type and length in metres.

W Total number of persons on board.

* In addition to designator P report, information on cargo other than dangerous goods is collected from all ships entering or leaving the ports of European Union countries in the Gulf of Finland. Ships are not required to report the information on cargo other than dangerous goods. Information is asked from ships only if it cannot be obtained by other means.

X Characteristics and estimated quantity of bunker fuel for ships carrying more than 5000 tons of bunker and navigational status.

All VHF, telephone, radar, AIS and other relevant information will be recorded and the records stored for 30 days.

3.3 *Geographical position for submitting reports*

3.3.1 The Gulf of Finland mandatory ship reporting system area is divided into three areas of monitoring responsibility with a borderline. This borderline is referred as Central Reporting Line and it consists of two parts.

The western part is drawn through the midpoints of the separation zones of the traffic separation schemes off Kõpu, Hankoniemi, Porkkala and Kalbådagrund to 59°59′.15 N, 026°30′.00 E.

The eastern part of the Central Reporting Line is drawn from the point 59°57′.00 N, 026°30′.00 E to 60°05′.00 N, 026°30′.00 E and further through the borderline of the Russian territorial sea and the outer limit of the Finnish Exclusive Economic Zone eastwards until the point 60°08′.90 N, 026°49′.00 E. From this point the Central Reporting Line continues through the limit of the Exclusive Economic Zone (EEZ) of Finland and the EEZ of Russia further to the point 60°10′.30 N, 026°57′.50 E to 60°10′.30 N, 027°10′.90 E and to 60°12′.00 N, 027°17′.60 E.

Monitoring of the GOFREP area north of the Central Reporting Line is the responsibility of Helsinki Traffic, and south of the Central Reporting Line in the area west of longitude 26°30′.00 E is the monitoring area of Tallinn Traffic and east of the longitude 26°30′.00 E south of the Central Reporting Line is the monitoring area of St. Petersburg Traffic. Thus,

- the vessels entering the mandatory ship reporting area north of the Central Reporting Line report to Helsinki Traffic,
- south of the Central Reporting Line east of longitude 26°30′.00 E report to St. Petersburg Traffic, and
- south of the Central Reporting Line west of longitude 26°30′.00 E or from Väinameri report to Tallinn Traffic.

3.3.2 Ships shall submit a Full Report:

.1 when entering the GOFREP area from the west or from Väinameri,

.2 on departure from a port or latest before entering the reporting area,

.3 on departure from a port if it shall not enter the reporting area at all,

.4 before departing from Russian port areas.

A Full Report on departure from a port is given to the Traffic Centre of the country whose port the vessel is departing in the Gulf of Finland traffic area.

3.3.3 Ships that are registered in domestic traffic navigating exclusively inside the inner territorial waters are not required to make a Full Report when departing from a port in the Gulf of Finland.

3.3.4 Ships shall submit a Short Report:

.1 on entering the GOFREP area from the Estonian or Finnish VTS areas in the Gulf of Finland,

.2 on crossing the Western or Väinameri Reporting Line inward-bound to Gulf of Finland,

.3 on crossing the Central Reporting Line,

.4 whenever there is a change in the vessel's navigational status, excluding the change of status when berthing or unberthing.

A Short Report is given on VHF when crossing the Central Reporting Line to the Traffic Centre of the country to which monitoring area the vessel is proceeding.

3.4 *Crossing traffic*

3.4.1 Reports to the nearest shore station should be made on departure from a port within the coverage area. Recognizing that ferries crossing between Helsinki and Tallinn generally operate according to published schedules, special reporting arrangements can be made on a ship-by-ship basis, subject to the approval of **both** HELSINKI TRAFFIC and TALLINN TRAFFIC.

3.4.2 Further reports should be made to the relevant shore station whenever there is a change of navigational status or circumstance, particularly in relation to items Q and R of the reporting format.

3.4.3 In the area between Helsinki and Tallinn lighthouses there is a heavy crossing traffic in summer consisting mostly of high-speed craft and recreational craft. In the area between Porkkala lighthouse and Naissaar there are recreational sailing activities in summer.

3.5 *Authority*

3.5.1 The shore-based Authorities are:

Estonia:	Estonian Maritime Administration
Finland:	Finnish Maritime Administration
Russian Federation:	Russian Maritime Administration

3.5.2 The Estonian, Finnish and Russian Authorities monitor shipping within the mandatory ship reporting area of the Gulf of Finland by radar. This does not relieve shipmasters of their responsibility for the navigation of their ship.

4 Information to be provided to participating ships and procedures to be followed

4.1 *Information provided*

4.1.1 Each Authority provides information to shipping about specific and urgent situations which could cause conflicting traffic movements and other information concerning safety of navigation, for instance information about weather, ice, water level, navigational problems or other hazards. Information is broadcast on the following frequencies when necessary or on request.

Station	Frequency	Times	Additional broadcasts in wintertimes
Tallinn	Main channel 61 Reserve channel 81	on request or when needed	on request or when needed
Helsinki	Main channel 60 Reserve channel 80	on request or when needed	on request or when needed
St. Petersburg	Main channel 74 Reserve channel 10	on request or when needed	on request or when needed

4.1.2 Information broadcasts will be preceded by an announcement on VHF channel 16 on which channel it will be made. All ships navigating in the area should listen to the announced broadcast.

4.1.3 If necessary, individual information can be provided to a ship, particularly in relation to positioning and navigational assistance or local conditions. If a ship needs to anchor due to breakdown or emergency, the operator can recommend suitable anchorage in the area.

4.2 *Ice routeing in winter*

4.2.1 During severe ice conditions the traffic separation schemes may be declared not valid. Such a decision is agreed jointly by the National Icebreaking Authorities and communicated to shipping with the daily ice reports. The decision may include all or a named traffic separation scheme.

4.2.2 During the period when the Gulf of Finland is covered by ice, ships reporting to the Centre will receive information on the recommended route through the ice and/or are requested to contact the national co-ordinating icebreaker for further instructions. The icebreaker gives the route according to the ice situation to the ships which fulfil the national ice class regulations and which are fit for winter navigation.

4.3 *Deviations*

4.3.1 If a ship participating in the mandatory ship reporting system fails to appear on the radar screen or fails to communicate with the Authority or an emergency is reported, MRCCs or MRSCs in the area are responsible for initiating a search for the ship in accordance with the rules laid down for the search and rescue service, including the involvement of other participating ships known to be in that particular area.

5 Radio communication required for the system, frequencies on which reports should be transmitted and information to be reported

5.1 The radiocommunications equipment required for the system is that defined in the GMDSS for sea area A1.

5.2 Ships are required to maintain a continuous listening watch in the area and to report and take any action required by the maritime Authorities to reduce risks.

5.3 Common call and information channels:

channel 16 call and distress

5.4 The reports can be made verbally on VHF, by AIS or by facsimile as follows:

- Full Report in advance is to be sent by facsimile or e-mail.
- Short Report is to be made verbally on VHF.
- Full Report is made by non-verbal means (facsimile, AIS or e-mail) or verbally on VHF.

5.5 Confidential information may be transmitted by other means.

5.6 The language used for communication shall be English, using the IMO Standard Marine Communication Phrases, where necessary.

6 Relevant rules and regulations in force in the area of the system

6.1 *Regulations for preventing collisions at sea*

The International Regulations for Preventing Collisions at Sea, 1972 are applicable throughout the reporting area.

6.2 *Traffic separation schemes*

The traffic separation schemes in the Gulf of Finland have been adopted by IMO and rule 10 of the International Regulations for Preventing Collisions at Sea applies.

6.3 *Pilotage*

Pilotage is mandatory in national waters under national laws.

6.4 *Dangerous and hazardous cargoes*

6.4.1 Ships carrying dangerous or hazardous cargoes and bound to or from any port within the ship reporting area must comply with the international and national regulations. The ship reporting system does not relieve ship's masters of their responsibility to give the nationally required reports and information to customs authorities.

6.4.2 Discharges of oil and ship-generated waste are monitored by the joint Estonian, Finnish and Russian Authorities. Ships causing pollution within the area can be prosecuted and fined.

7 Shore-based facilities to support operation of the system

The joint Estonian, Finnish and Russian Authorities have radar, information processing and retrieval system, VHF radio and Automatic Identification System (AIS) facilities. The frequencies used in AIS-NET are AIS1 and AIS2.

7.1 *HELSINKI TRAFFIC*

7.1.1 *System capability*

7.1.1.1 The control centre is situated at the Helsinki VTS in Helsinki. The operator can control, monitor and display the status of all the VTS sensors from the consoles. The VTS Centre will at all times be manned by two operators.

7.1.1.2 HELSINKI TRAFFIC maintains a continuous watch on traffic in the Gulf of Finland on channels 60 and 16. Operators add reported vessel information to the associated database and can display supporting information on the screen. The system is capable of providing an automatic alarm to identify any track which strays into an unauthorized area. Recording equipment automatically stores information from all tracks, which can either be replayed in the system or from the recorded resource. Records are made by an authorized method that can be used as evidence. Operators have access to different ship registers and hazardous cargo data.

7.1.2 *Radar facilities*

7.1.2.1 The surveillance sensors can observe targets of at least 300 gross tonnage and a minimum height of 10 metres in the given traffic area.

7.1.3 *Radio communication facilities*

7.1.3.1 Radiocommunication terminals are sited in the consoles of HELSINKI TRAFFIC operation room. VHF radio transceivers are located at Hanko, Porkkala, Harmaja, Emäsalo and Orrengrund.

The VHF channels used are:

- channel 60 main channel
- channel 80 reserve channel

7.1.4 *AIS facilities*

7.1.4.1 HELSINKI TRAFFIC can continually receive the messages broadcasted by ships fitted with transponders to gain information on their identity and position. This information is displayed as an icon on an electronic chart covering the Gulf of Finland mandatory ship reporting area.

7.1.5 *Personnel qualifications and training*

7.1.5.1 HELSINKI TRAFFIC is staffed with personnel trained according to national and international recommendations.

7.1.5.2 The training of the personnel comprises an overall study of the navigation safety measures, the relevant international (IMO) and national provisions with respect to safety of navigation. The training also includes thorough real-time simulations in different ship bridge simulators. The trainees are trained as well in navigating ships through the VTS area as servicing shipping from the VTS Centre.

7.2 *TALLINN TRAFFIC*

7.2.1 *System capability*

7.2.1.1 The system is managed from the Tallinn VTS Centre. There are two operator's positions with expansion capabilities and equipment for technical supervision of the systems.

7.2.1.2 TALLINN TRAFFIC maintains a continuous watch over traffic on the Gulf of Finland on channels 61 and 16. Operators add the reported vessel information to the associated database and can display supporting information on screen. The system is capable of providing an automatic alarm to identify any track that strays into the unauthorized area. Recording equipment automatically stores information from all tracks, which can either be replayed on the system or from the recorded resource. Records are made according to an authorized method that can be used as evidence.

7.2.2 *Radar facilities*

7.2.2.1 The surveillance sensors can observe targets of at least 300 gross tonnage and a minimum height of 10 metres in the given traffic area.

7.2.3 *Radio communication facilities*

7.2.3.1 VHF radio transceivers cover all the TALLINN TRAFFIC area of responsibility. The working channels are as follows:

- channel 61 main channel
- channel 81 reserve channel

7.2.4 *AIS facilities*

7.2.4.1 AIS system covers all the TALLINN TRAFFIC area of responsibility. The relevant information can be displayed at the operator's working positions on the screens and database.

7.2.5 *Personnel qualifications and training*

7.2.5.1 TALLINN TRAFFIC is staffed with personnel trained according to national and international recommendations.

7.2.5.2 The training of the personnel comprises an overall study of the navigation safety measures, the relevant international (IMO) and national provisions with respect to safety of navigation. The training also includes thorough real-time simulations.

7.3 ***ST. PETERSBURG TRAFFIC***

7.3.1 *System capability*

7.3.1.1 The Centre is situated at VTMIS Centre located in Petrodvorets. The Centre is linked with shore-based VHF station located at Gogland Island. VHF range covers the waters close to the border.

7.3.1.2 ST. PETERSBURG TRAFFIC maintains a continuous watch on traffic on the Gulf of Finland on channels 74 and 16. Operators add reported vessel information to the associated database and can display supporting information on screen. The system is capable of providing an automatic alarm to identify any track which strays into an unauthorized area. Recording equipment automatically stores information from all tracks, which can either be replayed on the system or from the recorded resource.

7.3.2 *Radar facilities*

7.3.2.1 The nearest radar sensor to the ship reporting system is placed on Gogland Island with antenna height 80 metres above sea level; it can observe targets at least 300 gross tonnage at the distances up to 026°30′ E.

7.3.3 *Radio communication facilities*

7.3.3.1 Radiocommunication terminals are sited in consoles of ST. PETERSBURG TRAFFIC operation rooms. VHF radio transceivers are located at Gogland.

The VHF channels used are:

- channel 74 main channel
- channel 10 reserve channel

7.3.4 *AIS facilities*

7.3.4.1 ST. PETERSBURG TRAFFIC can monitor ships sailing in the eastern part of the Gulf of Finland to the east of 026°30′ E and equipped with universal AIS shipborne stations.

7.3.5 *Personnel qualifications and training*

7.3.5.1 ST. PETERSBURG TRAFFIC is staffed with personnel trained according to national and international recommendations.

7.3.5.2 The training of the personnel comprises an overall study of the navigation safety measures, the relevant international (IMO) and national provisions with respect to safety of navigation. The training also includes thorough real-time simulations.

8 Alternative communication if the communication facilities of the shore-based Authorities fail

8.1 The system is designed with sufficient system redundancy to cope with normal equipment failure.

9 Measures to be taken if a ship fails to comply with the requirements of the system

9.1 The primary objective of the system is to facilitate the exchange of information between the ship station and the shore station and to support safe navigation and the protection of the marine environment. All means will be used to encourage and promote the full participation of ships required to submit reports under SOLAS regulation V/11. If reports are not submitted and the offending ship can be positively identified, then information will be passed to the relevant Flag State Authorities for investigation and possible prosecution in accordance with national legislation.

Appendix 1

Designators used in the Gulf of Finland mandatory ship reporting system and the format of the reports

Designator	Function	Information required
A	Ship	Vessel's name, call sign and IMO identification. MMSI may be reported.
C	Position	Geographical position by two six-digit groups; *or*
D	Position	Bearing and distance in nautical miles from a clearly identified landmark
E	Course	True course in three-digit group
F	Speed	Speed in knots with one decimal
H	Entry	Time (UTC) and point of entry into the GOFREP area
I	Destination and ETA	Destination and expected time of arrival
O	Draught	Vessel's present draught in metres with one decimal
P	Cargo	Dangerous goods on board, main classes and total quantity in metric tons with up to two decimals. The amount of classes 1 and 7, if any, shall be reported separately.*
Q	Deficiencies	Brief details of defects or restrictions of manoeuvrability
R	Pollution	Description of pollution or dangerous goods lost overboard
T	Owner or agent	Contact information of agent in the Gulf of Finland
U	Size and type	Ship's type and length in metres
W	Persons	Total number of persons on board
X	Bunkers and navigational status	Characteristics and estimated quantity of bunker fuel for ships carrying more than 5000 tons of bunker and navigational status

A Short Report consists of designators A, C *or* D and E. Vessels may additionally be requested to report designator F.

A Full Report consists of designators A, C *or* D, E, I, O, P, T, U, W and X. Vessels may additionally be requested to report designators F or H.

Vessels not equipped with AIS, entering the GOFREP area from the Northern Baltic or Väinameri, are recommended to give a Full Report to the relevant Traffic Centre by fax or e-mail at least one hour before entering the area. In any case, a Full Report shall be given prior to entering the GOFREP area.

If there are any circumstances affecting normal navigation in accordance with the provisions of the SOLAS and MARPOL Conventions, the master of the vessel in question is obliged to report designator Q or R, whichever is relevant under the prevailing circumstances. This report shall be made without delay.

* In addition to designator P report, information on cargo other than dangerous goods is collected from all ships entering or leaving the ports of European Union countries in the Gulf of Finland. Ships are not required to report the information on cargo other than dangerous goods. Information is asked from ships only if it cannot be obtained by other means.

Appendix 2

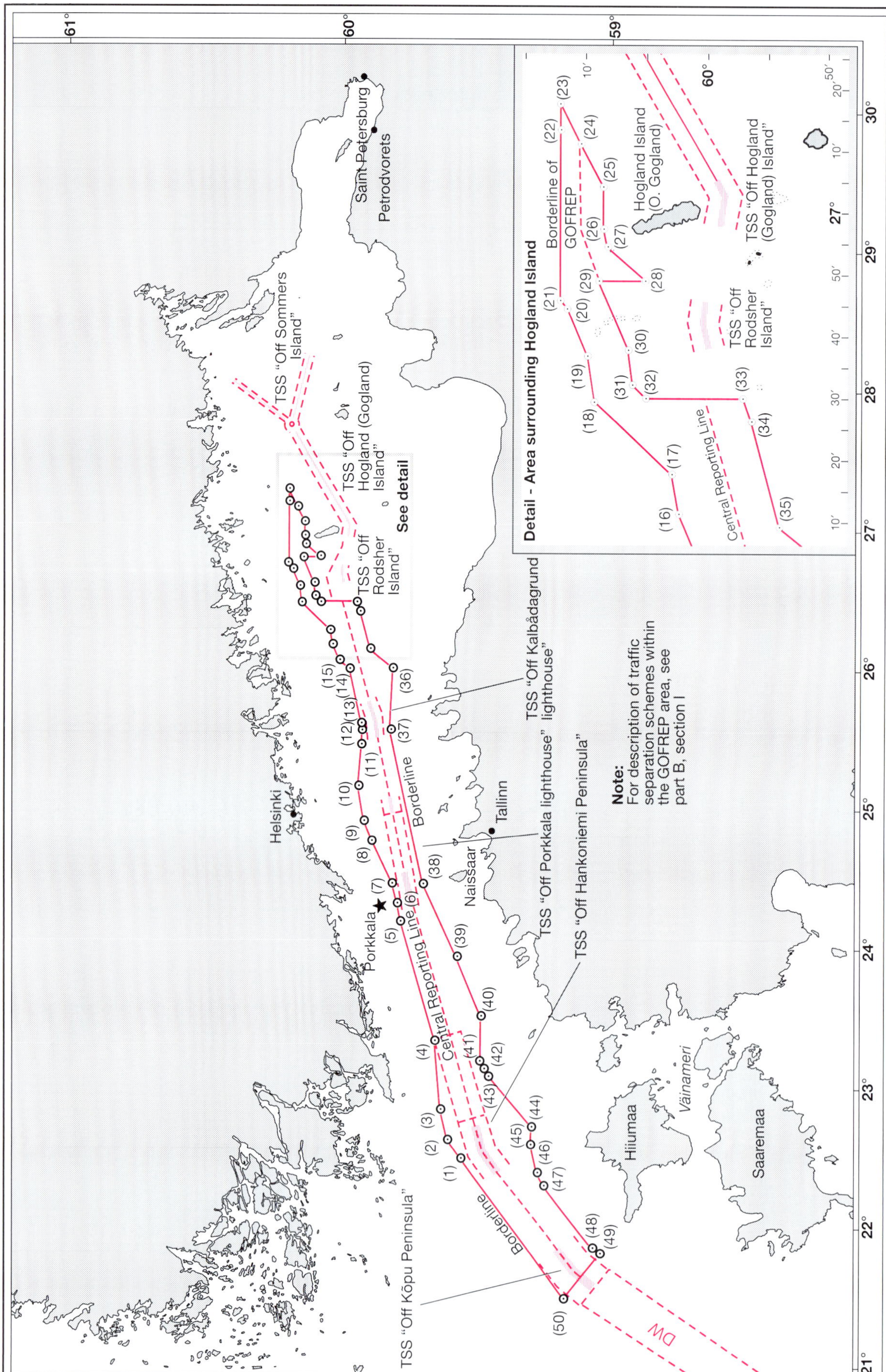

Detail - Area surrounding Hogland Island
Borderline of GOFREP
Hogland Island (O. Gogland)
TSS "Off Hogland (Gogland) Island"
TSS "Off Rodsher Island"
Central Reporting Line
Saint Petersburg
Petrodvorets
TSS "Off Sommers Island"
TSS "Off Hogland (Gogland) Island"
See detail
TSS "Off Rodsher Island"
Helsinki
Porkkala
Borderline
Naissaar
Tallinn
TSS "Off Kalbådagrund lighthouse"
TSS "Off Porkkala lighthouse"
TSS "Off Hankoniemi Peninsula"
Central Reporting Line
Hiiumaa
Väinameri
Saaremaa
Borderline
TSS "Off Kõpu Peninsula"
DW
Note:
For description of traffic separation schemes within the GOFREP area, see part B, section I

ON THE APPROACHES TO THE POLISH PORTS IN THE GULF OF GDAŃSK (GDANREP)

A ship reporting system (GDANREP) is established in the Gulf of Gdańsk in the territorial and internal waters of Poland.

1 Categories of ships required to participate in the system

1.1 Ships of the following categories are required to participate in the system proceeding to or from Polish ports or passing through the reporting area between Polish ports in the Gulf of Gdańsk, or ships visiting the area:

- all passenger ships as defined in chapter I of SOLAS 1974, as amended;
- ships of 150 gross tonnage and above;
- all vessels engaged in towing.

2 Geographical coverage of the system and the number and edition of the reference chart used for the delineation of the system

2.1 The operational area of the mandatory ship reporting system covers the territorial and internal waters of Poland in the Gulf of Gdańsk, south of parallel 54°45′ N, between the Reporting Line and the Polish coastline.

2.2 The reference chart is Polish chart No. 151 (INT 1291) published by the Hydrographic Office of the Polish Navy (2004 edition). Chart datum is World Geodetic System 1984 (WGS 84) datum.

2.3 For the purpose of this system, "Reporting Line" means the line joining the following geographical positions:

(1)	54°45′.00 N,	018°32′.56 E	(3)	54°36′.20 N,	019°24′.20 E
(2)	54°45′.00 N,	019°06′.10 E	(4)	54°27′.49 N,	019°38′.30 E

2.4 For the purpose of this system, reporting points are situated in the following geographical positions:

(5)	54°35′.58 N,	018°52′.82 E	(9)	54°31′.70 N,	018°40′.70 E
(6)	54°35′.23 N,	018°53′.76 E	(10)	54°28′.10 N,	018°42′.90 E
(7)	54°36′.76 N,	019°04′.67 E	(11)	54°25′.30 N,	018°54′.80 E
(8)	54°36′.66 N,	019°07′.51 E			

3 Format, content of reports, times and geographical positions for submitting reports, Authority to whom reports should be sent and available services

Reports should be made using VHF voice transmissions. A ship may elect, for reasons of commercial confidentiality, to communicate, in compliance with the relevant national regulations, that section of the report which provides information on cargo by non-verbal means prior to entering the ship reporting area.

3.1 *Format*

Designators to be used in the GDANREP area are derived from the format-type given in paragraph 2 of the appendix to resolution A.851(20).

System identifier: GDANREP (SP)(PR)(FR)

3.2 *Content*

A full report from a ship to the shore-based Authority by voice should contain the following information:

3.2.1 *Sailing Plan (SP)*

A	Name of the ship, call sign, IMO identification number (if applicable), MMSI number, flag
C *or* D	Position (expressed in latitude and longitude *or* bearing to and distance from a landmark)
E and F	Course and speed of the ship
G	Name of last port of call
I	Destination, ETA and ETD

O Maximum present draught

P Cargo and, if dangerous or polluting goods are present on board, quantity and UN numbers and IMO hazard classes or pollution category thereof, as appropriate

Q *or* R Defects, damage, deficiencies or other limitations (vessels towing are to report length of tow and name of object in tow) or any other circumstances affecting normal navigation in accordance with the provisions of the SOLAS and MARPOL Conventions

T Contact information of ship's agent or owner

W Total number of persons on board

X Miscellaneous remarks, amount and nature of bunkers if over 5000 tons, navigational status

3.2.2 *Position Report (PR)*

A Name of the ship, call sign, IMO identification number (or MMSI for transponder reports)

C *or* D Position (expressed in latitude and longitude *or* bearing to and distance from a landmark)

3.2.3 *Final Report (FR)*

A Name of the ship, call sign, IMO identification number (or MMSI for transponder reports)

C *or* D Position (expressed in latitude and longitude *or* bearing to and distance from a landmark)

3.2.4 *Other Reports*

When an incident or accident which can affect the safety of the ship, safety of navigation or any incident giving rise to pollution, or threat of pollution, to the marine environment occurs within the ship reporting system area, the vessel(s) shall immediately report to the shore-based Authority the type, time, and location of the incident, extent of damage or pollution, and whether assistance is needed. The vessel(s) shall provide without delay any additional information related to the incident or accident as requested by the shore-based Authority, given, when appropriate, in the format-type of detailed report as given in paragraph 3 of the appendix to resolution A.851(20).

Note: On receipt of a position message, the system operators will establish the relationship between the ship's position and the information supplied by the position-fixing equipment available to them. Information on course and speed will help operators to identify one ship among a group of ships.

All VHF, telephone, radar, AIS and other relevant information is recorded and the records are stored for 30 days.

3.3 *Times and geographical position for submitting reports*

Participating vessels are to report to the shore-based Authorities the information required in paragraph 3.2 in the following schedule:

3.3.1 The ship shall transmit the Sailing Plan (SP) on entry into the ship reporting system area by crossing the Reporting Line.

3.3.2 The ship shall transmit the Position Report (PR) on passing the reporting points.

3.3.3 The ship shall transmit the Final Report (FR) when finally exiting from the ship reporting system area by crossing the Reporting Line.

3.3.4 In the case of incidents or accidents as described in paragraph 3.2.4, the ship(s) shall transmit the Other Report(s) immediately to the shore-based Authority. The vessel(s) shall provide any additional information related to the incident or accident as requested by the shore-based Authority.

3.4 *Authority to whom reports should be sent and available services*

The shore-based Authority is Director of Maritime Office in Gdynia, Poland. The ships participating in the system shall transmit reports by radio to VTS Centre "Gulf of Gdańsk". The Authority monitors shipping within the mandatory ship reporting area of the Gulf of Gdańsk by radar and AIS. This does not relieve shipmasters of their responsibility for the navigation of their ship.

4 Information to be provided to participating ships and procedures to be followed

4.1 *Information provided*

4.1.1 Authority provides information to shipping about specific and urgent situations which could cause conflicting traffic movements and other information concerning safety of navigation, for instance:

- information on weather conditions, ice, water level;
- information on navigational conditions, including navigational warnings (status of aids to navigation, presence of other ships and, if necessary, their position, etc.);
- recommended route to be followed and status of areas temporarily closed for navigation.

4.1.2 Information is broadcasted by VTS Centre "Gulf of Gdańsk" station on the working channel or on the reserve channel, following the announcement on the working channel in the form of routine bulletins or when necessary or on request. Scheduled times of the routine weather bulletins and navigational warnings broadcasts are available in the relevant nautical publications.

4.1.3 Participating ships shall maintain listening watch on the designated VTS working channel.

4.1.4 Information broadcasts will be preceded by an announcement, on VHF channel 16, on which channel it will be made. All ships navigating in the area should listen to the announced broadcast.

4.1.5 If necessary, individual information can be provided to a ship on the working channel, particularly in relation to positioning and navigational assistance or local conditions. If a ship needs to anchor due to breakdown or emergency, the operator can recommend suitable anchorage in the area.

4.2 *Ice routeing in winter*

During severe ice conditions, the traffic separation schemes may be declared not valid. Mariners will be informed of the cancellation through Notices to Mariners and by VHF broadcasts from the VTS Centre. Ships reporting to the Centre will receive information on the recommended route through the ice and/or are requested to contact the regional ice-breaking co-ordinator for further instructions.

4.3 *Deviations*

If a ship participating in the mandatory ship reporting system fails to appear on the radar screen or fails to communicate with the Authority, or if an emergency is reported, MRCC in the area is responsible for initiating a search for the ship in accordance with the rules laid down for the search and rescue service, including the involvement of other participating ships known to be in that particular area.

5 Radiocommunication required for the system, frequencies on which reports should be transmitted and information to be reported

5.1 The radiocommunications equipment required for the system is that defined in the GMDSS for sea area A1.

5.2 Reports shall be made by voice on VHF radio, using the primary VTS working channel.

5.3 When submitting reports, the system identifier GDANREP can be omitted.

5.4 The voice call-sign of the VTS Centre "Gulf of Gdańsk" is "VTS Zatoka".

5.5 The VHF working channels of the VTS Centre "Gulf of Gdańsk" are:

Primary	channel 71	call and short report information
Reserve	channel 66	as designated by VTS
Other	channel 16	call and distress

5.6 Ships are required to maintain a continuous listening watch in the area on the VTS working channel and to report and take any action required by the maritime Authorities to reduce risks.

5.7 Confidential information may be transmitted by other means, including electronically, in compliance with relevant national regulations.

5.8 The language used for communication shall be English or Polish, using the IMO Standard Marine Communication Phrases, where necessary.

6 Relevant rules and regulations in force in the area of the system

6.1 *Regulations for preventing collisions at sea*

The International Regulations for Preventing Collisions at Sea, 1972, as amended, are applicable throughout the reporting area.

6.2 *Traffic separation schemes*

The traffic separation schemes in the Gulf of Gdańsk have been adopted by IMO and rule 10 of the International Regulations for Preventing Collisions at Sea, 1972 applies.

6.3 *Pilotage*

Pilotage is mandatory in national waters under national laws.

6.4 *National regulations*

Relevant local regulations issued under authority of the Director of Maritime Office in Gdynia, including Port Regulations, are in force in the Polish internal waters and are promulgated in the nautical publications.

6.5 *Dangerous and polluting cargoes*

Ships carrying dangerous or polluting cargoes and bound to or from any port within the ship reporting area must comply with the international and national regulations. The ship reporting system does not relieve shipmasters of their responsibility to give the nationally required reports and information to any other relevant authorities. Discharges of oil and ship-generated waste are monitored by the Authority. Ships causing pollution within the area can be prosecuted and fined.

7 Shore-based facilities to support operation of the system

7.1 VTS "Gulf of Gdańsk" is equipped with a radar network, VHF communications network, VHF direction-finding, Automatic Identification System (AIS) facilities, hydro-meteorological sensors and information processing and retrieval system. Its functions are data collection and evaluation, provision of information, navigation assistance, and provision of maritime safety-related information to allied services.

7.2 VTS Centre maintains a continuous 24-hour watch and is manned by two operators at all times. The VTS Centre is staffed with personnel trained according to national and international recommendations.

7.3 VTS Centre shares traffic image and ship reporting data with the MRCC in Gdynia and other allied services.

8 Information concerning the applicable procedures if the communication facilities of the shore-based Authority fail

The system is designed with sufficient system redundancy to cope with normal equipment failure, with multiple receivers on each channel. Should a VTS Centre suffer an irretrievable breakdown and call off itself from the system until the failure is repaired, it could be relieved by one of the Harbour Master's Traffic Control, which jointly use the VTS traffic image and reporting data and is operated by the shore-based Authority.

9 Description of plans for providing a response to an emergency that poses a risk to the safety of life at sea or threatens the marine environment

9.1 *SAR plan*

The national maritime SAR plan establishes the MRCC in Gdynia, which is responsible in the event of an emergency that poses risk to the safety of life at sea and for deploying SAR units operating in the reporting area.

9.2 *National contingency plan*

The Director of Maritime Office in Gdynia is the Authority responsible for prevention and control of pollution produced by oil and other harmful substances in the reporting area waters. Given the extent of the damage that can be caused by oil spills, there is a National Contingency Plan to deal with them, upon which various Authorities co-operate under operational co-ordination of the MRCC.

10 Measures to be taken if a ship fails to comply with the requirements of the system

10.1 The primary objective of the system is to enhance the safe navigation and the protection of the marine environment through the exchange of information between the ship and the shore. All means will be used to encourage and promote the full participation of ships required to submit reports under SOLAS regulation V/11.

10.2 If reports are not submitted and the offending ship can be positively identified, then information will be passed to the relevant Flag State Authorities for investigation and possible prosecution in accordance with national legislation. Information will be passed also to Port State Control, while at the same time an investigation will be launched with a view to possible legal action being taken in accordance with national legislation.

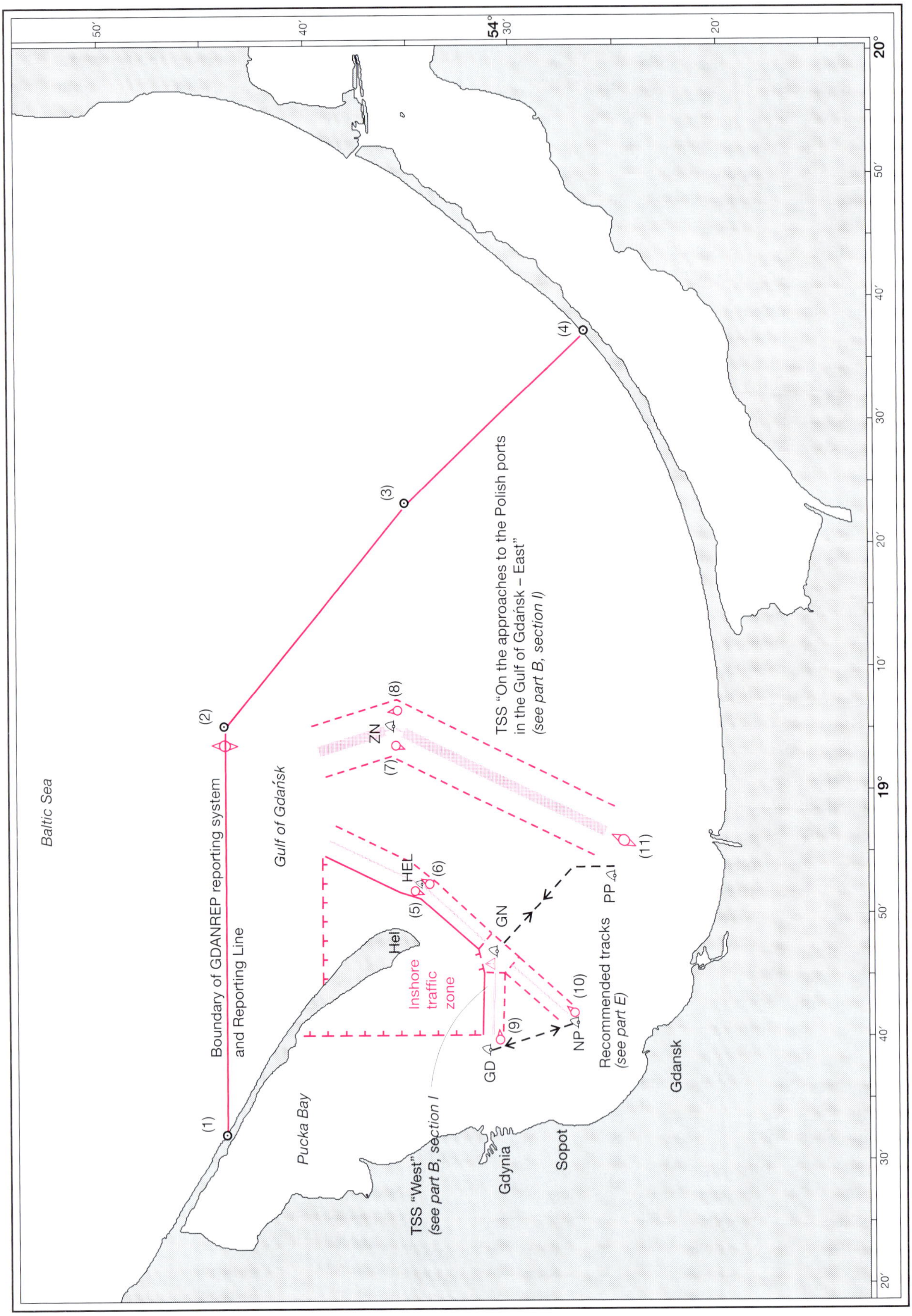

ON THE APPROACHES TO THE POLISH PORTS IN THE GULF OF GDAŃSK

IN THE SOUND BETWEEN DENMARK AND SWEDEN (SOUNDREP)*

1 Categories of ships required to participate in the system

1.1 *Ships participating in the ship reporting system*

Ships of 300 gross tonnage and upwards proceeding to or from ports or anchorages in The Sound or passing through the reporting area.

Pursuant to SOLAS 1974 Convention, as amended, the SOUNDREP does not apply to warships, naval auxiliaries, or other ships owned or operated by a Contracting Government and used only on Government non-commercial service. However, such ships are encouraged to participate in the reporting system.

2 Geographical coverage of the system and the number and edition of the reference chart used for delineation of the system

2.1 The mandatory ship reporting system SOUNDREP is operated by Sound VTS. The call sign is "Sound Traffic".

2.2 The operational area of SOUNDREP covers the northern, central and southern part of The Sound as shown on the chartlet given in appendix 1. The area includes the routeing systems, in the north the TSS "In the Sound" and in the south the TSS "Off Falsterborev", both adopted by the Organization.

2.2.1 *Reporting and border line North*

Denmark:
(1) 56°06′.58 N, 012°11′.00 E (Rågeleje)
(2) 56°14′.00 N, 012°11′.00 E (At sea, North of Rågeleje)

Sweden:
(3) 56°18′.08 N, 012°17′.39 E (At sea, West of Kullen)
(4) 56°18′.08 N, 012°26′.88 E (Kullen lighthouse)

2.2.2 *Reporting and border line South*

Denmark:
(5) 55°17′.44 N, 012°27′.28 E (Stevns lighthouse)
(6) 55°10′.00 N, 012°27′.28 E (At sea, South of Stevns)

Sweden:
(7) 55°10′.00 N, 012°54′.50 E (At sea, South of Falsterbo)

2.2.3 *Reporting and border line East*

Sweden:
(7) 55°10′.00 N, 012°54′.50 E (At sea, South of Falsterbo)
(8) 55°22′.89 N, 013°01′.93 E (Fredshög)

2.2.4 *Reporting and border line West*

Denmark:
(9) 55°19′.81 N, 012°27′.30 E (Mandehoved)
(10) 55°33′.28 N, 012°35′.53 E (Aflandshage)

2.2.5 *Sector division*

The SOUNDREP area is divided into two sectors at latitude 55° 50′.00 N; sector 1 northerly and sector 2 southerly. Each sector has an assigned VHF channel as shown in appendix 2.

* Date of implementation of new reporting system: 0000 hours UTC on 1 September 2011.

2.3 The reference charts (datum: World Geodetic System 1984 (WGS 84)) which include the operational area of SOUNDREP are:

.1 Danish charts 102 (7th edition May 2009), 104 (5th edition August 2009), 131 (1st edition November 2008), 132 (19th edition August 2009) and 133 (13th edition September 2009); and

.2 Swedish charts 921 (4th edition 2009) and 922 (22nd edition 2009).

3 Format, content of reports, times and geographical positions for submitting reports, Authority to whom reports should be sent and available services

3.1 *Procedures of reporting*

3.1.1 The SOUNDREP report must be initiated (see paragraph 3.1.4) to Sound VTS, using VHF voice transmission. However, ships can fulfil most of the reporting requirements of the reporting system by the use of non-verbal means such as AIS (Automatic Information System) class A as approved by the Organization, and by e-mail or other alternative methods, prior to entering the ship reporting area (see also paragraph 3.4.1, Note (c)). Additional details are given in appendix 3. For contact information, see appendix 2.

3.1.2 The use of correct and updated AIS information can accomplish the reporting requirements for designators A (part of), B, C, E, F, I, O, P and W.

3.1.3 E-mail or other alternative methods, prior to entering the ship reporting area, can accomplish the reporting requirements for designators L, T and X. Such non-verbal part report must also state designator A (see also paragraph 3.4.1, Note (c)). Additional details are given in appendix 3.

3.1.4 A ship which fulfils the reporting requirements of the SOUNDREP mandatory ship reporting system by the use of non-verbal means must, as a minimum, carry out a VHF voice transmission to communicate the name of the ship (part of designator A) and the report line of entry to the Sound VTS when actually entering the area. The same procedure must be followed before departing a port or leaving an anchorage in the SOUNDREP area. Additional details are given in appendix 3.

3.1.5 Designators U and Q, if applicable, shall at all times be given using VHF voice transmission to Sound VTS when entering the area. Additional details are given in appendix 3.

3.1.6 To prevent overloading the VHF channels for reporting by verbal voice transmissions and to avoid interference with essential navigational duties, and by this hampering the safety of navigation in the area, a ship unable to accomplish the reporting requirements for designators L, T and X by e-mail or other alternative methods prior to entering the ship reporting area can report these designators by the use of radio telephone or mobile phone to Sound VTS. Designator A must additionally be included in this part reporting.

3.2 Verbal reporting is not required when a ship is passing the SOUNDREP sector line at latitude 55° 50′.00 N. However, change of VHF frequency is required according to appendix 2.

3.3 *Format*

3.3.1 The mandatory ship report shall be drafted in accordance with the format shown in appendix 3. The information requested from ships is derived from the Standard Reporting Format shown in paragraph 2 of the appendix to resolution A.851(20).

3.4 *Content*

3.4.1 A report from a ship to the SOUNDREP by non-verbal means or by voice transmission must contain the following information:

A	Name of the ship, call sign and, if available, IMO identification number and MMSI number.
B	Date and time
C	Position expressed in latitude and longitude
E	True course
F	Speed
I	Destination and ETA

L	Route information on the intended route through The Sound
O	Maximum present draught
P	Cargo; and quantity and IMO class of dangerous goods, if applicable (see Note (c) below)
Q	Defects and deficiencies or other limitations
T	Contact details for the communication of cargo information (see Note (c) below)
U	Air draught when exceeding 35 metres
W	Total number of persons on board
X	Type and estimated quantity of bunker fuel, for ships of 1000 gross tonnage and above

Note:

(a) On receipt of a report, operators of the Sound VTS will establish the relation to the ship's position and the information supplied by the facilities available to them.

(b) The master of the ship must forthwith inform the Sound VTS concerned of any change to the information notified, including designator Q.

(c) Information on dangerous cargo and contact details for the communication of cargo information (designators P and T of the reporting format) is only requested when such information has not been notified to the competent authority via SafeSeaNet in an European Union (EU) Member State in accordance with the requirements of Article 13 (for ships leaving or entering an EU port) in Directive 2002/59/EC on establishing Community vessel traffic monitoring and information system and amended by Directive 2009/17/EC, prior to entering the operational SOUNDREP area. Additional details are given in appendix 3.

3.5 *Geographical position for submitting reports*

3.5.1 Ships entering the SOUNDREP operational area shall submit a report when crossing the entrance lines or on departure from a port or anchorage within the operational area.

3.5.2 Further reports should be made whenever there is a change in navigational status or circumstance, particularly in relation to designator Q of the reporting format.

3.6 *Crossing traffic*

3.6.1 Recognizing that ferries crossing between Helsingør and Helsingborg operate according to published schedules, special reporting arrangements can be made on a ship to ship basis. Ferries leaving the ports Helsingør in Denmark and Helsingborg in Sweden, operating according to published schedules, are normally not requested to report to the Sound VTS.

3.7 *Authority*

The VTS Authority for the SOUNDREP is Sound VTS, with call sign "Sound Traffic". Additional details are given in appendix 2.

4 Information to be provided to ships and procedures to be followed

4.1 Ships are required to keep a continuous listening watch in the area on the relevant VHF sector channel and VHF channel 16.

4.2 Sound VTS will provide an information service to shipping about specific and urgent situations which could cause conflicting traffic movements as well as other information concerning safety of navigation; for instance, information about weather, current, ice, water level, navigational problems or other hazards.

4.2.1 If necessary, Sound VTS can provide individual information to a ship, particularly in relation to positioning and navigational information or local conditions, by using the IMO Standard Marine Communication Phrases (IMO SMCP), section A1/6 for VTS message markers. The message markers can be of ADVICE, WARNING, INFORMATION, QUESTION, ANSWER, REQUEST and INTENTION.

4.2.2 Information of general interest to shipping in the area will be broadcast by Sound VTS on a VHF channel as specified by the VTS operator or will be given on request. A broadcast will be preceded by an announcement on VHF channel 16. All ships navigating in the area should listen to the announced broadcast.

4.3 If a ship needs to anchor due to breakdown, low visibility, adverse weather, changes in the indicated depth of water, etc., Sound VTS can recommend suitable anchorages or other place of refuge within the operational area.

5 Communication required for the SOUNDREP system

5.1 The language used for communication shall be English, using IMO Standard Marine Communication Phrases, where necessary.

5.2 Details of communication and contact information are given in appendix 2.

6 Rules, regulations and recommendation in force in the area of the system

6.1 *Regulations for preventing collisions at sea*

The International Regulations for Preventing Collisions at Sea (COLREG), 1972 are applicable throughout the operational area of SOUNDREP.

6.2 *Traffic separation scheme "In the Sound"*

The traffic separation scheme "In the Sound", situated to the north in the narrows of The Sound, was adopted by the Organization, and Rule 10 of the International Regulations for Preventing Collisions at Sea therefore applies.

6.3 *Traffic separation scheme "Off Falsterborev"*

The separation scheme "Off Falsterborev", situated in the southern part of The Sound, was adopted by the Organization, and Rule 10 of the International Regulations for Preventing Collisions at Sea therefore applies.

6.4 *IMO Recommendation on navigation through the entrances to the Baltic Sea – The Sound*

SN.1/Circ. 263, section 1.9 and IMO publication on Ships' Routeing, part C, on Amendments to Recommendation on navigation through the entrances to the Baltic Sea, adopted at MSC 83 in October 2007, recommends for The Sound that loaded oil tankers with a draught of 7 metres or more, loaded chemical tankers and gas carriers, irrespective of size, and ships carrying a shipment of irradiated nuclear fuel, plutonium or high-level radioactive wastes (INF Code materials), when navigating The Sound between a line connecting Svinbådan lighthouse and Hornbæk Harbour and a line connecting Skanör Harbour and Aflandshage, should use the pilotage services established by the Governments of Denmark and Sweden.

6.5 *Mandatory pilotage*

Harbours within the SOUNDREP area are covered by provisions about mandatory pilotage for certain ships bound for or coming from Danish and Swedish ports.

6.6 *Air draught when exceeding 35 metres*

The navigable Drogden channel is located beside a major airport. In order to ensure safety of navigation in the dredged channel of Drogden and to reduce the risk of collision between an aircraft that serves the airport and a ship or other floating equipment, a reporting obligation has been established. Additional details are given in appendix 3, designator U.

6.6.1 The safety procedure that has been established is that, for all ships, including ships with a tow, with an air draught exceeding 35 metres, Sound VTS shall notify the air traffic control, stating the maximum air draught of the ship or floating equipment. The notification shall be given at least 30 minutes prior to the expected time (UTC) for passage of:

- Nordre Røse lighthouse at position 55°38′.17 N, 012°41′.21 E; and
- light buoy No. 9 at position 55°36′.15 N, 012°41′.79 E.

Sound VTS will transfer the information to the air traffic control.

7 Shore-based facilities to support the operation of the system

7.1 *System capability*

7.1.1 The Sound VTS centre is situated at Malmö, Sweden.

7.1.2 The Sound VTS system comprises several remote sensor sites. The sites provide surveillance of the SOUNDREP area, using a combination of radar and AIS. An integrated network of ten radar sensors integrated with AIS provides surveillance of the area.

7.1.3 All the sensors mentioned below will be controlled or monitored by the VTS operators.

7.1.4 Recording equipment automatically stores information from all tracks, which can be replayed. In case of incidents, the VTS authority can use records as evidence. VTS operators have access to different ship registers, pilot information and hazardous cargo data.

7.1.5 An integrated database is available for the operators in handling information.

7.2 *Radar and other sensors*

Information necessary to evaluate the traffic activities within the operational area of SOUNDREP is compiled via remotely controlled sensors comprising:

- Sensors for water level and current at Drogden and Flintrännan;
- High-resolution radar systems; and
- VHF communications systems, including DSC call (see appendix 2).

7.3 *Radio communication equipment*

Redundant VHF system with DSC functionality (see appendix 2).

7.4 *AIS facilities*

Sound VTS is linked to both the Danish and Swedish national shore-based AIS network and can continually receive messages broadcast by ships with transponders to gain information on their identity and position. The information is displayed as part of the VTS system and is covering the ship reporting area.

7.5 *Personnel qualifications and training*

7.5.1 The VTS centre is staffed with personnel all educated and experienced as officers in charge of a navigational watch according to national and international requirements.

7.5.2 Training of VTS personnel will meet the standards recommended by IMO in MSC/Circ. 1065 on IALA Standards for training and certification of VTS personnel.

7.5.3 Refresher training is carried out on a regular basis.

8 Information concerning the applicable procedures if the communication facilities of the shore-based Authority fail

8.1 The system is designed with sufficient system redundancy to cope with normal equipment failure.

8.2 In the event of radio communication system failure at the VTS centre, communication will be maintained via a redundant standby VHF system. If the radar system or other essential equipment suffers a breakdown, information of reduced operational capability will be given by Sound VTS or as national navigational warnings.

9 Measures to be taken if a ship fails to comply with the requirements of the system

9.1 The objective of the VTS Authority is to facilitate the exchange of information between the shipping and the shore in order to ensure safe passages of the bridges, support safety of navigation and the protection of the marine environment.

9.2 All means will be used to encourage and promote the full participation of ships required to submit reports under SOLAS regulation V/11. If reports are not submitted and the offending ship can be positively identified, then information will be passed to the relevant Flag State Authority for investigation and possible prosecution in accordance with national legislation. Information will also be made available to Port State Control inspectors.

Appendix 1

SOUNDREP operational area

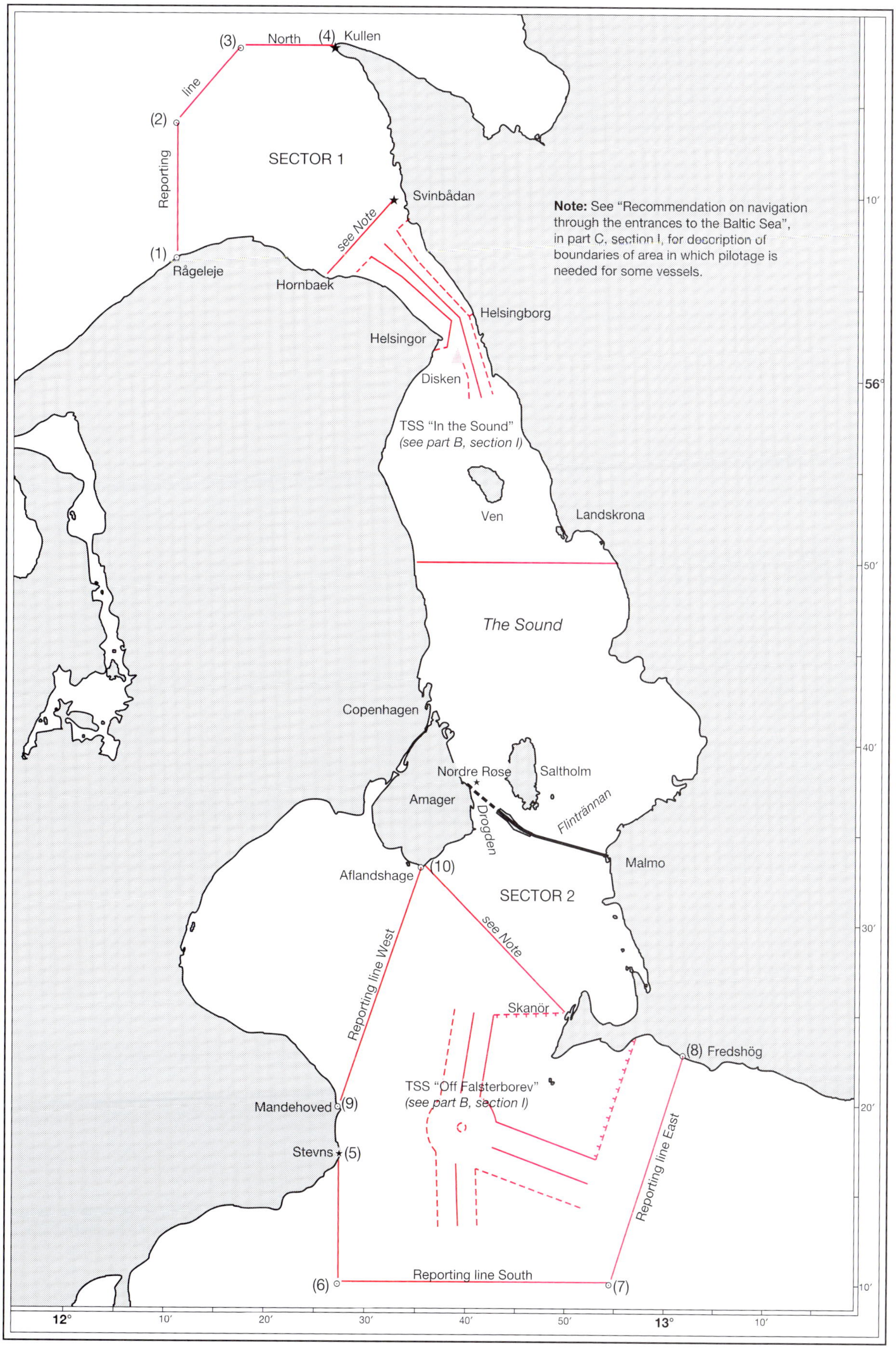

G

Appendix 2

Contact information and assigned VHF channels for sectors in the mandatory ship reporting system "In The Sound between Denmark and Sweden (SOUNDREP)"

SOUNDREP, radio call sign:	**"Sound Traffic"**

VHF Channels	**Operational use**
VHF channel 73	Sound VTS – Sector 1 North
VHF channel 71	Sound VTS – Sector 2 South
VHF channel 79	Sound VTS – Broadcast 1, individual assistance
VHF channel 68	Sound VTS – Broadcast 2, individual assistance and reserve channel

The Sound VTS operating SOUNDREP is located in Malmö, Sweden:

24-hour contact information:

(1) Sound VTS is monitoring VHF channels 73, 71 and 16 continuously.

(2) Duty officer phone: +46 40 20 43 17 or
+46 40 20 43 34

(3) Fax: +46 40 20 43 45

(4) E-mail: contact@soundvts.org

Address:
Sound VTS
Hans Michelsensgata 9
Box 855
S-201 80 Malmö
Sweden

Appendix 3

Drafting of reports to the mandatory ship reporting system "In The Sound between Denmark and Sweden (SOUNDREP)"

Designator	AIS	Function	Information required
A	Yes, and VHF	Ship	Name of the ship (VHF); call sign and, if available, IMO identification number and MMSI number (AIS)
B	Yes	Date and time of event	A 6-digit group giving day of month and hours and minutes in Universal Co-ordinated Time (UTC).
C	Yes	Position	A 5-digit group giving latitude in degrees and minutes, decimal, suffixed with N and a 6-digit group giving longitude in degrees and minutes, decimal, suffixed with E.
E	Yes	True course	A 3-digit group
F	Yes	Speed in knots and tenths of knots	A 3-digit group
I	Yes	Destination and ETA	The name of next port of call given in UN/LOCODE. For details see in IMO SN/Circ.244 and; www.unece.org/cefact/locode/service/main.htm. Date and time group expressed as in (B)
L	No	Route information	A brief description of the intended route as planned by the master. Ships navigating in The Sound have options on deciding route in the following areas (see appendix 1); (a) Disken shoal (b) Ven island (c) Drogden channel (d) Flintrännan channel The route information should be given coded by using the following local designators: • DW – Disken, west of • DE – Disken, east of • VW – Ven, west of • VE – Ven, east of • D – Drogden • F – Flintrännan See examples below.
O	Yes	Maximum present draught in metres	A 2-digit or 3-digit group giving the present maximum draught in metres (e.g.: 6.1 or 10.4).
P	Yes	Cargo on board	Cargo; and quantity and IMO class of dangerous goods, if applicable (see 3.4.1, Note (c)).
Q	VHF	Defects and deficiencies or other limitations	Details of defects and deficiencies affecting the equipment of the ship or any other circumstances affecting normal navigation and manoeuvrability.

Designator	AIS	Function	Information required
T	No	Ship's representative and/or owner	Address and particulars from which detailed information on the cargo may be obtained.
U	VHF	Ship's size	Information of maximum air draught when exceeding 35 metres, required for all ships, including ships towing or other floating equipment. This information shall be given by voice transmissions when entering the SOUNDREP area, irrespectively of, if the information also is given by, e.g., AIS; details in paragraph 6.6.
W	Yes	Total number of persons on board	State number.
X	No	Miscellaneous	Type and estimated quantity of bunker fuel, for ships of 1000 gross tonnage and above.

Examples of routes as given under designator L

A northbound ship leaving Malmö Port planning to sail east of Ven, TSS "In The Sound" (UN/LOCODE format for Malmö Port is SE MMA):

L: SE MMA, VE

A southbound ship in transit planning to sail TSS "In The Sound", east of Disken, west of Ven, Drogden channel and TSS "Off Falsterborev":

L: DE, VW, D

IN THE STOREBÆLT (GREAT BELT) TRAFFIC AREA (BELTREP)*

1 Categories of ships required to participate in the system

1.1 Ships passing through or proceeding to and from ports and anchorages in the BELTREP area are required to participate in the ship reporting system as follows:

1.1.1 ships with a gross tonnage of 50 and above;

1.1.2 all ships with an air draught of 15 metres or more; and

1.1.3 pleasure craft with a length less than 15 metres or with a gross tonnage less than 50 **are exempted** from participation.

2 Geographical coverage of the system and the number and edition of the reference charts used for delineation of the system

2.1 The mandatory ship reporting system BELTREP is operated by Great Belt VTS. The call sign is "Belt Traffic".

2.2 The operational area of BELTREP covers the central and northern part of the Storebælt (Great Belt) and the Hatter Barn area north of Storebælt (Great Belt) at the entrance to the Baltic Sea, as shown below and on the chartlet given in appendix 1-A. The area includes the routeing systems at Hatter Barn, in the Storebælt (Great Belt) area and Langelandsbælt, all adopted by the Organization. The BELTREP area also includes the central part of route Tango. Datum: World Geodetic System 1984 (WGS 84):

2.2.1 *Report-line and borderline West (RW)*

Fyn:	(1)	55°36′.00 N, 010°38′.00 E	(Korshavn)
Samsø:	(2)	55°47′.00 N, 010°38′.00 E	(East coast of Samsø)

2.2.2 *Report-line and borderline North (RN)*

Samsø:	(2)	55°47′.00 N, 010°38′.00 E	(East coast of Samsø)
	(3)	56°00′.00 N, 010°56′.00 E	(At sea near Marthe Flak)
Sjælland:	(4)	56°00′.00 N, 011°17′.00 E	(Sjællands Odde)

2.2.3 *Report-line and borderline South (RS)*

Stigsnæs:	(5)	55°12′.00 N, 011°15′.40 E	(Gulfhavn)
Omø:	(6)	55°08′.40 N, 011°09′.00 E	(Ørespids, Omø)
	(7)	55°05′.00 N, 011°09′.00 E	(At sea south of Ørespids)
Langeland E:	(8)	55°05′.00 N, 010°56′.10 E	(Snøde Øre)

2.2.4 *Report-line and borderline South-west (RSW)*

Langeland W:	(9)	55°00′.00 N, 010°48′.70 E	(South of Korsebølle Rev)
Thurø Rev:	(10)	55°01′.20 N, 010°44′.00 E	(Thurø Rev Lightbuoy)

2.2.5 *Sector division*

The BELTREP area is divided into two sectors at latitude (11) 55° 35′.00 N; sector 1 northerly and sector 2 southerly. Each sector has an assigned VHF channel as shown in appendix 2.

2.3 The reference charts (datum: World Geodetic System 1984 (WGS 84)) which include the operational area of BELTREP are Danish charts 112 (15th edition, 2010), 128 (10th edition, 2009), 141 (21st edition, 2010), 142 (18th edition, 2010), 143 (19th edition, 2009) and 160 (7th edition, 2007).

3 Format, content of reports, times and geographical positions for submitting reports, Authority to whom reports should be sent and available services

3.1 *Procedures of reporting*

3.1.1 All BELTREP reports must be made to Great Belt VTS, using VHF voice transmissions. However, ships are encouraged to fulfil certain reporting requirements of the reporting system by the use of correct and updated

* Date of implementation of amended reporting system: 0000 hours UTC on 1 July 2013.

AIS information (Automatic Identification System) class A as approved by the Organization and by non-verbal means as e-mail or similar, prior to entering the ship reporting area. Details are given in appendix 3.

3.1.2 The use of correct and updated AIS information can accomplish the reporting requirements for designators A, B, C, E, F, G and I, O and W. Details are given in appendix 3.

3.1.3 To minimize the time reporting on the VHF radio channels and to avoid interference with essential navigational duties, ships are encouraged to forward the reporting requirements for designators L, P, T and X by e-mail or similar prior to entering the ship reporting area. Such non-verbal partial reports must also state designators A and H. Reporting designators L, P, T and X prior to entry using mobile phone is also accepted as a means of communication. Details are given in subparagraph 3.5 and appendix 3.

3.1.4 A ship which fulfils the reporting requirements of the BELTREP mandatory ship reporting system by the use of correct and updated AIS information and prior non-verbal means must, as a minimum, carry out a VHF voice transmission to communicate the name of the ship (part of designator A), air draught and deadweight tonnage (designator U) and the report-line of entry to the Great Belt VTS when actually entering the area. The same procedure must be followed before departing a port or leaving an anchorage in the BELTREP area. Details are given in appendix 3.

3.1.5 Designator Q or R, if applicable, shall at all times be given using VHF voice transmission to Great Belt VTS. Details are given in appendix 3.

3.2 Verbal reporting is not required when a ship passes the BELTREP sector line at latitude 55° 35′.00 N. However, sector change of VHF frequency is required according to appendix 2.

3.3 *Format*

3.3.1 The mandatory ship report shall be drafted in accordance with the format shown in appendix 3. The information requested from ships is derived from the Standard Reporting Format shown in paragraph 2 of the appendix to resolution A.851(20).

3.4 *Content*

3.4.1 A report from a ship to BELTREP by AIS, non-verbal means or by voice transmission or combinations thereof must contain the following information; details are given in appendix 3:

A	name of the ship, call sign, MMSI number and, if available, IMO identification number;
B	date and time;
C	position expressed in latitude and longitude;
E	true course;
F	speed;
G *and* I	last port of call, destination and ETA;
H	date, time (UTC) and report-line of entry into the BELTREP area;
L	route information on the intended route through the BELTREP area;
O	maximum present draught;
P	cargo and, if dangerous goods are present on board, their quantity and IMO class. Dangerous goods information must be summarized in total tonnes per IMO class;
Q *or* R	defects, deficiencies, limitations – pollution or dangerous goods lost overboard;
T	address for the communication of cargo information;
U	air draught, deadweight tonnage;
W	total number of persons on board; and
X	type and estimated quantity of bunker fuel, for ships of 1000 gross tonnage and above. Must be summarized in total tonnes per type.

Note:

(a) The master of the ship must forthwith inform the Great Belt VTS concerned of any change in navigational status or in previous information notified, particularly in relation to designator Q or R.

3.5 *Geographical position for submitting reports*

3.5.1 Ships entering the BELTREP operational area shall submit a report when crossing the report-line or on departure from a port or anchorage within the operational area.

3.5.2 Previously forwarded reports can be submitted at any time after entering the Danish Exclusive Economic Zone (EEZ) and until in reach of VHF range of Great Belt VTS at an approximate distance of 20 nautical miles from the BELTREP area. As the Great Belt VTS must be able to timely handle incoming prior reporting, it will not be possible to undertake pre entry reports within the 20 nautical miles VHF range. The reporting option is then verbal reporting by VHF when crossing the report-line of entry. Details of areas are shown on the chartlet in appendix 1-B. The Danish EEZ border lines are shown in nautical charts.

3.5.3 Ships departing a port or leaving an anchorage within the 20 nautical miles range of the BELTREP area, or in the BELTREP area, may submit a pre-entry report for designators H, L, P, T and X if transmitted one hour before departure for enabling the Great Belt VTS to timely handle incoming prior reports.

3.6 *Crossing traffic*

3.6.1 Ferries frequently cross route Tango in sector 1, including high-speed ferries. The ferries generally operate according to published schedules; special reporting arrangements can be authorized.

3.7 *Authority*

The Admiral Danish Fleet is the VTS Authority for Great Belt VTS, which operates the BELTREP system with call sign "Belt Traffic". Details are in appendix 2.

4 Information to be provided to ships and procedures to be followed

4.1 Ships are required to keep a continuous listening watch in the BELTREP area on the relevant VHF sector channels and VHF channel 16.

4.2 Great Belt VTS will provide information service to ships about specific and urgent situations which could cause conflicting traffic movements as well as other information concerning safety of navigation; for instance, information about weather, current, ice, water level, navigational problems or other hazards.

4.2.1 Information of general interest to ships in the area will be broadcast by the Great Belt VTS on a VHF channel as specified by the VTS operator or will be given upon request. A broadcast will be preceded by an announcement on VHF channel 16 and sector channels. All ships navigating in the area should listen to the announced broadcast.

4.2.2 If necessary, Great Belt VTS can provide individual information to a ship, particularly in relation to positioning or local conditions.

4.2.3 If deemed necessary by the Great Belt VTS or upon request of a ship, navigational assistance can be provided. Great Belt VTS will inform the identifiable ship when the navigational assistance starts and subsequently terminates.

4.2.4 The following IMO Standard Marine Communication Phrases (IMO SMCP), section A1/6, for VTS message markers can be used: ADVICE, WARNING, INFORMATION, QUESTION, ANSWER, REQUEST and INTENTION.

4.3 If a ship needs to anchor due to breakdown, low visibility, adverse weather, changes in the indicated depth of water, etc., Great Belt VTS can recommend suitable anchorages or other places of refuge within the operational area. The anchorages in the vicinity of the Storebælt (Great Belt) bridges are marked on the nautical charts covering the area and are shown on the chartlet in appendix 1-A.

5 Communication required for the BELTREP system

5.1 The language used for communication shall be English, using IMO Standard Marine Communication Phrases, when deemed necessary by Great Belt VTS.

5.2 Ship-to-ship communication of navigational intentions should be carried out on the BELTREP working channels, enabling the Great Belt VTS and other ships to be kept informed.

5.3 Details of communication and contact information are given in appendix 2.

6 Rules, regulations and recommendation in force in the area of the system

6.1 *Regulations for preventing collisions at sea*

The International Regulations for Preventing Collisions at Sea (COLREGs) are applicable throughout the operational area of BELTREP.

6.2 *Traffic separation scheme "At Hatter Barn" (TSS-T5)*

6.2.1 The separation scheme "At Hatter Barn" is situated in Samsø Bælt, north of the Storebælt (Great Belt), between the islands of Sjælland and Samsø. It has been adopted by the IMO, and rule 10 of the International Regulations for Preventing Collisions at Sea applies.

6.2.2 The minimum depth in the traffic separation scheme is 15 metres at mean sea level. Ships with a draught of more than 13 metres should use the deep-water route "Between Hatter Rev and Hatter Barn", which lies north-west of the traffic separation scheme.

6.3 *Deep-water route "Between Hatter Rev and Hatter Barn" (DW-T3)*

6.3.1 The IMO-adopted deep-water route "Between Hatter Rev and Hatter Barn" has a minimum depth of water below mean sea level of 19 metres. Ships which are not obliged by reason of their draught (13 metres or less) to use the deep-water route should use the traffic separation scheme which lies south-east of the deep-water route, where there is a minimum depth of water below mean sea level of 15 metres.

6.3.2 Ships should be aware that other ships sailing in the deep-water route can be constrained by draught and exhibit signals according to COLREGs.

6.4 *Traffic separation scheme "Between Korsoer and Sprogoe" (TSS-T6)*

6.4.1 The traffic separation scheme "Between Korsoer and Sprogoe", situated in the narrows of the Eastern Channel in Storebælt (Great Belt) between the islands of Fyn and Sjælland, has been adopted by the IMO, and rule 10 of the International Regulations for Preventing Collisions at Sea applies.

6.4.2 The minimum free water depth in the northbound traffic lane is 17 metres and in the southbound traffic lane is 19 metres, both below mean sea level.

6.4.3 There is a recommended speed limit of 20 knots in the traffic separation scheme.

6.5 *The Great Belt Bridges – Safety regulations*

6.5.1 Passage through the marked spans at the West Bridge (a combined road and rail bridge) is allowed only for ships below 1000 tonnes deadweight and with an air draught of less than 18.00 metres. This passage has route designator BW.

6.5.2 Passage through the traffic separation scheme under the East Bridge (a suspension bridge for road traffic) is allowed only for ships with an air draught of less than 65.00 metres. This passage has route designator BE and includes route Tango.

6.6 *Deep-water route "Off the east coast of Langeland" (DW-T4)*

6.6.1 The deep-water route "Off the east coast of Langeland" has a minimum depth of water below mean sea level of 19 metres. Ships with draughts in excess of 10 metres are recommended to use the deep-water route because of navigational difficulties for such ships in following the national recommended route Hotel which lies to the east of the deep-water route.

6.6.2 Ships should be aware that other ships sailing in the deep-water route can be constrained by draught and should exhibit signals according to COLREGs.

6.7 *Route Hotel*

6.7.1 East of the deep-water route "Off the east coast of Langeland", the national route Hotel is established, which has a minimum depth of 12 metres below mean sea level. Ships with a draught of 10 metres or less should follow route Hotel.

6.8 *IMO Recommendation on navigation through the entrances to the Baltic Sea*

6.8.1 The recent amendment of the IMO Recommendation on navigation through the entrances to the Baltic Sea was adopted by MSC in October 2007 and promulgated in SN.1/Circ.263, section 1.9 and is given in the IMO publication Ships' Routeing, part C. It recommends, among other things, that ships with a draught of 11 metres or more navigating route Tango or ships, irrespective of size or draught, carrying a shipment of irradiated nuclear fuel, plutonium or high-level radioactive wastes (INF Code cargoes) should use the pilotage services established locally by the coastal States for passing ships.

6.8.2 Shipmasters should, in due time, when planning the passage, carefully note the content as regards route Tango in the IMO Recommendation on Navigation through the entrances to the Baltic Sea.

6.9 *Mandatory pilotage*

6.9.1 Harbours within the BELTREP area are covered by provisions on the subject of mandatory pilotage for certain ships bound for or coming from Danish harbours.

7 Shore-based facilities to support the operation of the system

7.1 *System capability*

7.1.1 The VTS centre is situated at the Naval Logistic Support Regional Centre at Korsør. The VTS system comprises several remote sensor sites. The sites provide surveillance of the VTS area, using a combination of radar, radio direction-finding, Automatic Identification System (AIS) and electro-optic sensors. An integrated network system of eight radar sensors integrated with AIS provides surveillance of the VTS area.

7.1.2 All the sensors mentioned will be controlled or monitored by the VTS operators.

7.1.3 There are a number of operator consoles in the control centre, one of which is intended for system maintenance and diagnostic purposes, which allows these activities to be carried out without disruption of normal operations. The operator can, from each of the consoles, control and display the status of the sensors. The VTS centre will, at all times, be manned with a duty officer and three operators.

7.1.4 Recording equipment automatically stores information from all tracks, which can be replayed. In case of incidents, the VTS authority can use records as evidence. VTS operators have access to different ship registers, pilot information and hazardous cargo data.

7.2 *Radar, electro-optic facilities and other sensors*

7.2.1 Information necessary to evaluate the traffic activities within the operational area of BELTREP is compiled via VTS area remote-controlled sensors comprising:

- high-resolution radar systems;
- infra-red sensor systems;
- daylight TV systems;
- VHF communications systems; and
- DF systems.

7.3 *Radiocommunication facilities*

7.3.1 Radiocommunication equipment in the VTS centre consists of six VHF radios, including DSC facilities. The VHF channels used are given in appendix 2.

7.4 *AIS facilities*

7.4.1 BELTREP is linked to the national shore-based AIS network and can continually monitor AIS information on ships, such as identity and position. The information is displayed as part of the VTS system and covers the VTS area.

7.5 *Personnel qualifications and training*

7.5.1 The VTS centre is staffed with civilian personnel, all experienced as officers at a competency level required in the International Convention on Standards of Training, Certification and Watchkeeping for Seafarers, chapter II, section A-II/1 or A-II/2.

7.5.2 Training of personnel will meet the standards recommended by IMO. Furthermore, it will comprise an overall study of the navigation safety measures established in Danish waters and, in particular, the operational area of BELTREP, including a study of relevant international and national provisions with respect to safety of navigation. The training also includes real-time training in simulators.

7.5.3 Refresher training is carried out at least every third year.

8 Information concerning the applicable procedures if the communication facilities of the shore-based Authority fail

8.1 The system is designed with sufficient system redundancy to cope with normal equipment failure.

8.2 In the event that the radiocommunication system or the radar system at the VTS centre breaks down, communication will be maintained via a standby VHF system. To continue the VTS operation in order to avoid collisions in the bridge area, Great Belt VTS has an emergency back-up VTS centre at Sprogø covering sector 2. The VTS emergency centre is equipped with radar, VHF radio sets and CCTV cameras.

8.3 If the radar system or other essential equipment suffers a breakdown, information of reduced operational capability will be given by Great Belt VTS or broadcast as national navigational warnings.

9 Measures to be taken if a ship fails to comply with the requirements of the system

9.1 The objective of Great Belt VTS is to facilitate the exchange of information between the ship and the shore in order to ensure safe passages of the bridges, to support safety of navigation and to protect the marine environment.

9.2 Great Belt VTS seeks to prevent ship collisions with the bridges crossing Storebælt (Great Belt). If a ship appears to be on a collision course with one of the bridges, Great Belt VTS will arrange for an emergency stop for road and rail traffic on the bridges.

9.3 All means will be used to encourage and promote the full participation of ships required to submit reports under SOLAS regulation V/11. If reports are not submitted or contraventions are made of the safety regulations in sections 6.5.1 and 6.5.2 for passing the bridges and the offending ship can be positively identified, then information will be passed to the relevant Flag State Authority for investigation and possible prosecution in accordance with national legislation. Information will also be made available to Port State Control inspectors.

Appendix 1-A

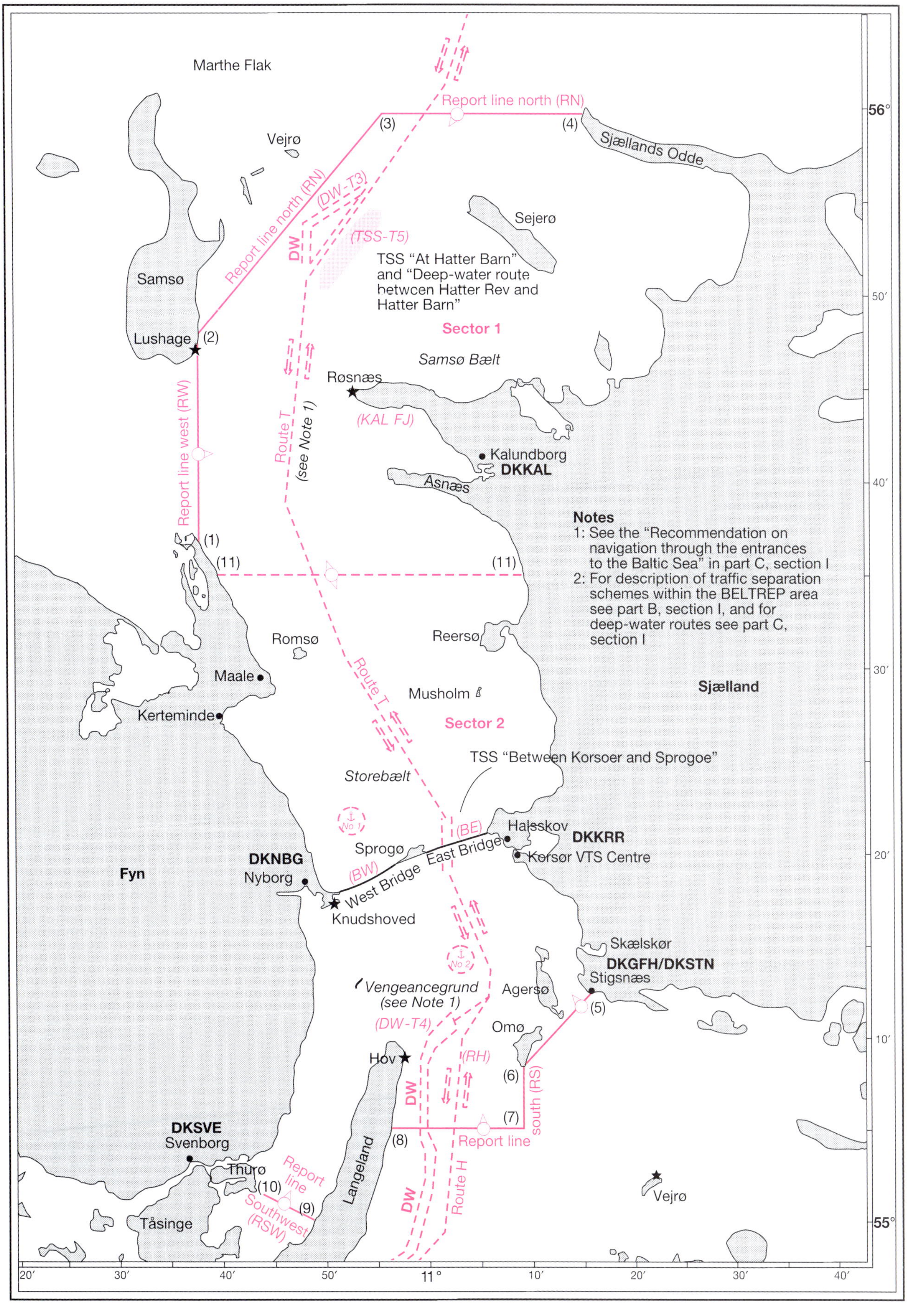

Marthe Flak
Report line north (RN)
56°
(3)
(4)
Sjællands Odde
Vejrø
Report line north (RN)
(DW-T3)
DW
(TSS-T5)
Sejerø
TSS "At Hatter Barn" and "Deep-water route between Hatter Rev and Hatter Barn"
Samsø
50′
Sector 1
Lushage
(2)
Samsø Bælt
Røsnæs
(KAL FJ)
Route T (see Note 1)
Report line west (RW)
Kalundborg
DKKAL
Asnæs
40′
Notes
1: See the "Recommendation on navigation through the entrances to the Baltic Sea" in part C, section I
2: For description of traffic separation schemes within the BELTREP area see part B, section I, and for deep-water routes see part C, section I
(1)
(11)
(11)
Romsø
Reersø
30′
Maale
Sjælland
Route T
Musholm
Kerteminde
Sector 2
TSS "Between Korsoer and Sprogoe"
Storebælt
Halsskov
(BE)
DKKRR
Sprogø
East Bridge
Korsør VTS Centre
20′
DKNBG
Fyn
Nyborg
(BW)
West Bridge
Knudshoved
Skælskør
DKGFH/DKSTN
Stigsnæs
Vengeancegrund (see Note 1)
Agersø
(5)
(DW-T4)
Omø
10′
Hov
(RH)
(6)
DW
south (RS)
(7)
DKSVE
Svenborg
(8)
Report line
Thurø
Report line
(10)
Langeland
Route H
Vejrø
Southwest (RSW)
(9)
DW
Tåsinge
55°
20′
30′
40′
50′
11°
10′
20′
30′
40′

Appendix 1-B

Pre-entry reporting areas – Danish EEZ

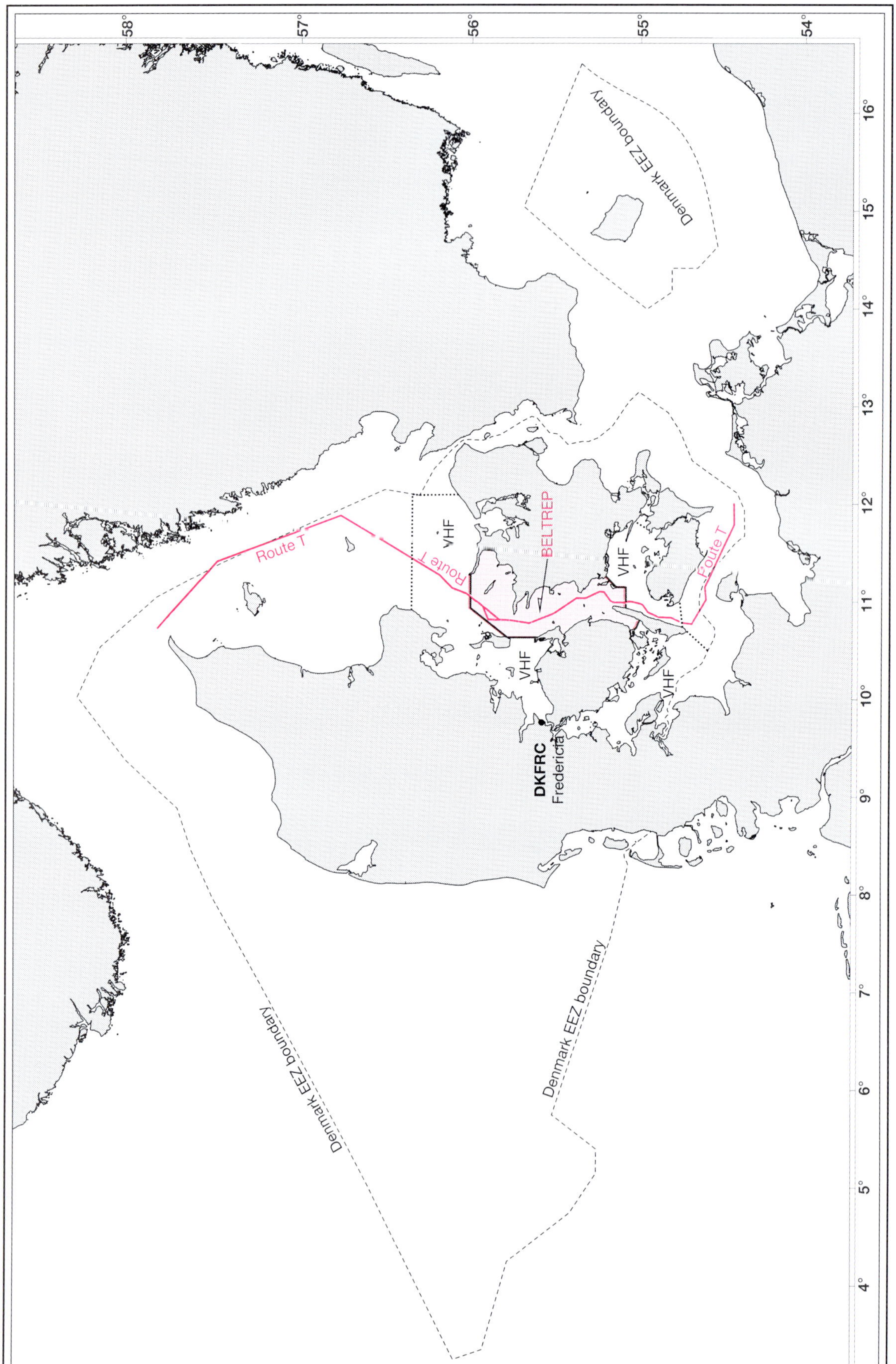

Appendix 2

Contact information and assigned VHF channels for sectors in the mandatory ship reporting system "BELTREP"

BELTREP radio call sign:	**"Belt Traffic"**

VHF channels	**Operational use**
VHF channel 74	Great Belt VTS – Sector 1 North
VHF channel 11	Great Belt VTS – Sector 2 South
VHF channel 10	Great Belt VTS – Broadcast, individual assistance, reserve channel
VHF channel 16	Great Belt VTS – Continuous monitoring

The Great Belt VTS operating BELTREP is located in Korsør at the bridge area:

24-hour contact information:

(1) Great Belt VTS is monitoring VHF channels 74, 11 and 16 continuously.

(2) Duty officer phone: +45 58 37 68 68

(3) Fax: +45 58 37 28 19

(4) MMSI: 002190001

(5) E-mail: beltrep@sok.dk
Web page: www.beltrep.org

Address:
Great Belt VTS
Sylowsvej 8
DK-4220 Korsør
Denmark

Appendix 3

Drafting of reports to the mandatory ship reporting system "BELTREP"

Summary:

Reporting is to be done by VHF, but can also be accomplished partly by the use of AIS and pre-entry non-verbal means as, e.g., e-mail.

- Correct and updated AIS information can accomplish reporting of designators A, B, C, E, F, G and I, O and W.
- Non-verbal means can accomplish reporting of designators (A, H), L, P, T and X.
- VHF must, as a minimum, be used for accomplishing designators A (part of) and U.

The scheme below gives the optimal use of reporting combined by AIS, non-verbal and VHF.

1 Desig-nator	**2 AIS**	**3 Non-verbal (e.g. e-mail)**	**4 VHF**	**5 Function**	**6 Information required**
A	Yes	Yes	Yes	Ship	(1) Name of ship: AIS, non-verbal, VHF (2) MMSI number: AIS (3) Call sign: AIS – and when available – (4) IMO number: AIS, non-verbal
	Yes	–	–	Date and time	A 6-digit group event giving day of month and hours and minutes in Universal Co-ordinated Time (UTC).
C	Yes	–	–	Position	A 5-digit group giving latitude in degrees and minutes, decimal, suffixed with N and a 6-digit group giving longitude in degrees and minutes, decimal, suffixed with E.
E	Yes	–	–	True course	A 3-digit group
F	Yes	–	–	Speed in knots and tenths of knots	A 3-digit group
G *and* I	Yes	–	–	Last port of call Destination and ETA	The name of last port of call and next port of call; both given in UN/LOCODE by AIS. For details and procedures see IMO SN/Circ.244 and www.unece.org/cefact/locode/service/main.htm. ETA date and time group expressed as in (B)
H	–	Yes	–	Date, time (UTC) and report-line of entry into the BELTREP area	This information is **only** required if reporting designators L, P, T and X are transmitted non-verbally (e.g. e-mail) prior to entry of the BELTREP

1 Desig- nator	2 AIS	3 Non-verbal (e.g. e-mail)	4 VHF	5 Function	6 Information required
L	–	Yes	–	Route information in the BELTREP area	A brief description of the intended route in the BELTREP area as planned by the master and stated by coded designators as given below (see also chartlet in appendix 1-A for references): Report-lines: RN – *Report-line North* RW – *Report-line West* RS – *Report-line South* RSW – *Report-line South-west* Routeing systems: DW-T3 – *Deep-water route "Between Hatter Rev and Hatter Barn"* TSS-T5 – *Separation scheme "At Hatter Barn"* Bridges: BE – *East bridge/Route Tango* BW – *West bridge* Routeing system: DW-T4 – *Deep-water route "Off east coast of Langeland"* Route: RH – *Route Hotel* Anchorage: KAL FJ – *Kalundborg Fjord* See examples below.
O	Yes	–	–	Maximum present draught in metres	A 2-digit or 3-digit group giving the present maximum draught in metres (e.g. 6.1 or 10.4).
P	–	Yes	–	Cargo on board	Cargo and, if dangerous goods present on board, their quantity and IMO class. Dangerous goods information must be summarized in total tonnes per IMO class when transmitted.
Q *or* R	–	–	Yes	Defects and deficiencies Pollution or dangerous goods overboard	Q: Details of defects and deficiencies affecting the equipment of the ship or any other circumstances affecting normal navigation and manoeuvrability. R: Pollution or dangerous goods lost overboard.
T	–	Yes	–	Ship's representative and/or owner	Address and particulars from which detailed information on the cargo may be obtained.

1 Designator	2 AIS	3 Non-verbal (e.g. e-mail)	4 VHF	5 Function	6 Information required
U	–	–	Yes	Ship's size	Information of maximum air draught and deadweight tonnage, required for all ships, including ship's tow or other floating equipment. This information shall be given by voice transmissions when entering the BELTREP area, irrespective of whether the information has also been given by, e.g., non-verbal means.
W	Yes	–	–	Total number of persons on board	State the number
X	–	Yes	–	Miscellaneous	Type and estimated quantity of bunker fuel, for ships of 1000 gross tonnage and above. Must be summarized in total tonnes per type when transmitted.

Examples of reporting route, coded in the format as given under designator L

(1) A northbound ship leaving the port of Gulfhavn planning to sail north route Tango via deep-water route "Between Hatter Rev and Hatter Barn", leaving at report-line North (UN/LOCODE format for Gulfhavn is DK GFH):

L: DK GFH, BE, DW-T3, RN

(2) A southbound ship in passage and planning to enter at report-line North, sailing through TSS "At Hatter Barn", then route Tango, route Hotel and leaving at report-line South:

L: RN, TSS-T5, BE, RH, RS

(3) A northbound ship entering via deep-water route "Off the east coast of Langeland", route Tango, East Bridge and leaving through report-line West, bound for the port of Fredericia:

L: RS, DW-T4, BE, RW

(4) A ship entering at report-line North sailing via TSS "At Hatter Barn", route Tango and then anchoring in Kalundborg Fjord:

L: RN, TSS-T5, KAL FJ

WEST EUROPEAN TANKER REPORTING SYSTEM (WETREP)

The West European Tanker Reporting System (WETREP) is established in the Western European Particularly Sensitive Sea Area.

1 Categories of ships required to participate in the system

1.1 Ships required to participate in the mandatory ship reporting system WETREP:

Every kind of oil tanker of more than 600 tonnes deadweight, carrying a cargo of:

- heavy crude oil, meaning crude oils with a density at 15°C of higher than 900 kg/m^3;
- heavy fuel oils, meaning fuel oils with a density at 15°C of higher than 900 kg/m^3, or a kinematic viscosity at 50°C of higher than 180 mm^2/s;
- bitumen and tar and their emulsions.

1.2 Pursuant to SOLAS, the mandatory ship reporting system WETREP does not apply to any warship, naval auxiliary or other vessel owned or operated by a contracting government and used, for the time being, only on government non-commercial service.

2 Geographical coverage of the system, and number and edition of the reference chart used for the delineation of the system

2.1 The area covered by the reporting system WETREP is defined within the following co-ordinates and is also shown in the chartlet attached at appendix 3:

Number	Latitude	Longitude
1 (UK)	58° 30′ N	UK coast
2 (UK)	58° 30′ N	000°
3 (UK)	62° N	000°
4 (UK)	62° N	003° W
5 (UK + Irl)	56° 30′ N	012° W
6 (Irl)	54° 40′ 40″.91 N	015° W
7 (Irl)	50° 56′ 45″.36 N	015° W
8 (Irl + UK + F)	48° 27′ N	006° 25′ W
9 (F)	48° 27′ N	008° W
10 (F + S)	44° 52′ N	003° 10′ W
11 (S)	44° 52′ N	010° W
12 (S)	44° 14′ N	011° 34′ W
13 (S)	42° 55′ N	012° 18′ W
14 (S + P)	41° 50′ N	011° 34′ W
15 (P)	37° N	009° 49′ W
16 (P)	36° 20′ N	009° 00′ W
17 (P)	36° 20′ N	007° 47′ W
18 (P)	Guadiana River mouth 37° 10′ N	007° 25′ W
19 (B)	51° 22′ 25″ N	003° 21′ 52″.5 E (border between B and NL)
20 (UK)	52° 12′ N	UK east coast
21 (Irl)	52° 10′ 3″ N	006° 21′ 8″ W
22 (UK)	52° 01′ 52″ N	005° 04′ 18″ W
23 (UK)	54° 51′ 43″ N	005° 08′ 47″ W
24 (UK)	54° 40′ 39″ N	005° 34′ 34″ W

2.2 The reference chart is Admiralty chart No. 4011 (World Geodetic System 1984 datum (WGS 84)).

3 Format, contents of report, times and geographical positions for submitting report, Authorities to whom the reports must be sent and available services

3.1 *Format*

3.1.1 WETREP reports shall be sent to the nearest participating coastal or communication station listed in appendix 1 and shall be drafted in accordance with the format as shown in appendix 2.

3.1.2 The format of the report described below is in accordance with resolution A.851(20) appendix, paragraph 2.

3.2 *Contents of report*

3.2.1 The report required from participating ships contains information that is essential to achieve the objectives of the system:

.1 the ship's name, call sign, IMO number/MMSI number and position are needed for establishing the identity of the ship and its initial position (letters A, B and C);

.2 the ship's course, speed and destination are important in order to maintain track of the ship so as to be able to implement search and rescue measures if a report from a ship fails to appear; to be able to instigate measures for the safe navigation of the ship; and to prevent pollution in the areas where weather conditions are severe (letters E, F, G and I). Proprietary information obtained as a requirement of the mandatory ship reporting system WETREP will be protected under this system consistent with the Guidelines and Criteria for Ship Reporting Systems, as amended (resolution A.851(20));

.3 the number of persons on board and other relevant information are important in relation to the allocation of resources in a search and rescue operation (letters P, T and W); and

.4 in accordance with the provisions of the SOLAS and MARPOL Conventions, ships will provide information on defects, damage, deficiencies or other limitations (under "Q") as well as additional information (under "X").

3.3 *Time and geographical position for submitting report*

3.3.1 Ships must report:

.1 on entry into the Reporting Area as defined in paragraph 2; or

.2 immediately on departing from a port, terminal or anchorage within the Reporting Area; or

.3 when they deviate from routeing to their original declared destination port/terminal/anchorage or position "for orders" given at time of entry into the Reporting Area; or

.4 when deviation from planned route is necessary due to weather or equipment malfunction or a change in the navigational status; and

.5 when finally exiting from the Reporting Area.

3.3.2 Ships need not report if, while on normal passage routeing during transit of the Reporting Area, the boundary of the Reporting Area is crossed on other occasions apart from the initial entry and final exit.

3.4 *Shore-based Authorities to whom reports are sent*

3.4.1 Upon entering the WETREP reporting area, ships will notify the co-ordination centre of the responsible Authority of the Coastal State participating in the system. The vessel traffic services, RCC, coastal radio station or other facilities to whom the reports must be sent are listed in appendix 1.

3.4.2 Should the ship be unable to send the report to the nearest coastal radio station or other facility, the report shall be sent to the next-nearest coastal radio station or other facility as listed in appendix 1.

3.4.3 Reports may be sent by any modern communication form, including Inmarsat-C, telefax and e-mail, as appropriate.

4 Information to be given to participating ships and procedures to be followed

4.1 If requested, coastal States can provide ships with information of importance for the safety of navigation in the ship reporting area, from broadcasting devices set up in the coastal States.

4.2 If necessary, individual information can be provided to a ship in relation to the special local conditions.

5 Communications required for the system, frequencies on which reports should be transmitted and information to be reported

5.1 The vessel traffic services, RCC, coastal radio station or other facilities to whom the reports must be sent are listed in appendix 1.

5.2 The reports required from a ship entering and navigating in the Reporting Area shall begin with the word "WETREP" and shall contain a two-letter abbreviation for identification of the report (Sailing Plan, Final Report or Deviation Report). Telegrams so prefixed are dispatched free of charge to ships.

5.3 Dependent on the type of report, the following information shall be included as referred to under paragraph 6 of appendix 2:

A: Ship identification (ship name, call sign, IMO identification number and MMSI number)

B: Date time group

C: Position

E: True course

F: Speed

G: Name of last port of call

I: Name of next port of call with the ETA

P: Oil cargo type(s), quantity, grade(s) and density. If those tankers carry other hazardous cargo simultaneously: the type, quantity and IMO class of that cargo, as appropriate

Q: To be used in cases of defects or deficiency affecting normal navigation

T: Address for the communication of cargo information

W: Number of persons on board

X: Various information applicable for those tankers:

- characteristics and estimated quantity of bunker fuel, for tankers carrying more than 5000 tonnes of bunker fuel
- navigational status, (for example, under way with engines, restricted in ability to manoeuvre, etc.)

5.4 Reports shall be in a format consistent with IMO resolution A.851(20).

5.5 Reports shall be free of charge for reporting ships.

6 Relevant rules and regulations in force in the area of the system

6.1 *Regulations for preventing collisions at sea*

The International Regulations for Preventing Collisions at Sea, 1972 (COLREGs), as amended, apply throughout the area covered by the system.*

G

* Ships carrying dangerous or polluting goods coming from or bound for a port within the reporting area must comply with the European Community Directive on *Vessel Traffic Monitoring* (2002/59/EC).

6.2 *Traffic separation schemes and other routeing measures*

6.2.1 The following IMO-adopted traffic separation schemes:
West of the Scilly Isles
South of the Scilly Isles
Off Land's End, between Seven Stones and Longships
Off Ushant
Off Casquets
In the Strait of Dover and adjacent waters
At West Hinder
Off Fastnet Rock
Off Smalls
Off Tuskar Rock
Off Skerries
In Liverpool Bay
In the North Channel
Off Neist Point in the Minches
Off Finisterre
Off Cape Roca
Off Cape S. Vicente

6.2.2 The following IMO-adopted deep-water routes:
Deep-water route leading to the port of Antifer
Deep-water route forming part of the north-eastbound traffic lane of the "Strait of Dover and adjacent waters" traffic separation scheme
Deep-water route west of the Hebrides

6.2.3 The following IMO-adopted areas to be avoided:
In the region of the Rochebonne Shelf
Around the CS4 buoy in the Dover Strait
Around the F3 station within the separation scheme "In the Strait of Dover and adjacent waters"
In the SUNK outer precautionary area
In the region of the Orkney Islands
In the region of The Fair Isle
In the region of the Shetland Islands
Between The Smalls lighthouse and Grassholme Island
In the region of the Berlengas Islands

6.2.4 The following other IMO-adopted routeing measures:
Recommended directions of traffic flow within the precautionary area around the Foxtrot3 station in the Dover Strait
Recommended routes in the Fair Isle Channel
Recommendations on navigation around the United Kingdom coast

6.2.5 The following IMO-adopted mandatory ship reporting systems:
Off "Les Casquets" and the adjacent coastal area
In the Dover Strait/Pas de Calais
Off Ushant
Off Finisterre
Off the coast of Portugal

6.2.6 The following coastal vessel traffic services (VTS):
Coast of Portugal VTS
Corsen VTS
Dover, Channel Navigation Information Service (CNIS)
Finisterre VTS
Gris-Nez VTS

7 Shore-based facilities to support the operation of the system

7.1 The vessel traffic services, RCC, coastal radio stations or other facilities to whom the reports must be sent are listed in appendix 1.

7.2 The vessel traffic services, RCC, coastal radio stations or other facilities that form a part of the service will at all times be manned.

7.3 *All communications facilities*

7.3.1 All IMO-approved communication methods are accepted and available as detailed in appendix 1.

7.4 *Staff training and qualification*

7.4.1 Personnel are trained according to national and international recommendations. The training of personnel comprises an overall study of the navigation safety measures, the relevant international (IMO) and national provisions with respect to the safety of navigation.

8 Procedures to be followed if shore-based communications fail

Should the ship be unable to send the report to the nearest coastal radio station or other facility, the report shall be sent to the next-nearest coastal radio station or other facility as listed in appendix 1.

9 Measures to be taken if a ship fails to comply with the requirements of the system

The objectives of the system are to initiate SAR and measures to prevent pollution as fast and effectively as possible if an emergency is reported or a report from a ship fails to appear, and it is impossible to establish communication with the ship. All means will be used to obtain the full participation of ships required to submit reports. If reports are not submitted and the offending ship can be positively identified, then information will be passed on to the relevant flag State Authorities for investigation and possible prosecution in accordance with national legislation. The mandatory ship reporting system WETREP is for the exchange of information only and does not provide any additional authority for mandating changes in the vessel's operations. This reporting system will be implemented consistent with UNCLOS, SOLAS and other relevant international instruments so that the reporting system will not provide the basis to impinge on a transiting vessel's passage through the Reporting Area.

Appendix 1

Vessel Traffic Services, RCC, coast radio station or other facilities to whom the reports must be submitted (Geographical positions refer to the World Geodetic System 1984 (WGS 84))

Position co-ordinates

BELGIUM

MRCC – SAR Oostende: 51°14′ N, 002°55′ E

Tel: +32 59 70 10 00
Tel.: +32 59 70 11 00
Fax: +32 59 70 36 05
Telex: 82125

VHF: 9, 16, 67, 70
MF: 2182
MMSI: 00 205 99 81

FRANCE

MRCC Gris-Nez: 50°52′ N, 001°35′ E

Tel.: +33 3 21 87 21 87
Fax: +33 3 21 87 78 55
Telex: 130680

Inmarsat-C: 422799256
VHF: 16, 70
MMSI: 002275100

MRCC Corsen: 48°25′ N, 004°47′ W

Tel.: +33 2 98 89 31 31
Fax: +33 2 98 89 65 75
Telex: 940086

Inmarsat-C: Nil
VHF: 16, 70
MMSI: 002275300

IRELAND

MRCC Dublin

Tel: +353 1 6620922/23
Fax: +353 1 6620795
e-mail: mrccdublin@irishcoastguard.ie

Communications may be sent to MRCC Dublin via:

MRSC Valentia (EJK) 51°56′ N, 010°21′ W

MRSC Malin Head (EJM) 55°22′ N, 007°21′ W

PORTUGAL

Roca Control: 38°41′.508 N, 009°17′.915 W

Tel: +351 214464838
Fax: +351 214464839
E-mail: oper.vts@imapor.pt
VHF: 22 & 79
MMSI: 002633030

Position co-ordinates

SPAIN

MRCC Madrid		40°24′ N, 003°43′ W
Tel:	+34 91 7559133	
Fax:	+34 91 5261440	
Telex:	+5241210, +5241224	
e-mail:	cncs@sasemar.es	
MRCC Finisterre:		42°42′ N, 008°59′ W
Tel:	+34 981 767500	
Fax:	+34 981 767740	
Telex:	+5282268, +5286207	
e-mail:	finister@sasemar.es	
VHF:	16 & 11	
MF:	2182	
MMSI:	002240993	
MRCC Bilbao		43°20′.8 N, 003°01′ W
Tel:	+34 944 839286	
Fax:	+34 944 839161	
e-mail:	bilbao@sasemar.es#	
VHF:	16 & 10	
MMSI:	002241021	

UNITED KINGDOM

MRCC Falmouth
Tel: +(0)1326 317575
Fax: +(0)1326 318342
Telex: +51 42981
Inmarsat-A and Inmarsat-C
e-mail: falmouthcoastguard@mcga.gov.uk

Sea Area A2 – MF DSC Coast Stations

		(MMSI)
MRCC Aberdeen	57°25′ N, 001°51′ W	002320004
MRCC Clyde	55°58′ N, 004°48′ W	002320022
MRCC Falmouth	50°08′ N, 005°07′ W	002320014
MRSC Holyhead	53°19′ N, 004°38′ W	002320018
MRSC Humber	54°05′ N, 001°10′ W	002320007
Cullercoats	55°04′ N, 001°28′ W	(sub-station)
MRSC Milford Haven	51°41′ N, 005°03′ W	002320017
MRCC Shetland	60°09′ N, 001°08′ W	002320001
MRSC Stornoway	58°13′ N, 006°20′ W	002320024

G

Appendix 2

West European Tanker Reporting System (WETREP)

Rules for drafting of reports

1 Ships on voyage to and from the Western European Reporting Area shall send reports:

.1 on entry into the Reporting Area; or

.2 immediately on departing from a port, terminal or anchorage within the Reporting Area; or

.3 when they deviate from routeing to their original declared destination port/terminal/anchorage or position "for orders" given at time of entry into Reporting Area; or

.4 when deviation from planned route is necessary due to weather or equipment malfunction or where information under entry "Q" is necessary; and

.5 when finally exiting from the Reporting Area.

2 Ships need not report if, while on normal passage routeing during transit of the Reporting Area, the boundary of the Reporting Area is crossed on other occasions apart from the initial entry and final exit.

3 Upon entering the WETREP reporting area, ships will notify the co-ordination centre of the responsible Authority of the Coastal State participating in the system. The vessel traffic services, RCC, coastal radio station or other facilities to whom the reports must be sent are listed in appendix 1.

4 Should the ship be unable to send the report to the nearest coastal radio station or other facility, the report shall be sent to the next-nearest coastal radio station or other facility as listed in appendix 1.

5 Each report shall begin with the word WETREP and a 2-letter abbreviation for identification of the report. Messages so prefixed are dispatched free of charge to ships.

6 The reports shall be drawn up in accordance with the following table. The designators A, B, C, E, F, G, I, P, T, W and X are mandatory for a sailing plan report, A, B, C, E and F for a final report, A, B, C, E, F, and I for a deviation report. The designator Q shall also be included at any time where defects, including breakdown, damage, deficiencies, or circumstances affecting normal navigation, should occur within the Reporting Area.

Designator	Function	Text
Name of system	Code word	"WETREP"
	Type of report: Sailing Plan Final Report Deviation Report	One of the following 2-letter identifiers: "SP" (Sailing Plan) "FR" (Final Report – on finally leaving the Reporting Area) containing only **A**, **B**, **C**, **E** & **F** "DR" (Deviation Report) containing only **A**, **B**, **C**, **E**, **F**, and **I**
A	Ship	Name and call sign (ship name, call sign, IMO identification number and MMSI Number) (e.g.: NONESUCH/KTOI)
B	Date Time group corresponding to the position under designator C given in UTC (Co-ordinated Universal Time)	A 6-digit group followed by a Z, the first 2 digits giving date of month, the next 2 digits giving hours and the last 2 digits minutes. The Z indicates that the time is given in UTC (e.g. 081340Z).
C	Position by latitude and longitude	A 4-digit group giving latitude in degrees and minutes suffixed with N, and a 5-digit group giving longitude in degrees and minutes suffixed with W or E (e.g. 5512N 03420W)
E	Course	True course. A 3-digit group (e.g. 083).

Designator	Function	Text
F	Speed	Speed in knots. A 2-digit group (e.g. 14).
G	Name of last port of call	The name of the last port of call (e.g. New York)
I	Destination and ETA (UTC)	The name of the destination followed by expected time of arrival, expressed as under designator B. (e.g. Milford Haven 181400Z)
P	Cargo	Oil cargo type(s), quantity, grade(s) and density of heavy crude oil, heavy fuel oil and bitumen and tar. If those tankers carry other hazardous cargo simultaneously: the type, quantity and IMO class of that cargo, as appropriate.
Q	Defect, damage, deficiency, limitations	Brief details of defects, including breakdown, damage, deficiencies or other circumstances affecting normal navigation
T	Address for the communication of cargo information	Name, telephone number and either facsimile, e-mail address or URL
W	Total number of persons on board	State the number
X	Various information	Various information applicable for those tankers: – characteristics and estimated quantity of bunker fuel, for tankers carrying more than 5000 tonnes of bunker fuel, – navigational status (for example, under way with engines, at anchor, not under command, restricted in ability to manoeuvre, constrained by draught, moored, aground, etc.).

7 **Sailing Plan** (*"SP"*) to be sent as a first report:

a) On entering the Reporting Area as defined in paragraph 2.1.

(b) Immediately on departing from a port located within the Reporting Area.

Example:

Name of station to which the report is being sent

WETREP – SP
A. NONESUCH/KTOI
B. 161520Z
C. 4105N 01115W
E. 026
F. 15
G. RAS TANNURAH
I. ROTTERDAM 230230Z
P. 56,000 TONNES HEAVY FUEL OILS
T. J. Smith, 00 47 22 31 56 10, Facsimile 00 47 22 31 56 11
W. 23
X. NONE, NONE

8 **Final Report** (*"FR"*) to be sent:

(a) On leaving the Reporting Area.

(b) On arrival in a port situated within the Reporting Area.

Example:

Name of station to which the report is being sent

WETREP – FR
A. NONESUCH/KTOI
B. 201520Z
C. 5145N 00238E
E. 044
F. 16

9 **Deviation Report** (*"DR"*) to be sent:

(a) When they deviate from routeing to their original declared destination/port/terminal/anchorage or position "for orders" given at time of entry into the Reporting Area.

(b) When deviation from planned route is necessary due to weather or equipment malfunction or a change in navigational status.

Example:

Name of station to which the report is being sent

WETREP – DR
A. NONESUCH/KTOI
B. 201520Z
C. 4957N 00207W
E. 073
F. 14
I. ROTTERDAM 270230Z
X. NONE, SATISFACTORY

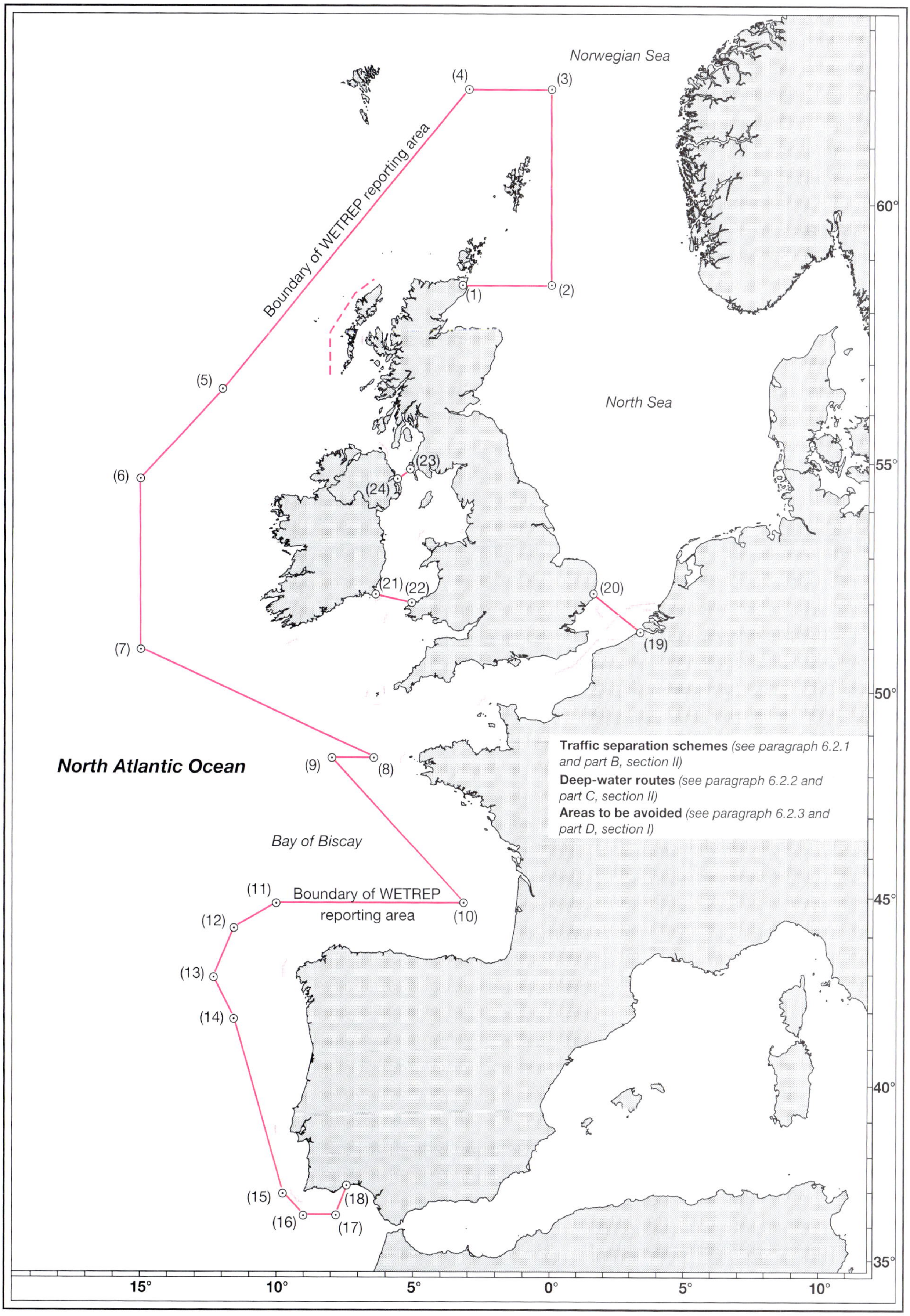
Norwegian Sea
North Sea
North Atlantic Ocean
Bay of Biscay
Boundary of WETREP reporting area
Boundary of WETREP
reporting area
(1)
(2)
(3)
(4)
(5)
(6)
(7)
(8)
(9)
(10)
(11)
(12)
(13)
(14)
(15)
(16)
(17)
(18)
(19)
(20)
(21)
(22)
(23)
(24)
60°
55°
50°
45°
40°
35°
15°
10°
5°
0°
5°
10°
Traffic separation schemes (see paragraph 6.2.1 and part B, section II)
Deep-water routes (see paragraph 6.2.2 and part C, section II)
Areas to be avoided (see paragraph 6.2.3 and part D, section I)

SUMMARY

1 Ships required to report

In the reporting system WETREP, every kind of oil tanker of more than 600 tonnes deadweight, carrying a cargo of:

- heavy crude oil, meaning crude oils with a density at 15°C of higher than 900 kg/m^3;
- heavy fuel oils, meaning fuel oils with a density at 15°C of higher than 900 kg/m^3, or a kinematic viscosity at 50°C of higher than 180 mm^2/s;
- bitumen and tar and their emulsions.

2 Position for submitting reports

Ships on voyage to and from the Western European Reporting Area shall send reports:

.1 on entry into the Reporting Area; or

.2 immediately on departing from a port, terminal or anchorage within the Reporting Area; or

.3 when they deviate from routeing to their original declared destination port/terminal/anchorage or position "for orders" given at time of entry into the Reporting Area; or

.4 when deviation from planned route is necessary due to weather or equipment malfunction or a change in the navigational status; and

.5 when finally exiting from the Reporting Area.

Ships need not report if, while on normal passage routeing during transit of the Reporting Area, the boundary of the Reporting Area is crossed on other occasions apart from the initial entry and final exit.

3 Reference chart

United Kingdom Hydrographic Office chart No. 4011 (World Geodetic System 1984 datum (WGS 84)).

4 Reporting format

System identifier: WETREP

Data to be transmitted in WETREP:

A: Ship identification (ship name, call sign, IMO identification number and MMSI number)

B: Date time group

C: Position

E: True course

F: Speed

G: Name of last port of call

I: Name of next port of call with ETA

P: Oil cargo type(s), quantity, grade(s) and density (If those tankers carry other hazardous cargo simultaneously, the type, quantity and IMO class of that cargo, as appropriate)

Q: To be used in cases of defects or deficiency affecting normal navigation

T: Address for the communication of cargo information

W: Number of persons on board

X: Various information applicable for those tankers:

- characteristics and estimated quantity of bunker fuel, for tankers carrying more than 5000 tonnes of bunker fuel
- navigational status (for example, under way with engines, restricted in ability to manoeuvre, etc.)

5 Authority receiving the report

5.1 Upon entering the WETREP reporting area, ships will notify the co-ordination centre of the responsible Authority of the Coastal State participating in the system. The vessel traffic services, RCC, coastal radio station or other facilities to whom the reports must be sent are listed in appendix 1.

5.2 Should the ship be unable to send the report to the nearest coastal radio station or other facility, the report shall be sent to the next-nearest coastal radio station or other facility as listed in appendix 1.

6 Communication

Reports may be sent by any modern communication form, including Inmarsat-C, telefax and e-mail as appropriate.

G

OFF USHANT (OUESSREP)

Note: See also mandatory ship reporting system "West European Tanker Reporting System".

1 Categories of ships required to participate in the system

Ships of more than 300 gross tonnage are required to participate in the system. This threshold is that used within the framework of the MAREP system, recently amended with regard to the categories of ships included (IMO document SN/Circ. 167, annex, page 4 – Recommendations on navigation through the English Channel and the Dover Strait[*]).

2 Geographical coverage of the system and the number and edition of the reference chart used for the delineation of the system

The reporting system covers a circular area 40 miles in radius centred on the Ile d'Ouessant (Stiff radar tower). The TSS covers the entire area. However, the Corsen/Ouessant vessel traffic service gathers all information relating to traffic within the area for which the MRCC Corsen is responsible, bounded as follows:

- to the south: parallel 47°47′.90 N, (via the Pointe de Penmarc'h)
- to the west: meridian 008°00′.00 W,
- to the north: a line connecting the positions
  48°50′.00 N, 008°00′.00 W
  49°30′.00 N, 004°00′.00 W
  48°53′.00 N, 002°20′.00 W
  48°49′.00 N, 001°49′.00 W
  48°37′.50 N, 001°34′.00 W (Baie de Mont St. Michel)

The reference chart which includes all the area of coverage for the system is the French chart No. 6989 of the Navy Hydrographic and Oceanographic Service.

3 Format and contents of report, times and geographical positions for submitting report, Authority to whom reports should be sent and available services

The reports required from ships entering the area covered by the system are position reports similar to the MAREP POSREP-type reports sent to the VTS by ships reporting within the scheme.

A ship may elect, for reasons of commercial confidentiality, to communicate that section of the report which provides information on cargo by non-verbal means prior to entering the system.

The information given below is derived from the format-type given in paragraph 2 of the appendix to the annex to resolution A.648(16)[†] of IMO.

3.1 *Content*

The report required should include:

A Name, call sign, IMO number (or MMSI number for reporting by transponder);

B Date and time;

C *or* D Position in latitude and longitude *or* true bearing and distance from a clearly identified landmark;

E True course;

F Speed;

G Port of departure;

I Port of destination and expected time of arrival;

[*] This has been amended by SN.1/Circ. 263 (see part F of this book; implemented 1 May 2008).

[†] Resolution A.648(16) has been revoked by A.851(20).

O	Present draught;
P	Cargo and, if dangerous goods are on board, IMO class and quantity;
Q *or* R	Defect, damage and/or deficiencies affecting ship's structure, cargo or equipment, or any other circumstance affecting normal navigation, in accordance with the SOLAS or MARPOL Conventions;
T	Address for provision of information concerning a cargo of dangerous goods;
W	Number of persons on board;
X	Miscellaneous: – Estimated quantity of bunker fuel and characteristics for ships carrying over 5000 tonnes of bunker fuel; – Navigation conditions.

3.2 *Recipient of report*

The shore-based authority is the Corsen/Ouessant vessel traffic service (voice communication call sign USHANT TRAFFIC) installed at the CROSS Corsen site. The Regional Centre for Surveillance and Rescue Operations – CROSS Corsen – is a service provided by the Department of Maritime Affairs, a department of the Ministry of Equipment, Transport and Tourism. It combines the maritime rescue co-ordination centre (MRCC) and the VTS as well as carrying out functions for the French Administration (monitoring fishing, monitoring pollution).

The VTS broadcasts a regular information bulletin at H + 10 min and H + 40 min. This bulletin includes:

- information on traffic
- urgent warnings to mariners concerning the area
- special weather bulletins.

In addition, a regular weather bulletin is broadcast every three hours from 0150 hours UTC. This information is broadcast in French and in English on VHF channel 79 after a call on channel 16.

If necessary, the VTS is capable of providing individual information to a ship, in particular with regard to positioning and navigational assistance.

4 Information to be provided to participating ships and procedures to be followed

The VTS processes the requests for anchoring made by the ships in the area for which the MRCC Corsen is responsible.

Detected and identified ships are monitored by radar, which in no way releases the masters from responsibility for their navigation.

The vessel traffic services in the Channel inform each other of the transit of ships, in particular those having hazardous cargoes. First, the identification for a southbound ship which has reported in accordance with the MAREP recommendations to the VTS at Jobourg is transmitted to the VTS at Corsen/Ouessant, which then sets up an HPA at the north-east racon radio beacon of the Ushant traffic separation scheme.

5 Communication requirements for the system, frequencies on which reports should be transmitted and information to be reported

The radiocommunications equipment required for the system is that defined in the GMDSS for sea area A1.

The ship reports will be made by voice on VHF radio. The channels defined are channel 13, monitored permanently by the VTS, as well as channels 79 and 80, which are also used to broadcast safety information. However, information of commercial confidentiality may be transmitted by non-verbal means.

The frequencies mentioned above will be used pending modifications made necessary by the use of an automatic identification system for which the draft definition of operational standards is under review.

In some cases, it could be decided to use the medium-frequency band for communication with ships, according to procedures which will be specified subsequently.

6 Relevant rules and regulations in force in the area of the system

The International Regulations for Preventing Collisions at Sea are applicable throughout the area of coverage of the system.

The "Off Ushant" traffic separation scheme has been approved by IMO and therefore rule 10 applies (document MSC XXXVIII/22, annex VII, pages 7 and 8).

In addition to the international regulatory scheme there are national regulations regarding vessel traffic and ship reporting. These are specifically:

- Decree No. 84/93 of the port-admiral for the Atlantic of 11 October 1993 regulating navigation in the "Off Ushant" TSS, the associated inshore traffic area and the fairways and waters of Fromveur, Four, Helle and Raz de Sein. Repealing a previous decree of 14 December 1978, it makes reporting mandatory for ships intending to use the north-eastbound lane of the TSS (situated in territorial waters) as well as inshore fairways. This decree repeats the provisions of the MSC document concerning the conditions for entry to the north-eastbound lane.

  The conditions for entry to the fairways and waterways are also specified.

- Joint prefectorial decree 326 Cherbourg/18/81 Brest of 13 May 1981 regulating navigation in the approaches to the French coast in the Channel and the Atlantic in order to prevent accidental marine pollution.

  This decree, concerning ships having hazardous cargoes, stipulates in particular:

  - for ships intending to enter French territorial waters, mandatory ship reporting with a 6-hour advance warning. In addition to information concerning the identity of the ship, the report must specify the place and time of entry into French waters, the port arrived from and the destination, the cargo and the state of manoeuvrability and navigational capacities,
  - a mandatory channel 16 VHF watch while travelling through territorial waters,
  - navigation at less than 7 miles from the coast is forbidden for ships of more than 1600 gross tonnage,
  - mandatory reporting to the French shipping authorities of any damage occurring at less than 50 miles from the French coast.

  Within the area of applicability of the system, the provisions of this decree apply more specifically in the following cases:

  - transit, via the north-eastbound lane of the TSS, of a ship having a cargo which is not prohibited in this lane but which comes under the decree,
  - traffic coming from or going towards the Port de Brest with hazardous cargoes.

- Decree No. 54/84 of the port-admiral for the Atlantic of 31 July 1984 regulating entry, movement and berthing of foreign ships in the internal waters of the second maritime region.

In addition to these provisions of a regulatory nature, also relevant are the Franco-British MAREP recommendations regarding ships of more than 300 gross tonnage and in particular those facing specific difficulties.

Application of these recommendations for the Ouessant area is as follows for the VTS:

- for northbound traffic, taking account of the information transmitted by ships approaching the TSS, plotting and radar monitoring and sending to the Jobourg VTS of MAREP information for ships having hazardous cargoes or facing specific difficulties in order to allow this VTS to set up an arrival forecast for the ship at the Casquets TSS;
- for southbound traffic, prior receipt, by the Jobourg VTS, of MAREP information concerning hazardous shipping or shipping facing specific difficulties and which have reported to Les Casquets. Plotting and radar monitoring of the ships identified.

7 Shore-based facilities to support operation of the system

The Corsen/Ouessant vessel traffic service is set up at the Regional Centre for Surveillance and Rescue Operations at Corsen. This service has radar and radio facilities.

7.1 *Radar facilities*

The surveillance radar type THOMSON TRS 3405 is installed at the Stiff tower at Ouessant. The installation includes three transmitter/receivers, a main antenna and a stand-by antenna. The nominal range of the radar is 64 miles. The antenna is positioned at 110 metres above the chart zero. Technical staff are permanently on duty at the tower. Radar messages are sent to the centre at Corsen via a radio-relay system where they are processed and then used by the staff on watch. The watch is carried out using visual display screens. The operators work using synthetic radar display. Each ship detected in the area of applicability has its echo noted as an automatically referenced radar track. Additional information is collected by the operators for each track identified. The vessel traffic service is equipped with a system for processing and storing radar data that allows statistics and course calculations to be printed. A complete reorganization of the processing and display chain will be carried out in the near future. The extraction and follow-up performances of the new system will be improved. Aids for the operators will form part of the new equipment. The operator will be alerted automatically as soon as violations or unusual behaviour is detected. It is also intended to add the Lloyd's file, on CD-ROM, to the "ships" file. It will be possible to obtain the record of a ship's track rapidly, to print texts and courses automatically and to write messages. Other databases will be used on office-type computers.

7.2 *Radiocommunications facilities*

Surveillance staff use the radio equipment installed at the Stiff tower in the Corsen centre. The vessel traffic service has the use of four single-channel VHF transmitter/receivers. If necessary, the VTS may, from time to time, use the VHF and MHF radio equipment belonging to the MRCC. These are VHF installations at Stiff, at the Pointe du Raz and at the Corsen site.

The VTS is also equipped with VHF air and UHF installations, allowing links with aircraft carrying out surveillance missions.

A renovation of the equipment is being undertaken. With regard to radio facilities, it will include the installation of channel 70 digital selective calling VHF equipment at Stiff and at the Pointe du Raz.

The vessel traffic service operators use VHF radio direction-finding equipment precise to within 0.5°. One is installed at the Pointe du Raz, the other at the Phare de Creac'h lighthouse. On each radio direction-finder it is possible to select two different tracks.

8 Alternative communication if the communication facilities of the shore-based Authority fail

The vessel traffic service VHF radiocommunications equipment is installed at Ouessant. It includes four single-channel transmitter/receivers plus a multi-channel transmitter/receiver on stand-by. A multi-channel transmitter/receiver normally dedicated to the MRCC Corsen completes the installation.

In the event that the radio-relay system between Stiff and Corsen breaks down, two emergency multi-channel VHF transmitter/receivers installed at the Corsen site can be used.

If none of the VTS VHF equipment is operational at the Corsen Centre, it would still be possible for the naval staff on watch at Stiff to intervene, as that staff has its own radio equipment and would be able to maintain contact with the ships. It should be noted that, in the event that the surveillance radar breaks down, this watch would take over temporarily from the vessel traffic service at Corsen/Ushant, pending the arrival, by the most rapid means (helicopter), of the VTS staff on Ile d'Ouessant. A breakdown involving several of the VTS VHF radios would not remove all possibility of contact between the VTS and the ships. There is therefore no reason to provide for a specific procedure in this event.

If it became necessary to establish an MHF link in the event of a breakdown at the MHF installation at the Corsen Centre, the inshore radio station, Le Conquet Radio, would be called upon.

SUMMARY

1 General

1.1 *Vessels concerned:* all vessels having a gross registered tonnage equal to or exceeding 300 tons.

1.2 *Area on entering which the vessels should report:* on entering a circular area 40 miles in radius centred on the Ile d'Ouessant (Stiff radar tower).

1.3 *Reference chart:* chart No. 6989 of the French Navy Hydrographic and Oceanographic Service.

1.4 *Reporting format* (in accordance with resolution A.648(16)*, General principles for ship reporting systems and ship reporting requirements, including guidelines for reporting incidents involving dangerous goods, harmful substances and/or marine pollutants):

Name of system: OUESSREP

The report required should include:

A Name, call sign, IMO Number (or MMSI number for reporting by transponder);

B Date and time;

C *or* D Position in latitude and longitude *or* true bearing and distance from a clearly identified landmark;

E True course;

F Speed;

G Port of departure;

I Port of destination and expected time of arrival;

O Present draught;

P Cargo and, if dangerous goods are on board, IMO class and quantity;

Q *or* R Defect, damage and/or deficiencies affecting ship's structure, cargo or equipment, or any other circumstance affecting normal navigation, in accordance with the SOLAS or MARPOL Conventions;

T Address for provision of information concerning a cargo of dangerous goods;

W Number of persons on board;

X Miscellaneous:

- Estimated quantity of bunker fuel and characteristics for ships carrying over 5000 tonnes of bunker fuel;
- Navigation conditions.

1.5 *Authority to whom the report should be sent:* Regional Centre for Surveillance and Rescue Operations at Corsen/Ouessant (CROSS Corsen), call sign USHANT TRAFFIC. (In addition to the vessel traffic service (VTS), the Centre carries out the functions of a rescue co-ordination centre (RCC), call sign CROSS CORSEN.)

1.6 *Communication facilities*

The reports will be transmitted by radiotelephone in VHF on channel 13 or, in the event of failure, on channel 79, according to the information given by the Centre.

It is proposed that the reports be transmitted in the future by automatic means when the relevant standards have been put in place by the Organization.

* Resolution A.648(16) has been revoked by A.851(20).

OFF USHANT

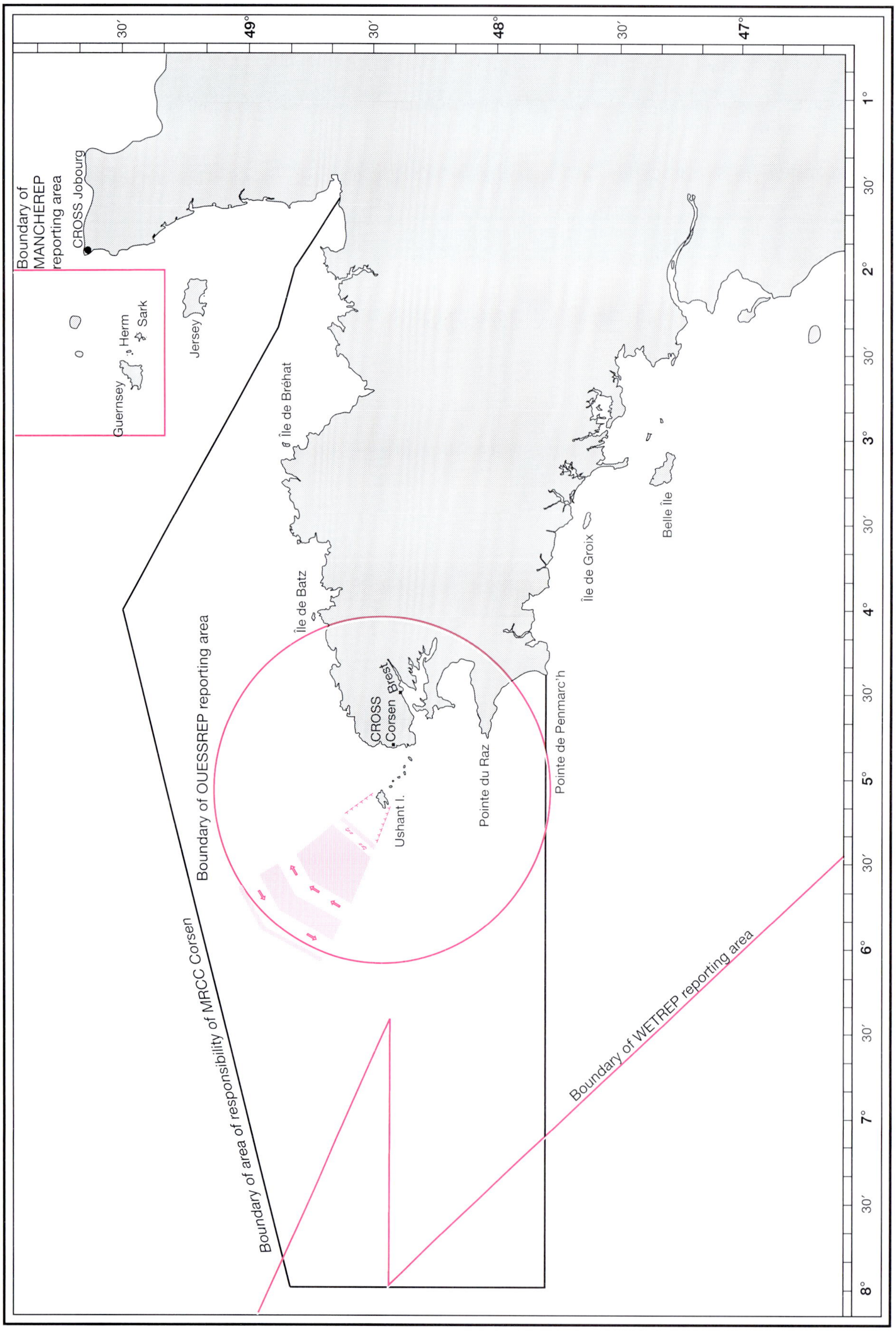

Boundary of MANCHEREP reporting area
CROSS Jobourg
Guernsey
Herm
Sark
Jersey
Île de Bréhat
Île de Batz
Boundary of OUESSREP reporting area
CROSS Corsen
Brest
Ushant I.
Pointe du Raz
Pointe de Penmarc'h
Île de Groix
Belle Île
Boundary of area of responsibility of MRCC Corsen
Boundary of WETREP reporting area
49°
48°
47°
30′
1°
2°
3°
4°
5°
6°
7°
8°

OFF LES CASQUETS AND THE ADJACENT COASTAL AREA (MANCHEREP)

Note: See also mandatory ship reporting system "West European Tanker Reporting System".

1 Categories of ships required to participate in the system

The new system applies to ships of over 300 gross tonnage, in line with the MAREP, OUESSREP and CALDOVREP systems already in place in The Channel or west of The Channel.

Within the coverage zone, these provisions replace the MAREP system in force for ships of 300 gross tonnage and over. However, ships of less than 300 gross tonnage will have to continue to make reports in accordance with the provisions of the voluntary system in the following circumstances:

- when they are not in control of their manoeuvres, or moored in the traffic separation scheme or the coastal area;
- when their capacity to manoeuvre is limited; or
- when their aids to navigation are defective.

Outside the zone, the provisions of the MAREP system remain unchanged.

2 Geographical coverage of the system and the number and edition of the reference chart used for the delineation of the system

The reporting system covers the TSS off Les Casquets and the adjacent coastal navigation area.

Thus, the area covered is bounded by a line connecting the following four points:

(A)	50°10′.0 N,	002°58′.0 W	(C)	49°20′.0 N,	002°00′.0 W
(B)	50°10′.0 N,	002°00′.0 W	(D)	49°20′.0 N,	002°58′.0 W

The call should be made 2 nautical miles before entering the area (chart annexed).

2.1 *Traffic crossing on regular routes*

Ships making regular voyages from a port situated within the coverage area or in an adjacent area must send their reports to Jobourg. However, since ferries generally sail in accordance with fixed schedules, it will be possible for arrangements to be made on a case-by-case basis between ships and the Jobourg VTS.

2.2 *Reference chart*

The marine reference chart including all the area covered by the system is French chart No. 7311 of the Naval Hydrographical and Oceanographic Service (International chart No. 1071).

3 Format and content of reports, Authority to which reports should be sent, services available

The MANCHEREP reports required of ships entering the area covered by the system are position reports of the OUESSREP and CALDOVREP type which are sent to the VTS by ships identifying themselves in the traffic separation schemes off Ouessant and the Pas de Calais.

A ship may elect, for reasons of commercial confidentiality, to communicate that section of the report which provides information on cargo by non-verbal means prior to entering the system.

The requirements listed below are taken from the standard reporting format set out in paragraph 2 of the appendix to resolution A.851(20).

3.1 *Content*

The report required should include:

A Name, call sign, IMO number (or MMSI number for reporting by transponder);

B Date and time;

C *or* D	Position in latitude and longitude *or* true bearing and distance from a clearly identified landmark;
E	True course;
F	Speed;
G	Port of departure;
I	Port of destination and expected time of arrival;
O	Present draught;
P	Cargo and, if dangerous goods are on board, IMO class and quantity;
Q *or* R	Defect, damage and/or deficiencies affecting ship's structure, cargo or equipment, or any other circumstance affecting normal navigation, in accordance with the SOLAS or MARPOL Conventions;
T	Address for provision of information concerning a cargo of dangerous goods;
W	Number of persons on board;
X	Miscellaneous: – Estimated quantity of bunker fuel and characteristics for ships carrying over 5000 tonnes of bunker fuel; – Navigation conditions.

When they receive a position report message, the VTS operators do their best to correlate the position of the ship with the information available to them:

- radar echo at position indicated
- direction-finding data
- description of the environment given by the officer of the watch
- position in relation to other ships (in case of dense traffic)
- course and speed.

Information on course and speed is thus an additional element enabling the VTS operators to correlate the announced position and if necessary to pick a ship out from within a group.

In addition, in accordance with the provisions of the SOLAS and MARPOL Conventions, ships will be required to give information on any defects, damage, deficiencies or other limitations, as well as, if appropriate, information on pollution or cargo losses.

3.2 *Recipient of report*

The shore-based Authority for the whole area is the Jobourg Vessel Traffic Service (VTS) (call sign JOBOURG TRAFFIC) operating from the premises of the Regional Operational Centre for Surveillance and Rescue (CROSS Jobourg). This is a service of the Ministry of Equipment, Transport and Housing which is similar to the MRCC and the VTS.

The VTS broadcasts a regular information bulletin on ship traffic at 20 minutes and 50 minutes past the hour. This bulletin indicates:

- information on traffic
- urgent warnings to mariners concerning the area
- special weather bulletins.

This information is broadcast in French and English on VHF channel 80 following a call on VHF channel 16.

The VTS also broadcasts regular weather reports in French (07h00, 15h00 and 19h00 French time) and special reports in French and English at 3 minutes past the hour from coastal transmitters situated at Granville, Jobourg, Port en Bessin and Antifer.

In addition, if required, the VTS can provide personalized information on a ship, notably as an aid to positioning.

4 Information to be provided to ships and procedures to be followed

Ships detected and identified are tracked on radar. This tracking in no way exempts masters from their navigational responsibilities.

They are informed about traffic conditions in the traffic separation scheme, about the beaconing situation and about weather conditions; on request, they can receive personalized assistance.

The Channel vessel traffic services keep each other informed of transits by ships, particularly ships carrying hazardous cargoes.

5 Radiocommunications required for the system, frequencies on which reports should be transmitted and information to be reported

The communication requirements for the system are those defined for sea area A1 in the framework of the GMDSS.

Ship reporting is effected by radiotelephony on metric waves. The channels selected are VHF channel 13, on which there is continuous watch by the VTS, and channel 80, which is also used for broadcasting safety information.

The above-mentioned frequency plan will be used pending the modifications made necessary by the use of AIS transponders, which can also be used for transmitting reports.

If for any reason a ship finds it impossible to communicate with the VTS by VHF, it should use any other means of communication it may have available.

6 Rules and regulations in force in the area of the system

The International Regulations for Preventing Collisions at Sea (COLREGs) apply throughout the area covered by the system.

Since the traffic separation scheme off Les Casquets is approved by IMO, regulation 10 applies therein.

Ships carrying dangerous goods coming from or bound for a port within the reporting zone must comply with the European Community directive HAZMAT (EC Directive 93/75).

In addition to these international regulations, the joint order issued by the Maritime Prefect for the Atlantic and the Maritime Prefect for The Channel and North Sea (No. 92/97 Brest, No. 03/97 Cherbourg) regulates shipping in the approaches to the French North Sea, Channel and Atlantic coasts with a view to preventing accidental marine pollution.

These regulations provide, in particular, that ships carrying oil (MARPOL 73 Annex I), dangerous liquid substances (MARPOL Annex II), noxious substances (MARPOL Annex III) or dangerous goods (IMDG Code), which are intending to pass through or to stay in French territorial waters, must give advance warning by sending a message to the appropriate CROSS five hours before entering those territorial waters, or six hours before setting sail.

The message sent to the CROSS must indicate what movements the ship plans to make in territorial waters and the condition of its manoeuvring and navigational capabilities.

The same regulations require a watch to be kept on channel 16 VHF or other specific frequencies in certain areas, and also require that notification be given of any accident occurring less than 50 miles from the French coast and that the necessary measures be taken by the maritime authorities to reduce risks.

The United Kingdom has established a pollution control area under the Merchant Shipping (Prevention of Pollution) (Limits) Regulations, 1996. The reporting zone comes partially within these limits. Polluting ships within the zone may be prosecuted and sentenced to a heavy fine.

7 Shore-based facilities to support the operation of the system

7.1 *Shore-based facilities*

The Jobourg Vessel Traffic Service operates from the premises of the Jobourg Regional Operational Centre for Surveillance and Rescue. This service has both radar and radio facilities.

7.2 *Radar facilities*

A radar monitoring system of the THOMSON TRS 3405 type is installed at the Jobourg centre. This facility has two transmitter/receivers. The main antenna is situated 202 metres above zero on the charts. An emergency radar facility of the THOMSON TRS 3410 type is also in service. The nominal range of the radar is 64 miles. The centre is manned by technical staff around the clock.

The radar data are processed and then interpreted by the personnel on duty. Watch is maintained on display consoles.

The echo of every ship detected in the area of coverage is noted as an automatically referenced radar track. Any additional information is keyed in by the operators for each track identified. The vessel traffic service is equipped with a system for processing and filing radar data which permits the publication of statistics and trajectography.

7.3 *Radiocommunication facilities*

The personnel on watch duty use radio facilities installed at the Jobourg centre. The vessel traffic service has four dedicated transmitter/receivers for its exclusive use.

In addition, the VTS can if necessary make occasional use of the VHF radio facilities of the MRCC. These are both local and off-site VHF facilities.

The VTS is also equipped with MHF facilities and with aeronautical VHF, which enables it to establish contact with aircraft carrying out monitoring missions.

The operators of the vessel traffic service use direction finders which are accurate to within one half of a degree. One of these is installed at Jobourg and the other at the Roches Douvres lighthouse. On each of these direction finders it is possible to select two different channels simultaneously.

7.4 *Information exchange*

Lastly, a database shared by all three Channel vessel traffic services makes it possible to exchange information on ships identified, so that procedures for contacts between the VTS and the ships can be simplified.

8 Alternative communication if the communication facilities of the shore-based Authority fail

The VHF radiocommunication facilities of the vessel traffic service are installed in Jobourg. They consist of four single-channel transmitter/receivers and one emergency multi-channel transmitter/receiver. One multi-channel transmitter/receiver normally dedicated to the Jobourg MRCC supplements the VTS facilities.

Failure of several of the VHF radio facilities of the VTS would not eliminate all possibility of contact between the VTS and ships. There is thus no need to make provision for any special procedure in such a case.

If need should arise for an MF link in the event of failure of the facilities at the Jobourg centre, a call would be made to the Ouessant VTS coastal radio station.

In the event of simultaneous breakdown of both radar monitoring facilities, the harbour master's office of Aurigny Island would take over the vessel traffic service off Les Casquets until such time as repairs had been completed.

Appendix

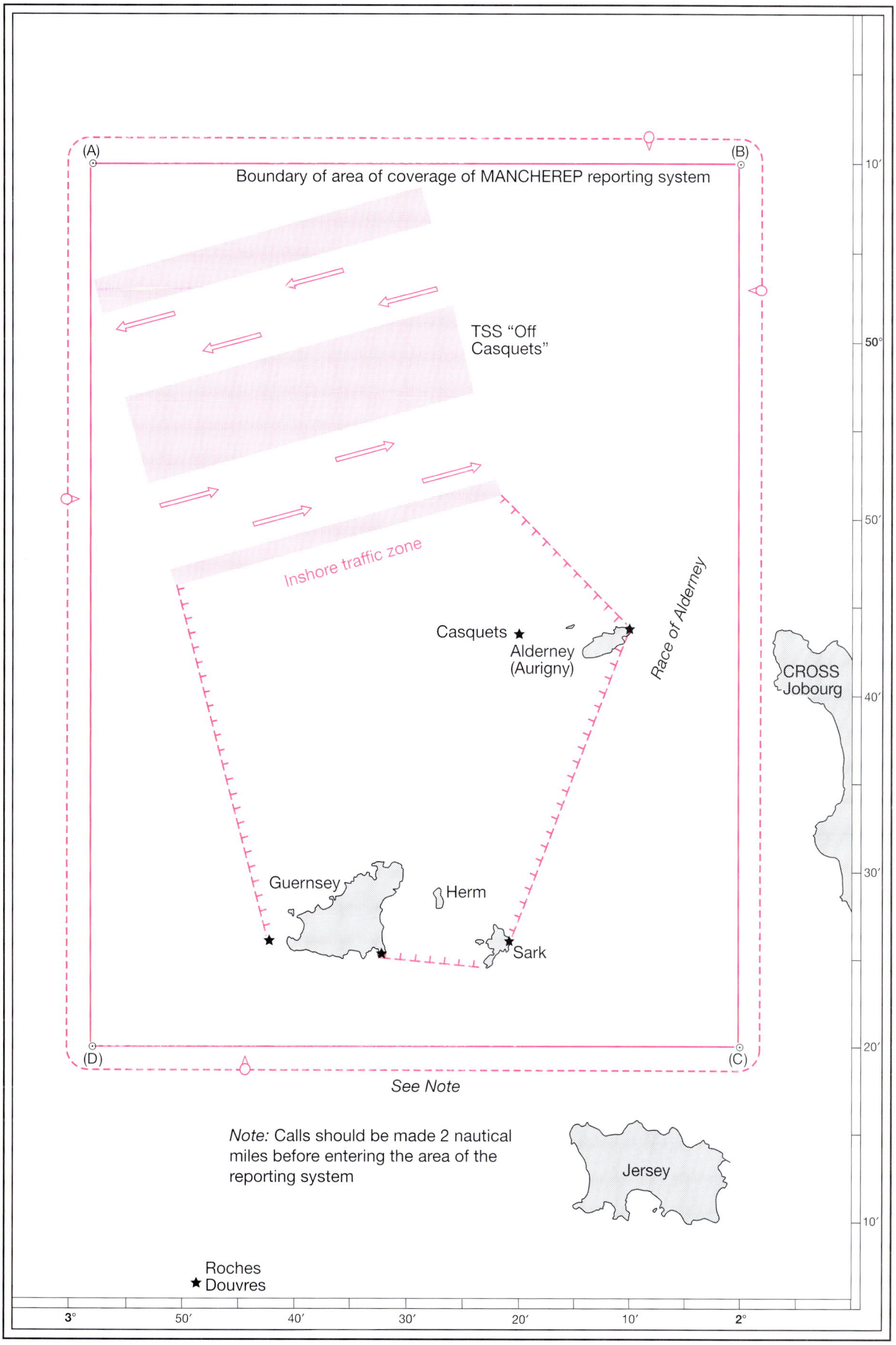

(A)
(B)
(C)
(D)
Boundary of area of coverage of MANCHEREP reporting system
TSS "Off Casquets"
Inshore traffic zone
Casquets
Alderney (Aurigny)
Race of Alderney
CROSS Jobourg
Guernsey
Herm
Sark
See Note
Note: Calls should be made 2 nautical miles before entering the area of the reporting system
Jersey
Roches Douvres
10′
50°
50′
40′
30′
20′
10′
3°
50′
40′
30′
20′
10′
2°

IN THE DOVER STRAIT/PAS DE CALAIS (CALDOVREP)

Note: See also mandatory ship reporting system "West European Tanker Reporting System".

1 Categories of ships required to participate in the system

Ships of 300 gross tonnage and over are required to participate in the system. This threshold is the same as used in the existing voluntary MAREP scheme (SN/Circ.167, annex, page 4, amending paragraph 7 of the Recommendations on navigation through the English Channel and Dover Strait (see part F)).

Within the coverage area, these arrangements replace the existing MAREP scheme for ships of 300 gross tonnage and over. However, ships of less than 300 gross tonnage should continue to make reports under the existing voluntary arrangements in circumstances where they:

- are "not under command" or at anchor in the TSS or its ITZs;
- are "restricted in their ability to manoeuvre"; or
- have defective navigational aids.

The MAREP arrangements outside the coverage area of this system remain unchanged.

2 Geographical coverage of the system and the number and edition of the reference chart used for the delineation of the system

The system covers a 65-mile stretch of the Dover Strait/Pas de Calais and is bounded by a line to the east drawn from North Foreland to the border between France and Belgium; and by a line to the west drawn from the Royal Sovereign Light Tower, through the Bassurelle Light Buoy (at its assigned position of 50°32′.80 N, 000°57′.80 E) to the coast of France.

The reference charts are British Admiralty charts 2449 (1998 edition, scale 1:150 000) and 2451 (1991 edition, scale 1:150 000), and also chart 7312 of the French Navy Hydrographic and Oceanographic Service (INT 1072) (1994 edition, scale 1:375 000). Also relevant is the British Admiralty chart 5500 – *Mariner's Routeing Guide English Channel and Southern North Sea* and the French Navy Hydrographic and Oceanographic Service (SHOM) chart 8001 – *Guide pour la préparation de la traversée de la Manche*.

The area of the reporting system is covered by modern hydrographic surveys and areas of unstable sea-bed are regularly resurveyed to ensure navigational safety.

3 Format and content of reports, times and geographical positions for submitting reports, Authority to whom reports should be sent and available services

The reports required from ships entering the area covered by the system are position reports similar to the existing MAREP/POSREP arrangements. The short title for the ship report is CALDOVREP.

Reports should be made using VHF voice transmissions. However, when reporting to DOVER COASTGUARD, ships can fulfil the reporting requirements of a CALDOVREP through the use of automatic ship identification transponders approved by the Organization.

A ship may elect, for reasons of commercial confidentiality, to communicate that section of the report which provides information on cargo by non-verbal means prior to entering the system.

3.1 *Format*

The information given below is derived from the format-type given in paragraph 2 of the appendix to resolution A.851(20).

3.2 *Content*

The report required should include:

A Name, call sign, IMO Number (or MMSI number for reporting by transponder);

B Date and time;

C *or* D	Position in latitude and longitude *or* true bearing and distance from a clearly identified landmark;
E	True course;
F	Speed;
G	Port of departure;
I	Port of destination and expected time of arrival;
O	Present draught;
P	Cargo and, if dangerous goods are on board, IMO class and quantity;
Q *or* R	Defect, damage and/or deficiencies affecting ship's structure, cargo or equipment, or any other circumstance affecting normal navigation, in accordance with the SOLAS or MARPOL Conventions;
T	Address for provision of information concerning a cargo of dangerous goods;
W	Number of persons on board;
X	Miscellaneous: – Estimated quantity of bunker fuel and characteristics for ships carrying over 5000 tonnes of bunker fuel; – Navigation conditions.

Note: On receipt of a position message, the VTS operators will establish the relationship between the ship's position and the information supplied by the position-fixing equipment available to them. Information on course and speed will help operators to identify one ship among a group of ships. This will be achieved automatically if a transponder is used.

3.3 *Geographical position for submitting reports*

North-eastbound traffic should report to GRIS NEZ TRAFFIC on the French coast 2 nautical miles before crossing the line from the Royal Sovereign Light Tower, through the Bassurelle Light Buoy (at its assigned position of 50°32′.80 N, 000°57′.80 E) to the coast of France.

South-westbound traffic should report to the shore at DOVER COASTGUARD on the English coast when within VHF range of North Foreland and not later than when crossing the line drawn from North Foreland to the border between France and Belgium (see appendix).

3.3.1 *Crossing traffic*

Reports to the nearer of the two shore stations should be made on departure from a port within the coverage area. Recognizing that cross-Channel ferries generally operate according to published schedules, special reporting arrangements can be made on a ship-by-ship basis, subject to the approval of **both** GRIS NEZ TRAFFIC and DOVER COASTGUARD.

Further reports should be made to the relevant shore station whenever there is a change of navigational circumstance, particularly in relation to items Q and R of the reporting format.

3.4 *Authority*

The shore-based Authorities are the Regional Centre for Surveillance and Rescue Operations, CROSS Gris Nez (call sign: GRIS NEZ TRAFFIC) – provided by the French Ministry with responsibility for maritime navigation, and the Maritime Rescue Co-ordination Centre, MRCC Dover (call sign: DOVER COASTGUARD) – provided by HM Coastguard, which is part of the United Kingdom's Department of the Environment, Transport and the Regions.

Both Gris Nez and Dover sites monitor shipping in the TSS in the Dover Strait/Pas de Calais using radar, and each provides regular information about weather and navigational hazards as part of the joint Channel Navigation Information Service (CNIS). Information is broadcast at the following times and on the following frequencies:

Station	Frequency	Times	Additional broadcasts in times of poor visibility
Gris Nez	VHF channel 79	$H + 10$	$H + 25$
(call sign: GRIS NEZ TRAFFIC)			
Dover	VHF channel 11	$H + 40$	$H + 55$
(call sign: DOVER COASTGUARD)			

Information broadcasts will be preceded by an announcement on VHF channel 16 and broadcasts from both stations will end with a reminder about the time of the next broadcast and the VHF frequency on which it will be made.

4 Information to be provided to participating ships

If necessary, individual information can be provided to a ship, particularly in relation to positioning and navigational assistance.

5 Radiocommunications requirements for the system, frequencies on which reports should be transmitted and information to be reported

The radiocommunications equipment required for the system is that defined in the GMDSS for sea area A1.

The ship reports can be made by voice on VHF radio using channel 13 (GRIS NEZ TRAFFIC) or channel 11 (DOVER COASTGUARD).

Ship reports to DOVER COASTGUARD can alternatively be made by automatic ship-identification transponder, where available, using a suitably adapted DSC facility on VHF channel 70, or by equipment conforming to the standards adopted for the Universal AIS Transponder.

Confidential information may be transmitted by other means.

6 Relevant rules and regulations in force in the area of the system

The International Regulations for Preventing Collisions at Sea, 1972 (as amended) apply throughout the reporting area. In particular, rule 10 of those Regulations applies to the IMO-adopted TSS.

Ships carrying dangerous or hazardous cargoes and bound to or from any port within the proposed reporting area must comply with the European HAZMAT Directive (EC Directive 93/75).

In addition to these international requirements, the Joint Decree of the Préfét maritime de l'Atlantique and the Préfét maritime de la Manche et de la Mer du Nord (No. 92/97 – Brest, No. 03/97 – Cherbourg) control navigation in the approaches to the French coast in the North Sea, the English Channel and the Atlantic in order to prevent accidental marine pollution. The Regulations make provision, in particular, for ships transporting hydrocarbons (MARPOL Annex I), harmful liquid substances (MARPOL Annex II), noxious substances (MARPOL Annex III), or dangerous goods (IMDG Code), preparing to pass through or remain in French territorial waters, to send an advance report to the appropriate CROSS five hours before entering territorial waters, or six hours before departure. The message sent to the CROSS must make clear the ship's intended movements in territorial waters and the status of its ability to manoeuvre and navigate.

The same Regulations require ships to monitor VHF channel 16 or other specific frequencies in certain areas, and require the reporting of any accident within 50 miles of the French coast and the taking of any action required by the maritime Authorities to reduce risks.

The United Kingdom has established a pollution control zone under the Merchant Shipping (Prevention of Pollution) (Limits) Regulations 1996. The proposed reporting area is included within those limits. Ships causing pollution within the area can be prosecuted and fined more than £250,000.

7 Shore-based facilities to support operation of the system

DOVER COASTGUARD

The Channel Navigation Information Service (CNIS) has radar, an information processing and retrieval system (IPRS), access to the United Kingdom's HM Coastguard operational radiocommunications, VHF direction-finding (DF), radio VHF Digital Selective Calling (DSC), and Automatic Identification System (AIS) facilities. The CNIS supports the primary responsibilities of preserving safety of life at sea and co-ordinating responses to incidents.

7.1 *CNIS facility*

The CNIS processing and display system receives inputs from the radar and VHF DF equipment, processes the information and presents it on any or all of six displays. Each display shows processed images (tracks) from any of the three radar inputs overlaid on a synthetic map of a selected area. New targets entering radar range are automatically tagged with a unique track number. The position, course and speed information of up to 300 tracks is automatically updated and recorded, for each of the three radars, throughout the vessel's passage through the CNIS area, giving the CNIS a 900-track capability.

DOVER COASTGUARD maintain a continuous watch on traffic in the Dover Strait/Pas de Calais. Operators can add vessel information to the associated IPRS database (such as name and cargo) and can display that supporting information on a separate screen. CNIS is capable of providing an automatic alarm to identify any track which strays into an unauthorised area. VHF DF vectors appear when a VHF radio transmits on the frequency selected on the VHF DF equipment. Recording equipment automatically stores information from all tracks, which can either be replayed on the system or specific track movements can be plotted onto an A0-size sheet of paper. CNIS operators have access to Lloyd's Register and hazardous cargo data on a separate computer.

7.2 *Radar facilities*

Three surveillance radars cover the CNIS area and the area of the mandatory ship reporting system. These are TERMA dual X-band systems, each comprising main and back-up transceivers (type 232075) and a single antenna. The radars are located at:

- Margate – The antenna is 118 metres above mean ordnance datum and covers the area from the southern area of the North Sea to Dover;
- Dover – The antenna is 125 metres above mean ordnance datum and covers the area from North Foreland to Hastings; and
- Fairlight – The antenna is 126 metres above mean ordnance datum and covers the area from Dover to the western boundary of the CNIS area.

Data from the Margate and Fairlight radars are transmitted to DOVER COASTGUARD via microwave links. The radars have a maximum operational range of 75 nautical miles, although the operational range of each radar is limited by radar video units to 35 nautical miles to prevent the track table from filling up with vessels which are not entering the CNIS area.

7.3 *VHF DF facilities*

The CNIS automatically displays vectors generated from the DF systems at Dover, Fairlight, North Foreland, Mont St. Frieux and Cap Gris Nez. All of the DF systems may be set to one of a number of the VHF channels used in the area. In parallel, channel 16 receivers monitor the distress channel, should a distress call be sent.

7.4 *Radiocommunication facilities*

Radiocommunications terminals are sited in the consoles of the MRCC Dover Operations Room. VHF radio receivers are located at Dover, while their associated transmitters are at West Hougham (near Folkestone) to gain optimum coverage of 13 VHF channels. MF is also fitted at Dover. Other VHF transmitters are fitted at Fairlight and North Foreland radio sites and are controlled via land lines. The VHF channels used are:

- VHF Air (AM) on 132.65 MHz
- channel 0 (SAR);

- channel 6 (inter-ship/scene of search for SAR);
- channel 9 (pilotage) – receive only;
- channel 10 (counter-pollution);
- channel 11 (port operations and CNIS) – continuously monitored;
- channel 12 (Thames port control) – receive only;
- channel 13 (inter-ship and port operations);
- channel 14 (Thames port control) – receive only;
- channel 16 (international distress) – continuously monitored;
- channel 30 (special operations);
- channel 67 (small ship safety) – secondary SAR;
- channel 69 (inter-ship, port operations and CNIS)
- channel 73 (channel 0 back-up);
- channel 74 (Dover port control);
- channel 80 (marinas);
- channel 99 (Coastguard private channel).

7.5 *VHF DSC facilities*

A VHF channel 70 digital selective calling system has been installed as part of the GMDSS requirement. Its purpose is to provide rapid distress alerting between vessels and the shore, routine calling of vessels and AIS facilities. DSC communications are available to all operator positions at DOVER COASTGUARD. DSC takes priority over all other operations.

7.6 *AIS facilities*

DOVER COASTGUARD can interrogate ships fitted with transponders to gain information on their identity and position. This information is displayed as an icon on an electronic charting package covering the CNIS area.

GRIS NEZ TRAFFIC

Similar facilities to those at DOVER COASTGUARD are also available at GRIS NEZ TRAFFIC. The two centres act in partnership in the operation of the CNIS. GRIS NEZ TRAFFIC specifically has the following facilities.

7.7 *Radar facilities*

GRIS NEZ TRAFFIC is equipped with two radar installations, at:

- Cap Gris Nez; and
- Mont St. Frieux.

The two radar installations are linked to a single processing system, giving a complete visual display of the area covered.

7.8 *Particular features*

The system at GRIS NEZ TRAFFIC allows the simultaneous monitoring of 1000 tracks, which can be recorded and saved for up to a year. Advanced functions include alarms signalling risk scenarios, the identification of tracks infringing rule 10 of the COLREGs, the monitoring of ships which make abrupt changes of course and speed, the observation of ships entering prohibited areas, and the monitoring of ships at anchor. All situations can be recorded, archived, and replayed either on screen or in the form of a print-out.

7.9 *Radiocommunication facilities*

CROSS Gris Nez is equipped with four VHF radio installations, allowing coverage of the whole of the reporting area. Each station can send or receive on:

- VHF DSC channel 70 (continuously monitored)
- channel 16 (continuously monitored)
- channel 13 (on which ships are requested to send their reports – again, continuously monitored)

One station (Cap Gris Nez) has facilities to send and receive information on MF, both through radiotelegraphy and DSC on a frequency of 2187.5 kHz, which is continually monitored.

7.10 *Direction-finding equipment*

GRIS NEZ TRAFFIC is equipped with two VHF radio direction-finders installed at Cap Gris Nez and Mont St. Frieux, allowing VHF calls to be located precisely. Each installation can monitor two frequencies simultaneously within an accuracy of 0.5°.

7.11 *Personnel*

Both DOVER COASTGUARD and GRIS NEZ TRAFFIC are staffed by personnel experienced in the management of ship reporting systems.

8 Alternative communication if the shore-based facilities fail

The CNIS is designed with sufficient system redundancy to cope with normal equipment failure. Radars have dual transmitter/receivers, controlled either from MRCC Dover or the radar site. Radiocommunications are controlled at the MRCC. In the event of a failure there, each transmitter/receiver can be operated from the radar site. Limited coverage can also be achieved using emergency 25 W transceivers, or 5 W portable radios at DOVER COASTGUARD. If CNIS operations are jeopardised at either DOVER COASTGUARD or GRIS NEZ TRAFFIC, then the other site can assume total control.

9 Measures to be taken if a ship fails to comply with the requirements of the system

The primary objective of the system is to facilitate the exchange of information between the ship and the shore and so support safe navigation and the protection of the marine environment. All means will be used to encourage and promote the full participation of ships required to submit reports under SOLAS regulation V/8-1. If reports are not submitted and the offending ship can be positively identified, then information will be passed to the relevant Flag State Authorities for investigation and possible prosecution in accordance with national legislation. Information will also be made available to Port State Control inspectors.

SUMMARY

1 Categories of ships to report

All ships of 300 gross tonnage and over.

2 When and where to report

North-eastbound traffic: To GRIS NEZ TRAFFIC on the French coast 2 nautical miles before crossing the line from the Royal Sovereign Light Tower, through the Bassurelle Buoy (at its assigned position of 50°32′.80 N, 000°57′.80 E*) to the French coast.

South-westbound traffic: To DOVER COASTGUARD on the English coast when within VHF range of North Foreland, and not later than when crossing the line drawn from North Foreland to the border between France and Belgium.

Report to the nearer of the two shore stations on departure from a port within the area covered.

3 How to report

By voice on VHF radio, using channel 13 (GRIS NEZ TRAFFIC) or channel 11 (DOVER COASTGUARD).

Alternatively to DOVER COASTGUARD by automatic ship-identification transponder, or using equipment conforming to the standards adopted for the Universal AIS Transponder.

Confidential information may be transmitted by other means.

4 Reporting format

The report required should include:

A	Name, call sign, IMO Number (or MMSI number for reporting by transponder);
B	Date and time;
C *or* D	Position in latitude and longitude *or* true bearing and distance from a clearly identified landmark;
E	True course;
F	Speed;
G	Port of departure;
I	Port of destination and expected time of arrival;
O	Present draught;
P	Cargo and, if dangerous goods are on board, IMO class and quantity;
Q *or* R	Defect, damage and/or deficiencies affecting ship's structure, cargo or equipment, or any other circumstance affecting normal navigation, in accordance with the SOLAS or MARPOL Conventions;
T	Address for provision of information concerning a cargo of dangerous goods;
W	Number of persons on board;
X	Miscellaneous: – Estimated quantity of bunker fuel and characteristics for ships carrying over 5000 tonnes of bunker fuel; – Navigation conditions.

* This is relative to European datum 1950.

Appendix

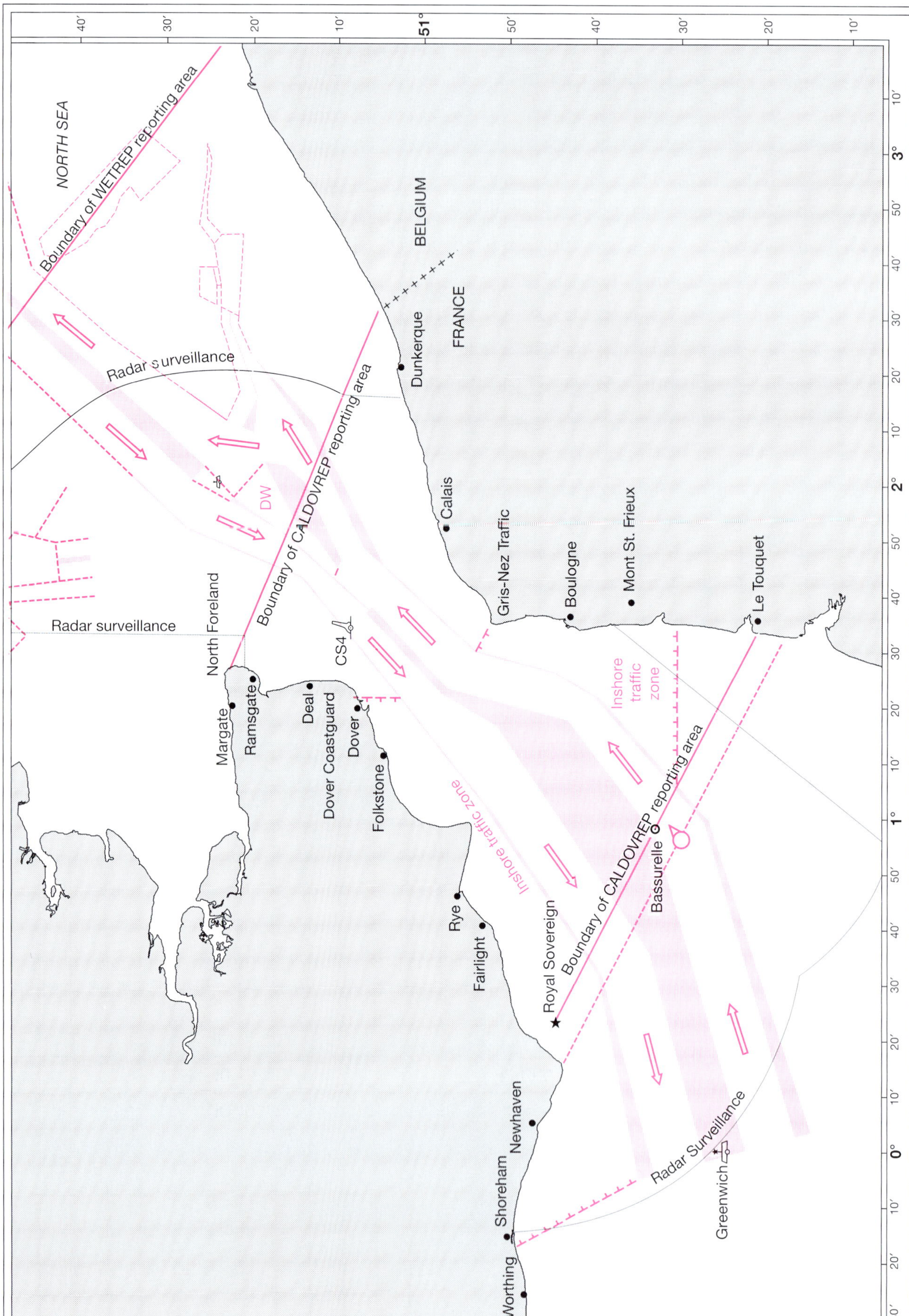
NORTH SEA
Boundary of WETREP reporting area
Radar surveillance
BELGIUM
FRANCE
Dunkerque
Boundary of CALDOVREP reporting area
DW
Calais
Gris-Nez Traffic
Boulogne
Mont St. Frieux
Le Touquet
Radar surveillance
North Foreland
CS4
Margate
Ramsgate
Deal
Dover Coastguard
Dover
Folkstone
Inshore traffic zone
Inshore traffic zone
Boundary of CALDOVREP reporting area
Bassurelle
Rye
Fairlight
Royal Sovereign
Newhaven
Shoreham
Worthing
Radar Surveillance
Greenwich
51°
3°
2°
1°
0°

IN THE BARENTS AREA (BARENTS SRS)*

1 Categories of ships required to participate in the system

1.1 The following categories of ships passing through or proceeding to and from ports and anchorages in the Barents SRS area are required to participate in the ship reporting system:

.1 all ships with a gross tonnage of 5000 and above;

.2 all tankers;

.3 all ships carrying hazardous cargoes (paragraph 1.2 refers);

.4 a vessel towing when the length of the tow exceeds 200 metres; and

.5 any ship not under command, restricted in their ability to manoeuvre or having defective navigational aids.

1.2 The meaning of "hazardous cargoes" is as follows:

.1 goods classified in the International Maritime Dangerous Goods (IMDG Code);

.2 substances classified in chapter 17 of the International Code for the Construction and Equipment of Ships Carrying Dangerous Chemicals in Bulk (IBC Code) and chapter 19 of the International Code for the Construction and Equipment of Ships Carrying Liquefied Gases in Bulk (IGC Code);

.3 "oils" as defined in MARPOL Annex I;

.4 "noxious liquid substances" as defined in MARPOL Annex II;

.5 "harmful substances" as defined in MARPOL Annex III; and

.6 radioactive materials specified in the Code for the Safe Carriage of Irradiated Nuclear Fuel, Plutonium and High-Level Radioactive Wastes in Flasks on Board Ships (INF Code).

1.3 Ships not listed above may participate in the ship reporting system (SRS) on a voluntary basis.

2 Geographical coverage of the system and the numbers and editions of the reference charts used for delineation of the system

2.1 The geographical area covered by the reporting system Barents SRS is defined within the following co-ordinates and is also shown in the chartlet attached at appendix 1.

Number	Latitude	Longitude
A – Norway	67° 10′.00 N	Norwegian coast
B – Norway	67° 10′.00 N	008° 00′.00 E
C – Norway	68° 15′.00 N	009° 30′.00 E
D – Norway	71° 15′.00 N	019° 00′.00 E
E – Norway	71° 50′.00 N	024° 00′.00 E
F – Norway	71° 50′.00 N	028° 00′.00 E
G – Russian Federation	71° 00′.00 N	033° 20′.00 E
H – Russian Federation	the Russian Federation coast	033° 20′.00 E

* Date of implementation of new reporting system: 0000 hours UTC on 1 June 2013.

2.2 The reference charts which include the operational area of Barents SRS are:

2.2.1 *Norwegian charts*

No.	Title	Scale	Datum	Edition
514	Barentshavet	1:2 000 000	WGS 84	2011
311	From Støtt to Andenes	1:350 000	ED 50	1960
321	From Andenes to Grøtsund	1:200 000	ED 50	1936
322	Fugløybanken–Lopphavet	1:200 000	ED 50	1970
323	From Sørøya to Nordkapp	1:200 000	ED 50	1962
324	From Nordkapp to Kjølnes	1:200 000	ED 50	1959
325	From Slettnes to Grense Jakobselv	1:200 000	ED 50	1929

Note: Position co-ordinates referred to the WGS 84 datum should be plotted direct onto these charts, as the difference between the WGS 84 and ED 50 datum is of no practical significance at the actual scale. The geographical positions listed in this document are given in the WGS 84 datum.

2.2.2 *Russian Federation charts*

No.	Title	Scale	Datum	Edition
10100	South part of Barents Sea	1:2 000 000	Pulkovo 1942	2002
11024	From North Cape to Rybachyy Inlet	1:500 000	Pulkovo 1942	2003
11114	From Rybachyy Inlet to Kanin Nos	1:500 000	Pulkovo 1942	1999
12000	From Varde to Cape Teriberskyy	1:200 000	Pulkovo 1942	2002
12050	From Cape Tsypnavolok to Cape Voroniy	1:200 000	Pulkovo 1942	2006
12100	From Cape Kulneset to Cape Tsypnavolok	1:200 000	Pulkovo 1942	2004

Note: Position co-ordinates in WGS 84 datum should be moved 0.4 seconds southward and 11.3 seconds eastward to agree with these charts.

3 Format, content of reports, times and geographical positions for submitting reports, Authority to whom reports should be sent and available services

3.1 *Procedures of reporting*

3.1.1 All Barents SRS reports must be sent to either Vardø VTS Centre or Murmansk VTS Centre. Ships within the Norwegian monitoring area report to Vardø VTS Centre and ships within the Russian Federation monitoring area report to Murmansk VTS Centre. Reports shall be given using AIS (Automatic Information System), Norwegian shiprep website, e-mail, fax, SATCom, mobile phone, VHF voice or by a combination of these communication means. Details are given in appendices 2 and 3.

3.1.2 The use of correct and updated AIS information can accomplish the reporting requirements for designators A, B, C, E, F, I, O and W. Details are given in appendix 3.

3.2 *Format*

3.2.1 The mandatory ship report shall be drafted in accordance with the format shown in appendix 3, as well as resolution A.851(20).

3.3 *Content*

3.3.1 A report from a ship to Barents SRS by AIS, by non-verbal means or by voice communication or combinations thereof must contain the following information; details are given in appendix 3.

A Name of ship, call sign, IMO identification number and MMSI

B Date and time

C Position expressed in latitude and longitude

E True course

F Speed in knots

H Date, time (UTC) and point of entry into Barents SRS area

I Destination and ETA

O Maximum present draught

P Hazardous cargo, class and quantity

Q Brief details of defects or restrictions in manoeuvrability

T Contact information (shipowner and representative)

W Total number of persons on board

X Characteristics and total quantity of bunkers, in metric tonnes

Note: The master of the ship must forthwith inform the Barents SRS VTS Centre concerned of any change in navigational status or in previous information notified, particularly in relation to designator Q.

3.3.2 Proprietary information obtained as a requirement of the mandatory ship reporting system Barents SRS will be protected under this system consistent with the *General principles for ship reporting systems and ship reporting requirements, including guidelines for reporting incidents involving dangerous goods, harmful substances and/or marine pollutants* (resolution A.851(20)).

3.4 *Geographical position for submitting reports*

3.4.1 Ships entering the Barents SRS operational area shall submit a report when entering into the area or on departure from a port or anchorage within the operational area.

3.4.2 Reports forwarded prior to entering the area can be submitted at any time after entering the Norwegian Economic Zone or the Russian Federation Exclusive Economic Zone and until one hour before entering the Barents SRS operational area. As the Vessel Traffic Services must be able to handle incoming prior reporting, it will not be possible to undertake pre entry reports any later than one hour prior to entering the area.

3.4.3 Ships departing a port or leaving an anchorage within the Barents SRS area may also submit a pre-entry report for designators H, P, T, Q and X if transmitted one hour prior to departure.

3.5 *Authority*

3.5.1 The Federal Agency of Maritime and River Transport and the Norwegian Coastal Administration are the VTS authorities for Murmansk VTS Centre and Vardø VTS Centre, respectively, which operate the Barents SRS ship reporting system.

4 Information to be provided to ships and procedures to be followed

4.1 Ships in the Barents SRS area are required to keep a continuous listening watch on VHF channel 16.

4.2 If requested, the VTS Centre concerned shall provide ships with information about positioning, weather forecast, navigational warnings and other hazards in the ship reporting area, from broadcasting devices set up in the coastal States or by other available communication means concurred by involved participants.

4.3 If necessary, the VTS Centre can provide individual information to a ship, particularly in relation to positioning or local conditions.

4.4 If a ship needs to anchor due to breakdown, low visibility, adverse weather, etc., the VTS Centre concerned can recommend suitable anchorages or other places of refuge within the operational area.

5 Communication required for the Barents SRS system

5.1 The language used for communication shall be English, using IMO Standard Marine Communication Phrases, when deemed necessary by the VTS Centre concerned.

5.2 Details of communication and contact information are given in appendix 2.

6 Rules, regulations and recommendations in force in the area of the system

6.1 *Regulations for preventing collisions at sea*

The Convention on the International Regulations for Preventing Collisions at Sea, 1972, as amended (COLREG) is applicable throughout the operational area of Barents SRS.

6.2 *Traffic separation schemes*

The traffic separation schemes off the coast of Norway from Vardø to Røst are in the operational area of Barents SRS. They have been adopted by IMO, and rule 10 of the International Regulations for Preventing Collisions at Sea applies.

6.3 *Hazardous cargo*

6.3.1 The meaning of "hazardous cargo" is stated in paragraph 1.2 and in resolution MSC.43(64), paragraph 1.4.

6.3.2 Ships carrying hazardous cargoes within the SRS operational area must comply with international and national regulations. The SRS does not relieve ship masters of their responsibility to provide nationally required reports and information to customs authorities.

6.3.3 Discharges of oil and ship-generated waste are monitored jointly by the Russian Federation and Norwegian Authorities.

7 Shore-based facilities to support the operation of the system

7.1 *Sensors, system and communication facilities*

7.1.1 Murmansk VTS Centre and Vardø VTS Centre are equipped with multiple-source information processing and retrieval systems, VHF radio, Automatic Identification System (AIS) and Long-Range Identification and Tracking (LRIT) facilities.

7.1.2 Both Centres have recording equipment to store information regarding a ship's transit. In case of an incident, the VTS Authority can use records as evidence.

7.2 *Personnel qualifications and training*

7.2.1 The Murmansk VTS Centre and Vardø VTS Centre are both operated by trained and experienced personnel according to national requirements and recommendations by IMO.

7.3 *Manning*

7.3.1 Murmansk VTS Centre and Vardø VTS Centre are both manned 24 hours per day, 365 (366) days per year.

8 Information concerning the applicable procedures if the communication facilities of the shore-based Authority fail

8.1 The Murmansk VTS Centre and Vardø VTS Centre are both designed with sufficient system redundancy to cope with normal equipment failure.

8.2 If essential equipment suffers breakdown, and sufficient operational capability cannot be maintained by backup systems, information on reduced operational capability will be given by the affected VTS Centre as needed or will be broadcasted as a national navigational warning.

9 Measures to be taken if a ship fails to comply with the requirements of the system

9.1 The main objective of the system is to facilitate the exchange of information between the ships and the shore in order to support safe navigation and to protect the marine environment. The system will also contribute to providing information to relevant SAR authorities.

9.2 All means will be used to encourage and promote the full participation of ships required to submit reports under SOLAS regulation V/11. If reports are not submitted and the offending ship can be positively identified, then information will be passed on to the relevant flag State Authorities for investigation and possible prosecution in accordance with national legislation. The mandatory ship reporting system Barents SRS is for the exchange of information only and does not provide any additional authority for mandating changes in the vessel's operations. The reporting system will be implemented consistent with UNCLOS, SOLAS and other relevant international instruments so that the reporting system will not provide the basis to impinge on a transiting vessel's passage through the Reporting Area.

Appendix 1

Chart of the Barents SRS operational area

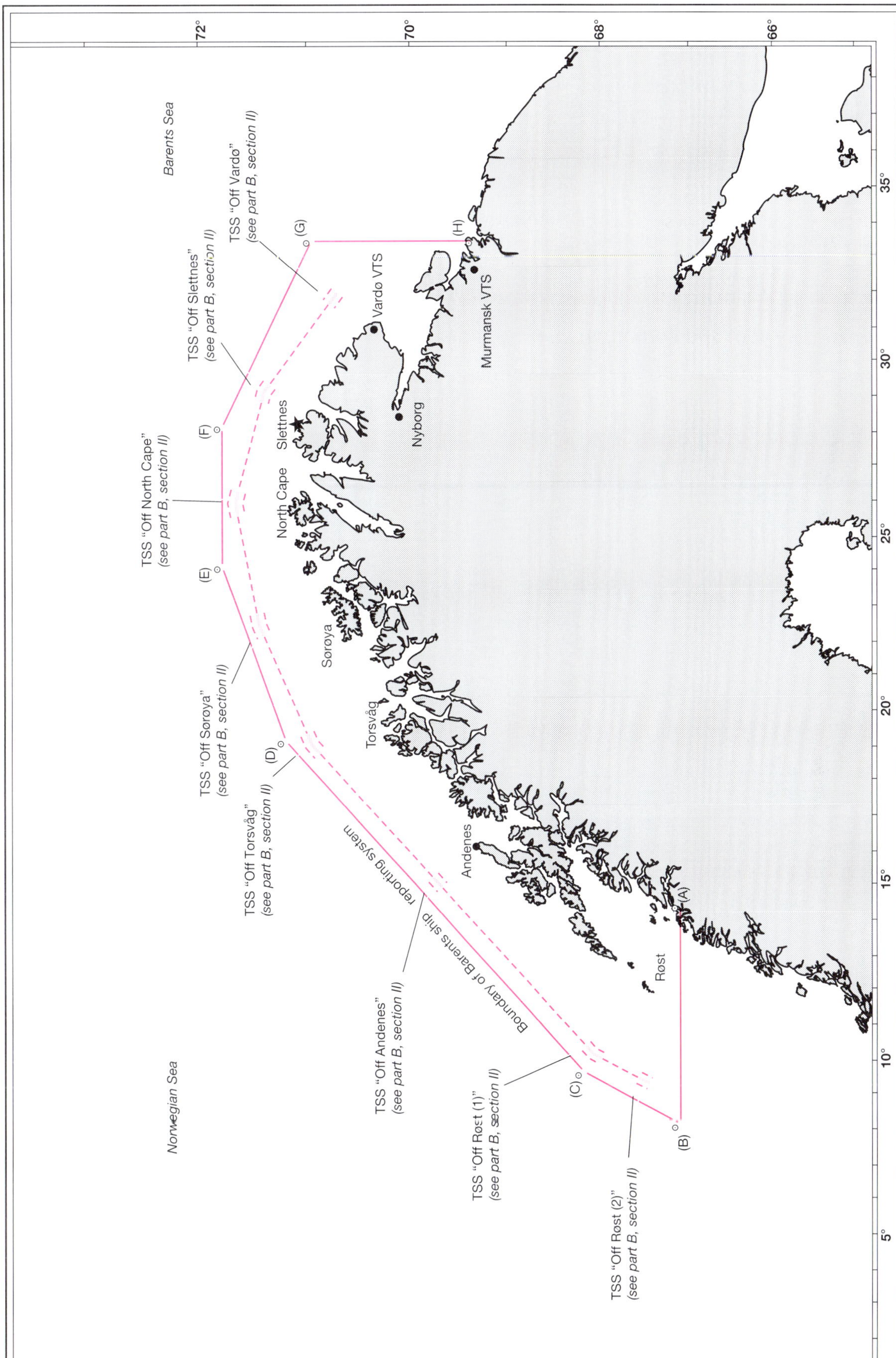

Appendix 2

Contact information and other relevant information in relation to the VTS centres to which the reports must be submitted

1 Contact information

1.1 Murmansk VTS Centre can be contacted by e-mail, VHF or fax

VHF:	Call "Murmansk Traffic" (channel 12)
MMSI:	002734484 or 002734466
E-mail:	vts@mf-rmp.ru
Fax:	+7 8152 479026

1.2 Vardø VTS Centre can be contacted by VHF, e-mail, fax or telephone

VHF:	Call Norwegian Coastal Radio Station and request "NOR VTS" (channel 16)
MMSI:	002573550
E-mail:	nor.vts@kystverket.no
Fax:	+47 78 98 98 99
Telephone:	+47 78 98 98 98

2 Submission of reports

2.1 Ships within the Russian Federation monitoring area or the Russian Federation Exclusive Economic Zone report to Murmansk VTS Centre primarily by e-mail, fax and AIS, alternatively VHF or a combination of these communication means.

2.2 Ships within the Norwegian monitoring area or Norwegian Economic Zone report to Vardø VTS Centre primarily by the Norwegian Ship Reporting System at website www.shiprep.no. Alternatively by AIS, e-mail, fax, telephone and VHF or a combination of these communication means.

Appendix 3

Drafting of reports to the mandatory ship reporting system "Barents SRS"

Summary

Reporting can be done by non-verbal means by the use of AIS and pre-entry non-verbal means such as, for example, e-mail, fax or the website www.shiprep.no. If a ship is unable to make use of the non-verbal means or to submit a report at least one hour prior to entering the area, reporting is to be done by VHF or by telephone (if outside VHF range).

- Correct and updated AIS information can accomplish reporting of designators A, B, C, E, F, I, O and W.
- Non-verbal means can accomplish reporting of designators A, H, P, Q, T and X.

The scheme below gives the preferred method of reporting combined by AIS, non-verbal means and VHF, as well as information required for each designator.

Desig-nator	AIS	Non-verbal	VHF	Function	Information required
A	Yes	Yes	Yes	Ship	(1) Name of ship (2) MMSI Number (3) Call sign and – when available – (4) IMO Number (5) Additional contact information.
B	Yes	–	–	Date and time	A 6-digit group giving day of month and hours and minutes in Universal Co-ordinated Time (UTC).
C	Yes	–	–	Position	A 5-digit group giving latitude in degrees and minutes, decimal, suffixed with N (north) and a 6 digit group giving longitude in degrees and minutes, decimal, suffixed with E (east) or W (west).
E	Yes	–	–	True course	A 3-digit group.
F	Yes	–	–	Speed in knots and tenths of knots	A 3-digit group.
I	Yes	–	–	Destination and ETA	The name of next port of call, given in UN/LOCODE, by AIS. For details and procedures, see IMO SN/Circ.244 and www.unece.org/cefact/locode/service/main.htm. ETA date and time group expressed as in (B).
H	–	Yes	–	Date, time and point of entry into the Barents SRS area	This information is only required if reporting designators P, T and X are transmitted non-verbally (e.g. e-mail) prior to entry of the Barents SRS area. Entry date and time expressed as in (B) and position expressed as in (C).
O	Yes	–	–	Maximum present draught in metres	A 2-digit or 3-digit group giving the present maximum draught in metres (e.g. 6.1 or 10.4).

G

Designator	AIS	Non-verbal	VHF	Function	Information required
P	–	Yes	–	Cargo on board	Cargo and, if hazardous goods are present on board, their quantity and IMO class (inclusive of UN code). Hazardous goods information must be summarized in total tonnes per IMO class when transmitted.
Q	–	Yes	–	Defects and deficiencies	Details of defects and deficiencies affecting the equipment of the ship or any other circumstances affecting normal navigation and manoeuvrability.
T	–	Yes	–	Ship's owner and representative	Address and particulars from which detailed information on the cargo may be obtained.
W	Yes	–	–	Total number of persons on board	State the number.
X	–	Yes	–	Miscellaneous	Type and estimated quantity of bunker fuel in metric tonnes. Must be summarized in total tonnes per type when transmitted.

OFF THE SOUTH-WEST COAST OF ICELAND (TRANSREP)

1 Categories of ships required to participate in the system

1.1 Ships of the following categories are required to participate in the system:

.1 ships calling at ports located within the eastern ATBA off the south and south-west coast of Iceland; and

.2 ships of less than 5000 gross tonnage permitted to transit the eastern ATBA south of latitude 63° 45′ N when engaged on voyages between Icelandic ports and not carrying dangerous or noxious cargoes in bulk or in cargo tanks.

.3 ships of up to 20,000 gross tonnage, en route to or from Faxaflói Bay, which neither carry dangerous goods nor noxious materials in bulk or cargo tanks and which may transit the Eastern ATBA south of latitude 63° 45′ N; and

.4 passenger ships of unlimited size, which may only transit the inner route (Húllið Passage) and the Eastern ATBA during the period 1 May to 1 October.

Pursuant to SOLAS 1974, the mandatory ship reporting system does not apply to any warship, naval auxiliary, coast guard vessel, or other vessel owned or operated by a contracting government and used, for the time being, only on government non-commercial service. However, such ships are encouraged to participate in the reporting system. The mandatory ship reporting system does not apply to fishing vessels with fishing rights within Iceland's exclusive economic zone (EEZ) and research vessels.

2 Geographical coverage of the system and the number and edition of the reference charts used for the delineation of the system

The reporting system covers the area to be avoided (the eastern area) off the south and south-west coast of Iceland located entirely within Icelandic territorial waters, and is bounded by lines connecting the following geographical positions:

(1)	63°24′.13 N,	019°07′.83 W	(Dyrhólaey light)
(2)	63°10′.00 N,	020°38′.00 W	(south of Surtsey Island)
(3)	63°40′.90 N,	022°40′.20 W	(south of Reykjanes Point)
(4)	63°45′.80 N,	022°44′.40 W	(south-west of Reykjanes Point)
(5)	63°47′.00 N,	022°47′.60 W	(Húllið Passage south-east part)
(6)	63°48′.00 N,	022°48′.40 W	(Húllið Passage north-east part)
(7)	63°49′.20 N,	022°47′.30 W	(south-west of Litla-Sandvik)
(8)	64°01′.70 N,	022°58′.30 W	(Off Sandgerði)
(9)	64°07′.20 N,	022°47′.50 W	(north-west of Garðskagi Point)
(10)	64°07′.20 N,	022°41′.40 W	(north of Garðskagi Point)
(11)	64°04′.92 N,	022°41′.40 W	(Garðskagi light)

The reference chart, which includes all the area of coverage for the system, is Icelandic chart 31 (INT 1103) *Dyrhólaey – Snæfellsnes* (May 2008 edition), based on datum WGS 84.

3 Format, contents of report, times and geographical positions for submitting reports, Authority to whom reports must be sent and available services

The ship report, short title "TRANSREP", shall be made to the shore-based Authority, Icelandic Maritime Traffic Service (MTS), located in Reykjavík. Reports should be made using VHF voice transmissions.

3.1 *Format*

The ship report to the shore-based Authority shall be in accordance with the format shown in paragraph 5.5. The information requested from ships is derived from the standard reporting format and procedures set out in paragraph 2 of the appendix to resolution A.851(20).

3.2 *Content*

The report required from a ship to the shore-based Authority contains only information which is essential to meet the objectives of the system:

Information considered to be essential:

A	Name of ship, call sign and IMO Number
C *or* D	Position (latitude and longitude *or* in relation to a landmark)
E	Course
F	Speed
G	Port of departure
H	Date, time and point of entry into system
I	Port of destination
K	Date, time and point of exit from system or departure from a harbour within the ATBA
L	Intended track within the ATBA

In the event of defect, pollution or goods lost overboard, additional information may be requested.

3.3 *Geographical position for submitting reports*

Ships entering the ATBA shall report to the Maritime Traffic Service their estimated time of crossing the area limits, specified in paragraph 2, four hours prior to entering the area or when departing from harbours in Faxaflói Bay. Ships leaving harbours within the ATBA shall report on departure.

3.4 *Authority*

The shore-based Authority is the Icelandic Maritime Traffic Service (MTS), which is operated by the Icelandic Coast Guard.

4 Information to be provided to ships and procedures to be followed

Detected and identified ships are monitored by AIS, which in no way releases their master from his responsibility for safe navigation.

Following the reception of a report, the Maritime Traffic Service can, on request, provide:

- information on navigational conditions; and
- information on weather conditions.

5 Radiocommunication required for the system, frequencies on which reports should be transmitted and information to be reported

.1 TRANSREP will be based on VHF voice radiocommunications.

.2 The call to the shore-based Authority shall be made on VHF channel 70 (16).

.3 However, a ship which cannot use VHF channel 70 (16) in order to transmit the reports should use MF DSC or INMARSAT.

.4 The language used for communication shall be English, using the IMO Standard Marine Communication Phrases, where necessary.

.5 Information to be reported:

A	Name of ship, call sign and IMO Number
C *or* D	Position (latitude and longitude *or* in relation to a landmark)
E	Course
F	Speed

G	Port of departure
H	Date, time and point of entry into system
I	Port of destination
K	Date, time and point of exit from system or departure from a harbour within the ATBA
L	Intended track within the ATBA

6 Rules and regulations in force in the area of the system

Relevant laws in force include domestic legislation and regulations to implement the Convention on the International Regulations for Preventing Collisions at Sea, 1972, the International Convention for the Safety of Life at Sea, 1974, and the International Convention for the Prevention of Pollution from Ships, 1973/1978.

7 Shore-based facilities to support operation of the system

The Icelandic Maritime Traffic Service (MTS).

- The MTS is equipped with AIS covering the whole of the ATBA;
- VHF, MF, HF and INMARSAT communication equipment;
- Telephone, telefax and e-mail communication facilities, and
- Personnel operating the system: The MTS is manned by Coast Guard personnel on a 24-hour basis.

8 Alternative communication if the communication facilities of the shore-based Authority fail

TRANSREP is planned with a sufficient system redundancy to cope with normal equipment failure.

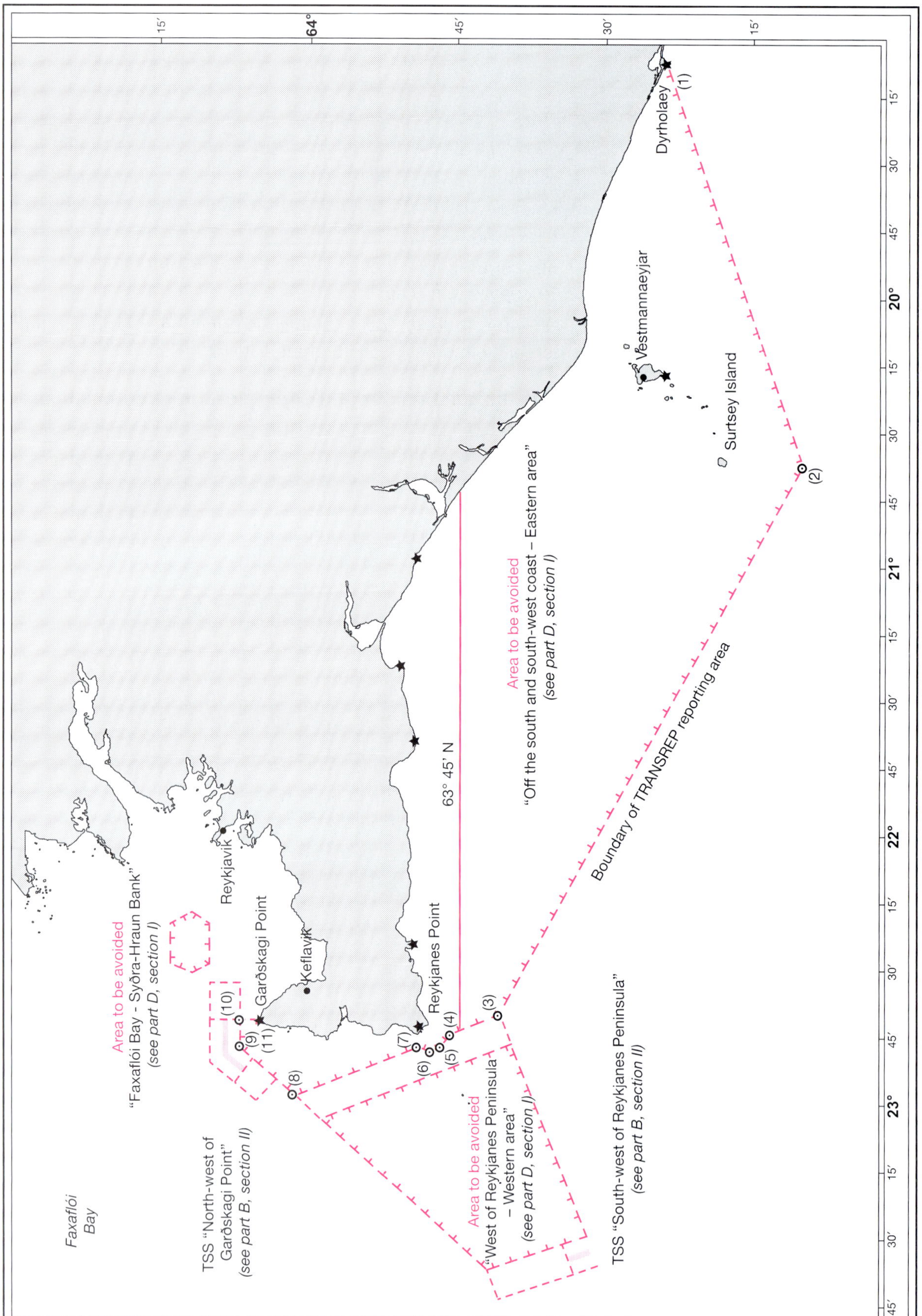

OFF THE SOUTH-WEST COAST OF ICELAND

IN THE "OFF FINISTERRE" TRAFFIC SEPARATION SCHEME AREA (FINREP)

Note: See also mandatory ship reporting system "West European Tanker Reporting System".

1 Categories of ships required to participate in the system

Ships of the following general categories are required to participate in the reporting system:

.1 All ships of 50 metres or more in length overall.

.2 All ships, regardless of length, carrying hazardous and/or potentially polluting cargo, as defined in paragraph 1.4 of resolution MSC.43(64).

.3 Ships engaged in towing or pushing another vessel where the combined length of the ship and tow or pushed vessel exceeds 50 metres.

.4 Any category of vessel less than 50 metres in length overall which is using the appropriate traffic lane or separation zone in order to engage in fishing.

.5 Any category of ship less than 50 metres in length overall which is using the appropriate traffic lane or separation zone in an emergency in order to avoid immediate danger.

2 Geographical coverage of the system and the number and edition of the reference chart used for the delineation of the system

2.1 The reporting system covers the area (appendix 1) between the coast and the following lines:

.1 a bearing of 130° (T) to Cape Villano lighthouse;

.2 a bearing of 075° (T) to Cape Finisterre lighthouse; and

.3 the meridian of longitude 010°15′ W.

This area includes the traffic separation scheme "Off Finisterre" and associated inshore traffic zones adopted by IMO resolution A.767(18), as amended by resolution A.957(23).

2.2 The reference chart which includes all of the area of coverage for the system is number 41 of the Catalogue of Nautical Charts of the Spanish Hydrographic Office, European edition (Potsdam) published in April 1978, 6th impression June 2002 and corrected by Notices to Mariners of November 2002, including Cape Estaca de Bares to Rio Lima.

3 Format and content of reports, times and geographical positions for submitting reports, Authority to whom reports should be sent, available services

The ship report, short title "FINREP", shall be made to the ship reporting centre located at Finisterre.

3.1 *Format*

The information requested from ships shall be provided in the standard reporting format given in paragraph 2 of the appendix to the annex to IMO resolution A.648(16).

A ship may elect, for reasons of commercial confidentiality, to communicate that section of the FINREP ENTRY report which provides information on cargo (line P) by non-verbal means prior to entering the system.

3.2 *Content*

The report from a ship to the VTS should contain only information which is essential to achieve the objectives of the system:

.1 Information considered essential:

A	Name of the ship, call sign, IMO identification number.
C *or* D	Position.
G and I	Last and next port of call.
P	Hazardous cargo, class and quantity, if applicable.
Q *or* R	Breakdown, damage and/or deficiencies affecting the structure, cargo or equipment of the ship or any other circumstances affecting normal navigation, in accordance with the provisions of the SOLAS and MARPOL Conventions.

G

.2 Information considered necessary:

E and F Course and speed of the ship.

Note: On receipt of a position message, operators of the VTS will establish the relation between the ship's position and the information supplied by the facilities available to them. The information on heading and speed will facilitate the VTS operator's task of identifying a ship within a group.

3.3 *Geographical position for submitting reports*

Ships entering the area of coverage shall report to the Finisterre Traffic VTS when crossing the limits mentioned in paragraph 2.1 or when leaving the ports or anchorages in the area.

To facilitate the positioning of ships and to ensure compliance with the International Regulations for Preventing Collisions at Sea, 1972, and especially rule 10 thereof, radio beacons with a range of more than 32 nautical miles have been installed on the coast, located at Mount Xastas, Cape Finisterre and Cape Villano.

3.4 *Authority*

The shore-based Authority is Finisterre VTS, which forms part of the Area Search and Rescue and Pollution Control Co-ordination Centre (CZCS Finisterre).

The CZCS Finisterre is a Co-ordination Centre under the authority of the Spanish Government Search and Rescue and Maritime Safety Division. The Division, administered by the Ministry of Development, is entrusted, amongst other responsibilities, with providing services relating to maritime search and rescue, vessel traffic control and assistance, and prevention and control of pollution of the marine environment.

3.5 *Services offered*

Finisterre VTS broadcasts regular information regarding warnings to mariners and traffic, navigational and weather conditions in the area, in Spanish and in English.

4 Information to be provided to participating ships and procedures to be followed

In addition to the general information stated above, Finisterre Traffic can provide a particular vessel with information regarding her position, course and speed or the identification of the traffic in her vicinity. The ship should request this additional information.

5 Radiocommunication equipment required for the system, frequencies on which reports should be transmitted and information to be reported

The radiocommunication equipment required for the system is that defined in the GMDSS for sea areas A1 and A2.

.1 The system will be based on VHF voice communications and will be interactive, with an interchange of data between ships and the ship reporting centre. The channels defined are channels 16 and 11, with channel 74 as a supplementary option.

.2 In special circumstances, the hectometric waveband may also be used for the interchange of information between the ship and the Vessel Traffic Service.

.3 Information of commercial confidentiality may be transmitted by non-verbal means. Details are as follows:

Fax: + 34 81 76 77 40 (available by auto-link)
Telex: 82268
Radiotelex selective call: 0993
  Answerback: SAFIS
Frequencies scanned: 4179 kHz, 6269 kHz, 8297.6 kHz, 8298.1 kHz, 12 520 kHz, 16 688.5 kHz

.4 The language used for reports in the system will be English, using the IMO Standard Marine Communication Phrases (SMCPs) where necessary, or Spanish if appropriate.

.5 Communications associated with reporting in accordance with the requirements of this system will be free of charge.

6 Rules and regulations in force in the area of the system

6.1 The International Regulations for Preventing Collisions at Sea (COLREG), 1972 are applicable throughout the area of coverage of the proposed system.

6.2 The TSS "Off Finisterre" has been approved by IMO and therefore rule 10 of COLREG applies.

7 Shore-based facilities to support operation of the system

7.1 The Finisterre VTS (FINISTERRE TRAFFIC) is provided with the following facilities:

.1 Telephone, facsimile and telex communications;

.2 two sets of VHF radiocommunication equipment with digital selective calling (DSC);

.3 one set of radiocommunication equipment in MF/HF bands with DSC;

.4 two sets of radiocommunication equipment with radiotelex in MF/HF bands;

.5 three real-time display consoles for S- and X-band radar signals and raw video from remote radar stations;

.6 two display consoles for monitoring and viewing; and

.7 one VHF radio direction-finder in marine and aeronautical bands.

7.2 The remote station at Malpica is provided with the following facilities:

.1 two sets of VHF radiocommunication equipment (marine band);

.2 one set of VHF radiocommunication equipment (aeronautical band);

.3 one duplicate X-band radar facility;

.4 one duplicate S-band radar facility;

.5 one weather station;

.6 one VHF marine and aeronautical band direction-finder; and

.7 one MF/HF marine band direction-finder.

7.3 The remote station at Mount Xastas-Torinan is provided with the following facilities:

.1 two sets of VHF radiocommunication equipment (marine band);

.2 one set of VHF radiocommunication equipment (aeronautical band);

.3 one X-band radar facility;

.4 one S-band radar facility;

.5 one weather station;

.6 one VHF marine and aeronautical band direction-finder; and

.7 one MF/HF marine band direction-finder.

7.4 The remote station at Cape Corrubedo is provided with the following facilities:

.1 two sets of VHF radiocommunication equipment (marine band);

.2 one set of VHF radiocommunication equipment (aeronautical band);

.3 one duplicate X-band radar facility;

.4 one weather station;

.5 one VHF marine and aeronautical band direction-finder; and

.6 one MF/HF marine band direction-finder.

7.5 The relay station at Mount Aro is provided with a microwave relay station for relaying telecontrol, radar, direction-finding and communications signals.

8 Alternative communication if the communication facilities of the shore-based Authority fail

8.1 The system is designed to avoid, as far as possible, any irretrievable breakdown of equipment which would hinder the functioning of the services normally provided by the Finisterre VTS.

8.2 The most important items of equipment and power sources are duplicated and the facilities are provided with emergency generating sets as well as with UPS units. A maintenance team, on call 24 hours a day, stands ready to repair, to the extent possible, any breakdowns which may occur.

8.3 The location of radar antennae ensures that, in the event of failure of the facility, coverage by another station will be provided.

8.4 In addition, the coast radio stations at Ortegal, La Coruña, Finisterre and Vigo, operated by the Telephone Company, can be used as an alternative so as to ensure VHF/MF communication with ships in case of need.

Appendix 1

Traffic separation scheme "Off Finisterre" – area of mandatory reporting

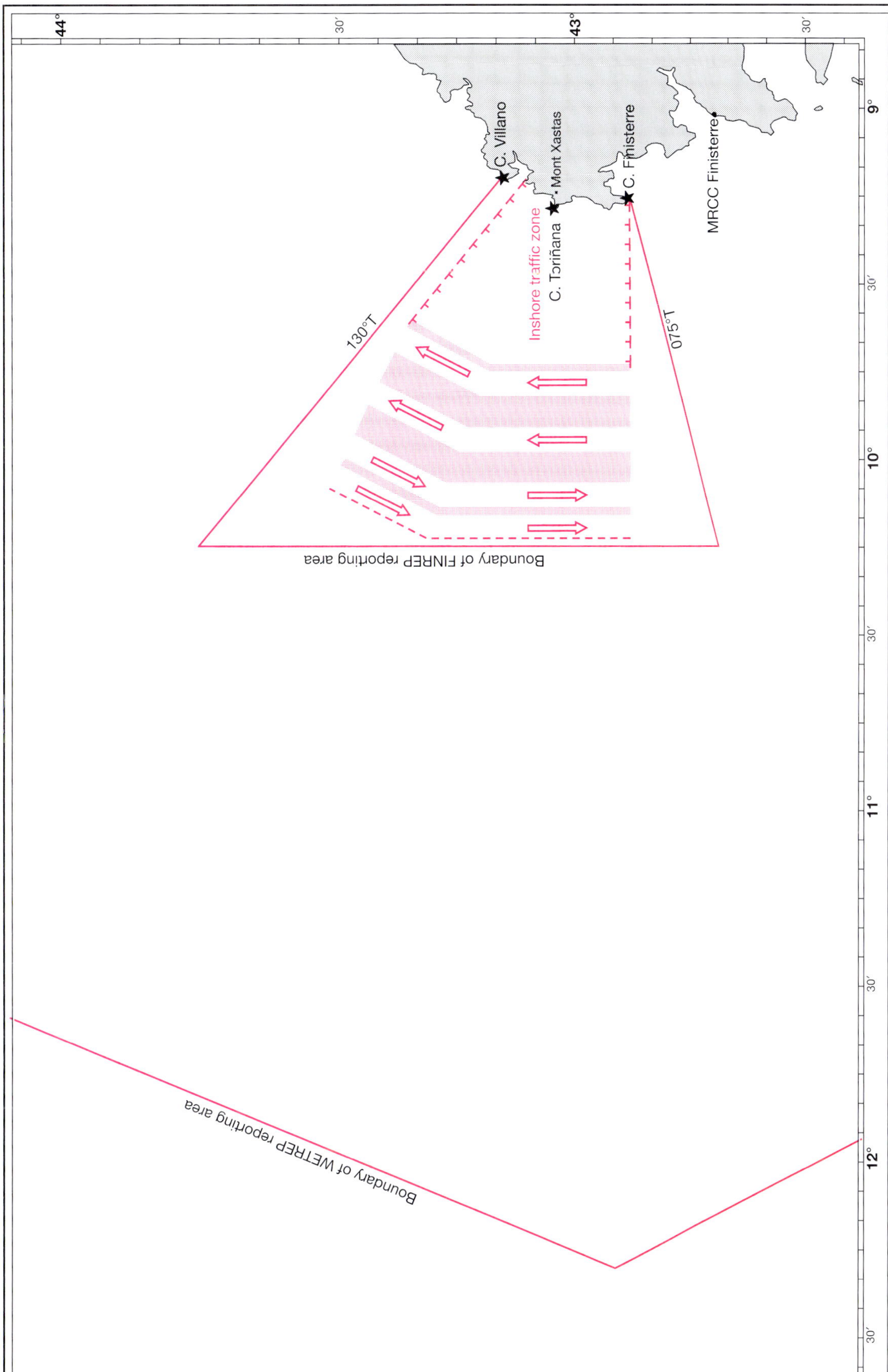

OFF THE COAST OF PORTUGAL (COPREP)

1 Categories of ships required to participate in the system

The following vessels are required to participate in the COPREP system:

(a) all vessels of 300 gross tonnage or above;

(b) all vessels carrying dangerous, hazardous and/or potentially polluting cargo;

(c) all passenger vessels;

(d) vessels engaged in towing or pushing where the combined length of the vessel and tow or pushed vessel is more than 100 metres LOA; and

(e) fishing vessels with an LOA of 24 metres or above.

Any other type of vessel is invited to voluntarily participate in the system.

2 Geographical coverage of the system and the number and edition of the reference chart used for delineation of the system

2.1 *Geographical coverage of the system*

The ship reporting system area is bounded by the shore and:

(a) In the North: by latitude 39°45′ N

(b) In the West and South: by a line joining the following geographical positions:

(i) 39°45′ N, 010°14′ W

(ii) 38°41′ N, 010°14′ W

(iii) 36°30′ N, 009°35′ W

(iv) 36°15′ N, 008°30′ W

(c) In the East: by longitude 008°30′ W

2.2 *Reference chart*

The reference chart is "Cabo Finisterra a Casablanca", number 21101, Catalogue of Nautical Charts of the Portuguese Hydrographic Office, 4th impression – April 2002 (**Note:** This chart is based on World Geodetic System 1984 datum).

3 Reports and procedures (format and content of reports, Authority to which reports should be sent)

3.1 *Format*

The format of information required in the COPREP reports is derived from the format given in resolution A.851(20) – General Principles for Ship Reporting Systems and Reporting Requirements, including Guidelines for Reporting Incidents involving Dangerous Goods, Harmful Substances and/or Marine Pollutants.

3.2 *Content*

Vessels required to participate in the system shall make a report, with the short title "COPREP", to Roca Control and it shall contain the following information, which is considered essential for the purpose of the system:

DESIGNATOR	INFORMATION REQUIRED
A	Ship's name and callsign IMO identification or MMSI number on request
C	Position (latitude – longitude), *or*
D	Distance and bearing from a landmark
E	True course in a three-digit group

DESIGNATOR	INFORMATION REQUIRED
F	Speed in knots
G	Last port of call
H	Time (UTC) and point of entry in the reporting sector
I	Next port of call and ETA
P	Hazardous cargo, IMO class or UN Number and quantity
Q *or* R	Breakdown, damage and/or deficiencies affecting the structure, cargo or equipment of the vessel or any other circumstances affecting normal navigation, in accordance with the provisions of the SOLAS and MARPOL Conventions
W	Total number of persons on board (when requested)
X	Miscellaneous remarks (when requested)

Any vessel may elect, for reasons of commercial confidentiality, to communicate the information regarding cargo (designator P of the report) by non-verbal means prior to entering the system.

3.3 *Time and geographical position for submitting reports*

3.3.1 Ships must submit a report:

(a) on entering the reporting area as defined in paragraph 2.1; or

(b) immediately after leaving a port, terminal or anchorage situated in the reporting area; or

(c) when deviating from the route leading to the originally declared destination, port, terminal, anchorage or position "for orders" given on entry into the reporting area; or

(d) when it is necessary to deviate from the planned route owing to weather conditions, damaged equipment or a change in navigational status; or

(e) when something is detected that could affect safety of navigation in the area; or

(f) on finally leaving the reporting area; or

(g) when requested by COPREP operator.

3.3.2 Ships who have submitted a voluntary report with the same designator letters prior to entering the reporting area are only required to submit a mandatory report:

(a) if there are any changes in previously submitted information;

(b) with designator letters "A" and "H" when entering the reporting area.

3.4 *Shore-based Authority*

The shore-based Authority for the COPREP mandatory ship reporting system, to which these reports should be sent, is ROCA CONTROL (identified in paragraph 7).

4 Information to be provided to the participating ship and the procedures to be followed

ROCA CONTROL is an information service. Ships are provided with information broadcasts on weather, hazards affecting the safety of navigation and other traffic in the area.

These broadcasts include:

(a) traffic information;

(b) hampered vessels, such as vessels not under command or vessels restricted in their ability to manoeuvre;

(c) adverse weather conditions;

(d) weather warnings and forecast;

(e) displaced or defective aids to navigation;

(f) radar assistance; and

(g) information on local harbours.

Information is broadcast on request or whenever necessary. Information broadcasts on ROCA CONTROL VHF main channel are preceded by an announcement on VHF channel 16. Information may be more frequent on occasions of adverse weather conditions, reduced visibility and imminent incident or accident.

The VTS centre is linked to MRCC LISBON and pollution control authorities in order to allow a prompt response to any emerging distress or urgent situation.

5 Communication requirements for the system, including frequencies on which reports should be transmitted and information to be reported

The communications required for the COPREP reporting system are as follows:

(a) The call to the shore-based authority shall be made on the VHF channel assigned to Vessel Traffic Service in the Portuguese Coast, or by the other available means based on the following contact information:

Call:	Roca Control
Telephone:	351-214464830
Fax:	351-214464839
E-mail:	oper.vts@imarpor.pt
VHF channels:	
Primary channels:	22 and 79; Secondary channel: 69
Call sign:	CSG229
MMSI:	00 263 3030

(b) The language used for communication shall be Portuguese or English, using the IMO Standard Marine Communication Phrases where necessary.

(c) Information of commercial confidentiality may be transmitted by non-verbal means.

6 Rules and regulations in force in the area of the system

Portugal has taken appropriate action to implement international conventions to which it is a party, including, where appropriate, adopting domestic legislation and promulgating regulations through domestic law. Relevant laws in force include domestic legislation and international regulations such as:

(a) Convention on the International Regulations for Preventing Collisions at Sea (COLREG), 1972, as amended;

(b) International Convention for the Safety of Life at Sea (SOLAS), 1974, as amended;

(c) International Convention on the Prevention of Pollution from Ships (MARPOL 73/78); and

(d) Directive 2002/59/CE.

7 Shore-based facilities and personnel qualifications and training required to support the operation of the system

7.1 *Shore-based facilities*

ROCA CONTROL maintains a continuous 24-hour watch over the COPREP area. The facilities of the Roca Control are the following:

(a) Eight coastal radars:

- (i) Long-range SCANTER primary radars
- (ii) Focus of long-distance sea side coverage
- (iii) Special high-gain 21″ antennas
- (iv) Surveillance of all the continental Portuguese coast
- (v) Video from selected radar and combined radar data available to main centre's VTS operator;

(b) Eight harbour radars:
   - (i) Short-range primary radars (for 3 of those)
   - (ii) Surveillance of the harbour's approach area (for 5 of those)
   - (iii) Video from selected radar and combined radar data available to main centre's VTS operator;

(c) Eleven AIS sites:
   - (i) Automatic identification of ships:
     - IMO standards
     - 3 types of information: ship static, dynamic and voyage
   - (ii) Based on GPS positioning
   - (iii) AIS position data merged with radar data at operator display (TDS)
   - (iv) Ship identification correlated with National Maritime Ship Database;

(d) Eleven voice radio communication sites:
   - (i) VHF voice radio communication with ships and aeronautical emergency channel
   - (ii) Complete coverage of continental Portuguese coast
   - (iii) VTS operators are able to communicate within the coverage area
   - (iv) Telephone and electronic communication between harbours and VTS control centres;

(e) Eleven VHF direction-finder sites:
   - (i) Azimuthing of radio communication
   - (ii) Complete coverage of continental Portuguese coast
   - (iii) Data from all sites available for the VTS operators
   - (iv) RDF data is presented on operator displays (TDS);

(f) Six meteorological sites with:
   - (i) Anemometer, thermometer, barometer, hygrometer, rainfall indicator, visibility sensors
   - (ii) Meteorological data of all sites will be presented to the VTS operators.

7.2 *Personnel qualifications and training*

The training given to ROCA CONTROL staff complies with the national and international recommendations and includes a general study of navigational safety measures and the relevant national and international (IMO) provisions/requirements to support the operation of the system.

8 Alternative procedures if the communication facilities of the shore-based Authority fail

The system is designed to avoid, as far as possible, any irretrievable breakdown of equipment which would hinder the functioning of the services normally provided by ROCA CONTROL.

The most important items of equipment and power sources are duplicated and the facilities are provided with emergency generating sets as well as with Uninterruptible Power Supply (UPS) units. A maintenance team is available 24 hours a day to attend to any breakdown.

The system is also designed in such a manner that, if one station fails, the adjacent station can provide the necessary coverage.

9 Actions to take in the event of emergency or ship's non-compliance with the system requirements

The main objectives of the system are to improve ships' safety in and off the Portuguese coastal waters, to support the organization of search and rescue and to protect and improve the marine environment in the coast, developing the actions as fast and effectively as possible if an emergency is reported or a report from a ship fails to appear, and it is impossible to establish communication with the ship. All means will be used to obtain the full participation of ships required to submit reports.

The mandatory ship reporting system COPREP is for the exchange of information only, and does not provide any additional authority for mandating changes in the ship's operations. This reporting system will be implemented consistent with UNCLOS, SOLAS and other relevant international instruments so that the reporting system will not constitute a basis for preventing the passage of a ship through the reporting area.

Infringements of these regulations shall be punishable under Portuguese law, or reported to the ship's flag State in accordance with IMO resolution A.432(XI) Compliance with the Convention on the International Regulations for Preventing Collisions at Sea, 1972, as amended.

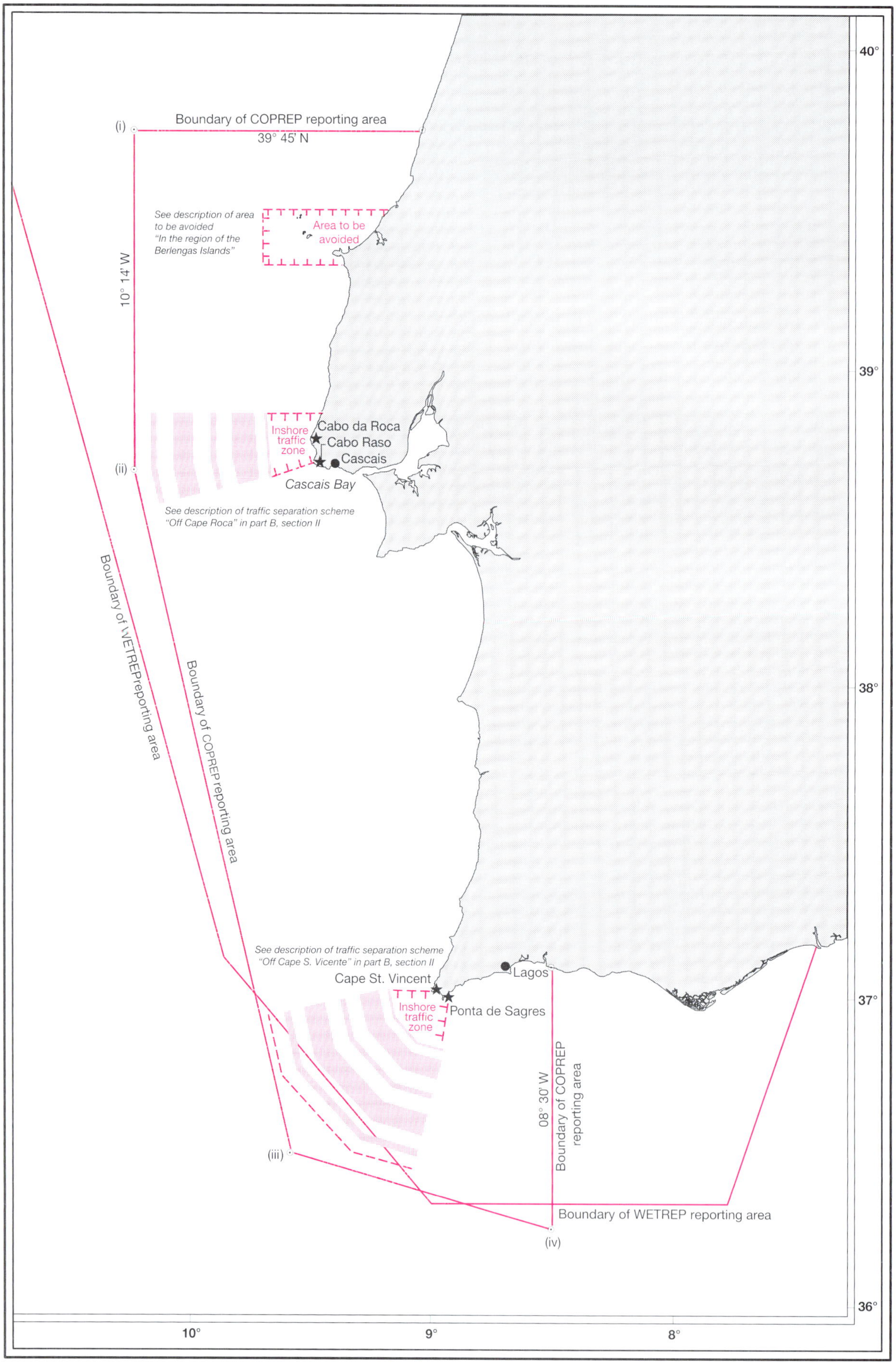

OFF THE COAST OF PORTUGAL

IN THE STRAIT OF GIBRALTAR (GIBREP)

1 Categories of ships required to participate in the system

Ships of the following general categories are required to participate in the reporting system:

.1 all ships of 300 gross tonnage and over;

.2 all ships, regardless of gross tonnage, carrying hazardous and/or potentially polluting cargo, as defined in paragraph 1.4 of resolution MSC.43(64);

.3 ships engaged in towing or pushing another vessel, regardless of gross tonnage;

.4 any category of vessel less than 300 gross tonnage which is using the appropriate traffic lane or separation zone in order to engage in fishing; and

.5 any category of ships less than 300 gross tonnage which is using the appropriate traffic separation zone in an emergency in order to avoid immediate danger.

Exemption

Recognizing that regular cross-Strait ferries, including passenger high-speed craft, generally operate according to published schedules, special reporting arrangements can be made on a ship-by-ship basis, subject to the approval of both TARIFA TRAFFIC and TANGIER TRAFFIC.

2 Geographical coverage of the system and the number and edition of the reference chart used for the delineation of the system

2.1 The reporting system will cover the area (see the appendix) between longitudes 005°58′.00 W and 005°15′.00 W. This area includes the amended traffic separation scheme "In the Strait of Gibraltar".

2.2 The reference charts which include all the area of coverage for the system are Spanish Hydrographic Office 105, French marine hydrographic and oceanographic service (SHOM) 7042 (INT 3150), and British Admiralty chart 142.

3 Format, content of report, times and geographical positions for submitting reports, Authority to whom reports should be sent, available services

The ship report (short title "GIBREP") shall be made to the ship reporting centres located at TARIFA and TANGIER. Reports should be made using VHF voice transmissions.

3.1 *Format*

The information requested from ships shall be provided in the standard reporting format, given in paragraph 2 of the appendix to IMO resolution A.851(20).

A ship may elect, for reasons of commercial confidentiality, to communicate that section of the GIBREP ENTRY report which provides information on cargo (line P) by non-verbal means prior to entering the system.

3.2 *Content*

The report from a ship to the VTS should contain only information which is essential to achieve the objectives of the system:

A	Name of the ship, call sign, IMO identification number;
B	Date and time of event;
C *or* D	Position in latitude and longitude *or* true bearing and distance from a clearly identified landmark;
E	True course;
F	Speed in knots;
G	Port of departure;
I	Port of destination and expected time of arrival;
P	Cargo and quantity and, if dangerous goods are on board, IMO classes and quantities;

Q *or* R Defect, damage and/or deficiencies affecting the structure, cargo or equipment of the ship or any other circumstances affecting normal navigation, in accordance with the provisions of relevant IMO Conventions;

T Address for provision of information concerning a cargo of dangerous goods;

W Total number of persons on board;

X Miscellaneous:

- Estimated quantity of bunker fuel and characteristics for ships carrying over 5000 tonnes of bunker fuel;
- Navigation conditions.

Note: On receipt of a position message, operators of the VTS will establish the relation between the ship's position and the information supplied by the facilities available to them. The information on heading and speed will facilitate the VTS operator's task of identifying a ship within a group.

3.3 *Geographical position for submitting report*

Westbound traffic should report to TARIFA TRAFFIC on the Spanish coast when crossing the meridian 005°15′.00 W (see the appendix).

Eastbound traffic should report to TANGIER TRAFFIC on the Moroccan coast when crossing the meridian 005°58′.00 W (see the appendix).

Reports to the nearer of the two shore stations should be made on departure from the limits of a port or anchorage within the coverage area, except vessels departing from Tangier-Med ports and its anchorage areas, which should report to TANGIER TRAFFIC (see the appendix).

Further reports should be made to the relevant shore station whenever there is a change of navigational circumstances, particularly in relation to items Q and R of the reporting format detailed in section 3.2.

3.4 *Authority*

The shore-based Authorities are:

.1 The Maritime Rescue Co-ordination Centre, MRCC TARIFA (Call sign: TARIFA TRAFFIC) under the authority of the Spanish Government Search and Rescue and Maritime Safety Division. The Division, administered by the Ministry of Development, is entrusted, amongst other responsibilities, with providing services relating to maritime search and rescue, vessel traffic services and assistance, and prevention and control of pollution of the marine environment; and

.2 The Centre de Surveillance du Trafic Maritime de Tanger (CSTM Tanger, Call sign: TANGIER TRAFFIC) is under the authority of the Moroccan Merchant Marine Directorate. The Directorate, administered by the Ministry of Equipment and Transports, is entrusted, amongst other responsibilities, in co-operation with governmental bodies, with providing services related to maritime search and rescue (SAR), vessel traffic services and assistance, and the prevention and control of pollution of the marine environment.

3.5 *Services offered*

Both TARIFA and TANGIER Centres monitor navigation in the traffic separation scheme "In the Strait of Gibraltar", using radar and AIS.

Each of them provides regular information about weather and navigational conditions; this information is broadcast at and on the following times and frequencies:

Station	Frequency	Broadcasting hours (UTC)
Tarifa Call sign: TARIFA TRAFFIC)	VHF channel 10	00h15; 04h15; 08h15; 12h15; 16h15; 20h15
Tangier (Call sign: TANGIER TRAFFIC)	VHF channel 69	02h15; 06h15; 10h15; 14h15; 18h15; 22h15

Information broadcasts will be preceded by an announcement on VHF channel 16 and broadcasts from both stations will end with a reminder about the time of the next broadcast and the VHF frequency on which it will be made.

When deemed necessary, navigational hazards, brought to the knowledge of any Centre, could be broadcast at any time.

4 Information to be provided to participating ships and procedures to be followed

In addition to the general information stated above, TARIFA TRAFFIC and TANGIER TRAFFIC could provide a particular vessel with information regarding her position, course, speed and/or the identification of the traffic in her vicinity, provided that it has been brought to the knowledge of the Centre. The ship should request this additional information.

5 Radiocommunication equipment required for the system, frequencies on which report should be transmitted and information to be reported

The radiocommunication equipment required for the system is that defined in the GMDSS for sea areas A1 and A2:

.1 The ship's reports can be made by voice on VHF radio, using:

  .1 Channel 10 for reporting to TARIFA TRAFFIC, with channel 67 as a supplementary option; and

  .2 Channel 69 for reporting to TANGIER TRAFFIC, with channel 68 as a supplementary option.

.2 In special circumstances, the hectometric waveband may also be used for the interchange of information between the ship and the VTS;

.3 Information of commercial confidentiality may be transmitted by non-verbal means. Details are as follows:

TARIFA TRAFFIC
Fax: + 34 956 68 06 06
E-mail: tarifa@sasemar.es
Inmarsat telex: 422423126

TANGIER TRAFFIC
Fax: + 212 539 93 45 71
E-mail: tangiervts@dmm.gov.ma
Inmarsat telex: 424241310

.4 The language used for reports in the system will be English, using the IMO Standard Marine Communication Phrases (SMCPs) where necessary, or Spanish, French or Arabic, if appropriate.

.5 Communications associated with reporting in accordance with the requirements of this system will be free of charge.

6 Rules and regulations in force in the area of the system

6.1 The International Regulations for Preventing Collisions at Sea (COLREG) 1972 (as amended) are applicable throughout the area of coverage of the system; and

6.2 The amended traffic separation scheme "In the Strait of Gibraltar" has been approved by IMO and therefore rule 10 of COLREG applies.

7 Shore-based facilities to support operation of the system

7.1 *Tarifa Traffic*

Tarifa Traffic has radar, communication equipments in different bands and frequencies, VHF direction-finding, AIS and DSC located in local and in remote sites to enable an appropriate coverage of the area.

Traffic surveillance is provided by a tracking system in which the AIS and VHF direction-finding are integrated. Vessel tracks are continuously recorded and can be plotted on paper.

Besides, the Tarifa Traffic Centre is equipped with data processing and retrieval systems, and normal communications such as telephone, fax and e-mail terminals.

A continuous listening watch is kept on VHF channel 16 and on the working channels.

7.2 *Tangier Traffic*

TANGIER VTS is an integrated system, using facilities such as radars, communication equipments in different bands and frequencies, VHF direction-finding, AIS and DSC located either in local site at Ras Parort and in remote site at Ras Cires, in order to enable an appropriate coverage of the area.

TANGIER TRAFFIC system allows the simultaneous monitoring of 1000 tracks, which can be recorded and saved. Advanced functions include alarms signalling risk scenarios, the identification of tracks infringing COLREG rules, particularly rule 10, and the monitoring of ships at anchor. All situations can be recorded, archived and replayed either on screen or in the form of printout.

A continuous listening watch is kept on VHF channel 16 and on the working channels.

8 Alternative communication in case of failure of the shore-based communication facilities

8.1 The system is designed to avoid, as far as possible, any irretrievable breakdown of equipment which would hinder the functioning of the services normally provided;

8.2 The most important items of equipment and power sources are duplicated and the facilities are provided with emergency generating sets as well as with UPS units. A maintenance team, on call 24 hours a day, stands ready to repair, to the extent possible, any breakdowns which may occur; and

8.3 If operations are jeopardized at either TARIFA TRAFFIC or TANGIER TRAFFIC, then the other centre will try to provide the service.

9 Measures to be taken if a ship fails to comply with the requirements of the system

The primary objective of the system is to facilitate the exchange of information between the ship and the shore and so support safe navigation and the protection of the marine environment. All means will be used to encourage and promote the full participation of ships required to submit reports under SOLAS regulation V/11. If reports are not submitted and the offending ship can be positively identified, then information will be passed to the relevant flag State Authorities for investigation and possible prosecution in accordance with national legislation. Information will also be made available to Port State Control Officers.

Appendix

Geographical coverage of system – lines and points of notification

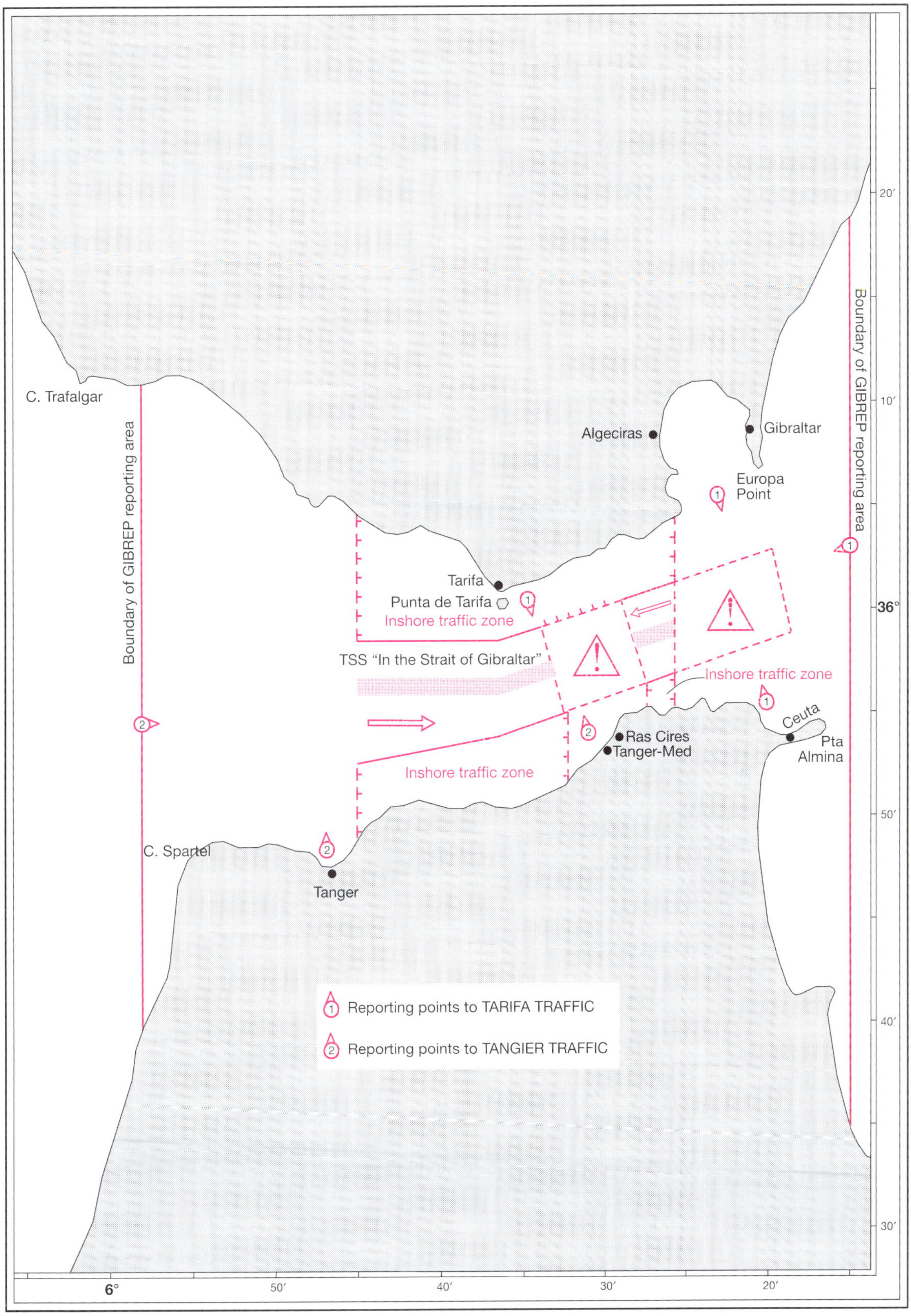

G

IN THE STRAIT OF BONIFACIO (BONIFREP)

Note: See "Routeing measures in the Strait of Bonifacio" in part E and "Recommendation on navigation through the Strait of Bonifacio" in part F.

1 Categories of ships required to participate in the system

Ships of 300 gross tonnage and over are required to participate in the system.

2 Geographical coverage of the system and reference chart

The reporting system covers a circular area with a radius of 20 nautical miles centred on Bonifacio. The reference chart is the French chart No. 7024 of the SHOM (Hydrographic and Oceanographic Service of the French Navy) (International chart No. 3350).

3 Format and contents of the report, times and geographical positions for submitting report, Authority to whom reports should be sent, available services

3.1 *Content*

The report required shall include:

- information considered essential:
  - the name of the ship, her call sign or IMO identification number (letter A)
  - time and position (letters C *or* D)
  - course and speed (letters E *and* F)
  - draught (letter O)
- additional information, if appropriate:
  - cargo (in case of transport of petroleum products, dangerous or polluting substances) (letter P)
  - defects or damage (letter Q)

In addition, in accordance with provisions of SOLAS and MARPOL Conventions, ships must report information on any defect, damage, deficiency or limitations as well as, if necessary, information relating to pollution incidents or loss of cargo. Possession of this information enables the operators to broadcast safety messages to other ship traffic and to ensure more effective tracking of the trajectories of ships concerned.

Ships shall transmit their reports on entering the precautionary areas defined in the documents about routeing measures in the Strait of Bonifacio, or when passing the following lines:

Eastbound:

- A line linking the beacon of Cap de Feno in Corsica to point 41°19′.18 N, 009°06′.51 E (west end of the north limit of the two-way route)
- A line linking the beacon of Capo Testa in Sardinia to point 41°16′.75 N, 009°06′.18 E (west end of the south limit of the two-way route).

Westbound:

- A line linking Pointe de Rondinara in Corsica to point 41°22′.55 N, 009°22′.38 E (east end of the north limit of the two-way route)
- A line linking Punta Galera in Sardinia to point 41°21′.58 N, 009°23′.30 E (east end of the south limit of the two-way route)

3.2 *Recipient of report*

The shore-based authorities are La Maddalena Coast Guard Station (Sardinia, Italy) and Pertusato Naval Signal Station (Corsica, France), common call sign: BONIFACIO TRAFFIC.

4 Information to be provided to ships and procedures to be followed

Detected and identified ships are monitored by radar, which in no way releases their master from their responsibility for safe navigation.

Following receiving a report, Bonifacio Traffic will provide:

- information on navigational conditions (status of aids to navigation, presence of other ships and their position at the moment of contact); and
- information on weather conditions.

5 Radiocommunications required for the system, frequencies on which reports should be transmitted and information to be reported

5.1 The radiocommunication equipment required for the system is VHF. Ship reports shall be transmitted by voice on VHF channel 10, back-up VHF channel 16, both permanently watched by the station. An IMO circular will provide for another back-up VHF channel, if necessary, after 1 February 1999. Use of an automatic identification system will be implemented in accordance with IMO decisions.

5.2 The report required from a ship is mentioned in paragraph 3.1 above and in the appendix "Summary". The language used shall be English or languages indicated in nautical publications.

5.3 Information of commercial confidentiality may be transmitted by non-verbal means. Detail of fax call number to be published in nautical information documents.

6 Rules and regulations in force in the area of the system

6.1 The International Regulations for Preventing Collisions at Sea (COLREGs) are applicable throughout the area of coverage of the system.

6.2 The IMO resolution A.766(18) about navigation in the Strait of Bonifacio, adopted on 4 November 1993, remains in force as far as it recommends each flag State to prohibit or at least strongly discourage the transit by certain categories of ships (operative paragraph 1). Its ship reporting provisions are replaced by those of the present instrument.

6.3 The regulation (arrêté) of the Préfet maritime for Mediterranean region n° 23/83 dated 6 May 1983 rules navigation in the approaches of the French coast in order to prevent accidental marine pollution, for ships carrying hazardous or polluting cargoes. This instrument has the following provisions:

.1 for ships intending to enter French territorial waters, mandatory ship reporting with a six-hour advance warning. In addition to information concerning the identity of the ship, the report must specify the place and time of entry into French waters, the port arrived from and the destination, the cargo and the status of manoeuvrability and navigational capacities;

.2 mandatory watch on VHF channel 16 while travelling through territorial waters; and

.3 mandatory reporting of any damage occurring at less than 50 miles from the French coast.

6.4 French regulations (arrêté) of the Préfet maritime n° 1/83 dated 15 February 1983 and 7/93 dated 5 March 1993 and Italian decree of the Minister of Merchant Marine dated 26 February 1993 prohibit transit through the Strait of Bonifacio for French and Italian ships carrying oil products or hazardous goods. They will remain in force.

7 Shore-based facilities to support operation of the system

7.1 Stations will be equipped with radar installations assisted by computer, covering the whole area.

7.2 Stations will be equipped with a duplicated VHF equipment.

7.3 Personnel operating the system: stations will be manned by Naval personnel on a 24-hour basis. Duty officers are qualified Senior Chief Petty-Officers.

8 Alternative communication if the communication facilities of the shore-based Authority fail

Each station will assure relief of the other one in case of failure.

Appendix

Summary

(Ship reporting system)

1 General

1.1 *Vessels concerned*

All ships of 300 gross tonnage and over.

1.2 *Area on entering which vessels shall report*

Ships shall transmit their reports on entering the precautionary areas defined in the documents about routeing measures in the Strait of Bonifacio, or when passing the following lines:

Eastbound:

- A line linking the beacon of Cap de Feno in Corsica to geographical position 41°19′.18 N, 009°06′.51 E (west end of the north limit of the two-way route)
- A line linking the beacon of Capo Testa in Sardinia to geographical position 41°16′.75 N, 009°06′.18 E (west end of the south limit of the two-way route).

Westbound:

- A line linking Pointe de Rondinara in Corsica to geographical position 41°22′.55 N, 009°22′.38 E (east end of the north limit of the two-way route)
- A line linking Punta Galera in Sardinia to geographical position 41°21′.58 N, 009°23′.30 E (east end of the south limit of the two-way route)

1.3 *Reference chart*

French (SHOM) chart No. 7024 (International chart No. 3350).

2 Reporting format

(In accordance with resolution A.851(20) – General principles for ship reporting systems and ship reporting requirements, including guidelines for reporting incidents involving dangerous goods, harmful substances and/or marine pollutants)

Name of system: BONIFREP

Data to be transmitted:

Heading	*Information*
A	Name + call sign + IMO Number
C *or* D	Time and position
E *and* F	Course and speed
O	Draught
P	Cargo (in case of transport of oil products, hazardous or polluting substances)
Q	Defect or damage (if relevant)
R	Polluting/dangerous goods lost overboard (if relevant)

In the event of defect, pollution or goods lost overboard, additional information may be requested.

3 Authority to whom the report shall be sent

Pertusato Naval Signal Station (France) – La Maddalena Coast Guard Station (Italy); common call sign: BONIFACIO TRAFFIC.

4 Communications facilities

The reports are to be transmitted on VHF channel 10 (or on channel 16 if not possible).

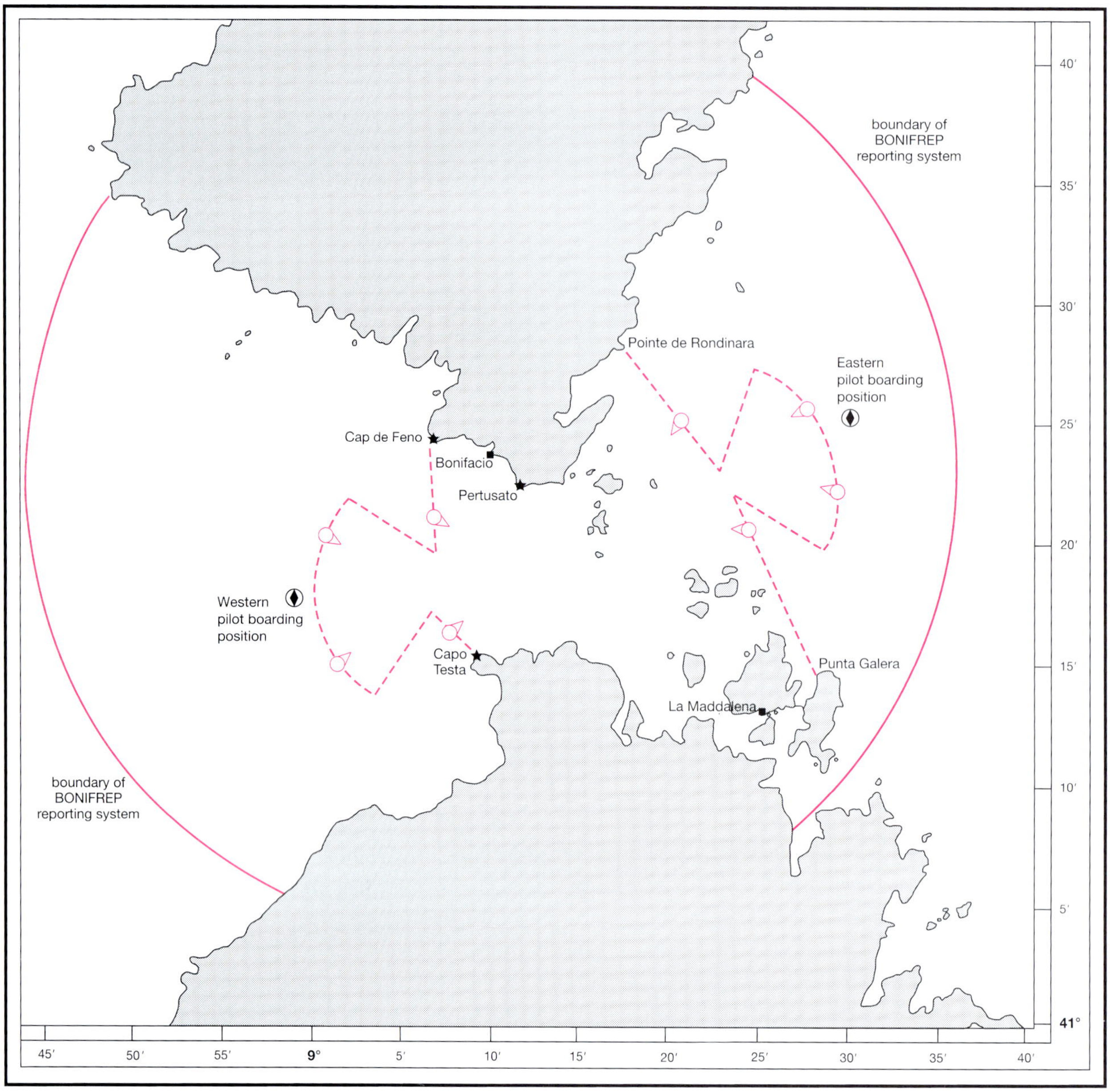

IN THE STRAIT OF BONIFACIO

IN THE ADRIATIC SEA (ADRIREP)

1 Categories of ships required to participate in the system

1.1 Ships of the following categories are required to participate in the system:

- all oil tanker ships of 150 gross tonnage and above;
- all ships of 300 gross tonnage and above, carrying on board, as cargo, dangerous or polluting goods, in bulk or in packages.

1.2 For the purpose of this system:

- "dangerous goods" means goods classified in the IMDG Code, in chapter 17 of the IBC Code and in chapter 19 of the IGC Code;
- "polluting goods" means oils as defined in MARPOL Annex I, noxious liquid substances as defined in MARPOL Annex II, harmful substances as defined in MARPOL Annex III.

2 Geographical coverage of the system and the number and edition of the reference chart used for the delineation of the system

2.1 The operational area of the mandatory ship reporting system covers the whole Adriatic Sea, north from the latitude 40°25′.00 N as shown in the attached chartlet as annex 1: the area is divided into five sectors, each of them assigned to a competent authority, operating on a VHF channel as shown in the attached table as annex 2.

2.2 The reference charts including the operational area of the ADRIATIC TRAFFIC system are the Italian chart No. 435 (INT 306) of the Italian Navy Hydrographic Institute (1993 edition, datum ED 50) and the Croatian chart No. 101 of the Hydrographic Institute of the Republic of Croatia (1998 edition, datum Besselov ellipsoid).

3 Format and contents of the report, times and geographical positions for submitting reports, Authorities to whom reports shall be sent, available services

The formats for reporting are derived from the one attached as appendix to resolution A.851(20).

3.1 *First report*

3.1.1 The first report of ADRIREP (FR) shall be sent by radio to the competent authorities in accordance with the format shown in annex 3.

3.1.2 The first report shall contain the following information, in order to meet the objectives of ADRIATIC TRAFFIC:

- ship's name, call sign, IMO identification number and flag;
- date and time of the report;
- present position;
- course;
- speed;
- port of departure;
- destination and estimated time of arrival;
- estimated time of arrival at the next check point;
- ship's draught;
- the general category of hazardous cargo as defined by the IMDG, IBC, IGC Codes and MARPOL Annex I;
- ship's representative and/or owner available on 24-hour basis;

- ship's type, deadweight, gross tonnage and length overall;
- total number of persons on board; and
- any other relevant information.

3.1.3 In the last section of the first report, in accordance with provisions of SOLAS and MARPOL Conventions, ships shall also report information on any defect, damage, deficiency or limitations as well as, if necessary, information related to pollution incident or loss of cargo. The possession of this information will enable the operators of the shore-based competent authority to broadcast safety messages to other ships and to ensure more effective tracking of the trajectories of ships concerned.

3.2 *Position report*

3.2.1 The position report of ADRIREP (PR) shall be sent by radio to the competent authorities in accordance with the format shown in annex 4.

3.2.2 The position report shall contain the following information, in order to meet the objectives of the ADRIATIC TRAFFIC:

- ship's name, call sign, IMO identification number and flag;
- date and time of the report;
- present position;
- course;
- speed;
- port of departure;
- destination and estimated time of arrival;
- estimated time of arrival at the next check point;
- any other relevant information.

3.2.3 The present format shall be supplemented by any other information which differs from the one provided by the previous report.

3.3 *Times and geographical positions for submitting reports*

3.3.1 *Sailing the Adriatic Sea northwards*

.1 The ship shall transmit the first report to the competent shore-based authority of the interested sector when:

- entering the Adriatic Sea by crossing northwards the parallel 40°25′.00 N,;
- entering the Adriatic Sea by leaving a port inside the area covered by the system.

.2 The ship shall transmit the position report to the competent shore-based authorities when:

- entering a new sector by crossing northwards its southern borderline, as per annex 2;
- entering the port of destination in the area covered by the system.

3.3.2 *Sailing the Adriatic Sea southwards*

.1 The ship shall transmit the first report to the competent shore-based authority of the interested sector when leaving a port inside the area covered by the system.

.2 The shore-based authority to whom the first report shall be transmitted is that of the country of the port the ship is leaving.

.3 The recipient of the report will inform the maritime authority of the ship's destination (if in the area covered by the system), Brindisi Coast Guard and the other shore-based authorities in between, if any.

.4 The ship shall transmit the position reports to the competent shore-based authorities when:

- entering a new sector by crossing southwards its northern borderline, as per annex 2;
- entering the port of destination in the area covered by the system.

3.3.3 *Crossing the Adriatic Sea*

3.3.3.1 The ship shall send the position report to the closest shore-based authority of the country the ship is leaving, which shall inform the maritime authority of the port of destination.

3.3.4 *Special cases*

.1 A ship which, sailing northwards or southwards, enters Sector 5 shall transmit the report to, alternatively, one of the competent authorities as per annex 2, according to where the ship is going to or coming from.

.2 A ship crossing southwards the latitude 40°25′.00 N, and going out either of Sector 1 or of the area covered by the system shall transmit an additional final position report to Brindisi Coast Guard.

3.4 *Authorities to whom the reports should be sent*

3.4.1 The ships participating in the system shall transmit by radio the report to the shore-based authorities as in annex 2.

4 Information to be provided to participating ships and procedures to be followed

4.1 The shore-based authority which receives the first report (01/FR) shall inform the maritime authority of the ship's destination (if in the area covered by the system) and the other shore-based authorities in between, if any.

4.2 The competent shore-based authority of Sector 5 (as per paragraph 3.3.4) which receives the position report from the ship entering the sector will also inform the other two shore-based authorities about the entrance of the abovementioned ship.

4.3 Once received a report, the ADRIATIC TRAFFIC competent authority will provide the ship with:

- information on navigational conditions (status of aids to navigation, presence of other ships and, if necessary, their position, etc.);
- information on weather conditions; and
- any other relevant information.

5 Radiocommunication required for the system, frequencies on which reports should be transmitted and information to be reported

5.1 ADRIATIC TRAFFIC will be based on VHF voice radiocommunications.

5.2 The call to the appropriate shore-based authority shall be made on the VHF channel assigned to the sector in which the ship is located, as per annex 2.

5.3 However, a ship which cannot use the frequencies listed in annex 2 in order to transmit the reports should use, via coast station, any other available communication equipment (e.g. MF, HF or Inmarsat) on which communication might be established.

5.4 The language used for communication shall be English, using the IMO Standard Marine Communication Phrases, where necessary.

6 Rules and regulations in force in the area of the system

6.1 The International Regulations for Preventing Collisions at Sea (COLREGs) are applicable through the whole area covered by the system.

7 Shore-based facilities to support operation of the system

.1 Brindisi Coast Guard (Italy)

- telephone and telefax communication facilities;
- VHF communication equipment.

.2 MRCC Bar (Yugoslavia)

- telephone and telefax communication facilities;
- VHF, MF and HF communication equipment.

.3 MRCC Rijeka (Croatia)

- telephone and telefax communication facilities;
- VHF, MF, HF and Inmarsat-C communication equipment.

.4 MRSC Ancona (Italy)

- telephone and telefax communication facilities;
- VHF, MF and HF communication equipment.

.5 MRSC Venezia (Italy)

- telephone and telefax communication facilities;
- VHF, MF and HF communication equipment.

.6 MRSC Trieste (Italy)

- telephone and telefax communication facilities;
- VHF, MF and HF communication equipment.

.7 MRCC Koper (Slovenia)

- telephone and telefax communication facilities;
- VHF communication equipment.

8 Alternative communication if the communication facilities of the shore-based Authorities fail

8.1 ADRIATIC TRAFFIC is planned with a sufficient system redundancy to cope with normal equipment failure. Since the system is based on the VHF voice communication, each shore-based facility has got at least two VHF transmitters/receivers; in addition to that, in case of failing contacts by VHF, the shore-based authorities can operate and be contacted through phone, fax, Inmarsat-C and MF/HF facilities. In order to ensure the continuous 24-hour activity, the shore-based facilities have been located and manned with properly trained and dedicated personnel in the respective national MRCCs/MRSCs. Should a shore-based authority suffer an irretrievable breakdown and call off itself from the system until the failure is repaired, it could be relieved by one of the adjacent shore-based authorities.

9 Measures to be taken if a ship fails to comply with the requirements of the system

9.1 The primary objective of the system is to support safe navigation and the protection of the marine environment through the exchange of information between the ship and the shore. If a ship does not submit reports and can be positively identified, then information will be passed to the competent Flag State authorities for investigation and possible prosecution in accordance with national legislation. Information will be passed also to Port State Control inspectors.

Annex 1

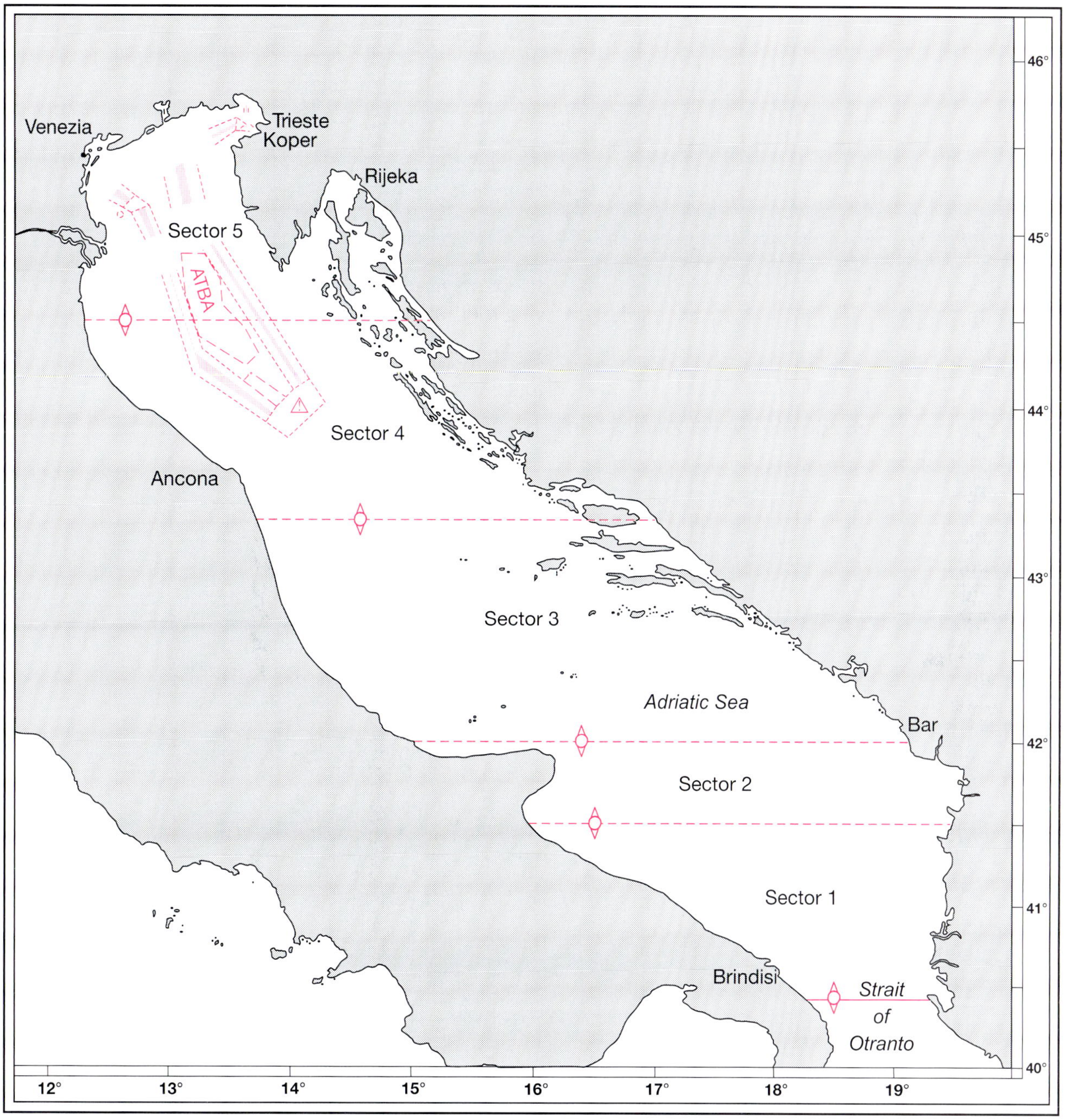
Venezia
Trieste
Koper
Rijeka
Sector 5
ATBA
Sector 4
Ancona
Sector 3
Adriatic Sea
Bar
Sector 2
Sector 1
Brindisi
Strait of Otranto
46°
45°
44°
43°
42°
41°
40°
12°
13°
14°
15°
16°
17°
18°
19°

Annex 2

Sector	Southern borderline	Northern borderline	Competent Authority	VHF frequencies
1	Latitude 40°25′.00 N	Latitude 41°30′.00 N	Brindisi Coast Guard (Italy)	Channel 10
2	Latitude 41°30′.00 N	Latitude 42°00′.00 N	Bar MRCC (Yugoslavia)	Channel 12
3	Latitude 42°00′.00 N	Latitude 43°20′.00 N	Rijeka MRCC (Croatia)	Channel 10
4	Latitude 43°20′.00 N	Latitude 44°30′.00 N	Ancona MRSC (Italy)	Channel 10
5	Latitude 44°30′.00 N	Coastline	Venezia MRSC (Italy)	Channel 10
5	Latitude 44°30′.00 N	Coastline	Trieste MRSC (Italy)	Channel 10
5	Latitude 44°30′.00 N	Coastline	Koper MRCC (Slovenia)	Channel 12

Annex 3

Format of "ADRIATIC TRAFFIC" ship reporting system First Report

	Message identifier:	ADRIREP
	Type of report:	01/FR (first report)
A	Ship	Name, call sign, IMO identification number and flag of the vessel
B	Date/time (UTC)	A six-digit group giving date of month (first two digits), hours and minutes (last 4 digits)
C	Present position	A four-digit group giving latitude in degrees and minutes suffixed with "N" or "S" and a five-digit group giving longitude in degrees and minutes suffixed with "E" or "W"
E	Course	A three-digit group giving the course in degrees
F	Speed	A three-digit group giving a speed in knots
G	Departure	Port of departure
I	Destination and estimated time of arrival	ETA in UTC expressed as in B above, followed by port of destination
N	Estimated time of arrival at the next check point	Date/time group expressed by a six-digit group, as in B above, followed by the parallel of the check point
O	Draught of the vessel	Draught expressed by a four-digit group indicating centimetres
P	Cargo information	The general category of hazardous cargo as defined by the IMDG, IBC, IGC Codes and MARPOL Annex I
T	Agent	Ship's representative and/or owner available on 24-hour basis
U	Size and type	Type, DWT, GT, and length overall in metres
W	Total number of persons on board	The total number of crew and other persons on board
X	Miscellaneous	Any other relevant information

Annex 4

Format of "ADRIATIC TRAFFIC" ship reporting system Position Report/Final Report

	Message identifier:	ADRIREP
	Type of report:	01/PR (position report) 02/PR 03/PR ER (final report)
A	Ship	Name, call sign, IMO identification number and flag of the vessel
B	Date/time (UTC)	A six-digit group giving date of month (first two digits), hours and minutes (last 4 digits)
C	Present position	A four-digit group giving latitude in degrees and minutes suffixed with "N" or "S" and a five-digit group giving longitude in degrees and minutes suffixed with "E" or "W"
E	Course	A three-digit group giving the course in degrees
F	Speed	A three-digit group giving a speed in knots
G	Departure	Port of departure
I	Destination and estimated time of arrival	ETA in UTC expressed as in B above, followed by port of destination
N	Estimated time of arrival at the next check point	Date/time group expressed by a six-digit group, as in B above, followed by the parallel of the check point
X	Miscellaneous	Any other relevant information

Note: The format of the position/final report shall contain, in addition to this format, any other field which differs from the information provided in the last report.

IN THE STRAITS OF MALACCA AND SINGAPORE (STRAITREP)

Note: See "Recommendatory measures for vessels crossing the traffic separation scheme and precautionary areas in the Singapore Strait during hours of darkness" in part E and "Rules for vessels navigating through the Straits of Malacca and Singapore" in part F.

1 Categories of ships required to participate in the system

1.1 Ships of the following categories are required to participate in the ship reporting system:

.1 vessels of 300 gross tonnage and above;

.2 vessels of 50 metres or more in length;

.3 vessels engaged in towing or pushing with a combined gross tonnage of 300 and above, or with a combined length of 50 metres or more;

.4 vessels of any tonnage carrying hazardous cargo, as defined in paragraph 1.4 of resolution MSC.43(64);

.5 all passenger vessels that are fitted with VHF, regardless of length or gross tonnage; and

.6 any category of vessels less than 50 metres in length or less than 300 gross tonnage which are fitted with VHF and, in an emergency, use the appropriate traffic lane or separation zone in order to avoid immediate danger.

2 Geographical coverage of the system and the number and edition of the reference chart used for the delineation of the system

2.1 The operational area of STRAITREP covers the Straits of Malacca and Singapore between longitudes 100°40′ E and 104°23′ E as shown in the chartlets attached as appendix 1 and appendix 2. The area includes the routeing system in the Straits of Malacca and Singapore. The area is divided into nine sectors; each has an assigned VHF channel as shown in appendix 3.

2.2 The reference charts which include the operational area of STRAITREP are the Malaysian Chart Series MAL 515, 521 and 523 of the Hydrographer, Royal Malaysian Navy or the equivalent charts published by the competent hydrographic authority.

3 Format, content of report, times and geographical positions for submitting reports, Authority to whom reports should be sent, and available services

The ship report (short title STRAITREP) shall be made to the VTS authorities as follows:

3.1 *Format*

The ship report shall be drafted in accordance with the format shown in appendix 4. The information requested from ships is derived from the Standard Reporting Format given in paragraph 2 of the appendix to IMO resolution A.851(20).

3.2 *Content*

The report required from a ship contains only information which is essential to meet the objectives of the STRAITREP:

.1 Information considered essential;

A	Name of ship, call sign, IMO identification number (if available);
C *or* D	Position;
P	Hazardous cargo, class (if applicable); and
Q *or* R	Breakdown, damage and/or deficiencies affecting the structure, cargo or equipment of the ship or any other circumstances affecting normal navigation in accordance with the provisions of the SOLAS and MARPOL Conventions.

.2 Information considered necessary when requested by VTS authority;

E *and* F Course and speed of ship.

Note: On receipt of a position message, operators of the VTS will establish the relation between the ship's position and the information supplied by the facilities available to them. The information on heading and speed will facilitate the VTS operator's task of identifying a ship within a group.

3.3 *Geographical position for submitting reports*

.1 Ships entering the operational area shall report when crossing the limits mentioned in paragraph 2.1 or when crossing a line joining Tanjung Piai (01°15′.50 N, 103°30′.75 E) and Pulau Karimun Kecil (01°09′.20 N, 103°24′.35 E) or when leaving port or anchorages in the area or before joining the traffic lane of the traffic separation scheme.

.2 Ships entering the operational area shall also report when approaching from the south via Selat Riau, abeam of Karang Galang light (01°09′.58 N, 104°11′.47 E), or via Selat Durian, when Pulau Jangkat beacon (00°57′.89 N, 103°42′.72 E) is abeam, and when approaching from the East Johor Strait, abeam of Eastern buoy (01°17′.87 N, 104°05′.99 E).

.3 A ship approaching from any direction other than those specified above shall, on reaching sector 7, sector 8 or sector 9 as appropriate, report by giving the vessel's position in terms of bearing and distance from one of the following reference points:

(i)	Pulau Iyu Kecil light	(01°11′.48 N,	103°21′.23 E)
(ii)	Sultan Shoal light	(01°14′.38 N,	103°38′.98 E)
(iii)	Raffles light	(01°09′.60 N,	103°44′.55 E)
(iv)	Sakijang light beacon	(01°13′.30 N,	103°51′.37 E)
(v)	Bedok light	(01°18′.54 N,	103°56′.06 E)
(vi)	Tanjung Stapa light	(01°20′.57 N,	104°08′.24 E)
(vii)	Horsburgh light	(01°19′.81 N,	104°24′.44 E)

As an alternative, the position can also be given in latitude and longitude.

3.4 *Authority*

The VTS authorities for the STRAITREP are as follows:

(i)	sector 1 to sector 5	Klang VTS;
(ii)	sector 6	Johor VTS; and
(iii)	sector 7 to sector 9	Singapore VTS.

4 Information to be provided to ships and procedures to be followed

4.1 STRAITREP also provides information to ships about specific and critical situations which could cause conflicting traffic movements and other information concerning safety of navigation.

4.2 Depending on the sector which a ship is in, every ship shall also maintain a VHF radiotelephone listening watch on the appropriate VHF channel. Information of general interest to ships will be broadcast on VHF channel 16 and any other channel as may be specified by the appropriate VTS authority. This broadcast will be preceded by an announcement on the appropriate VHF channel assigned to the sector.

5 Radiocommunications required for the system, frequencies on which reports should be transmitted and information to be reported

The radiocommunications required for the STRAITREP is as follows:

5.1 STRAITREP will be based on VHF voice radiocommunication and will be interactive. The call to the appropriate VTS authority shall be made on the VHF channel assigned to the particular sector in which the ship is located as indicated in appendix 3, and the report shall be transmitted on that channel or any other available channel as assigned by the appropriate VTS authorities.

5.2 The language used for communication shall be English, using the IMO Standard Marine Communication Phrases where necessary.

5.3 Information of commercial confidentiality may be transmitted by non-verbal means.

6 Rules and regulations in force in the area of the system

6.1 The International Regulations for Preventing Collisions at Sea, 1972 are applicable throughout the operational area of STRAITREP.

6.2 The Rules for Vessels Navigating through the Straits of Malacca and Singapore as approved by IMO are applicable throughout the area.

7 Shore-based facilities to support operation of the system

The facilities of the STRAITREP are as follows:

.1 Klang VTS

- telephone, facsimile and telex communication
- six sets of VHF radiocommunication equipment
- six real-time display consoles for X- and S-band radar signals from remote radar stations.

.2 Johor VTS

- telephone, facsimile and telex communication
- four sets of VHF radiocommunication equipment
- four real-time display consoles for X- and S-band radar signals from remote radar stations.

.3 Singapore VTS

- telephone, facsimile and telex communication
- eleven sets of VHF radiocommunication equipment
- four real-time display consoles for X-band radar signals from remote radar stations.
- four sets of VHF radio direction-finders in marine bands.

.4 Remote stations:

.4.1 *Pulau Angsa*

- one X-band radar facility
- one S-band radar facility
- VHF transmitters and receivers

.4.2 *Bukit Jugra*

- one X-band radar facility
- one S-band radar facility
- VHF transmitters and receivers

.4.3 *Cape Rachado*

- one X-band radar facility
- one S-band radar facility
- VHF transmitters and receivers

.4.4 *Pulau Undan*

- one X-band radar facility
- one S-band radar facility
- VHF transmitters and receivers

.4.5 *Bukit Segenting*

- one X-band radar facility
- one S-band radar facility
- VHF transmitters and receivers

.4.6 *Tanjung Piai*

- one X-band radar facility
- one S-band radar facility
- VHF transmitters and receivers

.4.7 *Bukit Pengerang*

- one X-band radar facility
- one S-band radar facility
- VHF transmitters and receivers

.4.8 *Sultan Shoal Lighthouse*

- VHF transmitters and receivers
- one X-band radar facility

.4.9 *Raffles Lighthouse*

- one X-band radar facility

.4.10 *St. John's Island*

- one X-band radar facility

.4.11 *Bedok Lighthouse*

- two sets of VHF/DF radio direction-finder

.4.12 *Bedok*

- one X-band radar facility

.4.13 *Horsburgh Lighthouse*

- VHF transmitters and receivers
- one X-band radar facility

.4.14 *Jurong Control*

- two sets of VHF/DF radio direction-finder.

8 Alternative communication if the communication facilities of the shore-based Authority fail

8.1 STRAITREP is designed to avoid, as far as possible, any irretrievable breakdown of equipment which would hinder the functioning of the services normally provided by the respective VTS authorities.

8.2 The most important items of equipment and power sources are duplicated and the facilities are provided with emergency generating sets as well as with Uninterruptible Power Supply (UPS) units. A maintenance team is available 24 hours a day to attend to any breakdown.

8.3 STRAITREP is also designed in such a manner that if one station fails, the adjacent station can provide the necessary coverage.

Appendix 1

STRAITREP operational area (sectors 1 to 9)

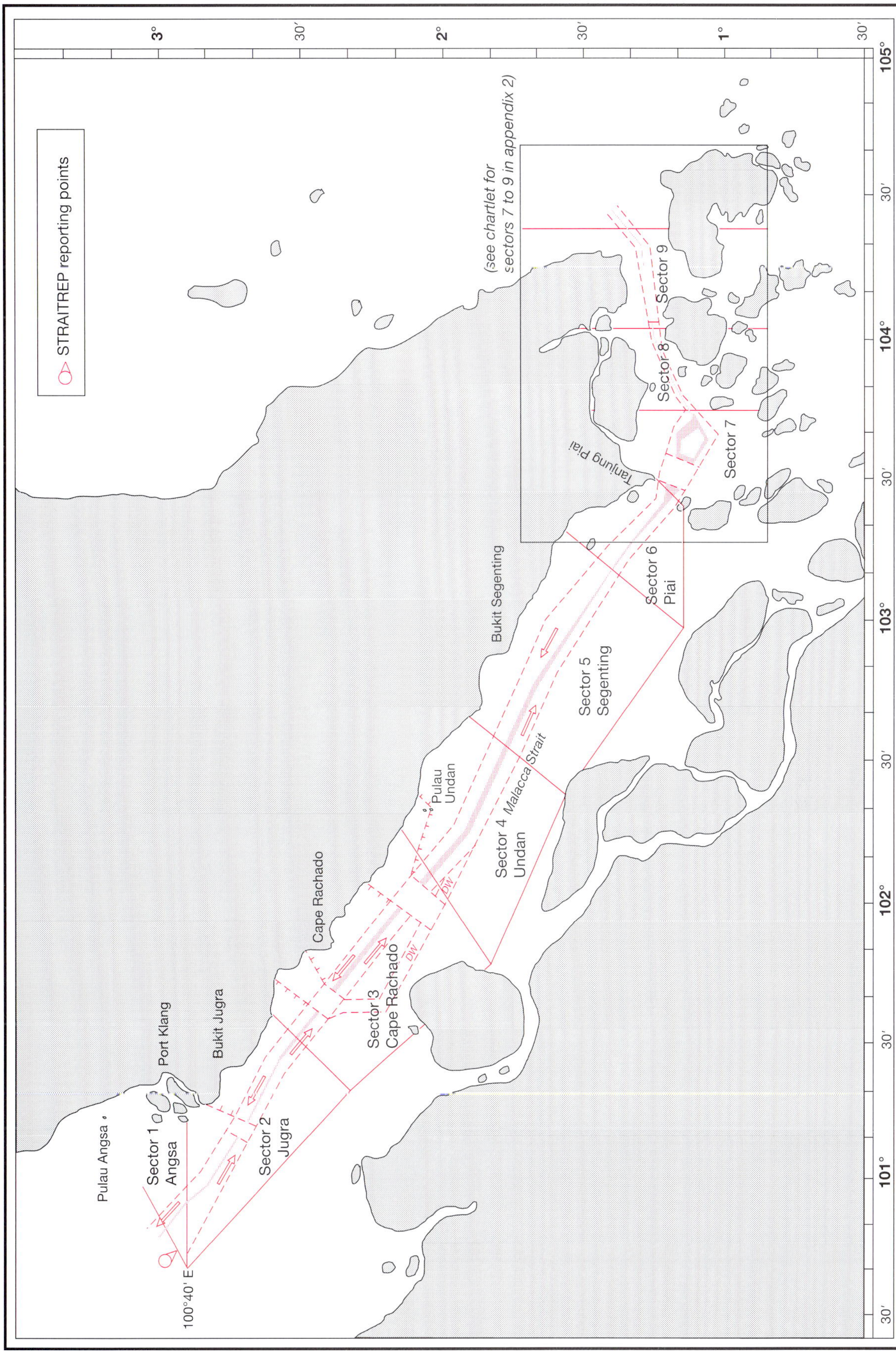

Appendix 2

STRAITREP operational area (sectors 7 to 9)

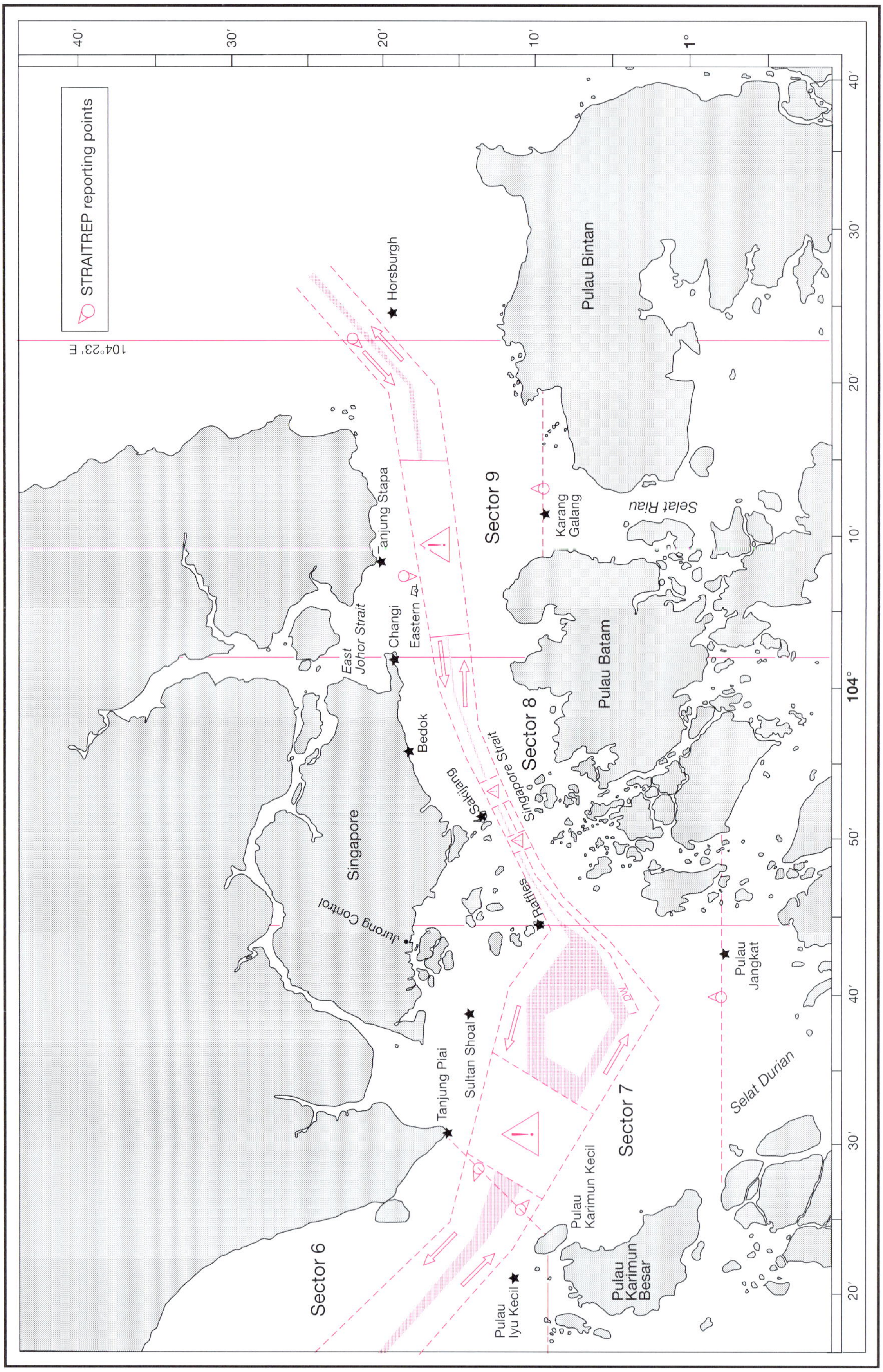

Appendix 3

Assigned VHF channels for sectors in the mandatory reporting system
In the Straits of Malacca and Singapore (STRAITREP)

Sector	VHF Channels	VTS Authorities
Sector 1	VHF channel 66	Klang VTS
Sector 2	VHF channel 88	Klang VTS
Sector 3	VHF channel 84	Klang VTS
Sector 4	VHF channel 61	Klang VTS
Sector 5	VHF channel 88	Klang VTS
Sector 6	VHF channel 88	Johor VTS
Sector 7	VHF channel 73	Singapore VTS
Sector 8	VHF channel 14	Singapore VTS
Sector 9	VHF channel 10	Singapore VTS

Appendix 4

Drafting of radio reports to the mandatory ship reporting system
In the Straits of Malacca and Singapore (STRAITREP)

Designator	Function	Information required
A	Ship	Name and call sign
C	Position	A 4-digit group giving latitude in degrees and minutes suffixed with N (north) or S (south) and a 5-digit group giving longitude in degrees and minutes suffixed with E (east) or W (west); *or*
D	Position	True bearing (first 3 digits) and distance given in nautical miles from a clearly identifiable point (state landmark)
E	True course	A 3-digit group
F	Speed in knots and tenths of knot	A 3-digit group
P	Hazardous cargo on board	Indicate "Yes" or "No" to whether vessel is carrying hazardous cargo. If "Yes", the class (if applicable).
Q	Defects/damage/deficiencies/ other limitations	Brief detail of defects, deficiencies or other limitations
R	Description of pollution or dangerous goods lost overboard	Brief detail of type of pollution (oil, chemicals, etc.) or dangerous goods lost overboard; position expressed as in (C) or (D)

IN THE TORRES STRAIT REGION AND THE INNER ROUTE OF THE GREAT BARRIER REEF (REEFREP)

1 Categories of ships required to participate in the system

Ships of the following general categories are required to participate in the reporting system:

.1 All ships of 50 metres or greater in overall length;

.2 All ships, regardless of length, carrying in bulk hazardous and/or potentially polluting cargo, in accordance with the definitions at resolution MSC.43(64), paragraph 1.4;

.3 Ships engaged in towing or pushing where either the towing or pushing vessel or the towed or pushed vessel is a vessel prescribed within the categories in subparagraphs .1 and .2.

2 Geographical coverage of the system and the number and edition of the reference chart used for the delineation of the system

2.1 The reporting system will cover the general area as shown in the chartlet at appendix 1. The area encompasses the Torres Strait between longitudes 141° 45′ E and 144° 00′ E, including the Endeavour Strait, and the waters of the Great Barrier Reef (GBR) between the Australian coast and the outer edge of the GBR, from the latitude of Cape York (10° 40′ S) south-eastwards to 21° 00′ S, 152° 55′ E. From this position, the REEFREP boundary extends as follows:

(a) to position 23° 42′ S, 153° 45′ E,

(b) thence to position 24° 30′ S, 153° 35′ E,

(c) thence westward on latitude 24° 30′ S to its intersection with the Queensland coastline at the low water mark, and

(d) thence generally north-westerly along the coastline to the latitude of Cape York (10° 40′ S).

2.2 The REEFREP area is shown on charts AUS 4620 (1996) and AUS 4635 (2010). A series of large-scale charts is provided for coastal navigation throughout the REEFREP area.

3 Format and content of report, times and geographical positions for submitting reports, Authority to whom reports should be sent and available services

The ship report, short title "REEFREP", will be made to the REEFREP VTS Centre (REEFCENTRE) located at Hay Point in Queensland. Examples of the format and content of all required reports are shown at appendix 2. A ship may elect, for reasons of commercial confidentiality, to communicate that section of the REEFREP ENTRY report which provides information on cargo (line P) by non-verbal means prior to entering the system. This can be achieved by including cargo information in the AUSREP Sailing Plan (SP) message.

3.1 *Entry and exit reports*

Ships will be required to provide a full REEFREP Position Report (PR) at least two hours prior to entering the REEFREP area from seaward or when sailing from a port within the area.

Ships will also be encouraged to provide a passage plan as described below when providing an Entry Report. However, it is recognized that, at this stage in their passage, they are unlikely to have a pilot on board and are therefore unable to provide a detailed passage plan.

When finally departing the REEFREP area, or entering a port within the area, the REEFREP system will associate the required PR and the designated reporting point and automatically recognize this report as an exit message.

3.2 *Passage plan reports*

Ships will be required to provide a passage plan, including information such as vessel details, pilot information, route/waypoint information, within one hour of entering the REEFREP area. The provision of accurate passage plans is critical to the dissemination of accurate ship traffic information and can be provided by one of the following means:

.1 Nominating the route using the chartlets which will be provided by pilots

.2 Nominating the waypoints, or

.3 Using the existing Mandatory Reporting Points as listed on the charts

3.3 *Intermediate position reports*

Automated Position Reporting via Inmarsat-C will be the primary mechanism for ships to provide position reports while transiting the REEFREP region. REEFCENTRE will generally carry out APR remotely without any intervention by ships' crews. However, a small proportion of vessels are fitted with first-generation Inmarsat-C terminals which do not support remote programming. Masters of ships fitted with these terminals, who choose to participate, will be required to program them onboard to send position reports automatically. Instructions relating to programming of these terminals can be obtained from REEFCENTRE.

Vessels can participate in Automated Position Reporting at any time by authorizing REEFCENTRE to download a Data Network Identifier (DNID) to the ship's Inmarsat-C terminal. Once the DNID is downloaded, REEFCENTRE is able to program the ship's Inmarsat-C terminal to transmit position reports automatically at regular intervals. Vessels can communicate authorization for DNID download either by Inmarsat-C or REEFREP VHF voice communication channels as described in appendix 2.

Vessels providing intermediate position reports via APR must still comply with the other VHF reporting requirements prescribed in section 2.4 (Entering and Leaving the REEFREP SRS), section 2.5 (Pilotage Reports) and section 2.6 (Special Reports) of the *AUSREP and REEFREP* booklet.

Where a ship is unable to provide intermediate position reports via APR as required by REEFCENTRE, they will be required to provide brief position reports as advised by the operator. The VHF position reports are limited to the identity of the vessel, position, any variation to the last reported speed and course and any further information the master considers might be of value to the system.

3.4 *Defect reports*

The following information is to be provided when a ship within the REEFREP area suffers damage, failure or breakdown affecting the safety of the ship, makes a marked deviation from a route, course or speed previously advised or requires to report safety-related information and reports of incidents involving Dangerous Goods (DG), Harmful Substances (HS) or Marine Pollutants (MP).

(a) Ship name and call sign.

(b) Position (latitude and longitude) and time.

(c) Name of next Mandatory Reporting Point or course, if not tracking between reporting points.

(d) Estimated time of arrival (ETA) at next Mandatory Reporting Point *or* speed (ship's anticipated average speed until next report, in knots & tenths of a knot).

(e) Description and details of any damage, failure or breakdown suffered:

(i) collision, grounding, fire, explosion, structural failure, flooding, cargo shifting.

(ii) failure or breakdown of steering gear, propulsion plant, electrical generating system, essential shipborne navigational aids.

(f) Details of any Safety Messages (navigational safety, abnormal weather, unserviceable aids to navigation) or DG/HS/MP incident reports using the recognized IMO reporting formats.

4 Information to be provided to participating ships and procedures to be followed

REEFCENTRE will provide information to shipping on potentially conflicting traffic movements from the analysis of incoming position reports, passage plans and other data sources.

The key information to be provided to shipping includes:

.1 Ship traffic information

.2 Navigational assistance

.3 Maritime safety information

4.1 *Ship traffic information:* The REEFREP VTS Centre will provide information to shipping on potentially conflicting traffic movements resulting from the analysis of incoming reports.

4.2 Certain sections of the route in the Torres Strait and the far northern sector of the Inner Route of the GBR present a particular navigational hazard in situations where large ships might be passing or overtaking, especially deeper draught ships. When the REEFREP VTS Centre considers that ships are approaching such sections, any relevant traffic information held by the Centre will be passed to them. Because of the extensive size of the REEFREP area it is not be intended to routinely broadcast traffic information across the whole area but to advise individual ships as necessary.

4.3 Traffic information, including other advice received from ships or local maritime authorities, which impacts on navigational safety will be passed to ships in relevant areas. Examples include concentrations of fishing vessels, unusual weather conditions, etc.

4.4 *Navigational assistance:* In circumstances where information available to REEFCENTRE may assist on-board decision-making, REEFREP may initiate interaction with an individual ship to provide this information. This may include circumstances where information available suggests a ship may be standing into shallow water (e.g. in areas of restricted navigation where there is radar coverage) or deviating from a recommended route. The types of assistance that may be provided are described further in NAV 49/INF.4.

4.5 Maritime safety information (MSI) in the form of navigational warnings (AUSCOAST Warnings) will continue to be issued in the appropriate broadcasts from MRCC AUSTRALIA. The REEFREP VTS Centre will maintain details of MSI for the REEFREP area for the information of participating ships.

5 Communication required for the system, frequencies on which reports should be transmitted and information to be reported

5.1 The system will be based on both Inmarsat-C communications and VHF voice communications. While, the use of Inmarsat-C is expected to become the main mechanism for ships to meet their position-reporting requirements and to provide other mandatory reports such as entry reports and passage plans, VHF voice communication provides an interactive mechanism for the interchange of data between ships and the REEFREP VTS Centre.

5.2 VHF channels 5, 18 and 19 in the international maritime mobile band have been allocated for the reporting points in the system.

5.3 Information of commercial confidentiality may be transmitted by non-verbal means.

5.4 The language used for reports in the system will be English, using the IMO Standard Marine Communication Phrases where necessary.

5.5 Communications associated with reporting in accordance with the requirements of this system will be free of charge

6 Rules and regulations in force in the area of the system

Compulsory pilotage rules apply in the northern section of the Inner Route (Cape York to Cairns) and in Hydrographers Passage. Other regulations apply domestic law in accordance with the terms of international conventions.

7 Shore-based facilities to support operation of the system

7.1 REEFCENTRE is located at Hay Point, on the central Queensland coast. The Centre is manned 24 hours per day, 365 days per year, and is equipped with a sophisticated traffic information management tool that integrates and assists in analysing all VHF communications, radar, AIS and APR data that is relayed to REEFCENTRE. The radar coverage is provided at the key entry and exit points to Torres Strait and the Inner Route.

7.2 The VTS Centre is equipped to provide a high standard of service to meet the system requirements and will be operated by trained and experienced personnel. Operator standards will be in accordance with "Guidelines on Recruitment, Qualification and Training of VTS Operators" (resolution A.857(20), annex 2).

7.3 The system will be operated to quality standards, with service levels being constantly monitored.

7.4 The entire area has full DGPS coverage redundancy, ensuring very high availability standards.

7.5 The REEFREP VTS Centre is also interfaced with the AUSREP system operated by RCC AUSTRALIA.

8 Alternative communication if the communication facilities of the shore-based Authority fail

In the event of failure of the system VHF communications, a report from a participating ship can be passed by any of the following methods:

.1 *Seaphone* through the commercial VHF coastal network;

.2 SATCOM; and

.3 HF radio through Townsville Radio (VIT).

9 Measures to be taken if a ship fails to comply with the requirements of the system

9.1 The primary objective of the system is to facilitate the exchange of information between the ship and the shore and so support safe navigation and the protection of the marine environment. All means will be used to encourage and promote the full participation of ships required to submit reports under SOLAS regulation V/11. If reports are not submitted and the ship can be positively identified, then information will be passed to the relevant flag State for investigation and possible prosecution in accordance with that State's legislation. A failure to report may also be investigated for breach of Australian laws relating to compulsory ship reporting.

Appendix 1

General area covered by the reporting system

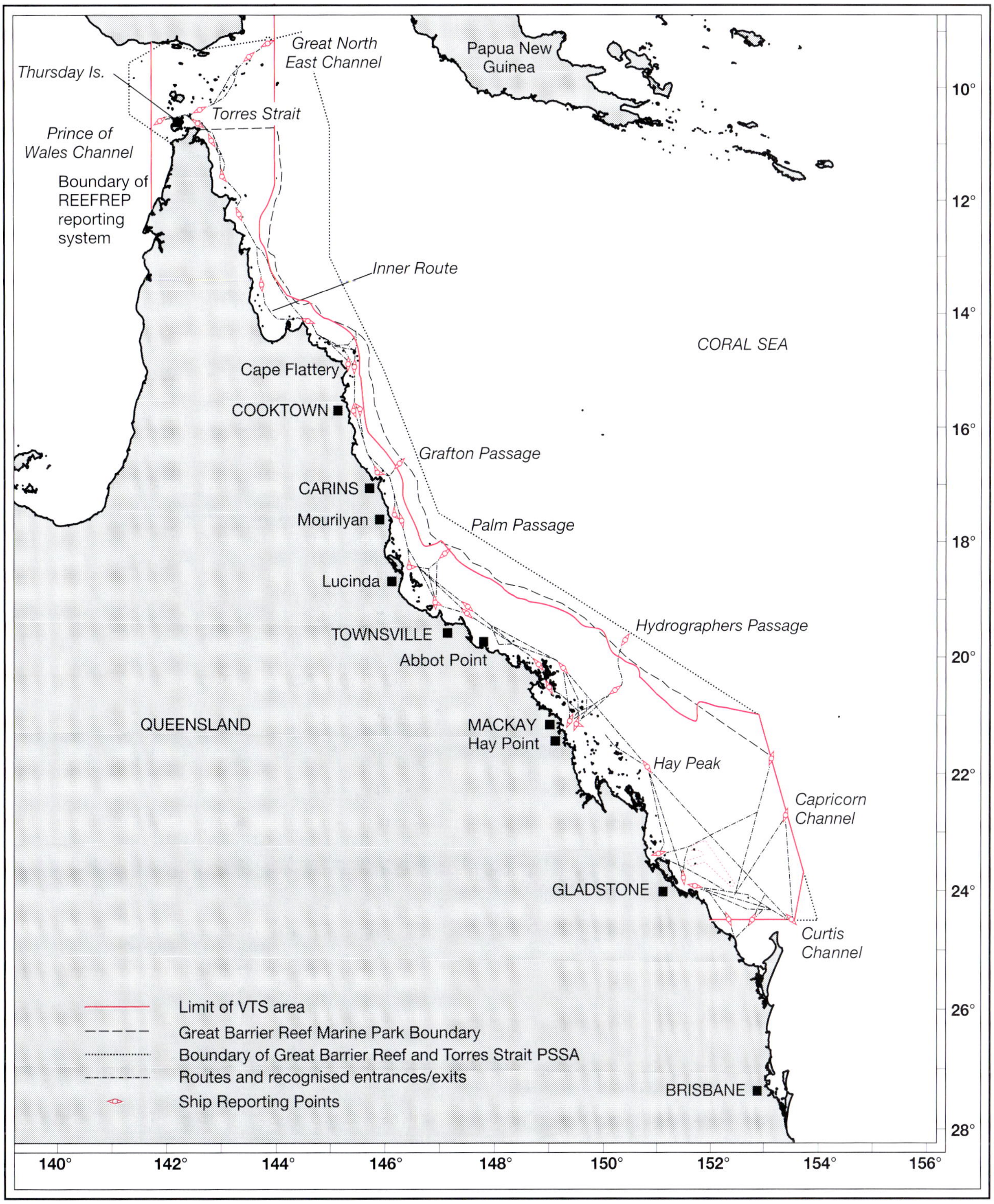

Appendix 2

Examples of reports for the REEFREP reporting system

REEFREP ENTRY (Full report)

Example 1: Ship sailing from a port within the reporting area, routeing through the area and departing the area through Grafton Passage bound for Pusan via Jomard Entrance.

Format		**Example**	
		REEFREP ENTRY	
A.	Ship's name and call sign	A.	MERIDIAN/VIPM
B.	Date/Time of position (UTC)	B.	020200Z
C.	Name of Reporting Point	C.	TOWNSVILLE
E.	Course (normally "VARIOUS")	E.	VARIOUS
F.	Speed	F.	15
G.	Departed (port, if outside reporting area)	G.	–
H.	Date/Time of entry in system and point of entry (not required if advised at C)		
J.	Pilot embarked or ordered	J.	NO*
L.	Intended route	L.	INNER ROUTE TO GRAFTON
O.	Draught	O.	10
P.	Cargo	P.	COAL
Q.	Defects/deficiencies (only if relevant)	Q.	NIL
U.	Ship type and length (metres)	U.	BULK CARRIER/250
X.	Remarks	X.	JOINING INNER ROUTE AT BREWER 020400Z

Example 2: Ship entering the reporting area northbound for Port Moresby, using Inner Route and Great North East Channel.

Format		**Example**	
		REEFREP ENTRY	
A.	Ship's name and call sign	A.	MERIDIAN/VIPM
B.	Date/Time of position (UTC)	B.	020200Z
C.	Name of Reporting Point	C.	HIGH PEAK
E.	Course (normally "VARIOUS")	E.	VARIOUS
F.	Speed	F.	15
G.	Departed (port, if outside reporting area)	G.	BRISBANE
H.	Date/Time of entry in system and point of entry (not required if advised at C)		
J.	Pilot embarked or ordered	J.	PILOT EMBARKED
L.	Intended route	L.	INNER ROUTE AND GREAT NORTH EAST CHANNEL
O.	Draught	O.	10
P.	Cargo	P.	GENERAL CARGO
Q.	Defects/deficiencies (only if relevant)		
U.	Ship type and length (metres)	U.	RESEARCH/65
X.	Remarks	X.	CONDUCTING RESEARCH ON PASSAGE

G

* Pilot not mandatory for this area of the GBR.

REEFREP REPORT

Example: Ship reporting at an intermediate reporting point within reporting area.

Format		Example
		REEFREP REPORT
A.	Ship's name and call sign	A. ENTERPRISE/VIPM
C.	Name of Reporting Point	C. CHARLOTTE
F.	Speed (if change from last report)	F. SPEED NOW 11.5
X.	Remarks	X. LARGE CONCENTRATION OF FISHING VESSELS VICINITY HANNAH ISLAND

REEFREP DEFECT

Example 1: Ship reporting defect within reporting area.

Format		Example
		REEFREP DEFECT
A.	Ship's name and call sign	A. ENTERPRISE/VIPM
B.	Date/Time of position	B. 030205Z
C.	Latitude/Longitude *or* Reporting Point	C. 1400S 14400E
Q.	Nature of defect/damage	Q. BOTH RADARS UNSERVICEABLE IN HEAVY RAIN SQUALLS; ALSO MINOR STEERING DEFECT
X.	Remarks	X. PROCEEDING TO ANCHOR 180 HANNAH ISLAND LT 1.0 TO EFFECT REPAIRS

Example 2: Ship defect repaired.

Format		Example
		REEFREP DEFECT
A.	Ship's name and call sign	A. ENTERPRISE/VIPM
B.	Date/Time of position	B. 030215Z
C.	Latitude/Longitude *or* Reporting Point	C. 1401S 14001E
F.	Speed	F. 8.5
X.	Remarks	X. DEFECT REPAIRED, REJOINING ROUTE

REEFREP EXIT

Example 1: Ship westbound reporting exit from reporting area at Torres Strait.

Format		Example
		REEFREP EXIT
A.	Ship's name and call sign	A. MITSUBISHI/XUGT
K.	Point of exit	K. COOK
I.	Destination (via route)	I. SINGAPORE VIA LOMBOK
X.	Remarks (must include "FINAL REPORT")	X. FINAL REPORT

Example 2: Ship reporting exit from reporting area at Palm Passage.

Format		Example	
		REEFREP EXIT	
A.	Ship's name and call sign	A.	IRON MAIDEN/RXTP
K.	Point of exit	K.	PALM
I.	Destination (via route)	I.	PUSAN VIA ROSSEL ISLAND
X.	Remarks (must include "FINAL REPORT")	X.	FINAL REPORT

Example 3: Ship reporting arrival at a port within reporting area (after transiting from another port also within the area).

Format		Example	
		REEFREP EXIT	
A.	Ship's name and call sign	A.	NORTHERN STAR/CPIM
K.	Point of exit	K.	CAIRNS
I.	Destination (via route) if outside REEFREP area		
X.	Remarks (must include "FINAL REPORT")	X.	ARRIVED CAIRNS, FINAL REPORT

Example 4: Ship eastbound reporting exit from reporting area at Great North East Channel.

Format		Example	
		REEFREP EXIT	
A.	Ship's name and call sign	A.	ENTERPRISE/VIPM
K.	Point of exit	K.	DARNLEY
I.	Destination (via route)	I.	PORT MORESBY DIRECT
X.	Remarks (must include "FINAL REPORT")	X.	FINAL REPORT

Appendix 3

Participating in APR via Inmarsat-C

APR information will only be used by the REEFREP system whilst the ship is in the REEFREP area. The DNID will remain downloaded until the master or company advises REEFCENTRE that the ship is no longer a regular visitor. It is important that this information is passed during the final visit to Australia, as the DNID has to be deleted whilst the Inmarsat-C terminal is logged into the particular satellite region.

A ship is deemed to be a regular visitor if it is operating on the Australian coastal trade or revisiting Australia from overseas within eighteen months. Infrequent visitors will have the DNID deleted from their terminals after sending a Final Report.

Vessels can communicate authorization for DNID download either by Inmarsat-C or REEFREP VHF voice communication channels as described below:

i Inmarsat*

By forwarding an APR message via Inmarsat to REEFCENTRE, the master authorizes download of a DNID into the Inmarsat-C terminal, and provides the following details for each Inmarsat-C installation:

- Vessel name, Call sign, Inmarsat-C Mobile Number (IMN), manufacturer, and model (example at Table 1).

ID	Message type	REEFREP/APR//
A	Ship name/Call sign	A/REEF CHAMPION/VJVJ//
B	Primary Inmarsat-C terminal details (Inmarsat-C Mobile Number (IMN), manufacturer, and model)	B/450309919/ THRANE & THRANE/3020B//
C	Secondary Inmarsat-C terminal details (Inmarsat-C Mobile Number (IMN), manufacturer, and model), where applicable.	C/450309920/ FURUNO/FELCOM12//

Table 1 – *Inmarsat-C Data Network Identifier (DNID)*

While reporting to REEFREP, masters must ensure that their INMARSAT equipment remains active in the "LOGIN" mode (Pacific Ocean Region (POR)) at all times.

ii REEFREP VHF voice communication channels

For example, at the first Reporting Point, the master (or his representative) verbally authorizes the DNID download and provides the following details for each Inmarsat-C installation:

- Inmarsat-C Mobile Number (IMN), manufacturer, and model. e.g.: 450306909, JRC, JUE75C

* APR messages sent to REEFCENTRE using Special Access Code (SAC) 861 via Perth LES using Inmarsat-C access code '222' will be reverse-charged to the SRS.

IN THE PAPAHĀNAUMOKUĀKEA MARINE NATIONAL MONUMENT PARTICULARLY SENSITIVE SEA AREA (PSSA) (CORAL SHIPREP)

A ship reporting system (CORAL SHIPREP) is established in the Papahānaumokuākea Marine National Monument Particularly Sensitive Sea Area (PSSA).

1 Categories of ships

1.1 *Ships required to participate in the system*

1.1.1 As a condition of entry to a United States port or place, all ships of 300 gross tonnage or greater, and all ships in the event of a developing emergency, and that are in transit through the reporting area are required to participate in CORAL SHIPREP, except for sovereign immune vessels which are exempt under SOLAS chapter V, regulation 1.

1.2 *Ships recommended to participate in the system*

1.2.1 All ships of 300 gross tonnage or greater, fishing vessels, and all ships in the event of a developing emergency, and that are in transit through the reporting area, are recommended to participate in CORAL SHIPREP.

2 Geographical coverage of the system and the numbers and edition of the reference charts used for the delineation of the system

2.1 The geographical coverage of CORAL SHIPREP is depicted by the geographical positions in the appendix.

2.2 The reference charts that include the ship reporting area are United States 19016 (2007 edition), 19019 (2007 edition), and 19022 (2007 edition). These charts are based on World Geodetic System 1984 datum (WGS 84) and astronomic datum.

3 Format, content of reports, times and geographical positions for submitting reports, Authorities to whom reports should* be sent, available services

3.1 *Format*

3.1.1 The ship report should be drafted in accordance with the format shown in paragraph 2 of the appendix to resolution A.851(20).

3.2 *Content*

3.2.1 The report for a ship entering the system should contain the following information:

System identifier: CORAL SHIPREP

A	Name of the ship, call sign, or IMO identification number
B	Date and time (UTC)
C *or* D	Position
E *and* F	Course and speed of ship
I	Destination
L	Intended route through the reporting area
O	Vessel draught
P	General categories of hazardous cargo on board
Q *or* R	Defects or deficiencies, if relevant
T	Contact information of ship's agent or owner

* For those ships that are required to report, the use of the word "should" in this text is to be read as "shall".

G

U	Ship size and type (e.g., length, tonnage, and type)
W	Total number of persons on board

3.2.2 The report for a ship leaving the system should contain the following information:

System identifier: CORAL SHIPREP

A	Name of the ship, call sign, or IMO identification number
B	Date and time (UTC)
C *or* D	Position

3.2.3 A ship may elect, for reasons of commercial confidentiality, to communicate that section of the report which provides information on general categories of hazardous cargo by non-verbal means prior to entering the reporting area.

3.3 *Geographical positions for submitting reports*

3.3.1 Each ship should submit a full report in accordance with paragraph 3.2.1 as soon as it crosses the boundary to enter the ship reporting system.

3.3.2 Each ship should submit a report in accordance with paragraph 3.2.2 as soon as it crosses the boundary to leave the ship reporting system.

3.3.3 Further reports should be made whenever there is a change in navigation status or circumstances, particularly in relation to item Q of the reporting format.

3.4 *Authority to whom reports should be sent*

3.4.1 The shore-based Authority is the United States Coast Guard's Communications Area Master Station Pacific (CAMSPAC). For ships of 300 gross tonnage and greater, an e-mail address to be used for reporting through Inmarsat-C will be provided in advance of implementation of this system through Notices to Mariners. In the event of a developing emergency, ships are urged to call the United States Coast Guard 14th District. Vessels unable to report in through Inmarsat-C should report to nwhi.notifications@noaa-gov.

4 Information to be provided to ship and procedures to be followed

4.1 The CORAL SHIPREP shore-based Authority will provide critical alerts and information to shipping about specific and urgent situations and other information that may affect safety of navigation within the IMO-adopted areas to be avoided and the Papahānaumokuākea Marine National Monument Particularly Sensitive Sea Area, as well as remind ships about the existence of the IMO-adopted areas to be avoided and necessity of navigating with extreme caution through the Particularly Sensitive Sea Area.

4.2 Navigational warnings and emergency broadcasts will be issued as NAVTEX messages or specifically directed at GMDSS-equipped vessels using Inmarsat-C.

5 Radio communication required for the system and frequencies on which reports should be transmitted

5.1 This system will be based on Inmarsat-C and an e-mail, and ships equipped with such capabilities should report through Inmarsat-C.

5.2 In the event of a developing emergency, a ship is urged to call the United States Coast Guard 14th District at 001-808-541-2500 to request a response and assistance.

5.3 For vessels unable to communicate through Inmarsat-C, reports should be made prior to, during, or after transiting through the reporting area to nwhi.notifications@noaa-gov.

5.4 Commercially sensitive information will be kept confidential and should be transmitted prior to entry into the reporting system. Such information may be sent to nwhi.notifications@noaa-gov.

5.5 The language used for reports to the system should be English, employing the IMO Standard Marine Communication Phrases, where necessary.

5.6 Communications associated with CORAL SHIPREP are, in accordance with SOLAS chapter V, regulation 11, free of charge to affected vessels.

6 Relevant rules and regulations in force in the area of the system

6.1 *International actions*

6.1.1 The United States has taken appropriate action to implement the international conventions to which it is party.

6.1.2 In recognition of the fragile environment in this area and potential hazards to navigation, the IMO has adopted several areas to be avoided to protect the North-Western Hawaiian Islands and has designated the area as a Particularly Sensitive Sea Areas where mariners should navigate with extreme caution.

6.1.3 The United States applies its laws in accordance with international law, which includes navigational rights under customary international law as reflected in the United Nations Convention on the Law of the Sea. No restrictions shall apply to or be enforced against foreign-flagged vessels unless in accordance with such law.

6.2 *Domestic actions*

6.2.1 The United States has taken considerable action to ensure maritime safety and to protect the fragile environment and cultural resources and areas of cultural importance significant to Native Hawaiians in the North-Western Hawaiian Islands. This area has been the subject of a variety of protective measures, including designation of this area as the North-Western Hawaiian Islands Marine National Monument (subsequently renamed the Papahānaumokuākea Marine National Monument) in recognition of its fragility and to protect the many species of coral, fish, birds, marine mammals, and other flora and fauna, as well as to protect historical and archaeological heritage resources, including cultural resources and areas of significant importance to Native Hawaiians.

6.2.2 Regulations in this area, *inter alia*, prohibit taking, possessing, injuring, or disturbing any resource; altering the seabed; anchoring or deserting a vessel; and possessing fishing gear unless stowed. All of these activities may be allowed by permit; however, permits cannot be issued for such things as releasing an introduced species. Activities such as discharging or depositing any material into the Monument, or discharging or depositing any material outside the Monument that subsequently injures Monument resources, except discharges incidental to vessel use, such as approved marine sanitation device effluent, cooling water, and engine exhaust, are also prohibited. The United States strictly regulates entry into the Monument and, for those vessels subject to United States jurisdiction, requires the mandatory use of vessel monitoring systems on those vessels that may be allowed into the Monument for specific purposes.

7 Shore-based facilities to support operation of the system

7.1 The shore-based Authority is the United States Coast Guard's Communications Area Master Station Pacific (CAMSPAC). CAMSPAC provides maritime distress communication services and safety and weather broadcasts to commercial and recreational mariners, and also provides secure voice communications and record message delivery services for all United States Coast Guard cutters, aircraft, and shore units. Additionally, CAMSPAC is one of the United States Coast Guard's Pacific Area's (PACAREA) Continuity of Operations sites. CAMSPAC delivers contingency and inter-agency communication services for Incident Commanders by deploying a state-of-the-art transportable communications centre. CAMSPAC is the Operational Commander of the United States Coast Guard's Pacific Area Communications System, consisting of communication stations in Honolulu Hawaii, Kodiak Alaska, and remote facilities in Guam. There are approximately 150 people assigned to CAMSPAC.

7.2 CORAL SHIPREP will use Inmarsat-C communications equipment. A computer server handles and sorts incoming reports and sends the return message. Incoming reports are text messages that arrive via either internet e-mail or telex. When the ship reporting system server receives a report, the server sends the ship a specific return message. Area co-ordinators will monitor and update the information to the server for inclusion in the outgoing message.

8 Alternative communication if the shore-based facilities fail

8.1 NAVTEX Broadcast Notice to Mariners may be used to notify mariners of the temporary failure of the system and can provide mariners with basic information necessary to navigate safely through this area.

8.2 For those ships reporting through Inmarsat-C, the standard protocol now used for such systems will be used to re-route incoming and outgoing communications through an alternative address and it is expected that this will minimize the system's downtime, though a short delay may occur.

9 Measures to be taken if a ship does not report

9.1 All means will be used to encourage and promote the full participation of the ships recommended to submit reports.

9.2 If reports are not submitted by those ships required to report and the ship can be positively identified, appropriate action will be taken – including interaction with the flag State – in accordance with customary international law as reflected in the 1982 United Nations Convention on the Law of the Sea.

Appendix

Geographical co-ordinates

Ship reporting system

(Reference charts: United States 19016, 2007 edition; 19019, 2007 edition; 19022, 2007 edition. These charts are based on World Geodetic System 1984 datum (WGS 84) and astronomic datum.)

1 Outer boundary

The outer boundary of the "CORAL SHIPREP" reporting area consists of lines connecting the following geographical positions:

Starting at	(1)	29°24′.21 N, 178°06′.45 W
a rhumb line to	(2)	29°12′.16 N, 177°04′.25 W
then a rhumb line to	(3)	28°43′.78 N, 175°13′.76 W
then a rhumb line to	(4)	27°00′.28 N, 173°25′.37 W
then a rhumb line to	(5)	26°44′.85 N, 171°28′.22 W
then a rhumb line to	(6)	26°23′.95 N, 170°20′.25 W
then a rhumb line to	(7)	25°56′.49 N, 167°32′.03 W
then a rhumb line to	(8)	24°50′.23 N, 165°58′.56 W
then a rhumb line to	(9)	24°02′.61 N, 161°42′.30 W
then an arc with a 60.25 NM radius centred at	(21)	23°03′.61 N, 161°55′.22 W
to a point	(10)	22°04′.59 N, 162°08′.14 W
then a rhumb line to	(11)	22°35′.32 N, 164°53′.46 W
then a rhumb line to	(12)	22°47′.86 N, 166°40′.44 W
then a rhumb line to	(13)	24°03′.30 N, 168°27′.53 W
then a rhumb line to	(14)	24°26′.59 N, 170°50′.37 W
then a rhumb line to	(15)	24°46′.49 N, 171°52′.87 W
then a rhumb line to	(16)	25°07′.23 N, 174°30′.23 W
then a rhumb line to	(17)	27°05′.50 N, 176°35′.40 W
then a rhumb line to	(18)	27°15′.11 N, 177°35′.26 W
then a rhumb line to	(19)	27°26′.10 N, 178°32′.23 W
then an arc with a 60.17 NM radius centred at	(20)	28°25′.23 N, 178°19′.51 W
then to point	(1)	29°24′.21 N, 178°06′.45 W

2 Inner boundary

The inner boundaries of the "CORAL SHIPREP" reporting area are coterminous with the outer boundaries of the IMO-adopted areas to be avoided "In the Region of the Papahānaumokuākea Marine National Monument", which consist of the following:

1 Those areas contained within circles of radius 50 nautical miles centred upon the following geographical positions:

(a) 28°25′.18 N, 178°19′.75 W (Kure Atoll)

(b) 28°14′.20 N, 177°22′.10 W (Midway Atoll)

(c) 27°50′.62 N, 175°50′.53 W (Pearl and Hermes Atoll)

(d) 26°03′.82 N, 173°58′.00 W (Lisianski Island)

(e) 25°46′.18 N, 171°43′.95 W (Laysan Island)

(f) 25°25′.45 N, 170°35′.32 W (Maro Reef)

(g) 25°19′.50 N, 170°00′.88 W (between Maro Reef and Raita Bank)

(h) 25°00′.00 N, 167°59′.92 W (Gardner Pinnacles)

(i) 23°45′.52 N, 166°14′.62 W (French Frigate Shoals)

(j) 23°34′.60 N, 164°42′.02 W (Necker Island)

(k) 23°03′.38 N, 161°55′.32 W (Nihoa Island)

2 Those areas contained between the following geographical co-ordinates:

		Begin co-ordinates	End co-ordinates
Area 1	Lisianski Island (N) → Laysan Island	26°53′.22 N, 173°49′.64 W	26°35′.58 N, 171°35′.60 W
	Lisianski Island (S) → Laysan Island	25°14′.42 N, 174°06′.36 W	24°57′.63 N, 171°57′.07 W
Area 2	Gardner Pinnacles (N) → French Frigate Shoals	25°38′.90 N, 167°25′.31 W	24°24′.80 N, 165°40′.89 W
	Gardner Pinnacles (S) → French Frigate Shoals	24°14′.27 N, 168°22′.13 W	23°05′.84 N, 166°47′.81 W

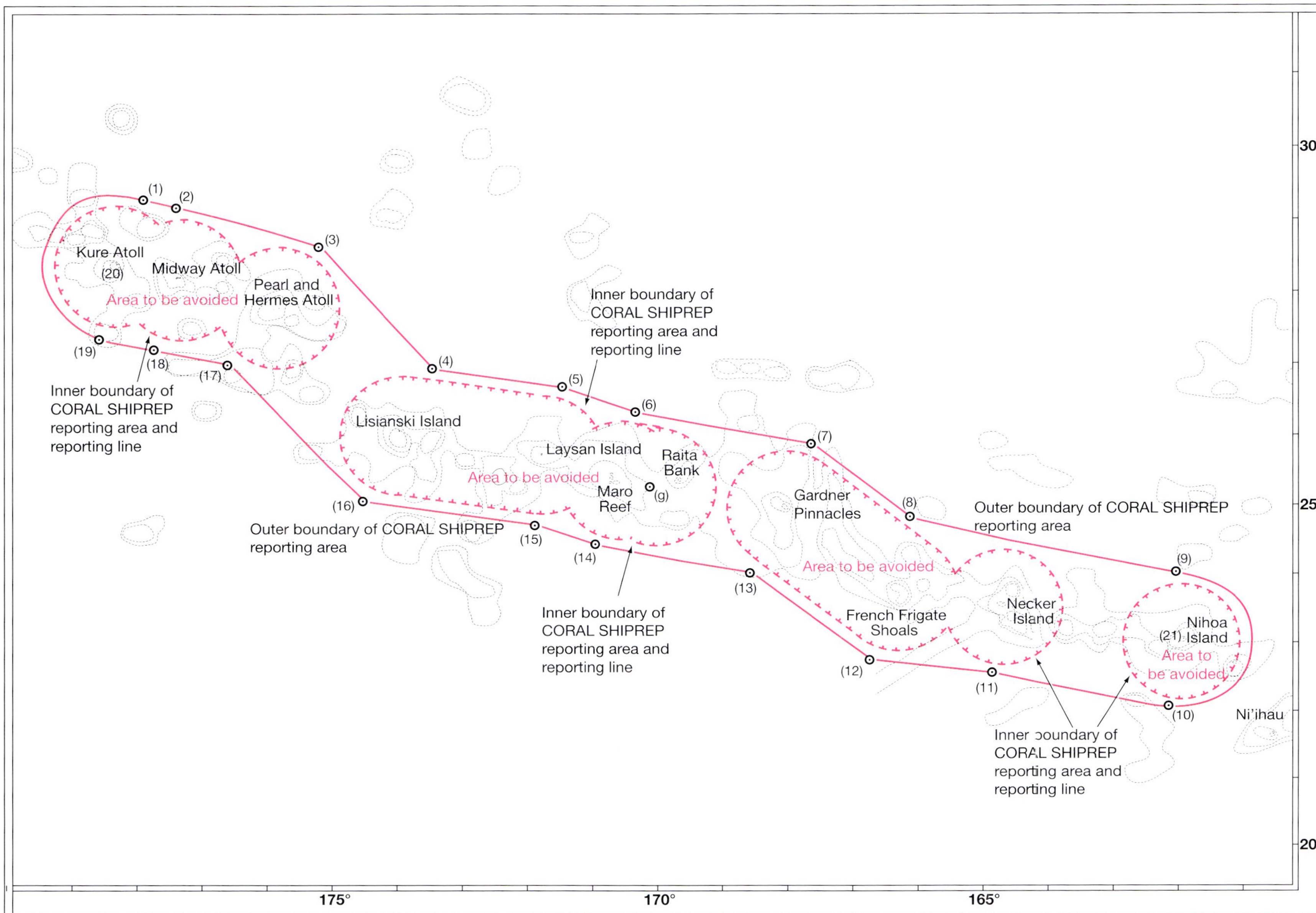

PAPAHĀNAUMOKUĀKEA MARINE NATIONAL MONUMENT PARTICULARLY SENSITIVE SEA AREA

IN THE GALAPAGOS PARTICULARLY SENSITIVE SEA AREA (PSSA) (GALREP)

1 Categories of ships required to participate in the system

All ships are required to participate in the mandatory ship reporting system.

2 Geographical coverage of the system and the number and edition of the reference chart used for delineation of the system

2.1 The operational area of GALREP covers the Galapagos area to be avoided and the Particularly Sensitive Sea Area as shown on the chartlet given in appendix 1.

2.1.1 The co-ordinates of the mandatory ship reporting system are as follows:

Point	Latitude	Longitude
A	02°30′ N	092°21′ W
D1	01°26′ N	089°03′ W
E1	00°01′ S	088°06′ W
F1	00°12′ S	088°01′ W
G1	00°35′ S	087°54′ W
H1	01°02′ S	087°53′ W
I1	02°34′ S	088°48′ W
J1	02°46′ S	089°30′ W
K1	02°42′ S	090°42′ W
L1	02°05′ S	092°18′ W
M1	01°32′ S	092°44′ W
L	01°49′ N	092°40′ W

2.2 The reference chart is I.O.A. 20 (2nd edition 1992, updated and reprinted in 2006), issued by the Ecuadorean Navy Oceanography Institute (INOCAR), based on WGS 84 datum.

3 Format and content of report, times and geographical positions for submitting reports, Authority to whom reports should be sent and available services

3.1 Reports may be sent by any modern means of communication, including Inmarsat-C, telephone, fax and e-mail, and other available means as described in appendix 2.

3.2 *Format*

3.2.1 The ship report shall be drafted in accordance with the format shown in appendix 3. The information requested from ships is derived from the Standard Reporting Format shown in paragraph 2 of the appendix to IMO resolution A.851(20).

3.3 *Content*

3.3.1 A full report from a ship should contain the following information:

A: Ship identification (name, call sign, IMO Number, MMSI number or registration number)

B: Date/time group

C: Position

E: True course

F: Speed

G: Name of last port of call

I: Destination and expected time of arrival

P: Type(s) of oil cargo, and quantity, quality and density. If these tankers are also carrying other hazardous material, the type, quantity and IMO classification should be stated, as appropriate.

Q: Used in the event of defects or deficiencies which affect normal navigation

T: Address for communication of information concerning cargo

W: Number of persons on board

X: Miscellaneous information concerning ships:

– estimated quantity and characteristics of liquid fuel

– navigational status (e.g., moving under own propulsion, limited manoeuvrability, etc.)

3.3.2 Every reporting message must begin with the word GALREP and include a two-letter prefix to enable identification, i.e., sailing plan "SP", final report "FR" or deviation report "DR". Messages using these prefixes will be cost-free to ships.

3.3.3 The reports must be written in accordance with the following table:

.1 Designators A, B, C, E, F, G, I, P, T, W and X are compulsory for sailing plans;

.2 Designators A, B, C, E and F must be used for final reports;

.3 Designators A, B, C, E, F and I must be used for deviation reports; and

.4 Designator Q is included whenever a problem arises in the reporting area, whether defects, damage, deficiencies or circumstances that affect normal navigation in the reporting area.

3.4 *Geographical positions for submitting reports*

3.4.1 A ship must give a full report at the following positions:

.1 on entering the reporting area;

.2 immediately after leaving a port or anchorage located in the Galapagos PSSA (the co-ordinates of which are at appendix 4);

.3 when deviating from the route leading to the port of destination or anchorage reported originally;

.4 when it is necessary to deviate from the planned route owing to weather conditions, damaged equipment or a change in navigational status; and

.5 on finally leaving the reporting area.

3.5 *Authority*

3.5.1 On entering the GALREP mandatory reporting area, ships must send a message to notify the Santa Cruz Maritime Rescue Sub-Centre via Puerto Ayora Radio or Baquerizo Moreno Radio. The Maritime Rescue Sub-Centres and coastal radio stations to which reports must be sent are shown in appendix 2.

3.5.2 If a ship is not able to send a message to Puerto Ayora Radio, it must send one to Baquerizo Moreno Radio, in accordance with the information given in appendix 2.

4 Information to be provided to ships and procedures to be followed

4.1 Ships are required to keep a continuous listening watch in the area.

4.2 The Puerto Ayora Maritime Rescue Sub-Centre will provide ships with the information necessary for safe navigation in the reporting area as required, using the radio transmission resources available in the area.

4.3 If necessary, a specific ship may be informed individually about particular local weather conditions.

5 Communication required for the system, frequencies on which reports should be transmitted and information reported

5.1 Radiocommunications required for the system is as follows:

The reports can be made by any modern means of communication, including Inmarsat-C, telephone, fax, and e-mail, and other available means as described in appendix 2.

5.2 Information of commercial confidential nature may be transmitted by non-verbal means.

5.3 The languages of communication used in this system are Spanish or English, using IMO Standard Marine Communication Phrases, where necessary.

6 Rules and regulations in force in the area of the system

6.1 *Vessel Traffic Services (VTS)*

Vessel traffic services are available at Puerto Ayora through Puerto Ayora Radio, which provides information for shipping in the Galapagos Particularly Sensitive Sea Area.

6.2 *SAR Plan*

6.2.1 The national maritime SAR plan establishes the Coast Guard Command as the Maritime Rescue Co-ordination Centre and DIGMER as the SAR co-ordination centre, with its headquarters under the supervision of the Director General for the Merchant Marine. The Galapagos PSSA comes under the jurisdiction of the Galapagos Archipelago administrative area, at the SAR co-ordination sub-centre for the island region, which is responsible for deploying Coast Guard units operating in that area.

6.2.2 The National Maritime Authority is responsible for prevention and control of pollution produced by oil and other harmful substances in Ecuador's waters and along its coasts. Given the extent of the damage that can be caused by oil spills, there is a national contingency plan to deal with them, whether at sea or along the coasts or rivers. The plan covers the mainland waters, the Galapagos island waters and the rivers of the western region. With regards to planning, implementation and control, geographical areas have been established corresponding to the maritime section of the island region, which includes the Galapagos PSSA, under the responsibility of the island naval operations command in co-ordination with the harbour masters' offices at Puerto Ayora, Puerto Baquerizo Moreno, Puerto Villamil and Seymour, and supported by the fleet air arm, the coast guard and the Galapagos National Park.

7 Shore-based facilities to support the operation of the system

7.1 *System capability*

7.1.1 The VTS, Maritime Rescue Sub-Centres, and coastal radio stations are shown in appendix 2; all have skilled personnel constantly on duty.

7.1.2 The accepted means of radiocommunication that are available are listed in appendix 2.

8 Information concerning the applicable procedures if the communication facilities of shore-based Authority fail

If a ship is not able to send a message to Puerto Ayora Radio, it must send one to Baquerizo Moreno Radio, in accordance with the information given in appendix 2.

9 Measures to be taken if a ship fails to comply with the requirements of the system

If a ship in breach of the mandatory ship reporting system can be identified, any enforcement actions taken shall not be incompatible with international law.

Appendix 1

Chart of area covered by the mandatory ship reporting system

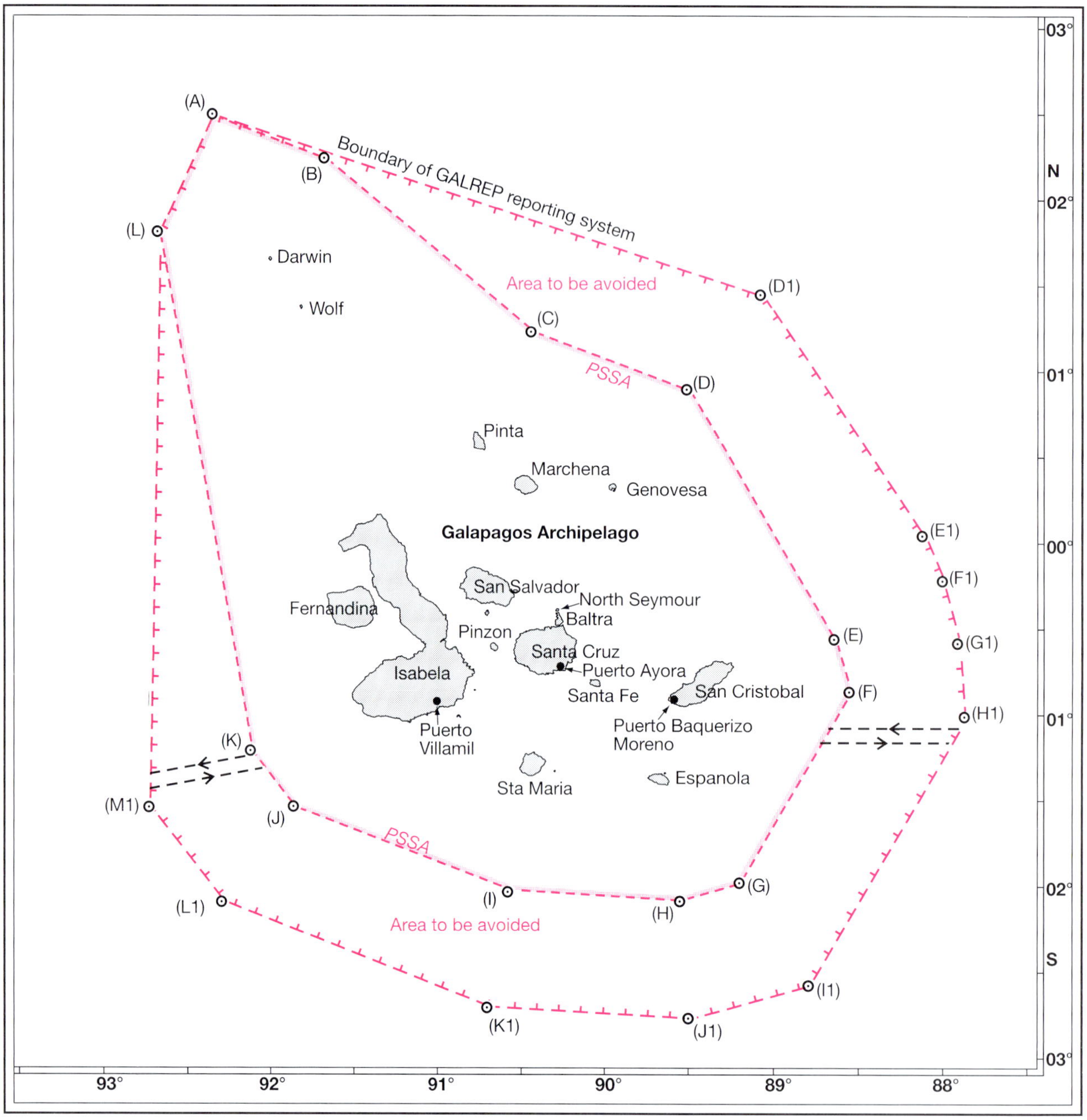

Appendix 2

Vessel traffic services, maritime rescue sub-centres, coastal radio stations and other establishments to which reports must be sent

ECUADOR – GALAPAGOS ISLANDS

SANTA CRUZ: PUERTO AYORA RADIO
Name: HCY
Geographical co-ordinates: 00°44′.59 S, 090°28′.29 W
MRSC – SAR Puerto Ayora: 00°44′.59 S, 090°28′.29 W
Tel.: +593 5 2527473
Fax: +593 5 2527473
E-mail: ayoraradio@islasantacruz.com

Inmarsat-C: 473575713

Inmarsat Mini-M:
Voice: 761609548
Fax: 761609549
Data: 761609550

VHF channels:

156.800 MHz	H-24	SIMPLEX	C-16
156.525 MHz	H-24	SIMPLEX	C-70

MF channels:

4125.0 kHz	H-24	SIMPLEX	C-421
2182.0 kHz	H-24	SIMPLEX	
2187.5 kHz	H-24	DSC SIMPLEX	

MMSI: 007354757.

PUERTO BAQUERIZO MORENO: BAQUERIZO MORENO RADIO

Name: HCW
Geographical co-ordinates: 00°54′ S, 089°37′ W
MRSC – SAR Puerto Baquerizo Moreno: 00°54′ S, 089°37′ W
Tel.: +593 5 2520346
Fax: +593 5 2520346
E-mail: capbaq@digmer.org

VHF channels:

156.800 MHz	H-24	SIMPLEX	C-16
156.525 MHz	H-24	SIMPLEX	C-70

MF channels:

4125.0 kHz	H-24	SIMPLEX	C-421
2182.0 kHz	H-24	SIMPLEX	
2187.5 kHz	H-24	DSC SIMPLEX	

MMSI: 007350090

Appendix 3

Designator	Function	Text
System name	Code word	GALREP
	Type of report: Sailing plan Final report Deviation report	One of the following 2-letter identifiers: SP FR (on *finally* leaving reporting area) to include only **A**, **B**, **C**, **E** and **F**. DR to include only **A**, **B**, **C**, **E**, **F** and **I**.
A	Ship	Name and call sign (Name of ship, call sign, IMO No. and MMSI No.) (e.g., TAURUS/HC4019/T-04-0561)
B	Date and time corresponding to position at C, expressed as UTC	A six-digit group followed by a Z. The first two digits indicate day of the month, the second two the hours and the last two the minutes. The Z indicates that the time is given in UTC (e.g., 081340Z).
C	Position (latitude and longitude)	A 4-digit group giving latitude in degrees and minutes, with the suffix N or S, and a 5-digit group giving longitude in degrees and minutes, with the suffix W (e.g., 0030S 08805W)
E	Course	True course. A 3-digit group (e.g., 270).
F	Speed	Speed in knots. A 2-digit group (e.g., 14).
G	Name of last port of call	Name of the last port of call (e.g., Guayaquil)
I	Destination and ETA (UTC)	Name of destination and date and time group as expressed in B (e.g., Puerto Ayora 082200Z)
P	Cargo	Type(s) of oil cargo, quantity, quality and density of heavy crude, heavy fuel, asphalt and coal tar. If the ships are carrying other potentially hazardous cargoes, indicate type, quantity and IMO classification (e.g., 10,000 TN DIESEL OIL).
Q	Defects, damage, deficiencies, limitations.	Brief details of defects, including damage, deficiencies and other circumstances that impair normal navigation
T	Address for the communication of cargo information	Name, telephone number, and either fax or e-mail
W	Total number of people on board	State how many
X	Miscellaneous	Miscellaneous information concerning these ships: – Characteristics and approximate quantity of bunker fuel for tankers carrying an amount of it greater than 5000 tonnes. – Navigational status (e.g., at anchor, moving under own propulsion, no steering, limited manoeuvrability, depth restriction, moored, aground, etc.)

Appendix 4

Particularly Sensitive Sea Area (PSSA)

Point	Latitude	Longitude
A	02°30′ N	092°21′ W
B	02°14′ N	091°40′ W
C	01°14′ N	090°26′ W
D	00°53′ N	089°30′ W
E	00°35′ S	088°38′ W
F	00°52′ S	088°34′ W
G	01°59′ S	089°13′ W
H	02°05′ S	089°34′ W
I	02°01′ S	090°35′ W
J	01°32′ S	091°52′ W
K	01°13′ S	092°07′ W
L	01°49′ N	092°40′ W

MANDATORY SHIP REPORTING SYSTEMS IN GREENLAND WATERS (GREENPOS AND COASTAL CONTROL)

Two systems are established, one – named GREENPOS – for ships on voyage to and from Greenland ports and places of call and one – named COASTAL CONTROL (KYSTKONTROL) – for ships in coastal trade between Greenland ports and Greenland places of call.

1 Categories of ships required to participate in the systems

1.1 Ships required to participate in the reporting system GREENPOS:
All ships, on voyage to or from Greenland ports and places of call.

1.2 Ships required to participate in the reporting system COASTAL CONTROL:
All ships of 20 gross tonnage and more, and fishing vessels, on voyage between Greenland ports and places of call.

2 Geographical coverage of the system and the number and edition of the reference chart used for the delineation of the system

2.1 The reporting system GREENPOS covers the area within the Continental Shelf or Exclusive Economic Zone off the coast of Greenland.

2.2 The reference charts are Danish charts Nos. 1000 (datum Qornoq 1927), 2000 and 3000 (datum unknown).

3 Format, content of reports, times and geographical positions for submitting reports, Authority to whom reports should be sent and available services

3.1 *Format*

3.1.1 The GREENPOS reports shall be sent to Island Commander Greenland/MRCC Groennedal and shall be drafted in accordance with the format shown in appendix 1.

3.1.2 The COASTAL CONTROL reports shall be sent to the relevant coast radio station and shall be drafted in accordance with the format shown in appendix 2.

3.1.3 The information requested from ships is derived from the Standard Reporting Format shown in resolution A.851(20).

3.2 *Content*

3.2.1 The report required from a ship participating in the two reporting systems contains only information which is essential to achieve the objectives of the systems, i.e.:

.1 the ship's name, call sign and position are needed for establishing the identity of the ship and its initial position (letters A, B, C *or* D);

.2 the ship's course and speed, destination, intended voyage and information about deficiencies and weather and ice conditions are important in order to maintain track of the ship so as to be able to implement search and rescue measures if a report from a ship fails to appear and to be able to service the safe navigation of the ship in the areas where weather and ice conditions can be extremely severe (letters E, F, I, L, Q and S);

.3 the number of persons on board and other relevant information are important in relation to the allocation of resources in a search and rescue operation (letter X).

3.3 *Position for submitting reports*

3.3.1 In the GREENPOS system, cf. the provisions of appendix 1, ships shall submit their reports when within the Continental Shelf or Exclusive Economic Zone off the coast of Greenland.

3.3.2 In the COASTAL CONTROL system, cf. the provisions of appendix 2, ships shall submit their reports when on voyage between Greenland ports and places of call.

3.3.3 Ships coming from an Atlantic voyage may remain in the GREENPOS system while on voyage between Greenland ports and Greenland places of call, when agreed upon by Island Commander Greenland.

3.4 *Authority*

3.4.1 Island Commander Greenland/MRCC Groennedal is the responsible Authority for the radio reporting systems and for initiating and carrying out maritime search and rescue operations in Greenland waters outside local areas. In local areas the police is the responsible Authority.

3.5 *Services offered*

3.5.1 If a report from a ship participating in the GREENPOS system fails to appear, and it is not possible to establish communication with the ship, or an emergency is reported, MRCC Groennedal is responsible for initiating a search for the ship in accordance with the rules laid down for the search and rescue service, including the involvement of other participating ships known to be in that particular area.

3.5.2 If a report fails to appear from a ship participating in the COASTAL CONTROL system, and it is not possible for the coast radio station to establish communication with the ship, or an emergency is reported, the police of the port of destination shall be informed. It is then the responsibility of the police to initiate a search in accordance with the rules laid down for the search and rescue service, including the involvement of other participating ships known to be in that particular area.

4 Information to be provided to the participating ship and procedures to be followed

4.1 Ships will be provided with information of importance for the safety of navigation in East Greenland waters from the NAVTEX transmitter Reykjavik and in West Greenland ports and places of call from the NAVTEX transmitter on Kook Islands (Igdlutaligssuaq/Telegraføen) at Nuuk/Godthåb.

4.2 If necessary, individual information can be provided to a ship, particularly in relation to special local conditions.

5 Communication required for the system, frequencies on which reports should be transmitted and information to be reported

GREENPOS

5.1 For ships entering and navigating in the reporting area, reports shall be addressed to Island Commander Greenland (GLK) via Naval Radio Station Groennedal (OVC), which can be contacted via all modern communication forms including Inmarsat-C, telefax and e-mail. Island Commander Greenland (GLK) is responsible for monitoring the voyage from the time of receiving the first Sailing Plan (SP) until the time of receiving the Final Report (FR).

5.2 The reports required from a ship entering and navigating in the reporting area shall begin with the word GREENPOS and shall contain a two-letter abbreviation for identification of the report (Sailing Plan, Position Report, Final Report or Deviation Report). Telegrams so prefixed are dispatched free of charge and as carrying the priority URGENT.

Dependent on the type of report, the following information shall be included as mentioned under paragraph 4 in appendix 1:

System identifier: GREENPOS

A	Ship's name and call sign;
B	Date Time Group (UTC);
C *or* D	Position;
E	True course;
F	Speed;
I	Destination and ETA (UTC);
L	Intended voyage;

G

Q	Defects and deficiencies;
S	Weather and ice conditions; and
X	Total number of persons on board and other relevant information.

COASTAL CONTROL

5.3 For each voyage between Greenland ports and places of call, reports shall be addressed to the coast radio station which is situated in the same control area as the contemplated destination (Aasiaat radio, Qaqortoq radio or Ammassalik radio), cf. appendix A. The coast radio stations can be contacted via all modern communication forms including Inmarsat-C, telefax and e-mail. The coast radio station is responsible for monitoring the voyage from the time of receiving the Sailing Plan (SP) until the time of receiving the subsequent Final Report (FR).

5.4 The reports required from a ship entering and navigating in the reporting area shall begin with the words COASTAL CONTROL and shall contain a two-letter abbreviation for identification of the report (Sailing Plan, Position Report, Final Report or Deviation Report). Telegrams so prefixed are dispatched free of charge and as carrying the priority URGENT.

Dependent on the type of report, the following information shall be included as mentioned under paragraph 4 in appendix 2:

System identifier: COASTAL CONTROL

A	Ship's name and call sign;
B	Date Time Group (LT);
C *or* D	Position;
E	True course;
F	Speed;
I	Destination and ETA (LT);
L	Intended voyage;
Q	Defects and deficiencies;
X	Total number of persons on board and other relevant information.

6 Relevant rules and regulations in force in the area of the proposed system

6.1 *International Regulations for Preventing Collisions at Sea*

The International Regulations for Preventing Collisions at Sea, 1972, as amended are applicable in Greenland waters.

7 Shore-based facilities to support operation of the system

7.1 Island Commander Greenland is the shore-based Authority which, on the basis of GREENPOS reports, is in possession of position, route, etc. for each ship on voyage to or from Greenland. The coast radio stations are, via COASTAL CONTROL reports, kept informed about all ships on voyage between Greenland ports or places of call.

7.2 Furthermore, information about ships and their characteristics can be obtained from the AMVER system operated by the United States Coast Guard.

7.3 The coast radio stations and Naval Radio Station Groennedal, which form part of the coast radio service, will at all times be manned.

8 Information concerning the applicable procedures if the communication facilities of the shore-based Authority fail

8.1 The coast radio service is designed with sufficient system redundancy to cope with normal equipment failure.

9 Measures to be taken if a ship fails to comply with the requirements of the system

9.1 The objective of the system is to enable Island Commander Greenland/MRCC Groennedal to initiate SAR measures as fast and effective as possible, if an emergency is reported or a report from a ship fails to appear, and it is impossible to establish communication with the ship. All means will be used to obtain the full participation of ships required to submit reports. If reports are not submitted and the offending ship can be positively identified, then information will be passed on to the relevant Flag State Authorities for investigation and possible prosecution in accordance with national legislation.

Appendix 1

Greenland Ship Reporting System (GREENPOS)

Rules for drafting of reports

1 Ships on voyage to and from Greenland ports and places of call shall send reports when within the Continental Shelf or Exclusive Economic Zone off the coast of Greenland. The reports shall be sent four times a day, between 0000–0030, 0600–0630, 1200–1230, and 1800–1830 UTC.

2 The reports shall be sent directly to Island Commander Greenland (GLK) via Naval Radio Station Groennedal (OVC), which maintains a continuous listening watch on 2182 kHz, or via a coast radio station. Naval Radio Station Groennedal (OVC) and coast radio stations can be contacted via all modern communication forms, including Inmarsat-C, telefax and e-mail.

3 Each report shall begin with the word GREENPOS and a two-letter abbreviation for identification of the report. Telegrams so prefixed are dispatched free of charge and as carrying the priority URGENT.

4 The reports shall be drawn up in accordance with the following diagram. Designators, which are not mandatory, can be included if necessary.

Designator	Mandatory for type of report	Information	Text
	All	Code word	"GREENPOS"
	All	*Type of report:* Sailing Plan Position Report Final Report Deviation Report	One of the following 2-letter identifiers: "SP" (Sailing Plan) "PR" (Position Report) "FR" (Final Report) "DR" (Deviation Report).
A	All	Ship	Name and call sign. (E.g.: AGNETHE NIELSEN/OULH)
B	All	Date Time Group corresponding to the position under designator C or D given in UTC (Co-ordinated Universal Time)	A 6-digit group followed by a "Z". The first 2 digits giving date of month, the next 2 digits giving hours and the last 2 digits minutes. The "Z" indicates that the time is given in UTC. (E.g.: 041330Z).
C	C *or* D for all	Position by latitude and longitude	A 4-digit group giving latitude in degrees and minutes suffixed with "N", and a 5-digit group giving longitude in degrees and minutes suffixed with "W". (E.g.: 5710N04112W).
D	C *or* D for all	Position by geographical name of place	Name of place *or* true bearing (3 digits) and distance in nautical miles (quote the word "distance") from an unambiguous known name of place. (E.g.: 165 distance 53 Cape Farewell).
E	SP, PR	True course	A 3-digit group (E.g.: 083).
F	SP, PR	Speed in knots	A 2-digit group (E.g.: 14).
I	SP	Destination and ETA (UTC)	The name of the destination followed by expected time of arrival, expressed as under designator B. (E.g.: Nanortalik 181400Z).

Designator	Mandatory for type of report	Information	Text
L	SP	Intended voyage	A brief description of the intended route, as estimated by the master. (E.g.: From present position by great circle until 100 n.m. south of Cape Farewell then along the ice edge to Qaqortoq).
Q		Defects and deficiencies	Brief details of defects and deficiencies of significance for the safety of the ship. (E.g.: Breakdown on radar and VHF).
S	All	Weather and ice conditions	Brief information about weather at the time of the report and about the ice situation since the last report. (E.g.: SW 5, ice edge observed from 6120N03905W).
X	SP	The total number of persons on board. Other relevant information.	Number of persons on board shall be given. (E.g.: POB 16). Any other information of importance to the safety of own or other ships. (E.g.: Going before the wind due to heavy icing).

5 ***Sailing Plan*** ("SP") to be sent as a first report:

(a) When entering the reporting area

(b) On last departure from Greenland port

(c) When a ship – not obliged to report – wishes to be covered by the GREENPOS system.

Example:

GLK GROENNEDAL
GREENPOS – SP
A. NONAME/NKFG
B. 071310Z
C. 5720N04510W
E. 330
F. 15
I. QAQORTOQ 080200Z
L. DIRECT IN OPEN WATERS
S. OVERCAST – SW 5 – NO ICE
X. POB 16.

6 ***Position Report*** (*"PR"*) to be sent 4 times a day:

At 0000–0030Z, 0600–0630Z, 1200–1230Z and 1800–1830Z.

Example:

GLK GROENNEDAL
GREENPOS – PR
A. NONAME/NKFG
B. 122310Z
C. 6024N05005W
E. 125
F. 10
S. CLEAR SKY – NW 5 – 1/10 ICE.

7 ***Final Report*** (*"FR"*) to be sent:

(a) When leaving the reporting area.

(b) On arrival at Greenland destination.

(c) When a ship – not obliged to report – wishes to be released from the ship reporting system.

Example:

GLK GROENNEDAL
GREENPOS – FR
A. NONAME/NKFG
B. 131700Z
C. 5705N03840W
S. E 6 – NO ICE.

8 ***Deviation Report*** (*"DR"*) to be sent:

When the position of the ship is or will be changed considerably compared with the position at which the ship, based on former reports, is expected to be.

Example:

GLK GROENNEDAL
GREENPOS – DR
A. NONAME/NKFG
B. 130800Z
C. 6005N04952W
L. HEADING TOWARDS ARSUK FIORD INSTEAD OF QAQORTOQ DUE TO ENGINE TROUBLE.

G

Appendix 2

Greenland Ship Reporting System (COASTAL CONTROL)
(KYSTKONTROL)

Rules for drafting of reports

1 Ships on voyages between Greenland ports and places of call shall send reports to the coast radio station which is situated in the same control area as the contemplated destination (Aasiaat Radio, Qaqortoq Radio or Ammassalik Radio), cf. appendix A. Coast radio stations can be contacted via all modern communication forms, including Inmarsat-C, telefax and e-mail. This coast radio station is responsible for monitoring the ship's voyage from the time of receiving the sailing plan until the time of receiving the subsequent final report.

2 The reports shall be sent to the coast radio station which is situated in the same control area as the contemplated destination (Aasiaat Radio, Qaqortoq Radio or Ammassalik Radio), cf. appendix A. Coast radio stations can be contacted via all modern communication forms, including Inmarsat-C, telefax and e-mail.

3 Each report shall begin with the words COASTAL CONTROL followed by a two-letter abbreviation for identification of the report. Telegrams so prefixed are dispatched free of charge and as carrying the priority URGENT.

4 The reports shall be drawn up in accordance with the following diagram. Designators, which are not mandatory, can be included if necessary.

Designator	Mandatory for type of report	Information	Text
	All	Code word	"COASTAL CONTROL"
	All	*Type of report:* Sailing Plan Position Report Deviation Report Final Report	One of the following 2-letter identifiers: "SP" (Sailing Plan – on departure) "PR" (Position Report) "DR" (Deviation Report) "FR" (Final Report – on arrival)
A	All	Ship	Name and call sign. (E.g.: AGNETHE NIELSEN/OULH)
B	All	Date Time Group corresponding to the position under designator C or D given in Local Time (LT)	A 6-digit group. The first 2 digits giving date of month, the next 2 digits giving hours and the last 2 digits minutes. (E.g.: 041330)
C	C *or* D for all	Position by latitude and longitude	A 4-digit group giving latitude in degrees and minutes suffixed with "N", and a 5-digit group giving longitude in degrees and minutes suffixed with "W". (E.g.: 5710N04112W).
D	C *or* D for all	Position by geographical name of place	Name of place *or* true bearing (3 digits) and distance in nautical miles (quote the word"distance") from an unambiguous known name of place. (E.g.: 165 distance 5 Paamiut).
E	PR	True course	A 3-digit group (E.g.: 083).
F	PR	Speed in knots	A 2-digit group (E.g.: 14).
I	SP	Destination and ETA (LT)	The name of the destination followed by expected time of arrival, expressed as under designator B. (E.g.: Nanortalik 181400).

Designator	Mandatory for type of report	Information	Text
L	SP	Intended voyage	A brief description of the intended route, as estimated by the master. (E.g.: From present position along the ice edge to Qaqortoq).
Q		Defects and deficiencies	Brief details of defects and deficiencies of significance for the safety of the ship. (E.g.: Breakdown on radar and VHF).
X	SP	The total number of persons on board. Other relevant information.	Number of persons on board shall be given. (E.g.: POB 16). Any other information of importance to the safety of own or other ships. (E.g.: Going before the wind due to heavy icing).

5 ***Sailing Plan*** (*"SP"*) to be sent as a first report by departure:

Example:

Coast Radio Station QAQORTOQ
COASTAL CONTROL – SP
A. NONAME/NKFG
B. 071310
D. NARSSAQ
I. QAQORTOQ 080200
L. DIRECT IN OPEN WATERS
X. POB 16.

6 ***Position Report*** (*"PR"*) If a voyage is of a longer duration than 24 hours and the ship is equipped with radio, a position report shall furthermore be sent at least once every 24 hours to the control station to which the departure report was addressed.

Example:

Coast Radio Station QAQORTOQ
COASTAL CONTROL – PR
A. NONAME/NKFG
B. 122310
D. OFF ARSUK
E. 310
F. 8

7 ***Deviation Report*** (*"DR"*) to be sent to the control station to which the departure report was addressed if there are changes from the information given in the departure report. A deviation report shall also be sent if the previous given time of arrival is overdue by more than one hour.

Example:
Coast Radio Station QAQORTOQ
COASTAL CONTROL – DR
A. NONAME/NKFG
B. 130800
D. ARRIVED IVITTUT AT 1500
L. AWAITING WEATHER IMPROVEMENT BEFORE CONTINUING TO PAAMIUT.
A NEW SAILING PLAN WILL BE SENT

8 ***Final Report*** ("*FR*") to be sent immediately upon arrival, to the control station to which the departure report was addressed.

Example:

Coast Radio Station QAQORTOQ
COASTAL CONTROL – FR
A. NONAME/NKFG
B. 131700
D. ARRIVED PAAMIUT

Appendix A

Ship control stations with associated control areas

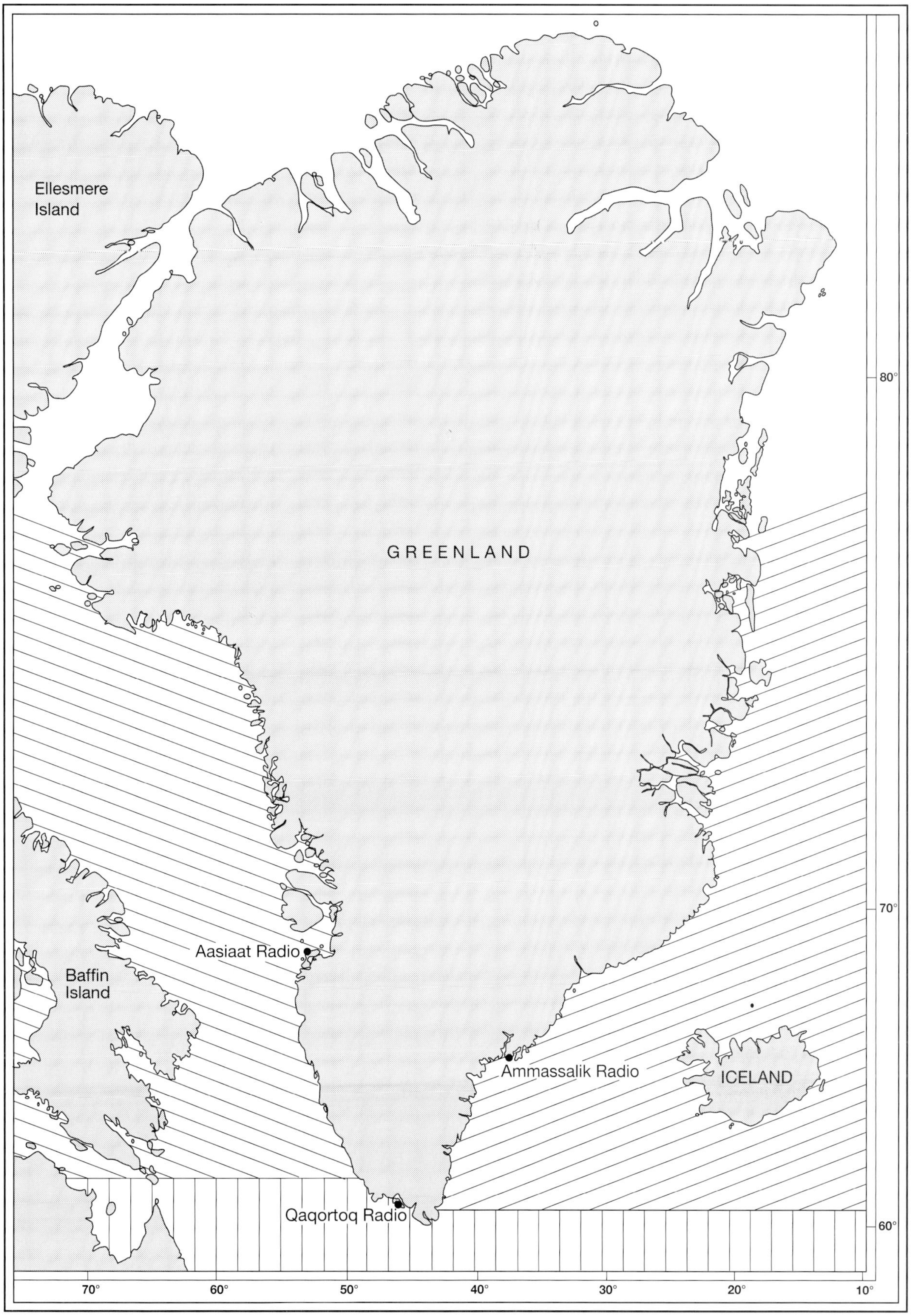

REPORTING SYSTEMS FOR PROTECTION OF ENDANGERED NORTH ATLANTIC RIGHT WHALES IN SEA AREAS OFF THE NORTH-EASTERN AND SOUTH-EASTERN COASTS OF THE UNITED STATES

1 Categories of ships required to participate in the systems

All ships of 300 gross tonnage or greater are required to participate in the reporting systems, except sovereign immune vessels which are exempt from reporting by SOLAS regulation V/8-1(c).

2 Geographical coverage of the systems and the number and edition of the reference charts used for the delineation of the systems

2.1 *North-eastern United States*

Geographical boundaries of the north-east area include the water of Cape Cod Bay, Massachusetts Bay, and the Great South Channel east and south-east of Massachusetts (appendix 1). Co-ordinates of the area are as follows: from a point on Cape Ann, Massachusetts at 42°39′.00 N, 070°37′.00 W; then north-east to 42°45′.00 N, 070°13′.00 W; then south-east to 42°10′.00 N, 068°31′.00 W; then south to 41°00′.00 N, 068°31′.00 W; then west to 41°00′.00 N, 069°17′.00 W; then north-east to 42°05′.00 N, 070°02′.00 W, then west to 42°04′.00 N, 070°10′.00 W; and then along the Massachusetts shoreline of Cape Cod Bay and Massachusetts Bay back to the point on Cape Ann at 42°39′.00 N, 070°37′.00 W. NOAA Chart 13009.

2.2 *South-eastern United States*

Geographical boundaries of the south-east area include coastal waters within about 25 nautical miles along a 90 nautical miles stretch of the Atlantic seaboard in Florida and Georgia (appendix 2). The area extends from the shoreline east to longitude 080°51′.60 W with the southern and northern boundary at latitudes 30°00′.00 N and 31°27′.00 N, respectively. NOAA Chart 11009.

3 Format, content of report, times and geographical positions for submitting reports, Authority to whom the reports should be sent, available services

3.1 *Format*

The format for reporting is as set forth in paragraph 2 of the appendix to resolution A.851(20). An example of a transmission between ship and shore is at appendix 3.

3.2 *Content*

Ships are required to provide the following information: the name of the ship; call sign or IMO identification number, if applicable; position when entering the system; course; speed; route; and destination. Commercially sensitive information received in conjunction with the reporting system shall be kept confidential.

3.3 *Geographical position for submitting reports*

Participating ships are required to report to a shore-based Authority only when entering the reporting area during a single voyage (that is, a voyage in which a ship is in the area to visit one or multiple ports or traverse the area before leaving for a port outside the reporting area); ships will not be required to report in again after leaving a port in the area or when exiting the system.

3.4 *Authority*

The Authority for both areas of the system is the United States Coast Guard.

4 Information to be provided to participating ships and procedures to be followed

Ships will be provided with the following information:

4.1 Mariners shall be informed that they are entering an area of critical importance for the protection of the highly endangered Right Whale; that such whales are present; and that ship strikes pose a serious threat to whales and may cause damage to ships. Communication systems between ship and shore are described in paragraphs 7 and 8, below.

4.2 To obtain seasonal Right Whale advisories which are broadcast periodically, mariners would also be advised to monitor Coast Guard Broadcast Notice to Mariners, NAVTEX, NOAA Weather Radio, and, in the north-eastern ship reporting system area only, the Cape Cod Canal Vessel Traffic Control and the Bay of Fundy Vessel Traffic Control. These advisories are based on surveys that are flown seasonally and in daylight and good weather conditions only. The sighting information may be useful only for brief periods as the whales move and surveys detect only a small percentage of the whales present.

4.3 Mariners would be advised to consult with NAVTEX, Inmarsat-C SafetyNET (satellite text broadcasts), the United States Coast Pilot, Notice to Mariners, the nautical charts for information on the boundaries of the Right Whale critical habitat and the national marine sanctuary, applicable regulations, and precautionary measures that mariners may take to reduce the risk of hitting Right Whales. Mariners will further be advised that information placards, videos, and other educational materials are available from shipping agents, port authorities, pilots, relevant State agencies, the Coast Guard, and the National Marine Fisheries Service.

4.4 In the message back to the ship, mariners will also be requested to report any whale sightings and dead, injured, or entangled marine mammals to the nearest local Coast Guard station.

4.5 Where available, specific and timely information on whale locations will be provided to ships.

5 Radiocommunications required for the systems, frequencies on which reports should be transmitted and the information to be reported

5.1 The reporting system in the north-eastern United States will operate independently of the system in the south-eastern United States. The system in the north-eastern United States will operate year-round, and the system in the south-eastern United States will operate from 15 November through 15 April.

5.2 The systems require ships to report in standard format, preferably through Inmarsat-C. For ships using Inmarsat-C, the message will be sent to the shore-based Authority described in paragraph 7.1 and a message will be automatically transmitted back to the ship, also via Inmarsat-C.

5.3 Ships not equipped with Inmarsat-C are required to report in standard format to the shore-based Authority described in paragraph 7.2, either through direct-printing telegraphy (Inmarsat-A/-B, HF, MF or VHF) or by telephony (Inmarsat-A/-B, MF, HF or VHF). Ships reporting through such direct-printing telegraphy systems will receive a message from the shore-based Authority described in paragraph 7.2.

5.4 The language used for reports in the systems is English, using the IMO Standard Marine Communication Phrases where necessary. Standard phrases in a prescribed format will be used in all direct-printing telegraphy and radiotelephony communications.

5.5 Commercially sensitive information will be kept confidential.

5.6 The United States will review the ship reporting systems no later than five years after their implementation date, to examine advances made in ship communication technologies and to ensure effective operation of the systems.

6 Rules and regulations in force in the areas of the systems

The United States has taken appropriate action to implement international conventions to which it is a party, including, where appropriate, adopting domestic legislation and promulgating regulations through domestic law. Relevant laws in force include domestic legislation and regulations to implement the International Convention on Collision Regulations, the Safety of Life at Sea Convention, the International Convention on the Prevention of Pollution from Ships, the International Convention on Oil Pollution Preparedness, Response and Co-operation, the Convention on the International Trade in Endangered Species of Wild Fauna and Flora, the International Convention for the Regulation of Whaling, and other treaties. Relevant domestic legislation includes the Ports and Waterways Safety Act, the Endangered Species Act, the Whaling Convention Act, the Marine Mammal Protection Act, the Marine Protection Resources and Sanctuaries Act, and a variety of other acts. In some cases, rules have been promulgated, including those relating specifically to Right Whales or governing ship operations. For example, a regulation has been promulgated which prohibits most approaches within 500 yards (460 metres) of a Northern Right Whale. This regulation, as well as other domestic law, is implemented and enforced consistent with international law.

7 Shore-based facilities to support operation of the systems

7.1 The shore-based Authority for those ships reporting via Inmarsat-C is the United States Coast Guard. The e-mail addresses to be used for this reporting will be provided well in advance of implementation of the systems through Notices to Mariners.

7.2 The small percentage of ships that do not have Inmarsat-C capabilities will be required to contact the nearest Coast Guard communication station through appropriate communication channels. The United States Coast Guard maintains communication stations along the United States east coast. Information about these stations can be found in the GMDSS Master Plan (GMDSS/Circ.7) or National Imagery and Mapping Agency (NIMA) Publication 117. Information received from the ships will be sent electronically to a central location for data storage, handling, and retrieval.

8 Alternative communications if the communication facilities of the shore-based Authority fail

Short-term failure of the reporting systems due to communications problems will not result in a loss of life, and will have minimal impact on the safety of vessels. NAVTEX Broadcast Notice to Mariners can be used to notify mariners of the temporary failure of the system and can provide mariners with basic information necessary to avoid Right Whales. Downtime is likely to be minimal and is not expected to result in increased ship strikes and whale mortality. For those ships reporting through Inmarsat-C or direct-printing radiotelegraphy, the standard protocol now used for such systems will be used to re-route incoming and outgoing communications through an alternate address, and it is expected that this will minimize the system's downtime, though some delay may occur.

The Coast-Guard-operated MF, HF, and VHF voice communications systems, by design, have built-in redundancies and overlapping coverage areas, and an individual equipment or site failure is unlikely to affect the ability of a mariner to contact a Coast Guard facility to make a required report.

Appendix 1

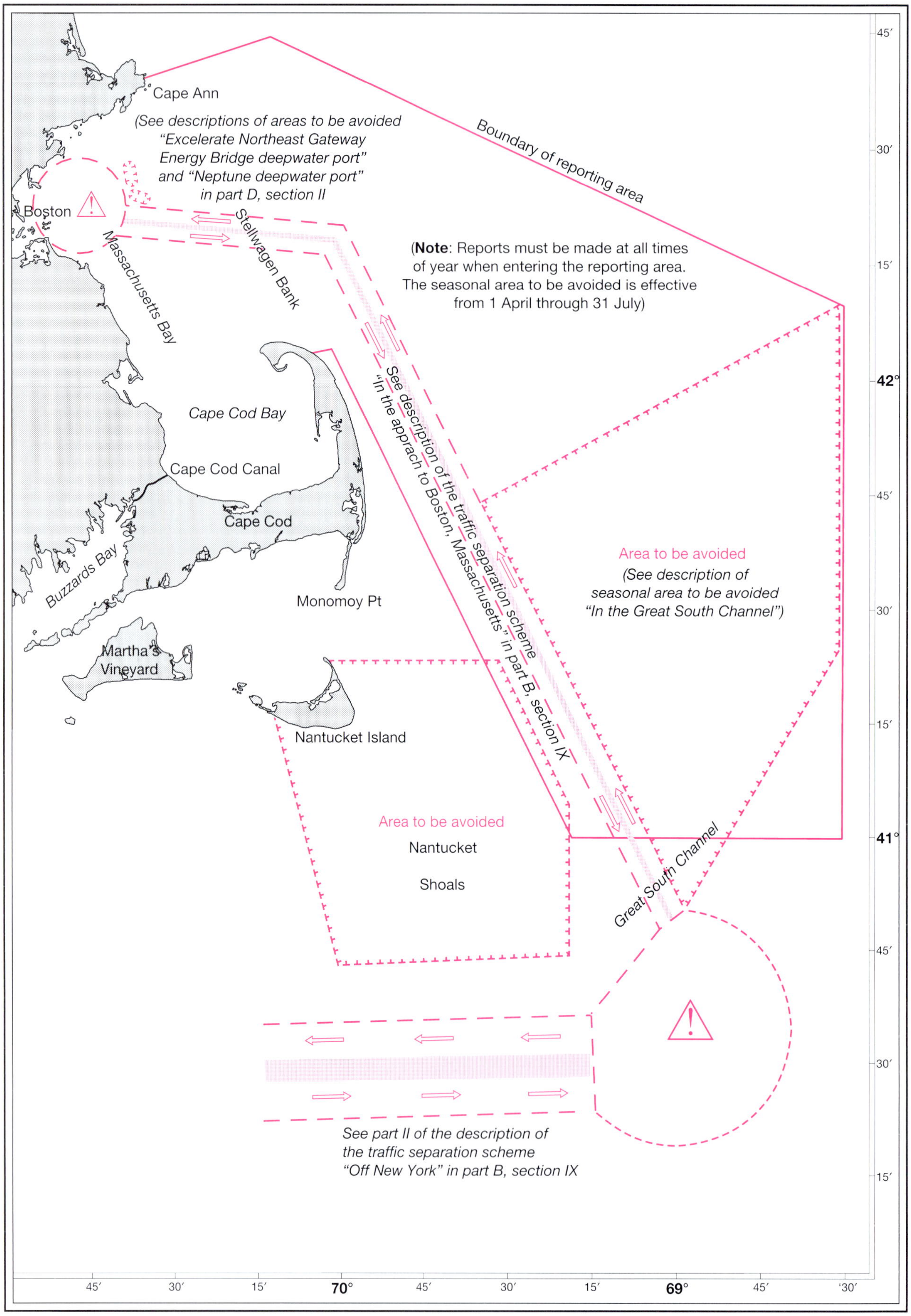
Cape Ann
(See descriptions of areas to be avoided "Excelerate Northeast Gateway Energy Bridge deepwater port" and "Neptune deepwater port" in part D, section II
Boundary of reporting area
Boston
Stellwagen Bank
Massachusetts Bay
(Note: Reports must be made at all times of year when entering the reporting area. The seasonal area to be avoided is effective from 1 April through 31 July)
Cape Cod Bay
Cape Cod Canal
Cape Cod
Buzzards Bay
Monomoy Pt
Martha's Vineyard
Nantucket Island
See description of the traffic separation scheme "In the appraoch to Boston, Massachusetts" in part B, section IX
Area to be avoided
(See description of seasonal area to be avoided "In the Great South Channel")
Area to be avoided
Nantucket
Shoals
Great South Channel
See part II of the description of the traffic separation scheme "Off New York" in part B, section IX
45′
30′
15′
42°
45′
30′
15′
41°
45′
30′
15′
45′
30′
15′
70°
45′
30′
15′
69°
45′
30′

Appendix 2

Note: reports must be made
when entering the area
from 15 November through 15 April
Boundary of reporting area
St. Catherines I.
Sapelo I.
St. Simons I.
Brunswick
Georgia
Cumberland I.
Florida
Amelia I.
40′
30′
20′
10′
31°
50′
40′
30′
20′
10′
30°
30′
20′
10′
81°
50′
40′
30′

Appendix 3

Example of message from the ship

A Ship name

B Call sign or IMO Identification Number

D Course

E Speed

H Entry

I Destination

L Route

Example of message back to the ship

00016April1999
From: Shore-based Authority
To: M/V Ship

You are entering an area where North Atlantic Right Whales exist. Right Whales are critically endangered and at risk from ship strikes. Whales can damage ships' sonar dome, propeller, and shaft. Recommend monitoring Coast Guard Broadcast Notice to Mariners, NAVTEX, NOAA Weather Radio, or, in the north-east only, Cape Cod Canal Vessel Traffic Control and Bay of Fundy Vessel Traffic Control for latest advisories and sightings reports. These advisories and reports are based on surveys which are conducted seasonally; however, such surveys locate only a small percentage of the whales, the information from them remains valid only for a short period of time because the whales move, and they cannot be conducted at night or in inclement weather.

Urge exercising prudent seamanship to avoid approaching Right Whales. Recommend consulting NAVTEX, Inmarsat-C SafetyNET, the United States Coast Pilot, and Notices to Mariners for information on precautionary measures that may be taken to reduce the risk of hitting Right Whales and for applicable regulations. Right Whale critical habitat and the Stellwagen Bank National Marine Sanctuary are also marked on charts.

Right Whale information placards, videos, and other educational material are available from shipping agents, port authorities, relevant State agencies, the United States Coast Guard, and the National Marine Fisheries Service. Mariners are requested to report Right Whale sightings, whale entanglements, or dead whales to the Coast Guard on VHF channel 16.

OFF CHENGSHAN JIAO PROMONTORY

1 Categories of ships required to participate in the system

The following vessels are required to participate in the system: fishing vessels with a length of 24 metres and above, cargo ships of 300 gross tonnage and above, and passenger ships as defined in chapter I of SOLAS 1974, as amended.

2 Geographical coverage of the system and the numbers and editions of the reference charts used for the delineation of the system

2.1 The waters covered by the ship reporting system is the water area with the VTS Centre (geographical position is 37°23′.65 N, 122°42′.12 E) as the centre and 24 miles as the radius.

2.2 The relevant charts are Chinese charts Nos. 9701, 9304 and 9305. Chart datum is World Geodetic System 1984 (WGS 84) datum.

3 Format, reporting time and geographical positions for submitting reports, Authority to whom the reports should be sent, available services

3.1 *Format*

The format for reporting is as set forth in paragraph 2 of the appendix to Assembly resolution A.851(20).

A	Name of ship, call sign, and IMO Number (if applicable)
C *or* D	Position (latitude and longitude *or* in relation to a landmark)
E	Course
F	Speed
G	Port of departure
I	Port of destination (optional)
Q	Defects and limitations (vessels towing are to report length of tow and name of object in tow)
U	Overall length and gross tonnage

3.2 *Content and geographical position for submitting reports*

3.2.1 Participating vessels are to report the information in paragraph 3.1 when entering the ship reporting system area. Reports are not required when a participating vessel leaves the area.

3.2.2 When a participating vessel leaves a port that is located within the reporting area, it shall report its name, position, departure time, and port of destination.

3.2.3 When a participating vessel arrives at a port or anchorage within the reporting area, it shall report, on arrival at its berth, its name, position, and arrival time.

3.2.4 When a traffic incident or a pollution incident occurs within the reporting area, the vessel(s) shall immediately report the type, time, and location of the incident, extent of damage or pollution, and whether assistance is needed. The vessel(s) shall provide any additional information related to the incident, as requested by the shore-based authority.

3.3 *Authority*

The competent authority is Yantai Maritime Safety Administration, China. The voice call sign is "CHENGSHAN JIAO VTS CENTRE".

4 Information to be provided to ships and procedures to be followed

4.1 The Chengshan Jiao VTS Centre, where appropriate, will provide participating vessels with information such as conflicting vessel traffic, abnormal weather conditions, and maritime safety information.

4.2 Participating vessels shall maintain a listening watch on the designated VTS frequency.

5 Radiocommunications required for the system, frequencies on which reports should be transmitted and the information to be reported

5.1 The working channels of the Chengshan Jiao VTS Centre are:

Primary – channels 8 or 9

Secondary – channel 65

Calling frequency – channel 16

5.2 The language used for reports in the system will be Chinese or English. IMO Standard Marine Communication Phrases in a prescribed format will be used in all direct-printing telegraphy and radiotelephony communications.

6 Rules and regulations in force in the area of the system

China has taken appropriate action to implement international conventions to which it is a party, including, where appropriate, adopting domestic legislation and promulgating regulations through domestic law. Relevant laws in force include domestic legislation and regulations to implement the Convention on the International Regulations for Preventing Collisions at Sea, 1972, the International Convention for the Safety of Life at Sea, 1974, and the International Convention for the Prevention of Pollution from Ships, 1973/1978.

7 Shore-based facilities to support operation of the system

7.1 Chengshan Jiao VTS Centre is comprised of radar, VHF communications, VHF-DF, information processing and display, information transmission, recording, replay, and hydro-meteorological sensors. Its functions are data collection and evaluation, provision of information, navigation assistance, and support to allied services.

7.2 Chengshan Jiao VTS Centre maintains a continuous 24-hour watch.

8 Alternative communications if the communication facilities of the shore-based Authority fail

Chengshan Jiao VTS Centre has built-in redundancies with multiple receivers on each channel. Alternative means of ship to shore communication are by HF (SSB), telex (facsimile), e-mail, or cellular telephone.

9 Measures to be taken if a ship fails to comply

Appropriate measures will be taken to enforce compliance with the system, consistent with international law.

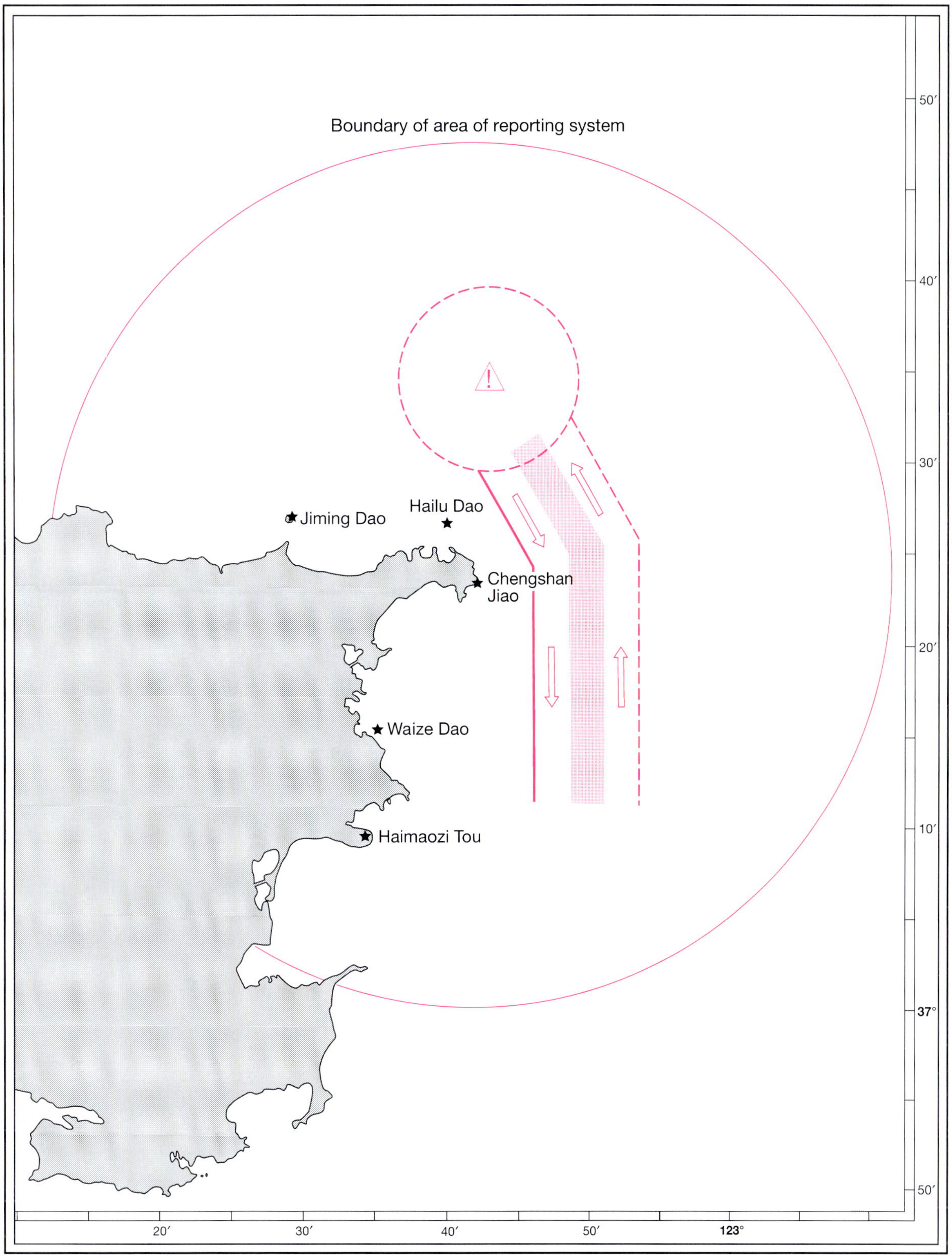

OFF CHENGSHAN JIAO PROMONTORY

THE CANARY ISLANDS (CANREP)

A mandatory reporting system for ships in the Canary Islands (CANREP) is established in the Canary Islands.

1 Types of ship required to take part in the system

1.1 Ships required to take part in the CANREP system:

Tankers of 600 tonnes deadweight and upwards, either transiting the Canary Islands or sailing to or from Canarian ports or involved in inter-island navigation, carrying the following:

.1 heavy-grade crude oils with a density greater than 900 kg/m^3 at 15°C;

.2 heavy fuel oils with a density greater than 900 kg/m^3 at 15°C or kinematic viscosity greater than 180 mm^2/s at 50°C; and

.3 bitumen, coal tar and their emulsions.

2 Geographical limits of the Canary Islands reporting area

2.1 The maritime area is bounded by a polygonal line connecting points along the outer limit of the territorial sea (12 nautical miles) that surrounds the archipelago, and having the following inflection points (see chartlet in appendix 3):

(1)	28°56′ N,	018°13′ W
(2)	29°04′ N,	017°47′ W
(3)	28°48′ N,	016°04′ W
(4)	28°22′ N,	015°19′ W
(5)	28°19′ N,	014°36′ W
(6)	29°37′ N,	013°39′ W
(7)	29°37′ N,	013°19′ W
(8)	29°17′ N,	013°06′ W
(9)	27°57′ N,	013°48′ W
(10)	27°32′ N,	015°35′ W
(11)	27°48′ N,	016°45′ W
(12)	27°48′ N,	017°11′ W
(13)	27°23′ N,	017°58′ W
(14)	27°36′ N,	018°25′ W

2.2 The reference chart is No. 209 of the Spanish Navy Hydrographical Institute (WGS 84 datum).

3 Format and content of reports, time and geographical position for submitting reports, Authority to which they must be sent, and available services

3.1 *Format*

3.1.1 CANREP reports must be sent to one of the Maritime Rescue Co-ordination Centres listed in appendix 1 and drafted in accordance with the format described in appendix 2.

3.1.2 The reporting format conforms with paragraph 2 of the appendix to resolution A.851(20).

3.2 *Content*

3.2.1 The reports to be submitted by participating ships must contain the information needed to achieve the system's aims:

.1 the ship's name, call sign, IMO or MMSI number and position are necessary in order to establish its identity and initial position (A, B and C);

.2 the ship's course, speed and destination are important for monitoring its track and launching search and rescue measures, should information about it fail to appear on the screen, for ensuring safe navigation, and for preventing pollution in areas where weather conditions are extreme (E, F, G and I);

.3 the number of people on board, and other relevant information, are important factors when it comes to assigning the resources for a search and rescue operation (P, T and W);

.4 in accordance with the relevant provisions of the SOLAS and MARPOL Conventions, ships are required to supply information on defects, damage, deficiencies and other limitations (under Q), as well as other information (under X).

3.3 *Time and geographical position for submitting reports*

3.3.1 Ships must submit a report:

.1 on entering the reporting area as defined in paragraph 2; or

.2 immediately after leaving a port, terminal or anchorage situated in the reporting area; or

.3 when deviating from the route leading to the originally declared destination, port, terminal, anchorage or position "for orders" given on entry into the reporting area; or

.4 when it is necessary to deviate from the planned route owing to weather conditions, damaged equipment or a change in navigational status; and

.5 on finally leaving the reporting area.

3.3.2 Ships are not required to send a report if, during normal sailing through the reporting area, they cross the area's boundary on other occasions apart from initial entry or final departure.

3.4 *Land-based Authorities to which reports must be sent*

3.4.1 On entering the CANREP reporting area, ships must report the fact to one of the MRCCs listed in appendix 1, according to the following criteria:

(i) Ships that enter the CANREP reporting area at a position east of the meridian of longitude 015°30′ W should notify the Las Palmas MRCC.

(ii) Ships that enter the reporting area at a position west of the meridian of longitude 015°30′ W should notify the Tenerife MRCC.

3.4.2 On leaving the CANREP reporting area, ships must report the fact to the same MRCC to which they reported on entry.

3.4.3 Reports must be completed in accordance with the format shown in appendix 2.

3.4.4 Reports may be sent by any means capable of being received by the media indicated in appendix 1.

4 Information to be provided to participating ships and procedures to be observed

4.1 When requested, the MRCCs listed in appendix 1 should provide ships with information vital to navigational safety in the ship's reporting area, using their broadcasting equipment.

4.2 If necessary, any ship may ask for information on its own behalf about specific local conditions.

5 Requirements regarding radiocommunications for the system, reporting frequencies and information to be reported

5.1 The Maritime Rescue Co-ordination Centres to which reports must be sent are listed in appendix 1.

5.2 The reports completed by a ship on entering and passing through the reporting area must begin with the word CANREP and include a two-letter abbreviation to indicate their type (sailing plan, final report or deviation report). Reports with these prefixes may be sent free of cost.

5.3 Depending on the type of report, the following information must be included, as described in paragraph 6 of appendix 2:

A: Ship's identity (name, call sign, IMO No. and MMSI No.);

B: Date and time;

C: Position;

E: True course;

F: Speed;

G: Name of last port of call;

I: Name of next port of call and estimated time of arrival;

P: Type(s) of cargo, quantity and IMO classification if carrying potentially dangerous goods;

Q: Used in the event of defects or deficiencies that impair normal navigation;

T: Address for communication of cargo information;

W: Number of people on board;

X: Miscellaneous information relating to tankers:

- estimated quantity and characteristics of bunker fuel for tankers carrying an amount of it greater than 5000 tonnes;
- navigational status (e.g. moving under own propulsion, limited manoeuvrability, etc.).

5.4 The reporting format must be consistent with resolution A.851(20).

6 Regulations in force in the area covered by the system

6.1 *Regulations on collision prevention*

The International Regulations for Preventing Collisions at Sea (COLREG) 1972, as amended, apply throughout the area covered by the system.

7 Shore-based establishments responsible for operation of the system

7.1 The MRCCs to which these reports must be sent are listed in appendix 1.

7.2 The MRCCs or any other establishment forming part of the service are to be manned constantly.

7.3 The training given to MRCC staff must comply with the national and international recommendations and include a general study of navigational safety measures and the relevant national and international (IMO) provisions.

7.4 All means of communication that can be received by the media indicated in appendix 1 are acceptable.

8 Action to take in the event of a ship's non-compliance with system requirements

8.1 The system's objectives are to initiate maritime search and rescue and anti-pollution measures as quickly and effectively as possible if an emergency is reported or if a ship that is supposed to report does not and no contact can be established with it. All possible means will be deployed to obtain the participation of the ships required to send in reports. Should these fail to materialize and the offending ship can be identified beyond doubt, the competent authorities in the relevant flag State will be informed with a view to their investigating the situation and possibly starting legal proceedings under their national legislation. The CANREP mandatory ship reporting system exists only for the exchange of information, and does not confer additional powers to impose change in a ship's operations. The reporting system will be implemented in accordance with the provisions of UNCLOS, the SOLAS Convention and other relevant international instruments, and the reporting system will not constitute a basis for preventing the passage of a ship in transit through the reporting area.

Appendix 1

Installations to which reports must be sent (positions refer to WGS 84 datum)

MRCC Tenerife 28°28′ N, 016°14′ W

Tel.: +34 900 202 111
E-mail: canrep.tenerife@sasemar.es
VHF channels: 16 and 70
MF channel: 2182 kHz

Automatic identification system (AIS)

MRCC Las Palmas 28°09′ N, 015°25′ W

Tel.: +34 900 202 112
E-mail: canrep.laspalmas@sasemar.es
VHF channels: 16 and 70
MF channel: 2182 kHz

Automatic identification system (AIS)

Appendix 2

Mandatory ship reporting system for the Canary Islands (CANREP)

Instructions for reports

1 Ships heading for the reporting area of the Canary Islands must send a report:

.1 on entering the reporting area; or

.2 immediately after leaving a port, terminal or anchorage situated in the reporting area; or

.3 when deviating from the route leading to the originally declared destination, port, terminal, anchorage or position "for orders" given on entry into the reporting area; or

.4 when it is necessary to deviate from the planned route owing to weather conditions, damaged equipment or when information under Q is required; and

.5 on finally leaving the reporting area.

2 Ships are not required to send a report if, during normal sailing through the reporting area, they cross the area's boundary on other occasions apart from initial entry or final departure.

3 On entering the CANREP reporting area, ships must report the fact to one of the MRCCs listed in appendix 1, according to the following criteria:

(i) Ships that enter the CANREP reporting area at a position east of the meridian of longitude 015°30′ W should notify the Las Palmas MRCC.

(ii) Ships that enter the reporting area at a position west of the meridian of longitude 015°30′ W should notify the Tenerife MRCC.

4 On leaving the CANREP reporting area, ships must report the fact to the same MRCC to which they reported on entry.

5 Every report must begin with the word CANREP and a two-letter abbreviation enabling the type of report to be identified. Messages with this prefix will be sent free of charge and treated as URGENT.

6 Reports must be in accordance with the following table. Sections A, B, C, E, F, G, I, P, T, W and X are compulsory for sailing plans, A, B, C, E and F for final reports, and A, B, C, E, F and I for deviation reports. The Q designation is included whenever a problem arises in the reporting area, be it defects, damage, deficiencies or circumstances that affect normal navigation.

Designator	Function	Text
Name of system	Code word	CANREP
	Type of report: Sailing plan: Final report: Deviation report:	One of the following 2-letter identifiers: SP FR (on *finally* leaving reporting area) to include only **A**, **B**, **C**, **E** and **F** DR to include only **A**, **B**, **C**, **E**, **F** and **I**
A	Ship	Name and call sign (Name of ship, call sign, IMO No. and MMSI No.), (e.g. NONESUCH/KTOI)
B	Date and time corresponding to position at C, expressed as UTC	A six-digit group followed by a Z. The first two digits indicate day of the month, the second two the hours and the last two the minutes. The Z indicates that the time is given in UTC (e.g. 081340Z).
C	Position (latitude and longitude)	A four-digit group giving latitude in degrees and minutes, with the suffix N, and a five-digit group giving longitude in degrees and minutes, with the suffix W (e.g. 2836N 01545W)
E	Course	True course. A three-digit group (e.g. 210).

Designator	Function	Text
F	Speed	Speed in knots. A two-digit group (e.g. 14).
G	Name of last port of call	Name of the last port of call (e.g. Strait of Gibraltar)
I	Destination and ETA (UTC)	Name of destination and date and time group as expressed in B (e.g. Cape Town 181400Z)
P	Cargo	Type(s) of cargo, and quantity and IMO classification if carrying potentially dangerous goods
Q	Defects, damage, deficiencies, limitations	Brief details of defects, including damage, deficiencies and other circumstances that impair normal navigation
T	Address for the communication of cargo information	Name, telephone number and fax, e-mail or URL
W	Total number of people on board	State number
X	Miscellaneous	Miscellaneous information concerning those tankers: – characteristics and approximate quantity of bunker fuel for tankers carrying an amount of it greater than 5000 tonnes – navigational status (e.g. moving under own propulsion, at anchor, no steering, limited manoeuvrability, depth restriction, moored, aground, etc.)

7 The ***sailing plan*** (*SP*) is sent as an initial report:

(a) When entering the reporting area, as defined in paragraph 2.1.

(b) On leaving the last port of call located in the reporting area.

Example:
Name of station to which report must be sent: CANREP – SP
A. GOLAR STIRLING/9001007
B. 261520Z
C. 2836N01545W
E. 210
F. 15
G. STRAIT OF GIBRALTAR
I. CAPE TOWN 230230Z
P. 56,000 TONNES HEAVY FUEL OILS
T. J Smith, 00 47 22 31 56 10, Fax 00 47 22 31 56 11
W. 23
X. NONE, NONE

8 The ***final report*** (*FR*) is sent:

(a) When leaving the reporting area.

(b) On arrival at a port of destination located in the reporting area.

Example:
Name of station to which report must be sent: CANREP – FR
A. GOLAR STIRLING/9001007
B. 261805Z
C. 2802N01614W
E. 175
F. 16

9 The ***deviation report*** (*DR*) is sent:

(a) When deviating from the route leading to the originally declared destination, port, terminal, anchorage or position "for orders" given on entry into reporting area.

(b) When it is necessary to deviate from the planned route owing to weather conditions, damage to equipment or a change in navigational status.

Example:
Name of station to which report must be sent: CANREP – DR
A. GOLAR STIRLING/9001007
B. 261605Z
C. 2821N01557W
E. 280
F. 14
I. SANTA CRUZ DE TENERIFE 261645Z
X. NONE, SATISFACTORY.

Appendix 3

Chartlet

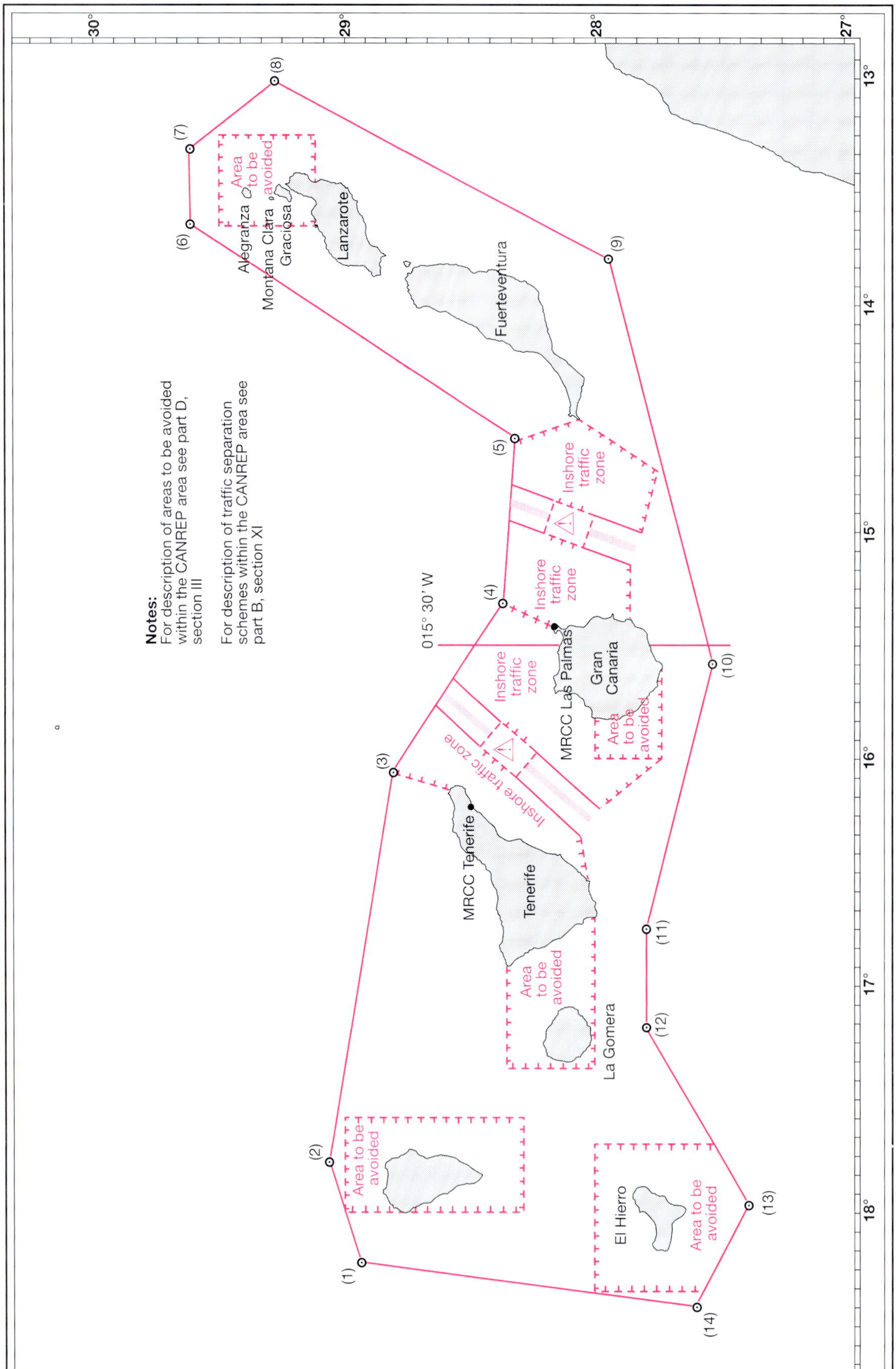

SUMMARY

1 Types of ship required to participate in the system

1.1 Ships required to take part in the CANREP mandatory ship reporting system:

Tankers of 600 tonnes deadweight and upwards, either transiting the Canary Islands or sailing to or from Canarian ports or involved in inter-island navigation, carrying the following:

.1 heavy-grade crude oils with a density greater than 900 kg/m^3 at 15°C;

.2 heavy fuel oils with a density greater than 900 kg/m^3 at 15°C or kinematic viscosity greater than 180 mm^2/s at 50°C; and

.3 bitumen, coal tar and their emulsions.

2 Geographical position for submitting reports

Ships travelling towards the Canary Island reporting area or leaving it must report:

.1 on entering the reporting area; or

.2 immediately after leaving a port, terminal or anchorage located in the reporting area; or

.3 when deviating from the route leading to the originally declared destination, port, terminal, anchorage or position "for orders" given on entry into the reporting area; or

.4 when it is necessary to deviate from the planned route owing to weather conditions, damaged equipment or a change in navigational status; and

.5 on finally leaving the reporting area.

3 Reference charts

The reference chart is No. 209 of the Spanish Navy Hydrographic Institute (WGS 84 datum).

4 Reporting format

A: Ship's identity (name, call sign, IMO No. and MMSI No.)

B: Date and time

C: Position

E: True course

F: Speed

G: Name of last port of call

I: Name of next port of call and estimated time of arrival

P: Type(s) of cargo, quantity and IMO classification if carrying potentially dangerous goods

Q: Used in the event of defects or deficiencies that affect normal navigation

T: Address for communication of information on cargo

W: Number of people on board

X: Various particulars relating to tankers:

- estimated quantity and characteristics of bunker fuel for tankers carrying an amount of it greater than 5000 tonnes
- navigational status (e.g. moving under own propulsion, limited manoeuvrability, etc.).

5 Shore-based Authorities to which reports must be sent

5.1 On entering the CANREP reporting area, ships must report the fact to one of the MRCCs listed in appendix 1, according to the following criteria:

(i) Ships entering the CANREP reporting area at a position east of the meridian of longitude 015°30′ W should notify the Las Palmas MRCC.

(ii) Ships entering the reporting area at a position west of the meridian of longitude 015°30′ W should notify the Tenerife MRCC.

5.2 On leaving the CANREP reporting area, ships must report the fact to the same MRCC to which they reported on entry.

6 Telecommunications

Reports may be sent cost-free by any means capable of being received by the media indicated in appendix 1.

Section II

Mandatory Routeing Systems and Mandatory No Anchoring Areas

Caution: The chartlets are for illustrative purposes only and must not be used for navigation. Mariners should consult the appropriate nautical publications and charts for up-to-date details on aids to navigation and other relevant information.

Warning: The geographical positions given in the descriptions of the routeing systems are only correct for charts using the same geodetic datum as the reference charts indicated under each description. Charts published by other hydrographic offices may use a different geodetic datum, as may new editions of the reference charts published after the adoption of the routeing system.

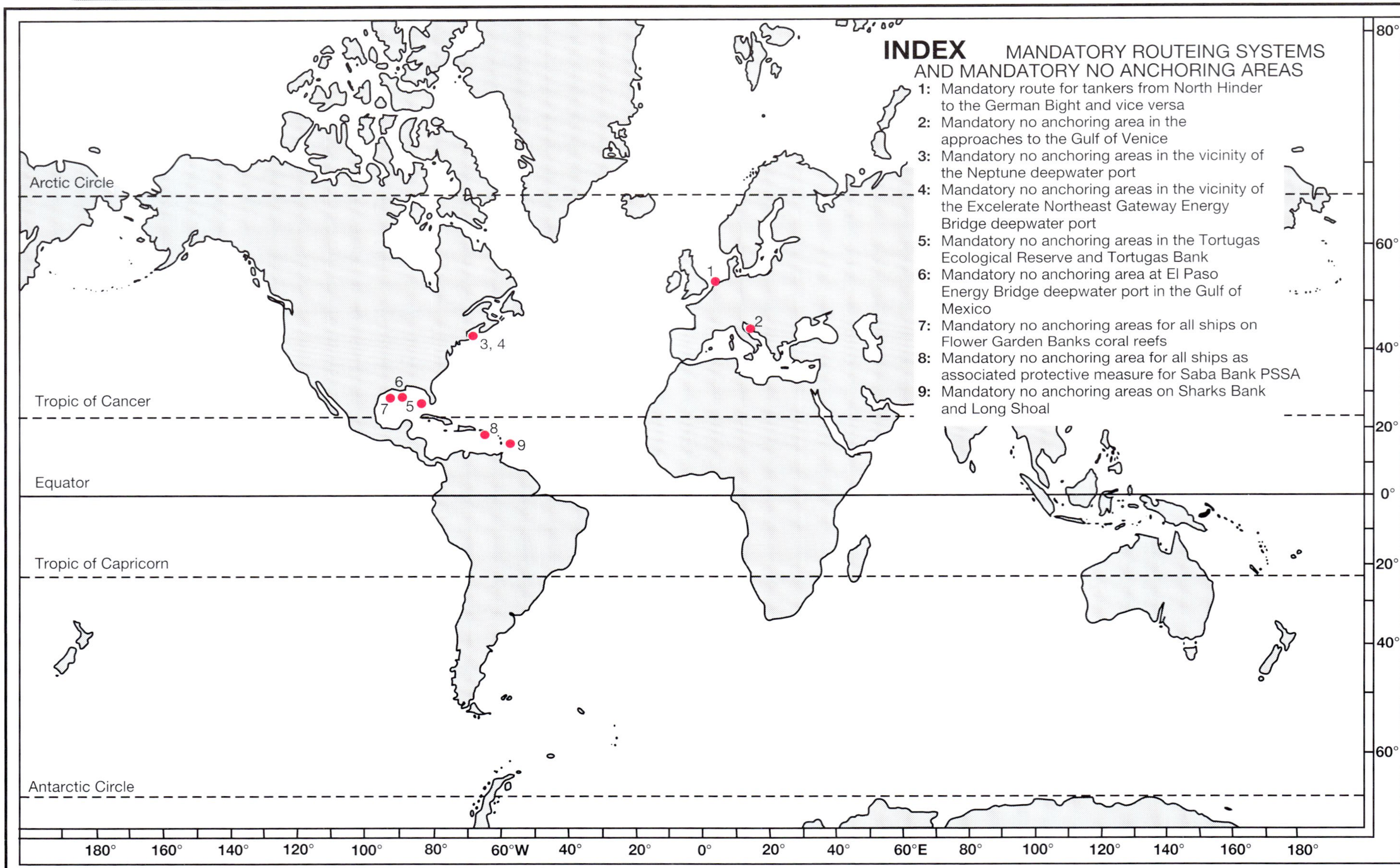
INDEX MANDATORY ROUTEING SYSTEMS AND MANDATORY NO ANCHORING AREAS
1: Mandatory route for tankers from North Hinder to the German Bight and vice versa
2: Mandatory no anchoring area in the approaches to the Gulf of Venice
3: Mandatory no anchoring areas in the vicinity of the Neptune deepwater port
4: Mandatory no anchoring areas in the vicinity of the Excelerate Northeast Gateway Energy Bridge deepwater port
5: Mandatory no anchoring areas in the Tortugas Ecological Reserve and Tortugas Bank
6: Mandatory no anchoring area at El Paso Energy Bridge deepwater port in the Gulf of Mexico
7: Mandatory no anchoring areas for all ships on Flower Garden Banks coral reefs
8: Mandatory no anchoring area for all ships as associated protective measure for Saba Bank PSSA
9: Mandatory no anchoring areas on Sharks Bank and Long Shoal
Arctic Circle
Tropic of Cancer
Equator
Tropic of Capricorn
Antarctic Circle
1
2
3, 4
5
6
7
8
9
80°
60°
40°
20°
0°
20°
40°
60°
180°
160°
140°
120°
100°
80°
60°W
40°
20°
0°
20°
40°
60°E
80°
100°
120°
140°
160°
180°

MANDATORY ROUTE FOR TANKERS FROM NORTH HINDER TO THE GERMAN BIGHT AND VICE VERSA

(Reference charts: International, British Admiralty, Netherlands Hydrographic Office and German Hydrographic Office

INT number	NL number	German number	BA number
1042	–	1001	2182B
1043	1014	1002	2182A
1045	1037	50	–
1046	1035	53	–
1412	–	–	–
1413	1353	87	–
1414	2593	84	2593
1415	2322	244	2322
1416	3371	–	3371
1419	1507	95	1507
1420	1505	96	1505
1509	–	202	1503
1510	–	193	1504
	1972	–	–
	1970*	–	–
		2910*	–
		103	–
		196	–
			1187
			1406
			1408

* Passage Planning Charts

Note: These charts are based on European datum.)

Description of the mandatory route

Deep-water route from North Hinder to traffic separation scheme "Off Brown Ridge"

(a) The deep-water route is bounded by a line connecting the following geographical positions:

(1)	52°55′.75 N,	003°14′.25 E	(4)	52°01′.23 N,	002°42′.47 E
(2)	52°09′.92 N,	002°35′.00 E	(5)	52°09′.58 N,	002°43′.33 E
(3)	51°54′.88 N,	002°33′.60 E	(6)	52°54′.17 N,	003°22′.00 E

Traffic separation scheme "Off Brown Ridge"

(b) A separation zone is bounded by a line connecting the following geographical positions:

(7)	53°03′.14 N,	003°21′.85 E	(9)	52°54′.81 N,	003°18′.87 E
(8)	52°55′.11 N,	003°17′.38 E	(10)	53°02′.84 N,	003°23′.34 E

(c) A traffic lane for northbound traffic is established between the separation zone in paragraph (b) above and a line connecting the following geographical positions:

(6)	52°54′.17 N,	003°22′.00 E	(11)	53°02′.20 N,	003°26′.48 E

(d) A traffic lane for southbound traffic is established between the separation zone in paragraph (b) above and a line connecting the following geographical positions:

(12)	53°03′.78 N,	003°18′.71 E	(1)	52°55′.75 N,	003°14′.25 E

Deep-water route from the traffic separation scheme "Off Brown Ridge" to the traffic separation scheme "West Friesland"

(e) The deep-water route is bounded by a line connecting the following geographical positions:

(11)	53°02′.20 N,	003°26′.48 E	(13)	53°22′.94 N,	003°28′.40 E
(12)	53°03′.78 N,	003°18′.71 E	(14)	53°19′.89 N,	003°39′.74 E

Traffic separation scheme "West Friesland"

(f) A separation zone is bounded by a line connecting the following geographical positions:

(15)	53°42′.99 N,	003°42′.12 E	(19)	53°46′.73 N,	004°20′.00 E
(16)	53°22′.12 N,	003°31′.47 E	(20)	53°56′.69 N,	004°36′.00 E
(17)	53°20′.67 N,	003°36′.85 E	(21)	53°59′.22 N,	004°36′.00 E
(18)	53°31′.12 N,	003°44′.72 E	(22)	53°57′.60 N,	004°15′.17 E

(g) A traffic lane for north-eastbound traffic is established between the separation zone in paragraph (f) above and a line connecting the following geographical positions:

(14)	53°19′.89 N,	003°39′.74 E	(24)	53°45′.90 N,	004°23′.32 E
(23)	53°30′.00 N,	003°47′.37 E	(25)	54°00′.00 N,	004°46′.00 E

(h) A traffic lane for south-westbound traffic is established between the separation zone in paragraph (f) above and a line connecting the following geographical positions:

(26)	53°57′.20 N,	004°10′.02 E	(13)	53°22′.94 N,	003°28′.40 E
(27)	53°43′.39 N,	003°38′.81 E			

Precautionary area "Friesland Junction"

(i) A precautionary area is established directly to the north of the traffic separation scheme "West Friesland". The area is bounded by a line connecting the following geographical positions:

(26)	53°57′.20 N,	004°10′.02 E	(29)	54°05′.59 N,	004°59′.32 E
(25)	54°00′.00 N,	004°46′.00 E	(30)	54°02′.57 N,	004°20′.92 E
(28)	54°01′.14 N,	005°00′.34 E	(31)	54°01′.91 N,	004°08′.96 E

Traffic separation scheme "East Friesland"

(j) A separation zone is bounded by a line connecting the following geographical positions:

(32)	54°02′.62 N,	005°00′.00 E	(35)	54°08′.97 N,	006°01′.33 E
(33)	54°04′.21 N,	005°20′.00 E	(36)	54°05′.69 N,	005°19′.66 E
(34)	54°08′.00 N,	006°01′.90 E	(37)	54°04′.11 N,	004°59′.66 E

(k) A traffic lane for north-eastbound traffic is established between the separation zone in paragraph (j) above and a line connecting the following geographical positions:

(28)	54°01′.14 N,	005°00′.34 E	(38)	54°06′.10 N,	006°03′.00 E

(l) A traffic lane for south-westbound traffic is established between the separation zone in paragraph (j) above and a line connecting the following geographical positions:

(39)	54°10′.90 N,	006°00′.20 E	(29)	54°05′.59 N,	004°59′.32 E
(40)	54°07′.17 N,	005°19′.32 E			

Note: The positions (38), (34), (35) and (39) coincide with the positions (15), (11), (8) and (14) of the traffic separation scheme "German Bight western approach".

Application and use of the route

The route is mandatory for use by the following classes of ships:

(a) tankers of 10,000 tons gross tonnage and upwards, carrying oil as defined under Annex I to the International Convention for the Prevention of Pollution from Ships, 1973, as modified by the Protocol of 1978 relating thereto (MARPOL 73/78);

(b) chemical tankers of 5000 tons gross tonnage and upwards, carrying noxious liquid substances in bulk assessed or provisionally assessed as Category X or Y of Annex II to the International

Convention for the Prevention of Pollution from Ships, 1973, as modified by the Protocol of 1978 relating thereto (MARPOL 73/78);

(c) chemical tankers and NLS tankers of 10,000 tons gross tonnage and upwards, carrying noxious liquid substances in bulk assessed or provisionally assessed as Category Z of Annex II to the International Convention for the Prevention of Pollution from Ships, 1973, as modified by the Protocol of 1978 relating thereto (MARPOL 73/78); and

(d) ships of 10,000 tons gross tonnage and upwards, carrying liquefied gases in bulk.

These ships shall avoid the sea area between the mandatory route and the adjacent Frisian Islands' coast, except when joining or leaving the route at the nearest point of the route to the port of departure or destination which permits a safe passage to or from that port.

The classes of ships referred to above shall use the mandatory route or part of it:

(i) when sailing from North Hinder to the Baltic or to North Sea ports of Norway, Sweden, Denmark, Germany or the Netherlands north of latitude 53° N and vice versa;

(ii) when sailing between North Sea ports of the Netherlands north and/or Germany, except in cases of adjacent port areas;

(iii) when sailing between United Kingdom or Continental North Sea ports south of latitude 53° N and Scandinavian and Baltic ports; and

(iv) when sailing between North Hinder, United Kingdom or Continental ports south of latitude 53° N and offshore and offshore-based loading facilities in the North Sea area. However, this provision does not apply to ships sailing between ports on the east coast of the United Kingdom, including Orkney and Shetland Islands.

Ships which, because of their draught, cannot safely navigate the mandatory route – in particular the southern part of it (the routeing measures a, b and c above) – are exempted from the requirements to use the southern part of the mandatory route and are strongly recommended to use the western route of the routeing system "Off Friesland" or part of it, as appropriate, instead.

This alternative western route is formed by the following routeing measures:

.1 Deep-water route from North Hinder to Indefatigable Bank via DR1 lightbuoy;

.2 TSS "Off Botney Ground"; and

.3 Deep-water route from the traffic separation scheme "Off Botney Ground" to the precautionary area "Friesland Junction".

Shipmasters should enter this deviation in the ship's log.

Joining or leaving the route

The classes of ships referred to above, when joining or leaving the route:

(a) shall do so at the nearest point of the route to the port of departure or destination which permits a safe passage to or from that port; and

(b) should be aware that oil and gas production facilities and mobile offshore drilling units may be encountered in the proximity of the route; safety zones of 500 metres (0.27 nautical mile) radius are established around all offshore structures.

Pilotage

Ships required to use the "Mandatory route for tankers from North Hinder to the German Bight and vice versa" are referred to resolution A.486(XII), adopted on 19 November 1981, "Recommendation on the use of adequately qualified deep-sea pilots in the North Sea, English Channel and Skagerrak".*

* It is anticipated that this resolution will be revoked and replaced by a resolution of similar title that will be considered for adoption at the 28th session of IMO Assembly in December 2013.

Notes:

1 It is recommended that an efficient electronic position-fixing device appropriate for the area should be carried on board.

2 Numerous offshore structures situated within the limits of the separation zones and/or situated in the proximity of the route are equipped with X- and S-band racons.

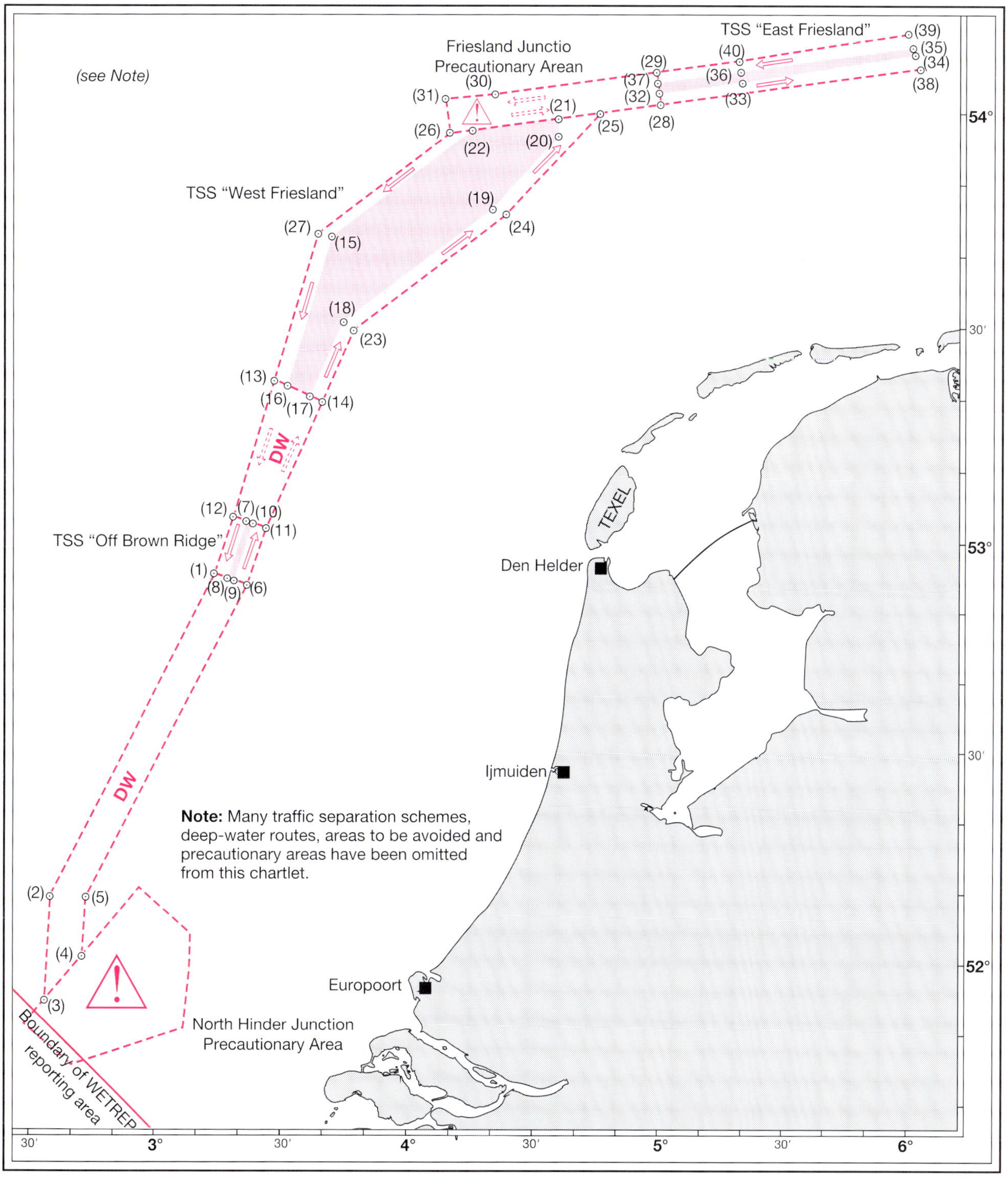

MANDATORY ROUTE FOR TANKERS FROM NORTH HINDER TO THE GERMAN BIGHT AND VICE VERSA

MANDATORY NO ANCHORING AREA IN THE APPROACHES TO THE GULF OF VENICE

Note: See mandatory ship reporting system "In the Adriatic Sea" in part G, section I.

(Reference chart: Italy 924, 2005 edition.
Note: This chart is based on Rome 1940 datum. The co-ordinates listed below are in WGS 84 datum)

Description of the mandatory no anchoring area

The area within the circle of 1.5 nautical miles centred on the following geographical position:

(1) 45°05′.30 N, 012°35′.10 E

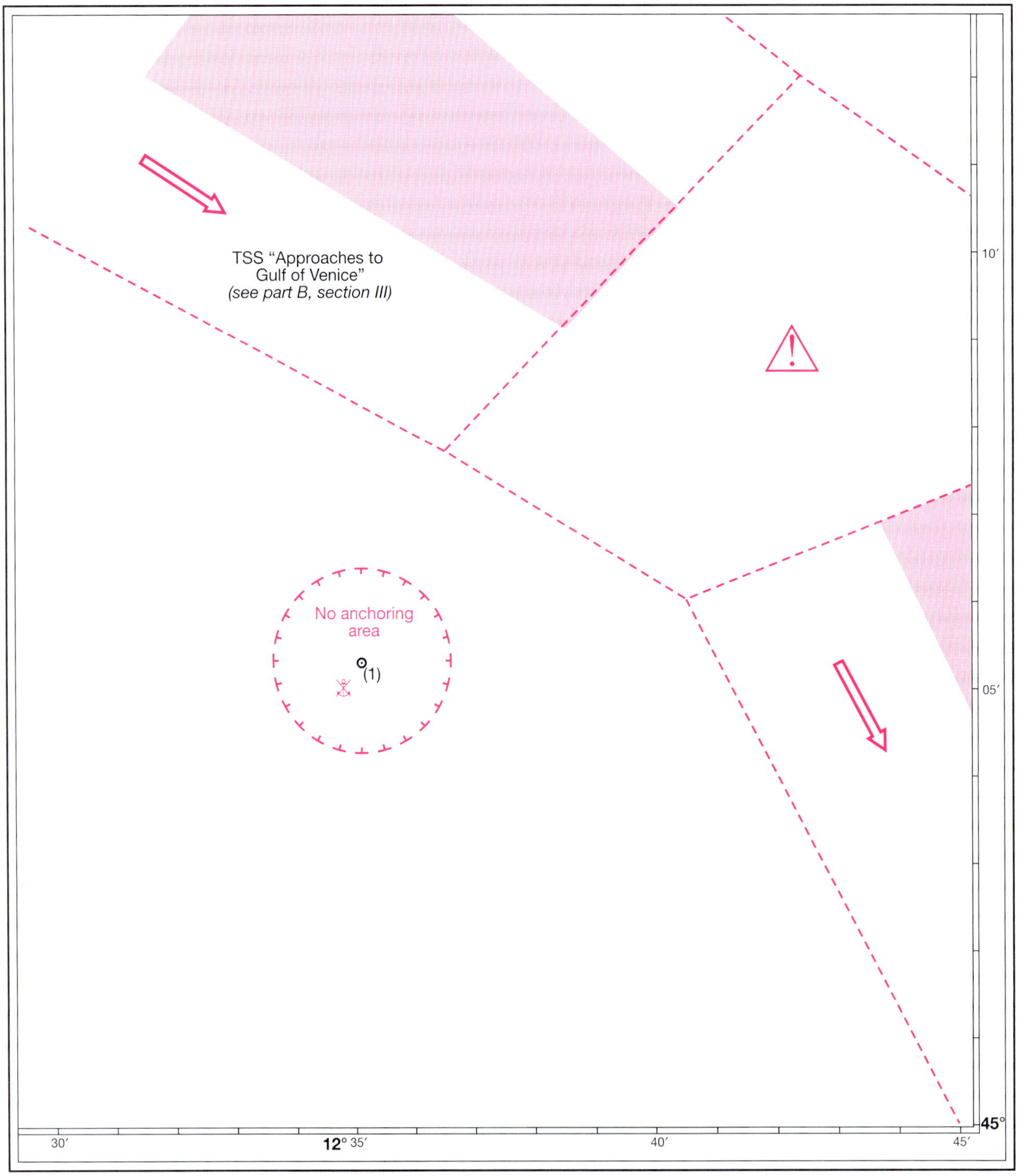

MANDATORY NO ANCHORING AREA IN THE APPROACHES TO THE GULF OF VENICE

MANDATORY NO ANCHORING AREAS IN THE VICINITY OF THE NEPTUNE DEEPWATER PORT IN THE WESTERN NORTH ATLANTIC OCEAN

(Reference charts: United States 13009, 2007 edition; 13200, 2008 edition; 13260, 2007 edition; 13267, 2007 edition.
Note: These charts are based on North American 1983 datum, which is equivalent to World Geodetic System 1984 datum (WGS 84).)

Description of the mandatory no anchoring areas

Two areas contained within a circle of radius 1000 metres centred upon the following geographical positions are designated as no anchoring areas for all ships:

Northern STL Buoy	42°29′.23 N,	070°36′.50 W,
Southern STL Buoy	42°27′.35 N,	070°36′.01 W

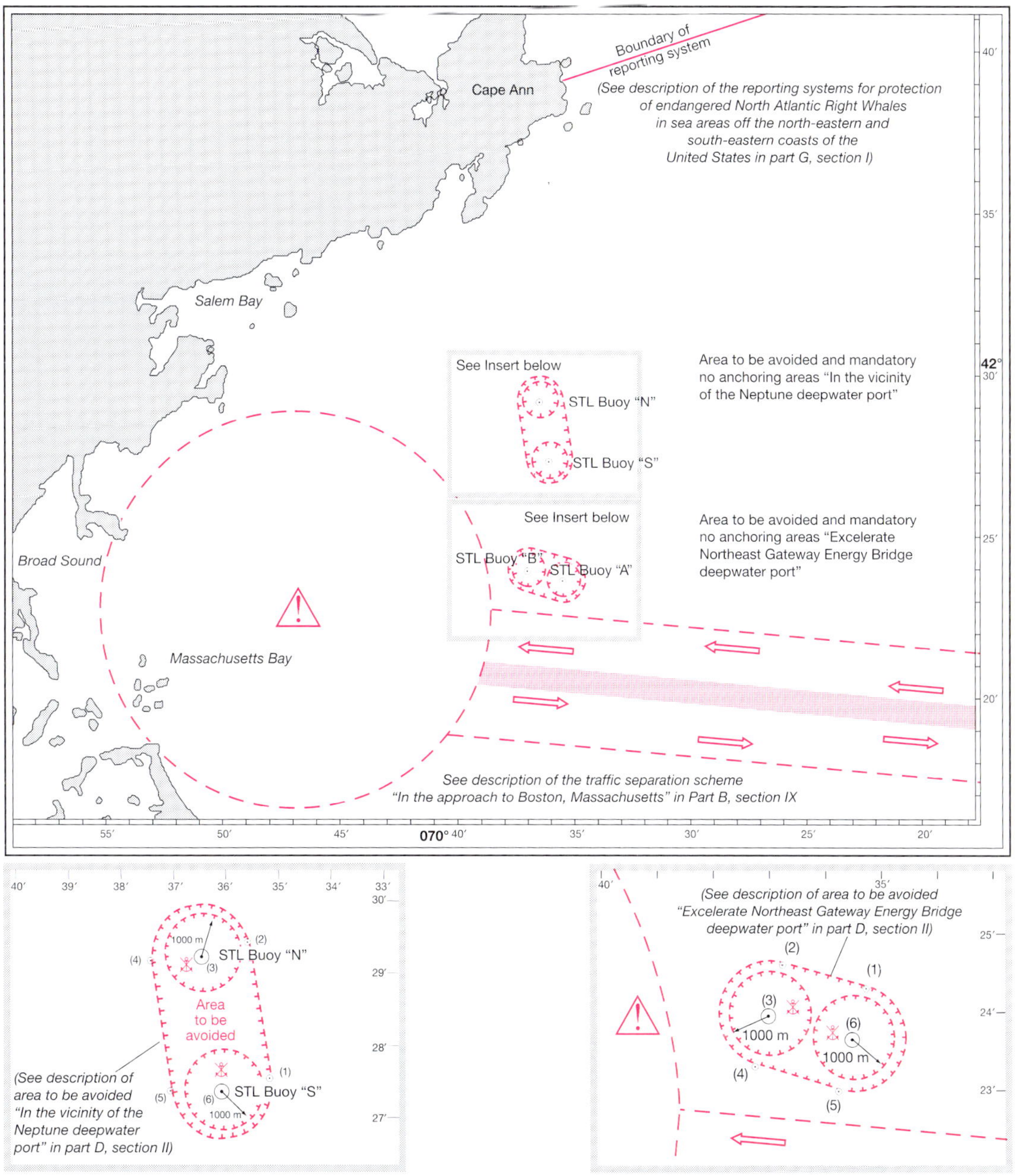

MANDATORY NO ANCHORING AREAS IN THE VICINITY OF THE NEPTUNE DEEPWATER PORT

MANDATORY NO ANCHORING AREAS IN THE VICINITY OF THE EXCELERATE NORTHEAST GATEWAY ENERGY BRIDGE DEEPWATER PORT IN THE ATLANTIC OCEAN

(Reference charts: United States 13009, 2007 edition; 13200, 2007 edition; 13246, 2006 edition; 13267, 2007 edition.
Note: These charts are based on North American 1983 datum, which is equivalent to World Geodetic System 1984 datum (WGS 84).)

Description of the mandatory no anchoring areas

Two areas contained within a circle of radius 1000 metres centred upon the following geographical positions are established as mandatory no anchoring areas:

STL Buoy "A"	42°23′.64 N,	070°35′.52 W
STL Buoy "B"	42°23′.94 N,	070°37′.01 W

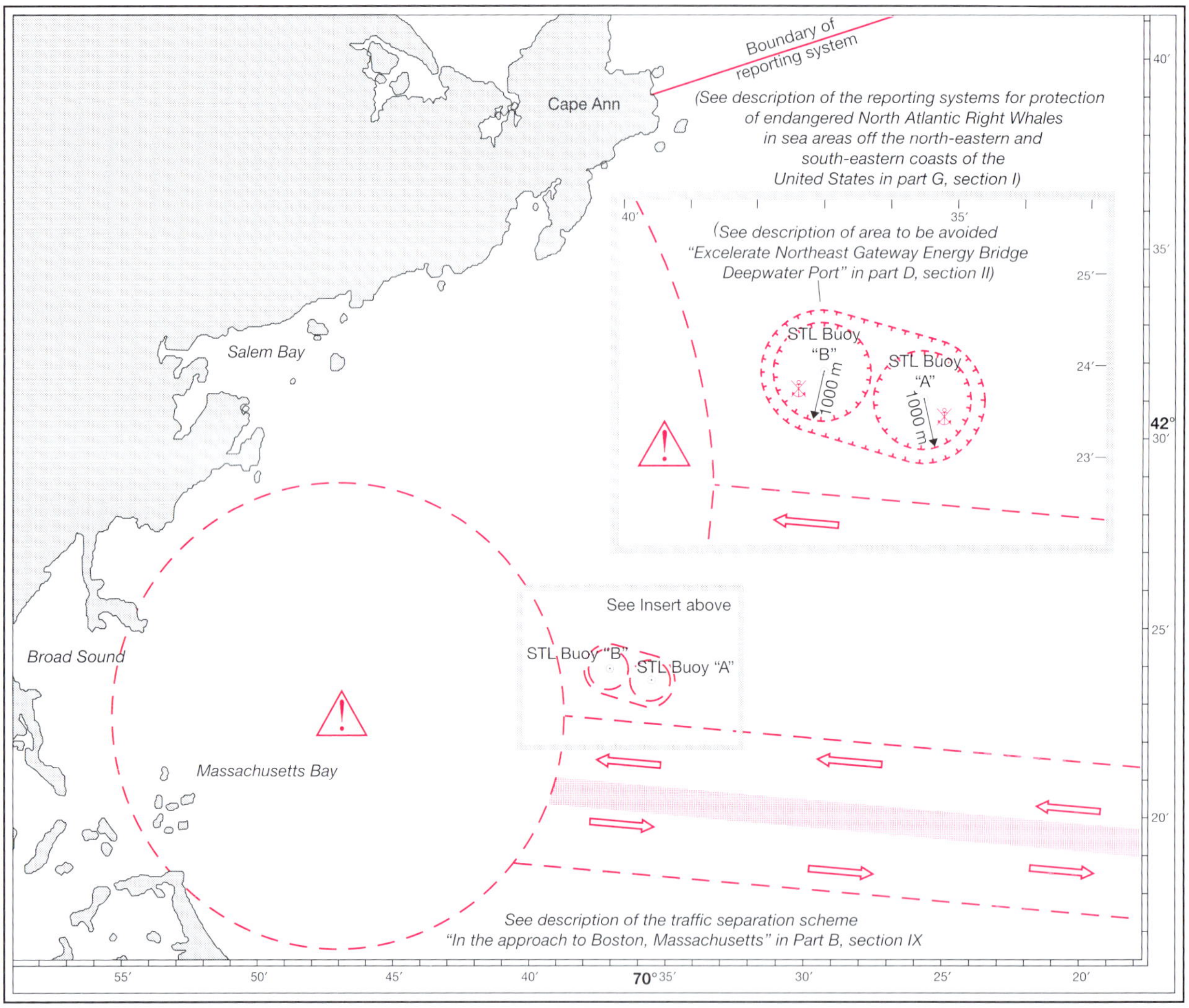

MANDATORY NO ANCHORING AREAS IN THE VICINITY OF THE EXCELERATE NORTHEAST GATEWAY ENERGY BRIDGE DEEPWATER PORT

MANDATORY NO ANCHORING AREAS IN THE TORTUGAS ECOLOGICAL RESERVE AND TORTUGAS BANK

(Reference chart: United States 11434, 1998 edition.
Note: This chart is based on North American 1983 datum.)

Description of the mandatory no anchoring areas

Northernmost area of the Tortugas Ecological Reserve

To avoid destruction of this unique, fragile and pristine coral reef ecosystem from anchoring, all ships shall avoid anchoring in the area bounded by a line connecting the following geographical positions which is designated as a mandatory no anchoring area:

(1)	24°46′.00 N,	083°06′.00 W	(6)	24°43′.00 N,	082°54′.00 W
(2)	24°46′.00 N,	082°54′.00 W	(7)	24°39′.00 N,	082°58′.00 W
(3)	24°45′.80 N,	082°48′.00 W	(8)	24°39′.00 N,	083°06′.00 W
(4)	24°43′.53 N,	082°48′.00 W	(9)	24°46′.00 N,	083°06′.00 W
(5)	24°43′.53 N,	082°52′.00 W			

Southernmost area of the Tortugas Ecological Reserve

To avoid destruction of this unique, fragile and pristine coral reef ecosystem from anchoring, all ships shall avoid anchoring in the area bounded by a line connecting the following geographical positions which is designated as a mandatory no anchoring area:

(10)	24°33′.00 N,	083°09′.00 W	(13)	24°18′.00 N,	083°09′.00 W
(11)	24°33′.00 N,	083°05′.00 W	(14)	24°33′.00 N,	083°09′.00 W
(12)	24°18′.00 N,	083°05′.00 W			

Tortugas Bank outside of the Tortugas Ecological Reserve

To avoid the destruction of this unique and fragile coral reef ecosystem from anchoring by large ships, ships 50 metres or more in length shall avoid anchoring in the area bounded by a line connecting the following geographical positions which is designated as a mandatory no anchoring area:

(15)	24°32′.00 N,	083°00′.05 W	(18)	24°39′.00 N,	083°00′.05 W
(16)	24°37′.00 N,	083°06′.00 W	(19)	24°32′.00 N,	083°00′.05 W
(17)	24°39′.00 N,	083°06′.00 W			

(chartlet overleaf)

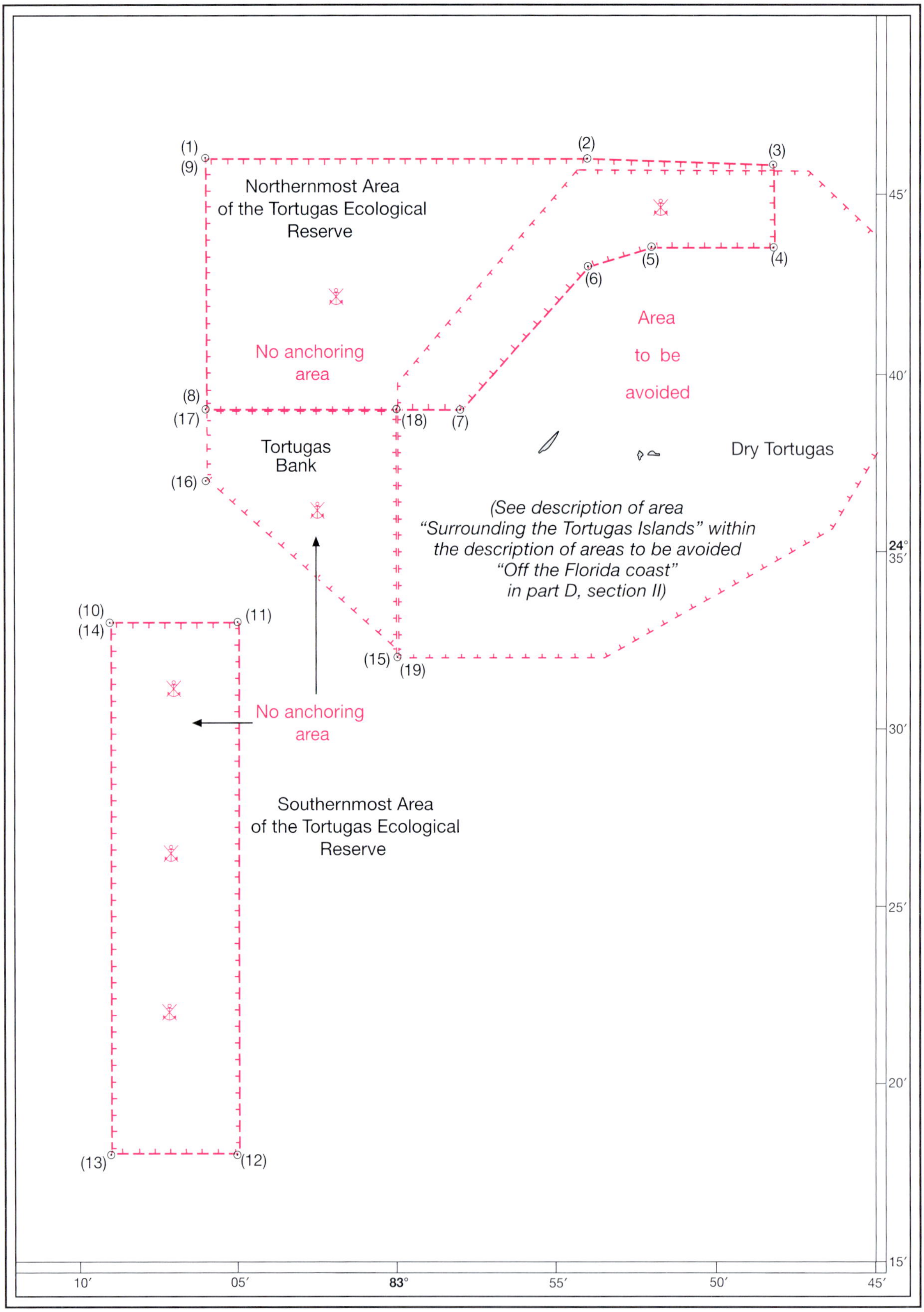

MANDATORY NO ANCHORING AREAS IN THE TORTUGAS ECOLOGICAL RESERVE AND TORTUGAS BANK

MANDATORY NO ANCHORING AREA AT EL PASO ENERGY BRIDGE DEEPWATER PORT IN THE GULF OF MEXICO

(Reference chart: United States 11340, 2003 edition.
Note: This chart is based on North American 1983 datum.)

Description of the mandatory no anchoring area

The area contained within a circle of radius 1500 metres centred on the following geographical position is designated as a mandatory no anchoring area:

28°05′.27 N, 093°03′.12 W

The mandatory no anchoring area applies to all vessels.

Appropriate charts will include the following notation:

The El Paso Energy Bridge Deepwater Port at 28°05′.27 N, 093°03′.12 W is surrounded by a Safety Zone of 500 metres radius. No vessel may enter the Safety Zone except those vessels intending to call or those assisting vessels at the Deepwater Port (DWP). There is a mandatory no anchoring area of 1500 metres radius centred at 28°05′.27 N, 093, 03°12 W. No vessel may anchor within this area. Further, there is an Area to be Avoided (ATBA) of 2000 metres radius also centred at 28°05′.27 N, 093°03′.12 W. The ATBA applies to all vessels not intending to call, or assisting vessels at the DWP.

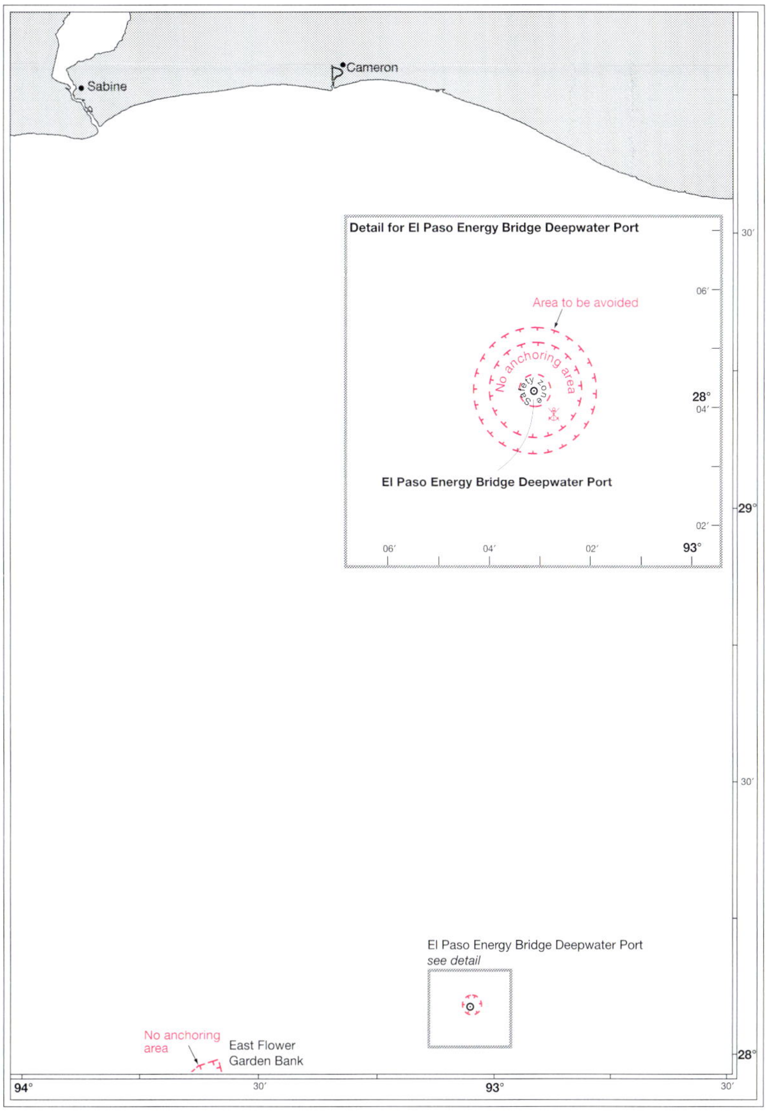

**MANDATORY NO ANCHORING AREA AT
EL PASO ENERGY BRIDGE DEEPWATER PORT IN THE GULF OF MEXICO**

MANDATORY NO ANCHORING AREAS FOR ALL SHIPS ON FLOWER GARDEN BANKS CORAL REEFS

EAST FLOWER GARDEN BANK

(Reference chart: United States 11340, 2000 edition.
Note: This chart is based on North American 1983 geodetic datum.)

(E-1)	27°52′.91 N,	093°37′.70 W	(E-7)	27°59′.03 N,	093°35′.17 W
(E-2)	27°53′.60 N,	093°38′.40 W	(E-8)	27°55′.39 N,	093°34′.26 W
(E-3)	27°55′.24 N,	093°38′.68 W	(E-9)	27°54′.08 N,	093°34′.32 W
(E-4)	27°57′.53 N,	093°38′.56 W	(E-10)	27°53′.46 N,	093°35′.09 W
(E-5)	27°58′.48 N,	093°37′.78 W	(E-11)	27°52′.88 N,	093°36′.96 W
(E-6)	27°59′.04 N,	093°35′.54 W			

WEST FLOWER GARDEN BANK

(Reference chart: United States 11340, 2000 edition.
Note: This chart is based on North American 1983 geodetic datum.)

(W-1)	27°49′.19 N,	093°50′.76 W	(W-8)	27°54′.60 N,	093°47′.18 W
(W-2)	27°50′.22 N,	093°52′.18 W	(W-9)	27°54′.26 N,	093°46′.83 W
(W-3)	27°51′.23 N,	093°52′.87 W	(W-10)	27°53′.61 N,	093°46′.86 W
(W-4)	27°51′.56 N,	093°52′.85 W	(W-11)	27°52′.97 N,	093°47′.26 W
(W-5)	27°52′.85 N,	093°52′.42 W	(W-12)	27°50′.69 N,	093°47′.38 W
(W-6)	27°55′.03 N,	093°49′.74 W	(W-13)	27°49′.20 N,	093°48′.72 W
(W-7)	27°54′.99 N,	093°48′.64 W			

STETSON BANK

(Reference charts: United States 11300, 1990 edition; 11330, 1998 edition; 11340, 2000 edition.
Note: These charts are based on North American 1983 geodetic datum.)

(S-1)	28°09′.52 N,	094°18′.53 W	(S-3)	28°10′.13 N,	094°17′.40 W
(S-2)	28°10′.17 N,	094°18′.50 W	(S-4)	28°09′.48 N,	094°17′.43 W

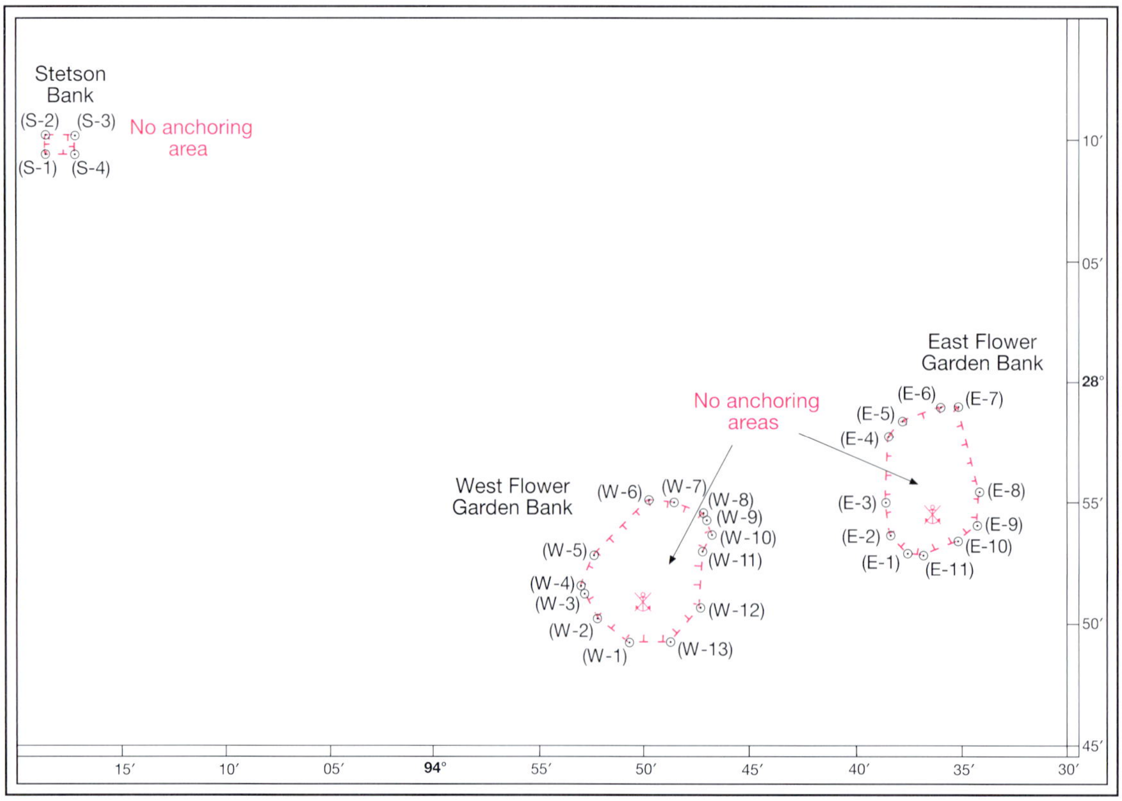

MANDATORY NO ANCHORING AREAS FOR ALL SHIPS ON FLOWER GARDEN BANKS CORAL REEFS

MANDATORY NO ANCHORING AREA FOR ALL SHIPS AS ASSOCIATED PROTECTIVE MEASURE (APM) FOR SABA BANK PSSA*

Note: See area to be avoided "By ships of 300 gross tonnage or over as associated protective measure (APM) for Saba Bank PSSA" in part D, section II.

(Reference chart: Netherlands 2020, edition November 2007.
Note: This chart is based on World Geodetic System 1984 datum (WGS 84).)

Description of the mandatory no anchoring area

A mandatory no anchoring area for all ships is established in the area designated as a Particularly Sensitive Sea Area and bounded by a line connecting the following geographical positions:

(1)	17°27′.06 N,	063°56′.14 W	(8)	17°30′.88 N,	063°10′.92 W
(2)	17°29′.00 N,	063°55′.09 W	(9)	17°23′.80 N,	063°11′.25 W
(3)	17°27′.94 N,	063°43′.32 W	(10)	17°16′.27 N,	063°15′.85 W
(4)	17°38′.03 N,	063°27′.41 W	(11)	17°13′.44 N,	063°26′.89 W
(5)	17°43′.35 N,	063°32′.74 W	(12)	17°10′.55 N,	063°41′.81 W
(6)	17°45′.98 N,	063°29′.98 W	(13)	17°20′.85 N,	063°49′.89 W
(7)	17°40′.34 N,	063°21′.10 W			

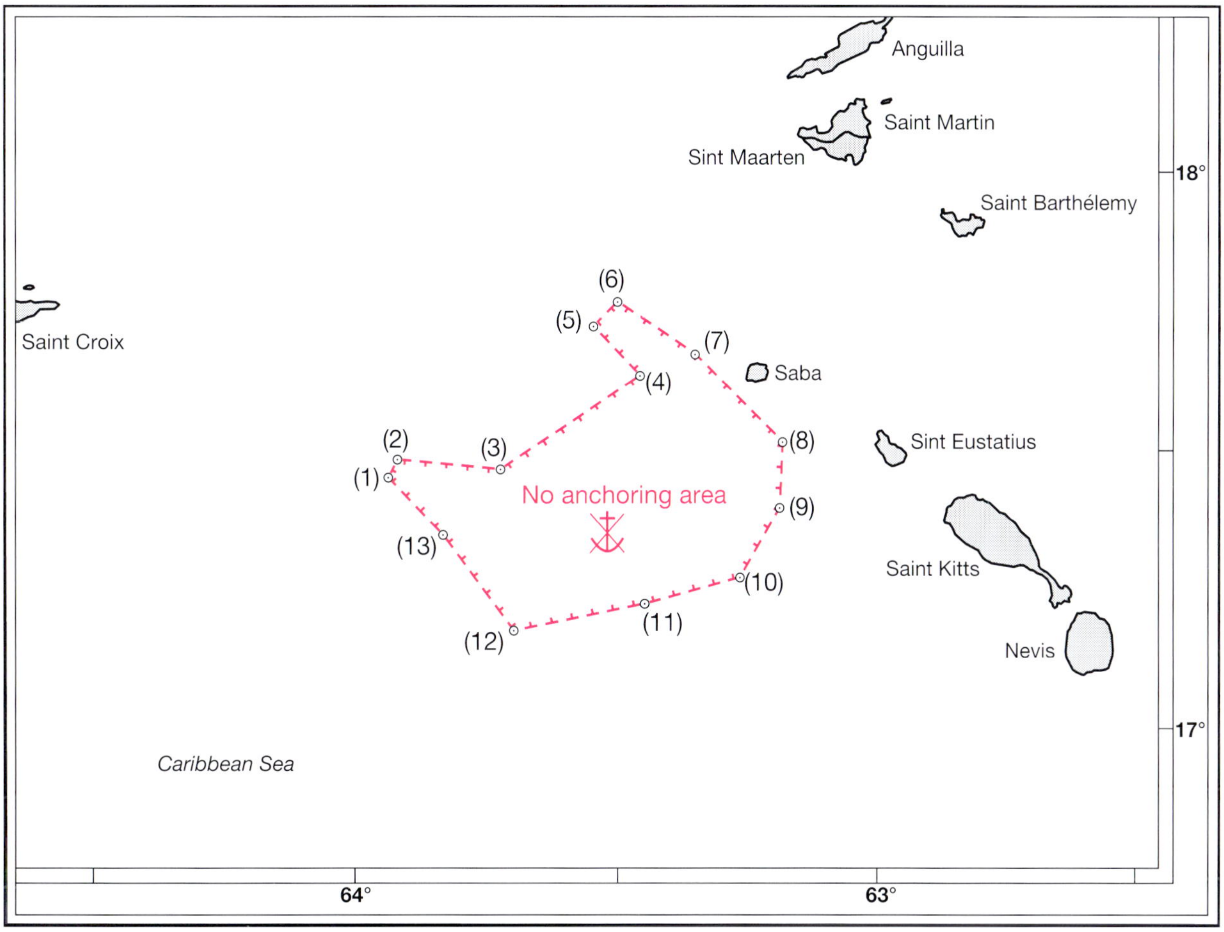

MANDATORY NO ANCHORING AREA FOR ALL SHIPS AS ASSOCIATED PROTECTIVE MEASURE (APM) FOR SABA BANK PSSA

G

* Date of implementation of new mandatory no anchoring area: 0000 hours UTC on 1 June 2013.

MANDATORY NO ANCHORING AREAS ON SHARKS BANK AND LONG SHOAL

(Reference chart: British Admiralty 502, January 2006 edition.
Note: This chart is based on World Geodetic System 1984 datum (WGS 84).)

Description of the mandatory no anchoring areas

Sharks Bank

To avoid destruction of this unique, fragile and pristine coral reef ecosystem from anchoring, all ships shall avoid anchoring in the area bounded by a line connecting the following geographical positions which is designated as a mandatory no anchoring area:

(1) 13° 05′ 18″.6 N, 059° 38′ 06″.1 W
(2) 13° 05′ 23″.6 N, 059° 37′ 56″.7 W
(3) 13° 05′ 16″.0 N, 059° 37′ 49″.3 W
(4) 13° 05′ 08″.6 N, 059° 37′ 57″.1 W

Long Shoal

To avoid destruction of this unique, fragile and pristine coral reef ecosystem from anchoring, ships 25 ft and greater shall avoid anchoring in the area bounded by a line connecting the following geographical positions which is designated as a mandatory no anchoring area:

(1) 13° 07′ 25″.4 N, 059° 38′ 40″.2 W
(2) 13° 07′ 22″.9 N, 059° 38′ 27″.4 W
(3) 13° 07′ 00″.7 N, 059° 38′ 30″.5 W
(4) 13° 07′ 00″.8 N, 059° 38′ 43″.3 W

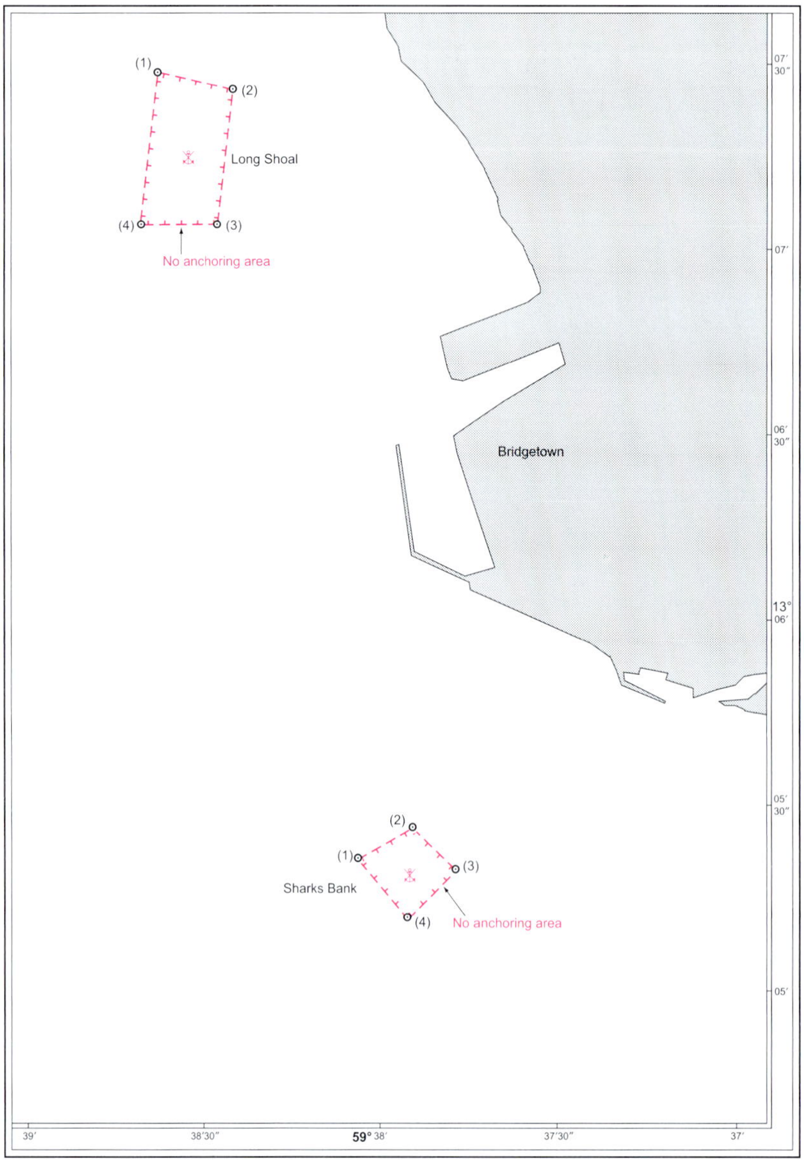

MANDATORY NO ANCHORING AREAS ON SHARKS BANK AND LONG SHOAL

G

Part H

Adoption, designation and substitution of Archipelagic Sea Lanes

H

H

GENERAL PROVISIONS FOR THE ADOPTION, DESIGNATION AND SUBSTITUTION OF ARCHIPELAGIC SEA LANES

Introduction

This Part takes into account the unique character of archipelagic sea lanes as a routeing system.

The legal regime for archipelagic sea lanes is contained in Part IV of the United Nations Convention on the Law of the Sea (UNCLOS). UNCLOS provides that designation and substitution of an archipelagic sea lane by an archipelagic State automatically includes a corresponding air route above the sea lane. Use of an air route above a designated archipelagic sea lane by civil aircraft engaged in international air navigation shall be in accordance with any relevant requirements of the International Civil Aviation Organization (ICAO). International air traffic services (ATS) routes above the archipelagic waters to be used by civil aircraft engaged in international air navigation are subject to the approval process of ICAO.

1 Objectives

1.1 The purpose of these provisions is to provide guidance for the preparation, consideration and adoption of proposals for the adoption, designation and substitution of archipelagic sea lanes.

2 Definitions and clarifications

2.1 The terms used in connection with matters relating to archipelagic sea lanes have the same meaning as in UNCLOS. These terms include:

.1 *Archipelagic State*

.2 *Archipelagic sea lane*

.3 *Archipelagic sea lanes passage*

.4 *Innocent passage*

2.2 The following terms are also used in connection with matters relating to archipelagic sea lanes:

.1 *All normal passage routes and navigational channels as required by UNCLOS*
All normal passage routes used as routes for international navigation or overflight through or over archipelagic waters and, within such routes, so far as ships are concerned, all normal navigational channels, provided that duplication of routes of similar convenience between the same entry and exit points shall not be necessary.

.2 *Partial archipelagic sea lanes proposal*
An archipelagic sea lanes proposal by an archipelagic State which does not meet the requirement to include all normal passage routes and navigational channels as required by UNCLOS.

3 Procedures and responsibilities

Procedures and functions of IMO

3.1 IMO is recognized as the competent international organization responsible for adopting archipelagic sea lanes in accordance with the relevant provisions of UNCLOS and these provisions.

3.2 When adopting a proposed archipelagic sea lane, IMO will ensure that the proposed sea lane is in accordance with the relevant provisions of UNCLOS and determine if the proposal is a partial archipelagic sea lanes proposal. IMO may adopt only such archipelagic sea lanes as may be agreed by the Government of the proposing archipelagic State.

3.3 Upon receipt of a proposal for designating archipelagic sea lanes and before consideration for adoption, the IMO shall ensure that the proposal is disseminated to all Governments and ICAO so as to provide them with sufficient opportunity to comment on the proposal.

3.4 Following a proposal to the IMO by an archipelagic State, other States may request that the archipelagic State propose additional sea lanes to include all other normal passage routes used as routes for international navigation or overflight through or over archipelagic waters as required by UNCLOS.

3.5 In order for IMO to ensure that sea lanes proposed for adoption include all normal passage routes, IMO shall retain continuing jurisdiction (i.e., competence) over the process of adopting archipelagic sea lanes until such time that sea lanes including all normal passage routes have been adopted as required by UNCLOS.

Responsibilities of Governments and recommended practices

3.6 The Government of an archipelagic State considering proposing archipelagic sea lanes should consult at an early stage with other user Governments and the IMO.

3.7 Subject to paragraph 3.9, the Government of an archipelagic State which wishes to designate archipelagic sea lanes shall propose to IMO for adoption archipelagic sea lanes including all normal passage routes and navigational channels as required by UNCLOS.

3.8 An archipelagic sea lanes proposal shall provide sea lanes suitable for the continuous and expeditious passage of foreign ships and aircraft in the normal mode through or over the archipelagic waters and the adjacent territorial sea. In proposing archipelagic sea lanes, the Government shall explain in its proposal the suitability of such sea lanes for such continuous and expeditious passage.

3.9 The proposal shall also indicate if it is a partial archipelagic sea lane proposal.

3.10 In proposing archipelagic sea lanes, Governments shall also include the number, edition and, where possible, the geodetic datum of the reference charts used for the proposed sea lanes, together with copies of the reference charts listed in the proposed sea lanes showing the axis of the proposed sea lanes.

3.11 It is recommended that in areas where the 10 per cent rule applies (see paragraph 6.3) the outer limits of the sea lane should, so far as practicable, be clearly indicated on the charts.

3.12 If IMO adopts a partial archipelagic sea lane proposal as a partial system of archipelagic sea lanes, the archipelagic State shall periodically inform IMO on its plans for conducting further surveys and studies that will result in the submission to IMO of proposals for adoption of all normal passage routes and navigational channels as required by UNCLOS, along with the general location of these lanes and time frame for this effort. In such a case, the archipelagic State is ultimately required to propose for adoption archipelagic sea lanes including all normal passage routes and navigational channels as required by UNCLOS.

3.13 After the adoption of the archipelagic sea lanes by IMO, the Government of the archipelagic State shall promulgate the designation of the sea lanes. The designation of the sea lanes shall be formally communicated to IMO.

3.14 Archipelagic sea lanes shall not come into effect until at least six months after the later of:

.1 designation of sea lanes as described in paragraph 3.13 and;

.2 publication of either Notices to Mariners to amend charts or revised charts to depict the sea lanes.

4 Criteria for consideration and adoption of proposals

4.1 Archipelagic sea lane proposals shall conform with the relevant provisions of UNCLOS, including Article 53, and the requirements of this Part.

4.2 The adequacy of aids to navigation, hydrographic surveys and nautical charts of the area, as well as the configuration of the archipelagic State, shall be considered.

4.3 Routeing measures in the vicinity shall also be considered.

5 Substitution of archipelagic sea lanes and traffic separation schemes

5.1 An archipelagic State may, when circumstances require, after giving due publicity thereto, substitute other sea lanes or traffic separation schemes for any sea lanes or traffic separation schemes previously designated or prescribed by it.

5.2 The provisions of this Part concerning the designation of archipelagic sea lanes apply equally to the substitution of archipelagic sea lanes.

5.3 The provisions of this Part and Part A of the IMO publication on ships' routeing concerning the prescription of traffic separation schemes apply equally to the substitution of traffic separation schemes.

6 Use of archipelagic sea lanes and normal passage routes

6.1 Ships and aircraft shall exercise in accordance with UNCLOS their right of archipelagic sea lanes passage in the normal mode solely for the purpose of continuous, expeditious and unobstructed transit between one part of the high seas or an exclusive economic zone and another part of the high seas or an exclusive economic zone.

6.2 Ships and aircraft in archipelagic sea lanes passage shall respect applicable sea lanes and the relevant provisions of UNCLOS, including Article 39. Ships shall also respect any traffic separation schemes in archipelagic sea lanes established in accordance with Part A of the IMO publication on ships' routeing.

6.3 Ships and aircraft in archipelagic sea lanes passage shall not deviate more than 25 nautical miles to either side of the axis lines defining archipelagic sea lanes, provided that such ships and aircraft shall not navigate closer to the coasts than 10 per cent of the distance between the nearest points on islands bordering the sea lane.

6.4 Within archipelagic sea lanes, traffic is not separated, except in traffic separation schemes.

6.5 Except for internal waters within archipelagic waters, ships of all States enjoy the right of innocent passage through archipelagic waters and the territorial sea.

6.6 If an archipelagic State does not designate sea lanes and air routes thereabove, the right of archipelagic sea lanes passage may be exercised through the routes normally used for international navigation.

6.7 Where a partial archipelagic sea lanes proposal has come into effect, the right of archipelagic sea lanes passage may continue to be exercised through all normal passage routes used as routes for international navigation or overflight in other parts of archipelagic waters in accordance with UNCLOS.

6.8 The right of archipelagic sea lanes passage shall not be suspended, hampered or obstructed.

6.9 The archipelagic State shall give appropriate publicity to any danger to navigation within archipelagic sea lanes of which it has knowledge.

7 Representation on charts

7.1 Axis lines of archipelagic sea lanes are shown on charts for the purpose of defining the sea lanes. Axis lines do not indicate any routes or recommended tracks as defined in Part A of the IMO publication on ships' routeing.

7.2 The axis of designated archipelagic sea lanes, including a listing of geographical co-ordinates with geodetic datum that define axis turning points, so far as practicable the outer limits of the sea lanes where the 10 per cent rule applies (see paragraphs 3.11 and 6.3), and any prescribed traffic separation schemes shall be clearly shown on all appropriate scale charts, to which due publicity shall be given, and referred to in complementary hydrographic publications.

7.3 The legends, symbols and notes appearing in paragraphs 7.4, 7.5, 7.6 and 7.7 are recommended by the International Hydrographic Organization as guidance for the representation of details of archipelagic sea lanes and associated measures on nautical charts. They are included to illustrate the information likely to be found on charts and as an aid to those designing archipelagic sea lanes proposed for adoption by IMO.

7.4 *Use of legends on charts and in notes*

Legend	**Use of legend**
Archipelagic Sea Lane	Not usually shown on charts but referred to in notes
ASL	Shown on charts in conjunction with symbol for axis line (paragraph 7.5)

7.5 *Symbol for axis line of archipelagic sea lanes*

Unless otherwise specified, symbols are printed on charts in colour, usually magenta.

	Description	Symbol	Note
1	Axis line of archipelagic sea lane	— – — –	1
2	Legend	ASL (see Note)	2
3	Turning point of axis line of archipelagic sea lane		3

Notes:

1 The axis line will be shown through other routeing measures without interruption, since it may not necessarily form the centre line of a routeing measure established in Archipelagic Sea Lanes, in accordance with Part A of the IMO publication on ships' routeing.

2 The legend *ASL (see Note)* should normally be used. The full legend *Archipelagic Sea Lane (see Note)* may, however, be used in cases where it is considered appropriate.

3 Turning points are indicated by joined pecked lines.

7.6 *Symbol for outer limits of archipelagic sea lanes*

Unless otherwise specified, symbols are printed on charts in colour, usually magenta.

	Description	Symbol	Note
1	Outer limit of achipelagic sea lane, including where 10% rule applies	▲ ▲ ▲	1

Note:

1 The solid triangle indicator points into the archipelagic sea lane. The full outer limit of archipelagic sea lane may be charted where it is considered appropriate.

7.7 *Cautionary and explanatory notes on charts*

The following note provides an example of the type of information which should be included in the note:

ASL – ARCHIPELAGIC SEA LANES

Archipelagic Sea Lanes as defined in UNCLOS have been designated in the area of this chart. Vessels exercising archipelagic sea lanes passage shall not deviate more than 25 miles from the charted axis line and shall not navigate, while in archipelagic sea lanes passage, within the areas indicated thus: ▲ ▲ ▲

Where a traffic separation scheme exists in a narrow channel in such a sea lane, rules for the use of traffic separation schemes apply. It should be noted that the axis line of the ASL does not indicate the deepest water, any route or recommended track.

Section I

Adopted Archipelagic Sea Lanes

1: Partial system of archipelagic sea lanes in Indonesian archipelagic waters

Caution: The chartlets are for illustrative purposes only and must not be used for navigation. Mariners should consult the appropriate nautical publications and charts for up-to-date details on aids to navigation and other relevant information.

Warning: The geographical positions given in the descriptions of the archipelagic sea lanes are only correct for charts using the same geodetic datum as the reference charts indicated under each scheme. Charts published by other hydrographic offices may use a different geodetic datum, as may new editions of the reference charts published after the adoption of the sea lanes.

H

PARTIAL SYSTEM OF ARCHIPELAGIC SEA LANES IN INDONESIAN ARCHIPELAGIC WATERS

Part I

Sea lane I: South China Sea – Natuna Sea – Karimata Strait – western Java Sea – Sunda Strait – Indian (Hindia) Ocean

(Reference charts (publisher, chart number and scale, points reflected on chart, geodetic datum):

Indonesian Navy Hydrographic Office, chart No. 2, September 1988, corrected to 17 February 1997, 1:4,000,000, (I-1) to (I-15), Bessel 1841;
Indonesian Navy Hydrographic Office, chart No. 38, February 1989, corrected to 11 May 1996, 1:1,000,000, (I-1) to (I-7), Bessel 1841;
Indonesian Navy Hydrographic Office, chart No. 66, June 1990, corrected to 15 September 1997, 1:1,000,000, (I-8) to (I-15), Bessel 1841;
Indonesian Navy Hydrographic Office, chart No. 147, March 1993, corrected to 6 March 1993, 1:500,000, (I-1) and (I-2), Bessel 1841;
Indonesian Navy Hydrographic Office, chart No. 148, December 1995, corrected to 9 December 1995, 1:500,000, (I-3) and (I-4), WGS 84;
Indonesian Navy Hydrographic Office, chart No. 149, September 1981, corrected to 15 February 1992, 1:500,000, (I-5) to (I-8), Bessel 1841;
Indonesian Navy Hydrographic Office, chart No. 78, March 1995, corrected to 15 September 1997, 1:200,000, (I-9) to (I-12), Bessel 1841;
Indonesian Navy Hydrographic Office, chart No. 71, March 1995, corrected to 11 March 1995, 1:200,000, (I-13) to (I-15), WGS 72)

Description of the archipelagic sea lane

The axis line connects the following geographical positions:

(I-1)	03°35′.00 N,	108°51′.00 E	(I-9)	05°12′.50 S,	106°54′.50 E
(I-2)	03°00′.00 N,	108°10′.00 E	(I-10)	05°17′.25 S,	106°44′.50 E
(I-3)	00°50′.00 N,	106°16′.33 E	(I-11)	05°17′.25 S,	106°27′.50 E
(I-4)	00°12′.33 S,	106°44′.00 E	(I-12)	05°15′.00 S,	106°12′.50 E
(I-5)	02°01′.00 S,	108°27′.00 E	(I-13)	05°57′.25 S,	105°46′.33 E
(I-6)	02°16′.00 S,	109°19′.50 E	(I-14)	06°18′.50 S,	105°33′.25 E
(I-7)	02°45′.00 S,	109°33′.00 E	(I-15)	06°24′.75 S,	104°41′.42 E
(I-8)	03°46′.75 S,	109°33′.00 E			

Notes for the use of this archipelagic sea lane:

(a) Geographical positions (I-1) to (I-3) define the axis line from the South China Sea through the Natuna Sea.

(b) Geographical positions (I-3) to (I-5) define the axis line from the Natuna Sea to the Karimata Strait.

(c) Geographical positions (I-5) to (I-7) define the axis line through the Karimata Strait.

(d) Geographical positions (I-7) to (I-12) define the axis line through the western Java Sea.

(e) Geographical positions (I-12) to (I-15) define the axis line through the Sunda Strait into the Indian (Hindia) Ocean.

Sea lane IA: Spur from North of Pulau Merapas to point (I-3)

(Reference charts (publisher, chart number and scale, points reflected on chart, geodetic datum):

Indonesian Navy Hydrographic Office, chart No. 38, February 1989, corrected to 11 May 1996, 1:1,000,000, (IA-1) to (I-3), Bessel 1841;
Indonesian Navy Hydrographic Office, chart No. 2, September 1988, corrected to 17 February 1997, 1:4,000,000, (IA-1) to (I-3), Bessel 1841)

Description of the archipelagic sea lane

The axis line connects the following geographical positions:

(IA-1)	01°52′.00 N, 104°55′.00 E	(I-3)	00°50′.00 N, 106°16′.33 E

Notes for the use of this archipelagic sea lane:

(a) Geographical positions (IA-1) to (I-3) define the axis line from the Singapore Strait through the Natuna Sea.

Part II

Sea lane II: Celebes (Sulawesi) Sea – Makasar Strait – Lombok Strait – Indian (Hindia) Ocean

(Reference charts (publisher, chart number and scale, points reflected on chart, geodetic datum):

Indonesian Navy Hydrographic Office, chart No. 2, September 1988, corrected to 17 February 1997, 1:4,000,000, (II-1) to (II-8), Bessel 1841;
Indonesian Navy Hydrographic Office, chart No. 121, October 1993, corrected to 7 July 1997, 1:1,000,000, (II-1) to (II-4), Bessel 1841;
Indonesian Navy Hydrographic Office, chart No. 111, August 1997, corrected to 4 August 1997, 1:1,000,000 (II-4) to (II-8), Bessel 1841;
Indonesian Navy Hydrographic Office, chart No. 128, October 1997, corrected to 20 October 1997, 1:500,000, (II-4) and (II-5), WGS 72;
Indonesian Navy Hydrographic Office, chart No. 113, July 1988, corrected to 2 July 1988, 1:500,000, (II-6) to (II-8), WGS 72;
Indonesian Navy Hydrographic Office, chart No. 291, June 1996, corrected to 20 July 1996, 1: 200,000, (II-7) and (II-8), WGS 72)

Description of the archipelagic sea lane

The axis line connects the following geographical positions:

(II-1)	00°57′.00 N, 119°33′.00 E	(II-5)	05°28′.00 S, 117°05′.00 E
(II-2)	00°00′.00 N, 119°00′.00 E	(II-6)	07°00′.00 S, 116°50′.00 E
(II-3)	02°40′.00 S, 118°17′.00 E	(II-7)	08°00′.00 S, 116°00′.00 E
(II-4)	03°45′.00 S, 118°17′.00 E	(II-8)	09°01′.00 S, 115°36′.00 E

Notes for the use of this archipelagic sea lane:

(a) Geographical positions (II-1) to (II-2) define the axis line from the Celebes (Sulawesi) Sea to the Makasar Strait.

(b) Geographical positions (II-3) to (II-6) define the axis line between Borneo (Kalimantan) and Celebes (Sulawesi) islands.

(c) Geographical positions (II-6) to (II-7) define the axis line through the Bali Sea.

(d) Geographical positions (II-7) to (II-8) define the axis line through Lombok Strait to the Indian (Hindia) Ocean

Part III

Sea lane IIIA: Pacific Ocean – Maluku Sea – Seram Sea – Banda Sea – Ombai Strait – Sawu Sea – Indian (Hindia) Ocean

(Reference charts (publisher, chart number and scale, points reflected on chart, geodetic datum):

Indonesian Navy Hydrographic Office, chart No. 3, March 1985, corrected to 13 October 1997, 1:4,000,000, (IIIA-1) to (IIIA-11), Bessel 1841;
Indonesian Navy Hydrographic Office, chart No. 403, September 1996, corrected to 14 September 1996, 1: 500,000, (IIIA-1) to (IIIA-3), Bessel 1841;
Indonesian Navy Hydrographic Office, chart No. 357, December 1985, corrected to 17 February 1997, 1:1,000,000, (IIIA-1) to (IIIA-3), Bessel 1841;
Indonesian Navy Hydrographic Office, chart No. 142, May 1991, corrected to 24 August 1996, 1:1,000,000, (IIIA-4) to (IIIA-8), Bessel 1841;
Indonesian Navy Hydrographic Office, chart No. 366, July 1993, corrected to 15 September 1997, 1:1,000,000, (IIIA-10) to (IIIA-13), Bessel 1841;
Indonesian Navy Hydrographic Office, chart No. 367, August 1993, corrected to 7 July 1997, 1:1,000,000, (IIIA-9) and (IIIA-10), Bessel 1841;
Indonesian Navy Hydrographic Office, chart No. 112, June 1991, corrected to 10 June 1995, 1:1,000,000, (IIIA-9) to (IIIA-13), Bessel 1841;
Indonesian Navy Hydrographic Office, chart No. 363, January 1990, corrected to 15 June 1996, 1:1,000,000, (IIIA-3) to (IIIA-6), Bessel 1841;
Indonesian Navy Hydrographic Office, chart No. 404, October 1993, corrected to 13 November 1993, 1: 500,000, (IIIA-4) and (IIIA-5), Bessel 1841)

Description of the archipelagic sea lane

The axis line connects the following geographical positions:

(IIIA-1)	03°27′.00 N,	127°40′.50 E
(IIIA-2)	01°40′.00 N,	126°57′.50 E
(IIIA-3)	01°12′.00 N,	126°54′.00 E
(IIIA-4)	00°09′.00 N,	126°20′.00 E
(IIIA-5)	01°53′.00 S,	127°02′.00 E
(IIIA-6)	02°37′.00 S,	126°30′.00 E
(IIIA-7)	02°53′.00 S,	125°30′.00 E
(IIIA-8)	03°20′.00 S,	125°30′.00 E
(IIIA-9)	08°25′.00 S,	125°20′.00 E
(IIIA-10)	09°03′.00 S,	123°34′.00 E
(IIIA-11)	09°23′.00 S,	122°55′.00 E
(IIIA-12)	10°12′.00 S,	121°18′.00 E
(IIIA-13)	10°44′.50 S,	120°45′.75 E

Notes for the use of this archipelagic sea lane:

(a) Geographical positions (IIIA-1) to (IIIA-5) define the axis line from the Pacific Ocean through the Maluku Sea.

(b) Geographical positions (IIIA-5) to (IIIA-7) define the axis line through the Seram Sea.

(c) Geographical positions (IIIA-7) to (IIIA-9) define the axis line through the western Banda Sea to the Ombai Strait.

(d) Geographical positions (IIIA-9) to (IIIA-13) define the axis line through the Ombai Strait and Sawu Sea between Sumba and Sawu Islands to the Indian (Hindia) Ocean.

Sea lane IIIE: Spur from point (IIIA-2) to (IIIE-2)

(Reference charts (publisher, chart number and scale, points reflected on chart, geodetic datum):

Indonesian Navy Hydrographic Office, chart No. 3, March 1985, corrected to 13 October 1997, 1:4,000,000, (IIIA-2) to (IIIE-2), Bessel 1841;
Indonesian Navy Hydrographic Office, chart No. 403, September 1996, corrected to 14 September 1996, 1:500,000, (IIIA-2) to (IIIE-2), Bessel 1841;
Indonesian Navy Hydrographic Office, chart No. 357, December 1985, corrected to 17 February 1997, 1:1,000,000, (IIIA-2) and (IIIE-1), Bessel 1841)

Description of the archipelagic sea lane

The axis line connects the following geographical positions:

(IIIA-2)	01°40′.00 N, 126°57′.50 E	(IIIE-2)	04°32′.20 N, 125°10′.40 E
(IIIE-1)	04°12′.10 N, 126°01′.00 E		

Notes for the use of this archipelagic sea lane:

(a) Geographical positions (IIIA-2) to (IIIE-2) define the axis line from the Maluku Sea to the Celebes (Sulawesi) Sea.

Sea lane IIIB: Spur from point (IIIA-8) to (IIIB-2); Banda Sea – Leti Strait – Timor Sea

(Reference charts (publisher, chart number and scale, points reflected on chart, geodetic datum):

Indonesian Navy Hydrographic Office, chart No. 3, March 1985, corrected to 13 October 1997, 1:4,000,000, (IIIA-8) to (IIIB-2), Bessel 1841;
Indonesian Navy Hydrographic Office, chart No. 142, May 1991, corrected to 24 August 1996, 1:1,000,000, (IIIA-8) and (IIIB-1), Bessel 1841;
Indonesian Navy Hydrographic Office, chart No. 367, August 1993, corrected to 7 July 1997, 1:1,000,000, (IIIB-2), Bessel 1841;
Indonesian Navy Hydrographic Office, chart No. 146, October 1993, corrected to 1 April 1995, 1:1,000,000, (IIIB-2), Bessel 1841)

Description of the archipelagic sea lane

The axis line connects the following geographical positions:

(IIIA-8)	03°20′.00 S, 125°30′.00 E	(IIIB-2)	08°31′.00 S, 127°33′.00 E
(IIIB-1)	04°00′.00 S, 125°40′.00 E		

Notes for the use of this archipelagic sea lane:

(a) Geographical positions (IIIA-8) to (IIIB-2) define the axis line through the Banda Sea and Leti Strait to the Timor Sea.

Sea lane IIIC: Spur from point (IIIA-8) to (IIIC-2); Banda Sea – Arafuru Sea

(Reference charts (publisher, chart number and scale, points reflected on chart, geodetic datum):

Indonesian Navy Hydrographic Office, chart No. 3, March 1985, corrected to 13 October 1997, 1:4,000,000, (IIIA-8) to (IIIC-2), Bessel 1841;
Indonesian Navy Hydrographic Office, chart No. 142, May 1991, corrected to 24 August 1996, 1:1,000,000, (IIIA-8) and (IIIB-1), Bessel 1841;
Indonesian Navy Hydrographic Office, chart No. 367, August 1993, corrected to 7 July 1997, 1:1,000,000, (IIIC-1) and (IIIC-2), Bessel 1841;
Indonesian Navy Hydrographic Office, chart No. 146, October 1993, corrected to 1 April 1995, 1:1,000,000, (IIIC-1) and (IIIC-2), Bessel 1841)

Description of the archipelagic sea lane

The axis line connects the following geographical positions:

(IIIA-8)	03°20′.00 S,	125°30′.00 E	(IIIC-1)	06°10′.00 S,	131°45′.00 E
(IIIB-1)	04°00′.00 S,	125°40′.00 E	(IIIC-2)	06°44′.00 S,	132°35′.00 E

Notes for the use of this archipelagic sea lane:

(a) Geographical positions (IIIA-8) to (IIIC-2) define the axis line through the Banda Sea to the Arafuru Sea.

Sea lane IIID: Spur from point (IIIA-11) TO (IIID-1); Sawu Sea – Sea between Sawu and Roti Islands – Indian (Hindia) Ocean

(Reference charts (publisher, chart number and scale, points reflected on chart, geodetic datum):

Indonesian Navy Hydrographic Office, chart No. 3, March 1985, corrected to 13 October 1997, 1:4,000,000, (IIIA-11) and (IIID-1), Bessel 1841;
Indonesian Navy Hydrographic Office, chart No. 112, June 1991, corrected to 10 June 1995, 1:1,000,000, (IIIA-11) and (IIID-1), Bessel 1841;
Indonesian Navy Hydrographic Office, chart No. 366, July 1993, corrected to 15 September 1997, 1:1,000,000, (IIIA-11) and (IIID-1), Bessel 1841)

Description of the archipelagic sea lane

The axis line connects the following geographical positions:

(IIIA-11)	09°23′.00 S,	122°55′.00 E	(IIID-1)	10°58′.00 S,	122°11′.00 E

Notes for the use of this archipelagic sea lane:

(a) Geographical positions (IIIA-11) to (IIID-1) define the axis line from the Sawu Sea to the Sea between Sawu and Roti Islands to the Indian (Hindia) Ocean.

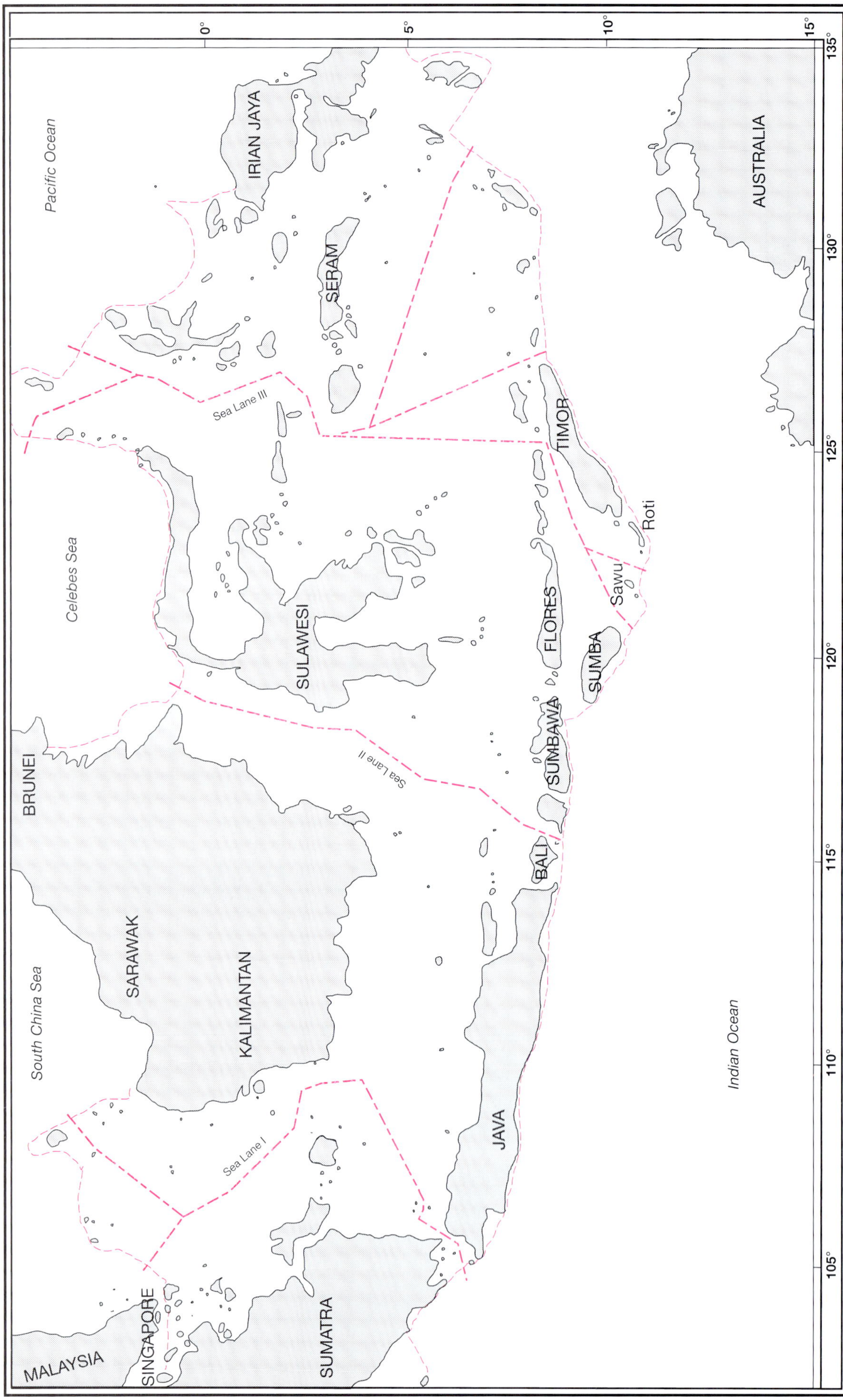

INDONESIAN ARCHIPELAGIC SEA LANES I, II AND III

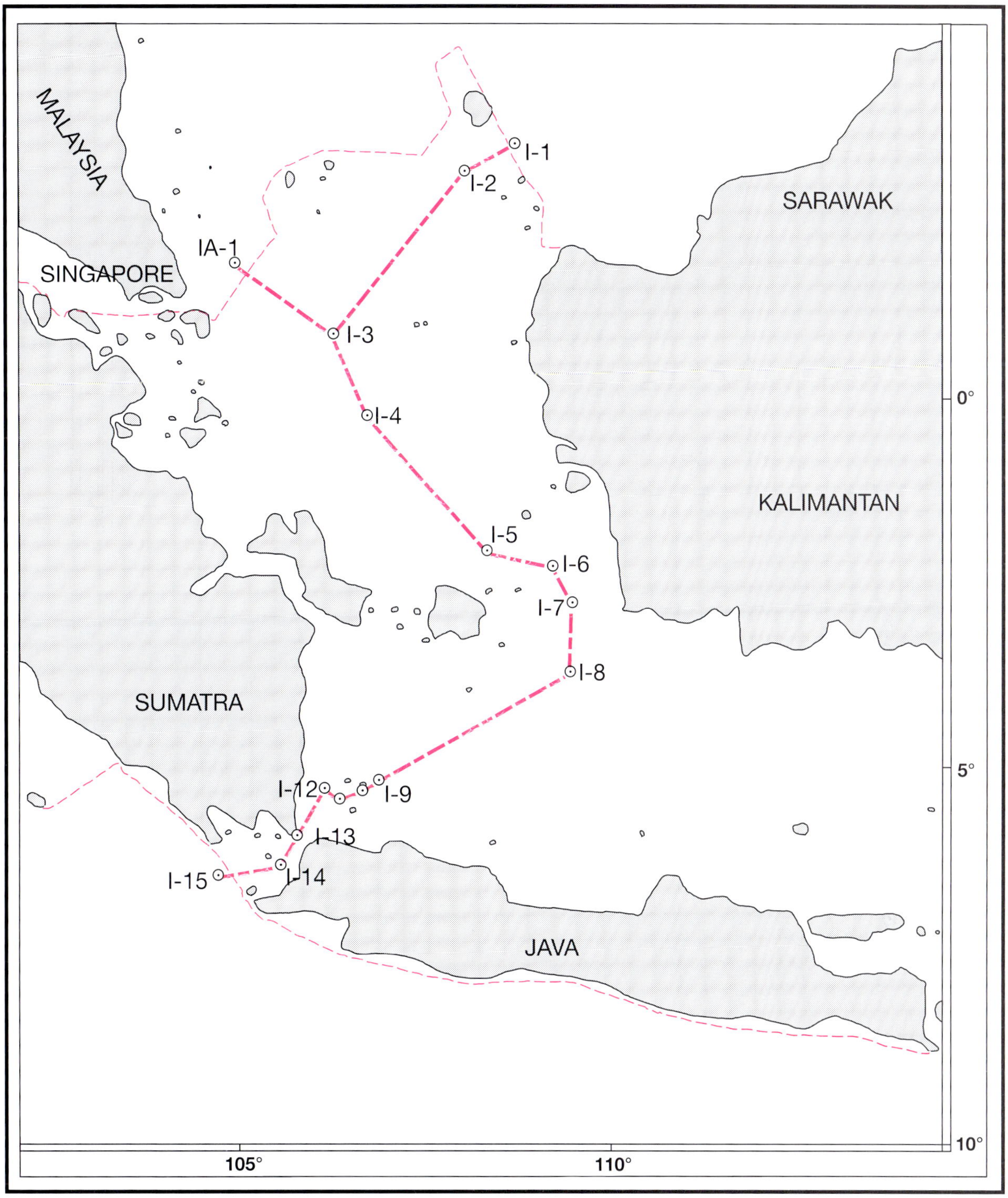

INDONESIAN ARCHIPELAGIC SEA LANE I

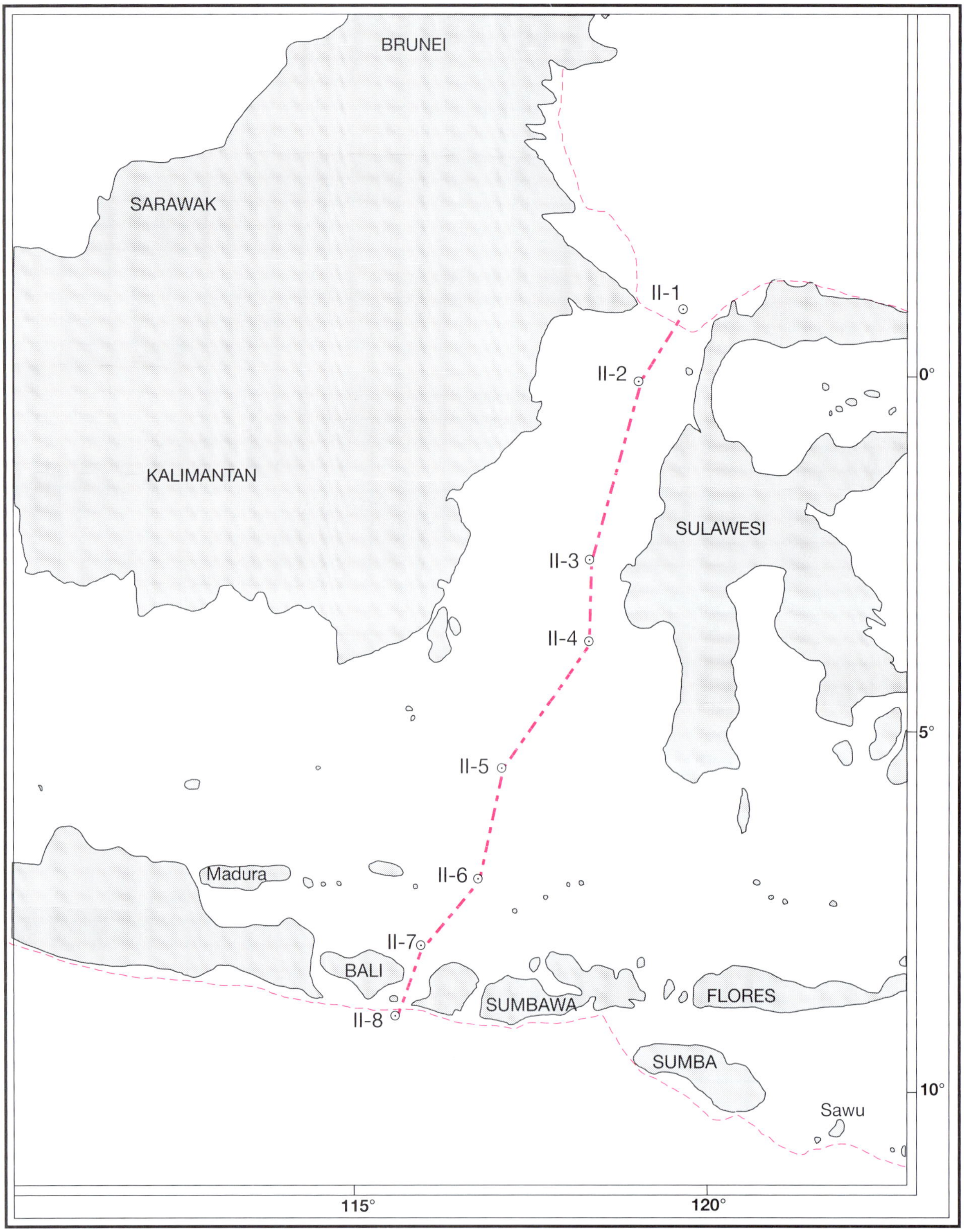

INDONESIAN ARCHIPELAGIC SEA LANE II

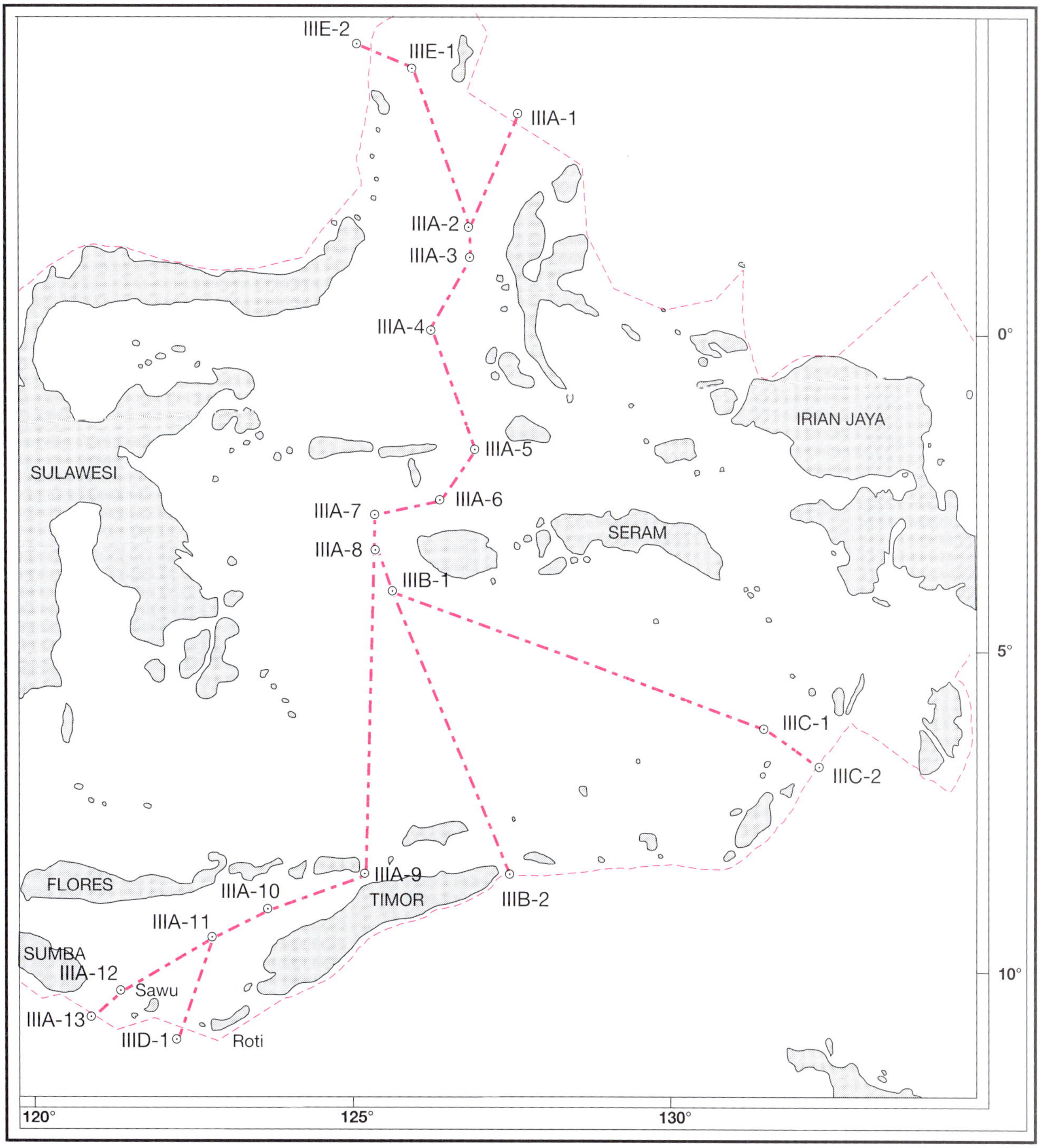

INDONESIAN ARCHIPELAGIC SEA LANE III

H

Notes

Notes

Notes

Notes

Notes

Notes

Notes

Notes